KU-289-135

Stanley Gibbons Stamp Catalogue

PART 6

FRANCE

First Edition 1979

STANLEY GIBBONS PUBLICATIONS LTD
391 Strand, London WC2R 0LX

Retail Price in UK £5·00

By Appointment to Her Majesty The Queen
Stanley Gibbons Ltd., London
Philatelists

1st Edition in this form – June 1979

ⓒ Stanley Gibbons Publications. Ltd 1979

ISSN: 0142–9809   ISBN: 0 85259 141 1

Stanley Gibbons Foreign Catalogue

The Stanley Gibbons Stamp Catalogue has been in continuous publication since 1865. From 1897 to 1945 Foreign Countries constituted Part II, then (1947–50) Parts II–VIII. From 1951 to 1970 rearranged as Part II *Europe and Colonies* and Part III *America, Asia and Africa*, then amalgamated 1970–71 as Sectional Catalogues, 12 of which were published. During 1972–78 recombined as alphabetical volumes, three for *Europe* and four for *Overseas*. Present division into 21 collecting groups began in 1979.

Copyright Notice

The layout and contents of this Catalogue are fully protected by copyright. Permission is hereby granted for copyright material to be quoted by publishers in newspapers, magazines and philatelic society publications and by stamp dealers in advertising matter, price lists and circulars distributed free, provided that acknowledgement of source is also given. Any reference to our catalogue numbers must include the identifying letters "S.G."

This permission does not extend to any book, catalogue, price list, album or other publication offered for sale unless prior permission has been obtained in writing from the Catalogue Editor in each instance. The illustrations also form part of the copyright and may not be reproduced in any circumstances.

Item No. 2835

Made and printed in Great Britain by Balding + Mansell, London and Wisbech

A Significant Step Forward

As publishers of one of the world's major stamp catalogues, Stanley Gibbons have a special responsibility to the collector. Backed by more than a century of service to philately the Catalogue has built a reputation for accuracy and thoroughness of which we are proud.

Past achievements, however praiseworthy, are insufficient. The Catalogue must grow and develop as the hobby itself grows and develops. Though on the surest of foundations it must nevertheless respond to current needs.

We believe that selective and more specialised collecting is today's trend. We have seen and supported the great growth in study circles and made use of the excellent research from innumerable students which these groups have encouraged. By carefully studying his stamps and exploring the exciting postal history associated with them the average collector can nowadays put together a satisfying collection that will repay him amply in numerous ways.

There is a trend, too, for study of areas neglected in the past and this is particularly the case with the stamps of foreign countries. Countless opportunities for research and discovery lie in the pages of the Foreign Catalogue and this is an added reason why collectors will welcome the new presentation now inaugurated.

The former *Europe* and *Overseas* volumes had between them grown to over 5000 pages of information and reference. We have divided this up into the significant collecting groups that correspond with the trends commented on above. By so doing, the individual specialist will be better served. Not only will he receive the pages he particularly wishes but the system becomes a flexible one, responding with more frequent editions where collector demand requires.

Much detailed discussion and planning have gone into the volume now in your hands. I am confident that this is another significant step forward in the evolution of the *Stanley Gibbons Stamp Catalogue* and I commend the work to you.

HOWARD O. FRASER
Chairman
Stanley Gibbons International Ltd.

Catalogue Revisions

The new division of countries in the *Stanley Gibbons Stamp Catalogue* allows us to present in one volume what is traditionally termed "France and Colonies", to which is added Andorra and Monaco for convenience. We are sure this will meet with the approval of the numerous collectors of this popular area.

The dividing line for the listings is a territory's attaining its independence: stamps issued after that date are in other Parts of the Foreign Catalogue.

We list here countries by their present name or the latest name used while a member of the French Group. We include issues of Autonomous Republics, occupation issues, and stamps from protectorates and mandated territories. Following the practice of the former *Overseas* volumes the current country name will be found to have subdivisions for territories of different name now absorbed by it. French Post Offices abroad are shown under the country in which the P.O. was located. The full list of contents (inside front cover) will readily explain the general layout.

For this edition all prices have been carefully studied and they have been revised, where necessary, to take account of the healthy international market which exists for stamps of the French Group. We now list the Philatelic Documents introduced by the French authorities in recent years and which are of great interest to many collectors.

Catalogue numbers altered

The following are alterations made to catalogue numbers used in the Third Edition of *Europe 1* (1977) and the Second Editions of *Overseas 1* and *2* (1976).

Old	New
France	
1647*g*	2065*a*
1648*a*	2065*b*
1648*b*	1648*a*
1648*c/f*	2065*c/f*
1648*g*	1648*b*
1649	2065*g*
1649*a*	1649
1649*b/f*	2065*h/l*
C15	C16
C16	C15
U12	U13
U13	U12
U18	U19
Algeria	
97/8	D97/8
French Polynesia	
210/16	211/17
Afars and Issas	
628/39	630/47
645/55	656/67

Stamps added to this edition

Items added to this catalogue, not previously published in Gibbons *Stamp Monthly* supplements.

France: 351a, 1710a

Indo-Chinese P.O.s (Kwangchow): 52a

New Caledonia: O530a, O531a/i

New Hebrides: F110a

Andorra: F262a

Monaco: 1149a, 1150a, 1151a/b, 1152a, 1153a, 1161a, 1162a, 1163a, 1165a, 1168, 1256, 1259, 1262, 1265

New issues: The first supplement to this catalogue appeared in Gibbons *Stamp Monthly* for April 1979.

Stanley Gibbons International Ltd.

Stanley Gibbons Ltd.
391 Strand, London WC2R 0LX. Sales and buying departments for popular stamps, albums, catalogues and accessories; mail order; new issues and approvals; postal history.
Retail Shop: 391 Strand, London WC2R 0LX.
Specialist and Rare Stamp Departments: Romano House, 399 Strand, London WC2R 0LX. Classic and rare material; Specialist Register; investment advice; the Gibbons Gallery of changing exhibitions.

Stanley Gibbons Publications Ltd.
Editorial Offices: Drury House, Russell Street, Drury Lane, London WC2B 5HD. The S.G. range of catalogues, books, albums and accessories; publications mail order service (hotline 01-836 0974).
Wholesale and Trade: Stangib House, Sarehole Road, Hall Green, Birmingham B28 8EE.

Stanley Gibbons Auctions Ltd.
Stanley Gibbons Magazines Ltd.
Drury House, Russell Street, Drury Lane, London WC2B 5HD.

Stanley Gibbons Currency Ltd.
Stanley Gibbons Antiquarian Books Ltd.
395 Strand, London WC2R 0LX.

Stanley Gibbons Mapsellers Ltd.
37 Southampton Street, London WC2E 7HE.

Stanley Gibbons Products Ltd.
Stangib House, Sarehole Road, Hall Green, Birmingham B28 8EE.

> ALL LONDON ADDRESSES: Telephone 01-836 8444; Telex 28883.
> BIRMINGHAM OFFICES: Telephone 021-777 7255; Telex 28883.

StanGib Ltd.
601 Franklin Avenue, Garden City, New York, NY 11530, U.S.A. Tel. 0101 516 746-4666 and 4667; Telex 96-7733.

Gibbons (Philatelists) Ltd.
Rockefeller Center, Suite 2906, 1270 Avenue of the Americas, New York, NY 10020, U.S.A. Tel. 0101 212 582-0165 and 0166; Telex 96-7733,

Stanley Gibbons Currency Inc.
P.O. Box 3034, San Bernadino, CA 92413, U.S.A. Tel. 0101 714 883 5849.

Stanley Gibbons Frankfurt G.m.b.H.
D-6000 Frankfurt am Main, Zeil 83, West Germany. Tel 010 49 611-287477; Telex 4189148.

Stanley Gibbons Monaco S.A.M.
2 Avenue Henry Dunant, Monte Carlo, Monaco. Tel. 010 3393 506862.

General Philatelic Information
and Guidelines to the Scope of the Foreign Catalogue

The notes which follow seek to reflect current practice in compiling the Foreign Catalogue.

It scarcely needs emphasising that the *Stanley Gibbons Stamp Catalogue* has a very long history and that the vast quantity of information it contains has been carefully built up by successive generations through the work of countless individuals. Philately itself is never static and the Catalogue has evolved and developed during this long time-span. Thus, while these notes are important for today's criteria, they may be less precise the farther back in the listings one travels. They are not intended to inaugurate some unwanted series of piecemeal alterations in a widely respected work, but it does seem to us useful that Catalogue users know as exactly as possible the policies currently in operation.

THE CATALOGUE IN GENERAL

Contents. The Catalogue is confined to adhesive postage stamps, including miniature sheets. For particular categories the rules are:

(*a*) Revenue (fiscal) stamps or telegraph stamps are listed only where they have been expressly authorised for postal duty.

(*b*) Stamps issued only precancelled are included, but normally issued stamps available additionally with precancel have no separate precancel listing unless the face value is changed.

(*c*) Stamps prepared for use but not issued, hitherto accorded full listing, are nowadays footnoted with a price (where possible).

(*d*) Bisects (trisects, etc.) are only listed where such usage was officially authorised.

(*e*) Stamps issued only on first day covers and not available separately are not listed but priced (on the cover) in a footnote.

(*f*) New printings, as such, are not listed, though stamps from them may qualify under another category, e.g. when a prominent new shade results.

(*g*) Official and unofficial reprints are dealt with by footnote.

(*h*) Only imperforates which are errors or are issued in quantities approaching the normal perforate versions are listed.

Exclusions. The following are excluded: (*a*) non-postal revenue or fiscal stamps; (*b*) postage stamps used fiscally; (*c*) local carriage labels and private local issues; (*d*) telegraph stamps; (*e*) bogus or phantom stamps; (*f*) railway or airline letter fee stamps, bus or road transport company labels; (*g*) cut-outs; (*h*) all types of non-postal labels; (*i*) documentary labels for the postal service, e.g. registration, recorded delivery, airmail etiquettes, etc.; (*j*) privately applied embellishments to official issues and privately commissioned items generally; (*k*) stamps for training postal officers; (*l*) specimen stamps.

Legitimate issues. In judging status, four broad considerations are applied to the stamps: (1) they must be issued by a legitimate postal authority; (2) they must be adhesives valid for proper postal use in prepaying the fee for the class of service for which they were issued; (3) except for such obvious categories as postage due and official stamps, they must be available to the general public in reasonable quantities at face value; (4) no artificial restrictions must have been imposed on their distribution. Note that covers from normal commercial usage are useful items of evidence.

For errors and varieties the criterion is legitimate (albeit inadvertent) sale over a post office counter in the normal course of business. Details of provenance are always important; printers' waste and fraudulently manufactured material is excluded.

Certificates. In assessing unlisted items due weight is given to Certificates from recognised Expert Committees and, where appropriate, we will usually ask to see them.

New issues. New issues are listed regularly in the Catalogue Supplement published in Gibbons *Stamp Monthly*, whence they are consolidated into the next available edition of the Catalogue.

Full listing. "Full listing" confers our recognition and implies allotting a catalogue number and (wherever possible) a price quotation. Stamps of each country are catalogued chronologically by date of issue. Subsidiary classes (e.g. postage due stamps) are integrated into one list with postage and commemorative stamps and distinguished by a letter prefix to the catalogue number.

Date of issue. Where local issue dates differ from dates of release by agencies, "date of issue" is the local date. Fortuitous stray usage before the officially intended date is disregarded in listing.

Catalogue numbers. The catalogue number appears in the extreme left column. The boldface Type numbers in the next column are merely cross-references to illustrations. Catalogue numbers in the Gibbons *Stamp Monthly* Supplement are provisional only and may need to be altered when the lists are consolidated. Miniature sheets only purchasable intact at a post office have a single **MS** number; sheetlets – individual stamps available – number each stamp separately.

Once published in the Catalogue, numbers are changed as little as possible; really serious renumbering is reserved for the occasions when a complete country or an entire issue is being rewritten. The edition first affected includes cross-reference tables of old and new numbers.

Our catalogue numbers are universally recognised in specifying stamps and as a hallmark of status.

Illustrations. Stamps are illustrated at three-quarters linear size. Stamps not illustrated are the same size and format as the value shown, unless otherwise indicated. Stamps issued only as miniature sheets have the stamp alone illustrated but sheet size is also quoted. Overprints, surcharges and watermarks are normally actual size. Illustrations of varieties are often enlarged to show the detail.

CONTACTING THE CATALOGUE EDITOR
The editor is always interested in hearing from people who have new information which will improve or correct the Catalogue. As a general rule he must see and examine the actual stamps before they can be considered for listing; photographs or photocopies are insufficient evidence. Neither he nor his staff give opinions as to the genuineness of stamps.

Submissions should be made in writing to the Catalogue Editor, Stanley Gibbons Publications Ltd., 391 Strand, London WC2R 0LX. The cost of return

Information (contd.)

postage for items submitted is appreciated, and this should include the registration fee if required.

Where information is solicited purely for the benefit of the enquirer, the editor cannot undertake to reply if the answer is already contained in these published notes or if return postage is omitted. Written communications are greatly preferred to enquiries by telephone and the editor regrets that he or his staff cannot see personal callers without a prior appointment being made.

The editor welcomes close contact with study circles and is interested, too, in finding reliable local correspondents who will verify and supplement official information in overseas countries where this is deficient.

TECHNICAL MATTERS

The meanings of the technical terms used in the Catalogue will be found in *Philatelic Terms Illustrated* by Russell Bennett and James Watson, published by Gibbons.

1. Printing

Printing errors. Errors in printing are of major interest to the Catalogue. Authenticated items meriting consideration would include: background, centre or frame inverted or omitted; centre or subject transposed; error of colour; error or omission of value; double prints and impressions; printed both sides; and so on. Designs *tête-beche*, whether intentionally or by accident, are listable. *Se-tenant* arrangements of stamps are recognised in the listings or footnotes. Gutter pairs (a pair of stamps separated by blank margin) are excluded unless they have some philatelic importance. Colours only partially omitted are not listed, neither are stamps printed on the gummed side.

Printing varieties. Listing is accorded to major changes in the printing base which lead to completely new types. In recess-printing this could be a design re-engraved; in photogravure or photolithography a screen altered in whole or in part. It can also encompass flat-bed and rotary printing if the results are readily distinguishable.

To be considered at all, varieties must be constant.

Early stamps, produced by primitive methods, were prone to numerous imperfections: the lists reflect this, recognising re-entries, retouches, broken frames, misshapen letters, and so on. Printing technology has, however, radically improved over the years, during which time photogravure and lithography have become predominant. Varieties nowadays are more in the nature of flaws and these, being too specialised for a general catalogue, are almost always outside the scope. We therefore do not list such items as: dry prints, kiss prints, doctor-blade flaws, blanket set-offs, doubling through blanket stretch, plate cracks and scratches, registration flaws (leading to colour shifts), lithographic ring flaws, and so on. Neither do we recognise fortuitous happenings like paper creases or confetti flaws.

Overprints (and surcharges). Overprints of different types qualify for separate listing. These include overprints in different colours; overprints from different printing processes such as litho and typo; overprints in totally different typefaces, etc.

Overprint errors and varieties. Major errors in machine-printed overprints are important and listable. They include: overprint inverted or omitted; overprint double (treble, etc.); overprint diagonal; overprint double, one inverted; pairs with one overprint omitted, e.g. from a radical shift to an adjoining stamp; error of colour; error of type fount; letters inverted or omitted, etc. If the overprint is handstamped, few of these would qualify and a distinction is drawn.

Varieties occurring in overprints will often take the form of broken letters, slight differences in spacing, rising spacers, etc. Only the most important would be considered for footnote mention.

James Watson's *Stamp Varieties Explained*, published by Gibbons, is recommended for study.

2. Paper

All stamps listed are deemed to be on "ordinary" paper of the wove type and white in colour; only departures from this are mentioned.

Types. Where classification so requires we distinguish such other types of paper as, for example, vertically and horizontally laid; wove and laid bâtonné; card(board); carton; cartridge; enamelled; glazed; GC (Grande Consommation); granite; native; pelure; porous; quadrillé; ribbed; rice; and silk thread.

Our chalky (chalk-surfaced) paper is specifically one which shows a black mark when touched with a silver wire. This and other coatings are easily lost or damaged through immersion in water.

The various makeshifts for normal paper are listed as appropriate. They include printing on: unfinished banknotes, war maps, ruled paper, Post Office forms, and the unprinted side of glossy magazines. The varieties of double paper and joined paper are recognised.

Descriptive terms. The fact that a paper is hand-made (and thus probably of uneven thickness) is mentioned where necessary. Such descriptive terms as "hard" and "soft"; "smooth" and "rough"; "thick", "medium" and "thin" are applied where there is philatelic merit in classifying papers.

Coloured, very white and toned papers. A coloured paper is one that is coloured right through (front and back of the stamp). In the Catalogue the colour of the paper is given in *italics*, thus:

black/*rose*=black design on rose paper.

Papers have been made specially white in recent years by, for example, a very heavy coating of chalk. We do not classify shades of whiteness of paper as distinct varieties. There does exist, however, a type of paper from early days called toned. This is off-white, often brownish or buffish, but it cannot be assigned any definite colour. A toning effect brought on by climate, incorrect storage or gum staining is disregarded here, as this was not the state of the paper when issued.

Safety devices. The Catalogue takes account of such safety devices as varnish lines, grills, burelage or imprinted patterns on the front or moiré on the back of stamps.

Modern developments. Two modern developments also affect the listings: printing on self-adhesive paper and the tendency, philatelic in origin, for conventional paper to be reinforced or replaced by different materials. Some examples are the use of foils in gold, silver, aluminium, palladium and steel; application of an imitation wood veneer; printing on plastic moulded in relief; and use of a plastic laminate to give a three-dimensional effect. Examples also occur of stamps impregnated with scent; printed on silk; and incorporating miniature gramophone records.

3. Perforation and Rouletting

Perforation gauge. The gauge of a perforation is the number of holes in a length of 2 cm. For correct classification the size of the holes (large or small) may need to be distinguished; in a few cases the actual number of holes on each edge of the stamp needs to be quoted.

Measurement. The Gibbons *Instanta* gauge is the standard for measuring perforations. The stamp is viewed against a dark background with the transparent gauge put on top of it. Though the gauge measures to decimal accuracy, perforations read from it are generally quoted in the Catalogue to the nearest half. For example:

Just over perf.$12\frac{3}{4}$ to just under perf.$13\frac{1}{4}$	=perf.13
Perf.$13\frac{1}{4}$ exactly, rounded up	=perf.$13\frac{1}{2}$
Just over perf.$13\frac{1}{4}$ to just under perf.$13\frac{3}{4}$	=perf.$13\frac{1}{2}$
Perf.$13\frac{3}{4}$ exactly, rounded up	=perf.14

However, where classification depends on it, actual quarter-perforations are quoted.

Notation. Where no perforation is quoted for an issue it is imperforate. Perforations are usually abbreviated (and spoken) as follows, though sometimes they may be spelled out for clarity. This notation for rectangular stamps (the majority) applies to diamond shapes if "top" is read as the edge to the top right.

P 14: perforated alike on all sides (read: "perf.14").

P 14×15: the first figure refers to top and bottom, the second to left and right sides (read: "perf.14 by 15"). This is a compound perforation. For an upright triangular stamp the first figure refers to the two sloping sides and the second to the base. In inverted triangulars the base is first and the second figure refers to the sloping sides.

P 14–15: perforation measuring anything between 14 and 15: the holes are irregularly spaced, thus the gauge may vary along a single line or even along a single edge of the stamp (read: "perf.14 to 15").

P 14 *irregular*: perforated 14 from a worn perforator, giving badly aligned holes irregularly spaced (read: "irregular perf.14").

P comp(ound) 14×15: two gauges in use but not necessarily on opposite sides of the stamp. It could be one side in one gauge and three in the other; or two adjacent sides with the same gauge. (Read: "perf. compound of 14 and 15".) For three gauges or more, abbreviated as "*P* 14, $14\frac{1}{2}$, 15 *or compound*" for example.

P 14, $14\frac{1}{2}$: perforated approximately $14\frac{1}{4}$ (read: "perf.14 or $14\frac{1}{2}$"). It does *not* mean two stamps, one perf.14 and the other perf.$14\frac{1}{2}$. This obsolescent notation is gradually being replaced in the Catalogue.

Imperf: imperforate (not perforated).

Imperf × P 14: imperforate at top and bottom and perf.14 at sides.

P 14 × *imperf*: perf.14 at top and bottom and imperforate at sides.

Such headings as "*P* 13×14 (*vert*) and *P* 14×13 (*horiz*)" indicate which perforations apply to which stamp format – vertical or horizontal.

Some stamps are additionally perforated so that a label or tab is detachable; others have been perforated suitably for use as two halves. Listings are normally for whole stamps, unless stated otherwise.

Other terms. Perforation almost always gives circular holes; where other shapes have been used they are specified, e.g. square holes; iozenge perf. Interrupted perfs. are brought about by the omission of pins at regular intervals. Perforations have occasionally been simulated by being printed as part of the design. With few exceptions, privately applied perforations are not listed.

Perforation errors and varieties. Authenticated errors, where a stamp normally perforated is accidentally issued imperforate, are listed provided no traces of perforation (blind holes or indentations) remain. They must be provided as pairs, both stamps wholly imperforate, and are only priced in that form.

Stamps merely imperforate between stamp and margin (fantails) are not listed.

Imperforate-between varieties are recognised, where one row of perfs has been missed. They are listed and priced in pairs:

Imperf between (*horiz pair*): a horizontal pair of stamps with perfs all around the edges but none between the stamps.

Imperf between (*vert pair*): a vertical pair of stamps with perfs all around the edges but none between the stamps.

Where several of the rows have escaped perforation the resulting varieties are listable. Thus:

Imperf vert (*horiz pair*): a horizontal pair of stamps perforated top and bottom; all three vertical directions are imperf – the two outer edges and between the stamps.

Imperf horiz (*vert pair*): a vertical pair perforated at left and right edges; all three horizontal directions are imperf – the top, bottom and between the stamps.

Straight edges. Large sheets cut up before issue to post offices can cause stamps with straight edges, i.e. imperf on one side or on two sides at right angles. They are not usually listable in this condition and are worth less than corresponding stamps properly perforated all round. This does not, however, apply to certain stamps, mainly from coils and booklets, where straight edges on various sides are the manufacturing norm affecting every stamp. The listings and notes make clear which sides are correctly imperf.

Malfunction. Varieties of double, misplaced or partial perforation caused by error or machine malfunction are not listable, neither are freaks, such as perforations placed diagonally from paper folds. Likewise disregarded are missing holes caused by broken pins, and perforations "fading out" down a sheet, the machinery progressively disengaging to leave blind perfs and indentations to the paper.

Centering. Well-centred stamps have designs surrounded by equal opposite margins. Where this condition affects the price the fact is stated.

Types of perforating. Where necessary for classification, perforation types are distinguished. These include:

Line perforation from one line of pins punching single rows of holes at a time.

Comb perforation from pins disposed across the sheet in comb formation, punching out holes at three sides of the stamp a row at a time.

Harrow perforation applied to a whole pane or sheet at one stroke.

Rotary perforation from toothed wheels operating across a sheet, then crosswise.

Sewing-machine perforation. The resultant condition, clean-cut or rough, is distinguished where required.

Pin-perforation is the commonly applied term for pin-roulette in which, instead of being punched out, round holes are pricked by sharp-pointed pins and no paper is removed.

Punctured stamps. Perforation holes can be punched into the face of the stamp. Patterns of small holes, often in the shape of initial letters, are privately applied devices against pilferage. These "perfins" are

Information (contd.)

outside the scope. Identification devices, when officially inspired, are listed or noted; they can be shapes, or letters or words formed from holes, sometimes converting one class of stamp into another.

Rouletting. In rouletting the paper is cut, for ease of separation, but none is removed. The gauge is measured, when needed, as for perforations. Traditional French terms descriptive of the type of cut are often used and types include:

Arc roulette (*percé en arc*). Cuts are minute, spaced arcs, each roughly a semicircle.

Cross roulette (*percé en croix*). Cuts are tiny diagonal crosses.

Line roulette (*percé en ligne* or *en ligne droite*). Short straight cuts parallel to the frame of the stamp. The commonest basic roulette. Where not further described, "roulette" means this type.

Rouletted in colour or *coloured roulette* (*percé en lignes colorées* or *en lignes de couleur*). Cuts with coloured edges, arising from notched rule inked simultaneously with the printing plate.

Saw-tooth roulette (*percé en scie*). Cuts applied zigzag fashion to resemble the teeth of a saw.

Serpentine roulette (*percé en serpentin*). Cuts as sharply wavy lines.

Zigzag roulettes (*percé en zigzags*). Short straight cuts at angles in alternate directions, producing sharp points on separation. U.S. usage favours "serrate(d) roulette" for this type.

Pin-roulette (originally *percé en points* and now *perforés trous d'epingle*) is commonly called pin-perforation in English.

4. Gum

All stamps listed are assumed to have gum of some kind; if they were issued without gum this is stated. Original gum (o.g.) means that which was present on the stamp as issued to the public. Deleterious climates and the presence of certain chemicals can cause gum to crack and, with early stamps, even make the paper deteriorate. Unscrupulous fakers are adept in removing it and regumming the stamp to meet the unreasoning demand often made for "full o.g." in cases where such a thing is virtually impossible.

Until recent times the gum used for stamps has been gum arabic, but various synthetic adhesives – tinted or invisible-looking – are coming into use. Stamps existing with more than one type of gum are not normally listed separately, though the fact is noted where it is of philatelic significance, e.g. in distinguishing reprints or new printings.

The distinct variety of grilled gum is, however, recognised. In this the paper is passed through a gum breaker prior to printing to prevent subsequent curling. As the patterned rollers were sufficient to impress a grill into the paper beneath the gum we can quote prices for both unused and used examples.

Self-adhesive stamps are issued on backing paper, from which they are peeled before affixing to mail. Unused examples are priced as for backing paper intact. Used examples are best kept on cover or on piece.

5. Watermarks

Stamps are on unwatermarked paper except where the heading to the set says otherwise.

Detection. Watermarks are detected for Catalogue description by one of four methods: (1) holding stamps to the light; (2) laying stamps face down on a dark background; (3) adding a few drops of petroleum ether 40/60 to the stamp laid face down in a watermark tray; or (4) by use of the Morley-Bright Detector, which works by revealing the thinning of the paper at the watermark. (Note that petroleum ether is highly inflammable in use and can damage photogravure stamps.)

Listable types. Stamps occurring on both watermarked and unwatermarked papers are different types and both receive full listing.

Single watermarks (devices occurring once on every stamp) can be modified in size and shape as between different issues; the types are noted but not usually separately listed. Fortuitous absence of watermark from a single stamp or its gross displacement would not be listable.

To overcome registration difficulties the device may be repeated at close intervals (a *multiple watermark*), single stamps thus showing parts of several devices. Similarly, a large *sheet watermark* (or *all-over watermark*) covering numerous stamps can be used. We give informative notes and illustrations for them. The designs may be such that

AS DESCRIBED (Read through front of stamp)		AS SEEN DURING WATERMARK DETECTION (Stamp face down and back examined)
GvR	Normal	ЯvϽ
ЯvϽ	Inverted	ϾʌЯ
ЯvϽ	Reversed	GvR
ϾʌЯ	Reversed and inverted	ЯvϽ
GvR	Sideways	ϾʌЯ
GvR	Sideways inverted	ЯvϽ

numbers of stamps in the sheet automatically lack watermark: this is not a listable variety. Multiple and all-over watermarks sometimes undergo modifications, but if the various types are difficult to distinguish from single stamps notes are given but not separate listings.

Papermakers' watermarks are noted where known but not listed separately, since most stamps in the sheet will lack them. Sheet watermarks which are nothing more than officially adopted papermakers' watermarks are, however, given normal listing.

Marginal watermarks, falling outside the pane of stamps, are ignored except where misplacement causes the adjoining row to be affected, in which case they are footnoted.

Watermark errors and varieties. Watermark errors are recognised as of major importance. They comprise stamps intended to be on unwatermarked paper but issued watermarked by mistake, or stamps printed on paper with the wrong watermark. Watermark varieties, on the other hand, such as broken or deformed bits on the dandy roll, are not listable.

Watermark positions. The diagram shows how watermark position is described in the Catalogue. Paper has a side intended for printing and watermarks are usually impressed so that they read normally when looked through from that printed side. However, since philatelists customarily detect watermarks by looking at the back of the stamp the watermark diagram also makes clear what is actually seen.

Illustrations in the Catalogue are of watermarks in normal positions (from the front of the stamps) and are actual size where possible.

Differences in watermark position are collectable as distinct varieties. In this Catalogue, however, only normal and sideways watermarks are listed (and "sideways inverted" is treated as "sideways"). Inverted and reversed watermarks have always been outside its scope: in the early days of flat-bed printing sheets of watermarked paper were fed indiscriminately through the press and the resulting watermark positions had no particular philatelic significance. Similarly, the special make-up of sheets for booklets can in some cases give equal quantities of normal and inverted watermarks.

6. Colours

Stamps in two or three colours have these named in order of appearance, from the centre moving outwards. Four colours or more are usually listed as multicoloured.

In compound colour names the second is the predominant one, thus:

orange-red = a red tending towards orange;

red-orange = an orange containing more red than usual.

Standard colours used. The 100 colours most used for stamp identification are given in the Stanley Gibbons Colour Guide; these, plus a further 100 variations for more specialised use, are included in the Stanley Gibbons Stamp Colour Key. The Catalogue has used the Guide and Key as standards for describing new issues for some years. The names are also introduced as lists are rewritten, though exceptions are made for those early issues where traditional names have become universally established.

Determining colours. When comparing actual stamps with colour samples in the Guide or Key, view in a good north daylight (or its best substitute: fluorescent "colour-matching" light). Sunshine is not recommended. Choose a solid portion of the stamp design; if

available, marginal markings such as solid bars of colour or colour check dots are helpful. Shading lines in the design can be misleading as they appear lighter than solid colour. Postmarked portions of a stamp appear darker than normal. If more than one colour is present, mask off the extraneous ones as the eye tends to mix them.

Errors of colour. Major colour errors in stamps or overprints which qualify for listing are: wrong colours; one colour inverted in relation to the rest; albinos (colourless impressions), where these have Expert Committee certificates; colours completely omitted, but only on unused stamps (if found on used stamps the information is footnoted).

Colours only partially omitted are not recognised. Colour shifts, however spectacular, are not listed.

Shades. Shades in philately refer to variations in the intensity of a colour or the presence of differing amounts of other colours. They are particularly significant when they can be linked to specific printings. In general, shades need to be quite marked to fall within the scope of this Catalogue; it does not favour nowadays listing the often numerous shades of a stamp, but chooses a single applicable colour name which will indicate particular groups of outstanding shades. Furthermore, the listings refer to colours as issued: they may deteriorate into something different through the passage of time.

Modern colour printing by lithography is prone to marked differences of shade, even within a single run, and variations can occur within the same sheet. Such shades are not listed.

Aniline colours. An aniline colour meant originally one derived from coal-tar; it now refers more widely to colour of a particular brightness suffused on the surface of a stamp and showing through clearly on the back.

Colours of overprints and surcharges. All overprints and surcharges are in black unless stated otherwise in the heading or after the description of the stamp.

7. Luminescence

Machines which sort mail electronically have been introduced in recent years. In consequence some countries have issued stamps on fluorescent or phosphorescent papers, while others have marked their stamps with phosphor bands.

The various papers can only be distinguished by ultraviolet lamps emitting particular wavelengths. They are separately listed only when the stamps have some other means of distinguishing them, visible without the use of these lamps. Where this is not so, the papers are recorded in footnotes or headings. (Collectors using the lamps, nevertheless, should exercise great care in their use as exposure to their light is extremely dangerous to the eyes.)

Phosphor bands are listable, since they are visible to the naked eye (by holding stamps at an angle to the light and looking along them, the bands appear dark). Stamps existing with and without phosphor bands or with differing numbers of bands are given separate listings. Varieties such as double bands, misplaced or omitted bands, bands printed on the wrong side, are not listed.

8. Coil Stamps

Stamps issued only in coil form are given full listing. If stamps are issued in both sheets and coils the coil stamps are listed separately only where there is some feature

Information (contd.)

(e.g. perforation) by which singles can be distinguished. Coil strips containing different stamps *se-tenant* are also listed.

Coil join pairs are too random and too easily faked to permit of listing; similarly ignored are coil stamps which have accidentally suffered an extra row of perforations from the claw mechanism in a malfunctioning vending machine.

9. Booklet Stamps

Stamp booklets are outside the scope of this Catalogue.

Single stamps from booklets are listed if they are distinguishable in some way (such as watermark or perforation) from similar sheet stamps. Listings of booklet panes themselves are given for certain countries and it is intended to extend this generally. These will absorb and replace present listings of pairs from booklet panes showing two different values *se-tenant* (and which will be found under the lower of the two values concerned). The particular perforations (straight edges) are covered by appropriate notes.

10. Forgeries and Fakes

Forgeries. Where space permits, notes are considered if they can give a concise description that will permit unequivocal detection of a forgery. Generalised warnings, lacking detail, are not nowadays inserted, since their value to the collector is problematic.

Fakes. Unwitting fakes are numerous, particularly "new shades" which are colour changelings brought about by exposure to sunlight, soaking in water contaminated with dyes from adherent paper, contact with oil and dirt from a pocketbook, and so on. Fraudulent operators, in addition, can offer to arrange: removal of hinge marks; repairs of thins on white or coloured papers; replacement of missing margins or perforations; reperforating in true or false gauges; removal of fiscal cancellations; rejoining of severed pairs, strips and blocks; and (a major hazard) regumming. Collectors can only be urged to purchase from reputable sources and to insist upon Expert Committee certification where there is any kind of doubt.

The Catalogue can consider footnotes about fakes where these are specific enough to assist in detection.

PRICES

Prices quoted in this Catalogue are the selling prices of Stanley Gibbons Ltd. at the time when the book went to press. They are for stamps in fine average condition; in issues where condition varies they may ask more for the superb and less for the sub-standard.

All prices are subject to change without prior notice and no guarantee is given to supply all stamps priced, since it is not possible to keep every catalogued item in stock.

Quotation of prices. The prices in the left-hand column are for unused stamps and those in the right-hand column are for used.

Prices are expressed in pounds and pence sterling. One pound comprises 100 pence (£1=100p).

The method of notation is as follows: pence in numerals (e.g. 5 denotes five pence); pounds and pence, up to £100, in numerals (e.g. 4·25 denotes four pounds and twenty-five pence); prices above £100 expressed in whole pounds with the "£" sign shown.

Unused stamps. Prices for stamps issued up to the end of the Second World War (1945) are for lightly hinged examples and more may be asked if they are in unmounted mint condition. Prices for all later unused stamps are for unmounted mint. Where not available in this condition, lightly hinged stamps supplied are often at a lower price.

Used stamps. The used prices are normally for stamps postally used but may be for stamps cancelled-to-order where this practice exists.

A pen-cancellation on early issues can sometimes correctly denote postal use. Instances are individually noted in the Catalogue in explanation of the used price given.

Prices quoted for bisects on cover or on large piece are for those dated during the period officially authorised.

Stamps not sold unused to the public but affixed by postal officials before use (e.g. some parcel post stamps) are priced used only.

Minimum price. The minimum price quoted is five pence. This represents a handling charge rather than a basis for valuing common stamps, for which the 5p price should not be reckoned automatically, since it covers a variation in real scarcity.

Set prices. Set prices are generally for one of each value, excluding shades and varieties, but including major colour changes. Where there are alternative shades, etc., the cheapest is usually included. The number of stamps in the set is always stated for clarity.

Repricing. Collectors will be aware that the market factors of supply and demand directly influence the prices quoted in this Catalogue. Whatever the scarcity of a particular stamp, if there is no one in the market who wishes to buy it it cannot be expected to achieve a high price. Conversely, the same item actively sought by numerous potential buyers may cause the price to rise.

All the prices in this Catalogue are examined during the preparation of each new edition by expert staff of Stanley Gibbons and repriced as necessary. They take many factors into account, including supply and demand, and are in close touch with the international stamp market and the auction world.

GUARANTEE

All stamps are guaranteed genuine originals in the following terms:

If not as described, and returned by the purchaser within six years, we undertake to refund the price paid to us and our liability will thereby be discharged. If any stamp is certified as genuine by the Expert Committee of the Royal Philatelic Society, London, or by B.P.A. Expertising Ltd., the purchaser shall not be entitled to make any claim against us for any error, omission or mistake in such certificate.

The recognised Expert Committees in this country are those of the Royal Philatelic Society, 41 Devonshire Place, London W1N 1PE, and B.P.A. Expertising Ltd., 1 Whitehall Place, London SW1A 2HE. They do not undertake valuations under any circumstances and fees are payable for their services.

France
100 Centimes=1 Franc

PRINTER. From 1849 to 1875 all stamps were typographed at the National Mint, Paris, under the direction of A. Hulot, *except where otherwise stated.*

SECOND REPUBLIC
24 February 1848–2 December 1852

See also Type **8** of France and Types F and G of French Colonies.

1 Ceres

(Die eng J. J. Barre)

1849 (1 Jan)–**52**. *T* **1**. *Yellow gum. Imperf.*
1	10 c. yellowish bistre/*yellowish* (12.9.50)		£500	£140
2	10 c. greenish bistre (1851)		£1100	£250
3	10 c. brownish bistre (1852)	..	£600	£160
4	15 c. green/*bluish green* (29.7.50)	..	£3500	£475
5	15 c. deep green (1852)	..	£5000	£950
6	20 c. black/*yellowish* (*paper coloured on surface only*) (1.1.49)	..	£140	23·00
7	20 c. black/*white* (1.1.49)	..	£200	28·00
8	20 c. grey-black (1.1.49)	..	£950	£325
9	20 c. black/*buff* (*paper coloured through*) (5.50)	..	£700	£175
10	25 c. greenish blue/*yellowish* (*fine impressions*) (1.7.50)	..	£1200	22·00
11	25 c. deep blue (11.50)	..	£1200	20·00
12	25 c. pale blue (8.51)	..	£1100	20·00
13	25 c. dull blue (*coarse impressions*) (3.52)	£1100		20·00
14	40 c. orange (3.2.50)	..	£700	£200
15	40 c. red-orange (1851)	..	£900	£250
16	1 f. orange-vermilion (1.1.49)	..	£16000	£6250
17	1 f. orange-brown (1.49)	..	£13000	£5000
18	1 f. carmine-brown (1.49)	..	£4500	£650
19	1 f. carmine (1.12.49)	..	£2000	£400

The 20 c. in blue was prepared but not issued.

An example of the 40 c. bisected and used as a 20 c. value, is known on a cover sent from Le Cheylard (Ardèche) in March 1855.

The "Vervelle" variety of No. 16, so called after the first owner of the sheet, is from an ungummed sheet of remainders discovered among the papers of the printer. Owing to the absence of gum they are lighter in shade than issued stamps. Price, *unused.* £5000.

Variety. Wider figure "4"

20	40 c. orange	..	£5500	£1400

The variety occurs twice in the bottom row only of each sheet of 300 stamps, and was caused by the re-engraving of two clichés of 20 c. introduced by error into the plate of the 40 c. One of these stamps has the wide "4" on both sides, the other on one side only.

Varieties. Tête-bêche (pair) in all shades
21	10 c. bistre	..	..	£20000	£4000
22	15 c. green	..	..	—	£38000
23	20 c. black	..	..	£2000	£1800
24	25 c. blue	..	..	£35000	£3000
25	1 f. orange	..	..	£80000	£55000
26	1 f. carmine (*shades*)	..	..	£35000	£6500

Of the 15 c. only one pair is known and of the 1 f. orange, only one each of the "Vervelle" and orange-brown shades.

SHADES. The shades listed above and in the following issues (up to 1871–76) represent in most cases "types" or "groups" rather than hard and fast colour varieties. While, therefore the shades merge into one another to some extent (and intermediate shades may be found which it is difficult to place in one or other of the groups), the types or "extremes" are well marked and can be identified with printings covering definite periods.

Prepared for use, but not issued
27	20 c. dull blue (June, 1850)	..	..	£425
	a. Tête-bêche (pair)	..		£12000
28	"25 c." surch in red on 20 c. blue	..		

The majority of the stamps offered as No. 27 are proofs or colour trials.

1862 (1–9 Sept). *Reprints available for postage.*
29	10 c. bistre	..	..	..	£120
30	15 c. green	..	..	..	£140
31	20 c. black/*toned*	..	..	90·00
32	25 c. blue	..	..	95·00
33	40 c. pale orange	..	..	£100
	a. Variety. Wider figure "4"	..	£3500
34	1 f. bright carmine	..	..	£130

Prepared for use, but not issued
35	20 c. blue	..	..	..	90·00
36	25 c. on 20 c. blue	..	..	£4250

The shades are mostly lighter and different in tone from those of originals, and except in the case of the 20 c. black, and the 1 franc are almost identical with those in use for the perforated Empire issue of the same date.

The 1 franc in the orange shades was not reprinted, and no *tête-bêche* pairs have been found in the reprints of the first issue. Only one copy of No. 36 has been reported.

2 Louis Napoléon, President

(Die eng J. J. Barre)

1852–53. *T* **2**. *Imperf.*
37	10 c. bistre-brown (12.52)	..	..	£7000	£250
37a	10 c. yellow-bistre/*yellowish* (1853)	£6500	£220
38	25 c. deep dull blue (9.52)	..	£800	25·00
39	25 c. pale blue (1853)	..	£700	20·00

1862 (1–9 Sept). *Reprints. Available for postage.*
40	10 c. dull bistre	..	..	..	£110
41	25 c. bright blue	..	..	90·00

The letter "B" below the bust is the initial of the engraver, M. Barre.

SECOND EMPIRE
2 December 1852–4 September 1870

IMPERF STAMPS As Types 3/5, 7, 8, 9, 10 and D11 are listed under French Colonies (General issues).

See also Type C of French Colonies

3 Napoléon III
Emperor of the French

Die I   Die II

Die II (which was employed for making up all 1 c. stamps, and all plates of the 10 c. and 20 c. constructed after Dec, 1860, including those of the perforated issue) may be distinguished from Die I mainly by (a) the different form of the lines forming the lock of hair between the eye and the ear and (b) the shading across the upper part of the neck which extends lower down than in Die I. All stamps of other values than the above are from Die I; also in the perforated issue.

Retouched varieties of the 20 c. (imperf and perf)

A. Small and very large corner ornaments

B. White dot too near first "E" of "EMPIRE", "R" of "FRANC" with thick downstroke

C. Corner ornament at left irregular, raised "P" in "EMPIRE", long left stroke to "A" of "FRANC", etc.

Retouch of the 25 c. (No. 73b)

D. Irregularities of lettering, "N" of "FRANC" with serifs, etc. (*Postmark obscures parts of letters in illustration*)

(Die eng J. J. Barre until 1855, then A. Barre)

1853 (3 Nov)–**1861.** *T 3. Imperf.*

42	1 c.	olive-green/*bluish* (1.11.60)		40·00	25·00
42a	1 c.	olive-green/*green*		45·00	28·00
43	1 c.	deep bronze-green/*bluish*		48·00	30·00
44	5 c.	deep green/*bluish* (15.12.54)		£350	45·00
45	5 c.	light green/*greenish* (5.60)		£180	28·00
46	10 c.	yell-ochre/*lem-yell* (Die I)(12.53)		£650	30·00
47	10 c.	brown-ochre/*yellowish* (Die I) (9.54)		£150	3·00
48	10 c.	orange-bistre/*cream* (Die I) (1.56)		£200	8·00
49	10 c.	pale yellow-buff/*cream (indistinct impressions)* (Die I) (3.57)		£150	3·00
50	10 c.	pale yellow-buff/*cream (fine impressions)* (Die I) (6.58)		£170	4·00
50a	10 c.	brownish bistre/*cream (coarse impressions)* (Die I) (9.59)		£140	3·00
50b	10 c.	yellowish bistre/*yellow (fine impressions)* (Die II) (10.60)		£200	15·00
50c	10 c.	brownish bistre/*cream (coarse impressions)* (Die II) ('61)		£180	15·00
51	20 c.	greyish blue/*greyish (fine impressions)* (Die I) (1.7.54)		65·00	40
52	20 c.	pale blue/*green* (Die I) (4.55)		£1750	85·00
53	20 c.	deep blue/*green* (Die I) (6.55)		£2000	90·00
54	20 c.	dark blue/*greyish* (Die I) (6.55)		£100	50
55	20 c.	dark royal blue/*bluish* (Die I) (11.55)		£120	60
56	20 c.	blue-black (Die I) (6.56)		£425	17·00
57	20 c.	bright blue/*bluish* (Die I) (11.57)		80·00	40
58	20 c.	blue/*azure* (Die I) (2.58)		£180	5·00
59	20 c.	dull blue/*bluish (coarse impressions)* (Die I) (3.59)		80·00	40
60	20 c.	dull blue/*green (coarse impressions)* (Die I) (3.61)		£1750	£110
61	20 c.	bright blue/*bluish (fine impressions)* (Die II) (11.60)		£140	2·00
62	20 c.	bright blue/*green (fine impressions)* (Die II) (4.61)		£1750	£125
62a	20 c.	dull blue/*bluish (coarse impressions)* (Die II) (8.61)		£140	2·00
63	25 c.	blue/*greyish* (3.11.53)		£650	£130
64	40 c.	orange/*cream* (8.9.53)		£650	6·00
65	40 c.	red-orange (1857)		£700	10·00
66	40 c.	orange/*straw* (1861)		£850	15·00
67	80 c.	carmine/*yellowish* (12.54)		£650	22·00
68	80 c.	deep carmine/*yellowish* ('55)		£700	24·00
69	80 c.	carmine-red/*yellowish* ('56)		£425	18·00
70	80 c.	rose-red/*yellowish* (7.4.60)		£400	18·00
71	80 c.	pale rose/*white* (4.60)		£375	18·00
71a	80 c.	deep rose/*white* (1860)		£425	22·00
72	1 f.	carmine (17.8.53)		£1250	£900
73	1 f.	deep carmine (1854)		£1400	£1000

Varieties. (a) Inscription of top label and corner ornaments redrawn

73a	20 c.	blue (6 *vars.*, 1862)		From	— 25·00
73b	25 c.	dull blue			£800 £220

(b) *With impression of the 1 f on back*

74	80 c.	rose		

Two examples of above are known.

(c) *Double impression of whole design*

74a	20 c.	pale blue/*green* (Die I)		
74b	40 c.	red-orange		
74c	80 c.	deep rose		

Varieties. Tête-bêche (pairs)

75	80 c.	carmine		£55000	£3500
76	80 c.	carmine-red		£12000	£2500
77	1 f.	carmine		£68000	£30000

The following stamps are known bisected and used for half their face value: 20 c. (Bordeaux February 1856, Villard de Lans January 1858, Vebron (Lozère) June 1861 to January 1862), 40 c. Mostaganem (Algeria May 1860) and 80 c. (Givors (Rhône)).

1862–63. *Reprints. Available for postage.*

78	25 c.	bright blue		90·00
78a	20 c.	carmine-red		£400
79	1 f.	carmine (9.3.63)		£300
		a. Tête-bêche (pair)		£4000

The shade of the 1 f., and the shape of the unshaded portion of the neck, differ slightly from those of the originals. The 20 c. tête-bêche, imperf, is now known to be only an essay.

1861 (Jan). *P 7 (unofficial). Used prices are for stamps on cover or on large pieces.*

80	1 c.	bronze-green/*blue*		—	£1500
81	5 c.	pale green /*greenish*		—	£600
82	10 c.	brownish bistre/*cream* (Die II)		—	£120
83	20 c.	blue (Die I)		—	35·00
83a	20 c.	blue (Die zz)			
83b	20 c.	bright blue/*green* (Die II)		—	£700
84	40 c.	orange		—	£100
85	80 c.	carmine		—	£250

This is an unofficial perforation, applied by Messrs. Susse to stamps perforated by them as stamp agents for the convenience of their clients. In 1875 the perforating machine was sold to a dealer in Paris. These stamps are also known rouletted and some of the values pin-perf, etc. from various towns and cities.

D 4

A. Thin figures. Accent on "à" nearly horizontal.
B. Thick figures. Accent nearly vertical.
C. Accent nearly vertical. Opening of "p" small.
D. Accent nearly horizontal. Opening of "p" large.
(See No. D185.)

(Ptd at the Imperial Printing Office, Paris, later known as the National Printing Office)

1859–63. *POSTAGE DUE. Imperf.*

(a) *Litho. Centre as A (1.1.59)*

D86	D 4	10 c. black		£3000	£100

(b) *Typo. Centre as B and C (1859–63)*

D87	D 4	10 c. black (19.2.59)		9·00	4·75
D88		15 c. black (1.1.63)		9·00	4·75

See also Nos. D212/17.

1862. P 14×13½.

86	**3**	1 c. bronze-green/*blue* (25.8.62)	..	28·00	13·00
87		1 c. olive-green/*greenish*	..	23·00	12·00
88		5 c. deep green/*greenish* (23.8.62)	..	55·00	3·50
89		5 c. yellow-green/*greenish*	..	45·00	3·00
91		10 c. bistre (19.8.62)	.. ..	£225	1·50
92		10 c. bistre brown	.. ..	£250	1·75
93		20 c. blue (13.8.62)	.. ..	50·00	30
94		20 c. deep blue ..	.. ..	70·00	40
95		20 c. blue/*bluish*	.. ..	45·00	30
96		40 c. orange (3.10.62)	.. ..	£300	2·00
97		40 c. orange-yellow	.. ..	£300	2·00
98		80 c. rose (27.9.62)	.. ..	£275	15·00
99		80 c. deep rose	.. ..	£300	20·00

For 5 c. green/*blue*, formerly listed in this set, see No. 134.

Varieties. (a) *Tête-bêche* (*pair*)

100	20 c. blue	.. .. ..	£1100	£450
101	80 c. rose	.. .. ..	£3500	£1300

(b) *Inscription of top label redrawn*

101*a*   20 c. blue   (7   *vars*—1862–63   (6), 1866 (1))   .. .. From   —   22·00

(c) *Imperf.* (*Rothschild*, July 1868)

101*b*	1 c. olive-green/*greenish*	.. ..	£125
101*c*	5 c. yellow-green/*greenish*	.. ..	£125

The above may be distinguished from Nos. 42 and 45 by the coarseness of the impression as well as by the shades.

4   **5**

Two Types of 10 c. and 20 c.

A.   Small stops

B.   Large stops

(Die eng Albert Barre)

1863–70. *Laureated types.* P 14×13½.

102	**4**	1 c. olive-green/(*bluish* (1.5.70)	..	7·00	4·75
103		1 c. olive-green/*green*	..	7·50	5·00
104		2 c. red-brown/*crimson* (1.1.63)	..	17·00	10·00
105		2 c. red-brown/*brownish buff*	..	17·00	11·00
106		2 c. chocolate/*cream*..	..	50·00	25·00
108		4 c. lilac-grey (10.8.63)	..	45·00	20·00
109		4 c. grey (1.67)	..	50·00	22·00
110		4 c. yellowish grey (1869)	..	55·00	25·00
112	**5**	10 c. bistre (A) (15.11.67)	..	80·00	1·75
113		10 c. brownish bistre (A)	..	90·00	1·75
		a. Type B (*shades*)(1.1.69)	..	70·00	1·75
114		20 c. blue (A) (4.4.67)	..	55·00	65
		a. Imperf (*used on cover*) (1869)	†	£3000	
115		20 c. deep blue (A)	..	60·00	60
		a. Type B (*shades*) (2.8.68)	..	45·00	45
116		30 c. brown (4.4.67)	.. ..	£175	7·00
117		30 c. deep brown	.. ..	£275	13·00
119		40 c. orange (8.68)	.. ..	£200	4·75
120		40 c. pale orange	.. ..	£250	5·00
121		80 c. bright rose (2.68)	.. ..	£200	7·50
122		80 c. pale rose..	.. ..	£200	10·00

All values except the 1 c. and 30 c. may be found bisected and used for half their value (1870–71). The 80 c. is found quartered and used as 20 c. These only have a value on letter or piece.

Distinguishing flaw

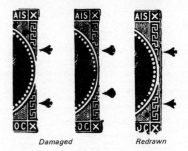

No. 122*a*   *Damaged*   *Redrawn*

Damaged   *Redrawn*

Damaged and redrawn frame-lines, Nos. 122*a*/*c*

See also Types B and D of French Colonies.

Varieties

(a) *Frame-line redrawn at left*

122*a*   **5**   20 c. blue (*one variety*)   .. .. £110   18·00

(b) *Frame-line at right damaged*

122*b*   **5**   20 c. blue (3 *vars*)   .. .. From £135   45·00

(c) *Frame-line at right redrawn*

122*c*   **5**   20 c. blue (3 *vars*)   .. .. From £135   45·00

(d) *Inscription at top retouched*

122*d*   **5**   20 c. blue (1 *var*)   .. .. ..   —   22·00

(e) *Tête-bêche* (*pair*)

123   **4**   4 c. grey (1869) £3500 £2750

(f) *Imperf.* (*Rothschild*, 1869)

124	**4**	2 c. red-brown	.. ..	90·00
125		4 c. grey	.. ..	70·00
126	**5**	10 c. bistre	.. ..	70·00
127		20 c. blue	.. ..	£140
128		30 c. brown	.. ..	70·00
129		40 c. orange	.. ..	£120
130		80 c. rose	.. ..	£230

These imperf varieties were issued by favour to Baron de Rothschild for his private use.

No. 114a is an imperf variety of the normal issue and differs slightly from No. 127 in shade.

J 6   6

(Eng M. Oudiné)

1868 (19 Dec)–**69**. *NEWSPAPER. With or without gum.*

(a) *Imperf.*

J131	J**6**	2 c. mauve			90·00	22·00
J132		2 c. blue			£200	90·00

(b) *P* 12½. (Jan 1869)

J133	J**6**	2 c. mauve			15·00	8·00
J134		2 c. blue			23·00	12·00
J135		2 c. rose			50·00	35·00
J136		5 c. mauve			£350	£250

These stamps represented a fiscal and postal charge combined. The 5 c. were for the Department of the Seine and Oise, and the 2 c. for all the other Departments.

The following stamps of Type J **6** were prepared, but not issued:—

					Imperf	*P* 12½
2 c. rose					£300	†
5 c. lilac					£2000	†
5 c. blue					£1000	£600
5 c. rose					£1000	£600

(Die eng Albert Barre)

1869 (Nov). *P* 14×13½.

131	6	5 f. lilac-grey/*greyish*			£2200	£425
	a.	"5" and "F" omitted			—	£17500
	b.	Double impression of background lines over "5"			£2500	£475
132		5 f. lilac/*pale lilac*			£2200	£425

The value "5" and "F", being overprinted separately, may be found in a different shade to that of the rest of the stamp, and vary considerably in the clearness or otherwise of the printing. This latter circumstance has given rise to the theory that different types exist.

THIRD REPUBLIC

4 September 1870–10 July 1940

10

1871 (Sept). *Prepared for use, but not issued. No.* 112 *surch as above, in blue*

133	5	10 on 10 c. bistre				£525

1871 (Dec). *As 1862 issue. P* 14×13½.

134	3	5 c. green/*blue*			£250	27·00

1870–71. *Issued in Paris during the Siege. From plates of* 1849–52 *issue. P* 14×13½.

135	1	10 c. bistre (11.10.70)			£120	22·00
136		10 c. yellow-bistre (1871)			£100	20·00
137		20 c. pale blue (11.10.70)			55·00	2·50
138		20 c. deep blue (1871)			65·00	3·00
139		20 c. blue/*yellow* (3.71)			90·00	6·00
140		40 c. orange (18.10.70)			£130	1·75
141		40 c. orange-yellow			£150	2·00
142		40 c. pale vermilion			£150	2·00

The 10 c. may be found bisected and used as 5 c. (Sept, '71). For 15 c. and 25 c., see Nos. 203/7.

Varieties. (i) *Wide figure "4"*

142a	1	40 c. orange			£750	60·00

(ii) *Tête-bêche (pairs)*

143	1	10 c. bistre			£1000	£600
144		20 c. blue			£850	£475
144a		20 c. blue/*yellowish*			£1000	£500

BALLOON POSTS. Mail carried by balloon during the siege of Paris, 1870–71, is listed at the end of France.

7 Ceres

8 Ceres

See also Type **9** of France and Types E and F of French Colonies.

The above differ from Type **1** and the corresponding imperf stamps of French Colonies (Types E and F) by the crown of laurel leaves which no longer projects from the top of the head.

I II

III

Three types of the 20 c.

I. The shading under the eye is made up of *finely dotted* lines and the eye appears almost closed.

II. The shading is made up of *continuous* lines, and the eye is open.

III. Similar to II, but inscriptions at top and bottom noticeably *taller*. The position of the head within the circle of pearls varies in Type III, a fact which gave rise to the former distinction between Type III and a so-called Type IV.

The worn impressions are the so-called "Tours" prints, fine impressions but with lines of background worn away, and shading on the cheek much shorter than normally. They are probably due to the cleaning of the stone, and are not a special printing at Tours, as was once believed.

(Drawn by L. Yon, except 20 c., Type I, by M. M. Dambourgez. Litho. M. Augé-Delile, at Bordeaux.)

1870 (13 Nov)–**71**. *Litho at Bordeaux. Imperf.*

145	7	1 c. olive-green/*greenish* (5.12.70)		30·00	30·00
146		1 c. deep olive-green/*greenish* (12.70)		28·00	28·00
147		1 c. bronze-green (1871)			32·00	32·00
148		1 c. deep olive-grn (*worn impression*)		32·00	32·00
149		2 c. deep chocolate (*fine impressions*) (A) (14.12.70)		£750	£550
149a		2 c. light choc. (*fine impressions*) (A)		£500	£400
150		2 c. chestnut/*cream* (*fine impressions*) (A) (12.70)		£600	£850
151		2 c. reddish brown/*yellowish* (*worn impressions on smooth paper*) (B)		£400	£350
152		2 c. red-brown (*coarse impressions*) (B) (1.71)		75·00	70·00
153		2 c. Venetian red (*coarse impressions*) (B) (2.71)		£750	£550
154		4 c. grey (13.12.70)			£100	£100
155		4 c. lilac-grey			£160	£130
156		4 c. yellowish grey			£125	£120
157	8	5 c. green (30.12.70)		95·00	55·00
158		5 c. deep green			£120	85·00
159		5 c. bluish green			£250	£110
160		10 c. bistre (*fine impressions*) (13.11.70)	£300	32·00
161		10 c. stone-brown (*fine impressions*)	£325	30·00
162		10 c. yellowish bistre			£300	30·00
163		10 c. yellow-ochre (*indistinct impressions*) (1.71)		£325	30·00
163a		10 c. pale orange-buff (*indistinct impressions*) (1.71)		£350	35·00
163b		10 c. red-bistre (*coarse impressions*)	£500	£170
164		20 c. blue (I) (15.11.70)		£3000	£250
165		20 c. pale blue (I)			£3250	£275
166		20 c. deep violet-blue (I)		£3750	£325
167		20 c. blue (II)(20.11.70)		£325	20·00
168		20 c. pale blue (II)			£325	20·00
169		20 c. deep blue (II)			£375	40·00
170		20 c. ultramarine (II)		£6000	£1250
171		20 c. blue (III) (13.12.70)		£325	8·00
172		20 c. pale blue (III)			£325	8·00
173		20 c. deep blue (III)			£375	15·00
174		20 c. slate-blue (III)			£475	35·00
174a		20 c. lilac-blue (III)			—	£250
175		30 c. brown (30.12.70)		£140	£110
176		30 c. deep brown			£600	£300
177		40 c. orange (9.12.70)		£140	50·00
178		40 c. orange-vermilion		£300	£100

179	**8**	40 c. lemon-yellow/*yellow*	..	..	£1500	£600
180		40 c. deep scarlet-vermilion	..	..	£2000	£850
181		40 c. light scarlet-vermilion	..	..	£750	£400
182		80 c. bright rose (10.12.70)	..	..	£200	£110
183		80 c. rose-carmine	..	..	£325	£150
184		80 c. carmine-red	..	..	£325	£150

Bordeaux was the seat of the French Government during the siege of Paris.

The 1 c., 2 c., 10 c. and 20 c. (three types) of above issue occur in two or more different settings, which may be distinguished by slight differences in the details of the design, as well as, in most cases, by the shades. The differences are due to retouching on the small key-stones from which the transfers were made to the printing stones.

In the case of the 2c., Nos. 149 and 150 (A) are distinguished from Nos. 151 to 153 (B) by the fact that in (B) the two pearls in the centre of the left-hand side of the inner circle, opposite the nose, are jointed, while in (A) they are not.

The 10 c. and 40 c. may be found bisected for use as 5 c. and 20 c. respectively, and the 80 c. quartered and used as 20 c. (Sept '71).

All values are known rouletted and pin-perforated.

1870 (15 Nov). *POSTAGE DUE. Litho at Bordeaux. Imperf. Centre as D.*

D185	D **4**	15 c. black	..	..	50·00	70·00

Following increases in postage rates during September 1871 many post offices surcharged the 15 c. postage due to make a 25 c. value. These provisional postage dues were produced by either manuscript or type surcharge and are rare on cover or piece.

As T 1 (*actual size*)

A.

B.

9 Ceres

See also Types E, F and G of French Colonies for imperf stamps.

Three states of 25 c.

II   III

State I. All corners normal.

State II. Spot of colour at left of upper right ornament.

State III. Three spots of colour: in upper left branch of upper left ornament and in both upper branches in upper right ornament.

(Die eng Albert Barre. Typo in Paris)

1871–76. *Tinted paper. P 14×13½.*

185	**9**	1 c. olive-green/*bluish* (11.72)	..	10·00	4·00
186		1 c. bronze-green/*greenish*	..	13·00	4·50
187		2 c. red-brown/*cream* (5.72)	..	20·00	4·00
188		2 c. deep red-brown/*cream* ('73)	..	30·00	6·50
189		4 c. grey (6.72)	..	75·00	12·00
190		4 c. yellowish grey	..	80·00	14·00
191		5 c. green/*blue* (10.6.72)	..	35·00	2·25
192		5 c. pale green/*greenish* (1873)	..	35·00	2·25
193		5 c. deep green/*greenish* (1876)	..	35·00	2·75

As 1849–52 issue

(a) Type A. *Thick figures of value*

194	**1**	10 c. bistre/*rose* (3.75)	..	75·00	3·00
195		15 c. yellow-bistre (6.73)	..	75·00	1·25
196		30 c. brown (9.72)	..	£110	1·75
197		30 c. pale brown	..	£120	2·50
198		30 c. grey-brown	..	£110	1·75
199		80 c. bright carmine (12.9.72)	..	£150	4·75
200		80 c. dull carmine	..	£150	5·50

Error on sheet of 10 c.

201	**1**	15 c. bistre/*rose* (3.75)	..	..	£1000	£1100
		a. In pair with normal	..	..	£1500	£1700

(b) Type B. *Thin figures of value*

202	**1**	10 c. bistre/*rose* (1.73)	..	..	60·00	3·00
203		15 c. bistre (1.9.71)	..	..	60·00	1·75
204		15 c. yellow-bistre (1873)	..	..	65·00	1·75
205		15 c. orange-bistre (1874)	..	..	60·00	1·75
206		25 c. pale blue (I) (5.9.71)	..	..	30·00	35
207		25 c. deep blue (I) (1872)	..	..	35·00	40
		a. Type II (*shades*) (1873)	..	..	£300	10·00
		b. Type III (*shades*)(1874)	..	..	25·00	40
		c. Type II and Type III *se-tenant* (pair)	..	..	£850	£500

Tête-bêche (*pairs*)

208	**1**	10 c. bistre/*rose*	..	..	£1000	£600
209		15 c. bistre	..	..	£8250	£2000
210		25 c. blue (I)	..	..	£1400	£900

With Sheet Watermark "LACROIX FRERES"

210a	**1**	5 c. green	..	..		

New plates were made for the 1 c. to 5 c. (Type **9**), but the other values were printed from the plates of the 1849–52 issue.

The 10 c. may be found bisected and used as 5 c. (Sept '71).

At least two of the plates of the 25 c. were extensively damaged and many interesting flaws and retouches may be found. Typical varieties are illustrated and listed below.

Retouches, etc.

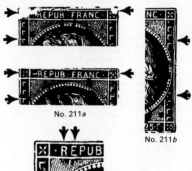

No. 211a

No. 211b

No. 211c

Thick tall narrow "R" wide "E", etc.

(a) *Damaged frame and corners at top*

211	**1**	25 c. blue	..	..	—	20·00

(b) *As last, redrawn* (1872)

211a	**1**	25 c. blue	..	..	—	40·00

(c) *Frame at right redrawn*

211b	**1**	25 c. blue	..	..	—	15·00

(d) *"REP" redrawn*

211c	**1**	25 c. blue	..	..	—	15·00

1871 (1 Sept)–**78.** *POSTAGE DUE. Typo in Paris. Imperf.*

D212	D4	25 c. black	..	..	35·00	14·00
D213		30 c. black (5.78)	..	..	55·00	40·00
D214		40 c. blue	..	..	£100	£130
D215		40 c. ultramarine	..	..	£1700	£2000
D216		60 c. ochre	..	..	£175	£400
D217		60 c. blue (1.5.78)	..	..	22·00	40·00

The 20 c. in *black* was prepared for use but not issued. Many of the above exist perforated unofficially.

PRINTERS. From 1876 till 1880 the stamps were typographed by the Bank of France. In 1880 the Government purchased all the plant and machinery, and has since conducted the manufacture. All issues to No. 462 were typographed.

IMPERF STAMPS. Many stamps of France, including modern issues, exist imperf in their original colours but were not valid for postage. Imperf stamps in other colours are colour trials.

(a)

(b)

10 Peace and Commerce
See also Type H of French Colonies for imperf stamps.
(Des J. A. Sage. Die eng E. Mouchon)

1876 (27 Mar)—**81**. *Tinted paper. P* 14×13½. *Two types.*

*(a) Letter "N" of "INV" under "B" of "*REPUBLIQUE*"*

212	**10**	1 c. green (8.11.76)	..	40·00	22·00
213		2 c. green (14.6.76)	.. ..	£375	£110
214		4 c. green (30.11.76)	..	38·00	17·00
215		5 c. green (27.3.76)	.. ..	£170	17·00
216		10 c. green (2.8.76)	..	£200	9·50
217		15 c. pale grey-lilac (6.76)	..	£200	7·00
218		15 c. grey-lilac	.. ..	£200	7·00
219		20 c. brown/*pale yellow* (10.76)	..	£150	6·50
220		25 c. ultramarine (13.6.76)	.. ..	£1800	35·00
		a. Type I and Type II *se-tenant* (pair)	£7500	£3250
221		30 c. cinnamon (7.76)	.. ..	£100	3·25
222		40 c. red/*pale yellow* (5.4.78)	..	£100	13·00
223		75 c. carmine (17.10.76)	.. ..	£200	5·00
224		1 f. olive-green(15.9.76)	..	£160	4·00

The 20 c. *blue* is a stamp prepared for use in Dec. 1876, but never issued. It was reprinted in 1887 in *deep blue* (imperf). It is found with a forged perforation. This reprint is always variety (*b*).

*(b) Letter "N" of "INV" under "U" of "*REPUBLIQUE*"*

225	**10**	2 c. green (14.9.76)..	.. ..	28·00	7·50
226		5 c. deep green (4.12.76)	.. ..	7·50	15
227		5 c. deep yellow-green	..	9·00	30
228		5 c. green	.. ..	7·50	12
229		5 c. blue-green	.. ..	7·50	12
230		5 c. pale green	..	7·50	12
231		10 c. green (6.12.76)	.. ..	£350	£110
232		15 c. grey-lilac (14.10.76)	..	£140	55
233		15 c. slate-lilac	.. ..	£140	55
234		25 c. ultramarine (20.7.76)	..	£110	15
235		25 c. blue	.. ..	£110	25
236		30 c. cinnamon (20.1.81)	..	14·00	25
237		30 c. yellow-brown (2.81)	..	14·00	25
238		75 c. rose (3.77)	.. ..	£475	38·00
239		1 f. pale yellow-green (9.77)	..	20·00	1·90
240		1 f. olive-green	.. ..	20·00	1·90
241		1 f. deep olive-green	..	22·00	2·25
242		1 f. grey-green	.. ..	20·00	2·25

The two varieties of type differ in the shapes of the numerals, as well as in the point above described.

1877–90. *Type (b) only. P* 14 × 13½.

243	**10**	1 c. black/*grey-blue* (16.6.77)	..	95	30
244		1 c. black/*grey*	..	80	25
245		1 c. black/*azure*	..	80	20
246		1 c. black/*Prussian blue* (10.80)	..	£2250	£1300
247		2 c. deep red-brown/*buff* (2.5.77)	..	1·25	65
248		2 c. pale red-brown/*buff*	..	1·25	40
249		3 c. ochre/*yellow* (1.6.78)	..	55·00	19·00
250		3 c. drab (6.80)	.. ..	1·10	55
251		3 c. grey (6.80)	.. ..	80	45
252		4 c. purple-brown/*grey* (9.77)	..	1·10	65
253		4 c. dull purple-brown/*grey*	..	1·25	65
254		4 c. plum/*grey*	.. ..	1·50	75
255		10 c. black/*pale lilac* (1.77)	..	10·00	30
256		10 c. black/*lilac*	..	11·00	40
257		15 c. blue/*toned* (5.78)	..	6·50	12
258		15 c. blue/*bluish*	..	6·50	12
259		15 c. deep blue/*bluish*	..	£100	1·25
260		20 c. red/*yellow-green* (16.11.84)	..	11·00	1·00
261		20 c. red/*deep green* (11.84)	..	13·00	1·10
262		25 c. black/*deep red* (20.10.78)	..	£225	9·50
263		25 c. bistre/*yellow*	..	80·00	1·25
264		25 c. yellow/*saffron*	..	90·00	2·00
265		25 c. ochre/*pale yellow*	..	90·00	2·00
266		25 c. black/*rose* (4.86)	..	13·00	25
267		25 c. black/*pale rose*	..	11·00	25ᵣ
268		35 c. deep brown/*yellow* (1.6.78)	..	£130	13·00
269		40 c. pale red/*yellow* (2.8.81)	..	17·00	55
270		40 c. red/*yellow*	..	18·00	70
271		50 c. pale rose (1.5.90)	..	40·00	40

272	**10**	50 c. deep rose (3.90)	..	38·00	40
273		50 c. carmine	..	38·00	40
274		75 c. brown/*pale orange* (15.10.90)..	55·00	13·00
275		75 c. brown/*deep orange*	..	55·00	14·00
276		75 c. dull brown/*deep orange*	..	55·00	14·00
277		5 f. lilac/*pale lilac* (6.77)	..	£150	32·00
278		5 f. mauve/*pale lilac*	..	£170	38·00

The 15 c. in *ochre* is a proof.
For the 10 c. and 50 c. in Type (*a*), see Nos. 284/6.

D 11	**11** "Blanc" type	**12** "Mouchon" type
(Des Georges Duval)	(Des Joseph Blanc. Eng E. Thomas)	(Des and eng Eugène Mouchon)

1881 (Aug)—**92**.. *POSTAGE DUE. P* 14×13½.

D279	D **11**	1 c. black (1.10.82)	..	15	15
D280		2 c. black (1.10.82)	.. ..	4·00	4·50
D281		3 c. black (1.10.82)	.. ..	4·50	4·75
D282		4 c. black (1.10.82)	.. ..	6·50	5·50
D283		5 c. black (1.10.82)	.. ..	15·00	4·00
D284		10 c. black (1.10.82)	.. ..	14·00	40
D285		15 c. black (1.10.82)	.. ..	9·00	2·25
D286		20 c. black (1.10.82)	..	40·00	25·00
D287		30 c. black	.. ..	28·00	7·00
D288		40 c. black (1.10.82)	..	17·00	9·50
D289		50 c. black (4.92)	.. ..	90·00	38·00
D290		60 c. black (5.84)	.. ..	90·00	10·00
D291		1 f. black (1.10.82)	..	£130	75·00
D292		1 f. reddish brown (3.84)	..	70·00	22·00
D293		2 f. black (1.10.82)	..	£225	£150
D294		2 f. reddish brown (5.84)	..	50·00	38·00
D295		5 f. black (1.10.82)	..	£450	£350
D296		5 f. reddish brown (3.84)	..	80·00	70·00

1892 (1 April). *Type (b). Quadrille paper. P* 14×13½.

279	**10**	15 c. pale blue	..	3·50	12
280		15 c. deep blue	.. ..	3·75	30
281		15 c. ultramarine	.. ..	3·75	30

1893–1941. *POSTAGE DUE. Colours changed and new values. P* 14 × 13½. *(a) Ordinary paper.*

D297	D**11**	5 c. pale blue (22.1.94)	..	10	5
D298		10 c. pale brown (24.12.93)	..	10	5
D299		15 c. pale green (2.94)	..	2·50	25
D300		20 c. olive-green (6.06)	..	65	10
D301		25 c. rosine (30.9.23)	..	90	55
D302		30 c. carmine (2.94)	..	10	5
D303		30 c. vermilion (7.95)	..	£160	16·00
D304		40 c. rosine (31.12.25)	..	2·00	70
D305		45 c. pale green (15.7.24)	..	90	45
D306		50 c. dull claret (4.95)	..	10	5
		a. *Deep purple*	..	10	5
D307		60 c. green (31.12.25)	..	15	8
D308		1 f. rose/*straw* (6.96)	..	£160	95·00
D309		1 f. claret/*straw* (12.20)	..	40	5
D310		1 f. claret/*white* (1935)	..	25	5
D311		2 f. vermilion (7.10)	..	55·00	15·00
D312		2 f. bright violet (8.2.26)	..	15	10
D313		3 f. magenta (12.26)	..	15	10
D314		5 f. red-orange (1941)	..	45	40

(b) Granite ("G.C.") paper (1917)

D315	D11	5 c. pale blue	..	50	15
D316		10 c. pale brown	..	25	15
D317		15 c. pale green	..	1·40	25
D318		20 c. olive-green	..	1·00	15
D319		30 c. pale carmine	..	20	15
D320		50 c. dull claret	..	15	15

1898–1900. *Plain paper. P* 14 × 13½.

282	**10**	5 c. bright yellow-green (a)(8.12.98)	2·75	25
283		5 c. bright yellow-green (b)(8.12.98)	4·50	30
284		10 c. black/*lilac* (a) (2.98)	..	5·00	90
285		50 c. carmine (a) (7.00)	..	38·00	13·00
286		50 c. carmine-rose (a)	..	38·00	13·00
287		2 f. brown/*pale blue* (a)(11.4.00) ..	32·00	14·00

1900 (4 Dec)–**24.** *P* 14×13½.

288	**11**	1 c. grey	.. ..	12	5
288*a*		1 c. grey-black (1921)	.. ..	12	5
289		2 c. claret ..	.. ..	12	5
290		3 c. orange-red ..	.. ..	20	5
291		3 c. lake-red (1906)	.. ..	4·50	1·25
292		4 c. brown ..	.. ..	1·10	20
292*a*		4 c. yellow-brown (1924)	.. ..	95	20
293		5 c. yellow-green ..	.. ..	30	5
294		5 c. blue-green (10.02)	.. ..	60	5
		a. Blue-green/yellow			
295		5 c. deep green (1924)	.. ..	25	5

Some values are known *imperf.*

(i) *Figures of value inserted at a second printing.* (Dec 1900)

296	**12**	10 c. carmine	.. ..	14·00	4·50
297		20 c. purple-brown ..	.. ..	35·00	3·50
298		25 c. blue ..	.. ..	65·00	3·25
299		30 c. mauve ..	.. ..	40·00	2·25

Some stamps are known without figures in corner, and all exist with misplaced figures.

(ii) *The entire stamp printed at one time*

300	**12**	10 c. carmine (1901)	.. ..	13·00	25
301		15 c. orange (12.00)	.. ..	3·50	10
302		25 c. blue (1901) ..	.. ..	55·00	45

13 "Olivier Merson" **(M 14)** **14** "Mouchon"
type "F.M."="Franchise type redrawn
 Militaire"

(Des Luc-Olivier Merson. Eng M. Thévenin)

1900 (4 Dec)–**1906.** *P* 14×13½.

303	**13**	40 c. red and pale blue	..	6·00	15
		a. Coloured background, omitted		£130	60·00
304		45 c. deep green and blue ('06)	..	6·50	40
305		50 c. cinnamon and lavender	..	50·00	35
		a. Coloured background omitted ..		£140	70·00
306		1 f. lake and yellow-green ..	..	12·00	10
		a. Coloured background omitted		£140	
306*b*		1 f. deep lake and yellow-green	..	12·00	10
307		2 f. deep lilac and buff ..		£375	22·00
308		5 f. deep blue and buff ..	..	28·00	1·25

1901–04. *MILITARY FRANK. Nos.* 301, 310 *and* 316 *optd with Type* M **14.**

M309	**12**	15 c. orange (6.01)	..	25·00	3·25
		a. Opt inverted ..	..	55·00	28·00
M310	**14**	15 c. pale red (4.03)	..	16·00	1·90
M311	**15**	15 c. slate-green (7.04)	..	16·00	2·25
		a. No stop after "M"	..	28·00	11·00

1902. *P* 14×13½.

309	**14**	10 c. carmine (July, '02)	..	11·00	12
310		15 c. pale red (Dec. '02)	..	3·25	10
311		20 c. purple-brown (May, '02)	..	42·00	5·50
312		25 c. blue (Aug. '02)	..	48·00	50
313		30 c. mauve (April, '02)	..	£120	4·50

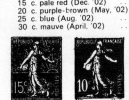

15 Sower **16** Sower **18** Sower,
 with ground without ground

(T **15**/**18.** Des O. Roty. Eng Eugène Mouchon)

1903. *P* 14×13½.

314	**15**	10 c. rose-carmine (6 May)	..	3·50	5
		a. Imperf (pair) ..	..	80·00	
315		10 c. deep carmine	..	4·00	10
316		15 c. slate-green (1 April)	..	95	5
317		20 c. purple-brown (29 June)	..	32·00	45
318		20 c. pale claret	..	35·00	50
319		25 c. blue (28 April)	..	40·00	50
320		25 c. pale blue	..	38·00	40

321	**15**	30 c. pale lilac (29 June)	..	90·00	2·00
		a. Imperf (pair) ..	..	£300	
322		30 c. indigo-lilac	..	£100	2·40

1906 (13 April). *P* 14×13½.

325	**16**	10 c. red	..	1·75	30
326		10 c. deep red	..	2·00	30

1906 (July). *MILITARY FRANK. No.* 314 *optd with Type* M **14.**

M327	**15**	10 c. rose-carmine ..	..	10·00	2·75
		a. No stop after "M" ..	..	28·00	13·00

A ... B

C ... D

In Types C and D the figures of value are thicker, as also is the wording; the word "POSTES" is particularly noticeable in this respect. In the 10 c. the oblique stroke of the figure "1" is much longer in Type C.

1906. *Thin figures as A and B. P* 14×13½.

328	**18**	10 c. red (28 July) ..	..	3·75	15
329		35 c. violet (8 Nov)	..	70·00	1·60

1907–13. *Thick figures as C and D. P* 14×13½.

331	**18**	5 c. deep green (5.3.07)	..	40	5
332		5 c. green	..	40	5
		a. Imperf (pair) ..	..	10·00	
333		10 c. scarlet (11.07)	..	48·00	9·50
334		10 c. deep red (12.07)	..	50	5
		a. Imperf (pair) ..	..	10·00	
335		10 c. orange-red (1909)	..	35	5
336		10 c. brick-red (1910)	..	1·60	35
337		20 c. brown-lake (12.07)	..	1·00	8
338		20 c. chocolate (12.07)	..	1·00	8
		a. Imperf (pair) ..	..	19·00	
339		25 c. deep blue (6.07)	..	90	25
340		25 c. indigo (6.07) ..	..	6·50	75
341		25 c. blue (6.07) ..	..	45	5
		a. Imperf (pair) ..	..	18·00	
342		25 c. pale blue (7.10)	..	45	5
343		30 c. orange (5.07) ..	..	5·50	30
344		30 c. yellow-orange (1909)	..	6·50	20
		a. Imperf (pair) ..	..	64·00	
345		35 c. violet (11.07) ..	..	5·00	12
		a. Imperf (pair) ..	..	64·00	
346		35 c. deep violet (1909)	..	5·00	25
347		35 c. lilac (1913) ..	..	5·00	45

1907 (Aug). *MILITARY FRANK. No.* 333 *optd with Type* M **14.**

M348	**18**	10 c. scarlet	..	25	10
		a. Opt inverted ..	..	28·00	22·00

D **19** **(19)** **20**

Stamps inscribed "RECOUVREMENTS" were employed to recover postage due from the sender in cases where the recipient refused delivery.

1908 (1 Oct)–**25.** *POSTAGE DUE. P* 14×13½.

D348	**D19**	1 c. olive	..	20	5
D349		10 c. violet	..	20	5
D350		20 c. bistre (12.19)	..	1·90	10
D351		30 c. bistre (11.09)	..	80	10
D352		50 c. red (11.09)	..	70·00	15·00
D353		60 c. red (30.9.25)	..	40	20

1914 (11 Aug). *Red Cross Fund. Surch with T* **19.**

351	**18**	10 c.+5 c. brick-red (C.) ..	..	1·75	1·25
		a. Surch inverted ..			

1914 (10 Sept). *Red Cross Fund. P* 14 × 13½.
352	**20**	10 c.+5 c. brick-red	.. ..	17·00	1·75
353		10 c.+5 c. scarlet	..	14·00	1·40

1916–19. *Types as before, but on greyish granite paper* ("G.C. *papier de Grande Consommation"*). *P* 14 × 13½.
353*a*	**11**	1 c. grey	.. ..	12	5
354		1 c. slate (1919)		12	5
355		2 c. claret (1917) ..	..	40	10
356		3 c. orange (1917)	..	20	5
357	**18**	5 c. blue-green	..	40	10
358		10 c. red	..	1·00	75
359	**15**	15 c. olive-green	..	80	5
360		15 c. slate-green (1917)	..	1·00	20
361		15 c. deep slate-green (1919)	..	2·00	40
362	**18**	20 c. chocolate (1917)	..	1·10	35
363		25 c. pale blue (1917)	..	1·10	30
364		25 c. blue ..	..	1·10	30
365		30 c. orange (1918)	..	9·00	75
365*a*		35 c. violet (1918) ..	..	7·50	80
366	**13**	40 c. red and pale blue	..	8·00	40
367		45 c. deep green and blue ..	..	7·50	95
368		50 c. cinnamon and lavender	..	65·00	75
369		1 f. lake and yellow	..	16·00	35

"GC PAPER". During the war as a measure of economy cheaper paper was used which is known as "GC paper" because the upper and lower margins of sheets bore these initials which signify "Grande Consommation" because it was intended to use this for values which called for large printings. However it was used for nearly all values in the period 1916 to 1920.

21 War Widow   **24** Front line Trench

22 Orphans   **25** Lion of Belfort

23 Woman replaces Man   **26** Spirit of War

(T **22** des by Surand, eng by Jarraud; others incl T **27** des by L. Dumoulin, eng by L. Ruffe)

1917 (Aug)–**19.** *War Orphans' Fund. P* 14 × 13½.
370	**21**	2 c.+3 c. brown-lake	..	1·25	1·25
371	**22**	5 c.+5 c. green (3.19)	..	4·50	2·50
372	**23**	15 c.+10 c. grey-green	..	10·00	9·00
373		25 c.+15 c. pale blue	..	45·00	25·00
374	**24**	35 c.+25 c. violet and slate	..	75·00	55·00
375	**25**	50 c.+50 c. brown	..	95·00	80·00
376	**26**	1 f.+1 f. carmine	..	£180	£140
377		5 f.+5 f. blue and black	..	£850	£500
370/377		*Set of 8*	..	£1200	£750

Nos. 375/7 should not be confused with Nos. 451/3 which are similar in appearance.

20 ^{c.}

(D **27**)   **27** Sinking Hospital Ship and Bombed Hospital

$$\frac{1}{2}$$

centime

(28)

1917 (23 Nov). *POSTAGE DUE. Surch as Type* D **27.**
D378	D **19**	20 c. on 30 c. bistre	..	2·50	75
D379		40 c. on 50 c. red	..	2·50	50

1918 (8 Aug). *Red Cross Fund. Cross in red. P* 14×13½.
378	**27**	15 c.+5 c. red and grey-green	..	50·00	17·00

1919 (Sept)–**22.** *T* **11** *surch with T* **28,** *in red.*
379		½ c. on 1 c. slate (G.C. *paper*)	..	8	8
379*a*		½ c. on 1 c. grey-black (*white paper*) ('22)		8	8

I.   II.   III. (*See No. 504*)

I. Short top bar to "3" (sheets of 300).
II. Top bar longer (sheets of 100).
III. Figure "0" narrower and more pointed, etc.

1920–26. *Colours changed and new values. P* 14 × 13½.
380	**18**	5 c. orange (15.7.21)	..	75	5
381		10 c. green, Type C (31.8.21) .	..	20	5
381*a*		10 c. green, Type A (1926) ..	..	13·00	11·00
382		30 c. scarlet (1.22)	..	3·50	70
382*a*		30 c. cerise (I) (1.25)	..	25	5
382*b*		30 c. cerise (II) (1925)	..	30	8
383	**15**	50 c. dark blue (1921)	..	9·50	12
384	**13**	60 c. violet and blue(1.6.20).	..	30	12
385	**15**	60 c. violet (17.6.24)	..	1·50	35
385*a*		65 c. carmine (2.7.24)	..	70	30
386		85 c. vermilion (7.24)	..	7·00	20
387	**13**	2 f. orange and blue-green (4.6.20) .	..	10·00	12
380/387		*Set of 12*	..	42·00	13·00

For 50 c. greenish blue in T **15**, see No. 592.

+5 ^{c.}
═

(29)

10 ^{c.}

30 Pasteur

CONGRES PHILATELIQUE
DE
BORDEAUX
1923

(30*a*)

1922 (1 Sept). *War Orphans' Fund. Nos.* 370/7 *surch as* T **29.**
388	**21**	+1 c. on 2 c.+3 c.		5	5
389	**22**	+2½ c. on 5 c.+5 c.		15	12
390	**23**	+5 c. on 15 c.+10 c.		25	20
391		+5 c. on 25 c.+15 c.		50	40
392	**24**	+5 c. on 35 c.+25 c.		1·60	80
393	**25**	+10 c. on 50 c.+50 c.		3·75	2·25
394	**26**	+25 c. on 1 f.+1 f. ..		6·50	4·50
395		+1 f. on 5 f.+5 f. ..		50·00	35·00
388/395		*Set of 8*	..	55·00	40·00

The object of the surcharges was to reduce the premium.

(Die eng Prud'homme)

1923 (25 May)–**26.** *P* 14 × 13½.
396	**30**	10 c. green	..	15	5
396*a*		15 c. green (19.9.24)	..	25	5
396*b*		20 c. green (22.1.26)	..	65	10
397		30 c. red	..	15	10
397*a*		30 c. green (11.26)	..	15	5
398		45 c. red (8.24)	..	65	40
399		50 c. blue	..	95	15
400		75 c. blue (7.24)	..	90	15
400*a*		90 c. red (11.26)	..	3·75	95
400*b*		1 f. blue (11.25)	..	7·50	5
400*c*		1 f. 25, blue (4.26)	..	7·50	2·00
400*d*		1 f. 50, blue (8.26)	..	2·50	5
396/400*d*		*Set of 12*	..	23·00	3·75

1923 (15 June). *Bordeaux Philatelic Congress. Optd with* T **30***a*.
400*e*	**13**	1 f. lake and yellow-green (B.)	..	£170	£170

31 Stadium and Arc de Triomphe   **35** Ronsard

(Des E. Becker. Eng G. Daussy (25 c., 30 c.), C. Parison (10 c., 50 c.))

1924. *Olympic Games. Designs inscr as in T* **31.** *P* 14 × 13½ (10 c., 25 c.) *or* 13½ × 14 (30 c., 50 c.).

401	10 c. green and yellow-green (1.4)	..	50	20
402	25 c. deep and dull carmine (1.4)	..	65	5
403	30 c. red and black (25.5)	..	5·00	3·50
404	50 c. ultramarine and blue (25.5)	..	6·00	60
401/404	*Set of 4*	.. ..	11·00	4·00

Designs: *Horiz*—25 c. Notre Dame and Pont Neuf. *Vert*—30 c. Milan de Crotone (statue), 50 c. The victor.

(Des V. Dautel. Eng A. Delzers)

1924 (6 Oct). *400th Birth Anniv of Ronsard. P* 14 × 13½.

405	**35**	75 c. blue/*bluish*	35	25

36

(Des E. Becker. Eng A. Mignon (Nos. 408, 410). Des L. Ruet. Eng H. Rapin (others))

1924–25. *International Exhibition of Modern Decorative Arts. Designs inscr as in T* **36.** *P* 13½ × 14, *or* 14 × 13½.

406	**36**	10 c. yellow and deep green (6.25) ..	25	15
407	–	15 c. green and deep green (30.4.25)	25	15
408	–	25 c. brown-lake and purple (8.12.24)	30	10
409	–	25 c. mauve and blue (11.5.25)	35	15
410	–	75 c. ultramarine & slate-bl (8.12.24)	1·10	45
411	**36**	75 c. blue and deep blue (6.25)	5·00	1·90
406/411		*Set of 6*	6·50	2·50

Designs: *Vert*—15 c. Stylised vase. *Horiz*—Nos. 408, 410, Potter and vase; No. 409, Castle and steps.

1925 (2 May). *Paris International Philatelic Exhibition. P* 14 × 13½.

412	**10**	5 f. carmine (*single*)	65·00	45·00
MS412*a*	140×220 mm No. 412 in block of four	£375	£325

The above were only sold against production of an entrance ticket costing 5 f.

I.   II.   I.   II.

I.   II.

Two types of 15 c., 20 c. and 75 c.:—
15 c. I. Top serif of "5" broad and ball low. II. Serif small and ball high.
20 c. I. Ball of "2" low and downstroke curved. II. Ball high and downstroke straight. Point close to frame-line.
75 c. I. One white line between points of "c" of value. II. Two white lines; "7" more rounded.

1925–31. *New colours and values. P* 14 × 13½.

413	**11**	7½ c. magenta (1926)*	..	20	10
413*a*		10 c. lilac (6.29)	..	1·90	8
414	**18**	15 c. purple-brown (I) (1.26)	..	8	5
414*a*		15 c. purple-brown (II) (1935)		15	5
415		20 c. bright magenta (I) (20.7.26) ..		8	5
415*a*		20 c. bright magenta (II) (1935)		12	5
415*b*		25 c. ochre-brown (6.27)		5	5
416		30 c. blue (7.25)	..	65	5
417		40 c. olive (8.25)	..	30	5
418		40 c. vermilion (25.5.26)	..	70	8
418*a*		40 c. violet (7.27)	..	1·10	8
418*b*		40 c. ultramarine (12.28)	..	65	5
419	**15**	45 c. violet (11.26)	..	1·75	25
420		50 c. sage-green (11.26)	..	1·60	10
421		50 c. vermilion (1.26)	..	8	5
422		65 c. sage-green (1.27)	..	1·90	40
423		75 c. bright magenta (I) (11.26)	..	1·10	15
423*a*		75 c. bright magenta (II)	..	£160	65·00
424		80 c. vermilion (27.7.25)	..	28·00	3·00
425		1 f. blue (8.26)	..	2·25	5
426	**18**	1 f. 05, vermilion (27.7.25)	..	3·00	1·00
427		1 f. 10, cerise (3.27)	..	4·75	45
428		1 f. 40, cerise (8.26)	..	7·00	4·50
428*a*		2 f. deep blue-green (1.1.31)	..	4·00	20
429	**13**	3 f. deep violet and blue (27.7.25)	..	11·00	2·25
430		3 f. mauve and carmine (20.8.27)		22·00	45
431		10 f. sage-green and red (8.26)	..	50·00	5·00
432		20 f. magenta and green (8.26)	..	£100	9·00

$$\overline{\overline{1}}^{F.} = 25^{c} = 55^{c} \equiv 1^{F}10$$

(D **40**)   (40)   (41)   (42)

1926. *POSTAGE DUE. Surch as Type* D **40.**

D433	D **19**	50 c. on 10 c. violet (16.8.26)	..	1·00	45
D434		60 c. on 1 c. olive (10.26)	..	1·50	75
D435		1 f. on 60 c. red (16.8.26)	..	4·75	1·75
D436		2 f. on 60 c. red (16.8.26)	..	4·75	2·10

1926 (Oct)–**27.** *Contemporary types, surch as T* **40/42.**

433	**40**	25 c. on 30 c. blue (No. 416)	8	5
434		25 c. on 35 c. violet (No. 345) (11.26)	8	5
436	**42**	50 c. on 60 c. violet (No. 385) (7.27)	45	15
437		50 c. on 65 c. carm (No. 385*a*) (8.27)	30	8
438	**40**	50 c. on 75 c. blue (No. 400) (11.26)	75	12
439		50 c. on 80 c. verm (No. 424) (1.27)	30	20
440		50 c. on 85 c. verm (No. 386) (2.27)	25	8
441	**42**	50 c. on 1 f. 05, verm (No. 426) (12.4.27)	70	15
442	**40**	50 c. on 1 f. 25, blue (No. 400*c*) (11.26)	45	12
443	**41**	55 c. on 60 c. violet (No. 385)*	70·00	23·00
444	**42**	90 c. on 1 f. 05, vermilion (No. 426)	2·25	1·10
445		1 f. 10 on 1 f. 40, cerise (No. 428) ..	40	15

* Nos. 413 and 443 were issued only precancelled. The prices in the unused column are for stamps with full gum and in the used column for stamps without gum.

1926–27. *War Orphans' Fund. P* 14 × 13½.

450	**21**	2 c.+1 c. plum (2.27)	..	20	20
451	**25**	50 c.+10 c. brown (2.27) ..	..	7·50	1·40
452	**26**	1 f.+25 c. carmine (1.27)	..	11·00	6·00
453		5 c.+1 f. blue and black (27.12.26)	38·00	25·00
450/453		*Set of 4*	50·00	30·00

D **43**   (43)

Poste Aérienne

1927 (Jan)–**31.** *POSTAGE DUE. P* 14 × 13½.

D454	D **43**	1 c. grey-green (11.28)	..	25	15
D455		10 c. rosine (3.31)	..	40	10
D456		30 c. bistre	..	75	10
D457		60 c. red	..	65	5
D458		1 f. bright violet	..	3·00	55
D459		1 f. greenish blue (7.31)	..	3·75	15
D460		2 f. pale blue	..	10·00	4·00
D461		2 f. sepia (7.31) ..	..	32·00	4·50
D454/461		*Set of 8*	45·00	8·50

1927 (4 June). *Strasbourg Philatelic Exhibition.* P 14 × 13½.
454 **18** 5 f. blue £130 £110
454a 10 f. red £130 £110
MS454b 110×140 mm 5 f.+10 f. and label
inscr "STRASBOURG 1927" £375 £325
Sold only in the exhibition (entrance fee 5 f.).

1927 (25 June). *AIR. First International Display of Aviation and Navigation, Marseilles.* Optd with T **43.**
455 **13** 2 f. red and blue-green (B.) .. 90·00 85·00
456 5 f. deep blue and buff .. 90·00 85·00
Nos. 455/6 exist with forged overprints.

44 Marcelin Berthelot   **45** Lafayette, Washington, Paris, and Lindbergh 'plane

(Des and die eng A. Mignon)

1927 (7 Sept). *Berthelot Birth Centenary.* P 14 × 13½.
457 **44** 90 c. rose-carmine 25 8

(Des and die eng A. Delzers)

1927 (15 Sept). *Visit of American Legion.* P 14 × 13½.
458 **45** 90 c. rose-carmine 40 25
459 1 f. 50, dull ultramarine 90 40

Caisse
d'Amortissement

Caisse
d'Amortissement

+10ᶜ **+25ᶜ** **+50ᶜ**

(**46**)   (**46**a)   (**47**)

1927 (26 Aug). *Sinking Fund.* T **18, 15** and **30**, surch.
460 **46** 40 c.+10 c. blue (R.) .. 2·25 1·60
461 **46**a 50 c.+25 c. blue-green (B.) .. 3·25 2·50
462 **47** 1 f. 50+50 c. orange .. .. 3·25 2·50

10 Fʀ.

48   (**49**)

(Des P. Turin. Eng A. Mignon. Recess)

1928 (15 May). *Sinking Fund.* P 14 × 13½.
463 **48** 1 f. 50+8 f. 50, blue .. .. 65·00 65·00
Three types exist, differing in the two horizontal frame lines above "f" over "8 50":—I. Lines unbroken; II. Both lines broken; III. Upper line broken.

1928 (23 Aug). *AIR. Surch as T* **49.**
464 **44** 10 f. on 90 c. rose-carmine .. £900 £900
  a. Surch inverted £4750 £4750
  b. Spaced 6½ mm between value
   and bar £1500 £1500
  c. As b. inverted .. £7000
465 **30** 10 f. on 1 f. 50, blue £4000 £4000
  a. Spaced 6½ mm between value
   and bar £5000 £5000
The above stamps were surcharged by authority of the French Consul-General in New York for use in prepayment of the special fee charged for conveyance of letters by aeroplane from the s.s. *Ile de France* to the shore. They have since been recognised by the French postal authorities.

1928 (1 Oct). *Sinking Fund.* T **18, 15** and **30** surch.
466 **46** 40 c.+10 c. pale violet (R.) .. 5·00 4·50
467 **46**a 50 c.+25 c. brown-red (B.) .. 11·00 9·50
468 **47** 1 f. 50+50 c. mauve .. .. 15·00 13·00

EXPOSITION
LE HAVRE
1929
PHILATÉLIQUE

50 Joan of Arc   (**51**)

(Des G. Barlangue. Eng A. Mignon. Typo)

1929 (Mar). *500th Anniv of Relief of Orleans.* P 14 × 13½.
469 **50** 50 c. blue 20 5

1929 (18 May). *International Philatelic Exhibition, Le Havre.* Optd with T **51.**
470 **13** 2 f. red and blue-green (B.) .. £225 £160
Sold only at the Exhibition (entrance fee 5 f.).

1929 (July). *MILITARY FRANK.* No. 421 optd with Type M **14.**
M471 **15** 50 c. vermilion .. .. .. 1·25 30
  a. No stop after "M" .. .. 15·00 6·00
  b. Stop before and after "F" .. 15·00 6·00

1929 (July). *POSTAGE DUE. Surch as Type* D **40.**
D471 D **43** 1 f. 20 on 2 f. pale blue (R.) .. 5·50 1·60
D472 5 f. on 1 f. bright violet .. 8·00 1·60

52 Reims Cathedral   **53** Mont St. Michel

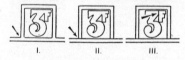

I.   II.   III.

(3 f.)

I
(5 f.)
II.

I.   (10 f.)   II.

Many other differences may be found, but the following comparisons are sufficient to distinguish between the various types:—
3 f. Type I. Horizontal line interrupted; Type II. Line continuous; Type III. "3" and "F" separated; Type IV. As III, but with dotted ground below central porch.
5 f. Heavier clouds and unbroken spire in Type II.
10 f. Type I. "E" of "POSTES" has downward serif to top bar; Type II. The top bar touches the "s" and is without serif; outer line of "o" broken at foot; Type III. As II, but outer line of "o" unbroken.

(Des—90 c. R. Prade; 2 f., 5 f. F. Bivel; 3 f. A. Verecque; 10 f., 20 f. H. Cheffer. Eng—90 c., 5 f. A. Mignon; 2 f. A. Delzers; 3 f. A. Dezarrois; 10 f., 20 f. H. Cheffer. Recess)

1929–33. *T* **52, 53** *and similar types.* *P* 13.

470a	90	c. magenta (18.9.33)	..	1·50	15
471	2	f. brown-lake (1.9.31)	.. ..	13·00	15
472	3	f. slate-blue (I) (17.11.30) ..	..	40·00	1·10
		a. Type II ('30)	.. ..	65·00	2·10
		b. Type III ('30)	.. ..	40·00	1·10
		c. Type IV ('31)	.. ..	£170	8·00
473	5	f. chocolate (I) (2.30)	.. · ..	9·50	12
		a. Type II ('31)	..	11·00	55
474	10	f. pale ultramarine (I) (18.7.29)	..	50·00	5·50
		a. Type II. *Blue* ('30)	..	55·00	9·50
		b. Type III. *Blue* ('31)	..	45·00	2·50
		c. Type III. *Bright ultramarine*		£1900	
475	20	f. deep red-brown (*p.* 13½) (15.5.29)		£110	14·00
		a. *P* 11. *Bright red-brown* ('30)	..	£450	90·00
		b. *P* 13½. *Deep red-brown* ('31)	..	£120	16·00

Designs: *Horiz*—90 c. Le Puy-en-Velay; 2 f. Arc de Triomphe; 10 f. Port de la Rochelle; 20 f. Pont du Gard.

1929 (1 Oct). *Sinking Fund.* *T* **18, 15** *and* **30** *surch.*

476	46	40 c.+10 c. green	..	9·50	6·50
477	46a	50 c.+25 c. magenta	..	11·00	9·50
478	47	1 f. 50+50 c. chestnut ..		20·00	13·00

54 Bay of Algiers   **55** "Le Sourire de Reims"

1930 (1 Jan). *Centenary of French Conquest of Algeria.* Typo. *P* 14 × 13½.

479	**54**	50 c. rose-red and bright blue	..	80	8

(Des L. P. Rigal. Eng A. Delzers. Recess)

1930 (15 Mar). *Sinking Fund.* *P* 13.

480	**55**	1 f. 50+3 f. 50, reddish purple	..	38·00	38·00

CONGRÈS
DU
B. I. T.
1930

(**56** "Bureau International du Travail")   **57** Notre-Dame de la Garde, Marseilles

1930 (23 Apr). *Session of the International Labour Office at Paris.* *Optd with T* **56.**

481	**15**	50 c. vermilion	.. .. ..	70	55
482	**30**	1 f. 50, blue	..	6·00	5·00

(Des P. A. Laurens. Eng A. Mignon. Recess)

1930–32. *AIR.* *P* 13.

483	**57**	1 f. 50, lake (8.6.30)	..	7·50	65
484		1 f. 50, blue (*shades*) (6.11.30)	..	7·50	65
		a. *Bright ultramarine* (1932)	..	£160	65·00

No. 484 was originally sold exclusively at the International Aero-Philatelic Exhibition, Paris, at 6 f. 50, including the entrance fee, but it was reissued at face value in 1931.

1930 (1 Oct). *Sinking Fund.* *T* **18** *and* **15** *(50 c.+25 c.) surch.*

485	**46**	40 c.+10 c. cerise	..	9·50	5·50
486	**46a**	50 c.+25 c. sepia	..	16·00	11·00
487	**46**	1 f. 50+50 c. violet	..	25·00	16·00

58 Woman of the Fachi Tribe   **59** "French Colonies"

I.   II.

Two Types of the 50 c.:—
I. With three downward lines at top of forehead.
II. Without lines.

(T **58.** Des Rigal. Eng Mignon. Typo. T **59.** Des J. de la Nézière. Photo Vaugirard)

1930–31. *International Colonial Exhibition.*
(*a*) *P* 14 × 13½

488	**58**	15 c. slate-black (17.11.30)		10	5
489		40 c. sepia (12.30)	..	30	5
490		50 c. carmine (I) (17.11.30)		10	5
		a. Type II ('31)	..	20	5
491		1 f. 50, blue (12.30)	..	4·50	12

(*b*) *P* 13½

492	**59**	1 f. 50, blue (24.4.31)	..	13·00	30
488/492		Set of 5	.. ..	16·00	50

60 "French Provinces"

UN FRANC
(D **61**)

(Des and eng A. Mignon. Recess)

1931 (1 Mar). *Sinking Fund.* *P* 13.

493	**60**	1 f. 50+3 f. 50, green	..	65·00	65·00

1931 (Aug). *POSTAGE DUE.* *Surch with Type* D **61.**

D494	D **43**	1 f. on 60 c. red	..	2·25	30

1931 (1 Oct). *Sinking Fund.* *T* **18** *and* **15** *(50 c.+25 c.) surch.*

494	**46**	40 c.+10 c. sage-green	..	19·00	16·00
495	**46a**	50 c.+25 c. pale violet	..	48·00	35·00
496	**46**	1 f. 50+50 c. carmine-red	..	48·00	35·00

               Small   Large

61 Peace   I. & II.   III.   IV.

Four Types of the 50 c.:—
I. Small "c", lines below buckle as I.
II. Large "c", lines as II.
III. Small "c", lines as II.
IV. Small "c", lines as IV.

(T **61.** Des P. A. Laurens. Die eng A. Delzers. Typo)

1932–39. *P* 14 × 13½.

497	**18**	1 c. olive-bistre (8.33)	..	5	5
497a		1 c. yellow-green ('36)	..	5	5
498		2 c. blackish green (3.33)	..	5	5
499		3 c. vermilion (9.33)	..	5	5
500		5 c. cerise (12.34)	..	5	5
501		10 c. bright ultramarine (9.32)	..	5	5
502	**61**	30 c. green (3.33)	..	15	5
503	**18**	30 c. brown-red (II) (17.11.37)	..	10	5
504		30 c. brown-red (III) (1938) (*See* 382 *a/b*)		25	20
505		35 c. green (13.9.37)	..	45	15
506	**61**	40 c. mauve (1.33)	..	8	5
507		45 c. yellow-brown (3.33)	..	50	25
508		50 c. rose-red (I) (9.32)	..	5	5
		a. Type II (1933)	..	40	8
		b. Type III (1935)	..	5	5
		c. Type IV (1935)	..	2·75	25
508d		55 c. violet (18.10.37)	..	25	5
508e		60 c. bistre (11.37)	..	5	5
509		65 c. dull purple (11.33)	..	20	5

509a	61	65 c. ultramarine (13.9.37)	..	8	5
510		75 c. sage-green (9.32)	.. ..	8	5
510a		80 c. orange (12.10.38)	..	5	5
511		90 c. scarlet (9.32)	..	14·00	70
511a		90 c. bright green (10.11.38)	..	5	5
511b		90 c. ultramarine (29.12.38)		10	5
512		1 f. orange (3.33)	..	35	5
512a		1 f. carmine-pink (31.12.37)	..	50	5
513		1 f. 25, olive (10.32)	..	25·00	95
513a		1 f. 25, carmine (20.1.39)	..	75	35
513b		1 f. 40, mauve (3.3.39)	..	2·25	1·25
514		1 f. 50, blue (10.32)	..	5	5
515		1 f. 75, rose-magenta (10.32)	..	1·40	5

1933–39. *MILITARY FRANK.* (a) *Nos. 508, 509a and 511b optd with Type M* **14**.

M516	61	50 c. rose-red (6.33)	..	50	10
		a. No stop after "M"	..	15·00	6·50
M517		65 c. ultramarine (R.) (11.37)		10	10
		a. No stop after "M"	..	9·50	7·00
M518		90 c. ultramarine (R.) (1939)		12	12

(b) *No. 511b optd "F" as in Type M* **14** *but without stop*

M519	61	90 c. ultramarine (1939)	..	1·10	1·10
		a. With stop after "F"	..	10·00	10·00

No. M519 was issued under military auspices for the use of Spanish refugees in France for Inland postage.

1933–37. *Surch with T* **28**.

515a	18	½ c. on 1 c. olive-bistre (12.33)	..	15	15
515b		½ c. on 1 c. yellow-brown (5.37)	..	20	20

62 Briand **63** Doumer **64** Victor Hugo

(Des H. Cheffer, G. Hourriez and J. Piel. Typo)

1933 (11 Dec). *P* 14 × 13½.

516	62	30 c. greenish blue	.. ..	9·50	3·25
517	63	75 c. mauve	.. ..	11·00	15
518	64	1 f. 25, claret	.. ..	80	15

65 Dove of Peace **66** J. M. Jacquard

(Des Daragnès. Typo)

1934 (20 Feb). *P* 14 × 13½.

519	65	1 f. 50, bright ultramarine	..	22·00	4·75

(Eng Ouvré. Recess)

1934 (14 Mar). *Death Centenary of Jacquard. P* 14 × 13.

520	66	40 c. grey-blue	.. ..	95	30

67 Jacques Cartier **68** Blériot's Monoplane

(Eng Ouvré. Recess)

1934. *Fourth Centenary of Cartier's Discovery of Canada. P* 13.

521	67	75 c. mauve (18 Aug)	.. ..	10·00	45
522		1 f. 50, blue (July)	..	21·00	95

(Eng Ouvré. Recess)

1934 (1 Sept). *AIR. 25th Anniv of Blériot's Channel Flight. P* 13.

523	68	2 f. 25, violet	.. ..	10·00	2·10

50ᶜ

(68a) **69** Breton River Scene

1934–37. *Nos. 513 and 512 surch as T* **68a**.

524	61	50 c. on 1 f. 25, olive (11.34)	..	1·60	12
524a		80 c. on 1 f. orange (R.) (10.37)	..	20	15

(Des Laboureur. Eng A. Delzers. Recess)

1935 (Feb). *P* 13.

525	69	2 f. bright green	.. ..	15·00	15

70 S.S. Normandie **71** St. Trophime, Arles

(Des and eng Decaris. Recess)

1935–36. *Maiden Voyage of S.S. Normandie. P* 13.

526	70	1 f. 50, deep blue (23.4.35)	..	7·50	40
526a		1 f. 50, sky-blue (26.5.36)	..	28·00	5·00

(Des and eng Decaris. Recess)

1935 (3 May). *P* 13.

527	71	3 f. 50, chocolate	.. ..	15·00	1·00

72 B. Delessert **73** Victor Hugo

(Des R. Gregoire. Eng A. Delzers. Recess)

1935 (20 May). *Opening of International Savings Bank Congress. P* 13.

528	72	75 c. green	.. ..	10·00	25

(Eng Ouvré. Recess)

1935 (30 May). *50th Death Anniv of Victor Hugo. P* 14 × 13.

529	73	1 f. 25, bright magenta	..	1·10	40

74 Cardinal Richelieu **75** Jacques Callot

(Eng Ouvré. Recess)

1935 (12 June). *Tercentenary of Founding of French Academy by Richelieu. P* 13.

530	74	1 f. 50, bright carmine	.. ..	10·00	45

1935 (19 Nov). *Death Tercentenary of Callot (engraver). Recess. P* 14 × 13.

531	75	75 c. red	.. ..	7·00	12

77 Symbolic of Art   **78** Aeroplane over Paris

(Des R. Grégoire and Ouvré. Eng Bouchery and Ouvré. Recess)

1935 (9 Dec). *Unemployed Intellectuals' Relief Fund.* P 13.
```
532  –  50 c.+10 c. deep ultramarine  ..  2·10   1·00
533 77  50 c.+ 2 f. red        ..  ..  25·00  19·00
```
Design: *Horiz*—No. 532, Help for intellectuals (inscr "POUR LES CHOMEURS INTELLECTUELS").

(Eng Ouvré. Recess)

1936 (17 Feb– 29 July). *AIR.* P 13.
```
534 78 85 c. green..    ..   ..   ..    95     20
535     1 f. 50, blue   ..   ..   ..   2·75   1·10
536     2 f. 25, bright violet ..  ..  7·00   2·25
537     2 f. 50, carmine  ..  ..   ..  7·00   2·25
538     3 f. ultramarine  ..  ..   ..  2·25    15
539     3 f. 50, red-brown  ..  ..  19·00   3·75
540    50 f. emerald-green (29.7.36)  .. £375  £110
534/540  Set of 7   ..   ..   ..  £375  £110
```

79 Aeroplane over Paris

(Recess. Institut de Gravure)

1936 (10 July). *AIR. Burelé background in second colour.* P 12½.
```
541 79  50 f. ultramarine (rose)  ..  .. £350  £110
```

80 Statue of Liberty   **81** André-Marie Ampère

(Eng Ouvré. Recess)

1936–37. *Nansen (Refugee) Fund.* P 13.
```
541a 80  50 c.+25 c. deep blue (1.7.37)  ..  2·25  1·75
542     75 c.+50 c. bright violet (25.2.36)  4·50  3·25
```

(Eng A. Delzers. Recess)

1936 (27 Feb). *Death Centenary of Ampère.* P 13.
```
543 81 75 c. brown ..  ..  ..  ..  10·00  30
```

82 Daudet's Mill, Fontvieille   **83** Children of the Unemployed

(Eng J. Piel. Recess)

1936 (27 Apr). P 13.
```
544 82 2 f. blue  ..  ..  ..  ..  80    5
```

(Des Gregoire. Eng J. Piel. Recess)

1936 (28 May). *Children of the Unemployed Fund.* P 13.
```
545 83 50 c.+10 c. dull scarlet  ..  ..  3·25  2·25
```

84 Pilâtre de Rozier   **85** Rouget de Lisle

86 "La Marseillaise"   **87** Canadian War Memorial, Vimy

(Des C. Kieffer. Eng J. Piel. Recess)

1936 (4 June). *150th Death Anniv of Pilâtre de Rozier.* P 13.
```
546 84 75 c. greenish blue ..  ..  .. 11·00  70
```

(Des after monuments by Bartholdi and Rude. Eng A. Delzers and J. Piel. Recess)

1936. *Death Centenary of Rouget de Lisle, Composer of the Marseillaise.* P 13.
```
547 85 20 c. blue-green (27.6.36) ..  ..  55  25
548 86 40 c. chocolate-brown  ..  ..  2·25  75
```

(Eng H. Cheffer. Recess)

1936 (26 July). *Unveiling of Canadian War Memorial, Vimy Ridge.* P 13.
```
549 87 75 c. red  ..  ..  ..  ..  4·50  50
550     1 f. 50, deep blue  ..  ..  7·50  3·00
```

88 Jean Jaurès as an Orator   **89** Jean Jaurès

(T **88** des Grégoire. Eng J. Piel; T **89** des and eng Ouvré. Recess)

1936 (30 July *Jaures Commemoration.* P 13.
```
551 88 40 c. red-brown  ..  ..  ..  1·10  20
552 89  1 f. 50, ultramarine  ..  ..  5·50  70
```

90   **91** S. Atlantic Flight

(Des G. Barlangue. Eng P. Munier and A. Delzers. Recess)

1936 (14 Aug). *100th Flight between France and S. America.* P 13.
553	**90**	1 f. 50, blue	..	..	6·50	90
554	**91**	10 f. myrtle-green	..	..	£160	48·00

92 Herald   **93** "World Exhibition"

(Eng Galanis and Daragnès. Typo)

1936 (15 Sept). *Paris International Exhibition.* P 14 × 13½.
555	**92**	20 c. mauve ..	..	..	8	5
556		30 c. blue-green	..	..	65	25
557		40 c. ultramarine	..	..	20	5
558		50 c. orange ..	..	..	10	5
559	**93**	90 c. carmine	..	..	4·75	3·50
560		1 f. 50, ultramarine	..	..	8·00	65
555/560		*Set of 6*	..	..	12·00	4·00

+20ᶜ
(95)

94 "Vision of Peace"

(Eng A. Delzers. Recess)

1936 (1 Oct). *Universal Peace Propaganda.* P 13
561	**94**	1 f. 50, blue ..	..	..	8·00	40

1936 (16 Oct). *Unemployed Intellectuals' Relief Fund. No. 533 surch with T **95**.*
562	**77** +20 c. on 50 c. +2 f. red	..	..	2·10	1·60

The surcharge reduces the Charity premium on the original stamp to 20 c.

96 Jacques Callot   **97** Ski-jumper

(Eng Ouvré and Hourriez (1 f. 50). Recess)

1936 (16 Nov). *Unemployed Intellectuals' Relief Fund. As T **96** (portraits inscr "POUR LES CHOMEURS INTEL-LECTUELS").* P 13.
563		20 c. +10 c. brown-lake	..	..	1·60	1·25
564		40 c. +10 c. bright yellow-green	..	..	1·60	1·25
565		50 c. +10 c. brown-red	..	..	2·50	1·25
566		1 f. 50+50 c. ultramarine	..	..	10·00	6·50
563/566		*Set of 4*	..	..	14·00	9·00

Portraits:—40 c. Hector Berlioz; 50 c. Victor Hugo; 1 f. 50 Louis Pasteur.

(Eng Degorce. Recess)

1937 (18 Jan). *Chamonix-Mont Blanc Skiing Week.* P 13.
567	**97**	1 f. 50, deep blue	..	..	4·00	35

98 Pierre Corneille   **99** France and Minerva

(Des and eng A. Delzers. Recess)

1937 (15 Feb). *300th Anniv of First Performance of "Le Cid".* P 13.
568	**98**	75 c. brown-lake	..	..	65	25

(Eng J. Piel. Recess)

1937 (15 Mar). *Paris International Exhibition.* P 13.
569	**99**	1 f. 50, greenish blue	..	..	80	30

100 Jean Mermoz   **101** Jean Mermoz Memorial

(Des G. Barlangue. Eng H. Cheffer. Recess)

1937 (22 Apr)**-38.** *Mermoz Commemoration.* P 13.
570	**100**	30 c. deep blue-green	..	..	20	12
571	**101**	3 f. violet	..	..	3·25	1·10
		a. Deep violet ('38)	..	..	9·00	1·10

102 Electric Train   **103** René Descartes

(Eng Ouvré and Degorce. Recess)

1937 (31 May). *XIII International Railway Congress, Paris. T **102** and similar type.* P 13.
572		30 c. green	..	..	40	30
573		1 f. 50, deep blue	..	..	4·75	2·75

Design:—1 f. 50, Stream-lined locomotive.

(Eng H. Cheffer. Recess)

1937 (10 June). *300th Anniv of Publication "Discours".* P 13. *(a) Wrongly inscr "DISCOURS SUR LA METHODE".*
574	**103**	90 c. scarlet	..	..	45	30

(b) Corrected to "DISCOURS DE LA METHODE"
575	**103**	90 c. scarlet	..	..	80	30

104 Anatole France   **107** Ramblers

(Eng A. Delzers and H. Cheffer. Recess)

1937 (16 June). *Unemployed Intellectuals' Relief Fund.* P 13.
576	**104**	30 c. +10 c. emerald-green	..	1·60	95
577		90 — c. +10 c. carmine	..	3·25	2·25

Design: Horiz—90 c. Auguste Rodin (inscr as in T **104**).

(Eng J. Piel. Recess)

1937 (16 June). *Postal Workers' Sports Fund. T **107** and similar horiz designs inscr "P.T.T. SPORTS & LOISIRS".* P 13.
578		20 c. +10 c. chocolate	..	..	1·25	1·10
579		40 c. +10 c. brown-lake	..	..	1·25	1·10
580		50 c. +10 c. brown-purple	..	..	1·25	1·10

Designs:—20 c. Tug-of-war; 40 c. Runners and discus thrower.

1937 (18 June). *International Philatelic Exhibition, Paris. As T* **1**, *printed in miniature sheets of four* (5¼ × 8⅝ *ins.*) *inscr* "PEXIP PARIS 1937" *between stamps. P* 14 × 13.

MS581	5 c. bistre and ultramarine		
	15 c. carmine and dull red		
	30 c. carmine and ultramarine		
	50 c. bistre and dull red	£110	95·00

Sold only at Exhibition (entrance fee 5 f.).

108 Pierre Loti and Constantinople   **109** "Victory" of Samothrace

(Eng G. Barlangue. Recess)

1937 (13 Aug). *Pierre Loti Memorial Fund. P* 13.

585	**108**	50 c.+20 c. carmine		2·00	1·40

(Eng A. Delzers. Recess)

1937 (20 Aug). *National Museums. P* 13.

586	**109**	30 c. green		45·00	21·00
		a. Error. Scarlet		£6500	
587		55 c. scarlet		45·00	21·00

Nos. 586/7 were sold at certain museums at 70 c. each above the face value.

110 "France" and Child   **111** France Congratulating U.S.A.

(Eng Ouvré. Recess)

1937–39. *Public Health Fund. P* 13.

588	**110**	65 c.+25 c. slate-purple (1.9.37)	75	55
588*a*		90 c.+30 c. turquoise-bl (20.1.39)	70	50

(Des G. Barlangue. Eng A. Delzers. Recess)

1937 (17 Sept). *150th Anniv of U.S. Constitution. P* 13.

589	**111**	1 f. 75, ultramarine		75	50

112 Iseran Pass   **113** Ceres

(Eng A. Delzers. Recess.)

1937 (4 Oct). *Opening of Col de l'Iseran Road. P* 13.

590	**112**	90 c. green		20	8

(Des C. Hourriez. Typo)

1938–40. *P* 14 × 13½.

591	**113**	1 f. 75, blue (2.2.38)		50	10
591*a*		2 f. carmine (22.3.39)		12	5
591*b*		2 f. 25, ultramarine (30.1.39)	2·10	8
591*c*		2 f. 50, green (20.1.39)		90	5
591*d*		2 f. 50, ultramarine (2.12.40)	45	15
591*e*		3 f. pale magenta (24.3.39)	40	5
591/591*e*		*Set of 6*		4·00	40

1938 (Feb). *P* 14 × 13½.

592	**15**	50 c. greenish blue		20	5

(Eng Gorvel and Piel. Recess)

1938–39. *Shipwrecked Mariners' Society. As T* **104**, *but portrait inscr* "JEAN CHARCOT, SOCIETE DES OEUVRES DE MER". *P* 13.

593	65 c.+35 c. blue-green (25.3.38)	65	65
593*a*	90 c.+35 c. bright purple (26.6.39)	4·50	3·50

(Eng A. Delzers. Recess)

1938 (2 Apr). *Birth Centenary of Gambetta. As T* **104**, *but portrait inscr* "LEON GAMBETTA 1838–1882". *P* 13.

594	55 c. violet		25	20

Designs: *Vert*—2 f. 15, Coal miners; 10 f. Vincennes. *Horiz*—90 c. Château de Pau; 2 f. Arc de Triomphe at Orange; 3 f. Papal Palace, Avignon; 5 f. Carcassonne; 20 f. St. Malo.

113*a* Champagne Girl

(Des André-Spitz (1 f. 75, 3 f.). Eng A. Rivaud (90 c.), A. Delzers (1 f. 75), H. Cheffer (2 f. 15, 20 f.), J. Piel (3 f., 5 f.) and P. Munier (2 f., 10 f.). Recess)

1938–39. *T* **113***a* *and pictorial designs as T* **52/3**. *P* 13.

594*a*	90 c. carmine/*blue* (25.8.39)		55	30
595	1 f. 75, bright blue (13.6.38)		2·00	1·00
596	2 f. sepia (15.12.38)		65	50
597	2 f. 15, slate-purple (20.4.38)	55	15
598	3 f. brown-lake (20.6.38)		3·75	1·10
599	5 f. blue (20.4.38)		25	15
600	10 f. purple/*blue* (16.5.38)		95	65
601	20 f. green (16.5.38)		20·00	5·50
594*a*/601	*Set of 8*		26·00	8·50

1938 (9 May). *Unemployed Intellectuals' Relief Fund. As Nos.* 563/6 *and* 576/7 (*portraits inscr* "POUR LES CHÔMEURS INTELLECTUELS"). *P* 13.

602	30 c.+10 c. brown-lake	1·25	1·10
603	35 c.+10 c. green	1·90	1·25
604	55 c.+10 c. violet	2·75	1·25
605	65 c.+10 c. bright blue	2·75	1·25
606	1 f.+10 c. carmine	2·75	1·25
607	1 f. 75+25 c. blue	4·75	2·10
602/607	*Set of 6*	14·00	7·50

Portraits: As T **96**—35 c. Callot; 55 c. Berlioz; 65 c. Victor Hugo; 1 f. 75 Louis Pasteur. As No. 577—1 f. Auguste Rodin. As T **104**—30 c. Anatole France.

114 Palais de Versailles   **115** Soldier in Trench

(Eng Degorce. Recess)

1938 (9 May). *French National Music Festivals. P* 13.

608	**114**	1 f. 75+75 c. deep blue	9·50	7·00

(Eng J. Piel. Recess)

1938 (16 May). *Infantry Monument Fund. P* 13.

609	**115**	55 c.+70 c. slate-purple	1·75	1·50
610		65 c.+1 f. 10, greenish blue	1·75	1·50

ALBUM LISTS

Write for our latest lists of albums and accessories.

These will be sent free on request.

116 Medical Corps   **117** Saving a Goal
Monument at Lyons

(Eng Ouvré. Recess)

1938 (25 May). *Military Medical Corps' Monument Fund.*
P 13.
611 **116** 55 c.+45 c. red . .   . .   . . 5·50 4·00

(Des J. Bridge. Eng Degorce. Recess)

1938 (1 June). *World Football Cup. P* 13.
612 **117** 1 f. 75, bright blue   . .   . . 3·75 2·10

117a Clément Ader   **118** Jean de La Fontaine

(Eng Ouvré. Recess)

1938 (16 June). *Clément Ader (air pioneer). P* 13.
612a **117a** 50 f. bright blue . .   . . 55·00 30·00

(Eng Ouvré. Recess)

1938 (8 July). *Jean de la Fontaine (writer of fables). P* 13.
613 **118** 55 c. green   35   20

(Des A. Verecque. Eng A. Dezarrois. Recess)

1938 (10 July). *Reims Cathedral Restoration Fund. As T* **52,**
but inscr "REIMS 10. VII. 1938". *P* 13.
614   65 c.+35 c. bright blue   . .   . . 4·00 3·50

119 Houses of Parliament,   **120** "France" welcoming
"Friendship" and Arc de   Frenchmen repatriated
Triomphe   from Spain

(Eng H. Cheffer. Recess)

1938 (19 July). *Visit of King George VI and Queen Elizabeth*
to France. P 13.
615 **119** 1 f. 75, bright blue   50   35

(Des R. Gregoire. Eng A. Delzers. Recess)

1938 (8 Aug). *French Refugees' Fund. P* 13.
616 **120** 65 c.+60 c. carmine   . .   . . 2·50 1·75

121 Pierre and Marie Curie   **122** Arc de Triomphe
and Allied Soldiers

(Des J. de la Nézière. Eng J. Piel. Recess)

1938 (1 Sept). *International Anti-Cancer Fund.* 40*th Anniv*
of Discovery of Radium. P 13.
617 **121** 1 f. 75+50 c. bright blue . .   . . 3·75 2·75

(Eng Degorce. Recess)

1938 (8 Oct). 20*th Anniv of Armistice,* 1918. *P* 13.
618 **122** 65 c.+35 c. carmine   . .   . . 2·50 1·75

123 Mercury   **124** Nurse and Patient

(Des G. Hourriez. Typo)

1938–42. *Inscr* "REPUBLIQUE FRANCAISE". *P* 14 × 13½.
618a **123**   1 c. chocolate-brown (10.5.39) . .   5   5
619   2 c. deep blue-green (9.3.39) . .   5   5
620   5 c. bright carmine (10.38) . .   5   5
621   10 c. ultramarine (17.10.38) . .   5   5
622   15 c. red-orange (8.12.38) . .   5   5
622a   15 c. orange-brown (3.4.39) . .   8   8
623   20 c. mauve (17.10.38)   5   5
624   25 c. green (11.38)   5   5
625   30 c. scarlet (22.2.39)   5   5
626   40 c. bright violet (17.2.39)   5   5
627   45 c. emerald-green (17.1.39)   30   15
627a   50 c. blue (24.6.39)   . .   1·10   5
627b   50 c. green (25.1.41)   . .   15   5
627c   50 c. greenish blue (7.2.42)   10   5
628   60 c. red-orange (14.3.39)   10   5
629   70 c. rose-magenta (17.1.39)   12   5
629a   75 c. red-brown (20.7.39)   . . 2·25   65
618a/629a   *Set of* 17   . .   . .   . . 4·00 1·40
For similar stamps inscr "POSTES FRANCAISES", see
Nos. 750/3.

(Eng P. Munier. Recess)

1938 (1 Dec). *Students' Fund. P* 13.
630 **124** 65 c.+60 c. greenish blue   . . 2·50 2·00

125 Blind Radio Listener   **126** Monument to
Civilian War Victims, Lille

(Des and eng J. Piel. Recess)

1938 (26 Dec). "*Radio for the Blind*" *Fund. P* 13.
631 **125** 90 c.+25 c. purple   . .   . . 2·25 1·75

(Des and eng G. Barlangue. Recess)

1939 (1 Feb). *War Victims' Monument Fund. P* 13.
632 **126** 90 c.+35 c. sepia   . .   . . 2·75 2·25

127 Paul Cézanne   **128** Red Cross Nurse   **134** Niepce and Daguerre   **135** Eiffel Tower

(Eng Ouvré. Recess)

1939 (15 Mar). *Cézanne Centenary. P* 13.
633 **127** 2 f. 25, turquoise-blue .. .. 2·10   90

(Des André Spitz. Eng A. Delzers. Recess)

1939 (24 Mar). *75th Anniv of Red Cross Society. Cross in red. P* 13.
634 **128** 90 c.+35 c. turquoise-blue and
greenish black .. .. 2·50   1·90

(Des and eng A. Delzers. Recess)

1939 (24 Apr). *Photographic Centenary. P* 13.
640 **134** 2 f. 25, blue .. .. .. 2·25   1·25

(Des and eng H. Cheffer. Recess)

1939 (5 May). *50th Anniv of Erection of Eiffel Tower. P* 13.
641 **135** 90 c.+50 c. bright purple .. 2·75   1·90

129 Military Engineer   **130** Ministry of Posts, Telegraphs and Telephones   **136** Iris   **137** Marly Water Works

(Eng J. Piel. Recess)

1939 (3 Apr). *To the Glory of French Military Engineers. P* 13.
635 **129** 70 c.+50 c. scarlet .. .. 2·75   2·50

(Des J. Schultz-Dal. Eng J. Piel. Recess)

1939 (8 Apr). *P.T.T. Orphans' Fund. P* 13.
636 **130** 90 c.+35 c. turquoise blue .. 5·00   3·50

(Des and die eng G. Hourriez. Typo)

1939–41. *P·*14 × 13½.
642 **136** 80 c. red-brown (2.12.40) .. 5   5
643   1 f. green (24.5.39) .. 20   5
643a   1 f. carmine-red (20.6.40) .. 5   5
643b   1 f. 30, ultramarine (8.1.40) .. 8   5
643c   1 f. 50, red-orange (25.1.41) .. 15   10
642/643c *Set of* 5 50   25
For new colours and values, see Nos. 861/8.

(Eng H. Cheffer. Recess)

1939 (22 May). *International Water Exhibition, Liege. P* 13.
644 **137** 2 f. 25, ultramarine .. .. 2·50   80

131 *Clemenceau*

(Des and eng Decaris. Recess)

1939 (18 Apr). *Laying down Keel of Battleship "Clemenceau". P* 13.
637 **131** 90 c. bright ultramarine 25   20

138 Balzac

(40 c. des A. Spitz eng A. Delzers; others des and eng J. Piel (70 c.), A. Delzers (90 c.), G. Barlangue (2 f. 25). Recess)

1939 (5 June). *Unemployed Intellectuals' Relief Fund. As T* **138** (*portraits inscr "POUR LES CHOMEURS INTEL-LECTUELS"*). *P* 13.
645   40 c.+10 c. scarlet 80   75
646   90 c.+10 c. slate-purple 95   75
647   90 c.+10 c. bright purple .. .. 1·10   90
648   2 f. 25+25 c. ultramarine .. .. 2·25   1·40
645/648 *Set of* 4 .. .. 4·50   3·50
Portraits: *Vert*—40 c. Puvis de Chavannes. *Horiz*—70 c. Claude Debussy; 2 f. 25, Claude Bernard.
See also Nos. 667b/d.

132 French Pavilion, New York Exhibition   **133** Mother and Child

(Des and eng P. Munier. Recess)

1939–40. *New York World's Fair. P* 13.
638 **132** 2 f. 25, bright ultramarine (18.4.39) 1·75   80
638a   2 f. 50, bright ultramarine (10.6.40) 1·50   1·00

(Des Grégoire. Eng J. Piel. Recess)

1939 (24 Apr). *Children of the Unemployed Fund. P* 13.
639 **133** 90 c.+35 c. scarlet .. .. 1·50   95

139 St. Gregory of Tours   **140** Mother and Children

(Eng C. P. Dufresne. Recess)
1939 (10 June). *1400th Anniv of Birth of St. Gregory of Tours.* P 13.
649 **139** 90 c. scarlet   35   25

(Des André Spitz. Eng E. Feltesse and J. Piel. Recess)
1939 (15 June). *Birth-rate Development Fund.* T **140** and similar type, inscr "POUR LA NATALITE". P 13.
650   70 c.+80 c. violet, blue and green   ..   1·40   1·40
651   90 c.+60 c. brown, purple and sepia ..   1·40   1·40
Design:—70 c. Mother and children admiring infant in cot.

141 Oath of the "Tennis Court"   **142** Strasbourg Cathedral

(Des André Spitz after L. David. Eng A. Delzers. Recess)
1939 (20 June). *150th Anniv of French Revolution.* P 13.
652 **141** 90 c. slate-green   25   20

(Des André Spitz. Eng G. Gandon. Recess)
1939 (23 June). *5th Centenary of Completion of Strasbourg Cathedral Spire.* P 13.
653 **142** 70 c. brown-lake   35   20

143 Porte Chaussée, Verdun   **144** "The Letter"

(Eng Ouvré. Recess)
1939 (23 June). *23rd Anniv of Battle of Verdun.* P 13.
654 **143** 90 c. olive-grey   45   35

(Eng by J. Piel after Fragonard. Recess)
1939 (6 July). *Postal Museum Fund.* P 13.
655 **144** 40 c.+60 c. brown and purple   ..   1·90   1·50

145 Statue to Sailors lost at Sea   **146** Languedoc

(Eng by Degorce after statue by Desruelles. Recess)
1939 (20 July). *Boulogne Monument Fund.* P 13.
656 **145** 70 c.+30 c. plum ..   ..   ..   2·75   2·10

(Des J. Julien. Eng P. Munier. Recess)
1939 (25 Dec). P 13.
657 **146** 70 c. black/*blue*   20   20

147 Lyons   **148** French Soldier and Strasbourg Cathedral

(Eng Ouvré. Recess)
1939 (25 Dec). P 13.
658 **147** 90 c. slate-purple   20   20

(Eng R. Serres and H. Cheffer. Recess)
1940 12 Feb). *Soldiers' Comforts Fund.* T **148** and similar type, inscr "POUR NOS SOLDATS". P 13.
659   40 c.+60 c. slate-purple   ..   55   45
660   1 f.+50 c. greenish blue   ..   55   45
Design :—1 f. Veteran French Colonial Soldier and African Village.

149 French Colonial Empire   **150** Marshal Joffre

(Eng J. Piel. Recess)
1940 (5 Apr). *Overseas Propaganda Fund.* P 13.
661 **149** 1 f.+25 c. scarlet ..   ..   ..   1·40   95

(Des André Spitz (2 f. 50). Eng H. Cheffer, Ouvré, J. Piel and A. Delzers. Recess)
1940 (1 May). *War Charities. As T* **150** (inscr "OEUVRES DE GUERRE"). P 13.
662   80 c.+45 c. reddish brown   ..   90   90
663   1 f.+50 c. violet   90   90
664   1 f. 50+50 c. lake-red   ..   90   80
665   2 f. 50+50 c. blue   95   90
662/665   Set of 4   ..   ..   ..   3·25   3·25
Designs: *Horiz*—1 f. 50, Portrait of Gen Galliéni; 2 f. 50, Ploughing. *Vert*—1 f. Portrait of Marshal Foch.

151 Nurse and Wounded Soldier

(Des and eng P. Munier (80 c.). Des A. Spitz, eng A. Delzers, (1 f.). Recess)
1940 (10 June). *Red Cross Fund.* T **151** and similar type inscr "CROIX ROUGE FRANCAISE". Cross in red. P 13.
666   80 c.+1 f. green   ..   ..   1·75   1·75
667   1 f.+2 f. purple-brown   ..   1·75   1·75
Design:—80 c. Doctor, nurse, soldier and family.

FRENCH STATE
10 July 1940—20 August 1944

152 G. Guynemer   **153** Nurse, Wounded
(pilot)   Soldier and Family

(Eng Ouvré. Recess)

1940 (12 Nov). *P* 13.
667a **152** 50 f. ultramarine .. .. .. 4·50 2·75

1940 (12 Nov). *Unemployed Intellectuals' Relief Fund. Designs inscr as in T* **138.** *P* 13.
667b 80 c.+10 c. violet-brown 70 70
667c 1 f.+10 c. bright purple 70 70
667d 2 f. 50+25 c. ultramarine 70 70
Portraits: *Horiz*—80 c. Debussy; 1 f. Balzac; 2 f. 50, Bernard.

(Des André Spitz. Eng J. Piel. Recess)

1940 (12 Nov). *War Victims' Fund. P* 13.
667e **153** 1 f.+2 f. brown-violet 40 30

154 Harvesting

(Eng J. Piel, P. Munier, Degorce and H. Cheffer. Recess)

1940 (2 Dec). *National Relief Fund. As T* **154** (*horiz designs, inscr* "SECOURS NATIONAL"). *P* 13.
668 80 c.+2 f. sepia 75 65
669 1 f.+2 f. red-brown 75 65
670 1 f. 50+2 f. violet 75 65
671 2 f. 50+2 f. green 75 65
668/671 *Set of* 4 .. .. .. 2·75 2·25
Designs:—1 f. Sowing; 1 f. 50, Gathering Grapes; 2 f. 50, Cattle.

1940–41. *Variously surch in red or black* (*No.* 679). *Two bars cancel original value except on Nos.* 682 *and* 684/5.
672 **18** 30 (c.) on 35 c. green (25.1.41) .. 5 5
673 **61** 50 (c.) on 55 c. violet (25.1.41) .. 5 5
674 50 (c.) on 65 c. ultramarine (25.1.41) .. 5 5
675 50 (c.) on 75 c. sage-green (4.3.41) .. 5 5
676 **123** 50 (c.) on 75 c. red-brown (15.4.41) .. 5 5
677 **61** 50 (c.) on 80 c. orange (4.3.41) .. 5 5
678 50 (c.) on 90 c. ultramarine (8.3.41) .. 5 5
679 1 f. on 1 f. 25 carm (Bk.) (18.3.41) .. 5 5
680 1 f. on 1 f. 40, mauve (4.3.41) .. 5 5
681 1 f. on 1 f. 50, blue (8.3.41) .. 10 10
682 **113** 1 f. on 1 f. 75, bright blue (2.12.40) .. 5 5
683 – 1 f. on 2 f. 15, slate-purple (No. 597) (2.12.40) .. 5 5
684 **113** 1 f. on 2 f. 25, ultram (25.1.41) .. 5 5
685 1 f. on 2 f. 50, green (4.3.41) .. 10 10
686 – 2 f. 50 on 5 f. bl (No. 599) (17.5.41) .. 12 12
687 5 f. on 10 f. purple/*blue* (No. 600) (15.4.41) .. 1·00 1·00
688 – 10 f. on 20 f. green (No. 601) (4.3.41) .. 45 45
689 **117a** 20 f. on 50 f. bright blue (23.1.41) .. 15·00 15·00
672/689 *Set of* 18 .. .. .. 16·00 16·00

155 Marshal Pétain   **156** Prisoners of War

(Eng J. Piel. Recess)

1941. *P* 13.
690 **155** 40 c. red-brown (25.1) 20 20
691 80 c. blue-green (25.1) 30 25
692 1 f. carmine (1.1) 10 10
693 2 f. 50, ultramarine (25.1) 50 50
690/693 *Set of* 4 .. .. .. 1·00 1·00

(Eng P. Munier and Degorce (1 f.) Recess)

1941 (1 Jan). *Prisoners of War Fund. As T* **156** *inscr* "POUR NOS PRISONNIERS DE GUERRE"). *P* 13.
696 80 c.+5 f. green 65 65
697 1 f.+5 f. brown-lake 65 65
Design: *Vert*—1 f. Group of soldiers.

157 Frédéric Mistral   **158** Science against Cancer

(Des M. E. Fabré. Eng C. Mazelin. Recess)

1941 (20 Feb). *Frédéric Mistral* (*poet*). *P* 14×13.
698 **157** 1 f. brown-lake 10 10

(Eng G. Barlangue. Recess)

1941 (20 Feb). *Anti-Cancer Fund. P* 13.
699 **158** 2 f. 50+50 c. black, blue & brown .. 65 65

159 Beaune Hospital   **+10ᶜ** (159a)

(Eng Feltesse (5 f., 15 f.), G. Barlangue (10 f.) and Mazelin (20 f.). Recess)

1941–2. *Views. T* **159** *and similar horiz designs. P* 13.
700 **159** 5 f. sepia (17.5.41) 15 5
701 – 10 f. violet (17.5.41) 10 5
702 **159** 15 f. lake (23.3.42) 15 12
703 – 20 f. sepia (4.3.41) 35 35
700/703 *Set of* 4 .. .. .. 70 50
Designs:—5 f. is inscr "POSTES/RF."; 10 f. Angers; 20 f. Ramparts of St. Louis, Aigues-Mortes.

1941 (4 Mar). *National Relief Fund. Surch with T* **159a**, *in blue.* (20 f.). Recess)
704 **155** 1 f.+10 c. carmine 10 8

160   **162** Liner *Pasteur*

(Eng Ouvré and Serres (2 f. 50). Recess)

1941 (4 Mar). *Winter Relief Fund. T* **160** *and similar horiz design. P* 13.
705 1 f.+2 f. slate-purple 45 30
706 2 f. 50+7 f. 50, blue 65 50
Design:—2 f. 50, "Charity" helping pauper.

(Des and eng Decaris. Recess)

1941 (17 May). *Seamen's Dependents Relief Fund. P* 13.
707 **162** 1 f.+1 f. on 70 c. dark bl-grn (R.) 10 10

1941 (17 July). *As No.* 661, *but without* "R.F." *and dated* "1941".
708 **149** 1 f.+1 f. green, purple, indigo & mag 30 30

163   **164**   Marshal Pétain   **165**

(Des Frost, Lemagny, and Bersier. Die eng Frost, Hourriez and J. Piel. Typo)

1941–42. P 14 × 13½.

709	**163**	20 c. purple (4.12.41)	..	5	5
710		30 c. scarlet (25.10.41)	..	5	5
711		40 c. ultramarine (30.10.41)	..	5	5
712	**164**	50 c. green (26.11.41)	..	5	5
713		60 c. violet (19.2.42)		5	5
714		70 c. blue (4.12.41)	..	5	5
715		70 c. red-orange (21.1.42)	..	5	5
716		80 c. chocolate (13.9.41)	..	5	5
717		80 c. emerald-green (27.1.42)		5	5
718		1 f. scarlet (12.8.41)		5	5
719		1 f. 20, red-brown (21.1.42)		5	5
720	**165**	1 f. 50, rose (17.12.41)		5	5
721		1 f. 50, red-brown (14.2.42)		5	5
722		2 f. blue-green (27.12.41)		5	5
723		2 f. 40, carmine (20.3.42)		5	5
724		2 f. 50, bright blue (20.10.41)	..	25	15
725		3 f. red-orange (14.10.41)		5	5
725a	**164**	4 f. violet-blue (15.12.42)		5	5
725b		4 f. 50, yellow-green (15.12.42)	..	20	15
709/725b		Set of 19 ..	..	85	60

See also Nos. 740/1.

166 Fisherman   **167** Arms of Nancy

(Des Lemagny. Eng P. Gandon. Recess)

1941 (23 Oct). *National Seamen's Relief Fund.* P 13.

726	**166**	1 f.+9 f. dark blue-green..	..	55	55

(Des and eng G. Barlangue, H. Cheffer, Degorce, Feltesse, J. Piel (80 c., 10 f.), R. Serres, Cottet, Ouvré, Ch. P. Dufresne, P. Gandon and P. Munier. Recess)

1941 (15 Dec). *National Relief Fund. As T **167** (coats-of-arms of various cities).* P 14 × 13.

727		20 c.+30 c. black	..	95	95
728		40 c.+60 c. red-brown	..	95	95
729		50 c.+70 c. greenish blue	..	95	95
730		70 c.+80 c. claret	..	95	95
731		80 c.+1 f. carmine	..	95	95
732		1 f.+1 f. black	..	95	95
733		1 f. 50+2 f. blue	..	95	95
734		2 f.+2 f. violet	..	95	95
735		2 f. 50+3 f. emerald-green ..		95	95
736		3 f.+5 f. red-brown ..		95	95
737		5 f.+6 f. ultramarine	..	95	95
738		10 f.+10 f. rose-red ..		95	95
727/738		Set of 12 ..	..	10·00	10·00

Designs:—Nos. 728/38 respectively show the Arms of Lille, Rouen, Bordeaux, Toulouse, Clermont-Ferrand, Marseilles, Lyons, Rennes, Reims, Montpellier and Paris.
For similar stamps see Designs Index, under "Arms"

168 Jean-François de La Pérouse   **169** Potez 63-11 Bombers

(Des Lemagny. Eng P. Munier. Recess)

1942 (23 Mar). *Birth Bicentenary of La Pérouse (navigator and explorer) and National Relief Fund.* P 13.

739	**168**	2 f. 50+7 f. 50, blue	..	50	50

(Des Lemagny. Eng P. Gandon. Recess)

1942. *As T **164**, but 18 × 21½ mm.* P 14 × 13.

740	**164**	4 f. ultramarine (31.3)	..	12	8
741		4 f. 50, deep green (12.5) ..		8	5

(Eng Henry Cheffer. Recess)

1942 (4 Apr). *Air Force Dependents Relief Fund.* P 13.

742	**169**	1 f. 50+3 f. 50, violet	..	20	20

170 Alexis Emannuel Chabrier   **171** Symbolical of French Colonial Empire

(Eng Ouvré. Recess)

1942 (18 May). *Birth Centenary of Chabrier (composer) and Musicians' Mutual Assistance Fund.* P 13.

743	**170**	2 f.+3 f. sepia	..	..	45	45

(Eng Gandon. Recess)

1942 (18 May). *Empire Fortnight and National Relief Fund.* P 13.

744	**171**	1 f. 50+8 f. 50, black	..	..	40	40

172 Marshal Pétain   **173**

(Des Bouguenec. Eng C. Mazelin. Recess)

1942. *P 14 × 13 (5 f.) or 13 (50 f.).*

745	**172**	5 f. blue-green (8.6)	..	..	5	5
746	**173**	50 f. black (25.7)	..	..	1·25	95

174 Jean de Vienne   **175** Jules Massenet

(Des and eng R. Serres. Recess)

1942 (16 June). *600th Birth Anniv of Jean de Vienne (admiral) and Seamen's Relief Fund.* P 13.

748	**174**	1 f. 50+8 f. 50, purple-brown	..	50	50

(Des Lemagny. Eng A. Delzers. Recess)

1942 (22 June). *Birth Centenary of Massenet (composer).* P 14 × 13.

749	**175**	4 f. blue-green	..	15	10

1942. *Inscr "POSTES FRANÇAISES". Typo.* P 14 × 13½.

750	**123**	10 c.ultramarine (15 Dec) ..		5	5
751		30 c. scarlet (15 Dec)	..	5	5
752		40 c. violet (15 Dec)	..	5	5
753		50 c. greenish blue (6 Aug)	..	5	5
750/753		Set of 4	..	..	10	10

(176)   **177** Stendhal (Marie Henri Beyle)   **178** André Blondel

1942 (14 Sept). *National Relief Fund. Surch with T* **176.** P 14 × 13½.
754 **165** 1 f. 50+50, ultramarine (R.)   ..   5   5

(Des Lemagny after Dedreux-Dorcy. Eng Hourriez. Recess)

1942 (14 Sept). *Death Centenary of Stendhal (novelist). P* 13.
755 **177** 4 f. sepia and red   20   20

(Des and eng J. Piel. Recess)

1942 (14 Sept). *André Blondel (physicist). P* 13.
756 **178** 4 f. blue   20   20

(Des E. Faure (60 c.), Folmer (1 f. 50). Eng J. Piel (60 c.), Degorce (1 f. 50). Des and eng P. Munier (50 c.), R. Serres (80 c.), Feltesse (1 f.), Ch. P. Dufresne (1 f. 20), H. Cheffer (2 f.), Mazelin (2 f. 40), A. Delzers (3 f.), G. Barlangue (4 f.), Ouvré (4 f. 50), Gandon (5 f.). Recess)

1942 (5 Oct). *National Relief Fund. As T* **169** *(2nd series). P* 14 × 13.
757   50 c.+60 c. black (Chambéry)   ..   95   95
758   60 c.+70 c. blue-green (La Rochelle)   95   95
759   80 c.+1 f. rose (Poitiers)   ..   95   95
760   1 f.+1 f. 30, green (Orleans)   ..   95   95
761   1 f. 20+1 f. 50, claret (Grenoble)   ..   95   95
762   1 f. 50+1 f. 80, blue (Angers)   ..   95   95
763   2 f.+2 f. 30, carmine (Dijon)   ..   95   95
764   2 f. 40+2 f. 80, grey-green (Limoges)   95   95
765   3 f.+3 f. 50, violet (Le Havre)   ..   95   95
766   4 f.+5 f. ultramarine (Nantes)   ..   95   95
767   4 f. 50+6 f. red (Nice)   ..   95   95
768   5 f.+7 f. lilac (St. Etienne)   95   95
757/768   *Set of* 12 ..   ..   ..   10·00   10·00
For similar stamps see Designs Index, under "Arms"

179 Legionary and Grenadiers

180 Belfry, Arras Town Hall

(Des Eric. Eng Gandon. Recess)

1942 (12 Oct). *Tricolour Legion. P* 13.
769 **179** 1 f. 20+8 f. 80, blue   ..   ..   1·60   1·60
770   1 f. 20+8 f. 80, scarlet   ..   ..   1·60   1·60
Nos. 769 and 770 were printed in sheets of five horizontal rows of five stamps comprising the following:—Rows 1/2, No. 769; Row 3, albino impressions; Rows 4/5, No. 770.

(Des and eng G. Barlangue. Recess)

1942 (8 Dec). *P* 13.
771 **180** 10 f. green   10   8

1943 (8 Feb). *National Relief Fund. P* 13.
772 **173** 1 f.+10 f. blue   ..   ..   1·90   1·90
773   1 f.+10 f. scarlet   ..   ..   1·90   1·90
774 **155** 2 f.+12 f. blue   ..   ..   1·90   1·90
775   2 f.+12 f. scarlet ..   ..   ..   1·90   1·90
                 Strip of 4   8·00   8·00
772/775   *Set of* 4 *singles*   ..   ..   6·50   6·50
Nos. 772/5 were printed in sheets of five horizontal rows, each row arranged in this order; Nos. 774, 772, a stamp-size label with battle-axe design, 773, 775.

182 Arms of Lyonnais

183 "Work"

184 Marshal Pétain

(Des Dufresne, Piel, Cortot and Louis. Die eng Ouvré, Piel and Cortot (15 f. and 20 f.). Typo)

1943. *As T* **182** *(provincial coats-of-arms). P* 14 × 13½.
776   5 f. scarlet, ultram & yellow (15.5.43)   10   5
777   10 f. black and yellow-brown (25.3.43)   12   8
778   15 f. yellow, ultram & scarlet (15.5.43)   75   70
779   20 f. yellow, ultram and brown (1.5.43)   55   45
776/779   *Set of* 4   ..   ..   ..   1·40   1·10
Arms *(inscr)*:—10 f. "Bretagne"; 15 f. "Provence"; 20 f. "Ile-de-France".
For similar stamps see Designs Index, under "Arms".

(1 f. 20 and 5 f. des and eng Ch. Mazelin, 1 f. 50, des Lemagny, eng R. Serres. 2 f. 40 and 4 f. des R. Cami. 2 f. 40, eng P. Munier. 4 f. eng Feltesse. Recess.)

1943 (7 June). *National Relief Fund. T* **183/4** *and similar vert designs. P* 13.
780   1 f. 20+1 f. 40, purple   ..   4·50   4·50
781   1 f. 50+2 f. 50, scarlet   ..   4·50   4·50
782   2 f. 40+7 f. brown   ..   ..   4·50   4·50
783   4 f.+10 f. violet   ..   ..   4·50   4·50
784   5 f.+15 f. red-brown   ..   ..   4·50   4·50
               Strip of 5   25·00   25·00
780/784   *Set of* 5 *singles*   ..   20·00   20·00
Designs:—1 f. 20, Marshal Pétain bareheaded; 2 f. 40, *inscr* "Famille"; 4 f. *inscr* "Patrie".
Nos. 780/4 were printed in sheets of 25 (5×5). Each horizontal row contains one stamp of each denomination, in order of value.

185 Lavoisier   186 Lake Lérie and the Meije Peak   D 187 Wheat Sheaves

(Eng Ouvré after a painting by L. David. Recess)

1943 (5 July). *Bicentenary of Birth of Lavoisier (chemist). P* 14 × 13.
785 **185** 4 f. blue   10   10

(Eng Gandon. Recess)

1943 (5 July). *P* 13.
786 **186** 20 f. green   30   30

(Des P. Gandon. Die eng H. Cortot. Typo)

1943–46. *POSTAGE DUE. Inscr* "CHIFFRE-TAXE" P 14 × 13½.
D787 D **187** 10 c. blackish brown   ..   5   5
D788   30 c. bright purple   5   5
D789   50 c. green   5   5
D790   1 f. blue   5   5
D791   1 f. 50, scarlet   5   5
D792   2 f. greenish blue   5   5
D793   3 f. brown-red   5   5
D794   4 f. violet ('46)   ..   ..   1·00   65
D795   5 f. pink   15   10
D796   10 f. orange ('46)   85   15
D797   20 f. olive-bistre ('46)   ..   1·50   20
D787/797   *Set of* 11 ..   ..   ..   3·00   1·25

187 Nicholas Rolin and Guisone de Salins   188 Victims of Bombed Towns

(Eng H. Cheffer. Recess)

1943 (21 July). *500th Anniv of Beaune Hospital. P* 13.
787 **187** 4 f. blue   20   20

(Eng Gandon. Recess)

1943 (23 Aug). *National Relief Fund.* 13
788 **188** 1 f. 50+3 f. 50, black .. 35 35

198 Gounod   **200** Arms of Flanders

(Des Ciry. Eng Dufresne. Recess)
1944 (27 Mar). *50th Death Anniv of Gounod* (*composer*). P 14 × 13½.
812 **198** 1 f. 50+3 f. 50, sepia 12 12

189 Prisoners' Families' Relief Work   **190** Bayard

(Des R. Louis. Die eng M. Cortot. Typo)
1944 (27 Mar). *As T* **200** (*provincial coats-of-arms*). P 14×13½.

(Des E. Faure and R. H. Munsch (2 f. 40), Eng J. Piel. Recess)

814	5 f. black, orange and carmine (27.3)	5 5
815	10 f. yellow, scarlet and brown (27.3) ..	8 5
816	15 f. yellow, blue and brown (24.4) ..	35 30
817	20 f. yellow, scarlet and blue (24.4) ..	40 40
814/817	Set of 4	75 75

1943 (27 Sept). *Prisoners' Families' Relief Fund. As T* **189** (*inscr* "FAMILLE DU PRISONNIER"). P 13.
789 1 f. 50+8 f. 50, purple-brown .. 40 40
790 2 f. 40+7 f. 60, green 40 40
Design: *Vert*—1 f. 50. Prisoner's family.

Arms (*inscr*):—10 f. "Languedoc"; 15 f. "Orléanais"; 20 f. "Normandie".
For similar stamps see Designs Index, under "Arms".

(Des and eng G. Barlangue (60 c.), A. Ouvré (1 f. 20), Degorce (1 f. 50), R. Serres (2 f. 40), P. Munier (4 f.) and Ouvré (5 f.). Recess)

1943 (25 Oct). *National Relief Fund. As T* **190** (*16th-century Celebrities*). P 13.
791 60 c.+80 c. blue-green 75 75
792 1 f. 20+1 f. 50, black 75 75
793 1 f. 50+3 f. ultramarine 75 75
794 2 f. 40+4 f. carmine-red 75 75
795 4 f.+6 f. red-brown 75 75
796 5 f.+10 f. green 75 75
791/796 *Set of 6* .. .. 4·00 4·00
Designs:—60 c. Montaigne; 1 f. 20, Francois Clouet; 1 f. 50, Ambroise Paré; 4 f. Sully; 5 f. Henry IV.

201 Marshal Pétain

202 Pétain gives France Workers' Charter

(T **201**. Des A. Lavrillier. Eng C. Mazelin. As T **202**. Eng Gandon (2 f.), Decaris (4 f.). All recess)

1944 (24 Apr). *Pétain's 88th Birthday.* P 13.
818 **201** 1 f. 50+3 f. 50, purple-brown .. 1·75 1·75
819 — 2 f.+3 f. blue 35 35
820 **202** 4 f.+6 f. carmine 35 35
Design as T **202** (*inscr*):—2 f. "Le Marechal institua la Corporation Paysanne". (*Trans* "The Marshal set up the Peasant Corporation").

191 Picardy   **196** Admiral de Tourville   **197** Branly

(60 c., des A. Delzers, eng G. Barlangue; 1 f. 20, des Decaris, eng Feltesse; 2 f. 40, des Lemagny, eng Dufresne. Des and eng 1 f. 50, C. Mazelin; 4 f. Cottet; 5 f. Decaris. Recess)

1943 (27 Dec). *National Relief Fund. As T* **191** (*provincial costumes*). P 13.
797 60 c.+1 f. 30, purple-brown 90 90
798 1 f. 20+2 f. violet 90 90
799 1 f. 50+4 f. greenish blue 90 90
800 2 f. 40+5 f. carmine 90 90
801 4 f.+6 f. blue 90 90
802 5 f.+7 f. scarlet 90 90
797/802 *Set of 6* .. .. 5·00 5·00
Designs (*inscr*):—1 f. 20, "Bretagne"; 1 f. 50, "Ile de France"; 2 f. 40, "Bourgogne"; 4 f. "Auvergne"; 5 f. "Provence".
The stamps issued by the French Committee of National Liberation formerly listed here will now be found under Nos. 82/9 of French Colonies.

203 Mobile Post Office   **204** Château of Chenonceaux

(Des Lemagny. Eng J. Piel. Recess)
1944 (21 Feb). *Birth Tercentenary of Admiral de Tourville.* P 13.
810 **196** 4 f.+6 f. brown-lake 40 40

(Eng M. Pelletan. Recess)
1944 (10 June). *Centenary of Mobile P.O s.* P 13.
821 **203** 1 f. 50, green 8 8

(Des and eng Decaris. Recess)
1944 (21 Feb). *Birth Centenary of Branly* (*physicist*). P 14 × 13.
811 **197** 4 f. ultramarine 10 5

(Eng G. Barlangue. Recess)
1944. P 13.
822 **204** 15 f. purple-brown (10 June) .. 20 20
823 25 f. black (30 Oct) 20 20
No. 822 is inscribed "FRANCE" instead of "RF".

205 Louis XIV   **206** Old-fashioned and Modern Locomotives   **207** Claude Chappe

(50 c. des M. Ciry, eng Mazelin; 1 f. 20, 2 f. des and eng P. Munier. Des and eng Gandon (80 c., 4 f.), Decaris (1 f. 50). Recess)

1944 (31 July). *National Relief Fund. As T 205 (various 17th-Century Celebrities). P 13.*

824	50	c.+1 f. 50, carmine	35	35
825	80	c.+2 f. 20, green	35	35
826	1	f. 20+2 f. 80, black	35	35
827	1	f. 50+3 f. 50, ultramarine	35	35
828	2	f.+4 f. red-brown	35	35
829	4	f.+6 f. orange-red	35	35
824/829		*Set of 6*	2·00	2·00

Designs:—50 c. Molière; 80 c. Hardouin-Mansart; 1 f. 20, Pascal; 1 f. 50, Le Grand Condé; 2 f. Colbert.

(Des Lemagny. Eng R. Serres. Recess)

1944 (14 Aug). *National Relief Fund. Centenary of Paris-Orléans and Paris-Rouen Railways. P 13.*

830	206	4 f.+6 f. black	20	20

(Des and eng R. Serres. Recess)

1944 (14 Aug). *150th Anniv of Invention of Semaphore Telegraph. P 14 × 13.*

831	207	4 f. blue	10	10

LIBERATION PERIOD, 1944

Stamps issued by the French Committee of National Liberation were first put on sale after the landing in Corsica in 1943 and later in the liberated areas in the south of France and, from November 1944, throughout France and in many of the French Colonies. These are listed under French Colonies (General Issues).

208 Gallic Cock   **209** "Marianne"

(Litho. Imbert, Algiers)

1944. *P 12.*

832	208	10 c. yellow-green	5	5
833		30 c. purple	5	5
834		40 c. blue	5	5
835		50 c. red	5	5
836	209	60 c. sepia	5	5
837		70 c. magenta	5	5
838		80 c. yellow-green	20	20
839		1 f. violet	5	5
840		1 f. 20, lake	5	5
841		1 f. 50, blue	5	5
842	208	2 f. grey-blue	5	5
843	209	2 f. 40, vermilion	30	30
844		3 f. blue-green	8	8
845		4 f. light blue	8	8
846		4 f. 50, black	8	8
847		5 f. violet-blue	95	95
848	208	10 f. violet	90	90
849		15 f. bistre-brown	90	90
850		20 f. deep green	95	95
832/850		*Set of 19*	4·50	4·50

The above series was first put on sale in Corsica after the Allied landing, and was later put on sale in Paris on 15 November, 1944.

210 Arc de Triomphe, Paris   **211** "Marianne"
(Typo. Bureau of Engraving and Printing, Washington)

1944 (June). *Design and value in same colour. P 11.*

851	210	5 c. bright purple	5	5
852		10 c. grey	5	5
853		25 c. red-brown	5	5
854		50 c. yellow-olive	5	5
855		1 f. emerald	5	5
856		1 f. 50, rose	5	5
857		2 f. 50, violet	5	5
858		4 f. blue	5	5
859		5 f. black	5	5
860		10 f. orange	5·50	5·00
851/860		*Set of 10*	5·50	5·00

Nos. 851–860 were brought to France when the Allies landed in Normandy and used in liberated areas as the armies advanced. They were first put on sale in Paris on 5 October, 1944.
See also Nos. 936/45.

PROVISIONAL GOVERNMENT

25 August 1944–26 October 1946

From 25 August 1944, the date of the Liberation of Paris, the Provisional Government, which had been set up in Algiers and then transferred to France, was recognised as the Government of France. A new Constitution, adopted by referendum, came into force on 27 October 1946.

1944. *New colours and values. P 14 × 13½.*

861	136	80 c. yellow-green (30.9)	5	5
862		1 f. greenish blue (18.9)	5	5
863		1 f. 20, violet (30.9)	5	5
864		1 f. 50, red-brown (5.9)	5	5
865		2 f. chocolate (30.10)	5	5
866		2 f. 40, carmine (7.10)	8	5
867		3 f. orange (1.11)	5	5
868		4 f. ultramarine (18.10)	5	5
861/868		*Set of 8*	35	30

(Des E. Dulac. Recess De La Rue, London)

1944–45. *P 11½ × 12½.*

869	211	10 c. blue (9.7.45)	5	5
870		30 c. yellow-brown (7.4.45)	5	5
871		40 c. deep blue (17.3.45)	5	5
872		50 c. orange-red (17.3.45)	5	5
873		60 c. grey-blue (17.3.45)	5	5
874		70 c. purple-brown (7.4.45)	5	5
875		80 c. emerald (17.3.45)	5	5
876		1 f. lilac (17.3.45)	5	5
877		1 f. 20, bronze-green (17.3.45)	5	5
878		1 f. 50, rose (16.9.44)	5	5
879		2 f. sepia (17.3.45)	5	5
880		2 f. 40, scarlet (17.3.45)	5	5
881		3 f. olive-green (17.3.45)	5	5
882		4 f. ultramarine (17.3.45)	5	5
883		4 f. 50, grey (7.4.45)	5	5
884		5 f. orange (7.4.45)	5	5
885		10 f. pale yellow-green (7.4.45)	8	5
886		15 f. claret (7.4.45)	15	15
887		20 f. brown-orange (9.7.45)	45	30
888		50 f. violet (15.11.45)	1·25	80
869/888		*Set of 20*	2·50	2·00

No. 880 imperf comes from a block of four in a miniature sheet which was not issued.

A regular new issue supplement to this catalogue appears each month in

STAMP MONTHLY

—from your newsagent or by postal subscription
—details on request.

212 St. Denis Basilica   **213** Marshal Bugeaud

(Eng Barlangue. Recess)

1944 (20 Nov). *8th Centenary of St. Denis Basilica.* *P* 13.
889 **212** 2 f. 40, red-brown ..   8   8

(Eng Decaris. Recess)

1944 (20 Nov). *Centenary of Battle of Isly.* *P* 13.
890 **213** 4 f. blue-green   10   10

214 Angoulème   **(214***a***)**   **215** Arms of De
Cathedral   Villayer

(50 c. des J. J. Dufour, eng Dufresne; 1 f. 20, des Lucas, eng Cottet. Des and eng C. Mazelin (80 c., 1 f. 50), Cottet (4 f.). Recess)

1944 (20 Nov). *Cathedrals of France. First Issue.* *T* **214** (*and similar designs*). *P* 13.
891   50 c.+1 f. 50, black   ..   10   10
892   80 c.+2 f. 20, purple (Chartres)   12   12
893   1 f. 20+2 f. 80, lake (Amiens)   20   20
894   1 f. 50+3 f. 50, blue (Beauvais)   25   25
895   4 f.+6 f. red (Albi)   25   25
891/895   *Set of* 5   80   85

1944 (27 Nov). *Nos. 750/3 optd with T* **214***a*.
896 **123** 10 c. ultramarine   ..   5   5
897   30 c. scarlet   ..   5   5
898   40 c. violet   ..   5   5
899   50 c. greenish blue   ..   5   5
896/899   *Set of* 4   10   10

(Des R. Louis. Eng H. Cortot. Recess)

1944 (9 Dec). *Stamp Day.* *P* 13.
900 **215** 1 f. 50+3 f. 50, brown ..   5   5

216 "France" exhorting Resistance Forces

(Eng Gandon. Recess)

1945 (16 Jan). *Liberation.* *P* 13.
901 **216** 4 f. blue   5   5

217 Shield and   **218** Ceres   **219** Marianne
Broken Chains

(Des A. Rivaud (T **217**), Mazelin (T **218**), Gandon (T **219/20**). Die eng Cortot (Nos 902/26), Gandon (Nos. 927/35))

220 Marianne

1945–46. (*a*) *Typo.* *P* 14 × 13½.
902 **217** 10 c. blackish brown (19.2.45)   5   5
903   30 c. green (19.2.45)   5   5
904   40 c. magenta (1.2.45)   ..   5   5
905   50 c. violet-blue (12.2.45)   5   5
906 **218** 60 c. ultramarine (19.2.45)   5   5
907   80 c. yellow-green (26.2.45)   5   5
908   90 c. blue-green (8.4.46)*   5   5
909   1 f. carmine-red (1.2.45)   5   5
910   1 f. 20, brownish black (19.2.45) ..   5   5
911   1 f. 50, bright purple (2.7.45)   5   5
912 **219** 1 f. 50, carmine (15.2.45)   5   5
913   2 f. blue-green (26.2.45)   5   5
914 **218** 2 f. yellow-green (12.8.46)   5   5
915 **219** 2 f. 40, scarlet (2.7.45)   10   5
916 **218** 2 f. 50, chocolate (21.2.46)   5   5
917 **219** 3 f. deep brown (26.2.45)   5   5
918   3 f. carmine (20.3.46)   ..   5   5
919   4 f. blue (14.6.45)   ..   5   5
920   4 f. bright violet (25.7.45)   5   5
921   5 f. green (7.4.45)   ..   5   5
922   6 f. ultramarine (14.6.45)   10   5
923   6 f. rose-red (14.4.46)   ..   5   5
924   10 f. orange (14.6.45)   ..   8   5
925   10 f. blue (11.2.46)   ..   15   10
926   15 f. bright purple (14.6.45)   60   35
902/926   *Set of* 25   ..   ..   1·25   75
*No. 908 was issued only precancelled, the unused price being for stamps with full gum.
For Types **218** and **219** typographed in new colours and values, see Nos. **997**, etc.

(*b*) *Recess.* *P* 14 × 13
927 **219** 4 f. blue (15.2.45)   ..   5   5
928   10 f. blue (15.3.46)   ..   15   5
929   15 f. bright purple (15.5.46)   95   15
930   20 f. blue-green (4.3.46)   ..   40   5
931   25 f. scarlet (15.3.46)   ..   95   20
927/931   *Set of* 5   ..   ..   2·25   35
For 15 f. scarlet and 25 f. blue see Nos. 1063/4.

(*c*) *Recess.* *P* 13.
932 **220** 20 f. green (14.5.45)   ..   45   20
933   25 f. violet (14.5.45)   ..   75   45
934   50 f. red-brown (1.4.45)   ..   60   35
935   100 f. carmine (7.4.45)   ..   1·75   1·00
932/935   *Set of* 4   ..   ..   3·25   2·75

1945 (12 Feb). *Value in black.* *P* 11.
936 **210** 30 c. orange   5   5
937   40 c. grey   5   5
938   50 c. olive   5   5
939   60 c. violet   5   5
940   80 c. yellow-green   5   5
941   1 f. 20, brown   5   5
942   1 f. 50, scarlet   5   5
943   2 f. orange-yellow   ..   5   5
944   2 f. 40, carmine   5   5
945   3 f. bright purple   5   5
936/945   *Set of* 10   25   20

221 Arms of
Strasbourg

222 Patient in
Deck Chair

(Des R. Louis. Eng P. Munier (2 f. 50) and J. Piel (4 f.) Recess)
1945 (5 Mar). *Liberation of Metz and Strasbourg.* P 14 × 13.
946 — 2 f. 40, blue (Metz) 5 5
947 **221** 4 f. sepia (Strasbourg) 5 5

(Des Barlangue. Die eng Cortot. Typo)
1945 (16 May). *Anti-Tuberculosis Fund.* Perf. 14 × 13½.
948 **222** 2 f.+1 f. red-orange 5 5

223 Refugee Employee
and Family

224 Sarah
Bernhardt

(Eng Serres. Recess)
1945 (16 May). *Postal Employees War Victims' Fund.* P 13.
949 **223** 4 f.+6 f. purple-brown 5 5

(Des Bastien-Lepage. Eng C. Mazelin. Recess)
1945 (16 May). *Birth Centenary of Sarah Bernhardt.* P 13.
950 **224** 4 f.+1 f. purple-brown 10 10

225 Alsatian and Lorrainer
in Native Dress

226 Children in
Country

(Des Lemagny. Eng Serres. Recess)
1945 (16 May). *Liberation of Alsace-Lorraine.* P 13.
951 **225** 4 f. red-brown 10 10

(Eng Ouvré. Recess)
1945 (9 July). *Fresh Air Crusade.* P 13.
952 **226** 4 f.+2 f. blue-green 8 8

1945 (17 Sept). As No. 661, but incorporating Cross of
Lorraine and inscr "1945". Recess. P 13.
953 **149** 2 f. greenish blue 5 5

227 Destruction of Oradour

228 Louis XI

(Eng Serres. Recess)
1945 (13 Oct). *Destruction of Oradour-sur-Glane.* P 13.
954 **227** 4 f.+2 f. sepia 10 10

(Eng Serres. Recess)
1945 (13 Oct). *Stamp Day.* P 13.
955 **228** 2 f.+3 f. blue 10 10

229 Dunkirk

230 Alfred Fournier

(Eng Barlangue (1 f. 50), Mazelin (2 f.), Piel (2 f. 40) and
Munier (4 f.). Recess)
1945 (5 Nov). *Devastated Towns.* T **229** (and similar views).
P 13.
956 1 f. 50+1 f. 50, red 8 8
957 2 f.+2 f. violet (Rouen) 8 8
958 2 f. 40+2 f. 60, blue (Caen) 8 8
959 4 f.+4 f. black (St. Malo) 8 8
956/959 Set of 4 .. .. .. 20 20

(Des Lemagny. Eng Dufresne Recess)
1946 (4 Feb)–**47**. *Prophylaxis Fund.* P 13.
960 **230** 2 f.+3 f. brown-lake 10 10
961 2 f.+3 f. indigo (20.10.47) .. 20 20

231 Henri Becquerel   (232)   **233** "Les Invalides"

(Eng P. Munier. Recess)
1946 (4 Feb). P 13.
962 **231** 2 f.+3 f. violet 10 10

1946 (21 Feb). Surch with T **232**.
963 **222** 3 f. on 2 f.+1 f. red-orange .. 5 5

(Eng G. Barlangue. Recess)
1946 (11 Mar). *War Invalids Relief Fund.* P 13.
964 **233** 4 f.+6 f. red-brown 15 15

234 Warships   235 "The Letter"

(Eng C. Mazelin. Recess)

1946 (8 Apr). *Naval Charities. P* 13.
965 **234** 2 f.+3 f. black 12   12

(Eng H. Cheffer after Chardin. Recess)

1946 (25 May). *Postal Museum Fund. P* 13.
966 **235** 2 f.+3 f. brown-lake 20   20

M 236

(Des and die eng R. Louis and Hourriez. Typo)

1946. *MILITARY FRANK. No value indicated. P* 14 × 13½.
M967 M **236** (–) Deep grey-green (6.6) .. 35   20
M968   (–) Carmine-red (1.10) .. 12   5

236 Iris   237 Jupiter carrying off Egine

(Eng Gandon. Recess)

1946–47. *AIR. P* 13.
967   –   40 f. blue-green (1.7.46) .. 25   5
968 **236** 50 f. pink (27.5.46) 25   5
969 **237** 100 f. ultramarine (20.1.47) .. 70   12
970   –   200 f. red (27.5.46) .. .. 1·10   25
967/970   Set of 4 .. .. 2·00   30
Designs: *Vert*—40 f. Centaur. *Horiz*—200 f. Apollo and chariot.

239 Arms of Corsica   241 Fouquet de la Varane

(Des R. Louis. Eng Cortot (10 c., 60 c.), Hourriez (30 c., 50 c.). Typo)

1946 (26 June–July) *As T* **239** (*provincial coats-of-arms*).
P 14 × 13½.
971   10 c. black and ultramarine 5   5
972   30 c. black, red and yellow 5   5
973   50 c. brown, yellow and red (8.7) .. 5   5
974   60 c. carmine, ultramarine and black .. 5   5
971/974   Set of 4 12   12
Arms (*inscr*):—30 c. "Alsace"; 50 c. "Lorraine" 60 c. "Nice".
For similar stamps see Designs Index, under "Arms".

(Eng R. Serres. Recess)

1946 (29 June). *Stamp Day. P* 13.
975 **241** 3 f.+2 f. sepia 20   20

242 Vézelay   243 Cannes

244 Luxembourg Palace   245 Roc-Amadour

246 Pointe du Raz   247 Stanislas Place, Nancy

(Des and eng Cottet (5 f.), Gandon (6 f.), Decaris (10 f.), E. Mazelin (15 f.), Cheffer (20 f.) and Serres (25 f.). Recess)

1946–48. *P* 13.
976 **242** 5 f. mauve (20.7.46) 5   5
977 **243** 6 f. scarlet (10.2.47) 12   8
978 **244** 10 f. blue (29.7.46) 8   5
979   12 f. carmine (10.5.48) 12   12
980 **245** 15 f. brown-purple (21.10.46) .. 25   5
980*a* **244** 15 f. scarlet (8.12.48) 12   12
981 **246** 20 f. slate-blue (21.10.46) .. 12   5
982 **247** 25 f. sepia (10.2.47) 20   5
982*a*   25 f. deep blue (9.12.48) 20   12
976/982*a*   Set of 9 .. .. .. 1·00   60
No. 978 is inscribed "RF" instead of "FRANCE".

248 "Peace"   249 Woman Releasing Dove   D 250 Wheat Sheaves

France 1946

(Eng Gandon and Decaris. Recess)
1946 (29 July). *Peace Conference. P 13.*
983 **248** 3 f. blue-green 5 5
984 **249** 10 f. blue 10 5

(Des P. Gandon. Die eng H. Cortot. Typo)
1946–53. *POSTAGE DUE. Inscr* "TIMBRE TAXE". *P* 14×13½.
D985 D **250** 10 c. blackish brown (18.2.47) 65 40
D986 30 c. bright purple (19.2.47) 50 40
D987 50 c. green (13.3.47) .. :: 2·00 1·00
D988 1 f. blue (18.1.47) 5 5
D989 2 f. greenish blue (5.12.46) .. 5 5
D990 3 f. brown-red (23.4.47) .. 5 5
D991 4 f. violet (11.9.46) 5 5
D992 5 f. pink (10.3.47) 5 5
D993 10 f. orange-red (2.6.47) .. 10 5
D994 20 f. olive-brown (4.6.47) .. 45 10
D995 50 f. deep green (1950) .. 1·10 40
D996 100 f. green (2.53) .. .. 13·00 65
D985/996 *Set of 12* .. .. .. 16·00 3·00

FOURTH REPUBLIC
27 October 1946–4 October 1958

250 François Villon

251

(Des and eng Decaris (2 f., 5 f.), Gandon and Piel (3 f.),
G. Barlangue (4 f.), Ouvré (6 f.), Lemagny and Dufresne (10 f.).
Recess)
1946 (28 Oct). *National Relief Fund. As T 250* (*vert portraits
of* 15th-century historical figures). *P 13.*
985 2 f.+1 f. greenish blue 45 45
986 3 f.+1 f. indigo 45 45
987 4 f +3 f. brown-lake 45 45
988 5 f.+4 f. ultramarine 45 45
989 6 f.+5 f. chocolate 4ᶠ 45
990 10 f.+6 f. red-orange 45 45
985/990 *Set of 6* .. .. .. 2·50 2·50
Portraits:—3 f. Jean Fouquet; 4 f. Philippe de Commynes;
5 f. Joan of Arc; 6 f. Jean Gerson; 10 f. Charles VII.

(Des and eng Decaris. Recess)
1946 (19 Nov). *U.N.E.S.C.O. Conference, Paris. P 13.*
991 **251** 10 f. blue 15 15

252 St. Julien Cathedral,
Le Mans

253 Louvois

(Eng 1 f. P. Munier; 3 f. Ch. Mazelin; 4 f. G. Barlangue; 6 f.
Decaris; 10 f. J. Piel. Recess)
1947 (6 Jan). *National Relief Fund. Cathedrals of France*
(2nd issue). *Various Cathedrals as T 214 and 252. P 13*
992 1 f.+1 f. carmine 8 8
993 3 f +2 f. blue-black 10 10
994 4 f.+3 f. brown-red 20 20
995 6 f.+4 f. blue 40 40
996 10 f.+6 f. blue-green 45 45
992/996 *Set of 5* .. .. .. 1·00 1·00
Designs: *Vert*—1 f. St. Sernin, Toulouse; 3 f. Notre-Dame du
Port, Clermont-Ferrand; 10 f. Notre-Dame, Paris. *Horiz*—4 f.
St. Front, Périgueux.

1947–51. *New values and colours changed. Typo. P* 14×13½.
997 **218** 1 f. 30, blue (8.4.47) 8 8
997a **219** 2 f. 50, brown (9.48)* .. .. 1·10 50
998 3 f. green (25.7.47) 10 5
999 3 f. magenta (10.5.48) 10 5
1000 3 f. 50, brown-red (8.4 47) .. 10 5
1001 4 f. turquoise-green (10.5.48) .. 15 5
1001a 4 f. brown-orange (14.12.48) .. 25 10
1002 4 f. 50, blue (23.1.47) 5 5
1003 5 f. carmine (3.1.47) 5 5
1004 5 f. blue (25.7.47) 8 5
1004a 5 f. yellow-green (14.12.48) .. 12 5
1004b 5 f. violet (1.5.51) 25 5
1005 6 f. carmine-red (12.7.47) .. 15 5
1005a 6 f. green (1.5.51) .. .. 2·10 10
1006 8 f. light blue (21.9.48) 12 5
1007 10 f. reddish violet (10.5.48) .. 15 5
1007a 12 f. ultramarine (27.1.49) .. 30 5
1007b 12 f. red-orange (1.5.51) .. 30 5
1007c 15 f. rose-carmine (10.1.49) .. 30 5
1007d 15 f. blue (1.5.51) 15 5
1007e 18 f. carmine (1.5.51) .. .. 3·50 20
997/1007e *Set of 21* .. .. .. 8·50 1·10
*No. 997a was issued only precancelled, the unused price
being for stamps with full gum.
The 5 f. carmine was sold at P.O's at 10 per cent below face
value and its franking power was therefore only 4 f. 50.

(Des and eng R. Serres. Recess)
1947 (15 Mar). *Stamp Day. P 13.*
1008 **253** 4 f. 50+5 f. 50, carmine .. 75 75

Designs: *Horiz*—4 f. 50,
La Conciergerie; 6 f. La
Cité; 10 f. Place de la
Concorde.

254 The Louvre Colonnade

255 Seagull over "Ile de la Cité"

(Eng Ouvré, J. Piel, H. Cheffer, Cottet and Gandon. Recess)
1947 (7 May). *Twelfth Congress of the U.P.U. P 13.*
(a) *POSTAGE. As T 254* (*views of Paris*).
1009 3 f. 50, purple-brown 20 20
1010 4 f. 50, bluish grey 20 20
1011 6 f. scarlet 30 30
1012 10 f. ultramarine 30 30
(b) *AIR*
1013 **255** 500 f. slate-green .. .. 14·00 11·00
1009/1013 *Set of 5* .. .. .. 14·00 11·00

256 Auguste Pavie

257 Fénelon

(Eng Ouvré. Recess)

1947 (30 May). *Pavie (explorer) Centenary. P* 13.
1014 **256** 4 f. 50, blackish violet 10 10

(Eng C. Mazelin. Recess)

1947 (12 July). *Fénelon, Archbishop of Cambrai. P* 13.
1015 **257** 4 f. 50, purple-brown 10 10

258 St. Nazaire Monument **259**

(Des G. Joly. Eng C. Mazelin. Recess)

1947 (2 Aug). *5th Anniv of British Commando Raid at St. Nazaire. P* 13.
1016 **258** 6 f.+4 f. indigo 12 10

(Eng Piel. Recess)

1947 (2 Aug). *Boy Scouts' Jamboree. P* 13.
1017 **259** 5 f. brown 12 12

260 Milestone on **261** "Resistance" **(262)**
Road of Liberty

(Des Mazelin. Eng Dufresne. Recess)

1947 (10 Sept). *Road Maintenance Fund. P* 13.
1018 **260** 6 f.+4 f. blue-green 15 15

(Des Lemagny. Eng Dufresne. Recess)

1947 (10 Nov). *Resistance Movement. P* 13
1019 **261** 5 f. blackish violet 12 12

1947 (15 Nov). *Surch with T* **262.**
1020 **218** 1 f. on 1 f. 30, blue (R.) 5 5

263 Conques Abbey **264** Louis Braille

(Des and eng Gandon. Recess)

1947–48. *P* 13.
1021 **263** 15 f. brown-red (18.12.47) .. 20 10
1022 18 f. blue (10.5.48) 20 10
No. 1022 is inscribed "FRANCE".

(Des and eng R. Serres. Recess)

1948 (19 Jan). *Louis Braille (inventor of system of writing and printing for the blind). P* 13.
1023 **264** 6 f.+4 f. bright violet 20 20

265 A. de Saint-Exupéry **266** Aeroplane and "Æolus"
(pilot and writer)

(Des and eng Pierre Gandon. Recess)

1948 (19 Jan). *AIR. As T* **265** *(portraits of famous airmen). P* 13.
1024 50 f.+30 f. brown-purple .. 50 50
1025 100 f.+70 f. blue (Dagnaux) .. 1·00 75

(Des and eng Pierre Gandon. Recess)

1948 (23 Feb). *AIR. Clément Ader (air pioneer). P* 13.
1026 **266** 40 f.+10 f. deep blue 45 40

267 Etienne Arago **268** Lamartine

(Des and eng R. Serres. Recess)

1948 (6 Mar). *Stamp Day and Centenary of First French Adhesive Postage Stamps. P* 13.
1027 **267** 6 f.+4 f. blackish violet 25 25

(Des Lemagny (1 f., 20 f.), Gandon, Mazelin, Cheffer, Piel, Ouvré and Serres. Eng Cottet, Mazelin (3 f., 4 f.), Cheffer, Piel, Ouvré, Serres and Feltesse. Recess)

1948 (5 Apr). *National Relief Fund and Centenary of 1848 Revolution. As T* **268** *(various portraits inscr* "1848/1948"). *P* 13.
1028 1 f.+1 f. green 40 40
1029 3 f.+2 f. brown-red 50 50
1030 4 f.+3 f. purple 50 50
1031 5 f.+4 f. greenish blue .. 65 65
1032 6 f.+5 f. blackish blue .. 65 65
1033 10 f.+6 f. carmine 65 65
1034 15 f.+7 f. indigo .. .. 1·25 1·25
1035 20 f.+8 f. violet .. .. 1·50 1·50
1028/1035 *Set of* 8 .. .. 5·50 5·50
Portraits: *Vert*—Lamartine; Ledru-Rollin; Louis Blanc; A. M. Albert; P. J. Proudhon; Blanqui, Barbès and Mgr Affre.

269 Dr. Calmette **270** General Leclerc

(Des and eng H. C. Cheffer. Recess)

1948 (18 June). *First International B.C.G. (Vaccine) Congress. P* 13.
1036 **269** 6 f.+4 f. greenish slate 15 12

(Des and eng R. Serres. Recess)

1948 (3 July). *General Leclerc Memorial. P* 13.
1037 **270** 6 f. black 10 10

271 Chateaubriand   272 Génissiat Barrage

(Des Lemagny. Eng Barlangue. Recess)

1948 (3 July). *Death Centenary of Chateaubriand.* P 13.
1038 **271** 18 f. blue   25   15

(Des and eng Barlangue. Recess)

1948 (21 Sept). *Inauguration of Génissiat Barrage.* P 13.
1039 **272** 12 f. carmine   25   20

273 Aerial View   274 Paul Langevin   (275)
of Chaillot Palace

(Des and eng Decaris (12 f.) and Piel (18 f.). Recess)

1948 (21 Sept). *U.N. Assembly, Paris.* T 273 *and similar design showing Chaillot Palace from ground level.* P 13.
1040   12 f. carmine   20   20
1041   18 f. indigo   25   25

(Des and eng Mazelin (5 f.) and Gandon (8 f.). Recess)

1948 (17 Nov). *Transfer of Ashes of Paul Langevin and Jean Perrin to the Pantheon.* T 274 *and similar portrait.* P 14 × 13.
1042   5 f. plum   10   8
1043   8 f. greenish blue (Jean Perrin)   ..   10   8

1949 (17 Jan). *No.* 1005 *surch with* T 275.
1044 **219** 5 f. on 6 f. carmine-red   ..   5   5

276 Ploughing   277 Arms of   278 Duc de
         Burgundy   Choiseul

(Eng Decaris (3 f. and 8 f.), Cheffer (5 f.) and Gandon (10 f.). Recess)

1949 (14 Feb). *Workers. Designs as* T 276. P 13.
1045   3 f. + 1 f. claret   15   10
1046   5 f. + 3 f. blue   20   12
1047   8 f. + 4 f. indigo   30   25
1048   10 f. + 6 f. scarlet   40   25
1045/1048 *Set of* 4   95   65
   Designs:—5 f. Fisherman; 8 f. Miner; 10 f. Industrial worker.

(Des R. Louis. Die eng J. Piel (10 c.), H. Cortot (50 c., 2 f., 4 f.) and Hourriez (1 f.). Typo)

1949. *As* T 277 *(provincial coats-of-arms).* P 14 × 13½.
1049   10 c. yellow, scarlet & ultram (21.3) ..   5   5
1050   50 c. yellow, scarlet & ultram (11.5) ..   5   5
1051   1 f. scarlet and brown (11.5)   ..   5   5
1052   2 f. scarlet, yellow and green (11.5) ..   10   5
1053   4 f. ultramarine, yellow & scarlet (11.5)   20   5
1049/1053 *Set of* 5   40   12
Arms (*inscr*):—50c. "Guyenne"; 1f. "Savoie"; 2f "Auvergne"; 4 f. "Anjou".
For similar stamps see Designs Index, under "Arms".

(Eng R. Serres. Recess)

1949 (26 Mar). *Stamp Day.* P 13.
1054 **278** 15 f. + 5 f. green   70   70

279 Lille   280 Polar Scene

279a Paris

(Des Decaris. Eng Decaris and Combet (1,000 f.) or Decaris (others). Recess)

1949–50. *AIR. As* T 279 *(various cities) and* T 279a. P 13.
1055   100 f. brown-purple (25.4.49)   ..   45   5
1056   200 f. green (23.6.49)   ..   ..   2·75   30
1057   300 f. violet (23.6.49)   ..   ..   6·50   4·00
1058   500 f. vermilion (18.7.49) ..   ..   16·00   1·40
1059   1000 f. slate-purple & blk/bl (16.1.50) 40·00   9·50
1055/1059 *Set of* 5 ..   ..   ..   60·00   14·00
   Designs:—200 f. Bordeaux; 300 f. Lyons; 500 f. Marseilles.

(Des and eng Gandon. Recess)

1949 (2 May). *Polar Expeditions.* P 13.
1060 **280** 15 f. indigo   30   30

1949 (9 May). *French Stamp Centenary. Recess. (a) Imperf.*
1061 **1** 15 f. scarlet ..   ..   ..   1·75   1·75
1062   25 f. blue   ..   ..   ..   1·75   1·75

(b) P 14 × 13

1063 **219** 15 f. scarlet ..   ..   ..   1·75   1·75
1064   25 f. blue ..   ..   ..   1·75   1·75
         Strip of 4   7·50   7·50
Nos. 1061/64 were printed in sheets of 40 (10 × 4) giving 10 vertical strips showing the above stamps in the order listed. The imperf are separated from the perf stamps by a label inscr "CENTENAIRE DU TIMBRE-POST 1849 1949" in brown.

281 Collegiate Church   282 Emblems of U.S.A. and France
of St. Barnard, Romans

(Des A. Spitz. Eng Mazelin. Recess)

1949 (14 May). *600th Anniv of Cession of Dauphiny to King of France.* P 13.
1065 **281** 12 f. red-brown   20   12

(Des Lubes. Eng Gandon. Recess)

1949 (14 May). *Franco-American Amity.* P 13.
1066 **282** 25 f. red and blue   40   35

284 St. Wandrille Abbey   **285** Jean Racine

(Des and eng Gandon (20 f., 30 f. indigo), H. Cheffer (T **284**), Cottet (40 f.), and P. Munier (50 f.). Recess)

1949–51. *Views as T* **284.** *P* 13.
1067	–	20 f. brown-red (20.7.49)	..	15	5
1068	**284**	25 f. blue (18.5.49)	..	20	5
1068a		30 f. turquoise-blue (1.5.51)	..	2·25	1·40
1068b		30 f. indigo (23.6.51)	..	40	5
1069	–	40 f. slate-green (23.5.49)	..	90	5
1070	–	50 f. brown-purple (3.6.49)	..	65	5
1067/1070		*Set of 6*	..	3·00	1·50

Designs:—20 f. St. Bertrand de Comminges; 30 f. indigo, Arbois (Jura); 40 f. Valley of the Meuse (Ardennes); 50 f. Mt. Gerbier-de-Jonc, Vivarais.

(Des Spitz. Eng Ouvré. Recess)

1949 (24 May). *250th Anniv of Death of Jean Racine (dramatist). P* 13.
1071	**285**	12 f. brown-purple	..	20	20

1949 (1 June). *French Stamp Centenary ("CITEX"). T* **1** *with dates "1849 1949" below, repeated ten times (2 × 5) with "1849–1949" centred above. Recess. Imperf (border P* 13.)
MS1071a 280×155 mm 10 f. (+100 f.)
orange-red. *Complete sheet of ten* .. £225 £225

286 Claude Chappe   **287** Alexander III Bridge and "Petit Palais"

(Des and eng Ouvré (10 f.), Barlangue (25 f.), Munier (50 f.) and Gandon (100 f.). Des Spitz and eng Cottet (15 f.). Recess)

1949 (13 June). *International Telephone and Telegraph Congress, Paris. As T* **286** *(various portraits inscr "C.I.T.T. PARIS 1949") and* **287.** *P* 13. (*a*) *POSTAGE. Inscr "POSTES"*
1072	10 f. vermilion	..	..	50	30
1073	15 f. blackish violet	..	..	80	30
1074	25 f. lake	..	..	1·50	1·25
1075	50 f. blue	..	..	1·90	95

(*b*) *AIR. Inscr "POSTE AERIENNE"*
1076	**287**	100 f. brown-red	..	2·50	1·90
1072/1076		*Set of 5*	..	6·00	4·25

Designs:—15 f. Arago and Ampère; 25 f. Emile Baudot; 50 f. General Ferrié.

288 Allegory of Commerce   **289** Allegory

(Des Spitz. Eng Munier. Recess)

1949 (18 Oct). *French Chambers of Commerce. P* 13.
1077	**288**	15 f. carmine	..	..	20	15

(Des Spitz. Eng Cottet. Recess)

1949 (7 Nov). *75th Anniv of U.P.U. P* 13.
1078	**289**	5 f. green	..	..	15	12
1079		15 f. scarlet	..	..	25	20
1080		25 f. blue	..	..	65	40

290 Montesquieu   **291** "Spring"

(Des Lemagny, eng Dufresne (5 f.). Des and eng Mazelin (8 f.), Cheffer (10 f.), Barlangue (12 f.), Serres (15 f.), Ouvré (25 f.). Recess)

1949 (14 Nov). *National Relief Fund. As T* **290** (*18th-century Celebrities*). *P* 13.
1081	5 f.+1 f. green	..	..	1·75	1·75
1082	8 f.+2 f. indigo (Voltaire)	..	..	1·75	1·75
1083	10 f.+3 f. red-brown (Watteau)	..	1·75	1·75
1084	12 f.+4 f. violet (Buffon)	..	..	1·75	1·75
1085	15 f.+5 f. carmine (Dupleix)	..	2·00	2·00
1086	25 f.+10 f. blue (Turgot)	..	..	2·25	2·25
1081/1086	*Set of 6* ..	..	..	10·00	10·00

(Des J. Piel after Bouchardon. Recess)

1949 (19 Dec). *National Relief Fund. T* **291** *and similar types showing the Seasons. P* 13.
1087	5 f.+1 f. blue-green and green	..	80	80
1088	8 f.+2 f. yellow and reddish brown	..	80	80
1089	12 f.+3 f. violet	..	..	1·10	1·10
1090	15 f.+4 f. blue	..	..	1·10	1·10
1087/1090	*Set of 4* ..	..	..	3·25	3·25

Seasons:—8 f. "Summer"; 12 f. "Autumn"; 15 f. "Winter".

292 Postman   **293** Raymond Poincaré

(Des and eng Decaris. Recess)

1950 (11 Mar). *Stamp Day. P* 13.
1091	**292**	12 f.+3 f. blue	..	..	1·90	1·40

(Des and eng Gandon. Recess)

1950 (27 May). *Honouring Raymond Poincaré. P* 13.
1092	**293**	15 f. deep blue	..	..	20	20

294 Charles Péguy   **295** François Rabelais.

(Des and eng Gandon. Recess)
1950 (12 June). *Honouring Charles Péguy (writer).* *P* 13.
1093 **294** 12 f. brown-purple 20 20

(Des and eng Decaris. Recess)
1950 (26 June). *Honouring François Rabelais (writer).* *P* 13.
1094 **295** 12 f. brown-lake 20 20

296 André Chénier   **297** Châteaudun

(Eng Barlangue (5 f.), Cottet (8 f.). Des and eng Cheffer (10 f.).
Des Lemagny, eng Dufresne (12 f.). Des and eng Mazelin
(15 f.). Eng Ouvré (20 f.). Recess)
1950 (10 July). *National Relief Fund.* *As T* **296** *(revolutionary
celebrites).* *Frames in slate-blue.* *P* 13.
  1095   5 f.+2 f. reddish purple .. .. 3·25 3·25
  1096   8 f.+3 f. purple-brown .. .. 3·25 3·25
  1097 10 f.+4 f. carmine .. .. .. 3·25 3·25
  1098 12 f.+5 f. orange-brown .. .. 3·50 3·50
  1099 15 f.+6 f. green .. .. .. 3·50 3·50
  1100 20 f.+10 f. blue .. .. 3·75 3·75
1095/1100 *Set of 6* .. .. 18·00 18·00
Portraits:—8 f. Louis David; 10 f. Lazare Carnot; 12 f. Danton;
15 f. Robespierre; 20 f. Hoche.

(Des and eng 8 f. Gandon, 12 f. Decaris. Recess)
1950–51. *T* **297** *and similar view.* *P* 13.
1101   8 f. purple-brown & yell-brn (25.11.50) 20 20
1102 12 f. purple-brown (20.1.51) 20 20
View:—12 f. Palace of Fontainebleau.

298 Madame   **299** "L'Amour"   **300** T.P.O.
Récamier   (after Falconet)   Sorting Van

(Des Lemagny. Eng Mazelin (12 f.), Ouvré (15 f.). Recess)
1950. *T* **298** *and similar portrait.* *P* 13.
1103 12 f. green (9 Dec) 20 20
1104 15 f. blue (25 Nov) 20 20
Portrait:—15 f. Madame de Sévigné.

(Des and eng J. Piel. Recess)
1950 (22 Dec). *Red Cross Fund.* *T* **299** *and similar type.*
Cross in red. *P* 13.
1105   8 f.+2 f. slate-blue .. .. 1·75 1·75
1106 15 f.+5 f. brown-purple .. .. 1·75 1·75
Design:—8 f. Bust of Alexander Brongniart (after Houdon).

(Des and eng Decaris. Recess)
1951 (10 Mar). *Stamp Day.* *P* 13.
1107 **300** 12 f.+3 f. slate-violet .. .. 1·75 1·75

301 J. Ferry (statesman)   **302** Shuttle

(Des and eng Cottet. Recess)
1951 (17 Mar). *P* 13.
1108 **301** 15 f. scarlet 35 30

(Des and eng Decaris. Recess)
1951 (9 Apr). *Textile Industry.* *P* 13.
1109 **302** 25 f. blue 55 50

303 De La Salle   **304** Anchor and Map

(Des and eng Gandon. Recess)
1951 (28 Apr). *Birth Tercentenary of Jean Baptiste de La
Salle (educational reformer).* *P* 13.
1110 **303** 15 f. brown-purple 25 20

(Des Louis. Eng Munier. Recess)
1951 (12 May). *50th Anniv of Formation of Colonial Troops.*
P 13.
1111 **304** 15 f. blue 35 30

305 Vincent D'Indy   **306** A. de Musset

(Des and eng Decaris. Recess)
1951 (15 May). *Birth Centenary of Vincent D'Indy (composer).*
P 13.
1112 **305** 25 f. green .. .. .. 1·10 70

(Des Lemagny. Eng Dufresne (5 f.). Des and eng Cheffer (8 f.),
Munier (10 f.), Mazelin (12 f.), Ouvré (15 f.) and Decaris
(30 f.). Recess)
1951 (2 June). *National Relief Fund.* *As T* **306** *(19th-century
celebrities).* *Frames in sepia.* *P* 13.
1113   5 f.+1 f. green .. .. .. 3·25 3·25
1114   8 f.+2 f. purple .. .. .. 3·50 3·50
1115 10 f.+3 f. blue-green .. .. 3·50 3·50
1116 12 f.+4 f. slate-purple .. .. 3·50 3·50
1117 15 f.+5 f. brown-red .. .. 3·50 3·50
1118 30 f.+10 f. blue .. .. .. 5·00 5·00
1113/1118 *Set of 6* .. .. .. 20·00 20·00
Portraits: 8 f. Delacroix; 10 f. Gay-Lussac; 12 f. Surcouf;
15 f. Talleyrand; 30 f. Napoléon.

307 Nocard, Bouley and Chauveau

308 Picqué, Roussin and Villemin

(Des and eng Serres. Recess)

1951 (8 June). *French Veterinary Research. P* 13.
1119 **307** 12 f. bright purple 40 30

(Des Serres. Eng Mazelin. Recess)

1951 (17 June). *Military Health Service. P* 13.
1120 **308** 15 f. brown-purple 40 25

(Des R. Louis. Die eng J. Piel (10 c., 1 f.), Hourriez (50 c.), Fenneteaux (2 f.) and A. Frères (3 f.). Typo)

1951 (June). *As T* **277** *(provincial coats-of-arms). P* 14×13½.
1121   10 c. yellow, ultramarine and scarlet .. 5 5
1122   50 c. black, scarlet and green .. 10 5
1123   1 f. scarlet, yellow and ultramarine 12 5
1124   2 f. yellow, ultramarine and scarlet .. 20 5
1125   3 f. yellow, ultramarine and scarlet .. 50 10
1121/1125 Set of 5 .. .. 85 25
Arms (inscr):—10 c. "Artois"; 50 c. "Limousin"; 1 f. "Béarn"; 2 f. "Touraine"; 3 f. "Franche-Comté".
For similar stamps see Designs Index, under "Arms".
Dates of issue:—2 f., 21 June, at Philatelic Exhibition, Tours Other values, 25 June.

309 St. Nicholas

310 Seal of the Mercantile Guild

311 M. Noguès

(Des Lemagny. Eng Pheulpin. Recess)

1951 (23 June). *Popular Pictorial Art Exhibition, Epinal. Multicoloured centre. P* 13.
1126 **309** 15 f. blue 35 25

(Des R. Louis. Eng J. Piel. Recess)

1951 (7 July). *Bimillenary of Paris. P* 13.
1127 **310** 15 f. purple-brown, blue & scarlet 30 20

(Des and eng Gandon. Recess)

1951 (13 Oct). *P* 13.
1128 **311** 12 f. indigo and pale blue .. 40 30

312 C. Baudelaire

313 Eiffel Tower and Chaillot Palace

(Des Lemagny. Eng Pheulpin (8 f.), Dufresne (12 f.) and Barlangue (15 f.). Recess)

1951 (27 Oct). *Famous French Poets. Portraits as T* **312**. *P* 13.
1129   8 f. violet 20 20
1130   12 f. lavender-grey (P. Verlaine) .. 30 30
1131   15 f. blue-green (A. Rimbaud) .. 35 35

(Des and eng Decaris. Recess)

1951 (6 Nov). *United Nations General Assembly. P* 13.
1132 **313** 18 f. scarlet 50 40
1133   30 f. bright blue 65 45

314 G. Clemenceau (statesman)

315 Château Clos-Vougeot

(Des and eng Decaris. Recess)

1951 (12 Nov). *110th Anniv of Clemenceau's Birth and 33rd Anniv of Armistice. P* 13.
1134 **314** 15 f. blackish brown 20 20

(Des and eng Gandon. Recess)

1951 (17 Nov). *Fourth Centenary of Château Clos-Vougeot. P* 13.
1135 **315** 30 f. deep brown and brown .. 1·00 50

316 15th-century Child

317 Observatory, Pic du Midi de Bigorre

(Des and eng J. Piel. Recess)

1951 (15 Dec). *Red Cross Fund. T* **316** *and similar design. Cross in red. P* 13.
1136   12 f.+3 f. purple-brown .. .. 1·90 1·90
1137   15 f.+5 f. deep blue .. .. 1·90 1·90
Portrait: Vert—15 f. 18th-century child (De La Tour).

(Des and eng Serres (40 f.), Barlangue (50 f.). Recess)

1951 (22 Dec). *P* 13.
1138 **317** 1 f. deep violet .. .. 1·25 8
1139   50 f. purple-brown .. .. 1·10 5
Design: Vert—50 f. Church of St. Etienne, Caen.

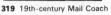

319 19th-century Mail Coach

320 Marshal de Lattre de Tassigny

(Des and eng Cheffer. Recess)

1952 (8 Mar). *Stamp Day. P* 13.
1140 **319** 12 f.+3 f. deep blue-green .. 2·10 1·75

(Des R. Serres. Eng Decaris. Recess)

1952–54. *P* 13.
1140a **320** 12 f. indigo & deep ultram (5.6.54) 1·10 65
1141   15 f. purple-brown (8.5.52) .. 50 20

321 Gate of France, Vaucouleurs   **322** French Monument, Narvik

(Des and eng Barlangue. Recess)
1952 (11 May). *P* 13.
1142 **321** 12 f. blackish brown   95   55

(Des and eng Cheffer. Recess)
1952 (28 May). *Battle of Narvik Commemoration.* *P* 13.
1143 **322** 30 f. deep blue   ..   ..   ..   1·40   70

323 Chambord Château   **324** Council of Europe Building, Strasbourg

(Des and eng Gandon. Recess)
1952 (30 May). *P* 13.
1144 **323** 20 f. violet   30   5

(Des and eng Decaris. Recess)
1952 (31 May). *Council of Europe Assembly, Strasbourg. P* 13.
1145 **324** 30 f. green   ..   ..   ..   4·50   2·75

325 Bir Hakeim Monument   **326** Abbey of the Holy Cross, Poitiers

(Des and eng Cheffer. Recess)
1952 (14 June). *Tenth Anniv of Battle of Bir Hakeim. P* 13.
1146 **325** 30 f. carmine-lake   ..   ..   1·50   1·00

(Des and eng Serres. Recess)
1952 (21 June). *Fourteenth Centenary of Abbey of the Holy Cross, Poitiers. P* 13.
1147 **326** 15 f. vermilion   25   20

327 Médaille Militaire in 1852 and 1952   **328** Garabit Viaduct

(Des and eng R. Serres. Recess)
1952 (5 July). *Centenary of Médaille Militaire. P* 13.
1148 **327** 15 f. brown, yellow and green   ..   30   25

(Des and eng P. Munier. Recess)
1952 (5 July). *P* 13.
1149 **328** 15 f. indigo   30   25

329 Leonardo, Amboise Château and town of Vinci   **330** Flaubert (after E. Giraud)

(Des and eng Decaris. Recess)
1952 (9 July). *Fifth Birth Centenary of Leonardo da Vinci. P* 13.
1150 **329** 30 f. deep ultramarine   ..   ..   3·25   1·90

(Des Lemagny (8 f., 12 f., 15 f.), eng Dufresne (8 f., 12 f.), Mazelin (15 f.). Des and eng Pheulpin (18 f.), Cottet 20 f.) and Gandon (30 f.). Recess)
1952 (18 Oct). *National Relief Fund. As T* **330** *(nineteenth-century celebrities). P* 13.
1151   8 f.+2 f. deep blue and black-brown   2·75   2·75
1152   12 f.+3 f. ultramarine & black-brown   2·75   2·75
1153   15 f.+4 f. deep blue-green & black-brn   2·75   2·75
1154   18 f.+5 f. black-brown   2·75   2·75
1155   20 f.+6 f. carmine-red & black-brown   3·25   3·25
1156   30 f.+7 f. reddish violet & black-brown   3·25   3·25
1151/1156   Set of 6 ..   ..   ..   17·00   17·00
Portraits:—12 f. Manet; 15 f. Saint-Saens; 18 f. H. Poincaré; 20 f. Haussmann (after Yvon); 30 f. Thiers.

331 R. Laënnec (physician)   **332** "Cherub" (bas-relief)

(Des and eng Mazelin. Recess)
1952 (7 Nov). *P* 13.
1157 **331** 12 f. deep green   30   20

(Des and eng J. Piel. Recess)
1952 (13 Dec). *Red Cross Fund. T* **332** *and similar horiz design showing sculptures from the Basin of Diana, Versailles. Cross in red. P* 13.
1158   12 f.+3 f. deep bluish green   ..   2·10   2·10
1159   15 f.+5 f. indigo   ..   ..   ..   2·10   2·10
Design:—15 f. "Cherub" (facing left).

STAMP MONTHLY
—finest and most informative magazine for all collectors. Obtainable from your newsagent or by postal subscription—details on request.

333 Versailles Gateway **334** Count D'Argenson

338 Olivier de Serres **339** Cyclists and Map

(Des after Utrillo. Eng Cheffer. Recess)

1952–54. P 13.
| 1160 | **333** | 18 f. maroon (20.12.52) | | 95 | 70 |
| 1160a | | 18 f. indigo, blue & blk-brn (10.7.54) | | 3·25 | 1·75 |

(Des and eng Serres. Recess)

1953 (14 Mar). *Stamp Day.* P 13.
| 1161 | **334** | 12 f.+3 f. deep blue | | 1·90 | 1·90 |

335 "Gargantua" **336** Mannequin **337** Mannequin
(Rabelais) Modelling and Place
Gloves Vendôme, Paris

(Des Cheffer (6 f.), Cottet (8 f.), Spitz (12 f.), Cami (18 f.),
Gandon (others). Eng Cheffer (6 f., 12 f.), Cami (8 f., 18 f.),
Mazelin (25 f. Tapestry, 75 f.), Piel (30 f. T **337**, 50 f.),
Gandon (25 f. T **336**, 30 f. Books, 40 f.). Recess)

1953–55. As T **335**/**7**. *National Industries and Literary
Figures.* P 13.
1162	6 f. carmine-lake & rose-red (27.5.53)	8	5
1163	8 f. blue and indigo (19.9.53)	10	5
1164	12 f. deep bluish grn & choc (19.9.53)	10	5
1165	18 f. black-brown & purple-brn (6.6.53)	40	20
1166	25 f. dp brown, carm & red-brn (6.5.54)	1·50	5
1166a	25 f. dp brt blue & brown-blk (26.3.55)	40	5
1167	30 f. reddish violet & indigo (24.4.53)	45	15
1167a	30 f. indigo & dp bluish green (6.5.54)	20	5
1168	40 f. brown and chocolate (6.5.54)	35	5
1169	50 f. brown, deep blue-green and deep		
	bright blue (6.5.54)	40	5
1170	75 f. lake and carmine (6.5.54)	2·25	20
1162/1170	*Set of 11*	6·00	80

Designs: *Vert*—6 f. T **335**, 8 f. "Célimène" (Molière); 12 f.
"Figaro" (Beaumarchais); 18 f. "Hernani" (Victor Hugo); 25 f.
No. 1166, Tapestry; No. 1166a, T **336**; 30 f., No. 1167, T **337**;
No. 1167a, Rare books and bookbinding; 40 f. Porcelain and
cut-glass; 50 f. Jewellery and gold plate; 75 f. Flowers and
perfumes.

(Des and eng R. Serres. Recess)

1953–54. *General Leclerc Commemoration. As T **270** but
inscr "GENERAL LECLERC/MARECHAL DE FRANCE".*
P 13.
| 1171 | 8 f. red-brown (13.6.53) | | 40 | 30 |
| 1171a | 12 f. dp blue-grn & dp grn (12.6.54) | 1·10 | 70 |

**HAVE YOU READ THE NOTES AT THE
BEGINNING OF THIS CATALOGUE?**

These often provide answers to the enquiries we
receive.

(Des A. Spitz. (18 f., 30 f.). Eng Cottet (18 f.), Barlangue (30 f.).
Des and eng Pheulpin (8 f.), R. Serres (12 f.), P. Munier
(15 f.), Mazelin (20 f.). Recess)

1953 (9 July). *National Relief Fund. Portraits as T **338**.* P 13.
1172	8 f.+2 f. bright blue		2·75	2·75
1173	12 f.+3 f. deep bluish green		2·75	2·75
1174	15 f.+4 f. lake-brown		3·25	3·25
1175	18 f.+5 f. deep blue		3·25	3·25
1176	20 f.+6 f. deep violet		3·25	3·25
1177	30 f.+7 f. chocolate		3·75	3·75
1172/1177	*Set of 6*		17·00	17·00

Portraits:—8 f. St. Bernard; 15 f. Rameau; 18 f. Monge;
20 f. Michelet; 30 f. Marshal Lyautey.

(Des R. Louis. Die-eng A. Frères (50 c., 1 f.), Fenneteaux
(70 c.), Miermont (80 c.), J. Piel (2 f., 3 f.). Typo)

1953. *As T **280** (various provincial coats-of-arms).* P 14 × 13½.
1178	50 c. yellow, red and ultramarine		20	12
1179	70 c. yellow, ultramarine and red		20	12
1180	80 c. yellow, red and ultramarine		20	12
1181	1 f. yellow, vermilion and black		8	5
1182	2 f. yellow, ultramarine and brown		8	5
1183	3 f. yellow, ultramarine and red		20	5
1178/1183	*Set of 6*		85	45

Arms (*inscr*):—50 c. "Picardie"; 70 c. "Gascogne"; 80 c.
"Berri"; 1 f. "Poitou"; 2 f. "Champagne"; 3 f. "Dauphine".
For similar designs see Designs Index, under "Arms".
Dates of issue: 23 July, 50 c., 1 f., 2 f., 3 f. 29 Sept., 70 c., 80 c.

(Des and eng Decaris Recess)

1953 (26 July). *Fiftieth Anniv of "Tour de France" Cycle Race.*
P 13.
| 1184 | **339** | 12 f. black, blue and brown-lake | 40 | 30 |

340 Swimming **341** Mme. Vigée-Lebrun
and Daughter (self-portrait)

(Des Jacquemin. Eng Dufresne (20 f.), Serres (25 f.), Mazelin
(30 f.), J. Piel (40 f.), Munier (50 f.), Cottet (75 f.). Recess)

1953 (28 Nov). *Horiz sports designs as T **340**.* P 13.
1185	20 f. black-brown and scarlet		40	5
1186	25 f. deep brown and slate-green		90	10
1187	30 f. deep brown and deep bright blue	40	10
1188	40 f. indigo and deep brown		1·10	10
1189	50 f. black-brown and deep emerald		1·25	5
1190	75 f. brown-carmine and yellow-orange	8·50	4·75
1185/1190	*Set of 6*		11·00	4·75

Designs:—25 f. Running; 30 f. Fencing; 40 f. Canoeing;
50 f. Rowing; 75 f. Horse-jumping.

(Eng J. Piel. Recess)

1953 (12 Dec). *Red Cross Fund. T **341** and similar vert
design. Cross in red.* P 13.
| 1191 | 12 f.+3 f. purple-brown | | 3·25 | 3·25 |
| 1192 | 15 f.+5 f. indigo | | 3·75 | 3·75 |

Design:—15 f. "The Return from the Baptism" (L. Le Nain).

15ᶠ

(342)   **343** *Magister*

1953 (14 Dec). *No.* 1007e *surch with T* **342.**
1193 **219** 15 f. on 18 f. carmine   ..   65   10

(Des P. Lengellé. Eng Dufresne (100 f.), J. Piel (200 f.), Gandon
(500 f.), R. Serres (1000 f.). Recess)

1954 (16 Jan). *AIR. T* **343** *and similar horiz designs. P* 13.
1194	100	f. red-brown and blue	65	5
1195	200	f. deep purple and ultramarine	1·90	5
1196	500	f. scarlet and yellow-orange	55·00	5·00
1197	1000	f. indigo, maroon & turquoise-blue	48·00	5·50

Designs:—100 f. *Mystère IV* (jet fighter); 200 f. *Noratlas*
(cargo 'plane); 1000 f. *Provence* (transport 'plane).
For similar stamp to No. 1195, see No. 1457.

344 Harvester   **345** Gallic Cock   **346** Lavallette

(Des Muller (T **344**). P Poulain (T **345**). Die eng J. Piel (T **344**),
A. Frères (T **345**). Typo)

1954 (Feb)–59. *P* 14 × 13½.
1198	**344**	4	f. turquoise-blue* ..	15	5
1198a	**345**	5	f. olive-brown* (5.8.57)	15	5
1198b	**344**	6	f. orange-brown (5.7.57)	5	5
1199		8	f. brown-lake*	2·40	20
1199a	**345**	8	f. violet* (1.3.59)	20	5
			aa. Error. Precancel omitted		
1199b		10	f. bright blue* (5.8.57)	20	8
1199c	**344**	10	f. emerald (12.1.59) ..	40	5
1200	**345**	12	f. cerise* ..	1·60	20
1200a	**344**	12	f. bright purple (5.7.57)	15	5
1200b	**345**	15	f. reddish purple* (5.8.57)	55	30
1200c		20	f. yellow-green* (1.3.59)	55	20
1201		24	f. blue-green*	5·50	1·90
1201a		30	f. orange-red* (5.8.57)	1·60	45
1201b		40	f. brown-red* (1.3.59)	2·75	1·60
1201c		45	f. deep green* (5.8.57)	9·50	3·75
1201d		55	f. emerald* (1.3.59) ..	7·00	5·00
1198/1201d			*Set of* 16 ..	27·00	12·00

* These stamps were issued only precancelled, tne unused
prices being for stamps with full gum.
See also Nos. 1470/3.

(Des and eng J. Piel. Recess)

1954 (20 Mar). *Stamp Day. P* 13.
1202 **346** 12 f.+3 f. deep green & purple-brn   2·75   2·50

347 Exhibition   **348** "D-Day"
    Buildings

(Des and eng Decaris. Recess)
1954 (22 May). *50th Anniv of Paris Fair. P* 13.
1203 **347** 15 f. lake and blue   25   20

(Des and eng R. Serres. Recess)
1954 (5 June). *Tenth Anniv of Liberation. P* 13.
1204 **348** 15 f. vermilion and deep ultramarine   30   20

349 Lourdes   **350** Jumièges Abbey

(Des and eng Cottet (6 f.), Decaris (8 f.), Cheffer (12 f. No.
1208), Pheulpin (18 f.). Des A. Spitz (10 f., 12 f. No. 1209),
Lemagny (20 f.). Eng J. Piel (10 f.), Dufresne (12 f. No.
1209), P. Munier (20 f.). Recess)

1954–58. *Views as T* **349.** *P* 13.
1205	6	f. indigo, blue & dp blue-grn (12.6.54)	12	5
1206	8	f. deep blue-green and blue (5.6.54)	12	5
1207	10	f. brown and light blue (3.7.54) ..	8	5
1208	12	f. deep lilac & reddish violet (12.6.54)	8	5
1209	12	f. brown and chocolate (26.3.55) ..	75	50
1210	18	f. indigo, blue & dp bl-grn (19.6.54)	30	15
1211	20	f. black-brown, chestnut and tur-		
		quoise-blue (3.7.54)	25	5
1211a	20	f. olive-brn & turq-bl (27.2.58)	20	5
1205/1211a		*Set of* 8 ..	1·50	80

Designs: *Horiz*—8 f. Seine Valley at Andelys; 10 f. Royan;
12 f. No. 1209, Limoges; 18 f. Cheverny Château; 20 f. (No.
1211) Ajaccio; 20 f. (No. 1211a), T **349**. *Vert*—12 f. No. 1208,
Quimper.

(Des and eng Cottet. Recess)

1954 (13 June). *Thirteenth Centenary of Jumieges Abbey. P* 13.
1212 **350** 12 f. indigo, dp blue & dp blue-grn   75   55

351 Abbey Church of   **352** Stenay
    St. Philibert, Tournus

(Des and eng Decaris. Recess)

1954 (18 June). *First Conference of Romanesque Studies,
Tournus. P* 13.
1213 **351** 30 f. blue and indigo   ..   ..   4·50   2·50

(Des A. Spitz. Eng Pheulpin. Recess)

1954 (26 June). *Third Centenary of Return of Stenay to France.
P* 13.
1214 **352** 15 f. brown and black-brown   ..   55   35

353 St. Louis   **354** Villandry Château.

(Des Lemagny (12 f.), Cami (15 f.). Eng Dufresne (12 f., 15 f.). Des and eng R. Serres (18 f.), Cheffer (20 f.), P. Munier (25 f.), Pheulpin (30 f.). Recess)

1954 (10 July). *National Relief Fund. Portraits as T* **353**. *P* 13.

1215	12 f.+4 f. blue		11·00	11·00
1216	15 f.+5 f. deep violet		11·00	11·00
1217	18 f.+6 f. blackish brown		11·00	11·00
1218	20 f.+7 f. scarlet		12·00	12·00
1219	25 f.+8 f. indigo		12·00	12·00
1220	30 f.+10 f. maroon		12·00	12·00
1215/1220	*Set of* 6		60·00	60·00

Portraits:—15 f. Bossuet; 18 f. Sadi Carnot; 20 f. A. Bourdelle; 25 f. Dr. E. Roux; 30 f. Paul Valery.

(Des and eng Cami. Recess)

1954 (17 July). *Four Centuries of Renaissance Gardens. P* 13.
1221 **354** 18 f. deep blue-green and blue   2·75   1·90

355 Cadet and Flag   **356** Napoleon Conferring Decorations

(Des and eng Mazelin. Recess)

1954 (1 Aug). *150th Anniv of St. Cyr Military Academy. P* 13.
1222 **355** 15 f. indigo, deep blue & carmine red   80   40

(Des Lalau. Eng Cheffer. Recess)

1954 (14 Aug). *150th Anniv of First Presentation of Legion of Honour. P* 13.
1223 **356** 12 f. vermilion   80   40

357 "Basis of Metric System"   **359** "Young Girl with Doves" (J.-B. Greuze)   **360** Saint-Simon

(Des and eng Decaris. Recess)

1954 (4 Oct). *150th Anniv of Introduction of Metric System. P* 13.
1224 **357** 30 f. blackish brown and indigo   4·50   2·75

(Des R. Louis. Die eng A. Freres (50 c., 70 c.), Fenneteaux (80 c.), Miermont (1 f.), Aufschneider (2 f.), J. Piel (3 f., 5 f.). Typo)

1954. *As T* **280** (*provincial coats-of-arms*).
1225	50 c. yellow, ultramarine and black	8	5
1226	70 c. yellow, red and emerald	8	5
1227	80 c. yellow, ultramarine and red	15	10

1228	1 f. yellow, ultramarine and red	5	5
1229	2 f. yellow, red and black	5	5
1230	3 f. yellow, red and brown	5	5
1231	5 f. yellow and ultramarine	5	5
1225/1231	*Set of* 7	45	35

Arms (*inscr*):—50 c., "Maine"; 70 c. "Navarre"; 80 c. "Nivernais"; 1 f. "Bourbonnais"; 2 f. "Angoumois"; 3 f. "Aunis"; 5 f. "Saintonge".
For similar stamps see Designs Index, under "Arms".
Dates of issue: 3 Nov, 50 c. to 1 f.; 11 Nov, 2 f., 3 f., 5 f.

(Eng J. Piel. Recess)

1954 (18 Dec). *Red Cross Fund. T* **359** *and similar vert design. Cross in red. P* 13.
1232	12 f.+3 f. indigo and deep grey-blue	3·25	3·25
1233	15 f.+5 f. brown and deep brown	3·25	3·25

Design:—12 f. "The Sick Child" (E. Carriere).

(Des and eng Decaris. Recess)

1955 (5 Feb). *200th Anniv of Death of Saint-Simon* (*writer*). *P* 13.
1234 **360** 12 f. brown-purple and black-brown   55   40

361 "Industry", "Agriculture" and Rotary Emblem

(Des and eng R. Serres. Recess)

1955 (23 Feb). *50th Anniv of Rotary International. P* 13.
1235 **361** 30 f. yellow-orange, blue & dp brt bl   55   45

362 "France"   Two types of 18 f.

I   II

(Des Muller. Die eng J. Piel. Typo)

1955–59. *P* 14 × 13½.
1236	**362**	6 f. brown-red (12.7.55)		1·75	1·10
1237		12 f. green (7.7.55)		1·10	80
1238		15 f. carmine (24.2.55)		20	5
1238a		18 f. deep green (I) (22.5.58)		25	5
		ab. Type II		20	5
1238b		20 f. ultramarine (22.6.57)		20	5
1238c		25 f. scarlet (5.1.59)		40	5
1236/1238c		*Set of* 7		3·50	1·90

363 Thimonnier and Sewing-machines

(Des and eng Hertenberger (5 f.), Cottet (10 f.), Cheffer (12 f.), Decaris (18 f.), Gandon (25 f.), Mazelin (30 f.). Recess)

1955 (5 Mar). *French Inventors* (*1st series*). *Horiz designs as T* **363**. *P* 13.
1239	5 f. deep bright blue and light blue		40	20
1240	10 f. chocolate and chestnut		40	20
1241	12 f. deep grey-green		50	40
1242	18 f. deep bright blue and violet-grey		1·25	95
1243	25 f. deep violet and plum		1·40	70
1244	30 f. vermilion and carmine-red		1·40	70
1239/1244	*Set of* 6		5·00	2·75

Designs:—5 f. Le Bon (gaslight); 12 f. Appert (food canning); 18 f. Sainte-Claire Deville (aluminium); 25 f. Martin (steel); 30 f. Chardonnet (artificial silk).

364 Paris Balloon Post, 1870   **365** Florian and Pastoral Scene

(Des and eng R. Serres. Recess)

1955 (19 Mar). *Stamp Day.* P 13.
1245 **364** 12 f.+3 f. chocolate, bronze-green
     and deep turquoise-blue ..   3·50   2·50

(Des Lalau. Eng Hertenberger. Recess)

1955 (2 Apr). *200th Anniversary of Birth of Florian (fabulist).*
P 13.
1246 **365** 12 f. deep turquoise-blue   45   30

366 Eiffel Tower and   **367** Observation Tower
    Television Aerials   and Fence

(Des and eng Decaris. Recess)

1955 (16 Apr). *Television Development.* P 13.
1247 **366** 15 f. deep bright blue and indigo..   35   20

(Des and eng Decaris. Recess)

1955 (23 Apr). *Tenth Anniv of Liberation of Concentration
Camps.* P 13.
1248 **367** 12 f. brownish black & violet grey   35   30

368 Electric Train   **369** The "Jacquemart"
                       (Campanile), Moulins

(Des and eng Decaris. Recess)

1955 (11 May). *Electrification of Valenciennes-Thionville
Railway Line.* P 13.
1249 **368** 12 f. blackish brown & violet-grey   45   30

(Des and eng Cottet. Recess)

1955 (28 May). P 13.
1250 **369** 12 f. black-brown..   ..   70   40

370 Jules Verne and   **371** Maryse Bastié
Capt. Nemo on the *Nautilus*   (airwoman)

(Des and eng Pheulpin. Recess)

1955 (3 June). *50th Death Anniv of Jules Verne. (author).*
P 13.
1251 **370** 30 f. indigo   ..   ..   3·50   2·75

(Des and eng Gandon. Recess)

1955 (4 June). *AIR. Maryse Bastié Commemoration* P 13.
1252 **371** 50 f. deep claret and carmine ..   3·50   2·25

372 Vauban   **373** A. and L. Lumière

(Des Muller (12 f.), Spitz (15 f., 18 f.), Lemagny (25 f., 30 f.),
Cheffer (50 f.). Eng Munier, (12 f.), Dufresne (15 f.),
Hertenberger (18 f.), Mazelin (25 f.), Cottet (30 f.), Cheffer
(50 f.). Recess)

1955 (11 June). *National Relief Fund. Portraits as T* **72.**
P 13.
1253   12 f.+5 f. bright violet   ..   8·00   8·00
1254   15 f.+6 f. deep blue   ..   8·00   8·00
1255   18 f.+7 f. deep green   ..   9·00   9·00
1256   25 f.+8 f. violet-grey   ..   9·50   9·50
1257   30 f.+9 f. brown-purple   ..   9·50   9·50
1258   50 f.+15 f. turquoise-blue   ..   9·50   9·50
1253/1258   *Set of 6* ..   ..   ..   40·00   40·00
Portraits:—12 f. King Philippe-Auguste; 15 f. Malherbe;
25 f. Vergennes; 30 f. Laplace; 50 f. Renoir.

(Des Muller. Eng Munier. Recess)

1955 (12 June). *60th Anniv of French Cinema Industry.* P 13.
1259 **373** 30 f. lake-brown ..   ..   2·75   2·00

374 Jacques Cœur   **375** La Capricieuse
   (merchant prince)

(Des Ciry. Eng Pheulpin. Recess)

1955 (18 June). P 13.
1260 **374** 12 f. deep violet ..   ..   ..   1·40   75

(Des and eng Decaris. Recess)

1955 (9 July). *Centenary of Voyage of "La Capricieuse".* P 13.
1261 **375** 30 f. deep blue & dp turquoise-blue 3·50   2·25

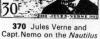 

376 Marseilles   **377** Gérard de Nerval

(Des Spitz, eng Munier (10 f.). Des Lemagny, eng Dufresne
(20 f.). Des and eng Pheulpin (6 f.), Cheffer (8 f.), Mazelin
(12 f.), Cottet (15 f.), Cami (18 f.), Decaris (25 f.). Recess)

1955 (15 Oct)–**57.** *T* **376** *and similar designs.* P 13.
1262   6 f. carmine-lake   5   5
1263   8 f. indigo   5   5
1264   10 f. deep bright blue   5   5
1265   12 f. blackish brown and violet-grey..   5   5

1265a 15 f. indigo and blue (11.2.56)   20   20
1266   18 f. indigo and slate-green   20   5
1267   20 f. reddish violet & dp violet (1.11.55) 20 5
1268   25 f. red-brown and chestnut   20   5
1268a 35 f. deep bluish green and blackish
           green (19.7.57) ..   50   15
1268b 70 f. black and grey-green (19.7.57) .. 1·40 40
1262/1268b Set of 10 ..   ..   ..   2·50 1·00
  Designs: *Horiz*—6 f., 35 f. Bordeaux; 10 f. Nice; 12 f., 70 f.
Valentré Bridge, Cahors; 18 f. Uzerche; 20 f. Mount Pelé, Martinique; 25 f. Ramparts of Brouage. *Vert*—15 f. Douai Belfry.

(Des and eng P. Munier. Recess)

1955 (11 Nov). *Death Centenary of De Nerval* (*writer*). *P* 13.
1269 **377** 12 f. black-brown and brown-lake   35   20

(Des R. Louis). Die eng Fenneteaux (50 c.), A. Frères (70 c.),
   Aufschneider (80 c.), Miermont (1 f.). Typo)

1955 (19 Nov). *As T* **280** (*various provincial coats-of-arms*).
  P 14 × 13½.
1270   50 c. yellow, red, green and black ..   5   5
1271   70 c. yellow, ultramarine and red   ..   5   5
1272   80 c. yellow, red and brown ..   5   5
1273   1 f. yellow, red and ultramarine   ..   5   5
1270/1273 Set of 4   12   10
Arms (*inscr*):—50 c. "Comté de Foix"; 70 c. "Marche";
80 c. "Roussillon"; 1 f. "Comtat Venaissin".
For similar stamps see Designs Index, under "Arms".

379 "Child and Cage"   **380**
(after Pigalle)

(Des and eng J. Piel. Recess)

1955 (17 Dec). *Red Cross Fund.* *T* **379** *and similar vert*
design. Cross in red. *P* 13.
1274   12 f+3 f. brown-purple   ..   ..   1·90 1·90
1275   15 f.+5 f. indigo ..   ..   ..   1·90 1·90
Design:—15 f. "Child and goose" (Greek sculpture).

(Des Lemagny. Eng Dufresne. Recess)

1956 (14 Jan). *National Déportation Memorial.* *P* 13.
1276 **380** 15 f. sepia and red-brown   ..   15   15

381 Colonel Driant   **382** Trench Warfare

(Des and eng Decaris. Recess)

1956 (21 Feb). *Birth Centenary of Colonel Driant.* *P* 13.
1277·**381** 15 f. deep blue   20   20

(Des and eng Decaris. Recess)

1956 (3 Mar). *40th Anniv of Battle of Verdun.* *P* 13.
1278 **382** 30 f. indigo and blackish olive .. 70 45

383 Francis of Taxis   **384** J. H. Fabre (entomologist)

(Des and eng Pheulpin. Recess)

1956 (17 Mar). *Stamp Day.* *P* 13.
1279 **383** 12 f.+3 f. blackish brn, green & blue 1·10 1·10

(Des Fabre. Eng Cami (12 f.). Des and eng Hertenberger
  (15 f.). Serres (18 f.), Gandon (30 f.). Recess)

1956 (7 Apr). *French Scientists.* *T* **384** *and similar horiz*
portraits. *P* 13.
1280   12 f. chocolate and orange-brown ..   25   20
1281   15 f. black and violet-grey   ..   40   20
1282   18 f. deep bright blue   ..   .. 1·10 70
1283   30 f. deep turquoise and slate-green .. 1·10 70
1280/1283 Set of 4 ..   .. 2·50 1·50
Portraits:—15 f. C. Tellier (refrigeration engineer); 18 f.
C. Flammarion (astronomer); 30 f. P. Sabatier (chemist).

385 Grand Trianon, Versailles   **386** "Latin America"
                                          and "France"

(Des and eng P. Munier. Recess)

1956 (14 Apr). *P* 13.
1284 **385** 12 f. red-brown, green and black .. 90 55

(Des C. Serveau. Eng J. Piel. Recess)

1956 (21 Apr). *Franco-Latin American Friendship.* *P* 13.
1285 **386** 30 f. red-brown and sepia   1·10 75

387 "Reims" and   **388** Order of Malta
"Florence"   and Leper Colony

(Des and eng Lemagny. Recess)

1956 (5 May). *Reims-Florence Friendship.* *P* 13.
1286 **387** 12 f. green and black   ..   55   25

(Des and eng Serres. Recess)

1956 (12 May). *Order of Malta Leprosy Relief.* *P* 13.
1287 **388** 12 f. scarlet, chestnut & blackish brn 30 20

389 St. Yves de Tréguier   **390** Marshal Franchet
                                        d'Esperey

(Des C. Mazelin. Recess)
1956 (19 May). *St. Yves de Tréguier Commemoration. P* 13.
1288 **389** 15 f. black and deep grey .. 20 20

(Des and eng Decaris. Recess)
1956 (26 May). *Centenary of Birth of Marshal Franchet d'Esperey. P* 13.
1289 **390** 30 f. brown-purple .. 65 40

391 Monument　　**392** Budé　　**393** Pelota

(Des Spitz. Eng Munier. Recess)
1956 (2 June). *Centenary of Montceau-les-Mines. P* 13.
1290 **391** 12 f. blackish brown .. 25 · 20

(Des Lemagny (Nos. 1291, 1294), Muller (1292), Decaris (1293), Spitz (1296), Ciry (1296). Eng Mazelin (1291), Dufresne (1292), Decaris (1293), Hertenberger (1294), Pheulpin (1295), Cottet (1296). Recess)
1956 (9 June). *National Relief Fund. T* **392** *and similar vert portraits. P* 13.
1291 12 f.+3 f. blue (Type **392**) .. 1·90 1·90
1292 12 f.+3 f. violet-grey (Goujon) .. 1·90 1·90
1293 12 f.+3 f. vermilion (Champlain) .. 1·90 1·90
1294 15 f.+5 f. green (Chardin) .. 1·90 1·90
1295 15 f.+5 f. chocolate (Barres) .. 2·25 2·25
1296 15 f.+5 f. bright bluish violet (Ravel) .. 2·25 2·25
1291/1296 *Set of* 6 .. .. .. 11·00 11·00

(Des R. Serres. Eng Dufresne (30 f.), R. Serres (40 f.), J. Piel (50 f.), Gandon (75 f.). Recess)
1956 (7 July). *Various vert sports designs as T* **393**. *P* 13.
1297 30 f. black and grey 30 5
1298 40 f. brown-purple and deep brown .. 35 12
1299 50 f. violet and purple .. 40 5
1300 75 f. deep blue-green, black and indigo 95 40
1297/1300 *Set of* 4 .. .. .. 1·90 55
Designs:—30 f. Basket-ball; 50 f. Rugby; 75 f. Alpine climbing.

394　　**395** Donzère-Mondragon Barrage

(Des Gonzague. Eng J. Piel. Typo (15 f.), recess (30 f.))
1956 (15 Sept). *Europa. P* 13.
1301 **394** 15 f. lake and rose-pink .. 50 5
1302 30 f. ultramarine and pale blue .. 1·50 30

(Des and eng Cami (12 f.), Cottet (18 f.), Gandon (30 f.). Recess)
1956 (6 Oct). *Technical Achievements. T* **395** *and similar designs. P* 13.
1303 12 f. violet-grey and chocolate .. 35 30
1304 18 f. indigo 60 35
1305 30 f. deep blue and indigo .. 1·10 65
Design: *Vert*—18 f. Aiguille du Midi cable railway. *Horiz*—30 f. Port of Strasbourg.

396 A. A. Parmentier　　**397** Petrarch
(agronomist)

(Des and eng Cheffer. Recess)
1956 (27 Oct). *Parmentier Commemoration. P* 13.
1306 **396** 12 f. deep brown and red-brown .. 30 20

(Des Muller (8 f.), Ciry (15 f.), Lalau (30 f.). Eng Pheulpin (8 f.), Cottet (15 f.), Dufresne (30 f.). Des and eng Mazelin (12 f.), Decaris (18 f.), Cheffer (20 f.). Recess)
1956 (10 Nov). *Famous Men. T* **397** *and similar vert portraits. P* 13.
1307 8 f. deep green 25 20
1308 12 f. maroon (Lully) 25 20
1309 15 f. deep orange-red (Rousseau) .. 40 25
1310 18 f. bright blue (Franklin) .. 1·40 90
1311 20 f. bright violet (Chopin) .. 1·40 45
1312 30 f. turquoise-blue (Van Gogh) .. 1·40 90
1307/1312 *Set of* 6 .. .. .. 4·50 2·50

398 Pierre de Coubertin　　**399** "Jeune Paysan"
(reviver of Olympic Games)　　(after Le Nain)

(Des and eng Serres. Recess)
1956 (24 Nov). *Coubertin Commemoration. P* 13.
1313 **398** 30 f. purple and violet-grey .. 80 50

(Des and eng J. Piel. Recess)
1956 (8 Dec). *Red Cross Fund. T* **399** *and similar vert design. Cross in red. P* 13.
1314 12 f.+3 f. brown-olive .. .. 1·10 1·10
1315 15 f.+5 f. lake .. .. 1·10 1·10
Design:—15 f. "Gilles" (after Watteau).

400 Pigeon and Loft　　**401** Caravelle

(Des and eng Gandon. Recess)
1957 (12 Jan). *Pigeon-fanciers' Commemoration. P* 13.
1316 **400** 15 f. dp blue, indigo & blackish pur 25 20

(Des and eng Gandon. Recess)
1957 (26 Jan)—**59**. *AIR. T* **401** *and similar horiz designs. P* 13.
1318 300 f. olive-brown & turq-bl (16.2.59) 2·25 90
1319 500 f. black and deep blue .. .. 9·00 90
1320 1000 f. blk, reddish vio & sepia (11.1.58) 23·00 11·00
Designs:—300 f. "Paris" (jet training aircraft); 1,000 f. "L'Alouette" (helicopter).

402 Victor Schoelcher (slavery abolitionist) **403** 18th-Century Felucca

(Des and eng Pheulpin. Recess)

1957 (16 Feb). *Schoelcher Commemoration.* P 13.
1321 **402** 18 f. magenta 25 20

(Des and eng Decaris. Recess)

1957 (16 Mar). *Stamp Day.* P 13.
1322 **403** 12 f.+3 f. brownish blk & vio-grey 1·00 90

404 "La Baigneuse" (after Falconet) and Sèvres Porcelain **405** Planté and Accumulators

(Des and eng P. Munier. Recess)

1957 (25 Mar). *200th Anniv of National Porcelain Industry at Sèvres.* P 13.
1323 **404** 30 f. violet-blue and bright blue .. 40 30

(Des Ciry. Eng Mazelin (8 f.). Des and eng Cheffer (12 f.), Hertenberger (18 f.), Pheulpin (30 f.). Recess)

1957 (13 Apr). *French Inventors (2nd series). Various horiz designs as T **405**.* P 13.
1324   8 f. brown-purple and black-brown .. 25 25
1325   12 f. black, deep blue and green .. 25 25
1326   18 f. lake and rose-red 80 80
1327   30 f. blackish green and green .. 1·00 1·00
1324/1327   *Set of 4* .. .. 2·00 2·00
Designs:—12 f. Béclère (radiology); 18 f. Terrillon (anti-septics); 30 f. Oehmichen (helicopter).

406 Uzès Château **407** Jean Moulin

(Des and eng Serres. Recess)

1957 (27 Apr). P 13.
1328 **406** 12 f. black, bistre-brown and indigo 20 15

(Des Lemagny (12 f.), Spitz (18 f.). Eng Munier (12 f.), Cheffer (18 f.). Des and eng Cottet (8 f.), Decaris (10 f.), Cami (20 f.). Recess)

1957 (18 May). *Heroes of the Resistance (First series). T **407** and similar vert portraits.* P 13.
1329   8 f. chocolate 30 20
1330   10 f. violet-blue and black 20 20
1331   12 f. blackish green and chocolate .. 30 20
1332   18 f. black and reddish violet .. 95 70
1333   20 f. deep blue and turquoise-blue .. 45 25
1329/1333   *Set of 5* .. .. 2·00 1·40
Portraits:—10 f. H. d'Estienne D'Orves; 12 f. R. Keller; 18 f. P. Brossolette; 20 f. J.-B. Lebas.
See also Nos. 1381/4, 1418/22, 1478/82 and 1519/22.

408 Le Quesnoy **409** Emblems of Auditing

(Des and eng Pheulpin. Recess)

1957 (1 June). P 13.
1334 **408**   8 f. blackish green (1 June) .. 5 5
1335   15 f. brownish black and deep bluish green (19 July) .. 8 5

(Des Serveau. Eng Piel. Recess)

1957 (1 June). *150th Anniv of the Court of Accounts.* P 13.
1336 **409** 12 f. deep blue and olive-green .. 15 15

410 Joinville **411** "Public Works"

(Des Lalau (No. 1337), Muller (1338), Lemagny (1339). Eng Cami (1337), Serres (1338), Pheulpin (1339), Des and eng Mazelin (1340), Lemagny (1341), Cottet (1342). Recess)

1957 (15 June). *National Relief Fund. T **410** and similar vert portraits.* P 13.
1337   12 f.+3 f. deep olive-brown & sage-grn 1·40 1·40
1338   12 f.+3 f. blackish green & turq-blue 1·50 1·50
1339   15 f.+5 f. lake and vermilion .. 1·60 1·60
1340   15 f.+5 f. indigo and deep bright blue 1·60 1·60
1341   18 f.+7 f. blackish green & dp blue-grn 1·75 1·75
1342   18 f.+7 f. deep chocolate and brown 1·75 1·75
1337/1342   *Set of 6* .. .. 8·50 8·50
Portraits:—No. 1337, T **410**; 1338, Bernard Palissy; 1339, Quentin de la Tour; 1340, Lamennais; 1341, George Sand; 1342, Jules Guesde.

(Des Serveau. Eng Piel Recess)

1957 (20 June). *French Public Works.* P 13.
1343 **411** 30 f. yellow-brown, blackish brown and blackish green 30 25

412 Port of Brest **413** Léo Lagrange (founder) and Stadium

(Des and eng Cheffer. Recess)

1957 (6 July). P 13.
1344 **412** 12 f. grey-green and bistre-brown 35 25

(Des and eng Decaris. Recess)

1957 (31 Aug). *Universities World Games.* P 13.
1345 **413** 18 f. black and violet-grey .. 25 20

414 Auguste Comte

415 "Agriculture and Industry"

(Des and eng Mazelin. Recess)

1957 (14 Sept). *Death Centenary of Auguste Comte (philosopher).* P 13.
1346 **414** 35 f. deep olive-brown & red-brown   45   45

(Des and eng Decaris. Recess)

1957 (16 Sept). *Europa.* P 13.
1347 **415** 20 f. brown and deep green   20   5
1348   35 f. sepia and greenish blue   40   20

416 Roman Theatre, Lyons   **417** Sens River, Guadeloupe

(Des Spitz. Eng Mazelin. Recess)

1957 (5 Oct). *Bimillenary of Lyons.* P 13.
1349 **416** 20 f. maroon and chestnut   30   20

(Des and eng Serres (8 f.417), Munier (10 f., 30 f.), Mazelin (18 f.), Cami (15 f., 25 f.), Pheulpin (65 f., 85 f.), Des Spitz. Eng Cottet (35 f.), Serres (50 f.). Recess)

1957 (19 Oct)–59. *Tourist Publicity Series.* T **417** and similar pictorial designs. P 13.
1350   8 f. brown and green   5   5
1351   8 f. chocolate and bistre-brown   5   5
1351*a*   15 f. sepia, green, grey & bl (11.10.58)   15   12
1352   18 f. chocolate and indigo   12   5
1353   25 f. chocolate and violet-grey   15   5
1353*a*   30 f. black-green (7.2.59)   45   5
1354   35 f. cerise and carmine-lake   20   5
1355   50 f. sepia and grey-green   20   5
1356   65 f. deep bright blue and indigo   45   5
1356*a*   85 f. brown-purple (7.2.59)   95   5
1356*b*   100 f. violet (7.2.59)   1·75   5
1350/1356*b*   *Set of 11*   4·00   20
Designs: *Horiz*—10 f., 30 f. Palais de l'Élysée, Paris; 15 f. Château de Foix; 25 f. Château de Valençay; 50 f. Les Antiques, Saint Rémy; 65 f., 85 f. Evian-les-Bains; 100 f. T **417**. *Vert*—18 f. Beynac-Cazenac (Dordogne); 35 f. Rouen Cathedral.

418 Copernicus   **419** L-J. Thénard

(Des and eng Piel (8 f.), Decaris (12 f.), Hertenberger (15 f.). Des Lalau. Eng Mazelin (10 f.). Munier (18 f.). Des Spitz. Eng Serres (25 f.). Des Lemagny. Eng Hertenberger (35 f.). Recess)

1957 (9 Nov). *Famous Men.* T **418** and similar vert portraits. P 13.
1357   8 f. blackish brown   20   12

1358   10 f. deep bluish green   20   20
1359   12 f. deep reddish violet   30   25
1360   15 f. orange-brown and deep brown   30   15
1361   18 f. deep blue   70   45
1362   25 f. maroon and deep lilac   50   25
1363   35 f. deep blue   75   65
1357/1363   *Set of 7*   2·50   1·50
Portraits:—10 f. Michelangelo; 12 f. Cervantes; 15 f. Rembrandt; 18 f. Newton; 25 f. Mozart; 35 f. Goethe.
See also Nos. 1367/74.

(Des and eng Gandon. Recess)

1957 (30 Nov). *Death Centenary of Thénard (chemist).* P 13.
1364 **419** 15 f. blackish green and bistre   20   20

420 "The Blind Man and the Beggar" (after J. Callot)   **421** Rural Postal Service

(Des and eng J. Piel. Recess)

1957 (7 Dec). *Red Cross Fund.* T **420** and similar vert design. Cross in red. P 13.
1365   15 f+7 f. deep bright blue   1·10   1·10
1366   20 f.+8 f. chocolate   1·10   1·10
Design:—20 f. "The Beggar and the One-eyed Woman" (after J. Callot).

(Des Spitz. Eng Cottet (8 f.), Pheulpin (12 f.), Mazelin (15 f.), Munier (35 f.). Recess)

1958 (25 Jan). *French Doctors.* Vert portraits as T **418**. P 13.
1367   8 f. bistre-brown (Pinel)   30   20
1368   12 f. blue-violet (Widal)   30   20
1369   15 f. deep blue (Nicolle)   30   25
1370   35 f. black (Leriche)   65   35
1367/1370   *Set of 4*   1·40   90

(Des and eng Decaris (8 f., 12 f.), Cottet (15 f.), Combet (35 f.). Recess)

1958 (15 Feb). *French Scientists.* Vert portraits as T **418**. P 13.
1371   8 f. bluish violet and greenish blue   30   25
1372   12 f. violet-grey and sepia   30   25
1373   15 f. bronze-green and deep green   50   30
1374   35 f. brown-red and lake   75   45
1371/1374   *Set of 4*   1·75   1·00
Portraits:—8 f. Lagrange (mathematician); 12 f. Le Verrier (astronomer); 15 f. Foucault (physicist); 35 f. Berthollet (chemist).

(Des and eng Gandon. Recess)

1958 (15 Mar). *Stamp Day.* P 13.
1375 **421** 15 f.+5 f. deep olive, yellow-green and brown   70   65

422 Le Havre   **423** French Pavilion

(Des Combet. Eng Combet (12 f., 15 f.), Munier (18 f.), Mazelin (25 f.). Recess)

1958 (29 Mar). *Municipal Reconstruction.* T **422** and similar designs. P 13.
1376   12 f. rose-carmine and olive-green   20   20
1377   15 f. bistre-brown and reddish violet   35   25
1378   18 f. indigo and ultramarine   30   25
1379   25 f. olive-brown, turq-grn & dp blue   30   30
1376/1379   *Set of 4*   1·00   90
Designs: *Vert*—12 f. Maubeuge; 18 f. Saint-Dié. *Horiz*—25 f. Sete.

(Des Serveau. Eng Piel. Recess)

1958 (12 Apr). *Brussels International Exhibition.* P 13.
1380 **423** 35 f. deep bluish green, blue and
    olive-brown   25   20

(Des Decaris. Eng Decaris (8 f., 15 f.), Pheulpin (12 f. 20 f.).
Recess)

1958 (19 Apr). *Heroes of the Resistance (Second issue).*
Various vert portraits as T **407.** P 13.
1381   8 f. brownish black and violet   ..   20   15
1382   12 f. deep bluish green and bright blue   20   15
1383   15 f. violet-grey and sepia   ..   75   45
1384   20 f. blue and olive-brown   65   45
1381/1384   *Set of* 4 ..   ..   ..   1·50   1·00
    Portraits:—8 f. Jean Cavaillès; 12 f. Fred Scamaroni; 15 f.
Simone Michel-Lévy; 20 f. Jacques Bingen.

424 Boule

425 Senlis Cathedral

(Des and eng R. Serres. Recess)

1958 (26 Apr). *French Traditional Games. Designs as T* **424.** P 13.
1385   12 f. brown and red   30   25
1386   15 f. dp bronze-green, blue-green & blue   30   20
1387   18 f. brown and deep bluish green   ..   50   35
1388   25 f. indigo and brown   50   30
1385/1388   *Set of* 4 ..   ..   ..   1·50   1·00
    Designs:—*Horiz*—15 f. Nautical jousting. *Vert*—18 f.
Archery; 25 f. Breton wrestling.

(Des Spitz Eng Mazelin. Recess)

1958 (17 May). *Senlis Cathedral Commemoration.* P 13.
1389 **425** 15 f. blue and indigo   20   20

(Des and eng Hertenberger (1390), Mazelin (1392), Munier
(1394). Nos. 1391 des Lalau, eng Combet, 1393 des
Lemagny, eng Pheulpin, 1395 des Ciry, eng Cottet. Recess)

1958 (7 June). *Red Cross Fund. French Celebrities. Various
vert portraits as T* **410.** P 13.
1390   12 f.+4 f. dp yellow-grn (Du Bellay)   95   95
1391   12 f.+4 f. deep blue (Jean Bart)   ..   95   95
1392   15 f.+5 f. brown-purple (Diderot)   ..   95   95
1393   15 f.+5 f. ultramarine (Courbet)   ..   95   95
1394   20 f.+8 f. vermilion (Carpeaux)   ..   1·25   1·25
1395   35 f.+15 f. dp bluish green (Toulouse-
    Lautrec)   ..   ..   1·25   1·25
1390/1395   *Set of* 6 ..   ..   ..   4·75   4·75

426 Fragment of the
Bayeux Tapestry

426a "Europa"

(Des and eng Cami. Recess)

1958 (21 June). P 13.
1396 **426** 15 f. carmine-red and blue   ..   30   20

(Des A. van der Vossen. Eng Gandon. Recess)

1958 (13 Sept). *Europa.* P 13.
1397 **426a** 20 f. carmine-red   40   5
1398   35 f. ultramarine   45   15

FIFTH REPUBLIC, 4 October 1958

427 Town Halls of Paris and Rome   **428** U.N.E.S.C.O.
                                        Headquarters, Paris

(Des and eng Decaris. Recess)

1958 (11 Oct). *Paris-Rome Friendship.* P 13.
1399 **427** 35 f. violet-grey, lt bl & carm-red   40   25

(Des and eng Hertenberger. Recess)

1958 (1 Nov). *Inauguration of U.N.E.S.C.O. Headquarters
Building, Paris. T* **428** *and a similar horiz design.* P 13.
1400   20 f. bistre and deep turquoise-blue   ..   15   10
1401   35 f. orange-red and black green   ..   20   20
    Design:—35 f. Different aerial view of H.Q. building.

429 Flanders Grave   **430** Arms of   **431** St. Vincent
                   Marseilles   de Paul

(Des and eng Gandon. Recess)

1958 (11 Nov). *40th Anniv of First World War Armistice.* P 13.
1402 **429** 15 f. blue, green & deep bluish green   15   12

(Des R. Louis. Die eng Fenneteaux (50 c.), Miermont (70 c.),
Aufschneider (80 c., 5 f.), Frères (1 f., 3 f.), Barre (2 f.).
Typo)

1958 (15 Nov)–59. *As T* **430** *(various town coats-of-arms).*
P 14 × 13½.
1403   50 c. blue and deep violet-blue   ..   5   5
1404   70 c. red, yellow, ultramarine and brown   5   5
1405   80 c. red, yellow and ultramarine   ..   5   5
1406   1 f. red, yellow and ultramarine   ..   5   5
1407   2 f. scarlet, green and ultramarine   ..   5   5
1408   3 f. red, yellow, green and black   ..   5   5
1409   5 f. red and sepia   5   5
1410   15 f. red, ultram, yell & grn (7.3.59)   10   5
1403/1410   *Set of* 8   25   15
    Arms (*inscr*):—70 c. "Lyon"; 80 c. "Toulouse"; 1 f. "Bor-
deaux"; 2 f. "Nice"; 3 f. "Nantes"; 5 f. "Lille"; 15 f. "Alger".
    For similar stamps see Designs Index, under "Arms".

(Des and eng J. Piel. Recess)

1958 (6 Dec). *Red Cross Fund. T* **431** *and similar vert
portrait. Cross in red.* P 13.
1411   15 f.+7 f. deep grey-green   65   65
1412   20 f.+8 f. deep violet   65   65
    Portrait:—20 f. J. H. Dunant (founder of Red Cross).

432 Arc du   **433** Symbols of Learning and
Carrousel and   "Academic Palms"
Flowers

(Des and eng Gandon. Recess)
1959 (17 Jan). *Paris Flower Festival. P* 13.
1413 **432** 15 f. multicoloured   15   10

(Des and eng Decaris. Recess)
1959 (24 Jan). *150th Anniv of the "Academic Palms". P* 13.
1414 **433** 20 f. black, violet and lake   ..   12   10

434 Father Charles de Foucauld   **435** Mail 'plane
(missionary)   making night-landing
(Des and eng Mazelin. Recess)
1959 (31 Jan). *De Foucauld Commemoration. P* 13.
1415 **434** 50 f. brown-purple, brown, bl & blk   50   40

(Des and eng Gandon. Recess)
1959 (21 Mar). *Stamp Day. P* 13.
1416 **435** 20 f.+5 f. red, sepia, yellow-green
         and black-green   40   40
See also No. 1644.

436 Miner's Lamp,   **437** "Five Martyrs"
Picks and School Building

(Des and eng Combet. Recess)
1959 (11 Apr). *175th Anniv of School of Mines. P* 13.
1417 **436** 20 f. turquoise-blue, brownish black
         and brown-red   15   12

(Des Serres. Eng Serres (No. 1418), Pheulpin (No. 1419),
Mazelin (No. 1420), Cami (No. 1421), Munier (No. 1422).
Recess)
1959 (25 Apr). *Heroes of the Resistance* (*Third series*).
T **437** *and various vert portraits as T* **407**. *P* 13.
1418   15 f. black and deep violet   ..   20   15
1419   15 f. reddish violet and bright purple ..   30   20
1420   20 f. brown and chestnut   30   20
1421   20 f. turquoise-blue and deep green   ..   45   30
1422   30 f. deep violet and bright purple   ..   45   30
1418/1422   Set of 5 ..   ..   1·50   1·00
Portraits:—No. 1419, Yvonne Le Roux; No. 1420, Martin
Bret; No. 1421, Médéric-Védy; No. 1422, Moutardier.

438 Foum el Gherza Dam   **439** C. Goujon and
                            C. Rozanoff (test pilots)

(Des Combet. Eng Munier (15. f.), Combet (20 f., 50 f.),
Durrens (30 f.). Recess)
1959 (23 May). *French Technical Achievements. Various
pictorial designs as T* **438**. *P* 13.
1423   15 f. turquoise-blue and olive-brown ..   15   15
1424   20 f. brown-purple, cerise and chestnut   30   20
1425   30 f. bistre-brown, turquoise and dp bl   25   20
1426   50 f. grey-blue and olive-green   ..   35   20
1423/1426   Set of 4   95   65

Designs: *Vert*—20 f. Marcoule Atomic Power Station;
30 f. Oil derrick and pipe-line at Hassi-Messaoud, Sahara.
Horiz—50 f. National Centre of Industry and Technology, Paris.

(Des and eng Munier. Recess)
1959 (13 June). *Goujon and Rozanoff Commemoration. P* 13.
1427 **439** 20 f. chestnut, red and light blue ..   20   20

440 Villehardouin (chronicler)   **441** M. Desbordes-Valmore

(Des Decaris. Eng Cottet (1428), Hertenberger (1429),
Mazelin (1430), Decaris (1431), Munier (1432), Pheulpin
(1433). Recess)
1959 (13 June). *Red Cross Fund. T* **440** *and similar horiz
portraits. P* 13.
1428   15 f.+5 f. blue-violet   70   70
1429   15 f.+5 f. blackish green   70   70
1430   20 f.+10 f. bistre   90   90
1431   20 f.+10 f. grey   90   90
1432   30 f.+10 f. lake   95   95
1433   30 f.+10 f. chestnut   95   95
1428/1433   Set of 6 ....   4·75   4·75
Portraits:—No. 1428, *T* **440**; 1429, Le Notre (Royal gardener);
1430, D'Alembert (philosopher); 1431, D'Angers (sculptor);
1432, Bichat (physiologist); 1433, Bartholdi (sculptor).

(Des and eng Gandon. Recess)
1959 (20 June). *Death Centenary of Marceline Desbordes-
Valmore* (*poetess*). *P* 13.
1434 **441** 30 f. chocolate, blue & dp bluish grn   20   15

442 "Marianne" in   **443** Tancarville Bridge
Ship of State

(Des A. Regagnon. Eng J. Piel. Typo)
1959 (27 July). *P* 14 × 13½.
1437 **442** 25 f. brown-red and black   ..   25   5

(Des and eng Combet. Recess)
1959 (1 Aug). *Inauguration of Tancarville Bridge. P* 13.
1438 **443** 30 f. blackish grn, choc & dp blue   20   12

444 Jean Jaurès   **444a** "Europa"

(Des and eng Decaris. Recess)
1959 (12 Sept). *Birth Centenary of Jaurès* (*socialist leader*).
P 13.
1439 **444** 50 f. chocolate   25   20

(Des W. Brudi. Eng Frères. Recess)
1959 (19 Sept). *Europa. P* 13.
1440 **444a** 25 f. emerald   ..   ..   '..   25   10
1441   50 f. violet   35   15

445 "Giving blood" **446** Clasped Hands of Friendship

(Des and eng Decaris. Recess)

1959 (17 Oct). *Blood Donors' Commemoration.* P 13.
1442 **445** 20 f. deep grey and lake . . 12 10

(Des Serveau. Eng Piel. Recess)

1959 (24 Oct). *300th Anniv of the Treaty of the Pyrénées.* P 13.
1443 **446** 50 f. orange-red, cerise and blue. . 35 25

447 Youth throwing away Crutches **448** Henri Bergson

(Des Spitz. Eng Cami. Recess)

1959 (31 Oct). *Infantile Paralysis Relief Campaign.* P 13.
1444 **447** 20 f. deep blue 12 12

(Des and eng Serres. Recess)

1959 (7 Nov). *Birth Centenary of Bergson (philosopher).* P 13.
1445 **448** 50 f. orange-brown 30 20

449 Avesnes-sur-Helpe **450** Abbé C. M. de l'Epée (teacher of deaf mutes)

(Des Serveau. Eng Durrens (20 f.), Piel (30 f.). Recess)

1959 (14 Nov). *T 449 and similar horiz design.* P 13.
1446 20 f. blue, chocolate and black . . 12 10
1447 30 f. chocolate, brown-purple and blue 20 12
Design:—30 f. Perpignan Castle.

(Des and eng J. Piel. Recess)

1959 (5 Dec). *Red Cross Fund. T 450 and similar vert portrait. Cross in red.* P 13.
1448 20 f.+10 f. brown-purple and black. . 65 65
1449 25 f.+10 f. black and blue 65 65
Portrait:—25 f. V. Hauy (teacher of the blind).

FREJUS

+5ᶠ

451 N.A.T.O. Head-quarters, Paris (452)

(Des and eng Mazelin. Recess)

1959 (12 Dec). *Tenth Anniv of North Atlantic Treaty Organisation.* P 13.
1450 **451** 50 f. chocolate, green & ultramarine 60 40

1959 (13 Dec). *Fréjus Disaster Fund. No. 1437 surch with T 452.*
1451 **442** 25 f.+5 f. brown-red and black . . 25 20

New currency. 100 (old) francs=1 (new) franc

453 Sower **454** Laon Cathedral

(Des O. Roty (T **453**). Die eng. J. Piel. Typo)

1960 (2 Jan)–**61.** *Various types and Arms types as T 430, but with values in new currency.* P 14 × 13½.
1452 — 5 c. red and sepia . . . . 3·25 5
1453 **344** 10 c. emerald 12 5
1454 — 15 c. red, ultramarine, yell & grn 12 5
1455 **453** 20 c. carmine and turquoise . . 12 5
1456 **442** 25 c. ultramarine and red . . 1·10 5
1456a **453** 30 c. violet-blue & indigo (23.2.61) 1·00 20
1452/1456a Set of 6 . . . . 5·00 20
Arms:—5 c. "Lille"; 15 c. "Alger".

(No. 1457b des and eng Gandon)

1960 (11 Jan)–**65.** *AIR. As Nos. 1195 and 1318/20 but with values in new currency and new design (No. 1457b).*
1457 2 f. deep purple and ultramarine . . 95 5
  a. Deep purple omitted ('63) . . 1·60 10
1457b 2 f. indigo & greenish blue (12.6.65) 80 5
1458 3 f. olive-brown and turquoise-blue 1·25 5
1459 5 f. black and deep blue . . 2·25 15
1460 10 f. black, reddish violet and sepia . . 5·00 70
1457/1460 Set of 5 . . . . 11·00 1·00
Design:—No. 1457b, Mystère "20" jetliner.
No. 1457a comes from printings between November 1963 and November 1964 which had the purple colour completely omitted. This was restored in a printing in March 1965. Some printings made in 1962 appear to be without the purple colour and these should not be confused with No. 1457a.

(Des and eng Cami (15 c.), Gandon (30 c.), Pheulpin (50 c.), Mazelin (85 c.), Munier (85 c.), Hertenberger (1 f.). Des Spitz. Eng Cami (45 c.). Recess)

1960 (16 Jan). *Tourist Publicity Series. T 454 and similar pictorial designs.* P 13.
1461 15 c. indigo and light blue 12 5
1462 30 c. deep maroon, blue-grn & ultram 35 5
1463 45 c. reddish violet, purple and sepia. . 30 5
1464 50 c. maroon and deep bronze-green . . 30 5
1465 65 c. olive-brown, grey-green & lt blue 30 5
1466 85 c. sepia, green and blue 55 5
1467 1 f. bluish violet, dp grn & turq-blue 50 5
1461/1467 Set of 7 . . . . 2·25 20
Designs: Horiz—30 c. Fougères Château; 65 c. Valley of the Sioule; 85 c. Chaumont Viaduct. Vert—45 c. Kerrata Gorges, Algeria; 50 c. Tlemcen Mosque, Algeria; 1 f. Cilaos Church and Great Bénard Mountains, Réunion.
See also Nos. 1485/7.

455 Pierre de Nolhac **456** St.-Étienne Museum

(Des and eng Pheulpin. Recess)

1960 (13 Feb). *De Nolhac (historian) Centenary.* P 13.
1468 **455** 20 c. deep olive-brown 20 12

(Des and eng Durrens. Recess)

1960 (20 Feb). *Museum of Art and Industry, St.-Etienne.* P 13.
1469 **456** 30 c. chocolate, carm-red & slate-bl 25 15

1960 (25 Feb). *As T **345** but with values in new currency. Typo.* P 14 × 13½.

1470	**345**	8 c. violet*	50	5
1471		20 c. deep yellow-green*	1·60	5
1472		40 c. brown-red†	3·25	95
1473		55 c. emerald*	9·00	5·50
1470/1473		Set of 4	13·00	6·00

* These stamps were only issued precancelled, the unused prices being for stamps with full gum.

D **457** Wheat Sheaves

457 Assembly Emblem and View of Cannes

(Des P. Gandon. Die eng H. Cortot. Typo)

1960 (Feb). *POSTAGE DUE. New currency* P 14 × 13½.

D1474	D **457**	5 c. cerise	65	12
D1475		10 c. orange-red	75	15
D1476		20 c. olive-brown	1·10	12
D1477		50 c. deep slate-green	4·00	40
D1478		1 f. green	9·50	45
D1474/1478		Set of 5	14·00	1·00

(Des and eng Decaris. Recess)

1960 (5 Mar). *Fifth Meeting of European Mayors Assembly.* P 13.

1474 **457** 50 c. chestnut and green .. 65 40

458 Cable-laying Ship

459 Girl of Savoy

(Des and eng Serres. Recess)

1960 (12 Mar). *Stamp Day.* P 13.

1475 **458** 20 c.+5 c. blue and turquoise-blue 55 55

(Des Serveau. Eng Piel (30 c.), Combet (50 c.). Recess)

1960 (24 Mar). *Centenary of Attachment of Savoy and Nice to France. T **459** and similar horiz design.* P 13.

1476		30 c. deep bronze-green	30	20
1477		50 c. chocolate, rose-red and yellow	40	25

Design:—50 c. Girl of Nice.

(Des Spitz. Eng Pheulpin (Nos. 1478, 1482), Cottet (No. 1479), Mazelin (No. 1480), Munier (No. 1481). Recess)

1960 (26 Mar). *Heroes of the Resistance (Fourth series). Various portraits as T **407**.* P 13.

1478		20 c. black and bistre-brown	75	45
1479		20 c. lake and carmine	75	45
1480		25 c. reddish violet and violet	75	45
1481		30 c. blue and indigo	90	65
1482		50 c. red-brown and bronze-green	1·25	90
1478/1482		Set of 5	4·00	2·50

Portraits:—No. 1478, Debeaumarché; No. 1479, Masse; No. 1480, Ripoche; No. 1481, Vieljeux; No. 1482, Abbé Bonpain.

460 Child Refugee

461 "Road to Learning"

(Des and eng Decaris Recess)

1960 (7 Apr). *World Refugee Year.* P 13.

1483 **460** 25 c.+10 c. indigo, bistre-brown and emerald 25 20

(Des and eng Hertenberger. Recess)

1960 (21 May). *150th Anniv of Normal School, Strasbourg.* P 13.

1484 **461** 20 c. reddish violet, bright purple and black 15 10

(Des and eng Gandon (15 c.), Mazelin (20 c.), Serres (30 c.), Combet (50 c.). Recess)

1960–61. *Pictorial designs similar to T **454**.* P 13.

1485		15 c. deep sepia, grey & bl (24.9.60)	15	12
1485a		20 c. blue, bluish green & buff (6.5.61)	15	12
1486		30 c. sepia, bluish green & blue (21.5.60)	30	20
1487		50 c. ol-brn, bluish grn & red (28.5.60)	40	25
1485/1487		Set of 4	90	65

Designs: *Horiz*—15 c. Lisieux Basilica; 20 c. Bagnoles de l'Orne; 30 c. Château de Blois; 50 c. La Bourboule.

462 L'Hospital (statesman)

463 "Marianne"

(Des Mazelin. Eng Cami (1488), Mazelin (1489), Munier (1490), Combet (1491), Durrens (1492), Hertenberger (1493) Recess)

1960 (13 June). *Red Cross Fund. T **462** and similar horiz designs.* P 13.

1488		10 c.+5 c. reddish violet and crimson	1·25	1·25
1489		20 c.+10 c. deep bluish green & green	1·40	1·40
1490		20 c.+10 c. olive-brown and chocolate	1·50	1·50
1491		30 c.+10 c. deep blue and bluish violet	1·50	1·50
1492		30 c.+10 c. crimson and rose-red	1·50	1·50
1493		50 c.+15 c. indigo and deep slate	1·60	1·60
1488/1493		Set of 6	9·00	9·00

Designs:—No. 1489, Boileau (poet); 1490, Turenne (military leader); 1491, Bizet (composer); 1492, Charcot (neurologist); 1493, Degas (painter).

(Des A. Decaris. Die eng J. Piel. Typo)

1960 (15 June). P 14 × 13½.

1494	**463**	25 c. grey and claret	12	5
		a. Grey omitted	38·00	
		b. Claret omitted	38·00	

464 Cross of Lorraine

465 Jean Bouin and Olympic Stadium

(Des C. Haley. Eng C. Durrens. Recess)

1960 (18 June). *20th Anniv of De Gaulle's Appeal.* P 13.

1495 **464** 20 c. red-brown, yellow-grn & sepia 15 12

(Des and eng Decaris. Recess)

1960 (9 July). *Olympic Games.* P 13.

1496 **465** 20 c. sepia, lake and blue 15 12

465a Conference Emblem

466 Madame de Staël (after Gerard)

(Des Rahikainen. Eng Combet. Recess)

1960 (17 Sept). *Europa. P* 13.
1497 **465a** 25 c. turquoise-green and emerald   15   5
1498   50 c. bright purple and crimson . .   25   12

(Des R. Louis. Die eng A. Frères (1 c., 5 c. (1499a), 12 c., 15 c., 30 c.). A. Barre (2 c., 5 c. (1499), 18 c.), Fenneteaux (10 c.). Typo)

1960–65. *Arms designs as T* **430.** *P* 14 × 13½.
1498a   1 c. deep violet-blue & yell (25.1.64)   5   5
1498b   2 c. yellow, green & dp vio-bl (25.1.64)   5   5
1499   5 c. red, yellow, ultram & grn (15.10.60)   12   5
1499a   5 c. red, yellow and ultram (23.7.62)   5   5
1499b   10 c. ultram, yellow & brn-red (14.1.63)   5   5
1499c   12 c. red, yellow and black (16.5.64) . .   5   5
1499d   15 c. yellow, ultramarine & red (23.7.62)   5   5
1499e   18 c. green, blue, yell & red (16.5.64)   10   5
1499f   30 c. red and ultramarine (16.1.65) . .   15   5
1498a/1499f Set of 9   60   10
Arms (*inscr*):—1 c. "Niort"; 2 c. "Guéret"; No. 1499, "Oran";· No. 1499a, "Amiens"; 10 c. "Troyes"; 12 c. "Agen"; 15 c. "Nevers"; 18 c. "Saint-Denis (Réunion)"; 30 c. "Paris".
For similar stamps, see Designs Index under "Arms".
For 10 c. "Troyes" with phosphor bands, see No.1867p.

(Des and eng Mazelin. Recess)

1960 (22 Oct). *Madame de Staël* (*writer*). *P* 13.
1500 **466** 30 c. olive-brown and maroon   . .   20   15

467 Gen. Estienne, Plane and Tank

468 Marc Sangnier (patriot)

(Des and eng Combet. Recess)

1960 (5 Nov). *General Estienne Centenary. P* 13.
1501 **467** 15 c. brownish black & reddish lilac   12   12

(Des and eng Cami. Recess)

1960 (5 Nov). *Sangnier Commemoration. P* 13.
1502 **468** 12 c. black, violet and blue   . .   12   10

469 Order of the Liberation

470 Puffins at Les Sept Iles

(Des and eng Durrens. Recess)

1960 (11 Nov). *20th Anniv of Order of the Liberation. P* 13.
1503 **469** 20 c. blue-green and black   . .   20   12

(Des and eng Gandon. Recess)

1960 (12 Nov). *Nature Protection. T* **470** *and similar horiz design. P* 13.
1504   30 c. multicoloured   20   12
1505   50 c. multicoloured   45   20
Design:—50 c. Bee-eaters of Camargue

471 A. Honnorat

472 Mace of St. Martin's Brotherhood

(Des and eng Munier. Recess)

1960 (19 Nov). *Tenth Anniv of Death of Honnorat* (*philanthropist*). *P* 13.
1506 **471** 30 c. black, green and blue   . .   20   12

(Des and eng Piel. Recess)

1960 (3 Dec). *Red Cross Fund. T* **472** *and similar vert design. Cross in red. P* 13.
1507   20 c.+10 c. lake   95   95
1508   25 c.+10 c. blue   95   95
Design:—25 c. St. Martin (after 16th-century wood-carving).

473 St. Barbe and College

474 Lapwings

(Des and eng Hertenberger. Recess)

1960 (3 Dec). *500th Anniv of St. Barbe College. P* 13.
1509 **473** 30 c. red, blue, sepia and bistre . .   25   20

(Des Mazelin. Eng Gandon (20 c.). Des and eng Gandon (45 c.). Recess)

1960 (17 Dec). *Bird Migration. T* **474** *and similar horiz design inscr* "ETUDE DES MIGRATIONS". *P* 13.
1510   20 c. multicoloured   20   12
1511   45 c. multicoloured   50   45
Design:—45 c. European green winged teal

475 "Mediterranean" (after Maillol)

(Des and eng Decaris. Recess)

1961 (18 Feb). *Maillol* (*sculptor*) *Centenary. P* 13.
1512 **475** 20 c. indigo and carmine-red   . .   15   10

476 "Marianne"

477 Orly Airport

France

1961

(Des J. Cocteau. Eng Decaris. Recess)

1961 (23 Feb). *P* 13.
1513 **476** 20 c. carmine-red and blue .. 8 5
     a. Carmine-red omitted .. 40·00

(Des and eng Combet. Recess)

1961 (25 Feb). *Opening of New Installations at Orly Airport, Paris. P* 13.
1514 **477** 50 c. turquoise-blue, blue and black 35 20

478 Georges Méliès

479 Postman of Paris "Little Post", 1760

(Des and eng Cottet. Recess)

1961 (11 Mar). *Birth Centenary of Méliès* (*cinematograph pioneer*). *P* 13.
1515 **478** 50 c. indigo, drab and reddish violet 45 35

(Des and eng Serres. Recess)

1961 (18 Mar). *Stamp Day and Red Cross Fund. P* 13.
1516 **479** 20 c. + 5 c. blk-grn, carm & chestnut 25 20

480 Jean Nicot and Tobacco Flowers and Leaves

481 Father Lacordaire (after Chassériau)

(Des and eng Combet. Recess)

1961 (25 Mar). *Fourth Centenary of Introduction of Tobacco into France. P* 13.
1517 **480** 30 c. red, chestnut and olive-green 20 15

(Des and eng Durrens. Recess)

1961 (25 Mar). *Father Lacordaire Centenary. P* 13.
1518 **481** 30 c. sepia and bistre-brown .. 20 15

(Des Spitz. Eng Cottet (Nos. 1519/20), Pheulpin (Nos. 1521/2). Recess)

1961 (22 Apr). *Heroes of the Resistance* (*Fifth series*). *Various vert portraits as T* **407**. *P* 13.
1519 20 c. reddish violet and blue (Renouvin) 30 20
1520 20 c. blue and bronze-green (Dubray) 45 30
1521 30 c. black and chestnut (Gateaud) .. 30 20
1522 30 c. ind & vio-blue (Mother Elisabeth) 70 45
1519/1522 *Set of 4* .. .. 1·50 1·00

482 Dove, Globe and Olive Branch

483 Deauville, 1861

(Des and eng Combet. Recess)

1961 (6 May). *World Federation of Old Soldiers' Meeting, Paris. P* 13.
1523 **482** 50 c. lake, blue and green .. 25 20

(Des and eng Cami. Recess)

1961 (13 May). *Centenary of Deauville. P* 13.
1524 **483** 50 c. lake 50 45

484 Du Guesclin (Constable of France)

485 Champmesle ("Roxane")

(Des Mazelin. Eng Pheulpin (1525), Mazelin (1526, 1530), Combet (1527), Durrens (1528), Bétemps (1529). Recess)

1961 (20 May). *Red Cross Fund. T* **484** *and similar horiz designs. P* 13.
1525 15 c. + 5 c. black and brown-purple .. 1·00 1·00
1526 20 c. + 10 c. black-green and blue .. 1·00 1·00
1527 20 c. + 10 c. crimson and red .. 1·00 1·00
1528 30 c. + 10 c. black and chestnut .. 1·00 1·00
1529 45 c. + 10 c. chocolate & dp bluish grn 1·10 1·10
1530 50 c. + 15 c. reddish violet and lake .. 1·10 1·10
1525/1530 *Set of 6* .. .. 5·50 5·50
    Designs:—No. 1526, Puget (sculptor); 1527, Coulomb (physicist); 1528, General Drouot; 1529, Daumier (caricaturist); 1530, Apollinaire (writer).

(Des Decaris. Eng Durrens (Nos. 1531, 1534), Decaris (others). Recess)

1961 (10 June). *French Actors and Actresses T* **485** *and similar vert portraits. P* 13.
1531 20 c. chocolate, green and crimson .. 20 15
1532 30 c. brown, scarlet and crimson .. 25 20
1533 30 c. black-green, yellow-green & crim 25 20
1534 50 c. chestnut, turquoise-green & crim 45 30
1535 50 c. chocolate, olive and crimson .. 45 30
1531/1535 *Set of 5* .. .. 1·50 1·00
    Portraits:—No. 1532, Talma ("Oreste"); No. 1533, Rachel ("Phèdre"); No. 1534, Raimu ("César"); No. 1535, Gerard Philipe ("Le Cid").

486 Mont Dore, Snow Crystal and Cable Railway

487 Thann

488 Pierre Fauchard

(Des and eng Combet. Recess)

1961 (1 July). *Mont Dore Commemoration. P* 13.
1536 **486** 20 c. bright purple and orange .. 15 10

(Des and eng Gandon. Recess)

1961 (1 July). *8th Centenary of Thann. P* 13.
1537 **487** 20 c. violet, chocolate & black-grn 35 20

(Des and eng Decaris. Recess)

1961 (1 July). *Fauchard Bicentenary. P* 13.
1538 **488** 50 c. black and bluish green .. 30 20

489 Doves   **490** Sully-sur-Loire

(Des T. Kurpershoek. Eng Combet. Recess)

1961 (16 Sept). *Europa.* P 13.
1539	**489**	25 c. vermilion	10	5
1540		50 c. ultramarine	20	12

(Des Serveau (30 c., 1543, 65 c.), eng Piel (30 c., 1543, 65 c.). Des and eng Cami, after Ambrogiani (15 c), Mazelin (20 c., 30 c., 1544), Pheulpin (45 c., 85 c., 1 f., 1550), Durrens (50 c.), Combet (1 f., 1549). Recess)

1961 (7 Oct.)—**62.** *Tourist Publicity.* T **490** *and similar horiz designs.* P 13.
1541	15 c. slate, purple and greenish blue		5	5
1542	20 c. brown & dp bluish grn (24.2.62)		15	10
1543	30 c. ultramarine, slate-green & sepia		12	5
1544	30 c. black, blue-grey & green (9.6.62)		25	20
1545	45 c. chestnut, dp blue-green & dp blue		20	5
1546	50 c. slate-green, turquoise and green		20	5
1547	65 c. ultram, chestnut & blackish grn		25	5
1548	85 c. indigo, chestnut & slate-green		35	5
1549	1 f. brown, blue and blackish green		1·25	5
1550	1 f. orange-brown, deep bluish green and blue (3.9.62)		45	5
1541/1550	*Set of* 10		3·00	60

Views: *Horiz*—15 c. Saint-Paul; 30 c. (No. 1543), Arcachon; 30 c. (No. 1544), Law Courts, Rennes; 45 c. T **490**; 50 c. Cognac; 65 c. Dinan; 85 c. Calais; 1 f. (No. 1549), Medea, Algeria; 1 f. (No. 1550), Le Touquet–Paris–Plage, golf-bag and aircraft. *Vert*—20 c. Laval, Mayenne.
See also Nos. 1619/23, 1654/7, 1684/8, 1755/61, 1814/18, 1883/5, 1929/33, 1958/61, 2005/8, 2042/4, 2062/4, 2115/20, 2187/92 and 2258/64.

491 "14th July" (R. de la Fresnaye)

(Des Gandon. Eng Cottet (1 f.). Des and eng Gandon (others). Recess)

1961 (10 Nov). *French Art.* T **491** *and similar horiz paintings.* P 13 × 12.
1551	50 c. black, brown, grey and blue	1·75	1·00
1552	65 c. blue, green and violet	2·10	1·25
1553	85 c. red, bistre and deep blue	1·90	1·50
1554	1 f. multicoloured	2·50	1·90
1551/1554	*Set of* 4	7·50	5·00

Paintings:—50 c. "The Messenger" (Braque); 65 c. "Blue Nudes" (Matisse); 85 c. "The Cardplayers" (Cézanne).
See also Nos. 1590/2, 1603/6, 1637/9, 1671/4, 1710/14, 1742/5, 1786/9, 1819/22, 1877/80, 1908/10, 1944/7, 1985/8, 2033/6, 2108/12, 2159/60 and 2243.

493 "It is so sweet to love"   **494** Liner *France*
(wood-carving from Rouault's "Miserere")

(Eng J. Piel. Recess)

1961 (2 Dec). *Red Cross Fund.* T **493** *and similar vert design. Cross in red.* P 13.
1555	20 c.+10 c. black & dp brown-purple	1·00	1·00
1556	25 c.+10 c. black & dp brown-purple	1·00	1·00

Design:—25 c. "The blind leading the blind" (from Rouault's "Miserere").

(Des and eng Hertenberger. Recess)

1962 (11 Jan). *Maiden Voyage of Liner "France".* P 13.
1557	**494**	30 c. black, red and blue	20	20

495 Skier at Speed   **496** M. Bourdet

(Des and eng Gandon. Recess)

1962 (27 Jan). *World Ski Championships, Chamonix.* T **495** *and similar vert design.* P 13.
1558	30 c. violet and blue	20	20
1559	50 c. deep bluish green, blue & violet	30	20

Design:—50 c. Slalom-racer

(Des and eng Pheulpin. Recess)

1962 (17 Feb). *60th Anniv of Birth of Maurice Bourdet (journalist and radio commentator).* P 13.
1560	**496**	30 c. grey	20	15

497 Dr. P.-F. Bretonneau   **498** Gallic Cock

(Des and eng Combet. Recess)

1962 (17 Feb). *Centenary of Death of Dr. Pierre-Fidele Bretonneau (medical scientist).* P 13.
1561	**497**	50 c. reddish violet and blue	30	20

(Des and eng Decaris. Recess)

1962 (12 Mar)—**65.** P 13.
1562	**498**	25 c. red, blue and yellow-brown	15	5
1562*a*		30 c. red, dp grn & yell-brn (15.1.65)	30	5

No. 1562 with red or green numerals on the back and No. 1562*a* with red numerals come from coils.
During 1962 and 1963 experimental printings of No. 1562 were made on fluorescent papers. The first series of trials, using a locally produced paper, were unsuccessful, and examples only show patches of fluorescence under the lamp. In the following year more successful tests were carried out on a stock of JB fluorescent paper obtained from Germany.

499 Royal Messenger   **500** Vannes
of late Middle Ages

France 1962

(Des and eng Cami. Recess)

1962 (17 Mar). *Stamp Day. P* 13.
1563 **499** 20 c.+5 c. choc, brt bl & carm-red   35   30

(Des and eng Pheulpin. Recess)

1962 (24 Mar). *P* 13.
1564 **500** 30 c. deep ultramarine   25   15

501 Globe and Stage Set

502 Harbour Installations

504 Emblem and Swamp

503 Mount Valerien Memorial

(Des and eng Durrens. Recess)

1962 (24 Mar). *World Theatre Day. P* 13.
1565 **501** 50 c. carm-lake, dp grn & ochre   35   30

(Des and eng Combet. Recess)

1962 (24 Mar). *300th Anniv of Cession of Dunkirk to France.
P* 13.
1566 **502** 95 c. brt purple, bistre & blue-grn   70   10

(Des and eng Decaris. Recess)

1962 (7 Apr). *Resistance Fighters' Memorials* (1*st Series*).
T **503** *and similar designs. P* 13.
1567   20 c. blackish green and drab   ..   20   15
1568   30 c. indigo   25   20
1569   50 c. indigo and light blue   ..   30   30
Memorials: *Vert*—30 c. Vercors; 50 c. Ile de Sein.
See also Nos. 1609/10.

(Des and eng Cottet. Recess)

1962 (14 Apr). *Malaria Eradication. P* 13.
1570 **504** 50 c. carm-red, dp blue & dp green   30   25

505 Nurses and Child

506 Gliders and Stork

(Des and eng Decaris. Recess)

1962 (5 May). *National Hospitals Week. P* 13.
1571 **505** 30 c. red-brown, grey & blue-green   15   15

(Des and eng Combet. Recess)

1962 (12 May). *Civil and Sports Aviation. T* **506** *and similar
horiz design. P* 13.
1572   15 c. chocolate and chestnut   ..   10   8
1573   20 c. crimson and bright purple   ..   12   12
Design:—20 c. Early aircraft and modern light planes.

507 Emblem of School of Horology

508 "Selecting a tapestry"

(Des and eng. Durrens. Recess)

1962 (19 May). *Centenary of School of Horology, Besancon.
P* 13.
1574 **507** 50 c. deep violet, yellow-brown
     and carmine   40   30

(Des and eng Hertenberger. Recess)

1962 (26 May). *Tercentenary of Manufacture of Gobelin
Tapestries. P* 13.
1575 **508** 50 c. deep bluish green, red and
     yellow-green   35   25

509 Pascal

510 Denis Papin (inventor)

(Des R. Schardner. Eng Mazelin. Recess)

1962 (26 May). *Death Tercentenary of Pascal* (*philosopher*).
P 13.
1576 **509** 50 c. orange-red & deep bronze-grn   35   30

(Des Serveau. Eng Cami (1577/8), Durrens (1579/80),
Combet (1581/2). Recess)

1962 (2 June). *Red Cross Fund. T* **510** *and similar vert
designs. P* 13.
1577   15 c.+5 c. dp sepia & dp bluish green   70   70
1578   20 c.+10 c. bistre-brown and claret   70   70
1579   20 c.+10 c. slate-blue and grey   ..   1·00   1·00
1580   30 c.+10 c. indigo and light blue   ..   1·00   1·00
1581   45 c.+15 c. brown-purple & orge-brn   1·00   1·00
1582   50 c.+20 c. black and greenish blue   1·25   1·25
1577/1582   Set of 6   ..   ..   ..   5·00   5·00
   Designs:—20 c. (1578), Edme Bouchardon (sculptor);
20 c. (1579), Joseph Lakanal (politician); 30 c. Gustave
Charpentier (composer); 45 c. Edouard Estaunié (writer); 50 c.
Hyacinthe Vincent (scientist).

511 "Modern" Rose

512 Europa "Tree"

(Des and eng Gandon. Recess)

1962 (8 Sept). *Rose Culture. T* **511** *and similar vert design.
P* 13.
1583   20 c. carmine-red, green and yell-olive   15   12
1584   30 c. rose, black-green and yellow-olive   25   20
Design:—30 c. "Old-fashioned" rose.

(Des Lex Weyer. Eng Piel. Recess)

1962 (15 Sept). *Europa. P* 13.
1585 **512** 25 c. violet 12 5
1586 50 c. chestnut 25 12

513 Telecommunications Centre, Pleumeur-Bodou

514 "Rosalie Fragonard" (after Fragonard)

(Des and eng Combet (25 c.), Durrens (Nos. 1587/8). Recess)

1962 (29 Sept)–**63**. *First Trans-Atlantic Telecommunications Satellite Link. T* **513** *and similar horiz designs. P* 13.
1587 25 c. yellow-brown, bluish grn & bl-grey 12 5
1588 50 c. ultramarine, grey-green & dp blue 25 20
1589 50 c. chocolate and deep blue (8.6.63) 25 20
Designs:—No. 1588, "Telstar" satellite, globe and television receiver; No. 1589, Radio-telescope, Nancay (Cher).

(Des and eng Gandon (65 c.), Cottet (others). Recess)

1962 (9 Nov). *French Art. Paintings as T* **491**. *P* 13 × 12 *or* 12 × 13 (1 *f*.).
1590 50 c. multicoloured .. .. 2·10 1·25
1591 65 c. multicoloured .. .. 1·40 1·10
1592 1 f. multicoloured .. .. 2·50 2·10
Paintings: *Horiz*—50 c. "Bonjour, Monsieur Courbet" (Courbet); 65 c. "Madame Manet on a Blue Sofa" (Manet). *Vert*—1 f. "Officer of the Imperial Horse Guards" (Géricault).

(Des and eng J. Piel. Recess)

1962 (8 Dec). *Red Cross Fund. T* **514** *and similar vert portrait. Cross in red. P* 13.
1593 20 c.+10 c. chocolate .. 55 55
1594 25 c.+10 c. deep bluish green .. 55 55
Portrait: 25 c. "Child as Pierrot" (after Fragonard).

515 Bathyscaphe "Archimède"

516 Flowers and Nantes Château

(Des and eng Decaris. Recess)

1963 (26 Jan). *Record Undersea Dive. P* 13.
1595 **515** 30 c. black and deep blue .. 20 15

(Des and eng Pheulpin. Recess)

1963 (9 Feb). *Nantes Flower Show. P* 13.
1596 **516** 30 c. ultramarine, red and deep green 20 15

517 Jacques Amyot (Bishop of Auxerre)

518 Roman Post Chariot

(Des Decaris. Eng Mazelin (1598, 1601), Decaris (1597, 1599), Hertenberger (1600, 1602). Recess)

1963. *Red Cross Fund. T* **517** *and similar horiz designs inscr* "1963". *P* 13.
1597 20 c.+10 c. brown-purple, red-violet and slate-purple (23 Feb) .. 50 50

1598 20 c.+10 c. chocolate, chestnut and blue (25 May) 65 65
1599 30 c.+10 c. deep bluish green and maroon (23 Feb) .. 50 50
1600 30 c.+10 c. olive-black, olive-green and brown-purple (25 May) .. 65 65
1601 50 c.+20 c. olive, ochre and blue (23 Feb) 65 65
1602 50 c.+20 c. black-brown, slate-blue and chocolate (25 May) .. 90 90
1597/1602 *Set of* 6 .. .. .. 3·50 3·50
Designs:—No. 1597, T **517**; 1598, Étienne Méhul (composer); 1599, Pierre de Marivaux (dramatist); 1600, N.-L. Vauquelin (chemist); 1601, Jacques Daviel (oculist); 1602, Alfred de Vigny (poet).

(Des and eng Gandon (50 c., 85 c.), Durrens (95 c.), Combet (1 f.). Recess)

1963. *French Art. Paintings as T* **491**. *P* 12 × 13.
1603 50 c. multicoloured (2.3) .. 1·90 1·25
1604 85 c. multicoloured (12.11) .. 1·25 80
1605 95 c. multicoloured (12.11) .. 70 45
1606 1 f. multicoloured (2.3) .. 4·00 3·25
1603/1606 *Set of* 4 .. .. .. 7·00 5·25
Designs: *Vert*—50 c. "Jacob's Struggle with the Angel" (Delacroix); 85 c. "The Married Couple of the Eiffel Tower" (Chagall); 95 c. "The Fur Merchants" (stained glass window, Chartres Cathedral); 1 f. "St. Peter and the Miracle of the Fishes" (stained glass window, Church of St. Foy de Conches).

(Des and eng Piel. Recess)

1963 (16 Mar). *Stamp Day. P* 13.
1607 **518** 20 c.+5 c. dull purple & yell-brn 20 20

519 Woman reaching for Campaign Emblem

520 Glières Memorial

(Des and eng Cottet. Recess)

1963 (21 Mar). *Freedom from Hunger. P* 13.
1608 **519** 50 c. orange-brown and black-green 30 25

(Des and eng Cami. Recess)

1963 (23 Mar). *Resistance Fighters' Memorials* (2nd Series). *T* **520** *and similar vert design. P* 13.
1609 30 c. olive-brown and chocolate .. 20 20
1610 50 c. blue-black 25 25
Design:—50 c. Deportees Memorial, Ile de la Cité (Paris).

521 Beethoven (West Germany)

522 Hôtel des Postes, Paris

(Des Serveau. Eng Piel (No. 1611), Cottet (Nos. 1612/3), Mazelin (No. 1614), Combet (No. 1615). Recess)

1963 (27 Apr). *Celebrities of European Economic Community Countries. T* **521** *and similar horiz designs. P* 13.
1611 20 c. indigo, yellow-brown & blue-grn 20 20
1612 20 c. black, reddish violet and claret .. 20 20
1613 20 c. indigo, brown-purple & yell-olive 20 20
1614 20 c. chocolate, brown-pur & yell-brn 20 20
1615 30 c. sepia, violet and yellow-brown .. 25 25
1611/1615 *Set of* 5 .. .. .. 95 95
Portraits and views:—No. 1611, T **521** (Birth-place and modern Bonn); No. 1612, Emile Verhaeren (Belgium: Family grave and residence, Roisin); No. 1613, Giuseppe Mazzini (Italy: Marcus Aurelius statue and Appian Way, Rome); No. 1614, Emile Mayrisch (Luxembourg: Colpach Château and Steel Plant, Esch); No. 1615, Hugo de Groot (Netherlands: Palace of Peace, The Hague, and St. Agatha's Church, Delft).

France

(Des and eng Gandon. Recess)

1963 (4 May). *Paris Postal Conference Centenary.* P 13.
1616 **522** 50 c. sepia   25   20

REPUBLIQUE FRANÇAISE CAEN 1963

523 College Building

524 St. Peter's Church
and Castle Keep, Caen

(Des and eng Hertenberger. Recess)

1963 (18 May). *400th Anniv of Louis the Great College, Paris.*
P 13.
1617 **523** 30 c. black-green   15   12

(Des and eng Pheulpin. Recess)

1963 (1 June). *36th French Philatelic Societies' Federation
Congress, Caen.* P 13.
1618 **524** 30 c. brown and grey-blue   .. 20   15

(Des Lambert. Eng Hertenberger (30 c.). Des and eng Cami
(50 c.). Des Lambert. Eng Durrens (60 c.). Des and eng
Pheulpin (85 c.). Des Spitz. Eng Mazelin (95 c.). Recess)

1963 (15 June). *Tourist Publicity. Designs similar to T* **490**
but inscr "1963". P 13.
1619   30 c. ochre, indigo and green 12   5
1620   50 c. orange-red, blue & dp bluish grn 25   5
1621   60 c. brown-red, dp bluish green & blue 30   10
1622   85 c. maroon, greenish blue & yell-grn 50   10
1623   95 c. black   45   12
1619/1623   Set of 5 ..   .. 1·50   35
Designs: *Horiz*—30 c. Amboise Château; 50 c. Cote d'Azur,
Var; 85 c. Vittel. *Vert*—60 c. Saint Flour; 95 c. Church and
cloisters, Moissac.

525 Water-skiing

526 "Co-operation"

(Des and eng Gandon. Recess)

1963 (31 Aug). *World Water-skiing Championships, Vichy.*
P 13.
1624 **525** 30 c. black, red & dp bluish green 15   10

(Des A. Holm. Eng Durrens. Recess)

1963 (14 Sept). *Europa.* P 13.
1625 **526** 25 c. red-brown 15   12
1626   50 c. deep emerald   30   15

527 "Child with
Grapes" (Angers)

528 "Philately"

(Des and eng J. Piel. Recess)

1963 (7 Dec). *Red Cross Fund. T* **527** *and similar vert
design. Cross in red* P 13.
1627   20 c.+10 c. black   35   35
1628   25 c.+10 c. deep b uish green   .. 35   35
Design:—25 c. "The Piper" (Manet)

(Des and eng Gandon. Recess)

1963 (14 Dec). *"PHILATEC 1964" International Stamp
Exhibition, Paris* (1st issue). P 13.
1629 **528** 25 c. carm, dp bluish grn & dp grey 12   5
See also Nos. 1640/3 and 1651.

529 Radio-T.V. Centre

530 Emblems of C.P. Services

(Des and eng Combet. Recess)

1963 (15 Dec). *Opening of Radio-T.V. Centre, Paris.* P 13.
1630 **529** 20 c. blue-grey,yell-olive&chestnut 10   5

(Des Louis. Eng Frères. Recess)

1964 (8 Feb). *Civil Protection.* P 13.
1631 **530** 30 c. blue, red and yellow-orange .. 12   8

531 Paralytic at work
in Invalid-chair

532 18th-century Courier

(Des and eng Decaris. Recess)

1964 (22 Feb). *Professional Rehabilitation of Paralytics.* P 13.
1632 **531** 30 c. brown, chestnut & blue-green 12   10

(Des and eng Cami (after C. Parrocel). Recess)

1964 (14 Mar). *Stamp Day.* P 13.
1633 **532** 20 c.+5 c. deep bluish green   .. 20   15

533 "Deportation"

534 Pres. René Coty

535 "Blanc" 2 c.
stamp of 1900

(Des B. Aldebert. Eng Combet (20 c.). Des and eng Combet
(after sculpture by Watkin) (50 c.). Recess)

1964 (21 Mar). *20th Anniv of Liberation* (1st issue). *T* **533**
and similar vert design. P 13.
1634   20 c.+5 c. deep slate   15   15
1635   50 c.+5 c. deep bluish green   .. 30   30
Design:—50 c. "Resistance" (memorial).
See also Nos. 1652/3 and 1658.

(Des and eng J. Piel. Recess)

1964 (25 Apr). *Pres. Coty Commemoration. P* 13.
1636 **534** 30 c.+10 c. deep sepia and lake ..   20   20

(Des and eng Cottet (No. 1638), Gandon (others). Recess)

1964. *French Art. Paintings as T* **491.** *P* 12 × 13.
1637 1 f. multicoloured (25.4)   2·10   1·10
1638 1 f. ultramarine, green, sepia & buff (4.7) 1·60   85
1639 1 f. multicoloured (31.10)   60   45
Designs: *Vert*—No. 1637, Jean le Bon (attributed to Girard of Orleans); No. 1638, Tomb plaque of Geoffroy IV (12th-century *champlevé* (grooved) enamel from Limousin); No. 1639, "The Lady with the Unicorn" (15th-century tapestry).

(Des and eng Piel (25 c.), Durrens (30 c.). Recess)

1964 (9 May). "PHILATEC 1964" *International Stamp Exhibition, Paris* (2nd issue). *T* **535** *and similar vert designs P* 13.
1640 30 c. blue, sepia and orange-brown ..   15   15
1641 25 c. claret and bistre   15   15
1642 25 c. blue and bistre   15   15
1643 30 c. carmine, sepia and turquoise   15   15
    a. Horiz strip of 4+label. Nos. 1640/3 70   70
Designs:—No. 1640, "Postal Mechanization" (letter-sorting equipment and parcel conveyor); No. 1641, T **535;** No. 1642, "Mouchon" 25 c. stamp of 1900; No. 1643, "Tele-communications" (telephone dial, teleprinter and T.V. tower). Nos. 1640/3 were printed in sheets of 20 (4 × 5) giving 5 horizontal strips showing the above stamps, with a *se-tenant* stamp-size "Philatec" label in the centre, in the order listed.

(Des and eng Gandon. Recess)

1964 (9 May). *25th Anniv of Night Airmail Service. As T* **435** *but additionally inscr* "25 E ANNIVERSAIRE" *and colours changed. P* 13.
1644 **435** 25 c. black, brown-red, yellow-green and deep blue   12   8

536 Stained Glass Window

537 Calvin

(Des and eng Durrens. Recess)

1964 (23 May). *800th Anniv of Nòtre Dame, Paris. P* 12 × 13.
1645 **536** 60 c. multicoloured   55   45

(Des and eng Cottet. Recess)

1964 (23 May). *400th Anniv of Death of Calvin* (reformer). *P* 13.
1646 **537** 30 c.+10 c. brown, sepia and deep bluish green   25   25

538 Gallic Coin

D **539** Poppies

539 Pope Sylvester II

(Des C. Durens. Eng Frères. Typo)

1964 (25 May)**–76.** *P* 13½ × 14.
1647 **538** 10 c. brown and emerald   55   5
1647a   15 c. yell-brn & orge (17.10.66)   30   5
1647b   22 c. vio & light bl-grn (10.3.69)   20   5
1647c   25 c. brown and reddish violet   30   5
1647d   26 c. brown and purple (1.7.71)   12   5
1647e   30 c. brown & yellow-brn (1.7./1)   20   5
1647f   35 c. ultram & carm-red (10.3.76)   40   10
1648   45 c. brown & blue-grn (1.7.71)   50   10
1648a   50 c. brown and light blue ..   45   10
1648b   70 c. lake-brown & bright blue (10.3.69)   1·25   55
1649   90 c. brown and red (1.7.71)   55   20
1647/1649 *Set of* 11 ..   4·00 1·25
The stamps were only issued precancelled, the unused prices being for stamps with full gum.
For stamps as T **538**, but inscribed "FRANCE", see Nos. 2065a/1.

(Des Combet. Dies eng Freres (5 c.), Aufschneider (10 c.), Jumelet (20, 40 c.), Barre (50 c.), Miermont (others). Typo)

1964 (25 May)**–71.** *POSTAGE DUE. Type D* **539** *and similar vert designs. P* 14 × 13½.
D1650   5 c. red, grn & bright pur (18.1.65)   5   5
D1651 10 c. blue, grn & bright pur (18.1.65)   5   5
D1652 15 c. red, green and brown ..   5   5
D1653 20 c. pur, light grn & bl-grn (15.3.71) 5   5
D1654 30 c. blue, green and brown ..   8   5
D1655 40 c. yellow, cerise & bl-grn (15.3.71) 10   5
D1656 50 c. carmine, green & ultram (18.1.65) 12   5
D1657   1 f. reddish vio, grn & ult (18.1.65) 70   30
D1650/1657 *Set of* 8   1·00   50
Designs:—5 c. Knapweed; 10 c. Gentian; 20 c. Little periwinkle; 30 c. Forget-me-not; 40 c. Columbine; 50 c. Clover; 1 f. Soldanella.

(Des Spitz. Eng Mazelin. Recess)

1964 (30 May). *Pope Sylvester II Commemoration. P* 13.
1650 **539** 30 c.+10 c. reddish purple & grey   25   25

540 Rocket and Horseman

(Des and eng Decaris. Recess)

1964 (5 June). "PHILATEC 1964" *International Stamp Exhibition, Paris* (3rd issue). *P* 13 × 12½.
1651 **540** 1 f. ultram, carmine-red & brown 9·50 9·50
MS1651a 145 × 285 mm. No. 1651 issued in sheets of 8 stamps (2 blocks of 4), with stamp-size *se-tenant* labels bearing the "PHILATEC" emblem.   *Price un* £90; *us* £80.
The No. 1651 was sold at 4 f., including entrance fee to the Exhibition.

541 Landings in Normandy and Provence

A regular new issue supplement to this catalogue appears each month in

STAMP MONTHLY

—from your newsagent or by postal subscription
—details on request.

(Des and eng Pheulpin. Recess)

1964. *20th Anniv of Liberation* (*2nd issue*). *T* **541** *and similar horiz design. P* 13.

1652	**541**	30 c.+5 c. sepia, orange-brown and slate-blue (6.6)	20	20
1653	–	30 c.+5 c. claret, sepia and chestnut (22.8)	25	25

Design:—No. 1653, Taking prisoners in Paris, and tank in Strasbourg.

(Des and eng Combet (40 c., 1 f. 25), Pheulpin (70 c.), Durrens (1 f. 30). Recess)

1964 (13 June)—**71.** *Tourist Publicity. Designs similar to T* **490**, *but inscr* "1964", *P* 13.

1654	40 c. chocolate, deep bluish green and orange-brown (6.2.65)		20	5
	a. Pur-brn, grey-grn & orge-brn. (2.71)		30	5
1655	70 c. maroon, deep bluish green & indigo		30	5
1656	1 f. 25, deep grey-green, blue & bistre		65	20
1657	1 f. 30, chestnut, chocolate and yellow-brown (6.2.65)		50	10
1654/1657	*Set of* 4		1·75	40

Designs: *Horiz*—40 c., 1 f. 25, Notre-Dame Chapel, Haut-Ronchamp (Haute-Saone). *Vert*—70 c. Caesar's Tower, Provins; 1 f. 30, Joux Château (Doubs).

No. 1654*a* comes from coils of 1,000 and is inscribed in red with duplicate serial numbers on the back of every tenth stamp.

542 De Gaulle's Appeal of 18th June, 1940

543 Judo

(Des and eng Combet. Recess)

1964 (18 June). *20th Anniv of Liberation* (*3rd issue*). *P* 12 × 13.

1658	**542**	25 c.+5 c. black, red and blue	30	30

(Des and eng Bétemps. Recess)

1964 (4 July). *Olympic Games, Tokyo. P* 13.

1659	**543**	50 c. brown-purple and deep blue	25	12

544 G. Mandel

545 Soldiers departing for the Marne by taxi-cab

546 Europa "Flower"

(Des Serveau. Eng Piel. Recess)

1964 (4 July). *20th Anniv of Death of Georges Mandel* (*statesman*). *P* 13.

1660	**544**	30 c. brown-purple	15	15

(Des and die eng R. Louis and G. Aufschneider. Typo)

1964 (20 July). *MILITARY FRANK. No value indicated. P* 13 × 14.

M1661	M **545**	(–) Ultramarine, red, yell & brn	20	12

Use of Military Frank stamps ceased in June 1972.

(Des and eng Hertenberger. Recess)

1964 (5 Sept). *50th Anniv of Victory of the Marne. P* 13.

1661	**545**	30 c. black, red and blue	20	12

(Des and eng Bétemps. Recess)

1964 (12 Sept). *Europa. P* 13.

1662	**546**	25 c. lake, yellow-brown and green	12	5
1663		50 c. lake, yellow-green and violet	25	12

547 "Co-operation" **548** J. N. Corvisart (physician) **549** La Rochefoucauld

(Des and eng Decaris. Recess)

1964 (6 Nov). *French, African and Malagasy Co-operation. P* 13.

1664	**547**	25 c. chocolate, black and brown	12	5

(Des and eng Piel. Recess)

1964 (12 Dec). *Red Cross Fund. T* **548** *and similar vert design. Cross in red. P* 13.

1665	20 c.+10 c. black		25	15
1666	25 c.+10 c. black		25	15

Portrait:—25 c. D. Larrey (military surgeon).

(Des Serveau. Eng Piel (1667). Des Cottet. Eng Mazelin (1669). Des and eng Gandon (1668). Cottet (1670). Recess)

1965. *Red Cross Fund. T* **549** *and similar vert designs inscr* "1965". *P* 13.

1667	30 c.+10 c. blue & chestnut (13 Feb)		30	30
1668	30 c.+10 c. brown & carmine (20 Feb)		30	30
1669	40 c.+10 c. slate and brown (13 Feb)		35	35
1670	40 c.+10 c. brown, turquoise-blue and brown-red (20 Feb)		35	35
1667/1670	*Set of* 4		1·25	1·25

Portraits:—No. 1667, *T* **549**; 1668, Nicolas Poussin (painter); 1669, Paul Dukas (composer); 1670, Charles d'Orléans.

(Des and eng Durrens (No. 1671), Cottet (No. 1672), Pheulpin (No. 1673), Gandon (No. 1674). Recess)

1965. *French Art. Designs as T* **491.** *P* 12 × 13 (*vert*) *or* 13 × 12 (*horiz*).

1671	1 f. multicoloured (12.3)		45	40
	a. Green omitted		35·00	
1672	1 f. multicoloured (25.9)		35	25
1673	1 f. multicoloured (30.10)		35	25
1674	1 f. black, rose-red and light red (6.11)		35	25
1671/1674	*Set of* 4		1·40	1·00

Designs: *Vert*—No. 1671, "L'Anglaise du 'Star' au Havre" (Toulouse-Lautrec); No. 1673, "The Apocalypse" (14th-century tapestry); No. 1674, "The Red Violin" (R. Dufy). *Horiz*—No. 1672, "Hunting with Falcons" (miniature from manuscript *Les Très Riches Heures du Duc de Berry*, by the Limbourg brothers); No. 1674, "The Red Violin" (R. Dufy).

550 Packet-steamer *La Guienne* **551** Deportees

(Des and eng Cami. Recess)

1965 (27 Mar). *Stamp Day. P* 13.
1675 **550** 25 c.+10 c. black, deep bluish
green and blue 30 30

(Des and eng J. Combet. Recess)

1965 (1 Apr). *20th Anniv of Return of Deportees. P* 13.
1676 **551** 40 c. deep bluish green 25 20

552 Youth Club   **553** Girl with Bouquet

(Des and eng Béquet. Recess)

1965 (10 Apr). *20th Anniv of Youth Clubs ("Maisons des Jeunes et de la Culture"). P* 13.
1677 **552** 25 c. indigo, chocolate and deep
bluish green 20 10

(Des and eng Decaris. Recess)

1965 (24 Apr). *"Welcome and Friendship" Campaign. P* 13.
1678 **553** 60 c. red, orange-red and deep
bluish green 25 20

554 Allied Flags and   **555** I.T.U. Emblem,
Broken Swastika   "Syncom", Morse Key and
                            Pleumeur-Bodou Centre

(Des and eng Durrens. Recess)

1965 (8 May). *20th Anniv of Victory in World War II. P* 13.
1679 **554** 40 c. red, blue and black 20 10

(Des and eng Decaris. Recess)

1965 (17 May). *I.T.U. Centenary. P* 13.
1680 **555** 60 c. brown, black and blue . . 25 20

556 Croix de Guerre   **557** Bourges Cathedral

(Des and eng Bétemps. Recess)

1965 (22 May). *50th Anniv of the Croix de Guerre. P* 13.
1681 **556** 40 c. bistre-brown, scar & blue-grn 20 15

(Des Spitz. Eng Frères. Recess)

1965 (5 June). *National Congress of Philatelic Societies, Bourges. P* 13.
1682 **557** 40 c. red-brown and blue . . 20 12

558 Stained Glass Window

(Des and eng Combet. Recess)

1965 (5 June). *800th Anniv of Sens Cathedral. P* 13 × 12.
1683 **558** 1 f. multicoloured 35 25
    a. Green omitted . . . . 40·00

(Des and eng Pheulpin (50 c.), Combet (60 c.), Gandon (75 c.),
Cami (95 c.), Bétemps (1 f.). Recess)

1965. *Tourist Publicity. Designs similar to T* **490,** *but inscr "1965". P* 13.
1684   50 c. grey-blue, deep bluish green and
       bistre (19.6.65) 20 5
1685   60 c. purple-brn & greenish bl (17.7.65) 25 5
1686   75 c. chocolate, dp green & bl (10.7.65) 60 25
1687   95 c. bistre-brn, grn & new bl (10.7.65) 45 10
1688   1 f. grey, yellow-green and yellow-
       brown (10.7.65) 40 5
1684/1688   *Set of 5* . . . . . . 1·60 30
Designs: *Horiz*—50 c. Moustiers Ste. Marie (Basses-Alpes);
95 c. Landscape, Vendée; 1 f. Monoliths, Carnac. *Vert*—60 c.
Yachting, Aix-les-Bains; 75 c. Tarn gorges.

559 Mont Blanc   **560** Europa "Sprig"
from Chamonix

(Des and eng Cottet. Recess)

1965 (17 July). *Opening of Mont Blanc Road Tunnel. P* 13.
1689 **559** 30 c. Royal blue, grnish blue & plum 20 5

(Des H. Karlsson. Eng C. Haley. Recess)

1965 (25 Sept). *Europa. P* 13.
1690 **560** 30 c. vermilion 15 5
1691   60 c. bluish grey 25 15

561 Étienne Régnault **562** "One Million **563** Atomic Reactor
and *Le Taureau*   Hectares"   and Emblems

(T **561/2** des and eng Decaris. Recess)

1965 (2 Oct). *Tercentenary of Colonisation of Réunion. P* 13.
1692 **561** 30 c. grey-blue and lake 12 8

1965 (2 Oct). *Reafforestation. P* 13.
1693 **562** 25 c. brown, yellow-green and
             blackish green 12 8

France 1965

(Des and eng Combet. Recess)

1965 (9 Oct). *20th Anniv of Atomic Energy Commission.*
P 13.
1694 **563** 60 c. black and blue   25   20

564 Aviation School,
Salon-de-Provence

(Des and eng C. Haley. Recess)

1965 (6 Nov). *30th Anniv of Aviation School.* P 13.
1695 **564** 25 c. myrtle - green, indigo and
     greenish blue   10   5

565 Rocket "Diamant"   **566** "Le Bébé à la Cuiller"
(Des and eng Durrens. Recess)

1965 (30 Nov). *Launching of First French Satellite.* T **565** *and
similar horiz design.* P 13.
1696   30 c. new blue, greenish blue & indigo   12   12
1697   60 c. new blue, greenish blue & indigo   25   20
Design:—60 c. Satellite "A1". Nos. 1696/7 were printed
in sheets of 32 (4×8) giving 16 horiz strips with a half stamp-
size *se-tenant* label in the centre inscr "MISE SUR ORBITE
DU PREMIER SATELLITE FRANCAIS 26 NOVEMBRE 1965".
(*Price per strip, un or us.* 40p.)

(Des and eng Piel. Recess)

1965 (11 Dec). *Red Cross Fund. Paintings by Renoir.*
T **566** *and similar vert design. Cross in red.* P 13.
1698   25 c.+10 c. indigo   20   15
1699   30 c.+10 c. red-brown   20   15
Design:—30 c. "Coco écrivant" (portrait of Renoir's small
son writing).

567 Arms of Auch   **568** St. Pierre Fourier and
                   Basilica, Mattaincourt (Vosges)

(Des M. Louis. Dies eng A. Barre (5 c.), A. Freres (25 c.). Typo)

1966 (22 Jan)**–69.** T **567** *and similar vert design.* P 14 × 13.
1700   5 c. vermilion and ultramarine   ..   5   5
     a. Perf 13 (1969)   15   5
1701   25 c. blue and chestnut   5   5
Arms (*inscr*)—25 c. "Mont-de-Marsan".
No. 1700a comes from coils only and every tenth stamp in
the roll has red numerals on the back. No. 1701 also exists
from coils with numerals on the back.

(Des Pheulpin. Eng Bétemps (1703), Cottet (1705/6),
Combet (1707) and Pheulpin (others). Recess)

1966 (12 Feb–July). *Red Cross Fund.* T **568** *and similar
horiz designs inscr* "1966". P 13.
1702   30 c.+10 c. sepia & deep bluish green   20   20
1703   30 c.+10 c. purple-brown & emerald   20   20
1704   30 c.+10 c. indigo, yellow-brn & grn   20   20
1705   30 c.+10 c. slate-blue & lt brn (25.6)   20   20

1706   30 c.+10 c. bistre-brown and deep
         bluish green (9.7)   20   20
1707   30 c.+10 c. black & bistre-brown (9.7)   20   20
1702/1707   *Set of* 6 ..   ..   ..   1·00   1·00
Designs:—No. 1702, T **568**; 1703, F. Mansard (architect)
and Carnavalet House, Paris; 1704, M. Proust (writer) and
St. Hilaire Bridge, Iliers (Eure-et-Loir): 1705, G. Fauré (composer), statuary and music; 1706, Hippolyte Taine (philosopher)
and birth-place; 1707, Elie Metchnikoff (scientist), microscope
and Pasteur Institute.

569 Satellite "D1"
(Des and eng Durrens. Recess)

1966 (18 Feb). *Launching of Satellite* "D1". P 13.
1708 **569** 60 c. carmine, deep blue and tur-
          quoise-green   20   20

570 Engraving a Die   **571** "Knight" and
(Des and eng Béquet. Recess)   Chess-board

1966 (19 Mar). *Stamp Day.* P 13.
1709 **570** 25 c.+10 c. chocolate, slate and
           orange-brown   20   20,
(Des and eng Combet (No. 1710), Durrens (No. 1711),
Bétemps (No. 1712), Decaris (No. 1713), Gandon (No. 1714).
Recess)

1966. *French Art. Designs as* T **491**. P 13 × 12 *or* 12 × 13
    (*No.* 1713).
1710   1 f. multicoloured (26.3)   30   25
     a. Green omitted   ..   ..
1711   1 f. multicoloured (25.6)   35   35
1712   1 f. multicoloured (22.10)   30   25
1713   1 f. multicoloured (19.11)   35   30
1714   1 f. multicoloured (10.12)   35   30
1710/1714   *Set of* 5   ..   ..   ..   1·50   1·25
Designs: *Horiz*—No. 1710, Detail of Vix Crater (wine-bowl);
No. 1711, "The New-born Child" (G. de la Tour); No. 1712,
"Baptism of Judas" (stained glass window, Sainte Chapelle,
Paris); No. 1714, "Crispin and Scapin" (after H. Daumier).
Vert—No. 1713, "The Moon and the Bull" (Lurçat tapestry).
On No. 1710a the background is black only, and the figures of
value are white.
A miniature sheet showing three stages of production of
No. 1711 was issued for the Postal Museum. Imperf and
without gum. it had no postal validity.

(Des Serveau. Eng Piel. Recess)

1966 (2 Apr). *International Chess Festival, Le Havre.* P 13.
1715 **571** 60 c. bluish grey, bistre-brown and
          violet   30   20

572 Pont St. Esprit Bridge   **573** St. Michel

(Des and eng Combet. Recess)

1966 (23 Apr). *700th Anniv of Pont St. Esprit.* *P* 13.
1716 **572** 25 c. black and greenish blue .. 12 8

(Des and eng Gandon. Recess)

1966 (30 Apr). *Millenary of Mont. St. Michel.* *P* 13.
1717 **573** 25 c. purple-brown, red, emerald and
pale yellow 15 5

574 King Stanislas, Arms and Palace **575** Niort

(Des J. M. Petey. Eng R. Cottet. Recess)

1966 (6 May). *Bicentenary of Union of Lorraine and Barrois
with France.* *P* 13.
1718 **574** 25 c. purple-brown, grey-green and
grey-blue 12 5

(Des and eng Cami. Recess)

1966 (28 May). *National Congress of Philatelic Societies,
Niort.* *P* 13.
1719 **575** 40 c. slate-blue, myrtle-green and
greenish blue 20 12

576 "Angel of Verdun" **577** Fontenelle

(Des P. Lambert. Eng Bétemps. Recess)

1966 (28 May). *50th Anniv of Verdun Victory.* *P* 13.
1720 **576** 30 c.+5 c. greenish blue, blue and
myrtle-green 20 20

(Des and eng Gandon. Recess)

1966 (4 June). *Tercentenary of Academy of Sciences.* *P* 13.
1721 **577** 60 c. chocolate and lake 25 15

578 William the Conqueror, Castle and Landings

(Des and eng C. Haley. Recess)

1966 (4 June). *900th Anniv of Battle of Hastings.* *P* 13.
1722 **578** 60 c. chestnut and blue 30 20

579 Globe and Railway Track **580** Oléron Bridge

(Des and eng C. Durrens. Recess)

1966 (11 June). *19th International Railway Congress, Paris.*
P 13.
1723 **579** 60 c. chocolate, greenish bl & crim 20 15

(Des and eng C. Durrens. Recess)

1966 (18 June). *Opening of Oléron Bridge.* *P* 13.
1724 **580** 25 c. brown, greenish blue & blue 12 5

581 Europa "Ship" **582** Vercingétorix

(Des G. and J. Bender. Eng J. Combet. Recess)

1966 (24 Sept). *Europa.* *P* 13.
1725 **581** 30 c. greenish blue 12 5
1726 60 c. scarlet 20 12

(Des and eng Decaris. Recess)

1966 (5 Nov). *History of France* (*First Series*). *T* **582** *and
similar designs inscr* "1966". *P* 13.
1727 40 c. purple-brown, slate-bl & myrtle grn 15 10
1728 60 c. purple-brown and black .. 15 10
1729 60 c. cerise, purple-brown & reddish vio 25 15
Celebrities: *Vert*—40 c. (No. 1728); Clovis; 60 c. Charlemagne.
See also Nos. 1769/71, 1809/11, 1850/2, 1896/8, 1922/4,
1975/7 and 2017/19.

583 Route Map **584** Château de Val

(Des and eng J. Combet. Recess)

1966 (11 Nov). *Centenary of Paris Pneumatic Post.* *P* 13.
1730 **583** 1 f. 60, Prussian blue, brn-lake & choc 70 40

(Des and eng P. Béquet. Recess)

1966 (19 Nov). *Chateau de Val.* *P* 13.
1731 **584** 2 f. 30, chocolate, green and greenish blue 95 8

585 Rance Barrage **586** Nurse tending
wounded Soldier (1859)

(Des and eng C. Haley. Recess)

1966 (3 Dec). *Inauguration of Rance River Tidal Power
Station.* *P* 13.
1732 **585** 60 c. slate, green & orange-brown 25 12

(Des and eng J. Piel. Recess)

1966 (10 Dec). *Red Cross Fund.* T **586** *and similar vert design. Cross in red.* P 13.
1733 25 c.+10 c. deep bluish green .. 25 25
1734 30 c.+10 c. indigo 25 25
Design:—30 c. Nurse tending young girl (1966).

587 Arms of Saint-Lô   **588** Beaumarchais (playwright)

(Des M. Louis. Photo)

1966 (17 Dec). P 13.
1735 **587** 20 c. multicoloured 5 5

No. 1735 with red figures on the reverse comes from coils, every tenth stamp being numbered.
For No. 1735 with 3 phosphor bands, see No. 1867ap.

(Des C. Durrens. Eng J. Combet (1736), C. Durrens (1737/38), R. Cottet (1739). Recess)

1967. *Red Cross Fund.* T **588** *and similar vert designs inscr* "1967". P 13.
1736 30 c.+10 c. violet & lake-brn (4 Feb) 20 20
1737 30 c.+10 c. greenish bl & ind (4 Feb) 20 20
1738 30 c.+10 c. dull purple and yellow-
    brown (24 June) 20 20
1739 30 c.+10 c. reddish violet and deep
    bluish violet (24 June) .. 20 20
1736/1739 Set of 4 .. .. 70 70
Designs:—No. 1737, Emile Zola (writer); 1738, A. Camus (writer); 1739, St. François de Sales (reformer).

589 Congress Emblem   **590** Postman of the
                               Second Empire

(Des and eng P. Béquet. Recess)

1967 (4 Mar). *Third International Congress of European Broadcasting Union* ("U.E.R."). P 13.
1740 **589** 40 c. crimson and deep ultramarine 15 12

(Des and eng Bétemps. Recess)

1967 (8 Apr). *Stamp Day.* P 13.
1741 **590** 25 c.+10 c. green, red & slate-blue 20 20

(Des and eng Pheulpin (No. 1742), Cottet (No. 1743), Gandon (No. 1744), Combet (No. 1745). Recess)

1967. *French Art. Designs as* T **491.** P 13 × 12 (*horiz*) or 12 × 13 (*vert*).
1742 1 f. multicoloured (15.4) 40 30
1743 1 f. multicoloured (1.7) 40 30
1744 1 f. yellow-brown, blue & black (9.9) 40 30
1745 1 f. multicoloured (7.10) 40 30
1742/1745 Set of 4 .. .. .. 1·50 1·00
Designs: *Horiz*—No. 1742, "Old Juniet's Trap" (after H. Rousseau); No. 1745, "The Window-makers" (stained glass window, St. Madeleine's Church, Troyes). *Vert*—No. 1743, "François I" (after Jean Clouet); No. 1744, "The Bather" (Ingres).

591 Winter Olympics   **592** French Pavilion
      Emblem

(Des Excoffon. Photo)

1967 (22 Apr). *Publicity for Winter Olympic Games, Grenoble* (1968). P 13.
1746 **591** 60 c. red, light blue and new blue.. 25 12

(Des and eng Durrens. Recess)

1967 (22 Apr). *World Fair, Montreal.* P 13.
1747 **592** 60 c. turquoise-green & greenish blue 25 12

593 Cogwheels   **594** Nungesser and Coli,
                      and "The White Bird" (aircraft)

(Des O. Bonnevalle. Eng Cami. Recess)

1967 (29 Apr). *Europa.* P 13.
1748 **593** 30 c. blue and grey 12 5
1749 60 c. bistre-brown and light blue .. 20 15

(Des C. Serveau. Eng C. Durrens. Recess)

1967 (6 May). *40th Anniv of Trans-Atlantic Flight Attempt by Nungesser and Coli.* P 13.
1750 **594** 40 c. slate-blue, orange-brn & mar 15 10

595 Great Bridge, Bordeaux   **596** Gouin
                                       Mansion, Tours

(Des and eng Combet. Recess)

1967 (6 May). *Inauguration of Great Bridge, Bordeaux.* P 13.
1751 **595** 25 c. black, olive and brown .. 12 5

(Des and eng Cottet. Recess)

1967 (13 May). *National Congress of Philatelic Societies, Tours.* P 13.
1752 **596** 40 c. red-brown, violet-blue & red 20 12

597 Gaston Ramon (vaccine pioneer) and College Gates

(Des and eng Haley. Recess)

1967 (27 May). *Bicentenary of Alfort Veterinary School.* P 13.
1753 **597** 25 c. red-brown, green and blue .. 12 8

598 Esnault-Pelterie, Rocket and Satellite

(Des and eng Gandon. Recess)

1967 (27 May). *Tenth Death Anniv of Robert Esnault-Pelterie (rocket pioneer).* P 13.
1754 **598** 60 c. slate-blue & deep violet-blue 25 15

(Des and eng Bétemps (50 c.), Haley (60 c.), Cami (70 c.), Béquet (75 c., 1 f. 50), Combet (95 c.). Des Spitz. Eng Monvoisin (1 f.). Recess)

1967. *Tourist Publicity. Designs similar to T **490**, but inscr "1967".* P 13.
1755 **50** 50 c. sepia, grey-blue & blue (8 July) 20 5
1756 60 c. chocolate, Prussian bl & bl (8 July) 20 5
1757 70 c. brown, blue & carmine (17 June) 30 5
1758 75 c. greenish blue, lake and orange-brown (22 July) 30 15
1759 95 c. reddish violet, blackish green and light blue (8 July) 35 15
1760 1 f. indigo (10 June) 35 5
1761 1 f. 50, brown-red, blue and blue-green (10 June) 55 10
1755/1761 Set of 7 .. .. .. 1·90 55
Designs: *Vert*—50 c. Town Hall, St. Quentin (Aisne); 60 c. Clock-tower and gateway, Vire (Calvados); 1 f. Rodez Cathedral; 1 f. 50, Morlaix—views and carved buttress. *Horiz*—70 c. St. Germain-en-Laye Château; 75 c. La Baule; 95 c. Boulogne-sur-Mer.

599 Orchids

600 Scales of Justice

(Des and eng Pheulpin after Sainson. Recess)

1967 (29 July). *Orléans Flower Show.* P 13.
1762 **599** 40 c. carmine, bright purple and deep reddish violet 15 12

(Des and eng Decaris. Recess)

1967 (2 Sept). *Ninth International Accountancy Congress, Paris,* P 13.
1763 **600** 60 c. orange-brown, greenish blue and maroon 20 12

601 Servicemen and Cross of Lorraine

602 Marie Curie and Pitchblende

(Des and eng Combet. Recess)

1967 (7 Oct). *25th Anniv of Battle of Bir-Hakeim.* P 13.
1764 **601** 25 c. deep ultram, new bl & brn 10 5

(Des and eng Pheulpin. Recess)

1967 (21 Oct). *Birth Centenary of Marie Curie.* P 13.
1765 **602** 60 c. ultramarine and bright blue .. 20 20

603 Lions Emblem   **604** "République"

(Des and eng Durrens. Recess)

1967 (28 Oct). *50th Anniv of Lions International.* P 13.
1766 **603** 40 c. bluish violet and brown-lake 20 10

(Des Cheffer. Eng Durrens. Recess)

1967–69. P 13.
1767 **604** 25 c. Prussian blue (4.11.67) .. 40 10
1768 30 c. bright purple (4.11.67) .. 45 5
1768a 30 c. emerald (11.1.69) 20 5
1768b 40 c. cerise (11.1.69) 20 5
1767/1768b Set of 4 .. .. .. 1·10 12
For No. 1768a printed by typography, see No. 1843, and for No. 1768b with phosphor lines, see No. 1869p.
Nos. 1767/8b with red numerals on the back come from coils. Only every tenth stamp in the roll is numbered.

(Des and eng Decaris. Recess)

1967 (10 Nov). *History of France (Second Series). Designs as T **582**, but inscr "1967".* P 13.
1769 40 c. ultramarine, grey-blue & new blue 15 10
1770 40 c. black and slate 15 10
1771 60 c. myrtle-green and chocolate .. 20 10
Designs: *Horiz*—No. 1769, Hugues Capet elected King of France. *Vert*—No. 1770, Philippe Auguste at Bouvines; No. 1771, Saint-Louis receiving poor.

605 "Flautist"

606 Anniversary Medal

(Des and eng Gandon. Recess)

1967 (16 Dec). *Red Cross Fund. Ivories in Dieppe Museum. T **605** and similar vert design. Cross in red.* P 13.
1772 25 c.+10 c. purple-brown and deep reddish violet 20 20
1773 30 c.+10 c. purple-brown and myrtle-green ("Violinist") 20 20

(Des Cottet, after Tuloup. Eng Forget. Recess)

1968 (6 Jan). *50th Anniv of Postal Cheques Service.* P 13.
1774 **606** 40 c. yellow-bistre & blackish green 15 10

607 Cross-country Skiing and Ski-jumping

608 Road Signs

609 Rural Postman of 1830

(Des Combet. Eng Frères (30 c.), Fenneteaux (75 c.),
Combet (others). Recess)

1968 (27 Jan). *Winter Olympic Games, Grenoble.* *T 607 and
similar vert designs. P 13.*
1775	**30** c.+10 c. brown, slate and vermilion	15	15
1776	**40** c.+10 c. bright purple, bistre & pur	20	20
1777	**60** c.+20 c. vermilion, reddish purple		
	and blackish green	30	30
1778	**75** c.+25 c. deep purple-brown, yellow-		
	green and bright purple	40	40
1779	**95** c.+35 c. red-brown, magenta and		
	greenish blue	55	55
1775/1779	Set of 5	1·40	1·40

Designs:—40 c. Ice-hockey; 60 c. Olympic flame; 75 c.
Figure-skating; 95 c. Slalom.

(Des and eng. J. Combet. Recess)

1968 (24 Feb). *Road Safety. P 13.*
1780 **608** 25 c. red, turquoise-blue & purple   10   8

(Des and eng Béquet. Recess)

1968 (16 Mar). *Stamp Day. P 13.*
1781 **609** 25 c.+10 c. indigo, bright blue
and carmine   20   20

610 F. Couperin (composer)   **611** Congress Palace,
and Concert Instruments   Royan

(Des Serveau. Eng Pheulpin (1782), Cottet (1783), Bétemps
(1784), Durrens (1785). Recess)

1968. *Red Cross Fund. T 610 and similar horiz portrait
designs inscr "1968". P 13.*
1782	**30** c.+10 c. reddish lilac and reddish		
	violet (23.3.68)	20	20
1783	**30** c.+10 c. chocolate and slate-green		
	(23.3.68)	20	20
1784	**30** c.+10 c. brown-red and bistre-		
	brown (6.7.68)	20	20
1785	**30** c.+10 c. brown-purple and reddish		
	lilac (6.7.68)	20	20
1782/1785	Set of 4	70	70

Designs:—No. 1782, *T* **610**; 1783, General Desaix and
death scene at Marengo; 1784, Saint Pol Roux (poet) and
"Evocation of Golgotha"; 1785, Paul Claudel (poet) and
"Joan of Arc".

(Des and eng Combet (No. 1788), Cottet (No. 1789),
Durrens (others). Recess)

1968. *French Art. Designs as T* **491**. *P 13 × 12 (horiz) or
12 × 13 (vert).*
1786	**1** f. multicoloured (13.4)	40	30
1787	**1** f. multicoloured (21.9)	45	30
1788	**1** f. brownish olive and red (26.10)	45	30
1789	**1** f. multicoloured (9.11)	45	30
1786/1789	Set of 4	1·60	1·00

Designs: *Horiz*—No. 1786, Wall painting, Lascaux; No. 1787,
"Arearea" (Gauguin). *Vert*—No. 1788, "La Danse" (relief by
Bourdelle in Champs-Elysées Theatre, Paris); No. 1789,
"Portrait of a Model" (Renoir).

(Des and eng C. Haley. Recess)

1968 (13 Apr). *World Co-operation Languages Conference,
Royan. P 13.*
1790 **611** 40 c. greenish blue, bistre-brown
and myrtle-green   15   8

612 Europa "Key"   **613** Alain R. Le Sage

(Des H. Schwarzenbach. Eng Béquet. Recess)

1968 (27 Apr). *Europa. P 13.*
1791	**612** 30 c. orange-brown & bright purple	12	5
1792	**60** c. claret and brown	20	15

(Des and eng Pheulpin. Recess)

1968 (4 May). *300th Birth Anniv of Le Sage (writer). P 13.*
1793 **613** 40 c. purple and new blue   15   8

(Des and eng Pheulpin. Recess)

1968 (4 May). *Tourist Publicity. Design similar to T* **490**, *but
inscr "1968". P 13.*
1794   60 c. slate-blue, brown-purple and
myrtle-green   20   12
Design: *Horiz*—60 c. Langeais Château.

614 Pierre Larousse   **615** Forest Trees
(encyclopedist)

(Des and eng Gandon. Recess)

1968 (11 May). *Larousse Commemoration. P 13.*
1795 **614** 40 c. chocolate and reddish violet   15   5

(Des and eng Monvoisin, after Wrede. Recess)

1968 (18 May). *Link of Black and Rambouillet Forests. P 13.*
1796 **615** 25 c. light brown, myrtle-green and
greenish blue   12   8

616 Presentation of the   **617** Louis XIV, and Arms of
Keys, and Map   Flanders and France

(Des Spitz. Eng Cottet. Recess)

1968 (25 May). *650th Anniv of Papal Enclave, Valréas. P 13.*
1797 **616** 60 c. reddish violet, bistre and
purple-brown   25   20

(Des and eng Cami. Recess)

1968 (29 June). *300th Anniv of (First) Treaty of Aix-la-
Chapelle. P 13.*
1798 **617** 40 c. lake, bistre and olive-grey   20   8

618 Martrou Bridge, Rochefort   **619** Letord "Lorraine" Military
Biplane and Route-map

(Des and eng C. Haley. Recess)

1968 (20 July). *Inauguration of Martrou Bridge. P 13.*
1799 **618** 25 c. black, chocolate and new blue   10   5

(Des and eng Gandon. Recess)

1968 (17 Aug). *50th Anniv of First Regular Internal Airmail
Service. P 13.*
1800 **619** 25 c. indigo, new blue and red   10   8

620 Tower of Constance, Aigues-Mortes

621 Cathedral and Old Bridge, Béziers

(Des and eng Decaris. Recess)
1968 (31 Aug). *Bicentenary of Release of Huguenot Prisoners. P* 13.
1801 **620** 25 c. brown-purple, olive-brown and new blue   12   5

(Des and eng Bétemps. Recess)
1968 (7 Sept). *National Congress of Philatelic Societies, Béziers. P* 13.
1802 **621** 40 c. ochre, myrtle-green & indigo   15   8

622 "Victory" and White Tower, Salonika

623 Louis XV and Arms of Corsica and France

(Des and eng Gandon. Recess)
1968 (28 Sept). *50th Anniv of Armistice on Salonika Front. P* 13.
1803 **622** 40 c. purple and bright purple   15   5

(Des and eng Cami. Recess)
1968 (5 Oct). *Bicentenary of Union of Corsica and France. P* 13.
1804 **623** 25 c. blue, emerald and black   12   5

624 Relay-racing

626 "Ball of the Little White Beds" (Paris Opera), Leon Bailby and Hospital Beds

625 Polar Landscape

(Des and eng Bétemps. Recess)
1968 (12 Oct). *Olympic Games, Mexico. P* 13.
1805 **624** 40 c. bright blue, blue-green and bistre-brown   20   20

(Des and eng Durrens. Recess)
1968 (19 Oct). *French Polar Exploration. P* 13.
1806 **625** 40 c. lt turq-bl, brn-red & grnish bl   20   8

(Des and eng Decaris. Recess)
1968 (26 Oct). *"Little White Beds" Children's Hospital Charity; 50th Anniv. P* 13.
1807 **626** 40 c. brown-lake, orange-brown and light brown   20   12

627 "Angel of Victory" over Arc de Triomphe

628 "Spring"

(Des and eng Gandon. Recess)
1968 (9 Nov). *50th Anniv of Armistice on Western Front. P* 13.
1808 **627** 25 c. blue and deep carmine   ..   10   5

(Des and eng Decaris. Recess)
1968 (16 Nov). *History of France (Third Series). Designs as T* **582**, *but inscr* "1968". *P* 13.
1809   40 c. green, grey and brown-red   ..   15   8
1810   40 c. ultramarine, green & bistre-brown   15   8
1811   60 c. yellow-brown, slate-bl & ultram   25   12
Designs: *Horiz*—No. 1809, Philip the Good presiding over States-General. *Vert*—No. 1810, Death of Du Guesclin; No. 1811, Joan of Arc.

(Des and eng Gandon, from paintings by N. Mignard. Recess)
1968 (14 Dec). *Red Cross Fund. T* **628** *and similar vert design. Cross in red. P* 13.
1812   25 c.+10 c. indigo and violet   ..   25   25
1813   30 c.+10 c. deep carmine & yell-brn   25   25
Design:—30 c. "Autumn".
See also Nos. 1853/4.

(Des and eng Bétemps (45 c.), Durrens (70 c.), Combet (80 c.), Decaris (85 c.), Haley (1 f. 15). Recess)
1969. *Tourist Publicity. Designs similar to T* **490**, *but inscr* "1969".
1814   45 c. olive, chestnut and new blue (15.2)   25   5
1815   70 c. lt brown, indigo & new blue (5.4)   35   12
1816   80 c. lake-brown, mar & bistre (15.2)   35   5
1817   85 c. grey, new bl & myrtle-grn (21.6)   35   20
1818   1 f. 15, light brown, olive-brown and new blue (15.2)   ..   45   25
1814/1818 Set of 5 ..   ..   ..   1·50   60
Designs: *Horiz*—45 c. Brou Church, Bourg-en-Bresse (Ain); 70 c. Hautefort Château; 80 c. Vouglans Dam, Jura; 85 c. Chantilly Château; 1 f. 15, La Trinité-sur-Mer, Morbihan.

(Des and eng Combet (No. 1819); Bétemps (No. 1820), Durrens (No. 1821), Gandon (No. 1822). Recess)
1969. *French Art. Designs as T* **491**. *P* 13 × 12 *(No.* 1821) *or* 12 × 13.
1819   1 f. bistre-brown and black (22.2)   ..   50   30
1820   1 f. multicoloured (3.5)   50   30
1821   1 f. multicoloured (28.6)   50   30
1822   1 f. multicoloured (8.11)   50   30
1819/1822 Set of 4 ..   ..   ..   1·75   1·00
Designs: *Vert*—No. 1819, "February" (bas-relief, Amiens Cathedral); No. 1820, "Philippe le Bon" (Rogier de la Pasture, called Van der Weyden); No. 1822, "The Circus" (Georges Seurat). *Horiz*—No. 1821, "Savin and Cyprien appearing before Ladicus" (Romanesque painting, Church of St. Savin, Vienne).

629 "Concorde" in Flight   **630** Postal Horse-bus of 1890

(Des and eng Durrens. Recess)

1969 (2 Mar). *AIR. First Flight of "Concorde". P* 13.
.1823 **629** 1 f. indigo and light greenish blue   1·40   20

(Des and eng Béquet. Recess)

1969 (15 Mar). *Stamp Day. P* 13.
1824 **630** 30 c.+10 c. myrtle-green, purple-
brown and black 25 20

631 A. Roussel (composer)   **632** Irises

(Des Serveau. Eng Cami (1825, 1828), Haley (1826), Pheulpin (1827, 1829), Bétemps (1830). Recess)

1969. *Red Cross Fund. Celebrities. T* **631** *and similar vert designs. P* 13.
1825 50 c.+10 c. deep ultramarine (22.3) 30 30
1826 50 c.+10 c. brown-red (22.3) .. 30 30
1827 50 c.+10 c. deep slate (22.3) 30 30
1828 50 c.+10 c. chocolate (10.5) .. 30 30
1829 50 c.+10 c. purple (17.5) .. 30 30
1830 50 c.+10 c. turquoise-green (17.5) .. 30 30
1825/1830 *Set of* 6 .. .. .. 1·60 1·60
Portraits:—No. 1825, **T** 631; 1826, General Marceau; 1827, C. A. Sainte-Beuve (writer); 1828, Marshal Lannes; 1829, G. Cuvier (anatomist and naturalist); 1830, A. Gide (writer).

(Des Pheulpin. Photo)

1969 (12 Apr). *International Flower Show, Paris. P* 13.
1831 **632** 45 c. multicoloured 20 12

633 Colonnade

(Des L. Gasbarra and G. Belli. Eng Béquet. Recess)

1969 (26 Apr). *Europa. P* 13.
1832 **633** 40 c. magenta 15 5
1833 70 c. turquoise-blue 25 15

634 Battle of the Garigliano (Italy)

(Des and eng Gandon (Nos. 1837/40). Des Gandon. Eng Haley (No. 1834), Béquet (1835), Durrens (1836). Recess)

1969. *"Resistance and Liberation". 25th Annivs. T* **634** *and similar designs. P* 13.
1834 45 c. black and bluish violet (10.5).. 20 10
1835 45 c. deep ultramarine, Prussian blue
and slate (31.5) 20 10
1836 45 c. slate, slate-bl & myrtle-grn (7.6) 20 10
1837 45 c. blackish brown and slate (23.8) 20 12
1838 45 c. indigo, blue and red (18.10) .. 20 15
1839 45 c.+10 c. olive and slate (23.8) .. 25 20
1840 70 c.+10 c. olive, mar & lt brn (22.11) 40 30
1834/1840 *Set of* 7 .. .. 1·40 1·00
Designs: *Horiz*—No. 1834, **T** 634; No. 1837, Troops storming beach (Provence Landings); 1838, French pilot, Soviet mechanic and fighter aircraft (Normandy-Niemen Squadron); 1839, General Leclerc, troops and Les Invalides (Liberation of Paris); 1840, As No. 1839, but showing Strasbourg Cathedral (Liberation of Strasbourg). *Vert*—1835, Parachutists and Commandos ("D-Day Landings"); 1836, Memorial and Resistance fighters (Battle of Mont Mouchet).

635 "Miners" (I.L.O. Monument,   **636** Chalons-sur-Marne
Geneva) and Albert Thomas
(founder)

(Des and eng C. Haley. Recess)

1969 (10 May). *50th Anniv of International Labour Organization. P* 13.
1841 **635** 70 c. bistre-brn, grey-bl & pur-brn 30 12

(Des and eng Pheulpin. Recess)

1969 (24 May). *National Congress of Philatelic Societies, Chalons-sur-Marne. P* 13.
1842 **636** 45 c. ochre, deep blue and green .. 20 10

1969 (7 July). *As No. 1768a, but printed by typography. P* 14 × 13.
1843 **604** 30 c. emerald 15 5
For this stamp with phosphor bands, see No. 1868p.

637 Canoeing

638 Napoleon as Young Officer,   **639** "Diamond Crystal"
and Birthplace   in Rain Drop

(Des and eng J. Combet. Recess)

1969 (2 Aug). *World Kayak-Canoeing Championships, Bourg-St. Maurice. P* 13.
1844 **637** 70 c. orange-brown, yellow-olive
and greenish blue 40 12

(Des and eng C. Haley. Recess)
1969 (16 Aug). *Birth Bicentenary of Napo. on Bonaparte.*
P 13.
1845 **638** 70 c. green, reddish violet & lt blue   40   15

(Des and eng J. Combet. Recess)
1969 (27 Sept). *European Water Charter. P* 13.
1846 **639** 70 c. black, light blue-green & blue   30   15

640 Mouflon   **641** Aerial View of College

(Des and eng R. Cami. Recess)
1969 (11 Oct). *Nature Conservation. P* 13.
1847 **640** 45 c. black, orange-brown & ol-grn   20   15

(Des and eng Derrey. Recess)
1969 (18 Oct). *College of Arts and Manufactures, Chatenay-Malabry. P* 13.
1848 **641** 70 c. yellow-green, yellow-orange
          and deep green   30   15

642 Le Redoutable   **643** Gerbault aboard *Firecrest*

(Des and eng R. Cami. Recess)
1969 (25 Oct). *First French Nuclear Submarine, "Le Redoutable". P* 13.
1849 **642** 70 c. myrtle-green, emerald & blue   30   15

(Des and eng Decaris. Recess)
1969 (8 Nov). *History of France (Fourth Series). Designs as T* **582**, *but inscr* "1969". *P* 13.
1850   80 c. myrtle-green, chocolate and bistre   35   12
1851   80 c. orange-brown, black and ochre . .   35   12
1852   80 c. ultramarine, black and violet . .   35   12
Designs: *Horiz*—No. 1850, Louis XI and Charles the Bold; No. 1852, Henry IV and Edict of Nantes. *Vert*—No. 1851, Bayard at the Battle of Brescia.

(Des and eng Gandon. Recess)
1969 (13 Dec). *Red Cross Fund. Paintings by N. Mignard as T* **628**. *Cross in red. P* 13.
1853   40 c.+15 c. light brown & chocolate   30   30
1854   40 c.+15 c. greenish blue & reddish vio   30   30
Designs:—No. 1853, "Summer"; No. 1854, "Winter".

(Des and eng Decaris. Recess)
1970 (10 Jan). *Alain Gerbault's World Voyage*, 1923–29.
P 13.
1855 **643** 70 c. indigo, grey and new blue . .   40   12

644 Gendarmerie Badge and Activities

(Des and eng Haley. Recess)
1970 (31 Jan). *National Gendarmerie. P* 13.
1856 **644** 45 c. dp blue, myrtle-grn & yell-brn   25   12

645 L. Le Vau (architect)   **646** Handball Player

(Des Serveau. Eng Durrens (1857), Haley (1858), Béquet (1859), Bétemps (1860), Pheulpin (1861), Combet (1862). Recess)
1970. *Red Cross Fund. T* **645** *and similar horiz designs, inscr* "1970". *P* 13.
1857   40 c.+10 c. brown-lake (14.2)   . .   30   30
1858   40 c.+10 c. turquoise-blue (14.2)   . .   30   30
1859   40 c.+10 c. slate-green (14.2)   . .   30   30
1860   40 c.+10 c. chocolate (11.4)   . .   30   30
1861   40 c.+10 c. slate (11.4)   . .   30   30
1862   40 c.+10 c. ultramarine (11.4)   . .   30   30
1857/1862 (*Set of* 6 . .   . .   1·60   1·60
Designs:—No. 1857, *T* **645**; 1858, Prosper Mérimée (writer); 1859, Philibert de l'Orme (architect); 1860, Edouard Branly (scientist); 1861, Maurice de Broglie (physicist); 1862, Alexandre Dumas (père) (writer).

(Des and eng Bétemps. Recess)
1970 (21 Feb). *Seventh World Handball Championships.*
P 13.
1863 **646** 80 c. myrtle-green   40   15

647 Marshal Alphonse Juin and Les Invalides, Paris

(Des and eng Gandon. Recess)
1970 (28 Feb). *Marshal Juin Commemoration. P* 13.
1864 **647** 45 c. chocolate and light blue . .   30   10

648 Hovertrain *Orleans* 1–80   **649** Postman of 1830 and
                                              Paris Scene

(Des and eng Combet. Recess)
1970 (7 Mar). *First "Hovertrain" in Service.* P 13.
1865 **648** 80 c. drab and reddish violet .. 35 20

(Des and eng Béquet. Recess)
1970 (14 Mar). *Stamp Day.* P 13.
1866 **649** 40 c.+10 c. black, ultramarine and
carmine-red 35 20

PHOSPHOR BAND STAMPS. Starting in March 1970, Nos. 1867p/9p were issued on an experimental basis in the town of Clermont-Ferrand. The phosphor band is similar in appearance to that used by the British Post Office, but reacts to Long Wave ultra-violet light with a yellow or orange glow.
The phosphor-lined stamps are for use with automatic sorting machinery which segregated "slow" from "fast" mail. In the original issue the "fast" mail (40 c. or 30 c. plus 10 c.) had an even number of bands and the "slow" (30 c. or three 10 c.) an odd number. The use of phosphor-lined stamps was later extended to other regions.

1970 (March)–**72.** *Phosphor issue. Various issues with bands of phosphor on the face of the stamp.* P 14×13½ (10 c.), 14×13 (30 c.) or 13 (others).
1867p 10 c. ultram, yell & brn-red (No. 1499b)
(3 bands) 5 5
1867ap 20 c. mult (No. 1735) (3 bands)(1.2.72) 5 5
1868p 30 c. emerald (No. 1843) (1 band) .. 8 5
1869p 40 c. cerise (No. 1768b) (2 bands) .. 3·50 3·00
See also Nos. 1904/6a.

650 P-J Pelletier and J-B Caventou
with Formula

651 Flamingo

(Des and eng C. Haley. Recess)
1970 (21 Mar). *150th Anniv of Discovery of Quinine.* P 13.
1870 **650** 50 c. deep myrtle-green, magenta
and light greenish blue .. 35 8

(Des and eng Cami. Recess)
1970 (21 Mar). *European Nature Conservation Year.* P 13.
1871 **651** 45 c. magenta, slate and olive-green 30 10

652 Rocket and Dish-aerial

653 "Health and Sickness"

(Des and eng Combet. Recess)
1970 (28 Mar). *Launching of "Diamant B" Rocket from Guyana.* P 13.
1872 **652** 45 c. blue-green 25 10

(Des and eng Decaris. Recess)
1970 (4 Apr). *W.H.O. "Fight Cancer" Day* (7th April). P 13.
1873 **653** 40 c.+10 c. mag, ol-brn & new bl 25 20

654 "Flaming Sun"

(Des L. le Brocquy. Eng Bétemps. Recess)
1970 (2 May). *Europa.* P 13.
1874 **654** 40 c. carmine 15 5
1875 80 c. light greenish blue 30 15

655 Marshal de Lattre de Tassigny and
Armistice Meeting

(Des and eng Bétemps. Recess)
1970 (8 May). *25th Anniv of Berlin Armistice.* P 13.
1876 **655** 40 c.+10 c. deep blue, violet-blue
and greenish blue 25 10

(Des and eng Pheulpin (Nos. 1877; 1879), Lacaque (1878), Gandon (1880). Recess)
1970. *French Art. Designs as T* **491.** *P* 12×13 (*Nos.* 1877, 1880) or 13×12 (others).
1877 1 f. multicoloured (9.5) 50 30
1878 1 f. chestnut (4.7) 50 30
1879 1 f. multicoloured (10.10) .. 50 30
1880 1 f. multicoloured (14.11) .. 50 30
1877/1880 Set of 4 .. .. 1·90 1·00
Designs: *Vert*—No. 1877, 15th-century Savoy "primitive" painting on wood; 1880, "The Ballet-dancer" (Degas). *Horiz*—1878, "The Triumph of Flora" (sculpture by J. B. Carpeaux; 1879, "Diana's Return from the Hunt" (F. Boucher).

656 Arms of Lens,
Miner's Lamp and Pithead

657 "République"
and Périgueux

(Des and eng Combet. Recess)
1970 (16 May). *43rd French Federation of Philatelic Societies Congress, Lens.* P 13.
1881 **656** 40 c. carmine 20 8

(Des Cheffer. Eng Durrens. Label des and eng Jumelet. Recess)
1970 (13 June). *Transfer of French Govt Printing Works to Périgueux.* P 13.
1882 **657** 40 c. cerise 45 25
The above stamp and label were issued together *se-tenant* in sheets for which special printing plates had been laid down. The stamp is virtually indistinguishable from the normal 40 c. definitive, No. 1768b.

(Des and eng Durrens (95 c.), Béquet (others). Recess)

1970 (20 June). *Tourist Publicity. Horiz designs as T* **490,** *but inscr* "1970". *P* 13.
1883	50 c. bright purple, new bl & blackish grn	20	5
1884	95 c. chocolate, brown-red & yell-olive	40	25
1885	1 f. blackish grn, new bl & dp carmine	40	5

Designs:—50 c. Diamond Rock, Martinique; 95 c. Chancelade Abbey (Dordogne); 1 f. Gosier Island, Guadeloupe.

658 Javelin-thrower in Wheel-chair   **659** Hand and Broken Chain   **660** Observatory and Nebula

(Des and eng Decaris. Recess)

1970 (27 June). *World Games for the Physically Handicapped, St. Étienne. P* 13.
1886 **658** 45 c. carmine, bright grn & bright bl   20   10

(Des and eng Haley, after S. Sourdille. Recess)

1970 (27 June). *25th Anniversary of Liberation from Concentration Camps. P* 13.
1887 **659** 45 c. light brn, deep ultram & blue   20   8

(Des and eng Combet. Recess)

1970 (4 July). *Haute-Provence Observatory. P* 13.
1888 **660** 1 f. 30, bluish vio, deep bl & dp grn   50   25

661 Pole-vaulting   **662** Daurat and Vanier, and Plane making Night-landing

(Des and eng Bétemps. Recess)

1970 (11 Sept). *First European Junior Athletic Championships, Paris. P* 13.
1889 **661** 45 c. indigo, new blue & bright pur   20   10

(Des and eng Gandon (5 f.), Pheulpin (20 f.), J. Combet (others). Recess)

1970 (19 Sept)–**73.** *AIR. Pioneer Aviators. T* **662** *and similar horiz designs. P* 13.
1890	5 f. deep blackish brown, emerald and deep greenish blue (17.4.71)	1·10	12
1891	10 f. slate-blue, reddish violet and carmine (10.6.72)	2·50	40
1892	15 f. slate, magenta & choc (24.2.73)	3·50	60
1893	20 f. indigo and new blue	4·50	60
1890/1893	Set of 4	10·00	1·60

Designs:—10 f. Hélène Boucher, Maryse Hilsz and aircraft; 15 f. Henri Guillaumet, Paul Codos and flying-boat; 20 f. Jean Mermoz, A. de Saint-Exupéry and "Concorde".

663 Bath-house, Arc-et-Senans (Doubs)   **664** U.N. Emblem, New York Headquarters and Palais des Nations, Geneva

(Des and eng C. Haley. Recess)

1970 (26 Sept). *Royal Salt Springs, Chaux (founded by N. Ledoux). P* 13.
1895 **663** 80 c. deep chocolate, myrtle-grn & bl   40   15

(Des and eng Decaris. Recess)

1970 (17 Oct). *History of France (Fifth Series). Horiz designs similar to T* **582,** *but inscr* "1970". *P* 13.
1896	45 c. magenta, slate and black	20	12
1897	45 c. chestnut, myrtle-green and light olive-yellow	20	12
1898	45 c. slate, chestnut and yellow-orange	20	12

Designs:—No. 1896, Richelieu; 1897, Louis XIV, 1898, Louis XV at Battle of Fontenoy (after painting by H. Vernet).

(Des and eng Decaris. Recess)

1970 (24 Oct). *25th Anniv of United Nations. P* 13.
1899 **664** 80 c. deep reddish violet, yell-olive and bright blue   40   20

665 Bordeaux and "Ceres" Stamp

(Des and eng Durrens. Recess)

1970 (7 Nov). *Centenary of Bordeaux "Ceres" Stamp Issue. P* 13.
1900 **665** 80 c. bluish violet and slate-blue   40   25

666 Col. Denfert-Rochereau and "Lion of Belfort" (after Bartholdi)

(Des and eng Cami. Recess)

1970 (14 Nov). *Siege of Belfort Centenary. P* 13.
1901 **666** 45 c. deep ultram, chestnut & olive   20   12

667 "Lord and Lady" (*Circa* 1500)   **668** "Marianne"   **669** Balloon leaving Paris

(Des and eng Gandon. Recess)

1970 (12 Dec). *Red Cross Fund. Frescoes from Dissay Chapel, Vienne. T 667 and similar vert design. Cross in red. P 13.*
1902 40 c.+15 c. green 65 55
1903 40 c.+15 c. brown-red 65 55
Design:—No.1903, "Angel with instruments of mortification"

(Des P. Béquet. Eng J. Miermont. Typo. Des and eng P. Béquet. Recess)

1971 (2 Jan) **–76.** (*a*) *Typo. P* 14×13.
1904 **668** 45 c. blue (6.2.71) 15 5
1904*a* 60 c. emerald (5.10.74) .. 80 5
 ap. One phosphor band .. 45 5
1904*b* 80 c. emerald (*One phosphor band*) (31.7.76) 20 5

 (*b*) *Recess. P* 13.
1905 **668** 50 c. cerise (2.1.71) .. 15 5
 p. Three phosphor bands (4.1.71) 20 5
1905*a* 60 c. emerald (*One phosphor band*) (5.10.74) .. 75 5
1905*b* 80 c. carmine (5.10.74) .. 1·60 55
 bp. Three phosphor bands .. 30 5
1905*c* 80 c. emerald (*One phosphor band*) (31.7.76) .. 20 5
1905*d* 1 f. carmine (*Three phosphor bands*) (31.7.76) 25 10

 (*c*) *Recess. P* 13×*imperf* (*coils*).
1906 **668** 80 c. emerald (*One phosphor band*) (1976) 25 10
1906*a* 1 f. carmine (*Three phosphor bands*) (1976) 30 10
 Nos. 1905/*b* and 1906/*a* with red numerals on the back are from coils.

Nos. 1904*b*, 1905*b* and 1905*d* were also issued with tropical gum, which can be distinguished from normal gum by its matt appearance.

(Des and eng Béquet. Recess)

1971 (17 Jan). *AIR. Centenary of Paris Balloon Post. P* 13.
1907 **669** 95 c. multicoloured 75 55

(Des and eng Lacaque (1908), Gandon (1909), Cami (1910), Recess)

1971. *French Art. Vert designs as T 491. P* 12×13.
1908 1 f. chocolate (23.1) 50 30
1909 1 f. multicoloured (3.4) .. 60 30
1910 1 f. multicoloured (5.6) .. 60 30
 Designs:—No. 1908, "St. Matthew" (sculpture, Strasbourg Cathedral); 1909, "The Winnower" (Millet); 1910, "Songe Creux" (G. Rouault).

670 Ice-skaters

(Des and eng Forget. Recess)

1971 (20 Feb). *World Ice-skating Championships, Lyon. P* 13.
1911 **670** 80 c. ultram, light blue and indigo 40 20

(Des and eng Combet. Recess)

1971 (6 Mar). *"Oceanexpo" Int Exhibition, Bordeaux. P* 13.
1912 **671** 80 c. deep turquoise-green & indigo 40 15

ALBUM LISTS
Write for our latest lists of albums and accessories.
These will be sent free on request.

672 General D. Brosset, and Fourvière Basilica, Lyon

673 Field Post Office, World War I

(Des Pheulpin. Eng Béquet (No. 1915), Pheulpin (others). Recess)

1971. *Red Cross Fund. Celebrities. T 672 and similar horiz designs, inscr "1971". P* 13.
1913 50 c.+10 c. olive-brn & slate-grn (6.3) 75 65
1914 50 c.+10 c. red-brown & chocolate (6.3) 75 65
1915 50 c.+10 c. olive-brn & brn-red (10.5) 75 65
1916 50 c.+10 c. reddish lilac & dp ult (29.5) 75 65
1917 50 c.+10 c. reddish pur & plum (16.10) 75 65
1918 50 c.+10 c. turq-blue & indigo (16.10) 75 65
1913/1918 *Set of 6* .. .. .. 4·00 3·50
 Designs:—No. 1913, T **672**; 1914, Esprit Auber (composer), and manuscript of "Fra Diavolo"; 1915, Victor Grignard (chemist), and Nobel Prize for Chemistry; 1916, Henri Farman (aviation pioneer), and early flight; 1917, General C. Delestraint (Resistance leader), and "Secret Army" proclamation; 1918, J. Robert-Houdin (magician), and levitation act.

(Des and eng Béquet. Recess)

1971 (27 Mar). *Stamp Day. P* 13.
1919 **673** 50 c.+10 c. blue, brn & bistre-brn 40 25

674 Cape-Horner *Antoinette*

675 Izard (Pyrenean chamois)

(Des Chapelet. Eng Durrens. Recess)

1971 (10 Apr). *French Sailing Ships. P* 13.
1920 **674** 80 c. reddish violet, indigo & new bl 40 25
 See also Nos. 1967, 2011 and 2100.

(Des and eng Haley. Recess)

1971 (24 Apr). *Inauguration of Western Pyrenees National Park. P* 13.
1921 **675** 65 c. chocolate, new blue & olive-brn 35 15

(Des and eng Decaris. Recess)

1971. *History of France (Sixth Series). Horiz designs similar to T 582, but inscr "1971". P* 13.
1922 45 c. plum, new bl & orange-red (8.5) 25 10
1923 45 c. brn-red, ol-brn & new bl (18.9) 25 12
1924 65 c. chocolate, reddish purple and Prussian blue (10.7) 30 20
 Designs:—No. 1922, Cardinal, noble and commoner (Opening of the States-General, 1789); 1923, Battle of Valmy, 1792; 1924, Fall of the Bastille, 1789.

676 Basilica of Santa Maria, Venice

677 View of Grenoble

(Des and eng Bétemps (50 c.). Des H. Haflidason. Eng
Bétemps (80 c.). Recess)

1971 (8 May). *Europa. T 676 and another horiz design. P 13.*
1925	50 c. bistre and grey-blue	..	25	8
1926	80 c. bright purple (Europa chain)	..	35	15

(Des and eng Combet. Recess)

1971 (29 May). 44*th French Federation of Philatelic Societies
Congress, Grenoble. P 13.*
1927	**677**	50 c. red, rose and bistre	..	..	20	5

678 A.F.R.
Emblem and Town

679 Bourbon Palace, Paris

(Des and eng Haley. Recess)

1971 (5 June). 25*th Anniv of Rural Family Aid* (1970). *P 13.*
1928	**678**	40 c. blue, violet and green	..	15	8

(Des and eng Bétemps (60 c.), Haley (65 c.), Lacaque (90 c.),
Béquet (1 f. 10), Durrens (1 f. 40). Recess)

1971. *Tourist Publicity. Various designs similar to T 490, but
inscr "1971". P 13.*
1929	60 c. black, light blue & dp green (19.6)	20	5
1930	65 c. black, violet & yellow-ochre (3.7)	25	5
1931	90 c. brown, green and ochre (3.7)	..	30	5
1932	1 f. 10, light brown, greenish blue and		
	myrtle-green (12.6)	35	10
1933	1 f. 40, mar, new bl & myrtle-grn (12.6)	50	12
1929/1933	*Set of 5*	1·40	30

Designs:—*Vert*—60 c. Sainte Chapelle, Riom; 65 c. Church
and fountain, Dole; 90 c. Gate-tower and houses, Riquewihr;
1 f. 40, Ardèche gorges. *Horiz*—1 f. 10, Fortress, Sedan.

(Des and eng Decaris. Recess)

1971 (28 Aug). 59*th Inter-Parliamentary Union Conference,
Paris. P 13.*
1934	**679**	90 c. ultramarine	..	..	..	40	15

680 Embroidery and
Instrument-making

681 Réunion Chameleon

(Des and eng Decaris. Recess)

1971 (16 Oct). 40*th Anniv of First Meeting of Crafts Guilds
Association. P 13.*
1935	**680**	90 c. light purple and carmine	..	50	15

(Des P. Lambert. Photo)

1971 (6 Nov). *Nature Conservation. P 13.*
1936	**681**	60 c. bright grn, brn & greenish yell	65	30

STAMP MONTHLY

—finest and most informative magazine for all
collectors. Obtainable from your newsagent or
by postal subscription—details on request.

682 De Gaulle
in Uniform
(June 1940)

683 Baron Portal (First President)
and First Assembly

(Des Bétemps. Eng Lacaque (Nos. 1937, 1940). Des and eng
Béquet (others). Recess)

1971 (9 Nov). *General Charles de Gaulle Commemoration and
First Death Anniv. T 682 and similar vert designs. P 13.*
1937	50 c. black	..	..	..	20	10
1938	50 c. blue	..	..	..	20	10
1939	50 c. red	..	..	..	20	10
1940	50 c. black	..	..	..	20	10
	a. Horiz strip of 4+label. Nos. 1937/40	85	60

Designs:—No. 1937, Type **682,** No. 1938, De Gaulle at
Brazzaville, 1944; No. 1939, Liberation of Paris, 1944; No.
1940, De Gaulle as President of the French Republic, 1970.
Nos. 1937/40 were issued in sheets of 20 stamps giving
5 horiz *se-tenant* strips with a stamp-sized label showing the
Cross of Lorraine in the centre of each horiz strip.

(Des and eng Béquet. Recess)

1971 (13 Nov). 150*th Anniv of National Academy of Medicine.
P 13.*
1941	**683**	45 c. plum and bright purple	..	20	12

684 "Young Girl with
Little Dog" (Greuze)

685 Penguin, Map and
Ships

(Des and eng Gandon. Recess)

1971 (11 Dec). *Red Cross Fund. Paintings by J-B. Greuze.
T 684 and similar vert design. Cross in red. P 13.*
1942	30 c.+10 c. ultramarine	..	55	55
1943	50 c.+10 c. lake ("The Dead Bird")	..	55	55

(Des and eng C. Durrens (No. 1944), R. Cami (1946), P. Gandon
(others). Recess)

1972. *French Art. Multicoloured paintings as T 491. P 13×12
(No. 1947) or 12×13 (others).*
1944	1 f. "L'Étude" (portrait of a young girl)		
	(Fragonard) (*vert*) (22.1)	60	30
1945	1 f. "Women in a Garden" (C. Monet)		
	(*vert*) (17.6)	60	30
1946	2 f. "St. Peter presenting Pierre de		
	Bourbon" (Master of Moulins) (*vert*)		
	(14.10)	1·40	45
1947	2 f. "The Barges" (A. Derain) (16.12) ..	1·50	45
1944/1947	*Set of 4*	3·50	1·40

(Des and eng P. Béquet. Recess)

1972 (29 Jan). *Bicentenary of Discovery of Crozet Islands and
Kerguelen (French Southern and Antarctic Territories). P 13.*
1948	**685**	90 c. black, blue and orange-brown	65	25

686 Skier and Emblem   **687** Aristide Bergès
(hydro-electric engineer)

690 Great   **691** "Com-   **692** "Tree of
Horned Owl   munications"   Hearts"

(Des and eng P. Forget. Recess)

1972. *Nature Conservation.* T **690** *and similar design. P* 13.
1962	60 c. blue-black, emerald and blue (27.5)			50	30
1963	65 c. light brn, bistre-brn & slate (15.4)			50	30

Design: *Horiz*—60 c. Salmon.

(Des and eng C. Haley. Recess (50 c.). Des P. Huovinen and
P. Lambert. Photo (90 c.))

1972 (22 Apr). *Europa.* T **691** *and another vert design with
similar inscr. P* 13.
1964	50 c. dull purple, yellow & bistre-brown	20	5
1965	90 c. multicoloured	45	15

Design:—50 c. Aix-la-Chapelle Cathedral.

(Des F. Belle. Eng G. Bétemps. Recess)

1972 (5 May). *20th Anniv of Post Office Employees' Blood
Donors Association. P* 13.
1966	**692** 40 c. red	20	10

(Des and eng G. Bétemps. Recess)

1972 (5 Feb). *Winter Olympic Games, Sapporo, Japan.
P* 13.
1949	**686** 90 c. red and deep olive	50	20

(Des P. Béquet. Eng J. Combet (No. 1950), C. Hertenberger
(1952), M. Monvoisin (1953), P. Béquet (others). Recess)

1972. *Red Cross Fund. Celebrities.* T **687** *and similar vert
designs. P* 13.
1950	50 c.+10 c. black, emerald and blackish green (19.2)	65	65
1951	50 c.+10 c. black, light bl & deep ultram (19.2)	65	65
1952	50 c.+10 c. blk, bright pur & plum (24.6)	65	65
1953	50 c.+10 c. black, red and crimson (1.7)	65	65
1954	50 c.+10 c. black, chestnut and blackish brown (9.9)	75	75
1955	50 c.+10 c. blk, orge & orge-red (9.9)	75	75
1950/1955	*Set of* 6	3·50	3·50

Portraits:—No. 1950, T **687**; 1951, Paul de Chomedey,
Sieur de Maisonneuve (founder of Montreal); 1952, Edouard
Belin (communications scientist); 1953, Louis Blériot (pioneer
airman); 1954, Théophile Gautier (writer); 1955, Admiral
Francois de Grasse.

693 Newfoundland Banks   **694** St.-Brieuc Cathedral
Fishing-boat   (from lithograph of 1840)
Côte d'Emeraude

(Des R. Chapelet. Eng C. Durrens. Recess)

1972 (6 May). *French Sailing Ships. P* 13.
1967	**693** 90 c. ultram, myrtle-grn & yell-orge	50	20

(Des and eng E. Lacaque. Recess)

1972 (20 May). *45th French Federation of Philatelic Societies
Congress, St.-Brieuc. P* 13.
1968	**694** 50 c. cerise	20	10

688 Rural Postman of 1894   **689** Heart and W.H.O.
Emblems

(Des and eng J. Pheulpin. Recess)

1972 (18 Mar). *Stamp Day. P* 13.
1956	**688** 50 c.+10 c. light blue, drab & yellow	40	30

(Des and eng J. Gauthier. Recess)

1972 (8 Apr). *World Heart Month. P* 13.
1957	**689** 45 c. carmine, yellow-orange & slate	30	15

(Des Sainson. Eng C. Durrens (1 f.). Des and eng C. Haley
(1 f. 20), P. Gandon (2 f.), J. Pheulpin (3 f. 50). Recess)

1972. *Tourist Publicity. Various designs similar to* T **490**, *but
inscr* "1972". *P* 13.
1958	1 f. red-brown and yellow (30.9)	40	5
1959	1 f. 20, slate-blue & bistre-brown (29.4)	45	8
1960	2 f. maroon and blackish green (2.9)	55	5
1961	3 f. 50, ol-brn, carm & greenish bl (8.4)	1·25	15
1958/1961	*Set of* 4	2·25	20

Designs: *Vert*—1 f. Stag and forest, Sologne Nature Reserve.
Horiz—1 f. 20, Charlieu Abbey; 2 f. Bazoches-du-Morvand
Château; 3 f. 50, St. Just Cathedral, Narbonne.

695 Hand and Code   **696** Old and New
Emblem   Communications

1972 (3 June). *Postal Code Campaign. Typo. P* 14×13.
1969	**695** 30 c. carmine-red, black and emerald	12	5
1970	50 c. yellow, black and carmine-red	15	5

(Des and eng G. Bétemps. Recess)

1972 (1 July). *21st World Congress of Post Office Trade Union Federation (I.P.T.T.), Paris.* P 13.
1971 **696** 45 c. ultramarine and slate . . 20 8

697 Hurdling   **698** Hikers on Road

(Des and eng G. Bétemps. Recess)

1972 (8 July). *Olympic Games, Munich.* P 13.
1972 **697** 1 f. brown-olive 50 20

(Des Le Foll. Photo)

1972 (15 July). *"Walking Tourism Year".* P 13.
1973 **698** 40 c. multicoloured 80 25

699 Cycling   **700** J.-F. Champollion and Hieroglyphics

(Des and eng G. Bétemps. Recess)

1972 (22 July). *World Cycling Championships.* P 13.
1974 **699** 1 f. sepia, purple and grey 1 00 40

(Des and eng A. Decaris. Recess)

1972. *History of France* (7th series). *The Directory. Vert designs, similar to T* **582**, *but dated "1972".* P 13.
1975   45 c. magenta, olive and blackish green (7.10) 20 12
1976   60 c. indigo, red and black (10.11) . . 30 15
1977   65 c. purple-brown, orange-brown and ultramarine (10.11) . . 30 15
Designs:—45 c. "Incroyables et Merveilleuses" (fashionable Parisians), 1794; 60 c. Napoleon Bonaparte at the Bridge of Arcole, 1796; 65 c. Discovery of antiquities, Egyptian Expedition, 1798.

(Des and eng C. Durrens. Recess)

1972 (14 Oct). *150th Anniv of Champollion's Translation of Egyptian Hieroglyphics.* P 13.
1978 **700** 90 c. lake-brown, ultramarine & blk 45 20

701 Nicolas Desgenettes (military physician)   **702** St. Theresa and Porch of Notre Dame, Alençon

(Des and eng P. Gandon. Recess)

1972 (16 Dec). *Red Cross Fund. Doctors of the 1st Empire. T* **701** *and similar vert portrait. Cross in red.* P 13.
1979   30 c.+10 c. dull green & bronze-grn . . 45 40
1980   50 c.+10 c. scarlet and brown-lake . . 45 40
Design:—50 c. François Broussais (pathologist).

(Des P. Lambert. Eng G. Bétemps. Recess)

1973 (6 Jan). *Birth Centenary of St. Theresa of Lisieux.* P 13.
1981 **702** 1 f. indigo and turquoise-blue . . 55 20

703 Anthurium   **704** National Colours of France and West Germany

(Des P. Lambert. Photo)

1973 (20 Jan). *Martinique Flower Cultivation.* P 13.
1982 **703** 50 c. multicoloured 20 5

(Des H. & H. Schillinger. Photo)

1973 (22 Jan). *10th Anniv of Franco-German Co-operation Treaty.* P 13.
1983 **704** 50 c. multicoloured 20 10

705 Polish Immigrants   **706** Admiral G. de Coligny (Protestant leader)

(Des and eng P. Béquet, after an idea by R. Juskowiak). Recess)

1973 (3 Feb). *50th Anniv of Polish Immigration.* P 13.
1984 **705** 40 c. carmine, myrtle-gm & pur-brn 20 10

(Des and eng C. Haley (No. 1985), P. Béquet (1986), J. Combet (1987), P. Gandon (1988). Recess)

1973. *French Art. Vert designs, similar to T* **491**. P 12×13.
1985   2 f. multicoloured (10.2) . . . . 1·00 45
1986   2 f. carmine-red and yellow (28.4) . . 1·00 45
1987   2 f. maroon and brown (26.5) . . 1·00 45
1988   2 f. multicoloured (22.9) . . 80 45
1985/1988   *Set of* 4 . . . . . . 3·50 1·60
Designs:—No. 1985, "The Last Supper" (carved capital, St. Austremoine Church, Issoire); 1986, "Study of a Kneeling Woman" (Charles le Brun); 1987, Wood-carving, Moutier d'Ahun; 1988, "La Finette" (girl with lute) (Watteau).

(Des J. Gauthier. Eng J. Pheulpin (No. 1992), C. Jumelet (1993), J. Gauthier (others). Recess)

1973. *Red Cross Fund. Celebrities' Anniversaries. T* **706** *and similar vert designs.* P 13.
1989   50 c.+10 c. slate-blue, bistre-brown & plum (17.2) 55 50
1990   50 c.+10 c. magenta, slate & orge (28.4) 55 50
1991   50 c.+10 c. olive, bright pur & yell (26.5) 55 50
1992   50 c.+10 c. lake, bright pur & bistre (2.6) 55 50

1993	50 c.+10 c. slate, bright purple and cinnamon (9.6)	55 50
1994	50 c.+10 c. sepia, lilac and blue (6.10)	55 50
1995	50 c.+10 c. indigo, bright purple and sepia (17.11)	55 50
1989/1995	Set of 7	3·50 3·00

Designs:—No. 1989, T **706** (400th death anniv (1972));
1990, Ernest Renan (philologist and writer) (150th birth
anniv); 1991, Santos-Dumont (pioneer aviator) (birth centenary); 1992, Colette (writer) (birth centenary); 1993,
Duguay-Trouin (naval hero) (300th birth anniv); 1994,
Louis Pasteur (scientist) (150th birth anniv (1972)); 1995,
Tony Garnier (architect) (25th death anniv).

707 Mail Coach, *circa* 1835

708 Tuileries Palace and New Telephone Exchange

(Des and eng E. Lacaque. Recess)

1973 (24 Mar). *Stamp Day. P* 13.
1996 **707** 50 c.+10 c. turquoise-blue .. 30 20

(Des P. Lengelle. Eng P. Gandon (3 f.). Des and eng P. Forget
(others). Recess)

1973. *French Technical Achievements. T* **708** *and similar
horiz designs. P* 13.
1997 45 c. ultram, drab & grey-grn (15.5) 25 8
1998 90 c. black, blue and purple (27.10) .. 35 12
1999 3 f. black, light bl & blackish grn (7.4) 1·40 75
Designs:—90 c. François I Lock, Le Havre; 3 f. European
"A 300 B" airbus.

709 Town Hall, Brussels

710 Guadeloupe Raccoon

(Des and eng P. Forget. Recess (50 c.). Des L. F. Anisdahl and
P. Lambert (90 c.). Photo)

1973 (14 Apr). *Europa. T* **709** *and design with similar inscr.
P* 13.
2000 50 c. purple-brown and magenta .. 20 5
2001 90 c. multicoloured 35 12
Design: *Horiz*—90 c. Europa "posthorn".

(Des and eng R. Cami. Recess)

1973. *Nature Conservation. T* **710** *and similar horiz design.
P* 13.
2002 40 c. maroon, bright purple & olive (23.6) 20 10
2003 60 c. black, turquoise-blue and red (12.5) 30 20
Design:—60 c. Alsace storks.

STAMP MONTHLY

—finest and most informative magazine for all
collectors. Obtainable from your newsagent or
by postal subscription—details on request.

711 Masonic Emblem

712 Globe and "Heart"

(Des and eng G. Bétemps. Recess)

1973 (12 May). *Bicentenary of Masonic Grand Orient Lodge
of France. P* 13.
2004 **711** 90 c. ultramarine and bright purple 40 20

(Des and eng M. Monvoisin (60 c.), C. Hertenberger (65 c.),
J. Pheulpin (90 c.), C. Guillame (1 f.). Recess)

1973. *Tourist Publicity. Various designs similar to T* **490**, *but
inscr* "1973". *P* 13.
2005 60 c. indigo, grey-green & light bl (8.9) 20 5
2006 65 c. reddish violet and rose-red (19.5) 25 10
2007 90 c. purple-brown, deep blue & greenish blue (18.8) 35 8
2008 1 f. myrtle-green, orge-brn & lt bl (23.6) 35 10
2005/2008 Set of 4 .. .. 1·00 30
Designs: *Vert*—60 c. Waterfall, Doubs; 1 f. Clos-Lucé
Palace, Amboise. *Horiz*—65 c. Palace of the Dukes of Burgundy,
Dijon; 90 c. Gien Château.

(Des and eng J. Combet. Recess)

1973 (26 May). *50th Anniv of Academy of Overseas Sciences.
P* 13.
2009 **712** 1 f. blackish green, lake-brown & pur 40 15

713 Racing-car at Speed

715 Bell-tower, Toulouse

714 Five-masted Barque *France II*

(Des and eng G. Bétemps. Recess)

1973 (2 June). *50th Anniv of Le Mans 24-hour Endurance
Race. P* 13.
2010 **713** 60 c. blue and chocolate 30 15

(Des R. Chapelet. Eng C. Durrens. Recess)

1973 (9 June). *French Sailing Ships. P* 13.
2011 **714** 90 c. greenish blue, indigo and blue 35 12

(Des and eng C. Durrens. Recess)

1973 (9 June). *46th French Federation of Philatelic Societies
Congress, Toulouse. P* 13.
2012 **715** 50 c. brown-red and reddish violet 25 8

716 Dr. G. Hansen

717 Eugène Ducretet (radio pioneer)

718 Molière as "Sganarelle"

721 "Mary Magdalene"

722 Weathervane

723 Figure and Human Rights Emblem

(Des and eng C. Haley. Recess)

1973 (29 Sept). *Centenary of Identification of Leprosy Bacillus by Hansen. P* 13.
2013 **716** 45 c. orange-brown, olive & bl-grn   20   8

(Des and eng J. Combet. Recess)

1973 (6 Oct). *75th Anniv of Eiffel Tower-Panthéon Experimental Radio Link. P* 13.
2014 **717** 1 f. yellow-green and carmine   . .   40   12

(Des and eng J. Derrey. Recess)

1973 (20 Oct). *300th Death Anniv of Molière (playwright). P* 13.
2015 **718** 1 f. bistre-brown and carmine-red . .   40   15

(Des and eng P. Gandon. Recess)

1973 (1 Dec). *Red Cross Fund. Tomb Figures, Tonnerre. T* **721** *and similar vert design. Cross and inscr in red. P* 13.
2021   30 c.+10 c. myrtle-green   25   25
2022   50 c.+10 c. black (Female saint)   . .   35   35

(Des and eng P. Béquet. Recess)

1973 (1 Dec). *50th Anniv of French Chambers of Agriculture. P* 13.
2023 **722** 65 c. black, ultramarine and green   25   12

(Des and eng P. Béquet. Recess)

1973 (8 Dec). *25th Anniv of Declaration of Human Rights. P* 13.
2024 **723** 45 c. deep red-brown, red-orange and brown-red   20   5

719 Pierre Bourgoin (parachutist) and Philippe Kieffer (Marine commando)

720 Eternal Flame, Arc de Triomphe

724 Façade of Museum

725 Exhibition Emblem

(Des and eng J. Pheulpin. Recess)

1973 (27 Oct). *Heroes of World War II. P* 13.
2016 **719** 1 f. claret, ultramarine and red   . .   35   15

(Des and eng A. Decaris. Recess)

1973. *History of France* (8th series). *The Years of Napoleon. Designs similar to T* **582**, *but dated "1973". P* 13.
2017   45 c. maroon, grey and new blue (3.11)   20   8
2018   60 c. red-brown,   bistre-brown   and myrtle-green (24.11)   . .   25   12
2019   1 f. carmine-red, bistre & dp grn (10.11)   40   20
Designs: *Horiz*—45 c. Napoleon and Portalis (Preparation of Civil Code, 1800–04); 60 c. Paris Industrial Exhibition, Les Invalides, 1806. *Vert*—1 f. "The Coronation of Napoleon,

(Des and eng J. Pheulpin. Recess)

1973 (19 Dec). *Opening of New Postal Museum Building. P* 13.
2025 **724** 50 c. bistre, brown-purple & brown   20   20

(Des and eng J. Combet. Recess)

1974 (19 Jan). *"ARPHILA 75" International Stamp Exhibition, Paris* (1975). *P* 13.
2026 **725** 50 c. brown, new blue & bright purple   20   5

(Des and eng C. Durrens. Recess)

1973 (10 Nov). *50th Anniv of Tomb of the Unknown Soldier, Arc de Triomphe. P* 13.
2020 **720** 40 c. red, blue and deep reddish lilac   20   10

A regular new issue supplement to this catalogue appears each month in

STAMP MONTHLY

—from your newsagent or by postal subscription
—details on request.

726 St. Louis-Marie Grignion de Montfort

727 Automatic Letter-sorting

(Des and eng J. Combet. Recess)

1974. *Red Cross Fund. Celebrities. T* **726** *and similar vert designs. P* 13.
2027   50 c.+10 c. bistre-brown, green and brown-lake (23.2)   . .   75   75

2028 50 c.+10 c. brown-lake, bright purple
and deep ultramarine (20.7)   50   50
2029 80 c.+15 c. bright purple, deep dull
purple and blue (16.11) ..   50   50
2030 80 c.+15 c. deep turquoise-blue, blue-
black & bright pur (16.11)   50   50
2027/2030 *Set of* 4 ..   ..   ..   2·00   2·00
Designs:—No. 2028, Francis Poulenc (composer); 2029, Jean Giraudoux (writer); 2030, Jules Barbey d'Aurevilly (writer).

(Des and eng C. Guillame. Recess)
1974 (9 Mar). *Stamp Day. P* 13.
2031 **727** 50 c.+10 c. bistre-brn, brn-red & ol   25   15

728 "Concorde" over Airport   **729** French Alps and Edelweiss

(Des P. Forget and P. Lengelle. Eng P. Forget. Recess)
1974 (16 Mar). *Opening of Charles de Gaulle Airport, Roissy. P* 13.
2032 **728** 60 c. reddish violet and olive-drab   25   20

(Des and eng R. Cami (2033), P. Gandon (2035). Recess. Des J. Miro (2034), P. Forget (2036). Photo)
1974. *"Arphila* 1975" *Stamp Exhibition. French Art. Designs similar to T* **491**. *Multicoloured. P* 13×12 (2035) *or* 12×13 (*others*).
2033 2 f. "Cardinal Richelieu" (P. de
Champaigne) (23.3)   80   45
2034 2 f. "Abstract after Original Work" (J.
Miro) (14.9)   75   45
2035 2 f. "Loing Canal" (A. Sisley) (*horiz*)
(9.11)   75   45
2036 2 f. "Homage to Nicolas Fouquet" (E. de
Mathieu) (16.11)   75   45
2033/2036 *Set of* 4 ..   ..   ..   2·75   1·50
The stamps were issued in sheets together with narrow *se-tenant* labels publicising the exhibition.

(Des and eng M. Monvoisin. Recess)
1974 (30 Mar). *Centenary of French Alpine Club. P* 13.
2037 **729** 65 c. bluish vio, slate-grn & new bl   30   15

730 "The Brazen Age" (Rodin)   **731** Shipwreck and Modern Lifeboat

(Des and eng G. Bétemps. Recess)
1974 (20 Apr). *Europa. Sculptures. T* **730** *and similar design. P* 13.
2038 50 c. black and bright purple   20   5
2039 90 c. purple-brown and bistre   ..   35   25
Design: *Horiz*—90 c. "The Expression" (reclining woman) (A. Maillol).

THE WORLD CENTRE FOR FINE STAMPS IS 391 STRAND

(Des R. Chapelet. Eng C. Durrens. Recess)
1974 (27 Apr). *French Lifeboat Service. P* 13.
2040 **731** 90 c. indigo, red and bistre   ..   40   15

732 Council Headquarters, Strasbourg

(Des and eng P. Forget. Recess)
1974 (4 May). *25th Anniv of Council of Europe. P* 13.
2041 **732** 45 c. grey-blue, new blue & ol-brn   20   8

733 "Cornucopia of St. Florent" (Corsica)   **734** European Bison

(Des and eng R. Quillivic (2 f.), J. Combet (3 f.), C. Durrens (others). Recess)
1974. *Tourist Publicity. T* **733** *and views as T* **490**. *P* 13.
2042 65 c. agate and deep green (22.6)   ..   20   5
2043 1 f. 10, deep bluish green & agate (7.9)   30   15
2044 2 f. bright purple and deep violet-blue
(12.10)   55   10
2045 3 f. verm, yellowish green and new blue
(11.5)   95   20
2042/2045 *Set of* 4 ..   ..   ..   1·75   45
Designs: *Horiz*—65 c. Salers; 1 f. 10, Lot valley. *Vert*—2 f. Basilica of St. Nicolas-de-Port.

(Des and eng R. Cami. Recess)
1974. *Nature Conservation. T* **734** *and similar horiz design. P* 13.
2046 40 c. deep dull pur, new bl & bistre (25.5)   25   5
2047 65 c. ol-grey, brt grn & slate-blk (19.10)   25   12
Design:—65 c. Giant Armadillo of Guiana.

735 Normandy Landings   **736** Colmar

(Des and eng C. Haley (2048, 2050), J. Pheulpin (2049), M. Monvoisin (2051). Recess)
1974. *30th Anniv of Liberation. T* **735** *and similar designs. P* 13.
2048 45 c. carmine-lake, bl-blk & emer (8.6)   20   8
2049 1 f. carmine-lake, olive-brown and
slate-lilac (25.5)   35   15
2050 1 f. deep ol-brn, blk & brt scar (23.11)   45   20

2051   1 f.+10 c. olive-brown, blue-black and
            deep turquoise-green (15.6)   ..   40   35
2048/2051   *Set of 4* ..   ..   1·25   70
Designs: *Horiz*—No. 2050, Resistance medal and torch;
2051, Order of Liberation and honoured towns. *Vert*—No.
2049, General Koenig and liberation monuments.

(Des and eng E. Lacaque. Recess)

1974 (1 June). *47th Congress of French Philatelic Societies.*
P 13.
2052 **736** 50 c. lake, bright mauve and deep
            reddish lilac   20   5

737 "Chess"   **738** Commemorative
                             Medallion

(Des P. Lambert. Eng M. Monvoisin. Recess)

1974 (8 June). *World Chess Championships, Nice. P* 13.
2053 **737** 1 f. rose-carmine, choc & royal bl   40   20

(Des and eng P. Béquet. Recess)

1974 (15 June). *300th Anniv of "Hôtel des Invalides". P* 13.
2054 **738** 40 c. bl-blk, chestnut & greenish bl   20   5

739 French Turbotrain   **740** "Nuclear Power"

(Des and eng C. Haley. Recess)

1974 (31 Aug). *Completion of Turbotrain T.G.V. 001. project.*
P 13.
2055 **739** 60 c. orge-verm, blk & deep turq-bl   45   15

(Des and eng J. Gauthier. Recess)

1974 (21 Sept). *Completion of Phénix Nuclear Generator*
P 13.
2056 **740** 65 c. deep   olive-brown,   bright
            magenta and orange-vermilion   20   ˙10

741 Peacocks with Letter

(Des and eng P. Béquet. Recess)

1974 (5 Oct). *Centenary of Universal Postal Union. P* 13.
2057 **741** 1 f. 20, carm-red, dp dull gm & ultram   40   25

742 Copernicus and   **743** Children playing
Heliocentric System   on Beach

(Des and eng C. Andréotto. Recess)

1974 (12 Oct). *500th Birth Anniv of Copernicus* (1973). *P* 13.
2058 **742** 1 f. 20, deep magenta, deep olive-
            sepia and slate-black   40   20

(Des P. Lambert. Eng C. Guillame (60 c.). Eng M. Monvoisin
(80 c.). Recess)

1974 (30 Nov). *Red Cross Fund. Seasons. T* **743** *and similar*
vert design. P 13.
2059   60 c.+15 c. scarlet, brown and new blue   30   20
2060   80 c.+15 c. scarlet, olive-brown & indigo   35   30
Design:—80 c. Child in garden looking through window.
See also Nos. 2098/9.

744 Dr. Albert   **745** Herons   **746** Edmond Michelet
Schweitzer   (politician)

(Des and eng E. Lacaque. Recess)

1975 (11 Jan). *Birth Centenary of Dr. Albert Schweitzer. P* 13.
2061 **744** 80 c.+20 c. reddish brown, carmine-
            vermilion and deep grey-green   40   40

(Des and eng J. Gauthier (85 c.), R. Quillivic (1 f. 20,), C. Durrens
(1 f. 40,). Recess)

1975. *Tourist Publicity. Designs similar to T* **490***. P* 13.
2062   85 c. deep greenish blue and deep olive-
            brown (25.1)   20   10
2063   1 f. 20, bistre-brown, reddish brown
            and new blue (18.1)   30   10
2064   1 f. 40, deep violet-blue, brown and
            dull yellowish green (11.1)   ..   35   12
Designs: *Vert*—1 f. 20, St. Pol-de-Léon. *Horiz*—85 c.
Law Courts, Rouen; 1 f. 40, Chateau de Rochechouart.

(Des and eng R. Cami. Recess)

1975 (15 Feb). *Nature Conservation. P* 13.
2065 **745** 70 c. sepia and new blue   30   15

1975 (16 Feb)**-76.** *As T* **538***, but inscribed* "FRANCE".
2065*a* 42 c. carmine and dull orange   ..   25   10
2065*b* 48 c. Venetian red and greenish blue   30   10
2065*c* 50 c. light brown & blue-green (1.1.76)   25   10
2065*d* 52 c. brown and bright rose-red (1.7.76)   20   10
2065*e* 60 c. brown and reddish lilac (1.1.76) ..   35   12
2065*f* 62 c. brown and deep magenta (1.7.76)   25   15
2065*g* 70 c. rose-carmine and bright magenta ..   50   15
2065*h* 90 c. brown and salmon pink (1.1.76) ..   50   20
2065*i* 95 c. brown and olive sepia (1.7.76) ..   40   20
2065*j* 1 f. 35, lake-brown and light green   ..   70   30
2065*k* 1 f. 60, brown and violet (1.1.76)   ..   90   35
2065*l* 1 f. 70, brown & dp ultramarine (1.7.76)   65   30
2065*a*//   *Set of 12*   ..   ..   ..   4·75   2·00
The stamps were only issued precancelled, the unused prices
being for stamps with full gum.

France

(Des and eng P. Gandon. Recess)

1975. *Red Cross Fund. Celebrities.* T **746** *and similar designs.*
P 13.

2066	**80** c.+20, blue-black and blue (22.2)..	40	40
2067	**80** c.+20, black and blue-black (10.5)..	40	40
2068	**80** c.+20, black and blue-black (28.6)..	40	40
2069	**80** c.+20, black, greenish blue and blue-black (15.11)	40	40
2066/2069	*Set of 4*	1·50	1·50

Designs: *Vert*—No. 2067, Robert Schuman (statesman);
2068, Eugene Thomas (former Telecommunications Minister).
Horiz—No. 2069 André Siegfried (geographer and humanist).

747 Eye   **748** Postman's Badge

(Des and eng C. Guillame (2 f.). Des B. Knoblauch (1 f.).
N. Nandan (3 f.), C. Bridoux (4 f.). Eng Govt Ptg Wks.
Recess)

1975. *"Arphila 1975." Stamp Exhibition, Paris.* T **747** *and similar horiz designs.* P 13.

2070	**1** f. yell-orge, plum and bright scar (1.3)	40	15
2071	**2** f. slate-grn, lake & deep yell-grn (22.3)	70	25
2072	**3** f. dp grn, blkish grn & brn-lake (19.4)	1·00	40
2073	**4** f. slate-grn, scar & yell-orge (17.5)	1·40	55
2070/2073	*Set of 4*	3·25	1·25

MS2074 152×143 mm.

2 f. Prussian blue and carmine (*Type* **747**)
3 f. Prussian blue, carmine-lake and new blue (as No. 2071)
4 f. new bl, Prussian bl & carm (as No. 2072)
6 f. Prussian bl, new bl & carm (as No. 2073) } 7·00 7·00

Designs:—2 f. Capital; 3 f. "Arphila 75, Paris"; 4 f. Head of Ceres.

(Des J. Pheulpin. Photo)

1975 (8 Mar). *Stamp Day.* P 13.
2075 **748** 80 c.+20 c. black, greenish yellow and bright yellow-blue 35   30

749 President G. Pompidou   **750** "Paul as Harlequin" (Picasso)

(Des and eng P. Gandon. Recess)

1975 (2 Apr). *President Georges Pompidou Commemoration.* P 13.
2076 **749** 80 c. black and grey-blue 20   8

(Des P. Forget. Photo)

1975 (26 Apr). *Europa.* T **750** *and similar multicoloured design.* P 13.

2077	**80** c. Type **750**	30	8
2078	**1** f. 20, "In the Square" or "Woman Leaning on Balcony" (Van Dongen) (*horiz*)	40	15

751 Machine Tools and Emblem   **752** First Assembly at Luxembourg Palace

(Des and eng A. Decaris. Recess)

1975 (3 May). *1st World Machine-Tools Exhibition, Paris.* P 13.
2079 **751** 1 f. 20, blk, deep carm-red & bright greenish blue 40   15

(Des and eng A. Decaris. Recess)

1975 (24 May). *Centenary of the French Senate.* P 13.
2080 **752** 1 f. 20, olive-bistre, olive-brn & lake   40   15

753 Symbols, Signatures and Seals

(Des and eng C. Haley. Recess)

1975 (31 May). *Centenary of Metre Convention.* P 13.
2081 **753** 1 f. deep purple, deep mag & lake-brn   30   12

754 "Gazelle" Helicopter   **755** Youth and Health Symbols

(Des P. Lengelle. Eng P. Forget. Recess)

1975 (31 May). *Development of the Gazelle Helicopter.* P 13.
2082 **754** 1 f. 30, yellowish grn & dp ultram   40   20

(Des and eng C. Andréotto. Recess)

1975 (21 June). *Students' Health Foundation.* P 13.
2083 **755** 70 f. black, purple and bright scarlet   25   10

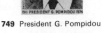

756 Underground Train   **757** Brussang Theatre and M. Pottecher (founder)

(Des and eng G. Bétemps. Recess)

1975 (21 June). *Opening of Metro Regional Express Service.* P 13.
2084 **756** 1 f. Prussian blue and new blue ..   45   12

(Des and eng E. Lacaque. Recess)

1975 (9 Aug). *80th Anniv of Peoples Theatre, Brussang.* P 13.
2085 **757** 85 c. deep rose-lilac, olive-sepia and deep turquoise-blue 20   12

758 Picardy Rose   **759** Concentration Camp Victims   **760** "Ballon d'Alsace (Mine-clearers Monument)

763 Rainbow over Womens' Faces   **764** French and Russian Flags

(Des J. M. Lallemand. Eng J. Pheulpin (85 c.). Des D. Bonin. Eng C. Durrens (1 f.). Des S. Karl-Marquet. Eng C. Haley (1 f. 15,). Des M. Bassot. Eng P. Forget (1 f. 30,). Des P. Lambert. Eng M. Monvoisin (1 f. 90,). Des C. Salembier. Eng E. Lacaque (2 f. 80,). Recess)

1975. Regions of France. T **758** and similar designs. P 13.
2086   85 c. orge, turq-bl & new bl (15.11)   25   12
2087   1 f. brown-lake, bright scarlet and yellow-ochre (25.10)   ..   30   10
2088   1 f. 15, emer, grnish bl & bistre (6.9)   40   12
2089   1 f. 30, blk, rosine & Prussian bl (4.10)   40   15
2090   1 f. 90, deep turquoise-blue, olive-bistre and grey-black (6.12)   55   15
2091   2 f. 80, dull blue, carmine and black (horiz) (13.12)   80   30
2086/2091   Set of 6 ..   ..   ..   2·50   85
Designs: Vert—1 f. Bourgogne agriculture emblems; 1 f. 15, Loire scene; 1 f. 30, Bouquet of carnations. Auvergne, 1 f. 90, Allegory, Poitou-Charentes. Horiz—2 f. 80, "Nord—Pas-de-Calais".
See also Nos. 2102/6, 2152/7 and 2246/8.

(Des and eng J. Combet. Recess)
1975 (27 Sept). 30th Anniv of Concentration Camps' Liberation. P 13.
2092 **759** 1 f. olive-grey, new blue & rose-red   30   12

(Des and eng C. Haley. Recess)
1975 (11 Oct). 30th Anniv of Mine Clearance Service. P 13.
2093 **760** 70 c. olive-grey, bistre and blue   ..   20   10

761 "Urban Development"   **762** St. Nazaire Bridge

(Des M. Deviers. Eng C. Durrens. Recess)
1975 (18 Oct). New Towns. P 13.
2094 **761** 1 f. 70, new bl, emer & chestnut   55   20

(Des and eng R. Quillivic. Recess)
1975 (8 Nov). Opening of St. Nazaire Bridge. P 13.
2095 **762** 1 f. 40, blue-black, greenish blue and deep turquoise-green   45   12

ALBUM LISTS
Write for our latest lists of albums and accessories.
These will be sent free on request.

(Des G. Lacroix. Photo)
1975 (8 Nov). International Women's Year. P 13.
2096 **763** 1 f. 20, multicoloured   30   20

(Des R. Dessirier. Eng C. Durrens. Recess)
1975 (22 Nov). 50th Anniv of Franco-Soviet Diplomatic Relations. P 13.
2097 **764** 1 f. 20, orange-yellow, verm & bl   40   20

(Des P. Lambert. Eng C. Guillame (60 c.). Eng M. Monvoisin (80 c.). Recess)
1975 (29 Nov). Red Cross Fund. Seasons. Vert designs similar to T **743**. P 13.
2098   60 c.+15 c. scarlet and yellowish green   30   20
2099   80 c.+20 c. olive-brown, salmon & scar   35   30
Designs: 60 c. Child on swing; 80 c. Rabbits under umbrella.

765 Frigate La Melpomene   **766** "Concorde"

(Des R. Chapelet. Eng C. Durrens. Recess)
1975 (6 Dec). French Sailing Ships. P 13.
2100 **765** 90 c. slate-blue, reddish orange and deep carmine   25   15

(Des P. Langelle. Eng P. Forget. Recess)
1976 (10 Jan). AIR. First Commercial Flight of "Concorde", Paris–Rio de Janeiro. P 13.
2101 **766** 1 f. 70, black, new blue and vermilion   50   25

(Des J.-P. Champdavoine. Eng J. Pheulpin (25 c.). Des R. Barrau. Eng M. Monvoisin (60 c.). Des Y. Cheffer-Delouis. Eng C. Haley (70 c.). Des O. Baillais. Eng C. Guillame (1 f. 25,). Recess. Des P. Davila (2 f. 20,). Photo)
1976. Regions of France. Designs similar to T **758**. P 13.
2102   25 c. emerald and new blue (31.1)   ..   10   5
2103   60 c. yellish grn, royal bl & mar (22.5)   20   5
2104   70 c. ultramarine, deep yellowish green and grey-black (22.5)   25   10
2105   1 f. 25, bl, yell-brn & deep grn (16.10)   35   8

2106   2 f. 20, multicoloured (10.1)   ..   55   25
2102/2106 Set of 5 ..   ..   ..   1·25   45
Designs: *Horiz*—25 c. Industrial complex in the Central Region; 60 c. "Aquitaine"; 2 f. 20, Scene in Pyrenees. *Vert*—70 c. "Limousin"; 1 f. 25, "Guyane".

(Des and eng M. Monvoisin (2108), G. Bétemps (2109), J. Combet (2111), P. Béquet (2113). Des J. Carzou. Eng C. Durrens (2112). Recess. Des R. Delaunay (2110). Photo)

1976. *French Art. Designs similar to T 491. P 13 (2108) 12×13 (2109/10) or 13×12 (2111/13)*
2108   2 f. grey-blue and blue (24.1)   55   40
2109   2 f. stone and sepia (6.3)   55   40
2110   2 f. multicoloured (24.7)   55   40
2111   2 f. multicoloured (4.9)   55   30
2112   2 f. multicoloured (18.9)   55   30
2113   2 f. multicoloured (18.12)   55   30
2108/2113 Set of 6   ..   ..   ..   3·00   2·00
Designs: *Vert*—No. 2108, "The Two Saints" (wood-carving), Sant-Genis-des-Fontaihes; 2109, "Venus of Brassem-pouy" (ivory sculpture); 2110, "La Joie de Vivre" (Robert Delaunay). *Horiz*—No. 2111, Rameses II in war chariot (wall-carving); 2112, Painting by Carzou; 2113, "Still Life with Fruit" (Maurice de Vlaminck).

767 French Stamp Design of 1876

768 Old Rouen

(Des and eng G. Bétemps. Recess)

1976 (13 Mar). *International Stamp Day. P* 13.
2114 **767** 80 c.+20 c. deep reddish lilac & blk   30   30

(Des and eng C. Durrens (1 f.), J. Pheulpin (1 f. 10), C. Guillame (1 f. 40,), J. Combet (2 f.), M. Monvoisin (3 f.). Des M.-N. Goffin. Eng E. Lacaque (1 f. 70,), Recess)

1976. *Tourist Publicity. Designs similar to T 490. P* 13.
2115   1 f. ol-brn, slate-grn & carm-verm (10.7)   20   5
2116   1 f. 10, deep ultramarine (13.11)   ..   25   10
2117   1 f. 40, new blue, deep grn & brn (25.9)   40   10
2118   1 f. 70, brown-purple, bronze-green and new blue (9.10)   45   10
2119   2 f. deep mag, lake-brn & ochre (10.7)   50   5
2120   3 f. yellow-brown, deep slate-blue and yellowish green (10.4)   75   8
2115/2120 Set of 6 ..   ..   ..   2·50   45
Designs: *Horiz*—1 f. Chateau Bonaquil; 1 f. 40, Basque coast, Biarritz; 3 f. Chateau de Malmaison. *Vert*—1 f. 10, Lodève Cathedral; 1 f. 70, Thiers; 2 f. Ussel.

(Des and eng P. Gandon. Recess)

1976 (24 Apr). *49th Congress of French Philatelic Societies. P* 13.
2121 **768** 80 c. deep yellow-grn & orge-brn   25   10

769 Warships and Naval Emblem

770 Youth

(Des and eng A. Decaris. Recess)

1976 (24 Apr). *50th Anniv of Central Marine Officers' Reserve Association. P* 13.
2122 **769** 1 f. olive-yellow, deep ultramarine and deep carmine-red   30   12

(Des and eng C. Andréotto. Recess)

1976 (27 Apr). *"Juvarouen 1976". Youth Stamp Exhibition, Rouen. P* 13.
2123 **770** 60 c. indigo, turquoise-blue and deep carmine-red   20   8

771 Strasbourg Jug

(Des O. Baillais. Photo)

1976 (8 May). *Europa. T* **771** *and similar square design. Multi-coloured. P* 13.
2124   80 c. Type **771**   20   10
2125   1 f. 20, Sèvres plate   30   15

772 Vergennes and Franklin

773 Marshal Moncey

(Des and eng R. Quillivic. Recess)

1976 (15 May). *Bicentenary of American Revolution. P* 13.
2126 **772** 1 f. 20, blue-black, carm-red & bl   40   15

(Des R. Dessirier. Eng E. Lacaque (2128/9). Des P. Lambert. Eng E. Lacaque (2132). Des and eng C. Andréotto (others). Recess)

1976. *Red Cross Fund. Celebrities. T* **773** *and similar vert designs. P* 13.
2127   80 c.+20 c. deep reddish purple, black and orange-brown (22.5)   ..   30   30
2128   80 c.+20 c. olive-brn & deep brn (22.7)   30   30
2129   80 c.+20 c. mag & dp yellish grn (28.8)   30   30
2130   1 f.+20 c. blue-black, pale grnish blue and blue (6.9)   35   35
2131   1 f.+20 c. deep ultramarine, magenta and blackish purple (25.9)   ..   35   35
2132   1 f.+20 c. slate and brown-red (6.11)   35   35
2127/2132 Set of 6 ..   ..   ..   1·75   1·75
Designs:—No. 2128, Max Jacob (poet); 2129, Mounet-Sully (tragedian); 2130, General Daumesnil; 2131, Eugene Fromentin (writer and painter); 2132, Anna de Noailles.

A regular new issue supplement to this catalogue appears each month in

STAMP MONTHLY

—from your newsagent or by postal subscription
—details on request.

774 People talking   **775** Verdun Memorial   **776** Tronçais Forest

(Des E. Authe. Photo)

1976 (12 June). *"Communication". P* 13.
2133 **774** 1 f. 20, black, bistre-yell & rosine   30   15

(Des C. Durrens. Eng P. Forget. Recess)

1976 (12 June). *60th Anniv of Verdun Offensive. P* 13.
2134 **775** 1 f. rosine, sepia & deep grey-green   30   12

(Des and eng A. Decaris. Recess)

1976 (19 June). *Nature Conservation. P* 13.
2135 **776** 70 c. brown, deep grn & grnish bl   20   12

777 Cross of Lorraine Emblem   **778** Satellite "Symphonie"

(Des and eng C. Durrens. Recess)

1976 (19 June). *30th Anniv of Free French Association. P* 13.
2136 **777** 1 f. scarlet, deep ultramarine & blue   30   12

(Des and eng J. Combet. Recess)

1976 (26 June). *Launch of "Symphonie No. 1" Satellite. P* 13.
2137 **778** 1 f. 40, ol-brn, choc & brt reddish vio   30   20

779 Carnival Figures   **780** Sailing

(Des and eng G. Bétemps. Recess)

1976 (10 July). *"La Fete" (Summer Festivals Exhibition, Tuileries, Paris). P* 13.
2138 **779** 1 f. rosine, bright grn & deep ultram   30   12

(Des and eng P. Béquet. Recess)

1976 (17 July). *Olympic Games, Montreal. P* 13.
2139 **780** 1 f. 20, deep violet-blue, deep ultramarine and new blue   35   15

781 Officers in Military and Civilian Dress   **782** Early and Modern Telephones

(Des and eng P. Forget. Recess)

1976 (18 July). *Centenary of Reserve Officers Corps. P* 13.
2140 **781** 1 f. slate, lake and blue   30   12

(Des and eng J. Combet. Recess)

1976 (25 Sept). *Telephone Centenary. P* 13.
2141 **782** 1 f. slate, lake-brown and new blue   30   8

783 Bronze Statue and Emblem   **784** Police and Emblems

(Des P. Lambert. Eng G. Bétemps. Recess)

1976 (2 Oct). *10th Anniv of International Tourist Film Association. P* 13.
2142 **783** 1 f. 40, ol-brn, salmon & blkish grn   40   20

(Des and eng G. Bétemps. Recess)

1976 (9 Oct). *10th Anniv of National Police Force. P* 13.
2143 **784** 1 f. 10, brn-ol, scar-verm & royal bl   30   12

785 Symbol of Nuclear Science   **786** Fair Emblems

(Des J. Gauthier. Photo)

1976 (22 Oct). *European Research into Nuclear Science. P* 13.
2144 **785** 1 f. 40, multicoloured   40   15

(Des and eng J. Gauthier. Recess)

1976 (20 Nov). *50th Anniv of French Fairs and Exhibitions Federation. P* 13.
2145 **786** 1 f. 50, deep ultramarine, deep bluish green and yellow-brown ..   40   12

787 St. Barbara   **788** "Douane" Symbol

(Des and eng P. Gandon. Recess)

1976 (20 Nov). *Red Cross Fund. Statuettes from Brou Church. T* **787** *and similar vert design. P* 13.
2146   80 c.+20 c. violet and red   ..   30   30
2147   1 f.+25 c. deep purple-brown and red   35   35
Design:—1 f. Cumaean Sybil.

(Des B. Lallemand. Photo)

1976 (27 Nov). *French Customs Service. P* 13.
2148   **788** 1 f. 10, multicoloured   ..   30   12

789 Museum and *Duchesse Anne*

(Des and eng A. Decaris. Recess)

1976 (4 Dec). *Atlantic Museum, Port-Louis. P* 13.
2149   **789** 1 f. 45, olive-brown, greenish blue
       and blackish green   ..   40   20

(Des M.-A. Douyère (1 f. 45), M. Pelz (1 f. 50), J.-L. Castellano (2 f. 10), M. Houssin (2 f. 40), M. Gros (2 f. 50), J. Monnet (2 f. 75), R. Irolla (3 f. 20), B. Onipenko (3 f. 90), Eng C. Guillame (2 f. 10), J. Pheulpin (2 f. 40), P. Béquet (2 f. 75), C. Haley (3 f. 20), C. Andréotto (3 f. 90). Photo (1 f. 45, 1 f. 50, 2 f. 50) or recess (others)

1977. *Regions of France. Designs similar to T* **758.** *P* 13.
2150   1 f. 45, magenta and emerald (5.2)   ..   40   12
2151   1 f. 50, multicoloured (29.1)   ..   40   12
2152   2 f. 10, lemon, dp bl & greenish bl (8.1)   55   15
2153   2 f. 40, brown, green & violet-bl (19.2) ..   65   12
2154   2 f. 50, multicoloured (15.1)   ..   70   20
2155   2 f. 75, deep bluish green (22.1)   ..   75   25
2156   3 f. 20, ochre, bottle grn & new bl (16.4)   80   30
2157   3 f. 90, maroon, bistre & new blue (26.2) 1·10   40
2150/2157 *Set of 8* ..   ..   5·00 1·50
Designs: *Vert*—1 f. 50, Banana tree (Martinique); 2 f. 10, Arms and transport (Franche-Comté); 2 f. 50, Fruit and yachts (Languedoc-Roussillon); 3 f. 20, Champagne and scenery (Champagne-Ardenne); 3 f. 90, Village church (Alsace). *Horiz*—1 f. 45, Birds and flowers (Réunion); 2 f. 40, Coastline (Bretagne); 2 f. 75, Mountains (Rhône-Alpes).

790 Centre Building

(Des and eng J. Combet. Recess)

1977 (5 Feb). *Opening of Georges-Pompidou National Centre of Arts and Culture, Paris. P* 13.
2158   **790** 1 f. brown-red, new bl & blackish grn   30   .8

(Des and eng P. Gandon (No. 2159), E. Lacaque (2160). Recess)

1977. *French Art. Designs similar to T* **491.** *P* 13×12 (*No.* 2159) *or* 12×13 (2160).
2159   2 f. multicoloured (12.2)   55   25
2160   2 f. multicoloured (5.11)   40   20
Designs: *Horiz*—No. 2159, "Mantes Bridge" (Corot). *Vert*—2160, "Virgin and Child" (detail, Rubens).

791 Dunkirk Harbour   **792** Torch and
                                     Dagger Emblem

(Des and eng C. Haley. Recess)

1977 (12 Feb). *Dunkirk Port Extensions. P* 13.
2161   **791** 50 c. blue, indigo and sepia   12   5

(Des P. Lambert. Eng C. Jumelet. Recess)

1977 (5 Mar). *90th Anniv of "Le Souvenir Français" (French War Graves Organization). P* 13.
2162   **792** 80 c. sepia, scarlet and bright blue   ..   20   10

793 Marckolsheim Post   **794** "Pisces"
       Relay Sign

(Des and eng M. Monvoisin. Recess)

1977 (26 Mar). *Stamp Day. P* 13.
2163   **793** 1 f. + 20 c, slate-blue and new blue ..   35   35

(Des and eng G. Bétemps. Recess)

1977 (1 Apr)–**78.** *Signs of the Zodiac. T* **794** *and similar horiz designs. P* 13.
2164   54 c. bluish violet   10   5
2165   58 c. bright green (17.1.78)   ..   10   5
2166   61 c. new blue (1.7.78)   ..   10   5
2167   68 c. chocolate   10   5
2168   73 c. scarlet (17.1.78)   ..   10   5
2169   78 c. orange-vermilion (1.7.78)   ..   15   5
2170   1 f. 05, bright mauve   ..   20   5
2171   1 f. 15, bright orange (17.1.78)   ..   20   10
2172   1 f. 25, brown-olive (1.7.78)   25   10
2173   1 f. 85, bottle green   35   12
2174   2 f. blue-green (17.1.78)   ..   40   15
2175   2 f. 10, bright magenta (1.7.78)   ..   50   15
2164/2175 *Set of 12* ..   ..   2·25   85
Designs:—58 c. Cancer; 61 c. Sagittarius; 68 c. Taurus; 73 c. Aries; 78 c. Libra; 1 f. 05, Scorpio; 1 f. 15, Capricorn; 1 f. 25, Leo; 1 f. 85, Aquarius; 2 f. Virgo; 2 f. 10, Gemini.
    The stamps were only issued precancelled, the unused prices being for stamps with full gum.

795 "Geometric Design"
(Victor Vasarely)

(Des and eng J. Pheulpin. Recess (No. 2176). From original design by P.-Y. Trémois. Photo (2177). From original design by R. Excoffon. Eng G. Bétemps. Recess (2178))

1977. "Philatelic Creations". Works by Art by Modern Artists. T **795** and similar designs. P 12×13 (Nos. 2176, 2177) or 13 ×12 (2178).

2176	3 f. myrtle-green and pale lavender (7.4)	80	35
2177	3 f. black and carmine-vermilion (17.9) ..	65	30
2178	3 f. multicoloured (17.12)	65	30

Designs: Horiz—No. 2178, Abstract in blue. Vert—2177, Profile heads of man and hawk.
See also Nos. 2249/50.

796 Flowers and Ornamental Garden

(Des H. Sainson. Eng J. Pheulpin. Recess)

1977 (23 Apr). 150th Anniv of National Horticultural Society. P 13.
2179 **796** 1 f. 70, lake, choc and bronze-grn .. 45 20

797 Provençal Village   **798** Stylised Plant

(Des and eng R. Quillivic. Recess)

1977 (23 Apr). Europa. T **797** and similar horiz design. P 13.
2180 1 f. lake-brown, olive-brown and new
       blue 25 5
2181 1 f. 40, slate-blk, bistre-brn & bronze-grn 40 12
Design:—1 f. 40, Breton port.

(Des O. Baillais. Eng J. Pheulpin. Recess)

1977 (7 May). International Flower Show, Nantes. P 13.
2182 **798** 1 f. 40, dp mauve, lem & greenish bl 40 15

799 Battle of Cambrai   **800** Church, School and Map

(Des O. Baillais. Eng C. Guillame. Recess)

1977 (14 May). 300th Anniv of Reunification of Cambrai with France. P 13.
2183 **799** 80 c. mauve, chocolate and new blue 20 8

(Des P. Lambert. Eng J. Combet. Recess)

1977 (14 May). 100th Anniv of French Catholic Institutions. P 13.
2184 **800** 1 f. 10, chocolate, bistre-brn & slate.. 30 8

801 Modern Constructions   **802** Annecy

(Des and eng C. Guillame. Recess)

1977 (21 May). Meeting of European Civil Engineering Federation. Paris. P 13.
2185 **801** 1 f. 10, dull scarlet, ol-bistre & ultram 30 10

(Des P. and C. Jacquet. Eng C. Durrens. Recess)

1977 (28 May). 50th Congress of French Philatelic Societies. P 13.
2186 **802** 1 f. chocolate, blackish grn & brn-ol ·30 10

(Des M. Deviers (1 f. 25), C. Andréotto (1 f. 40), M. N. Goffin (1 f. 45), J. Chesnot (1 f. 50), C. Haley (1 f. 90), J. Devillers (2 f. 40). Eng P. Béquet (1 f. 25), C. Andréotto (1 f. 40), M. N. Goffin (1 f. 45), P. Forget (1 f. 50), C. Haley (1 f. 90), M. Monvoisin (2 f. 40). Recess)

1977. Tourist Publicity. Designs similar to T **490.** P 13.

2187	1 f. 25, slate, blackish brn & brn-rd (1.10)	25	8
2188	1 f. 40, dp turqu bl, mar & brt mag (17.9)	30	8
2189	1 f. 45, ol-brn, chestnut & cobalt (16.7)	30	12
2190	1 f. 50, olive-brn, scar & chestnut (4.6) ..	30	12
2191	1 f. 90, pale greenish yellow & blk (9.7)	40	15
2192	2 f. 40, yellow-brown, deep grey-green		
	and blue-black (24.9) ..	50	8
2187/2192	Set of 6	1·75	55

Designs: *Horiz*—1 f. 25, Prémontrés Abbey, Pont-à-Mousson; 1 f. 50, Statue and cloisters, Fontenay Abbey, Côte d'Or; 2 f. 40, Château de Vitré. *Vert*—1 f. 40, Abbey Tower of Saint-Amand-les-Eaux, Nord; 1 f. 45, Church at Dorat, Haute-Vienne; 1 f. 90, Bayeux Cathedral.

803 School Building

(Des R. Dessirier. Eng C. Andréotto. Recess)

1977 (4 June). *Polytechnic School, Palaiseau. P* 13.
2193 **803** 1 f. 70, dp grey-green, red & ultram . .   45   15

804 *Spirit of St. Louis* and *Oiseau Blanc*

(Des and eng P. Forget. Recess)

1977 (4 June). *AIR. 50th Anniv of North Atlantic Flights. P* 13.
2194 **804** 1 f. 90, indigo, olive-grn & dp turq-bl   40   15

805 French Football Cup and Players

(Des and eng G. Bétemps. Recess)

1977 (11 June). *60th Anniv of French Football Cup. P* 13.
2195 **805** 80 c. bistre-brown, new blue and red   20   8

806 De Gaulle Memorial   **807** "Map of France"

(Des C. Durrens. Photo and embossed)

1977 (18 June). *5th Anniv of General de Gaulle Memorial. P* 13.
2196 **806** 1 f. multicoloured   20   8

(Des and eng G. Bétemps. Recess)

1977 (18 June). *25th Anniv of Junior Chambers of Commerce. P* 13.
2197 **807** 1 f. 10, ultramarine and red   30   12

808 Battle of Nancy   **809** Seal of Burgundy

(Des and eng A. Decaris. Recess)

1977 (25 June). *500th Anniv of Battle of Nancy. P* 13.
2198 **808** 1 f. 10, dark slate and blue   30   12

(Des and eng M. Monvoisin. Recess)

1977 (2 July). *500th Anniv of Union of Burgundy with France. P* 13.
2199 **809** 1 f. 25, deep grey-green & olive-sepia   30   12

810 Compass on Globe   **811** Red Cicada

(Des and eng A. Decaris. Recess)

1977 (8 July). *10th Anniv of International Association of French Language Parliaments. P* 13.
2200 **810** 1 f. 40, red and ultramarine   35   12

(Des Y. Schach-Duc. Photo)

1977 (10 Sept). *Nature Conservation. P* 13.
2201 **811** 80 c. multicoloured   20   12

812 Hand and Examples of Craftsmanship   **813** Edouard Herriot (statesman)

(Des and eng E. Lacaque. Recess)

1977 (1 Oct). *French Craftsmanship. P* 13.
2202 **812** 1 f. 40, chocolate and olive-brown ..   40   12

(Des and eng P. Gandon (No. 2203), R. Quillivic (2204), E. Lacaque (2205), P. Forget (2206). Recess)

1977. *Red Cross Fund. Celebrities. T* **813** *and similar vert designs. P* 13.
2203   1 f. + 20 c. black (8.10)   35   35
2204   1 f. + 20 c. ol-brn & myrtle-grn (15.10) ..   35   35
2205   1 f. + 20 c. chocolate, bistre and slate-
     green (12.11)   ..   35   35
2206   1 f. + 20 c. indigo, lt blue & carm (3.12) ..   35   35
2203/2206   *Set of* 4   ..   ..   1·25   1·25
Designs:—No. 2204, Abbé Breuil (archaeologist); 2205, Guillaume de Machault (poet); 2206, Charles Cros (poet).

814 "Agriculture   **815** "Old Man"   **816** "Sabine"
and Industry"

(Des and eng A. Decaris. Recess)

1977 (22 Oct). *30th Anniv of Economic and Social Council. P* 13.
2207 **814** 80 c. bistre, olive-sepia and chocolate   20   10

(Des and eng P. Béquet. Recess)

1977 (26 Nov). *Red Cross Fund. Carved Christmas Crib Figures from Provence. T* **815** *and similar vert design. P* 13.
2208   80 c. + 20 c. slate-black and red   30   30
2209   1 f. + 25 c. bottle green and red   ..   35   35
Design:—1 f. "Old Woman".

(Des and eng P. Gandon. Recess)

1977 (17 Dec)–**78**. *Without phosphor bands* (1 c. *to* 5 c.) *or with phosphor bands (others).* (a) *P* 13.
2210 **816**   1 c. slate-black (31.3.78)   ..   5   5
2211   2 c. bright ultramarine (31.3.78) ..   5   5
2212   5 c. bottle green (31.3.78)   5   5
2213   10 c. brown-red (1 band) (31.3.78)   5   5
2214   15 c. dp turq bl (1 band) (31.3.78) ..   5   5
2215   20 c. brt blue-grn (1 band) (31.3.78)   5   5
2216   30 c. brt orange (1 band) (31.3.78) ..   8   5
2217   50 c. reddish vio (1 band) (31.3.78)   10   5
2218   80 c. emerald (1 band)   ..   15   5
      a. Without phosphor (3.6.78)   ..   15   5
2219   80 c. olive-yellow (1 band) (3.6.78)   15   5
2220   1 f. bright scarlet (2 bands)   ..   20   5
      a. Without phosphor (3.6.78)   ..   20   5
2221   1 f. emerald (1 band) (3.6.78)   ..   20   5
2222   1 f. 20, brt scar (2 bands) (3.6.78)   25   5
2223   1 f. 40, new bl (2 bands) (31.3.78)   30   5
2224   1 f. 70, greenish blue (2 bands)
      (3.6.78)   35   5
2225   2 f. brt yell-grn (2 bands) (31.3.78)   40   5
2226   2 f. 10, brt purple (2 bands) (3.6.78)   40   5
2227   3 f. reddish brn (2 bands) (3.6.78)   65   5
2210/2227   *Set of* 20 ..   ..   ..   3·50   90

(b) *P* 13 × *imperf* (*coils*).
2228   80 c. emerald (1 band) (1978)   15   5
2229   1 f. brt scarlet (2 bands) (1978) ..   20   5
2230   1 f. emerald (1 band) (1978)   20   5
2231   1 f. 20, brt scarlet (2 bands) (1978)   20   5
Nos. 2218a and 2220a were issued for use in the French Overseas Departments.

Nos. 2210 to 2231 were also issued with tropical gum. See note following No. 1906*a*.

817 Table Tennis

(Des and eng R. Quillivic. Recess)

1977 (17 Dec). *50th Anniv of French Table Tennis Federation. P* 13.
2240 **817** 1 f. 10, blue-green, purple & brt orge   25   12

818 Percheron

(Des J. Birr. Photo (1 f. 70). Des and eng P. Forget (1 f. 80))

1978. *Nature Conservation. P* 13.
2241   1 f. 70, multicoloured (7.1)   ..   35   12
2242   1 f. 80, bistre-brown, olive-green and
     bright yellow-green (14.10)   ..   35   12
Design: *Vert* (22 × 36 mm)—1 f. 80, osprey.

(Des E. Lacaque, from original engraving in Louvre. Recess)

1978 (14 Jan). *French Art. Vert design similar to T* **491.** *P* 12 × 13.
2243   2 f. black   40   20
Design:—Tournament under Louis XIV, Les Tuileries, 1662.

819 Flags of France and   **820** College
Sweden of 1878   Building

(Des O. Baillais. Eng P. Béquet. Recess)

1978 (19 Jan). *Centenary of Return of St. Barthelemy Island to France. P* 13.
2244 **819** 1 f. 10, lake-brown, choc & dp mag ..   25   10

(Des and eng P. Béquet. Recess)

1978 (19 Jan). *Centenary of National Telecommunications College. P* 13.
2245 **820** 80 c. deep turquoise-blue   25   10

(Des J.-J. Pons (1 f. 40), D. Houillère (1 f. 70). Eng G. Bétemps
(1 f. 40). Recess (1 f. 40) or photo (others))

1978. *Regions of France. Designs similar to T* **758.** *P* 13.
2246	1 f. vermilion, new blue and black (4.3)	30	10
2247	1 f. 40, ultram, salmon & emer (21.1)	30	10
2248	1 f. 70, gold, carmine-red & black (1.4)	35	12

Designs: *Vert*—1 f. Symbol of Ile de France. *Horiz*—1 f. 40,
Flower and port (Haute-Normandie); 1 f. 70, old Norman boat
(Basse-Normandie).

(Eng C. Durrens. From original design by B. Buffet (No. 2249).
Eng P. Forget. From original design by Y. Brayer (No. 2250).
Recess)

1978. *"Philatelic Creations". Horiz design similar to T* **795.**
P 13×12.
2249	3 f. multicoloured (4.2)	65	30
2250	3 f. multicoloured (9.12)	65	30

Designs:—2249, "Hôtel de la Monnaie and Seine Bridge, Paris"
(B. Buffet); 2250, "Camargue Horses" (Y. Brayer).

821 Marie Noel
(poet)

822 Jigsaw Map
of France

(Des and eng M-N. Goffin (No. 2251), J. Gauthier (2252),
J. Combet (2253), J. Jubert (2254), E. Lacaque (2255). Des
R. Halpern. Eng E. Lacaque (2256). Recess)

1978. *Red Cross Fund. Celebrities. T* **821** *and similar vert
designs. P* 13.
2251	1 f.+20 c, indigo and new blue (11.2)	25	25
2252	1 f.+20 c, brn-ol, orge-brn & ind (18.2)	25	25
2253	1 f.+20 c, brt mauve & bluish vio (25.3)	25	25
2254	1 f.+20 c, dp grey-green & ol-brn (15.4)	25	25
2255	1 f.+20 c, brt magenta & carm-lake (1.7)	25	25
2256	1 f.+20 c, slate-blk, ol-sep & red (16.9)	25	25
2251/2256	Set of 6	1·40	1·40

Designs:—No. 2252, Georges Bernanos (writer); 2253,
Leconte de Lisle (poet); 2254, Leo Tolstoy (novelist); 2255,
Voltaire and J.-J. Rousseau; 2256, Claude Bernard (physician).

(Des and eng G. Bétemps. Recess)

1978 (11 Feb). *15th Anniv of Regional Planning Boards. P* 13.
2257	822	1 f. 10, bright green and bluish violet	25	10

(Des M.-N. Goffin (2258), A. Decaris (2259), J.-M. Winckler
(2260), J. Gauthier (2261), P. Andrieu (2262), C. Guillame
(2263), C. Durrens (2264). Eng M.-N. Goffin (2258),
A. Decaris (2259), C. Durrens (2260, 2264), J. Gauthier (2261),
J. Combet (2262), C. Guillame (2263). Recess)

1978. *Tourist Publicity. Designs similar to T* **490.** *P* 13.
2258	50 c. greenish blue, deep dull blue and slate green (4.3)	10	5
2259	80 c. dp turquoise bl & blackish ol (27.5)	15	5
2260	1 f. slate-black (10.6)	20	5
2261	1 f. 10, reddish violet, bistre-brown and new blue (25.3)	25	10
2262	1 f. 10, brown, slate-black and deep yellow-green (17.6)	25	10
2263	1 f. 25, red-brown and scarlet (18.2)	25	10
2264	1 f. 70, slate-black & reddish brn (3.6)	35	10
2258/2264	Set of 7	1·40	50

Designs: *Vert*—50 c. Verdon Gorge; 1 f. Church of St. Saturnin,
Puy-de-Dôme. *Horiz*—80 c. Pont Neuf, Paris; 1 f. 10 (No.2261),
Notre-Dame du Bec-Hellouin Abbey; 1 f. 10 (2262), Château
d'Esquelbecq; 1 f. 25, Abbey Church of Aubazine; 1 f. 70,
Fontevraud Abbey.

823 Head of Girl

824 Postman
emptying Pillar
Box, 1900

(Des H. Sainson. Eng J. Pheulpin. Recess)

1978 (25 Feb). *"Juvexniort" Youth Philately Exhibition, Niort.*
P 13.
2265	823	80 c. olive-brown, choc & brt mag	15	8

(Des and eng P. Forget. Recess)

1978 (8 Apr). *Stamp Day. P* 13.
2266	824	1 f.+20 c. olive-green and indigo	25	25

825 Underwater Scene

826 Floral Arch
and Garden

1978 (15 Apr). *Port Cros National Park. Photo. P* 13.
2267	825	1 f. 25, multicoloured	25	12

(Des P. Lambert. Eng P. Forget. Recess)

1978 (22 Apr). *"Make France Bloom". P* 13.
2268	826	1 f. 70, bright rose-red, new blue and bronze-green	35	12

827 Hands encircling Sun

828 War
Memorial, Notre
Dame de Lorette

(Des and eng J. Jubert. Recess)

1978 (22 Apr). *Energy Conservation. P* 13.
2269	827	1 f. orange-yellow, olive-brn & bistre	20	5

(Des and eng C. Haley. Recess)

1978 (6 May). *Hill of Notre Dame de Lorette (War Cemetery).*
P 13.
2270	828	2 f. lake-brown and bistre	40	15

829 Fontaine des
Innocents, Paris

830 Hôtel De
Mauroy, Troyes

(Des and eng M. Monvoisin. Recess)

1978 (6 May). *Europa. Fountains. T* **829** *and similar vert design.*
P 13.
2271 1 f. black, bistre-brown and ultramarine   20   5
2272 1 f. 40, sepia, deep olive and new blue ..   30   10
Design:—1 f. 40, Fontaine du Parc Floral, Paris.

(Des and eng J. Combet. Recess)

1978 (13 May). *51st Congress of French Philatelic Societies.*
P 13.
2273 **830** 1 f. black, brown-lake and ultramarine   20   10

831 Tennis Player and Stadium   **832** Open Hand

(Des J. Lovera. Eng P. Béquet. Recess)

1978 (27 May). *50th Anniv of Roland Garros Tennis Stadium.*
P 13.
2274 **831** 1 f. slate-black, chestnut & new blue   20   8

(Des and eng R. Quillivic. Recess)

1978 (9 Sept). *Handicrafts. P* 13.
2275 **832** 1 f. 30, chocolate, deep yellow-green
       and deep rose-red   25   10

833 Citadel and
Church

834 Emblem

(Des and eng M. Monvoisin. Recess)

1978 (23 Sept). *300th Anniv of Reunion of Franche-Comté with*
France. P 13.
2276 **833** 1 f. 20, slate-green, new bl & yell-gr   25   12

(Des and eng P. Gandon. Recess)

1978 (23 Sept). *400th Anniv of Establishment of State Printing*
Office. P 13.
2277 **834** 1 f. dp bluish green, black & new blue   20   8

835 Valenciennes and
Maubeuge

836 Sower

(Des M. Caussin. Eng M. Monvoisin. Recess)

1978 (30th Sept). *300th Anniv of Return of Valenciennes and*
Maubeuge to France. P 13.
2278 **835** 1 f. 20, red-brn, brt vio & grey-blk   ..   25   10

(Des C. Bridoux. Eng C. Haley. Recess)

1978 (7 Oct). *50th Anniv of Académie de Philatélie. P* 13.
2279 **836** 1 f. new blue, brt purple & bluish vio   20   8

837 Morane-Saulnier
"MS6" and Route

838 Gymnasts, Stork and
Strasbourg Cathedral

(Des and eng J. Combet. Recess)

1978 (14 Oct). *AIR. 65th Anniv of First Airmail Flight*
Villacoublay-Pauillac. P 13.
2280 **837** 1 f. 50, choc, new bl & blackish grn ..   30   10

(Des and eng J. Gauthier. Recess)

1978 (21 Oct). *19th World Gymnastics Championships,*
Strasbourg. P 13.
2281 **838** 1 f. crimson, bistre-brown & orge-brn   20   8

839 Sporting
Activities

840 "Freedom
holding Dying
Warrior" (A.
Greck)

France   1978

(Des and eng C. Andréotto. Recess)

1978 (21 Oct). *Sport for All.* *P* 13.
2282 **839** 1 f. reddish violet, magenta & new bl   20   8

(Des and eng P. Béquet. Recess)

1978 (11 Nov). *Polish War Veterans' Monument.* *P* 13.
2283 **840** 1 f. 70, lake, orange-verm & turq-grn   35   12

843 "The Hare and the Tortoise"   **844** Human Figures balanced on Globe

841 Railway Carriage, Rethondes, and Armistice Monument   **842** Symbols of Readaptation

(Des and eng C. Andréotto. Recess)

(Des and eng G. Bétemps. Recess)

1978 (2 Dec). *Red Cross Fund. Fables of La Fontaine.* *T* **843** and similar vert design. *P* 13.
2286   1 f.+25 c. bistre-brown, scarlet-vermilion and deep yellow-green   25   12
2287   1 f. 20+30 c. deep yellow-green, scarlet-vermilion and bistre-brown   30   12
Design:—1 f. 20, "The Town and the Country Mouse".

1978 (11 Nov). *60th Anniv of Armistice.* *P* 13.
2284 **841** 1 f. 20, blue-black   25   12

(Des O. Baillais. Eng C. Guillame. Recess)

(Des and eng G. Bétemps. Recess)

1978 (18 Nov). *Help for Convalescents.* *P* 13.
2285 **842** 1 f. bright scarlet, dp brn & dull orge   20   8

1978 (9 Dec). *30th Anniv of Declaration of Human Rights.* *P* 13.
2288 **844** 1 f. 70, Prussian blue & reddish brn ..   35   15

Leading the field is Gibbons world-famous *Stamp Monthly* offering you an attractive magazine that contains so much for stamp enthusiasts everywhere. Just look at some of the interesting features:

- Latest information on all new issues.
- Well written, lavishly illustrated articles.
- The all-important Supplement to the Stanley Gibbons Catalogue.
- The Crown Agents Gazette with latest news and lists of forthcoming issues.
- Regular Stamp Market, Great Britain and Through the Magnifying Glass features.
- A vast and varied selection of advertisements from the stamp trade.
- Large size format—297 × 210 mm.

As a collector you cannot afford to be without *Stamp Monthly*. Enter a subscription, and keep in touch with all events in this ever popular hobby by courtesy of Gibbons—the First Name in Stamps.

France COUNCIL OF EUROPE, U.N.E.S.C.O.

COUNCIL OF EUROPE STAMPS

Until 25 March, 1960, these stamps could be used only by delegates and officials of the Council of Europe on official correspondence at Strasbourg. From that date they could be used on all correspondence posted within the Council of Europe building.

CONSEIL
DE L'EUROPE
(C **1**)

C **2** Council Flag

1958 (14 Jan). *No.* 1354 *optd with Type* C **1**.   1·10   2·00
C1   35 f. cerise and carmine-lake   ..   ..

(Des and eng Decaris.   Recess)

1958–59. *P* 13.
C2	C **2**	8 f. ultram, red-orge & mar (10.10.58)	12	12
C3		20 f. ultram, yell & yell-brn (11.10.58)	20	15
C4		25 f. ultramarine, bright purple & deep bronze-green (1.6.59) ..	30	20
C5		35 f. ultramarine and red (13.10.58)	40	40
C6		50 f. ultramarine & brt pur (1.6.59)	80	80
C2/6		*Set of* 5	1·75	1·50

New currency. 100 (old) francs=1 (new) franc

1963 (3 Jan)**–76.** *P* 13.
C 7	C **2**	20 c. ultramarine, yellow & yell brn ..	20	15
C 8		25 c. ultram, brt pur & dp bronze-grn ..	45	40
C 9		25 c. ultramarine, yellow, red and deep green (16.1.65) ..	25	20
C10		30 c. ultram, yell & red (16.1.65)	25	20
C11		40 c. ultram, yell, red & blk (24.3.69)..	20	20
C12		50 c. ultramarine & bright purple	70	60
C13		50 c. ult, yell, red & bl-grn (20.2.71) ..	30	25
C14		60 c. ultram, yell, red & vio (16.1.65)..	40	30
C15		70 c. ultramarine, yellow, red and purple-brown (24.3.69)	1·00	75
C7/15		*Set of* 9	3·50	2·50

1975 (22 Nov)**–76.** *As Type* C **2**, *but inscribed "FRANCE".*
C16	60 c. multicoloured	20	20
C17	80 c. yellow, ultramarine & dp carmine	30	25
C18	1 f. multicoloured (16.10.76)	50	45
C19	1 f. 20, multicoloured ..	50	45
C16/19	*Set of* 4	1·40	1·25

C **3** New Council of Europe
Building, Strasbourg

C **4** New Council of Europe
Building with Human Rights
Symbol

(Des and eng E. Lacaque.   Recess)

1977 (22 Jan).   *P* 13.
C20	C **3**	80 c. carmine-red, yellow-brn & brn	20	20
C21		1 f. chestnut, new blue & myrtle-grn	20	20
C22		1 f. 40, slate, myrtle-grn & bistre-brn	30	30

1978 (14 Oct). *25th Anniv of European Convention on Human Rights. P* 13.
C23	C **4**	1 f. 20, slate-blk, brt pur & dp dull grn	50	45
C24		1 f. 70, dp turq-bl, new bl & emer	60	50

U.N.E.S.C.O. STAMPS

For use on correspondence posted within the U.N.E.S.C.O. headquarters building.

U **1** Buddha and Hermes

(Des and eng Hertenberger.   Recess)

1961 (23 Jan)**–65.**   *P* 13.
U1	U **1**	20 c. bistre, ultramarine and sepia ..	20	15
U2		25 c. maroon, bluish green and black	20	20
U3		30 c. orange-brown & sepia (23.1.65)	25	20
U4		50 c. brown-red, bluish violet & black	65	50
U5		60 c. chestnut, mag & turq-bl (23.1.65)	40	40
U1/5		*Set of* 5	1·50	1·40

U **2** Open Book and Globe   U **3** "Human Rights"

(Des and eng Combet)

1966 (17 Dec).   *P* 13.
U6	U **2**	25 c. blackish brown .. .	15	15
U7		30 c. brown-red	20	20
U8		60 c. green	35	35

(Des and eng P. Béquet.   Recess)

1969 (8 Mar)**–75.**   *P* 13.
U 9	U **3**	30 c. red, myrtle-green & chocolate ..	12	12
U10		40 c. red, magenta and chocolate ..	20	20
U11		50 c. red, ultram & brown (13.2.71) ..	25	25
U12		70 c. red, reddish violet & slate-blue ..	1·00	70
U9/12		*Set of* 4	1·40	1·10

1975 (15 Nov).   *As Type U* **3**, *but inscribed "FRANCE".*
U13	60 c. scarlet, emerald & purple-brown	20	20
U14	80 c. scarlet, orange-brn & lake-brn ..	30	25
U15	1 f. 20, scarlet, indigo & brown-pur	50	45

U **4** "Leaf"

(Des R. Ibach.   Eng C. Durrens.   Recess)

1976 (23 Oct)**–78.**   *P* 13.
U16	U **4**	80 c. dp turq-bl, bistre & slate-pur ..	20	20
U17		1 f. orange, yellowish grn & new bl ..	20	20
U18		1 f. 20, ultramarine, brown-red and bright green (14.10.78) ..	25	25
U19		1 f. 40, chestnut, deep magenta and deep olive-brown	30	30
U20		1 f. 70, scarlet-vermilion, emerald and yellow brown (14.10.78) ..	45	45

PHILATELIC DOCUMENTS

Following the opening of the French Postal Museum, in December 1973, the Postal Administration introduced, with each new issue of stamps, a "Philatelic Document", the income from which was to help cover running costs of the Museum.

The documents are produced by the National Printing Works, Périgueux. They are printed on high quality paper, size 210×297 mm, and include the text of the official announcement of the stamp issue, connected illustrations, a single-coloured proof specimen and the actual stamp with first day cancellation. The "Document" also carries the embossed seal of the French Government Printing Works. Each document is sold for 8 f. plus the face value of the issue, and their sale is limited to 8 weeks, starting on the date of issue.

11-78

Type	Cat. no.	Issue			Price
00-73	2025	Opening of Postal Museum	..	..	5·00
01-74	2026	"Arphila 75" International Stamp			
		Exhibition	..	..	5·50
02-74	2027	Red Cross Fund. St. L.-M. Grignion			
		de Montfort	..	..	9·00
03-74	2031	Stamp Day	..	..	9·00
04-74	2032	Opening of Charles de Gaulle Airport	..		8·00
05-74	2033	"Arphila 75" – "Cardinal Richelieu"			
		(P. de Champaigne)	..	..	8·00
06-74	2037	Centenary of French Alpine Club	..		7·00
07-74	2038/9	Europa	..	..	7·00
08-74	2040	French Lifeboat Service	..	..	7·50
09-74	2041	25th Anniv of Council of Europe	..		8·00
10-74	2045	Tourist Publicity. St. Florent	..	..	6·50
11-74	2046	Nature Conservation	..	..	8·00
12-74	2049	General Koenig	..	..	7·50
13-74	2052	47th Congress of French Philatelic			
		Societies, Colmar	..	..	7·00
14-74	2048	30th Anniv of Normandy Landing	..		8·00
15-74	2053	World Chess Championships	..	..	9·00
16-74	2054	300th Anniv of "Hôtel des Invalides"	..		8·00
17-74	2051	Order of Liberation	..	..	8·00
18-74	2042	Tourist Publicity. Salers	..	..	8·00
19-74	2028	Red Cross Fund. Francis Poulenc	..		5·00

Type	Cat. no.	Issue			Price
20-74	2055	Completion of Turbotrain Project	..		5·50
21-74	2043	Tourist Publicity. Lot Valley	..	..	4·50
22-74	2034	"Arphila 75" – "Abstract after			
		Original Work" (Miro)	..	..	6·50
23-74	2056	Completion of Phénix Nuclear			
		Generator	..	..	5·50
24-74	2057	Centenary of U.P.U.	..	..	7·50
25-74	1904a,				
	1905a/b	"Marianne"	..	..	9·00
26-74	2058	500th Birth Anniv of Copernicus	..		7·50
27-74	2044	Tourist Publicity. Basilica of			
		St. Nicolas-de-Port	..	..	8·00
28-74	2047	Nature Conservation	..	..	7·00
29-74	2035	"Arphila 75" – "Loing Canal" (Sisley)			6·50
30-74	2036	"Arphila 75" – "Homage to Nicolas			
		Fouquet" (de Mathieu)	..	..	6·50
31-74	2029	Red Cross Fund. Jean Giraudoux	..		7·50
32-74	2030	Red Cross Fund. Jules Barbey			
		d'Aurevilly	..	..	7·50
33-74	2050	Resistance Medal	..	..	7·50
34-74	2059/60	Red Cross Fund. Seasons	..	..	7·50
01-75	2064	Tourist Publicity. Château de			
		Rochechouart	..	..	6·50

France Philatelic Documents

Type	Cat. no.	Issue	Price
02-75	2061	Birth Centenary of Dr. Albert Schweitzer	6·50
03-75	2063	Tourist Publicity. St. Pol-de-Léon	7·00
04-75	2062	Tourist Publicity. Palace of Justice, Rouen	5·50
05-75	2065	Nature Conservation	6·50
06-75	2066	Red Cross Fund. Edmond Michelet	5·50
07-75	2070	"Arphila 75"	6·50
08-75	2075	Stamp Day	6·50
09-75	2071	"Arphila 75"	6·50
10-75	2076	President Georges Pompidou Commemoration	5·50
11-75	2072	"Arphila 75"	6·50
12-75	2077/8	Europa	5·50
13-75	2079	1st World Machine-Tools Exhibition ..	5·00
14-75	2067	Red Cross Fund. Robert Schuman	5·00
15-75	2073	"Arphila 75"	6·50
16-75	2080	Centenary of the French Senate	5·00
17-75	2081	Centenary of Metre Conversion	5·00
18-75	2082	Development of Gazelle Helicopter ..	5·00
MS2074		"Arphila 75"	18·00
19-75	2083	Students' Health Foundation ..	5·50
20-75	2084	Opening of Metro Regional Express Service	5·50
21-75	2068	Red Cross Fund. Eugene Thomas ..	5·00
22-75	2085	80th Anniv of Peoples Theatre, Brussang	5·00
23-75	2088	Regions of France. Loire ..	5·00
24-75	2092	30th Anniv of Concentration Camps' Liberation	5·00
25-75	2089	Regions of France. Auvergne ..	4·75
26-75	2093	30th Anniv of Mine Clearance Service	4·75
27-75	2094	New Towns	5·00
28-75	2087	Regions of France. Burgundy ..	5·00
29-75	2096	International Women's Year ..	4·50
30-75	2095	Opening of St. Nazaire Bridge ..	4·75
31-75	2086	Regions of France. Picardy ..	4·75
32-75	2069	Red Cross Fund. Andre Siegfried	4·75
33-75	2097	50th Anniv of Franco-Soviet Diplomatic Relations ..	4·50
34-75	2098/9	Red Cross Fund. Seasons ..	5·50
35-75	2090	Regions of France. Poitou-Charentes	4·50
36-75	2100	French Sailing Ships	5·00
37-75	2091	Regions of France. Nord – Pas-de-Calais	4·50
01-76	2101	First Commercial Flight of "Concorde", Paris–Rio de Janeiro ..	6·50
02-76	2106	Regions of France. Midi-Pyrenees	4·75
03-76	2108	French Art. Wood carving, St. Genis-des-Fontaines ..	5·00
04-76	2102	Regions of France. Centre ..	3·75
05-76	2109	French Art. "Venus of Brassempouy" ..	5·00
06-76	2114	Stamp Day	5·00
07-76	2120	Tourist Publicity. Château de Malmaison	3·75
08-76	2122	50th Anniv of Central Marine Officers' Reserve Association	4·00
09-76	2121	49th Congress of French Philatelic Societies	3·75
10-76	2123	"Juvarouen 1976" Youth Stamp Exhibition	4·00
11-76	2124/5	Europa	3·75
12-76	2126	Bicentenary of American Revolution (double size)	6·50
13-76	2127	Red Cross Fund. Marshal Moncey	3·50
14-76	2103	Regions of France. Aquitaine ..	3·75
15-76	2104	Regions of France. Limousin ..	3·75
16-76	2134	60th Anniv of Verdun Offensive	3·75
17-76	2133	"Communication"	4·00
18-76	2136	30th Anniv of Free French Association	4·50
19-76	2135	Nature Conservation	4·50
20-76	2137	Launch of "Symphonie No. 1" Satellite	4·25
21-76	2115	Tourist Publicity. Château de Bonaguil	4·50
22-76	2119	Tourist Publicity. Ussel ..	4·00
23-76	2138	"La Fête" (Summer Festivals Exhibition, Tuileries, Paris) ..	3·75
24-76	2139	Olympic Games, Montreal ..	4·50
25-76	2140	Centenary of Reserve Officers Corps ..	3·75
26-76	2128	Red Cross Fund. Max Jacob ..	3·75
27-76	2110	French Art. "La Joie de Vivre" (Robert Delaunay) ..	4·50
28-76	1904b, 1905c/d, 1906/a	"Marianne"	5·00
29-76	2129	Red Cross Fund. Mounet-Sully	2·75
30-76	2130	Red Cross Fund. General Daumesnil ..	2·75

Type	Cat. no.	Issue	Price
31-76	2111	French Art. Rameses II in war chariot	3·75
32-76	2112	French Art. Painting by Carzou (double size)	4·50
33-76	2131	Red Cross Fund. Eugene Fromentin ..	3·25
34-76	2117	Tourist Publicity. Basque Coast, Biarritz	3·25
35-76	2141	Centenary of Telephone ..	3·50
36-76	2142	10th Anniv of International Tourist Film Association	3·25
37-76	2118	Tourist Publicity. Thiers ..	3·25
38-76	2143	10th Anniv of National Police Force ..	3·25
39-76	2105	Regions of France. Guyane ..	3·50
40-76	2144	European Research into Nuclear Science	3·25
41-76	2132	Red Cross Fund. Anna de Noailles ..	3·00
42-76	2116	Tourist Publicity. Lodève Cathedral ..	2·50
43-76	2145	50th Anniv of French Fairs and Exhibitions Federation ..	3·00
44-76	2146/7	Red Cross Fund. Statuettes from Brou Church	3·75
45-76	2148	French Customs Service ..	2·50
46-76	2149	Atlantic Museum, Port-Louis ..	2·75
47-76	2113	French Art. "Still Life with Fruit" (Maurice de Vlaminck) ..	3·75
01-77	2152	Regions of France. Franche-Comté ..	3·75
02-77	2154	Regions of France. Languedoc-Roussillon	3·75
03-77	2155	Regions of France. Rhône-Alpes	3·75
04-77	2151	Regions of France. Martinique ..	3·25
05-77	2158	Georges-Pompidou National Centre of Art and Culture ..	5·00
06-77	2150	Regions of France. Réunion ..	3·25
07-77	2159	French Art. "Mantes Bridge" (Corot) ..	3·50
08-77	2161	Dunkirk Port Extensions ..	3·00
09-77	2153	Regions of France. Bretagne ..	3·25
10-77	2157	Regions of France. Alsace ..	3·50
11-77	2163	Stamp Day	3·00
12-77	2162	"Le Souvenir Français" ..	2·75
13-77	2176	"Philatelic Creations". "Geometric Design" (Vasarely) ..	3·50
14-77	2156	Regions of France. Champagne-Ardenne	3·50
15-77	2180/1	Europa	3·00
16-77	2179	150th Anniv of National Horticultural Society	3·00
17-77	2182	International Flower Show, Nantes ..	3·00
18-77	2183	300th Anniv of Reunification of Cambrai with France ..	2·75
19-77	2184	100th Anniv of French Catholic Institutions	3·00
20-77	2185	Meeting of European Civil Engineering Federation, Paris ..	3·00
21-77	2186	50th Congress of French Philatelic Societies	3·00
22-77	2194	50th Anniv of North Atlantic Crossings	3·75
23-77	2193	Polytechnic School, Palaiseau ..	3·25
24-77	2190	Tourist Publicity. Fontenay Abbey ..	3·00
25-77	2195	60th Anniv of French Football Cup	3·00
26-77	2196	5th Anniv of General de Gaulle Memorial	3·25
27-77	2197	25th Anniv of Junior Chambers of Commerce	2·50
28-77	2198	500th Anniv of Battle of Nancy ..	2·50
29-77	2199	500th Anniv of Union of Burgundy with France	2·75
30-77	2220	10th Anniv of International Association of French Language Parliaments	2·75
31-77	2191	Tourist Publicity. Bayeux Cathedral ..	3·25
32-77	2189	Tourist Publicity. Church at Dorat	3·00
33-77	2201	Nature Conservation	2·75
34-77	2188	Tourist Publicity. Abbey of St. Amand-les-Eaux ..	2·75
35-77	2177	"Philatelic Creations". Work by P.-Y. Trémois ..	3·75
36-77	2192	Tourist Publicity. Château de Vitré ..	3·25
37-77	2187	Tourist Publicity. Prémontrés Abbey ..	3·00
38-77	2202	French Craftsmanship	3·00
39-77	2203	Red Cross Fund. Edouard Herriot	2·75
40-77	2204	Red Cross Fund. Abbé Breuil ..	2·75
41-77	2207	30th Anniv of Economic and Social Council	2·25
42-77	2160	French Art. "Virgin and Child" (Rubens)	3·00

Type Cat. no.	Issue	Price
43-77 2205	Red Cross Fund. Guillaume de Machault	2·75
44-77 2208/9	Red Cross Fund. Carved Christmas Crib Figures from Provence	3·25
45-77 2206	Red Cross Fund. Charles Cros	2·75
46-77 2218/20	"Sabine"	3·50
47-77 2178	"Philatelic Creations". Work by R. Excoffon	3·75
48-77 2240	50th Anniv of French Table Tennis Federation	3·00
01-78 2241	Nature Conservation	3·25
02-78 2243	French Art. Tournament under Louis XIV	3·00
03-78 2244	Centenary of Return of St. Barthelemy Island to France	3·00
04-78 2245	Centenary of National Telecommunications College	2·25
05-78 2247	Regions of France. Haute-Normandie	2·75
06-78 2249	"Philatelic Creations". Work by B. Buffet	3·00
07-78 2251	Red Cross Fund. Marie Noel	3·25
08-78 2257	15th Anniv of Regional Planning Boards	3·00
09-78 2252	Red Cross Fund. Georges Bernanos	3·25
10-78 2263	Tourist Publicity. Abbey Church of Aubazine	3·00
11-78 2265	"Juvexniort" Youth Philately Exhibition	2·25
12-78 2246	Regions of France. Ile de France	2·75
13-78 2258	Tourist Publicity. Verdon Gorge	2·50
14-78 2253	Red Cross Fund. Leconte de Lisle	3·25
15-78 2261	Tourist Publicity. Notre Dame du Bec-Hellouin Abbey	2·75
16-78 2210/7, 2223, 2225, 2227 "Sabine"		4·50
17-78 2248	Regions of France. Basse-Normandie	3·25
18-78 2266	Stamp Day	3·25
19-78 2254	Red Cross Fund. Leo Tolstoy	3·25
20-78 2267	Port Cros National Park	3·00
21-78 2269	Energy Conservation	3·00

Type Cat. no.	Issue	Price
22-78 2268	"Make France Bloom"	3·25
23-78 2270	Notre Dame de Lorette, War Cemetery	3·25
24-78 2271/2	Europa	3·25
25-78 2273	51st Congress of French Philatelic Societies	2·75
26-78 2259	Tourist Publicity. Pont Neuf, Paris	2·25
27-78 2274	50th Anniv of Roland Garros Tennis Stadium	2·75
28-78 2264	Tourist Publicity. Fontrevaud Abbey	3·00
29-78 2219, 2221, 2222, 2224, 2226 "Sabine"		3·25
30-78 2260	Tourist Publicity. Church of St. Saturnin	2·75
31-78 2262	Tourist Publicity. Château d'Esquelbecq	3·00
32-78 2255	Red Cross Fund. Voltaire and J.-J. Rousseau	3·25
33-78 2275	Handicrafts	3·00
34-78 2256	Red Cross Fund. Claude Bernard	3·25
35-78 2277	State Printing Office	2·75
36-78 2276	300th Anniv of Reunion of Franche-Comte with France	3·00
37-78 2278	300th Anniv of Return of Valenciennes and Maubeuge	3·00
38-78 2279	50th Anniv of Academie de Philatelie	2·75
39-78 2242	Nature Conservation	3·25
40-78 2280	50th Anniv of First Airmail Flight Villacoublay-Pauillac	3·00
41-78 2281	19th World Gymnastics Championships, Strasbourg	3·00
42-78 2282	Sport for All	3·00
43-78 2283	Polish War Veterans' War Memorial	3·25
44-78 2284	60th Anniv of Armistice	3·00
45-78 2285	Help for Convalescents	3·00
46-78 2286/7	Red Cross Fund. Fables of La Fontaine	3·00
47-78 2250	"Philatelic Creations". Work by Y. Brayer	3·00
48-78 2288	30th Anniv of Declaration of Human Rights	3·25

Leading the field is Gibbons world-famous *Stamp Monthly* offering you an attractive magazine that contains so much for stamp enthusiasts everywhere. Just look at some of the interesting features:

- Latest information on all new issues.
- Well written, lavishly illustrated articles.
- The all-important Supplement to the Stanley Gibbons Catalogue.
- The Crown Agents Gazette with latest news and lists of forthcoming issues.
- Regular Stamp Market, Great Britain and Through the Magnifying Glass features.
- A vast and varied selection of advertisements from the stamp trade.
- Large size format—297 × 210mm.

As a collector you cannot afford to be without *Stamp Monthly*. Enter a subscription, and keep in touch with all events in this ever popular hobby by courtesy of Gibbons — the First Name in Stamps.

INDEX TO STAMP DESIGNS

A. DEFINITIVE ISSUES

Most of the definitive stamp designs have allegorical themes, some of which, i.e. 'Marianne', are used repeatedly. Many of these designs are known and identified by their designers and in the following list designers' names are shown in *italics*. The cross-references include issues which have the basic design overprinted or surcharged. Where the same design appears on more than one stamp in an issue only the first stamps is referenced.

B. AIRMAIL ISSUES

The following is a checklist of definitive and commemorative stamps specifically issued for the conveyance of mail by air. All of the issues, except Nos. 464/5, are inscribed "POSTE AERIENNE".

455/6, 464/5, 483/4*a*, 523, 534/40, 541, 967/70, 1013, 1024/5, 1026, 1055/9, 1076, 1194/7, 1252, 1318/20, 1457/60, 1823, 1890/3, 1907, 2101, 2194.

C. PICTORIAL, PORTRAIT, CHARITY AND COMMEMORATIVE ISSUES

This index provides in a condensed form a key to the numerous portrait and pictorial stamps of France from 1914 onwards. In order to save space, portrait stamps are usually listed under surnames only, views under the name of the town or city, and other issues under the main French inscription. Where the same design or subject appears on more than one stamp, only the first stamp of each series is indicated. As a rule accents are omitted unless they appear on the stamps.

France Design Index

Leading the field is Gibbons world-famous *Stamp Monthly* offering you an attractive magazine that contains so much for stamp enthusiasts everywhere. Just look at some of the interesting features:

- Latest information on all new issues.
- Well written, lavishly illustrated articles.
- The all-important Supplement to the Stanley Gibbons Catalogue.
- The Crown Agents Gazette with latest news and lists of forthcoming issues.
- Regular Stamp Market, Great Britain and Through the Magnifying Glass features.
- A vast and varied selection of advertisements from the stamp trade.
- Large size format—297 × 210mm.

As a collector you cannot afford to be without *Stamp Monthly*. Enter a subscription, and keep in touch with all events in this ever popular hobby by courtesy of Gibbons — the First Name in Stamps.

PARIS BALLOON POSTS, 1870–71

During the siege of Paris in the Franco-Prussian War, mail and newspapers were carried by balloons and these are of great interest to philatelists. The balloons were operated by the "Compagnie des Aérostiers" (which applied their own cachet on the back of the mail), by the postal administration and also privately with official permission to carry mail. In all 56 mail-carrying flights took place and all but five arrived safely.

Many factors have to be taken into account to establish the value of an ordinary cover. The principal elements are (a) whether it is possible to identify the name of the balloon from the postal markings; (b) the stamps with which it is franked; (c) its destination; (d) scarce cancellations or cachets. Apart from covers there were letter journals, journals, news agency letters, official circulars, military post, etc., and these are listed but there were also other items such as private circulars, scarce cancellations and cachets and mail entrusted to aeronauts which are outside the scope of our list.

An unofficial printed letter despatched by balloon 'Le Général Faidherbe'

I. Ordinary Covers without Identification

Franked with two 10 c. T **5**, one 20 c. T **5**, one 20 c. Nos. 190/2 or one 10 c. T **5** (postcards) .. .. *Price* 50·00

II. Ordinary Covers franked as above with positive Identification

Name of Balloon	Despatch Postmarks	Arrival Cachets	Price
Neptune*	18–22.9.70	23–25.9.70	£1300
La Ville de Florence ..	23–24.9.70	27–28.9.70	£120
Les Etats-Unis	25–28.9.70	29.9–3.10.70	85·00
Céleste	29.7.30	Before 7.10.70	75·00
Unnamed and unmanned ..	27–29.9.70 (cards)	None or 15–22.10.70 ..	70·00
Armand Barbès*	30.9–6.10.70	Before 11.10.70	70·00
Unnamed	30.9–8.10.70	La Courneuve	60·00
Washington	7–11.10.70	12–14.10.70	60·00
Louis Blanc*	7–11.10.70	12–14.10.70	60·00
	Very difficult to distinguish mail on these two flights		
Godefroy-Cavaignac ..	12–13.10.70	15–18.10.70	60·00
Jean-Bart I	11–14 (1st colln.) 10.70	15–19.10.70 ..	60·00
Jules-Favre I	14–15.10.70	17–19.10.70 ..	60·00
Jean-Bart II	14–15.10.70	17–19.10.70 ..	60·00
Victor Hugo*	16–18 (1st colln.) 10.70	20–22.10.70 ..	60·00
Lafayette	18.10.70 (later collns.) ..	19–23.10.70 ..	70·00
Garibaldi*	19–21.10.70	23.10–3.11.70 ..	65·00
Montgolfier	22–23.10.70	None (captured) ..	£700
Vauban	24–26.10.70	29.10–6.11.70 ..	65·00
Colonel Charras* ..	27–29 (2nd colln.) 10.70 ..	30.10–2.11.70 ..	60·00
Fulton	29 (later collns.) 10.70–1.11.70	3–4.11.70	65·00
Ferdinand-Flocon* ..	2–3.11.70	5–6.11.70	70·00
Galilé	2–4 (1st colln.) 11.70 ..	None (captured) ..	70·00
Ville de Chateaudun* ..	4 (other collns.)–6 (1st colln.). 11.70	7–10.11.70	70·00
Gironde	6–8 (1st colln.) 11.70 ..	9–11.11.70	70·00
Daguerre	8 (later collns.)–11.11.70 ..	None or 20–29.11.70 ..	75·00
Général Uhrich* ..	12–18.11.70	20–27.11.70	60·00
Archimède	19–20.11.70	Before 30.11.70 ..	70·00
Ville d'Orléans* ..	21–24.11.70	12.70–1.71 (Recovered from sea)	80·00
		Do. (Landed in Norway) ..	75·00
Jacquard	24–28.11.70	3–28.12.70	£800
Jules-Favre II* ..	28–30.11.70	Before 5.12.70	70·00
Franklin	1–4.12.70	5–6.12.70	70·00
Denis-Papin	5–6.12.70	7.12.70	£325
Armée de Bretagne* ..	5–6.12.70	8–10.12.70	70·00
Général Renault* ..	7–10.12.70	Before 15.12.70 ..	70·00
Ville de Paris* ..	10 (7th colln.)–13.12.70 ..	None (captured) ..	80·00

Parmentier	..	..	..	.. 14–16.12.70	..	..	.. 22–31.12.70 .. .. .. 70·00
Davy	..	..	.◦	.. 17.12.70	..	..	.. 18–21.12.70 .. .. .. 90·00
Général Chanzy*	..	..	..	.. 18 (1st to 6th collns.) 12.70		..	None (captured) £500
Lavoisier	..	..	..	.. 18 (7th colln.)–21.12.70	..	..	22–28.12.70 .. .. .. 75·00
La Délivrance*	..	..	..	.. 22.12.70	..	..	.. 23–26.12.70 .. .. .. 75·00
Tourville	..	..	..	.. 23–26.12.70 ..	..	..	27–29.12.70 .. .. .. 75·00
Bayard	..	..	..	.. 27–28.12.70 ..	..	..	30.12.70–3.1.71 .. .. 75·00
Armée de la Loire*	..	..	..	.. 29–30.12.70	..	..	1–3.1.71 .. .. .. 75·00
Newton	..	..	..	.. 31.12.70–3.1.71	..	..	Before 9.1.71 .. .. .. 75·00
Duquesne	..	..	..	.. 4–8.1.71	..	..	10–18.1.71 .. .. .. 75·00
Gambetta*	..	..	..	.. 9.1.71	..	..	11–17.1.71 .. .. .. 75·00
Kepler	..	..	..	.. 10.1.71	..	..	11–13.1.71 .. .. .. 75·00
Général Faidherbe*	..	..	..	.. 11–12.1.71	..	..	13–15.1.71 .. .. .. 75·00
Vaucanson	..	..	..	.. 13–14.1.71	..	..	15–17.1.71 .. .. .. 75·00
Poste de Paris*	..	..	..	.. 15–17.1.71	..	..	21–29.1.71 .. .. .. 75·00
Général Bourbaki*	..	..	..	.. 18–19.1.71	..	..	23–31.1.71 .. .. .. 75·00
Général Daumesnil	..	..	..	.. 20–21.1.71	..	..	22–23.1.71 .. .. .. 80·00
Torricelli	..	..	..	.. 22–23.1.71	..	..	29–30.1.71 .. .. .. 75·00
Richard Wallace*	..	..	..	.. 24–26.1.71	..	..	From 7.2.71 (Recovered from sea) .. £750
Général Cambronne	..	..	..	.. 27.1.71	..	..	28.1–4.2.71 .. .. .. £250

* Balloons operated by "Compagnie des Aérostriers"

Notes. The *Jean-Bart I* was also known as the *Guillaume Tell* and the *Christophe Colomb,* whilst the *Jean-Bart II* was also called *Lafayette.* On the other hand the balloon listed as *Lafayette* was also known as the *Republique Universelle.*

III. Covers franked with rarer Stamps

The value of covers under Sections I or II is increased by the following amounts if franked with the stamps listed below:—

			Price				Price				Price
10 c.	T **3**, imperf.		£700	20 c.	T **3**, perf.		£100	4 c.	T **5**		£400
20 c.	Do.		£550	40 c.	Do.		£180	30 c.	T **5**		40·00
40 c.	Do.		£750	80 c.	Do.		£350	40 c.	T **5**		70·00
1 c.	T **3**, perf.		£550	1 c.	T **5**		£300	80 c.	T **5**		£200
5 c.	Do.		£120	2 c.	T **5**		£400	10 c.	Nos. 135/6		50·00
10 c.	Do.		£150					40 c.	Nos. 140/2		60·00

IV. Destinations

The value of covers when addressed to certain foreign countries and franked accordingly, are as follows:—

	Price from
20 c. to occupied France without arrival cachet (normal)	60·00
20 c. to occupied France with French arrival cachet	90·00
20 c. to occupied France with German arrival cachet	£180
20 c. to Corsica or Monaco	£250
20 c. to Algeria	80·00
25 c. to Luxembourg	£700
30 c. to Belgium, Great Britain and Switzerland	60·00
40 c. or 50 c. to Germany without arrival cachet	85·00
40 c. or 50 c. to Germany with arrival cachet	£225
40 c. to Egypt, Italy, Netherlands, Portugal, Spain or to Turkey by sea	£120
40 c. to Rumania	£600
50 c. to Denmark, Reunion or Senegal	£550
60 c. to Austria	£150
70 c. to Netherlands Antilles, Norway or U.S.A. (also 80 c.)	£500
70 c. to Sweden	£700
80 c. to Turkey by land	£325
80 c. to Argentina, Brazil, Chile, Mexico, Panama or Russia	£600
80 c. to Cape of Good Hope, China, Haiti, Japan, Malaya, Mauritius, Philippine Is. or Puerto Rico	£850
1 f. to Peru	£850

Clear arrival cachets on most of the scarcer items increase the value considerably.

V. Letter Journals

These contain a printed portion giving news of the siege and a blank area for correspondence.

		Price
(a) *La Gazette des Absents* (32 issues)		
No. 1 by *Montgolfier*		£1000
No. 1 by others		£400
No. 10 by *Ville d'Orléans* recovered from sea with PP cachet		90·00
No. 10 by *Ville d'Orléans* landed in Norway		85·00
No. 11 by *Jacquard*		£900
No. 11 by others		£350
No. 31 by *Richard Wallace*		£900
No. 31 by *Général Cambronne* (arrival up to 4.2.71)		£350
No. 32 by *Richard Wallace*		£900
No. 32 by *Général Cambronne* (arrival up to 4.2.71)		£350
Others (flown)	*From*	£100
Nos. 4, 7, 13, 14, 15 to 20 with printed supplement		75·00
Unflown copies (new condition)		20·00
(b) *La Dépéche-Ballon* (27 issues)		
No. 1		£350
No. 8 by *Ville d'Orléans* recovered from sea with PP cachet		£125
No. 8 by *Ville d'Orléans* landed in Norway		£150
No. 9 by *Jacquard*		£900
No. 26 by *Richard Wallace*		£950
No. 27 by *Général Cambronne*		£400
Others (flown)	*From*	85·00
Unflown copies (new condition)	*From*	25·00

(c) *Other Letter Journals*
  Le Ballon-Poste on pink paper (21 issues)

Nos. 1 to 4	Each	£300
No. 8 by *Jacquard*		£1000
Others (flown)	From	£120
On salmon paper (31 October)		£750
La Cloche 26 and 30 November	Each	£500
L'Echo des Etrangers (5 issues)	Each	£1250
L'Electeur Libre (29 November)		£1000
L'Enveloppe-Gazette (13 issues) 7 to 19 December	Each	£1250
Le Journal-Ballon (4 issues)	Each	£750
Le Journal-Poste (17 issues)		
Nos. 12, 13, 14, 16 with envelope showing name of journal	Each	£600
Nos. 3 to 7 with supplement	Each	£500
Others (flown)	From	£200
Le Moniteur Aérien (2 issues)	Each	£1500
Le Montgolfier (15 November)		£1600
Le Soir (17 issues)	Each	£600
Unflown copies of the above journals (new condition)	From	30·00

VI. Journals

Certain Paris newspapers printed special editions on pelure paper intended for despatch by balloon. There was no space available for correspondence.

		Price
La Chronique Illustrée (21 December) with envelope		£1200
Les Dernières Nouvelles (3 issues) with envelope	Each	£1000
Le Gaulois, large format (13 issues)	Each	£1200
Le Gaulois, small format (2 issues)	Each	£1300
Le Journal des Debats (5 issues)	Each	£1300
Journal Le Français (2 issues) with envelope	Each	£1400
Le Journal Officiel (7 issues flown) with band	Each	£1300
Le National (1 issue) with envelope		£750
Les Nouvelles du Matin (3 December)		£1000
Les Nouvelles du Soir (24 October)		£1000
Paris Journal		£1200
Le Petit Journal (7 issues) with envelope	Each	£1000
Le Petit Journal, reproduction photo (4 issues) with envelope	Each	£1200
La Revue des Deux Mondes (1 issue) with envelope		£1200
Le Siècle (2 issues) with envelope	Each	£1200
Unflown copies of the above journals (new condition)	From	20·00
Other journals which are not known to have been flown:		
L'Ami de la France, Le Journal d'Outre-Mer, Le Moniteur des Communes, Les Nouvelles (new condition)	From	20·00

VII. News Agency Letters

Press notices published by Press Agencies

Agence Fournier, with envelope		£700
Dernières Nouvelles (Havas), 20, 23, 26 September, with envelope	Each	£900
Correspondance Havas (French edition)		£150
Correspondance Havas (German edition)		£275
Gazette de Francfort		£800
Nouvelle Press Bible de Vienne		£1000

VIII. Official Circulars

Circulaire de la Compagnie du Chemin de fer P.L.M...		£900
Conseil Général des Hospices		£950
Ministère des Finances aux Directeurs des Manufactures		£850
Circulaire du Directeur général des Manufactures de l'Etat		£850
Circulaire de l'Assistance Publique		£850
Circulaire de la Direction Générale des Douanes		£950
Unflown copies of any of the above (new condition)	Each	50·00

IX. Military Post Cachets

(a) *Army of the Rhine*
  Cancelled AR, ARAL, ARAM, ARAN and dated cachet of the Rhine Army   From   £400

(b) *French Army*
  Cancelled AFA to AFJ and AFM or with dated cachet of the French Army, Bureau A, 14th Corps   From   £450

There were also other means of carrying messages which can be of interest to the specialist but are outside the scope of this list. They include the use of pigeon post, which called forth a very early example of the use of micro-photography; *Papillons de Metz*, the use of small paper or silk balloons to which packages were attached at Metz; and *Boules de Moulins*, a kind of zinc ball containing messages which were centred at Moulins-sur-Allier for putting into the Seine, in the hope that they would be picked up in Paris.

ALBUM LISTS

Please write for our latest lists of albums and accessories. These will be sent free on request.

FRENCH POST OFFICES ABROAD

The following table covers those offices of the French Postal Administration, situated in foreign countries, which, during some period of their existence, used the stamps of France.

Offices in the French colonial empire are excluded, as are those in Algeria, together with the post offices open in Tunisia after the Treaty of Bardo (12 May 1881).

In the table the French names actually used by the offices are shown in capitals, followed by the modern equivalent, where this is necessary.

The postal markings used by these post offices varied, but many utilized the numbers assigned to them in their cancellations. The original system, known as the "petit chiffres" (small figures), was introduced in 1852, but, due to the expansion of the network, it became necessary to reorganise the system in 1862. The second series, known as the "grand chiffres" (large figures) continued until 1876, when most of the numeral cancellations were replaced by circular date stamps. Not all offices were issued with numeral cancellations during the "grand chiffres" period.

The information given in this table has been adapted from *Catalogue Specialise des Timbres de France; tome* I and is used with the permission of Editions Yvert et Tellier.

| | | | P.O. Numbers | | |
Office	Opened	Closed	Small Series	Large Series	
ALEXANDRETTA (Iskenderun) Turkish Empire					
(Turkey)	Oct 1852	Aug 1914	3766	5079	(a)
ALEXANDRIE (Alexandria) Egypt	6 May 1837	31 Mar 1931	3704	5080	(b)
BEYROUTH (Beirut) Turkish Empire (Lebanon)	1840	Aug 1914	3706	5082	(a)
LE CAIRE (Cairo) Egypt	Nov 1865	11 Mar 1875	—	5119	
CANDIE (Herakleion) Crete (Greece)	July 1897	1913	—	—	(c)
LA CANEE (Khenia) Crete (Greece)	July 1897	1913	—	—	(c)
CAVALLE (Kavalla) Turkish Empire (Greece)	1 Jan 1874	Aug 1914	—	5156	(a)
CONSTANTINOPLE—PERA Turkish Empire					
(Turkey)	1799	1920	3707	5083	(a)
—GALATA	July 1879	July 1923	—	5243	(a)
—STAMBOUL	1880	July 1923	—	5278	(a)
DARDANELLES (Canakkale) Turkish Empire (Turkey)	1835	July 1923	3708	5084	(a)
DEDEAGH (Alexandroupolis) Turkish Empire					
(Greece)	1 Jan 1874	Aug 1914	—	5155	(a)
ENOS Turkish Empire (Turkey)	Jan 1874	Apr 1875	—	5153	
FINANARANTSOA Madagascar	After 1880	1896	—	—	(d)
GALATZ (Galati) Moldavia (Rumania)	Nov 1857	16 Jan 1875	4008	5085	
GALLIPOLI Turkish Empire (Turkey)	June 1852	Feb 1872	3767	5086	
LA GOULETTE Tunisia	Nov 1867	1 July 1888	—	5121	
HIERAPETRA Crete (Greece)	July 1897	Dec 1899	—	—	
IBRAILA (Bràila) Wallachia (Rumania)	Nov 1857	16 Jan 1875	4009	5087	
INEBOLI (Inebolu) Turkish Empire (Turkey)	Aug 1857	Aug 1876	4010	5088	
JAFFA Turkish Empire (Israel)	June 1852	Aug 1914	3768	5089	(a)
JERUSALEM Turkish Empire (Israel)	Aug 1900	Aug 1914	—	—	(a)
KERASSUNDE (Giresun) Turkish Empire (Turkey)	Aug 1857	Aug 1914	4011	5090	(a)
KUSTENDJE (Constanta) Turkish Empire (Rumania)	1 Sept 1869	April 1879	—	5139	
LAGOS (Port-Lagos) Turkish Empire (Greece)	Jan 1874	April 1875	—	5154	
LATTAQUIE (Latakia) Turkish Empire (Syria)	June 1852	Aug 1914	3769	5091	(a)
MAHANORO Madagascar	After 1880	1896	—	—	(d)
MAJUNGA Madagascar	After 1880	1896	—	—	(d)
MERSINA (Mersin) Turkish Empire (Turkey)	June 1852	Aug 1914	3770	5092	(a)
METELIN (Mytilene) Turkish Empire (Greece)	June 1852	April 1872	3771	5093	
MONACO Monaco	June 1860	3 June 1885	4222	2387	
MONTE-CARLO Monaco	10 Dec 1884	30 June 1885	—	7571	
NOSSIE-VEY Madagascar	After 1880	1896	—	—	(d)
ORDOU Turkish Empire (Turkey)	May 1869	Aug 1876	—	5097	

Office	Opened	Closed	Small Series	P.O. Numbers Large Series	
PORT-LAGOS Turkish Empire (Greece)	1880	1898	—	5271	(a)
PORT-SAID Egypt	18 Mar 1867	31 Mar 1931	—	5129	(b)
RETHYMNO Crete (Greece)	July 1897	1913	—	—	(c)
RHODES Turkish Empire (Greece)	June 1852	July 1923	3772	5094	(a)
RODOSTO (Tekirdağ) Turkish Empire (Turkey)	Feb 1872	Aug 1876	—	5086	
SALONIQUE (Salonika) Turkish Empire (Greece)	Nov 1857	Aug 1914	4012	5095	(a)
SAMSOUN (Samsun) Turkish Empire (Turkey)	Nov 1857	Aug 1914	4013	5096	(a)
SAN NICOLO (Ayios Nikolaos) Crete (Greece)	July 1897	Dec 1899	—	—	
SFAX Tunisia	Jan 1881	1 July 1888	—	5262	
SHANGHAI China	Nov 1862	31 Dec 1922	—	5104	(e)
SINOPE Turkish Empire (Turkey)	Nov 1857	May 1869	4014	5097	
SITIA Crete (Greece)	July 1897	Dec 1899	—	—	
SMYRNE (Izmir) Turkish Empire (Turkey)	1835	Aug 1914	3709	5098	(a)
SUEZ Egypt	27 Oct 1862	Dec 1888	—	5105	
SULINA Turkish Empire (Rumania)	Nov 1857	April 1879	4015	5099	
TAMATAVE Madagascar	After 1880	1896	—	—	(d)
TANANARIVE Madagascar	After 1880	1896	—	—	(d)
TANGER (Tangier) Morocco	Nov 1862	1 Oct 1913	—	5106	
TIEN-TSIN (Tientsin) China	16 Mar 1889	31 Dec 1922	—	—	(e)
TREBIZONDE (Trabzon) Turkish Empire (Turkey)	Nov 1857	Aug 1914	4016	5100	(a)
TRIPOLI Turkish Empire (Libya)	1880	1912	—	5264	
TRIPOLI Turkish Empire (Lebanon)	1852	Aug 1914	3773	5101	(a)
TULSCHA (Tulcea) Turkish Empire (Rumania)	1857	April 1879	4017	5102	
TUNIS Tunisia	1852	1 July 1888	—	5107	
VARNA Turkish Empire (Bulgaria)	Nov 1857	Aug 1878	4018	5103	
VATOMANDRY Madagascar	After 1880	1896	—	—	(d)
VOHEMAR Madgascar	After 1880	1896	—	—	(d)
VOLO Turkish Empire (Greece)	Nov 1857	1881	4019	—	
YOKOHAMA Japan	June 1865	April 1880	—	5118	
ZANZIBAR Zanzibar (Tanzania)	Jan 1889	31 July 1904	—	—	(f)

NOTES.

(a) These offices used the issues of French Post Offices in the Turkish Empire from 5 Aug 1885, often concurrently with the stamps of France.

(b) These offices used the issues of French Post Offices in Egypt from 1899.

(c) These offices used the issues of French Post Offices in Crete from Oct 1902.

(d) The French Post Offices in Madagascar used the stamps of France from 1892 until their transfer to the colonial administration in 1896.

(e) These offices used the issues of French Post Offices in China from 1894.

(f) This office used the issues of French Post Office in Zanzibar from 1894, except for a short period in July 1904 when French stamps were utilized.

ALBUM LISTS

Please write for our latest lists of albums and accessories. These will be sent free on request.

French Colonies
GENERAL ISSUES
100 Centimes=1 Franc

PRINTERS. The stamps for the General Issues of French Colonies were printed at the same works as those of the contemporary issues for France.

A. Eagle

(Die eng M. Barre. Typo)

1859–65. *Tinted paper. Imperf.*
1	A	1 c. bronze-green (1.5.62)	..	6·50	7·00
2		5 c. yellow-green (1.5.62)	..	7·00	5·50
3		10 c. bistre (1.6.59)	..	8·00	2·75
		a. Stamp turned sideways with top to left (pair)	.. ..	£325	£160
		b. Bistre-brown	..	8·00	2·75
4		20 c. pale blue (20.8.65)	..	10·00	5·50
		a. Blue (1870)	..	10·00	5·50
		b. Deep blue (1870)	..	10·00	5·50
5		40 c. orange (1.7.59)	..	6·50	3·50
		a. Pale orange-vermilion	..	6·50	3·50
6		80 c. bright rose (7.8.65)	..	22·00	21·00
		a. Deep carmine (1870)	..	22·00	21·00

This issue exists unofficially *pin-perf.*
Reprints were made in 1887 without gum in sheets of 16 (4 × 4).

B. Laureated   C. Empire   D. Laureated

1871–72. *As Types 3/5 of France. Tinted paper. Typo. Imperf.*
7	B	1 c. bronze-green (11.71)	..	25·00	21·00
8	C	5 c. green (1.72)	..	£275	£200
9	D	30 c. bistre-brown (11.71)	..	50·00	14·00
		a. Deep brown (1872)	..	50·00	14·00
10		80 c. rose-carmine (12.71)	..	£275	40·00

The 1 c. to 30 c. exist unofficially *pin-perf.*
Reprints were made in 1887 of the 1 c. and 30 c. without gum.

E. Ceres F. Ceres (small figures) G. Ceres (large figures)

1871–76. *As Type 9 of France. Typo. Imperf.*
11	E	1 c. bronze-green/azure (10.73)	..	6·50	7·00
12		2 c. brown/buff (10.8.76)	..	£170	£250
13		4 c. grey (12.7.76)	..	£3500	£225
14		5 c. green/bluish (7.72)	..	6·50	4·50
		a. Green/pale green (1875)	..	6·50	4·50

As Type 1 of France. Thin figures.
15	F	10 c. bistre (1871)	..	£110	50·00
		a. Tête-bêche (pair)	..	£10000	£7500
16		15 c. bistre (7.72)	..	95·00	5·50
17		20 c. blue (1871)	..	£170	50·00
		a. Tête-bêche (pair)	..	—	£5500
18		25 c. blue (7.72)	..	55·00	5·50
19		40 c. orange (1871)	..	80·00	4·25
		a. Wide "4" (see France No. 20)	..	£1000	£200
		b. Pale orange	..	£150	19·00

Stamps as Type 1 of France were printed from the same plates. Used copies can generally be sorted by the postmarks. Distinguishing features are the worn impressions, stouter paper and white instead of yellow gum.
Reprints were made in 1887 without gum of the 10 c. in *yellow* and the 10 c. and 25 c. in *blue* or *deep blue.*
The 4 c., No. 13, should only be purchased from experts as it is easily confused with Nos. 154/6 of France. It is, of course, typographed, whilst the French stamps are lithographed.

1872–77. *As Type 1 of France. Thick figures. Typo. Imperf.*
20	G	10 c. brown/rose (10.76)	..	70·00	5·50
21		15 c. bistre (1.77)	..	£190	45·00
22		30 c. drab (12.72)	..	35·00	7·50
		a. Grey-brown	..	35·00	7·50
23		80 c. pale rose (7.73)	..	£140	55·00
		a. Deep rose	..	£140	55·00

Nos. 11/23a exist unofficially *pin-perf.*

H. Peace and Commerce   J. Commerce

(a) Letter "N" of "INV" under "B" of "REPUBLIQUE".
(b) Letter "N" of "INV" under "U" of "REPUBLIQUE".

1877–78. *As Type 10 of France. Typo. Imperf.*
24	H	1 c. green (a) (9.77)	..	11·00	14·00
25		2 c. green (b) (6.77)	..	5·50	4·50
26		4 c. green (b) (6.77)	..	7·00	5·50
27		5 c. green (b) (6.77)	..	8·00	2·25
		a. Deep green/pale green (1878)	..	9·50	4·50
28		10 c. green (b) (1877)	..	35·00	4·50
29		15 c. grey (b) (12.77)	..	95·00	32·00
30		20 c. brown/pale yellow (b) (5.77)	..	25·00	2·50
31		25 c. blue (b) (1878)	..	£2250	75·00
		a. Ultramarine	..	16·00	4·50
32		30 c. cinnamon (a) (1878)	..	14·00	14·00
33		35 c. black/yellow (b) (1878)	..	17·00	11·00
		a. Black/orange	..	17·00	11·00
34		40 c. red/yellow (a) (4.77)	..	10·00	9·00
35		75 c. carmine (a) (7.77)	..	28·00	25·00
		a. Rosine (1878)	..	38·00	38·00
36		1 f. olive-green (a) (6.77)	..	13·00	7·00

This issue exists unofficially *pin-perf.*
Reprints were made in 1887 without gum, all Type (b) and in different shades.
The 20 c. *blue* was prepared but never issued.

1878–80. *Colours changed. All Type (b). Imperf*
37	H	1 c. black/azure (6.78)	..	8·00	8·00
38		2 c. brown/buff (6.78)	..	7·00	5·50
39		4 c. purple-brown/grey (6.78)	..	9·50	9·50
40		10 c. black/lilac (5.79)	..	38·00	9·00
41		15 c. blue/pale blue (1.79)	..	14·00	5·50
42		20 c. red/green (8.79)	..	32·00	5·50
43		25 c. black/red (5.79)	..	£190	£140
44		25 c. ochre/yellow (6.80)	..	£200	13·00

Reprints were made in 1887 without gum and in different shades.
The 3 c. ochre, 3 c. grey, 25 c. black/rose and 5 f. lilac were not issued for colonial use and are simply stamps of France but *imperf.*

(Des and die eng A. Dubois. Typo)

1881 (May)**–86.** *P 14 × 13½.*
45	J	1 c. black/azure	..	70	70
46		2 c. brown/buff	..	80	80
		a. Deep brown/buff	..	80	80
47		4 c. purple-brown/grey	..	80	80
		a. Dull purple-brown/grey	..	80	80

48	J	5 c. green/*green*	..	..	..	95	50
		a. Green/*pale green*				95	50
49		10 c. black/*lilac*	..	..	..	1·90	1·10
		. a. Black/*pale grey*	..			1·90	1·10
50		15 c. blue/*pale blue* (1881)	..		2·75	50
		a. Deep blue/*pale blue*				2·75	50
51		20 c. red/*green*	..	..	..	9·00	4·00
		a. Red/*deep green*	..		9·00	4·00
52		25 c. ochre/*yellow*	..	..	2·50	1·00
53		25 c. black/*rose* (5.86)	..		2·50	50
54		30 c. cinnamon/*drab*	..	..	7·50	5·00
55		35 c. black/*orange*	..	..	9·00	7·50
		a. Black/*yellow*				9·00	7·50
56		40 c. red/*yellow*	..	..	10·00	7·00
		a. Red/*buff*				10·00	7·00
57		75 c. rose-carmine/*rose*	..		21·00	13·00
58		1 f. olive-green/*toned*	..		14·00	8·00

K. Map of France   L. Colonies offering France Aid

(Des Bodiniet. Eng C. Hervé. Litho)

1943. *Aid to Resistance Movement.* P 12.

82	K	50 c.+·4 f. 50, yellow-green	..	..	20	25
83		1 f. 50+8 f. 50, carmine		..	20	25
84		3 f.+12 f. greenish blue		..	20	25
85		5 f.+15 f. grey	..	..	20	25
86	L	9 f.+41 f. purple	..	..	20	25
82/86		*Set of 5*	..	..	90	1·10

U

1884 (Mar)–**85.** *POSTAGE DUE. As Type* D **3** *of France.* Typo. *Imperf.*

D59	U	1 c. black (10.85)	..	..	90	90
D60		2 c. black (10.85)	..		90	90
D61		3 c. black (10.85)	..		90	90
D62		4 c. black (10.85)	..		1·00	75
D63		5 c. black	..	..	1·25	1·00
D64		10 c. black	..	..	1·90	1·50
D65		15 c. black	..	..	2·50	1·90
D66		20 c. black	..	..	2·50	2·50
D67		30 c. black	..	..	3·00	1·90
D68		40 c. black	..	..	5·00	1·90
D69		60 c. black	..	..	9·50	5·00
D70		1 f. brown (4.84)	..		7·50	6·50
D71		2 f. brown (4.84)	..		6·50	5·00
D72		5 f. brown (4.84)	..		22·00	20·00

1893 (Sept)–**1906.** *POSTAGE DUE. Typo. Imperf.*

D73	U	5 c. pale blue	..	..	15	15
D74		10 c. grey-brown	..	..	15	15
D75		15 c. pale green	..	..	15	15
D76		20 c. olive-green (1906)	..		15	15
D77		30 c. carmine	..	..	30	20
D78		50 c. dull claret	..	..	30	25
D79		60 c. brown/*buff*	..		95	50
D80		1 f. rose/*buff*	..		4·75	4·50
D81		1 f. red/*buff* (1905)	..		1·25	80

For Nos. D78 and D80 overprinted "Colis Postaux", see Nos. P19 and P21 of Ivory Coast.

The 1881–86 regular issue was the last to have currency in all the French Colonies. Variations in exchange rates in some Colonies made it necessary for them to have their individual issues, first by surcharges on the general issues, but from 1892 the "tablet" definitive type was introduced. The Postage Due stamps continued to be used until superseded by individual issues as required.

French Committee of National Liberation

The following stamps were issued by the French Committee of National Liberation and put on sale first after the landing in Corsica, later in liberated areas in the south of France and from November 1944 throughout France and in many of the French Colonies.

M. Resisters   O

N   V

(Litho E. Imbert)

1943. *Aid to Resistance Movement. Zigzag roulette.*

87	M	1 f. 50+98 f. 50, deep blue and grey	..	6·50	6·50

Printed in sheets of 10 (5 × 2) *se-tenant* at top and bottom with grey ornamental labels and Cross of Lorraine in deep blue.

(Eng C. Hervé. Litho)

1943. *French Solidarity Fund.* P 12.

88	N	10 f.+40 f. blue	..	..	95	1·10

(Des M. Patton. Eng C. Hervé. Litho)

1944 (25 May). *AIR. Aviation Fund.* P 12.

89	O	10 f.+40 f. grey-green	..	..	1·10	1·25

(Typo in London)

1945–46. *POSTAGE DUE. P 11½.*

D 90	V	10 c. blue	..	..	..	5	5
D 91		15 c. yellow-green	..	..	5	5
D 92		25 c. orange	..	..	5	5
D 93		50 c. greenish black	..		15	15
D 94		60 c. red-brown	..	..	15	15
D 95		1 f. claret	..	..	5	5
D 96		2 f. red	..	..	15	15
D 97		4 f. grey	..	..	40	40
D 98		5 f. ultramarine	..	..	40	40
D 99		10 f. violet	..	..	1·90	1·60
D100		20 f. brown	..	..	75	80
D101		50 f. green	..	..	1·00	1·25
D90/101		*Set of 12*	..	..	4·75	5·00

ALBUM LISTS

Please write for our latest lists of albums and accessories. These will be sent free on request.

Algeria

100 Centimes = 1 Franc

I. FRENCH DEPARTMENT

A French expedition to Algeria forced the Bey of Algiers to capitulate on 5 July 1830; but a long war against the Arabs of the interior did not end till the surrender of their leader, Abd-el-Kader, on 23 December 1847. From then on, in spite of further risings of the natives, many Europeans were settled in Algeria. Until 1924 French stamps were used without overprint.

PRINTERS. All the stamps of Algeria until 1958 were printed at the Government Printing Works, Paris, *unless otherwise stated.*

IMPERFORATE STAMPS. Many stamps exist imperforate in their issued colours but they were not valid for postage. Imperforate stamps in other colours are colour trials.

ALGÉRIE

(1)

ALGÉRIE

(2)

1924 (8 May)–**25**. Stamps of France, 1900–25, optd as T **1** or **2**.

1	**11**	½ c. on 1 c. slate (R.)			5	5
		a. Opt treble			25·00	
2		1 c. grey (R.)			5	5
3		2 c. claret			5	5
4		3 c. orange-red (6.24)			5	5
5		4 c. brown (B.) (7.24)			5	5
6	**18**	5 c. orange (B.)			5	5
7	**11**	5 c. blue-green (6.25)			5	5
8	**30**	10 c. green			5	5
9	**18**	10 c. green (1.25)			5	5
10	**15**	15 c. sage-green			5	5
11	**30**	15 c. green (6.25)			5	5
12	**18**	15 c. chocolate (B.) (11.25)			5	5
13		20 c. purple-brown (B.)			5	5
14		25 c. blue (R.)			5	5
15	**30**	30 c. scarlet (B.)			5	5
16	**18**	30 c. blue (R.) (9.25)			5	5
17		30 c. rosine (4.25) *			8	5
18		35 c. violet			5	5
19	**13**	40 c. red and pale blue			8	5
20	**18**	40 c. olive (R.) (6.25)			12	10
21	**13**	45 c. green and pale blue (R.)			10	8
		a. Opt double			40·00	
22	**30**	45 c. red (B.) (2.25)			5	5
23		50 c. blue (R.)			5	5
24	**15**	60 c. mauve (7.24)			8	5
		a. Opt inverted			—	£150
25		65 c. carmine (B.) (1.25)			8	5
26	**30**	75 c. blue (R.) (7.24)			15	5
		a. Opt double			25·00	
27	**15**	80 c. scarlet (12.25)			20	8
28		85 c. scarlet (B.) (7.24)			15	5
29	**13**	1 f. lake and yellow-green			35	5
30	**18**	1 f. 05, scarlet (11.25)			30	12
31	**13**	2 f. red and blue-green			25	12
32		3 f. violet and blue (12.25)			75	25
33		5 f. blue and buff (R.)			3·75	2·75
1/33		Set of 33			6·50	3·50

The overprint is T **2** on the 2 f., and similar but larger on the other oblong stamps, except on the 5 f., where it is similar to T **1**, but larger.

*No. 17 was only issued pre-cancelled and the price in the unused column is for stamps with full gum.

D **3**

D **4**

1926 (1 May)–**28**. POSTAGE DUE. Typo. P 14×13½.

D34	D **3**	5 c. blue			5	5
D35		10 c. brown			5	5
D36		20 c. olive-green			8	8
D37		25 c. rosine			20	20
D38		30 c. carmine			8	5
D39		45 c. green			20	20
D40		50 c. dull claret			5	5
D41		60 c. green (2.28)			65	20
D42		1 f. claret/*straw*			5	5
D43		2 f. magenta (7.27)			12	12
D44		3 f. deep blue (7.27)			5	5
D34/44		Set of 11			1·40	1·00

See also Nos. D249/52.

1926 (May)–**27**. POSTAGE DUE. Typo. P 14×13½.

D45	D **4**	1 c. olive-green (6.26)			5	5
D46		10 c. violet			20	12
D47		30 c. bistre			12	8
D48		60 c. red			10	8
D49		1 f. bright violet (11.27)			4·25	1·00
D50		2 f. pale blue (7.27)			3·50	40
D45/50		Set of 6			7·50	1·50

Stamps of Type D **4** were employed to recover postage due from the sender in cases where the recipient refused delivery.

3 Street in the Casbah   **4** Mosque of Sidi Abderahman   **5** Grand Mosque

6 The Bay of Algiers   (7)

(Des Watremetz (**3**), A. Montader (**4**), Anthony (**5**) and Brouty (**6**). Typo)

1926 (June)–**41**. P 14×13½.

34	**3**	1 c. olive			5	5
35		2 c. claret			5	5
36		3 c. brown-orange			5	5
37		5 c. green			5	5
38		10 c. bright mauve			5	5
39	**4**	15 c. chestnut			5	5
40		20 c. green			5	5
41		20 c. carmine (11.26)			5	5
42		20 c. yellow-green (1941) *			8	8
43		25 c. green			5	5
44		25 c. light blue (11.27)			10	5
45		25 c. deep ultramarine (1939)			5	5
46		30 c. light blue			10	5
47		30 c. green (11.27)			30	20
48		35 c. violet			40	35
49		40 c. olive-green			5	5
50	**5**	45 c. plum			10	5
51		50 c. blue (7.26)			5	5
		a. *Indigo*			5	5
53		50 c. scarlet (7.30)			5	5
54		60 c. yellow-green (7.26)			5	5
55		65 c. sepia (8.27)			75	60
56	**3**	65 c. bright blue (1938)			5	5

 $\dfrac{1}{2}$

centime

(7)

57	**5**	75 c. carmine (7.26)			15	15
58		75 c. light blue (10.29)			1·10	5
59		80 c. red-orange (8.26)			15	15
60		90 c. red (8.27)			2·75	1·00
61	**6**	1 f. maroon and green			25	5
62	**5**	1 f. 05, brown (8.26)			12	12
63		1 f. 10, bright magenta (8.27)			2·25	55
64	**6**	1 f. 25, ultramarine and blue (8.26)			30	30
65		1 f. 50, ultramarine and blue (8.27)			75	5
66		2 f. chocolate and blue-green (10.26)			95	5
67		3 f. vermilion and bright mauve (8.26)			1·50	45
68		5 f. mauve and scarlet (8.26)			3·25	1·00
69		10 f. carmine and brown (7.27)			19·00	13·00
70		20 f. yellow-green & bright violet (7.27)			1·40	1·25
34/70		Set of 36			23·00	12·00

*No. 42 pre-cancelled only. See note after No. 33.
For stamps as T **5**, but without "REPUBLIQUE FRAN-ÇAISE", see Nos. 178/9, and for stamp as T **6**, but inscribed "CENTENAIRE-ALGERIE", see France, No. 479.

1926. *Surch with T* **7**.

71	**3**	½ c. on 1 c. olive (R.)		5	5

(8)	(9)	(D 10)

1927 (Jan). *Wounded Soldiers of Moroccan War Charity issue. Surch as T* **8**.

72	**3**	5 c.+5 c. green		12	12
73		10 c.+10 c. bright mauve		12	12
74	**4**	15 c.+15 c. chestnut		12	12
75		20 c.+20 c. carmine		12	12
76		25 c.+25 c. green		12	12
77		30 c.+30 c. light blue		12	12
78		35 c.+35 c. violet		12	12
79		40 c.+40 c. olive-green		12	12
80	**5**	50 c.+50 c. deep blue (R.)		12	12
		a. Surch double (R.+Bk.)		65·00	65·00
81		80 c.+80 c. red-orange		12	12
82	**6**	1 f.+1 f. maroon and green		12	12
83		2 f.+2 f. chocolate and blue-green		7·00	7·00
84		5 f.+5 f. mauve and scarlet		7·00	7·00
72/84		Set of 13		14·00	14·00

1927 (May). *Surch* (*a*) *with or* (*b*) *without bars as T* **9**.

85	**4**	10 on 35 c. violet (*a*)		5	5
86		25 on 30 c. light blue (*a*)		5	5
87		30 on 25 c. green (*b*)		5	5
88	**5**	65 on 60 c. yellow-green (*b*)		40	35
89		90 on 80 c. red-orange (*b*)		15	10
90		1 f. 10 on 1 f. 05, brown (*a*)		12	5
91	**6**	1 f. 50 on 1 f. 25, ultramarine & blue (*a*)		95	35
85/91		Set of 7		1·60	1·25

1927 (June). *POSTAGE DUE. Surch as Type* D **10**, *without bars.*

D92	D **3**	60 on 20 c. olive-green		40	12
D93		2 f. on 45 c. green		50	30
D94		3 f. on 25 c. rosine		15	12

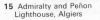

(D 11)	(D 12)	(10)

1927 (June)–**32**. *POSTAGE DUE. Surch as Types* D **11** *or* D **12**, *with bars.*

D95	D **4**	10 c.on 30 c. bistre (10.32)		70	70
D96		1 f. on 1 c. olive green		30	20
D97		1 f. on 60 c. red (10.32)		5·00	5
D98		2 f. on 10 c. violet		2·75	2·75
D96/98		Set of 4		8·00	3·25

1927 (Nov). *No. 5, surch with T* **10**.

92	**11**	5 c. on 4 c. brown		5	5

Minor variations in the shape of the "5" have been noted.

11 Railway Terminus, Oran   **12** Bay of Algiers, after painting by Verecque

(Recess Institut de Gravure, Paris)

1930 (Mar). *Centenary of French Occupation. As T* **11** (*inscr* "CENTENAIRE DE L'ALGERIE"). *P* 12½.

93		5 c.+5 c. orange		2·25	2·25
94		10 c.+10 c. olive-green		2·25	2·25
95		15 c.+15 c. sepia		2·25	2·25
96		25 c.+25 c. slate		2·25	2·25
97		30 c.+30 c. scarlet		2·25	2·25
98		40 c.+40 c. yellow-green		2·25	2·25
99		50 c.+50 c. ultramarine		2·25	2·25
100		75 c.+75 c. bright purple		2·25	2·25
101		1 f.+1 f. vermilion		2·25	2·25
102		1 f. 50+1 f. 50, deep ultramarine		2·25	2·25
103		2 f.+2 f. carmine		2·25	2·25
104		3 f.+3 f. deep green		2·25	2·25
105		5 f.+5 f. carmine and deep green		3·50	3·50
		a. Centre inverted		£130	
93/105		Set of 13		27·00	27·00

Designs: *Horiz*—10 c. Constantine; 15 c. The Admiralty, Algiers; 25 c. Algiers; 30 c. Ruins of Timgad; 40 c. Ruins of Djemila; 1 f. 50 Tolga; 2 f. Touaregs; 3 f. Native Quarter, Algiers; 5 f. The Mosque, Algiers. *Vert*—50 c. Ruins of Djemila; 75 c. Tlemçen; 1 f. Ghardaia; 1 f. 50 Tolga; 2 f. Touaregs; 3 f. Native Quarter, Algiers; 5 f. The Mosque, Algiers.

(Recess Institut de Gravure)

1930 (4 May). *North African International Philatelic Exhibition. P* 12½.

106	**12**	10 f.+10 f. purple-brown		5·50	5·50
		a. Perf 11		5·50	5·50

The premium included the cost of entry into the Exhibition.

13 Colomb Bechar-Oued   **14** Arc de Triomphe, Lambèse

15 Admiralty and Peñon Lighthouse, Algiers   **16** Moslem Cemetery, Tlemçen

(Eng H. Cheffer (A and **14**), Das (**13**), J. Piel (B), G. Hourriez (**15**), Feltesse (C and **16**) and A. Delzers (D). Recess)

1936–40. *T* 13/16 *and similar designs. P* 13.

107	A	1 c. ultramarine		5	5
108	**13**	2 c. purple		5	5

109	**14**	3 c. green			5	5
110	B	5 c. bright magenta			5	5
111	**15**	10 c. emerald-green			5	5
112	C	15 c. scarlet			5	5
113	**16**	20 c. green			5	5
114	D	25 c. purple			20	5
115	B	30 c. emerald-green			12	5
116	C	40 c. maroon			5	5
117	**16**	45 c. blue			40	30
118	**13**	50 c. scarlet			25	5
119	A	65 c. red-brown			95	80
120		65 c. rose-carmine (1937)			12	5
121		70 c. red-brown (1939)			5	5
122	**13**	75 c. slate			12	5
123	**14**	90 c. scarlet			40	35
124		90 c. scarlet* (1939)			5	5
125	D	1 f. brown			10	5
126	**15**	1 f. 25, bright violet			20	12
127		1 f. 25, rose-carmine (1939)			5	5
128	**13**	1 f. 50, turquoise-blue			50	12
129		1 f. 50, rose-carmine (1940)			15	5
130	B	1 f. 75, orange-red			5	5
131	**14**	2 f. maroon			5	5
132	A	2 f. 25, emerald-green			4·50	3·50
133	D	2 f. 25, turquoise-blue* (1939)			5	5
134	B	2 f. 50, ultramarine (1940)			12	12
135	**16**	3 f. rose-magenta			5	5
136	D	3 f. 50, turquoise-blue			90	80
137	**15**	5 f. slate			5	5
138	**13**	10 f. orange-red			8	5
139	C	20 f. turquoise-blue			20	20
107/139		*Set of 33*			9·00	7·00

Designs: *Horiz*—A, A halt in the Sahara; B, Ghardaia, Mzab; C, Marabouts, Touggourt; D, El Kebir Mosque, Algiers.
*Nos. 124 and 133 have figures of value in colour on white background.
For 1 f. 50, rose-carmine, as No. 129, but without "RF" in side panels, see No. 180.

17 Exhibition Pavilion

18 Constantine in 1837

(T **17**/8 Des M. Racim. Eng J. Piel. Recess)

1937. *Paris International Exhibition.* P 13.

140	**17**	40 c. green			30	20
141		50 c. rose-carmine			8	5
142		1 f. 50, blue			35	15
143		1 f. 75, brownish black			40	35
140/143		*Set of 4*			1·00	65

1937. *Centenary of Capture of Constantine.* P 13.

144	**18**	65 c. carmine			20	5
145		1 f. brown			1·90	20
146		1 f. 75, greenish blue			10	8
147		2 f. 15, bright purple			5	5
144/147		*Set of 4*			2·00	35

19 Ruins of Roman Villa

(Eng J. Piel. Recess)

1938 (Oct). *Centenary of Philippeville.* P 13.

148	**19**	30 c. green			25	20

149	**19**	65 c. ultramarine			5	5
150		75 c. purple			30	25
151		3 f. carmine			1·10	1·10
152		5 f. brown			1·40	95
148/152		*Set of 5*			2·75	2·25

(20)

1938 (11 Nov). *20th Anniv of Armistice Day. No. 132 such with T* **20**.

153		65 c.+35 c. on 2 f. 25, emerald-green (R.)		20	20
		a. Surch inverted			48·00	

(21)

1938. *No. 118 surch with T* **21**.

154	**15**	25 c. on 50 c. scarlet			5	5
		a. Surch inverted			9·50	7·00
		b. Surch double			11·00	8·00
		c. Pair, one without surch			22·00	

22 Caillié, Lavigerie and Duveyrier

(Des and eng J. Piel and M. Racim. Recess)

1939. *Sahara Pioneers' Monument Fund.* P 13.

155	**22**	30 c.+20 c. emerald-green			30	30
156		90 c.+60 c. carmine			30	30
157		2 f. 25+75 c. ultramarine			3·50	3·50
158		5 f.+5 f. black			7·00	7·00
155/158		*Set of 4*			10·00	10·00

23 Vessel in Algiers Harbour (24)

(Des L. Carré. Eng J. Piel. Recess)

1939. *New York World's Fair.* P 13.

159	**23**	20 c. emerald-green			40	30
160		40 c. bright purple			40	30
161		90 c. sepia			12	5
162		1 f. 25, rose-carmine			1·50	45
163		2 f. 25, bright blue			40	40
159/163		*Set of 5*			2·50	1·40

1939–40. *Surch as T* **24**.

164	**3**	1 f. on 90 c. scarlet (bars 5¾ mm)		5	5
		a. Surch inverted			8·00	
		b. Surch double			14·00	
		c. Pair, one without surch				
165		1 f. on 90 c. scarlet (bars 7 mm) (1940)	75	5
		a. Surch inverted			7·50	
		b. Pair, one without surch				

+60c

25 Algerian Soldiers	**26** Algiers	(**27**)	**31** Arms of Constantine

32 Arms of Oran **33** Arms of Algiers

(Des L. Carré. Photo)

1940 (Jan). *Soldiers' Dependents' Relief Fund. Design surch as in T* **25**. *P* 12.

166	**25**	1 f.+1 f. blue (R.)	..	..	25	25
		a. Surch double	..	..	32·00	
167		1 f.+2 f. brown-lake	..	..	25	25
168		1 f.+4 f. green (R.)	..	..	30	30
169		1 f.+9 f. brown (R.)	..	..	35	35
166/169		*Set of 4*	..	..	1·00	1·00

(Des and die eng J. Piel and A. Bodiniet. Typo)

1941. *P* 14×13½.

170	**26**	30 c. ultramarine		..	5	5
171		70 c. blackish brown	..		5	5
172		1 f. carmine	..	..	5	5
170/172		*Set of 3*		..	12	12

For 30 c. ultramarine, as No. 170, but without "RF" in bottom left-hand corner, see No. 177.

1941–42. (*a*) *Surch as T* **24**.

173	**3**	50 on 65 c. bright blue		..	10	5
		a. Surch inverted	..	..	7·50	
		b. Pair, one without surch	..	..	21·00	

(*b*) *No. 124 surch with T* **27**

173c	**14**	90 c.+60 c. scarlet (1942)		..	5	5
		d. Surch double	..	..	21·00	

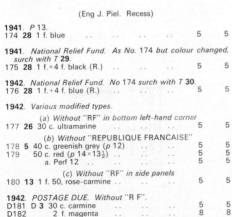

28 Marshal Pétain	(**29**)	(**30**)

+4f   **SECOURS NATIONAL** **+4f**

(Eng J. Piel. Recess)

1941. *P* 13.

174	**28**	1 f. blue	..	..	5	5

1941. *National Relief Fund. As No.* 174 *but colour changed, surch with T* **29**.

175	**28**	1 f.+4 f. black (R.)	..	..	5	5

1942. *National Relief Fund. No* 174 *surch with T* **30**.

176	**28**	1 f.+4 f. blue (R.)	..	..	5	5

1942. *Various modified types.*

(*a*) *Without "RF" in bottom left-hand corner*

177	**26**	30 c. ultramarine		..	5	5

(*b*) *Without "REPUBLIQUE FRANCAISE"*

178	**5**	40 c. greenish grey (*p* 12)	..	..	5	5
179		50 c. red (*p* 14×13½)	..	..	5	5
		a. Perf 12	..	..	5	5

(*c*) *Without "RF" in side panels*

180	**13**	1 f. 50, rose-carmine	..	..	5	5

1942. *POSTAGE DUE. Without* "R F".

D181	D **3**	30 c. carmine	..	..	5	5
D182		2 f. magenta	..	..	8	8

1942–45. (*a*) *Local printing with* "Berliot" *imprint. Photo. P* 12.

181	**31**	40 c. violet (1943)	5	5
182	**32**	60 c. carmine (1943)	5	5
183	**31**	1 f. 20, yellow-green (1943)	5	5
184	**33**	1 f. 50, carmine	5	5
185	**32**	2 f. blue	5	5
186	**31**	2 f. 40, carmine (1943)	5	5
187	**33**	3 f. blue	5	5
188	**31**	4 f. blue (1943)	5	5
189	**32**	5 f. yellow-green (1943)	5	5
181/189		*Set of 9*	40	40

(*b*) *Paris printing without imprint. Typo. P* 14×13½

190	**33**	10 c. brown-lilac (1945)	5	5
191	**32**	30 c. blue-green (1945)	5	5
192	**31**	40 c. brown-lilac (1945)	5	5
193	**32**	60 c. carmine (1945)	5	5
194	**31**	70 c. blue (1945)	5	5
195	**33**	80 c. green (11.42)	5	5
196	**31**	1 f. 20, blue-green (1945)	5	5
197	**33**	1 f. 50, carmine (11.42)	5	5
198	**32**	2 f. blue (1945)	5	5
199	**31**	2 f. 40, carmine (1945)	5	5
200	**33**	3 f. blue (1945)	5	5
201	**32**	4 f. 50, plum (11.42)	5	5
190/201		*Set of 12*	55	55

34 Marshal Pétain	**35** Allegories of Victory	**36** Allegories of Victory

(Des Bouguenec. Eng C. Mazelin. Recess)

1942. *P* 14×13.

202	**34**	1 f. 50, orange-red	5	5

(Des Fernez and Bodiniet (T **36**). Die eng C. Hervé. Litho Victor Heintz, Algiers)

1943. *P* 12.

203	**35**	1 f. 50, carmine	5	5
204	**36**	1 f. 50, blue	5	5

2f

(**37**)   **38** Summer Palace, Algiers

1943. *Surch with T* **37**.

205	**32**	2 f. on 5 f. red-orange	5	5
		a. Surch double	40·00	
		b. Surch omitted	70·00	

(Die eng C. Hervé. Litho)

1943 (1 Dec). *P* 12.

206	**38**	15 f. grey	55	50
207		20 f. yellow-green	40	12
208		50 f. brown-lake	20	20

209	**38**	100 f. blue		75	65
210		200 f. olive-brown		1·25	65
206/210		Set of 5		3·00	2·00

39 Mother and Children

40 "Marianne"

41 Gallic Cock

(Des L. Fernez. Die eng C. Hervé. Litho)

1943 (1 Dec). *War Prisoners' Relief Fund. P* 12.

211	**39**	50 c.+4 f. 50, pink		15	15
212		1 f. 50+8 f. 50, emerald-green		15	15
213		3 f.+12 f. blue		15	15
214		5 f.+15 f. brown-purple		15	15
211/214		Set of 4		55	55

(Des L. Fernez. Die eng C. Hervé. Litho)

1944. *P* 12.

215	**40**	10 c. grey		5	5
216		30 c. lilac		5	5
217		50 c. scarlet		5	5
218		80 c. emerald-green		5	5
219		1 f. 20, rose-lilac		5	5
220		1 f. 50, blue		5	5
221		2 f. 40, rose-red		5	5
222		3 f. violet		5	5
223		4 f. 50, olive-black		5	5
215/223		Set of 9		40	40

(Des "H.R." Die eng C. Hervé. Litho)

1944-45. *P* 12.

224	**41**	40 c. carmine (1945)		5	5
225		1 f. green		5	5
226		2 f. red		5	5
277	**50**	4 f. 50, ultramarine and scarlet		5	5
278		5 f. black and greenish blue (3.11.48)		5	5
229		10 f. greenish black		20	12
224/229		Set of 6		40	35

TAXE P. C. V. DOUANE

20 Fr. (D 42)

T 0f·30 (42)

0.50 (D 43)

1944. *POSTAGE DUE. No.* 208 *surch with Type* D **42**.

D230	**38**	20 f. on 50 f. brown-lake		8	8
		a. Surch double		13·00	

1944. *No.* 39 *surch with T* **42**.

230	**4**	30 c. on 15 c. chestnut*		5	5
		a. Surch inverted		3·25	2·50
		b. Surch double		5·50	

*No. 230 pre-cancelled only. See note after No. 70.

1944. *POSTAGE DUE. No.* 42 *surch with Type* D **43**.

D231	**4**	50 c. on 20 c. yellow-green (R.)		5	5
		a. Surch inverted		1·25	
		b. Surch double		4·50	

1945-47. *Various types of France optd.* "ALGÉRIE", *as T* **1**.

(a) *Shield and Broken Chains*

231	**217**	40 c. magenta (21.2.45)		5	5
232		50 c. violet-blue (R.)		5	5

(b) *Ceres*

233	**218**	60 c. ultramarine (R.) (1946)		5	5
234		1 f. carmine-red (1946)		5	5
235		1 f. 50, bright purple (1947)		5	5

(c) *Iris* (1946)

236	**136**	80 c. yellow-green		5	5
237		1 f. greenish blue		5	5
238		1 f. 20, violet		8	8
239		2 f. chocolate		5	5
240		2 f. 40, carmine		5	5
241		3 f. orange		5	5

(d) *Marianne*

242	**219**	2 f. blue-green (R.)		5	5
243		3 f. carmine (1946)		5	5
244		4 f. 50, blue (R.) (1947)		20	5
245		5 f. green		5	5
246		10 f. blue (1946)		15	15

(e) *Arms of Corsica and Lorraine* (4.47)

247	**239**	10 c. black and ultramarine (R.)		5	5
248	–	50 c. brown, yellow and red (B.)		10	5
231/248		Set of 18		1·10	95

1945-47. *POSTAGE DUE. As Nos.* D34/44. (a) *Litho P* 12

D249	D **3**	1 f. 50, magenta		12	10
D250		2 f. greenish blue		12	10
D251		5 f. carmine		10	10

(b) *Typo. P* 14×13½

D252	D **3**	5 f. green (1947)		45	30
D249/252		Set of 4		70	55

0f·50

RF (43) **RF** (44) **2ᶠ** (45) **46** Aeroplane over Algiers

1945 (2 July). *Airmen and Dependents Fund. As No.* 742 *of France but colour changed, optd* "ALGÉRIE" *as T* **1**, *in black and further optd with T* **43** *and surch, in red.*

249	**169**	1 f. 50+3 f. 50, grey-blue		8	8
		a. "ALGÉRIE" omitted		95·00	
		b. "R F" omitted		£110	

1945 (Sept). *Postal Employees War Victims' Fund. No.* 949 *of France optd* "ALGÉRIE" *as T* **1**.

250	**223**	4 f.+6 f. purple-brown		5	5

1945 (15 Oct). *Stamp Day. As No.* 955 *of France but colour changed, optd* "ALGÉRIE" *as T* **1**.

251	**228**	2 f.+3 f. brown-purple (B.)		15	15
		a. Opt omitted		£190	

1946 (Jan). *No.* 197 *surch with T* **44**.

252	**33**	50 c. on 1 f. 50, carmine		5	5
		a. Surch inverted		7·00	

1946 (May). *Iris type of France optd* "ALGÉRIE" *as T* **1** *and surch with T* **45**.

253	**136**	2 f. on 1 f. 50, red-brown		5	5
		a. "2F" omitted		70·00	

I.

II.

Type I: Cross-bars of "F" of "RF" without serifs; "P" of "POSTES" 3½ mm. from end of coloured panel.

Type II: "F" with prominent sloping serifs; "P" 4½ mm. from end of panel.

(Eng Feltesse. Recess)

1946 (20 June). *AIR. P* 13.

254	**46**	5 f. scarlet	..	..	5	5
255		10 f. blue	..	..	5	5
256		15 f. green	..	..	15	5
257		20 f. brown (I)	..	35·00	32·00	
		a. Type II	..	..	10	5
258		25 f. violet	..	..	15	5
259		40 f. black	..	..	30	5
254/259		*Set of* 6			70	25

1946 (29 June). *Stamp Day. As No.* 975 *of France* (*De la Varane*), *but colour changed, optd* "ALGÉRIE" *as T* **1**.

260	**241**	3 f.+2 f. red (B.)	..	15	15

POSTES ALGERIE

47 Children at a Spring   48 Boy gazing Skywards

(Des O. Ferru, F. Fauck (4 f., 8 f.) and A. Boutet. Eng Feltesse, Barlangue, Mazelin and C. P. Dufresne. Recess)

1946 (2 Oct). *National Fellowship. T* **47/8** *and similar designs inscr* "SOLIDARITE ALGERIENNE". *P* 13.

261		3 f.+17 f. blue-green	..	..	50	50
262		4 f.+21 f. rose-red	..	..	50	50
263		8 f.+27 f. bright purple	..	1·25	1·25	
264		10 f.+35 f. blue	..	..	50	50
261/264		*Set of* 4	..	..	2·50	2·50

Designs: *Vert*—8 f. Laurel-crowned head. *Horiz*—10 f. Soldier looking at Algerian coastline.

1947 (18 Jan). *AIR. No.* 254 *surch* "—10%".

265	**46**	"—10%" on 5 f. scarlet	..	5	5

1947 (15 Mar). *Stamp Day. As No.* 1008 *of France* (*Louvois*) *but colour changed, optd* "ALGÉRIE" *as T* **1**.

266	**253**	4 f. 50+5 f. 50, blue (R.)	..	20	20

49 Arms of Constantine   50 Arms of Algiers   51 Arms of Oran

1947–49. *Typo. P* 14×13½.

267	**49**	10 c. green and scarlet	..	..	5	5
268	**50**	50 c. black and orange	..		5	5
269	**51**	1 f. ultramarine and yellow	..		5	5
270	**49**	1 f. 30, black and greenish blue	..	15	15	
271	**50**	1 f. 50, violet and yellow	..		5	5
272	**51**	2 f. black and emerald	..		5	5
273	**49**	2 f. 50, black and scarlet	..	15	12	
274	**50**	3 f. carmine and emerald	..		5	5
275	**51**	3 f. 50, green and purple	..		5	5
276	**49**	4 f. brown and emerald	..		5	5
277	**50**	4 f. 50, ultramarine and scarlet	..		5	5
278		5 f. black and greenish blue (3.11.48)		5	5	
279	**51**	6 f. brown and scarlet	..		5	5
280		8 f. brown and ultramarine (3.11.48)		5	5	
281	**49**	10 f. rose and sepia (3.11.48)	..	15	5	
282	**50**	15 f. black and red (3.49)	..	15	5
267/282		*Set of* 16	..	..	1·10	90

For similar designs see Nos. 364/8 and 381/3.

1947. *POSTAGE DUE. Nos.* D985/6 *of France* (*inscr* "TIMBRE TAXE"), *optd* "ALGÉRIE" *as T* **1**.

D283	D **10**	10 c. blackish brown	..	..	5	5
D284		30 c. bright purple	..	..	5	5

✦
18 Juin 1940
+10 ^Fr._

(52)

1947 (18 June). *AIR. Seventh Anniv of De Gaulle's Call to Arms. No.* 255 *surch with T* **52**.

283	**46**	10 f.+10 f. blue (R.)	..	25	25

See also No. 286.

ALGÉRIE

+10^f

D 53   (53)   (54)

(Des M. Racim. Eng H. Cortot. Recess)

1947–55. *POSTAGE DUE. P* 14×13.

D285	D **53**	20 c. red	..	..	8	5
D286		60 c. ultramarine	..	..	15	15
D287		1 f. brown	..	..	5	5
D288		1 f. 50, grey-olive	..	..	25	20
D289		2 f. carmine	..	..	5	5
D290		3 f. violet	..	..	5	5
D291		5 f. ultramarine	..	..	5	5
D292		6 f. black	..	..	8	8
D293		10 f. bright purple	..	..	8	5
D294		15 f. bronze-green (22.8.55)	..	30	30	
D295		20 f. emerald-green	..		12	10
D296		30 f. orange-red (1.2.55)	..		25	20
D297		50 f. blue-black (1951)	..		55	45
D298		100 f. blue (15.6.53)	..		2·00	1·50
D285/298		*Set of* 14	..	..	3·50	3·00

1947 (13 Nov). *Resistance Movement. As No.* 1019 *of France but colour changed, surch with T* **53**.

284	**261**	5 f.+10 f. slate-grey (R.)	..	20	20

1948 (6 Mar). *Stamp Day. As No.* 1027 *of France* (*Arago*), *but colour changed, optd with T* **54**.

285	**267**	6 f.+4 f. blue-green (G.)	..	30	25

✦
18 JUIN 1940
+10 ^Fr.

(55)

POSTES·ALGERIE

57 Battleship *Richelieu*

+4^f

ALGÉRIE

(56)

1948 (18 June). *AIR. Eighth Anniv of De Gaulle's Call to Arms. No.* 254 *surch with T* **55**.

286	**46**	5 f.+10 f. scarlet (B.)	..	25	25

1948 (Dec). *General Leclerc Memorial. As No.* 1037 *of France but colour changed, surch with T* **56**.
287 **270** 6 f.+4 f. red (B.) 20 20

(Des Berliot. Eng Dufresne (10 f.))

1949 (15 Jan). *Naval Welfare Fund. T* **57** *and similar type inscr* "OEUVRES SOCIALES DE LA MARINE". *P* 13.
288 10 f.+15 f. deep blue .. .. .. 1·90 1·90
289 18 f.+22 f. scarlet .. .. .. 1·90 1·90
Design:—18 f. Aircraft-carrier *Arromanches*.

58 Storks over   **(59)**   **60** French Colonials
Minaret

(Des and eng P. Gandon. Recess)

1949–53. *AIR. T* **58** *and similar horiz design. P* 13.
290 **58** 50 f. green (7.3.49) .. .. 1·10 15
291 — 100 f. brown-purple (7.2.49) .. 75 12
292 **58** 200 f. vermilion (16.11.49) .. .. 2·25 1·50
293 — 500 f. ultramarine (12.10.53) .. 8·00 6·00
290/293 *Set of 4* .. .. .. 11·00 7·00
Design:—100 f., 500 f. Aeroplane over valley dwellings.

1949 (26 Mar). *Stamp Day. As No.* 1954 *of France* (*Choiseul*), *but colour changed, optd with T* **59**.
294 **278** 15 f.+5 f. magenta (B.) 55 55

(Des and eng Decaris. Recess)

1949 (24 Oct). *75th Anniv of U.P.U. P* 13.
295 **60** 5 f. green 45 45
296 15 f. scarlet 50 50
297 25 f. blue .. .. 1·60 95

61 Statue of   **62** Grapes   **63** Foreign
Duke of Orleans   Legionary

(Des Sayous. Eng Barlangue. Recess)

1949 (10 Nov). *AIR. 25th Anniv of First Algerian Stamp. P* 13.
298 **61** 15 f.+20 f. purple-brown .. .. 1·50 1·50

1950 (25 Feb). *As T* **62** (*fruits*). *Recess. P* 13.
299 20 f. purple, green and deep purple .. 50 10
300 25 f. brown, green and black 55 12
301 40 f. orange, yellow-green and brown .. 95 20
Designs:—25 f. Dates; 40 f. Oranges and lemons.

1950 (11 Mar). *Stamp Day. As No.* 1091 *of France* (*Postman*) *but colour changed, optd with T* **54**.
302 **292** 12 f.+3 f. blackish brown (G.) .. 45 45

(Des Marin. Eng Barlangue. Recess)

1950 (30 Apr). *Foreign Legion Welfare Fund. P* 13.
303 **63** 15 f.+5 f. deep green.. .. .. 50 50

64 R. P. de Foucauld and   **65** Colonel C. d'Ornano
Gen. Laperrine

(Des M. Racim. Eng H. Cortot (25 f.), Dufresne (40 f.). Recess)

1950 (21 Aug). *50th Anniv of the French in the Sahara* (25 f.) *and Unveiling of Monument to Abd-el-Kader* (40 f.). *T* **64** *and similar horiz design.*
304 25 f.+5 f. black and blackish olive .. 1·60 1·60
305 40 f.+10 f. purple-brown and red-brown .. 1·60 1·60
Design:—40 f. Emir Abd-el-Kader and Marshal Bugeaud.

(Des R. Jeanne. Eng Dufresne. Recess)

1951 (11 Jan). *Colonel C. d'Ornano Monument Fund. P* 13.
306 **65** 15 f.+5 f. purple, red-brown and black 30 30

1951 (10 Mar). *Stamp Day. As No.* 1107 *of France* (*Sorting Van*), *but colour changed, optd* "ALGÉRIE" *as T* **1**.
307 **300** 12 f.+3 f. red-brown 35 35

66 Apollo of   **67** Algerian War   **68** Médaille
Cherchel   Memorial   Militaire

(Des and eng J. Piel. Recess)

1952. *T* **66** *and similar vert designs. P* 14×13.
308 **66** 10 f. blackish brown (10.1) 12 5
309 — 12 f. orange-brown (10.3) 20 5
310 — 15 f. deep blue (8.2) 10 5
311 — 18 f. carmine (10.3) 20 10
312 — 20 f. green (10.3) 12 5
313 **66** 30 f. deep blue (10.3) 30 12
308/313 *Set of 6* 95 40
Statues:—15 f., 20 f. Boy and eagle, 12 f., 18 f. Isis of Cherchel.

1952 (8 Mar). *Stamp Day. As No.* 1140 *of France* (*Mail Coach*), *but colour changed, optd with T* **59**.
314 **319** 12 f.+3 f. indigo (B.) 75 75

(Des and eng A. Decaris. Recess)

1952 (11 Apr). *African Army Commemoration. P* 13.
315 **67** 12 f. deep green 20 12

(Des R. Louis. Eng J. Piel. Recess)

1952 (5 July). *Centenary of Médaille Militaire. P* 13.
316 **68** 15 f.+5 f. dp brown, lemon & emerald 65 65

HAVE YOU READ THE NOTES AT THE BEGINNING OF THIS CATALOGUE?

These often provide answers to the enquiries we receive.

+
5^F

ALGÉRIE

69 Fossil (*Berberice-*   **(70)**
ras sekikensis)

1952 (11 Aug). *Nineteenth International Geological Congress,
Algiers. Recess. P 13.*
317 **69** 15 f. carmine-red   30   25
318   —   30 f. bright blue   40   30
Design: *Horiz*—30 f. Phonolite Dyke, Hoggar (inscr as in
T **69**).

1952 (15 Sept). *Tenth Anniv of Battle of Bir-Hakeim. As No.
1146 of France but colour changed, surch with T **70**.*
319   30 f. +5 f. ultramarine   55   55

72 Bou-Nara   **73** Members of Corps
                     and Camel

(Des H. Razous. Eng Cottet (8 f.), Barlangue (12 f.). Recess)

1952 (15 Nov). *Red Cross. T **72** and similar horiz design.
P 13.*
320   8 f. +2 f. red and deep blue   65   65
321   12 f. +3 f. red   80   80
Design:—8 f. El-Oued and Map of Algeria.

(Des R. Thiriet. Eng Dufresne. Recess)

1952 (30 Nov). *50th Anniv of Sahara Corps. P 13.*
322 **73** 12 f. orange-brown   30   20

1953 (14 Mar). *Stamp Day. As No. 1161 of France (Count
D'Argenson), but colour changed, optd "ALGÉRIE" as T 1.*
323 **334** 12 f. +3 f. reddish violet   50   50

74 "Victory" of Cirta   **75** E. Millon

(Des and eng Mazelin. Recess)

1953 (18 Dec). *Army Welfare Fund. P 13.*
324 **74** 15 f. +5 f. red-brown & blackish brown   30   30

(Des and eng R. Serres. Recess)

1954 (4 Jan). *Military Health Service. T **75** and similar
portraits. P 13.*
325   25 f. black-brown and deep bluish green   50   5
326   40 f. brown-lake and chestnut   65   20
327   50 f. indigo and ultramarine   65   5
Portraits: *Vert*—40 f. Dr. F. Maillot. *Horiz*—50 f. Dr. A.
Laveran.

1954 (20 Mar). *Stamp Day. As No. 1202 of France (Lavalette),
but colour changed, optd "ALGÉRIE" as T 1.*
328 **346** 12 f. +3 f. scarlet   30   30

76 French and   **77** Foreign Legionary   **78**
     Algerian
     Soldiers

1954 (27 Mar). *Old Soldiers' Welfare Fund. Recess. P 13.*
329 **76** 15 f. +5 f. blackish brown   15   15

(Des Marin. Eng Dufresne. Recess)

1954 (30 Apr). *Foreign Legion Welfare Fund. P 13.*
330 **77** 15 f. +5 f. deep emerald   40   40

(Des B. Sarraillon. Eng Pheulpin. Recess)

1954 (8 May). *Third International Congress of Mediterranean
Citrus Fruit Culture. P 13.*
331 **78** 15 f. light blue and indigo   20   15

1954 (6 June). *Tenth Anniv of Liberation. As No. 1204 of
France but colour changed, optd "ALGÉRIE" as T 1.*
332 **348** 15 f. carmine   20   20

79 Darguinah Hydro-   **30** Courtyard of
     electric Station   Bardo Museum

(Des H. Razous. Eng Dufresne. Recess)

1954 (19 June). *Inauguration of River Agrioun Hydro-electric
Installations. P 13.*
333 **79** 15 f. bright purple   25   20
Two types of 12 f.
I. "POSTES" and "ALGERIE" in brown-orange.
II. Redrawn and inscriptions in white.

(Des B. Sarraillon. Typo)

1954–57. *P 14×13½.*
334 **80** 10 f. bistre-brown and pale brown
         (10.10.55)   5   5
335   12 f. brown-orange and red-brown (I)
         (15.11.54)   10   5
336   12 f. brown-orange and red-brown (II)
         (22.5.56)   5   5

337 **80** 15 f. blue and pale blue (1.7.54)   10   5
338   18 f. carmine-red and red (1.9.57)   20   5
339   20 f. green and pale green (20.2.57) ..   12   12
340   25 f. deep reddish lilac and deep mauve
     (10.10.55)   20   5
334/340   *Set of 7*   80   40

1954 (17 Aug). *150th Anniv of First Presentation of Legion of Honour. As No.* 1223 *of France but colour changed, optd* "ALGÉRIE" *as T* **1**.
341 **356** 12 f. deep green (R.)   30   25

85 Ruins of Tipasa   **86** Widows and Children

(Des B. Sarraillon. Eng R. Serres. Recess)

1955 (31 May). *Bimillenary of Tipasa. P* 13.
353 **85** 50 f. lake-brown   30   5

1955 (13 June). *50th Anniv of Rotary International. As No.* 1235 *of France but colour changed, optd* "ALGÉRIE" *as T* **1**.
354   30 f. blue (R.)   30   20
     a. Pair, one without opt   ..

1955 (3 Oct)–**57**. *As Nos.* 1238 *and* 1238b *of France* ("*France*" *type*), *but inscr* "ALGÉRIE".
355 **362** 15 f. carmine-rose   10   5
356   20 f. ultramarine (2.12.57)   12   5

(Des H. Racim. Eng C. Mazelin. Recess)

1955 (5 Nov). *War Victims' Welfare Fund. P* 13.
357 **86** 15 f.+5 f. indigo and light blue   ..   25   25

81 Red Cross Nurses   **82** St. Augustine

(Des A. Splitz (12 f.), J. Piel (15 f.). Eng J. Piel. Recess)

1954 (30 Oct). *Red Cross Fund. T* **81** *and similar horiz design. P* 13.
342   12 f.+3 f. indigo and red   ..   1·00   1·00
343   15 f.+5 f. deep reddish violet and red   ..   1·00   1·00
Design:—15 f. J. H. Dunant and ruins of Djemila.

(Des and eng A. Decaris. Recess)

1954 (12 Nov). *1600th Birth Anniv of St. Augustine. P* 13.
344 **82** 15 f. chocolate   20   20

87 Grande Kabylie   **88**

(Des F. M. de Buzon. Eng P. Gandon. Recess)

1955 (17 Dec). *P* 13.
358 **87** 100 f. indigo and blue   ..   80   5

(Des A Boutet. Eng G. Barlangue. Recess)

1956 (3 Mar). *Anti-Cancer Fund. P* 13.
359 **88** 15 f.+5 f. deep brown   ..   20   20

1956 (17 Mar). *Stamp Day. As No.* 1279 *of France* (*Francis of Taxis*), *but colour changed, optd* "ALGÉRIE" *as T* **1**.
360 **383** 12 f.+3 f. red   20   20

83 Earthquake Vic-   **84** Statue of Aesculapius and
tims and Ruins   El Kettar Hospital

(Des M. Racim. Eng C. Mazelin (12 f., 15 f.), J. Pheulpin (18 f., 20 f.), R. Serres (25 f., 30 f.). Recess)

1954 (5 Dec). *Orleansville Earthquake Victims' Relief Fund. T* **83** *and similar designs inscr* "SEISME D'ORLEANS-VILLE". *P* 13.
345 **83** 12 f.+4 f. chocolate   75   75
346   15 f.+5 f. deep bright blue   ..   75   75
347   18 f.+6 f. bright reddish purple   ..   75   75
348   —   20 f.+7 f. deep violet   75   75
349   25 f.+8 f. lake   75   75
350   —   30 f.+10 f. turquoise-blue   ..   75   75
345/350   *Set of 6*   ..   ..   4·00   4·00
Designs: *Horiz*—18 f., 20 f. Red Cross workers and injured; 25 f., 30 f. Stretcher-bearers.

1955 (19 Mar). *Stamp Day. As No.* 1245 *of France* (*Balloon Post*), *but colour changed, optd* "ALGÉRIE" *as T* **1**.
351 **364** 12 f.+3 f. deep bright blue   30   30

89 Foreign Legion Retire-   **90** Marshal Franchet
ment Home, Sidi Bel Abbès   d'Esperey (after J. Ebstein)

(Des Pierre. Eng J. Pheulpin. Recess)

(Des B. Sarraillon. Eng J. Pheulpin. Recess)

1955 (3 Apr). *30th French Medical Congress. P* 13.
352 **84** 15 f. scarlet   15   15

1956 (29 Apr). *Foreign Legion Welfare Fund. P* 13.
361 **89** 15 f.+5 f. deep bluish green   40   40

(Des and eng A. Decaris. Recess)

1956 (25 May). *Birth Centenary of Marshal Franchet d'Esperey. P* 13.
362 **90** 15 f. indigo and blue 25 25

91 Marshal Leclerc and Memorial   **92** Oran

(Des and eng R. Serres. Recess)

1956 (29 Nov). *Marshal Leclerc Commemoration. P* 13.
363 **91** 15 f. red-brown and sepia 20 20

1956–58. *Various coats-of-arms as T* **49/51.** *Typo. P* 14×13½.
364   1 f. green and scarlet (12.56) ..   5   5
365   3 f. ultramarine and emerald (8.3.58) .. 20   8
366   5 f. bright blue and yellow (29.6.57) ..   5   5
367   6 f. green and orange-red (9.12.57) .. 20 15
368   12 f. ultramarine and vermilion (1.3.58).. 20 15
364/368 *Set of* 5 .. .. 65 45
Designs:—1 f. Bône; 3 f. Mostaganem; 5 f. Tlemcen; 6 f. Algiers; 12 f. Orleansville.
For similar designs see Nos. 381/3.

(Des and eng H. Cheffer. Recess)

1956 (16 Dec)**–58.** *P* 13.
369 **92** 30 f. deep purple 15   5
370   35 f. rose-carmine (19.5.58) 35 20

1957 (16 Mar). *Stamp Day. As No.* 1322 *of France (Felucca), but colour changed, optd with T* **54**.
371 **403** 12 f.+3 f. deep purple 40 40

93 Electric Train crossing Viaduct   **94** Fennec

(Des B. Sarraillon. Eng J. Pheulpin. Recess)

1957 (25 Mar). *Electrification of Bône-Tebessa Railway Line. P* 13.
372 **93** 40 f. deep bluish green and emerald .. 15   5

(Des and eng C. Mazelin. Recess)

1957 (6 Apr). *Red Cross Fund. T* **94** *and similar horiz design. P* 13.
373   12 f.+3 f. reddish brown and red .. 1·50 1·50
374   15 f.+5 f. sepia and red (Storks) .. 1·50 1·50

18 JUIN 1940
+ 5ᶠ

(95)

1957 (18 June). *Seventeenth Anniv of Gen. de Gaulle's Call to Arms. As No.* 363 *but colours changed and surch as T* **95**.
375 **91** 15 f.+5 f. red and carmine-red (B.) .. 25 25

96 Beni Bahdel Barrage, Tlemcen   **97** "Horseman Crossing Ford" (after Delacroix)

(Des and eng J. Pheulpin. Recess)

1957 (29 June). *AIR. P* 13.
376 **96** 200 f. deep red .. .. .. 2·00 40

(Des and eng J. Piel. Recess)

1957 (30 Nov). *Army Welfare Fund. Designs as T* **97** *inscr* "OEUVRES SOCIALES DE L'ARMEE". *P* 13.
377   15 f.+5 f. brown-red .. .. .. 1·50 1·50
378   20 f.+5 f. green .. .. .. 1·50 1·50
379   35 f.+10 f. blue .. .. .. 1·50 1·50
Designs: *Horiz*—20 f. "Lakeside view" (after Fromentin). *Vert*—35 f. "Arab dancer" (after Chasseriau).

1958 (15 Mar). *Stamp Day. As No.* 1375 *(Rural Posts) of France, but colour changed, optd with T* **54**.
380 **421** 15 f.+5 f. chestnut (B.) 35 35

1958. *Various coats-of-arms as T* **49/51**, *but inscr* "REPUBLIQUE FRANCAISE" *instead of* "R.F." *at foot. Typo. P* 14×13½.
381   2 f. orange-red and bright blue (5.6.58) 15 15
382   6 f. green and orange-red (7.58) .. 20 15
383   10 f. maroon and emerald (26.5.58) .. 20 15
Designs:—2 f. Tizi Ouzou; 6 f. Algiers; 10 f. Sétif.

99 *Strelitzia reginae*   **100**

(Des Mme. Garcin. Eng R. Cami. Recess)

1958 (14 June). *Algerian Child Welfare Fund. P* 13.
384 **99** 20 f.+5 f. orange, violet and dp green 80 80

1958 (20 July). *Marshal de Lattre Foundation. P* 13.
385 **100** 20 f.+5 f. rose-red, emerald & ultram 40 40

Stamps of France were used in Algeria from 22 July 1958 until Algeria became independent.

On 1 November 1954, an Algerian rising against French rule began; intervention by President De Gaulle led eventually to a cease-fire on 18 March 1962. An exodus of French settlers was followed by a referendum in favour of independence, which took effect on 3 July 1962.

O.A.S. OVERPRINTS. In February 1962, fifteen French stamps (Nos. 1462/4, 1539/41, 1543, 1545/9 and 1557/9) were overprinted "ALGÈRIE/FRANÇAISE/13 Mai 1958" at Oran, and put on sale in the city and in surrounding towns. The issue was made under the authority of the O.A.S. (Organisation Armeé Secrète), opposed to Algerian independence, which was at the time in effective control of Oran.

Cambodia

100 Cents = 1 Piastre

The land of the Khmer people, called Kambuja in its Indianized form, was originally in the middle Mekong valley. About the year 627 the Khmers conquered the country of Funan to the south, and founded a kingdom, where the temple of Angkor Vat was later built. This kingdom reached the height of its power and civilisation late in the 14th century, before Siamese invasions caused the abandonment of Angkor in 1432. Continual wars with Siam led to a long decline, until in 1847, Cambodia accepted the suzerainty both of Siam and Annam.

On 11 August 1863 Cambodia was forced to become a French protectorate, which became part of the Union of Indo-China in 1887.

In 1941–45 Cambodia was occupied by Japanese forces and in March 1944 King Norodom Sihanouk proclaimed its independence. After the surrender of Japan, French rule was restored, and Cambodia became an autonomous state within the French Union on 7 January 1946.

PRINTERS All the stamps of Cambodia were printed at the Government Printing Works, Paris, *unless otherwise stated.*

IMPERFORATE STAMPS. Many stamps exist imperforate in their issued colours, but these were not valid for postage. Imperforate stamps in other colours are colour trials.

1951 (3 Nov)–*52. Recess. P* 13.

1	1	10 c. blue-green and deep blue-green (1.2.52)		45	45
2		20 c. chestnut and lake (1.2.52)		30	15
3		30 c. indigo and reddish violet (1.2.52)		30	15
4		40 c. turquoise-blue & ultram (1.2.52)		30	15
5	2	50 c. dull green & deep blue-grn (1.2.52)		30	15
6	3	80 c. blue-green and indigo (2.11.52)		55	55
7	2	1 p. reddish violet and indigo (1.2.52)		80	80
8	3	1 p. 10, vermillion and lake (2.11.52)		80	80
9	1	1 p. 50, carmine and lake		90	80
10	2	1 p. 50, deep blue and indigo (1.2.52)		90	80
11	3	1 p. 50, purple-brown & choc (1.2.52)		90	90
12		1 p. 90, blue and indigo (2.11.52)		1·40	1·25
13	2	2 p. chestnut and lake (1.2.52)		1·25	75
14	3	3 p. chestnut and lake (2.11.52)		1·75	1·25
15	1	5 p. reddish violet and indigo (1.2.52)		5·50	2·75
16	2	10 p. indigo and reddish violet (1.2.52)		11·00	5·50
17	3	15 p. reddish violet & dp violet (2.11.52)		14·00	8·00
1/17		Set of 17		35·00	23·00
MS17*a*		Three sheets each 130×90 mm. Nos. 15/7. (1.2.52). *Price for three sheets*		55·00	55·00

KINGDOM

(within the French Union)

King Norodom Sihanouk

26 April 1941–2 March 1955

(4)

1952 (20 Oct). *Students' Aid Fund. Nos.* 8, 12, 14 *and* 15, *surch as T* **4**.

18	3	1 p. 10+40 c. vermilion and lake		1·90	1·90
19		1 p. 90+60 c. blue and indigo		1·90	1·90
20		3 p.+1 p. chestnut and lake		1·90	1·90
21	1	5 p.+2 p. reddish violet and indigo		1·90	1·90
18/21		Set of 4		7·00	7·00

5 "Kinnari"

1953 (13 Apr–1 Oct). *AIR. Recess. P* 13.

22	5	50 c. green		50	50
23		3 p. brown-lake (1.7)		65	50
24		3 p. 30, reddish violet		80	65
25		4 p. blue and black-brown (1.7)		1·00	65
26		5 p. 10, ochre, red and brown		1·25	90
27		6 p. 50, brt purple & black-brown (1.7)		1·25	1·40
28		9 p. emerald and magenta (1.7)		1·90	1·90
29		11 p. 50, orange, red, magenta, emerald and black (1.7)		3·50	2·75
30		30 p. ochre, brown and deep blue-green		5·50	3·50
22/30		Set of 9		15·00	15·00
MS30*a*		Three sheets each 129×100 mm. Nos. 22, 24, 26 and 30 (sold at 50 p.); Nos. 23, 25 and 29 (sold at 25 p.); Nos. 27/8 (sold at 20 p.). (1.10.53). *Price for three sheets*		90·00	90·00

1 "Apsara" or Dancing Nymph

3 King Norodom Sihanouk

2 Throne Room, Phnom-Penh

6 Arms of Cambodia

7 "Postal Transport"

1954 (24 Sept)–55. *Insr.* "ROYAUME DE CAMBODGE".
Recess. P 13.

31	– 10 c. carmine-red	.. .. ..	5	5
32	– 20 c. deep green	.. ..	5	5
33	– 30 c. indigo	.. ..	5	5
34	– 40 c. deep violet	.. ..	5	5
35	– 50 c. brown-purple	.. ..	5	5
36	– 70 c. chocolate (10.12.54)	.. ..	12	12
37	– 1 p. red-violet (10.12.54)	.. ..	12	12
38	– 1 p. 50, red (10.12.54)	.. ..	12	12
39	6 2 p. red (30.10.54)	.. ..	25	25
40	2 p. 50, deep green (30.10.54)	..	40	40
41	7 2 p. 50, green (9.11.54)	..	50	40
42	6 3 p. deep bright blue (30.10.54)	..	75	65
43	7 4 p. black-brown (9.11.54)	..	75	75
44	6 4 p. 50, deep violet (30.10.54)	..	90	75
45	7 5 p. rose-red (9.11.54)	.. ..	1·00	75
46	6 6 p. chocolate (30 10 54)	.. ..	1·25	75

47	7 10 p. deep violet (9.11.54)	.. ..	1·25	1·00
48	15 p. blue (9.11.54)	.. ..	1·50	1·40
49	– 20 p. ultramarine (10.12.54)	..	3·50	2·25
50	– 30 p. blue-green (10.12.54)	..	5·00	4·00
31/50	*Set of 20*	.. ..	15·00	13·00

MS50*a* Three sheets each 120×120 mm. Nos. 31/5 (sold at 2 p.); Nos. 39/40, 42, 44 and 46 (sold at 20 p.); Nos. 41, 43, 45 and 47/8 (sold at 40 p.) and one sheet 160×92 mm containing Nos. 36/8 and 49/50 (sold at 60 p.). (13.4.55). *Price for four sheets* .. 70·00 70·00

Designs: *Vert.*—View of Phnom Daun Penh. 10 c. to 50 c. *Horiz.*—East Gate, Temple of Angkor, 70 c., 1 p., 1 p. 50, 20 p., 30 p.

Cambodia left the French Union on 25 September 1955.

PHILATELIC TERMS ILLUSTRATED

This successful STAMP MONTHLY series has now been brought together in a snappy black and yellow binding and published as a useful addition to Stanley Gibbons range of essential handbooks for keen stamp collectors. Within its 192 pages this handy limp-bound volume houses a veritable mine of useful information on the words and phrases used in philately. It describes and illustrates printing processes and watermarks, papers and perforations, errors and varieties . . . and it does all this IN COLOUR. Indeed, there are 92 full page plates in colour, plus many black and white illustrations, making it

FANTASTIC VALUE AT ONLY £1·95 POST PAID FROM

**Stanley Gibbons Publications Ltd
391 Strand, London WC2R 0LX**

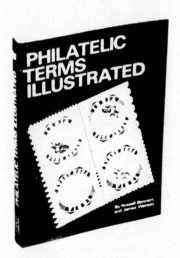

Cameroun

100 Centimes = 1 Franc

In 1914–16 the German colony of Kamerun was occupied by British and French forces and on 4 March 1916 was provisionally divided between France and Britain, the latter receiving a strip of territory along the Nigerian border. This arrangement was recognised by the peace settlement of 1919, with the proviso that what had been the German protectorate before 1911 was to be administered by the two powers under League of Nations mandates. In 1946 the mandates were changed to trusteeships under the United Nations.

The stamps issued in the British area are listed in the *British Commonwealth Catalogue*.

PRINTERS. All the stamps of Cameroun were printed at the Government Printing Works, Paris, *unless otherwise stated.*

IMPERFORATE STAMPS. Many stamps exist imperforate in their issued colours but were not valid for postage. Imperforate stamps in other colours are colour trials.

A. FRENCH OCCUPATION
September 1914–20 July 1922

Corps Expéditionnaire
Franco-Anglais
CAMEROUN

(1)

1915 (10 Nov). *Stamps of Gabon of 1910–17 (except 10 c., which is No. 37), optd as T 1, reading up on vert stamps.*

1	1 c. brown and orange	..	..	22·00	7·00
2	2 c. black and chocolate	..	..	40·00	38·00
3	4 c. violet and dull blue	..	..	40·00	38·00
4	5 c. olive-grey and emerald	..	..	6·50	3·25
	a. Opt double	..	..	£1200	
5	10 c. red and rose-lake	..	..	6·50	3·25
	a. Error. On Gabon No. 53	..	..	£3750	£3750
6	20 c. chocolate and violet	..	..	45·00	40·00
7	25 c. chocolate and dull blue	..	..	13·00	4·50
8	30 c. scarlet and grey	..	..	38·00	35·00
9	35 c. green and violet	..	..	9·50	4·50
	a. Opt double	..	..	£350	£350
10	40 c. ultramarine and brown	..	..	45·00	38·00
	a. "Franco-Anglais" omitted	..	..		
11	45 c. violet and carmine	..	..	48·00	40·00
12	50 c. grey and blue-green	..	..	48·00	38·00
13	75 c. chocolate and orange-vermilion	..	65·00	38·00
14	1 f. bistre and brown	..	..	55·00	40·00
15	2 f. brown and carmine	..	..	55·00	40·00

Inverted "s" in "Corps" exists on all values.

Occupation
Française
du Cameroun

(2)

CAMEROUN
Occupation
Française.

(3)

1916 (Jan). *Stamps of Congo optd locally as T 2 (vert on 20 c. to 2 f.).*

(a) On stamps of Middle Congo, 1907–17

16	1 c. olive and brown	..	..	19·00	19·00
17	2 c. violet and brown	..	..	22·00	19·00
18	4 c. blue and brown	..	..	22·00	19·00
19	5 c. green and blue	..	..	7·00	4·00
20	35 c. chocolate and blue	..	..	28·00	19·00
21	45 c. violet and salmon	..	..	16·00	16·00

(b) On stamps of French Congo, 1900–4

22	15 c. dull violet and olive-green	..	..	16·00	16·00
	a. Opt inverted	..	..	25·00	25·00
23	20 c. green and pale red	..	..	38·00	19·00
24	30 c. carmine and yellow	..	..	22·00	13·00
25	40 c. chestnut and green	..	..	16·00	16·00
26	50 c. deep violet and lilac	..	..	17·00	16·00
27	75 c. claret and orange	..	..	17·00	13·00
28	1 f. drab and slate	..	..	28·00	19·00
29	2 f. carmine and grey-brown	..	..	28·00	19·00
16/29	*Set of 14*	..	..	£300	£225

The overprint reads down on Nos. 20/21. On Nos. 23/29 it reads up or down (same prices) but pairs with overprint *tête-bêche* are rare.

1916–17. *Stamps of Congo (Middle Congo issue of 1907–17), optd in Paris with T 3 (1 c. to 20 c.) or with first two lines 7 mm apart (others).*

30	**1**	1 c. olive and brown	..	5	5
		a. No stop	..	90	90
31		2 c. violet and brown	..	5	5
		a. No stop	..	90	90
32		4 c. blue and brown	..	5	5
33		5 c. green and blue	..	5	5
34		10 c. carmine and blue	..	20	15
34a		15 c. purple and carmine (1917)	..	25	12
35		20 c. pale brown and blue	..	8	8
36	**2**	25 c. blue and grey-green	..	12	10
		a. Opt triple	..	65·00	
		b. Inverted "s"	..	1·25	1·25
		c. No stop	..	1·50	1·50
37		30 c. salmon-pink and green	..	10	8
		a. Opt double	..	25·00	
		b. Inverted "s"	..	1·25	1·25
		c. No stop	..	1·50	1·50
38		35 c. chocolate and blue	..	12	10
		a. Inverted "s"	..	1·25	1·25
		b. No stop	..	1·50	1·50
39		40 c. dull green and pale brown	..	20	15
		a. Inverted "s"	..	1·25	1·25
		b. No stop	..	1·50	1·50
40		45 c. violet and salmon	..	25	20
		a. Inverted "s"	..	1·50	1·50
		b. No stop	..	1·50	1·50
41		50 c. green and salmon	..	25	20
		a. Inverted "s"	..	1·50	1·50
		b. No stop	..	1·50	1·50
42		75 c. brown and blue	..	40	25
		a. Inverted "s"	..	1·50	1·50
43	**3**	1 f. deep green and pale violet	..	25	20
		a. Inverted "s"	..	1·50	1·50
		b. No stop	..	3·25	3·25
44		2 f. violet and grey-green	..	1·75	1·10
		a. Inverted "s"	..	7·00	7·00
45		5 f. blue and pink	..	1·75	1·50
		a. Inverted "s"	..	9·00	9·00
		b. No stop	..		
30/45		*Set of 17*	..	5·50	4·00

All values except the 15 c. exist on chalk-surfaced paper (same prices).

CAMEROUN

(4)

1921 (15 July). *Stamps of Congo (Middle Congo types of 1907–17) but colours changed, optd in Paris with T 4.*

46	1 c. orange and olive-green	..	..	5	5
47	2 c. carmine and brown	..	..	5	5
	a. Opt "CAMEROUN" omitted	..	38·00	
48	4 c. green and grey	..	..	5	5
	a. Opt "CAMEROUN" omitted	..	38·00	
49	5 c. orange and red	..	..	5	5
	a. Opt double	..	..	£130	
50	10 c. pale green and green	..	..	5	5
51	15 c. orange and blue	..	..	5	5
	a. Opt "CAMEROUN" omitted	..	75·00	

52	20 c. grey and dull purple	..	5	5
53	25 c. orange and slate	..	8	8
	a. Opt "CAMEROUN" omitted		90·00	
54	30 c. red and carmine	..	8	5
55	35 c. ultramarine and grey	..	12	12
56	40 c. orange and olive-green	..	10	8
57	45 c. carmine and brown ..	..	10	8
58	50 c. ultramarine and blue	..	5	5
	a. Opt "CAMEROUN" omitted		38·00	
59	75 c. green and claret	..	10	10
60	1 f. orange and slate	..	30	30
61	2 f. carmine and olive-green	..	1·10	90
62	5 f. grey and vermilion ..	..	1·40	1·25
46/62	Set of 17	..	3·50	3·00

No. 47a differs from No. 2a of Chad in that the centre is carmine instead of pink.

B. FRENCH MANDATED TERRITORY
20 July 1922–12 December 1946

1924 (June)–**25**. Stamps of 1921 surch with new value, and bars obliterating original value.

63	25 c. on 15 c. orange and blue (1.2.25)	..	12	12
64	25 c. on 2 f. carmine and olive-green	..	12	12
65	25 c. on 5 f. grey and vermilion ..	..	12	12
66	"65" on 45 c. carmine and brown (1.2.25)		35	35
67	"85" on 75 c. green and claret (1.2.25)	..	40	40
63/67	Set of 5	.. ..	1·00	1·00

5 Cattle fording River

6 Tapping Rubber-trees

7 Liana Suspension Bridge

D 8 Felling Mahogany Tree

(Des J. Kerhor. Eng G. Daussy. Typo)

1925 (1 May)–**26**. P 14 × 13½ (horiz) or 13½ × 14 (vert).

68	**5**	1 c. magenta and yellow-white ..	..	5	5
69		2 c. green and carmine/greenish	..	5	5
70		4 c. black and pale blue	..	5	5
71		5 c. bright violet and yellow	..	5	5
72		10 c. orange and purple/yellow ..	..	5	5
73		15 c. yellow-green and green	..	5	5
74	**6**	20 c. chestnut and olive	..	5	5
75		25 c. black and yellow-green	..	10	5
76		30 c. scarlet and pale green	..	5	5
77		35 c. black and brown	..	5	5
78		40 c. bright violet and orange	..	20	15
79		45 c. carmine and rose-red	..	5	5
80		50 c. carmine and yellow-green	..	5	5
81		60 c. black and mauve ..	..	5	5
82		65 c. brown and deep blue	..	5	5
83		75 c. bright and deep blue	..	10	5
84		85 c. light blue and rose-red	..	10	5
85	**7**	1 f. brown and deep blue	..	12	10
86		2 f. red-orange and olive-green	..	45	12
		a. Error. Black and brown/azure	..	£400	
		b. Value omitted	..	28·00	
		c. Value double	..	16·00	
87		5 f. black and brown/azure	..	65	25
68/87		Set of 20	.. ..	1·50	95

(Des J. Kerhor. Eng G. Daussy. Typo)

1925 (20 May)–**27**. POSTAGE DUE. P 14 × 13½.

D 88	**D 8**	2 c. black and light blue ..		5	5
D 89		4 c. purple and yellow-olive	..	5	5
D 90		5 c. black and lilac	..	8	8
D 91		10 c. black and red	..	10	10
D 92		15 c. black and drab	..	12	12
D 93		20 c. black and olive-green	..	15	15
D 94		25 c. black and yellow	..	20	20
D 95		30 c. orange and blue	..	25	25
D 96		50 c. black and brown	..	30	30
D 97		60 c. carmine and green	..	40	40
D 98		1 f. green and red/greenish	..	40	40
D 99		2 f. mauve and red (10.10.27)		65	65
D100		3 f. brt blue & red-brn (10.10.27)		90	90
D88/100		Set of 13	..	3·25	3·25

1927–38. New values and colours. P 14 × 13½ or 13½ × 14.

88	**5**	15 c. red and lilac (14.11.27)		15	15
89	**6**	20 c. green (1.3.26)	..	5	5
90		20 c. brown and lake (28.2.27)		5	5
91		30 c. green and deep olive (14.11.27)		5	5
91a		35 c. yellow-green and green (1938)	..	15	15
92		45 c. chestnut and mauve (14.11.27) ..		50	40
93		55 c. carmine and bright blue (1938) ..		20	20
		a. Value omitted	..	20·00	
94		60 c. carmine (1.3.26)	..	5	5
95		75 c. magenta and chestnut (5.9.27)	..	8	5
95a		80 c. brown and carmine (1938)	..	20	20
96		90 c. rose-red and carmine (28.2.27) ..		40	20
97	**7**	1 f. blue (1.3.26)	..	10	5
98		1 f. magenta and brown (14.11.27) ..		10	10
99		1 f. brown and green (25.3.29)	..	30	20
100		1 f. 10, brown and carmine (25.9.28)		90	75
100a		1 f. 25, blue and brown (25.9.33) ..		95	50
101		1 f. 50, blue (28.2.27)	..	20	5
101a		1 f. 75, orange and brown (25.9.33)	..	25	20
101b		1 f. 75, blue and deep blue (1938) ..		20	15
		c. Value double	..	14·00	
102		3 f. magenta and brown (19.12.27) ..		1·40	25
		a. Value double	..	17·00	
103		10 f. mauve and orange (20.12.26)	..	2·50	1·25
		a. Value omitted	..	55·00	
104		20 f. green and carmine (20.12.26)	..	4·50	2·10
88/104		Set of 22	.. ..	12·00	6·50

=

1ᶠ25

(8)

1926 (14 June). Surch with T 8.

105	**7**	1 f. 25 on 1 f. blue (R.)	..	5	5

9 French Colonial Races

10 Native Women

11 "France the Civiliser"

12 French Colonial Commerce

(Des J. de la Nézière, Mme Cayon-Rouan, A. Parent and G. François resp. Recess)

1931 (13 Apr). *International Colonial Exhibition, Paris. Inscr "CAMEROUN" in black. P 12½.*

106	**9**	40 c. green	65	50
		a. "CAMEROUN" omitted	6·50	
107	**10**	50 c. mauve	1·00	90
		a. "CAMEROUN" omitted	32·00	
108	**11**	90 c. vermilion	1·00	75
		a. "CAMEROUN" omitted	6·50	
109	**12**	1 f. 50, blue	1·00	90
		a. "CAMEROUN" omitted	6·50	
106/109		*Set of* 4	3·25	2·75

13 Commerce

14 Sailing Ships

15 Berber, Negress and Annamite   **16** Agriculture

17 France extends Torch of Civilisation   **18** Diane de Poitiers

(Des Jean Goujon (**13**), Robichon (**14**), Mme Cayon-Rouan (**15**), A. Decaris (**16**, **18**), Barlangue (**17**). Eng Cottet (**13**), Feltesse (**14**), Munier (**15**), A. Decaris (**16**, **18**), Delzers (**17**). Recess)

1937 (15 Apr). *International Exhibition, Paris. P 13.*

110	**13**	20 c. bright violet	25	25
111	**14**	30 c. green	20	20
112	**15**	40 c. carmine	20	20
113	**16**	50 c. brown	12	12
114	**17**	90 c. scarlet	25	25
115	**18**	1 f. 50, blue	20	20
110/115		*Set of* 6	1·10	1·10
MS115a		120×100 mm. **16** 3 f. orange-red and black. Imperf	1·00	1·00

19 Pierre and Marie Curie

20

(Des J. de la Nézière. Eng J. Piel. Recess)

1938 (24 Oct). *International Anti-Cancer Fund. P 13.*

116	**19**	1 f. 75+50 c. ultramarine	1·75	1·50

(Des and eng A. Decaris. Recess Institut de Gravure, Paris)

1939 (10 May). *New York World's Fair. P 12½.*

117	**20**	1 f. 25, lake	15	15
118		2 f. 25, ultramarine	15	15

21 Lamido Woman

22 Banyo Waterfall

23 Elephants

24 African Boatman

(Eng Degorce (**21**, **24**), H. Cheffèr (**22**), A. Decaris (**23**). Recess)

1939 (12 June)–**40**. *P 13.*

119	**21**	2 c. black-brown	5	5
120		3 c. magenta	5	5
121		4 c. ultramarine	5	5
122		5 c. brown-lake	5	5
123		10 c. green	5	5
124		15 c. scarlet	5	5
125		20 c. purple	5	5
126	**22**	25 c. black-brown	12	12
127		30 c. red-orange	8	5
128		40 c. ultramarine	10	10
129		45 c. myrtle-green	40	30
130		50 c. brown-lake	10	10
131		60 c. turquoise-blue	10	10
132		70 c. purple	55	55
133	**23**	80 c. turquoise-blue	40	35
134		90 c. turquoise-blue	15	5
135		1 f. carmine	20	20
135a		1 f. chocolate (15.4.40)	20	12
136		1 f. 25, carmine	55	55
137		1 f. 40, red-orange	25	20
138		1 f. 50, chocolate	12	12
139		1 f. 60, black-brown	50	45
140		1 f. 75, blue	10	10
141		2 f. green	5	5
142		2 f. 25, blue	15	15
143		2 f. 50, bright purple	25	20
144		3 f. deep violet	10	5
145	**24**	5 f. black-brown	20	15
146		10 f. bright purple	30	25
147		20 f. green	45	30
119/147		*Set of* 30	5·00	4·50

D **25** African Idols

25 Storming the Bastille

(Eng A. Decaris. Recess)

1939 (12 June). *POSTAGE DUE. P* 14 ×13.

D148	D **25**	5 c. bright purple			5	5
D149		10 c. turquoise-blue			15	15
D150		15 c. carmine			5	5
D151		20 c. black-brown			5	5
D152		30 c. ultramarine			5	5
D153		50 c. green			5	5
D154		60 c. deep purple			5	5
D155		1 f. deep violet			15	15
D156		2 f. red-orange			30	30
D157		3 f. blue			30	30
D148/157	Set of 10				1·10	1·10

(Des and eng Ouvré. Design photo, remainder typo Vaugirard, Paris)

1939 (5 July). *150th Anniv of French Revolution. Name and value in black. P* 13½ ×13.

148	**25**	45 c. +25 c. green			1·90	1·90
149		70 c. +30 c. brown			1·90	1·90
150		90 c. +35 c. red-orange			1·90	1·90
151		1 f. 25+1 f. carmine			2·25	2·25
152		2 f. 25+2 f. blue			2·25	2·25
148/152	Set of 5				9·00	9·00

VICHY ISSUES. A number of stamps were prepared by the Pétain Government of Unoccupied France for use in Cameroun but were not placed on sale there.

CAMEROUN FRANCAIS

CAMEROUN FRANCAIS

27-8-40

(26)

27.8.40

(27)

1940 (2–26 Oct). *Adherence to General de Gaulle. Variously optd as T* 26 *or* 27 (*horiz designs*).

153	**21**	2 c. black-brown (R.)			5	5
		a. Black opt			£350	
154		3 c. magenta			5	5
155		4 c. ultramarine (R.)			10	10
		a. Black opt			£325	
156		5 c. brown-lake			35	35
157		10 c. green (R.)			5	5
158		15 c. scarlet			15	15
159		20 c. purple (R.)			1·50	1·25
160	**22**	25 c. black-brown			10	5
		a. Opt inverted			50·00	
161		30 c. red-orange			1·25	75
162		40 c. ultramarine			50	25
163		45 c. myrtle-green			40	20
164	**6**	50 c. carmine and yellow-green			12	5
		a. Opt inverted			48·00	
165	**22**	60 c. turquoise-blue			65	40
166		70 c. purple			12	12
167	**23**	80 c. turquoise-blue (R.)			65	50
168		90 c. turquoise-blue (R.)			15	15
169	**20**	1 f. 25, lake			65	65
170	**23**	1 f. 25, carmine			25	20
171		1 f. 40, red-orange			40	30
172		1 f. 50, chocolate			15	15
173		1 f. 60, black-brown (R.)			25	25
174		1 f. 75, blue (R.)			25	25
		a. Opt inverted			38·00	

175	**20**	2 f. 25, ultramarine			65	65
176	**23**	2 f. 25, blue (R.)			15	12
177		2 f. 50, bright purple			15	12
178	**7**	5 f. black and brown/*azure*			2·50	2·00
179	**24**	5 f. black-brown			3·25	2·50
180	**7**	10 f. mauve and orange			3·75	3·25
181	**24**	10 f. bright purple			8·00	5·00
182	**7**	20 f. green and carmine			9·00	7·00
183	**24**	20 f. green			45·00	45·00
153/183	Set of 31				70·00	65·00

The overprint settings consisted of mixed type and many varieties exist, including mixed numerals, closed "4", wrong fount "C" in "CAMEROUN", broken "B" for "R", etc.

OEUVRES DE GUERRE

(28)

(29)

1940 (21 Oct). *War Relief Fund. Surch as T* 28.

184	**7**	1 f. 25+2 f. blue and brown			2·75	2·75
185		1 f. 75+3 f. orange and brown			2·75	2·75
186		2 f. +5 f. red-orange and olive-green			2·75	2·75

Exist without "S" in "OEUVRES". (*Price each £4 un or us.*)

1940 (28 Nov). *Spitfire Fund. Surch with T* 29.

187	**22**	25 c. +5 f. black-brown			25·00	22·00
188		45 c. +5 f. myrtle-green			25·00	22·00
189		60 c. +5 f. turquoise-blue			32·00	25·00
190		70 c. +5 f. purple			32·00	25·00
187/190	Set of 4				£100	85·00

(29*a*)

1941 (25 Feb). *Spitfire Fund. Surch with T* 29*a*.

190*a*	**20**	1 f. 25+10 f. lake			22·00	15·00
190*b*		2 f. 25+10 f. ultramarine			22·00	15·00

Nos. 190*a/b* exist with "a" of "Général" inverted and also with "e" of "de" inverted (*Price each £75 un or us*).

29*b* 'Plane over Map

29*c* Flying Boat

29*d* 'Plane over Harbour

+ **10 Frs.**
AMBULANCE
LAQUINTINIE

(30)

(T **29***b/c* des J. Douy. T **29***d* des Ouvré. Photo Vaugirard)

1941 (17 Mar). *AIR. Prepared by Vichy Govt but issued by Free French. P* 13½.

190*c*	**29***b*	25 c. brown-red			5	5
190*d*		50 c. green			5	5
190*e*		1 f. purple			5	5

190*f*	**29***c*	2 f. olive-green	..	..	.. 5 5
190*g*		3 f. brown	..	..	.. 5 5
190*h*		4 f. deep blue	..	..	.. 5 5
190*i*		6 f. myrtle-green	..		.. 5 5
190*j*		7 f. purple	..	..	.. 5 5
190*k*	12	f. yellow-orange	..		.. 1·25 1·25
190*l*	20	f. rose-red	..	..	.. 20 20
190*m*	**29***d* 50	f. ultramarine	..	..	.. 30 30
190*c*/190*m*		Set of 11	..	..	.. 2·00 2·00

1941 (3 June). *Laquintinie Hospital Fund. Surch with T* **30**.

191	**20**	1 f. 25+10 f. lake (B.)	..	.. 3·75 2·75
192		2 f. 25+10 f. ultramarine	..	.. 3·75 2·75

31 Cross of Lorraine, Sword and Shield

32 Airliner

(Des E. Dulac. Photo Harrison & Sons)

1942. *Free French Issue.* (*a*) POSTAGE. *P* 14×14½.

193	**31**	5 c. brown	..	..	.. 5 5
194		10 c. blue	..	..	.. 5 5
195		25 c. emerald-green	..	..	.. 5 5
196		30 c. red-orange	..	..	.. 5 5
197		40 c. slate-green	..	..	.. 5 5
198		80 c. maroon	..	..	.. 5 5
199		1 f. magenta	..	..	.. 5 5
200		1 f. 50, scarlet	..	..	.. 5 5
201		2 f. grey-black	..	..	.. 5 5
		a. Error. Deep green	..	.. 55·00
202		2 f. 50, ultramarine	..	..	.. 5
203		4 f. violet	..	..	.. 12 12
204		5 f. yellow-bistre	..	..	.. 20 15
		a. Error. Carmine	..	.. 55·00
205		10 f. red-brown	..	..	.. 25 12
206		20 f. blue-green	..	..	.. 45 15
		a. Error. Blue	..	.. 45·00
		b. Error. Carmine	..	.. 45·00
		c. Error. Orange	..	.. 45·00

(*b*) AIR. *P* 14½×14

207	**32**	1 f. red-orange	..	..	.. 5 5
208		1 f. 50, scarlet	..	..	.. 5 5
209		5 f. maroon	..	..	.. 5 5
210		10 f. black	..	..	.. 12 12
211		25 f. ultramarine	..	..	.. 20 20
212		50 f. green	..	..	.. 25 25
213	100	f. claret	..	..	.. 40 40
193/213		Set of 21	..	..	.. 2·40 2·00

(Des E. Dulac. Photo Harrison)

1944 (Dec). *Mutual Aid and Red Cross Funds. P* 14½×14.

214	**33**	5 f.+20 f. rose	..	..	.. 45 45

1945. *Surch with new values and bars.*

215	**31**	50 c. on 5 c. brown (R.)	..	.. 5 5
216		60 c. on 5 c. brown (R.)	..	.. 5 5
		a. Surch inverted	..	.. 21·00
217		70 c. on 5 c. brown (R.)	..	.. 8 8
218		1 f. 20 on 5 c. brown (R.)	..	.. 5 5
219		2 f. 40 on 25 c. emerald-green	.. 5 5
220		3 f. on 25 c. emerald-green	..	12 12
221		4 f. 50 on 25 c. emerald-green	25 25
222		15 f. on 2 f. 50, ultramarine (R.)	25 25
215/222		Set of 8	..	..	.. 65 65

1945. *Recess. P* 13.

223	**34**	2 f. black	..	..	.. 5 5
224		25 f. blue-green	..	..	.. 15 15

35 "Victory"

(Des and eng A. Decaris. Recess Institut de Gravure)

1946 (8 May). *AIR. Victory. P* 12½.

225	**35**	8 f. brown-purple	..	..	.. 10 10

36 Chad

(Des and eng A. Decaris. Recess Institut de Gravure)

1946 (6 June). *AIR. From Chad to the Rhine. As T* **36** (*inscr* "DU TCHAD AU RHIN"). *P* 12½.

226	**35**	5 f. greenish blue (T **36**)	..	12 12
227		10 f. purple (Koufra)	..	.. 15 15
228		15 f. rose-red (Mareth)	..	20 20
229		20 f. ultramarine (Normandy)	.. 20 20
230		25 f. brown-red (Paris)	..	.. 25 25
231		50 f. blackish olive (Strasbourg)	30 30
226/231		Set of 6	..	..	.. 1·10 1·10

33

34 Félix Eboué

37 Zebu and Herdsman   **38** Tikar Women

39 Africans carrying Bananas (23×37 *mm*)
40 Bowman (23×37 *mm*)

41 Lamido Horsemen   **45** Aeroplane, African and Mask

42 Native Head (23×37 mm)

43 Birds in Flight over Mountain Ranges

44 African Horsemen and Aeroplane (49×27 mm)
45a Aeroplane over Piton d'Humsiki (27×48 mm)

(Des and eng G. Barlangue (**37**, **38**, **43**), A. Decaris (**39**/**41**, **44**), G. Bétemps (**42**, **45**), P. Gandon (**45a**). Recess Institut de Gravure, Paris)

1946–53. P 12½. (a) POSTAGE.

232	**37**	10 c. blue-green	..	..	5	5
233		30 c. brown-orange	..	..	5	5
234		40 c. ultramarine	..	..	5	5
235	**38**	50 c. olive-brown	..	..	5	5
236		60 c. purple	..	..	5	5
237		80 c. chestnut	..	..	5	5
238	**39**	1 f. red-orange	..	..	5	5
239		1 f. 20, bright green	..	..	5	5
240		1 f. 50, lake	..	..	30	30
241	**40**	2 f. black	..	..	5	5
242		3 f. carmine	..	..	5	5
243		3 f. 60, brown-red	..	..	15	12
244		4 f. blue	..	..	5	5
245	**41**	5 f. lake ..	..	..	12	5
246		6 f. ultramarine	..	..	12	5
247		10 f. greenish slate	..	..	12	5
248	**42**	15 f. greenish blue	..	..	40	5
249		20 f. dull green	..	..	35	5
250		25 f. black	..	..	55	5

(b) AIR

251	**43**	50 f. greenish grey (10.2.47)	..		45	30
252	**44**	100 f. red-brown (10.2.47)	..		95	12
253	**45**	200 f. blackish olive (10.2.47)	..		1·75	45
253a	**45a**	500 f. indigo, deep ultramarine and deep lilac (16.2.53)	..		4·50	95
232/253a		Set of 23 ..	..	..	9·00	3·00

STAMP MONTHLY

—finest and most informative magazine for all collectors. Obtainable from your newsagent or by postal subscription—details on request.

C. FRENCH TRUST TERRITORY
13 December 1946–31 December 1959

D 46   **46** People of Five Races, Aircraft and Globe

(Recess Institut de Gravure, Paris)

1947. POSTAGE DUE. P 13.

D254	**D 46**	10 c. scarlet	..	..	..	5	5
D255		30 c. orange	..	..	..	5	5
D256		50 c. black	..	..	..	5	5
D257		1 f. carmine	..	..	..	5	5
D258		2 f. emerald-green	..	..	..	5	5
D259		3 f. magenta	..	..		5	5
D260		4 f. ultramarine	..	..		10	10
D261		5 f. red-brown	..	..		12	12
D262		10 f. greenish blue	..	..		20	20
D263		20 f. sepia	..	..		35	30
D254/263		Set of 10 ..	..	..	..	1·00	90

(Des and eng R. Serres. Recess)

1949 (4 July). AIR. 75th Anniv of Universal Postal Union. P 13.

254	**46**	25 f. multicoloured	..	..	..	1·10	1·00

47 Doctor and Patient   **48**

(Des and eng R. Serres. Recess)

1950 (15 May). Colonial Welfare Fund. P 13.

255	**47**	10 f.+2 f. green and blue-green	..	80	80

(Des R. Serres. Recess)

1952 (1 Dec). Centenary of Médaille Militaire. Name and value typo, in black. P 13.

256	**48**	15 f. carmine-lake, yellow and green	..	90	55

49 Edéa Barrage

(Des and eng C. Hertenberger. Recess)

1953 (18 Nov). AIR. Opening of Edéa Barrage. P 13.

257	**49**	15 f. blue, brown-lake & black-brown	80	40

50 "D-Day"

(Des and eng R. Serres. Recess)

1954 (6 June). *AIR. 10th Anniv of Liberation. P* 13.
258 50 15 f. emerald and deep turquoise .. 95 75

51 Dr. Jamot and Students

(Des and eng J. Pheulpin. Recess)

1954 (29 Nov). *AIR. 75th Birthday of Dr. Jamot* (*physician*). *P* 13.
259 51 15 f. blackish brown, indigo & dp bl-grn 95 80

52 Porters
Carrying Bananas   53 Transporting Logs

(Des C. Mazelin. Eng R. Serres (40 f.). Des and eng R. Cami
(8 f., 15 f.), J. Pheulpin (50 f.), C. Hertenberger (100 f.),
H. Cheffer (200 f.). Recess)

1954–55. *Various designs. P* 13. (*a*) *POSTAGE. As T* 52
(29.11.54).
260   8 f. bluish violet, orange & bright purple 12   5
261   15 f. black-brown, yellow and red   ..   30   8
262   40 f. orange-brown, mag & blackish brn   30   5
(*b*) *AIR. As T* 53 (24.1.55)
263   50 f. olive-green, brown & blackish brn   50   8
264   100 f. blackish brown, brown & turquoise 1·25   20
265   200 f. chocolate, deep blue & slate-green 1·90   30
260/265 Set of 6   ..   ..   4·00   70
Designs: *Vert*—8 f., As T 52. 40 f. Woman gathering
coffee. *Horiz*—100 f. Aeroplane over giraffes; 200 f. Douala
Port.

54 Native Cattle   55 Coffee

(Des and eng R. Cottet. Recess)

1956 (4 June). *Economic and Social Development Fund.
T* 54 *and similar horiz designs inscr* "F.I.D.E.S." *P* 13.
266   5 f. orange-brown and blackish brown.. 15   10
267   15 f. turquoise-blue, violet-grey & black 20   5
268   20 f. turquoise-blue and deep blue   ..   30   15
269   25 f. deep bright blue   40   25
266/269 Set of 4   95   50
Designs:—15 f. R. Wouri bridge; 20 f. Technical education;
25 f. Mobile medical unit.

(Des and eng R. Serres. Recess)

1956 (22 Oct). *P* 13.
270 55 15 f. vermilion and carmine-red   ..   15   8

56 Woman, Child and Flag   57 "Human Rights"

(Des and eng R. Cottet. Recess)

1958 (10 May). *First Anniv of First Cameroun Government.
P* 13.
271 56 20 f. brown, green, red, yellow & ultram 30   5

(Des and eng R. Cami. Recess)

1958 (10 Dec). *10th Anniv of Declaration of Human Rights.
P* 13.
272 57 20 f. chocolate and brown-red   ..   35   25

58 *Randia malleifera*   59 Loading Bananas on Ship

(Des M. Rolland. Photo)

1959 (5 Jan). *Tropical Flora. P* 12½.
273 58 20 f. multicoloured   25   12

(Des and eng C. Durrens. Recess)

1959 (23 Mar). *T* 59 *and similar design. P* 13.
274   20 f. orange, brown, blue & dp bluish grn   20   5
275   25 f. grey-green, red-brown & purple-brn   25   8
Design: *Vert*—25 f. Bunch of bananas, and Africans on
jungle path.

A National Assembly was elected in 1959 and the French
trust territory of Cameroun became an independent republic on
1 January 1960.

A regular new issue supplement to this
catalogue appears each month in

STAMP MONTHLY

—from your newsagent or by postal subscription
—details on request.

Chad

100 Centimes = 1 Franc

A. FRENCH COLONY

Lake Chad was first explored by British explorers in 1823, but French influence reached there with the expeditions of Paul Crampel in 1890–91 and Emile Gentil in 1896–97. It was then within the empire of the Sudanese military adventurer and slave-dealer Rabah. After Rabah's defeat and death at the hands of a French expedition, Chad became a French military territory on 5 September 1900.

Chad became part of the French Congo and was integrated with Ubangi-Shari in 1906. The stamps of French Congo were used until 1915 and those of Ubangi-Shari-Chad (see under Central African Republic), from 1915 to 1922. Chad became a separate Colony on 17 March 1920.

PRINTERS. All the stamps of Chad, other than those in lithography, were printed at the Government Printing Works, Paris, *unless otherwise stated.*

IMPERFORATE STAMPS. Many stamps exist imperforate in their issued colours but they were not valid for postage. Imperforate stamps in other colours are colour trials.

TCHAD

(1)

1922 (Nov). *Types of Middle Congo, colours changed, optd with T* **1.**

1	1 c. bright rose and violet	.. ..	5	5
	a. Opt omitted	..	32·00	
2	2 c. brown and pink	..	5	5
	a. Opt omitted†	..	50·00	
3	4 c. slate-blue and violet	..	5	5
4	5 c. brown and green	..	15	15
5	10 c. green and blue-green	..	25	25
6	15 c. violet and rose	..	30	30
7	20 c. green and violet	..	95	95
8	25 c. brown and chocolate	..	1·75	1·75
9	30 c. carmine	.. ..	20	20
10	35 c. slate-blue and pink	..	50	50
11	40 c. purple-brown and green	..	50	50
12	45 c. violet and green	..	40	40
13	50 c. blue and pale blue	..	40	40
14	60 on 75 c. violet/*rose*	..	55	55
	a. Opt omitted	..	40·00	
	b. "60" omitted	..	40·00	
15	75 c. bright rose and violet	..	30	30
16	1 f. slate-blue and rose ..	..	2·25	2·25
17	2 f. slate-blue and violet	..	3·25	3·25
18	5 f. slate-blue and brown	..	2·25	2·25
1/18	*Set of* 18	.. ..	13·00	13·00

† See footnote relating to No. 47a of Cameroun.

1924 (Sept)–**33.** *Stamps of* 1922 *and similar stamps optd with Ubangi-Shari (Central African Republic) T* **5** (1 *c. to* 20 *c.) or* **6** *(others).*

19	1 c. bright rose and violet	..	5	5
	a. T **1** opt omitted	..	22·00	
	b. T **1** opt double	..	19·00	
	c. Violet (background) omitted	..	19·00	
20	2 c. brown and pink	..	5	5
	a. T **1** opt omitted	..	22·00	
	b. T **1** opt double	..	19·00	
21	4 c. slate-blue and violet	..	5	5
22	5 c. brown and green	..	8	8
	a. T **1** opt omitted	..	32·00	
	b. T **5** opt in blue	..	12	12
	c. Do. T **1** opt omitted	..	25·00	
23	10 c. green and blue-green	..	5	5
	a. T **5** opt in blue	..	10	10
24	10 c. orange-vermilion and grey (1.12.25)	5	5
	a. T **1** opt omitted	..	22·00	
	b. T **5** opt omitted	..	22·00	

25	15 c. violet and rose	.. .. ..	10	10
26	20 c. green and violet	.. ..	10	10
	a. T **1** opt omitted	.. ..	28·00	
27	25 c. brown and chocolate	..	10	10
	a. T **6** opt double	..	16·00	
28	30 c. carmine	.. ..	5	5
29	30 c. grey and blue (R.) (1.12.25)	5	5
30	30 c. olive-green and green (14.11.27)	..	15	15
	a. T **6** opt omitted	..	35·00	
31	35 c. slate-blue and pink ..	..	5	5
32	40 c. purple-brown and green	..	15	15
	a. T **6** opt double (Bk.+R.)	..	40·00	
33	45 c. violet and green	..	10	10
	a. T **6** opt double (Bk.+B.)	..	40·00	
34	50 c. blue and pale blue (R.)	..	10	10
	a. T **6** opt inverted	..	40·00	
35	50 c. green and purple (1.12.25) ..	..	15	15
36	60 on 75 c. violet/*rose*	..	5	5
	a. "60" omitted	..	28·00	
37	65 c. red-brown and blue (2.4.28)	..	30	30
	a. T **6** opt omitted	..	23·00	
38	75 c. bright rose and violet (B.) ..	..	10	10
39	75 c. blue and pale blue (R.) (1.6.25)	..	8	8
	a. T **1** opt omitted†	..	23·00	
40	75 c. claret and brown (25.9.28) ..	..	45	45
41	90 c. carmine and rose-red (22.3.30)	..	1·40	1·40
42	1 f. slate-blue and rose (B.)	..	25	25
43	1 f. 10, green and ultramarine (25.9.28)	40	40
44	1 f. 25, red-brown & ultram (25.9.33)	..	1·40	1·40
45	1 f. 50, ultramarine and blue (22.3.30) ..	1·40	1·40
46	1 f. 75, chocolate and magenta (25.9.33)	10·00	10·00
47	2 f. slate-blue and violet (B.)	..	40	40
48	3 f. magenta/*rose*(22.3.30)	..	1·50	1·50
49	5 f. slate-blue and brown (B.) ..	..	40	40
19/49	*Set of* 31	.. ..	18·00	18·00

† See footnote relating to No. 62a of Ubangi-Shari (Central African Republic).

1925–27. *Stamps as* 1924–33 *but colours changed, with opt T* **1** *in black and opt Ubangi-Shari T* **6** *in black or colours shown, further surch as Ubangi-Shari T* **7/10,** *in black.*

(a) In figures only (1.2.25)

50	65 on 1 f. chocolate and olive-green (R.)	25	25
51	85 on 1 f. chocolate and olive-green (R.)	25	25

(b) In figures with bars over old values

52	90 on 75 c. carmine & rose-red (11.4.27)	25	25
53	1 f. 25 on 1 f. blue and ultramarine (B.+R.) (14.6.26)	5	5
	a. T **6** opt omitted	.. ..	25·00	
54	1 f. 50 on 1 f. ultramarine and greenish blue (11.4.27)	30	30
55	3 f. on 5 f. chestnut & carmine (19.12.27)	80	80
	a. No stop after "F"	..	2·25	2·25
56	10 f. on 5 f. green and rose (21.3.27)	2·50	2·50
	a. "10 F" omitted	..	50·00	
57	20 f. on 5 f. violet and vermilion (21.3.27)	3·00	3·00
	a. No stop after "F"	..	6·50	6·50
50/57	*Set of* 8		6·50	6·50

On No. 53 the Type **6** overprint is in blue and the surcharge in red.

TCHAD

A. E. F.

(D 2)

1928 (4 Apr). *POSTAGE DUE. Type D* **11** *of France optd with Type D* **2.** *P* $14 \times 13\frac{1}{2}$.

D58	5 c. light blue ..	.. ..	5	5
D59	10 c. brown	.. .. ..	5	5
D60	20 c. olive-green	.. .. ..	10	10

D61	25 c. rosine				12	12
D62	30 c. rose				15	15
D63	45 c. green				20	.20
D64	50 c. claret				30	30
	a. No stop after "F"				1·60	1·60
D65	60 c. yellow-brown/*cream*				30	30
D66	1 f. maroon/*cream*				30	30
D67	2 f. rose-red				80	80
D68	3 f. bright violet				50	50
D58/68	*Set of* 11				4·00	4·00

D 3 Village of Straw-huts

D 4 Pirogue on Lake Chad

(Des J. Kerhor. Eng G. Daussy. Typo)

1930 (17 Feb). *POSTAGE DUE. P* 14×13½ (D **3**) *or* 13½×14 (D **4**).

D69	D **3**	5 c. drab and deep blue			5	5
D70		10 c. chocolate and scarlet			10	10
D71		20 c. chocolate and green			20	20
D72		25 c. chocolate and light blue			25	25
D73		30 c. blue-green and yellow-brown			25	25
D74		45 c. drab and blue-green			30	30
D75		50 c. chocolate and magenta			30	30
D76		60 c. black and lilac-blue			50	50
D77	D **4**	1 f. slate-black and yellow-brown			50	50
D78		2 f. chocolate and mauve			70	70
D79		3 f. chocolate and scarlet			7·50	7·50
D69/79	*Set of* 11				9·50	9·50

1931 (13 Apr). *International Colonial Exhibition, Paris. As T* **9/12** *of Cameroun.*

58	40 c. green				90	90
59	50 c. mauve				90	90
60	90 c. vermilion				90	90
61	1 f. 50, blue				90	90
58/61	*Set of* 4				2·50	2·50

From 16 March 1936 to 1959, stamps of French Equatorial Africa were used in Chad.

B. CHAD REPUBLIC

The Chad Republic was created as an autonomous state of the French Union on 28 November 1958.

2 "Birth of the Republic"

3 Flag, Map and U.N. Emblem

(Des and eng J. Combet. Recess)

1959 (28 Nov). *First Anniv of Republic. T* **2** *and similar vert design. P* 13.

62	15 f. lake, green, yellow and bright blue		20	10
63	25 f. lake and blackish green		25	10

Design:—25 f. Map and birds.

1960 (21 May). *10th Anniv of African Technical Co-operation Commission. As T* **62** *of Cameroun.*

64	50 f. violet and bright purple		55	50

Chad became an independent republic on 11 August 1960.

Stamp monthly

Gibbons' own monthly magazine, essential reading for **every** collector !
Detailed monthly New Issue Guide to update all Gibbons catalogues for you—and a special Stamp Market feature on price changes.
Informative articles cover all facets of philately, with regular notes on new discoveries, stamp designs, postmarks, market trends and news and views of the world of stamps.
Britain's LARGEST circulation of any stamp magazine—that fact speaks for itself !
Monthly from all dealers and newsagents or by post direct from Stanley Gibbons Magazines Ltd—subscription rates on application.

Comoro Islands

100 Centimes = 1 Franc

The Comoro Archipelago consists of the islands of Anjouan, Great Comoro, Mayotte and Mohéli, lying between Madagascar and Mozambique. France took possession of Mayotte as a colony in 1843 and the Sultans of Anjouan, Great Comoro and Mohéli placed themselves under French protection in 1886. In 1891 the protected islands became French colonies, and from 1898 to 1912 they were French dependencies. On 25 July 1912 the islands were again given the status of French colonies, until 23 February 1914 when the whole archipelago was subordinated to the Governor-General of Madagascar. From 1914 to 1950 the stamps of Madagascar were used in the islands.

PRINTERS. All stamps were printed at the Government Printing Works, Paris, *unless otherwise stated.*

IMPERFORATE STAMPS. Stamps exist imperforate in their issued colours but they were not valid for postage. Imperforate stamps in other colours are colour trials.

ANJOUAN

X. "Tablet" Type

		(2)	(3)

In Type A the space between "0" and "5" is $1\frac{1}{2}$ mm and between "1" and "0" $2\frac{1}{2}$ mm. In Type B the spacing is 2 mm and 3 mm respectively.

1892. (Nov). *Inscr* "SULTANAT D'ANJOUAN" *in red* (1, 5, 15, 25, 75 c. *and 1 f.) or blue (others).* P 14×13½.

1	X	1 c. black/*azure*		30	30
2		2 c. brown/*buff*		30	30
3		4 c. purple-brown/*grey*		60	35
4		5 c. green/*pale green*		1·00	80
5		10 c. black/*lilac*		1·10	1·00
6		15 c. blue		1·25	1·00
7		20 c. red/*green*		2·00	1·50
8		25 c. black/*rose*		2·00	1·50
9		30 c. cinnamon/*drab*		3·50	3·50
10		40 c. red/*yellow*		6·00	5·00
11		50 c. carmine/*rose*		5·50	4·00
12		75 c. brown/*orange*		5·00	3·50
13		1 f. olive-green/*toned*		14·00	12·00
1/13		*Set of 13*		40·00	32·00

1900 (Dec)–**07.** *Colours changed and new values.* *Inscr in blue* (10 c.) *or red* (others). P 14×13½.

14	X	10 c. rose-red		3·50	3·00
15		15 c. grey		2·00	1·75
16		25 c. blue		3·00	3·00
17		35 c. black/*yellow* (7.06)		1·75	1·25
18		45 c. black/*green* (10.07)		25·00	20·00
19		50 c. brown/*azure*		4·00	3·50
14/19		*Set of 6*		36·00	30·00

1912 (Nov). *Surch with T 2 or 3.*

A. *Narrow spacing.* B. *Wide spacing*

			A		B	
20	X	05 on 2 c. brown/*buff*	12	12	1·60	1·60
21		05 on 4 c. purple-brn/*grey* (R.)	12	12	1·60	1·60
		a. Pair, one without surch	—	—	†	
22		05 on 15 c. blue (R.)	12	12	1·60	1·60
		a. Pair, one without surch	—	—	†	
23		05 on 20 c. red/*green*	12	12	1·60	1·60
		a. Pair, one without surch	—	—	†	

			A		B	
24	X	05 on 25 c. black/*rose* (R.)	12	12	1·60	1·60
25		05 on 30 c. cinna/*drab* (R.)	15	15	1·60	1·60
26		10 on 40 c. red/*yellow*	15	15	8·00	8·00
27		10 on 45 c. black/*green* (R.)	20	20	9·50	9·50
28		10 on 50 c. carmine/*rose*	45	45	20·00	20·00
29		10 on 75 c. brown/*orange*	30	30	14·00	14·00
30		10 on 1 f. olive-green/*toned*	30	30	20·00	20·00
		a. Pair, one without surch	—	—	†	
20/30		*Set of 11*		1·90	1·90	75·00 75·00

GREAT COMORO

1897 (Nov). *Inscr* "GRANDE COMORE", *in red* (1, 5, 15, 25, 75 c., 1 f.) *or blue* (others). P 14×13½.

1	X	1 c. black/*azure*		8	8
2		2 c. brown/*buff*		15	12
3		4 c. purple-brown/*grey*		30	30
4		5 c. green/*pale green*		30	30
5		10 c. black/*lilac*		1·00	80
6		15 c. blue		2·50	2·00
7		20 c. red/*green*		2·50	2·00
8		25 c. black/*rose*		2·75	2·00
9		30 c. cinnamon/*drab*		3·25	2·25
10		40 c. red/*yellow*		3·50	2·75
11		50 c. carmine/*rose*		5·50	3·50
12		75 c. brown/*orange*		6·50	5·00
13		1 f. olive-green/*toned*		5·00	3·50
1/13		*Set of 13*		30·00	22·00

1900 (Dec)–**07.** *Colours changed. Inscr in blue* (10 c.) *or red* (others). P 14×13½.

14	X	10 c. rose-red		2·50	2·50
15		15 c. grey		2·50	2·50
16		25 c. blue		3·75	1·90
17		35 c. black/*yellow* (7.06)		3·75	2·50
18		45 c. black/*green* (11.07)		18·00	15·00
19		50 c. brown/*azure*		7·50	7·00
14/19		*Set of 6*		35·00	28·00

1912 (Nov). *Surch as T 2 and 3 of Anjouan.*

A. *Narrow spacing.* B. *Wide spacing*

			A		B	
20	X	05 on 2 c. brown/*buff*	20	20	90	90
21		05 on 4 c. pur-brn/*grey* (R.)	15	15	90	90
22		05 on 15 c. blue (R.)	12	12	90	90
23		05 on 20 c. red/*green*	15	15	1·90	1·90
24		05 on 25 c. black/*rose* (R.)	20	20	1·60	1·60
25		05 on 30 c. cinna/*drab* (R.)	20	20	1·60	1·60
26		10 on 40 c. red/*yellow*	20	20	11·00	11·00
27		10 on 45 c. black/*green* (R.)	20	20	9·50	9·50
28		10 on 60 c. carmine/*rose*	30	30	9·50	9·50
29		10 on 75 c. brown/*orange*	30	30	19·00	19·00
20/29		*Set of 10*		1·75	1·75	50·00 50·00

For note re spacing see Anjouan.

MAYOTTE

1892 (Nov)–**99.** *Inscr* "MAYOTTE". *Name in red* (1, 5, 15, 25, 75 c. *and 1 f.) or blue* (others). P 14×13½.

1	X	1 c. black/*azure*		8	8
2		2 c. brown/*buff*		12	12
		a. Name double		50·00	50·00
3		4 c. purple-brown/*grey*		25	25
4		5 c. green/*pale green*		45	35
5		10 c. black/*lilac*		60	45
6		15 c. blue		2·00	1·50
7		20 c. red/*green*		2·00	1·75
8		25 c. black/*rose*		1·25	1·00
9		30 c. cinnamon/*drab*		2·00	1·75
10		40 c. red/*yellow*		2·00	1·75

11	X	50 c. carmine/*rose*			3·25	2·25
12		75 c. brown/*orange*			3·50	2·75
13		1 f. olive-green/*toned*			2·50	2·25
14		5 f. mauve/*pale lilac* (1899)			16·00	15·00
1/14		*Set of 14*			35·00	30·00

1900 (Dec)–**07**. *Colours changed and new values. Name in blue* (10 c.) *or red* (*others*). *P* 14×13½.

15	X	10 c. rose-red			9·00	7·00
16		15 c. grey			18·00	16·00
17		25 c. blue			1·60	1·25
18		35 c. black/*yellow* (7.06)			1·25	1·10
19		45 c. black/*green* (10.07)			2·50	1·75
20		50 c. brown/*azure*			2·75	2·75
15/20		*Set of 6*			32·00	27·00

1912 (Nov). *Surch as T* **2** *and* **3** *of Anjouan.*

A. Narrow spacing. B. Wide spacing

			A	B		
21	X	05 on 2 c. brown/*buff*	25	25	2·50	2·50
		a. Pair, one without surch	—	†		
22		05 on 4 c. purple-brn/*grey* (R.)	20	20	1·60	1·60
23		05 on 15 c. blue (R.)	15	15	1·25	1·25
24		05 on 20 c. red/*green*	20	20	1·60	1·60
25		05 on 25 c. black/*rose* (R.)	20	20	1·60	1·60
		a. Surch double	38·00	—	£375	—
26		05 on 30 c. cinna/*drab* (R.)	20	20	1·25	1·25
27		10 on 40 c. red/*yellow*	20	20	10·00	10·00
		a. Surch double	38·00	—	£450	—
28		10 on 45 c. black/*green* (R.)	10	10	7·50	7·50
		a. Surch double	38·00	—	£450	—
29		10 on 50 c. carmine/*rose*	45	45	13·00	13·00
30		10 on 75 c. brown/*orange*	30	30	13·00	13·00
31		10 on 1 f. olive-green/*toned*	30	30	25·00	25·00
21/31		*Set of 11*	2·25	2·25	70·00	70·00

MOHÉLI

1906–07. *Inscr* "MOHÉLI" *in blue* (2, 4, 10, 20, 30, 40 c. *and* 5 f.) *or red* (*others*). *P* 14×13½.

1	X	1 c. black/*azure*			40	40
2		2 c. brown/*buff*			45	40
3		4 c. purple-brown/*grey*			50	50
4		5 c. yellow-green			55	40
5		10 c. rose-red			75	50
6		20 c. red/*green*			1·50	90
7		25 c. blue			1·50	90
8		30 c. cinnamon/*drab*			3·25	1·80
9		35 c. black/*yellow*			1·25	65
10		40 c. red			2·50	1·75
11		45 c. black/*green* (1907)			·11·00	9·50
12		50 c. brown/*azure*			4·50	2·50
13		75 c. brown/*orange*			4·50	4·50
14		1 f. olive-green/*toned*			4·50	2·50
15		2 f. violet/*rose*			7·00	5·50
16		5 f. mauve/*pale lilac*			25·00	24·00
1/16		*Set of 16*			65·00	50·00

1912 (Nov). *Surch as T* **2** *and* **3** *of Anjouan.*

A. Narrow spacing. B. Wide spacing

			A	B		
17	X	05 on 4 c. purple-brn/*grey* (R.)	20	20	2·50	2·50
18		05 on 20 c. red/*green*	65	65	9·00	9·00
19		05 on 30 c. cinna/*drab* (R.)	25	25	9·00	9·00
20		10 on 40 c. red/*yellow*	20	20	25·00	25·00
21		10 on 45 c. black/*green* (R.)	20	20	11·00	11·00
		a. Name double	45·00	—	†	
22		10 on 50 c. brown/*azure* (R.)	35	35	22·00	22·00
17/22		*Set of 6*	1·60	1·60	70·00	70·00

For note *re* spacing, see Anjouan.

A regular new issue supplement to this catalogue appears each month in

STAMP MONTHLY

—from your newsagent or by postal subscription
—details on request.

COMORO ISLANDS
(General Issues)

On 9 May 1946 the Comoro Archipelago was given administrative autonomy within the French Republic.

1 Anjouan Bay   **2** Native Woman

3 Mosque at Moroni

4 Ouani Mosque, Anjouan (22½×36 *mm*)

5 Coelacanth (36×22½ *mm*)

6 Mutsamudu Village   D **9** Mosque in Anjouan

7 Natives and Mosque de Vendredi (48×27 *mm*)
8 Ouani Mosque, Anjouan (48×27 *mm*)

(Postage. Des Barlangue (T **1**, **4**), Mahias (T **2/3**). Eng Barlangue (T **1**, **4**), Dufresne (T **2**) and Munier (T **3**). Air. Des and eng P. Gandon (T **5**), J. Pheulpin (T **6**) and R. Serres (T **7/8**). Recess)

1950 (15 May)–**54**. *P* 13. (*a*) *POSTAGE.*

1	1	10 c. blue				5	5
2		50 c. yellowish green				5	5
3		1 f. brown				5	5
4	2	2 f. emerald-green				10	10
5		5 f. bright violet				10	10
6		6 f. plum				15	15
7	3	7 f. scarlet				15	15
8		10 f. green				15	15
9		11 f. blue				20	20
10	4	15 f. purple-brown (1.12.52)				25	20
11		20 f. lake-brown (1.12.52)				30	25
12	5	40 f. indigo & turquoise-blue (20.9.54)			5·00	3·75

(*b*) *AIR*

13	6	50 f. lake and green				95	45
14	7	100 f. chocolate and scarlet				1·60	45
15	8	200 f. lake-brown, deep blue-green and reddish violet (15.1.53)			6·50	3·25
1/15		*Set of 15*				14·00	8·50

(Des Giat. Eng E. Feltesse. Recess)

1950 (15 May). *POSTAGE DUE. P* 14×13.

D16	D **9**	50 c. bright green				12	12
D17		1 f. brownish black				12	12

1952 (1 Dec). *Centenary of Médaille Militaire. As T* **48** *of Cameroun.*

16   15 f. blue, yellow and green   ...   .. 11·00 11·00

1954 (6 June). *AIR. 10th Anniv of Liberation. As T* **50** *of Cameroun.*

17   15 f. brown-red and deep brown..   .. 8·00   7·00

D **10** Coelacanth   **9** Village Pump

(Des and eng P. Camors. Recess)

1954 (13 Aug). *POSTAGE DUE. P* 13.
D18 D **10** 5 f. sepia and deep green   .. 12   12
D19   10 f. violet-grey and red-brown .. 20   20
D20   20 f. indigo and light blue 30   30

(Des and eng H. Cheffer. Recess)

1956 (25 Apr). *Economic and Social Development Fund. P* 13.
18 **9** 9 f. bluish violet 35   20

10 "Human Rights"   **11** Radio Station, Dzaoudzi

(Des and eng R. Cami. Recess)

1958 (10 Dec). *Tenth Anniv of Declaration of Human Rights. P* 13.
19 **10** 20 f. bronze-green and blue   .. 3·50   3·50

1959 (5 Jan). *Tropical Flora. Multicoloured design as T* **58** *of Cameroun.*
20 **10** f. Colvillea (*horiz*)   ..   .. 1·50   1·00

(Des P. Chapelet. Eng J. Combet. Recess)

1960 (23 Dec). *Inauguration of Comoro Broadcasting Service. T* **11** *and similar design. P* 13.
21   20 f. green, bluish violet and brown-purple   45   40
22   25 f. emerald, red-brown and ultramarine   50   50
Design:—25 f. Radio mast and map.

12 Bull Mouth Helmet   **13** Marine Plants

(Des R. Chapelet. Photo Hélio-Comoy)

1962 (13 Jan–27 Oct). *Multicoloured.*

(*a*) *POSTAGE. Seashells as T* **12**. *P* 13.
23   50 c. Type **12** 20   20
24   1 f. Conoidal harp   20   20
25   2 f. White murex   25   25
26   5 f. Green turban (27.10)   50   50
27   20 f. Scorpion conch (27.10)   ..   .. 1·10   1·10
28   25 f. Pacific triton   ..   ..   .. 1·50   1·50

(*b*) *AIR. Marine plants as T* **13**. *P* 12½×13½
29   100 f. Type **13** (27.10) ,..   ..   .. 2·25   2·25
30   500 f. Stoney-coral   ..   ..   .. 9·00   7·50
23/30 *Set of 8*   ..   .. 14·00 12·00

1962 (7 Apr). *Malaria Eradication. As T* **11** *of Central African Republic.*
31   25 f.+5 f. rose-carmine   ..   ..   .. 1·10   1·10

13*a* "Telstar" Satellite and part of Globe

(Des C. Durrens. Eng P. Béquet. Recess)

1962 (5 Dec). *AIR. First Trans-Atlantic Television Satellite Link. P* 13.
32 **13***a* 25 f. bright purple, purple and violet   2·10   1·10

14 Emblem in Hands, and   **14***a* Centenary
Globe   Emblem

(Des and eng J. Derrey. Recess)

1963 (21 Mar). *Freedom from Hunger. P* 13.
33 **14** 20 f. deep bluish green and chocolate   1·60   1·40

(Des and eng J. Combet. Recess)

1963 (2 Sept). *Red Cross Centenary. P* 13.
34 **14***a* 50 f. red, grey and bright emerald   .. 2·50   2·25

15 Globe and Scales of Justice   **16** Tobacco Pouch

(Des and eng A. Decaris. Recess)

1963 (10 Dec). 15th Anniv of Declaration of Human Rights. P 13.
35 **15** 15 f. green and carmine-red .. .. 2·50 2·25

(Des and eng J. Combet. Recess)

1963 (27 Dec). Handicrafts. T **16** and similar vert designs. P 13. (a) POSTAGE.
36 3 f. ochre, carmine-red and emerald .. 10 10
37 4 f. deep grey-green, brown-pur & orge 15 15
38 10 f. chocolate, green and chestnut .. 30 30
(b) AIR. Inscr "POSTE AERIENNE". Size 27×48 mm
39 65 f. carmine-red, yellow-brown & green 1·60 95
40 200 f. claret, red and turquoise .. .. 3·25 1·90
36/40 Set of 5 .. .. 5·00 3·00
Designs:—4 f. Perfume-burner; 10 f. Lamp-bracket; 65 f. Baskets; 200 f. Filigree pendant.

20 "Syncom" Communications Satellite, Telegraph Poles and Morse Key

21 Hammer-head Shark

(Des and eng J. Combet. Recess)

1965 (17 May). AIR. I.T.U. Centenary. P 13.
48 **20** 50 f. turquoise-blue, yellow-olive & slate 6·50 5·00

(Des and eng J. Combet. Recess)

1965 (2 Dec). Marine Life. T **21** and similar designs. P 13.
49 1 f. myrtle-green, orange & reddish violet 15 15
50 12 f. black, indigo and carmine 35 30
51 20 f. brown-red and bluish green .. 50 45
52 25 f. purple-brown, vermilion & bluish grn 55 50
49/52 Set of 4 .. .. 1·40 1·25
Designs: Vert—1 f. Spiny lobster; 25 f. Grouper. Horiz—20 f. Scaly turtle.

16a "Philately"

17 Pirogue

(Des and eng P. Gandon. Recess)

1964 (31 Mar). "PHILATEC 1964" International Stamp Exhibition, Paris. P 13.
41 **16a** 50 f. red, green and deep blue .. 1·10 1·10

(Des R. Chapelet. Photo So.Ge.Im.)

1964 (7 Aug). Native Craft. T **17** and similar vert designs. Multicoloured. (a) POSTAGE. Size 22×37 mm. P 13×12½.
42 15 f. Type **17** 50 50
43 30 f. Boutre felucca .. .. 1·00 1·00
(b) AIR. Inscr "POSTE AERIENNE". Size 27×48½ mm. P 13.
44 50 f. Mayotte pirogue .. .. 1·10 50
45 85 f. Schooner .. .. .. 1·60 1·10
42/45 Set of 4 .. .. .. 4·00 2·75

21a Rocket "Diamant"

(Des and eng C. Durrens. Recess)

1966 (17 Jan). AIR. Launching of First French Satellite. T **21a** and similar horiz design. P 13.
53 25 f. plum, reddish violet and ultramarine 1·40 1·40
54 30 f. plum, reddish violet and ultramarine 1·75 1·75
Design:—30 f. Satellite "A1".
Nos. 53/4 were printed together in sheets of 16, giving 8 horiz strips containing one of each value separated by a half stamp-size inscr label. (Price per strip un or us £3·50)

18 Boxing (ancient bronze plaque)

19 Medal

21b Satellite "D1"

(Des and eng C. Haley. Recess)

1964 (10 Oct). AIR. Olympic Games, Tokyo. P 13.
46 **18** 100 f. bronze-green, chestnut & choc .. 1·90 1·90

(Des P. Lambert. Photo So.Ge.Im.)

1964 (10 Dec). AIR. Star of Great Comoro. P 13.
47 **19** 500 f. multicoloured .. .. .. 7·00 5·00

(Des and eng C. Durrens. Recess)

1966 (16 May). AIR. Launching of Satellite "D1". P 13.
55 **21b** 30 f. maroon, myrtle-green and orange 1·25 95

22 Lake Salé   23 Comoro Sunbird

(Des R. Chapelet. Photo So.Ge.Im.)

1966 (19 Dec). *Comoro Views. T **22** and similar multicoloured designs. (a) POSTAGE. P* 12½×13.
56   15 f. Type **22**   30   20
57   25 f. Itsandra Hotel, Moroni   35   20

(b) AIR. Inscr "POSTE AERIENNE". P 13
58   50 f. The Battery, Dzaoudzi (48×27 mm)   75   65
59   200 f. Ksar Fort, Mutsamudu (27×48 mm)   2·75   1·75
56/59   Set of 4   .. .. 3·75   2·50

(Des P. Lambert. Photo So.Ge.Im.)

1967 (20 June). *Birds. T **23** and similar multicoloured designs.*
(a) POSTAGE. P 12½×13
60   2 f. Type **23**   50   50
61   10 f. Kingfisher 65   65
62   15 f. Fody   75   75
63   30 f. Cuckoo-roller   .. .. 1·25   1·25

(b) AIR. Inscr "POSTE AERIENNE". P 13
64   75 f. Flycatcher (27×48 mm)   .. 1·60   65
65   100 f. Blue-cheeked bee-eater (27×48 mm)   1·90   75
60/65   Set of 6   .. .. .. 6·00   4·00

24 Nurse tending   25 Slalom Skiing
Child

(Des and eng P. Forget. Recess)

1967 (3 July). *Comoro Red Cross. P* 13.
66 **24** 25 f.+5 f. purple-brown, red & blue-grn   65   65

(Des and eng P. Forget. Recess)

1968 (29 Apr). *AIR. Winter Olympic Games, Grenoble. P* 13.
67 **25** 70 f. purple-brown, greenish bl & bl-grn   90   65

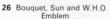

26 Bouquet, Sun and W.H.O.   27 Powder Blue Surgeon
Emblem

(Des and eng A. Decaris. Recess)

1968 (4 May). *20th Anniv of World Health Organization. P* 13.
68 **26** 40 f. crimson, violet and blue-green   .. 55   50

(Des and eng J. Derrey. Recess)

1968 (1 Aug). *Fishes. T **27** and similar horiz designs. P* 13.
(a) POSTAGE. Size 36×21½ mm
69   20 f. violet-blue, yellow and brown-red   .. 50   50
70   25 f. ultramarine, orange & turquoise-blue   65   65

(b) AIR. Inscr "POSTE AERIENNE". Size 48×27 mm
71   50 f. yellow-ochre, indigo and purple   .. 1·25   1·10
72   90 f. yellow-ochre, grey-green & emerald   2·25   1·75
Designs:—25 f. Imperial angelfish; 50 f. Moorish idol; 90 f.
Yellow-banded sweetlips.

28 Human Rights   29 Swimming
Emblem

(Des and eng A. Decaris. Recess)

1968 (10 Aug). *Human Rights Year. P* 13.
73 **28** 60 f. blue-green, chocolate and orange   90   90

(Des G. Bétemps. Photo Delrieu)

1968 (28 Dec). *AIR. Olympic Games, Mexico* (1968). *P* 12½.
74 **29** 65 f. multicoloured   .. .. .. 1·00   80

30 Prayer Mat and   31 Vanilla Flower
Worshipper

(Des and eng C. Guillame. Recess)

1969 (27 Feb). *Msoila Prayer Mats. T **30** and similar horiz designs. P* 13.
75   20 f. carmine, blue-green and violet   .. 20   15
76   30 f. blue-green, violet and carmine   .. 25   20
77   45 f. violet, carmine and blue-green   .. 40   30
Designs:—As T **30**, but worshipper stooping (30 f.) or
kneeling upright (45 f.).

(Des P. Lambert. Photo So.Ge.Im.)

1969 (5 Mar). *Flowers. T **31** and similar multicoloured designs.*
(a) POSTAGE. Size 36½×23 mm. P 12½×13
78   10 f. Type **31**   20   15
79   15 f. Ylang-ylang blossom   25   20

(b) AIR. Inscr "POSTE AERIENNE". Size 27×49 mm. P 13
80   50 f. Heliconia 75   65
81   85 f. Tuberose ..   .. 1·10   95
82   200 f. Orchid   ..   .. .. 2·25   1·60
78/82   Set of 5   .. .. 4·00   3·00

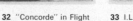

32 "Concorde" in Flight   33 I.L.O. Building, Geneva

(Des and eng C. Durrens. Recess)

1969 (17 Apr). *AIR. First Flight of "Concorde". P* 13.
83 **32** 100 f. plum and orange-brown .. 5·50 4·50

(Des and eng J. Derrey. Recess)

1969 (24 Nov). 50*th Anniversary of International Labour Organization. P* 13.
84 **33** 5 f. grey, emerald and salmon 15 12

38 White Egret

(Des C. Guillame. Photo)

1971 (12 Mar). *Birds. T* **38** *and similar vert designs. Multicoloured. P* 12½×13.
94	5 f. Type **38**	..	..	..	15	12
95	10 f. Comoro pigeon	..	..	..	20	15
96	15 f. Green-backed heron	..	..	25	20
97	25 f. Sganzin's wart pigeon	..	..	40	30
98	35 f. *Humblotia flavirostris*	..	..	70	50
99	40 f. Allen's gallinule	..	..	..	80	65
94/99	*Set of 6*	..	..	..	2·25	1·75

34 Poinsettia

35 "EXPO" Panorama

(Des P. Lambert. Photo Delrieu)

1970 (5 Mar). *Flowers. P* 12½×12.
85 **34** 25 f. multicoloured 40 30

1970 (20 May). *New U.P.U. Headquarters Building, Berne. As T* **156** *of Cameroun.*
86 65 f. lake-brown, blue-green and violet .. 95 65

(Des P. Lambert. Photo)

1970 (13 Sept). *AIR. World Fair "EXPO 70", Osaka, Japan. T* **35** *and similar vert design. Multicoloured. P* 13.
87 60 f. Type **35** 75 50
88 90 f. Geisha and map of Japan 75 50

39 Sunset, Moutsamoudou (Anjouan)

36 Chiromani Costume,
Anjouan

37 Mosque de
Vendredi, Moroni

(Des P. Lambert. Photo)

1970 (30 Oct). *Comoro Costumes. T* **36** *and similar vert design. Multicoloured. P* 12½×13.
89 20 f. Type **36** 30 25
90 25 f. Bouiboui, Great Comoro 40 30

(Des P. Lambert. Eng E. Lacaque. Recess)

1970 (18 Dec). *P* 12½×13.
91 **37** 5 f. turquoise-blue, blue-green & cerise 20 12
92 10 f. reddish violet, blue-green & purple 25 20
93 40 f. red-brown, blue-green and red .. 45 40

40 Map of Comoro Archipelago

(Des P. Lambert. Photo (15 f. to 85 f.). Des and eng P. Béquet. Recess (100 f.))

1971 (3 May). *AIR. Comoro Landscapes. P* 13. (*a*) *T* **39** *and similar horiz designs. Multicoloured.*
100	15 f. Type **39** ..	..	..	20	10
101	20 f. Sada village (Mayotte)	..	30	20
102	65 f. Ruined palace, Iconi (Great Comoro)	..	65	35
103	85 f. Off-shore islands, Moumatchoua, (Mohéli) ..	..	..	75	45

(*b*) *T* **40**
104 100 f. brown-red, blue-green & ultram 1·50 75
100/104 *Set of 5* .. .. 3·00 1·60
See also Nos. 124/8, 132/6, 157/60 and 168/71.

STAMP MONTHLY

—finest and most informative magazine for all collectors. Obtainable from your newsagent or by postal subscription—details on request.

41 Pyrostegia venusta

42 Conus lithoglyphus

(Des S. Gauthier. Photo)

1971 (12 July). *Tropical Plants. T* **41** *and similar multicoloured designs. P* 13. (*a*) *POSTAGE. Size as T* **41**.
105	1 f. Type **41**	..	..	10	10
106	3 f. *Allamanda cathartica* (*horiz*)		15	12
107	20 f. *Plumeria rubra*	..	..	50	35

(*b*) *AIR. Inscr* "POSTE AERIENNE". *Size* 27 × 48 *mm*
108	60 f. *Hibiscus schizopetalus*	..	..	90	50
109	85 f. *Acalypha sanderii* ..		..	1·10	75
105/109	*Set of* 5	..	..	2·50	1·50

(Des P. Lambert. Photo)

1971 (4 Oct). *Seashells. T* **42** *and similar horiz designs. Multicoloured. P* 13.
110	5 f. Type **42**	..	..	12	10
111	10 f. *Conus litteratus*	..	..	15	12
112	20 f. *Conus aulicus*	..	..	25	20
113	35 f. *Nerita polita*	..	..	40	30
114	60 f. *Cypraea caputserpentis*	..	65	65
110/114	*Set of* 5	..	..	1·40	1·25

43 De Gaulle in Uniform (June 1940)

44 Mural, Airport Lounge

(Des G. Bétemps. Eng J. Miermont (20 f.), G. Bétemps (35 f.). Recess)

1971 (9 Nov). *First Death Anniv of Gen. Charles de Gaulle. T* **43** *and similar vert design. P* 13.
115	20 f. black and bright purple	..	..	40	20
116	35 f. black and bright purple	..	..	50	45
Design:—35 f. De Gaulle as President of France (1970).

(Des and eng N. Hanniquet. Recess (100 f.). Photo (others))

1972 (31 Mar). *AIR. Inauguration of New Airport, Moroni. T* **44** *and similar horiz designs. P* 13.
117	65 f. multicoloured	..	45	40
118	85 f. multicoloured	..	65	40
119	100 f. myrtle-green, lt brown & new blue	1·00	65
Designs:—85 f. Mural similar to T **44**; 100 f. Airport buildings.

HAVE YOU READ THE NOTES AT THE BEGINNING OF THIS CATALOGUE?

These often provide answers to the enquiries we receive.

45 Eiffel Tower, Paris, and Telecommunications Centre, Moroni

(Des and eng N. Hanniquet. Recess)

1972 (24 Apr). *AIR. Inauguration of Paris–Moroni Radio-Telephone Link. T* **45** *and similar horiz design. P* 13.
120	35 f. red, slate-purple and light blue	..	25	15
121	75 f. lake, violet and new blue	..	50	30
Design:—75 f. Telephone conversation.

46 Underwater Spear-fishing

(Des and eng J. Combet. Recess)

1972 (5 July). *AIR. Aquatic Sports. P* 13.
122	**46**	70 f. lake, blue-green and deep blue	..	90	70

47 Pasteur, Crucibles and Microscope

48 Pres. Said Mohamed Cheikh

(Des and eng R. Quillivic. Recess)

1972 (2 Aug). *150th Birth Anniv of Louis Pasteur. P* 13 × 12½.
123	**47**	65 f. slate-blue, olive-brn & red-orge	75	65

(Des P. Lambert. Photo (20 f. to 60 f.). Des P. Béquet. Eng E. Lacaque. Recess (100 f.))

1972 (15 Nov). *AIR. Anjouan Landscapes. P* 13. (*a*) *Horiz views similar to T* **39**. *Multicoloured.*
124	20 f. Fortress wall, Cape Sima ..		..	20	15
125	35 f. Bambao Palace	..	..	30	25
126	40 f. Palace, Domoni	..	..	40	30
127	60 f. Gomajou Island	..	..	50	45

(*b*) *Horiz map design as T* **40**
128	100 f. myrtle-green, new blue & brn-lake	1·10	75
124/128	*Set of* 5	..	..	..	2·25	1·75
Design:—100 f. Map of Anjouan.

(Photo Delrieu)

1973 (16 Mar). *AIR. Said Mohamed Cheikh, President of Comoro Council, Commemoration. P* 13.

129	**48**	20 f. multicoloured	..	..	20	15
130		35 f. multicoloured	..	..	30	15

120ᶠ

Mission Internationale pour l'étude du Cœlacanthe

(49)

1973 (30 Apr). *AIR. International Coelacanth Study Expedition. No. 72 surch with T* **49**.

131	120 f. on 90 f. yellow-ochre, grey-green and emerald	..	1·25	95

(Des and eng P. Béquet. Recess (135 f.). Des P. Lambert. Photo (others))

1973 (28 June). *Great Comoro Landscapes. P* 13.

(*a*) *POSTAGE. Horiz views similar to T* **39**. *Multicoloured*

132	10 f. Goulaivoini	..	..	..	12	10
133	20 f. Mitsamiouli	..	..		25	20
134	35 f. Foumbouni	..	..		45	40
135	50 f. Moroni	..	..		55	50

(*b*) *AIR. Vert map design as T* **40**

136	135 f. dull purple, greenish blue & violet	1·60	1·25
132/135	*Set of* 5	2·75	2·25

Design:—135 f. Map of Great Comoro.

50 Bank

51 Volcanic Eruption

(Des P. Lambert. Photo)

1973 (10 July). *Moroni Buildings. T* **50** *and similar horiz designs. Multicoloured. P* 13.

137	5 f. Type **50**	..	..	8	5
138	15 f. Post Office	..	..	15	12
139	20 f. Prefecture	..	..	..	25	20

(Des G. Bétemps. Photo)

1973 (16 July). *AIR. Karthala Volcano Eruption (Sept* 1972). *P* 13.

140	**51**	120 f. multicoloured	..	1·25	1·00

52 Dr. G. A. Hansen

53 Pablo Picasso (artist)

(Des P. Lambert. Eng C. Guillame. Recess)

1973 (5 Sept). *AIR. Centenary of Hansen's Identification of Leprosy Bacillus. P* 13.

141	**52**	100 f. myrtle-green, dull pur & ultram	1·10	95

(Des P. Lambert. Eng C. Guillame. Recess)

1973 (5 Sept). *AIR. 500th Birth Anniv of Nicholas Copernicus (astronomer). Vert design as T* **52**. *P* 13.

142	150 f. dull purple, turquoise-bl & ultram	1·75	1·25

Design:—150 f. Copernicus and solar system.

(Des P. Sampoux. Photo Delrieu)

1973 (30 Sept). *AIR. Picasso Commemoration. P* 13.

143	**53**	200 f. multicoloured	..	..	2·00	1·50
MS144	100×131 mm. **53** 100 f. multicoloured	1·25	1·25

54 Zaouiyat Chaduli Mosque   **55** Star and Ribbon

1973 (20 Oct). *Mosques. T* **54** *and similar multicoloured design. Photo. P* 13.

145	20 f. Type **54**	..	..	20	20
146	35 f. Salimata Hamissi Mosque (*horiz*)	..	40	40

1974 (7 Jan). *AIR. Order of Star of Anjouan. Photo. P* 13.

147	**55** 500 f. gold, new blue & reddish brown	4·50	3·75

56 Said Omar Ben Soumeth   **57** Doorway of Mausoleum
(Grand Mufti of the Comoros)

(Photo Delrieu)

1974 (31 Jan). *AIR. T* **56** *and similar multicoloured design. P* 13×13½ *(135 f.) or* 13½×13 *(200 f.)*.

148	135 f. Type **56**	..	..	1·00	90
149	200 f. Ben Soumeth seated (*vert*)	..	1·75	1·25

(Des and eng J. Pheulpin. Recess)

1974 (16 Mar). *Mausoleum of Shaikh Said Mohamed. T* **57** *and similar horiz design. P* 13.

150	5 f. bistre-brown, black & yellow-green	40	35
151	50 f. bistre-brown, black & yellow-green	55	45

Design:—50 f. Mausoleum.

HAVE YOU READ THE NOTES AT THE BEGINNING OF THIS CATALOGUE?

These often provide answers to the enquiries we receive.

58 Wooden Combs   **59** Mother and Child

(Des P. Lambert. Photo)

1974 (10 May). *Comoro Handicrafts.* (1st series). *T* **58** *and similar multicoloured designs.* P 13.

152	15 f. Type **58**			20	15
153	20 f. Three-legged table			25	20
154	35 f. Koran lectern (*horiz*)			40	35
155	75 f. Sugar-cane press (*horiz*)			75	65
152/155	*Set of 4*			1·40	1·25

See also Nos. 164/7.

(Des P. Lambert. Eng E. Lacaque. Recess)

1974 (10 Aug). *Comoro Red Cross Fund.* P 13.
156 **59** 35 f.+10 f. red-brown and vermilion .. 40 40

(Des and eng P. Béquet. Recess (120 f.). Des P. Lambert. Photo (others))

1974 (31 Aug). AIR. *Mayotte Landscapes.* P 13.

(*a*) *Horiz views similar to T* **39**. *Multicoloured*
157	20 f. Moya beach			20	15
158	35 f. Chiconi			35	30
159	90 f. Mamutzu harbour			95	75

(*b*) *Vert map design as T* **40**
160	120 f. deep yellow-green and bright blue	1·10	95
157/160	*Set of 4*		2·40	2·00

Design:—120 f. Map of Mayotte.

60 U.P.U. Emblem and Globe

(Des and eng R. Quillivic. Recess)

1974 (9 Oct). *Centenary of Universal Postal Union.* P 13.
161 **60** 30 f. lake, olive-brown and emerald .. 30 30

61 Aircraft taking off

(Des and eng G. Bétemps. Recess)

1975 (10 Jan). AIR. *Inauguration of Direct Moroni–Hahaya– Paris Air Service.* P 13.
162 **61** 135 f. new blue, yellow-green and red   1·25   1·00

62 Rotary Emblem, Moroni Clubhouse and Map

(Des J. Chesnot. Photo Delrieu)

1975 (23 Feb). AIR. *70th Anniv of Rotary International and 10th Anniv of Moroni Rotary Club.* P 13½.
163 **62** 250 f. multicoloured .. .. .. 2·25   1·90

63 Bracelet

(Des and eng M. Monvoisin. Recess)

1975 (28 Feb). *Comoro Handicrafts* (2nd series). *T* **63** *and similar horiz designs.* P 13.
164	20 f. orange-brown and bright purple	..	25	20
165	35 f. orange-brown and yellow-green	..	40	35
166	120 f. orange-brown and new blue	..	1·25	1·10
167	135 f. chestnut and cerise	..	1·40	1·25
164/167	*Set of 4*	..	3·00	2·75

Designs:—35 f. Diadem; 120 f. Sabre; 135 f. Dagger.

(Des and eng P. Béquet. Recess· (230 f.). Des P. Lambert. Photo (others))

1975 (26 May). *Mohéli Landscapes.* P 13.

(*a*) *POSTAGE. Horiz views similar to T* **39**. *Multicoloured*
168	30 f. Mohani village		30	25
169	50 f. Djoezi village		55	40
170	55 f. Chirazian tombs		65	45

(*b*) *AIR. Map design as T* **40**, *but horiz*
171	230 f. deep green, new blue & orange-brn	2·75	2·25
168/171	*Set of 4*	4·00	3·00

Design:—230 f. Map of Mohéli.

64 Coelacanth and Skin-diver

(Des and eng G. Bétemps. Recess)

1975 (27 June). *Coelacanth Expedition.* P 13.
172 **64** 50 f. bistre-brown, new blue & lake-brn   75   65

Following a referendum in the islands, in December 1974, and a *coup d'état* in 1975, the independent State of Comoro (consisting of Grand Comoro, Mohéli and Anjouan) was established, and was recognised by France on 1 January 1976. Mayotte, however, finally voted for the status of an Overseas Department of France.

Congo

100 Centimes = 1 Franc

PRINTERS. All stamps were printed at the Government Printing Works, Paris, *unless otherwise stated.*

IMPERFORATE STAMPS. Stamps exist imperforate in their issued colours but they were not valid for postage. Imperforate stamps in other colours are colour trials.

A. FRENCH CONGO

The explorer Savorgnan de Brazza made a treaty with the King of the Bateke, who ceded his rights to France, in 1880, and Brazzaville was founded. De Brazza secured Pointe Noire and Loango, on the coast, for France by 1882 and in 1888 Paul Crampel opened up the region between the French Congo and Lake Chad. The French Congo, to which Gabon was joined, and which included the Chad and Ubangi-Shari territories, was created a Colony on 11 December 1888. The colony, at first Gabon-Congo, was given the title of "Congo Français" on 20 April 1891.

Congo français   **COngo Français**

5c.   **5 c.**

(1)   (2)

1891–92. Type J of French Colonies (*General Issues*) surch. P 14×13½.

(a) As T **1**

1	5 c. on 1 c. black/*azure* (R.) (2.9.91)		£1200	£1000
2	5 c. on 1 c. black/*azure* (2.9.91)		35·00	18·00
	a. Surch double (Bk.)		45·00	40·00
	b. Surch double (Bk.+R.)		£1700	£1500
3	5 c. on 15 c. blue (24.3.91)		55·00	20·00
	a. Surch double		70·00	50·00
	b. Surch vert			
4	5 c. on 25 c. black/*rose* (4.12.91)		18·00	7·50
	a. Surch inverted		30·00	15·00
	b. Surch vert			

(b) As T **2**

5	5 c. on 20 c. red/*green* (13.5.92)		£225	£100
	a. Surch double		—	£250
6	5 c. on 25 c. black/*rose* (9.7.92)		25·00	10·00
	a. Surch vert		25·00	10·00
	b. Vert surch double			
7	10 c. on 25 c. black/*rose* (9.7.92)		30·00	10·00
	a. Surch double		45·00	20·00
	b. Surch inverted		30·00	10·00
	c. Surch vert		30·00	10·00
8	10 c. on 40 c. red/*yellow* (13.5.92)		£500	80·00
	a. Surch double		—	£300
9	15 c. on 25 c. black/*rose* (5.8.92)		32·00	7·50
	a. Surch double		40·00	18·00
	b. Surch inverted		32·00	7·50
	c. Surch vert		32·00	7·50

(c) As T **1** *but vert and no stop after "c"* (20.9.92)

10	5 c. on 25 c. black/*rose*		20·00	12·00
11	10 c. on 25 c. black/*rose*		32·00	10·00
12	15 c. on 25 c. black/*rose*		35·00	10·00

The 5 c. on 1 c. were first surcharged in red as Type **1**, but the type was reset for the black surcharge. The "5" and "c" are 4 mm apart in the red surcharge and 1 mm in the black.

There were two printings of No. 3, but they are practically indistinguishable.

The vertical surcharges exist reading up or down, the value being about the same for each.

P 3

1891. PARCEL POST. *Type-set. Imperf.*

P13	P **3**	10 c. black/*blue*		30·00	18·00
		a. Tête-bêche (pair)		£125	£100

5 c   **Congo français Timbre posé**   **COLIS POSTAUX**   **Congo Francais**   **Valeur 15**

(3)   (P 4)   (5)

1892. Type U of French Colonies (*General issues*), handstamped locally as T **3**. *Imperf.*

13	5 c. on 5 c. black (R.) (9.11)		25·00	22·00
14	5 c. on 20 c. black (R.) (9.11)		25·00	22·00
15	5 c. on 30 c. black (R.) (9.11)		30·00	25·00
16	10 c. on 30 c. black (8.9)		30·00	22·00
	a. Surch horiz		£250	£250

Nos. 13/16 exist with surcharge reading up or down and the prices are the same for each. In the 10 c. the word "Timbres" is in the plural.

1892 (Nov)–**1900.** Type X of Anjouan inscr "CONGO FRANCAIS". *Name in red* (1, 5, 10, 25, 50 (*No.* 31), 75 c. *and* 1 f.) *or blue* (*others*). P 14×13½.

17	1 c. black/*azure*			15	15
	a. Name double				
18	2 c. brown/*buff*			25	25
	a. Name in red and black			25·00	25·00
19	4 c. purple-brown/*grey*			35	35
	a. Name in black and blue			28·00	28·00
20	5 c. green/*pale green*			75	75
21	10 c. black/*lilac*			2·25	1·50
	a. Name double			90·00	90·00
22	10 c. rose-red (12.00)			50	30
23	15 c. blue			8·00	2·75
24	15 c. grey (12.00)			1·50	1·25
25	20 c. red/*green*			3·00	2·75
26	25 c. black/*rose*			2·75	2·50
27	25 c. blue (12.00)			2·00	1·75
28	30 c. cinnamon/*drab*			3·00	2·75
29	40 c. red/*yellow*			6·00	4·50
30	50 c. carmine/*rose*			7·00	4·75
31	50 c. brown/*azure* (12.00)			1·60	1·25
	a. Name double			£100	£100
32	75 c. brown/*orange*			5·50	4·75
33	1 f. olive-green/*toned*			8·50	4·75
17/33	Set of 17			50·00	35·00

1893. *PARCEL POST. Receipt stamp of France handstamped with Type P* **4.**
P34   10 c. grey   ..   ..   16·00   12·00

1900 (8 July). *Brazzaville Provisionals. Type X of Anjouan surch as T* **5.** *P* 14×13½.
34   5 on 20 c. red/*green*   ..   ..   ..   — £1600
35   15 on 30 c. cinnamon/*drab*   ..   ..   — £650
   a. Surch double   ..   ..   — £1400
Nos. 34/5 were authorised by the Lieutenant-Governor by decree of 9 July. They were withdrawn on 12 July.

6   Leopard in Ambush

7   Thistle Branch

8   Bakalois Woman

10   Coconut Palms, Libreville

9   Rose Branch

11   Olive Branch

(Des Paul Merwart. Eng B. Damman. Typo by M. Chassepot)

1900 (May)**–4**. *P* 11. (*a*) *W* **7**.
36 **6**	1 c. deep purple and sepia	..	10	5
	a. Background and value inverted	..	8·00	8·00
	b. Value tablet double	..		
	c. *Red-brown and grey* (5.04)	..	10	5
37	2 c. brown and yellow ..	..	10	5
	a. Imperf (pair)	..	13·00	13·00
	b. *Error. Red and pale red*	..	30·00	30·00
38	4 c. vermilion and grey ..	..	20	5
	a. Background and value inverted	..	9·50	9·50
	b. *Error. Red and pale red*	..	£150	
39	5 c. green and grey-green	..	25	5
	a. Imperf (pair)	..	25·00	25·00
40	10 c. red and pale red	..	1·00	40
	a. Imperf (pair)	..	25·00	25·00

41 **6**	15 c. dull violet and olive-green	..	25	12
	a. Imperf (pair)	..	19·00	19·00

(*b*) *W* **9**
42 **8**	20 c. green and pale red	..	25	12
43	25 c. blue and pale blue	..	50	15
	a. *Blue and greenish blue*	..	50	15
44	30 c. carmine and yellow	..	50	25
45	40 c. chestnut and green	..	65	30
	a. Imperf (pair)	..	19·00	19·00
	b. Background and value inverted	..	22·00	22·00
46	50 c. deep violet and lilac	..	90	75
47	75 c. claret and orange ..	..	2·25	1·40
	a. Imperf (pair)	..	19·00	19·00
	b. *Red and orange* ..	..	2·50	3·50

(*c*) *W* **11**
48 **10**	1 f. drab and slate-green	..	3·25	2·50
	a. Imperf (pair)	..	23·00	23·00
	b. Background and value inverted	..	50·00	50·00
	c. Value misplaced and inverted	..	25·00	25·00
49	2 f. carmine and grey-brown	..	6·50	3·75
	a. Imperf (pair)	..	40·00	40·00
	b. *Pink and grey-brown*	..	6·50	3·75
50	5 f. orange and black ..	..	14·00	13·00
	a. Imperf (pair)	..	£100	£100
	b. Error. Wmk T **9** ..	..	55·00	
	c. Background and value inverted	..	75·00	75·00
	d. Value misplaced and inverted	..	50·00	50·00
	e. Value tablet double	..	65·00	65·00
	f. *Ochre and black* ..	..	£130	
36/50	*Set of* 15 ..	..	..	27·00	20·00

(12)   (13)

1903 (13 July). *Stamps of* 1900–4 *surch with T* **12** *or* **13**.
51	5 c. on 30 c. carmine and yellow	..	70·00	32·00
	a. Surch inverted	..	£400	
52	0,10 on 2 f. carmine and grey-brown	..	90·00	35·00
	a. Surch inverted	..	£400	
	b. Surch double	..		

B. MIDDLE CONGO

By decree of 29 December 1903, the French Congo Colony was divided, as from 1 July 1904, into Middle Congo (Moyen Congo), Gabon, Ubangi-Shari and Chad. Middle Congo was the area which now forms the Congo Republic.

1   Leopard in Ambush

STAMP MONTHLY

—finest and most informative magazine for all collectors. Obtainable from your newsagent or by postal subscription—details on request.

$1^f 25$

2 Bakalois Woman   **3** Coconut Palms, Libreville

(Designs adapted from those of French Congo. Eng J. Puyplat. Typo)

1907–17. *Frames in first colour. P* 14×13½ (*T* **1**) *or* 13½×14 (*others*).

1	**1**	1 c. olive and brown	..	5	5
2		2 c. violet and brown	..	5	5
3		4 c. blue and brown	..	5	5
4		5 c. green and blue	..	8	5
5		10 c. carmine and blue	..	10	8
6		15 c. dull purple and pink (1917)	..	20	15
7		20 c. pale brown and blue	..	65	45
8	**2**	25 c. blue and grey-green	..	10	8
9		30 c. salmon-pink and green	..	20	20
10		35 c. chocolate and blue	..	20	20
11		40 c. dull green and pale brown	..	15	15
12		45 c. violet and salmon	..	90	65
13		50 c. green and salmon	..	20	20
14		75 c. brown and blue	..	1·50	1·10
15	**3**	1 f. deep green and pale violet	..	1·90	1·75
16		2 f. violet and grey-green	..	1·25	1·25
17		5 f. blue and pink	..	5·00	4·50
1/17		*Set of* 17	..	11·00	10·00

All values, *except* the 15, 35 and 45 c., exist on chalk-surfaced paper.

See also Nos. 21/5.

For stamps in different colours see "Opt omitted" errors of Cameroun, Central African Republic and Chad.

(4)   (5)

1916. *Surch locally with T* **4**. (*a*) *In centre of stamp*.

18	**1**	10 c.+5 c. carmine and blue	..	20	15
		a. Surch inverted	..	16·00	16·00
		b. Surch double	..	16·00	16·00
		c. Surch double, one inverted	..	19·00	19·00
		d. Pair, one without surch	..	6·00	6·00

(*b*) *In left lower corner*

19	**1**	10 c.+5 c. carmine and blue	..	40	40
		a. Surch double	..	14·00	14·00

No. 19 was surcharged at Bangui for use there.

1916. *Surch with T* **5**, *in red. Chalk-surfaced paper.*

20	**1**	10 c.+5 c. carmine and blue	..	12	12

1922 (1 Jan). *New colours. P* 14×13½ (*T* **1**) *or* 13½×14 (*T* **2**).

21	**1**	5 c. yellow and blue	..	10	10
22		10 c. green and blue-green	..	40	40
23	**2**	25 c. green and grey	..	15	15
24		30 c. carmine	..	15	15
25		50 c. blue and green	..	15	15
21/25		*Set of* 5	..	90	90

AFRIQUE ÉQUATORIALE FRANÇAISE

(6)

AFRIQUE EQUATORIALE FRANÇAISE

(7)

25c = 65   90 =   90 =   =

(8)   (9)   (10)   (11)

1924 (June)–**27**. *Stamps as T* 2/3, *some with colours changed, optd with T* **7** *in blue* (*Nos.* 28/9) *or black* (*others*), *and further surch.*

(*a*) *With T* **8** *and obliterating bars. Chalk-surfaced paper* (*No. 26*) (6.24)

26	**3**	25 c. on 2 f. violet and grey-green	..	10	10
27		25 c. on 5 f. blue and pink (B.)	..	10	10

(*b*) *As T* **9** (1.2.25)

28	**3**	65 on 1 f. red and brown	..	15	15
		a. Opt T **7** omitted	..	32·00	
29		85 on 1 f. red and brown	..	15	15
		a. Opt T **7** double	..	14·00	

(*c*) *With T* **10** (11.4.27)

30	**2**	90 on 75 c. scarlet and rose-red	..	15	15

(*d*) *As T* **11** (1926–27)

31	**3**	1 f. 25 on 1 f. blue and ultramarine (R.) (14.6.26)	..	5	5
		a. Surch T **11** omitted	..	11·00	
32		1 f. 50 on 1 f. ultramarine & bl (11.4.27)	30	20
		a. Surch T **11** omitted	..	16·00	
33		3 f. on 5 f. chestnut and rose (19.12.27)	45	30
		a. Surch T **11** omitted	..	30·00	
34		10 f. on 5 f. rose-red and green (11.4.27)	2·25	1·75
35		20 f. on 5 f. brown and purple (11.4.27)	2·25	1·90
26/35		*Set of* 10	..	5·50	4·50

1924 (Nov)–**30**. *Stamps as T* 1/3, *some with colours changed, optd with T* **6** (1 c. to 20 c.) *or* **7**.

36	**1**	1 c. olive and brown	..	5	5
		a. Opt double	..	16·00	16·00
37		2 c. violet and brown	..	5	5
38		4 c. blue and brown	..	5	5
39		5 c. yellow and blue	..	5	5
40		10 c. green and blue-green (R.)	..	5	5
41		10 c. carmine and grey (1.12.25)	..	5	5
42		15 c. purple and pink (B.)	..	8	8
		a. Opt double	..	14·00	14·00
43		20 c. brown and blue	..	5	5
44		20 c. green and pale green (1.3.26)	..	5	5
45		20 c. brown and magenta (6.27)	..	5	5
46	**2**	25 c. green and grey	..	8	8
47		30 c. carmine (B.)	..	10	8
48		30 c. grey and mauve (R.) (1.12.25)	..	5	5
49		30 c. olive-green and green (14.11.27)	..	25	20
50		35 c. chocolate and blue (B.)	..	5	5
51		40 c. sage-green and brown	..	12	10
		a. Opt double	..	28·00	28·00
52		45 c. violet and salmon (B.)	..	12	10
		a. Opt inverted	..	16·00	15·00
53		50 c. blue and green (R.)	..	5	5
54		50 c. yellow and black (1.12.25)	..	5	5
		a. Opt omitted	..	32·00	
55		65 c. brown-red and blue (19.12.27)	..	55	50
56		75 c. brown and blue	..	8	8
		a. Opt double (Blk.+R.)	..	28·00	
		b. Opt quadruple (2 Blk.+2 R.)	..	32·00	
57		90 c. scarlet and bright rose (22.3.30)	65	65
58	**3**	1 f. green and violet	..	15	12
		a. Opt double	..	40·00	38·00
59		1 f. 10, mauve and chocolate (25.9.28)	55	50
60		1 f. 50, ultramarine and blue (22.3.30)	1·25	1·00
61		2 f. violet and grey-green	..	20	15
62		3 f. magenta/*rose* (22.3.30)	..	1·60	1·50
63		5 f. blue and pink	..	60	40
36/63		*Set of* 28	..	6·50	5·50

Of the 1924 values the 2. 4, 20, 40, 75 c., 1, 2 and 5 f. exist on chalk-surfaced paper, the 40, 75 c. and 1 f. do not exist on ordinary paper.

For similar stamps in other colours see "Opt omitted" errors of Central African Republic and Chad.

MOYEN-CONGO

A. E. F.
(D 12)

1928 (2 Apr) *POSTAGE DUE. Type D 11 of France optd with Type D 12. P 14×13½.*

D64	5 c. light blue			8	8
D65	10 c. brown			8	8
D66	20 c. olive-green			12	12
D67	25 c. rosine			12	12
D68	30 c. rose			12	12
D69	45 c. green			20	20
D70	50 c. claret			25	25
D71	60 c. yellow-brown/*cream*			30	30
D72	1 f. maroon/*cream*			40	40
D73	2 f. rose-red			45	45
D74	3 f. bright violet			1·00	1·00
D64/74	*Set of 11*			2·75	2·75

D 13 Village

D 14 Steamer on the R. Congo

(Des J. Piel. Typo)

1930 (17 Feb). *POSTAGE DUE. P 14×13½.*

D75	D 13	5 c. drab and deep blue		15	15
D76		10 c. chocolate and scarlet		30	30
D77		20 c. chocolate and green		75	75
D78		25 c. chocolate and light blue		75	75
D79		30 c. blue-green and yellow-brown		1·10	1·00
D80		45 c. drab and blue-green		1·10	1·00
D81		50 c. chocolate and magenta		1·10	1·10
D82		60 c. black and lilac		1·60	1·40
D83	D 14	1 f. slate-black and yellow-brown		1·90	1·60
D84		2 f. chocolate and magenta		1·90	1·60
D85		3 f. chocolate and scarlet		1·90	1·60
D75/85		*Set of 11*		11·00	10·00

1931 (13 Apr). *International Colonial Exhibition, Paris. As T 9/12 of Cameroun.*

65	40 c. black and green			95	70
66	50 c. black and mauve			30	30
67	90 c. black and vermilion			50	45
68	1 f. 50, black and blue			75	45
65/68	*Set of 4*			2·25	1·50

15 Mindouli Viaduct

16 Pasteur Institute, Brazzaville

(Des Herviault. Photo Vaugirard, Paris)

1933 (1 May–25 Sept). *T 15/16 and similar horiz design. P 13½.*

69	15	1 c. chocolate		5	5
70		2 c. greenish blue		5	5
71		4 c. bronze-green		5	5
72		5 c. claret		5	5
73		10 c. deep blue-green		5	5
74		15 c. purple		8	8
75		20 c. red/*rose*		1·50	1·10
76		25 c. orange		10	8

77	15	30 c. green			40	30
78	16	40 c. red-brown			25	20
79		45 c. black/*green*			40	25
80		50 c. slate-purple			15	15
81		65 c. red/*green*			20	15
82		75 c. black/*rose*			1·90	1·60
83		90 c. rosine			20	20
84		1 f. vermilion			20	10
85		1 f. 25, green (25.9)			30	30
86		1 f. 50, blue			1·40	65
87	–	1 f. 75, violet (25.9)			40	35
88	–	2 f. myrtle-green			30	25
89	–	3 f. black/*red*			65	65
90	–	5 f. blackish blue			2·75	2·75
91	–	10 f. black			8·00	5·50
92	–	20 f. brown			5·50	3·75
69/92		*Set of 24*			22·00	17·00

Design: 1 f. 75 to 20 f. Govt Building, Brazzaville.

The above issue overprinted "AFRIQUE EQUATORIALE FRANÇAISE" and with "MOYEN CONGO" obliterated by bars, will be found listed under French Equatorial Africa.

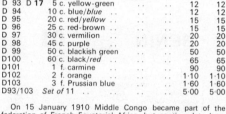

D 17 "Le Djoué"

(Des Herviault. Photo Vaugirard, Paris)

1933 (1 May). *POSTAGE DUE. P 13½.*

D 93	D 17	5 c. yellow-green			12	12
D 94		10 c. blue/*blue*			12	12
D 95		20 c. red/*yellow*			15	15
D 96		25 c. red-brown			15	15
D 97		30 c. vermilion			20	20
D 98		45 c. purple			20	20
D 99		50 c. blackish green			50	50
D100		60 c. black/*red*			65	65
D101		1 f. carmine			90	90
D102		2 f. orange			1·10	1·10
D103		3 f. Prussian blue			1·60	1·60
D93/103		*Set of 11*			5·00	5·00

On 15 January 1910 Middle Congo became part of the federation of French Equatorial Africa, but continued to have its own stamps until 16 March 1937, after which the stamps of French Equatorial Africa were used there until 1959.

C. CONGO REPUBLIC

Middle Congo became the Congo Republic, an autonomous state of the French Union, on 28 November 1958.

1 "Birth of the Republic"

(Des and eng R. Cami. Recess)

1959 (28 Nov). *First Anniv of Republic. P 13.*

1	1	25 f. brown-purple, yell, brn & bronze-grn	35	10

1960 (21 May). *10th Anniv of African Technical Co-operation Commission. As T 62 of Cameroun.*

2	50 f. lake and deep bluish green		65	55

Congo Republic became an independent state on 15 August 1960.

Dahomey

100 Centimes = 1 Franc

The African kingdom of Dahomey was at the height of its power under King Guezo (1818–58), with an elite Corps of Amazons forming a quarter of his army. The King of Porto-Novo placed himself under French protection in 1863 and this protectorate was re-established in 1882. Cotonou had been acquired by France in a treaty of 1878. Stamps inscribed "Benin" were issued for these areas, which were styled the Establishments of Benin in 1893.

A. BENIN

FRENCH PROTECTORATE

PRINTERS. All the stamps of Benin and Dahomey were printed at the Government Printing Works, Paris, *unless otherwise stated.*

IMPERFORATE STAMPS. Stamps exist imperforate in their issued colours, but they were not valid for postage. Imperforate stamps in other colours are colour trials.

BENIN   01

(1)   (2)

1892 (Sept). *French Colonies Type* J *("Commerce").* P 14×13½. *Handstamped with T* **1**.

1	1 c. black/*azure* ..	..	..	..	30·00	28·00
2	2 c. brown/*buff* ..	..	..	..	28·00	28·00
3	4 c. purple-brown/*grey* ..	..	..	9·00	9·00
4	5 c. green/*pale green*	..	..	..	3·50	3·00
	a. Blue opt	..	..	..	£400	£100
5	10 c. black/*lilac* ..	..	..	..	15·00	12·00
6	15 c. blue/*pale blue*	..	..	..	6·00	2·50
	a. Blue opt	..	..	..	£400	£100
	b. Red opt	..	..	..	18·00	10·00
7	20 c. red/*green*	..	..	..	50·00	40·00
8	25 c. black/*rose* ..	..	..	..	18·00	11·00
9	30 c. cinnamon/*drab*	..	..	..	35·00	25·00
10	35 c. black/*orange*	..	..	..	38·00	32·00
11	40 c. red/*yellow* ..	..	..	..	32·00	28·00
12	75 c. rose-carmine/*rose* ..	..	..	85·00	75·00
13	1 f. olive-green/*toned* ..	..	..	85·00	75·00

Specialists recognize three different types of this handstamp:

Type A. Without accent. Measures slightly less than 15 mm in length. During use developed a break in the lower curve of the "B".

Type B. Without accent. Measures slightly more than 15 mm in length. During use developed a break at the foot of the diagonal in the first "N".

Type C. As Type **1**.

These different handstamps exist on all values. Our prices are for stamps handstamped with Type C. Types A and B, especially early states, are rare. Nos. 4a and 6a/b only exist with Type A handstamp.

The handstamps can also be found diagonal, inverted, double, etc.

1892 (Sept–Oct). *Nos.* 4 *and* 6 *surch as T* **2**, *in red.*

14	01 on 5 c. green/*pale green* (Oct)	..	50·00	35·00
15	40 on 15 c. blue/*pale blue*	..	40·00	11·00
16	75 on 15 c. blue/*pale blue*	..	£175	£100
	a. Black surch	..	..	£550	£375

Nos. 14/16a only exist genuine on stamps with "BENIN" handstamp Type A.

1893 (Mar). *French Colonies Type* X *("Tablet") inscr* "GOLFE DE BENIN", *in red* (1, 5, 15, 25, 75 *c. and* 1 *f.*) *or blue* (*others*). *P* 14×13½.

17	1 c. black/*azure* ..	..	..	65	65
18	2 c. brown/*buff* ..	..	..	75	75
19	4 c. purple-brown/*grey* ..	..	60	60
20	5 c. green/*pale green*	..	..	1·00	75
21	10 c. black/*liliac* ..	..	..	1·10	85
22	15 c. blue (*quadrillé paper*)	..	5·00	3·50
23	20 c. red/*green*	..	..	3·25	1·75
24	25 c. black/*rose* ..	..	..	7·50	3·50
25	30 c. cinnamon/*drab*	..	..	3·25	3·00
26	40 c. red/*yellow* ..	..	..	75	50
27	50 c. carmine/*rose*	..	..	60	60
28	75 c. brown/*orange*	..	..	1·75	1·25
29	1 f. olive-green/*toned* ..	..	10·00	8·00
17/29	*Set of* 13	..	..	32·00	22·00

1894. *French Colonies Type* X *("Tablet") inscr* "BENIN" *only. Inscr in red* (1, 5, 15, 25, 75 *c. and* 1 *f.*) *or blue* (*others*). *P* 14×13½.

33	1 c. black/*azure* ..	..	..	60	60
34	2 c. brown/*buff* ..	..	..	60	60
35	4 c. purple-brown/*grey* ..	..	60	60
36	5 c. green/*pale green*	..	..	60	60
37	10 c. black/*lilac* ..	..	..	1·10	85
38	15 c. blue (*quadrillé paper*)	..	1·25	75
39	20 c. red/*green*	..	..	1·50	1·25
40	25 c. black/*rose* ..	..	..	1·25	90
41	30 c. cinnamon/*drab*	..	..	1·00	90
42	40 c. red/*yellow* ..	..	..	3·25	1·75
43	50 c. carmine/*rose*	..	..	3·50	3·00
44	75 c. brown/*orange*	..	..	3·00	1·25
45	1 f. olive-green/*toned* ..	..	60	60
33/45	*Set of* 13	..	..	15·00	11·00

1894. *POSTAGE DUE. French Colonies Type* U *handstamped with T* **1**. *Imperf.*

D46	5 c. black	..	..	30·00	16·00
D47	10 c. black	..	..	30·00	16·00
D48	20 c. black	..	..	30·00	16·00
D49	30 c. black	..	..	30·00	16·00
D46/49	*Set of* 4	..	..	£110	60·00

Nos. D46/9 exist with either Type A or Type B handstamps, our prices being for Type A.

The handstamp comes either horizontally or vertically on all values.

King Behanzin of Dahomey came into conflict with the French, who hindered his slave-trading, in 1889. After campaigns in which the Amazons played a conspicuous part the Dahomeyans were defeated. Ouidah and adjacent areas were annexed by France on 3 December 1892 and the rest of Dahomey became a French protectorate. Against opposition from Britain and Germany the French secured a common border in the north with French Sudan. The colony of Dahomey and Dependencies was formed in 1899.

B. DAHOMEY AND DEPENDENCIES

FRENCH COLONY

1899–1905. *French Colonies Type* X *inscr* "DAHOMEY ET DEPENDANCES", *in red* (1, 5, 15, 25, 50 *c.* (*No.* 12), 75 *c.*, 1, 2 *f.*) *or blue* (*others*). *P* 14×13½.

1	1 c. black/*azure* (1901) ..	..	..	8	5
2	2 c. brown/*buff* (1905) ..	..	..	12	12
3	4 c. purple-brown/*grey* (1905) ..	..	25	25
4	5 c. pale yellow-green (1905) ..	..	50	50
5	10 c. rose-red (12.1900) ..	..	75	70
6	15 c. grey (12.1900) ..	..	..	60	30
7	20 c. red/*green* (1905) ..	..	2·75	2·75
8	25 c. black/*rose* ..	..	..	2·50	2·00
9	25 c. blue (12.1900) ..	..	..	2·75	2·50

10	30 c. cinnamon/*drab* (1905)	..	..	2·75	2·75
11	40 c. red/*yellow* (1905)	..	..	3·25	3·25
12	50 c. brown and carmine/*azure* (12.1900)		3·25	2·75
13	50 c. brown and blue/*azure* (1905)			5·00	5·00
14	75 c. brown/*orange* (1905)	..	..	13·00	12·00
15	1 f. olive-green/*toned* (1905)	..		6·50	6·00
16	2 f. violet/*rose* (1905)	..	..	18·00	18·00
17	5 f. mauve/*pale blue* (1905)	..		30·00	24·00
1/17	*Set of 17*	..	..	85·00	75·00

1 General Faidherbe   **2** Palm Trees

3 Dr. N. Eugène Balay

(Des J. Puyplat. Typo)

1906–7. *Name in blue* (10 *c.*, 5 *f.*) *or red* (*others*). *P* 14×13½ (*horiz*) *or* 13½×14 (*vert*).

18	**1**	1 c. slate	..	..	..	12	12
19		2 c. chocolate	..	..	..	12	12
20		4 c. chocolate/*blue*	..	..	40	25
21		5 c. green	..	..	..	1·25	25
22		10 c. rose	..	..	..	3·25	40
23	**2**	20 c. black/*bluish*	..	..	2·50	2·00
24		25 c. blue	..	..	..	2·50	1·90
25		30 c. chocolate/*flesh*	..	..	3·25	2·25
26		35 c. black/*yellow*	..	..	19·00	2·50
27		45 c. chocolate/*green* (1907)	..	3·25	2·50
28		50 c. deep violet	..	..	3·75	3·25
29		75 c. green/*orange*	..	..	3·75	2·50
30	**3**	1 f. black/*azure*	..	..	4·50	2·75
31		2 f. blue/*rose*	..	..	25·00	25·00
32		5 f. red/*straw*	..	..	22·00	22·00
18/32		*Set of 15*	..	..	85·00	60·00

D 4 Dakar and   **(4)**   **(5)**   **6** Climbing
West Africans   Palm-tree

(Des J. Puyplat. Typo)

1906. *POSTAGE DUE. Name in blue* (10 *c.*, 30 *c.*) *or red* (*others*). *P* 13½×14.

D33	**D 4**	5 c. green/*toned*	..	..	50	50
D34		10 c. maroon		..	90	90
D35		15 c. blue/*bluish*		..	1·90	1·90
D36		20 c. black/*yellow*		..	1·10	1·10
D37		30 c. red/*cream*		..	1·25	1·25
D38		50 c. violet	..	..	4·50	4·50
D39		60 c. black/*buff*	..	..	2·50	2·50
D40		1 f. black/*flesh*	..	..	6·50	6·50
D33/40		*Set of 8*	..	..	17·00	17·00

1912 (Nov). *Nos. 2/14 surch as T* **4** *and* **5.**

A. Narrow spacing. B. Wide spacing

		A		B	
33	X 05 on 2 c. brown/*buff* ..	10	10	1·50	1·50
34	05 on 4 c. pur-brn/*grey* (R.)	15	15	1·00	1·00
35	05 on 15 c. grey (R.)	10	10	1·60	1·60
36	05 on 20 c. red/*green* ..	10	10	1·25	1·25
37	05 on 25 c. blue (R.)	10	10	1·90	1·90
38	05 on 30 c. cinnamon/*drab* (R.)	20	12	1·40	1·40
39	10 on 40 c. red/*yellow* ..	20	12	13·00	8·00
40	10 on 50 c. brn & bl/*azure* (R.) (No. 13)	20			
40a	10 on 50 c. brn & carm/*azure* (R.) (No. 12)	£225	£250	£1500	£1500
41	10 on 75 c. brown/*orange*	1·10	1·10	50·00	50·00

In Type A the space between "0" and "5" is 1½ mm and between "1" and "0" 2½ mm. In Type B the spacing is 2 mm and 3 mm respectively.

(Des J. de la Nézière, eng A. Mignon. Typo)

1913 (Oct)–**25.** *Ordinary or chalk-surfaced paper. P* 13½×14.

42	**6**	1 c. black and violet	..	..	5	5
43		2 c. rose and chocolate		..	5	5
44		4 c. brown and black	..	..	5	5
45		5 c. green and yellow-green	..	5	5
46		10 c. rose and orange-red	..	12	10
47		15 c. purple and chestnut (7.17)		5	5
48		20 c. chocolate and grey	..	5	5
		a. Sepia and slate-grey (1925)	15	10
49		25 c. blue and ultramarine	..	15	12
50		30 c. violet and chocolate	..	40	40
51		35 c. black and brown	..	15	12
52		40 c. orange and black	..	5	5
53		45 c. ultramarine and grey	..	5	5
54		50 c. brown and chocolate	..	70	70
55		75 c. violet and blue	..	..	5	5
56		1 f. black and green	..	..	12	12
57		2 f. chocolate and orange-yellow	15	15
58		5 f. Prussian blue and violet	..	30	30
42/58		*Set of 17*	..	..	2·50	2·50

For 5 f. chocolate and ultramarine, see No. 73a. See also Nos. 60/4 and 75/95.

The 10 c., 30 c. and 50 c. are known bisected and used as half these values between September 1920 and November 1921, with covers recorded from several offices. Horizontal, vertical and diagonal bisects occur.

D 7   **(7)**

1914 (June). *POSTAGE DUE. Typo. P* 14×13½.

D59	**D 7**	5 c. green	..	..	5	5
D60		10 c. carmine	..	..	5	5
D61		15 c. grey	..	..	10	10
D62		20 c. brown	..	..	10	10
D63		30 c. blue	..	..	12	12
D64		50 c. black	..	..	25	25
D65		60 c. orange	..	..	40	40
D66		1 f. violet	..	..	35	35
D59/66		*Set of 8*	..	..	1·25	1·25

The 50 c. is known bisected and used as a 25 c. postage stamp at Ouidah in November 1920.

Dahomey 1915

1915 (Mar). *Surch with T 7, in red.*
59	**6**	10 c. + 5 c. rose and orange-red	20	15
		a. Surch triple		

1922 (1 Jan). *Colours changed. P 13½ × 14.*
60	**6**	5 c. violet and purple	5	5
61		10 c. green and pale green . .	5	5
62		25 c. orange and purple	5	5
63		30 c. carmine and red	30	30
64		50 c. blue and ultramarine . .	10	10
60/64		*Set of 5*	50	50

25ᶜ 60 60 90 90
=   =   =   =   =

(8)   (9)   (10)

1922–27. *Stamps as T 6, some with colours changed, surch.*

(a) As T 8 with bars obliterating old value
65	**6**	25 c. on 2 f. chocolate & orge-yell (6.24)	5	5

(b) As T 9
66	**6**	60 on 75 c. violet/*rose* (9.22) . .	5	5
		a. Surch double	10·00	
67		65 on 15 c. purple and chestnut (1.2.25)	20	20
		a. Small "5" at left		
68		85 on 15 c. purple and chestnut (1.2.25)	20	20

(c) As T 10
69	**6**	90 c. on 75 c. brown-red & carm (28.2.27)	30	30
70		1 f. 25 on 1 f. brt blue & bl (R.) (14.6.26)	5	5
71		1 f. 50 on 1 f. light blue & blue (28.2.27)	35	35
72		3 f. on 5 f. verm & sage-grn (19.12.27)	1·60	1·60
73		10 f. on 5 f. chocolate & ultram (7.2.27)	1·40	1·40
		a. Surch omitted	90·00	
74		20 f. on 5 f. green and red (7.2.27) . .	1·40	1·40
65/74		*Set of 10*	5·00	5·00

A 65 c. on 45 c. surcharge is a Togo issue, with "TOGO" overprint omitted in error.

1925–39. *New values and colours changed. P 13½ × 14.*
75	**6**	10 c. olive and red (15.4.25) . .	5	5
76		20 c. green (1.3.26)	5	5
77		20 c. black and magenta (6.27) . .	5	5
78		30 c. violet and yellow (1.2.26) . .	5	5
79		30 c. green and olive-green (14.11.27)	5	5
80		35 c. green and blue-green (16.5.38) . .	5	5
81		50 c. blue and brown-red (1.2.26) . .	5	5
82		55 c. chocolate and green (16.5.38) . .	5	5
83		60 c. violet/*rose* (16.11.25) . .	5	5
84		65 c. olive-green and brown (1.3.26) . .	5	5
85		80 c. ultramarine and chestnut (16.5.38)	5	5
86		85 c. bright rose and blue (1.3.26) . .	10	10
87		90 c. brown-red and carmine (5.5.30) . .	5	5
87a		90 c. vermilion and brown (1939) . .	5	5
88		1 f. bright blue and blue (1.3.26) . .	15	15
89		1 f. vermilion and brown (30.4.28) . .	20	12
90		1 f. red and brown-red (1938) . .	12	10
91		1 f. 10, brown & bright violet (25.9.28)	40	40
92		1 f. 25, chocolate and blue (25.9.33)	3·50	1·10
93		1 f. 50, light blue and blue (5.5.30) . .	12	12
94		1 f. 75, red-brown & choc (25.9.33)	65	45
94a		1 f. 75, ultramarine and blue (1938) . .	5	5
95		3 f. magenta/*rose* (5.5.30) . .	30	20
75/95		*Set of 23*	5·50	3·00

1927 (10 Oct). *POSTAGE DUE. Surch as Type D 11.*
D96	**D 7**	2 f. on 1 f. magenta . .	70	70
D97		3 f. on 1 f. chestnut . .	75	75

2ᶠ·

(D 11)   11 René Caillié

1931 (13 Apr). *International Colonial Exhibition, Paris. As T 9 to 12 of Cameroun.*
96		40 c. green	95	95
97		50 c. mauve	95	95
98		90 c. vermilion	95	95
99		1 f. 50, blue	95	95
96/99		*Set of 4*	3·50	3·50

1937 (15 Apr). *International Exhibition, Paris. As T 13 to 18 of Cameroun.*
100		20 c. bright violet	15	15
101		30 c. green	20	20
102		40 c. carmine	20	20
103		50 c. brown	20	20
104		90 c. scarlet	20	20
105		1 f. 50, blue	20	20
100/105		*Set of 6*	85	85
MS105a		120 × 100 mm. 3 f. ultramarine and		
		black (as T 16). Imperf . .	90	90
		b. Error. Inscription inverted . .	£225	£225

1938 (24 Oct). *International Anti-Cancer Fund. As T 19 of Cameroun.*
106		1 f. 75 + 50 c. ultramarine	2·00	2·00

(Des and eng R. Cottet. Recess Institut de Gravure, Paris)

1939 (5 Apr). *Death Centenary of R. Caillié (explorer). P 12½.*
107	**11**	90 c. orange	25	25
108		2 f. violet	25	25
109		2 f. 25, blue	30	30

1939 (10 May). *New York World's Fair. As T 20 of Cameroun.*
110		1 f. 25, lake	15	15
111		2 f. 25, ultramarine	15	15

1939 (5 July). *150th Anniv of French Revolution. As T 25 of Cameroun. Name and value in black.*
112		45 c. + 25 c. green	1·60	1·60
113		70 c. + 30 c. brown	1·60	1·60
114		90 c. + 35 c. red-orange	1·60	1·60
115		1 f. 25 + 1 f. carmine	1·60	1·60
116		2 f. 25 + 2 f. blue	1·60	1·60
112/116		*Set of 5*	7·00	7·00

12 African Landscape

(Des D. Paul. Recess Institut de Gravure)

1940 (8 Feb). *AIR. P 12½.*
117	**12**	1 f. 90, bright blue	5	5
118		2 f. 90, rose-red	5	5
119		4 f. 50, green	10	10
120		4 f. 90, olive-bistre	12	12
121		6 f. 90, orange	25	25
117/121		*Set of 5*	50	50

PUZZLED?
Then you need
PHILATELIC TERMS ILLUSTRATED
to tell you all you need to know about printing methods, papers, errors, varieties, watermarks, perforations, etc. 192 pages, almost half in full colour, soft cover. £1·95 post paid.

VICHY GOVERNMENT

Nos. 122/143*i* were issued by the Pétain régime in Unoccupied France. A number of other issues exist, but we only list those items which were available in Dahomey.

13 Native Poling Canoe **14** Village on Piles

(Des and eng A. Decaris (2 c. to 15 c.), N. Degorce (20 c. to 70 c.), P. Gandon (2 f. 50 to 20 f.). Des Dassonville. Eng R. Feltesse (80 c. to 2 f.). Recess)

1941. *P* 13.

122	**13**	2 c. scarlet		5	5
123		3 c. deep blue		5	5
124		5 c. brown-violet		5	5
125		10 c. green		5	5
126		15 c. black		5	5
127	**14**	20 c. violet-brown		5	5
128		30 c. deep violet		5	5
129		40 c. scarlet		5	5
130		50 c. slate-green		10	10
131		60 c. black		5	5
132		70 c. magenta		5	5
133	–	80 c. brown-black		8	8
134	–	1 f. violet		12	12
135	–	1 f. 30, brown-violet		12	12
136	–	1 f. 40, green		15	15
137	–	1 f. 50, rose-carmine		20	20
138	–	2 f. brown-orange		25	25
139	–	2 f. 50, deep blue		20	20
140	–	3 f. scarlet		25	25
141	–	5 f. slate-green		15	15
142	–	10 f. violet-brown		25	25
143	–	20 f. black		40	40
122/143		*Set of* 22		2·50	2·50

Designs: *Vert*—80 c. to 2 f. Boat on Lake Nokoué; 2 f. 50 to 20 f. Dahomey warrior.

50 c. and 60 c. values as Type **14**, but without "RF" were prepared in 1944, but not issued in Dahomey.

SECOURS
+ 3 fr.
NATIONAL

(14*a*) D **14** Native Head

1941. *National Defence Fund. Surch as T* **14***a*.

143*a*	**6**	+1 f. on 50 c. blue and brown-red	20	20
143*b*		+2 f. on 80 c. ultramarine & chestnut	1·40	1·40
143*c*		+2 f. on 1 f. 50, light blue and blue	1·60	1·60
143*d*		+3 f. on 2 f. chocolate & orange-yellow	1·60	1·60
143*a*/143*d*		*Set of* 4	4·50	4·50

(Des and eng C. Hertenberger. Recess)

1941. *POSTAGE DUE. P* 14×13.

D143	D **14**	5 c. black	5	5
D144		10 c. lilac-rose	5	5
D145		15 c. deep blue	5	5
D146		20 c. yellow-green	5	5
D147		30 c. orange	5	5
D148		50 c. violet-brown	10	10
D149		60 c. slate-green	12	12

D150	D **14**	1 f. rose-red	20	20
D151		2 f. yellow	20	20
D152		3 f. deep purple	25	25
D143/152		*Set of* 10	1·00	1·00

10 c., 15 c. and 20 c. values without "RF" were prepared in 1943/44, but not issues in Dahomey.

14*b* Village on Piles and Marshal Pétain

(Des and eng Degorce. Recess Institut de Gravure, Paris)

1942. *Marshal Pétain issue. P* 12½ × 12.

143*e*	**14***b*	1 f. deep green	10	10
143*f*		2 f. 50, deep blue	10	10

14*c* Maternity Hospital, Dakar **14***d* "Vocation"

(Nos. 143*g*/*h* des J. Douy. Photo Vaugirard. No. 143*i* des C. Mazelin. Recess Institut de Gravure, Paris)

1942 (22 June). *AIR. Colonial Child Welfare Fund. T* **14***c and similar horiz designs. P* 13½ × 12½ *or* 13 (*No.* 143*i*).

143*g*		1 f. 50+3 f. 50, green		12
143*h*		2 f.+6 f. red-brown		12
143*i*		3 f.+9 f. carmine-red		12

Designs:—2 f. Dispensary, Mopti; 3 f. "Child welfare" (48½ × 27 *mm*).

(Des J. Douy. Eng J. Piel. Recess Institut de Gravure, Paris)

1942 (22 June). *AIR. "Imperial Fortnight". P* 12½ × 13½.

143*j*	**14***d*	1 f. 20+1 f. 80, blue and red		10

14*e* Camel Caravan

(Des and eng D. Paul. Typo and recess)

1942 (19 Oct). *AIR. P* 12½ × 12.

143*k*	**14***e*	50 f. grey-blue and yellow-green	40	40
		l. Pale blue and yellow-green	45	45

Other values in this and a similar design were not issued in Dahomey.

Dahomey remained under the Vichy Government until November 1942. From 1944 ro 1960 the general issues for French West Africa were used in Dahomey.

C. AUTONOMOUS REPUBLIC OF DAHOMEY

Dahomey became an autonomous republic within the French Community on 4 December 1958.

15 Ganvie Village

16 Conseil de l'Entente Emblem

(Des and eng R. Cottet (25 f.), A. Decaris (others). Recess)

1960. *T* **15** *and similar horiz designs.* *P* 13.

(*a*) *POSTAGE* (1 Mar)
144	**15**	25 f. chocolate, red and blue	25	5

(*b*) *AIR. Inscr* "POSTE AERIENNE" (1 Apr)
145	—	100 f. chocolate, ochre and indigo	75	20
146	—	500 f. brown-red, bistre & dp blue-grn	3·25	80

Designs:—100 f. Somba fort; 500 f. Royal Court, Abomey.

1960 (16 May). *10th Anniv of African Technical Co-operation Commission. As T* **62** *of Cameroun.*
147	5 f. ultramarine and bright purple	25	20

(Photo Comoy, Paris)

1960 (29 May). *First Anniv of Conseil de l'Entente.* *P* 13.
148	**16**	25 f. multicoloured	40	30

Dahomey became an independent republic on 1 August 1960.

PHILATELIC TERMS ILLUSTRATED

This successful STAMP MONTHLY series has now been brought together in a snappy black and yellow binding and published as a useful addition to Stanley Gibbons range of essential handbooks for keen stamp collectors.
Within its 192 pages this handy limp-bound volume houses a veritable mine of useful information on the words and phrases used in philately. It describes and illustrates printing processes and watermarks, papers and perforations, errors and varieties . . . and it does all this IN COLOUR. Indeed, there are 92 full page plates in colour, plus many black and white illustrations, making it

FANTASTIC VALUE AT ONLY £1·95 POST PAID FROM

Stanley Gibbons Publications Ltd
391 Strand, London WC2R 0LX

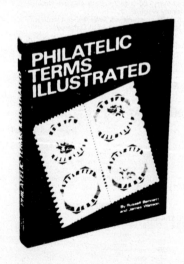

Fezzan

100 Centimes = 1 Franc

Free French troops advancing from Chad took Murzuk, the chief town of Fezzan, the southern part of Libya, on 16 January 1943. From 1943 to 1951 Fezzan was under French military administration.

MILITARY ADMINISTRATION

(a) Issues for Fezzan and Ghadamès

FEZZAN

Occupation Française

1 fr.

(1)

1943 (16 May). *Optd as T 1 or surch in addition with bars obliterating old inscriptions and values, by V. Heintz, Algiers.*

(a) POSTAGE

No. 247 of Italy optd only

1	**103**	50 c. bright violet	..	..	17·00	17·00
		a. Opt double	..	..		

Stamps of Libya surch. No wmk. P 14.

2	**4**	0 f. 50 on 5 c. green and black	..	50·00	45·00
3	**5**	1 f. on 10 c. rose and black ..		70·00	65·00
4	**6**	2 f. on 30 c. sepia and black (R.)	..	£110	£100
		a. Surch double	..	..	£350	
5	**9**	3 f. on 20 c. green	..	..	22·00	22·00
6	**5**	3 f. 50 on 25 c. blue & deep blue (R.)	32·00	28·00
7	**6**	5 f. on 50 c. olive and black (R.)	..	5·00	5·00
		a. Surch double	..	..	£120	
		b. Surch triple	..	..		
8		10 f. on 1 l. 25, ultramarine & ind (R.)	£450	£400
		a. Surch double	..	..	£900	
9	**9**	20 f. on 1 l. 75, orange (R.) ..	..	£1200	£1100
10	**7**	50 f. on 75 c. scarlet and purple (R.)..	£1400	£1400

(b) AIR

No. 271 of Italy optd.

11	**110**	50 c. sepia	..	..	28·00	28·00
		a. Opt double	..	..	£325	
		b. Opt triple	..	..		

No. 72 of Libya surch

12	**18**	7 f. 50 on 50 c. deep carmine	..	25·00	25·00
		a. Surch double	..	..		
		b. Surch triple	..	..		
		c. Two bars instead of three	..	85·00	75·00

(c) POSTAGE DUE

Postage Due stamps of Libya surch

D13	D **6**	0 f. 50 on 5 c. chocolate	..	..	£500	£500
D14		1 f. on 10 c. blue	..	..	£500	£500
		a. Surch double (Bk.+R.) ..	..		
D15		2 f. on 25 c. green ..	..		£500	£500
D16		3 f. on 50 c. bright violet	..	£500	£500
D17	D **7**	5 f. on 1 l. orange	..	..	£2500	£2500

(2)

R.F. I Fr FEZZAN

(3)

1943 (10 June). *Handstamped at Sebha.*

(a) POSTAGE

No. 247 of Italy with T 2

13	**103**	0 f. 50 on 50 c. violet	..	..	—	£140

No. 53 of Libya with T 3

14	**5**	1 f. on 25 c. blue and deep blue	..	—	£120

(b) AIR

No. 271 of Italy with T 2.

15	**110**	0 f. 50 on 50 c. sepia ..	..	..	—	£325

1943 (16 July). *Parcel Post stamps of Libya handstamped at Sebha across each half with T 3.*

16	P **2**	1 f. on 5 c. brown	..	..	—	£175
17	P **4**	1 f. on 10 c. blue	..	..	—	£175
18		1 f. on 50 c. orange	..	..	—	£175
19		1 f. on 1 l. violet	..	..	—	£175
20		1 f. on 2 l. green	..	..	—	£1200
21		1 f. on 3 l. yellow-bistre	..	—	£1200
22		1 f. on 4 l. grey-black	..	..	—	£1200

Two sets can be made of the above issue as each half is different. The prices apply to either half.

When the above stamps were exhausted mail was endorsed to the effect that stamps were lacking and cancelled "P. P." (Port Payé) and signed by the postal clerk. Thereafter until 1946 the area came under Algerian postal administration and Algerian stamps were used.

4 Fort of Sebha   **6** Map and Fort of Sebha
5 Turkish Fort and Mosque
at Murzuk (36×21½ mm)

(Des A. Boutet. Eng Cortot, Dufresne and Cottet. Recess)

1946 (29 Oct). *P 13.*

23	**4**	10 c. black	..	..	..	5	5
24		50 c. carmine	..	..		5	5
25		1 f. brown	..	..	..	5	5
26		1 f. 50, green ..	..	..	5	5
27		2 f. ultramarine	..	..		5	5
28	**5**	2 f. 50, violet ..	..	..	8	8
29		3 f. scarlet	..	..	..	15	20
30		5 f. brown	..	..	..	15	15
31		6 f. green	..	..	..	15	15
32		10 f. blue	..	..	..	15	20
33	**6**	15 f. violet	..	..	..	20	25
34		20 f. red	..	..	..	30	35
35		25 f. purple-brown	..	..	30	35
36		40 f. green	..	..	..	30	40
37		50 f. blue	..	..	..	40	50
23/37		*Set of 15*	..	..	..	2·25	2·50

(b) Issues for Fezzan only

7 Fezzan Airfield   **8** Aeroplane over Fezzan

(Des A. Boutet. Eng Feltesse and Dufresne. Recess)

1948 (5 Mar). *AIR. P* 13.
38 **7** 100 f. red	.. .. ..	1·25	1·25
39 **8** 200 f. blue	.. .. ..	2·25	2·25

14 Camel Breeding   **15** Ahmed Bey

(Des H. Razous. Eng A. Frères (30 c. to 2 f.), Cottet (4 f. to 8 f.), Feltesse (10 f. to 15 f.), C. Mazelin (20 f. to 50 f.), Dufresne (100 f.), Pheulpin (200 f.). Recess)

1951 (25 June). *T* **14/15** *and similar designs. P* 13.

(a) POSTAGE
59 **14**	30 c. brown	.. .. ..	8	8
60	1 f. blue	.. .. ..	12	12
61	2 f. carmine	.. ..	12	12
62 —	4 f. red	.. .. ..	12	12
63 —	5 f. bright green	.. ..	12	12
64 —	8 f. blue	.. .. ..	25	25
65 —	10 f. blackish brown	..	80	80
66 —	12 f. green	.. ..	90	90
67 —	15 f. scarlet	.. ..	1·25	1·25
68 **15**	20 f. blackish brown	..	1·25	1·25
69	25 f. pale blue and deep blue	..	1·00	1·00
70	50 f. orange-brown and indigo	..	1·50	1·50

(b) AIR. Inscr "POSTE AERIENNE"
71 —	100 f. deep blue	.. ..	2·50	2·50
72 —	200 f. scarlet	.. ..	4·00	4·00
59/72	*Set of* 14	.. ..	13·00	13·00

Designs: *Horiz*—4 f. to 8 f. Arab hoeing; 100 f. Brak Oasis; 200 f. Sebha Fort. *Vert*—10 f. to 15 f. Artesian well.

On 24 December 1951 Fezzan became part of the Kingdom of Libya.

9 Djerma   **10** Well at Gorda

(Des A. Boutet. Eng Cortot (1 f., 2 f.), Dufresne (4 f., 5 f.), Feltesse (8 f., 10 f., 12 f.), Serres (others). Recess)

1949. *T* **9/10** *and similar horiz designs. P* 13.
40 **9**	1 f. black	.. ..	..	10	10
41	2 f. rose-pink	.. ..		10	10
42 —	4 f. reddish brown	..	..	30	30
43 —	5 f. emerald-green	..	..	40	40
44 **10**	8 f. blue	.. ..	..	40	40
45	10 f. brown	.. ..	..	85	85
46	12 f. deep green	..	..	1·60	1·60
47 —	15 f. scarlet	..	..	1·90	1·90
48 —	20 f. brownish black	..	..	80	80
49 —	25 f. blue	.. ..	..	80	80
50 —	50 f. brown-red	..	..	90	90
40/50	*Set of* 11	..	..	7·50	7·50

Designs:—4 f. 5 f., Beni-Khettab tombs; 15 f. 20 f. Colonel Colonna d'Ornano and fort; 25 f., 50 f. General Leclerc and map of Europe and N. Africa.

CIVIL ADMINISTRATION

11 "Charity"   **12** Mother and Child   D **13** Brak Oasis

(Des and eng A. Boutet (both), Cottet (15 f.) and B. Munier (25 f.) Recess)

1950. *Charity. P* 13.
51 **11**	15 f. +5 f. lake	..	..	80	1·00
52 **12**	25 f. +5 f. blue	..	..	80	1·00

(Des H. Razous. Eng Feltesse. Recess)

1950. *POSTAGE DUE. P* 13.
D53	D **13**	1 f. black	.. ..	15	15
D54		2 f. emerald-green	..	20	20
D55		3 f. brown-lake	..	20	20
D56		5 f. violet	.. ..	25	25
D57		10 f. scarlet	..	70	70
D58		20 f. blue	.. ..	80	80
D53/58		*Set of* 6	.. ..	2·00	2·00

HAVE YOU READ THE NOTES AT THE BEGINNING OF THIS CATALOGUE?

These often provide answers to the enquiries we receive.

GHADAMÈS

FRENCH MILITARY ADMINISTRATION

From 1949 to 1951 the French issued separate stamps for Ghadamès, in the corner of Libya near Tunisia and Algeria. This had been administered from 1943 as part of Fezzan.

1 Cross of Agadem

(Des Besson. Eng Cortot. Recess)

1949 (12 Apr). *P* 13. (*a*) *POSTAGE.*
1 **1**	4 f. brown and sepia	..	..	30	30
2	5 f. deep green and turquoise-blue		30	30
3	8 f. orange-brown and sepia	..		90	90
4	10 f. ultramarine and indigo	..		1·00	90
5	12 f. bright purple and violet	..		2·50	2·25
6	15 f. red-brown and brown	..		2·25	2·00
7	20 f. emerald-green and sepia	..		2·25	2·00
8	25 f. blue and sepia	..		2·25	2·00

(*b*) *AIR. Inscr* "POSTE AERIENNE"
9 **1**	50 f. carmine-pink and purple	..		3·50	3·50
10	50 f. brown-purple and sepia	..		4·00	4·00
1/10	*Set of* 10	.. ..	..	17·00	17·00

On 24 December 1951 Ghadamès became part of the Kingdom of Libya.

Free French Forces in the Levant

(SYRIA AND LEBANON)

100 Centimes = 1 Franc

After British and Free French troops had occupied Syria and Lebanon in June 1941, the following stamps were issued for the use of Free French forces in those areas.

100 Centimes =1 Franc

(1)

1942. *No. 252 of Syria surch with T* **1.**
1	50 c. on 4 p. orange	.. .. ..	1·25	1·25
	a. Surch inverted	.. ..		

1942. *Nos. 251 and 212 of Lebanon surch as T* **1**, *in red.*
2	1 f. on 5 p. greenish blue ..	..	1·25	1·25
3	2 f. 50 on 12½ p. ultramarine	.. ..	1·25	1·25

(2)

1942. *AIR.* **269/70** *of Syria surch as T* **2.**
4	4 f. on 50 p. black (R.) ..	.. ..	70	70
5	6 f. 50 on 50 p. black (R.)	.. ..	70	70
6	8 f. on 50 p. black (O.)	.. ..	70	70
7	10 f. on 100 p. magenta	.. ..	70	70
4/7	*Set of 4*	.. ..	2·50	2·50

3 Camelry and Ruins at Palmyra

(Des R. Soriano. Litho, Beirut)

1942. *P* 11½. (*a*) *POSTAGE. Buff background.*
8	**3**	1 f. lake	8	8
9		1 f. 50, violet	8	8
10		2 f. orange	8	8
11		2 f. 50, sepia	8	8
12		3 f. blue	8	8
13		4 f. green	10	10
14		5 f. claret	10	10

(*b*) *AIR*
15	**4**	6 f. 50, rose-carmine	25	25
16		10 f. purple and blue	25	25
8/16		*Set of 9*	1·00	1·00
MS17		106×16 mm. Nos. 15/16. No gum ..	4·75	
		a. Imperf	4·50	

(5)

1942. *AIR. No.* 15 *surch with T* **5** *in the colour of the stamp.*
17	**4**	4 f. on 6 f. 50, rose-carmine ..	.. 40	40

(6)

(7)

1943. (*a*) *POSTAGE. Surch as T* **6** *with premium.*
18	**3**	1 f.+9 f. lake	1·40	1·40
19		5 f.+20 f. claret	1·40	1·40

(*b*) *AIR. Surch as T* **7** *with premium*
20	**4**	6 f. 50+48 f. 50, rose-carmine ..	.. 4·50	4·50
21		10 f.+100 f. purple and blue ..	.. 4·50	4·50
18/21		*Set of 4*	.. 11·00	11·00

(8)

1943. *AIR. No.* 12 *surch with T* **8.**
22	**3**	4 f. on 3 f. blue and buff	.. ..	40	40

4 Wings bearing Lorraine Crosses

By an Anglo-French agreement of 13 December 1945 all British and French troops left Syria and Lebanon by 15 April 1946.

ALBUM LISTS

Please write for our latest lists of albums and accessories. These will be sent free on request.

French Equatorial Africa

100 Centimes = 1 Franc

On 15 January 1910 the French colonies of Gabon, Middle Congo and Ubangi–Shari–Chad were federated to form French Equatorial Africa. Each colony continued to issue its own stamps until the first issues for the federation appeared in 1936.

PRINTERS. All issues were printed at the French Government Printing Works, Paris, *unless otherwise stated.*

IMPERFORATE STAMPS. Many stamps exist imperforate in their issued colours, but these were not valid for postage. Imperforate stamps in other colours are colour trials.

4 Berber, Negress and Annamite

5 Agriculture

AFRIQUE ÉQUATORIALE FRANÇAISE

(1)

1936 (16 Mar). *Optd with T 1 or similar types.*

(a) On 1933 *issue of Congo* (*Middle Congo*)

1	1 c. chocolate	..	..	..	5	5
2	2 c. greenish blue				5	5
3	4 c. bronze-green				8	5
4	5 c. claret	..		..	10	5
5	10 c. deep blue-green				30	20
6	15 c. purple	..		..	30	20
7	20 c. red/*rose*				15	12
8	25 c. orange	..		..	65	40
9	40 c. red-brown				60	40
10	50 c. slate-purple	..			45	40
11	75 c. black/*rose*	..			90	65
12	90 c. rosine	..			55	40
13	1 f. 50, blue	..			30	25
14	5 f. blackish blue			..	11·00	7·00
15	10 f. black	..		..	6·50	5·00
16	20 f. brown	..		..	7·00	5·00

(b) On 1932–33 *issue of Gabon*

17	1 c. claret	..			5	5
18	2 c. black/*rose*	..			5	5
19	4 c. green	..			15	10
20	5 c. greenish blue				12	5
21	10 c. scarlet/*yellow*				15	5
22	40 c. purple	..			35	12
23	50 c. chocolate-brown				30	12
24	1 f. yellow-green/*blue*	..			6·50	2·50
25	1 f. 50, blue	..			45	10
26	2 f. chestnut	..			3·75	2·00
1/26	*Set of 26*	..			35·00	23·00

6 France extends Torch of Civilisation

7 Diane de Poitiers

(Des J. Goujon (T **2**), Robichon (T **3**), Canyon-Rouan (T **4**), A. Decaris (T **5, 7**), G. Barlangue (T **6**). Eng R. Cottet (T **2**), E. Feltesse (T **3**), P. Munier (T **4**), A. Decaris (T **5, 7**), A. Delzers (T **6**). Recess)

1937 (15 Apr). *International Exhibition, Paris. P* 13.

27	2	20 c. bright violet	..		..	50	50
28	3	30 c. green				50	50
29	4	40 c. carmine	..		..	50	50
30	5	50 c. brown and blue	..			30	30
31	6	90 c. scarlet	..		..	50	50
32	7	1 f. 50, blue	..		..	50	50
27/32		*Set of 6*			..	2·50	2·50
MS33		120 × 100 mm. **7** 3 f. brown-red. Imperf				1·25	1·25
		a. Error. Inscription inverted	..			£140	

2 Commerce

3 Sailing Ships

8 Logging near Mayumba

9 Chad Family

10 Count Savorgnan de Brazza

11 Flying-boat over Pointe-Noire

STAMP MONTHLY
—finest and most informative magazine for all collectors. Obtainable from your newsagent or by postal subscription—details on request.

12 Savoia "S 73" Aircraft over Stanley Pool

D 13

Two types of 25 c.:—

I   II

(Des J. Douy. Photo Vaugirard, Paris)

1937 (3 May)–**40.** (a) *POSTAGE.* T **8/9** *and various portraits as T* **10**. P 13½×13.

34	**8**	1 c. chocolate and yellow		5	5
35		2 c. violet and green		5	5
36		3 c. blue and yellow (15.4.40)		5	5
37		4 c. magenta and pale blue		5	5
38		5 c. deep and pale green		5	5
39	**9**	10 c. magenta and pale blue		5	5
40		15 c. blue and flesh		5	5
41		20 c. chocolate and yellow		5	5
42		25 c. red and pale blue (I)		10	5
43		25 c. red and pale blue (II)		20	12
44	**10**	30 c. deep and pale green		5	5
45		30 c. blue and flesh (15.4.40)		5	5
46	**9**	35 c. green and yellow-green (16.5.38)		20	12
47	**10**	40 c. blue and pale blue		5	5
48		45 c. blue and pale green		80	50
49		45 c. green and pale green (15.4.40)		10	5
50		50 c. chocolate and yellow		5	5
51		55 c. violet and pale blue (16.5.38)		10	8
52		60 c. purple and blue (26.3.40)		5	5
53	–	65 c. blue and pale green		5	5
54	–	70 c. violet and orange (26.3.40)		8	8
55	–	75 c. olive-black and yellow		1·00	65
56	–	80 c. chocolate and yellow (16.5.38)		5	5
57	–	90 c. red and orange		5	5
58	–	1 f. violet and pale green		30	12
59	**10**	1 f. carmine and orange (16.5.38)		45	12
60	–	1 f. blue-green and blue (26.3.40)		8	8
61	–	1 f. 25, red and orange		25	25
62	–	1 f. 40, brown & blue-green (5.3.40)		8	8
63	–	1 f. 50, blue and pale blue		20	15
64	–	1 f. 60, violet and orange (5.3.40)		8	8
65	–	1 f. 75, chocolate and yellow		30	15
66	–	1 f. 75, bright and pale blue (16.5.38)		5	5
67	–	2 f. green and pale green		30	20
68	–	2 f. 15, violet and yellow (6.7.38)		10	5
69	–	2 f. 25, blue and pale blue (4.12.39)		20	20
70	–	2 f. 50, purple and orange (5.3.40)		8	8
71	–	3 f. blue and flesh		10	5
72	–	5 f. green and pale green		25	20
73	–	10 f. violet and pale blue		45	30
74	–	20 f. olive-black and yellow		50	40
34/74		*Set of 41*		6·50	4·50

Designs: 65 c. to 1 f. (No. 58), 1 f. 75 (No. 66), Emile Gentil; 1 f. 25 to 1 f. 75 (No. 65), 2 f. Paul Crampel; 2 f. 15 to 20 f. Victor Liotard.

10, 15, 60 c. and 1 f. 50 stamps as Nos. 39/40, 52 and 63, but without "RF" were prepared in 1943/4, but not issued in the colony.

(b) *AIR.* P 13½×13.

75	**11**	1 f. 50, olive-black and lemon		5	5
76		2 f. bright magenta and pale blue		8	8
77		2 f. 50, green and flesh		10	10
78		3 f. 75, chocolate and green		10	10
79	**12**	4 f. 50, scarlet and pale blue		10	10
80		6 f. 50, blue and pale green		20	20
81	**12**	8 f. 50, lake and orange		20	20
82		10 f. 75, violet and pale green		20	20
75/82		*Set of 8*		90	90

12 stamps in these designs, but without "RF", were prepared in 1943, but not placed on sale in the colony.

(c) *POSTAGE DUE.* P 13

D83	D **13**	5 c. pale blue and deep purple		5	5
D84		10 c. flesh and red		5	5
D85		20 c. pale green and green		5	5
D86		25 c. flesh and red-brown		5	5
D87		30 c. pale blue and red		5	5
D88		45 c. pale green and bright magenta		10	10
D89		50 c. flesh and deep olive-green		10	10
D90		60 c. yellow and deep purple		15	15
D91		1 f. yellow and brown		15	15
D92		2 f. flesh and blue		30	30
D93		3 f. pale blue and red-brown		30	30
D83/93		*Set of 11*		1·25	1·25

14 Pierre and Marie Curie   (15)

(Des J. de la Nézière. Eng J. Piel. Recess)

1938 (24 Oct). *International Anti-Cancer Fund.* P 13.

94	**14**	1 f. 75+50 c. ultramarine		4·00	4·00

1938 (7 Nov). *Social Welfare. Nos. 53 and 66 surch as T* **15**.

95		65 c.+35 c. blue and pale green (R.)		45	35
96		1 f. 75+50 c. bright blue and pale blue		45	35

16 Bouët-Willaumez and *La Malouine*   **17**

(Des J. Douy. Photo Vaugirard, Paris)

1938 (5 Dec). *Centenary of Landing of Bouët-Willaumez in Gabon.* P 13½.

97	**16**	65 c. chocolate		25	25
98		1 f. carmine		25	25
99		1 f. 75 c. greenish blue		35	35
100		2 f. deep violet		35	35
97/100		*Set of 4*		1·10	1·10

(Des and eng A. Decaris. Recess Institut de Gravure, Paris)

1939 (10 May). *New York World's Fair.* P 12.

101	**17**	1 f. 25, lake		40	40
102		2 f. 25, ultramarine		40	40

18 Storming the Bastille

(Des and eng A. Ouvré. Photo and typo Vaugirard, Paris)

1939 (5 July). *150th Anniv of French Revolution.* P 13½×13.

(a) POSTAGE

103	**18**	45 c.+25 c. green and black	3·25	3·25
104		70 c.+30 c. brown and black	3·25	3·25
105		90 c.+35 c. red-orange and black	3·25	3·25
106		1 f. 25+1 f. carmine and black	3·25	3·25
107		2 f. 25+2 f. blue and black	3·25	3·25

(b) AIR

108	**18**	4 f. 50+4 f. black and orange	5·50	5·50
103/108		*Set of 6*	20·00	20·00

VICHY ISSUES. A number of stamps were produced by the Pétain Government of France between 1940 and 1944, but none of these issues were placed on sale in French Equatorial Africa.

AFRIQUE FRANÇAISE
LIBRE
(19)

LIBRE
(20)

Afrique Française
Libre
(21)

LIBRE
24-10-40
(22)

1940. *Adherence to General de Gaulle.*

A. *Stamps of 1936–40*

(a) T 8 and 9 optd with T 19

109	1 c. chocolate and yellow (R.)		15	15
110	2 c. violet and green (R.)		20	20
111	3 c. blue and yellow (R.)		20	20
	a. Opt double		19·00	
112	5 c. deep and pale green (R.)		20	20
	a. Black opt		38·00	38·00
113	10 c. magenta and pale blue		30	30
114	15 c. blue and flesh (R.)		25	25
115	20 c. chocolate and yellow (R.)		30	30
116	25 c. red and pale blue		1·10	1·10
117	35 c. green and yellow-green (R.)		25	25
109/117	*Set of 9*		2·50	2·50

There were two printings of this overprint and each position in the two settings of 50 can be identified by minor variations such as individual letters of a different type or size, broken letters, etc.
Stamp No. 6 on the stamps with black surcharge (10 c. and 25 c.) has the "I" of "LIBRE" omitted.

(b) No. 3 optd with T 20

118	4 c. bronze-green		2·25	1·90

(c) As T 10 (portraits) optd with T 20

119	30 c. deep and pale green (R.)		2·50	2·00
	a. Black opt		40	25
120	30 c. blue and flesh (R.)		2·25	2·00
	a. Black opt		1·40	1·40
121	40 c. red and pale blue		12	10
	a. Opt double			
122	45 c. green and pale green (R.)		15	12
	a. Black opt		12	10
	b. Black opt double			
123	50 c. chocolate and yellow (R.)		1·00	85
	a. Black opt		55	50
	b. Black opt double		19·00	
124	55 c. violet and pale blue (R.)		20	15
	a. Black opt		12	10
	b. Black opt double			
	c. Black opt double, one inverted			
125	60 c. purple and blue		10	5
126	65 c. blue and pale green		12	12
	a. Opt double			
127	70 c. violet and orange		15	10
	a. Opt double			
128	75 c. olive-black and yellow		7·50	7·50
129	80 c. chocolate and yellow		8	5
	a. Opt double			
130	90 c. red and orange		20	20
	a. Opt double			
	b. Opt double, one inverted			
131	1 f. carmine and orange		30	20

132	1 f. blue-green and blue (R)		1·10	1·10
	a. Black opt		1·25	90
133	1 f. 40, brown and yellow-green		5	5
	a. Opt double			
134	1 f. 50, blue and pale blue		12	12
	a. Opt double			
135	1 f. 60, violet and orange		10	5
136	1 f. 75, chocolate and yellow		25	12
137	2 f. 15, violet and yellow		15	10
	a. Opt double			
138	2 f. 25, blue and pale blue (R.)		25	25
	a. Opt double			
	b. Black opt		30	30
	c. Black opt double			
139	2 f. 50, purple and orange		15	15
	a. Opt double			
140	3 f. blue and flesh (R.)		25	25
	a. Black opt		40	30
	b. Black opt double			
141	5 f. green and pale green (R.)		65	65
	a. Black opt		25·00	13·00
142	10 f. violet and pale blue (R.)		35	30
	a. Black opt		17·00	13·00
143	20 f. olive-black and yellow (R.)		35	35
	a. Black opt		1·75	1·75
118/143	*Set of 26 (cheapest)*		15·50	15·50

Nos. 120/140. Variety small "L" in "LIBRE" from the first printing exists in all values (No. 33 in sheet).

(d) Portrait types optd with T 20, and surch

144	75 c. on 50 c. chocolate and yellow		5	5
	a. Surch double			
145	1 f. on 65 c. blue and pale green (R.)		5	5
	a. Surch double		1·40	

(e) T 8 and T 9 optd with T 21

146	1 c. chocolate and yellow		25	25
147	2 c. violet and green		25	25
148	3 c. blue and yellow		25	25
149	5 c. deep and pale green		25	25
150	10 c. magenta and pale blue		25	25
151	15 c. blue and flesh		25	25
152	20 c. chocolate and yellow		25	25
153	25 c. red and pale blue		50	50
154	35 c. green and yellow-green		50	50
	a. Opt double			

(f) AIR. T 11/12. (i) Optd with T 21

155	1 f. 50, olive-black and lemon		65·00	55·00
	a. Opt double			
156	2 f. 50, green and flesh		20	20
	a. Opt inverted		65·00	55·00
	b. Opt double			
157	3 f. 75, chocolate and green		55·00	55·00
158	4 f. 50, scarlet and pale blue		30	30
	a. Opt double			
159	6 f. 50, blue and pale green		45	45
160	8 f. 50, lake and orange		30	30

(ii) Optd with T 21 and surch

161	10 f. on 2 f. 50, green and flesh		28·00	25·00
162	50 f. on 10 f. 75, violet and pale green (R.)		1·90	1·90
146/162	*Set of 17*		£140	£140

There were two settings of the overprint on Nos. 146/160 except 155 and 157, one with 1½ mm between the lines of the overprint and the other spaced 2½ mm. There are numerous minor varieties of overprint. On stamp No. 25 in all values with the 1½ mm setting the words "Afrique" and "Française" are widely spaced (3 mm).

B. *Stamp of Congo (Middle Congo)*
No. 71, optd with T 19

163	4 c. bronze-green (R.)		10·00	9·00

1940. *Arrival of General de Gaulle in Brazzaville. Nos. 56, 59/60 and 63 optd with T 22.*

164	80 c. chocolate and yellow		3·50	2·75
165	1 f. carmine and orange		3·50	2·75
166	1 f. blue-green and blue		3·50	2·75
167	1 f. 50, blue and pale blue		3·50	2·75
164/167	*Set of 4*		13·00	10·00

Nos. 164/7 were only sold affixed to postcards.

HAVE YOU READ THE NOTES AT THE BEGINNING OF THIS CATALOGUE?

These often provide answers to the enquiries we receive.

23 Phoenix   **24** Passenger Aircraft

(Des E. Dulac. Photo Harrison)

1941. *Free French Issue.* (*a*) *POSTAGE.* P 14×14½.

168	**23**	5 c. brown			5	5
169		10 c. blue			5	5
170		25 c. emerald-green			5	5
171		30 c. red-orange			5	5
172		40 c. slate-green			5	5
173		80 c. maroon			5	5
174		1 f. magenta			5	5
175		1 f. 50, scarlet			5	5
176		2 f. grey-black			8	5
177		2 f. 50, ultramarine			5	5
178		4 f. violet			12	5
179		5 f. yellow-bistre			8	8
180		10 f. red-brown			12	10
181		20 f. blue-green			20	15

(*b*) *AIR.* P 14½×14

182	**24**	1 f. red-orange			12	10
183		1 f. 50, scarlet			15	12
184		5 f. maroon			30	15
185		10 f. black			30	15
186		25 f. ultramarine			30	20
187		50 f. green			20	15
188		100 f. claret			35	20
168/188		*Set of 21*			2·50	1·75

25 Count Savorgnan de Brazza and Stanley Pool

(Photo Harrison)

1941. *De Brazza Memorial Fund.* P 14½×14.

189	**25**	1 f.+2 f. brown and red		12	12

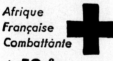

Afrique Française Combattante

+ 50 fr.

(26)

1943 (28 June). *Free French Funds. Nos. 69, 73 and 82 surch as T 26 in red.* (*a*) *POSTAGE.*

190	2 f. 25+50 f. blue and pale blue		2·50	2·50
191	10 f.+100 f. violet and pale blue		7·50	7·50

(*b*) *AIR*

192	10 f. 75+200 f. violet and pale green		40·00	40·00

RÉSISTANCE

+ 10 fr.

(27)

1944. *French Aid Fund. Surch as T 27, in red.*

(*a*) *Horizontally on Nos.* 164 *and* 167

193	80 c.+10 f. chocolate and yellow		3·25	3·25
194	1 f. 50+15 f. blue and pale blue		3·25	3·25

(*b*) *Vertically on* 1941 *Free French issue*

195	**23**	5 c.+10 f. brown		1·40	1·40
196		10 c.+10 f. blue		1·40	1·40
197		25 c.+10 f. emerald-green		1·40	1·40
198		30 c.+10 f. red-orange		1·40	1·40
199		40 c.+10 f. slate-green		1·40	1·40
200		1 f.+10 f. magenta		1·40	1·40
201		2 f.+20 f. grey-black		1·40	1·40
202		2 f. 50+25 f. ultramarine		1·40	1·40
203		4 f.+40 f. violet		1·40	1·40
204		5 f.+50 f. yellow-bistre		1·40	1·40
205		10 f.+100 f. red-brown		1·60	1·60
206		20 f.+200 f. blue-green		1·60	1·60
193/206		*Set of 14*		21·00	21·00

LIBÉRATION

+ 10 fr.

(28)

1944. *French Aid Fund. Surch as T 28 in red.*

(*a*) *Horizontally on Nos.* 164 *and* 167

207	80 c.+10 f. chocolate and yellow		3·25	3·25
208	1 f. 50+15 f. blue and pale blue		3·25	3·25

(*b*) *Vertically on* 1941 *Free French issue*

209	**23**	5 c.+10 f. brown		1·60	1·60
210		10 c.+10 f. blue		1·60	1·60
211		25 c.+10 f. emerald-green		1·60	1·60
212		30 c.+10 f. red-orange		1·60	1·60
213		40 c.+10 f. slate-green		1·60	1·60
214		1 f.+10 f. magenta		1·60	1·60
215		2 f.+20 f. grey-black		1·60	1·60
216		2 f. 50+25 f. ultramarine		1·60	1·60
207/216		*Set of 10*		17·00	17·00

29   (**30**)

(Des E. Dulac. Photo Harrison)

1944. *Mutual Aid and Red Cross Funds.* P 14½×14.

217	**29**	5 f.+20 f. blue	20	20

1945. *Nos. 168, 170 and 177 surch as T 30.*

218	**23**	50 c. on 5 c. brown (R.)		10	10
219		60 c. on 5 c. brown (R.)		10	10
220		70 c. on 5 c. brown (R.)		5	5
221		1 f. 20 on 5 c. brown (R.)		5	5
222		2 f. 40 on 25 c. emerald-green		12	12
223		3 f. on 25 c. emerald-green		25	25
224		4 f. 50 on 25 c. emerald-green		20	20
225		15 f. on 2 f. 50, ultramarine (R.)		20	20
218/225		*Set of 8*		1·00	1·00

31 Félix Eboué   **32** "Victory"

1945. *Recess. P* 13.
226	**31**	2 f. black	..	..	5	5
227		25 f. blue-green	..	..	35	35

(Des and eng A. Decaris. Recess Institut de Gravure, Paris)

1945 (8 May). *AIR. Victory. P* 12½.
228	**32**	8 f. carmine	..	..	20	20

33 Legionaries by
Lake Chad

(Des and eng A. Decaris. Recess Institut de Gravure, Paris)

1946 (6 June). *AIR. From Chad to the Rhine. T* **33** *and similar horiz designs. P* 12½.
229	5 f. purple	..	..	15	15
230	10 f. blackish green	..	..	15	15
231	15 f. blue	..	..	30	30
232	20 f. brown-red	..	..	35	35
233	25 f. brownish black	..	..	40	40
234	50 f. claret	..	..	45	45
229/234	*Set of 6*	..	..	1·50	1·50

Designs:—10 f. Battle of Koufra; 15 f. Tank battle, Mareth; 20 f. Normandy landings; 25 f. Liberation of Paris; 50 f. Liberation of Strasbourg.

34 Rhinoceros

35 Palms and
Cataract

36 Boatman

37 Aeroplane over Beach

(Des and eng R. Serres (100 f.), P. Gandon (others). Recess Institut de Gravure, Paris)

1947 (10 Feb). *P* 12½. (a) *POSTAGE.*
235	**34**	10 c. blue	..	..	5	5
236		30 c. blackish violet	..	..	5	5
237		40 c. red-orange	..	..	5	5
238	**35**	50 c. ultramarine	..	..	5	5
239		60 c. carmine-lake	..	..	5	5
240		80 c. olive-green	..	..	10	5
241	–	1 f. red-orange	..	..	5	5
242	–	1 f. 20, claret	..	..	12	12
243	–	1 f. 50, blue-green	..	..	20	15

244	–	2 f. violet-brown	..	..	5	5
245	–	3 f. carmine	..	..	5	5
246	–	3 f. 60, red-brown	..	..	45	40
247	–	4 f. blue	..	..	5	5
248	**36**	5 f. purple-brown	..	..	15	5
249		6 f. blue	..	..	10	5
250		10 f. black	..	..	15	5
251	–	15 f. yellow-brown	..	..	35	5
252	–	20 f. claret	..	..	20	5
253	–	25 f. black	..	..	30	5

(b) AIR. Inscr "POSTE AERIENNE"
254	–	50 f. red-brown	..	..	55	15
255	**37**	100 f. grey-green	..	..	1·00	20
256	–	200 f. blue	..	..	1·90	35
235/256		*Set of 22*	..	..	5·00	2·00

Designs: *As T* **35**—1 f., 1 f. 20, 1 f. 50, River view; 2 f. to 4 f. Tropical forest. *As T* **36**—15, 20, 25 f. Bakongo girl. *As T* **37**—50 f. Savoia "S 82" aircraft over village; 200 f. Aeroplane over column of porters.

D 38

39 People of Five Races,
Globe and Aeroplane

(Recess Institut de Gravure, Paris)

1947 (10 Feb). *POSTAGE DUE. P* 13.
D257	**D 38**	10 c. scarlet	..	..	5	5
D258		30 c. orange	..	..	5	5
D259		50 c. black	..	..	5	5
D260		1 f. scarlet	..	..	5	5
D261		2 f. emerald-green	..	..	5	5
D262		3 f. magenta	..	..	8	8
D263		4 f. ultramarine	..	..	8	8
D264		5 f. red-brown	..	..	15	15
D265		10 f. greenish blue	..	..	20	20
D266		20 f. sepia	..	..	30	30
D257/266		*Set of 10*	..	..	95	95

(Des and eng R. Serres. Recess)

1949 (4 July). *AIR. 75th Anniv of Universal Postal Union. P* 13.
267	**39**	25 f. blue-green	..	..	2·25	2·25

40 Doctor and
Patient

(Des and eng R. Serres. Photo)

1950 (15 May). *Colonial Welfare Fund. P* 13.
268	**40**	10 f.+2 f. purple and blue-green	..	1·10	1·10

PUZZLED ?

Then you need
PHILATELIC TERMS ILLUSTRATED
to tell you all you need to know about printing methods, papers, errors, varieties, watermarks, perforations, etc. 192 pages, almost half in full colour, soft cover. £1·95 post paid.

41 De Brazza   **42** De Brazza and Landscape

(Des and eng C. Hertenberger (10 f.), R. Serres (15 f.). Recess)

1951 (5 Nov). *Birth Centenary of Count Savorgnan de Brazza (explorer)*. *P* 13. (*a*) *POSTAGE*.
269 **41** 10 f. blue-green and indigo 20 5

(*b*) *AIR*
270 **42** 15 f. scarlet, indigo and chocolate .. 30 5

43 Monseigneur Augouard   **44**

(Des and eng R. Serres. Recess)

1952 (1 Dec). *AIR*. *Birth Centenary of Mgr. Augouard (first Bishop of the Congo)*. *P* 13.
271 **43** 15 f. black-brown, brown-purple & olive   80   50

(Des R. Serres. Recess and typo)

1952 (1 Dec). *Centenary of Médaille Militaire*. *P* 13
272 **44** 15 f. multicoloured .. .. .. 1·25 95

45 Native Craft

(Des and eng R. Serres (50 f.), P. Gandon (100 f., 500 f.), A. Decaris (200 f.). Recess)

1953 (16 Feb)–**55**. *AIR*. *T* **45** *and similar horiz designs*. *P* 13.
273   50 f. yell-brn, slate-grn & ind (24.1.55)   45   8
274   100 f. slate-grn, turq & brn-blk (24.1.55)   1·25   12
275   200 f. deep orange-red and lake (24.1.55)   1·90   30
276   500 f. deep blue, black & deep blue-green   9·50   1·10
Designs:—50 f. Logs in river; 200 f. Native driver and docks; 500 f. Anhingas (snake-birds).

ALBUM LISTS

Write for our latest lists of albums and accessories.
These will be sent free on request.

46 Normandy Landings, 1944

(Des and eng R. Serres. Recess)

1954 (6 June). *AIR*. *10th Anniv of Liberation*. *P* 13.
277 **46** 15 f. purple-brown and violet .. 75   75

47 Lieut.-Governor Cureau

(Des and eng R. Cami. Recess)

1954 (20 Sept). *P* 13.
278 **47** 15 f. red-brown and bronze-green .. 40   12

48 Félix Eboué

(Des and eng R. Serres. Recess)

1955 (2 May). *AIR*. *Governor-General Eboué Commemoration*. *P* 13.
279 **48** 15 f. blackish brn, red-brn & vio-grey   75   45

49 Lizard   **50** Boali Waterfall and Power Station

(Des and eng G. Bétemps. Recess)

1955 (2 May). *Nature Protection*. *P* 13.
280 **49** 8 f. deep green and maroon 35   12

(Des and eng A. Decaris. Recess)

1956 (25 Apr). *Economic and Social Development Fund*. *T* **50** *and similar horiz designs inscr* "F.I.D.E.S." *P* 13.
281   5 f. brown-purple and blackish brown ..   5   5
282   10 f. deep bluish green and black .. 10   5
283   15 f. deep grey-blue and indigo .. 12   5
284   20 f. brown-orange and brown-red .. 15   5
281/284   Set of 4 40   15
Designs:—10 f. Cotton production, Chad; 15 f. Brazzaville Hospital, Middle Congo; 20 f. Libreville Harbour, Gabon.

51 Coffee

(Des and eng R. Serres. Recess)

1956 (22 Oct). *P* 13.
285 **51** 10 f. blue-violet and deep lilac   20   5

52 Riverside Hospital   53 Gen. Faidherbe and African Trooper

(Des and eng R. Serres. Recess)

1957 (11 Mar). *Order of Malta Leprosy Relief. P* 13.
286 **52** 15 f. blue-green, green and scarlet   40   12

(Des and eng R. Serres. Recess)

1957 (22 July). *AIR. Centenary of African Troops. P* 13.
287 **53** 15 f. purple-brown and chestnut   45   40

54 Lion and Lioness

55 Regional Bureau,
Brazzaville

(Des H. Cheffer. Eng J. Pheulpin (3 f.). Des and eng R. Cottet (1 f.), P. Gandon (2 f.), A. Decaris (4 f.). Recess)

1957 (4 Nov). *T* **54** *and similar designs. P* 13.
288   1 f. chocolate and blue-green   5   5
289   2 f. yellow-olive and deep blue-green   5   5
290   3 f. black, blue and deep blue-green   5   5
291   4 f. brown-purple and violet-grey   5   5
288/291   Set of 4   15   12
Designs: *Horiz*—1 f. Eland. *Vert*—3 f. Elephant; 4 f. Great Kudu.

(Des and eng A. Decaris. Recess)

1958 (19 May). *10th Anniv of World Health Organization. P* 13.
292 **55** 20 f. chestnut and slate-green   20   20

56 *Eudania*   57 "Human Rights"

(Des M. Rolland. Photo Vaugirard, Paris)

1958 (7 July). *Flowers. T* **56** *and similar vert design. P* 12½.
293   10 f. yellow, green and deep violet   12   8
294   25 f. vermilion, yellow and green   25   10
Design:—25 f. *Spathodea.*

(Des and eng R. Cami. Recess)

1958 (10 Dec). *10th Anniv of Declaration of Human Rights. P* 13.
295 **57** 20 f. turquoise-blue and blue   40   30

The four constituent colonies of French Equatorial Africa became autonomous republics in 1958. Gabon, Congo Republic, Central African Republic and Chad were declared independent states of the French Community in 1960.

stamp monthly

Gibbons' own monthly magazine, essential reading for **every** collector !
Detailed monthly New Issue Guide to update all Gibbons catalogues for you—and a special Stamp Market feature on price changes.
Informative articles cover all facets of philately, with regular notes on new discoveries, stamp designs, postmarks, market trends and news and views of the world of stamps. Britain's LARGEST circulation of any stamp magazine— that fact speaks for itself !
Monthly from all dealers and newsagents or by post direct from Stanley Gibbons Magazines Ltd—subscription rates on application.

French Guiana

100 Centimes = 1 Franc

PRINTERS. All issues were printed at the French Government Printing Works, Paris, *unless otherwise stated.*

IMPERFORATE STAMPS. Many stamps exist imperforate in their issued colours, but these were not valid for postage. Imperforate stamps in other colours are colour trials.

A. FRENCH COLONY

French traders settled at Cayenne around 1635 and in 1674 the area passed to the French crown. A mismanaged attempt at colonization in 1763–65 resulted in the death of over 11,000 of the settlers. During the French Revolution it was a place of exile for royalist supporters who escaped the Terror. From 1809 to 1817 the colony was under British and Portuguese rule. The boundaries with Surinam and Brazil were settled by arbitration in 1891 and 1900.

Déc. 1886.	Avril 1887.	DÉC. 1887.
GUY. FRANÇ.	GUY. FRANÇ.	GUY. FRANÇ.
0ᶠ05	**0ᶠ25**	**5ᶜ**
(1)	(2)	(3)

Three types of surcharge:

I. As T **1**. Height of surcharge 10½ mm.
II. As T **1**. Height of surcharge 12 mm.
III. As T **1**, but with "f" omitted. Height of surcharge 12½ mm.

1886 (Dec). *Nos. 25 and 46 of French Colonies (General Issues), surch with T* **1**. *No gum.*

1 H	0 f. 05 on 2 c. green (I)		£100	£100
	a. Surch double			
2	0 f. 05 on 2 c. green (II)		90·00	90·00
3	0 f. 05 on 2 c. green (III)		£125	£125
4 J	0 f. 05 on 2 c. brown/*buff* (II)		£110	£110
5	0 f. 05 on 2 c. brown/*buff* (III)		75·00	75·00

Varieties are known in which the accent over "e" of "Déc." and the stops after "Déc." "GUY." or "FRANC." have failed to print.

1887 (23 Apr). *Nos. 25, 33a and 22 of French Colonies (General Issues), surch with T* **2**. *No gum.*

6 H	0 f. 05 on 2 c. green		20·00	18·00
	a. "f" in surch omitted		25·00	25·00
7	0 f. 20 on 35 c. black/*orange*		55·00	55·00
	a. "f" in surch omitted		75·00	75·00
	b. "Av" of "Avril" inverted		9·00	9·00
	ba. "Av" inverted, surch double			
8 G	0 f. 25 on 30 c. drab		6·50	6·00
	a. "f" in surch omitted		8·00	8·00
	b. Surch double			

Nos. 6a, 7a and 8a are compositor's errors and not a surcharge type. No. 7b is a similar error which occurred during surcharging. Nos. 7 and 7b are known *se-tenant* in vertical pairs, and are rare thus.

1887 (21 Dec). *Nos. 22 and 32 of French Colonies (General Issues) surch with T* **3**.

9 G	5 c. on 30 c. drab		25·00	22·00
	a. Surch inverted		£175	£175
10 H	5 c. on 30 c. cinnamon		£350	£325
	a. Surch inverted			

Février 1888 — GUY. FRANÇ **5**	Fevrier 1888 — GUY. FRANÇ **10**	*GUYANE*
(4)	(5)	(6)

1888 (Feb). *Nos. 32 and 35/a of French Colonies (General Issues), surch with T* **4** *or* **5**.

11 G	5 on 30 c. drab		25·00	25·00
	a. Surch inverted		80·00	80·00
	b. Surch double			
12 H	10 on 75 c. rosine		42·00	40·00
13	10 on 75 c. carmine		45·00	42·00

1892 (20 Feb). *Stamps of French Colonies (General Issues), optd with T* **6**.

(a) On Ceres type (large figures). Imperf

14 G	30 c. drab		22·00	22·00

(b) On Peace and Commerce type. Imperf

15 H	2 c. green		£175	£160
16	35 c. black/*orange*		£500	£400
17	40 c. red/*yellow*		20·00	18·00
18	75 c. carmine		20·00	18·00
	a. Opt inverted		70·00	65·00
19	1 f. olive-green		30·00	28·00
	a. Opt inverted		85·00	80·00
	b. Opt double		85·00	
	c. Opt triple			

(c) On Commerce type. P 14 × 13½

20 J	1 c. black/*azure*		7·00	5·00
21	2 c. brown/*buff*		5·50	5·00
22	4 c. purple-brown/*grey*		5·50	5·00
23	5 c. green/*pale green*		5·50	
	a. Opt inverted		16·00	
	b. Opt double		16·00	
24	10 c. black/*lilac*		9·50	7·00
25	15 c. blue/*pale blue*		7·00	6·00
26	20 c. red/*green*		7·00	7·00
27	25 c. black/*rose*		12·50	4·50
	a. Opt double		22·00	
	b. Opt triple		28·00	
28	30 c. cinnamon/*drab*		6·00	5·00
29	35 c. black/*orange*		32·00	32·00
30	40 c. red/*yellow*		25·00	20·00
31	75 c. rose-carmine/*rose*		22·00	20·00
32	1 f. olive-green/*toned*		40·00	35·00

Most of these overprints were typographed, but some values also exist with a similar handstamp.

These stamps come with or without a stop after "GUYANE".

1892 (Nov). *French Colonies Type* X *("Tablet") inscr* "GUYANE". *Name in red* (1, 5, 15, 25, 75 *c. and* 1 *f.*) *or blue (others). P* 14 × 13½.

38	1 c. black/*azure*		15	12
39	2 c. brown/*buff*		15	12
40	4 c. purple-brown/*grey*		15	10
	a. Name double		30·00	30·00
41	5 c. green/*pale green*		1·50	1·00
42	10 c. black/*lilac*		1·25	50
43	15 c. blue		4·00	25
44	20 c. red/*green*		2·75	1·75
45	25 c. black/*rose*		2·00	35
46	30 c. cinnamon/*drab*		2·50	1·60
47	40 c. red/*yellow*		2·50	1·60
48	50 c. carmine/*rose*		3·50	1·90
49	75 c. brown/*yellow*		5·00	2·75
50	1 f. olive-green/*toned*		2·50	1·60
38/50	Set of 13		25·00	12·00

DÉC. 92.

0'05

(7)

8 Ant-eater

9
Gold-washer

10 Plantation of Coconut
palms, Cayenne

1892 (5 Dec). *No. 25 surch with T* **7**.
51	J	0.05 on 15 c. blue/*pale blue*	4·00	4·00
		a. Surch double	30·00	30·00

1900 (Dec)–**04**. *Type X. Colours changed. Name in blue*
(10 c.) or red (others). P 14×13½.
52	5 c. bright yellow-green (1904)		12	5
53	10 c. rose-red		80	25
54	15 c. grey		21·00	18·00
55	25 c. blue		2·75	3·25
56	50 c. brown/*azure*		3·75	3·00
57	2 f. violet/*rose*(10.02)		45·00	1·10
52/57	*Set of* 6		65·00	23·00

(Des Paul Merwart. Eng J. Puyplat)

1904 (Dec)–**07**. *P* 13½×14 (*T* **8**) *or* 14×13½.
58	**8**	1 c. black		5	5
59		2 c. pale blue		5	5
60		4 c. chocolate		5	5
61		5 c. green		12	8
62		10 c. rose-red		5	5
63		15 c. violet		20	15
64	**9**	20 c. chocolate		5	5
65		25 c. deep blue		20	10
66		30 c. black		15	10
66a		35 c. black/*yellow* (1906)		5	5
67		40 c. rose-red		5	5
68		45 c. grey-brown (1907)		10	5
69		50 c. bright lilac		50	40
70		75 c. green		10	10
71	**10**	1 f. rose-red		5	5
72		2 f. deep blue		10	5
73		5 f. black		95	80
58/73		*Set of* 17		2·50	2·00

05
(11)

10
(12)

1912 (Nov). *Surch as T* **11/12**.
A. Narrow spacing. B. Wide spacing
			A		B	
74	X	05 on 2 c. brown/*buff*		8	8	2·50	2·50
75		05 on 4 c. purple-brown/*grey* (R.)		5	5	1·25	1·25
76		05 on 20 c. red/*green*		10	10	1·60	1·60
77		05 on 25 c. black/*rose* (R.)		40	40	5·50	5·50
78		05 on 30 c. cinnamon/*drab* (R.)		20	20	2·50	2·50
79		10 on 40 c. red/*yellow*		10	10	32·00	32·00
80		10 on 50 c. carmine		35	35	65·00	65·00
		a. Surch double		70·00		—	—
74/80		*Set of* 7		1·10	1·10	£100	£100

In Type A the space between "0" and "5" is 1½ mm and
between "1" and "0" 2½ mm. In Type B the spacing is 2 mm
and 3 mm respectively.

+ 5
(13)

+ 5ᶜ
(14)

0,01 =
(15)

1915 (Mar). *Red Cross. No.* 62 *surch with T* **13**, *in red*.
81	**8**	10 c.+5 c. rose-red		2·75	1·90
		a. Surch inverted		22·00	16·00
		b. Surch double		16·00	14·00

1915. *Red Cross. No.* 62 *surch in Paris with T* **14**, *in red*.
82	**8**	10 c.+5 c. rose-red		8	8

1922 (1 Jan). *As* 1904–7. *New colours*.
83	**8**	5 c. orange		5	5
84		10 c. green		5	5
85	**9**	25 c. violet		10	8
86		30 c. carmine		5	5
87		40 c. black		10	8
88		50 c. blue		5	5
83/88		*Set of* 6		35	30

1922 (Dec). *No.* 63 *surch as T* **15**.
89	**8**	0,01 on 15 c. violet		5	5
		a. Surch double		5	
90		0,02 on 15 c. violet (B.)		5	5
		a. Surch inverted		11·00	
91		0,04 on 15 c. violet (G.)		5	5
		a. Surch double		13·00	
92		0,05 on 15 c. violet (R.)		5	5
89/92		*Set of* 4		15	15

DIX
FRANCS
DIX
FRANCS
(16)

1923 (20 Dec). *Surch as T* **16**, *in blue*.
93	**10**	10 f. on 1 f. green/*yellow*		2·50	2·50
94		20 f. on 5 f. mauve/*rose*		2·50	2·50

= 25ᶜ
(17)

= 90
(18)

1924 (June)–**27**. *Stamps as T* **8/10**, *some with colours changed, surch as T* **17/18**.
95	**8**	25 c. on 15 c. violet (1.2.25)		5	5
		a. Surch triple		13·00	
96	**10**	25 c. on 2 f. deep blue		5	5
		a. Surch double		15·00	
		b. Surch triple		18·00	
97	**9**	65 on 45 c. grey-brown (R.) (1.2.25)		12	12
98		85 on 45 c. grey-brown (R.) (1.2.25)		12	12
99		90 on 75 c. red (11.4.27)		12	12
100	**10**	1 f. 05 on 2 f. bistre-brown (19.12.27)		15	15
101		1 f. 25 on 1 f. blue/*azure* (R.) (14.6.26)		12	12
102		1 f. 50 on 1 f. light blue (11.4.27)		20	20
103		3 f. on 5 f. bright violet (19.12.27)		20	20
95/103		*Set of* 9		1·00	1·00

1924 (31 July)–**28**. *As* 1904–7. *New colours and values.*
P 13½×14 (10 c.) *or* 14×13½ (*others*).
104	**8**	10 c. vermilion/*azure* (16.11.25)		5	5
105	**9**	30 c. orange (16.11.25)		5	5
106		30 c. blue-green/*greenish* (25.9.28)		10	10
107		50 c. grey (16.11.25)		5	5
108		60 c. violet/*rose* (16.11.25)		5	5
109		65 c. blue-green (1.3.26)		8	5
110		85 c. purple (1.3.26)		5	5
111	**10**	1 f. blue/*azure* (16.11.25)		5	5
112		1 f. blue/*yellow-green* (25.9.28)		40	40
113		1 f. 10, rose (25.9.28)		15	15

114	**10**	2 f. red/*yellow* (1.3.26)			20	20
115		10 f. green/*yellow*			2·50	2·40
116		20 f. carmine			3·00	2·75
104/116		*Set of 13*			6·00	5·75

GUYANE
FRANÇAISE
15
centimes
à percevoir

(D 19)　　　　　　**20** Carib Archer

21 Shooting the Rapids,　　**22** Government Building,
R. Maroni　　　　　　　　　　　Cayenne

1925 (Apr)–**27**. *POSTAGE DUE. Postage Due stamps of France, Type* D **11**, *optd* "GUYANE FRANÇAISE", *or surch in addition, as Type* D **10**. *P* 14×13½.

D117		5 c. pale blue			5	5
D118		10 c. pale brown			5	5
D119		15 c. on 20 c. olive-green			5	5
	a.	Blue surch			9·00	
D120		20 c. olive-green			5	5
D121		25 c. on 5 c. pale blue			8	5
D122		30 c. on 20 c. olive-green			12	5
D123		45 c. on 10 c. pale brown			8	5
D124		50 c. dull claret			12	10
D125		60 c. on 5 c. pale blue			12	12
D126		1 f. on 20 c. olive-green			25	20
D127		2 f. on 50 c. dull claret			25	25
D128		3 f. magenta (10.10.27)			1·60	1·40
D117/128		*Set of 12*			2·50	2·25

(Des R. Tillet. Dies eng A. Delzers (**20**), C. Hourriez (**21**), A. Mignon (**22**). Typo)

1929 (4 Feb)–**40**. *P* 13½×14 (*T* **20**) *or* 14×13½ (*others*).

117	**20**	1 c. greenish blue and lilac			5	5
118		2 c. blue-green and carmine			5	5
119		3 c. green and violet (1939)			5	5
120		4 c. magenta and sepia			5	5
121		5 c. vermilion and greenish blue			5	5
122		10 c. sepia and magenta			5	5
123		15 c. vermilion and brown			5	5
124		20 c. sage-green and blue			5	5
125		25 c. chocolate and carmine			5	5
126	**21**	30 c. yellow-green and green			8	8
127		30 c. chocolate & yellow-green (1939)		5	5
128		35 c. sage-green & greenish bl (1938)		10	10
129		40 c. drab and red-brown			5	5
130		45 c. chocolate and yellow-green			12	12
131		45 c. yellow-green & olive-grn (1939)		5	5
132		50 c. drab and blue			5	5
133		55 c. carmine and ultramarine (1938)		10	10
134		60 c. green and vermilion (1939)			5	5
135		65 c. green and vermilion			10	10
136		70 c. blue-green and blue (1938)			8	8
137		75 c. greenish blue and blue			20	20
138		80 c. ultramarine and black (1938)			8	8
139		90 c. vermilion and carmine			8	8
140		90 c. chocolate and mauve (1939)			8	8
141		1 f. chocolate and mauve			12	12
142		1 f. rose-red and carmine (1938)			40	15
143		1 f. ultramarine and black (1939)			5	5
144	**22**	1 f. 05, sage-green and vermilion			90	70
145		1 f. 10, magenta and sepia			90	70
146		1 f. 25, green and chocolate (25.9.33)		10	10

147	**22**	1 f. 25, rose-red and carmine (1939)		8	8
148		1 f. 40, magenta & chocolate (1939)		8	5
149		1 f. 50, light blue and blue			5	5
150		1 f. 60, green and chocolate (1939)		8	5
151		1 f. 75, chocolate & carmine (25.9.33)		30	25
152		1 f. 75, ultramarine and blue (1938)		8	8
153		2 f. carmine and green			5	5
154		2 f. 25, ultramarine and blue (1939)		8	5
155		2 f. 50, chocolate and scarlet (1939)		5	5
156		3 f. mauve and red-brown			5	5
157		5 f. yellow-green and violet			8	5
158		10 f. blue and sepia			12	8
159		20 f. vermilion and blue			15	15
117/159		*Set of 43*			5·00	4·00

The 15 c., 1 f. and 1 f. 50 without "RF" cypher were prepared in 1944 by the Vichy authorities, but were not issued in the colony.

D 23 Palm Trees　　　　**D 24** Creole Girl

(Dies eng A. Mignon. Typo)

1929 (14 Oct). *POSTAGE DUE. P* 13½×14.

D160	D **23**	5 c. greenish blue and blue		5	5
D161		10 c. greenish blue and brown		5	5
D162		20 c. carmine and green			5	5
D163		30 c. carmine and sepia			5	5
D164		50 c. sepia and carmine			5	5
D165		60 c. sepia and carmine			12	12
D166	D **24**	1 f. brown-red and blue			20	20
D167		2 f. green and carmine			30	30
D168		3 f. slate and mauve			50	50
D160/168		*Set of 9*			1·25	1·25

1931 (13 Apr). *International Colonial Exhibition, Paris. As T* **17/20** *of French Sudan.*

160	40 c. black and green			80	80
161	50 c. black and mauve			80	80
162	90 c. black and vermilion			80	80
163	1 f. 50, black and blue			80	80
160/163	*Set of 4*			3·00	3·00

25 Cayenne

(Des Herviault. Eng Le Guernigou. Photo Vaugirard)

1933 (20 Nov). *AIR. P* 13½.

164	**25**	50 c. red-brown			5	5
165		1 f. green			5	5
166		1 f. 50, blue			5	5
167		2 f. orange			5	5
168		3 f. black			5	5
169		5 f. violet			5	5
170		10 f. olive			5	5
171		20 f. scarlet			10	10
164/171		*Set of 8*			40	40

The 50 c. without "RF" cypher was prepared by the Vichy authorities in 1942, but not issued in the Colony.

26 Cayenne recaptured by   27 Local Products
   D'Estrées, 1676

(Des A. Decaris and A. Delzers. Recess)

1935 (21 Oct). *West Indies Tercentenary. P* 13.
172	**26**	40 c. sepia			95	65
173		50 c. scarlet			1·90	1·10
174		1 f. 50, ultramarine			95	75
175	**27**	1 f. 75, carmine			2·50	2·25
176		5 f. brown			2·25	1·90
177		10 f. emerald-green			2·25	1·90
172/177		*Set of* 6			10·00	7·00

1937 (15 Apr). *International Exhibition, Paris. As T* **2**/**7** *of French Equatorial Africa.*
178	20 c. bright violet				15	15
179	30 c. green				15	15
180	40 c. carmine				15	15
181	50 c. brown				15	15
182	90 c. scarlet				15	15
183	1 f. 50, blue				15	15
178/183	*Set of* 6				80	80
MS183*a*	120×100 mm. 3 f. violet (as *T* **3**).					
	Imperf				95	95
	b. Error. Country inscription inverted	£400				

1938 (24 Oct). *International Anti-Cancer Fund. As T* **14** *of French Equatorial Africa.*
184	1 f. 75+50 c. ultramarine			1·90	1·90

1939 (10 May). *New York World's Fair. As T* **17** *of French Equatorial Africa.*
185	1 f. 25, lake				20	20
186	2 f. 25, ultramarine				20	20

1939 (5 July). *150th Anniv of French Revolution. As T* **18** *of French Equatorial Africa.* (*a*) POSTAGE.
187	45 c.+25 c. green and black			1·90	1·90
188	70 c.+30 c. brown and black			1·90	1·90
189	90 c.+35 c. red-orange and black			1·90	1·90
190	1 f. 25+1 f. carmine and black			1·90	1·90
191	2 f. 25+2 f. blue and black			1·90	1·90

(*b*) AIR
192	5 f.+4 f. black and orange			3·25	3·25
187/192	*Set of* 6			8·00	8·00

VICHY GOVERNMENT

Nos. 192*a*/*b* were issued by the Pétain régime in Unoccupied France. A number of other issues exist, but we list only those items which were available in French Guiana.

28 View of Cayenne and
   Marshal Pétain

(Des J. Piel. Eng A. Degorce. Recess Institut de Gravure, Paris)

1941. *P* 12½×12.
192*a*	**28**	1 f. purple				8	8
192*b*		2 f. 50, blue				8	8

FREE FRENCH ADMINISTRATION

1944. *Mutual Aid and Red Cross Funds. As T* **29** *of French Equatorial Africa.*
193	5 f.+20 f. maroon				10	10

1945. *Félix Eboué. As T* **31** *of French Equatorial Africa.*
194	2 f. black				5	5
195	25 f. blue-green				12	10

28*a* Arms of French Guiana

(Litho De La Rue)

1945. *P* 12.
196	**28***a*	10 c. indigo			5	5
197		30 c. orange-brown			5	5
198		40 c. greenish blue			5	5
199		50 c. claret			5	5
200		60 c. orange-yellow			5	5
201		70 c. grey-brown			5	5
202		80 c. green			5	5
203		1 f. light blue			5	5
204		1 f. 20, lilac			5	5
205		1 f. 50, orange			10	10
206		2 f. black			8	8
207		2 f. 40, red			8	8
208		3 f. pink			10	10
209		4 f. ultramarine			12	12
210		4 f. 50, yellow-green			12	12
211		5 f. yellow-brown			15	15
212		10 f. violet			15	15
213		15 f. carmine			12	12
214		20 f. olive-green			15	15

1945. *AIR. As T* **24** *of French Equatorial Africa.*
215	50 f. green				20	20
216	100 f. claret				40	40
196/216	*Set of* 21				2·00	2·00

B. FRENCH OVERSEAS DEPARTMENT

On 19 March 1946 French Guiana became an Overseas Department of the French Republic.

1946 (8 May). *AIR. Victory. As T* **32** *of French Equatorial Africa.*
217	8 f. black				25	25

1946 (6 June). *AIR. From Chad to the Rhine. As Nos.* 229/34 *of French Equatorial Africa.*
218	5 f. blue				12	12
219	10 f. carmine				12	12
220	15 f. brown-purple				20	20
221	20 f. blackish green				20	20
222	25 f. purple				20	20
223	50 f. mauve				25	25
218/223	*Set of* 6				1·00	1·00

29 Hammock   32 Cayenne Girl

30 Riverside Village **31** Pirogue Canoe

33 Toco Toucans **34** Parakeet and Macaws

35 Steller's Sea Eagles **D 36**

(Des M. Soubrier (10 c. to 1 f. 50). Eng C. Dufresne (10 c. to 50 c.), E. Feltesse (60 c. to 1 f. 50). Des and eng C. Mazelin (2 f. to 6 f.), P. Gandon (10 f. to 100 f.). Des P. Gandon. Eng C. Barlangue (200 f.). Recess)

1947 (2 June). *P* 13. (*a*) POSTAGE.

224	29	10 c. blue-green	..	..	5	5
225		30 c. red	..	..	5	5
226		50 c. brown-purple	..	..	5	5
227	30	60 c. bluish slate	..	..	5	5
228		1 f. brown-lake	..	..	5	5
229		1 f. 50, sepia	..	..	5	5
230	31	2 f. green	..	..	8	5
231		2 f. 50, blue	..	..	8	5
232		3 f. brown-lake	..	..	10	8
233	32	4 f. chocolate	..	..	20	15
234		5 f. blue	..	..	20	15
235		6 f. brown-lake	..	..	20	15
236	33	10 f. blue	..	..	75	65
237		15 f. sepia	..	..	80	65
238		20 f. brown-lake	..	..	1·10	95
239	34	25 f. bright green	..	..	1·40	1·25
240		40 f. sepia	..	..	1·40	1·25

(*b*) AIR. *T* 35 *and similar designs*

241	50 f. dull green	..	..	2·75	2·75
242	100 f. brown-lake	..	..	3·25	3·25
243	200 f. indigo	..	..	5·00	5·00
224/243	*Set of* 20	..	..	16·00	15·00

Designs: *Vert*—100 f. Aeroplane over Peccary and palms. *Horiz*—200 f. Aeroplane and Toucans.

(Des M. Soubrier, eng R. Cortot. Recess)

1947 (2 June). POSTAGE DUE. *P* 14×13.

D244	D 36	10 c. carmine	..	..	5	5
D245		30 c. olive-green	..	..	5	5
D246		50 c. black	..	..	5	5
D247		1 f. ultramarine	..	..	5	5
D248		2 f. brown-lake	..	..	5	5
D249		3 f. bright violet	..	..	5	5
D250		4 f. rose-red	..	..	12	12
D251		5 f. purple	..	..	12	12
D252		10 f. emerald	..	..	30	30
D253		20 f. bright purple	..	..	30	30
D244/253	*Set of* 10	..	..	1·00	1·00

Stamps of France are now used in French Guiana.

ISSUES OF COMPAGNIE DES TRANSPORTS AERIENS GUYANAIS

The following stamps were issued by the Company during part of 1921 to prepay,the 75 c. airmail fee for letters carried on their internal flights, under contract with the postal authorities.

St. Laurent du Maroni—Cayenne Route

1 **2**

1921 (July). *AIR. St. Laurent du Maroni issue. Typo from woodblock. Roul or imperf.*

1	**1**	75 c. violet/*cream* (9.7)	..	..	£450	£450
2		75 c. red/*bluish* (8.7)	..	..	£275	£250

These stamps are usually found showing part of the red oval control mark. They were cancelled by a m/s signature in red, and "AVION" handstamp in black.

(Typo Imp Chiris, Cayenne)

1921 (8 July). *AIR. Cayenne issue. Black impression. Imperf.*

3	**2**	75 c. on *salmon*	..	..	£200	£130
4		75 c. on *bluish*	..	..	£200	£140
5		75 c. on *grey*	..	..	£225	£140

St. Laurent du Maroni—Cayenne—Inini Route

3 **4**

(Des Tillet. Typo Imp Chiris, Cayenne)

1921 (Sept). *AIR. Black impression. Imperf.*

6	**3**	75 c. on *salmon*	..	..	£1500	£1500
7		75 c. on *bluish*	..	..	£250	£140
		a. Tête-bêche (pair)	..			
8		75 c. on *grey*	..	..	£200	£150
		a. Tête-bêche (pair)	..			

General Issue

(Typo Imp Chiris, Cayenne)

1921 (Sept). *AIR. Black impression. Imperf.*

9	**4**	75 c. on *salmon*	..	..	£200	£150
10		75 c. on *rose*	..	..	£275	£190
11		75 c. on *yellow*	..	..	£325	£250
12		75 c. on *grey*	..	..	£550	£500

The normal cancellation used on Nos. 3/12 was a large "AVION" handstamp.

These issues did not continue in use after October, 1921. After this date the airmail fee was prepaid by additional postage stamps.

ININI

The territory of Inini, situated in the interior of French Guiana, was connected to the coast by waterways only navigable by local craft. The administration of the area was separated from the colony on 6 July 1930.

100 Centimes = 1 Franc

TERRITOIRE
DE L'ININI   Territoire de l'ININI

(1)   (2)

1932 (7 April)–40. *T 20/2 of French Guiana optd. P 13½ × 14 (1 c. to 25 c.) or 14 × 13½ (others)*.

1	**1**	1 c. greenish blue and lilac	..	5	5
2		2 c. blue-green and carmine	..	5	5
3		3 c. green and violet (1940)	..	5	5
4		4 c. magenta and sepia (5.12.38)	..	5	5
5		5 c. vermilion and greenish blue..	..	5	5
6		10 c. sepia and claret	..	5	5
7		15 c. vermilion and brown	..	5	5
8		20 c. sage-green and blue	..	5	5
9		25 c. chocolate and carmine	..	8	8
10	**2**	30 c. yellow-green and green	..	10	10
11		30 c. chocolate and yellow-green (1940)		5	5
12		35 c. sage-green & greenish blue (6.7.38)		5	5
13		40 c. drab and red-brown	..	5	5
14		45 c. yellow-green & olive-green (1940)	..	8	8
15		50 c. drab and blue	..	5	5
16		55 c. carmine and ultramarine (6.7.38)		30	30
17		60 c. green and vermilion (1940) ..	..	5	5
18		65 c. green and vermilion (6.7.38)	..	10	10
19		70 c. blue-green and blue (1940)	..	10	10
20		75 c. greenish blue and black (B.)	..	35	35
21		80 c. ultramarine and black (R.) (6.7.38)	..	8	8
22		90 c. vermilion and carmine	..	8	8
23		90 c. chocolate and mauve (1939)	..	10	10
24		1 f. chocolate and mauve	..	2·50	2·25
25		1 f. rose-red and carmine (5. 12. 38)	..	8	8
26		1 f. ultramarine and black (1940)	..	5	5
27		1 f. 25, green and chocolate (25.9.33)	..	5	5
28		1 f. 25, rose-red and carmine (1939)	..	10	10
29		1 f. 40, magenta and chocolate (1940) ..		10	10
30		1 f. 50, light blue and blue	..	8	8
31		1 f. 60, green and chocolate (1940)	..	12	12
32		1 f. 75, chocolate and carmine (25.9.33)		3·50	2·50
33		1 f. 75, ultramarine and blue (5.12.38)	..	12	12
34		2 f. carmine and green	..	5	5
35		2 f. 25, ultramarine and blue (1939)	..	10	10
36	**2**	2 f. 50, chocolate and scarlet (1940)	..	12	12
37		3 f. mauve and red-brown	..	5	5
38		5 f. yellow-green and violet	..	8	8
39		10 f. blue and sepia (R.)	..	8	8
40		20 f. vermilion and blue	..	10	10
1/40		*Set of 40*	..	8·50	7·25

The overprint on T 22 (1 f. 25 to 20 f.) of French Guiana is as T 2, but closer set.

TERRITOIRE
DE L'ININI

(D 3)

1932 (7 Apr). *POSTAGE DUE. Types D 23/4 of French Guiana optd as Type D 3 (1 f. to 3 f.) or similar opt. P 13½ × 14.*

D41	5 c. greenish blue and blue	..	5	5
D42	10 c. greenish blue and brown ..		5	5
D43	20 c. carmine and green	..	5	5
D44	30 c. carmine and sepia	..	5	5
D45	50 c. sepia and mauve ..	..	10	10
D46	60 c. sepia and carmine	..	10	10
D47	1 f. brown and blue ..	..	12	12
D48	2 f. green and carmine	..	20	20
D49	3 f. slate and mauve ..	..	20	20
	a. Red opt ..	..	90	90
D41/49	*Set of 9* ..	..	85	85

1937 (15 Apr). *International Exhibition, Paris. Sheet 120 × 100 mm. As T 3 of French Equatorial Africa.*

MS50	3 f. brown-red ..	..	1·90	1 90
	a. Error. Inscription inverted ..		£450	

1939 (10 May). *New York World's Fair. As T 17 of French Equatorial Africa.*

51	1 f. 25, lake	..	75	75
52	2 f. 25, ultramarine	..	75	75

1939 (5 July). *150th Anniv of French Revolution. As T 18 of French Equatorial Africa.*

53	45 c. +25 c. green and black	..	2·25	2·25
54	70 c. +30 c. brown and black	..	2·25	2·25
55	90 c. +35 c. red-orange and black	..	2·25	2·25
56	1 f. 25 +1 f. carmine and black	..	2·25	2·25
57	2 f. 25 +2 f. blue and black	..	2·25	2·25
53/57	*Set of 5* ..	..	10·00	10·00

During 1941/44 a number of stamps were produced for Inini by the Vichy Government, but none of these were issued in the Territory.

The Territory of Inini was re-united to French Guiana on 19 March 1946.

stamp monthly

Gibbons' own monthly magazine, essential reading for **every** collector!
Detailed monthly New Issue Guide to update all Gibbons catalogues for you—and a special Stamp Market feature on price changes.
Informative articles cover all facets of philately, with regular notes on new discoveries, stamp designs, postmarks, market trends and news and views of the world of stamps.
Britain's LARGEST circulation of any stamp magazine— that fact speaks for itself!
Monthly from all dealers and newsagents or by post direct from Stanley Gibbons Magazines Ltd—subscription rates on application.

French Guinea

100 Centimes =1 Franc

Between 1848 and 1865 the French signed treaties with the chiefs of the Guinea coastal tribes, establishing protectorates over their territories. The area of French influence was further increased in 1887 when the Emir of Futa Jallon asked for French protection. The protectorates were administered from Senegal, and their boundaries were finally fixed by conventions with Great Britain (1882 and 1889) and Portugal (1886). French Guinea became a separate colony on 12 December 1891. Its area was extended in 1899 to include part of the Upper Niger basin, formerly part of French Sudan.

PRINTERS. All stamps of French Guinea were printed at the Government Printing Works, Paris, *unless otherwise stated.*

IMPERFORATE STAMPS. Stamps exist imperforate in their issued colours, but these were not valid for postage. Imperforate stamps in other colours are colour trials.

1892 (Nov). *French Colonies Type X inscr "GUINEE FRANCAISE". Names in red (1, 5, 15, 25, 75 c. and 1 f.), or blue (others). P* 14×13½.

1	X	1 c. black/*azure*	..	..	12	12
2		2 c. brown/*buff*	..	..	12	12
3		4 c. purple-brown/*grey*	..	..	25	25
4		5 c. green/*pale green*	..		1·25	1·00
5		10 c. black/*lilac*	..	..	75	50
6		15 c. blue (*quadrillé paper*)	..	1·00	75
7		20 c. red/*green*	..	..	3·00	2·50
8		25 c. black/*rose*	..	..	2·00	1·50
9		30 c. cinnamon/*drab*	..	..	5·50	4·50
10		40 c. red/*yellow*	..	..	5·50	4·00
		a. Name double	..	..	70·00	70·00
11		50 c. carmine/*rose*	..	..	7·50	10·00
12		75 c. brown/*yellow*	..	..	10·00	8·00
13		1 f. olive-green/*toned*	..	..	7·50	6·00
1/13		*Set of 13*	..	..	42·00	35·00

1900 (Dec). *Colours changed. Names in blue (10 c.) or red (others). P* 14×13½.

14	X	10 c. rose-red	..	..	9·00	6·50
15		15 c. grey	..	..	25·00	22·00
16		25 c. blue	..	..	3·75	3·25
17		50 c. brown/*azure*	..	..	5·00	4·50
14/17		*Set of 4*	..	..	38·00	32·00

1 Fulas Shepherd

D **2** Woman of Futa Jallon

1904 (24 Nov). *Typo. P* 14×13½.

18	**1**	1 c. black/*yellow-green*	..	..	12	8
19		2 c. purple-brown/*straw*	..	..	12	10
20		4 c. carmine/*azure*	..	..	25	20
21		5 c. green/*green*	..	..	25	20
22		10 c. rose-red	..	..	50	20
23		15 c. bright lilac/*rose*	..	..	1·25	75
24		20 c. carmine/*green*	..	..	2·50	2·10
25		25 c. blue	..	..	2·50	2·10
26		30 c. pale brown/*toned*	..	..	4·50	3·75
27		40 c. red/*straw*	..	..	5·50	4·50
28		50 c. pale brown/*pale green*	..	5·50	5·00
29		75 c. blue/*yellow*	..	..	6·50	6·50
30		1 f. olive-green/*toned*	..	..	8·00	7·00
31		2 f. red/*orange*	..	..	19·00	17·00
32		5 f. blue/*yellow-green*	..	..	25·00	23·00
18/32		*Set of 15*	..	..	75·00	65·00

1905 (Feb). *POSTAGE DUE. P* 14×13½.

D33	D **2**	5 c. blue	..	..	25	25
D34		10 c. brown	..	..	40	40
D35		15 c. green	..	.:	90	65
D36		30 c. rose	..	..	1·00	50
D37		50 c. black	..	..	1·90	1·40
D38		60 c. orange	..	..	2·50	1·90
D39		1 f. lilac	..	..	8·00	7·50
D33/39		*Set of 7*	..	..	13·00	11·00

1906–7. *As T* **3/5** *of Upper Senegal and Niger (see French Sudan), inscr "GUINÉE". Name in blue (10 c., 5 f.) or red (others). P* 14×13½ *(horiz) or* 13½×14 *(vert).*

33		1 c. slate	..	..	5	5
34		2 c. chocolate	..	..	12	10
35		4 c. chocolate/*blue*	..	..	20	15
36		5 c. green	..	..	65	45
37		10 c. rose	..	..	3·25	40
		a. Inscr double	..	..		
38		20 c. black/*bluish*	..	..	65	45
39		25 c. blue	..	..	1·40	1·10
		a. Imperf (pair)	..	..		
40		30 c. chocolate/*flesh*	..	..	90	70
41		35 c. black/*yellow* (1906)	..	40	25
43		45 c. chocolate/*green*	..	..	65	55
44		50 c. deep violet	..	..	2·00	1·75
45		75 c. green/*orange*	..	..	65	45
46		1 f. black/*azure*	..	..	4·50	3·50
47		2 f. blue/*rose*	..	..	9·00	7·50
48		5 f. red/*straw*	..	..	11·00	11·00
33/48		*Set of 15*	..	..	32·00	26·00

1906 (Nov)**–8.** *POSTAGE DUE. As Type D* **6** *of Upper Senegal and Niger (see French Sudan), inscr "GUINÉE" in blue (10 c., 30 c.), or red (others). P* 13½×14.

D49		5 c. green/*toned* (1907)	..	..	3·75	2·50
D50		10 c. maroon (1907)	..	..	1·25	95
D51		15 c. blue/*bluish* (5.08)	..	..	65	65
D52		20 c. black/*yellow*	..	..	65	65
D53		30 c. red/*cream* (5.08)	..	..	5·50	4·75
D54		50 c. violet (5.08)	..	..	5·00	4·50
D55		60 c. black/*buff* (5.08)	..	..	4·50	3·75
D56		1 f. black/*flesh* (5.08)	..	..	2·50	2·50
D49/56		*Set of 8*	..	..	21·00	18·00

05 10

(2)	(2a)

1912 (Aug). *Surch with T* **2/2a**. *(a) Type X.*

A. Narrow spacing. B. Wide spacing

				A		B	
49		05 on 2 c. brown/*buff*	..	20	20	19·00	19·00
50		05 on 4 c. purple-brown/*grey* (R.)	..	10	10	5·00	5·00
51		05 on 15 c. blue (R.)	..	10	10	7·50	7·50
52		05 on 20 c. red/*green*	..	65	65	48·00	48·00
53		05 on 30 c. cinnamon/*drab* (R.)	75	75	£130	£130
54		10 on 40 c. red/*yellow*	..	25	25	8·00	8·00
55		10 on 75 c. brown/*yellow*	1·10	1·10	40·00	40·00
		a. Surch double inverted	..	32·00	—	£550	—
49/55		*Set of 7*	..	2·75	2·75	£225	£225

(b) T **1**

56		05 on 2 c. purple-brown/*straw*		12	12	5·00	5·00
		a. Pair, one without surch	..	—	—	—	—
57		05 on 4 c. carmine/*azure*	..	12	12	5·00	5·00
58		05 on 15 c. bright lilac/*rose*	..	15	15	5·00	5·00
59		05 on 20 c. carmine/*green*	..	15	15	9·00	9·00
60		05 on 25 c. blue (R.)	..	15	15	17·00	17·00

157

61	05 on 30 c. pale brn/*toned* (R.)	15	15 25·00 25·00
62	10 on 40 c. red/*straw* ..	20	20 8·00 8·00
63	10 on 50 c. pale brown/*pale*		
	green (R.)	50	50 10·00 10·00
56/63	*Set of 8*	1·40	1·40 75·00 75·00

In Type A the space between "0" and "5" is 1½ mm and between "1" and "0" 2½ mm. In Type B the spacing is 2 mm and 3 mm respectively.

🔴5ᶜ

3 Ford at Kitim   (3*a*)

(Des J. de la Nézière. Eng J. Puyplat. Typo)

1913–17. *P* 13½×14.

64	**3**	1 c. blue and violet ..	5	5
65		2 c. chocolate and yellow-brown ..	5	5
		a. Centre double	16·00	
66		4 c. black and grey ..	5	5
67		5 c. blue-green and yellow-green ..	5	5
68		10 c. rose and orange-red ..	5	5
69		15 c. carmine and dull purple (1917) ..	5	5
70		20 c. violet and brown ..	5	5
71		25 c. blue and ultramarine ..	10	10
72		30 c. green and dull purple ..	5	5
73		35 c. rose and blue ..	5	5
74		40 c. grey and green ..	10	5
75		45 c. orange-red and brown ..	15	10
76		50 c. black and ultramarine ..	1·00	55
77		5 c. ultramarine and rose ..	25	15
78		1 f. black and violet ..	15	10
79		2 f. brown and dull orange ..	45	12
80		5 f. violet and black ..	1·90	1·60
64/80	*Set of 17*	4·00	3·00

The 5, 10, 15 and 25 c. values exist on chalk-surfaced paper. Some stamps of this issue can be found overprinted "VALEUR D'EXCHANGE". These were used as currency during 1920, and were not valid for postage.

1914 (Mar). *POSTAGE DUE. As Type* D **9** *of Upper Senegal and Niger (see French Sudan), inscr* "GUINÉE". *P* 14×13½.

D81	5 c. green	5	5
D82	10 c. carmine	5	5
D83	15 c. grey	5	5
D84	20 c. brown	5	5
D85	30 c. blue	5	5
D86	50 c. black	8	8
D87	60 c. orange	35	35
D88	1 f. violet	35	35
D81/88	*Set of 8*	90	90

1915 (May). *Surch with T* **3***a*, *in red. Ordinary or chalk-surfaced paper.*

81	**3**	10 c. +5 c. rose and orange-red ..	20	8

1922 (1 Jan)–**33.** *New values and colours changed.* *P* 13½×14.

83	**3**	5 c. green and purple ..	5	5
84		10 c. green and yellow-green ..	5	5
85		10 c. red and lilac (22.6.25) ..	5	5
86		15 c. yellow-green and green (7.9.25)	5	5
87		15 c. magenta and plum (5.9.27) ..	8	5
88		20 c. green (13.3.26) ..	10	5
89		20 c. sepia and lake (14.11.27) ..	5	5
90		25 c. violet and black ..	10	5
91		30 c. rose and orange-red ..	5	5
92		30 c. green and scarlet (22.6.25) ..	5	5
93		30 c. green and olive-green (25.9.28) ..	30	20
94		50 c. blue and ultramarine ..	8	5
95		50 c. olive and yellow-brown (22.6.25)	5	5
96		60 c. violet/*rose* (7.9.25) ..	5	5
97		65 c. blue and yellow-brown (13.3.26)	20	20
98		75 c. greenish blue and blue (22.6.25)	5	5

99	**3**	75 c. apple-green & magenta (14.11.27)	30	15
100		85 c. claret and olive-green (13.3.26) ..	8	8
101		90 c. magenta and brown-red (5.5.30)	1·10	90
102		1 f. 10, sepia and violet (25.9.28)	1·10	1·10
103		1 f. 25, red-brown and violet (25.9.33)	30	20
104		1 f. 50, light blue and blue (5.5.30) ..	70	45
105		1 f. 75, magenta & chocolate (25.9.33)	30	30
106		3 f. magenta/*rose* (5.5.30) ..	1·25	75
107		5 f. black and blue	40	35
83/107	*Set of 25*	6·00	5·00

The 60 c. is on chalk-surfaced paper.

1922–27. *Stamps as T* **3**, *some with colours changed, surch as T* **11**/**12** *of French Sudan.*

108	25 c. on 2 f. brown & orange (R.) (6.24)	5	5
109	25 c. on 5 f. black and blue (6.24) ..	5	5
110	60 on 75 c. violet/*rose* (28.9.22) ..	5	5
111	65 on 75 c. ultramarine and rose (1.2.25)	15	15
	a. Surch double (65+60) ..	35·00	
112	85 on 75 c. ultramarine and rose (1.2.25)	15	15
113	90 c. on 75 c. mag & brn-red (28.2.27)	30	30
114	1 f. 25 on 1 f. ultramarine & bl (14.6.26)	5	5
115	1 f. 50 on 1 f. light blue & blue (28.2.27)	25	25
116	3 f. on 5 f. slate & magenta (19.12.27)	70	70
117	10 f. on 5 f. green and blue (7.2.27) ..	1·40	1·40
118	20 f. on 5 f. sepia & mag/*rose* (7.2.27)	3·25	3·25
108/118	*Set of 11*	5·75	5·75

1927 (10 Oct). *POSTAGE DUE. As No.* D88 *(colour changed) surch as Type* D **13** *of French Sudan.*

D119	2 f. on 1 f. magenta	1·00	1·00
D120	3 f. on 1 f. chestnut	1·00	1·00

1931 (13 Apr). *International Colonial Exhibition, Paris. As T* **17**/**20** *of French Sudan.*

119	40 c. black and green ..	70	65
120	50 c. black and mauve ..	70	65
121	90 c. black and vermilion ..	65	50
122	1 f. 50, black and blue ..	50	30
	a. Inscr double	25·00	
119/122	*Set of 4*	2·25	1·90

1937 (15 Apr). *International Exhibition, Paris. As T* **2**/**7** *of French Equatorial Africa.*

123	20 c. bright violet	25	25
124	30 c. green	25	25
125	40 c. carmine	25	25
126	50 c. brown	25	25
127	90 c. scarlet	25	25
128	1 f. 50, blue	25	25
123/128	*Set of 6*	1·40	1·40
MS128*a*	120×100 mm. 3 f. turquoise-green and black-green (as T **4**). Imperf	80	80

4 Native Village   **5** Waterfall

6 Native Women   D **7**

(Des and eng E. Feltesse (2 c. to 15 c.), A. Degorce (20 c. to 50 c.), A. Decaris (others). Recess)

1938 (1 Mar)–**40.** *P* 13.

129	**4**	2 c. vermilion..		5	5
130		3 c. bright blue		5	5
131		4 c. green		5	5
132		5 c. carmine		5	5
133		10 c. greenish blue		5	5
134		15 c. slate-purple		5	5
135	–	20 c. carmine		5	5
136	–	25 c. greenish blue		5	5
137	–	30 c. bright blue		5	5
138	–	35 c. green		5	5
139	–	40 c. black-brown (15.4.40)		5	5
140	–	45 c. blue-green (15.4.40)		5	5
141	–	50 c. brown-lake		5	5
142	**5**	55 c. blue		5	5
143		60 c. ultramarine (26.3.40)		15	15
144		65 c. green		10	5
145		70 c. green (26.3.40)		15	15
146		80 c. purple		5	5
147		90 c. purple (4.12.39)		15	15
148		1 f. scarlet		40	30
149		1 f. black-brown (26.3.40)		5	5
150		1 f. 25, scarlet (4.12.39)		20	20
151		1 f. 40, brown (5.3.40)		20	20
152		1 f. 50, brown		40	30
153	**6**	1 f. 60, red (5.3.40)		12	12
154		1 f. 75, bright blue		8	5
155		2 f. rose-magenta		20	8
156		2 f. 25, bright blue (4.12.39)		20	20
157		2 f. 50, black-brown (5.3.40)		15	15
158		3 f. greenish blue		5	5
159		5 f. purple		12	5
160		10 f. blue-green		12	10
161		20 f. brown		30	20
129/161		*Set of 33*		3·50	3·00

Design: *Horiz*—20 c. to 50 c. Wooden pot-makers.
Stamps of 10, 20, 30, 40, 60., 1 f. 50 and 2 f. as this issue, but without "RF", were prepared in 1943–44, but not placed on sale in French Guinea.

(Des and eng H. Cheffer. Recess)

1938 (1 Mar). *POSTAGE DUE. P* 14×13.

D162	D **7**	5 c. dull violet		5	5
D163		10 c. carmine		5	5
D164		15 c. green		5	5
D165		20 c. brown-lake		5	5
D166		30 c. bright purple..		5	5
D167		50 c. brown		5	5
D168		60 c. greenish blue		5	5
D169		1 f. red		8	8
D170		2 f. bright blue		15	15
D171		3 f. black		15	15
D162/171		*Set of 10*		65	65

The 10 c. without "RF" was prepared in 1944, but not used.

1938 (24 Oct). *International Anti-Cancer Fund. As T* **14** *of French Equatorial Africa.*

162	1 f. 75+50 c. ultramarine			1·75	1·75

1939 (5 Apr). *Death Centenary of R. Caillié. As T* **21** *of French Sudan.*

163	90 c. orange			12	12
164	2 f. violet			15	15
165	2 f. 25, blue			12	12

1939 (10 May). *New York World's Fair. As T* **17** *of French Equatorial Africa.*

166	1 f. 25, lake			15	15
167	2 f. 25, ultramarine			15	15

1939 (5 July). *150th Anniv of French Revolution. As T* **18** *of French Equatorial Africa.*

168	45 c.+25 c. green and black			1·10	1·10
169	70 c.+30 c. brown and black			1·10	1·10
170	90 c.+35 c. red-orange and black			1·10	1·10
171	1 f. 25+1 f. carmine and black			1·10	1·10
172	2 f. 25+2 f. blue and black			1·10	1·10
168/172	*Set of 5*			5·00	5·00

1940 (8 Feb). *AIR. As T* **22** *of French Sudan.*

173	1 f. 90, bright blue			5	5
174	2 f. 90, rose-red			8	8
175	4 f. 50, green			10	10

176	4 f. 90, olive-bistre			12	12
177	6 f. 90, orange			15	15
173/177	*Set of 5*			45	45

VICHY GOVERNMENT

Nos. 178/87 were issued by the Pétain régime in Unoccupied France. A number of other issues exist, but we list only those items which were available in French Guinea.

1941. *National Defence Fund. Surch as T* **23** *of French Sudan.*

178	–	+1 f. on 50 c. brown-lake (No. 141)		12	12
179	**5**	+2 f. on 80 c. purple		1·00	1·00
180		+2 f. on 1 f. 50, brown		1·00	1·00
181	**6**	+3 f. on 2 f. rose-magenta		1·00	1·00
178/181		*Set of 4*		2·75	2·75

7 Ford at Kitim and Marshal Pétain

8 Dakar Maternity Hospital

9 "Child Welfare"

(Des and eng A. Degorce. Recess Institut de Gravure, Paris)

1941. *P* 12×12½.

182	**7**	1 f. deep green		5	5
183		2 f. 50, deep blue		5	5

(Des J. Douy. Photo Vaugirard, Paris (Nos. 184/5). Des C. Mazelin. Recess Institut de Gravure, Paris (No. 186))

1942 (22 June). *AIR. Colonial Child Welfare Fund. T* **8/9** *and similar design. P* 13 (*No.* 186) *or* 13½×12½ (*others*).

184	**8**	1 f. 50+3 f. 50, green			8
185		2 f.+6 f. red-brown			8
186	**9**	3 f.+9 f. carmine-red			10

Design: As T **8**—No. 185, Dispensary at Mopti.

1942 (22 Oct). *AIR. As T* **25** *of French Sudan, inscr* "GUINEE".

187	50 f. brown-olive and yellow-green			25	40

Seven other values from 50 c. to 20 f. exist, but were not used.

French Guinea had been included in French West Africa since 15 June 1895, but had still continued to have separate issues of stamps. It remained under the Vichy Government until November 1942. In 1944 the issues of French West Africa were introduced, and they remained in use until 1959.

STAMP MONTHLY

—finest and most informative magazine for all collectors. Obtainable from your newsagent or by postal subscription—details on request.

French Indian Settlements

1892. 100 Centimes = 1 Franc
1923. 24 Caches = 1 Fanon
8 Fanon = 1 Rupee

The French Indian Settlements were originally trading posts founded by the French India Company during the 17th and 18th centuries, and represent the remnants of a once considerable French presence in the sub-continent. The Settlements consisted of Pondicherry (founded 1683), Karikal (captured 1739) and Yanaon (founded *circa* 1750) on the Coromandel coast; Mahé (acquired 1725) on the Malabar coast; and Chandernagore, near Calcutta (acquired 1688). All were captured by the British during both the Seven Years War and the Revolutionary and Napoleonic Wars, but were restored to France by the treaties of 1763 and 1815.

PRINTERS. All issues were printed by the French Government Printing Works, Paris, *unless otherwise stated.*

IMPERFORATE STAMPS. Many stamps exist imperforate in their issued colours, but these were not valid for postage. Imperforate stamps in other colours are colour trials.

1892 (Nov). *French Colonies Type X ("Tablet") inscr "ETAB-LISSEMENTS DE L'INDE" in red (1, 5, 15, 25, 75 c., 1 f.) or blue (others). P 14 × 13½.*

1	1 c. black/*azure* ..	..	..	8	8
2	2 c. brown/*buff* ..			5	5
3	4 c. purple-brown/*grey* ..	..		12	10
4	5 c. green/*pale green*	..	..	80	20
5	10 c. black/*lilac* ..	..	..	1·50	50
6	15 c. blue (*quadrillé paper*)	..	..	1·25	75
7	20 c. red/*green* ..	..	..	80	60
8	25 c. black/*rose* ..	..	..	50	50
9	30 c. cinnamon/*drab* ..	..	..	7·50	6·50
10	40 c. red/*yellow* ..	..	..	1·00	75
11	50 c. carmine/*rose* ..	..	..	1·00	75
12	75 c. brown/*yellow* ..	..	..	1·25	1·25
13	1 f. olive-green/*toned* ..	..	..	1·50	1·50
1/13	*Set of 13* ..	..	..	15·00	12·00

1900 (Dec)–**07**. *French Colonies Type X. Colours changed and new values. Inscr in blue (10 c.) or red (others). P 14 × 13½.*

14	10 c. rose-red ..	..	..	50	40
15	15 c. grey ..	..	..	5·00	5·00
16	25 c. blue ..	..	..	2·25	1·75
17	35 c. black/*yellow* (7.06)	..	..	2·25	75
18	45 c. black/*green* (10.07)	..	..	50	25
19	50 c. brown/*azure* ..	..	..	1·50	1·25
14/19	*Set of 6* ..	..	..	11·00	8·50

0,05

(1)   2

1903 (6 Dec). *Nos. 8 and 11 surch at Pondicherry as T 1.*

20	0,05 on 25 c. black/*rose* (R.)	..	..	70·00	40·00
21	0,10 on 25 c. black/*rose* (R.)	..	..	70·00	48·00
	a. Second "0" narrower	..	..	£325	£325
22	0,15 on 25 c. black/*rose* (R.)	..	..	25·00	25·00
23	0,40 on 50 c. carmine/*rose*	..	..	£110	90·00
	a. Second "0" narrower	..	..	£400	£400

1903 (Dec). *Fiscal stamp bisected horizontally and upper half surch as in T 2.*

24	0,05 black and grey-blue ..	..	..	3·75	3·75
	a. Large "E" in "POSTES" ..	..	..	65·00	50·00

3 Brahma   **4** Temple near Pondicherry

(Dies eng E. Froment and J. Puyplat. Typo)

1914 (June). *Value and centre in black. P 13½ × 14 (T 3) or 14 × 13½ (T 4).*

26	**3**	1 c. grey	..	..	..	5	5
27		2 c. dull purple	..	..	..	5	5
28		3 c. yellow-brown	..	..	..	5	5
29		4 c. orange	..	..	..	8	8
30		5 c. blue-green	..	..	..	10	10
31		10 c. rose-carmine	..	..	..	8	8
32		15 c. violet	..	..	..	12	12
33		20 c. vermilion	..	..	..	20	20
34		25 c. blue	..	..	..	25	25
35		30 c. ultramarine	..	..	..	20	20
36	**4**	35 c. deep brown	..	..	..	20	20
37		40 c. vermilion	..	..	..	20	20
38		45 c. blue-green	..	..	..	20	20
39		50 c. deep carmine	..	..	..	12	12
40		75 c. blue	..	..	..	40	40
41		1 f. yellow	..	..	..	40	40
42		2 f. violet	..	..	..	75	75
43		5 f. ultramarine	..	..	..	30	30
26/43		*Set of 18*	..	..	..	3·25	3·25

See also Nos. 52/8 and 88/107.

✚   **5ᶜ**

(5)

1915. *Red Cross. T 3 surch at Pondicherry with T 5, in red.*

   (a) *Surch near top of design* (June)

44	10 c.+5 c. black and carmine	..	..	20	20
	a. Surch inverted	..	..	13·00	13·00

   (b) *Surch at foot of design* (15 Nov)

45	10 c.+5 c. black and carmine	..	..	35	35

✚

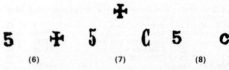

5   **✚**   **5**   **C 5**   **c**

(6)   (7)   (8)

1916. *Red Cross. T 3 surch. (a) With T 6 at Pondicherry, in red (June).*

48	10 c.+5 c. black and carmine	..	..	2·50	2·50
	a. Surch double	..	..	11·00	11·00
	b. Surch inverted	..	..	13·00	13·00

<table>
<tr><td colspan="4">(b) With T 7 (June)</td></tr>
</table>

49	10 c.+5 c. black and carmine	45	45
	a. Surch double	11·00	11·00
	b. Surch inverted	11·00	11·00

(c) As *T* **8** (20 July)

50	10 c.+5 c. black and carmine	12	12
	a. "e" for "c"	6·50	6·50
	b. Surch inverted	11·00	11·00
	c. Surch double	9·50	9·50

The spacing between "5" and "c" varies considerably.

✚5ᶜ   **0.01 ≡**

(9)   (10)

1916. *Red Cross. T* **3** *surch in Paris with T* **9**, *in red.*

51	10 c.+5 c. black and carmine	20	20

1922 (1 Jan). *New colours.*

52 **3**	2 c. purple and green	5	5
53	5 c. black and purple	5	5
54	10 c. black and green	10	10
55	25 c. red and ultramarine	10	10
56	30 c. black and carmine	12	12
57 **4**	50 c. blue and ultramarine	12	12
58	5 f. black and carmine	45	45
52/58	*Set of 7*	90	90

1922 (Dec). *No. 32 surch as T* **10**.

59 **3**	0,01 on 15 c. black and violet	5	5
60	0,02 on 15 c. black and violet (B.)	5	5
61	0,05 on 15 c. black and violet (R.)	5	5
59/61	*Set of 3*	10	10

I FANON

6 CACHES   **I 2 CACHES**

(11)   (12)

2

ROUPIES

(13)

1923 (Nov)–**28**. *New Currency. Surch as T* **11**/**13**.

62 **3**	1 ca. on 1 c. black and grey (R.)	5	5
	a. "1" and "c" widely spaced	1·25	1·25
63	2 ca. on 5 c. black and purple	8	8
64	3 ca. on 3 c. black and brown	8	8
65	4 ca. on 4 c. black and orange	10	8
66	6 ca. on 10 c. black and green	12	12
	a. Surch double		
67 **4**	6 ca. on 45 c. black and green (R.)	10	10
68 **3**	10 ca. on 20 c. green & carmine (22.10.28)	40	40
69	12 ca. on 15 c. black and violet	12	12
70	15 ca. on 20 c. black and vermilion	12	12
71 **4**	16 ca. on 35 c. yell-brn & brt bl (22.10.28)	35	35
72 **3**	18 ca. on 30 c. black and carmine	12	12
73 **4**	20 ca. on 45 c. rose and green (5.9.27)	20	20
74 **3**	1 fa. on 25 c. carmine & green (22.10.28)	40	40
75 **4**	1 fa. 3 ca. on 35 c. black & choc (R.)	12	12
76	1 fa. 6 ca. on 40 c. black & verm (R.)	12	12
77	1 fa. 12 ca. on 50 c. blue & ultram (B.)	12	12
78	1 fa. 12 ca. on 75 c. black and blue (B.)	12	12
	a. Surch double	25·00	
79	1 fa. 16 ca. on 75 c. green & lake (5.9.27)	55	45
80 **3**	2 fa. 9 ca. on 25 c. red & ultram (B.)	25	15
81 **4**	2 fa. 12 ca. on 1 f. sep & mve (22.10.28)	30	30
82	3 fa. 3 ca. on 1 f. black and yellow (R.)	30	30
	a. Surch double	25·00	
83	6 fa. 6 ca. on 2 f. black and violet (B.)	95	65
	a. Large figure "6" in "6 CACHES"	70·00	65·00
84	1 r. on 1 f. blue and green (R.) (3.5.26)	1·25	1·25
85	2 r. black and carmine (R.)	1·25	1·00
86	3 r. on 2 f. violet and grey (R.) (3.5.26)	2·75	1·90
87	5 r. on 5 f. blk & rose/*greenish* (3.5.26)	3·25	2·50
62/87	*Set of 26*	12·00	10·00

Nos. 68, 71, 74 and 81 have the original value obliterated by bars.

1923 (Nov)–**28**. *POSTAGE DUE. Postage Due stamps of France. Type* D **11**, *surch as T* **11** *or* **12**. *P 14×13½.*

D88	4 ca. on 20 c. violet-blue (10.28)	12	12
D89	6 ca. on 10 c. brown (B.)	12	12
D90	12 ca. on 25 c. carmine	12	12
D91	15 ca. on 20 c. olive-green (R.)	12	12
D92	1 fa. on 30 c. orange (10.28)	25	25
D93	1 fa. 6, on 30 c. carmine-red (B.)	20	20
D94	1 fa. 12, on 50 c. dull purple (B.)	25	25
D95	1 fa. 15, on 5 c. light blue	30	30
D96	1 fa. 16, on 5 c. black (R.) (10.28)	30	30
D97	3 fa. on 1 f. green (10.28)	50	50
D98	3 fa. 3, on 1 f. red-brown/*straw* (B.)	50	50
D88/98	*Set of 11*	2·50	2·50

Nos. D88, D92, D96/7 have the original value obliterated by bars.

1929 (16 Sept). *Inscr in new currency.*

88 **3**	1 ca. black and grey-black	5	5
89	2 ca. black and purple	5	5
90	3 ca. black and chocolate-brown	5	5
91	4 ca. black and orange-yellow	5	5
92	6 ca. green and grey-green	5	5
93	10 ca. green and carmine	8	8
94 **4**	12 ca. olive-green and green	8	5
95 **3**	16 ca. black and blue	12	10
96	18 ca. vermilion and carmine	12	10
97	20 ca. green and deep blue/*azure*	10	8
98 **4**	1 fa. carmine and grey-green	10	8
99	1 fa. 6 ca. black and orange	10	8
100	1 fa. 12 ca. blue and deep blue	10	8
101	1 fa. 16 ca. green and carmine	10	8
102	1 fa. 12 ca. chocolate and mauve	12	10
103	6 fa. 6 ca. black and violet	12	10
104	1 r. deep blue and grey-green	12	8
105	2 r. black and carmine	15	12
106	3 r. lilac and grey-black	40	25
107	5 r. black and carmine/*greenish*	50	30
88/107	*Set of 20*	2·25	1·75

D **14**

(Des G. Duval. Die eng Dujardin. Typo)

1929 (16 Sept). *POSTAGE DUE. P 14×13½.*

D108 D **14**	4 ca. carmine	5	5
D109	6 ca. blue	5	5
D110	12 ca. green	5	5
D111	1 fa. chocolate-brown	10	10
D112	1 fa. 12, violet-blue	15	15
D113	1 fa. 16, yellow-brown	20	20
D114	3 fa. mauve	30	30
D108/114	*Set of 7*	80	80

1931 (13 Apr). *International Colonial Exhibition, Paris. As T* **17**/**20** *of French Sudan.*

108	10 ca. black and deep green	50	50
109	12 ca. black and mauve	50	50
110	18 ca. black and orange-vermilion	50	50
111	1 fa. 12, black and deep blue	50	50
108/111	*Set of 4*	1·75	1·75

1937 (15 Apr). *International Exhibition, Paris. As T* **2**/**7** *of French Equatorial Africa.*

112	8 ca. bright violet	20	20
113	12 ca. green	20	20
114	16 ca. carmine	20	20
115	20 ca. brown	20	20
116	1 fa. 12, scarlet	20	20
117	2 fa. 12, blue	20	20
112/117	*Set of 6*	1·10	1·10
MS117*a*	120×100 mm. 5 fa. bright purple (as *T* **7**). Imerf	95	95

1938 (24 Oct). *International Anti-Cancer Fund. As T* **14** *of French Equatorial Africa.*

118	2 fa. 12 ca.+20 ca. ultramarine	2·25	2·25

1939 (10 May). *New York World's Fair. As T* **17** *of French Equatorial Africa.*

119	1 fa. 12, lake	.. ..	20 20
120	2 fa. 12, ultramarine	.. .. ..	35 35

1939 (5 July). *150th Anniv of French Revolution. As T* **18** *of French Equatorial Africa.*

121	18 ca.+10 ca. green and black ..	..	1·25 1·25
122	1 fa. 6 ca.+12 ca. brown and black	..	1·25 1·25
123	1 fa. 12 ca.+16 ca. red-orange & black		1·25 1·25
124	1 fa. 16 ca.+1 fa. 16 ca. carmine & black		1·25 1·25
125	2 fa. 12 ca.+3 fa. blue and black	..	1·25 1·25
121/125	*Set of 5*	.. ..	5·75 5·75

VICHY ISSUES. A number of stamps were prepared by the Pétain Government of Unoccupied France for use in the Territory, but as the Settlements were controlled by the Free French, none of these issues were placed on sale there.

FRANCE LIBRE

(15)

FRANCE LIBRE

(16)

1941. *Various issues optd at Pondicherry with T* **15** *(u) diagonally upwards, (h) horizontally, or with T* **16**.

(a) On Nos. 70, 72, 75 and 80

126	15u	15 ca. on 20 c. black & vermilion (R.)	13·00	13·00
127		18 ca. on 30 c. black and carmine (R.)	30	30
128	15h	1 fa. 3 on 35 c. black & chocolate (R.)	13·00	13·00
129	15u	1 fa. 3 on 35 c. black & chocolate (R.)	15·00	15·00
130	16	2 fa. 9 on 25 c. red & ultramarine (R.)	£225	£200
131		2 fa. 9 on 25 c. red & ultramarine (R.)	£225	£200
132	15u	2 fa. 9 on 25 c. red & ultramarine (R.)	£225	£200

(b) On Nos. 89/107

133	15u	2 ca. black and purple (R.)	1·25	1·10
134		3 ca. black & chocolate-brown (R.)	40	40
135		4 ca. black and orange-yellow (R.)	1·10	1·00
136		6 ca. green and grey-green (R.) ..	25	25
137		10 ca. green and carmine (B.) ..	40	30
138		10 ca. green and carmine (R.)	90·00	80·00
139		12 ca. olive-green and green (R.) ..	40	30
140		16 ca. black and blue (R.)	25	25
141		18 ca. vermilion and carmine (B.) ..	£150	£110
142		20 ca. green and blue/*azure* (R.) ..	40	30
143		1 fa. carmine and grey-green (B.)..	40	25
144		1 fa. 6, black and red (R.). . ..	40	25
145		1 fa. 12, blue and deep blue (R.) ..	75	65
146		1 fa. 16, green and carmine (R.) ..	40	25
147		2 fa. 12, chocolate and mauve (R.)	40	25
148		6 fa. 6, black and violet (R.) ..	40	30
149		1 r. deep blue and grey-green (R.)	40	25
150		2 r. black and carmine (R.) ..	40	25
151		3 r. lilac and grey-black (R.) ..	40	30
152		5 r. black & carmine/*greenish* (R.)	1·25	80

Nos. 133/52 exist with inverted overprints.

(c) On Nos. 112/17 (Paris Exhibition)

153	16	8 ca. bright violet (B.) ..	48·00	48·00
		a. Black opt	£170	£170
154	15h	8 ca. bright violet (R.)	1·25	1·25
		a. Opt inverted ..	35·00	32·00
155	15u	8 ca. bright violet (R.)	25·00	25·00
156		8 ca. bright violet (B.)	45·00	40·00
157		12 ca. green (R.) ..	65	65
		a. Opt inverted ..	35·00	32·00
158		16 ca. carmine (R.) ..	65	65
159		1 fa. 12, scarlet (B.) ..	65	65
160		2 fa. 12, blue (R.) . .	65	65
		a. Opt inverted		
MS160a	5 fa. bright purple (**MS**117a) (B)		£190	£170
MS160b	Wider opt (105 *mm long*) with serifs		£150	£130

(d) On Nos. 119/20 (New York Fair)

161	15u	1 fa. 12, lake (B.) ..	50	50
162		2 fa. 12, ultramarine (R.) ..	50	50

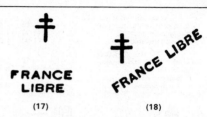

(17)   (18)

1942–43. *Various issues optd locally with "FRANCE LIBRE" and Cross of Lorraine as T* **17** *or* **18**.

(a) On pictorial issue of 1929 (Nos. 89, etc.)

163	17	2 ca. black and purple (R.+Bk.)* ..	18·00	14·00
164		2 ca. black and purple (Bk.) ..	20·00	16·00
165		2 ca. black and purple (R.) . .	12	12
166		3 ca. black and chocolate-brown (R.)	20	20
167		6 ca. green and grey-green (R.) ..	39·00	32·00
168		6 ca. green and grey-green (Bk.) ..	14·00	14·00
169		6 ca. green and grey-green (B.) ..	20	20
170	18	12 ca. olive-green and green (B.) ..	40	40
171	17	16 ca. black and blue (R.)	20	20
172		18 ca. vermilion and carmine (B.) ..	20	20
173		18 ca. on 30 c. blk & carm (No. 72) (B.)	65·00	45·00
174		20 ca. green and deep blue/*azure* (R.)	20	20
		a. Double opt (R.+B.)		80·00
175		20 ca. green and deep blue/*azure* (B.)	90	75
176	18	1 fa. carmine and grey-green (B.) ..	12	12
177		1 fa. 6, black and red (B.) ..	55·00	38·00
178		1 fa. 6, black and red (R.)	30	30
179		1 fa. 12, blue and deep blue (R.) ..	25	25
180		1 fa. 16, green and carmine (B.) ..	12	12
181		2 fa. 12, chocolate and mauve (B.)..	6·50	6·50
182		2 fa. 12, chocolate and mauve (R.)..	30	30
183		6 fa. 6, black and violet (R.) ..	50	50
184	1	r. deep blue and grey-green (R.)..	1·00	1·00
185	2	r. black and carmine (R.) ..	75	75
186	3	r. lilac and grey-black (B.) ..	28·00	25·00
187	3	r. lilac and grey-black (R.) ..	75	75
188	5	r. black and carmine/*green* (R.) ..	80	80

* On No. 163, the Cross is in red and "FRANCE LIBRE" in black.

There are two different spacings of T **17**, one with 11 mm between cross and words and the other 7 to 8 mm. Nos. 163, 164, 167, 168 and 174 exist only with the wide spacing, and Nos. 173 to 175 only with the narrow. In the other values, which come with both spacings, the wide spacing is much scarcer (No. 165, wide £14, Nos. 166, 169, 171 and 172, £9 each).

(b) On Nos. 112, etc (Paris Exhibition)

189	17	8 ca. bright violet (B.)	1·25	90
190	18	12 ca. green (B.)	1·00	1·00
191		16 ca. carmine (B.)	£325	£225
192		1 fa. 12, scarlet (B.)	15	15
193		2 fa. 12, blue (R.)	55	50

The overprint on No. 189 has the close spacing.

(c) On Nos. 119/20 (New York Fair)

194	18	1 fa. 12, lake (B.)	25	25
195		2 fa. 12, ultramarine (R.) ..	65	65

1942 (Dec). *No. 95 surch as T* **17** *and new value at foot.*

196	1 ca. on 16 ca. (R.)	..	13·00	7·50
197	4 ca. on 16 ca. (R.)	..	13·00	7·50
198	10 ca. on 16 ca. (R.)	..	7·50	2·50
199	15 ca. on 16 ca. (R.)	..	6·50	2·50
200	1 fa. 3 ca. on 16 ca. (R.) ..	..	13·00	6·50
201	2 fa. 9 ca. on 16 ca. (R.) ..	..	10·00	11·00
202	3 fa. 3 ca. on 16 ca. (R.) ..	..	7·50	3·25
196/202	*Set of 7*	..	65·00	35·00

$$= \dagger \; \text{I fa} \; \text{FRANCE LIBRE} \; \text{3 ca}$$

(19)

STAMP MONTHLY

—finest and most informative magazine for all collectors. Obtainable from your newsagent or by postal subscription—details on request.

1943. *Nos. 103/7 surch locally. (a) As T* **19**, *in red.*

203	1 ca. on 6 fa. 6, black and violet	..	2·25	1·60
204	1 ca. on 1 r. deep blue and grey-green		65	65
205	2 ca. on 1 r. deep blue and grey-green		12	12
206	4 ca. on 6 fa. 6, black and violet	..	2·75	1·50
207	4 ca. on 1 r. deep blue and grey-green		12	12
208	6 ca. on 2 r. black and carmine	..	12	12
209	10 ca. on 6 fa. 6, black and violet	..	50	12
210	10 ca. on 2 r. black and carmine	..	25	25
211	12 ca. on 2 r. black and carmine	..	12	12
212	15 ca. on 6 fa. 6, black and violet	..	75	30
213	15 ca. on 3 r. lilac and grey-black	..	12	12
214	16 ca. on 3 r. lilac and grey-black		12	12
215	1 fa. 3 on 6 fa. 6, black and violet	..	1·25	50
216	1 fa. 3 on 3 r. lilac and grey-black	..	12	12
217	1 fa. 6 on 5 r. black and carmine/*green*		25	25
218	1 fa. 12 on 5 r. black & carmine/*green*		25	12
219	1 fa. 16 on 5 r. black & carmine/*green*		25	25
220	2 fa. 9 on 6 fa. 6, black and violet	..	1·25	70
221	3 fa. 3 on 6 fa. 6, black and violet	..	1·25	70
203/221	*Set of 19*	.. ..	11·00	7·00

(b) As T **19**, *in red, but without "FRANCE LIBRE" and Cross*

222	1 ca. on 6 fa. 6, black and violet	..	4·50	3·25
223	4 ca. on 6 fa. 6, black and violet	..	4·50	3·25
224	10 ca. on 6 fa. 6, black and violet	..	1·25	95
225	15 ca. on 6 fa. 6, black and violet	..	1·25	95
226	1 fa. 3 on 6 fa. 6, black and violet	..	3·75	3·25
227	2 fa. 9 on 6 fa. 6, black and violet	..	4·00	3·25
228	3 fa. 3 on 6 fa. 6, black and violet	..	4·00	3·25
222/228	*Set of 7*	.. .. ..	21·00	16·00

200 complete sets made up of Nos. 70, 72, 75, 89/90, 92 and 94/117, overprinted "FRANCE TOUJOURS" and Cross of Lorraine, in a circle, were apparently officially authorised. (*Price for set of* 27 £1700 *used.*)

20 Lotus Flowers

21 Passenger Aircraft

(Des E. Dulac. Photo Harrison)

1942. *London issue. (a) POSTAGE. P* 14×14½.

229	**20**	2 ca. brown ..	..	5	5
230		3 ca. blue	..	5	5
231		4 ca. emerald-green..	..	5	5
232		6 ca. red-orange	..	5	5
233		12 ca. slate-green	..	5	5
234		16 ca. purple ..	..	5	5
235		20 ca. maroon	..	10	8
236		1 fa. scarlet ..	..	12	10
237		1 fa. 18, grey-black ..	..	12	10
238		6 fa. 6, ultramarine ..	..	15	10
239		1 r. violet ..	..	12	12
240		2 r. yellow-bistre ..	..	25	20
241		3 r. red-brown ..	..	30	25
242		5 r. blue-green ..	..	30	30

(b) AIR. P 14½×14

243	**21**	4 fa. red-orange	..	12	10
244		1 r. scarlet ..	..	12	12
245		2 r. maroon	..	20	20
246		5 r. black	..	25	25
247		8 r. ultramarine	..	45	35
248		10 r. green	..	45	40
229/248		*Set of 20*	..	3·00	2·75

These stamps did not become available in the Indian Settlements until some time later.

1944. *Mutual Aid and Red Cross Funds. As T* **29** *of French Equatorial Africa.*

249	3 fa.+1 r. 4 fa. bistre	.. ..	12	12

1945. *Félix Eboué. As T* **31** *of French Equatorial Africa.*

250	3 fa. 8, black	.. .. ..	5	5
251	5 r. 1 fa. 16, blue-green	..	20	20

1946 (8 May). *AIR. Victory. As T* **32** *of French Equatorial Africa.*

252	4 fa. blue-green ..	.. ..	15	15

1946 (6 June). *AIR. From Chad to the Rhine. As Nos.* 229/34 *of French Equatorial Africa.*

253	2 fa. 12, bistre-brown ..	..	15	15
254	5 fa. blue	.. ..	15	15
255	7 fa. 12, violet	.. ..	20	20
256	1 r. 2 fa. grey-green	.. ..	20	20
257	1 r. 12, brown-red	.. ..	20	20
258	3 r. 1 fa. maroon	.. ..	20	20
253/258	*Set of 6*	.. ..	1·00	1·00

22 Apsara

23 Aeroplane over Chindambaram Temple

(Des M. Rolland. Photo Vaugirard, Paris)

1948 (8 June)–**52**. *T* **22** *and similar vert designs. P* 13×13½.

259	**22**	1 ca. blackish olive ..	..	5	5
260		2 ca. red-brown	..	5	5
261		4 ca. dull violet/*cream*	..	5	5
262	–	6 ca. brown-orange ..	..	10	5
263	–	8 ca. slate ..	..	20	15
264	–	10 ca. green/*green*	..	20	15
265	–	12 ca. brown-purple ..	..	8	5
266	–	15 ca. greenish blue ..	..	8	8
267	–	18 ca. lake (30.6.52) ..	..	15	15
268	–	1 fa. bright violet/*rose*	..	12	10
269	–	1 fa. 6, brown-red ..	..	15	15
270	–	1 fa. 15, deep bluish violet (30.6.52)		45	45
271	–	2 fa. blue-green ..	..	12	8
272	–	2 fa. 2, blue/*cream* ..	..	20	15
273	–	2 fa. 12, brown ..	..	25	20
274	–	3 fa. orange-red ..	..	45	30
275	–	4 fa. bronze-green (30.6.52)	..	45	45
276	–	5 fa. purple/*rose* ..	..	35	30
277	–	7 fa. 12, sepia ..	..	30	30
278	–	1 r. 2 fa. black ..	..	80	80
279	–	1 r. 4 fa. 12, grey-green ..	..	90	80
259/279		*Set of 21*	..	5·00	4·50

Designs:—6, 8, 10 ca. Dvarabalagar standing erect; 12, 15 ca., 1 fa. Vishnu; 18 ca., 1 fa. 15, 4 fa. Brahmin idol; 1 fa. 6, 2 fa., 2 fa. 2, Dvarabalagar with leg raised; 2 fa. 12, 3, 5 fa. Temple Guardian; 7 fa. 12, 1 r. 2 fa., 1 r. 4 fa. 12, One of the Tigoupalagar.

A 3 r. air stamp, Type **23**, designed by M. Dassonville, was also prepared for issue with this set, but was never placed on sale in the French Settlements. It was withdrawn because the temple shown stood on Indian, and not French, territory. (*Price* £1·90 *unused.*)

ALBUM LISTS

Write for our latest lists of albums and accessories.

These will be sent free on request.

D 24   25 Aeroplane and Bas-relief

(Des M. Rolland. Photo Vaugirard, Paris)

1948 (June). *POSTAGE DUE. P* 13×13½.

D280	D 24	1 ca. violet	..	5	5
D281		2 ca. brown	..	5	5
D282		6 ca. blue-green	..	5	5
D283		12 ca. brown-red	..	5	5
D284		1 fa. magenta	..	5	5
D285		1 fa. 12, red-brown	..	10	10
D286		2 fa. blue	..	12	12
D287		2 fa. 12, brown-lake	..	20	20
D288		5 fa. blackish green	..	40	40
D289		1 r. slate-violet	..	45	45
D280/289		*Set of* 10 ..	..	1·40	1·40

(Des A. Brenet (1 r.), L. Scrépel (others). Photo Vaugirard, Paris)

1949 (24 Jan). *AIR. T* **25** *and similar designs. P* 13½×12½ *(horiz) or* 12½×13½ *(vert).*

281	1 r. carmine and yellow ..	..	..	95	65
282	2 r. deep green and green	..	..	1·60	1·25
283	5 r. reddish purple and blue	..	..	4·50	4·00

Designs: *Vert*—2 r. Wing and temple; 5 r. Bird and palm trees.

1949 (4 July). *AIR.* 75th *Anniv of Universal Postal Union. As T* **39** *of French Equatorial Africa.*

284	6 fa. carmine	..	..	1·40	1·40

1950 (15 May). *Colonial Welfare Fund. As T* **40** *of French Equatorial Africa.*

285	1 fa.+10 ca. blue and indigo	..	..	40	40

1952 (1 Dec). *Centenary of Médaille Militaire. As T* **44** *of French Equatorial Africa.*

286	1 fa. brown, yellow and green	..	50	50

1954 (6 June). *AIR.* 10th *Anniv of Liberation. As T* **46** *of French Equatorial Africa.*

287	1 fa. purple-brown and deep brown	..	95	95

Following a referendum in 1949 the administration of Chandernagore was transferred to India on 2 May 1950 and in 1954 it became part of West Bengal. The remaining four settlements voted to join India on 18 October 1954, the transfer being completed on 1 November. When the agreement was ratified in 1962 the four former settlements became a Union Territory of India.

PHILATELIC TERMS ILLUSTRATED

This successful STAMP MONTHLY series has now been brought together in a snappy black and yellow binding and published as a useful addition to Stanley Gibbons range of essential handbooks for keen stamp collectors.
Within its 192 pages this handy limp-bound volume houses a veritable mine of useful information on the words and phrases used in philately. It describes and illustrates printing processes and watermarks, papers and perforations, errors and varieties . . . and it does all this IN COLOUR. Indeed, there are 92 full page plates in colour, plus many black and white illustrations, making it

FANTASTIC VALUE AT ONLY £1·95 POST PAID FROM

Stanley Gibbons Publications Ltd
391 Strand, London WC2R 0LX

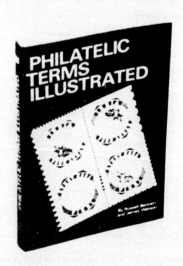

French Morocco

Morocco, which had been the Roman province of Mauretania. was conquered by Moslem invaders from the east in 710 Arab and Berber forces crossed into Spain in 711 and by 719 reached the Pyrenees. Moorish dynasties ruled much of Spain until 1212 and the Moors were not finally expelled from Granada, their last stronghold there, until 1492. A long period of warfare between rival dynasties in Morocco followed. Morocco shut itself in a mediaeval civilisation and the area where the sultan's rule was obeyed steadily decreased.

In the 19th century European powers began to cast acquisitive eyes on Morocco. A Spanish invasion took place in 1859–60 and in 1904 secret conventions provided for the partition of Morocco between Spain and France. Germany also claimed interests, until in 1911 these were given up in exchange for the acquisition of part of French Congo.

On 30 March 1912 the Sultan of Morocco was forced to accept a French protectorate over all the country except for a Spanish zone of protection in the north, and Tangier, which was given a special status.

A. FRENCH POST OFFICES

The first French Post Office was opened in 1862 at Tangier, using the stamps of France with obliteration "5106". Other offices were later opened at Casablanca, El Ksar el Kebir, Larache, Mazagan, Mogador, Rabat and Safi. Special stamps with surcharges on French issues in cèntimos and pesetas became necessary by 1891 because of the depreciation of the Spanish currency.

Postal Courier Services between various towns were operated by private French or Spanish concerns from 1891 to 1909. Stamps for these were issued but as they were of a local nature we do not list them.

TYPES OF FRANCE. Type **10** of France is illustrated above No. 15 of French P.O.s in Madagascar (see Malagasy Republic). Type D **11** of France is illustrated at the beginning of Lebanon.

TIMBRE

5	1	
CENTIMOS	**PESETA**	**POSTE**
(1)	(2)	(3)

1891 (1 Jan)–**1900**. *Peace and Commerce type of France surch as T* **1** *or* **2**. *Type* (b) *unless otherwise stated.*

1	10	5 c. on 5 c. deep green (C.)		1·40	75
		a. Surch in vermilion (4.95)		7·00	1·75
2		5 c. on 5 c. brt yell-grn (a) (Vm.) (1899)	6·00	5·00
3		5 c. on 5 c. brt yell-grn (b) (Vm.) (1899)	7·00	5·00
4		10 c. on 10 c. black/lilac (a) (C.) (1899)	7·50	3·50
		a. Error. 10 c. on 25 c. black/rose (C.)	£200	
5		10 c. on 10c. black/lilac (b) (C.) (1.1.93)	5·00	50
		a. Surch in vermilion (4.95)		25·00	2·00
6		20 c. on 20 c. red/yellow-green (1.1.93)	7·00	5·00
		a. Red/deep green (1.1 93)		7·00	5·00
7		25 c. on 25 c. black/rose (C.)		4·50	15
		a. Surch double		30·00	
		b. Surch in vermilion (4.95)		40·00	5·00
8		50 c. on 50 c. rose (b)		25·00	7·00
		a. Carmine		25·00	7·00
9		50 c. on 50 c. carmine-rose (a) (1900)	90·00	50·00
		a. Carmine		90·00	50·00
10		1 p. on 1 f. olive-green		20·00	15·00
11		2 p. on 2 f. brown/pale blue (a) (1900)	60·00	60·00
1/11		Set of 11		£200	£140

1893 (5 Feb). *Postage Due stamps of France handstamped with T* **3** *at Tangier for postal use.*

12	D **11**	5 c. black			£450	£200
13	\	10 c. black			£400	£150

There are two types of this handstamp on both values.

1896. *POSTAGE DUE. Postage Due stamps of France surch as T* **1** *or* **2**.

D14	D **11**	5 c. on 5 c. pale blue (C.)		80	80
		a. Surch in vermilion		1·50	1·50
D15		10 c. on 10 c. brown (C.)		1·75	80
		a. Surch in vermilion		3·25	1·75
D16		30 c. on 30 c. carmine		3·00	2·75
		a. Vermilion		3·00	2·75
D17		50 c. on 50 c. dull claret		3·25	2·75
		a. Deep purple		3·25	2·75
D18		1 p. on 1 f. reddish brown		65·00	58·00
D14/18	Set of 5			65·00	58·00

| 4 | 5 | 6 |

3
CENTIMOS   10 CENTIMOS
(6a)   (6b)   (6c)

1902 (Oct). *Surch as T* **6a** (*T* **4** *and* **6**) *or T* **6b** (*T* **5**). *Typo. P* 14 × 13½.

14	4	1 c. on 1 c. grey (R.) (1907)		12	8
		a. "CFNTIMOS"		6·50	6·50
		b. "GENTIMOS"		4·00	4·00
15		2 c. on 2 c. claret (1907)		20	15
		a. "CFNTIMOS"		8·00	8·00
		b. "GENTIMOS"		4·50	4·50
16		3 c. on 3 c. orange-red (1907)		20	20
		a. "CFNTIMOS"		8·00	8·00
		b. "GENTIMOS"		5·00	5·00
17		4 c. on 4 c. brown (1907)		2·40	1·75
		a. "CFNTIMOS"		10·00	10·00
		b. "GENTIMOS"		8·00	8·00
18		5 c. on 5 c. yellow-green (R.)		80	20
		a. Blue-green (1906)		95	20
		b. Do. "CFNTIMOS"		15·00	12·00
		c. Do. Surch double		—	40·00
19	5	10 c. on 10 c. carmine (12.02)		65	12
20		20 c. on 20 c. purple-brown (5.03)	5·00	2·75
21		25 c. on 25 c. blue (3.03)		5·00	30
22		35 c. on 35 c. lilac (1910)		8·50	5·50
23	6	50 c. on 50 c. brown and lavender	8·00	2·25
24		1 p. on 1 f. lake and yellow-green	21·00	16·00
25		2 p. on 2 f. deep lilac and buff		25·00	16·00
14/25	Set of 12			70·00	40·00

The 5, 10, 20 and 25 c. exist imperforate (price per pair un, each £10).

For 25 c. without surcharge, see No. 10a of French Post Offices in Tangier.

1903 (10 Oct). *Postage Due stamps of 1896 handstamped with T* **6c** (= "Port Payé") *at Tangier for postal use.*

26	D **11**	5 c. on 5 c. pale blue (D14)		£250	*
27		10 c. on 10 c. pale brown (D15a)	£500	*

* These were not to be postmarked in order not to obscure the handstamp.

Stamps of the Sower type of France overprinted "MAROC GOUVERNEMENT PROVISOIRE 1907" are a bogus issue.

| 1 | 1 |

| Type D **19** | (7) | (8) |
| of France | | |

1909–10. *POSTAGE DUE. Postage Due stamps of France, (Recouvrements), such as T* **1**.

D28	D **19**	1 c. on 1 c. olive (R.)	..	..	40	40
D29		10 c. on 10 c. violet	..	..	6·50	6·50
D30		30 c. on 30 c. bistre	..	..	7·50	7·50
D31		50 c. on 50 c. red	..	..	11·00	11·00
D28/31		*Set of 4*	..	..	23·00	23·00

1911–17. *Surch as T* **7** *or with T* **8** (1 *p.*).

28	**4**	1 c. on 1 c. grey (R.)	..	..	5	5
		a. 2 dots under figure	..	..	1·90	1·60
29		2 c. on 2 c. claret (B.)	..	..	8	8
		a. 2 dots under figure	..	..	5·00	4·50
30		3 c. on 3 c. orange (B.)	..	..	5	5
		a. 2 dots under figure	..	..	6·50	5·00
31		5 c. on 5 c. blue-green (R.)	..	..	10	5
		a. 2 dots under figure	..	..	6·50	5·00
32	**5**	10 c. on 10 c. carmine (B.)	..	..	5	5
		a. 2 dots under figures	..	..	6·50	5·00
		b. Imperf (pair)	..	..	56·00	
33		15 c. on 15 c. orange (B.) (1917)	..	45	40
34		20 c. on 20 c. purple-brown (B.)	..	70	60
		a. 2 dots under figures	..	..	21·00	14·00
35		25 c. on 25 c. blue (R.)	..	..	40	15
		a. 2 dots under figures	..	..	18·00	14·00
		b. Black surch	..	..	50·00	50·00
36		35 c. on 35 c. lilac (R.)	..	..	1·40	65
37	**6**	40 c. on 40 c. rose and blue (B.) (1917)	1·10	1·10
38		50 c. on 50 c. brown and lavender (R.)	..	5·00	3·50
39		1 p. on 1 f. lake and yellow-green (B.)	..	3·25	1·25
28/39		*Set of 12*	..	..	11·00	7·00

The 10 c. and 20 c. exist with figures widely spaced.

1911. *POSTAGE DUE. Postage Due stamps of France surch as* **T** *7*

D40	D **11**	5 c. on 5 c. pale blue (R.)	..	70	70
		a. 2 dots under figure	..	60·00	50·00
D41		10 c. on 10 c. pale brown (R.)	..	1·90	1·90
		a. 2 dots under figures	..	60·00	50·00
		b. Surch double	..	..	22·00	
D42		50 c. on 50 c. deep purple (B.)	..	2·50	2·50

1911. *POSTAGE DUE. Postage Due stamps of France, (Recouvrements), surch as T* **7**.

D43	D **19**	1 c. on 1 c. olive (R.)	..	25	25
D44		10 c. OR 10 c. violet (R.)	..	1·00	1·00
D45		30 c. on 30 c. bistre (R.)	..	1·25	1·25
D46		50 c. on 50 c. red (B.)	..	2·25	2·25
D43/46		*Set of 4*	..	..	4·25	4·25

B. SHERIFIAN POST

400 Moussonats = 1 Rial

The Sherifian (or Imperial) Post began in 1892, using various octagonal cachets for the various towns, but did not issue stamps until 1912. These were in use throughout Morocco until 1915, and in Tangier until 1919.

1 Aissouas Mosque, Tangier

(Des P. Legat. Litho Lecocq Mathorel and Chr. Bernard)

1912–13. *P* 11.

(a) Narrow margins. White paper (25.5.12)

1	**1**	1 m. light grey	..	..	..	95	75
2		2 m. lilac	..	..	..	95	75
3		5 m. bluish green	..	..	..	1·25	60
4		10 m. vermilion	..	..	..	1·90	60
5		25 m. blue	..	..	..	2·50	1·25
6		50 m. slate-purple	..	..	..	3·75	1·25
1/6		*Set of 6*	..	..	..	10·00	4·75

(b) Wide margins. Tinted paper (1913)

7	**1**	1 m. grey	..	..	..	15	15
8		2 m. brown-lilac	..	..	..	15	15
9		5 m. bluish green	..	..	..	30	30
10		10 m. vermilion	..	..	..	30	30
11		25 m. blue	..	..	..	80	80
12		50 m. slate-purple	..	..	..	80	80
7/12		*Set of 6*	..	..	..	2·10	2·10

The 2 m. exists with and without name of engraver at foot, the 5 m. and 10 m. always have the engraver's name and the rest are without it.

1913. *No. 6 surch in figures.*

| 13 | **1** | 05 on 50 m. slate-purple | .. | |
| 14 | | 0.10 on 50 m. slate-purple | .. | |

C. FRENCH PROTECTORATE

100 Centimes = 1 Franc

Sultan Mulay Hafid abdicated on 11 August 1912. He was succeeded by Sultan Mulay Yusuf, who died on 17 November 1927. The real ruler of the country was the French resident-general from 1912 to 1925, General (from 1921 Marshal) Louis Lyautey, whose achievement was to preserve the best Moroccan traditions whilst developing economic resources and pacifying unruly tribesmen. On 17 November 1927 Sultan Sidi Mohammed ben Yusuf was appointed Sultan. He became a supporter of the nationalist Istaqlal party which arose in 1944, and in 1953 was exiled. From 21 August 1953 to 30 October 1955 the pro-French Sidi Mohammed ben Arafa was Sultan.

PRINTERS. All the stamps of the French Protectorate were printed at the Government Printing Works, Paris, *unless otherwise stated.*

IMPERFORATE STAMPS. Many stamps exist imperforate in their issued colours but they were not valid for postage. Imperforate stamps in other colours are colour trials.

PROTECTORAT FRANÇAIS

PROTECTORAT FRANÇAIS

(8*a*)

(8*b*)

1914 (1 Aug)**–21.** *Stamps of French Post Offices surch as T* **7** *or* **8** *(peseta values), in blue or red and further optd with T* **8***a* *T* **4/5**) *or* **8***b* (*T* **6**), *in black.*

40	**4**	1 c. on 1 c. grey (R.)	..	..	10	5
		a. Slate (R.) (1921)	..	..	8	5
41		2 c. on 2 c. claret (B.)	..	..	5	5
42		3 c. on 3 c. orange (B.)	..	..	15	15
43		5 c. on 5 c. blue-green (R.)	..	..	5	5
		a. Imperf (pair)	..	..	50·00	
		b. T **7** omitted	..	..	55·00	55·00
44	**5**	10 c. on 10 c. carmine (B.)	..	..	5	5
		a. T **7** omitted	..	..	85·00	85·00
45		15 c. on 15 c. orange (B.) (1917)	..	5	5
		a. T **7** omitted	..	..	15·00	15·00
46		20 c. on 20 c. purple-brown (B.)	..	95	50
		a. "ROTECTORAT"	..	..	16·00	
		b. T **8***a* double	..	..	60·00	60·00
47		25 c. on 25 c. blue (R.)	..	..	25	5
		a. "ROTECTORAT"	..	..	16·00	
		b. T **7** omitted	..	..	50·00	50·00
48		25 c. on 25 c. violet-brown (B.) (1921)	15	5
		a. T **8***a* omitted	..	..	8·00	8·00
		b. T **8***a* double	..	..	32·00	32·00
		c. T **8***a* double (Bk. + R.)	..	..	28·00	28·00
49		30 c. on 30 c. violet-brown (B.) (1921)	2·75	2·75

50	**5**	35 c. on 35 c. lilac (R.)		1·10	40
51	**6**	40 c. on 40 c. rose and blue (B.) (1917)		3·25	1·90
		a. T **7** omitted		55·00	55·00
52		45 c. on 45 c. green and blue (R.) (1921)		9·00	7·00
53		50 c. on 50 c. brown and lavender (R.)		15	5
		a. T **8**a inverted		22·00	16·00
54		1 p. lake and yellow-green (B.)		30	5
		a. T **8** double		28·00	28·00
		b. T **8** double, one inverted		28·00	28·00
		c. T **8**b inverted		65·00	60·00
55		2 p. deep lilac and buff (R.)		75	25
		a. T **8** omitted		30·00	30·00
		b. T **8**b omitted		19·00	19·00
		c. T **8**b double		28·00	28·00
56		5 p. deep blue and buff (R.)		2·50	1·00

40/56 Set of 17 .. .. 19·00 13·00

The 10 c. and 20 c. exist with figures widely spaced.
Nos. 40/48 and 50 exist with inverted "S" in "FRANÇAIS".
Several values were reprinted in 1918 on greyish "G.C." paper.

1914–17. Red Cross Fund. Stamps of French Post Offices surcharged.

(9)	(10)	(10a)	(11)

(a) Oudjda issue. No. 32 handstamped with T **9**, in carmine
57 **5** 10 c.+5 c. carmine (9.14) .. £400 £325
This was applied in fugitive ink by a locally-made wooden handstamp.

T **10**. Cross composed of four pieces of printer's metal, two horizontal, two vertical.
T **11**. Cross composed of three pieces of printer's metal, one horizontal, two vertical.

(b) No. 32 surch with T **10** (inverted), in carmine
58 **5** 10 c.+5 c. carmine (9.14) .. £4000 £3500
This only exists with the surcharge inverted, a pane of 25 of No. 32 having been included with the supply of No. 44 used for making No. 59.

(c) No. 44 surch with T **10**, in carmine
59 **5** 10 c.+5 c. carmine (9.14) .. 65 65
    a. "5" with small straight top .. 6·50 5·00
    b. "c" omitted .. 11·00 11·00
    c. Surch double .. 18·00 18·00
    d. Surch double, one inverted .. 25·00 23·00
    e. Surch inverted .. 25·00 25·00

(d) No. 44 surch with T **10**a
60 **5** 10 c.+5 c. carmine (Verm.) (3.15) .. 3·25 3·25
    a. "5" with small straight top .. 9·00 7·00
    b. Surch double .. 23·00 20·00
    c. Surch double, one inverted .. 25·00 23·00
    d. Surch inverted .. 28·00 23·00
61 10 c.+5 c. carmine (C.) (9.15) .. 65·00 65·00
No. 61 was sold mainly in Casablanca.

(e) As No. 43 but without T **7**, surch with T **11**, in carmine
62 **4** 5 c.+5 c. blue-green (9.15) .. 45 40
This stamp without the red cross surcharge was never issued, except as an error of No. 43 (No. 43b).
The widely spaced "10" varieties occur on Nos. 59/61 and the inverted "S" on No. 60.

MAROC
مراكش

(12)	13	(14)

(f) Tangier issue. Red Cross stamp of France optd with T **12**, in black
63 **20** 10 c.+5 c. brick-red (13.3.15) .. 1·25 1·25

(g) Optd in black with T **8**a as in T **13**
64 **13** 10 c.+5 c. carmine (9.15) .. 50 50

(h) No. 32 surch with T **14**, in very deep red
65 **5** 10 c.+5 c. carmine (1917) .. 50 50
No. 65 was surcharged on a new printing in sheets of 150 containing no varieties. Earlier surcharges were made on panes of 25 with slight variations in the settings.

1915. POSTAGE DUE. Postage Due stamps of France surch as T **7** in blue or red and further optd with T **8**a, in black.

D66	D **11**	1 c. on 1 c. black (R.)		5	5
		a. T **7** double		25·00	
D67		5 c. on 5 c. pale blue (R.)		15	15
		a. T **8**a double		28·00	
D68		10 c. on 10 c. pale brown (R.)		30	30
		a. "ROTECTORAT"		8·00	5·50
D69		20 c. on 20 c. olive-green (R.)		30	30
D70		30 c. on 30 c. carmine (B.)		80	80
D71		50 c. on 50 c. deep purple (B.)		1·50	70

D66/71 Set of 6 .. .. 2·75 2·00
The widely spaced figure varieties exist on the 10 c. and 20 c. and all values occur with the inverted "S" variety. All values were reprinted on the greyish "G.C." paper.

1915. POSTAGE DUE. Postage Due stamps of France (Recouvrements), surch as T **7** in blue or red and further optd with T **8**a, in black.

D72	D **19**	1 c. on 1 c. olive (R.)		12	12
D73		10 c. on 10 c. violet (R.)		50	35
D74		30 c. on 30 c. bistre (R.)		50	40
D75		50 c. on 50 c. red (B.)		60	45

D72/75 Set of 4 .. .. 1·50 1·10
All values occur with the inverted "S" variety.

15 Tower of Hassan, Rabat	16 Fez

17 Chella	18 Marrakesh

19 Meknès	20 Volubilis

(Des J. de la Nézière. Eng A. Mignon (T **15**/16), A. Dezarrois (T **17**), A. Delzers (T **18**), C. Coppier (T **19**). Recess A. Oelzer & Co, Morocco)

1917 (1 Sept). P 13½×14 (vert) or 14×13½ (horiz).
76 **15** 1 c. grey-black .. 5 5
77 2 c. dull purple .. 10 5
78 3 c. chestnut .. 8 8

79	16	5 c. yellow-green				5	5
80		10 c. carmine-red				5	5
81		15 c. slate				5	5
82	17	20 c. dull claret				85	85
83		25 c. deep blue				75	10
84		30 c. deep lilac				90	60
85	18	35 c. orange				65	40
86		40 c. ultramarine				20	10
87		45 c. blue-green				3·75	2·25
88	19	50 c. chocolate				1·40	80
89		1 f. bluish slate				1·60	85
90	20	2 f. sepia				55·00	30·00
91		5 f. blackish green				11·00	9·00
92		10 f. black-brown				11·00	9·50
76/92		Set of 17				80·00	50·00

See also Nos. 123/48.

D 21   P 21

(Des J. de la Nézière. Eng C. Crespelle. Typo)

1917 (Sept)–**26.** POSTAGE DUE. P 14×13½.

D 93	D 21	1 c. black			5	5
D 94		5 c. blue			5	5
D 95		10 c. brown			5	5
D 96		20 c. green			30	20
D 97		30 c. red			5	5
D 98		50 c. chocolate			5	5
D 99		1 f. claret/straw (27.7.26)			12	10
D100		2 f. bright violet (27.7.26)			30	12
D93/100		Set of 8			90	60

See also Nos. D308/15 and D162/5 of Morocco.

(Des J. de la Nézière. Eng C. Crespelle. Typo)

1917. PARCEL POST. P 13½×14.

P101	P 21	5 c. green			12	8
P102		10 c. carmine			15	10
P103		20 c. red-brown			15	10
P104		25 c. blue			25	15
P105		40 c. brown			40	15
P106		50 c. red			70	15
P107		75 c. slate			75	45
P108		1 f. ultramarine			1·00	10
P109		2 f. grey			1·50	12
P110		5 f. violet			2·00	15
P111		10 f. black			2·50	15
P101/111		Set of 11			8·50	1·50

22 Aeroplane over Casablanca   **23** Ploughing with Camel and Donkey

Three Types of Imprint

I. Thick frame-line; "Helio-Vaugirard" hyphenated.
II. Thin frame-line; "Helio-Vaugirard" hyphenated.
III. Thin frame-line; "Helio Vaugirard" without hyphen and more widely spaced.

(Des J. de la Nézière. Photo Vaugirard)

1922 (1 Jan)–**27.** AIR. P 13½.

112	22	5 c. orange (III) (1.27)			5	5
113		25 c. ultramarine (II) (1.1.23)			12	8
		a. Type I			20	20
114		50 c. greenish blue (II) (1.1.23)			5	5
		a. Type I			25	20
115		75 c. blue (I)			16·00	3·00
116		75 c. green (III) (8.11.22)			5	5
		a. Type I			15	5
117		80 c. purple-brown (III) (1.27)			25	10
118		1 f. vermilion (I)			5	5
		a. Type I			2·00	15
119		1 f. 40, lake (III) (1.27)			30	20
120		1 f. 90, blue (III) (1.27)			40	30
121		2 f. violet (I)			25	15
		a. Blackish violet (I)			25	20
122		3 f. greenish black (III) (1.27)			45	25
112/122		Set of 11			15·00	3·75

(Photo Vaugirard)

1923 (Aug)–**27.** As 1917 types but printed in photogravure with imprint below design. P 13½.

123	15	1 c. grey-olive			5	5
124		2 c. claret			5	5
		a. Purple-brown (1.27)			5	5
125		3 c. yellow-brown			5	5
126	16	5 c. yellow			5	5
127		10 c. green			5	5
128		15 c. black			5	5
129	17	20 c. plum			5	5
130		20 c. claret (1.27)			10	10
131		25 c. light blue			5	5
132		30 c. scarlet			5	5
133		30 c. Prussian blue (1.27)			15	5
134	18	35 c. purple			5	5
		a. Greyish purple (1.27)			15	15
135		40 c. red-orange			5	5
136		45 c. green			5	5
137	19	50 c. greenish blue			5	5
138	18	50 c. blackish green (10.27)			12	5
139	19	60 c. mauve			8	5
140		75 c. pale dull purple (1.27)			12	12
		a. Claret (11.27)			8	8
141		1 f. brown			10	8
142		1 f. 05, purple-brown (1.27)			30	25
143		1 f. 40, carmine-rose (1.27)			10	10
144		1 f. 50, Prussian blue (1.27)			15	5
145	20	2 f. brown			25	20
146		3 f. brown-red (1.27)			25	25
147		5 f. deep green			80	50
148		10 f. black-brown			2·25	1·40
123/148		Set of 26			5·00	3·50

(Des Marchisio from photographs by Flandrin. Photo Vaugirard)

1928 (26 July). AIR. Flood Relief Fund. T 23 and similar horiz designs. P 13½.

149		5 c. blue			95	95
150		25 c. vermilion			95	95
151		50 c. scarlet			95	95
152		75 c. orange-brown			95	95
153		80 c. green			95	95
154		1 f. orange			95	95
155		1 f. 50, blue			95	95
156		2 f. chocolate			95	95
157		3 f. purple			95	95
158		5 f. grey-black			95	95
149/158		Set of 10			8·50	8·50

Sold at double face value.

Designs:—5 c. Moorish tribesmen; 25 c. Moor ploughing with camel and donkey; 50 c. Caravan nearing Safi; 75 c. Walls of Marrakesh; 80 c. Sheep grazing at Azrou; 1 f. Gateway at Fez; 1 f. 50, Aerial view of Tangier; 2 f. Aerial view of Casablanca; 3 f. Storks at Rabat; 5 f. "La Hedia", a Moorish entertainment.

STAMP MONTHLY

—finest and most informative magazine for all collectors. Obtainable from your newsagent or by postal subscription—details on request.

Designs: *Horiz*—1 c., 2 c. Sultan's Palace, Tangier (*a*), 3 c. to 5 c. Agadir Bay (*b*); 10 c. to 20 c. G.P.O., Casablanca (*c*); 25 c. to 40 c. Moulay Idriss (*d*); 45 c. to 65 c. Rabat (*e*); 1 f. 50 to 3 f. Ouarzazat (*c*). *Vert*—75 c. to 1 f. 25, Attarine College, Fez (*f*); 5 f. to 20 f. Saadian tombs, Marrakesh (*d*).

15ᶜ 15ᶜ 50ᶜ 50ᶜ

(24) (25)

1929 (29 Dec). *No.* 135 *surch with T* 24.
163 **18** 15 c. on 40 c. red-orange 25 25

1931 (Feb–Dec). *Stamps of* 1923–27 *surch as T* 25, *in blue.*
164 **17** 25 c. on 30 c. Prussian blue (Dec) .. 50 50
   a. Surch inverted .. .. .. 18·00 16·00
165 **19** 50 c. on 60 c. greenish mauve .. 12 5
   a. Surch inverted .. .. .. 20·00 16·00
166   1 f. on 1 f. 40, carmine-rose .. 50 30
   a. Surch inverted .. .. .. 20·00 16·00

29 Hassan Tower,   30 Marshal Lyautey
Rabat

(Des R. Belliot. Eng A. Delzers (50 c. to 1 f. 50) and A. Mignon. Recess)

1933 (1 Jan). *AIR. T* 29 *and similar type. P* 13.
193 **29** 50 c. blue 12 10
194   80 c. brown 10 5
195   1 f. 50, lake 10 5
196 – 2 f. 50, carmine .. .. 1·00 12
197 – 5 f. bright violet 60 40
198 – 10 f. blue-green 25 20
193/198 *Set of* 6 .. .. .. 2·00 85
Design:—2 f. 50 to 10 f. Casablanca.

1fr

(26)

1931 (Feb). *AIR. Nos.* 119/20 *surch as T* 26.
167 **22** 1 f. on 1 f. 40, lake (B.) 40 40
   a. Surch inverted .. .. 75·00 75·00
168   1 f. 50 on 1 f. 90, blue 40 40

(Des J. de la Nézière. Photo Vaugirard)

1935 (15 May). *Lyautey Memorial Fund. T* 30 *and similar type. P* 13½. (*a*) *POSTAGE.*
199 **30** 50 c. +50 c. orange-vermilion .. 2·50 2·50
200   1 f. +1 f. green .. .. 2·50 2·50
201   5 f. +5 f. brown .. .. 13·00 13·00
  (*b*) *AIR. Inscr* "POSTE AÉRIENNE"
202 – 1 f. 50 +1 f. 50, blue .. .. 6·50 5·50
199/202 *Set of* 4 .. .. .. 22·00 30·00
Design: *Horiz*—1 f. 50 Miniature profile portrait of Marshal Lyautey.

27 Sultan's Palace,   28 Saadian Tombs,
Tangier   Marrakesh

(Des R. Belliot. Eng A. Mignon (*a*), C. Hourriez (*b*), H. Cheffer (*c*), A. Delzers (*d*), A. Dezarrois (*e*) and J. Piel (*f*). Recess)

1933 (1 Jan)–**34**. *Views and frames as T* 27/8. *P* 13.
169   1 c. grey-black 5 5
170   2 c. magenta 5 5
171   3 c. chocolate 5 5
172   5 c. brown-lake 5 5
173 10 c. blue-green 5 5
174 15 c. black 5 5
175 20 c. maroon 5 5
176 25 c. blue 8 5
177 30 c. emerald-green 8 5
178 40 c. sepia 8 5
179 45 c. purple 5 5
180 50 c. deep blue-green 8 5
181 65 c. red 5 5
182 75 c. purple 5 5
183 90 c. vermilion 5 5
184   1 f. chocolate 20 5
185   1 f. 25, grey-black (9.34) .. 25 5
186   1 f. 50, deep ultramarine .. 10 5
187   1 f. 75, deep blue-green (9.34) .. 5 5
188   2 f. brown 60 5
189   3 f. carmine .. .. .. 9·50 1·60
190   5 f. brown-lake .. .. 1·25 25
191 10 f. black .. .. .. 1·75 1·40
192 20 f. slate-blue .. .. 2·00 1·60
169/192 *Set of* 24 .. .. .. 15·00 5·00

O.S.E.
+2ᶜ

(31 "Oeuvres Sociales de l'Enfance")

1938 (14 Mar). *Child Welfare Fund. Stamps of* 1933/34 *surch as T* 31. (*a*) *POSTAGE. As T* 27/8.
203   2 c. +2 c. magenta (B.) .. .. 1·10 1·10
204   3 c. +3 c. chocolate (B.) .. 1·10 1·10
205 20 c. +20 c. maroon (B.) .. 1·10 1·10
206 40 c. +40 c. sepia (R.) .. .. 1·10 1·10
207 65 c. +65 c. red (B.) .. .. 1·10 1·10
208   1 f. 25 +1 f. 25, grey-black (R.) .. 1·10 1·10
209   2 f. +2 f. brown (B.) .. .. 1·10 1·10
210   5 f. +5 f. brown-lake (B.) .. 1·10 1·10
  (*b*) *AIR. As T* 29
211 50 c. +50 c. blue (R.) .. .. 1·25 1·25
212 10 f. +10 f. blue-green (R.) .. 1·25 1·25
203/212 *Set of* 10 .. .. .. 10·00 10·00

40ᶜ

(32)

1939 (Feb). *No.* 180 *surch with T* 32.
213 40 c. on 50 c. deep blue-green (R.) .. 5 5

33 Mosque at Sefrou   34 Mosque at Salé   35 Horseman and Cedar-tree

36 Shepherd and Arganier Trees   37 Ramparts at Salé

38 Gazelles   39 Draa Valley

40 Fez   41 Storks and Minaret, Chella

42 Aeroplane over Morocco

(Des Quesnel (T **33**), H. Hourtal (T **34**), C. Josso (T **35**/**7**, **42**), A. Vaur (T **38**, **41**), J. Hainaut (T **39**), J. E. Laurent (T **40**). Eng. A. Ouvré (T **33**), G. Barlangue (T **34**), P. Gandon (T **35**/**7**, **42**), H. Cheffer (T **38**/**9**, **41**), J. Piel (T **40**). Recess)

1939 (17 July)–42. *P* 13. (*a*) *POSTAGE*.

214	**34**	1 c. purple				5	5
215	**33**	2 c. emerald-green				5	5
216		3 c. ultramarine				5	5

217	**34**	5 c. green				5	5
218	**33**	10 c. bright purple				5	5
219	**35**	15 c. green				5	5
220		20 c. sepia				5	5
221	**36**	30 c. blue				5	5
222		40 c. brown				5	5
223		45 c. blue-green				10	10
224	**37**	50 c. carmine				15	12
225		50 c. blue-green (1940)				5	5
226		60 c. greenish blue				20	12
227		60 c. brown (1940)				5	5
228	**38**	70 c. violet				5	5
229	**39**	75 c. slate-green				5	5
230		80 c. greenish blue (1940)				5	5
231		80 c. green (31.7.42)				5	5
232	**37**	90 c. ultramarine				5	5
233	**35**	1 f. brown				5	5
234	**39**	1 f. 20, purple (1942)				5	5
235		1 f. 25, brown-red				10	5
236	**37**	1 f. 40, purple				5	5
237		1 f. 50, brown-red (1940)				5	5
238		1 f. 50, rose (31.7.42)				5	5
239	**40**	2 f. blue-green				5	5
240		2 f. 25, bright blue				5	5
241	**34**	2 f. 40, scarlet (31.7.42)				5	5
242		2 f. 50, scarlet				10	8
243		2 f. 50, ultramarine (1940)				10	5
244	**40**	3 f. purple-brown				5	5
245	**34**	4 f. deep blue (31.7.42)				5	5
246	**39**	4 f. 50, slate-green (1942)				5	5
247	**38**	5 f. grey-blue				8	5
248		10 f. scarlet				15	15
249		15 f. grey-green (1942)				90	90
250		20 f. brown-purple				30	30
214/250		*Set of 37*				3·25	3·00

For typographed issue, see Nos. 291/307.

(*b*) *AIR*

251	**41**	80 c. blue-green				5	5
252		1 f. red-brown				5	5
253	**42**	1 f. 90, ultramarine				5	5
254		2 f. bright purple (22.3.40)				5	5
255		3 f. brown				5	5
256	**41**	5 f. bright violet				25	25
257	**42**	10 f. greenish blue				15	15
251/257		*Set of 7*				60	60

35⁰

(43)

1940. *Alternate horizontal rows of No.* 181 *surch with T* **43**.

258	35 c. on 65 c. red			30	15
	a. In pair with No. 181			50	40

Enfants de France au Maroc

+4 ᶠ

(44)   45 Allegories of Victory

1942 (Jan). *Fund for French Child Refugees in Morocco. As* 1939–42, *but surch as T* **44**.

259	**36**	45 c.+2 f. blue-green				95	95
260	**37**	90 c.+4 f. ultramarine				95	95
261	**39**	1 f. 25+6 f. brown-red				95	95
262	**34**	2 f. 50+8 f. scarlet				95	95
259/262		*Set of 4*				3·50	3·50

(Des L. Fernez, after Rude. Die eng C. Hervé. Litho Victor Heintz, Algiers)

1943. *P* 12.

263	**45**	1 f. 50, blue				5	5

46 Tower of Hassan

47 Aeroplane over Desert

(D 48)

(Eng C. Hervé. Litho Victor Heintz, Algiers)

1943–44. P 11½ or 12.

264	46	10 c. rose-lilac				5	5
265		30 c. blue				5	5
266		40 c. lake				5	5
267		50 c. blue-green				5	5
268		60 c. purple-brown				5	5
269		70 c. lilac				5	5
270		80 c. grey-green				5	5
271		1 f. carmine-lake				5	5
272		1 f. 20, violet				5	5
273		1 f. 50, red				5	5
274		2 f. pale blue-green				5	5
275		2 f. 40, carmine-rose				5	5
276		3 f. olive-brown				5	5
277		4 f. ultramarine				5	5
278		4 f. 50, slate-black				5	5
279		5 f. blue				5	5
280		10 f. orange-brown				10	10
281		15 f. slate-green				25	25
282		20 f. brown-purple				25	5
264/282		Set of 19				1·25	90

(Des R. Imbert and L. Schultz. Litho Lugat, Casablanca)

1944. AIR. P 11½.

283	47	50 c. blue-green				5	5
284		2 f. ultramarine				5	5
285		5 f. red				8	8
286		10 f. violet				8	8
287		50 f. black				25	25
288		100 f. blue and red				60	60
283/288		Set of 6				1·00	1·00

1944. POSTAGE DUE. Surch as Type D 48.

D289	D 21	50 c. on 30 c. red			65	65
D290		1 f. on 10 c. brown			95	75
D291		3 f. on 10 c. brown			2·00	1·50

ENTR'AIDE FRANÇAISE

+98ᶠ50

(48)

49 Aeroplane over Minarets

1944. AIR. Mutual Aid Fund. Surch with T 48.

289 47 1 f. 50+98 f. 50, red and blue .. 35 35

(Des C. Josso. Eng P. Gandon. Recess)

1945 (1 Sept). AIR. P 13.

290 49 50 f. purple-brown 25 25

(Designers as for Nos. 214/250. Die eng H. Cortot. Typo)

1945–47. As types of 1939–42, but designs redrawn slightly smaller and "CORTOT" at foot. P 13½×14 (vert) or 14×13½ (horiz).

291	33	10 c. lilac			5	5
292	36	40 c. chocolate			5	5
293	37	50 c. grey-green			5	5
294	35	1 f. chocolate (1946)			5	5
295	39	1 f. 20, purple-brown (1946)			5	5
296	33	1 f. 30, greenish blue (1947)			10	10
297	37	1 f. 50, red			5	5
298	40	2 f. grey-green			5	5
299		3 f. purple-brown			5	5
300	36	3 f. 50, brown-red (1947)			10	8
301	38	4 f. 50, magenta (6.2.47)			5	5
302		5 f. indigo			10	8
303	39	6 f. blue (1946)			5	5
304	38	10 f. red			20	20
305		15 f. grey-green			30	12
306		20 f. brown-purple			50	50
307		25 f. blackish brown			45	45
291/307		Set of 17			2·00	1·60

1945–52. POSTAGE DUE. As Type D 21 but with thinner figures. Typo. P 14×13½.

D308	D 21	1 f. brown-lake (1947)			15	12
D309		2 f. bright violet (1947)			20	12
D310		3 f. ultramarine			8	5
D311		4 f. orange			8	5
D312		5 f. yellow-green			15	5
D313		10 f. yellow-bistre			15	5
D314		20 f. carmine (1950)			30	20
D315		30 f. sepia (17.10.52)			50	40
D308/315		Set of 8			1·40	95

See also Nos. D162/5 of Morocco.

AIDEZ

LES

TUBERCULEUX

+1ᶠ

(50)

51 Mausoleum

1945. Anti-tuberculosis Fund. No. 298 surch with T 50.

308 40 2 f.+1 f. grey-green 5 5

(Des C. Josso. Eng Flandrin and Vechke. Recess)

1945. Solidarity Fund, Marshal Lyautey's Mausoleum. P 11½.

309 51 2 f.+3 f. blue 5 5
 a. Ultramarine 15 15

3ᶠ

+5ʳ

18 Juin 1940

18 Juin 1948

(52)

(53)

1946 (6 Apr). No. 308 surch with T 52.

310 40 3 f. on 2 f.+1 f. grey-green (R.) .. 5 5

1946 (18 June). AIR. Sixth Anniv of De Gaulle's Call to Arms. No. 285 surch with T 53.

311 47 5 f.+5 f. scarlet 15 15

A regular new issue supplement to this catalogue appears each month in

STAMP MONTHLY

—from your newsagent or by postal subscription
—details on request.

+5F50

54 Marshal Lyautey   (55)
Statue, Casablanca

61 The Gardens, Fez

62 Barracks in
the Oasis

(Des F. Cogne. Eng Flandrin and Vechke. Recess)

1946 (16 Dec). *Solidarity Fund. P* 13. (*a*) *POSTAGE.*
312 **54**   2 f.+10 f. black   30   30
313   3 f.+15 f. brown-red   35   35
314   10 f.+20 f. bright blue   70   70

   (*b*) *AIR. Inscr* "POSTE AERIENNE"
315 **54** 10 f.+30 f. green   40   40
312/315 *Set of 4*   1·60   1·60

(Des A. Vaur. Eng H. Cheffer. Design recess, surch typo)

1947 (15 Mar). *Stamp Day. Surch with T* **55** *in same colour as stamp. P* 13.
316 **38**   4 f. 50+5 f. 50, magenta   30   30

63 Todra Valley   **64** Moulay Idriss

56 Coastline and Symbols of Prosperity

65 La Medina Barracks   **66** Oudayas Kasbah, Rabat

1947. *25th Anniv of Establishment of Sherifian Phosphates Office. Recess. P* 13.
317 **56**   4 f. 50+5 f. 50, green   15   15

(Des C. Josso. Eng P. Gandon. Recess Lugat, Casablanca)

1947–54. *P* 13. (*a*) *POSTAGE.*
318 **57** 10 c. sepia   5   5
319   30 c. red-orange   5   5
320   30 c. violet (1948)   5   5
321   50 c. greenish blue   5   5
322   60 c. bright purple   5   5
323 **58**   1 f. black   5   5
324   1 f. 50, light blue   5   5
325 **59**   2 f. bright green   8   5
325*a* **58**   2 f. brown-purple (3.49)   5   5
326 **59**   3 f. brown-lake   5   5
327 **60**   4 f. violet   5   5
328   4 f. green (1948)   5   5
329 **61**   5 f. green   12   8
329*a* —   5 f. emerald-green (22.4.49)   8   5
330 **60**   6 f. vermilion   5   5
330*a* **61**   8 f. yellow-orange (3.49)   10   5
331   10 f. blue (10.47)   8   5
332   10 f. light blue (1948)   12   5
332*a* **62** 10 f. rose-carmine (12.48)   12   5
333 **58** 12 f. scarlet (1948)   15   5
334 **62** 15 f. green (10.47)   20   8
334*a* — 15 f. scarlet (12.4.49)   15   5
335 **62** 18 f. deep ultramarine (1948)   20   15
336   20 f. brown-red (10.47)   15   5
337   25 f. violet (10.47)   40   12
337*a* — 25 f. ultramarine (12.4.49)   30   5
337*b* — 25 f. deep reddish violet (1954)   25   15
337*c* **63** 30 f. blue (15.7.51)   30   8
337*d*   35 f. brown-lake (5.50)   25   5
337*e*   50 f. indigo (5.50)   25   5
318/337*e* *Set of 30*   3·50   1·75

   (*b*) *AIR*
338 **64**   9 f. carmine   8   5
339   40 f. indigo   20   5
340   50 f. brown-purple (10.47)   25   5
341 **65** 100 f. greenish blue   75   20
342   200 f. orange-red   1·25   40

57 The Terraces

58 Coastal Fortress

59 Barracks on the
Mountains

60 Marrakesh

342a **66** 300 f. violet (22.5.51) .. .. 6·00 3·50
338/342a Set of 6 .. .. 7·50 3·75
Designs: Horiz—No. 329a, Fortified oasis; Nos. 334a and 337a/b, Walled City.

67 "Energy"   **68** Marshal Lyautey's Mausoleum

(Des C. Josso. Eng P. Gandon. Recess Lugat, Casablanca)

1948 (9 Feb). Solidarity Fund. T **67** and similar designs inscr "SOLIDARITE 1947". P 13. (a) POSTAGE.
343 6 f.+9 f. brown-red 40 40
344 10 f.+20 f. blue 40 40

(b) AIR. Inscr "POSTE AÉRIENNE"
345 9 f.+16 f. green 45 45
346 20 f.+35 f. brown 45 45
343/346 Set of 4 .. .. .. 1·50 1·50
Designs: Vert—10 f. Red Cross unit ("Health"). Horiz—9 f. Ship at quayside and aeroplane ("Supplies"); 20 f. Aeroplane over landscape ("Agriculture").

1948 (6 Mar). Stamp Day. Inscr "JOURNÉE DU TIMBRE 1948". Recess. P 13.
347 **19** 6 f.+4 f. red-brown 25 25

(Des C. Josso. Eng P. Gandon. Recess)

1948 (18 May). AIR. Lyautey Exhibition, Paris. P 13.
348 **68** 10 f.+25 f. green 30 30

69 P.T.T. Clubhouse, Ifrane   **70** Warship and Coastline

(Des G. Goupil. Eng Barlangue. Recess)

1948 (7 June). AIR. P.T.T. Employees' Holiday Camp Fund. P 13.
349 **69** 6 f.+34 f. blue-green 45 45
350 9 f.+51 f. brown-lake 45 45

(Des C. Josso. Eng P. Gandon. Recess Lugat, Casablanca)

1948 (Aug). Naval Charities. P 13.
351 **70** 6 f.+9 f. violet 40 40

1948 (1 Dec). No. 250 such as T **52**, in red.
352 **38** 8 f. on 20 f. brown-purple 12 10

72 Wheat and View of Meknès

(Postage. Des and eng Josso. Air. Des Josso. Eng Gandon. Recess Lugat, Casablanca)

1949 (12 Apr). Solidarity Fund. T **72** and similar designs inscr "SOLIDARITÉ 1948". P 13. (a) POSTAGE.
353 1 f.+2 f. yellow-orange 20 20
354 2 f.+5 f. carmine 20 20
355 3 f.+7 f. greenish blue 20 20
356 5 f.+10 f. purple 20 20
MS356a 120×96 mm. Nos. 353/6 .. 3·75 3·75

(b) AIR. Inscr "POSTE AÉRIENNE"
357 5 f.+5 f. green 30 30
358 6 f.+9 f. scarlet 30 30
359 9 f.+16 f. brown-purple 30 30
360 15 f.+25 f. indigo 30 30
353/360 Set of 8 .. .. .. 1·75 1·75
MS360a 96×120 mm. Nos. 357/60 .. 3·75 3·75
Designs: Postage (horiz)—2 f. Olive grove and Taroudant; 3 f. Fishing scene and coastal town; 5 f. Plums and Aguedal gardens, Marrakesh. Air (vert)—Aeroplane over Agadir (5 f.); Fez (6 f.), Atlas valley (9 f.) and Draa valley (15 f.).

74 Gazelle Hunter   **75** Soldiers with Flag

(Des and eng Cortot. Recess Lugat, Casablanca)

1949 (1 May). Stamp Day and 50th Anniv of Mazagan-Marrakesh Local Stamp. P 13.
361 **74** 10 f.+5 f. carmine and brown-purple 25 25

(Des Delpy. Eng Serres. Recess Lugat, Casablanca)

1949. Army Welfare Fund. P 13.
362 **75** 10 f.+10 f. scarlet 30 30

76 Oudayas   **77** Nejjarine   **78** Gardens
Gate, Rabat   Fountain, Fez   at Meknès

(Des Delpy. Eng Feltesse (T **76**), Serres (T **77**) and Dufresne (T **78**). Recess)

1949 (July). P 14×13.
363 **76** 10 c. black 5 5
364 50 c. brown-lake 8 8
365 1 f. violet 5 5
366 **77** 2 f. carmine 5 5
367 3 f. deep blue 5 5
368 5 f. emerald-green 8 5
369 **78** 8 f. blue-green 10 5
370 10 f. scarlet 10 5
363/370 Set of 8 .. .. .. 50 35

ALBUM LISTS
Write for our latest lists of albums and accessories.
These will be sent free on request.

388	33	1 f. on 1 f. 30, greenish blue (B.)	..	5	5
389	60	5 f. on 6 f. vermilion (3.51)	..'	5	5
387/389		Set of 3	..	10	8

79 Post Office, Meknès

80 Aeroplane over Globe

84 General Leclerc

85 New Hospital, Meknès

(Des Goupil. Eng Piel. Recess Lugat, Casablanca)

1949 (3 Oct). 75th Anniv of U.P.U. P 13.

371	79	5 f. green	..	..	..	40	40
372		15 f. carmine ..	..	..	..	50	50
373		25 f. blue	..	..	..	70	70

(Des Perrot. Recess)

1950 (11 Mar). AIR. Stamp Day and 25th Anniv of First Mail Flight from Casablanca to Dakar. Air route in red. P 13.

| 374 | 80 | 15 f.+10 f. green and greenish blue | .. | 30 | 30 |

81 Carpets

83 Ruins of Sala-Colonia (Chella)

(Postage: Des Delpy, eng Delpy (1 f.), Serres (2 f.), Piel (3 f.) and Dufresne (5 f.). Air: Des and eng Josso. Recess)

1950 (11 Apr). Solidarity Fund. Various designs as T. 81 inscr "SOLIDARITE 1949". P 13. (a) POSTAGE.

375	1 f.+2 f. crimson	..	..	..	45	45
376	2 f.+5 f. greenish blue	..	..	45	45
377	3 f.+7 f. reddish violet	..	..	45	45
378	5 f.+10 f. red-brown	..	..	45	45
MS378a	96×120 mm. Nos. 375/8	..	3·75	3·75

(b) AIR. Inscr "POSTE AÉRIENNE"

379	5 f.+5 f. blue	..	..	..	30	30
380	6 f.+9 f. deep green	..	..	30	30
381	9 f.+16 f. sepia	..	..	30	30
382	15 f.+25 f. red-brown	..	..	30	30
375/382	Set of 8	..	..	2·75	2·75
MS382a	120×96 mm. Nos. 379/82 ..		3·75	3·75

Designs: Postage (vert)—2 f. Pottery; 3 f. Books; 5 f. Copper ware. Air (horiz)—Maps of Morocco:—N.W. (5 f.), N.E. (6 f.), S.W. (9 f.) and S.E. (15 f.).

(Postage: Des Pheulpin, eng Delpy. Air: Des Delpy, eng Dufresne. Recess)

1950 (25 Sept). Army Welfare Fund. T 83 and similar type inscr "OEUVRES SOCIALES DE L'ARMÉE". P 13. (a) POSTAGE.

| 383 | 83 | 10 f.+10 f. claret | .. | .. | 30 | 30 |
| 384 | | 15 f.+15 f. deep blue .. | .. | 30 | 30 |

(b) AIR. Inscr "POSTE AÉRIENNE"

385	—	10 f.+10 f. blackish brown	..	..	25	25
386	—	15 f.+15 f. turquoise-green	..	25	25
383/386		Set of 4	..	..	1·00	1·00

Design:—10 f., 15 f. Triumphal Arch of Caracalla, Volubilis

1950 (18 Nov)—**51**. Nos. 295/6 surch as T 43 and No. 330 surch as T 52.

| 387 | 39 | 1 f. on 1 f. 20, purple-brown .. | .. | 5 | 5 |

(Des Pheulpin. Eng Cogné. Recess)

1951 (28 Apr). General Leclerc Monument, Casablanca. P 13.

(a) POSTAGE

390	84	10 f. blue-green	..	..	..	30	30
391		15 f. magenta	..	..	..	30	30
392		25 f. deep blue	..	..	..	45	45

(b) AIR. Inscr "POSTE AERIENNE"

| 393 | 84 | 50 f. violet | .. | .. | .. | 50 | 50 |
| 390/393 | | Set of 4 | .. | .. | 1·40 | 1·40 |

(Des A. Delpy. Eng P. Munier (10 f.), Dufresne (15 f.), Barlangue (25 f.) and Pheulpin (50 f.). Recess)

1951 (4 June). Solidarity Fund. Various designs as T 85 inscr "SOLIDARITE 1950". P 13. (a) POSTAGE.

394	10 f. bright violet and indigo	..	..	20	20
395	15 f. lake-brown and deep green	..	30	30
396	25 f. deep blue and brown	..	..	35	35

(b) AIR. Inscr "POSTE AERIENNE"

| 397 | 50 f. blue-green and violet | .. | .. | 65 | 65 |
| 394/397 | Set of 4 | .. | .. | 1·40 | 1·40 |

Designs: Horiz—10 f. Loustau Hospital, Oujda; 25 f. New Hospital, Rabat; 50 f. Sanatorium, Ben Smine.

86 Fountain and Doves

87 Karaouine Mosque, Fez

88 Old Moroccan Courtyard

No. 403. Die I

No. 404. Die II

(Des Delpy. Eng Mazelin (T 86), R. Cottet (T 87), Pheulpin (15 f. Dies I and II), Serres (15 f. violet and 18 f.), Dufresne (T 88). Recess)

1951–54. P 14×13 or 13 (20 f.).

398	86	5 f. bright purple (2.52)	..	5	5
399	87	6 f. emerald-green (19.5.52)	..	5	5
400	86	8 f. deep brown (2.52)	..	..	5	5
401	87	10 f. carmine-red (23.6.53)	..	10	5
402		12 f. deep blue (17.10.52)	..	15	5
403	—	15 f. red-brown (I) (15.7.51)	..	50	5
404	—	15 f. red-brown (II) (17.11.51)	..	20	5

405	–	15 f. reddish violet (12.52)	20	5
406	**86**	15 f. blue-green (24.9.54)	20	8
407	–	18 f. scarlet (19.5.52)	30	20
408	**88**	20 f. greenish blue (19.5.52)	25	10
398/408		*Set of 11*	1·75	65

Designs as T **86/7**:—15 f. brown (2) Oudayas Courtyard,
15 f. violet, 18 f. Oudayas Point, Rabat.
For 5 f. and 15 f. smaller, see Nos. 434/5.

89 Casablanca Post Office
and Reproduction of T **22**

90 Saadian Capital

1952 (8 Mar). *AIR. Stamp Day and 30th Anniv of First Moroccan Air Stamps. Recess. P* 13.
409 **89** 15 f.+5 f. blue and red-brown ... 1·00 1·00

(Des and eng A. Delpy. Recess)

1952 (5 Apr). *Solidarity Fund. T* **90** *and similar vert designs showing capitals inscr "SOLIDARITE 1951". P* 13.

410	15 f. blue (Omeiyad)		60	60
411	20 f. red (Almohad)		60	60
412	25 f. violet (Merinid)		60	60
413	50 f. green		60	60
410/413	*Set of 4*		2·10	2·10

91 Ramparts at
Chella, Rabat

92 War Memorial
Casablanca

(Des A. Delpy. Eng Dufresne (10 f.), Cottet (40 f., 100 f.),
R. Serres (200 f.). Recess)

1952 (19 Apr). *AIR. As T* **91**. *P* 13.

414	10 f. deep bluish green		12	5
415	40 f. vermilion		30	12
416	100 f. brown		80	12
417	200 f. deep reddish violet		2·50	90
414/417	*Set of 4*		3·25	1·10

Designs: *Horiz*—40 f. Aeroplane over Marrakesh. *Vert*—
100 f. Fort in Anti-Atlas Mountains; 200 f. Aeroplane over Fez.

1952 (22 Sept). *Centenary of Médaille Militaire. Recess. P* 13.
418 **92** 15 f. red-brown, yellow and emerald ... 50 50

93 Jewellery from
Fez

94 Arab Courier and
Scribe

(Des A. Delpy. Eng Cottet (15 f.), Barlangue (20 f.), Mazelin
(25 f.) and Dufresne (50 f.). Recess)

1953 (27 Mar). *Solidarity Fund. T* **93** *and similar vert designs inscr "SOLIDARITE 1952". P* 13. (*a*) *POSTAGE*.

419	15 f. carmine-lake		60	60
420	20 f. purple-brown		60	60
421	25 f. deep blue		60	60

(*b*) *AIR. Inscr "POSTE AERIENNE"*

422	50 f. deep emerald		70	70
419/422	*Set of 4*		2·25	2·25

Designs:—15 f. Daggers from South Morocco; 25 f. Jewellery
from the Anti-Atlas; 50 f. Jewellery from North Morocco.

(Des E. Vales. Eng Mazelin. Recess)

1953 (16 May). *Stamp Day. P* 13.
423 **94** 15 f. purple-brown ... 40 40

95 Bine el Ouidane
Barrage

96 Mogador
Battlements

(Des A. Delpy. Eng Hertenberger. Recess)

1953 (3 Nov)—**54**. *Inauguration of Bine el Ouidane Barrage. P* 13.

424	**95**	15 f. indigo	35	35
424a		15 f. deep blue and chocolate (8.3.54)	20	8

(Des A. Delpy. Eng Dufresne (15 f.), C. Mazelin (30 f.). Recess)

1953 (4 Dec). *Army Welfare Fund. T* **96** *and another vert design inscr "OEUVRES SOCIALES DE L'ARMEE 1953". P* 13.

425	15 f. deep bluish green		40	40
426	30 f. red-brown (Moorish horsemen)		40	40

(97)

98 Meknès

1954. *Nos. 324 and 335 surch as T* **97**.

427	**58**	1 f. on 1 f. 50, light blue	5	5
428	**62**	15 f. on 18 f. deep ultramarine	15	15

(Des A. Delpy. Eng Pheulpin (10 f.), Mazelin (20 f.), R. Serres
(40 f.), Dufresne (50 f.). Recess)

1954 (8 Mar). *AIR. Solidarity Fund. As T* **98** (*horiz aerial views inscr "SOLIDARITE 1953"). P* 13.

429	10 f. brown-olive		45	45
430	20 f. deep reddish violet (Rabat)		45	45
431	40 f. red-brown (Casablanca)		60	60
432	50 f. deep blue-green (Fedala)		70	70
429/432	*Set of 4*		2·00	2·00

STAMP MONTHLY

—finest and most informative magazine for all
collectors. Obtainable from your newsagent or
by postal subscription—details on request.

103 Mazagan P.O.   **104** Map of Morocco

1955 (24 May). *Stamp Day. Recess. P* 13.
446 **103** 15 f. red   15   15

99 Mail Van and Postmen   **100** Sailing Vessel
          and Warship

(Des Josso. Eng Gandon. Recess)

1955 (11 June). *50th Anniv of Rotary International. P* 13.
447 **104** 15 f. blue and red-brown   ..   50   30

(Des A. Delpy. Eng Mazelin. Recess)

1954 (10 Apr). *Stamp Day. Inscr* "1954". *P* 13.
433 **99** 15 f. deep bluish green   ..   25   25

(Des A. Delpy. Typo)

1954. *Coil stamps. As Nos.* 398 *and* 405 *but designs redrawn size* 17 × 21½ *mm instead of* 12 × 22¾ *mm. P* 14 × 13½.
434 **86** 5 f. bright purple   12   10
435 – 15 f. reddish violet   20   15
Design: —15 f. Oudayas Point, Rabat.

(Des Milhau & Vechke. Eng Dufresne. Recess)

1954 (18 Oct). *AIR. Naval Welfare Fund. P* 13.
436 **100** 15 f. deep bluish green   ..   40   40
437   30 f. violet-blue   50   50

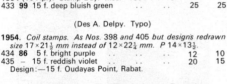

105 Bab el Mrissa,   **106** Mahakma,   **107** Bou Regreg
    Salé   Casablanca   Estuary

(Des A. Cadet (T **106**), A. Delpy (others). Eng Cheffer (T **105**), J. Piel (5 f., 6 f., 8 f.), Mazelin (10 f., 12 f., 15 f.), Dufresne (T **106**), Gandon (25 f.), Fenneteaux (30 f.), R. Serres (40 f.), Pheulpin (50 f.), A. Frères (75 f.). Recess)

1955 (10–25 Aug). *T* **105/6** *and similar designs. P* 14 × 13 (*small vert*) *or* 13 (*others*).
448 **105** 50 c. maroon (25.8)   5   5
449   1 f. blue (25.8)   5   5
450   2 f. bright purple (25.8)   ..   5   5
451   3 f. indigo (25.8)   5   5
452 – 5 f. vermilion   12   10
453 – 6 f. emerald (25.8)   ..   5   5
454 – 8 f. deep orange-brown (25.8)   12   12
455 – 10 f. slate-purple   ..   30   5
456 – 12 f. turquoise-blue (25.8) ..   8   5
457 – 15 f. claret   30   5
458 **106** 18 f. slate-green (25.8)   ..   30   25
459   20 f. brown-lake (25.8)   ..   12   5
460 – 25 f. deep bright blue   ..   55   8
461 – 30 f. emerald (25.8)   ..   50   12
462 – 40 f. deep orange-red (25.8)   20   8
463 – 50 f. sepia   ..   ..   1·40   15
464 – 75 f. turquoise-blue (25.8)   ..   40   20
448/464 *Set of* 17   ..   ..   4·25   1·25
Designs: *As T* **105**—5 f., 6 f., 8 f. Bab Chorfa, Fez; 10 f., 12 f., 15 f. Chella Minaret, Rabat. *As T* **106**: *Horiz*—25 f. Coastal castle, Safi; 30 f. Menara, Marrakesh; 40 f. Tafraout; 50 f. Portuguese cistern, Mazagan. *Vert*—75 f. Oudaya gardens, Rabat.

101 Marshal Lyautey   **102** Moroccan
    at Khenifra   Scholar

(Des A. Delpy. Eng R. Serres (50 f.), Mazelin (others). Recess)

1954 (17 Nov). *Birth Centenary of Marshal Lyautey. T* **101** *and similar designs inscr* "CENTENAIRE MARECHAL LYAUTEY". *P* 13.
438 5 f. indigo   65   65
439 15 f. deep green   65   65
440 30 f. brown-lake   95   95
441 50 f. deep brown   95   95
438/441 *Set of* 4   ..   ..   3·00   3·00
Designs: *Horiz*—5 f. Lyautey receiving Moroccan notables at Rabat. *Vert*—30 f. Lyautey in dockyard; 50 f. Portrait of Lyautey (after Laszlo).

(Des Delpy and Belin. Eng Munier (5 f.), Mazelin (15 f.), Dufresne (30 f.), Frères (50 f.). Recess)

1955 (16 Apr). *Solidarity Fund. T* **102** *and similar designs inscr* "CAMPAGNE DE SOLIDARITE 1954—1955". *P* 13.
442 5 f. indigo   30   30
443 15 f. claret   30   35
444 30 f. purple-brown   50   50
445 50 f. deep green   60   60
442/445 *Set of* 4   ..   ..   1·50   1·60
Designs: *Horiz*—5 f. French and Moroccan school-children; 30 f. Muslim School, Camp-Boulhaut. *Vert*—50 f. Moulay Idriss College, Fez.

(Des A. Delpy. Eng R. Serres (100 f.), Munier (200 f.). Miermont (500 f.). Recess)

1955 (10 Aug). *AIR. T* **107** *and similar designs. P* 13.
465 – 100 f. violet   50   8
466 **107** 200 f. carmine-red   ..   1·00   30
467 – 500 f. turquoise-blue   ..   3·00   1·25
Designs: *Vert*—100 f. Village in the Anti-Atlas. *Horiz*—500 f. Ksar es Souk.

The French Government again granted recognition to Sidi Mohammed ben Yusuf as Sultan of Morocco on 5 November 1955. The independence of Morocco was recognised by France on 2 March 1956 and the French protectorate then terminated.

French Polynesia

100 Centimes = 1 Franc

PRINTERS. All issues were printed by the French Government Printing Works, Paris, *unless otherwise stated.*

IMPERFORATE STAMPS. Many stamps exist imperforate in their issued colours, but these were not valid for postage. Imperforate stamps in other colours are colour trials.

A. TAHITI

The island of Tahiti, in the central Pacific, was discovered by Captain Samuel Wallis in 1767. It became a French protectorate in 1842 and a French colony in 1880.

(1)

(2)

1882 (9 June–Sept). *French Colonies (General issues) Type H ("Peace and Commerce"). Imperf. Surch at Papeete with T 1 and 2.*

1	1	25 c. on 35 c. black/*orange*	..	80·00	65·00
		a. Surch inverted	..	80·00	65·00
		b. Surch vert reading up or down		80·00	65·00
2	2	25 c. on 35 c. black/*orange* (6.9)	..	£1000	£900
		a. Surch inverted	..	£1000	£900
		b. Surch vert reading up or down		£1100	£1000
3	1	25 c. on 40 c. red/*yellow* (6.9)	..	£700	£750
		a. Surch inverted	..	£700	£750

(3)

(4)

1884 (12 June–July). *French Colonies (General issues) surch as T 2/4.*

(a) Type J ("Commerce"). P 14 × 13½.

4	3	5 c. on 20 c. red/*green*	..	35·00	25·00
		a. Surch inverted	..	35·00	25·00
		b. Surch vert reading up or down		35·00	25·00
5	4	10 c. on 20 c. red/*green* (30.7)	..	60·00	50·00
		a. Surch inverted	..	60·00	50·00
		b. Surch vert reading up or down		60·00	50·00

(b) Type H ("Peace and Commerce"). Imperf

6	2	25 c. on 1 f. olive-green/*toned* (30.7)	..	£150	£120
		a. Surch inverted	..	£150	£120
		b. Surch vert reading up or down		£150	£120

During June, July and August, 1884, local mail was hand-stamped with similar surcharges, applied directly onto the covers and cards.

(5)

1893

TAHITI

(6)

1893 (1 July). *French Colonies (General issues) Type J ("Commerce"). P 14 × 13½. Handstamped at Papeete with T 5.*

7	1 c. black/*azure* ..			..	£175	£150
8	2 c. brown/*buff* ..		..	..	£700	£450
9	4 c. purple-brown/*grey*	..	..	..	£300	£200
10	5 c. green/*pale green*		..	..	3·75	3·75
11	10 c. black/*lilac*		..	..	3·75	3·75
12	15 c. blue			..	4·00	3·50
13	20 c. red/*green*		..	..	5·00	4·75
14	25 c. ochre		..	..	£1200	£900
15	25 c. black/*rose*	..		..	4·00	3·75
16	35 c. black/*orange*		..	..	£450	£375
17	75 c. carmine/*rose*		..	..	5·50	5·00
18	1 f. olive-green/*toned*	..		..	10·00	8·00

This overprint is also found reading downwards diagonally from left to right.

1893 (1 July). POSTAGE DUE. *French Colonies (General issues) Type U. Imperf. Optd at Papeete with T 5.*

D19	1 c. black		..	..	70·00	70·00
D20	2 c. black		..	..	70·00	70·00
D21	3 c. black		..	..	70·00	70·00
D22	4 c. black		..	..	70·00	70·00
D23	5 c. black		..	..	75·00	75·00
D24	10 c. black		..	..	75·00	75·00
D25	15 c. black		..	..	75·00	75·00
D26	20 c. black		..	..	55·00	55·00
D27	30 c. black		..	..	75·00	75·00
D28	40 c. black		..	..	75·00	75·00
D29	60 c. black		..	..	75·00	75·00
D30	1 f. brown		..	..	£200	£200
D31	2 f. brown		..	..	£200	£200

1893 (27 Aug). *French Colonies (General issues) Type J ("Commerce"). P 14 × 13½. Optd at Papeete with T 6.*

32	1 c. black/*azure* ..		..	..	£175	£150
	a. Opt inverted		..	..	£275	
33	2 c. brown/*buff* ..		..	..	£700	£550
	a. Opt inverted		..	..	£750	
34	4 c. purple-brown/*grey*	..	..	..	£350	£300
	a. Opt inverted		..	..	£475	
35	5 c. green/*pale green*	..	..	..	£250	£200
	a. Opt inverted		..	..	£325	£300
36	10 c. black/*lilac* ..		..	..	60·00	55·00
	a. Opt inverted		..	..	£125	
37	15 c. blue		..	..	4·25	4·25
	a. Opt inverted		..	..	25·00	22·00
38	20 c. red/*green*		..	..	4·25	4·00
	a. Opt inverted		..	..	32·00	32·00
39	25 c. ochre		..	..	£6000	
40	25 c. black/*rose*	..	..	..	4·25	4·00
	a. Opt inverted		..	..	32·00	
41	35 c. black/*orange*		..	..	£500	£450
	a. Opt inverted		..	..	£650	
42	75 c. carmine/*rose*		..	..	4·25	4·00
	a. Opt inverted		..	..	35·00	
	b. Opt double ..		..	..	45·00	45·00
43	1 f. olive-green/*toned*	..	..	..	5·00	5·00
	a. Opt inverted		..	..	35·00	

1893 (27 Aug). POSTAGE DUE. *French Colonies (General issues) Type U. Imperf. Optd at Papeete with T 6.*

D44	1 c. black		..	..	£325	£325
	a. Opt inverted		..	..	£350	£350
D45	2 c. black		..	..	£100	£100
	a. Opt inverted		..	..	£125	£125
	b. Opt double		..	..	£125	£125

D46	3 c. black	.. .. ..	£100	£100	
	a. Opt double	.. ..	£125	£125	
D47	4 c. black	.. .. ..	£100	£100	
	a. Opt double	.. ..	£125	£125	
D48	5 c. black	.. ..	£100	£100	
	a. Opt double	.. ..	£125	£125	
D49	10 c. black	.. ..	£100	£100	
	a. Opt inverted	.. ..	£125	£125	
	b. Opt double	.. ..	£125	£125	
D50	15 c. black	.. ..	£100	£100	
	a. Opt inverted	.. ..	£125	£125	
	b. Opt double	.. ..	£125	£125	
D51	20 c. black	.. ..	55·00	55·00	
D52	30 c. black	.. ..	£100	£100	
	a. Opt inverted	.. ..	£125	£125	
D53	40 c. black	.. ..	£100	£100	
	a. Opt inverted	.. ..	£125	£125	
D54	60 c. black	.. ..	£100	£100	
	a. Opt inverted	.. ..	£125	£125	
D55	1 f. brown	.. ..	£100	£100	
	a. Opt inverted	.. ..	£125	£125	
D56	2 f. brown	.. ..	£100	£100	
	a. Opt inverted	.. ..	£125	£125	

After 1893 Tahiti used the stamps of French Oceanic Settlements, although the name Tahiti did make two brief reappearances on the following issues.

TAHITI

10

centimes

(7)

TAHITI

10

CENTIMES

(8)

✚

TAHITI

(9)

1903 (17 Mar–June). *Nos. 6, 8 and 10 of French Oceanic Settlements, surch at Papeete as T 7/8.*

57	**7** 10 c. on 15 c. blue (25.6)	.. ..	1·00	1·00
	a. Surch inverted	.. ..	7·00	7·00
	b. Surch double	.. ..	7·00	7·00
58	**8** 10 c. on 25 c. black/*rose* (C.) (31.3)	..	1·00	1·00
	a. Surch inverted	..	7·00	7·00
	b. Surch double	..	7·00	7·00
	c. Pair, one without surch	..	40·00	40·00
59	10 c. on 40 c. red/*yellow*	..	1·25	1·25
	a. Surch inverted	..	7·00	7·00
	b. Surch double	..	7·00	7·00

Nos. 57/9 exist with both types of figures "10" as shown in T 7 and 8. The same prices apply to either type.

1915 (23 Apr). *Red Cross. Nos. 6 and 16 of French Oceanic Settlements optd at Papeete with T 9, in red*

60	15 c. blue	.. ..	30·00	30·00
	a. Opt inverted	..	65·00	65·00
61	15 c. grey	.. ..	2·75	2·75
	a. Opt inverted	..	28·00	28·00

B. FRENCH OCEANIC SETTLEMENTS

In 1842 France embarked on a policy of annexation in the Pacific. In that year the Marquesas were annexed and Tahiti, together with the other Society Islands, became a protectorate. During 1844 Gambier Island was annexed and a protectorate declared over the Tuamotu group; annexation followed in 1881. The Austral or Tubuai Islands became a protectorate in 1889, being annexed in 1900.

In 1885 the islands received the collective title of Oceanic Settlements, later amended to French Oceanic Settlements.

1892 (Nov). *French Colonies Type X ("Tablet") inscr "ETABLISSEMENTS DE L'OCEANIE" in red (1, 5, 15, 25, 75 c., 1 f.) or blue (others). P 14×13½.*

1	1 c. black/*azure* ..	..	25	25
2	2 c. brown/*buff* ..	..	40	40
3	4 c. purple-brown/*grey* ..	..	65	50
4	5 c. green/*pale green*	..	1·50	1·00
5	10 c. black/*lilac*	..	3·25	1·90
6	15 c. blue (*quadrillé paper*)	..	2·50	1·25
7	20 c. red/*green*	.. ..	1·90	1·00

8	25 c. black/*rose* ..	..	6·50	3·75
9	30 c. cinnamon/*drab*	..	2·00	1·50
10	40 c. red/*yellow* ..	..	15·00	10·00
11	50 c. carmine/*rose*	..	1·25	95
12	75 c. brown/*orange*	..	1·40	1·00
13	1 f. olive-green/*toned*	..	2·00	1·60
1/13	*Set of 13*	..	35·00	23·00

1900 (Dec)–**07**. *Type X. Colours changed and new values. Inscr in blue (10 c.) or red (others). P 14×13½.*

14	5 c. bright yellow-green (1906)	..	30	20
15	10 c. rose-red	.. ..	30	20
16	15 c. grey	.. ..	65	40
17	25 c. blue	.. ..	1·50	90
18	35 c. black/*yellow* (7.06)	..	65	45
19	45 c. black/*green* (10.07)	..	40	45
20	50 c. brown/*azure* (6.03)	..	35·00	30·00
14/20	*Set of 7*	..	35·00	30·00

2 Tahitian Woman   3 Kanakas

E F O

1915

4 Valley of Fautaua   (5)

(Des J. de la Nézière. Eng H. Lemasson. Typo)

1913–15. *P 14×13½ (T 4) or 13½×14 (others).*

21	**2** 1 c. brown and violet ..	..	5	5
22	2 c. grey and brown ..	..	5	5
23	4 c. blue and orange ..	..	5	5
24	5 c. yellow-green and green ..	..	5	5
	a. Centre double ..	..	32·00	
25	10 c. orange and carmine ..	..	12	10
25a	15 c. black and orange (1915)	..	8	8
	b. Imperf (pair)	..	6·50	
26	20 c. violet and black ..	..	5	5
27	**3** 25 c. blue and ultramarine	..	5	5
28	30 c. brown and grey ..	..	40	40
29	35 c. carmine and green ..	..	8	5
30	40 c. green and black ..	..	10	8
31	45 c. red and orange ..	..	10	10
32	50 c. black and brown ..	..	1·40	1·25
33	75 c. violet and dull purple	..	20	20
34	**4** 1 f. black and carmine	..	25	25
35	2 f. green and brown ..	..	55	45
36	5 f. blue and violet ..	..	1·50	1·10
21/36	*Set of 17*	..	4·50	3·75

No. 25b was issued at Utuora in January 1919.
See also Nos. 46/62.

1915 (28 Apr). *No. 15 optd at Papeete with T 5.*

37	X 10 c. rose-red ..	..	35	30
	a. Overprint inverted ..	..	11·00	11·00
	b. No tongue to "E" ..	..	3·25	2·50

Variety b is found on the forty-sixth stamp of the setting of fifty.

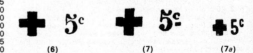

(6)   (7)   (7a)

French Polynesia OCEANIC SETTLEMENTS

1915 (19 May). *Red Cross. No.* 37 *surch at Papeete with T* **6**, *in red.*
38	X	10 c.+5 c. rose-red	2·75	2·75
		a. "e" for "c"	6·50	6·50
		b. No tongue to "E"	6·50	6·50
		c. Surcharge inverted	18·00	16·00

Variety a is found on the twenty-third stamp of the setting of fifty. There are several varieties in the figure "5".

1915 (2 Sept). *Red Cross. No.* 25 *surch with T* **6**, *in vermilion.*
39	2	10 c.+5 c. orange and carmine	1·10	1·10
		a. Variety. "e" for "c"	4·50	4·50
		b. "c" inverted	4·50	4·50
		c. Surcharge inverted	14·00	14·00

Varieties a and b are the seventeenth and fifth stamps respectively in the setting of twenty-five.

1915 (2 Oct). *Red Cross. No.* 25 *surch at Papeete with T* **7**, *in deep red.*
40	2	10 c.+5 c. orange and carmine	35	35
		a. Surch inverted	16·00	16·00
		b. Variety. "e" for "c"	2·75	2·75

The surcharge in this colour is set higher on the stamp, and also differs from T **6** by having a thick bar below the "c".

1916 (May). *Red Cross. No.* 25 *surch in Paris with T* **7a**, *in deep carmine.*
41	2	10 c.+5 c. orange and carmine	35	35

10

$$\frac{05}{1921}$$

10   **1921**

(8)   (9)   (10)

1916 (5 Aug). *No.* 25a *surch at Papeete with T* **8**.
42	2	10 c. on 15 c. black and orange	12	12

1921 (18 Mar). *Surch at Papeete as T* **9** (*Nos.* 43 *and* 45) *or* 10.
43	2	05 on 2 c. grey and brown	3·50	3·50
44	3	10 on 45 c. red and orange	3·25	3·25
45	2	25 on 15 c. black and orange	55	55

1922 (1 Jan)–**30**. *Colours changed and new values. P* 14×13½ (*T* **4**) *or* 13½×14 (*others*).
46	2	5 c. black and blue	5	5
47		10 c. yellow-green and green	5	5
48		10 c. purple and red/*azure* (1.2.26)	20	20
49		20 c. green (1.3.26)	5	5
50		20 c. sepia and lake (14.11.27)	12	12
51	3	25 c. carmine and violet	5	5
52		30 c. red and carmine	12	12
53		30 c. red and black (1.2.26)	20	20
54		30 c. green and greenish blue (14.11.27)	12	12
55		50 c. blue and ultramarine	8	8
56		50 c. ultramarine and grey (1.2.26)	5	5
57		60 c. black and green (21.12.25)	5	5
58		65 c. magenta and chocolate (19.12.27)	30	30
59		90 c. bright mauve and scarlet (22.3.30)	2·25	2·25
60	4	1 f. 10, chocolate & magenta (25.9.28)	20	20
61		1 f. 40, pale violet & yell-brn (25.3.29)	55	55
62		1 f. 50, light blue and blue (22.3.30)	2·40	2·40
46/62		*Set of* 17	6·00	6·00

65   **1ᶠ25** ≡

(10a)   (10b)

1923 (June)–**27**. *Surch as T* **10a**.
63	3	60 on 75 c. red-brown and blue	5	5
64	4	65 on 1 f. brown and blue (R.) (1.2.25)	20	20
65		85 on 1 f. brown and blue (R.) (1.2.25)	20	20
66	3	90 on 75 c. mauve and scarlet (28.2.27)	12	12
63/66		*Set of* 4	50	50

1924 (June)–**27**. *Surch as T* **10b**.
67	4	25 c. on 2 f. green and brown	12	12
68		25 c. on 5 f. blue and violet	12	12
69		1 f. 25 on 1 f. ultram & bl (R.) (14.6.26)	12	12
70		1 f. 50 on 1 f. light blue & blue (28.2.27)	20	20
71		20 f. on 5 f. magenta & orge-red (5.9.27)	3·50	2·50
67/71		*Set of* 5	3·75	3·75

Établs Français de l'Océanie

45 c.

1924

(11)

2 francs à percevoir

(D 12)

1924 (1 Aug). *Surch at Papeete with T* **11**.
72	2	45 c. on 10 c. orange and carmine	20	20
		a. Surch inverted	50·00	50·00

1926 (17 May)–**27**. *POSTAGE DUE. Type* D **11** *of France optd "Etabts/Français/de l'Océanie" or surch additionally as Type* D **12** (*No.* D80). *P* 14×13½.
D73	5 c. blue		5	5
D74	10 c. brown		10	10
D75	20 c. olive-green		12	12
D76	30 c. carmine		12	12
D77	40 c. rose		20	20
D78	60 c. green		20	20
D79	1 f. claret/*straw*		25	25
D80	2 f. on 1 f. vermilion		40	40
D81	2 f. magenta (10.10.27)		90	90
D73/81	*Set of* 9		2·10	2·10

TROIS FRANCS

(12)   13 Papetoia Bay

1926 (14 June). *Surch as T* **12**.
73	4	3 f. on 5 f. blue and drab	20	20
74		10 (DIX) f. on 5 f. black and green (R.)	65	50

(Des Ambo. Eng G. Hourriez. Typo)

1929 (25 Mar). *P* 14×13½.
75	13	3 f. sepia and green	1·25	1·25
76		5 f. sepia and light blue	2·25	2·25
77		10 f. sepia and red	5·00	5·00
78		20 f. sepia and mauve	7·00	7·00
75/78		*Set of* 4	14·00	14·00

D **14** Fautaua Falls   D **15** Polynesian Man

(Des Ambo (D **14**), Limouse (D **15**). Eng G. Hourriez. Typo)

1929 (14 Oct). *POSTAGE DUE. P* 13½ × 14.
D82	D **14**	5 c. chocolate and light blue		8	8
D83		10 c. green and vermilion		5	5
D84		30 c. carmine and chocolate		15	15
D85		50 c. chocolate and green		5	5
D86		60 c. green and mauve		35	35
D87	D **15**	1 f. magenta and greenish blue		20	20
D88		2 f. chocolate and carmine		10	10
D89		3 f. green and violet-blue		12	12
D82/89	*Set of 8*			1·00	1·00

1931 (13 Apr). *International Colonial Exhibition, Paris. As T* **17/20** *of French Sudan.*
79	40 c. black and green		65	65
80	50 c. black and mauve		65	65
81	90 c. black and vermilion		65	65
82	1 f. 50, black and blue		75	75
79/82	*Set of 4*		2·50	2·50

14 Spearing Fish   **15** Tahitian Girl

16 Native Gods   **17** Flying-boat

(Des Herviault. Eng A. Mignon, J. Piel and H. Cheffer. Photo Vaugirard, Paris)

1934 (19 Mar)–**39**. *P* 13½.
83	**14**	1 c. grey-black			5	5
84		2 c. claret			5	5
85		3 c. light blue (5.6.39)			5	5
86		4 c. orange			5	5
87		5 c. mauve			8	8
88		10 c. olive-brown			5	5
89		15 c. blue-green			5	5
90		20 c. scarlet			5	5
91	**15**	25 c. slate-blue			5	5
92		30 c. green			12	12
93		30 c. brown-red (5.6.39)			5	5
94	**16**	35 c. blue-green (16.5.38)			45	45
95	**15**	40 c. magenta			5	5
96		45 c. vermilion			80	80
97		45 c. blue-green (5.6.39)			12	12
98		50 c. violet			5	5
99		55 c. blue (16.5.38)			55	55
100		60 c. black (5.6.39)			5	5
101		65 c. chocolate			40	40
102		70 c. rose-pink (5.6.39)			8	8
103		75 c. olive-green			70	70
104		80 c. purple (16.5.38)			10	10
105		90 c. carmine			8	8
106	**16**	1 f. red-brown			5	5
107		1 f. 25, purple			80	80
108		1 f. 25, carmine (5.6.39)			5	5
109		1 f. 40, orange (5.6.39)			8	8
110		1 f. 50, blue			10	10
111		1 f. 60, violet (5.6.39)			8	8
112		1 f. 75, bronze-green			65	65
113		2 f. scarlet			5	5
114		2 f. 25, blue (5.6.39)			8	8
115		2 f. 50, black (5.6.39)			8	8
116		3 f. brown-orange (5.6.39)			8	8
117		5 f. magenta (5.6.39)			5	5
118		10 f. blue-green (5.6.39)			30	30
119		20 f. olive-brown (5.6.39)			45	45
83/119	*Set of 37*				6·50	6·50

The 10, 30 c., 1 f. 50, 10 f. and 20 f. without "RF" were produced in 1942/44 by the Vichy authorities but were not placed on sale in the Settlements.

(Des J. Douy. Eng A. Mignon. Photo Vaugirard, Paris)

1934 (5 Nov). *AIR. P* 13½.
120	**17**	5 f. blue-green		5	5

This value, together with similar 10, 20 and 50 f. stamps, all without "RF", was prepared in 1944 by the Vichy Government, but not issued.

1937 (1 Mar). *International Exhibition, Paris. As T* **2/7** *of French Equatorial Africa.*
121	20 c. bright violet			20	20
122	30 c. green			20	20
123	40 c. carmine			25	25
124	50 c. brown			25	25
125	90 c. scarlet			25	25
126	1 f. 50, blue			25	25
121/126	*Set of 6*			1·25	1·25
MS126a	120 × 100 mm. 3 f. emerald-green (as T **6**). Imperf (29.11)			95	95

1938 (20 Oct). *International Anti-Cancer Fund. As T* **14** *of French Equatorial Africa.*
127	1 f. 75+50 c. ultramarine		2·40	2·40

1939 (10 May). *New York World's Fair. As T* **17** *of French Equatorial Africa.*
128	1 f. 25, lake		25	25
129	2 f. 25, ultramarine		25	25

1939 (5 July). *150th Anniv of French Revolution. As T* **18** *of French Equatorial Africa.* (a) *POSTAGE.*
130	45 c.+25 c. green and black		1·75	1·75
131	70 c.+30 c. brown and black		1·75	1·75
132	90 c.+35 c. red-orange and black		1·75	1·75
133	1 f. 25+1 f. carmine and black		1·75	1·75
134	2 f. 25+2 f. blue and black		1·75	1·75

(b) *AIR*
135	5 f.+4 f. black and orange		3·75	3·75
130/135	*Set of 6*		10·00	10·00

VICHY ISSUES. A number of stamps were prepared by the Pétain Government of Unoccupied France for use in French Oceanic Settlements, but as the inhabitants declared for the Free French, these issues were not placed on sale in the territory.

FRANCE LIBRE

(**18**)   **19** Polynesian Travelling Canoe

1941. *Adherence to General de Gaulle. Optd with T* **18**.

(a) *POSTAGE*
(i) *Nos.* 75/8
136	**13**	3 f. sepia and green (R.)		65
137		5 f. sepia and light blue (R.)		1·00
138		10 f. sepia and bright rose (R.)		1·40
139		20 f. sepia and mauve (R.)		11·00

(ii) *Nos.* 106, 115/19
140	**16**	1 f. red-brown		50
141		2 f. 50, black (R.)		65
142		3 f. vermilion		75
143		5 f. magenta		75
144		10 f. blue-green (R.)		5·50
145		20 f. olive-brown (R.)		5·00

(b) *AIR*
146	**17**	5 f. blue-green (R.)		45	45
136/146	*Set of 11*				

(Des E. Dulac. Photo Harrison)

1942. *P* 14½ × 14. (a) *POSTAGE.*
147	**19**	5 c. brown		5	5
148		10 c. blue		5	5
149		25 c. emerald-green		5	5
150		30 c. red-orange		5	5
151		40 c. slate-green		5	5

152	**19**	80 c. maroon			5	5
153		1 f. magenta			5	5
154		1 f. 50, scarlet			8	8
155		2 f. grey-black			8	8
156		2 f. 50, ultramarine			25	20
157		4 f. violet			12	10
158		5 f. yellow-bistre			12	10
159		10 f. red-brown			15	12
160		20 f. blue-green			15	12

(b) AIR. As T **24** of French Equatorial Africa.

161		1 f. red-orange			8	8
162		1 f. 50, scarlet			8	8
163		5 f. maroon			12	12
164		10 f. black			30	30
165		25 f. ultramarine			30	30
166		50 f. green			20	20
167		100 f. claret			30	25
147/167		Set of 21			2·40	2·00

1944 (Dec). *Mutual Aid and Red Cross Funds. As T **29** of French Equatorial Africa.*

168	5 f.+20 f. greenish blue			10	10

50ᶜ **=**

(20)

1945. *Surch as T **20**.*

169	**19**	50 c. on 5 c. brown (R.)		8	8
170		60 c. on 5 c. brown (R.)		8	8
171		70 c. on 5 c. brown (R.)		8	8
172		1 f. 20 on 5 c. brown (R.)		8	8
173		2 f. 40 on 25 c. emerald-green		8	8
174		3 f. on 25 c. emerald-green		8	8
175		4 f. 50 on 25 c. emerald-green		20	20
176		15 f. on 2 f. 50, ultramarine (R.)		30	30
169/176		Set of 8		90	90

1945. *Eboué. As T **31** of French Equatorial Africa.*

177	2 f. black			8	8
178	25 f. blue-green			20	20

1946 (8 May). *AIR. Victory. As T **32** of French Equatorial Africa.*

179	8 f. green			30	30

1946 (6 June). *AIR. From Chad to the Rhine. As Nos. 229/34 of French Equatorial Africa.*

180	5 f. brown-red			25	25
181	10 f. yellow-brown			25	25
182	15 f. grey-green			25	25
183	20 f. rose-red			25	25
184	25 f. purple			25	25
185	50 f. black			45	45
180/185	Set of 6			1·50	1·50

21 Mooréa Coastline **22** Tahitian Girl

23 Frigate-bird over Mooréa **D 24**

(Des P. Gandon (9 f., 13 f., 50 f. to 200 f.), J. Boullaire (others). Eng G. Barlangue (10 c. to 40 c.), R. Serres (50 c. to 80 c.), C. Mazelin (2 f. to 4 f.), E. Feltesse (5, 6, 10 f.), J. Piel (15 f. to 25 f., 200 f.), P. Gandon (others). Recess)

1948 (1 Mar)–**55.** *P* 13. (a) *POSTAGE. Designs as T **21/22**.*

186	**21**	10 c. red-brown			5	5
187		30 c. blue-green			5	5
188		40 c. blue			5	5
189	–	50 c. brown-lake			5	5
190	–	60 c. olive			5	5
191	–	80 c. blue			5	5
192	–	1 f. brown-lake			5	5
193	–	1 f. 20, grey-blue			5	5
194	–	1 f. 50, blue			8	5
195	**22**	2 f. blackish brown			10	10
196		2 f. 40, brown-lake			15	15
197		3 f. violet			1·25	25
198		4 f. indigo			12	12
199		5 f. chocolate			20	20
200		6 f. grey-blue			20	20
201		9 f. black-brown, blk & red (1.10.55)		2·50	1·90
202	–	10 f. olive			35	12
203	–	15 f. vermilion			70	55
204	–	20 f. grey-blue			75	45
205	–	25 f. sepia			75	50

(b) *AIR. Horiz designs as T **23***

206		13 f. indigo and blue (1.10.55)		1·25	1·10
207	**23**	50 f. brown-lake			3·50	3·50
208	–	100 f. violet			3·25	1·90
209	–	200 f. greenish blue			7·50	5·50
186/209		Set of 24			22·00	16·00

Designs: *Horiz* (As T **21**)—1 f., 1 f. 20, 1 f. 50, Faa village; 5 f., 6 f., 10 f. Bora-Bora and pandanus pine; 15 f., 20 f., 25 f. Polynesian girls. (As T **23**)—13 f. Pahia Peak and palms; 100 f. Aeroplane over Mooréa; 200 f. Frigate-bird over Maupiti Island. *Vert* (As T **22**)—50 c., 60 c., 80 c. Kanaka fisherman; 9 f. Bora-Bora girl.

Nos. 201 and 206 were released in Paris on 26 Sept.

(Des and eng P. Munier. Recess)

1948 (1 Mar). *POSTAGE DUE. P* 14×13.

D210	**D 24**	10 c. green			5	5
D211		30 c. chocolate			5	5
D212		50 c. carmine			5	5
D213		1 f. ultramarine			5	5
D214		2 f. blue-green			5	5
D215		3 f. vermilion			12	12
D216		4 f. violet			20	20
D217		5 f. magenta			20	20
D218		10 f. indigo			45	45
D219		20 f. brown-lake			65	65
D210/219		Set of 10			1·75	1·75

1949 (11 Oct). *AIR. 75th Anniv of Universal Postal Union. As T **39** of French Equatorial Africa.*

210	10 f. blue		2·10	2·10

No. 210 was released in Paris on 4 July.

1950 (15 May). *Colonial Welfare Fund. As T **40** of French Equatorial Africa.*

211	10 f.+2 f. green and blue-green		50	50

1952 (1 Dec). *Centenary of Médaille Militaire. As T **44** of French Equatorial Africa.*

212	3 f. reddish violet, yellow and green		1·10	1·10

ALBUM LISTS Please write for our latest lists of albums and accessories. These will be sent free on request.

25 "Nafea" (after Gauguin) **26** Dry Dock, Papeete

(Des and eng P. Munier. Recess)

1953 (24 Sept). *AIR. 50th Death Anniv of Gauguin (painter). P* 13.
213 **25** 14 f. sepia, red and deep bluish green .. 19·00 19·00

1954 (23 June). *AIR. 10th Anniv of Liberation. As T **46** of French Equatorial Africa.*
214 3 f. emerald and deep turquoise 70 70
No. 214 was released in Paris on 6 June.

(Des and eng J. Pheulpin. Recess)

1956 (20 Oct). *Economic and Social Development Fund. P* 13.
215 **26** 3 f. greenish blue 30 30

(Des and eng C. Mazelin (T **1**, 13 f.), G. Bétemps (T **2**), R. Cottet (10 f., 20 f.), C. Hertenberger (16 f.), J. Pheulpin (T **3**), P. Gandon (100 f.) and R. Serres (200 f.). Des J. Boullaire. Eng A. Decaris (5 f., 17 f.). Recess)

1958 (Nov)–**60**. *Various designs as T* 1/3. *P* 13.

(*a*) POSTAGE

1	**1**	10 c. brown, green and deep bluish green	12	10
2		25 c. maroon, red and green-black ..	15	12
3		1 f. sepia, orange-red and blue ..	20	15
4		2 f. violet, chocolate and bistre-brown..	20	20
5	**2**	4 f. green-black, green and yellow ..	25	20
6	—	5 f. bistre-brown, reddish violet and green (16.5.60) ..	30	25
7	**2**	7 f. chestnut, green and yellow-orange	45	40
8	—	9 f. maroon, blue-green and orange ..	65	45
9	—	10 f. carmine-red, blue and chocolate ..	80	40
10	—	16 f. clar, yell-grn, bl-grn & bl (15.12.60)	80	55
11	—	17 f. brown, blue & blue-green (16.5.60)	1·00	70
12	—	20 f. brown, reddish violet and pink ..	1·10	80

(*b*) AIR. *Inscr* "POSTE AERIENNE"

13	—	13 f. red-brown, blue-green and drab ..	95	45
14	**3**	50 f. multicoloured	3·25	1·10
15	—	100 f. multicoloured	5·50	2·50
16	—	200 f. deep slate-blue and lilac ..	7·00	2·50
1/16		*Set of 16*	21·00	10·00

Designs : *Vert*—5 f. Spear-fishing; 10 f., 20 f. Polynesian girl on beach; (27×47½ mm) 13 f. Mother-of-pearl engraver; 100 f. "The White Horse" (after Gauguin). *Horiz*—16 f. Post Office, Papeete; 17 f. Tahitian dancers; (47½×27 mm) 200 f. Night-fishing off Moorea.

(Des and eng R. Cami. Recess)

1958 (3 Nov). *POSTAGE DUE. P* 14×13.

D17	**D 4**	1 f. bronze-green & dp purple-brown	12	12
D18		3 f. brown-red and indigo	20	20
D19		5 f. ultramarine and light brown ..	20	20

C. FRENCH POLYNESIA

In 1957 the Oceanic Settlements were renamed French Polynesia, and on November 1958 the inhabitants voted to become an Overseas Territory of the French Republic.

5 "Human Rights" **6** Artocarpus

(Des and eng R. Cami. Recess)

1958 (10 Dec). *10th Anniv of Declaration of Human Rights. P* 13.
17 **5** 7 f. deep blue-grey and ultramarine .. 3 25 3·25

(Des M. Rolland. Photo Vaugirard, Paris)

1959 (3 Jan). *P* 12½.
18 **6** 4 f. multicoloured 80 55

1 Girl playing Guitar **2** Polynesian

3 "The Women of Tahiti" (after Gauguin) **D 4** Polynesian Mask

7 Airliner over Papeete Airport **8** Saraca indica

(Des and eng C. Hertenberger. Recess)

1960 (15 Dec). *AIR. Inauguration of Papeete Airport. P* 13.
19 **7** 13 f. dp violet-blue, brt purple & yell-grn 75 45

(Des P. Lambert. Photo Delrieu)

1962 (12 July). *T 8 and similar vert design. Multicoloured.*
P 13½ × 13.
20	15 f. Type **8**	..	..	..	1·90	1·00
21	25 f. Hibiscus	..	..	..	2·50	1·50

9 Pacific Map and Palms

(Des P. Lambert. Photo Delrieu)

1962 (18 July). *Fifth South Pacific Conference, Pago-Pago.*
P 13 × 12.
22	**9**	20 f. multicoloured	..	..	2·25	1·40

10 "Telstar" Satellite

(Des C. Durrens. Eng P. Béquet. Recess)

1962 (5 Dec). *AIR. First Transatlantic Television Satellite Link.*
P 13.
23	**10**	50 f. ultramarine, brown-purple & brt pur	2·50	1·60

11 Squirrel Fish   **12** Football

(Des and eng C. Mazelin. Recess)

1962 (15 Dec). *Fishes. T 11 and similar horiz designs.
Multicoloured. P 13.*
24	5 f. Type **11**	..	..	..	65	30
25	10 f. One Spot Butterfly	..	..	95	40
26	30 f. Scorpion Fish	..	..	1·90	1·25
27	40 f. Cowfish	..	..	..	2·75	1·90
24/27	Set of 4	..	..	..	5·50	3·50

(Des C. Durrens. Photo Delrieu)

1963 (29 Aug). *First South Pacific Games, Suva, Fiji. T 12 and
similar design. P 12½.*
28	20 f. brown and ultramarine	..	..	1·60	95
29	50 f. ultramarine and cerise	..	..	2·50	1·60
Design:—50 f. Throwing the javelin.

13 Centenary   **14** Globe and Scales
Emblem   of Justice

(Des and eng J. Combet. Recess)

1963 (2 Sept). *Red Cross Centenary. P 13.*
30	**13**	15 f. red, grey and brown-purple	..	2·25	2·25

(Des and eng A. Decaris. Recess)

1963 (10 Dec). *15th Anniv of Declaration of Human Rights.*
P 13.
31	**14**	7 f. bluish violet and green	..	..	2·75	2·50

15 "Philately"

(Des and eng P. Gandon. Recess)

1964 (9 Apr). *"PHILATEC 1964" International Stamp
Exhibition, Paris. P 13.*
32	**15**	25 f. brown-red, black and deep emerald	2·75	2·50

16 Dancer   **17** Tahitian
                      Volunteers

(Des R. Serres. Eng C. Mazelin. Recess (T **16**). Des P.
Lambert. Photo So.Ge.Im. (15 f.))

1964 (14 May). *Tahitian Dancers. P 13. (a) POSTAGE.*
33	**16**	1 f. orange, sepia, bistre and blue	..	15	12
34		3 f. orange, sepia and reddish purple	..	25	20

                (b) AIR. Inscr "POSTE AERIENNE"
35	–	15 f. multicoloured	..	..	70	45
Design: *Vert (27 × 46½ mm)*—15 f. Dancer in full costume.

(Des J. Pheulpin (16 f. after G. Reboul-Salze). Photo So.Ge.Im.)

1964 (10 July). *Polynesia's War Effort in Second World War.
Multicoloured. (a) POSTAGE. P 13 × 12½.*
36	5 f. Type **17**	..	..	..	55	30

   (b) AIR. Inscr "POSTE AERIENNE". Size 48 × 27 mm. P 13
37	16 f. Badges and map of Tahiti	..	..	2·50	1·00

18 Tuamotu Lagoon (after J. D. Lajoux)

19 "Syncom" Communications Satellite, Telegraph Poles and Morse Key

22 Tropical Foliage

23 Aerial, Globe and Palm

(Des and eng A. Decaris, after S. Poroi (20 f.), R. Wilhelm (80 f.). Recess)

(Des P. Lambert. Photo So.Ge.Im.)

1964 (1 Dec). *Landscapes. T* **18** *and similar horiz designs. Multicoloured.*

(a) *POSTAGE. P* 12½ × 13

38	2 f. Type **18**	..	..	15	12
39	4 f. Bora-Bora (after Lajoux)	..	..	25	20
40	7 f. Papeete (after Sylvain)	..	..	45	30
41	8 f. Marquesas (Gauguin's grave)	..	50	30
42	20 f. Gambier (after Mazellier)	..	1·10	75

(b) *AIR. Size* 48 × 27 *mm. Inscr* "POSTE AERIENNE". *P* 13

43	23 f. Moorèa (after Sylvain)	..	..	1·00	55
38/43	*Set of 6*	..	..	..	3·00	2·00

(Des and eng J. Combet. Recess)

1965 (17 May). *AIR. I.T.U. Centenary. P* 13.

44 **19** 50 f. chestnut, blue and violet .. .. 9·50 5·50

20 Museum Buildings

(Des Dessirier. Eng J. Miermont. Recess)

1965. *AIR. Gauguin Museum. T* **20** *and similar horiz designs. P* 13.

45	25 f. olive-green (13.6)	..	..	1·60	75
46	40 f. turquoise-green (7.11)	..	..	2·25	1·10
47	75 f. chestnut (13.6)	..	..	4·50	2·50

Designs:—40 f. Statues and hut; 75 f. Gauguin.

21 Skin-diver with Harpoon

(Des and eng J. Combet. Recess)

1965 (1 Sept). *AIR. World Underwater Swimming Championships, Tuamoto. P* 13.

48 **21** 50 f. greenish blue, chestnut & dp green 13·00 9·50

1965 (29 Nov). *Schools Canteen Art. T* **22** *and similar design. P* 13. (a) *POSTAGE.*

49 **22** 20 f. crimson, myrtle-green & chocolate 1·60 95

(b) *AIR. Inscr* "POSTE AERIENNE"

50 80 f. red, new blue and chocolate .. 4·00 2·25

Design: *Vert* (27 × 48 *mm*)—80 f. Totem, and garland in harbour.

(Des Baille. Eng C. Haley. Recess)

1965 (29 Dec). *AIR. 50th Anniv of First Radio Link with France. P* 13.

51 **23** 60 f. chocolate, green and red-orange.. 3·25 1·90

24 Rocket "Diamant"

(Des and eng C. Durrens. Recess)

1966 (17 Jan). *AIR. Launching of First French Satellite. T* **24** *and similar horiz design. P* 13.

52	7 f. red-brown, brt purple & myrtle-green	1·25	1·25
53	10 f. red-brown, brt purple & myrtle-green	1·60	1·60

Design:—10 f. Satellite "A1".

Nos. 52/3 were printed together *se-tenant* within the sheet, separated by a half stamp-size label inscribed "MISE SUR ORBITE DU PREMIER SATELLITE FRANCAIS 26 NOVEMBRE 1965". (*Price for strip unused or used* £3·25)

25 Satellite "D1"

(Des and eng C. Durrens. Recess)

1966 (10 May). *AIR. Launching of Satellite* "D1". *P* 13.

54 **25** 20 f. claret, light brown and emerald .. 1·60 75

26 Papeete Port

(Des M. Monvoisin. Photo So.Ge.Im.)

1966 (30 June). *AIR. P* 13.
55 26 50 f. multicoloured .. .. .. 3·25 1·25

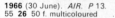

27 Pirogue

(Des P. Béquet, after Labaysse (10 f., 12 f.), after Mackenzie (11 f., 14 f.), after Sylvain (19 f., 22 f.). Recess)

1966 (30 Aug). *Polynesian Boats. T* **27** *and similar designs. P* 13.
56 10 f. lake, emerald and ultramarine .. 45 20
57 11 f. lake, green and blue .. 50 35
58 12 f. purple, emerald and blue .. 65 40
59 14 f. purple-brn, greenish bl & myrtle-grn 75 45
60 19 f. myrtle-green, vermilion and blue .. 90 45
61 22 f. turquoise-green, black and purple .. 1·25 65
56/61 *Set of* 6 .. .. .. 4·00 2·25
Designs: *Vert*—11 f. Schooner; 19 f. Early schooner. *Horiz*—12 f. Fishing launch; 14 f. Pirogues; 22 f. Coaster, *Oiseau des Iles II.*

28 Tahitian Dancer and Band

(Des H. Ouin ("Lacroix") (after A. Benichou). Photo So.Ge.Im.)

1966 (28 Nov). *AIR. "Vive, Tahiti!" (tourist publicity). P* 13.
62 **28** 13 f. multicoloured 95 45

29 High-jumping

30 Stone Pestle

(Des and eng J. Combet. Recess)

1966 (15 Dec). *Second South Pacific Games, Nouméa. T* **29** *and similar designs. Sportsmen in black. P* 13.
63 10 f. bistre and carmine-red .. 40 20
64 20 f. bright green and greenish blue .. 75 45

65 40 f. bright purple and emerald .. .. 1·40 90
66 60 f. new blue and yellow-brown .. 1·90 90
63/66 *Set of* 4 .. .. 3·00 2·25
Designs: *Vert*—20 f. Pole-vaulting; 40 f. Basket-ball. *Horiz*—60 f. Hurdling.

(Des Dessirier. Eng R. Cottet. Recess)

1967 (15 June). *50th Anniv of Oceanic Studies Society. P* 13.
67 **30** 50 f. indigo and red-orange 85 55

31 Spring Dance   32 Ear-ring

(Des J. Boullaire. Eng J. Derrey (5 f., 16 f.), J. Miermont (13 f.), C. Hertenberger (15 f.), P. Gandon (21 f.). Recess)

1967 (11 July). *July Festival. T* **31** *and similar designs. P* 13.
68 5 f. ultramarine, maroon and drab .. 30 15
69 13 f. brn-pur, brt reddish vio & myrtle-grn 50 20
70 15 f. dp brown, brown-purple & turq-grn 55 30
71 16 f. brown-purple, brt green & dp vio-bl 65 40
72 21 f. light brown, deep myrtle-green & blue 1·00 50
68/72 *Set of* 5 .. .. .. 2·75 1·40
Designs: *Vert*—13 f. Javelin-throwing; 16 f. Fruit-porters' race. *Horiz*—15 f. Horse-racing; 21 f. Pirogue-racing.

(Des and eng C. Haley. Recess)

1967 (19 Dec)–**68.** *Ancient Art of the Marquesas Islands. T* **32** *and similar vert designs. P* 13.
73 10 f. ultramarine, red and purple (28.2.68) 40 25
74 15 f. black and light emerald (28.2.68) .. 55 35
75 20 f. olive-brown, turquoise-green & lake 75 45
76 23 f. chocolate and yellow-ochre (28.2.68) 80 45
77 25 f. chocolate, light purple and blue .. 95 55
78 30 f. light brown and bright purple .. 1·10 80
79 35 f. bright blue and chocolate (28.2.68) .. 1·40 95
80 50 f. bistre-brown, lt blue & blackish green 1·75 1·25
73/80 *Set of* 8 .. .. 7·00 4·50
Designs:—10 f. Sculpture on mother-of-pearl; 15 f. Paddle-blade; 23 f. Receptacle for anointing-oil; 25 f. Hunting stirrups; 30 f. Fan handles; 35 f. Tattoed man; 50 f. "Tikis".

33 Ship's Stern and Canoe ("Wallis, 1767")

(Des Dessirier. Eng P. Forget (80 f.), J. Miermont (others). Recess)

1968 (6 Apr). *AIR. Bicentenary of Discovery of Tahiti. T* **33** *and similar designs. P* 13.
81 40 f. orange-brown, blue and emerald .. 1·60 80
82 60 f. red-orange, black and blue .. .. 2·25 1·25
83 80 f. salmon, lake and bright purple .. 2·75 1·60
MS84 180×100 mm. Nos. 81/3 .. .. 6·00 3·25
Designs: *Horiz*—60 f. Ship and witchdoctor ("Cook, 1769"). *Vert*—80 f. "Bougainville, 1768" (portrait).

34 Bouquet, Sun and W.H.O. Emblem

(Des and eng A. Decaris. Recess)

1968 (4 May). 20th Anniv of World Health Organization. P 13.
85 34 15 f. violet, crimson and blue-green .. 50 40
86 16 f. blue-green, purple and orange .. 55 40

39 "Concorde" in Flight   40 Polynesian with Guitar

(Des and eng C. Durrens. Recess)

1969 (17 Apr). AIR. First Flight of "Concorde". P 13.
93 39 40 f. chestnut and cerise .. .. 5·00 3·50

(Des M. Constantin. Photo So.Ge.Im.)

1969 (9 July). AIR. Pacific Area Travel Association (P.A.T.A.) Congress, Tahiti (1970) (1st issue). P 13.
94 40 25 f. multicoloured .. .. .. 1·10 50

35 "The Meal" (Gauguin)   36 Human Rights Emblem

(Photo Delrieu)

1968 (30 July). AIR. P 12 × 12½.
87 35 200 f. multicoloured .. .. .. 9·50 6·50

(Des and eng A. Decaris. Recess)

1968 (10 Aug). Human Rights Year. P 13.
88 36 15 f. red, new blue and brown .. 55 30
89 16 f. ultramarine, chocolate & brt purple 75 45

41 Diver and Fish

(Des H. Biais. Photo So.Ge.Im.)

1969 (5 Aug). AIR. World Underwater Hunting Champion-ships. T 41 and similar design. P 13.
95 48 f. black, bright purple and turquoise .. 1·75 1·00
96 52 f. black, red and light blue .. .. 2·25 1·25
Design: Vert—52 f. "Flag" fish.

37 Putting the Shot   38 Tiare Apetahi   42 Boxing

(Des and eng C. Haley. Recess)

1968 (12 Oct). AIR. Olympic Games, Mexico. P 13.
90 37 35 f. blue-green, brown-purple and lake 2·25 1·10

(Des P. Lambert. Photo So.Ge.Im.)

1969 (27 Mar). Flowers. T 38 and similar horiz design. Multicoloured. P 12½ × 13.
91 9 f. Type 38 .. .. 45 25
92 17 f. Tiare Tahiti 75 30

(Des and eng G. Bétemps. Recess)

1969 (13 Aug). Third South Pacific Games, Port Moresby, New Guinea. T 42 and similar designs. P 13.
97 9 f. bistre-brown and violet 40 25
98 17 f. bistre-brown and vermilion .. 55 30
99 18 f. bistre-brown and new blue .. 80 45
100 22 f. maroon and emerald .. .. 1·10 65
97/100 Set of 4 .. .. 2·50 1·50
Designs: Vert—17 f. High-jumping; 18 f. Running; 22 f. Long-jumping.

ALBUM LISTS

Please write for our latest lists of albums and accessories. These will be sent free on request.

43 "Bonaparte, Commander-in-Chief, Italy" (Rouillard)

44 I.L.O. Building, Geneva

(Photo Delrieu)

1969 (15 Oct). *AIR. Birth Bicentenary of Napoleon Bonaparte.* P 12½×12.
101 **43** 100 f. multicoloured .. .. .. 19·00 15·00

(Des and eng J. Derrey. Recess)

1969 (24 Nov). *50th Anniv of International Labour Organization* P 13.
102 **44** 17 f. light drab, emerald and salmon .. 70 30
103 18 f. ultramarine, chocolate and salmon 80 40

45 Territorial Assembly Building

46 Tiki holding P.A.T.A. Emblem

(Photo So.Ge.Im. (24 f.), Delrieu (others))

1969 (19 Dec). *Polynesian Buildings. T 45 and similar horiz designs. Multicoloured.* P 12½×13 (24 f.) or 12½×12 (others).
104 **45** Type **45** 40 20
105 14 f. Governor's Residence 50 25
106 17 f. Tourist Office 65 30
107 18 f. Maeva Hotel 75 40
108 24 f. Taharaa Hotel 90 45
104/108 *Set of 5* .. .. 3·00 1·50

(Des and eng C. Guillame, after L. Law (20 f.) or V. Adams (60 f.). Des C. Guillame, after J. Bovy. Eng M. Monvoisin (40 f.). Recess)

1970 (7 Apr). *P.A.T.A. Congress, Tahiti (2nd issue). T 46 and similar designs.* P 13.
109 20 f. greenish blue, agate and purple .. 75 30
110 40 f. ultramarine, bright purple & emerald 1·75 75
111 60 f. chocolate, new blue and lake-brown 2·25 1·10
Designs: *Horiz*—40 f. Globe, airliner and "tourists". *Vert*—60 f. Polynesian holding globe.

47 New U.P.U. Building, Berne

(Des and eng J. Gauthier. Recess)

1970 (20 May). *New U.P.U. Headquarters Building, Berne.* P 13.
112 **47** 18 f. light brown, dp violet & red-brown 75 30
113 20 f. slate-blue, olive-brown & brt pur 90 45

48 Tower of the Sun and Mt. Fuji

(Des H. Ouin ("Lacroix"). Photo)

1970 (15 Sept). *AIR. "EXPO 70" World Fair, Osaka, Japan. T 48 and similar multicoloured design.* P 13.
114 30 f. Type **48** .. : .. .. 1·60 75
115 50 f. Eiffel Tower and Torii Gate (*vert*) .. 2·75 1·50

49 Diver and Basket

50 I.E.Y. Emblem, Open Book and "The Thinker" (statue)

(Des C. Guillame, after F. Seli. Eng M. Monvoisin (27 f.), C. Guillame (others). Recess)

1970 (30 Sept). *AIR. Pearl-diving. T 49 and similar designs.* P 13.
116 2 f. lake-brown, indigo & greenish blue 20 10
117 5 f. ultramarine, orange & greenish blue 30 15
118 18 f. slate, orange and purple 75 40
119 27 f. lilac, brown and bright purple .. 1·10 65
120 50 f. orange, slate and lake-brown .. 2·00 1·10
116/120 *Set of 5* .. .. 4·00 2·25
Designs: *Vert*—5 f. Diver gathering oysters; 27 f. Pearl in opened oyster; 50 f. Women with pearl jewellery; *Horiz*—18 f. Opening oyster-shell.

(Des A. Peyrié. Eng P. Forget. Recess)

1970 (15 Oct). *AIR. International Education Year.* P 13.
121 **50** 50 f. grey-blue, brown-lake & new blue 95 50

51 "Polynesian Woman" (Y. de Saint-Front)

(Photo Delrieu)

1970 (14 Dec). *AIR. Paintings by Polynesian Artists* (1*st* series). *T* **51** *and similar multicoloured designs. P* 12½ ×12 (100 *f.*) *or* 12 ×12½ (*others*).

122	20 f. Type **51**	1·25	65
123	40 f. "Harbour Scene" (F. Fay)	2·50	1·25
124	60 f. "Niu" (abstract) (J. Guillois)	3·25	1·60
125	80 f. "Beach Hut" (J. Masson)	4·00	1·90
126	100 f. "Polynesian Girl" (J.-C. Bouloc) (vert)	5·50	2·75
122/126	*Set of 5*	15·00	7·50

See also Nos. 147/51, 160/4, 172/6, 189/93 and 205/9.

52 Games Emblem

53 Flame of Remembrance

(Des P. Lambert. Photo Delrieu)

1971 (21 Jan). *AIR. 4th South Pacific Games, Tahiti* (1*st* issue). *P* 12½.
127 **52** 20 f. multicoloured 75 40

(Des G. E. Bovy. Photo Delrieu)

1971 (19 Mar). *AIR. Erection of General de Gaulle Monument. P* 12½.
128 **53** 5 f. multicoloured 70 45

54 Volunteer, Crest and Tricolour

(Des G. E. Bovy. Photo Delrieu)

1971 (21 Apr). *AIR. 30th Anniv of Departure of "Free French" Tahitian Volunteers. P* 12½.
129 **54** 25 f. multicoloured .. .. .. 1·90 1·25

55 Marara Fisherman

(Des C. Guillame (10 f. after F. Seli). Photo)

1971 (11 May). *Water Sports. T* **55** *and similar multicoloured designs. P* 13. (*a*) POSTAGE.
130 10 f. Type **55** 55 30

(*b*) *AIR. Inscr* "POSTE AERIENNE"

131	15 f. Surfing (*vert*)	55	30
132	16 f. Skin-diving (*vert*) ..	65	40
133	20 f. Water-skiing with kite	75	45
130/133	*Set of 4*	2·25	1·40

56 Red Flower   57 Yachting

(Des C. Petras. Photo)

1971 (27 Aug). *"Day of the 1,000 Flowers". T* **56** *and similar multicoloured designs. P* 13 ×12½ (12 *f.*) *or* 12½ ×13 (*others*).

134	8 f. Type **56**	40	25
135	12 f. Hibiscus (*horiz*)	65	40
136	22 f. Porcelain rose	90	50

(Des P. Lambert. Photo Delrieu)

1971 (8 Sept). *AIR. 4th South Pacific Games, Tahiti* (2*nd* issue). *T* **57** *and similar square designs. P* 12½.

137	15 f. Type **57**	55	35
138	18 f. Golf	80	45
139	27 f. Archery	1·10	55
140	53 f. Tennis	2·00	95
137/140	*Set of 4*	4·00	2·00
MS141	138 ×170 mm. Nos. 137/40 ..	4·75	4·75

58 Water-skiing   59 De Gaulle in Uniform (1940)

(Des and eng G. Bétemps. Recess)

1971 (11 Oct). *First World Water-ski Championships, Papeete. T* **58** *and similar designs. P* 13.

142	10 f. red, turquoise-green & bistre-brown	45	25
143	20 f. red, brown and bright emerald	90	45
144	40 f. purple, red-brown and emerald	1·50	85

Designs: *Vert*—20 f. Ski-jumping. *Horiz*—40 f. Acrobatics on one ski.

(Des G. Bétemps. Eng J. Miermont (30 f.), G. Bétemps (50 f.). Recess)

1971 (9 Nov). *First Death Anniv of General De Gaulle. T* **59** *and similar vert portrait. P* 13.

145	30 f. black and bright purple	1·25	75
146	50 f. black and bright purple	1·90	1·00

Design:—50 f. De Gaulle as President of the French Republic, 1970.

(Photo Delrieu)

1971 (15 Dec). *AIR. Paintings by Polynesian Artists* (2*nd* series). *Multicoloured designs as T* **51**. *P* 13.

147	20 f. "Polynesian Village" (I. Wolf)	95	60
148	40 f. "Lagoon" (A. Dobrowolski)	1·25	1·00
149	60 f. "Polynesian Woman" (F. Seli) (*vert*)	2·25	1·60

150 80 f. "The Holy Family" (P. Heymann)
     (vert)   ..   .. 3·25   2·25
151 100 f. "Faces in a Crowd" (N. Michou-
     touchkine)   ..   ..   .. 3·75   2·50
147/151 Set of 5   ..   ..   .. 10·00   7·00

60 Cross Emblem

(Des P. Sampoux. Photo)

1971 (18 Dec). Second French Pacific Scouts and Guides
Rally, Taravao. P 13 × 12½.
152 **60** 28 f. multicoloured ..   ..   .. 1·10   55

61 Harbour, Papeete

(Des G. E. Bovy. Photo)

1972 (13 Jan). AIR. 10th Anniv of Papeete as an Autonomous
Port. P 13.
153 **61** 28 f. multicoloured ..   ..   .. 1·10   55

62 Figure-skating

(Des and eng J. Combet. Recess)

1972 (25 Jan). AIR. Winter Olympic Games, Sapporo,
Japan. P 13.
154 **62** 20 f. claret, blue-green & bluish violet   95   40

63 Commission Headquarters, Nouméa,
New Caledonia

(Des O. Baillais. Photo)

1972 (5 Feb). AIR. 25th Anniv of South Pacific Commission.
P 13.
155 **63** 21 f. multicoloured   75   40

64 Alcoholic behind   65 Floral Emblem
     Bars

(Des T. Roscol. Photo)

1972 (24 Mar). Campaign against Alcoholism. P 13.
156 **64** 20 f. multicoloured   75   55

(Des and eng C. Guillame, after F. Seli. Recess)

1972 (9 May). AIR. South Pacific Arts Festival, Fiji. P 13.
157 **65** 36 f. red-orange, green and new blue ..   1·25   65

66 Raft Kon-Tiki and Route-map

(Des P. Heyman. Photo)

1972 (18 Aug). AIR. 25th Anniv of Arrival of "Kon-Tiki"
Expedition in French Polynesia. P 13.
158 **66** 16 f. multicoloured   95   50

67 De Gaulle and Monument

(Des and eng J. Miermont. Recess)

1972 (9 Dec). AIR. Completion of De Gaulle Monument.
P 13.
159 **67** 100 f. slate   ..   .. 5·00   3·25

(Photo Delrieu)

1972 (14 Dec). AIR. Paintings by Polynesian Artists (3rd
series). Multicoloured designs as T 51. P 13.
160   20 f. "Horses" (G. Bovy)   95   50
161   40 f. "Harbour" (R. Juventin) (vert)   .. 1·25   75

162	60 f. "Landscape" (A. Brooke)	..	2·25	1·90
163	80 f. "Polynesians" (D. Adam) (*vert*)	..	3·25	2·50
164	100 f. "Dancers" (A. Pilioko) (*vert*)	..	3·75	3·25
160/164	*Set of* 5	..	10·00	8·00

68 St. Theresa and Lisieux Basilica

(Des and eng J. Combet. Recess)

1973 (23 Jan). *AIR. Birth Centenary of St. Theresa of Lisieux.* P 13.

165	**68**	85 f. multicoloured	..	..	3·75	2·25

69 Copernicus and Planetary System

(Des and eng M. Monvoisin. Recess)

1973 (7 Mar). *AIR. 500th Birth Anniv of Nicolas Copernicus (astronomer).* P 13.

166	**69**	100 f. bluish violet, brown & brt purple	4·00	2·50

70 Aeroplane and Flying Fish

(Des J. F. Favre. Photo)

1973 (3 Apr). *AIR. Inauguration of "Air France" Round-the-World Service via Tahiti.* P 13.

167	**70**	80 f. multicoloured	..	..	2·75	1·90

71 "DC-10" in Flight

(Des and eng C. Haley. Recess)

1973 (18 May). *AIR. Inauguration of "DC-10" Service.* P 13.

168	**71**	20 f. blue, myrtle-green and light blue	75	40

72 "Ta Matete" (Gauguin)

(Photo Delrieu)

1973 (7 June). *AIR. 125th Birth Anniv of Gauguin.* P 13.

169	**72**	200 f. multicoloured	..	..	6·50	3·75

73 Loti, Fisherman and Polynesian Girl

(Des and eng J. Combet. Recess)

1973 (4 July). *AIR. 50th Death Anniv of Pierre Loti* (*writer*). P 13.

170	**73**	60 f. multicoloured	..	..	1·90	1·10

74 Polynesian Mother and Child	**75** "Teeing-off"

(Des J. Manteuil. Photo)

1973 (26 Sept). *Opening of Tahitian Women's Union Crèche.* P 12½×13.

171	**74**	28 f. multicoloured	..	..	90	55

(Photo Delrieu)

1973 (13 Dec). *AIR. Paintings by Polynesian Artists* (*4th series*). *Multicoloured designs as T* **51**. P 13.

172	20 f. "Sun God" (J.-F. Favre) (*vert*)	..	65	50
173	40 f. "Polynesian Girl" (E. de Gennes)			
	(*vert*)	..	1·25	75
174	60 f. "Abstract" (A. Sidet) (*vert*)	..	1·90	1·60
175	80 f. "Bus Passengers" (F. Ravello) (*vert*)		2·75	1·90
176	100 f. "Boats" (J. Bourdin)	..	3·50	2·75
172/176	*Set of* 5	..	9·00	7·00

(Des from photographs by Sylvain. Photo Delrieu)

1974 (27 Feb). *Atimaono Golf Course, Tahiti. T* **75** *and similar vert design. Multicoloured. P* 13½.

177	16 f. Type **75**	..	..	55	45
178	24 f. View of golf course	..	..	95	55

76 "A Helping Hand"

(Des after H. Tcheou. Photo)

1974 (9 May). *Polynesian Animal Protection Society. P* 13.

179	**76**	21 f. multicoloured	..	65	40

77 Mountains and Lagoon

78 Bird, Fish, Leaf and Flower

(Des from photographs by Sylvain (2 f., 5 f., 6 f.), or by Christian (others). Photo)

1974 (22 May). *Polynesian Landscapes. T* **77** *and similar multicoloured designs. P* 13.

180	2 f. Type **77**	..	..	8	5
181	5 f. Beach games	..	..	15	10
182	6 f. Canoe fishing	..	..	20	15
183	10 f. Mountain peak (*vert*)	..	30	20
184	15 f. Schooner in sunset scene	..	50	30
185	20 f. Island and lagoon	..	..	65	40
180/185	*Set of 6*	..	..	1·75	1·10

(Des J. Saquet. Photo)

1974 (12 June). *AIR. Protection of Nature. P* 13.

186	**78**	12 f. multicoloured	..	50	20

79 Catamarans

80 Polynesian Woman

(Des J. Saquet. Photo)

1974 (22 July). *AIR. Second World Catamaran Sailing Championships, Papeete. P* 13.

187	**79**	100 f. multicoloured	..	2·50	1·25

(Des Caussin. Eng G. Aufschneider. Recess)

1974 (9 Oct). *Centenary of Universal Postal Union. P* 13.

188	**80**	65 f. multicoloured	..	1·25	1·10

(Photo Delrieu)

1974 (12 Dec). *AIR. Paintings by Polynesian Artists (5th series). Multicoloured designs as T* 51. *P* 13.

189	20 f. "Flower arrangement (R. Temarui-Masson) (*vert*)		50	40
190	40 f. "Palms on Beach" (M. Chardon) (*vert*)		75	50
191	60 f. "Portrait of a Man" (M-F. Avril) (*vert*)	..	1·60	1·10
192	80 f. "Polynesian Girl" (H. Robin) (*vert*)	2·25	1·50
193	100 f. "Lagoon at Night" (D. Farsi)	..	3·25	1·90
189/193	*Set of 5*	..	..	7·50	5·00

81 "The Travelling Gods"

(Des Dessirier. Eng J. Larrivière (50 f.), C. Jumelet (75 f.), P. Guédron (100 f.). Recess)

1975 (7 Feb). *AIR. "50 Years of Tahitian Aviation". T* **81** *and similar horiz designs. P* 13.

194	50 f. reddish violet, lake and chocolate	..	1·25	65
195	75 f. new blue, red and olive-green	..	1·90	95
196	100 f. chocolate, magenta and olive-green	2·50	1·25

Designs:—75 f. Tourville flying-boat; 100 f. Tourist airliner.

82 Polynesian Girl and French "Ceres" Stamp of 1870

83 Tahiti Lions' Emblem

(Des C. Bridoux. Eng J. Combet. Recess)

1975 (29 May). *AIR. "Arphila 75" International Stamp Exhibition, Paris. P* 13.

197	**82**	32 f. red, brown and black	..	75	45

(Des J. Saquet. Photo)

1975 (17 June). *15th Anniv of Tahiti Lions' Club. P* 13.

198	**83**	26 f. multicoloured	..	65	40

84 "Protect Nature"

(Des E. Coudurier. Litho Cartor)

1975 (9 July). *Nature Protection. P* 12.
199 **84** 19 f. deep ultramarine and green   45   25

88 "Concorde"

89 President Pompidou

1976 (21 Jan). *AIR. First Commercial Flight of "Concorde".
P* 13.
210 **88** 100 f. deep blue, new blue & magenta   2·50   2·25

(Des and eng P. Gandon. Recess)

1976 (16 Feb). *Pompidou Commemoration. P* 13.
211 **89** 49 f. slate and deep blue   95   5

85 Putting the Shot

86 Athlete and View of Montreal

(Des J. Chesnot. Photo)

1975 (1 Aug). *AIR. Fifth South Pacific Games, Guam.
T* **85** *and similar square designs. Multicoloured. P* 13.
200   25 f. Type **85**   55   30
201   30 f. Volleyball   70   40
202   40 f. Swimming   80   50

(Des and eng C. Guillame. Recess)

1975 (15 Oct). *AIR. Olympic Games, Montreal* (1976). *P* 13.
203 **86** 44 f. black, new blue and vermilion   95   65

90 Battle of the Saints

(Des and eng J. Combet. Recess)

1976 (15 Apr). *AIR. Bicentenary of American Revolution. T* **90** *and similar horiz design. P* 13.
212   24 f. turquoise-blue, yellow-brown & blk   40   20
213   31 f. claret, red and bistre   55   30
Design:— 31 f. Sea battle of The Chesapeake.

87 Airliner and Letters

(Des and eng M. Monvoisin. Recess)

1975 (5 Nov). *AIR. World U.P.U. Day. P* 13.
204 **87** 100 f. blue, olive and light brown   2·25   1·25

(Litho Cartor)

1975 (17 Dec). *AIR. Paintings by Polynesian Artists* (6th
series). *Multicoloured designs as T* 51. *P* 12½.
205   20 f. "Beach Scene" (R. Marcel-Marius)   50   30
206   40 f. "Rooftop Aerials" (M. Anglade)   75   45
207   60 f. "Street Scene" (J. Day)   1·25   80
208   80 f. "Tropical Waters" (J. Steimetz)
         (vert)   1·75   1·10
209   100 f. "Portrait of a Woman" (A. van der
         Heyde) (vert)   2·00   1·40
205/209   Set of 5   5·50   3·75

91 King Pomaré I

(Des P. Lambert. Litho Cartor)

1976 (28 Apr). *AIR. Pomaré Dynasty. T* **91** *and similar vert
designs. Multicoloured. P* 12½.
214   18 f. Type **91**   30   15
215   21 f. King Pomaré II   40   20
216   26 f. Queen Pomaré IV   50   20
217   30 f. King Pomaré V   55   30
214/217   Set of 4   1·60   80
See also Nos. 234/7.

92 Gerbault and *Firecrest*

93 Turtle (*Chelonia mydas*)

96 "The Dream" (Gauguin)

(Photo Government Printing Works, Paris)
1976 (17 Oct). *AIR. P* 13.
226 **96** 50 f. multicoloured .. .. .. 1·10 75

(Des J. Boullaire. Photo Delrieu)
1976 (25 May). 50*th Anniv of Alain Gerbault's Arrival at Bora-Bora. P* 13.
218 **92** 90 f. multicoloured .. .. 1·40 90

(Des P.-M. Yolande (18 f.), H. Sarah (42 f.). Litho Cartor)
1976 (24 June). *World Ecology Day. T* 93 *and similar vert design. Multicoloured. P* 12.
219 18 f. Type **93** 30 15
220 42 f. Doves in hand 70 40

97 Marquesas Pirogue

(Des H. K. Kane. Litho Edila)
1976 (16 Dec). *Ancient Pirogues. T* 97 *and similar horiz designs. Multicoloured. P* 13 × 12½.
227 25 f. Type **97** 45 25
228 30 f. Raiatea pirogue 55 30
229 75 f. Tahiti pirogue .. .. .. 1·25 65
230 100 f. Tuamotu pirogue .. .. .. 1·50 90
227/230 *Set of* 4 .. .. 3·50 1·90

94 Legs of Runner

(Des C. Bridoux. Eng J. Larrivière (26 f.), C. Jumelet (34 f.) Guédron (50 f.). Recess)
1976 (19 July). *AIR. Olympic Games, Montreal. T* 94 *and similar designs. P* 13.
221 26 f. chestnut, maroon and blue .. 40 20
222 34 f. maroon, chestnut and new blue .. 55 35
223 50 f. chestnut, blue and deep maroon .. 65 45
MS224 181 × 101 mm. Nos. 222/224 .. 1·75 1·75
Designs: *Vert* 34f. Runners. *Horiz*—50f. Olympic flame and flowers.

98 Murex steeriae

99 Acropora

(Des Ky Phungchaleun. Photo)
1977 (14 Apr). *AIR. Seashells. T* 98 *and similar vert designs. Multicoloured. P* 12½ × 13.
231 25 f. Type **98** 40 15
232 27 f. Conus gauguini 45 20
233 35 f. Conus marchionatus 60 25
See also Nos. 268/270.

95 A. Graham Bell, Early Telephone and Dish Aerial

(Des and eng C. Haley. Recess)
1976 (15 Sept). *Telephone Centenary, P* 13.
225 **95** 37 f. brown-lake, brt blue & orge brn .. 65 40

(Des P. Lambert. Litho Cartor)
1977 (19 Apr). *AIR. "Sovereigns of the Archipelago". Vert portraits as T* 91. *Multicoloured. P* 12½.
234 19 f. Maputeoa (Mangareva) 25 20
235 33 f. Tamatoa V (Raiatea) 45 35
236 39 f. Vaekehu (Marquesas) 55 40
237 43 f. Teuruarii III (Rurutu) 55 45
234/237 *Set of* 4 .. .. 1·60 1·25

(Des O. Baillais. Photo)

1977 (23 May). *AIR. 3rd Coral Reefs Symposium, Miami. T* **99** *and similar multicoloured design. P* 13×12½ (25 f.) *or* 12½×13 (33 f.).

238	25 f. Type **99**	..	..	35	25
239	33 f. Pocillopora (*vert*)	..		45	35

103 *Hibiscus tiliaceus*　　　104 Palm Tree

(Des P. Lambert. Photo)

1977 (15 Sept). *AIR. Polynesian Flowers. T* **103** *and similar vert design. Multicoloured. P* 12½×13.

258	8 f. Type **103**	..	..	..	10	5
259	12 f. Plumeria acuminata ..		..	15	12

(Des O. Baillais. Photo)

1977 (8 Nov). *AIR. Forest Conservation. P* 13.

260	**104**	32 f. multicoloured	..	..	45	30

O**100** Uru　　　101 Dancer

(Des Ky Phungchaleun. Litho Cartor)

1977 (9 June). *OFFICIAL. Native Fruits. Type O* **100** *and similar horiz designs. P* 12½×12.

O240	1 f. multicoloured	..	..	5	5
O241	2 f. multicoloured	..	..	5	5
O242	3 f. multicoloured	..	..	5	5
O243	5 f. multicoloured	..	..	5	5
O244	7 f. multicoloured	..	..	10	5
O245	8 f. multicoloured	..	..	12	10
O246	10 f. multicoloured	..	..	15	12
O247	15 f. multicoloured	..	..	20	15
O248	19 f. multicoloured	..	..	25	20
O249	20 f. multicoloured	..	..	30	20
O250	25 f. multicoloured	..	..	35	25
O251	35 f. multicoloured	..	..	45	35
O252	50 f. multicoloured	..	..	70	50
O253	100 f. multicoloured	..	..	1·25	95
O254	200 f. multicoloured	..	..	2·75	2·00
O240/O254	*Set of* 15	..	..	6·00	4·50

Designs:—2 f., 3 f., 5 f. Type O **100**; 7 f., 8 f., 10 f., 15 f Vi Tahiti; 19 f., 20 f., 25 f., 35 f. Avocat; 50 f., 100 f., 200 f. Vi Popaa.

1977 (18 June). *AIR. 5th Anniv of General de Gaulle Memorial. As T* **806** *of France.*

255	40 f. multicoloured	..	..	55	40

(Des Ky Phungchaleun. Litho Cartor)

1977 (14 July). *AIR. Polynesian Dancer. P* 12.

256	**101**	27 f. multicoloured	..	..	40	30

105 "Portrait of Rubens' Son, Albert"

(Des and eng C. Haley. Recess)

1977 (28 Nov). *AIR. 400th Birth Anniv of Peter Paul Rubens. P* 13.

261	**105**	100 f. carmine-lake and indigo	..	1·40	1·00

102 Lindbergh and *Spirit of St. Louis*

(Des J. Combet. Litho Cartor)

1977 (18 Aug). *AIR. 50th Anniv of Lindbergh's Transatlantic Flight. P* 12.

257	**102**	28 f. multicoloured	..	..	40	30

106 Cutter

(Des J. Combet. Photo)

1977 (22 Dec). *Sailing Ships. T* **106** *and similar horiz designs. Multicoloured. P* 13.

262	20 f. Type **106**	..	..	..	..	30	20
263	50 f. Schooner	..	..	..	..	65	45
264	85 f. Barque	..	..	..	..	1·10	75
265	120 f. Full-rigged three-master	..	..	1·75	1·10
262/265	*Set of* 4	..	..	..	..	3·50	2·25

THE WORLD CENTRE FOR FINE STAMPS IS 391 STRAND

107 Captain Cook and H.M.S. *Discovery*

(Des and eng C. Andréotto. Recess)

1978 (20 Jan). *AIR. Bicentenary of Discovery of Hawaii.* T **107** *and similar horiz design.* P 13.

266	33 f. dp mag, brn-red & dp ultram		45	35
267	39 f. emerald, brt greenish blue & dp mve		55	40

Design:—39 f. Captain Cook and H.M.S. *Resolution.*

(Des Ky Phungchaleun. Photo Delrieu)

1978 (13 Apr). *AIR. Seashells (2nd issue). Vert designs as* T **98**. *Multicoloured.* P 13.

268	22 f. *Erosaria obvelata*			40	20
269	24 f. *Cypraea ventriculus*			40	30
270	31 f. *Lambis robusta*			45	30

111 Fungia

112 *Hibiscus rosa sinensis*

(Des O. Baillais. Photo)

1978 (13 July). *AIR. Coral.* T **111** *and similar multicoloured design.* P 13×12½ (26 f.) *or* 12½×13 (34 f.).

274	26 f. Type **111**		40	30
275	34 f. Millepora (*vert*)		45	35

(Des O. Baillais. Photo)

1978 (23 Aug). *Flowers.* T **112** *and similar vert design. Multicoloured.* P 12½×13.

276	13 f. Type **112**		15	12
277	16 f. *Fagraea berteriana*		20	15

113 Polynesian Girl and Aerial

(Des J. M. Deligny. Eng J. Larrivière. Recess)

1978 (5 Sept). *AIR. Papenoo Ground Receiving Station.* P 13.

278	**113** 50 f. black and greenish blue		65	45

108 "Tahitian Woman and Boy" (Gauguin)

109 Microwave Antenna

(Photo Delrieu)

1978 (7 May). *AIR. 75th Death Anniv of Paul Gauguin.* P 13.

271	**108** 50 f. multicoloured		65	45

(Litho Edila)

1978 (17 May). *AIR. World Telecommunications Day.* P 13.

272	**109** 80 f. multicoloured		1·10	75

114 Bird and Rainbow over Tropical Island

115 Polynesian Girl on Beach

(Des T. Valerie. Photo)

1978 (8 Oct). *AIR. Nature Protection.* P 13.

279	**114** 23 f. multicoloured		40	30

(Des and eng R. Cottet (20 f.), G. Bétemps (28 f.), C. Mazelin (36 f.). Recess)

1978 (3 Nov). *30th Anniv of First French Polynesian Stamps.* T **115** *and similar vert designs as* 1958 *issue but inscr* "1958 1978". P 13.

280	20 f. orange-brown, violet and red		40	20
281	28 f. orange-brown, dp yell-grn & orge-yell		40	30
282	36 f. brown, vermilion and new blue		45	35
MS283	130×100 mm. Nos. 280/282 in different colours		1·10	75

Designs:—28 f. Polynesian (T **2**); 36 f. Girl playing guitar (T **1**).

110 Match Scene

(Des J. Combet. Photo)

1978 (1 June). *AIR. World Cup Football Championship, Argentina.* P 13.

273	**110** 28 f. multicoloured		40	30

116 *Tahiti*

(Des J. Combet. Litho Edila)

1978 (29 Dec). *Ships. T* **116** *and similar horiz designs.*
Multicoloured. P 13×12½.

284	15 f. Type **116**	..	..	..	20	15
285	30 f. *Monowai*	..	..	..	45	30
286	75 f. *Tahitien*	..	..	..	1·25	65
287	100 f. *Mariposa*	..	..	..	1·50	90
284/287	*Set of* 4	..	..	..	3·00	1·75

PHILATELIC TERMS
ILLUSTRATED

This successful STAMP MONTHLY series has
now been brought together in a snappy black
and yellow binding and published as a useful
addition to Stanley Gibbons range of essential
handbooks for keen stamp collectors.
Within its 192 pages this handy limp-bound
volume houses a veritable mine of useful
information on the words and phrases used in
philately. It describes and illustrates printing
processes and watermarks, papers and
perforations, errors and varieties . . . and it does
all this IN COLOUR. Indeed, there are 92 full
page plates in colour, plus many black and
white illustrations, making it

FANTASTIC VALUE AT ONLY £1·95
POST PAID FROM
Stanley Gibbons Publications Ltd
391 Strand, London WC2R 0LX

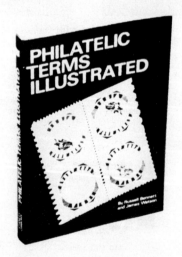

French Post Offices in China

1894. 100 Centimes=1 Franc
1907. 100 Cents=1 Piastre

A French Post Office was opened by the consular authorities in Shanghai in November 1862 and another at Tientsin on 16 March 1889. Unoverprinted stamps of France were used until 1894. French Post Offices were opened at Chefoo in November 1898; at Peking in December 1900; at Amoy in January 1902; and at Foochow and Ningpo in 1902. A Postal Agency was opened at Hankow in November 1898 and this became a Post Office in October 1902.

All overprints are on stamps of France, the "Tablet", Type X inscribed "INDO-CHINE" or the Type of Indo-China illustrated below.

X "Tablet" Type   6 "Grasset" Type

Chine **25** **16 Cents**

(1)   (2)   (3)

1894–1903. "Peace and Commerce" Type of France optd with *T* 1. *All Type (b) except where otherwise stated.*

1	**10**	5 c. deep green/*green* (b) (Vm.)	50	40
		a. Carmine opt	50	50
2		5 c. yellow-green (a) (C.) (1900)	50	25
3		5 c. yellow-green (b) (C.) (1900)	7·50	3·75
4		10 c. black/*lilac* (a) (C.) (1900)	2·50	2·10
5		10 c. black/*lilac* (b) (C.)	3·75	3·25
		a. Vermilion opt	3·25	2·50
6		15 c. blue (C.)	1·50	50
		a. Vermilion opt	1·10	45
7		15 c. blue/*bluish* (C.) (1903)	45·00	32·00
8		20 c. red/*green*	1·00	50
9		25 c. black/*rose* (C.)	90	25
		a. Vermilion opt	3·25	50
10		30 c. cinnamon	90	75
11		40 c. red/*yellow* (1900)	1·25	1·00
12	**10**	50 c. carmine (b)	2·50	1·50
		a. Pale carmine	2·25	1·25
13		50 c. carmine (a) (1900)	3·25	2·50
14		75 c. brown/*orange* (Vm.)	16·00	9·50
		a. Carmine opt	17·00	11·00
15		1 f. olive-green	2·50	75
		a. Opt double	55·00	
		b. Grey-green	2·50	75
16		2 f. brown/*pale blue* (a) (1900)	6·50	4·25
17		5 f. lilac/*pale lilac*	20·00	8·00
		a. Mauve/*pale lilac*	9·00	8·00

No. 7 was issued at Tientsin.
The 50 c. (b) and 5 f. with carmine overprint exist but were not issued.

1900 (25 Oct). *Provisional for Shanghai. No.* 15 *surch with T* 2.

18	**10**	25 on 1 f. olive-green	13·00	8·00

1901 (20 Apr). *Provisionals for Peking. No.* 9 *surch as T* 3, *in red.*

19	**10**	2 c. on 25 c. black/*rose*	£225	65·00
20		4 c. on 25 c. black/*rose*	£190	65·00
21		6 c. on 25 c. black/*rose*	£225	95·00
22		16 c. on 25 c. black/*rose*	65·00	40·00
		a. Surch in black	—	£1400

1901–7. *POSTAGE DUE. Postage Due stamps of France optd with T* 1.

D23	D **3**	5 c. pale blue (C.)	75	65
D24		10 c. pale brown (C.)	1·50	1·25
D25		15 c. pale green (C.)	1·50	1·25
D26		20 c. olive-green (1907)	1·25	1·25
D27		30 c. carmine	2·50	1·90
D28		50 c. dull claret	2·50	1·90
D23/28		*Set of 6*	9·00	7·50

CHINE   **CHINE**

仙六十   仙六十   **5**

(4)   (5)   (6)

(Surch at Hanoi)

1902 (Sept). *Type X inscr* "INDO-CHINE" *surch* "CHINE" *and value in Chinese only as in T* 4.

23	X	1 c. black/*azure*	35	35
24		2 c. brown/*buff*	65	50
25		4 c. purple-brown/*grey*	65	50
26		5 c. pale green	90	50
27		10 c. rose-red	50	50
28		15 c. grey	75	75
29		20 c. red/*green*	1·90	1·25
30		25 c. black/*rose*	2·50	1·25
31		30 c. cinnamon/*drab*	3·25	3·25
32		40 c. red/*yellow*	9·00	5·50
33		50 c. carmine/*rose*	11·00	9·50
34		75 c. brown/*orange*	8·50	6·50
35		1 f. olive-green/*toned*	12·00	6·50
36		5 f. mauve/*pale lilac*	17·00	14·00
23/36		*Set of 14*	60·00	45·00

This issue was in use for a short time at post offices in Canton, Chungking, Hoihow, Mengtsz and Pakhoi. It was replaced by individual sets for each of these places (see Indo-Chinese Post Offices) and in 1904 this issue was put on sale again with revised surcharge as *T* 5. (See Nos. 49/62.)

1902 (Oct)–**6.** "Blanc" (**11**), "Mouchon" (**14**) and "Merson" (**13**) *Types of France, inscr* "CHINE". *P* 14×13½.

37	**11**	5 c. yellow-green	30	30
		a. Blue-green (1906)	30	30
38	**14**	10 c. carmine (3.03)	30	30
39		15 c. pale red (3.03)	50	50
40		20 c. purple-brown (2.03)	1·00	1·00
41		25 c. blue (3.03)	75	30
42		30 c. mauve (5.03)	90	90
43	**13**	40 c. red and pale blue	2·25	2·25
44		50 c. brown and lavender	2·75	2·25
45		1 f. lake and yellow-green	3·75	1·90
46		2 f. deep lilac and buff	9·50	6·50
47		5 f. deep blue and buff	14·00	9·50
37/47		*Set of 11*	32·00	24·00

Nos. 37/47 are inscribed "POSTE FRANCAISE".

1903 (4 July). *Provisional for Shanghai. No.* 39 *surch with T* 6, *in blue.*

48	**14**	5 on 15 c. pale red	3·25	1·60
		a. Surch inverted	14·00	14·00

A
PERCEVOIR

(D 7)

A
PERCEVOIR

(D 8)

1903 (Sept). *POSTAGE DUE. Provisional issue handstamped at Peking as Type D 7.*

(a) *Stamps of 1894–1903*

A. In red B. In violet

D49	**10**	5 c. deep green/*green* (No. 1)	. . . . £1400	—	†
D50		5 c. brt yellow-green (a)	£700 £250	£700 £250	
D51		10 c. black/*lilac* (a)	£1600 £1300	£1600 £1300	
D52		15 c. blue	£700 £200	£700 £200	
D53		30 c. cinnamon . .	£400 22·00	£400 22·00	

(b) *Stamps of 1902–06*

D54	**11**	5 c. yellow-green . .	£400 £200	£400 £200	
D55	**14**	10 c. carmine . .	£160 38·00	£160 38·00	
D56		15 c. pale red . .	£170 40·00	£170 40·00	

The above were for use in Peking and Tientsin.
Two types of handstamp exist. One with the "A" above the space between "C" and "E" and the other with "A" above the second "E".

1903 (13 Oct). *POSTAGE DUE. Handstamped as Type D 8.*

(a) *Stamps of 1894–1903*

A. In red B. In violet

D57	**10**	5 c. deep green/*green* (No. 1)	. . . . £1400	—	†
D58		5 c. brt yellow-green (a)	£475 90·00	£475 90·00	
D59		10 c. black/*lilac* (a)	£1600 £1300	£1600 £1300	
D60		15 c. blue	£275 22·00	£275 22·00	
D61		30 c. cinnamon . .	£110 19·00	£110 19·00	

(b) *Stamps of 1902–06*

D62	**11**	5 c. yellow-green . .	£275 £110	£275 £110	
D63	**14**	10 c. carmine . .	80·00 11·00	80·00 11·00	
D64		15 c. pale red . .	£160 13·00	£160 13·00	

There are two types of handstamp. The first a rubber stamp with an open "C" and the second a leather stamp with an almost closed "C".

(Surch at Hanoi)

1904. *Type X inscr "INDO-CHINE" surch "CHINE" and value in Chinese only as in T 5.*

49	X	1 c. black/*azure*	40	25
50		2 c. brown/*buff*	1·50	1·10
51		4 c. purple-brown/*grey* . .	50	40
52		5 c. pale green	65	50
53		10 c. rose-red	1·40	1·10
54		20 c. red/*green*	1·40	1·10
55		25 c. black/*rose*	1·75	1·50
56		25 c. blue	1·50	1·10
57		30 c. cinnamon/*drab* . .	1·00	75
58		40 c. red/*yellow* . .	4·25	3·75
59		50 c. brown/*azure* . .	1·90	1·50
60		75 c. brown/*orange* . .	6·50	4·50
61		1 f. olive-green/*toned* . .	7·50	5·50
62		5 f. mauve/*pale lilac* . .	17·00 14·00	
49/62		*Set of 14*	42·00 32·00	

A variety exists on all the values in which the letter "C" of "CHINE" is slightly larger than the normal type.
Stamps with inverted surcharges or with surcharge incomplete in this and the following issue are of clandestine origin.

Two types of 15 c.: (I) as Type 5; (II) with Chinese characters above "CHINE". Type II are from a different printing and occur on the same sheet with Type I.

1904–05. *T 8 of Indo-China surch as in T 5.*

63	**8**	1 c. olive-green . .	25	25
64		2 c. claret/*yellow*	25	25
65		4 c. purple-brown/*grey* . .	£250	£180
66		5 c. deep green	50	50
67		10 c. rose	50	50
68		15 c. brown/*azure* (I) . .	50	50
69		15 c. brown/*azure* (II) . .	50	50
70		20 c. red/*green*	1·90	1·90
71		25 c. blue	1·00	65

72		40 c. black/*greyish*	90	65
73		1 f. pale olive-green	85·00 55·00	
74		2 f. brown/*yellow*	6·50	4·50
75		10 f. red/*green*	40·00 35·00	
63/75		*Set of 13*	£350	£250

The variety mentioned after No. 62 may be found on all values.

<pre>
    2 CENTS   2̄ CENTS
    仙二   分二
     (9)   (10)
</pre>

1907. *Stamps of 1902–06 such as T 9.*

76	**11**	2 c. on 5 c. yellow-green	5	5
77	**14**	a. Blue-green	5	5
77	**14**	4 c. on 10 c. carmine . .	10	10
78		6 c. on 15 c. pale red . .	25	12
79		8 c. on 20 c. purple-brown . .	75	55
		a. "8" inverted	9·50	9·50
80		10 c. on 25 c. blue	5	5
81	**13**	20 c. on 50 c. brown and lavender . .	40	40
		a. Surch treble . .	48·00 48·00	
82		40 c. on 1 f. lake and yellow-green . .	3·75	2·50
83		2 pi. on 5 f. deep blue and buff . .	4·00	2·50
		a. Surch double . .	£275	£275
76/83		*Set of 9*	8·50	5·50

1911–21. *As last but surch as T 10.*

84	**11**	2 c. on 5 c. blue-green	15	8
85	**14**	4 c. on 10 c. carmine	20	5
86		6 c. on 15 c. orange (1915) . .	40	15
87		8 c. on 20 c. purple-brown . .	25	10
88		10 c. on 25 c. blue (1921) . .	30	15
89		20 c. on 50 c. blue (1921) . .	11·00 10·00	
90	**13**	40 c. on 1 f. lake and yellow . .	55	25
91		$2 on 5 f. deep blue and buff (1921)	40·00 32·00	
84/91		*Set of 8*	48·00 38·00	

1911. *POSTAGE DUE. Postage Due stamps of France surch as T 10.*

D92	D 3	2 c. on 5 c. pale blue . .	30	20
		a. Surch double . .	13·00	
D93		4 c. on 10 c. brown . .	25	20
		a. Surch double . .	13·00	
D94		8 c. on 20 c. olive-green . .	40	35
		a. Surch double . .	13·00	
D95		20 c. on 50 c. dull claret . .	45	35
D92/95		*Set of 4*	1·25	1·00

1922 (Dec). *Types of 1902–06 in new colours surch with new values as T 10. P 14×13½.*

92	**11**	1 c. on 5 c. orange	65	40
93	**14**	2 c. on 10 c. green	1·25	65
94		3 c. on 15 c. orange . .	1·90	1·50
95		4 c. on 20 c. purple-brown . .	2·50	1·90
96		5 c. on 25 c. purple . .	1·25	65
97		6 c. on 30 c. red	2·50	1·90
98		10 c. on 50 c. blue . .	2·50	1·90
99	**13**	20 c. on 1 f. lake and yellow-green . .	6·50	5·00
100		40 c. on 2 f. red and blue-green . .	6·50	5·00
101		1 pi. on 5 f. blue and buff . .	38·00 38·00	
92/101		*Set of 10*	55·00 50·00	

1922. *POSTAGE DUE. As Nos. D92/5 but surch different values as T 10.*

D102	D 3	1 c. on 5 c. pale blue . .	15·00 14·00	
D103		2 c. on 10 c. brown . .	22·00 19·00	
D104		4 c. on 20 c. olive-green . .	22·00 19·00	
D105		10 c. on 50 c. dull claret . .	22·00 19·00	

The French post offices in China were closed down on 31 December 1922.

ALBUM LISTS

Please write for our latest lists of albums and accessories. These will be sent free on request.

French Post Offices in Crete

100 Centimes =1 Franc
25 Centimes =1 Piastre

French Post Offices were opened at Canea, Rethymnon, Candia, San Nicolo (Ayios Nikolaos), Sitia and Hierapetra in July 1897.

French stamps overprinted or surcharged

1902 (Oct)–**3**. *"Blanc"* **(11)**, *"Mouchon"* **(14)** and *"Merson"* **(13)**, *types of France, inscr* "CRETE". *P* 14×13½.

1	**11**	1 c. grey			40	40
2		2 c. claret			40	40
3		3 c. orange-red			40	40
4		4 c. brown			40	40
5		5 c. green			25	20
6	**14**	10 c. carmine (12.02)			50	30
7		15 c. pale red (2.03)			50	40
8		20 c. purple-brown (3.03)			65	50
9		25 c. blue (9.03)			75	65
10		30 c. mauve (5.03)			1·00	90
11	**13**	40 c. red and pale blue			1·90	1·40
12		50 c. brown and lavender			3·00	1·75
13		1 f. lake and yellow-green			4·50	3·75
14		2 f. deep lilac and buff			5·50	4·50
15		5 f. deep blue and buff			8·00	5·50
1/15		*Set of 15*			25·00	20·00

2

1 PIASTRE 1	**2 PIASTRES**
(1)	(2)

1903 (Feb–Mar). *Nos.* 9 *and* 12/15, *surch with values in Turkish currency, as T* **1/2**.

16	**14**	1 pi. on 25 c. blue (Mar)		5·00	5·00
17	**13**	2 pi. on 50 c. brown and lavender		9·50	9·50
18		4 pi. on 1 f. lake and green		17·00	16·00
19		8 pi. on 2 f. deep lilac and buff		25·00	20·00
20		20 pi. on 5 f. deep blue and buff		35·00	25·00
16/20		*Set of 5*		80·00	70·00

The French post offices at Ayios Nikolaos, Sitia and Hierapetra were closed at the end of 1899 and the three others on 13 October 1914.

PHILATELIC TERMS ILLUSTRATED

This successful STAMP MONTHLY series has now been brought together in a snappy black and yellow binding and published as a useful addition to Stanley Gibbons range of essential handbooks for keen stamp collectors. Within its 192 pages this handy limp-bound volume houses a veritable mine of useful information on the words and phrases used in philately. It describes and illustrates printing processes and watermarks, papers and perforations, errors and varieties . . . and it does all this IN COLOUR. Indeed, there are 92 full page plates in colour, plus many black and white illustrations, making it

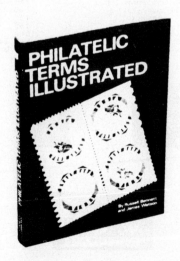

FANTASTIC VALUE AT ONLY £1·95 POST PAID FROM

Stanley Gibbons Publications Ltd
391 Strand, London WC2R 0LX

French Post Offices in Egypt

1899. 100 Centimes=1 Franc
1921. 10 Milliemes=1 Piastre

A. ALEXANDRIA

The French Post Office in Alexandria was opened in 1830 and from 1857 to 1876 used the stamps of France, with numbered cancellations "3704" (small figures) or "5080" (large figures).

Type **10** of France   (1)

ALEXANDRIE

1899–1900. *Peace and Commerce type of France optd with T* **1**. *Type (b) unless otherwise stated. P* 14×13½.

1	**10**	1 c. black/*blue* (C.)	25	25
		a. Opt double	19·00	
		b. Opt triple	19·00	
2		2 c. red-brown/*buff* (B.)	40	40
3		3 c. drab (B.)	50	25
4		4 c. purple-brown/*grey* (B.)	40	40
5		5 c. bright yellow-green (a) (C.)	65	50
6		5 c. bright yellow-green (b) (C.)	30·00	22·00
7		10 c. black/*lilac* (a) (C.)	1·25	1·10
8		10 c. black/*lilac* (b) (C.)	10·00	5·50
9		15 c. blue (C.)	1·25	75
10		20 c. red/*green*	2·50	1·40
11		25 c. black/*rose*	1·00	65
		a. Opt inverted	11·00	
		b. Opt double, one inverted	19·00	
12		30 c. cinnamon	3·25	1·90
13		40 c. red/*yellow*	2·50	2·50
14		50 c. carmine (a)	32·00	3·25
15		50 c. carmine (b)	4·50	3·25
16		1 f. olive-green	4·50	3·25
17		2 f. brown/*azure* (a) (1900)	19·00	16·00
18		5 f. bright mauve/*lilac*	25·00	24·00
1/18		*Set of 18*	£120	80·00

2   3

4

(Des J. Blanc, eng E. Thomas (T **2**). Des and eng E. Mouchon (T **3**), Des Luc-Olivier Merson, eng M. Thévenin (T **4**). Typo Government Ptg Works, Paris)

1902 (Oct)–**21**. *P* 14×13½.

19	**2**	1 c. grey	5	5
		a. *Slate* (1921)	10	10
20		2 c. claret	10	5
21		3 c. orange-red	10	5
22		4 c. brown	10	5
23		5 c. yellow-green	20	10
24		5 c. blue-green (1906)	8	5
25	**3**	10 c. carmine (12.02)	30	10
26		15 c. pale red (3.03)	30	25
27		15 c. orange (8.11)	20	12
28		20 c. purple-brown (2.03)	30	15
29		25 c. blue (3.03)	12	5
30		30 c. mauve (2.03)	1·10	65
31	**4**	40 c. red and pale blue	80	40
32		50 c. brown and lavender	1·25	45
33		1 f. lake and yellow-green	1·40	45
34		2 f. deep lilac and buff	2·75	2·25
35		5 f. deep blue and buff	3·75	3·25
19/35		*Set of 17*	11·00	7·50

+5ᶜ   **5 Mill.**   **15 Mill.**

(5)   (6)   (7)

1915 (May). *Red Cross Fund. No. 25 surch in Paris with T* **2**, *in red.*

36	**3**	10 c.+5 c. carmine	12	12

1921 (Apr)–**23**. *Surch locally as T* **6** *or* **7** *(Nos.* 47/51).

37	**2**	2 m. on 5 c. green	1·00	65
38		3 m. on 3 c. orange-red	1·10	80
		a. Wide "3"	13·00	11·00
		b. Error. On stamp of Port Said	20·00	20·00
39	**3**	4 m. on 10 c. carmine	75	65
40	**2**	5 m. on 1 c. grey	1·00	75
		a. On 1 c. *slate* (1923)	45	45
41		5 m. on 4 c. brown	1·00	1·00
42	**3**	6 m. on 15 c. orange	50	50
		a. Wide "6"	11·00	11·00
43		8 m. on 20 c. purple-brown	75	70
		a. Wide "8"	5·50	5·50
44		10 m. on 25 c. blue	40	25
		a. Surch double	4·50	4·50
		b. Surch inverted	4·50	4·50
45		12 m. on 30 c. mauve	3·25	2·75
46	**2**	15 m. on 2 c. claret	1·10	95
		a. Error. On stamp of Port Said	20·00	20·00
47	**4**	15 m. on 40 c. red and pale blue	3·25	2·50
48		15 m. on 50 c. brown and lavender	1·25	1·25
49		30 m. on 1 f. lake and yellow-green	40·00	35·00
50		60 m. on 2 f. deep lilac and buff	55·00	55·00
		a. Thick, broad figures "60"	£100	£100
51		150 m. on 5 f. deep blue and buff	75·00	75·00
37/51		*Set of 15*	£170	£160

Surch twice, with bar obliterating first surch

52	**4**	30 m. and 15 m. on 1 f. lake & yell-grn	£200	£200

6   **15**

MILLIÈMES   **MILLIÈMES**

(8)   (9)   Type D **3** of France

1921 (May)–**22**. *Surch in Paris as T* **8** *or* **9** *(Nos.* 61/4).

53	**2**	1 m. on 1 c. grey	45	45
54		2 m. on 5 c. green	25	25
55	**3**	4 m. on 10 c. carmine	65	55

French Post Offices—EGYPT

56	2	5 m. on 3 c. orange		1·25	1·00
57	3	6 m. on 15 c. orange		30	30
58		8 m. on 20 c. purple-brown		20	15
59		10 m. on 25 c. blue		20	15
60		10 m. on 30 c. mauve		55	50
61	4	15 m. on 50 c. brown and lavender		55	50
62		30 m. on 1 f. lake and yellow-green		50	35
63		60 m. on 2 f. deep lilac and buff		£450	£450
64		150 m. on 5 f. deep blue and buff		2·00	1·40

1922 (Jan). *POSTAGE DUE. Postage Due stamps of France surch as T 8, but wider vertical spacing.*

D65	D 3	2 m. on 5 c. pale blue		30	30
D66		4 m. on 10 c. brown		30	30
D67		10 m. on 30 c. carmine		30	30
D68		15 m. on 50 c. dull claret		45	45
D69		30 m. on 1 f. claret/*straw*		80	80
D65/69		*Set of 5*		1·90	1·90

1923. *Stamps as 1902–21, colours changed, surch as T 8 or 9 (2 f.).*

65	3	4 m. on 10 c. green		40	30
66		15 m. on 50 c. blue		50	30
67	4	60 m. on 2 f. red and blue		2·50	1·60
		a. "60" omitted		£130	

1925 (Apr–Aug). *Types of 1902–21 surch as T 8 or 9, but with bars obliterating original value.*

68	2	1 m. on 1 c. slate		12	12
69		2 m. on 5 c. orange		12	12
70		2 m. on 5 c. blue-green		30	30
71	3	4 m. on 10 c. green		12	12
72	2	5 m. on 3 c. orange-red		12	12
73	3	6 m. on 15 c. orange		20	20
74		8 m. on 20 c. purple-brown		12	12
75		10 m. on 25 c. blue		5	5
76		15 m. on 50 c. blue		25	20
77	4	30 m. on 1 f. lake and yellow-green		25	20
78		60 m. on 2 f. red and blue-green		75	65
79		150 m. on 5 f. deep blue and buff		70	55
68/79		*Set of 12*		2·75	2·50

1927–28. *Inscr "Mm." below value. P 14×13½.*

80	2	3 m. orange-red (11.28)		30	30
81	3	15 m. dull blue (2.9.27)		30	30
82		20 m. magenta (11.28)		95	65
83	4	50 m. red and blue-green		2·25	1·75
84		100 m. deep blue and buff		2·50	1·75
85		250 m. sage-green and red		4·50	3·25
80/85		*Set of 6*		9·50	7·00

+5 **Mm**

**Caisse
d'Amortissement**

(10)

D 11

1927 (Nov)–30. *Sinking Fund. As No. 81, colour changed, surch with T 10.*

86	3	15 m.+5 m. orange-red (B.)		40	40
87		15 m.+5 m. magenta (12.28)		75	75
88		15 m.+5 m. chestnut (1929)		1·10	1·10
89		15 m.+5 m. lilac (1930)		1·50	1·50
86/89		*Set of 4*		2·50	2·50

1928 (Feb)–30. *POSTAGE DUE. P 14×13½.*

D90	D 11	1 m. slate		45	45
D91		2 m. pale blue		30	30
D92		4 m. pale magenta		35	35
D93		5 m. olive-green		30	30
D94		10 m. carmine		35	35
D95		20 m. claret		30	30
D96		30 m. blue-green (1930)		80	80
D97		40 m. lilac		65	65
D90/97		*Set of 8*		3·00	3·00

Nos. D90/7 were issued for use in both Alexandria and Port Said.

B. PORT SAID

The French Post Office in Port Said was opened in June 1867 and used the stamps of France until 1899, with the numbered cancellation "5129" (large figures).

**VINGT-
CINQ**

PORT-SAÏD **25**c

(12) (14)

1899–1900. *Peace and Commerce type of France (see Alexandria) optd with T 12. Type (b) unless otherwise stated. P 14×13½.*

101	10	1 c. black/*blue* (C.)		35	25
102		2 c. red-brown/*buff* (B.)		40	40
103		3 c. drab (B.)		50	40
104		4 c. purple-brown/*grey* (B.)		50	40
105		5 c. bright yellow-green (a) (C.)		1·40	1·00
106		5 c. bright yellow-green (b) (C.)		11·00	2·50
107		10 c. black/*lilac* (a) (C.)		1·90	1·90
108		10 c. black/*lilac* (b) (C.)		14·00	9·50
109		15 c. pale blue (C.)		1·90	1·25
		a. Deep blue		1·90	1·25
110		20 c. red/*green*		2·50	1·25
111	10	25 c. black/*rose* (C.)		1·90	40
		a. Opt double		28·00	
112		30 c. cinnamon		1·90	1·40
		a. Opt inverted		28·00	28·00
113		40 c. red/*yellow*		2·50	1·50
114		50 c. carmine (a)		65·00	22·00
115		50 c. carmine (b)		3·75	2·50
		a. Opt double (b)		40·00	
116		1 f. olive-green		5·00	3·25
117		2 f. brown/*azure* (a) (1900)		16·00	10·00
118		5 f. bright mauve/*lilac*		23·00	17·00
101/118		*Set of 18*		£140	70·00

1899 (18 Nov). *No. 107 surch locally.*

(a) *With T 13 and 14, both in red*

119	10	25 c. on 10 c. black/*lilac*		90·00	38·00
		a. T 14 inverted		£250	£225

(b) *With T 13 in black and T 14 in red*

120	10	25 c. on 10 c. black/*lilac*		—	£650
		a. T 14 inverted		—	£700
		b. T 13 vert		—	£700
		c. T 13 vert and T 14 inverted		—	£700

(c) *With T 14, in red*

121	10	25 c. on 10 c. black/*lilac*		32·00	5·50
		a. Surch inverted		—	45·00

1902 (Oct)–20. *As T 2/4 of Alexandria, inscr "PORT-SAID"*

122	2	1 c. grey		12	10
		a. Slate (1920)		15	12
123		2 c. claret		12	10
124		3 c. orange-red		12	10
125		4 c. brown		20	12
126		5 c. yellow-green		65	50
		a. *Blue-green* (1905)		20	15
127	3	10 c. carmine (12.02)		30	15
128		15 c. pale red (3.03)		45	25
128a		15 c. orange (1920)		45	25
129		20 c. purple-brown (2.03)		40	20
130		25 c. blue (2.03)		45	25
131		30 c. mauve (2.03)		1·00	75
132	4	40 c. red and pale blue		95	65
133		50 c. brown and lavender		1·40	85
134		1 f. lake and yellow-green		1·60	1·25
135		2 f. deep lilac and buff		2·50	2·25
136		5 f. deep blue and buff		5·50	5·50
122/136		*Set of 16*		15·00	12·00

1915 (May). *Red Cross Fund. No. 127 surch in Paris with T 5 of Alexandria, in red.*

137	3	10 c.+5 c. carmine		40	40

French Post Offices—EGYPT

4
Millièmes
(15)

15
MILLIÈMES
(16)

1921–23. Stamps of 1902–20, surch locally as T **15** or **16** (Nos. 146/50).

138 2	2 m. on 5 c. green			1·40	1·40
	a. Surch inverted			7·50	7·50
139 3	4 m. on 10 c. carmine			1·40	1·40
	a. Surch inverted			7·50	7·50
140 2	5 m. on 3 c. orange-red			1·90	1·90
	a. Error. On stamp of Alexandria			70·00	70·00
	b. Surch inverted			7·50	7·50
	c. "Millièmes"			15·00	15·00
141	5 m. on 4 c. brown			1·60	1·60
	a. Surch inverted			11·00	11·00
142	10 m. on 4 c. brown			4·50	4·50
	a. Surch inverted			11·00	11·00
	b. Surch double			11·00	11·00
	c. "Millièmes"			15·00	15·00
143 3	10 m. on 25 c. blue			1·25	1·25
	a. Surch inverted			9·50	9·50
144	12 m. on 30 c. brown			8·00	8·00
145 2	15 m. on 4 c. brown			1·50	1·50
	a. Surch inverted			10·00	10·00
	b. Surch double			10·00	10·00
	c. "Millièmes"			15·00	15·00
146 4	15 m. on 40 c. red and pale blue			10·00	10·00
	a. "MILLtEMES"			25·00	25·00
	b. "MILL1EMES"			19·00	19·00
147 4	15 m. on 50 c. brown and lavender			16·00	16·00
	a. "MILLtEMES"			65·00	65·00
	b. "MILL1EMES"			55·00	55·00
148	30 m. on 1 f. lake and yellow-green			55·00	55·00
	a. "MILLtEMES"			£160	£160
	b. "MILL1EMES"			£140	£140
149	60 m. on 2 f. deep lilac and buff			18·00	18·00
	a. "MILLtEMES"			70·00	70·00
	b. "MILL1EMES"			50·00	50·00
150	150 m. on 5 f. deep blue and buff			55·00	55·00
	a. "MILLtEMES"			£160	£160
	b. "MILL1EMES"			£140	£140
138/150	Set of 13			£160	£160

1921–23. Stamps of 1902–20 surch in Paris as T **8** and **9** of Alexandria.

151 2	1 m. on 1 c. grey			20	20
	a. On 1 c. slate (1923)			20	20
152	2 m. on 5 c. green			20	20
153 3	4 m. on 10 c. carmine			50	50
154 2	5 m. on 3 c. orange			1·75	1·75
155 3	6 m. on 15 c. orange			55	55
156	6 m. on 15 c. pale red			2·50	2·50
157	8 m. on 20 c. purple-brown			40	40
158	10 m. on 25 c. blue			65	65
159	10 m. on 30 c. mauve			1·10	1·10
160 4	15 m. on 50 c. brown and lavender			95	95
161 3	15 m. on 30 c. blue			95	95
162 4	30 m. on 1 f. lake and yellow-green			1·10	1·10
163	60 m. on 2 f. lilac and buff			24·00	24·00
164	60 m. on 2 f. red and blue-green			1·60	1·60
	a. Surch omitted			£130	
165	150 m. on 5 f. deep blue and buff			1·50	1·50
151/165	Set of 15			34·00	34·00

1921. POSTAGE DUE. Postage Due Stamps of France (see Alexandria) surch as T **15**.

D166 D 3	12 m. on 10 c. brown			10·00	10·00
D167	15 m. on 5 c. blue			11·00	11·00
D168	30 m. on 20 c. olive			14·00	14·00
	a. Surch inverted			90·00	90·00
D169	30 m. on 50 c. dull claret			£800	£800

1921 (17 Nov). Stamps of 1902–20 surch locally as T **15** or **16** (Nos. 171/3).

166 2	5 m. on 1 c. grey			2·50	2·50
	a. On 1 c. slate			3·25	3·25
	b. Surch inverted			10·00	10·00
	c. Error. 2 m. on 1 c.			9·00	9·00
	d. On stamp of French Levant			16·00	16·00
	e. Do. With "5" inverted			£130	£130

167	5 m. on 2 c. claret			2·50	2·50
	a. Error. 2 m. on 2 c.			10·00	10·00
	b. Do. Surch inverted			17·00	17·00
	c. Error. 2 m. on 2 c. of French Levant			16·00	16·00
168	10 m. on 2 c. claret			1·90	1·90
169 3	15 m. on 15 c. pale red			9·50	9·50
	a. Surch inverted			15·00	15·00
	b. Error. 10 m. on 15 c.			21·00	21·00
170	15 m. on 20 c. purple-brown			9·50	9·50
	a. Surch inverted			17·00	17·00
171 4	30 m. on 50 c. brown and lavender			70·00	70·00
	a. "MILLIEMES"			£100	£100
172	60 m. on 50 c. brown and lavender			80·00	80·00
	a. "MILLIEMES"			£130	£130
173	150 m. on 50 c. brown and lavender			90·00	90·00
	a. "MILLIEMES"			£150	£150
166/173	Set of 8			£225	£225

2
MILLIÈMES
(D 17)

1921 (17 Nov). POSTAGE DUE. Postage Due stamps of France (see Alexandria) surch locally as Type D **17**.

D174 D 3	2 m. on 5 c. pale blue (C.)			10·00	10·00
	a. Surch in blue			70·00	70·00
D175 D 3	4 m. on 10 c. brown (B.)			11·00	11·00
	a. Error. 15 m. on 10 c.			£140	£140
D176	10 m. on 30 c. carmine (B.)			10·00	10·00
	a. Surch inverted			22·00	22·00
D177	15 m. on 50 c. dull claret (B.)			14·00	14·00
	a. Surch inverted			25·00	25·00
D174/177	Set of 4			40·00	40·00

All values exist with the following varieties: "MIILIEMES"; MILLIÈME"; with accent omitted; and with second "M" inverted (Price £40 each).

1924–25. Stamps of 1902–20 surch as T **8** and **9** of Alexandria but with bars obliterating original value.

174 2	1 m. on 1 c. slate			12	12
175	2 m. on 5 c. green			12	12
176 3	4 m. on 10 c. carmine			12	12
177 2	5 m. on 3 c. orange			12	12
178 3	6 m. on 15 c. orange			12	12
179	8 m. on 20 c. purple-brown			12	12
180	10 m. on 25 c. blue			20	20
181	15 m. on 50 c. blue			20	20
182 4	30 m. on 1 f. lake and yellow-green			25	25
183	60 m. on 2 f. red and blue-green			35	35
184	150 m. on 5 f. deep blue and buff			45	45
174/184	Set of 11			2·00	2·00

1927–28. As T **2/4** of Alexandria, inscr "PORT-SAID" and "Mm." below value.

185 2	3 m. orange-red (11.28)			25	25
186 3	15 m. dull blue (11.28)			30	30
187	20 m. magenta (11.28)			40	40
188 4	50 m. red and blue-green (2.28)			45	45
189	100 m. blue and buff (2.28)			70	70
190	250 m. green and carmine (2.28)			1·40	1·40
185/190	Set of 6			3·00	3·00

1927 (Dec)**–30.** Sinking Fund. As No. 186, colour changed, surch with T **10** of Alexandria.

191 3	15 m.+5 m. orange-red (B.)			40	40
192	15 m.+5 m. magenta (1928)			40	40
193	15 m.+5 m. chestnut (1929)			50	50
194	15 m.+5 m. lilac (1930)			95	95
191/194	Set of 4			2·00	2·00

For Postage Due stamps of 1928, see Alexandria.

Both French Post Offices in Egypt closed down on 31 March 1931.

French Post Offices in Ethiopia

100 Centimes = 1 Franc

French Post Offices operated at Harar, Addis Ababa and Diredawa in Ethiopia. Stamps of Obock, Djibouti and French Somali Coast were used there, including the Obock bisect No. 69a (*see* French Territory of the Afars and the Issas). Nos. 126/7 of Port Said (*see* French Post Offices in Egypt) and No. 14 of French Levant (*see* Foreign Post Offices in the Turkish Empire) are also known used in Ethiopia.

The following stamps, although inscribed "LEVANT", have face values in French instead of Turkish currency, and were issued specifically for use in Ethiopia.

2

1

(Des and eng E. Mouchon (T **1**). Des Luc-Olivier Merson, eng M. Thévenin (T **2**). Recess Govt Ptg Wks, Paris)

1906–8. *P* 14×13½.

25	1	25 c. blue	..	.. 11·00	9·50
26	2	50 c. brown and lavender (3.07)		.. 38·00	35·00
27		1 f. lake and yellow-green (1908)		.. 95·00	95·00

Nos. 1/3 also exist imperforate.

French Post Offices in Ethiopia closed in November 1908, after Ethiopia had joined the Universal Postal Union.

STAMPS OF
CHILE
1853–1866

GIBBONS CATALOGUE SUPPLEMENT IN EVERY ISSUE

Leading the field is Gibbons world-famous *Stamp Monthly* offering you an attractive magazine that contains so much for stamp enthusiasts everywhere. Just look at some of the interesting features :

- Latest information on all new issues.
- Well written, lavishly illustrated articles.
- The all-important Supplement to the Stanley Gibbons Catalogue.
- The Crown Agents Gazette with latest news and lists of forthcoming issues.
- Regular Stamp Market, Great Britain and Through the Magnifying Glass features.
- A vast and varied selection of advertisements from the stamp trade.
- Large size format—297 × 210mm.

As a collector you cannot afford to be without *Stamp Monthly*. Enter a subscription, and keep in touch with all events in this ever popular hobby by courtesy of Gibbons — the First Name in Stamps.

French Post Offices in Turkish Empire

1885. 25 Centimes=1 Piastre
1921. 40 Paras=1 Piastre

Types of France overprinted or surcharged

A. GENERAL ISSUES

2

1 PIASTRE 1 **1 PIASTRE 1** **PIASTRES**
(1)   (2)   (3)

1885 (5 Aug). *Stamps of 1876–77 (Type (b)), surch as T 1.*
1	**10**	1 pi. on 25 c. bistre/*yellow*	..	95·00	2·50
		a. Surch inverted	..	£550	£225
2		3 pi. on 75 c. carmine	..	5·00	2·25
3		4 pi. on 1 f. olive-green	..	3·75	1·25

1886–1901. *Stamps of 1877–1900 surch as T 1. Type (b) except where otherwise stated.*
4	**10**	1 pi. on 25 c. black/*rose* (C.) ('91)	..	40	12
		a. Surch in deep red (1886)	..	50	12
		b. Surch inverted	..	45·00	35·00
5		2 pi. on 50 c. rose (b) (1890)	..	3·50	30
		a. Surch at foot (1895)	..	10·00	1·25
6		2 pi. on 50 c. carmine-rose (a) (1901)	70·00	7·00
7		8 pi. on 2 f. brown/*pale blue* (1900)	..	7·00	4·50
8		20 pi. on 5 f. lilac (6.90)	..	17·00	8·00
		a. *Mauve*	..		

1902 (Oct)–**20.** *Types of France inscr "LEVANT". P 14 × 13½.*
(a) Without surch
9	**11**	1 c. grey	..	8	5
		a. *Slate* (1920)	..	10	10
10		2 c. claret	..	12	10
11		3 c. orange-red	..	10	10
		a. *Lake-red* (1908)	..	30	30
12		4 c. brown	..	30	25
13		5 c. yellow-green	..	20	10
		a. *Blue-green* (1905)	..	15	10
14	**14**	10 c. carmine (12.02)	..	20	8
15		15 c. pale red (2.03)	..	40	25
16		20 c. purple-brown (2.03)	..	40	25
17		30 c. deep lilac (5.03)	..	75	40
18	**13**	40 c. red and pale blue	..	75	40

(b) Surch as T 2 or 3
19	**14**	1 pi. on 25 c. blue (2.03)	..	15	5
		a. Second figure "1" omitted	..	5·50	5·00
		b. Surch double	..	8·00	6·00
20	**13**	2 pi. on 50 c. brown and lavender	..	30	15
		a. Background colour omitted	17·00	
21		4 pi. on 1 f. lake and yellow-green	..	50	30
22		8 pi. on 2 f. deep lilac and buff	..	3·75	2·25
23		20 pi. on 5 f. deep blue and buff	..	80	65

1 Piastre   **3 PIASTRES**

Beyrouth   **30 PARAS**
(4)   (5)

1905 (17 Jan). *Provisional issued at Beirut. No. 15 surch with T 4, in greenish black.*
24	**14**	1 pi. on 15 c. pale red	..	£350	60·00
		a. "Piastte" for "Piastre"	..	£1300	£200

1906–8. *New values as Nos. 9/18 for use in offices in Ethiopia.*
25	**14**	25 c. blue	..	..	11·00	9·50

26	**13**	50 c. brown and lavender (1907)	..	38·00	35·00
27		1 f. lake and yellow-green (1908)	..	95·00	95·00

1921–22. *New currency. Stamps of France surch as T 5.*
28	**18**	30 pa. on 5 c. green	..	..	15	10
29		30 pa. on 5 c. orange	..		15	10
30		1 pi. 20 pa. on 10 c. scarlet	..	15	15
31		1 pi. 20 pa. on 10 c. green	..	15	10
32		3 pi. 30 pa. on 25 c. blue	..	15	8
33		4 pi. 20 pa. on 30 c. orange	..	15	10
34	**15**	7 pi. 20 pa. on 50 c. blue	..	12	8
35	**13**	15 pi. on 1 f. lake and yellow-green	..	25	20
36		30 pi. on 2 f. red and blue-green	..	2·25	1·40
37		75 pi. on 5 f. blue and buff	..	1·50	65
28/37		*Set of 10*			

1923 (26 Mar). *Stamps of France handstamped as T 5 but thinner letters.*
38	**18**	1 pi. 20 pa. on 10 c. scarlet	..	10·00	10·00
39	**15**	3 pi. 30 pa. on 15 c. grey-green	..	4·50	4·50
		a. "3 PIASTRES" omitted	..	£190	£190
		b. "3" omitted	..	£190	£190
		c. "3" inserted by hand	..	£190	£190
40	**18**	7 pi. 20 pa. on 35 c. violet	..	4·50	4·50
		a. Error. 1 pi. 20 pa. on 35 c.	..	£150	£150

The French offices were closed down, owing to the Abrogation of the Capitulations, on 13 October 1914 but the post office in Constantinople opened again from August 1921 to July 1923.

B. KAVALLA

Cavalle   **2 Piastres 2**
(6)   (7)

1893–1900. *Stamps of 1876–1900 optd with T 6 or surch as T 7. Type (b) unless otherwise stated.*
41	**10**	5 c. blue-green (b) (C.)	..	3·25	2·50
		a. Opt in vermilion	..	..	5·50	5·00
42		5 c. yellow-green (a) (C.) (1900)	..	3·25	2·50
43		10 c. black/*lilac* (b) (B.)	..	3·75	3·25
44		10 c. black/*lilac* (a) (B.) (1898?)	35·00	32·00
45		15 c. blue (C.)	..	4·50	3·75
		a. Opt in vermilion (1895)	..	4·50	3·75
46		1 pi. on 25 c. black/*rose* (B.)	..	5·00	4·25
47		2 pi. on 50 c. rose (B.)	..	17·00	13·00
		a. *Carmine*	..	..	19·00	14·00
48		4 pi. on 1 f. olive-green (Vm.)	..	22·00	16·00
		a. Surch in carmine	..	16·00	11·00
		b. *Grey-green* (C.)	..	..	16·00	16·00
49		8 pi. on 2 f. brn/*pale bl* (a) (Bk.) (1900)	20·00	18·00

1902 (Oct)–**11.** *Types of France inscr "CAVALLE". P 14×13½.*
(a) Without surch
50	**11**	5 c. yellow-green	..	..	25	20
51	**14**	10 c. carmine (5.03)	..	..	30	25
52		15 c. pale red (5.03)	..	..	1·50	1·50
53		15 c. orange (1911)	..	..	40	25

(b) Surch as T 2 or 3
54	**14**	1 pi. on 25 c. blue (3.03)	..	65	50
55	**13**	2 pi. on 50 c. brown and lavender	..	1·10	90
56		4 pi. on 1 f. lake and yellow-green	..	1·90	1·50
57		8 pi. on 2 f. deep lilac and buff	..	3·00	2·75

This office was closed down in August 1914 after Kavalla had become a Greek town in 1913.

French Post Offices—TURKISH EMPIRE

C. DEDEAGATZ

Dédéagh

(8)

1893–1900. *Stamps of 1876–98 optd with T* **8** *or surch as T* **7.** *Type (b) unless otherwise stated.*

58	**10**	5 c. blue-green (b) (C.)	..	2·50	1·90
		a. Opt in vermilion (1895)	..	2·50	1·90
59		5 c. yellow-green (a) (R.) (1900)	..	2·50	2·50
60		10 c. black/*lilac* (b) (B.)	..	3·75	3·25
61		10 c. black/*lilac* (a) (B.) (1900)	..	7·50	5·00
		a. Opt double	..	28·00	
62		15 c. blue (C.)	..	5·00	3·25
		a. Surch in vermilion (1895)	..	5·50	3·75
63		1 pi. on 25 c. black/*rose* (B.)	..	5·50	5·00
64		2 pi. on 50 c. rose (B.)	..	10·00	8·00
		a. Carmine	..	11·00	8·00
65		4 pi. on 1 f. olive-green (C.) ..	..	13·00	8·00
66		8 pi. on 2 f. brn/*pale bl* (a) (Bk.) (1900)		19·00	16·00

1902 (Oct)–**11.** *Types of France inscr* "DEDEAGH". *P* 14 × 13½.

(a) Without surch

67	**11**	5 c. yellow-green	.. .. ..	20	15
		a. Green (1906)	.. ..	20	15
68	**14**	10 c. carmine (5.03) ..	.. ..	25	15
69		15 c. pale red (5.03)	.. ..	40	20
70		15 c. orange (1911) ..	.. ..	50	20

(b) Surch as T **2** *or* **3**

71	**14**	1 pi. on 25 c. blue (5.03)	.. ..	50	25
72	**13**	2 pi. on 50 c. brown and lavender	..	1·10	90
		a. Surch double	.. ..	25·00	
73		4 pi. on 1 f. lake and yellow-green	..	2·50	2·10
74		4 pi. on 2 f. deep lilac and buff	..	3·75	3·25

This office was closed down in August 1914 after Dedeagatz had become a Bulgarian town in 1913.

D. PORT LAGOS

Port-Lagos

(9)

1893 (1 Apr). *Stamps of 1876–90 optd with T* **9** *or surch as T* **7.** *Type (b) only.*

75	**10**	5 c. blue-green (C.)	..	5·00	3·75
76		10 c. black/*lilac* (B.) ..	..	9·00	5·50
77		15 c. blue (C.)	..	18·00	14·00
		a. Surch in vermilion	..	19·00	14·00
78		1 pi. on 25 c. black/*rose* (B.)	..	13·00	11·00
79		2 pi. on 50 c. rose (B.)	..	28·00	22·00
		a. Carmine	..	29·00	23·00
80		4 pi. on 1 f. olive-green (C.) ..	..	22·00	20·00

This office closed down in 1898.

E. VATHY (Samos)

Vathy

(10)

1893–1900. *Stamps of 1876–1900 optd with T* **10** *or surch as T* **7.** *Type (b) unless otherwise stated.*

81	**10**	5 c. blue-green (b) (C.)	..	2·10	1·90
82		5 c. yellow-green (a) (C.) (1900)	..	2·10	2·10
83		5 c. yellow-green (b) (C.) (1900)	..	17·00	13·00
84		10 c. black/*lilac* (a) (B.)	..	3·00	3·00
85		10 c. black/*lilac* (b) (B.)	..	9·50	5·50
86		15 c. blue (C.)	..	3·25	3·25
87		1 pi. on 25 c. black/*rose* (B.)	..	3·50	2·75
88		2 pi. on 50 c. rose (B.)	..	7·50	7·00
		a. Carmine	..	7·50	7·00
89		4 pi. on 1 f. olive-green (C.) ..	..	7·50	7·50
90		8 pi. on 2 f. brn/*pale bl* (a) (Bk.) (1900)		17·00	17·00
91		20 pi. on 5 f. mauve (Bk.) (1900)	..	28·00	25·00

This office was closed down in 1914 after Samos had become a Greek island in 1913.

stamp monthly

Gibbons' own monthly magazine, essential reading for **every** collector!

Detailed monthly New Issue Guide to update all Gibbons catalogues for you—and a special Stamp Market feature on price changes.

Informative articles cover all facets of philately, with regular notes on new discoveries, stamp designs, postmarks, market trends and news and views of the world of stamps. Britain's LARGEST circulation of any stamp magazine— that fact speaks for itself!

Monthly from all dealers and newsagents or by post direct from Stanley Gibbons Magazines Ltd—subscription rates on application.

French Post Office in Zanzibar

16 Annas = 1 Rupee
100 Centimes = 1 Franc

A French Post Office was opened in Zanzibar in January 1889 and the stamps of France were used there without overprint or surcharge until December 1893.

1Fr. **1Fr.** **1Fr.**

M   N   O

1894 (16 Mar). *Type* **10** *of France, variety* (*b*), *surch locally as T* **2**, *with value in Indian currency and corresponding value in French currency over original value.*

15	½ a. and 5 on 1 c. black/*azure* (Vm.) (A)	35·00	32·00
	a. Type B		42·00	42·00
16	1 a. and 10 on 3 c. grey (Vm.) (C)	32·00	32·00
	a. Type D		90·00	90·00
	b. Type E		70·00	70·00
17	2½ a. and 25 on 4 c. purple-brown/*grey* (F)	45·00	45·00
	a. Type G		80·00	80·00
	b. Type H		65·00	65·00
	c. Type I		£110	£110
18	5 a. and 50 on 20 c. red/*green* (J)	48·00	48·00
	a. Type K		65·00	65·00
	b. Type L		85·00	85·00
19	10 a. and 1 f. on 40 c. red/*yellow* (M)	80·00	80·00
	a. Type M. Stop omitted		£130	£130
	b. Type N		95·00	95·00
	c. Type O		£110	£110

Nos. 15/19 were surcharged in sheets of 25, the settings being made-up as follows:
½ a. and 5 on 1 c.—Type A 19, Type B 6.
1 a. and 10 on 3 c.—Type C 23, Type D 1, Type E 1.
2½ a. and 25 on 4 c.—Type F 16, Type G 4, Type H 3, Type I 2.
5 a. and 50 on 20 c.—Type J 19, Type K 5, Type L 1.
10 a. and 1 f. on 40 c.—Type M 13, Type N 10, Type O 2.

1/2
ANNA
(1)

Type **10** of France

(There are two varieties of this type: (*a*) has the letter "N" of "INV" in the imprint under the "B" of "REPUBLIQUE"; (*b*) has this "N" under the "U" of "REPUBLIQUE")

1894–95. *Type* **10** *of France, variety* (*b*), *surch as T* **1**.

1	**10**	½ a. on 5 c. deep green (Vm.)	75	50
		a. Surch in carmine	1·00	80
3		1 a. on 10 c. black/*lilac* (B.)	1·75	1·25
4		1½ a. on 15 c. blue/*toned* (C.) (1895)	3·25	2·50
		a. Surch in vermilion	6·00	3·75
		b. Do. "ANNAS" for "ANNA"	17·00	17·00
6		2 a. on 20 c. red/*green* (1895)	2·00	1·00
7		2½ a. on 25 c. black/*rose* (B.)	1·40	70
8		3 a. on 30 c. cinnamon (1895)	3·00	1·75
9		4 a. on 40 c. red/*yellow* (1895)	3·00	1·75
10		5 a. on 50 c. rose (B.)	4·50	3·75
		a. Carmine	4·50	3·75
11		7½ a. on 75 c. brown/*orange* (Vm.) ('95)	80·00	70·00
12		10 a. on 1 f. olive-green (C.)	6·50	5·50
		a. Surch in vermilion	7·50	6·00
14		50 a. on 5 f. mauve/*lilac* (1895)	60·00	55·00
1/14		*Set of 11*	£150	£130

1/2
ANNA
ZANZIBAR
(3)

Type D11
of France

1896–1900. *Type* **10** *of France, variety* (*b*) *except where stated, surch with T* **3**.

20	**10**	½ a. on 5 c. green (Vm.)	1·10	1·10
		a. Surch in carmine	1·25	1·25
22		½ a. on 5 c. yellow-grn (*a*) (C.) (1899)	1·10	1·10
23		½ a. on 5 c. yellow-grn (*b*) (C.) (1899)	1·10	1·10
24		1 a. on 10 c. black/*lilac* (*b*) (B.)	1·25	1·10
25		1 a. on 10 c. black/*lilac* (*a*) (B.) (1900)	2·10	2·10
26		1½ a. on 15 c. blue (Vm.)	75	70
		a. Surch in carmine	90	90
28		2 a. on 20 c. red/*green*	80	75
		a. "ZANZIBAR" double	20·00	20·00
29		2½ a. on 25 c. black/*rose* (B.)	85	85
		a. Surch inverted	23·00	
30		3 a. on 30 c. cinnamon	1·10	1·00
31		4 a. on 40 c. red/*yellow*	90	90
32		5 a. on 50 c. carmine (*b*) (B.)	5·50	3·75
33		5 a. on 50 c. carmine (*a*) (B.) (1900)	17·00	17·00
35		10 a. on 1 f. olive-green (Vm.)	2·50	2·00
		a. Surch in carmine	3·00	1·90
37		20 a. on 2 f. brown/*pale blue* (*a*) (1900)	3·75	3·75
		a. Error. "ZANZIBAS"	£130	£130
38		50 a. on 5 f. mauve/*pale lilac*	7·50	6·50
		a. Error. "ZANZIBAS"	£500	£500
		b. "ZANZIBAR" triple	20·00	
20/38		*Set of 15*	45·00	40·00

There were two printings of some values of the above, in the first of which the word "ZANZIBAR" was added to stamps of the 1894 issue, and in the other the whole surcharge was made at one printing.

ZANZIBAR
5 ANNAS
50
(2)

5 **5** **10** **10** **10**
A   B   C   D   E

25 **25** **25** **25**
F   G   H   I

50 **50** **50**
J   K   L

1897. *POSTAGE DUE. Type D 11 of France surch with T 3.*

D39	D 11	½ a. on 5 c. pale blue (C.)	2·75	2·00
D40		1 a. on 10 c. pale brown (B.) ..	2·50	1·75
		a. Surch inverted ..	20·00	20·00
D41		1½ a. on 15 c. pale green (C.)	4·00	2·50
D42		3 a. on 30 c. carmine	4·50	3·50
D43		5 a. on 50 c. dull claret (B.)	4·25	3·25
D39/43		*Set of 5*	16·00	12·00

Error. Surcharged with wrong value

D44	D 11	2½ a. on 50 c. dull claret (B.) ..	£170	£170
		a. Error corrected in red or black ink	£550	£550

PosteFrance
5
ZANZIBAR
Annas
50c

(4)

1897 (20 July). *Stamps of 1894–95 further surch locally with new figures of value (for both annas and centimes) and with "ZANZIBAR" (but without "Poste France") as in T 4, vertically downwards on the right side of the stamp—all in black.*

42	10	2½ and 25 on ½ a. (No. 1)	£200	50·00
43		2½ and 25 on 1 a. (No. 3)	£625	£225
44		2½ and 25 on 1½ a. (No. 4a) ..	£625	£225
45		5 and 50 on 3 a. (No. 8) ..	£625	£225
46		5 and 50 on 4 a. (No. 9) ..	£625	£250

1897 (20 July). *Printed on margins of sheets and the horizontal spaces between vertical panes of the regular issues as T 4, in black.*

47	10	2½ a. and 25 c. on *grn & white* (from 5 c.)	—	£300
48		2½ a. and 25 c. on *lilac* and white (from 10 c.)	—	£500
49		2½ a. and 25 c. on *blue* and white (from 15 c.)	—	£500
50		5 a. and 50 c. on *buff* and white (from 30 c.)	—	£500
51		5 a. and 50 c. on *straw* and white (from 40 c.)	—	£500
52		5 a. on 50 c. on white	—	£2000

Nos. 42/52 were surcharged in settings of 35 (25 stamps and 10 surcharges on the sheet margins and gutters). Specialists identify many minor differences of surcharge; there being 15 types of the 2½ a. and 25 c. and 10 of the 5 a. and 50 c., including those on the margins.

5  **6**

7

1/2
ANNA

(8)

1 1/2 ANNA

(9)

5
ANNAS

(10)

(T **5** des J. Blanc, eng E. Thomas, T **6** des and eng E. Mouchon, T **7** des Luc-Olivier Merson, eng M. Thévenin. Typo Govt Printing Works, Paris)

1902 (Oct)-03. *Surch with T 8 or as T 9/10 P14× 13½*

53	11	½ a. on 5 c. green (R.)	95	75
54	6	1 a. on 10 c. carmine (5.03) ..	1·25	1·10
55		1½ a. on 15 c. pale red (5.03) ..	2·50	2·25
56		2 a. on 20 c. purple-brown (5.03)	3·25	2·50
57		2½ a. on 25 c. blue (3.03)	2·75	2·50
58		3 a. on 30 c. mauve (5.03) ..	2·50	2·10
59	7	4 a. on 40 c. red and pale blue	4·50	4·00
60		5 a. on 50 c. cinnamon and lavender	3·25	2·75
61		10 a. on 1 f. lake and yellow-green	5·50	5·00
62		20 a. on 2 f. deep lilac and buff	11·00	11·00
63		50 a. on 5 f. deep blue and buff	16·00	16·00
53/63		*Set of 11*	48·00	45·00

Error. On sheet of 3 a. on 30 c.

64	6	5 a. on 30 c. mauve	55·00	55·00

25ᶜ **2½** **50** **5**

(11) (12)

2

1 fr 10 **25**

(13) (14)

1904 (19 July). (a) *Nos. 30/31 further surch locally with T 11, 12 or 13.*

65	10	"25 c 2½" on 4 a. on 40 c. red/yellow	—	£250
66		"50 5" on 3 a. on 30 c. cinnamon	—	£275
67		"50 5" on 4 a. on 40 c. red/yellow	—	£275
68		"1 fr 10" on 3 a. on 30 c. cinnamon	—	£400
69		"1 fr 10" on 4 a. on 40 c. red/yellow	—	£450

(b) *No. 53 surch with T 14 (value in annas thus reading, in conjunction with the original surcharge "2½")*

70	5	"2 25" on ½ a. on 5 c. green (R.)	—	22·00

25ᶜ **50ᶜ** **1 fr**

2½ **cinq** **dix**

(15) (16) (17)

(c) *Nos. 54 and 58 further surch with T 15, 16 or 17*

71	6	"25 c. 2½" on 1 a. on 10 c. carmine	—	25·00
		a. Surch T 15 double		
72		"25 c 2½" on 3 a. on 30 c. mauve	—	£400
73		"50 c cinq" on 3 a. on 30 c. mauve	—	£275
74		"1 fr dix" on 3 a. on 30 c. mauve	—	£325

Timbre **Affranchᵗ**

(18) (19)

(d) *Nos. D39/40 optd respectively with T 18 in upper right corner in red, and T 19 over word "TAXE", in black*

75	D 11	½ a. on 5 c. pale blue	—	90·00
76		1 a. on 10 c. pale brown	—	90·00

(e) *No. D41. optd with a red line at top and bottom obliterating the words "CHIFFRE" and "TAXE"*

77	D 11	1½ a. on 15 c. pale green	—	£170

This office closed down on 31 July 1904. Unoverprinted French stamps were again used there during the final month of operation.

French Southern and Antarctic Territories

100 Centimes=1 Franc

This French Overseas Territory, known as "Terres Australes et Antarctiques Françaises", was created on 6 August 1955. It consists of the Crozet Archipelago (annexed in 1772), the islands of St. Paul, New Amsterdam and Kerguelen (occupied in 1949), all in the Southern Indian Ocean, and Adélie Land, part of the Antarctic continent.

PRINTERS. All issues were printed by the French Government Printing Works, Paris, *unless otherwise stated.*

IMPERFORATE STAMPS. Many stamps exist imperforate in their issued colours, but these were not valid for postage. Imperforate stamps in other colours are colour trials.

TERRES AUSTRALES ET ANTARCTIQUES FRANÇAISES

(1)

1955 (2 Nov). *No. 324 of Madagascar optd with* T **1**.
1   15 f. blue and deep blue-green   .. ..   14·00   14·00

2 Gorfous Penguins

3 Sea-lion and Settlement

4 Emperor Penguins and South Pole

(Des and eng R. Serres (30 c.), R. Cottet (40 c.), P. Munier (T **2**), C. Durrens (4 f., 25 f.), H. Cheffer (T **3**), G. Bétemps (2 f., 10 f., 12 f., 15 f., 85 f.), R. Cami (T **4**), C. Hertenberger (200 f.). Recess. 20 f. Des S. Gauthier. Die-eng A. Barre. Typo)

1956 (25 Apr)–**60.** *T* 2/4 *and similar designs.* P 13.

(a) POSTAGE

2 –	30 c. red-brn, bluish grn & bl (7.12.59)	20	20
3 –	40 c. black, purple & turq-bl (7.12.59)	20	20
4 **2**	50 c. deep blue, ochre and black-brown	25	30
5 –	1 f. deep blue, orange and violet-grey	25	30
6 –	2 f. blk, chocolate & turq-bl (20.11.60)	35	35
7 –	4 f. purple-brn, dp grn & bl (20.11.60)	35	35
8 **3**	5 f. blue and light blue..	55	65
9 –	8 f. purple-brown and violet-grey	4·75	5·00
10 –	10 f. indigo	80	90
11 –	12 f. black and blue (7.12.59) ..	1·10	1·10
12 –	15 f. deep reddish purple and indigo ..	95	1·10
13 –	20 f. blue, yellow & pale blue (7.12.59)	3·75	3·75

14 –	25 f. black, yellow-brown and deep bluish green (20.11.60)	1·40	1·40
15 –	85 f. orange turq-bl & blk (20.11.60) ..	5·00	5·00

(b) AIR. Inscr "POSTE AERIENNE"

16 **4**	50 f. slate-green and olive-green ..	18·00	18·00
17	100 f. indigo and turquoise-blue ..	18·00	18·00
18 –	200 f. black, blue & brown-pur (7.12.59)	11·00	11·00
2/18	*Set of* 17	60·00	60·00

Designs: *Vert*—30 c. Sooty albatross; 2 f. Sheathbills; 12 f. Cormorants; 20 f. Territorial arms; 85 f. King penguin. *Horiz* (*as T* **3**)—40 c. Skuas; 4 f. Sea leopard; 10 f., 15 f., Sea-elephant; 25 f. Kerguelen seal: (*as T* **4**)—200 f. Albatross. See also Nos. 26/34.

5 Polar Camp and Meteorologist   **5a** *Pringlea*

(Des C. Hertenberger. Recess)

1957 (14 Nov). *International Geophysical Year.* P 13.

19 **5**	5 f. black and violet ..	..	..	1·90	1·90
20	10 f. bright scarlet ..	..	..	1·90	1·90
21	15 f. deep blue ..	..	..	1·90	1·90

(Des M. Rolland. Photo Vaugirard, Paris)

1959 (2 Feb). *P* 12½.
22 **5a** 10 f. multicoloured   .. ..   1·25   1·25

6 Yves-Joseph Kerguelen-Tremarec

(Des and eng C. Durrens. Recess)

1960 (19 Nov). *Kerguelen Archipelago Discovery Commemoration.* P 13.
23 **6** 25 f. chocolate, chestnut and deep blue   4.75   4·75

7 Jean Charcot, Compass and Ship

(Des and eng P. Gandon. Recess)

1961 (19 Dec). *25th Anniv of Disappearance of Jean Charcot.* *P* 13.
24 **7** 25 f. chocolate, red and green   .. ..   5·00   5·00

French Southern and Antarctic Territories 1962

1962 (24 Dec). *AIR. First Transatlantic Television Satellite Link. As T* **10** *of French Polynesia.*
25 50 f. blue-green, olive and blue .. .. 9·00 9·00

(Des P. Béquet. Eng A. Frères (5 f.), M. Monvoisin (12 f.), P. Béquet (others). Recess)

1962 (24 Dec)—**72.** *P* 13. (*a*) *POSTAGE. As T* **3.**
26 5 f. dp bluish violet & new bl (23.12.66) 1·60 1·60
27 8 f. indigo, brown-purple and blue .. 1·40 1·40
28 10 f. black, slate-blue and bistre (5.1.69) .. 3·50 3·50
29 12 f. deep bluish green, light greenish blue
       and yellowish bistre (5.1.69) .. 3·50 3·50
30 15 f. greenish blue, blk & ol-brn (24.12.69) 1·90 1·90
31 20 f. slate, orange & yellow-olive (31.1.68) 22·00 22·00
32 45 f. myrtle-grn, lake-brn & bl (30.12.72) 95 95

    (*b*) *AIR. As T* **4** *Inscr* "POSTE AERIENNE"
33 25 f. purple, chocolate & new bl (23.12.66) 7·00 7·00
34 50 f. black, brown-purple and blue .. 11·00 11·00
26/34 Set of 9 .. .. .. 48·00 48·00
Designs: *Horiz* (*As T* **3**)—5 f. Great blue whale; 8 f. Sealions in combat; 12 f. Phylica (tree), New Amsterdam Island; 15 f. Killer whale, Crozet Islands. (*As T* **4**)—50 f. Adélie penquins. *Vert* (*As T* **3**)—10 f. Great skuas; 20 f. Black-browed albatross; 45 f. Kerguelen cabbage. (*As T* **4**)—25 f. Ionospheric research pylon, Adélie Land.

11 Space Probe **12** Dumont D'Urville and Ships

(Des and eng J. Combet. Recess)

1967 (4 Mar). *Launching of First Space Probe, Adélie Land. P* 13.
43 **11** 20 f. black, purple and new blue .. 2·75 2·75

(Des and eng P. Béquet. Recess)

1968 (20 Jan). *Dumont D'Urville Commemoration. P* 13.
44 **12** 30 f. deep brown, deep blue & light blue 6·50 6·50

8 Crozet Archipelago **9** Observation Station

(Des P. Béquet. Eng J. Miermont. Recess)

1963 (16 Dec). *P* 13.
35 **8** 5 f. chestnut, black and light blue .. 3·25 3·25

(Des R. Serres; eng C. Mazelin (20 f.). Des and eng P. Béquet (100 f.). Recess)

1963 (16 Dec). *"International Year of the Quiet Sun". T* **9** *and similar design. P* 13. (*a*) *POSTAGE.*
36 **9** 20 f. slate-blue, chestnut & bluish violet 17·00 17·00

    (*b*) *AIR. Inscr* "POSTE AERIENNE"
37 – 100 f. red, blue and black .. .. 32·00 32·00
Design: *Vert* (27×48 *mm*)—100 f. Pylons and penguins.

13 Port-aux-Français, Kerguelen

(Des P. Béquet. Eng M. Monvoisin (40 f.), P. Béquet (50 f.). Recess)

1968 (21 Jan)—**69.** *AIR. T* **13** *and similar horiz design. P* 13.
45 40 f. deep slate and blue (5.1.69) .. .. 3·25 3·25
46 50 f. black, deep green and light blue .. 8·00 8·00
Design:—40 f. Aerial view of St. Paul Island.

10 Landfall of Dumont d'Urville

(Des (after Le Breton) and eng P. Béquet. Recess)

1965 (20 Jan). *AIR. Discovery of Adélie Land,* 1840. *P* 13.
38 **10** 50 f. indigo and light blue .. .. 32·00 32·00

1965 (17 May). *AIR. I.T.U. Centenary. As T* **19** *of French Polynesia.*
39 30 f. bistre-brown, magenta & greenish bl 70·00 70·00

1966 (2 Mar). *AIR. Launching of First French Satellite. As Nos.* 52/3 *of French Polynesia.*
40 25 f. slate-blue, myrtle-green & chocolate 7·50 7·50
41 30 f. slate-blue, myrtle-green & chocolate 7·50 7·50
Price for *se-tenant* pair separated by label, £19 *unused or used.*

1966 (27 Mar). *AIR. Launching of Satellite "D1". As T* **25** *of French Polynesia.*
42 50 f. reddish violet, deep purple & orange 13·00 13·00

14 Kerguelen and Rocket

(Des and eng C. Haley. Recess)

1968 (22 Apr). *AIR. Launching of "Dragon" Space Rockets. T* **14** *and similar horiz design. P* 13.
47 25 f. chocolate, myrtle-green & greenish bl 5·00 5·00
48 30 f. greenish blue, chocolate & myrtle-grn 5·00 5·00
Design:—30 f. Adélie Land and rocket.
Nos. 47/8 were issued together in horizontal pairs separated by a half stamp-size *se-tenant* label inscr "ETUDE DE L'ENVIRONNEMENT SPATIAL PAR FUSEES SONDES IONOSPHERIQUES DRAGON 1967–1968". (*Price for strip unused or used* £5)

1968 (4 May). *20th Anniv of World Health Organization. Design as T* **34** *of French Polynesia.*
49 30 f. new blue, orange-yellow and red .. 3·75 3·75

1968 (10 Aug). *Human Rights Year. Design as T* **36** *of French Polynesia.*
50 30 f. red, greenish blue and brown .. 3·50 3·50

15 Eiffel Tower, Paris, and Ship in Antarctica

(Des and eng P. Béquet. Recess)

1969 (13 Jan). *AIR. Fifth Antarctic Treaty Consultative Meeting. Paris. P* 13.
51 **15** 50 f. blue .. .. 4·00 4·00

16 Antarctic Scene

(Des and eng C. Durrens. Recess)

1969 (17 Mar). *French Polar Exploration. P* 13.
52 **16** 25 f. lt turq-bl, brn-red & greenish bl 2·25 2·25

1969 (2 Apr). *AIR. First Flight of "Concorde". As T* **39** *of French Polynesia.*
53 85 f. greenish blue and new blue .. 9·50 9·50

17 Possession Island, Crozet Archipelago

(Des and eng P. Béquet (500 f. after S. Gauthier). Recess)

1969 (24 Dec)—**71**. *AIR. T* **17** *and similar designs. P* 13.
54 50 f. slate-green, clar & new bl (22.12.70) 2·25 2·25
55 100 f. black, grey and new blue .. .. 3·25 3·25
56 200 f. choc, slate-grn & turq-bl (1.1.71) 5·00 5·00
57 500 f. turquoise-blue .. .. .. 9·00 9·00
54/57 *Set of* 4 .. .. 18·00 18·00
Designs: *Horiz*—100 f. Relief map of Kerguelen. *Vert*—200 f. Cape Geology Archipelago map; 500 f. Territorial arms.

1969 (25 Dec). *50th Anniv of International Labour Organization. As T* **44** *of French Polynesia.*
58 20 f. maroon, deep blue and orange-red 1·25 1·25

18 Relief Map of New Amsterdam Island

(Des P. Béquet. Eng C. Haley. Recess)

1970 (27 Mar). *AIR. 20th Anniv of Meteorological Station, New Amsterdam Island. P* 13.
59 **18** 30 f. brown .. .. 1·50 1·50

1970 (20 May). *New U.P.U. Headquarters Building, Berne. As T* **47** *of French Polynesia.*
60 50 f. olive-brown, dp reddish pur & new bl 2·50 2·50

19 *Chaenichthys rhinoceratus*

(Des and eng C. Haley. Recess)

1971 (1 Jan–22 Dec). *Fishes. T* **19** *and similar horiz designs. P* 13.
61 5 f. indigo, orange-yellow and emerald 25 25
62 10 f. brown, bluish violet and deep blue 40 40
63 20 f. blue-green, yellow-orange & maroon 65 65
64 22 f. claret, violet & olive-brown (22.12) 50 50
65 25 f. dp slate-blue, orange-yell & dp grn 75 75
66 30 f. dp slate, ultramarine & dp bistre-brn 1·10 1·10
67 35 f. multicoloured (22.12) 90 90
68 135 f. verm, ol-brn & greenish bl (22.12) 2·10 2·10
61/68 *Set of* 8 .. .. 6·00 6·00
Designs:—10 f. *Notothenia rossii;* 20 f. *Notothenia coriiceps;* 22 f. *Trematomus hansoni;* 25 f. *Notothenia macrocephala;* 30 f. *Notothenia cyanobrancha;* 35 f. *Trematomus bernacchii;* 135 f. *Zanchlorhynchus spinifer.*

20 Port-aux-Français, 1950

(Des P. Béquet. Eng R. Fenneteaux (40 f.), J. Miermont (50 f.). Recess)

1971 (9 Mar). *AIR. 20th Anniv of Port-aux-Français, Kerguelen. T* **20** *and similar horiz design. P* 13.
69 40 f. orange-brown, myrtle-grn & new bl 1·40 1·40
70 50 f. myrtle-green, new blue & yellow-brn 2·10 2·10
Design:—50 f. Port-aux-Français, 1970.

French Southern and Antarctic Territories 1971

Nos. 69/70 were issued together in sheets, with an intervening se-tenant half stamp-size label showing map of Kerguelen and commemorative inscription. (*Price for strip unused or used* £3·75.)

21 Treaty Emblem

(Des and eng P. Béquet. Recess)

1971 (22 Dec). *10th Anniv of Antarctic Treaty. P* 13.
71 21 75 f. red .. .. 14·00 14·00

22 *Christiansenia dreuxi*

23 Landing on Crozet Islands

(Des and eng C. Haley. Recess)

1972 (2 Jan–16 Dec). *Insects. T* **22** *and similar vert designs. P* 12½×13.
72 15 f. chocolate, deep reddish purple and
    vermilion (16.12) 45 45
73 22 f. lemon, deep ultramarine and slate-
    green (16.12) 55 55
74 25 f. reddish violet, bright purple & green 55 55
75 30 f. royal blue, yell, grn & bl (16.12) .. 75 75
76 40 f. black, orange-brown and chocolate 90 90
77 140 f. brown, bright green and blue .. 2·25 2·25
72/77 *Set of* 6 .. .. 5·00 5·00
Designs:—22 f. *Phtirocoris antarcticus;* 25 f. *Microzetia mirabilis;* 30 f. *Antarctophytosus atriceps;* 40 f. *Paractora dreuxi;* 140 f. *Pringleophaga kerguelenensis.*

(Des and eng P. Béquet. Recess)

1972. *AIR. Bicentenary of Discovery of Crozet Islands and Kerguelen. T* **23** *and similar horiz design. P* 13.
78 100 f. black (24.1) .. .. .. 2·50 2·50
79 250 f. black and brown (13.2) .. .. 4·50 4·50
Design:—250 f. Hoisting the flag on Kerguelen.

(Des G. Bétemps. Eng J. Miermont (50 f.), G. Bétemps (100 f.). Recess)

1972 (1 Feb). *First Death Anniv of General De Gaulle. As Nos.* 145/6 *of French Polynesia. P* 13.
80 50 f. black and emerald 95 95
81 100 f. black and emerald .. .. .. 2·00 2·00

24 M. S. *Galliéni*

(Des P. Béquet. Eng C. Haley. Recess)

1973 (25 Jan). *AIR. Antarctic Voyages of the "Galliéni". P* 13.
82 24 100 f. black and new blue .. .. 5·50 5·50

25 *Azorella selago*

(Des and eng P. Béquet (61 f.), C. Haley (87 f.). Recess)

1973 (13 Dec). *T* **25** *and similar horiz design. P* 13.
83 61 f. yellow-green, slate-green & yell-brn 75 75
84 87 f. myrtle-green, new blue & brown-red 95 95
Design:—87 f. *Acaena ascendens.*

26 *Le Mascarin*, 1772

(Des and eng P. Béquet. Recess)

1973 (13 Dec). *AIR. Antarctic Ships. T* **26** *and similar horiz designs. P* 13.
85 120 f. bistre-brown .. .. .. 1·25 1·25
86 145 f. ultramarine .. .. .. 1·50 1·50
87 150 f. deep slate-blue .. .. 1·60 1·60
88 185 f. orange-brown .. .. .. 1·90 1·90
85/88 *Set of* 4 .. .. 5·50 5·50
Ships:—145 f. *L'Astrolabe*, 1840; 150 f. *Le Rolland*, 1774; 185 f. *La Victoire*, 1522.
See also Nos. 93/4.

27 Part of Alfred Fauré Base

(Des and eng C. Haley. Recess)

1974 (7 Jan). *AIR. 10th Anniv of Alfred Fauré Base, Crozet Archipelago. T* **27** *and similar horiz designs. P* 13.
89 75 f. chocolate, greenish blue & ultram 1·25 1·25
90 110 f. chocolate, greenish blue & ultram 1·50 1·50
91 150 f. chocolate, greenish blue & ultram 2·00 2·00
Nos. 89/91 were issued together *se-tenant* in the form of a triptych, the three designs forming a composite view of the Base. (*Price for strip unused or used* £5·00.)

A regular new issue supplement to this catalogue appears each month in

STAMP MONTHLY

—from your newsagent or by postal subscription
—details on request.

28 Penguin, Globe and Letters

(Des and eng P. Béquet. Recess)

1974 (9 Oct). *AIR. Centenary of Universal Postal Union. P* 13.
92 **28** 150 f. brown, black and greenish blue.. 1·40 1·40

(Des and eng P. Béquet. Recess)

1974 (16 Dec). *AIR. Charcot's Antarctic Voyages. Horiz designs as T* **26**. *P* 13.
93 100 f. new blue 75 75
94 200 f. brown-purple .. .. .. 1·50 1·50
Ships:—100 f. *Le Français* (1903–5 voyage); 200 f. *Le Pourquoi Pas?* (1908–10 voyage).

29 Packet-boat *Sapmer*

(Des and eng C. Haley. Recess)

1974 (31 Dec). *25th Anniv of Postal Service. P* 13.
95 **29** 75 f. black, plum and new blue .. 80 80

30 Rockets over Kerguelen Islands

(Des and eng C. Haley. Recess)

1975 (26 Jan). *AIR. "ARAKS" Franco-Soviet Magnetosphere Research Project. T* **30** *and similar horiz design. P* 13.
96 45 f. rosine, indigo and reddish lilac .. 70 70
97 90 f. crimson, reddish lilac and indigo .. 70 70
Design:—90 f. Map of North Coast of U.S.S.R.
Nos. 96/7 were issued together *se-tenant* with an intervening half stamp-size label inscribed "OPERATION FRANCO-SOVIETIQUE ARAKS" etc. (*Price for strip unused or used* 75p.)

CURRENCY. On 1 January 1976 the CFA franc used in French Southern and Antarctic Territories was replaced by the French Metropolitan franc.

31 Antarctic Tern

32 *La Curieuse*

(Des P. Béquet. Eng C. Haley (40 c., 50 c.). Des and eng P. Béquet (90 c. to 1 f. 40). Des and eng C. Haley (1 f. 90 to 4 f.). Recess)

1976 (1 Jan). *P* 13. *(a) POSTAGE. T* **31** *and similar designs.*
98 40 c. black, turquoise and orange .. 20 20
99 50 c. agate, new blue and bright blue .. 25 25
100 90 c. blackish brown and new blue .. 35 35
101 1 f. blackish brown, new blue & vio-bl 40 40
102 1 f. 20, myrtle-grn, ultram & blackish brn 45 45
103 1 f. 40, indigo, blackish green & orange 55 55
    (b) AIR. T **32** *and similar horiz designs*
104 1 f. 90, greenish blue, ultramarine and red-brown (1.11) 75 75
105 2 f. 70, red-brown, blue and ultramarine (1.11) .. .. 1·10 1·10
106 4 f. violet-blue and red (1.11) .. .. 1·50 1·50
98/106 *Set of* 9 .. .. 5·00 5·00
Designs: *As T* **31**: *Horiz*—50 c. Antarctic petrel; 90 c. Seal; 1 f. Weddell's seal. *Vert*—1 f. 20, Kerguelen cormorant; 1 f. 40, Penguin. *As T* **32**—2 f. 70, *Commandant Charcot;* 4 f. *Marion-Dufresne.*

33 Dumont D'Urville Base, 1956

(Des and eng C. Haley. Recess)

1976 (1 Jan). *AIR. 20th Anniv of Dumont d'Urville Base, Adélie Land. T* **33** *and similar horiz design. P* 13.
107 1 f. 20, brown, orange-brown & turq-bl 50 50
108 4 f. orange-brown, turquoise-blue & brn 1·60 1·60
Design:—4 f. Dumont D'Urville Base, 1976.
Nos. 107/8 were issued together *se-tenant* with an intervening half stamp-size label inscribed "XX ANNIVERSAIRE DE LA BASE DUMONT D'URVILLE—TERRE ADELIE". (*Price for strip unused or used* £2·25.)

A regular new issue supplement to this catalogue appears each month in

STAMP MONTHLY
—from your newsagent or by postal subscription
—details on request.

38 Seaweed, *Macrocystis*

(Des and eng J. Delpech. Recess)

34 Kerguelen Island

(Des and eng P. Béquet, after Benard. Recess)

1976 (31 Dec). *AIR. Bicentenary of Cook's Passage to Kerguelen.* P 13.
110 **34** 3 f. 50, grey-black and blue .. .. 1·90 1·90

1977. *T* **38** *and similar designs.* P 13.
115 40 c. olive-brown and bistre 10 10
116 70 c. bronze-green, brown and black .. 20 20
117 1 f. indigo 30 30
118 1 f. 20, vermilion, greenish blue & royal bl 40 40
119 1 f. 40, scarlet-vermilion, turq-bl & slate 45 45
115/119 *Set of* 5 .. .. 1·25 1·25
Designs: *Horiz*—70 c. Seaweed, *Durvillea*; 1 f. 20, *Magga Dan*; 1 f. 40, *Thala Dan. Vert*—1 f. Oceanology.

39 Kerguelen Satellite

(Des and eng J. Gauthier. Recess)

1977. *AIR. Satellites. T* **39** *and similar horiz design.* P 13.
120 2 f. 70, multicoloured .. .. .. 1·10 1·10
121 3 f. royal blue and new blue .. .. 1·50 1·50
Design:—3 f. Adélie Land satellite.

35 Captain Cook   **36** First Ascent of
Mt Ross (5 Jan 1975)

(Des and eng P. Béquet. Recess)

1977 (3 Jan). *Cook Commemoration.* P 13.
109 **35** 70 c. ultramarine, reddish brown & lemon 1·25 1·25

(Des and eng J. Delpech. Recess)

1977 (3 Jan). *Ross Commemoration. T* **36** *and similar vert design.* P 13.
111 30 c. brown-red, olive-sepia and new blue 50 50
112 3 f. dp violet-blue, yellow-orge & new bl 2·00 2·00
Design:—3 f. Sir James Clark Ross.

40 Polar Explorer with   **41** Salmon and Breeding Tanks
Flags

(Des P. E. Victor. Eng J. Gauthier. Recess)

1977 (24 Dec). *30th Anniv of French Polar Expeditions.* P 13.
122 **40** 1 f. 90, orange, bright scarlet and
ultramarine 65 65

(Des and eng C. Andréotto. Recess)

1977 (24 Dec). *Antarctic Fauna. T* **41** *and similar designs.* P 13.

(a) POSTAGE.
123 50 c. bright violet and deep ultramarine .. 12 12
124 90 c. brown, greenish blue & dp turq-grn 20 20

(b) AIR. Inscr "POSTE AERIENNE"
125 10 f. deep brown, royal blue & bright
magenta .. .. 4·00 4·00
Designs: *Horiz*—90 c. Head of albatross. *Vert* (36×48 *mm*)—10 f. Sea lion and cub.

37 Blue Rorqual

(Des and eng P. Béquet. Recess)

1977 (1 Feb). *Marine Mammals. T* **37** *and similar horiz design.* P 13.
113 1 f. 10, Prussian blue and new blue .. 40 40
114 1 f. 50, indigo, greenish blue & br-ochre .. 65 65
Design:—1 f. 50, Commerson's dolphin.

42 R. Rallier du Baty

43 Memorial and Names of French Navigators

(Des and eng P. Béquet. Recess)

1978 (31 Dec). *R. Rallier du Baty Commemoration.* P 13.
126 **42** 1 f. 20, indigo and bistre 40 40

(Des J. Gauthier. Eng J. Pheulpin. Recess)

1978 (31 Dec). *French Navigators' Memorial, Hobart.* P 13.
127 **43** 1 f. ol-brn, dp bluish grn & greenish bl . . 30 30

44 "Argos" Satellite and Geophysical Laboratory

(Des and eng J. Gauthier. Recess)

1979 (1 Jan). *AIR. Satellite Research. T* **44** *and similar horiz design.* P 13.
128 70 c. greenish blue, bluish violet & yell-ol 20 20
129 1 f. 90, slate-black, yellow-ol & dp mve 65 65
Design:—1 f. 90, Satellite and Kerguelen receiving station.

45 Kerguelen Cormorant

(Des and eng C. Andréotto. Recess)

1979 (1 Jan). *Antarctic Fauna. T* **45** *and similar designs.* P 13.
(a) POSTAGE.
130 1 f. 40, blackish green, new blue and sepia 45 45

(b) AIR. *Inscr "POSTE AERIENNE"*
131 4 f. dp ultram, new bl & yellowish grn . . 1·50 1·50
132 10 f. olive-brown, yellowish green & black 4·00 4·00
Designs: *Vert* (27 × 48 mm)—10 f. Sea elephant. (36 × 48 mm)—4 f. As No. 125.

46 Squadron Escort Vessel *Forbin*

(Des and eng J. Delpech. Recess)

1979 (1 Jan). *Ships. T* **46** *and similar horiz design.* P 13.
133 40 c. blue-black, greenish blue & bottle grn 10 10
134 50 c. blue-black, greenish blue & bottle grn 12 12
Design:—50 c. Helicopter Carrier *Jeanne d'Arc.*

47 H.M.S. *Challenger* in the Antarctic (from engraving in "Illustrated London News")

(Des and eng P. Béquet. Recess)

1979 (1 Jan). *AIR. Expedition of the "Challenger",* 1872–6. P 13.
135 **47** 2 f. 70, black and new blue . . . . 1·10 1·10

ALBUM LISTS

Please write for our latest lists of albums and accessories. These will be sent free on request.

French Sudan

100 Centimes = 1 Franc

The area which became the French Sudan, around the upper waters of the Senegal and Niger rivers, was part of that belt of territory, stretching across Africa south of the Sahara Desert, which was known to the Arabs as Bilad-es-Sudan (Land of the Blacks).

PRINTERS. All issues were printed by the French Government Printing Works, Paris, *unless otherwise stated*.

IMPERFORATE STAMPS. Many stamps exist imperforate in their issued colours, but these were not valid for postage. Imperforate stamps in other colours are colour trials.

A. FRENCH SUDAN

Colonel Louis Faidherbe, appointed Governor of Senegal in 1854, conceived the plan of linking the territory around the Upper Senegal river with that around the Upper Niger within the French sphere of influence. The Muslim empires of Ahmadu and Samori, recently established, were subdued by the campaigns of Colonels J. S. Galliéni and Borgnis-Desbordes. French rights on the Upper Niger were recognised by the Berlin Conference on 26 February 1885, although control was not complete until the final defeat of Samori in 1898. The town of Tombouctou was taken on 16 December 1893.

SOUDAN F^ais

0,25

(1)

1894 (12 Apr). *Type J ("Commerce") of French Colonies (General issues) surch as T 1 at Bamako by lithography.* P 14×13½.

1	0.15 on 75 c. carmine	£750	£500
2	0.25 on 1 f. olive-green	£750	£400

French Colonies (General issues) Type H 75 c. rose-carmine exists with similar surcharge. This year was not authorised, and all known copies are cancelled 15 July 1894 at Médine.

1894 (May). *French Colonies Type X ("Tablet") inscr "SOUDAN FRANCAIS" in red (1, 5, 15, 25, 75 c., 1 f.) or blue (others).* P 14×13½.

3	1 c. black/azure		15	15
4	2 c. brown/buff		30	30
5	4 c. purple-brown/grey		55	40
6	5 c. green/pale green		1·25	75
7	10 c. black/lilac		2·75	2·50
8	15 c. blue (quadrillé paper)		50	40
9	20 c. red/green		5·00	3·75
	a. Bisected (10 c.) (on cover, Gaoua, Mar 1908)			
10	25 c. black/rose		5·00	3·75
11	30 c. cinnamon/drab		7·50	6·50
12	40 c. red/yellow		6·00	5·00
13	50 c. carmine/rose		8·50	7·50

14	75 c. brown/yellow		7·00	7·00
15	1 f. olive-green/toned		1·10	1·10
3/15	Set of 13		40·00	35·00

TAXE PERÇUE: *0.2½*
Manqué de Timbres dans la Colonie.

2

1894 (Aug). *Kayes Provisionals. Values in Manuscript. Imperf.*

16	**2** 15 c. black			— 75·00
17	25 c. black			— 75·00

Only these two values were officially authorised, although others to 1 f. are known.

1900 (Dec). *Type X. Colours changed. Inscr in blue (10 c.) or red (others).* P 14×13½.

18	10 c. rose-red		75	75
19	15 c. grey		1·40	1·40
20	25 c. blue		1·25	1·25
21	50 c. brown/azure		2·25	2·25
18/21	Set of 4		5·00	5·00

On 18 October 1899 the parts of the territory adjoining Senegal, French Guinea, Ivory Coast and Dahomey were detached from French Sudan and were added to the coastal colonies. The remainder became a protectorate known as the Territories of the Senegambia and the Niger.
Nos. 18/21 were printed in error after the division of French Sudan, and were not in regular issue. They were, however, allowed to pay postage in the area as administratively redistributed.

B. SENEGAMBIA AND NIGER

1903 (July). *Type X ("Tablet") inscr "SENEGAMBIE ET NIGER" in red (1, 5, 15, 25, 75 c., 1 f.) or blue (others).* P 14×13½.

22	1 c. black/azure		55	45
23	2 c. purple-brown/buff		65	45
24	4 c. purple-brown/grey		1·00	1·00
25	5 c. yellow-green		95	80
26	10 c. rose-red		1·25	1·10
27	15 c. grey		3·25	3·25
28	20 c. red/green		3·25	3·25
29	25 c. blue		4·75	4·00
30	30 c. cinnamon/drab		4·75	3·50
31	40 c. red/yellow		5·00	3·50
32	50 c. brown/azure (name in blue)		10·00	10·00
33	75 c. brown/orange		11·00	11·00
34	1 f. olive-green/toned		14·00	14·00
22/34	Set of 13		55·00	50·00

On 18 October 1904 the protectorate became the colony of Upper Senegal and Niger.

ALBUM LISTS   Please write for our latest lists of albums and accessories. These will be sent free on request.

C. UPPER SENEGAL AND NIGER

3 General Faidherbe   **4** Palm Trees

5 Dr. N. Eugène Balay   **D 6** Dakar and West Africans

(Des J. Puyplat. Typo)

1906–8. *Name in blue (10 c., 40 c., 5 f.) or red (others). P 13½×14 (T 4) or 14×13½ (others).*

35	3	1 c. slate	25	25
36		2 c. chocolate	25	25
37		4 c. chocolate/*blue*	25	25
38		5 c. green	75	50
39		10 c. rose	75	40
40		15 c. bright violet	65	65
41	4	20 c. black/*bluish*	75	75
42		25 c. blue	3·75	75
43		30 c. chocolate/*flesh*	1·25	1·10
44		35 c. black/*yellow*	75	50
45		40 c. carmine/*azure*	1·25	90
46		45 c. chocolate/*green* (1908)	1·90	1·25
47		50 c. deep violet	1·25	95
48		75 c. green/*orange*	1·90	1·90
49	5	1 f. black/*azure*	5·00	3·50
50		2 f. blue/*rose*	11·00	9·50
51		5 f. red/*straw*	19·00	18·00
35/51		*Set of 17*	45·00	38·00

(Des J. Puyplat. Typo)

1906. *POSTAGE DUE. Name in blue (10 c.) or red (others). P 13½×14.*

D52	D 6	5 c. green/*toned*	65	50
D53		10 c. maroon	1·60	1·40
D54		15 c. blue/*bluish*	2·50	1·90
D55		20 c. black/*yellow*	2·25	1·25
D56		50 c. violet	5·50	5·00
D57		60 c. black/*buff*	3·25	3·25
D58		1 f. black/*flesh*	6·50	5·50
D52/58		*Set of 7*	20·00	17·00

7 Touareg   **(8)**

(Des J. de la Nézière. Eng E. Froment. Typo)

1914–17. *P 13½×14.*

59	7	1 c. violet and grey-purple		5	5
60		2 c. grey-purple and grey		5	5
61		4 c. blue and black		5	5
62		5 c. green and yellow-green		5	5
63		10 c. carmine and orange-red		40	25
64		15 c. orange-yellow and chocolate (1917)		20	12
65		20 c. black and grey-purple		20	15
66		25 c. blue and ultramarine		20	20
67		30 c. chocolate and brown		15	12
		a. Brown and olive		5·00	5·00
68		35 c. violet and carmine		40	25
69		40 c. carmine and grey		30	20
70		45 c. yellow-brown and blue		30	25
71		50 c. green and black		30	30
72		75 c. brown and orange-yellow		25	25
73		1 f. grey-purple and brown		30	25
74		2 f. blue and green		55	50
75		5 f. black and violet		1·60	1·40
59/75		*Set of 17*		5·00	4·00

The 5, 10 and 15 c. exist on chalk-surfaced paper.

Stamps in other colours may be "opt omitted" errors from the later "SOUDAN FRANCAIS" overprinted issues.

This design was also used overprinted for Niger and Upper Volta and similar varieties will be found in these lists.

1915 (Apr). *Red Cross. Surch in Paris with T 8, in red.*

76	7	10 c.+5 c. carmine and orange-red		15	15

D 9

1915. *POSTAGE DUE. Typo. P 14×13½.*

D77	D 9	5 c. green		15	15
D78		10 c. carmine		15	15
D79		15 c. grey		15	15
D80		20 c. brown		15	15
D81		30 c. blue		45	40
D82		50 c. black		12	12
D83		60 c. orange		90	75
D84		1 f. violet		75	65
D77/84		*Set of 8*		2·50	2·25

For this design inscribed "SOUDAN FRANÇAIS" see Nos. D176/85.

On 4 December 1920 the colony reverted to the previous title of French Sudan.

D. FRENCH SUDAN

SOUDAN

FRANÇAIS

(10)

1921 (Dec). *T 7, some values in new colours, optd with T 10. P 13½×14.*

85		1 c. violet and purple		5	5
86		2 c. purple and grey		5	5
87		4 c. blue and black		5	5
88		5 c. chocolate and brown		5	5
		a. Opt omitted		25·00	
89		10 c. green and yellow-green		5	5
90		15 c. orange and maroon		5	5
91		20 c. black and purple		5	5
92		25 c. green and black		5	5
		a. Opt omitted			
93		30 c. carmine and orange-red		5	5
94		35 c. violet and carmine		5	5
95		40 c. carmine and grey		12	10
96		45 c. brown and blue		8	8
97		50 c. blue and ultramarine		12	12
		a. Opt omitted		45·00	
98		75 c. brown and yellow		12	12
99		1 f. purple and brown		15	10
100		2 f. blue and green		45	35
101		5 f. black and violet		1·00	80
85/101		*Set of 17*		2·25	2·00

1921 (Dec). *POSTAGE DUE. Nos.* D77/84 *optd as T* **10**.

D102	D **9**	5 c. green	.. .. ..	5	5
D103		10 c. carmine	.. .. ..	12	12
D104		15 c. drab ..	.. ..	12	12
D105		20 c. brown	.. ..	12	12
D106		30 c. blue ..	.. ..	15	15
D107		50 c. black	.. ..	30	30
D108		60 c. orange	.. ..	30	30
D109		1 f. violet	.. ..	35	35
D102/109		*Set of 8* ..	.. ..	1·40	1·40

65 = 65   90^c   2^{F.}

(11)   (12)   (D 13)

1922 (28 Sept)–**27**. *Stamps as T* **7**, *some with colours changed, surch as T* **11/12**.

110	25 c. on 45 c. brown and blue (1.2.25)		10	10
	a. Surch double	.. ..	13·00	
111	60 on 75 c. violet/*rose* ..	..	5	5
	a. Surch omitted	.. ..	25·00	
112	65 on 75 c. brown and yellow (1.2.25) ..		15	15
113	85 on 2 f. blue and green (1.2.25)		25	20
114	85 on 5 f. black and violet (1.2.25)	..	25	20
115	90 c. on 75 c. rose-red & carm (11.4.27)		40	20
116	1 f. 25 on 1 f. pale bl & bl (R.) (14.6.26)		15	15
117	1 f. 50 on 1 f. ultramarine & bl (11.4.27)		15	15
	a. Opt and surch omitted	..	45·00	
	b. Surch omitted	.. ..	25·00	
118	3 f. on 5 f. buff and dull rose (19.12.27)		70	40
119	10 f. on 5 f. green and carmine (21.3.27)		3·50	3·25
120	20 f. on 5 f. vermilion & violet (21.3.27)		4·50	3·75
110/120	*Set of 11*	..	9·00	8·00

1925 (1 May)–**30**. *As* 1921. *Colours changed and new values. Optd with T* **10**.

121	**7** 10 c. pale blue and magenta ..		5	5
	a. Opt omitted	.. ..	28·00	
122	15 c. green and yellow-green ..		5	5
123	15 c. magenta and chestnut (4.11.27) ..		12	12
124	30 c. black and blue-green (1.12.25) ..		5	5
	a. Opt omitted	..	35·00	
125	30 c. green and olive-green (25.9.28) ..		25	25
126	50 c. blue and orange (1.12.25)	..	8	5
	a. Opt omitted	..	35·00	
127	60 c. violet/*rose* (21.12.25)	..	5	5
	a. Opt double	.. ..	32·00	
128	65 c. blue and yellow-brown (2.4.28) ..		15	15
129	90 c. carmine and brown-red (5.5.30) ..		1·00	1·00
130	1 f. 10, magenta & violet-bl (25.9.28)		25	25
131	1 f. 50, blue (5.5.30)		1·10	1·10
	a. Opt omitted	..	28·00	
132	3 f. magenta/*rose* (5.5.30) ..		1·90	1·90
	a. Opt double	..	28·00	
121/132	*Set of 12*	..	4·50	4·50

1927 (10 Oct). *POSTAGE DUE. Surch as Type* D **13**.

D133	D **9** 2 f. on 1 f. magenta	..	90	90
D134	3 f. on 1 f. red-brown	..	90	90

(Des and eng A. Delzers (T **14**), J. Piel (T **15**), G. Hourriez. (T **16**). Typo)

1931 (9 Mar)–**39**. *P* 13½ × 14.

135	**14**	1 c. black and scarlet	..	5	5
136		2 c. vermilion and deep blue		5	5
137		3 c. black and scarlet (1939)		5	5
138		4 c. carmine and lilac		5	5
139		5 c. green and indigo	..	5	5
140		10 c. carmine and olive-green	..	5	5
141		15 c. violet and black	..	5	5
142		20 c. blue and red-brown	..	5	5
143		25 c. pink and magenta	..	5	5
144	**15**	30 c. yellow-green and green		8	5
145		30 c. vermilion and blue (1939)	..	5	5
146		35 c. green and olive-green (1938) ..		5	5
147		40 c. carmine and olive-green	..	5	5
148		45 c. vermilion and deep blue	..	10	8
149		45 c. green and olive-green (1939) ..		5	5
150		50 c. black and scarlet	..	5	5
151		55 c. carmine and bright blue (1938) ..		5	5
152		60 c. chocolate and blue (1939)	..	5	5
153		65 c. black and violet	.. ..	5	5
154		70 c. carmine and ultramarine (1939) ..		8	8
155		75 c. chocolate and blue	..	30	12
156		80 c. chocolate and carmine (1938) ..		5	5
157		90 c. vermilion and brown-red	..	5	5
158		90 c. black and violet	.. ..	5	5
159		1 f. green and deep ultramarine	..	1·40	15
160		1 f. carmine (1938) ..	..	65	10
161		1 f. chocolate and carmine (1939) ..		5	5
162	**16**	1 f. 25, magenta and violet (25.9.33)		10	8
163		1 f. 25, rose-red and scarlet (1938)..		8	8
164		1 f. 40, black and violet (1939)	..	8	8
165		1 f. 50, blue and indigo	.. ..	8	8
166		1 f. 60, blue and chocolate (1938) ..		8	8
167		1 f. 75, blue and chocolate (25.9.33)		5	5
168		1 f. 75, ultramarine (1938)		5	5
169		2 f. green and red-brown	.. ..	5	5
170		2 f. 25, ultramarine & violet-bl (1939)		10	10
171		2 f. 50, chocolate (1939)	.. ..	12	12
172		3 f. chocolate and blue-green	..	5	5
173		5 f. black and scarlet	..	25	12
174		10 f. green and indigo	..	30	30
175		20 f. chocolate and magenta..	..	40	40
135/175		*Set of 41*	..	5·00	3·00

10 c. and 30 c. values as T **14/15**, but without "RF", prepared in 1943/4, but not placed on sale in French Sudan.

1931 (9 Mar). *POSTAGE DUE. Inscr* "SOUDAN FRANÇAIS". *P* 14 × 13½.

D176	D **9**	5 c. green	.. .. ..	5	5
D177		10 c. carmine	.. ..	5	5
D178		15 c. drab ..	.. ..	5	5
D179		20 c. brown	.. ..	5	5
D180		30 c. blue ..	.. ..	5	5
D181		50 c. black	.. ..	5	5
D182		60 c. orange	.. ..	12	12
D183		1 f. violet	.. ..	20	20
D184		2 f. magenta	.. ..	20	20
D185		3 f. red-brown	.. ..	20	20
D176/185		*Set of 10* ..	.. ..	90	90

17 French Colonial Races

18 Women of Five Races

14 Sudanese Woman marketing

15 Djenné Gateway

16 Niger Boatman

19 "France the Civiliser"

20 French Colonial Commerce

French Sudan
1931

(Des J. de la Nèzière (T **17**), M. Cayon-Rouan (T **18**), A. Parent (T **19**), G. Francois (T **20**). Recess Institut de Gravure, Paris)

1931 (13 Apr). *International Colonial Exhibition, Paris.* P 12½.
186	**17**	40 c. black and green	..	45	45
187	**18**	50 c. black and mauve	..	45	45
188	**19**	90 c. black and vermilion	..	45	45
189	**20**	1 f. 50, black and blue	..	45	45
186/189		*Set of 4*	..	2·00	2·00

1937 (15 Apr). *International Exhibition, Paris.* As T **2**/**7** of French Equatorial Africa.
190	20 c. violet	..	20	20
191	30 c. green	..	20	20
192	40 c. carmine	..	20	20
193	50 c. brown	..	20	20
194	90 c. scarlet	..	20	20
195	1 f. 50, blue	..	20	20
190/195	*Set of 6*	..	1·10	1·10

MS196 120×100 mm. 3 f. magenta and black (as T **5**). Imperf .. 80 80

1938 (24 Oct). *International Anti-Cancer Fund.* As T **14** of French Equatorial Africa.
197 1 f. 75+50 c. ultramarine .. 2·25 2·25

21 René Caillé **22** Aeroplane over Jungle

(Des and eng R. Cottet. Recess Institut de Gravure, Paris)

1939 (5 Apr). *Death Centenary of René Caillé (explorer).* P 12½.
198	**21**	90 c. orange ..	12	12
199		2 f. violet	12	12
200		2 f. 25, blue	12	12

1939 (10 May). *New York World's Fair.* As T **17** of French Equatorial Africa.
201	1 f. 25, lake	12	12
202	2 f. 25, ultramarine	12	12

1939 (5 July). *150th Anniv of French Revolution.* As T **18** of French Equatorial Africa.
203	45 c.+25 c. green and black	..	1·40	1·40
204	70 c.+30 c. brown and black	..	1·40	1·40
205	90 c.+35 c. red-orange and black	1·40	1·40
206	1 f. 25+1 f. carmine and black	1·40	1·40
207	2 f. 25+2 f. blue and black	..	1·40	1·40
203/207	*Set of 5*	..	6·40	6·40

(Des D. Paul. Recess Institut de Gravure, Paris)

1940 (8 Feb). *AIR.* P 12½.
208	**22**	1 f. 90, bright blue ..	5	5
209		2 f. 90, rose-red	5	5
210		4 f. 50, green ..	12	12
211		4 f. 90, olive-bistre	12	12
212		6 f. 90, orange	12	12
208/212		*Set of 5*	40	40

VICHY GOVERNMENT

Nos. 213/19 were issued by the Pétain régime in Unoccupied France. A number of other sets exist, but we only list those items which were available in French Sudan.

SECOURS
+ **1 fr.**
NATIONAL

(23)

24 Gate at Djenné and Marshal Pétain

1941. *National Defence Fund.* Surch as T **23**.
213	**15**	+1 f. on 50 c. black and scarlet (R.) ..	15	15
214		+2 f. on 80 c. chocolate and carmine..	1·60	1·60
215	**16**	+2 f. on 1 f. 50, blue and indigo	..	1·60	1·60
216		+3 f. on 2 f. green and red-brown	..	1·60	1·60
213/216		*Set of 4*	..	4·50	4·50

(Des and eng A. Degorce. Recess Institut de Gravure, Paris)

1941. P 12×12½.
217	**24**	1 f. deep green	..	..	5
218		2 f. 50, deep blue	..	..	10

25 Aeroplane over Camel Caravan

(Des and eng D. Paul. Typo and recess)

1942 (19 Oct). *AIR. As T* **25** *but inscr* "SOUDAN". P 12½×12.
219 **25** 50 f. blue and yellow-green 25 30
Seven other values exist, but were not issued.

From 1944 to 1959 French Sudan used the stamps of French West Africa.

ALBUM LISTS

Please write for our latest lists of albums and accessories. These will be sent free on request.

French Territory of the Afars and the Issas

100 Centimes=1 Franc

PRINTERS. All issues were printed by the French Government Printing Works, Paris, *unless otherwise stated.*

IMPERFORATE STAMPS. Stamps exist imperforate in their issued colours, but these were not valid for postage. Imperforate stamps in other colours are colour trials.

A. OBOCK

The town of Obock, together with adjoining territory was purchased for France by the Consul in Aden during 1857. The cession was ratified by treaty with local Danakil chiefs in 1862 and formal possession of the area followed in 1883.

(1)   (2)

1892 (1 Feb). *French Colonies (General issues) Type J* ("Commerce"). *P* 14×13½. *Handstamped at Obock.*

(a) With T **1**

1	1 c. black/*azure*			5·50	5·00
2	2 c. brown/*buff*			5·50	5·00
3	4 c. purple-brown/*grey*			75·00	75·00
4	5 c. green/*pale green*			4·50	3·75
5	10 c. black/*lilac*			12·00	11·00
6	15 c. blue			10·00	8·50
7	25 c. black/*rose*			15·00	15·00
8	35 c. black/*orange*			95·00	95·00
9	40 c. red/*buff*			85·00	85·00
10	75 c. carmine/*rose*			95·00	95·00
11	1 f. olive-green/*toned*			£100	£100

The overprint on the 4 c. has been reprinted. In this reprint the letters "O" of "OBOCK" are 4 mm instead of 3½ mm in height.

(b) With T **2**

12	4 c. purple-brown/*grey*			3·25	3·00
13	5 c. green/*pale green*			3·25	3·00
14	10 c. black/*lilac*			4·50	4·25
15	15 c. blue			4·50	4·25
16	20 c. red/*green*			7·50	5·25
17	25 c. black/*rose*			2·75	2·50
18	40 c. red/*buff*			9·00	7·00
19	75 c. carmine/*rose*			75·00	50·00
20	1 f. olive-green/*toned*			10·00	9·00

The 1, 2, 30 and 35 c. handstamped with T **2** exist, but were never issued.

1892. *French Colonies (General issues) Type U. Imperf. Handstamped at Obock.*

(a) With T **1**

D21	5 c. black			£1500
D22	10 c. black			35·00 35·00
D23	30 c. black			70·00 70·00
D24	60 c. black			75·00 75·00

The overprint on the 5 c., No. D21, has been reprinted. On the original the overprint is 12½ mm wide by 3¾ mm high. On the reprint it is 12×13¼ mm.

(b) With T **2**

D25	1 c. black			6·50	6·00
D26	2 c. black			5·00	4·50
D27	3 c. black			5·00	4·50
D28	4 c. black			5·00	4·50
D29	5 c. black			1·25	1·25
D30	10 c. black			4·00	3·75
D31	15 c. black			3·50	2·75
D32	20 c. black			3·50	2·75
D33	30 c. black			4·50	4·00

D34	40 c. black			8·00	7·00
D35	60 c. black			9·00	8·50
D36	1 f. brown			35·00	32·00
D37	2 f. brown			35·00	32·00
D38	5 f. brown			75·00	75·00

(3)   (4)

1892 (29 Feb–Apr). *Nos.* 14, 15, 17 *and* 20 *handstamped with new value as T* **3/4**.

39	**3**	1 on 25 c. black/*rose* (R.)		1·50	1·50
40		2 on 10 c. black/*lilac* (R.) (6.4)		10·00	8·50
41		2 on 15 c. blue (R.)		2·50	2·00
42		4 on 15 c. blue		2·50	2·00
43		4 on 25 c. black/*rose* (25.3)		3·50	3·25
44		4 on 25 c. black/*rose* (R.) (25.3)		4·00	3·50
45		20 on 10 c. black/*lilac* (R.) (6.4)		18·00	15·00
46		30 on 10 c. black/*lilac* (R.) (6.4)		22·00	20·00
47		35 on 25 c. black/*rose* (25.3)		16·00	16·00
		a. "3" for "35"		£175	£175
48		75 on 1 f. olive-green/*toned* (25.3) (R.)		20·00	18·00
		a. "55" for "75"		£1200	£1200
		b. "57" for "75"		£1200	£1200
49	**4**	5 f. on 1 f. olive-green/*toned* (B.) (6.4)		£200	£200

1892 (Nov). *French Colonies Type X* ("Tablet") *inscr* "OBOCK" *in red* (1, 5, 15, 25, 75 *c.*, 1 *f.*) *or blue* (*others*). *P* 14×13½.

50	1 c. black/*azure*			65	40
51	2 c. brown/*buff*			20	15
52	4 c. purple-brown/*grey*			40	25
53	5 c. green/*pale green*			60	35
54	10 c. black/*lilac*			80	60
55	15 c. blue (*quadrillé paper*)			2·50	1·75
56	20 c. red/*green*			5·00	3·50
57	25 c. black/*rose*			4·50	3·50
58	30 c. cinnamon/*drab*			3·75	2·50
59	40 c. red/*yellow*			3·75	2·00
60	50 c. carmine/*rose*			4·00	2·50
61	75 c. brown/*orange*			4·25	2·50
	a. Name double			35·00	35·00
	b. Name inverted			£350	£350
62	1 f. olive-green/*toned*			4·50	3·50
50/62	*Set of 13*			30·00	20·00

5   6

ALBUM LISTS

Write for our latest lists of albums and accessories.

These will be sent free on request.

7

1893. *T 5 and same type in larger triangular design (length of sides 45 mm). Quadrillé paper. Imperf.*

63	2 f. slate-green	..	9·00	8·50
64	5 f. rose	..	22·00	20·00

The apparent perforation in the illustrations is part of the engraved design, and the same is the case in the following issue.

1894–1903. *Quadrillé paper. Imperf.* (a) *T 6.*

65	1 c. black and rose		35	35
66	2 c. claret and green	..	45	45
67	4 c. claret and orange	..	35	35
68	5 c. blue-green and brown	..	40	40
69	10 c. black and green	..	1·75	1·60
	a. Bisected (5 c.) (on cover) (12.7.01)	†	12·00
70	15 c. ultramarine and rose	..	1·60	1·25
71	20 c. orange and purple	..	1·60	1·25
	a. Bisected (10 c.) (on cover) (12.11.01)	†	8·00
72	25 c. black and blue	..	1·75	1·60
	a. Bisected (2 c.) (on cover) (13.6.03)*	†	7·00
	b. Bisected (5 c.) (on cover) (12.11.01)*	†	7·00
73	30 c. bistre and green	..	3·75	3·25
	a. Bisected (15 c.) (on cover) (2.7.01)	†	£175
74	40 c. red and blue-green	..	2·75	2·25
75	50 c. rose and blue	..	2·50	2·00
	a. Bisected (25 c.) (on cover) (2.7.01)	†	£300
76	75 c. lilac and orange	..	2·50	1·25
77	1 f. olive-green and purple	..	2·50	1·25
65/77	Set of 13	..	20·00	15·00

(b) *As T 7 (various sizes, length of sides shown in brackets)*

78	2 f. orange and lilac (37 mm)	..	22·00	18·00
79	5 f. rose and blue (42 mm)	..	16·00	14·00
80	10 f. lake and red (46 mm)	..	30·00	25·00
81	25 f. blue and brown (49 mm)	..	£150	£150
82	50 f. green and lake (49 mm)	..	£175	f175

*To form Nos. 72a/b the stamps were bisected vertically so that the cut fell between the figures of "25 c.". The left-hand half was then used as a 2 c. value, and the right as a 5 c.

During 1894 the administration was moved to Djibouti and the Obock Post Office was closed. Obock issues were used at Djibouti, both with and without overprints, and all the bisects listed in the 1894 set were issued there.

B. DJIBOUTI

The town of Djibouti was founded by Governor Leonce Lagarde of Obock in 1888, the year in which the French Somali Coast Protectorate was established. It became the capital of the protectorate in 1894. The boundaries of French Somali Coast were settled by treaties with Great Britain, Ethiopia and Italy between 1888 and 1901.

(8)

(9)

1893 (Dec). *No. 53 handstamped with T* **8** *(No.* 83) *or similarly without bar (No. 84) at Djibouti.*

83	X	5 c. green/*pale green*	..	30·00	28·00
84		5 c. green/*pale green*	..	£225	£125

No. 51 handstamped at Djibouti with T **9.** *Name in blue and value in black*

85	X	25 on 2 c. brown/*buff*	..	65·00	45·00
	a. "25" omitted	..	£200	£175
	b. "DJIBOUTI" omitted	..	£200	£175

(10)   **(11)**

No. 50 handstamped at Djibouti with T **10.** *Name in red and value in blue*

86	X	50 on 1 c. black/*azure*	..	75·00	55·00
	a. "5" for "50"	..	£200	£175
	b. "0" for "50"	..	£200	£175
	c. "DJIBOUTI" omitted	..	£200	£175

No. 64 surch or optd as T **11** *by handstamp at Djibouti*

87	1 f. on 5 f. rose (B.)	..	£175	£150
88	5 f. rose (B.)	..	£400	£350

12 Djibouti

13 French Gunboat

14 Crossing the Desert

(The apparent perforation, see T **12**, *is part of the design, and also appears on T* **13/14)**

1894–1902. *Quadrillé paper. Imperf.*

89	**12**	1 c. claret and black	..	40	40
		a. Thick card paper	..	2·00	2·00
90		2 c. black and claret	..	40	40
	·	a. Thick card paper	..	2·00	2·00

91	**12**	4 c. blue and purple-brown	1·75	1·50
		a. Thick card paper	5·00	5·00
92		5 c. red and blue-green	1·50	1·00
93		5 c. yellow-green (3.02)	1·75	1·50
94		10 c. green and brown	3·25	1·50
		a. Bisected (5 c.) (on cover) (12.7.01)	†	10·00
95	–	15 c. green and lilac .. ·	2·00	1·50
96	–	25 c. blue and rose	3·75	2·25
97	–	30 c. rose and olive-brown ..	3·50	2·50
		a. Bisected (15 c.) (on cover) (2.7.01)	†	20·00
98	–	40 c. blue and yellow (3.00)	10·00	8·50
99	–	50 c. carmine and blue	3·50	2·25
		a. Bisected (25 c.) (on cover) (2.7.01)	†	£120
100	–	75 c. orange and mauve	9·00	7·50
101	–	1 f. black and olive-green	4·00	3·00
102	–	2 f. rose and grey-brown	22·00	16·00
103	**13**	5 f. blue and rose	30·00	25·00
104	**14**	25 f. blue and rose	£225	£200
105		50 f. rose and blue	£225	£200

Designs: As T **12**—15 c. to 75 c. (various views of Djibouti) ; 1 f., 2 f. Djibouti Harbour.
Bisects of the 40 c. were not authorised.

(15)   **(16)**

1899 (10 June). *No. 91 handstamped with T **15** at Djibouti.*
106	**12**	0.40 on 4 c. blue and purple-brown ..	£700	5·00

Dangerous forgeries exist.

1902 (4 Jan–2 Feb). *Nos. 76 and 100/3 handstamped at Djibouti as T **16**.*
107	**6**	0.05 on 75 c. lilac and orange (B.) (2.2)	£400	£225
108	–	0.05 on 75 c. orange and mauve (B.)	16·00	9·50
		a. "0,05"	25·00	12·00
		b. Pair, one without surch ..	£300	
109	–	0,10 on 1 f. black and olive-green (B.)	19·00	15·00
110	–	0,40 on 2 f. rose and grey-brown (B.)	£160	£100
111	**13**	0,75 on 5 f. blue and rose	£170	£140

Nos. 107/8 have stop between "0" and "05"; all others, including No. 108a, have a comma in this position.

CENTIMES   **5** centimes

(17)   **(18)**

1902 (15 Apr). *Nos. 81/2, surch as T **17** at Djibouti.*
112		5 c. on 25 f. blue and brown		
113		10 c. on 50 f. green and lake	13·00	11·00
		a. "01" for "10"	17·00	14·00
		b. Surch double	50·00	45·00
		c. Surch double, one inverted	—	£500
			£550	

1902. *Nos. 98/9 surch at Djibouti as T **18**.*
114		5 c. on 40 c. blue and yellow (26.4) ..	1·25	1·10
		a. Surch double	22·00	22·00
115		10 c. on 50 c. carmine and blue (11.7) ..	4·75	4·75
		a. Surch inverted	80·00	80·00

HAVE YOU READ THE NOTES AT THE BEGINNING OF THIS CATALOGUE?
These often provide answers to the enquiries we receive.

---

10 CENTIMES DJIBOUTI

(19)

10 CENTIMES DJIBOUTI

(20)

10 CENTIMES DJIBOUTI

(21)

5 *centimes* **DJIBOUTI**

(22)

1902 (26 Apr–24 June). *Nos. 72, 78 and 80 surch with T **19/21** at Djibouti.*
116	**19**	10 c. on 25 c. black and blue (R.) ..	2·75	2·25
		a. Surch double	65·00	55·00
		b. Surch treble	£225	£225
		c. Surch inverted	55·00	55·00
117	**20**	10 c. on 25 c. black and blue (R.) ..	£7500	£5000
118		10 c. on 2 f. orange and lilac (27.5) ..	13·00	11·00
		a. Surch double	£110	£110
		b. Surch treble		
		c. "DJIBOUTI" inverted ..	70·00	60·00
119	**21**	10 c. on 10 f. lake and red (26.4) ..	7·50	6·50
		a. Surch double	65·00	55·00
		b. Surch treble	£225	£225

1902 (11 July). *No. 73 surch with T **22** at Djibouti.*
120		5 c. on 30 c. bistre and green	2·50	2·25
		a. Surch double	55·00	55·00
		b. Surch inverted	50·00	40·00

C. FRENCH SOMALI COAST

In 1902 the stamps of Djibouti were replaced by issues bearing the title of the protectorate only.

23 Mosque at Tajurah   **24** Mounted Somalis   **25** Somali Warriors

(Des P. Merwart. Eng B. Damman. Recess Chassepot, Paris)

1902 (Aug)–**03**. *Centres in first colour. P 11, 11½.*
121	**23**	1 c. orange and purple		12	12
122		2 c. green and bistre-brown ..		12	12
123		4 c. carmine and blue (12.02) ..		45	20
		a. Centre inverted		3·25	
124		5 c. yellow-green and blue-green ..		30	20
		a. Imperf between (pair) ..		75	
125		10 c. orange and carmine (12.02) ..		1·50	75
126		15 c. blue and orange (10.02) ..		1·25	75
127	**24**	20 c. green and dull lilac (12.02) ..		2·25	1·75
		a. Centre inverted		4·50	

128	**24**	25 c. pale blue (12.02)	.. ..	4·00	3·25
		a. Centre inverted ..		7·50	
129		25 c. blue and indigo (8.03) ..	..	5·00	3·75
130		30 c. black and red (12.02)	..	1·25	90
		a. Imperf between (pair) ..	..	1·75	
		b. Centre inverted ..	..	4·50	
131		40 c. blue and orange-yellow (12.02)		2·50	1·90
		a. Blue and orange		2·25	1·75
132		50 c. pale red and green (12.02)		10·00	10·00
133		75 c. mauve and orange (12.02)		90	90
		a. Imperf between (pair) ..		1·75	
134	**25**	1 f. purple and orange-red (12.02) ..		3·75	3·75
135		2 f. carmine and green (12.02)	..	7·00	6·50
		a. Engraver's name, etc. omitted	..	32·00	32·00
136		5 f. blue and orange (12.02)	..	3·75	3·25
121/136		Set of 16	..	40·00	35·00

Stamps can be found showing part of the sheet watermark "B F K RIVES".

Varieties are known in incorrect colours or with the colours reversed; these are probably printer's trials.

Other "centre inverted" errors exist on this and the following issue, but these are of clandestine origin; some are, however, known on cover.

1903 (15 Sept). *Centres in black. P 11, 11½.*

137	**23**	1 c. purple-brown ..	..	12	12
		a. Imperf between (pair) ..	..	40	
138		2 c. brown ..	..	20	20
139		4 c. red ..	..	20	20
		a. Imperf between (pair) ..	..	60	
		b. Crimson-lake ..	..	15	15
140		5 c. green ..	..	65	50
		a. Blue-green ..	..	25	20
141		10 c. carmine ..	..	1·75	65
		a. Red ..	..	1·00	50
142		15 c. yellow-brown ..	..	3·75	2·25
143	**24**	20 c. dull lilac ..	..	5·00	5·00
144		25 c. blue ..	..	1·90	1·75
145		40 c. orange ..	..	1·90	1·75
146		50 c. green ..	..	3·75	3·50
147		75 c. yellow-brown ..	..	2·25	1·90
148	**25**	1 f. orange-red ..	..	2·75	2·50
		a. Scarlet ..	..	2·75	2·50
149		2 f. green ..	..	1·60	1·60
		a. Engraver's name, etc. omitted	..	7·50	7·50
150		5 f. orange-red ..	..	2·50	3·25
		a. Yellow-buff ..	..	3·25	3·25
137/150		Set of 14 (cheapest) ..	..	26·00	23·00

See note below No. 136.

26 Mosque at Tajurah
27 Mounted Somalis
(27*a*)

(Des P. Merwart. Eng J. Puyplat. Typo)

1909 (Nov). *Centre in first colour. P 14×13½ (1 c. to 20 c.) or 13½×14.*

151	**26**	1 c. bistre-brown and maroon		12	10
152		2 c. olive and violet ..	..	12	10
153		4 c. pale blue and olive-brown		25	20
154		5 c. olive-green and green ..		40	5
155		10 c. orange and carmine ..		70	30
156		20 c. chestnut and black ..		1·60	1·25
157	**27**	25 c. blue and deep blue ..		1·00	75
158		30 c. scarlet and pale brown ..		1·25	1·10
159		35 c. green and violet ..		1·50	1·25
160		40 c. violet and rose ..	..	1·25	1·10
161		45 c. myrtle and brown ..		1·90	1·60
162		50 c. brown and maroon ..		1·90	1·75
163		75 c. green and vermilion ..		2·50	2·50

164	**25**	1 f. bistre-brown and violet..	..	5·00	5·00
165		2 f. rose and brown..	..	7·50	7·00
166		5 f. blue-green and purple-brown	..	11·00	11·00
151/166		Set of 16	..	35·00	32·00

The design of the "franc" values, though similar to T **25**, differs from it in details.

1915 (May). *Red Cross. No. 172 surch in Paris with T 27a, in red. Chalk-surfaced paper.*

167	**29**	10 c.+5 c. red and carmine	..	1·90	1·90

28 Drummer   29 Somali Woman

30 Railway Bridge at Holl-Holli   D 31 Somali Spears

(Des A. Montader. Eng C. Hourriez. Typo)

1915 (1 July)–**16**. *Centre in first colour. Chalk-surfaced paper (40 c. ordinary paper). P 13½×14 or 14×13½ (1 f. to 5 f.).*

168	**28**	1 c. brown and violet ..	..	5	5
169		2 c. indigo and yellow-bistre	..	5	5
170		4 c. red and grey-brown ..		5	5
171		5 c. green and yellow-green	..	10	10
172	**29**	10 c. red and carmine ..		10	10
173		15 c. rose and grey-lilac (1916)	..	10	10
174		20 c. grey-brown and orange	..	5	5
175		25 c. blue and ultramarine ..		5	5
176		30 c. blue-green and black ..		25	20
177		35 c. rose and pale green ..		5	5
178		40 c. grey-lilac and ultramarine (1916)	..	5	5
179		45 c. blue and chocolate ..		12	10
180		50 c. black and rose-pink ..		1·50	1·25
181		75 c. brown and deep lilac ..		10	10
182	**30**	1 f. red and pale brown ..		20	15
183		2 f. black and indigo-violet ..		45	30
184		5 f. black and rose-red ..		80	40
168/184		Set of 17	..	3·75	2·75

The 1, 2, 4, 5, 15, 20, 25, 75 c., 1 f., 2 f. and 5 f. also come on ordinary paper.

For stamps in new colours see Nos. 195/9 and· 214/30.

(Des A. Montader. Eng G. Hourriez. Typo)

1915 (July). *POSTAGE DUE. P 14×13½.*

D185	**D 31**	5 c. ultramarine ..	..	5	5
D186		10 c. lake ..	..	5	5
D187		15 c. black ..	..	8	8
D188		20 c. bright violet ..	..	12	12
D189		30 c. orange ..	..	20	20
D190		50 c. maroon ..	..	55	55
D191		60 c. yellow-green ..	..	75	75
D192		1 f. deep blue ..	..	1·00	1·00
D185/192		Set of 8	..	2·50	2·50

5 c. exists on both ordinary and chalk-surfaced paper, others on chalk-surfaced only.

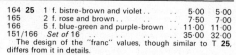

(32)

0,01

(33)

1922 (Apr). *Nos. 171 and 175 surch as T 32.*
193 **28** 10 on 5 c. green and yellow-green (G.)   5   5
194 **29** 50 on 25 c. blue and ultramarine (B.)   5   5
On No. 194 the original value is obliterated by a thick bar.

1922 (Apr)–**24**. *New colours. P* 13½×14.
195 **28** 5 c. brown-red and red   5   5
196 **29** 10 c. green and yellow-green (8.22) ..   8   8
197   25 c. blue-green and black ..   12   12
198   30 c. chocolate and carmine (8.22) ..   12   12
199   50 c. blue and ultramarine (9.24) ..   20   20
195/199 *Set of 5*   50   50

1922 (Dec). *No. 173 surch as T 33.*
200 **29** 0.01 on 15 c.   5   5
201   0.02 on 15 c. (B.)   5   5
202   0.04 on 15 c. (G.)   5   5
203   0.05 on 15 c. (R.)   5   5
200/203 *Set of 4*   12   12
Nos. 200/2 can be found on chalk-surfaced paper.

25ᶜ

=   **60**   **2ᶠ·**

(33a)   (33b)   (D 34)

1923 (June)–**27**. *Stamps as T 29/30, some with colours changed, surch as T 33a/b.*
204 **30** 25 c. on 5 f. black and carmine (6.24)   12   12
205 **29** 60 on 75 c. violet and sage-green ..   5   5
206   65 on 15 c. rose and grey-lilac (1.2.25)   15   15
207   85 on 40 c. grey-lilac and blue (1.2.25)   15   15
208   90 on 75 c. carmine (28.2.27) ..   75   75
209 **30** 1 f. 25 on 1 f. ultramarine and blue
      (R.) (14.6.26)   12   12
210   1 f. 50 on 1 f. blue & lt blue (28.2.27)   25   25
211   3 f. on 5 f. magenta & red (19.12.27)   75   75
212   10 f. on 5 f. brown & carmine (7.2.27)   1·60   1·60
213   20 f. on 5 f. rose & yellow-grn (7.2.27)   2·75   2·75
204/213 *Set of 10* .. .. ..   6·00   6·00
Nos. 204 and 206 are known on chalk-surfaced paper.

1925 (7 Sept)–**33**. *P* 13½×14.
214 **29** 10 c. green and scarlet   5   5
215   20 c. pale green and green (1.3.26) ..   5   5
216   20 c. carmine & myrtle-grn (14.11.27)   8   8
217   30 c. yellow-green and violet ..   5   5
218   30 c. olive-green and green (14.11.27)   5   5
219   50 c. purple and brown   5   5
    a. Centre double .. ..   22·00
220   60 c. purple and sage-green   5   5
221   65 c. olive-green and carmine (1.3.26)   5   5
222   75 c. bright blue and deep blue ..   5   5
223   75 c. chocolate and mauve (5.9.27) ..   20   20
224   85 c. green and maroon (1.3.26) ..   5   5
225   90 c. carmine and brown-red (5.5.30)   1·25   1·10
226 **30** 1 f. 10, ultram & red-brn (25.9.28)   95   95
227   1 f. 25, chocolate and blue (25.9.33)   1·60   1·40
228   1 f. 50, blue and light blue (5.5.30)   15   15
229   1 f. 75, red and olive-green (25.9.33)   75   75
230   3 f. magenta/*rose* (5.5.30) ..   1·25   1·25
214/230 *Set of 17* .. .. ..   6·00   5·75

1927 (10 Oct). *POSTAGE DUE. Surch as Type D 34.*
D231 D **31** 2 f. on 1 f. rose-red   95   95
D232   3 f. on 1 f. magenta   95   95

1931 (13 Apr). *International Colonial Exhibition, Paris. As T 17/20 of French Sudan.*
233   40 c. black and green .. ..   1·00   1·00
234   50 c. black and mauve .. ..   1·00   1·00

235   90 c. black and vermilion .. ..   1·00   1·00
236   1 f. 50, black and blue .. ..   1·00   1·00
233/236 *Set of 4* .. .. ..   3·50   3·50

1937 (15 Apr). *International Exhibition, Paris. As T 2/7 of French Equatorial Africa.*
237   20 c. violet   25   25
238   30 c. green   35   35
239   40 c. carmine   25   25
240   50 c. brown   30   30
241   90 c. scarlet   30   30
242   1 f. 50, blue   30   30
237/242 *Set of 6* .. .. ..   1·60   1·60
MS243 120×100 mm. 3 f. slate-violet (as T 3).
Imperf   95   95

1938 (24 Oct). *International Anti-Cancer Fund. As T 14 of French Equatorial Africa.*
244   1 f. 75×50 c. ultramarine ..   1·40   1·40

34 Mosque at   **35** Somali Warriors   **36** Governor L.
Djibouti   Lagarde

37 Djibouti

(Des J. Kerhor (T **36**). Eng G. Barlangue (T **34**), A. Ouvré (T **35**)
E. Feltesse (T **36**). Recess Institut de Gravure, Paris)

1938 (17 Nov)–**40**. *P* 12×12½ (*T* **34**/6) *or* 12½ (*T* **37**).
245 **34** 2 c. purple   5   5
246   3 c. olive-green   5   5
247   4 c. chocolate   5   5
248   5 c. carmine   5   5
249   10 c. ultramarine   5   5
250   15 c. black   5   5
251   20 c. orange-red   5   5
252 **35** 25 c. sepia   5   5
253   30 c. blue   5   5
254   35 c. olive-green   8   5
255 **34** 40 c. red-brown (15.4.40) ..   5   5
256   45 c. green (15.4.40) ..   5   5
257 **35** 50 c. scarlet   5   5
258   55 c. purple   10   5
259   60 c. black (26.3.40) ..   8   5
260   65 c. chestnut   5   5
261   70 c. violet (26.3.40)   30   30
262 **36** 80 c. black   35   20
263 **35** 90 c. mauve (4.12.39) ..   20   20
264 **36** 1 f. crimson   35   25
265   1 f. black (26.3.40)   5   5
266   1 f. 25, carmine (4.12.39) ..   15   15
267   1 f. 40, greenish blue (5.3.40)   15   15
268   1 f. 50, blue-green ..   10   8
269   1 f. 60, brown-lake (5.3.40) ..   15   15
270   1 f. 75, bright blue ..   8   8
271   2 f. orange-red   10   10
272   2 f. 25, bright blue (4.12.39)   15   15
273   2 f. 50, red-brown (5.3.40) ..   25   25
274   3 f. purple   12   12

French Afars and Issas SOMALI COAST 1938

275	**37**	5 f. red-brown and brown		40	40
276		10 f. light blue and indigo		40	40
277		20 f. blue and carmine		40	40
245/277		Set of 33		4·00	3·75

Stamps as the 40, 50 c. and 1 f. 50, but without "RF", were prepared by the Vichy Government in 1944, but were not placed on sale in French Somali Coast.

(Des A. Montader. Eng G. Hourriez. Recess Institut de Gravure, Paris)

1938 (17 Nov). POSTAGE DUE. As Type D **31** but figures altered and "INST. DE GRAV." below design. P 12½×13.

D278		5 c. ultramarine		5	5
D279		10 c. lake		5	5
D280		15 c. black		5	5
D281		20 c. bright violet		5	5
D282		30 c. orange-yellow		5	5
D283		50 c. chestnut		5	5
D284		60 c. yellow-green		5	5
D285		1 f. deep blue		30	30
D286		2 f. scarlet		8	8
D287		3 f. sepia		10	10
D278/287		Set of 10		75	75

The 30, 50, 60 c., 2 f. and 3 f. values were reissued without "RF" during 1944, but were not used in French Somali Coast.

1939 (10 May). New York World's Fair. As T **17** of French Equatorial Africa.

288		1 f. 25, lake		20	20
289		2 f. 25, ultramarine		20	20

1939 (5 July). 150th Anniv of French Revolution. As T **18** of French Equatorial Africa.

290		45 c.+25 c. green and black		1·60	1·60
291		70 c.+30 c. brown and black		1·60	1·60
292		90 c.+35 c. red-orange and black		1·60	1·60
293		1 f. 25+1 f. carmine and black		1·60	1·60
294		2 f. 25+2 f. blue and black		1·60	1·60
290/294		Set of 5		7·00	7·00

VICHY ISSUES. A number of stamps were produced by the Pétain Government of France between 1940 and 1944, but none of these issues were placed on sale in French Somali Coast.

1941. AIR. As T **24** of French Equatorial Africa, inscr "DJIBOUTI". P 14½×14.

295		1 f. red-orange		10	10
296		1 f. 50, scarlet		10	10
297		5 f. maroon		15	15
298		10 f. black		20	20
299		25 f. ultramarine		40	40
300		50 f. green		35	35
301		100 f. claret		65	65
295/301		Set of 7		1·75	1·75

France

FRANCE

LIBRE

(38)

France

Libre

(39)

FRANCE LIBRE

(40)

1942. Optd as T **38**, **39** or **40**; or additionally surch with new value.

302	**28**	1 c. brown and violet		15	15
303		2 c. indigo and yellow-bistre		20	20
304	**34**	2 c. purple		30	30
305		3 c. olive-green (R.)		30	30
306	**28**	4 c. red and grey-brown		5·00	5·00
307	**34**	4 c. chocolate		30	30
308	**28**	5 c. brown-red and red		20	20
309	**34**	5 c. carmine		30	30
310		10 c. ultramarine (R.)		10	10
311	**29**	15 c. rose and grey-lilac		1·25	1·25
312	**34**	15 c. black (R.)		30	30
313	**29**	20 c. carmine and myrtle-green		20	20
314	**34**	20 c. orange-red		30	30

315	**35**	25 c. sepia (R.)		45	45
316	**29**	30 c. olive-green and green		30	30
317	**35**	30 c. blue (R.)		8	8
318		35 c. olive-green (R.)		30	30
319	**34**	40 c. red-brown		8	8
320		45 c. green		30	30
321	**29**	50 c. purple and brown		15	15
322	**35**	50 c. on 65 c. chestnut		5	5
323		55 c. purple (R.)		30	30
324		60 c. black (R.)		15	15
325	**29**	65 c. olive-green and carmine		20	20
326	**35**	70 c. violet (R.)		10	10
		a. Opt inverted		38·00	
327	**36**	80 c. black (R.)		15	15
328	**35**	90 c. mauve (R.)		12	12
329	**36**	1 f. 25, carmine		15	15
330		1 f. 40, greenish blue (R.)		8	8
331	**30**	1 f. 50, blue and light blue (R.)		20	20
332	**36**	1 f. 50, blue-green		15	15
333		1 f. 60, brown-lake		15	15
334	**30**	1 f. 75, red and olive-green		1·40	1·40
335	**36**	1 f. 75, bright blue (R.)		90	90
336		2 f. orange-red		8	8
337		2 f. 25, bright blue (R.)		15	15
338		2 f. 50, red-brown		15	15
339		3 f. purple (R.)		15	15
340	**37**	5 f. red-brown and brown		95	95
341		10 f. light blue and indigo		32·00	32·00
342		20 f. blue and carmine		65	65
302/342		Set of 41		45·00	45·00

1942. POSTAGE DUE. Nos. D185/92 optd as T **38**, but with more space between lines of overprint.

D343	D **31**	5 c. ultramarine (R.)		12	12
D344		10 c. lake		12	12
D345		15 c. black (R.)		12	12
D346		20 c. bright violet		12	12
D347		30 c. orange		12	12
D348		50 c. maroon		12	12
D349		60 c. yellow-green		12	12
D350		1 f. deep blue (R.)		90	90
D343/350		Set of 8		1·50	1·50

1943. POSTAGE DUE. Nos. D278/87 optd as T **39**, but with more space between lines of overprint.

D351		5 c. ultramarine (R.)		10	10
D352		10 c. lake		10	10
D353		15 c. black (R.)		10	10
D354		20 c. bright violet		10	10
D355		30 c. orange-yellow		20	20
D356		50 c. chestnut		20	20
D357		60 c. yellow-green		10	10
D358		1 f. deep blue (R.)		10	10
D359		2 f. scarlet		95	95
D360		3 f. sepia (R.)		1·25	1·25
D351/360		Set of 10		3·00	3·00

41 Symbolical of Djibouti (42)

(Des E. Dulac. Photo Harrison)

1943. P 14½×14.

361	**41**	5 c. grey-blue		5	5
362		10 c. rose		5	5
363		25 c. emerald-green		5	5
364		30 c. grey-black		5	5
365		40 c. violet		5	5
366		80 c. maroon		5	5
367		1 f. light blue		5	5
368		1 f. 50, scarlet		5	5
369		2 f. bistre		8	8
370		2 f. 50, ultramarine		8	8
371		4 f. red-orange		10	10
372		5 f. magenta		12	10
373		10 f. pale ultramarine		15	15
374		20 f. blue-green		15	15
		a. Value omitted			
361/374		Set of 14		1·00	95

1944. *Mutual Aid and Red Cross Funds. As T* **29** *of French Equatorial Africa, inscr "DJIBOUTI".*
375　5 f.+20 f. emerald-green　　..　　..　25　　25

1945. *Félix Eboué. As T* **31** *of French Equatorial Africa.*
376　2 f. black　　..　　..　　..　　..　5　　5
377　25 f. blue-green ..　　..　　..　　20　　20

1945. *Surch as T* **42.**
378 **41**　50 c. on 5 c. grey-blue (R.) ..　　..　10　　10
379　　60 c. on 5 c. grey-blue (R.)　..　　..　5　　5
380　　70 c. on 5 c. grey-blue (R.) ..　　..　5　　5
　　　　a. Surch inverted　..　　..　　.. 35·00
381　　1 f. 20 on 5 c. grey-blue (R.)　..　5　　5
382　　2 f. 40 on 25 c. emerald-green　..　10　　10
　　　　a. Surch inverted　..　　.. 22·00
383　　3 f. on 25 c. emerald-green ..　　..　10　　10
384　　4 f. 50 on 25 c. emerald-green　..　10　　10
　　　　a. Surch inverted　..　　.. 22·00
385　15 f. on 2 f. 50, ultramarine (R.)　..　20　　20
378/385　*Set of 8*　..　　..　　..　　..　70　　70

1946 (8 May). *AIR. Victory. As T* **32** *of French Equatorial Africa.*
386　8 f. blue ..　　..　　..　　..　　20　　20

1946 (6 June). *AIR. From Chad to the Rhine. As Nos.* 229/34 *of French Equatorial Africa.*
387　5 f. olive-black ..　　..　　..　　..　40　　40
388　10 f. brown-red ..　　..　　..　　..　30　　30
389　15 f. purple-brown　..　　..　　..　30　　30
390　20 f. mauve　　..　　..　　..　　..　30　　30
391　25 f. emerald-green　..　　..　　..　45　　45
392　50 f. ultramarine　　..　　..　　..　65　　65
387/392　*Set of 6*　..　　..　　..　　.. 2·10　2·10

43 Danakil Tent　　　**44** Outpost at Khor-Angar

45 Somali　　　　　　　D 47

46 Government Palace, Djibouti

(Des Magnan (*POSTAGE*) and Planson (*AIR*). Photo Vaugirard, Paris)

1947 (6 Oct). (*a*) *POSTAGE. P* 13½.
393 **43**　10 c. orange and violet　　..　　..　5　　5
394　　30 c. orange and dull green ..　　..　5　　5
395　　40 c. orange and purple　　..　　..　5　　5
396 **44**　50 c. orange and green　　..　　..　5　　5
397　　60 c. yellow and purple-brown　..　5　　5
398　　80 c. orange and violet　　..　　..　5　　5
399　－　1 f. brown and blue　　..　　..　5　　5
400　－　1 f. 20, green and grey　　..　　12　　12
401　－　1 f. 50, blue and orange　　..　5　　5
402　－　2 f. mauve and grey　　..　　..　10　　5
403　－　3 f. blue and brown　　..　　..　10　　8
404　－　3 f. 60, brown-red and carmine　..　40　　35
405　－　4 f. brown and grey　　..　　..　20　　12
406　－　5 f. orange and purple-brown　..　10　　8
407　－　6 f. blue and grey-blue　..　　..　20　　15
408　－　10 f. purple and grey-blue　..　　15　　8
409　－　15 f. brown, blue and buff ..　　30　　20
410　－　20 f. deep blue, orange and light blue　40　　20
411　－　25 f. claret, blue and purple　..　50　　45

　　　　　　(*b*) *AIR. P* 12×13½ (*vert*) or 13½×12 (*horiz*)
412 **45**　50 f. red-brown and blue　　..　　.. 1·25　45
413　－　100 f. yellow and green　　..　　.. 1·60　80
414 **46**　200 f. green, yellow and blue　　.. 2·75　1·25
393/414　*Set of 22*　..　　..　　..　　.. 7·50　4·50
Designs: *Horiz* (As *T* **44**)—1 f. to 1 f. 50, Obock–Tajurah road; 2 f. to 4 f. (Woman carrying dish; 5 f. to 10 f. Somali village; 15 f. to 25 f. Mosque, Djibouti. (*As T* **46**)—100 f. Frontier post, Loyada.

(Des Planson. Photo Vaugirard, Paris)

1947 (6 Oct). *POSTAGE DUE. P* 13.
D415 **D 47**　10 c. mauve　　..　　..　　..　5　　5
D416　　30 c. sepia　　..　　..　　..　　5　　5
D417　　50 c. blue-green　..　　..　　..　5　　5
D418　　1 f. orange-brown　..　　..　　..　5　　5
D419　　2 f. claret　　..　　..　　..　　5　　5
D420　　3 f. red-brown　..　　..　　..　　5　　5
D421　　4 f. blue　　..　　..　　..　　..　5　　5
D422　　5 f. brown-red ..　　..　　..　　10　　10
D423　　10 f. olive-green ..　　..　　..　10　　10
D424　　20 f. violet-blue ..　　..　　..　25　　25
D415/424　*Set of 10* ..　　..　　..　　75　　75

1949 (4 July). *AIR. 75th Anniv of U.P.U. As T* **39** *of French Equatorial Africa.*
425　30 f. blue, blue-green, purple & brt green　1·90　1·90

1950 (15 May). *Colonial Welfare Fund. As T* **40** *of French Equatorial Africa.*
426　10 f.+2 f. vermilion and red-brown　..　95　　95

1952 (1 Dec). *Centenary of Médaille Militaire. As T* **44** *of French Equatorial Africa.*
427　15 f. deep violet, yellow and green　.. 1·00　1·00

1954 (6 June). *AIR. Tenth Anniv of Liberation. As T* **46** *of French Equatorial Africa.*
428　15 f. reddish violet and indigo ..　　.. 1·75　1·75

48 Ras-Bir Lighthouse　　　**49** Aerial Map of Djibouti

(Des and eng R. Cami (40 f.), C. Hertenberger (500 f.). Recess)
1956. *P* 13. (*a*) *POSTAGE.*
429 **48**　40 f. grey-blue and deep blue (4.6) ..　80　45
　　　　　　(*b*) *AIR*
430 **49**　500 f. bright purple & dp violet (20.2) 16·00　13·00

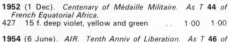

50 Djibouti

51 Wart Hog

52 Salt Caravan, Lake Assal

(Des and eng R. Cami. Recess)

1956 (4 June). *Economic and Social Development Fund.*
P 13.
431 **50** 15 f. reddish violet 30 12

(Des and eng R. Cami (30 c.), G. Bétemps (40 c.), C. Mazelin
(50 c.), C. Durrens (4 f., 10 f., 25 f., 75 f., 200 f.), C. Hertenberger (100 f.). Des C. Robin (1 f., 2 f., 3 f., 5 f., 15 f., 20 f.,
60 f., 500 f.). Eng G. Bétemps (1 f., 60 f.), C. Durrens (2 f.,
15 f., 20 f., 30 f.), J. Pheulpin (3 f., 5 f.), C. Mazelin (500 f.).
Recess)

1958 (7 July)–**62.** *Animals, fishes and birds.* P 13.
(a) POSTAGE. Designs as T 51
432   30 c. bistre-brown and red-brown .. 5 5
433   40 c. sepia and bistre 5 5
434   50 c. maroon, vio-grey & dp bluish grn 8 8
435   1 f. orange, lt blue & brown (21.11.59) 10 8
436   2 f. yellow, black, grn & bl (21.11.59) 10 8
437   3 f. deep chocolate & violet (21.11.59) 12 8
438   4 f. bis-brn, orge & turq-bl (21.11.59) 20 15
439   5 f. black & turquoise-blue (21.11.59) 25 15
440   10 f. claret, yellow-brown and deep
            bluish green (15.12.60) .. 40 30
441   15 f. yellow, blue-grn & mag (15.12.60) 45 30
442   20 f. brown-purple, red & bl (21.11.59) 55 40
443   25 f. violet-blue, red & emer (21.11.59) 80 55
444   30 f. black, orange-red & bl (15.12.60) 1·10 65
445   60 f. dp bluish green & blue (21.11.59) 1·50 1·10
446   75 f. yellow, dp ol-brn & grn (15.12.60) 2·00 1·60
(b) AIR. As T 52
447 100 f. chocolate, olive-green & ultram 1·50 75
448 200 f. choc, blk & brn-orge (15.12.60) 3·50 2·50
449 500 f. chestnut, red, blue & blk (6.1.62) 5·00 2·50
432/449 *Set of 18* .. .. 16·00 10·00
Designs: *Horiz*—40 c. Cheetah; 1 f. Parrot Fish; 3 f. Black
Marlin; 4 f. Coffer Fish; 5 f. Eagle Ray; 15 f. Bee-eater; 20 f.
Trigger-fish (*Balistapus undulatus*); 25 f. Trigger-fish (*Odonus
niger*); 30 f. Ibis; 60 f. Hammerhead Shark; 100 f. Gazelles and
aircraft; 200 f. Bustard. *Vert*—50 c. Gerenuk Gazelles; 2 f.
Angel-fish; 10 f. Flamingo; 75 f. Pelican.

52a Haemanthus

53 Governor Bernard

(Des M. Rolland. Photo Vaugirard, Paris)

1957 (7 July). P 12½.
450 **52a** 10 f. carmine-red, blue-green & yell 55 30

1958 (10 Dec). *Tenth Anniv of Declaration of Human Rights.*
As T **5** *of French Polynesia.*
451   20 f. reddish violet and blue 65 65

(Des and eng R. Serres. Recess)

1960 (18 Jan). *AIR. 25th Death Anniv of Governor Bernard.*
P 13.
452 **53** 55 f. deep chocolate, blue & carmine 70 45

54 Obock in 1862

(Des and eng G. Aufschneider. Recess)

1962 (11 Mar). *AIR. Centenary of Obock.* P 13.
453 **54** 100 f. red-brown and blue .. .. 1·25 75

55 Dragon Tree (*Dracæna*)

56 *Meleagrina
margaritifera*

(Des V. Ravelonanosy-Razafimbelo. Eng P. Béquet (2 f., 6 f.).
Des and eng J. Combet (others). Recess)

1962 (24 Mar). *Fauna and Flora. T* **55** *and similar designs.*
P 13.
454   2 f. blue-green, brown, orge-red & yell 45 25
455   4 f. chocolate and yellow-ochre .. 45 25
456   6 f. yellow, yell-grn, orge, bl & brn-pur 90 50
457   25 f. yellow-brown, green & dp brn-red 1·50 1·10
458   40 f. orange-brown, black and blue .. 1·50 1·40
459   50 f. bistre-brown, maroon & turq-bl 2·75 1·90
454/459 *Set of 6* .. .. 7·00 5·00
Designs: *Horiz*—4 f. Daman (marmot); 6 f. Large carangue
(fish); 25 f. Fennecs; 40 f. Tawny vulture. *Vert*—50 f. Mountain deer.

1962 (7 Apr). *Malaria Eradication. As T* **35** *of Gabon.*
460   25 f.+5 f. light greenish blue .. .. 1·90 1·90

(Des C. Robin and P. Lambert. Photo Hélio-Comoy)

1962 (24 Nov). *Shells of the Red Sea. Multicoloured.*
P 13½×12½ (60 f., 100 f.) or 13 (others). (*a*) *POSTAGE. As
T* **56.**
461   8 f. Type **56** 25 20
462   10 f. *Tridacna squamosa* (*horiz*) .. 25 20
463   25 f. *Strombus tricornis* (*horiz*) .. 70 40
464   30 f. *Trochus dentatus* 25 20
(b) AIR. Inscr "POSTE AERIENNE". Horiz (50×28 mm)
465   60 f. *Rostellaria magna* 75 50
466 100 f. *Lambris bryonia* .. .. 1·10 65
461/466 *Set of 6* .. .. .. 3·25 2·00

1963 (9 Feb). *AIR. First Trans-Atlantic Television Satellite
Link. As T* **10** *of French Polynesia.*
467   20 f. brown-purple & deep bluish green 20 20

1963 (2 Sept). *Red Cross Centenary. As T* **13** *of French
Polynesia.*
468   50 f. red, grey and light brown .. .. 1·90 1·90

61 Ghoubet Kharab

57 Madrepore **58** Houri Sailing Boat

(Des P. Lambert. Photo So.Ge.Im.)

1963 (30 Nov). *Corals. T **57** and similar designs. Multicoloured. (a) POSTAGE. P 13×12½.*
469 5 f. Type **57** 25 20
470 6 f. Tubipore 25 20

(b) AIR. Inscr "POSTE AERIENNE". Size 48×27 mm. P 13
471 40 f. Millepore 55 30
472 55 f. Meandrine 80 40
473 200 f. Ramose polyp .. .. .. 2·10 1·10
469/473 *Set of 5* .. .. 3·50 2·00

1963 (10 Dec). *15th Anniv of Declaration of Human Rights. As T **14** of French Polynesia.*
474 70 f. light blue and chocolate .. .. 2·50 2·50

1964 (7 Apr). *"PHILATEC 1964" International Stamp Exhibition, Paris. As T **15** of French Polynesia.*
475 80 f. brown, green and brown-purple .. 2 50 2 50

(Des G. Aufschneider and C. Robin, eng G. Aufschneider (15, 25 f.). Des C. Robin, eng C. Hertenberger (50, 85, 300 f.). Recess).

1964–65. *Local Sailing Craft. Multicoloured. P 13.*

*(a) POSTAGE. T **58** and similar horiz design (9 June, 1964)*
476 15 f. Type **58** 30 25
477 25 f. Sambouk sailing ship 55 45

(b) AIR. Inscr "POSTE AERIENNE". Size 48×27 mm
478 50 f. Building sambouks (18.12.64) .. 75 45
479 85 f. Zaroug sailing ship (18.9.64) .. 1·00 65
480 300 f. Zeima (6.3.65) .. .. .. 3·75 2·25
476/480 *Set of 5* .. .. 5·75 3·75

59 Rameses II and Nefertari Temple, Philae

60 "The Discus Thrower" (Ancient Greece)

(Des and eng J. Derrey. Recess)

1964 (28 Aug). *AIR. Nubian Monuments Preservation. P 13.*
481 **59** 25 f.+5 f. lt brn, dp bluish grn & carm 2 25 2 25

(Des and eng J. Combet. Recess)

1964 (10 Oct). *AIR. Olympic Games, Tokyo. P 13.*
482 **60** 90 f. bright purple, brown-red & black 2·75 2·50

1965 (17 May). *AIR. I.T.U. Centenary. As T **19** of French Polynesia.*
483 95 f. blue, orange-brown & bright purple 3·75 2·75

(Des C. Robin. Eng P. Béquet (6 f., 20 f.), C. Mazelin (45 f.), A. Frères (65 f.). Recess)

1965. *Landscapes. T **61** and similar horiz designs. P 13.*

(a) POSTAGE. Inscr "POSTES". Size 26×22 mm
484 6 f. lake-brown, ultramarine and blackish green (20.10) 20 15
485 20 f. yell-grn, ultram & red-brn (20.10) 25 20

(b) AIR. Size 47×26½ mm
486 45 f. orange-brown, greenish blue and deep blue (20.10) 50 30
487 65 f. purple-brown, yell-ochre & bl (16.7) 75 20
484/487 *Set of 4* .. .. 1·50 75
Views:—6 f. Dadwayya; 20 f. Tajurah; 45 f. Lake Abbé.

62 "Life and Death" **63** Senna

(Des and eng J. Derrey. Recess)

1965 (10 Dec). *Anti-Tuberculosis Campaign. P 13.*
488 **62** 25 f.+5 f. orange-brown, myrtle-green and turquoise-green 65 65

1966 (17 Jan). *AIR. Launching of First French Satellite. As Nos. 52/3 of French Polynesia.*
489 25 f. brown, bistre-brown and brown-red 65 65
490 30 f. brown, bistre-brown and brown-red 65 65
Price for se-tenant strip unused or used, 60p.

(Des C. Robin. Eng R. Cottet (5 f., 25 f.), C. Mazelin (8 f.), P. Forget (55 f.). Recess)

1966 (18 Mar). *Flowers. T **63** and similar designs. P 13.*

(a) POSTAGE
491 5 f. yellow-orge, myrtle-grn & lake-brn 20 15
492 8 f. red-orange, myrtle-green and brown 20 15
493 25 f. vermilion, grey-blue & myrtle-green 40 25

(b) AIR. Inscr "POSTE AERIENNE"
494 55 f. lake, bright green & blackish green 75 45
491/494 *Set of 4* .. .. 1·40 90
Flowers: *Vert*—8 f. Poinciana; 25 f. Aloes. *Horiz* (48½×27 mm)—55 f. Stapelia.

PUZZLED?
Then you need
PHILATELIC TERMS ILLUSTRATED
to tell you all you need to know about printing methods, papers, errors, varieties, watermarks, perforations, etc. 192 pages, almost half in full colour, soft cover. £1·95 post paid.

64 Feather Star and Flame Coral   **65** Giant Lizard

(Des P. Lambert, after Sillner. Photo So.Ge.Im.)

1966 (13 May–14 Oct). *AIR. Marine Life. T **64** and similar vert designs. Multicoloured. P 13.*

495	8 f. Type **64**		30	30
496	25 f. Regal Angel Fish		65	65
497	40 f. Purple Moon Angel Fish (14.10)	1·00	1·00
498	50 f. Cardinal Coral Fish		1·40	1·40
499	70 f. Squirrel Fish		1·90	1·90
500	80 f. Majestic Surgeon Fish (14.10)	1·90	1·90
501	100 f. Scorpion Fish (14.10)		2·25	2·25
495/501	Set of 7		8·50	8·50

1966 (10 June). *AIR. Launching of Satellite "D1". As T **25** of French Polynesia.*

502	48 f. green, chocolate and new blue	75	55

(Des and eng J. Combet. Recess)

1967 (8 May). *Somali Fauna. P 13.*

503	**65** 20 f. dull purple, orange-brn & red-brn	50	40

In a referendum held 19 March 1967 60% of the population voted for continued association with France, rather than independence. The name of the territory was changed by statute of 5 July 1967 to the French Territory of the Afars and the Issas, these being the principal tribes.

D. FRENCH TERRITORY OF THE AFARS AND THE ISSAS

66 Grey-headed Kingfisher   **67** Footballers

(Des P. Gandon. Eng P. Gandon (10 f., 200 f.), C. Hertenberger (15 f.), C. Haley (50 f.), G. Bétemps (55 f.). Des and eng J. Combet (60 f.). Recess)

1967. *Fauna. T **66** and similar designs. P 13 (60 f., 200 f.) or 13×12½ (others). (a) POSTAGE.*

504	10 f. blackish brown, ochre, yellow-olive and new blue (21.8)		50	50
505	15 f. multicoloured (25.9)		90	65
506	50 f. deep maroon, orange-brown and myrtle-green (25.9)		1·60	1·25
507	55 f. new bl, bluish vio & ol-grey (21.8)	2·10	1·60
508	60 f. orange, emer & myrtle-grn (25.9)	2·75	2·25

    (b) AIR. Inscr "POSTE AERIENNE"

509	200 f. sepia, yellow-bistre & new bl (21.8)	3·75	1·75
504/509	Set of 6			10·00	7·00

Designs: (*As T **66**) Horiz*—15 f. Oystercatcher; 50 f. Sandpipers; 55 f. Abyssinian roller. *Vert (22×36 mm)*—60 f. Ground-squirrel. *(27×48 mm)*—200 f. Tawny eagles.

(Des and eng P. Bèquet. Recess)

1967 (18 Dec)–**68**. *Sports. T **67** and similar designs. P 13.*

    (a) POSTAGE

510	25 f. brown, lt yellow-green & new blue	90	70
511	30 f. brown, greenish blue & brt purple	1·00	90

    (b) AIR. Inscr "POSTE AERIENNE"

512	48 f. mar, greenish bl & bis-brn (5.1.68)	95	65
513	85 f. choc, greenish bl & bis (15.3.68)	1·40	1·10
510/513	Set of 4			4·00	3·00

Designs: *Horiz*—30 f. Basketball. *Vert (27×48 mm)*—48 f. Parachute-jumping; 85 f. Aquatic sports.

1968 (4 May). *20th Anniv of World Health Organization. Design as T **34** of French Polynesia.*

514	15 f. purple-brn, yell-orge, red-orge & bl	45	40

68 Damerdjog Fort   **69** Broadcasting Station

70 Relief Map of Territory

(Des and eng M. Monvoisin. Recess)

1968 (17 May). *Administrative Outposts. T **68** and similar horiz designs. P 13.*

515	20 f. slate-blue, light brown & brt green	30	20
516	25 f. greenish blue, blue-green & lt brn	40	20
517	30 f. slate-blue, bistre-brown & orge-brn	45	30
518	40 f. slate-blue, bistre-brown & blue-grn	75	40
515/518	Set of 4		1·75	1·00

Forts:—25 f. Ali Adde; 30 f. Dorra; 40 f. Assamo.

1968 (10 Aug). *Human Rights Year. As T **36** of French Polynesia.*

519	1 f. vermilion, reddish violet & orge-yell	40	25
520	70 f. purple, myrtle-green and red-orange	90	70

(Des A. Peyriè. Eng G. Aufschneider (No. 529). Des and eng G. Aufschneider (40, 60 f.), M. Monvoisin (70 f.), C. Haley (500 f.), A. Decaris (others). Recess)

1968 (15 Nov)–**70**. *Buildings and Landmarks. P 13.*

    *(a) POSTAGE. Designs as T **69** or **70** (60 f.)*

521	1 f. slate-blue, greenish blue and brown-red (17.2.69)		5	5
522	2 f. slate-bl, bl-grn & new bl (17.2.69)	8	5
523	5 f. orange-brown, myrtle-green and greenish blue (17.2.69)		10	8
524	8 f. choc, slate-bl & emer (17.2.69)	12	8
525	15 f. sepia, myrtle-green and greenish blue (6.3.69)		45	30
526	40 f. slate, chestnut & turquoise (3.3.70)	45	20
527	60 f. brown-pur, bl & emer (18.12.68)	90	65
528	70 f. bistre-brown, myrtle-green and slate (30.5.69)		95	75
529	85 f. myrtle-green, new blue and red-brown (19.6.69)		1·25	75
530	85 f. slate, new blue and myrtle-green (30.1.70)		1·10	45

(b) AIR. Designs as T 70

531 100 f. myrtle-green, sepia and greenish
blue (6.3.69) .. .. 1·10 50
532 200 f. new bl, pur-brn & brt pur (8.5.69) 2·10 1·00
533 500 f. yellow-orange, purple-brown & bl 5·00 2·75
521/533 Set of 13 .. .. .. 12·00 7·00
Designs: Horiz (As T 69) — 2 f. Courts of Justice; 5 f. Chamber of Deputies; 8 f. Great Mosque; 40 f. Post Office, Djibouti; 70 f. Governor Lagarde's Residency, Obock; 85 f. (No. 529) Port Administration Building, Djibouti; 85 f. (No. 530) Airport. (As T 70) — 60 f. French High Commission, Djibouti. Vert (As T 69) — 15 f. Free French Monument. (As T 70) — 100 f. Djibouti Cathedral; 200 f. Sayed Hassan Mosque.

1969 (17 Apr). AIR. First Flight of "Concorde". As T 39 of French Polynesia. P 13.
534 100 f. brown-red and drab .. .. 4·00 2·75

71 Schistocerca gregaria (locust)

D 72 Nomadic Milk-jug

(Des and eng J. Pheulpin. Recess)

1969 (6 Oct). Anti-Locust Campaign. T 71 and similar horiz designs. P 13.
535 15 f. bistre-brown, slate and emerald .. 25 15
536 50 f. bistre-brn, myrtle-grn & greenish bl 65 40
537 55 f. bistre-brown, new blue & lake-brn 70 45
Designs: — 50 f. Spraying by helicopter; 55 f. Spraying by light aircraft.

1969 (24 Nov). 50th Anniv of International Labour Organization. As T 44 of French Polynesia. P 13.
538 30 f. mauve, slate and orange-red .. 50 45

(Des and eng M. Monvoisin. Recess)

1969 (15 Dec). POSTAGE DUE. P 14×13.
D539 D 72 1 f. slate, lake-brown & brt purple 5 5
D540 2 f. slate, lake-brown and emerald 5 5
D541 5 f. slate, lake-brown & new blue 5 5
D542 10 f. slate, lake-brown and brown 12 12
D539/542 Set of 4 .. ..- 25 25

73 Afar Dagger

74 Ionospheric Station

(Des A. Peyrié. Eng G. Aufschneider. Recess)

1970 (3 Apr). P 13.
543 73 10 f. orange-brown, apple-green and deep myrtle-green 15 12
544 15 f. orange-brown, apple-green & blue 15 12
545 20 f. orange-brown, apple-grn & verm 25 20
546 25 f. orange-brown, apple-green and reddish violet 40 20
543/546 Set of 4 .. .. .. 85 60
For 50 c. in smaller design, see No. 606.

(Des A. Peyrié. Eng M. Monvoisin. Recess)

1970 (8 May). AIR. Opening of Ionospheric Station, Arta. P 13.
547 74 70 f. carmine, brt emerald & new blue 1·10 75

1970 (20 May). New U.P.U. Headquarters Building, Berne. As T 47 of French Polynesia. P 13.
548 25 f. chocolate, blue-green and bistre .. 40 20

75 Clay-pigeon Shooting

76 "Fish" Sword-guard

(Des C. Robin. Eng E. Lacaque (48, 55 f.). Des and eng G. Bétemps (30 f.), C. Durrens (others). Recess)

1970. Sports. Designs as T 75. P 13.
549 30 f. chocolate, new blue & brt grn (5.6) 40 30
550 48 f. red-brown, brt pur & new bl (9.10) 55 30
551 50 f. red, violet and new blue (6.11) .. 70 45
552 55 f. lake-brown, bistre & new bl (9.10) 65 40
553 60 f. black, chestnut & yellow-olive (6.11) 75 45
549/553 Set of 5 .. .. .. 2·75 1·75
Designs: — Horiz — 48 f. Speed-boat racing; 50 f. Showjumping; 60 f. Pony-trekking. Vert — 55 f. Sailing.

(Des M. Monvoisin. Litho and embossed on gold foil Société Pierre Mariotte)

1970 (29 Sept). AIR. "EXPO 70" World Fair, Osaka, Japan. T 76 and similar vert design. P 12½.
554 100 f. slate-violet, brt blue & brt grn/gold 1·90 1·60
555 200 f. slate-violet, brt green & verm/gold 3·25 2·25
Design: — 200 f. "Horse" sword-guard.

77 Car Ferry

(Des A. Peyrié. Eng C. Jumelet. Recess)

1970 (25 Nov). Inauguration of Car Ferry, Tajurah. P 13.
556 77 48 f. chocolate, blue and blue-green .. 65 40

78 Dolerite Basalt

79 Manta birostris

1971. Minerals. T 78 and similar horiz designs. Multicoloured. Photo. P 13.
557 10 f. Type 78 (22.11) 15 10
558 15 f. Olivine basalt (8.10) 20 12

559	25 f. Volcanic geode (26.4)	.. ..	30	20
560	40 f. Diabase and Chrysolite (25.1)	..	55	30
557/560	*Set of 4*	.. .. ..	1·10	65

(Des P. Lambert. Photo French Govt Ptg Wks, Paris (40, 60 f.), Delrieu (others))

1971 (1 July)–73. *Marine Fauna. T 79 and similar multicoloured designs. (a) POSTAGE. Vert designs as T 79. P* 12×12½.

561	4 f. Type **79**	.. ..	15	12
562	5 f. *Coryphaena hippurus*	..	20	20
563	9 f. *Pristis pectinatus*	.. ..	30	25

(b) *AIR. Inscr "POSTE AERIENNE". Horiz designs* 46×27 *mm* (30 f.) *or* 48×27 *mm* (others). *P* 12½ (30 f.) *or* 13 (*others*)

564	30 f. *Scarus vetula*	.. ..	75	65
565	40 f. *Octopus macropus* (16.3.73)	..	50	40
566	60 f. *Halicore dugong* (16.3.73)	..	75	65
561/566	*Set of 6*	.. ..	2·40	2·00

1971 (9 Nov). *First Death Anniv of General de Gaulle. Vert portraits as Nos.* 145/6 *of French Polynesia. P* 13.

567	60 f. black and deep blue	..	75	65
568	85 f. black and deep blue	..	1·10	95

80 Aerial View of Port

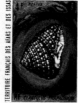

81 *Clanculus pharaonium*

(Des J. Pheulpin. Photo Delrieu)

1971 (26 Nov). *AIR. New Harbour, Djibouti. P* 12½.

569	**80** 100 f. multicoloured	.. ..	1·10	65

(Des P. Lambert. Photo)

1972 (8 Mar). *Seashells. T 81 and similar vert designs. Multicoloured. P* 12½×13.

570	4 f. Type **81**	..	12	5
571	9 f. *Cypraea pantherina*	.. ..	15	5
572	20 f. *Cypraecassis rufa*	.. ..	30	15
573	50 f. *Melo aethiopicus*	.. ..	60	30
570/573	*Set of 4*	.. ..	1·00	50

82 Lichtenstein's Sandgrouse

83 Swimming

(Des P. Lambert. Photo)

1972 (21 Apr–3 Nov). *AIR. Birds. T 82 and similar vert designs. Multicoloured. P* 13.

574	30 f. Type **82**	.. ..	50	40
575	49 f. Hoopoe	.. ..	75	50
576	66 f. Great snipe	.. ..	1·00	95
577	500 f. Francolin (3.11)	..	5·50	2·50
574/577	*Set of 4*	.. ..	7·00	3·75

(Des C. Jumelet. Eng J. Larrivière (5 f.), C. Jumelet (others). Recess)

1972 (8 June). *AIR. Olympic Games, Munich. T 83 and similar designs. P* 13.

578	5 f. purple-brown, blue-green and violet	15	12
579	10 f. purple-brown, myrtle-green & lake	20	15
580	55 f. light brown, blue and light emerald	65	35
581	60 f. violet, lake and blue-green.. ..	90	50
578/581	*Set of 4*	1·75	1·00

Designs: *Vert*—5 f. Running; 10 f. Basketball. *Horiz*—60 f. Olympic flame, rings and ancient frieze.

84 Pasteur and Experiment

(Des and eng R. Quillivic. Recess)

1972 (5 Oct). *AIR. Famous Medical Scientists. T 84 and similar horiz design. P* 13.

582	20 f. bistre-brown, turq-grn & cerise	30	25
583	100 f. purple-brown, blue-grn & lake-brn	1·10	75

Design:—100 f. Calmette and Guérin (B.C.G. pioneers).

85 Mosque, Map and Transport

(Des P. Lambert. Photo Delrieu)

1973 (15 Jan). *AIR. Visit of Pres. Pompidou. T 85 and similar multicoloured design. P* 13.

584	30 f. Type **85**	.. ..	80	75
585	200 f. Mosque and street scene, Djibouti (*vert*)	3·50	3·25

86 Oryx   **87** Flint Pick-heads

(Des O. Baillais. Photo)

1973 (26 Feb). *AIR. Wild Animals. T 86 and similar horiz designs. Multicoloured. P* 13.

587	30 f. Type **86**	.. .. ..	40	25
588	50 f. Dik-dik	.. ..	65	50
590	66 f. Caracal	.. ..	90	65

See also Nos. 603/5, 633/5, 648/9 and 662/4.

French Territory of Afars and Issas 1973

(Des C. Robin (20, 49 f.), R. Quillivic (others). Photo)

1973 (16 Mar–7 Sept). *AIR. Archaeological Discoveries. T* **87** *and similar multicoloured designs. P* 13.

592	20 f. Type **87**	..	40	25
593	40 f. Arrow-heads and blade (*horiz*) (7.9)	75	55
594	49 f. Biface flint tool	..	40	30
595	60 f. Flint axe-head and scraper (*horiz*) (7.9)		65	45
592/595	*Set of* 4	..	2·00	1·40

88 Shepherd watering Sheep

89 Nicolas Copernicus (500th Birth Anniv)

(Des P. Lambert, after Yacine (10 f.). Photo)

1973 (11 Apr). *Pastoral Economy. T* **88** *and similar horiz design. Multicoloured. P* 13.

596	9 f. Type **88**	..	15	10
597	10 f. Camel herd	..	15	10

(Des and eng P. Béquet. Recess)

1973 (9 May–12 Oct). *AIR. Anniversaries. T* **89** *and similar vert portraits. P* 13.

598	8 f. black, brown-purple & olive-brown	15	12
599	9 f. maroon, orange-brn & brn (12.10)	12	10
600	10 f. maroon, choc & carm-red (12.10)	15	12
601	49 f. mar, yell-grn & bottle grn (12.10)	65	45
602	85 f. deep ultramarine, blue and violet ..	1·10	90
598/602	*Set of* 5	2·00	1·50

Designs: — 9 f. Wilhelm Röntgen (X-ray pioneer) (50th death anniv); 10 f. Edward Jenner (smallpox vaccination pioneer) (150th death anniv); 49 f. Robert Koch (bacteriologist) (130th birth anniv); 85 f. Molière (playwright) (300th death anniv).
See also Nos. 607, 611, 615, 640, 646 and 647.

(Des O. Baillais. Photo)

1973 (12 Dec). *AIR. Wild Animals* (2nd series). *Multicoloured designs as T* **86**. *P* 13.

603	20 f. Baboon (*vert*)	..	25	15
604	50 f. Genet	..	65	45
605	66 f. Hare (*vert*)	..	90	65

90 Afar Dagger

91 Flamingoes

(Des A. Peyrié. Eng G. Aufschneider. Recess)

1974 (29 Jan). *P* 13.

606	**90**	30 f. maroon and blackish green	..	45	40

(Des and eng P. Béquet. Recess)

1974 (29 Jan). *AIR. Birth Centenary of Henri Farman* (*aviation pioneer*). *Vert design as T* **89**. *P* 13.

607	100 f. maroon, new blue and yellow-green	1·40	1·00

Design: — 100 f. Farman and biplane.

(Des P. Lambert. Photo)

1974 (22 Feb). *Lake Abbé. T* **91** *and similar horiz designs, showing rocks and flamingos. P* 13.

608	5 f. multicoloured	..	..	5	5
609	15 f. multicoloured	..	..	12	10
610	50 f. multicoloured	..	..	50	25

(Des and eng P. Béquet. Recess)

1974 (22 Mar). *AIR. Birth Centenary of Guglielmo Marconi* (*radio pioneer*). *Vert design as T* **89**. *P* 13.

611	55 f. indigo, olive-brown & greenish blue	70	55

Design: — 55 f. Marconi and "radio waves".

92 Underwater Hunting

(Des and eng J. Combet. Recess)

1974 (14 Apr). *AIR. Third Underwater Hunting Trophy. P* 13.

612	**92**	200 f. greenish blue, turq-grn & verm	2·25	1·75

On No. 612 part of the original inscription has been blocked out.

93 Various Animals

(Des and eng C. Haley. Recess)

1974 (26 Apr). *AIR. Balho Rock Paintings. P* 13.

613	**93**	200 f. black and carmine	..	2·25	1·90

94 Football and Emblem

(Des and eng G. Bétemps. Recess)

1974 (24 May). *World Cup Football Championship, West Germany. P* 13.

614	**94**	25 f. black and bright green	..	40	25

(Des and eng P. Béquet. Recess)

1974 (23 Aug). *AIR. 40th Death Anniv of Marie Curie* (*physicist*). *Vert design as T* **89**. *P* 13.

615	10 f. plum, new blue and bright purple	15	15

Design: — 10 f. Marie Curie and sample of radium.

95 U.P.U. Emblem and Letters   **97** *Oleo chrysophylla*

96 Sunrise over Lake

(Des and eng M. Monvoisin. Recess)

1974 (9 Oct). *Centenary of Universal Postal Union. P* 13.

616	**95**	20 f. bluish violet, new blue & indigo		25	20
617		100 f. orange-brn, pur-brn & crimson		1·25	1·10

(Des P. Lambert. Photo)

1974 (25 Oct). *AIR. Lake Assal. T* **96** *and similar horiz designs. Multicoloured. P* 13.

618	49 f. Type **96**		50	40
619	50 f. Rocky shore		55	50
620	85 f. Crystallization on dead wood		1·10	90

(Des C. Robin. Photo)

1974 (22 Nov). *Forest Plants. T* **97** *and similar vert designs. Multicoloured. P* 13.

621	10 f. Type **97**		15	12
622	15 f. *Fiscus* (tree)		20	20
623	20 f. *Solanum adoënse* (shrub)		30	25

40ᶠ

═

(98)

1975 (1 Jan). *No. 606 surch with T* **98**, *in red.*

624	**90**	40 f. on 30 f. maroon & blackish green	35	20

99 Treasury Building

(Des and eng A. Decaris. Recess)

1975 (7 Jan). *Administrative Buildings in Djibouti. T* **99** *and similar horiz design, each slate, brown-red and new blue. P* 13.

625	8 f. Type **99**		10	5
626	25 f. "Government City" complex		20	20

100 *Darioconus textile*

(Des and eng G. Bétemps. Recess)

1976 (10 Jan)–**77**. *Seashells. T* **100** *and similar horiz designs. P* 13.

627	5 f. brown and turquoise (21.1.75)	10	8
628	5 f. chestnut & greenish blue (17.11.76)	5	5
629	5 f. sepia, deep mauve and deep reddish violet (3.6.77)	5	5
630	10 f. brown and purple (21.1.75)	15	12
631	15 f. brown and new blue (21.1.75)	20	15
632	20 f. yellow-brown & reddish vio (21.1.75)	25	20
633	20 f. dp brown & brt blue-green (17.11.76)	20	15
634	30 f. yell-brn, mar & bronze-grn (16.3.77)	25	20
635	40 f. brown and yellow-green	50	45
636	45 f. yellow-brown, emer & bl (19.12.75)	50	40
637	55 f. dp brown & dp tur-bl (4.6.76)	45	30
638	60 f. black and orange-brown (4.6.76)	50	40
639	70 f. blackish brown, vio-bl & blk (16.3.77)	55	45
640	85 f. maroon, dull ultram & blk (3.6.77)	70	50
627/640	*Set of* 14	4·00	3·25

Designs:—5 f. (No. 627) T **100**; 5 f. (628) *Murex palmarosa*; 5 f. (629) *Cypraea tigris*; 10 f. *Conus sumatrensis*; 15 f. *Cypraea pulchra*; 20 f. (632), 45 f. *Murex scolopax*; 20 f. (633) *Cypraea exhusta*; 30 f. *Conus betulinus*; 40 f. *Ranella spinosa*; 55 f. *Cypraea erythraensis*; 60 f. *Conus taeniatus*; 70 f. *Conus striatus*; 85 f. *Cypraea mauritiana*.

(Des O. Baillais. Photo)

1975 (21 Feb). *Wild Animals* (*3rd series*). *Multicoloured designs as T* **86**. *P* 13.

641	50 f. Ichneumon		50	30
642	60 f. Porcupine (*vert*)		65	50
643	70 f. Zoril		75	50

101 *Hypolimnas misippus*   **102** *Columba guinea*

(Des O. Baillais. Photo)

1975 (21 Mar–25 Apr) *Butterflies* (*1st series*). *T* **101** *and similar square designs. Multicoloured. P* 13.

644	25 f. Type **101**		25	20
645	40 f. *Papilio nereus* (25.4)		40	30
646	70 f. *Papilio demoducus* (25.4)		75	50
647	100 f. *Papilio dardanus*		1·00	80
644/647	*Set of* 4		2·10	1·50

See also Nos. 666/7 and 675/6,

(Des Ky Phungchaleun. Photo)

1975 (23 May)–**76**. *Birds. Vert designs as T* **102**. *Multicoloured.*
P 13.

(*a*) *POSTAGE. Inscr* "POSTES".

648	20 f. *Vidua macroura* (21.11.75)	..	15	12
649	25 f. *Psittacula krameri* (13.10.76)	..	20	12
650	50 f. *Cinnyris venustus* (21.11.75)	..	45	30
651	60 f. *Ardea goliath* (21.11.75)	..	50	40
652	100 f. *Scopus umbretta* (19.12.75)	..	75	65
653	100 f. *Oena capensis* (13.10.76) ..	..	70	50
654	300 f. *Platalea alba* (15.6.76)	..	2·10	1·25

(*b*) *AIR. Inscr* "POSTE AERIENNE".

655	500 f. Type **102** ..	..	..	4·00	2·25
648/655	*Set of* 8	..	..	8·00	5·00

(Des P. Béquet. Eng P. Forget. Recess)

1975 (26 June). *AIR. 500th Birth Anniv of Michelangelo.*
Vert design as T **89**. *P* 13.
656   250 f. blackish brown, lt brn & bronze-grn   2·00   1·50
Design:— 250 f. Michelangelo and artist's materials.

(Des P. Béquet. Eng C. Haley. Recess)

1975 (24 July). *AIR. Birth Bicentenary of Ampère* (*physicist*).
Vert design as T **89**. *P* 13.
657   150 f. greenish blue, new blue & bis-brn ..   1·00   65
Design:—150 f. Ampère and electrical apparatus.

(Des P. Béquet. Eng C. Haley. Recess)

1975 (25 Sept). *AIR. 50th Death Anniv of Clément Ader*
(*aviation pioneer*). *Vert design as T* **89**. *P* 13.
658   50 f. bistre-brown, new blue & myrtle-grn   45   40
Design:—50 f. Ader and aircraft.

(Des O. Baillais. Photo)

1975 (24 Oct). *Wild Animals* (4th series). *Multicoloured*
designs as T **86**. *P* 13.

659	15 f. Grivets (*vert*)	..	..	..	20	15
660	200 f. Anteaters ..	..	..	..	1·75	1·25

103 Palm Trees

(Des C. Robin. Eng C. Haley. Recess)

1975 (19 Dec). *P* 13.
661 **103** 20 f. multicoloured   20   12

(Des O. Baillais. Photo)

1976 (4 Feb). *Wild Animals* (5th series). *Multicoloured designs*
as T **86**. *P* 13.

662	10 f. Hyena	...	..	..	10	·5
663	15 f. Wild ass (*vert*)	..	..	..	12	10
664	30 f. Antelope	..	..	..	..	25	20

THE WORLD CENTRE FOR
FINE STAMPS IS 391 STRAND

104 Alexander Graham Bell
and Satellite

(Des and eng P. Béquet. Recess)

1976 (10 Mar). *Telephone Centenary. P* 13.
665 **104** 200 f. blue, blackish green and orange   1·40   1·00

(Des P. Lambert. Photo)

1976 (5 May). *Butterflies* (2nd series). *Square designs as T* **101**.
Multicoloured. P 13.

666	65 f. *Holocerina smilax menieri* ..	..	45	30
667	100 f. *Balachowsky gonimbrasia* ..	..	70	55

105 Basketball

(Des Chesnot. Litho Edila)

1976 (7 July). *Olympic Games, Montreal. T* **105** *and similar*
square designs. Multicoloured. P 12½.

668	10 f. Type **105**	..	..	..	8	5
669	15 f. Cycling	..	..	..	12	10
670	40 f. Football	..	..	..	30	20
671	60 f. Running	..	..	..	45	30
668/671	*Set of* 4	..	..	..	85	60

106 *Pterois radiata*

(Des C. Robin. Photo)

1976 (10 Aug). *Marine Life. P* 13.
672 **106** 45 f. multicoloured   45   30

SET PRICES

Set prices are given for many issues generally
those containing five stamps or more. Definitive
sets include one of each value or major colour
change but do not cover different perforations, die
types or minor shades. Where a choice is possible
the catalogue set prices are based on the cheapest
versions of the stamps included in the listings.

107 *Naja nigricollis*

108 Motorcyclist on Course

(Des O. Baillais. Photo)

1976 (27 Sept). *Snakes. T 107 and similar design. Multicoloured. P 13.*

673	70 f. Type **107**	..	50	40
674	80 f. *Psammophis elegans* (*horiz*)	..	65	50

(Des P. Lambert. Photo)

1976 (15 Dec). *Diurnal Butterflies (3rd series).* Square designs as T **101**. *Multicoloured. P 13.*

675	50 f. *Acraea anemosa*	..	40	25
676	150 f. *Vanessa cardui*	..	1·00	75

(Des J. Chesnot. Litho Cartor)

1977 (27 Jan). *Moto-Cross. P 12×12½.*

677	**108**	200 f. multicoloured	1·50	1·00

109 Air Terminal

(Des J. Chesnot. Litho Cartor)

1977 (1 Mar). *AIR. Inauguration of New Djibouti Airport. P 12½.*

678	**109**	500 f. multicoloured	..	3·75	3·25

110 *Gaterin gaterinus*

(Des P. Lambert. Photo)

1977 (15 Apr). *Fishes. T 110 and similar horiz design. Multicoloured. P 13×12½.*

679	15 f. Type **110**	..	12	10
680	65 f. *Agrioposphyraena barracuda*	..	45	35

111 Edison and Phonograph

(Des and eng C. Guillame. Recess)

1977 (5 May). *AIR. Celebrities. T 111 and similar horiz design. P 13.*

681	55 f. brown-red, slate and bright green	..	65	50
682	75 f. rosine, red-brown and yellow-olive		95	75

Design:—75 f.Volta and electric train.

The French Territory of Afars and Issas attained independence, as the Republic of Djibouti, on 27 June 1977.

stamp
monthly

Gibbons' own monthly magazine, essential reading for **every** collector!

Detailed monthly New Issue Guide to update all Gibbons catalogues for you—and a special Stamp Market feature on price changes.

Informative articles cover all facets of philately, with regular notes on new discoveries, stamp designs, postmarks, market trends and news and views of the world of stamps. Britain's LARGEST circulation of any stamp magazine—that fact speaks for itself!

Monthly from all dealers and newsagents or by post direct from Stanley Gibbons Magazines Ltd—subscription rates on application.

French West Africa

100 Centimes = 1 Franc

On 15 June 1895 the French possessions in West Africa were grouped into the governorate-general of French West Africa, administered from Dakar.

Each colony or protectorate continued to issue its own stamps until 1944 when Dahomey, French Guinea, French Sudan, Ivory Coast, Mauritania, Niger, Senegal and Upper Volta were provided with the general issues inscribed French West Africa.

PRINTERS. All issues were printed by the French Government Printing Works, Paris, *unless otherwise stated.*

IMPERFORATE STAMPS. Stamps exist imperforate in their issued colours, but these were not valid for postage. Imperforate stamps in other colours are colour trials.

1944 (Dec). *Mutual Aid and Red Cross Funds. As T 29 of French Equatorial Africa.*

1	5 f.+20 f. purple	..	..	..	45	45

1945. *Eboué. As T 31 of French Equatorial Africa.*

2	2 f. black ..	..	..	..	5	5
3	25 f. blue-green	..	..	..	30	30

1 Soldiers

A O F

(2)

(Litho De La Rue)

1945. *P 11½ (30 c., 70 c., 1 f. 50, 2 f. 40, 4 f., 4 f. 50, 20 f.) or 12 (others).*

4	1	10 c. indigo and flesh	..	..	5	5
5		30 c. olive-green and cream	..	..	5	5
6		40 c. grey-blue and flesh	..	..	5	5
7		50 c. orange and blue-grey	..	..	5	5
8		60 c. brown-olive and blue-grey	..	..	5	5
9		70 c. magenta and cream	..	..	5	5
10		80 c. emerald-green and cream ..	..		5	5
11		1 f. purple and yellow-olive	..	..	5	5
12		1 f. 20, purple-brown and yellow-olive		55	55
13		1 f. 50, brown and rose	..	..	5	5
14		2 f. yellow and blue-grey	..	..	10	5
15		2 f. 40, scarlet and blue-grey ..	..		20	15
16		3 f. carmine and yellow-olive ..	..		5	5
17		4 f. ultramarine and rose	..	..	5	5
18		4 f. 50, chestnut and yellow-olive	..		5	5
19		5 f. violet and yellow-olive	..	..	5	5
20		10 f. green and rose	..	..	20	5
21		15 f. orange-brown and cream ..	..		45	20
22		20 f. blue-green and blue-grey ..	..		45	20
4/22		*Set of 19*	..	..	2·40	1·60

1945 (13 Oct). *Stamp Day. As No. 955 of France (Louis XI), but colour changed, optd with T 2.*

23	2 f.+3 f. red	..	..	..	8	8

1945. *AIR. As T 24 of French Equatorial Africa.*

24	5 f. 50, ultramarine	..	..	..	12	12
25	50 f. blue-green ..	..	..	..	70	10
26	100 f. claret	..	..	..	70	10

1946 (8 May). *AIR. Victory. As T 32 of French Equatorial Africa.*

27	8 f. mauve	..	..	..	15	15

1946 (6 June). *AIR. From Chad to the Rhine. As Nos. 229/34 of French Equatorial Africa.*

28	5 f. brown-lake ..	..	..	..	30	30
29	10 f. blue ..	..	..	..	30	30
30	15 f. mauve	..	..	..	40	40
31	20 f. blackish green	..	..		40	40
32	25 f. sepia	..	..	..	50	50
33	50 f. chocolate	..	..	..	70	70
28/33	*Set of 6*	..	..	..	2·40	2·40

3 War Dance

4 Girl and Bridge

5 Crocodile and Hippopotamus

6 Sudanese Carving

7 Sudanese Market

8 A. de St. Exupéry

D 10

9 Natives and Aeroplane

(Des Maudonnet. Eng P. Munier (8 f.). Des and eng C. Mazelin (10 c., 1 f., 15 f., 50 f.), P. Munier (30 c., 3 f. 60, 4 f., 25 f.), R. Serres (40 c., 50 c., 2 f., 3 f., 5 f., 10 f.), G. Bétemps (60 c., 80 c., 200 f.), P. Gandon (1 f. 20, 1 f. 50, 6 f., 20 f., 100 f.). Recess Institut de Gravure, Paris)

1947 (24 Mar). *P* 12½. (*a*) *POSTAGE. As T **3** to **7** (various designs).*

34	10 c. blue	..	..	5	5
35	30 c. brown-red	..	..	5	5
36	40 c. green	..	..	5	5
37	50 c. brown-red	..	..	5	5
38	60 c. olive-grey	..	..	10	10
39	80 c. lilac	..	..	10	10
40	1 f. claret	..	..	5	5
41	1 f. 20, green	..	..	20	20
42	1 f. 50, blue	..	..	20	20
43	2 f. orange-red	..	..	5	5
44	3 f. chocolate	..	..	10	5
45	3 f. 60, red	..	..	20	20
46	4 f. blue	..	..	5	5
47	5 f. green	..	..	5	5
48	6 f. blue	..	..	8	5
49	10 f. brown-red	..	..	15	5
50	15 f. purple-brown	..	..	20	5
51	20 f. chocolate	..	..	20	5
52	25 f. greenish black	..	..	40	5
34/52	*Set of* 19	..	..	2·00	1·40

Designs: *Horiz*—40 c. Canoe; 50 c. Niger landscape; 80 c. Dahomey weaver; 1 f. Donkey caravan; 10 f. Djenné Mosque; 15 f. Diesel rail-car. *Vert*—60 c. Coconuts; 1 f. 50, Palm trees; 3 f. Togo girl; 4 f. Dahomey labourer; 5 f. Mauritanian woman; 6 f. Guinea headdress; 20 f. Ivory Coast girl; 25 f. Niger washerwoman.

(*b*) *AIR. As T **8**/**9** (various designs)*

53	8 f. brown-red	..	..	12	10
54	50 f. violet	..	..	55	12
55	100 f. ultramarine	..	..	2·50	95
56	200 f. slate-grey	..	..	2·25	95
53/56	*Set of* 4	..	..	5·00	2·00

Designs: *Horiz*—50 f. Aeroplane over Dakar (Senegal); 100 f. Flight of Storks (Niger).

(Recess Institut de Gravure, Paris)

1947. *POSTAGE DUE. P* 13.

D57	D **10**	10 c. carmine	..	..	5	5
D58		30 c. orange	..	..	5	5
D59		50 c. black	..	..	5	5
D60		1 f. carmine	..	..	5	5
D61		2 f. green	..	..	5	5
D62		3 f. magenta	..	..	10	10
D63		4 f. blue	..	..	12	12
D64		5 f. red-brown	..	..	25	25
D65		10 f. greenish blue	..	..	45	45
D66		20 f. sepia	..	..	55	55
D57/66	*Set of* 10	..	..	..	1·50	1·50

1948. *As Nos.* 38 *and* 44, *but without* "TOGO" *imprint below design.*

67	60 c. olive-grey	..	..	12	5
68	3 f. chocolate	..	..	5	5

1949 (4 July). *AIR. 75th Anniv of Universal Postal Union. As T **39** of French Equatorial Africa.*

69	25 f. blue, purple, grey-green and red	..	1·90	1·90

1950 (15 May). *Colonial Welfare Fund. As T **40** of French Equatorial Africa.*

70	10 f.+2 f. brown-purple and red-brown	..	1·25	1·25

12 Logging Camp

(Des M. Debard. Eng J. Pheulpin (25 f.). Des and eng C. Mazelin (8 f.), J. Pheulpin (15 f.), R. Cottet (40, 200 f.), H. Cheffer (50 f.), C. Hertenberger (100 f.), R. Serres (500 f.). Recess)

1951 (5 Nov)–**58**. *P* 13. (*a*) *POSTAGE. Horiz designs as T **10**/**11**.*

71	8 f. indigo and brown (29.11.54)		25	10
72	15 f. dp bl-grn, blk-brn & brn (18.11.53)		25	5
73	20 f. blackish green & turq-bl (15.3.58)		30	5
74	25 f. sepia, blue & brown-purple (20.9.54)		30	5
75	40 f. carmine-lake (1.12.52)	..	40	5

(*b*) *AIR. As T **12***

76	50 f. dp orge-brn & bronze-grn (20.9.54)		55	5
77	100 f. black-brn, dp bl-grn & ind (20.9.54)		95	12
78	200 f. blackish green, deep turquoise and brown-lake (20.9.54)		2·75	55
79	500 f. blue-green, ultramarine and orange		6·50	95
71/79	*Set of* 9		11·00	1·75

Designs: (As *T* **10**/**11**)—8 f. Governor-General Ballay; 20 f. Abidjan Bridge; 25 f. Natives, animals and sailing canoe. (*As T* **12**)—100 f. Telephonist, aeroplane and pylons; 200 f. Baobab trees; 500 f. Vridi Canal, Abidjan.

1952 (1 Dec). *Centenary of Médaille Militaire. As T **44** of French Equatorial Africa.*

80	15 f. black-brown, yellow and green	..	1·00	1·00

1954 (6 June). *AIR. 10th Anniv of Liberation. As T **46** of French Equatorial Africa.*

81	15 f. bright blue and indigo	..	..	95	95

13 Chimpanzee

14

(Des and eng G. Bétemps (5 f.), R. Cottet (8 f.). Recess)

1955 (2 May). *Nature Protection. T **13** and horiz design inscr* "PROTECTION DE LA NATURE". *P* 13.

82	5 f. blackish brown and violet-grey	..	25	10
83	8 f. blackish brown and blue-green	..	20	10

Design:—8 f. Scaly ant-eater.

(Des and eng R. Cottet. Recess)

1955 (4 July). *50th Anniv of Rotary International. P* 13.

84	**14**	15 f. deep blue	..	..	20	12

10 Medical Research

11 T. Laplene and Map of Ivory Coast

15 Mossi Railway

16 Medical Station and Ambulances

(Des and eng R. Serres. Recess)

1955 (20 Feb–22 Oct). *Economic and Social Development Fund. T* **15** *and similar horiz designs inscr* "F.I.D.E.S." *P* 13×12½.

85	1 f. deep green and myrtle-green (22.10)	15	15
86	2 f. myrtle-green & greenish blue (22.10)	15	15
87	3 f. sepia and brown	20	15
88	4 f. carmine	20	20
89	15 f. blue and indigo (22.10)	20	5
90	17 f. deep blue and indigo (22.10)	25	15
91	20 f. brown-purple	25	15
92	30 f. brown-purple and deep lilac	25	15
85/92	*Set of* 8	1·50	1·00

Designs:—1 f. Date palms; 2 f. Milo River bridge; 4 f. Native cattle and herdsman; 15 f. Combine harvester; 17 f. Native woman and aerial view; 20 f. Palm oil factory; 30 f. Road between Abidjan and Abengourou.

1956 (22 Oct). *Coffee. As T* **51** *of French Equatorial Africa.*
93   15 f. deep bluish green and deep turquoise   12   5

(Des and eng C. Mazelin. Recess)

1957 (11 Mar). *Order of Malta Leprosy Relief. P* 13.
94 **16** 15 f. plum, brown-purple and scarlet ..   30   12

1957 (22 July). *AIR. Centenary of African Troops. As T* **53** *of French Equatorial Africa.*
95   15 f. light blue and indigo   40   40

  17 Map of Africa   **18** "Communication"

(Des and eng G. Bétemps. Recess)

1958 (11 Feb). *Sixth African International Tourist Congress. P* 13.
96 **17** 20 f. crimson and deep turquoise-green   30   15

(Des and eng C. Hertenberger. Recess)

1958 (15 Mar). *Stamp Day. P* 13.
97 **18** 15 f. chocolate, blue and orange   25   15
See also No. 126.

  19 Isle of Gorée and West African

(Des and eng J. Pheulpin (15 f.), P. Gandon (20 f.), C. Hertenberger (25 f.), A. Decaris (40 f.), P. Munier (50 f.), R. Cottet (100 f.). Recess)

1958 (17 Mar). *AIR. Centenary of Dakar. Various horiz designs as T* **19** *inscr* "CENTENAIRE DE DAKAR". *Multi-coloured. P* 13.

98	15 f. Type **19**	25	20
99	20 f. Map of Dakar, ships and aircraft..	25	20
100	25 f. Town construction	25	20
101	40 f. Council house	25	20

102	50 f. Groundnuts, artisan and ship at quayside ..	45	20
103	100 f. Bay of N'Gor	75	20
98/103	*Set of* 6	2·00	1·10
MS104	185×125 mm. Nos. 98/103 with view of Dakar	2·25	2·50

  20 Banana Plant and Fruit   O **21**

(Des and eng R. Serres. Recess)

1958 (19 May). *Banana Production. P* 13.
105 **20** 20 f. brt pur, dp bronze-grn & yell-ol   20   5

(Des R. Cottet. Typo)

1958 (2 June). *OFFICIAL. Type O* **21** *and similar designs inscr* "OFFICIEL". *P* 14×13½.

O106	O **21**	1 f. brown-purple	12	12
O107		3 f. blue-green	12	12
O108		5 f. red	10	5
O109		10 f. bright blue	10	5
O110	—	20 f. vermilion	12	5
O111	—	25 f. reddish violet	20	5
O112	—	30 f. green	25	20
O113	—	45 f. slate-black	30	20
O114	—	50 f. carmine-red	45	10
O115	—	65 f. ultramarine	55	20
O116	—	100 f. olive-brown	1·00	12
O117	—	200 f. deep green	2·25	40
O106/117	*Set of* 12 ..		5·00	1·50

Designs:—20 f. to 45 f. Head with female face; 50 f. to 200 f. Head with hooped headdress, diagonally on stamp.

1958 (7 July)–59. *Flowers. As T* **56** *of French Equatorial Africa.*

118	10 f. multicoloured	12	5
119	25 f. yellow, green and scarlet (5.1.59) ..	20	5
120	30 f. multicoloured	25	20
121	40 f. yellow, green & black-brn (5.1.59)	30	25
122	65 f. multicoloured	50	25
118/122	*Set of* 5 ..	1·25	70

Designs: *Vert*—10 f. *Gloriosa*; 25 f. *Adenopus*; 30 f. *Cyrtosperma*; 40 f. *Cistanche*; 65 f. *Crinum moorei*.

  22 Moro Naba Sagha and Map of Upper Volta

(Des and eng P. Munier. Recess)

1958 (1 Nov). 10*th Anniv of Upper Volta Scheme. P* 13.
123 **22** 20 f. sepia, violet, rose carmine & crim   20   15

PUZZLED?

Then you need

PHILATELIC TERMS ILLUSTRATED

to tell you all you need to know about printing methods, papers, errors, varieties, watermarks, perforations, etc. 192 pages, almost half in full colour, soft cover. £1·95 post paid.

23 Native Chief and Musician

(Des Mme Y. Durand-Ledret. Eng J. Pheulpin. Recess)

1958 (29 Nov). *AIR. Inauguration of Nouakchott, capital of Mauritania. P 13.*
124 **23** 20 f. black-brown, chestnut & vio-grey   30   20

1958 (10 Dec). *10th Anniv of Declaration of Human Rights. As T 57 of French Equatorial Africa.*
125   20 f. brown-purple and blue   40   40

1959 (21 Mar). *Stamp Day. As T 18 but inscr "DAKAR-ABIDJAN" instead of "AFRIQUE OCCIDENTALE FRAN-CAISE".*
126 **18** 20 f. slate-green, greenish blue and red   45   40
No. 126 was for use in Ivory Coast and Senegal only.

During 1958–59 the constituent parts of French West Africa became separate republics, issuing their own stamps.

PHILATELIC TERMS ILLUSTRATED

This successful STAMP MONTHLY series has now been brought together in a snappy black and yellow binding and published as a useful addition to Stanley Gibbons range of essential handbooks for keen stamp collectors. Within its 192 pages this handy limp-bound volume houses a veritable mine of useful information on the words and phrases used in philately. It describes and illustrates printing processes and watermarks, papers and perforations, errors and varieties . . . and it does all this IN COLOUR. Indeed, there are 92 full page plates in colour, plus many black and white illustrations, making it

FANTASTIC VALUE AT ONLY £1·95 POST PAID FROM
Stanley Gibbons Publications Ltd
391 Strand, London WC2R 0LX

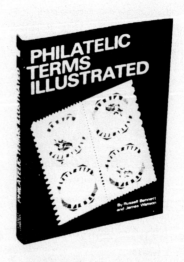

Guadeloupe

100 Centimes = 1 Franc

FRENCH COLONY

Guadeloupe was discovered by Columbus in 1493, being named by him in honour of Santa Maria de Guadelupe Monastery, Spain. It was seized by the French Antilles Company in 1635 and passed to the French crown in 1674. Until 1775 the islands were administered as a dependency of Martinique. The colony was occupied by Britain during hostilities in 1759–63, 1794–95 and 1810–16.

PRINTERS. All the stamps of Guadeloupe were printed at the Government Printing Works, Paris, *unless otherwise stated.*

IMPERFORATE STAMPS. Many stamps exist imperforate in their issued colours, but these were not valid for postage. Imperforate stamps in other colours are colour trials.

D 1　(2)　D 3

(Type-set at Basse-Terre)

1876 (20 Nov).–**79**. *POSTAGE DUE. Imperf.*

D1	D **1**	15 c. black/*blue* (1.1.79)	..	7·50	5·50
D2		25 c. black/*white*	..	£175	£150
D3		30 c. black/*white* (1.1.79)	..	15·00	12·00
D4		40 c. black/*blue* (end of 1877)	..	—	£6000
D5		40 c. black/*white* (1878)	..	£200	£175

The 30 c. has larger figures, and "centimes" abbreviated to "c".

The sheet consists of 20 varieties (5 rows of 4).

So-called reprints of the 25 c. and 40 c. were made in 1884, but inasmuch as the type was entirely reset and there are only 8 varieties (2 rows of 4), these can only be considered imitations. They are on whiter and thinner paper than the originals.

(Surch at Govt Ptg Works, Basse-Terre)

1884 (28 Feb). *Type H of French Colonies (General issues) surch as T 2. Imperf.*

6	20 on 30 dull brown	..	..	10·00	9·00
	a. Figures "20" double		..	35·00	32·00
	b. Larger figure "2"	..	..	35·00	32·00
7	25 on 35 c. black/*orange*	..	..	10·00	9·00
	a. Larger figure "2"	..	..	32·00	30·00
	b. Larger figure "5"	..	..	30·00	32·00

(Type-set at Basse-Terre)

1884 (16 July). *POSTAGE DUE. Imperf.*

D 8	D **3**	5 c. black/*white*	..	3·75	3·00
D 9		10 c. black/*blue*	..	11·00	7·50
D10		15 c. black/*lilac*	..	15·00	9·50
D11		20 c. black/*rose*	..	25·00	18·00
		a. Italic "2" in "20"	..	£150	£125
D12		30 c. black/*yellow*	..	25·00	22·00
		a. *Black/orange-yellow*	..	25·00	22·00
D13		35 c. black/*drab*	..	6·50	5·50
		a. "UADELOUPE"	..	28·00	25·00
D14		50 c. black/*green*	..	3·25	3·25
		a. *Black/yellow-green*	..	3·25	3·25
		b. *Black/blue-green*	..	£120	£120

Many other minor varieties similar to those of the postage issue of 1889 occur in the type and setting of this issue.

(4)　(5)　(6)

(Surch at Govt Ptg Works, Basse-Terre)

1889 (9 Jan). *Type J of French Colonies (General issues) surch as T 4.* P 14×13½.

8	3 c. on 20 c. red/*green*	..	..	60	60
9	15 c. on 20 c. red/*green*	..	..	6·00	5·50
10	25 c. on 20 c. red/*green*	..	..	5·50	4·50

The word "centimes" usually measures 10½ mm in length, but can be found measuring up to 12½ mm, depending on its position in the 25 subject surcharge plate.

(Surch at Govt Ptg Works, Basse-Terre)

1889. *Type J of French Colonies (General issues) surch as T 5.* P 14×13½.

11	5 c. on 1 c. black/*azure* (25.6)	..	2·25	2·25
	a. Surcharge inverted	..	£100	90·00
12	10 c. on 40 c. red/*yellow* (22.3)	..	5·00	4·50
	a. Surch double	..	75·00	
13	15 c. on 20 c. red/*green* (22.3)	..	4·50	4·00
	a. Surch double	..	75·00	
14	25 c. on 30 c. cinnamon/*drab* (22.3)	..	7·00	6·00
	a. Surch double	..	75·00	

The word "centimes" is normally 10½ mm in length, but can be found measuring up to 12½ mm, depending on the stamp's position in the surcharge plate of 25 subjects.

There are many varieties of this surcharge, differing in the corner ornaments of the frames, which are of two types found in various combinations. In the 10 c. surcharge, seven stamps in the setting show a wider "0" in "10".

(Surch at Govt Ptg Works, Basse-Terre)

1891. *Type J of French Colonies (General issues) surch as T 6.* P 14×13½.

15	5 c. on 10 c. black/*lilac* (11.1)	..	2·25	1·75
16	5 c. on 1 f. olive/*green* (Mar)	..	2·25	1·75
	a. Surch double	..		

GUADELOUPE

(7)

(Optd at Govt Ptg Works, Basse-Terre)

1891 (Sept). *Stamps of French Colonies (General issues) optd with T 7.* (a) *Type G. Imperf.*

19	30 c. drab	..	..	65·00	65·00
20	80 c. rose	..	..	£200	£200

(b) *Type J.* P 14×13½

21	1 c. black/*azure*	..	..	15	15
	a. Opt double	..	..	4·00	4·00
	b. Opt inverted	..	..	25·00	
22	2 c. brown/*buff*	..	..	30	20
	a. Opt double	..	..	4·00	4·00
23	4 c. purple-brown/*grey*	..	..	80	75
24	5 c. green/*pale green*	..	..	1·00	75
	a. Opt double	..	..	7·00	6·00
	b. Opt inverted	..	..	30·00	30·00
25	10 c. black/*lilac*	..	..	2·75	2·00
26	15 c. blue/*pale blue*	..	..	7·00	60
	a. Opt double	..	..	—	18·00

27	20 c. red/*green*				6·50	5·00
	a. Opt double				32·00	30·00
28	25 c. black/*rose*				7·00	60
	a. Opt double				32·00	30·00
	b. Opt inverted				30·00	30·00
29	30 c. cinnamon/*drab*				7·00	8·50
	a. Opt double				32·00	30·00
30	35 c. black/*orange*				14·00	12·00
31	40 c. red/*yellow*				9·00	8·00
	a. Opt double				£120	£120
32	75 c. rose-carmine/*rose*				25·00	22·00
33	1 f. olive-green/*toned*				15·00	14·00
21/33	*Set of 13*				90·00	70·00

Errors of Overprint

A. "GNADELOUPE". B. "GUADELOUEP".
C. "GUADELONPE". D. "GUADBLOUPE".

(*Same prices used or unused*)

				A	B	C	D
19	G	30 c.		£175	£550	£525	£525
20		80 c.		£900	£2250	£2250	£2250
21	J	1 c.		1·40	1·50	1·40	1·50
22		2 c.		1·50	1·75	1·75	1·75
23		4 c.		2·50	3·00	3·00	2·50
24		5 c.		3·75	4·00	4·00	3·75
25		10 c.		7·50	8·50	8·00	7·50
26		15 c.		15·00	15·00	15·00	15·00
27		20 c.		15·00	22·00	20·00	20·00
28		25 c.		16·00	28·00	25·00	25·00
29		30 c.		20·00	30·00	28·00	28·00
30		35 c.		85·00	75·00	55·00	65·00
31		40 c.		55·00	£120	£100	£100
32		75 c.		70·00	£125	£110	£110
33		1 f.		85·00	55·00	50·00	45·00

There were two printings of this overprint, utilising three settings. Error A occurs on one position of the 1st setting, error B on one position of the 3rd, error C on one stamp from the 2nd and one from the 3rd setting, and error D on one position from the 2nd and one from the 3rd. Settings 1 and 2 were used for the first printing and setting 3 for the second.

1892 (Nov). *French Colonies Type X inscr* "GUADELOUPE ET DEPENDANCES" *in red* (1, 5, 15, 25, 75 c., 1 f.) *or blue* (*others*). *P* 14×13½.

34	X	1 c. black/*azure*				20	10
35		2 c. brown/*buff*				15	10
36		2 c. purple-brown/*buff*				15	10
37		4 c. purple-brown/*grey*				20	12
38		5 c. green/*pale green*				50	8
39		10 c. black/*lilac*				1·75	35
40		15 c. blue (*quadrillé paper*)				1·50	8
41		20 c. red/*green*				80	50
42		25 c. black/*rose*				1·10	20
43		30 c. cinnamon/*drab*				3·00	2·25
44		40 c. red/*yellow*				3·25	2·00
45		50 c. carmine/*rose*				6·00	4·00
46		75 c. brown/*yellow*				5·50	4·25
		a. Brown/*orange*				5·75	4·50
47		1 f. olive-green/*toned*				5·50	4·75
34/47		*Set of 14*				26·00	20·00

1900 (Dec)–**01**. *Colours changed. Inscr in blue* (10 *c.*) *or red* (*others*). *P* 14×13½.

48	X	5 c. bright yellow-green (10.01)				50	15
49		10 c. rose-red				1·00	25
50		15 c. grey				1·75	12
51		25 c. blue				18·00	16·00
52		50 c. brown/*azure*				6·50	5·00
48/52		*Set of 5*				25·00	20·00

1903 (Aug). *Nos. 43/7 surch at Govt Printing Works, Basse-Terre, in sheets of 50.*

G & D

5

(10)

G & D

(11)

G & D

(12)

G & D

(13)

G & D

(14)

G & D

(15)

All 5 c. surcharges include the figure "5" as in T **10**, with "G & D" differing as in T **11/15**.

The setting of 50 was made up of T **10** (23, including one with "C" for "G" error), **11** (12), **12** (6), **13** (3), **14** (3) and **15** (3).

All types of the 5 c. surcharge exist, inverted, double or double, one inverted. Prices given are for the cheapest variety.

53	**10**	5 on 30 c. cinnamon/*drab*				75	75
		a. "C" for "G"				3·75	3·75
		b. Surch T **11**				75	75
		c. Surch T **12**				75	75
		d. Surch T **13**				75	75
		e. Surch T **14**				75	75
		f. Surch T **15**				75	75
		g. Surch inverted				6·50	6·50
		h. Surch double				22·00	22·00
		i. Surch double, one inverted				25·00	

G et D

10   **10**   **10**   **1 O**   **10**

(16)   (17)   (18)   (19)   (20)

All 10 c. surcharge include "G et D" as in T **16**, with figures "10" differing as in T **17/20**.

The setting of 50 was made up of T **16** (20, including one with "inverted 1" error), **17** (14, including one "C" for "G" error), **18** (9), **19** (6, including one "C" for "G" error) and **20** (1).

All types of the 10 c. surcharge exist inverted or double. Prices given are for the cheapest variety.

54	**16**	10 on 40 c. red/*yellow*				1·10	1·10
		a. "1" inverted				7·50	7·50
		b. Surch T **17**				1·10	1·10
		ba. "C" for "G"				4·50	4·50
		c. Surch T **18**				1·10	1·10
		d. Surch T **19**				1·10	1·10
		da. "C" for "G"				4·50	4·50
		e. Surch T **20**				1·10	1·10
		f. Surch inverted				7·50	7·50
		g. Surch double					

All 15 c. surcharges show figures "15", with "G & D" as in T **10/15**.

There were two settings of 50 for this surcharge. The first was of the same composition as that used for the 5 c. values, and is known with all types inverted or double. In the second setting one example of T **10** and one of T **15** occur inverted; on one example of T **15** the figures "15" only are inverted.

55	**10**	15 on 50 c. carmine/*rose*				1·75	1·75
		a. "C" for "G"				5·00	5·00
		ab. Pair, one with surch inverted					
		b. Surch T **11**				1·75	1·75
		c. Surch T **12**				1·90	1·90
		ca. Pair, one with surch inverted					
		d. Surch T **13**				2·50	2·50
		e. Surch T **14**				3·25	3·25
		f. Surch T **15**				3·25	3·25
		fa. "15" inverted				65·00	65·00
		g. Surch inverted				16·00	16·00
		h. Surch double				32·00	32·00

G et D   **G et D**

40   **40**

(21)   (22)

There were two settings of 50 for the 40 c. surcharge. The first consisted of T **21** (44, including one "C" for "G" error) and **22** (6, including one "C" for "G" error). This setting is known with surcharge inverted, double or triple. On the second setting 4 positions as T **21** and one as T **22** show figure "4" inverted.

56	**21**	40 on 1 f. olive-green/*toned*				1·90	1·90
		a. "C" for "G"				5·50	5·50
		b. "4" inverted				18·00	18·00
		c. Surch T **22**				3·25	3·25
		ca. "C" for "G"				5·50	5·50
		cb. "4" inverted				18·00	18·00
		d. Surch inverted				21·00	21·00
		e. Surch double				35·00	35·00
		f. Surch triple				40·00	40·00

1 fr. **1. fr.** **1 fr.**

(23)   (24)   (25)

1 fr.   **1 fr.**

(26)   (27)

The 1 f. surcharge combined the six types of "G & D", T **10/15**, with five versions of "1 fr.", T **23/7**.

There were two settings of this value. The first utilised the letters from the 5 c. surcharge and the same varieties exist as on that setting. The "1 fr." surcharge was used in various combinations with "G & D", the setting of 50 consisting of T **23** (18, including three "1 inverted" errors), **24** (19, including two "missing stop" varieties), **25** (2), **26** (10) and **27** (1). The first setting is known inverted. The second setting consists of T **23** and **25** only in various combinations with "G & D". It was made up of T **23** (46, including nine "1 inverted" errors) and **25** (4, including one "1 inverted").

57   1 f. on 75 c. brown/*yellow* (Surch
          T **23**+10)   .. .. ..   8·50   8·50
   a. "C" for "G" (2nd setting)   ..   18·00   18·00
   b. "1" inverted ..   ..   ..   25·00   25·00
   ba. "1" inverted and with value above
          "G & D" (2nd setting)   .   55·00   55·00
   c. Surch T **23**+11 (2nd setting)   7·50   7·50
   ca. "1" inverted (2nd setting)   ..   25·00   25·00
   d. Surch T **23**+12   ..   ..   7·50   7·50
   da. "1" inverted ..   ..   ..   25·00   25·00
   e. Surch T **23**+13   ..   ..   7·50   7·50
   ea. "1" inverted ..   ..   ..   25·00   25·00
   f. Surch T **23**+14   ..   ..   7·50   7·50
   g. Surch T **23**+15 (2nd setting)   7·50   7·50
   ga. "1" inverted (2nd setting)   ..   25·00   25·00
   h. Surch T **24**+10   ..   ..   7·50   7·50
   ha. No stop after "fr"   ..   ..   20·00   20·00
   i. Surch T **24**+11   ..   ..   7·50   7·50
   ia. No stop after "fr"   ..   ..   20·00   20·00
   j. Surch T **24**+15   ..   ..   11·00   11·00
   k. Surch T **25**+10   ..   ..   16·00   16·00
   l. Surch T **25**+12 with "1" inverted (2nd
          setting)   ..   ..   ..   25·00   25·00
   m. Surch T **26**+10   ..   ..   7·50   7·50
   ma. "C" for "G"   ..   ..   20·00   20·00
   n. Surch T **26**+11   ..   ..   12·00   12·00
   o. Surch T **26**+12   ..   ..   12·00   12·00
   p. Surch T **26**+15   ..   ..   23·00   23·00
   q. Surch T **27**+12   ..   ..   25·00   25·00
   r. Surch inverted   ..   ..   18·00   18·00

1903 (Aug). *No. 44 handstamped in two operations with* "G et D" *as T* **16** *and* "10" *as T* **19**.
58   10 on 40 c. red/*yellow* £110   £110

G & D
30

(D 28)

G & D
30

(D 29)

Two settings were used for the Postage Due surcharge. The first contained 48 examples of Type D **28** and 2 of Type D **29** (varieties D60a/ab and D62a/ab). The second setting was made up of 3 examples of Type D **29** and 47 of Type D **28**.

The "33 corrected to 30" varieties and the "30 sideways" errors only occur on the first setting. Of the two settings only the second is known inverted.

(Surch at Govt Ptg Wks, Basse-Terre)

1903 (Aug). *POSTAGE DUE. French Colonies* (*General issues*) *Type* U *surch. Imperf.*
D59 D **28** 30 on 60 c. brown/*buff*   ..   75·00   75·00
   a. "33" corrected to "30"   £2250   £2250
   b. Roman "G" ..   ..   ..   75·00   75·00
   c. Roman "D" ..   ..   ..   75·00   75·00
   d. "G" omitted £100   £100
   e. Surch inverted (2nd setting
          only) £130   £130
D60 D **29** 30 on 60 c. brown/*buff*   £130   £130
   a. "30" printed vertically   ..   £2250   £2250
   ab. "30" printed vertically, and
          "G & D" inverted   ..   £2250
   b. Surch inverted (2nd setting
          only) £275   £275
D61 D **28** 30 on 1 f. rose/*buff*   ..   80·00   80·00
   a. "33" corrected to "30"   £2000   £2000
   b. Roman "G" £130   £130
   c. Roman "D" ..   ..   ..   80·00   80·00
   d. "G" omitted £110   £110
   e. Surch inverted (2nd setting
          only) £175   £175
D62 D **29** 30 on 1 f. rose/*buff*   £160   £160
   a. "30" printed vertically   ..   £1900   £1900
   ab. "30" printed vertically, and
          "G & D" inverted   ..   £2250
   b. Surch inverted (2nd setting
          only) £325   £325

1903   1903   1903

(30)   (31)   (32)

1903   1903   **1903**

(33)   (34)   (35)

1 9 0 3   *1903*   1903

(36)   (37)   (38)

1903   *1903*   ᥱ06ᒥ

(39)   (40)   (41)

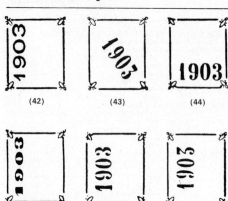

(42)   (43)   (44)

(45)   (46)   (47)

		A	B	C

i. Opt T **39** .. .. .. † † 38·00
j. Opt T **40** .. .. .. † † 38·00
k. Opt T **41** .. .. .. * † 38·00
l. Opt T **42** .. .. .. * 35·00 40·00
m. Opt T **43** .. .. .. * † 38·00
n. Opt T **44** .. .. .. * † 38·00
o. Opt T **45** .. .. .. * 15·00 †
p. Opt T **46** .. .. .. * 19·00 †
q. Opt T **47** .. .. .. * 19·00 †

D **48** Gustavia Bay, Island of St. Bartholomew

49 Mount Houllemont, Basse-Terre

50 La Soufrière

51 Pointe-à-Pitre, Grande Terre

Nos. 59/60 were overprinted in sheets of 50, using five different settings.
  Setting 1. In blue or red on both values. Made up of T **30** (47), **31** (2) and **32** (1).
  Setting 2. In blue or red on both values. Made up of T **31** (1), **32** (1), **33** (47) and **34** (1).
  Setting 3. In blue, red or black on the 40 on 1 f., and in red only on the 1 f. on 75 c. Made up of T **31** (1), **32** (2), **33** (1), **34** (45) and **35** (1).
  Setting 4. In red only on both values. Made up of T **36** (40), **37** (3), **38** (2), **39** (1), **40** (2), **41** (1), **42** (1), **43** (1) and **44** (1).
  Setting 5. In blue only on both values. Made up of T **42** (1), **45** (35), **46** (7) and **47** (7).

Both values are known with red overprint inverted. The 1 f. on 75 c. with red or blue overprint exists with overprint double and the 40 on 1 f. (blue overprint) can be found with overprint double, one inverted. These varieties are not known from Setting 1.

Most of the varieties listed under Nos. 56/7 also occur on these ''1903'' overprints. For the 1 f. on 75 c. value Setting 2 in blue or red can be found on both settings of the ''1 fr.'' surcharge. All the other overprint settings are on the first ''1 fr.'' setting only.

(Optd at Govt Ptg Wks, Basse-Terre)

1904 (Mar). *Nos. 56/7 further optd as T* **30**/**47**.
  A. *Black opt.* B. *Blue opt.* C. *Red opt*
  Prices are for unused only. Used stamps are worth 10% *more*

			A	B	C
59	40 on 1 f. ol-grn/*toned* (Opt T **30**)		÷	13·00	8·50
	a. Opt T **31**	.. .. ..	£200	22·00	19·00
	b. Opt T **32**	.. .. ..	£170	22·00	19·00
	c. Opt T **33**	.. .. ..	£200	8·00	11·00
	d. Opt T **34**	.. .. ..	80·00	9·50	9·50
	e. Opt T **35**	.. .. ..	£200	35·00	35·00
	f. Opt T **36**	.. .. ..	*	†	11·00
	g. Opt T **37**	.. .. ..	*	†	35·00
	h. Opt T **38**	.. .. ..	*	†	35·00
	i. Opt T **39**	.. .. ..	*	†	35·00
	j. Opt T **40**	.. .. ..	*	†	35·00
	k. Opt T **41**	.. .. ..	*	†	35·00
	l. Opt T **42**	.. .. ..	*	35·00	35·00
	m. Opt T **43**	.. .. ..	*	†	35·00
	n. Opt T **44**	.. .. ..	*	†	35·00
	o. Opt T **45**	.. .. ..	*	9·50	†
	p. Opt T **46**	.. .. ..	*	13·00	†
	q. Opt T **47**	.. .. ..	*	16·00	†
60	1 f. on 75 c. brn/*yell* (Opt T **30**)		*	15·00	15·00
	a. Opt T **31**	.. .. ..	*	25·00	22·00
	b. Opt T **32**	.. .. ..	*	25·00	22·00
	c. Opt T **33**	.. .. ..	*	15·00	15·00
	d. Opt T **34**	.. .. ..	*	19·00	15·00
	e. Opt T **35**	.. .. ..	*	†	38·00
	f. Opt T **36**	.. .. ..	*	†	15·00
	g. Opt T **37**	.. .. ..	*	†	38·00
	h. Opt T **38**	.. .. ..	*	†	28·00

(Eng J. Puyplat. Typo)

1905 (July) 06   *P* 14 · 13½
D63 D **48** 5 c. deep blue 5 5
D64   10 c. brown 8 8
D65   15 c. green 8 8
D66   20 c. brown/*yellow* (9.06) .. 8 8
D67   30 c. rose 8 8
D68   50 c. black 45 45
D69   60 c. orange-brown .. 15 15
D70   1 f. bright lilac 40 40
D63/70 *Set of 8* .. .. 1·25 1·25

(Eng J. Puyplat. Typo)

1905 (July)–**07**. *P* 14×13½.
61 **49** 1 c. black/*azure* 5 5
62   2 c. purple-brown/*straw* .. 5 5
63   4 c. brown/*pale grey* .. 5 5
64   5 c. green 12 10
65   10 c. carmine 12 5
66   15 c. bright lilac 5 5
67 **50** 20 c. red/*green* 5 5
68   25 c. blue 5 5
69   30 c. black 70 40
70   35 c. black/*yellow* (1906) .. 5 5
71   40 c. red/*straw* 10 5
72   45 c. grey-brown/*lilac* (1907) .. 5 5
73   50 c. olive-green/*straw* .. 90 55
74   75 c. carmine/*azure* .. 12 10
75 **51** 1 f. black/*green* 25 25
76   2 f. red/*orange* 30 30
77   5 f. blue/*orange* .. .. 1·10 1·10
61/77 *Set of 17* .. .. 3·75 3·00
  See also Nos. 83/94.

1912 (Nov). *Surch as T* **11**/**12** *of French Guiana*.
  A. Narrow spacing. B. Wide spacing

				A	B
78	X	05 on 4 c. purple-brown/*grey* (R.)		12	12 25·00 25·00
79		05 on 20 c. cinnamon/*drab* (R.)		15	15 40·00 40·00
80		10 on 40 c. red/*yellow*		30 ·	30 25·00 25·00

For note *re* spacing, see French Guiana.

1915 (May)–**17**. *Red Cross. Surch in Paris as T* **14** *of French Guiana, in red*.
81 **49** 10 c.+5 c. carmine 90 40
82   15 c.+5 c. lilac (1917) 50 40
  a. Surch double .. .. 16·00 16·00

1922 (1 Jan)–**27**. *New value and colours.* P 14×13½.

83	49	5 c. blue			5	5
84		10 c. green			5	5
85		10 c. scarlet/*azure* (20.5.25)			5	5
86	50	20 c. green (17.5.26)			5	5
87		25 c. sage-green			5	5
88		30 c. carmine			5	5
89		30 c. olive/*lilac* (1.12.25)			5	5
90		45 c. carmine (1.5.25)			5	5
91		50 c. blue			10	10
92		50 c. bright magenta (1.12.25)			5	5
93		65 c. dull blue (19.12.27)			5	5
94	51	1 f. light blue (1.12.25)			8	8
83/94		*Set of 12*			60	60

1924 (June)–**27**. *Surch as T* **11/12** *of French Sudan.*

95	51	25 c. on 5 f. blue/*orange*			5	5
96		65 on 1 f. olive-green (1.2.25)			12	12
97		85 on 1 f. olive-green (1.2.25)			15	15
98	50	90 c. on 75 c. carmine (28.2.27)			15	15
99	51	1 f. 05 on 2 f. red (B.) (14.2.26)			8	8
100		1 f. 25 on 1 f. light blue (R.) (14.6.26)			5	5
101		1 f. 50 on 1 f. blue (28.2.27)			15	15
102		3 f. on 5 f. red-brown (19.12.27)			15	15
103		10 f. on 5 f. carmine/*yellow* (28.2.27)			1·90	1·90
104		20 f. on 5 f. magenta/*rose* (28.2.27)			1·90	1·90
95/104		*Set of 10*			4·25	4·25

2
francs
à percevoir

(D 52)

53 Sugar-refinery

54 Saints Harbour

55 Pointe-à-Pitre Harbour

1926 (17 May)–**27**. *POSTAGE DUE. Surch as Type* D **52**.

D105	D **48**	2 f. on 1 f. grey			15	15
D106		3 f. on 1 f. ultramarine (10.10.27)			40	40

(T **53** des Michineau, **54** and **55** G. de Chambertrand. Dies eng C. Hourriez. Typo)

1928 (18 June)–**40**. P 14×13½.

105	53	1 c. mauve and yellow			5	5
106		2 c. scarlet and black			5	5
107		3 c. magenta and yellow (1940)			5	5
108		4 c. chestnut and yellow-olive			5	5
109		5 c. green and scarlet			5	5
110		10 c. blue and brown			5	5
111		15 c. black and scarlet			5	5
112		20 c. chocolate and mauve			5	5
113	54	25 c. olive and light blue			5	5
114		30 c. green and grey-green			5	5
115		35 c. blue-green (6.7.38)			5	5
116		40 c. mauve and yellow			5	5
117		45 c. slate and purple			8	8
118		45 c. blue-green & grey-green (1940)			8	8
119		50 c. vermilion and green			5	5
120		55 c. carmine and ultramarine (6.7.38)			5	5
121		60 c. carmine and ultramarine (1940)			5	5
122		65 c. scarlet and grey-black			5	5
123		70 c. scarlet and black (1940)			5	5
124		75 c. blue-green and carmine			8	12
125		90 c. brown and carmine (6.7.38)			5	5
126		90 c. carmine			40	40
127		90 c. light blue and rose (1939)			12	12

128	55	1 f. light blue and rose			80	40
129		1 f. orange and carmine (5.12.38)			12	12
130		1 f. brown and blue (1940)			5	5
131		1 f. 05, rose and light blue			20	20
132		1 f. 10, green and red-orange			55	50
133		1 f. 25, chocolate and blue (25.9.33)			5	5
134		1 f. 25, orange and carmine (1939)			10	10
135		1 f. 40, magenta & light blue (1940)			8	8
136		1 f. 50, light blue and blue			5	5
137		1 f. 60, orange and magenta (1940)			5	5
138		1 f. 75, orange and magenta (25.9.33)			75	55
139		1 f. 75, ultramarine (5.12.38)			95	75
140		2 f. chocolate and green			5	5
141		2 f. 25, ultramarine (1939)			8	8
142		2 f. 50, green and red-orange (1940)			8	8
143		3 f. black and chestnut			5	5
144		5 f. vermilion and blue			5	5
145		10 f. sepia and mauve			10	10
146		20 f. rose and green			20	20
105/146		*Set of 42*			6·50	4·75

The 10 c. in similar design, but without "RF", was prepared in 1944, but not issued.

D **56** Allée Dumanoir, Capesterre

(Des G. de Chambertrand. Eng C. Hourriez. Typo)

1928 .(18 June). *POSTAGE DUE.* P 14×13½.

D147	D **56**	2 c. mauve and sepia			5	5
D148		4 c. chestnut and blue			5	5
D149		5 c. chocolate and green			5	5
D150		10 c. yellow and mauve			5	5
D151		15 c. olive and carmine			5	5
D152		20 c. olive and orange			5	5
D153		25 c. green and lake			5	5
D154		30 c. bistre and slate-blue			5	5
D155		50 c. scarlet and chocolate			5	5
D156		60 c. black and blue			15	15
D157		1 f. scarlet and green			40	40
D158		2 f. scarlet and yellow-brown			25	25
D159		3 f. indigo and mauve			15	15
D147/159		*Set of 13*			1·25	1·25

The 60 c., 1 f. and 2 f. were prepared in 1944 without "RF", but were not issued.

1931 (13 Apr). *International Colonial Exhibition, Paris. As* T **17/20** *of French Sudan.*

147		40 c. black and green			50	50
148		15 c. black and mauve			50	50
149		90 c. black and vermilion			1·00	1·00
150		1 f. 50, black and blue			80	80
147/150		*Set of 4*			2·50	2·50

57 Richelieu founding Antilles Co., 1635

58 Victor Hughes and Corsairs, 1793

(Eng A. Mignon. Recess)

1935 (22 Oct). *West Indies Tercentenary.* P 13.

151	57	40 c. sepia			1·90	1·90
152		50 c. scarlet			1·90	1·90
153		1 f. 50, ultramarine			1·90	1·90

154	**58**	1 f. 75, magenta	1·90	1·90
155		5 f. brown	1·90	1·90
156		10 f. emerald-green	1·90	1·90
151/156		*Set of 6*	10·00	10·00

1937 (15 Apr). *International Exhibition, Paris. As T* **2/7** *of French Equatorial Africa.*

157	20 c. bright violet		20	20
158	30 c. green		20	20
159	40 c. carmine		20	20
160	50 c. brown		20	20
161	90 c. scarlet		20	20
162	1 f. 50, blue		20	20
157/162	*Set of 6*		1·10	1·10
MS162a	120×100 mm. 3 f. grey-blue (as *T* **3**)			
	Imperf		95	95
	b. Error. Inscription omitted	£425	£425

1938 (24 Oct). *International Anti-Cancer Fund. As T* **14** *of French Equatorial Africa.*

163	1 f. 75+50 c. ultramarine		2·10	2·10

1939 (10 May). *New York World's Fair. As T* **17** *of French Equatorial Africa.*

164	1 f. 25, lake		15	15
165	2 f. 25, ultramarine		15	15

1939 (5 July). *150th Anniv of French Revolution. As T* **18** *of French Equatorial Africa.*

166	45 c.+25 c. green and black		1·40	1·40
167	70 c.+30 c. brown and black		1·40	1·40
168	90 c.+35 c. red-orange and black		1·40	1·40
169	1 f. 25+1 f. carmine and black		1·40	1·40
170	2 f. 25+2 f. blue and black		1·40	1·40
166/170	*Set of 5*		6·50	6·50

VICHY ISSUES. A number of stamps were prepared by the Pétain Government of Unoccupied France for use in Guadeloupe, but were not placed on sale there.

4^F

(59)

50^c

(60)

V

Un franc

(61)

40^c

(62)

1943–44. *Surch locally with bars obliterating original values.*

(a) No. 99 *further surch with T* **59**

171	**51**	4 f. on 1 f. 05 on 2 f. red (1944)	30	30
		a. Surch T **59** double	16·00	

(b) As T **60**

172	**54**	40 c. on 35 c. blue-green (1944)	12	10
173		50 c. on 25 c. olive & light blue (1944)	5	5
174		50 c. on 65 c. scarlet and grey-black	12	12
175		1 f. on 90 c. carmine	20	20
176		1 f. on 90 c. light blue and rose	15	12

(c) With T **61**

177	**54**	1 f. on 65 c. scarlet & grey-blk (1944)	5	5
		a. Surch inverted	22·00	22·00
		b. Surch double	19·00	

(d) Nos. 164/5 *surch with T* **62**

178	–	40 c. on 1 f. 25, lake	15	15
179	–	40 c. on 2 f. 25, ultramarine	30	20
171/179		*Set of 9*	1·25	1·25

On No. 172 the original value is obliterated by a cross.

1944. *Mutual Aid and Red Cross Funds. As T* **29** *of French Equatorial Africa.*

180	5 f.+20 f. pale ultramarine		15	15

1945. *Eboué. As T* **31** *of French Equatorial Africa.*

181	2 f. black		5	5
182	25 f. blue-green		12	12

63

(Des E. Dulac. Litho De La Rue & Co)

1945. *P* 11½.

183	**63**	10 c. slate-blue and orange	5	5
184		30 c. yellow-green and orange	5	5
185		40 c. blue and red	5	5
186		50 c. orange-red and yellow-green	5	5
187		60 c. olive-grey and blue	5	5
188		70 c. grey and yellow-green	5	10
189		80 c. green and yellow	5	5
190		1 f. purple and green	5	5
191		1 f. 20, magenta and yellow-green	5	5
192		1 f. 50, brown and red	10	5
193		2 f. carmine and blue	10	5
194		2 f. 40, red and yellow-green	20	15
195		3 f. brown and grey-blue	5	5
196		4 f. ultramarine and orange	5	5
197		4 f. 50, brown-orange & yellow-green	5	5
198		5 f. violet and green	5	5
199		10 f. green and magenta	10	10
200		15 f. slate and orange	12	12
201		20 f. grey and orange	20	20
183/201		*Set of 19*	1·40	1·40

1945. *AIR. As T* **24** *of French Equatorial Africa.*

202	50 f. green		20	20
203	100 f. claret		30	30

FRENCH OVERSEAS DEPARTMENT

On 19 March 1946 Guadeloupe became an overseas department of the French Republic.

1946 (8 May). *AIR. Victory. As T* **32** *of French Equatorial Africa.*

204	8 f. red-brown		20	20

1946 (6 June). *AIR. From Chad to the Rhine. As Nos.* 229/34 *of French Equatorial Africa.*

205	5 f. blackish olive		25	25
206	10 f. indigo		25	25
207	15 f. purple		25	25
208	20 f. claret		25	25
209	25 f. brownish black		25	25
210	50 f. purple-brown		25	25
205/210	*Set of 6*		1·40	1·40

64 Woman and Port Basse-Terre

65 Cutting Sugar-Cane

66 Guadeloupe Woman

D **68** Palms and Houses

67 Aeroplane over Guadeloupe Woman and Boats

(Des and eng P. Munier (10 c. to 50 c., 25 f., 40 f., 200 f.),
R. Serres (60 c. to 1 f. 50, 4 f. to 6 f., 100 f.), A. Decaris
(others). Recess)

1947 (2 June). *P* 13. (*a*) *POSTAGE*.

211	64	10 c. brown-lake			5	5
212		30 c. blackish brown			5	5
213		50 c. emerald			5	5
214	65	60 c. sepia			5	5
215		1 f. carmine			5	5
216		1 f. 50, indigo			12	12
217	–	2 f. emerald			25	20
218	–	2 f. 50, carmine			15	15
219	–	3 f. blue			25	20
220	–	4 f. violet			20	20
221	–	5 f. emerald			20	15
222	–	6 f. scarlet			20	15
223	–	10 f. blue			20	15
224	–	15 f. brown-purple			40	30
225	–	20 f. rose-red			50	30
226	**66**	25 f. bright green			55	50
227		40 f. red-orange			70	65

(*b*) *AIR*. *Inscr* "POSTE AERIENNE"

228	–	50 f. purple			1 60	1·25
229	–	100 f. blue			1 60	1·25
230	**67**	200 f. orange-red			1·90	1·40
211/230		*Set of 20*			8·00	6·50

Designs: *Vert* (*As T* **65/6**)—2 f. to 3 f. Women carrying pineapples; 4 f. to 6 f. Woman in kerchief, facing left; 10 f. to 20 f. Picking coffee. *Horiz* (*As T* **67**)—50 f. Aeroplane over village scene; 100 f. Flying-boat landing in bay.

(Des and eng R. Serres. Recess)

1947 (2 June). *POSTAGE DUE. P* 14×13.

D231	D **68**	10 c. black			5	5
D232		30 c. blue-green			5	5
D233		50 c. ultramarine			5	5
D234		1 f. green			5	5
D235		2 f. blue			8	8
D236		3 f. blackish brown			8	8
D237		4 f. bright purple			20	20
D238		5 f. violet			20	20
D239		10 f. red-orange			25	25
D240		20 f. purple			30	30
D231/240		*Set of 10*			1·25	1·25

After supplies of the 1947 issues were exhausted, the stamps of France were used in Guadeloupe.

Leading the field is Gibbons world-famous *Stamp Monthly* offering you an attractive magazine that contains so much for stamp enthusiasts everywhere. Just look at some of the interesting features:

- Latest information on all new issues.
- Well written, lavishly illustrated articles.
- The all-important Supplement to the Stanley Gibbons Catalogue.
- The Crown Agents Gazette with latest news and lists of forthcoming issues.
- Regular Stamp Market, Great Britain and Through the Magnifying Glass features.
- A vast and varied selection of advertisements from the stamp trade.
- Large size format—297 × 210mm.

As a collector you cannot afford to be without *Stamp Monthly*. Enter a subscription, and keep in touch with all events in this ever popular hobby by courtesy of Gibbons — the First Name in Stamps.

Indo-China

1886. 100 Centimes = 1 Franc
1919. 100 Cents = 1 Piastre

French influence began to grow in Indo-China during the 18th century, receiving an impetus after the loss of French power in India. Missionaries were active in the area and the French bishop Pigneau de Béhaine helped Nguyen Anh to become King of Annam in 1801 and Emperor Gia-Long of Vietnam in 1802. Gia-Long's death was followed by a reaction in favour of the Confucians and French missionaries and their converts were persecuted and killed.

A joint Franco-Spanish punitive expedition under Admiral Rigault de Genouilly took Saigon in 1859, and in 1862 the Emperor Tu Duc ceded the eastern provinces of Cochin China to France. The King of Cambodia accepted a French protectorate in 1863 and in 1867 the remainder of Cochin China was occupied. French sovereignty over all Cochin China was recognised by the Treaty of Saigon in 1874.

China had claims of suzerainty over Annam and Tongking and these, combined with attacks on French ports by Chinese "Black Flag" pirates, led to war in 1884–85. China was defeated, and by the Treaty of Tientsin recognised the French protectorate over Annam and Tongking, which had been established by the Treaty of Hué signed with the Emperor Tu Duc in 1883.

By a decree of 17 October 1887 Cambodia, Cochin China, Annam and Tongking were formed into the Indochinese Union, and Laos was added in 1893, France having forced Siam to relinquish the suzerainty which she had held over parts of the territory.

A. COCHIN CHINA

(1) (2) C. CH. (3) (4)

1886 (16 May)–**87**. *French Colonies* (*General issues*) *Type J surch at Saigon as T* 1/3. *P* 14×13½.
1 **1** 5 on 25 c. ochre/*yellow* .. .. .. 35·00 22·00
2 **2** 5 on 2 c. brown/*buff* (1.87) .. .. 2·00 2·00
3 5 on 25 c. ochre/*yellow* (9.6.86) .. 2·00 2·00
4 **3** 5 on 25 c. black/*rose* (2.87) .. .. 7·00 6·00
  a. Surch inverted .. .. .. — 7·50
  b. Surch double .. .. ..
  c. Surch double, T 2+3 .. .. £250 £175
  d. Surch triple, 2×T 2+3

Nos. 4c/d come from a proof sheet of a 5 c. on 25 c. black/*rose* surcharge, as Type 2 which was unsatisfactory. This was then further surcharged as Type 3 and issued.

Nos. 1/4 were issued during shortages of the French Colonies (General issues) 5 c. values. During 1888 a further surcharge as Type 4 was prepared to meet an expected shortage of the 15 c. value. Type 4 was surcharged on Type J 30 c. cinnamon, it being intended to bisect the stamps along the diagonal line. Further supplies of the French Colonies (General issues) 15 c. were, however, received in time, and the surcharge was not issued. (*Price* £6 *un*).

Postage Due stamps with a diagonal surcharge "COCHIN-CHINE" were never officially issued.

Stamps of the French Colonies (General issues) continued in use until 1892, when they were replaced by Indo-China issues.

B. ANNAM AND TONGKING

A & T   A & T   A - T
  1   5   1

(1)   (2)   (3)

(Handstamped at Hanoi)

1888 (21 Jan). *French Colonies* (*General issues*) *Type J.* *P* 14×13½. (*a*) *Surch with T* 1 *or* 2.
1 1 on 2 c. brown/*buff* .. .. .. 6·00 5·50
2 1 on 4 c. purple-brown/*grey* .. .. 4·50 4·00
3 5 on 10 c. black/*lilac* .. .. .. 5·00 4·50

(*b*) *Surch as T* 3
4 1 on 2 c. brown/*buff* .. .. .. 50·00 45·00
5 1 on 4 c. purple-brown/*grey* .. 80·00 75·00
6 5 on 10 c. black/*lilac* .. .. .. 40·00 35·00

Nos. 1/6 were issued during a shortage of French Colonies (General issues) 5 c. stamps. A further surcharge as Type 2, but on the 2 c. brown/*buff*, was prepared but not issued.

The surcharges T 1 and 2 were printed from wooden handstamps. Specialists recognise eight different handstamps as Type 1 and four as Type 2. Because of their construction the handstamps often show signs of wear.

Annam and Tongking continued to use stamps of French Colonies (General issues) until 1892, when they were replaced by Indo-China issues.

C. INDO-CHINA

PRINTERS. All stamps of Indo-China, except Nos. 264 to 327, were printed at the Government Printing Works, Paris, *unless otherwise stated*.

IMPERFORATE STAMPS. Stamps exist imperforate in their issued colours, but these were not valid for postage. Imperforate stamps in other colours are colour trials.

INDO-CHINE   INDO-CHINE   INDO-CHINE 89
1889   1889
5   5   5
R – D   R – D   R   D

(1)   (2)   (3)

Figures "1889" 2½ mm (T 1) or 2 mm high (T 2)

The letters "R–D" are the initials of Messieurs Richaud, Governor of the Colony, and Démars, Director of Posts at Saigon.

1889. *Type J of French Colonies (General issues) surch at Saigon as T* 1/3. *P* 14×13½.

(a) Surch in red (8 Jan)

1	1	5 on 35 c. black/*orange*	..	.. ..	18·00 16·00
	a.	Surch inverted	..	..	£200 £180
	b.	Type **2**	..	..	35·00 32·00
	ba.	Surch inverted	..	..	£250 £225

(b) Surch in black (10 Jan)

2	3	5 on 35 c. black/*orange*	..	..	1·75 1·50
	a.	"89" omitted	..	..	55·00 48·00

Type **2** surcharge occurs at three positions in the pane of 25, the remainder being T **1**.

Nos. 1/2 were issued during a shortage of French Colonies (General issues) 5 c. stamps.

INDO-CHINE   **INDO-CHINE**

TIMBRE   **TIMBRE**

COLIS POSTAUX   **COLIS POSTAUX**   **Colis Postaux**

(P 4)   (P 5)   (P 6)

1891. *PARCEL POST. French Colonies (General issues) Type J. P* 14×13½.

(a) Optd with Type P **4**, *in red at Hanoi*
P4   10 c. black/*lilac* ..   ..   2·50   75

(b) Handstamped with Type P **5**, *in red at Hanoi*
P5   10 c. black/*lilac* ..   ..   75·00 65·00

The lines of type on the handstamp measure 12, 8½ and 16½ mm against similar measurements on Type P **4** of 10½, 6½ and 16 mm.

1892 (Nov)–**96.** *French Colonies Type X inscr* "INDO-CHINE" *in red* (1, 5, 15, 25, 75 c., 1 f.) *or blue (others). P* 14×13½.

6	1 c. black/*azure* ..	..	5	5
7	2 c. brown/*buff* ..	..	10	8
8	4 c. purple-brown/*grey* ..	..	12	8
	a. Name double	..		
9	5 c. green/*pale green*	..	10	5
10	10 c. black/*lilac* ..	..	60	12
11	15 c. blue (*quadrillé paper*)	..	4·50	5
12	20 c. red/*green*	..	1·25	65
13	25 c. black/*rose* ..	..	2·50	12
	a. Grey/*pale rose*	..	2·50	12
14	30 c. cinnamon/*drab*	..	3·25	1·75
15	40 c. red/*yellow* ..	..	3·25	75
16	50 c. carmine/*rose*	..	7·50	3·00
17	75 c. brown/*orange*	..	5·00	2·75
	a. Name inverted (1893)	..	£900	£800
	b. Pair, one with name omitted	..		
18	1 f. olive-green/*toned*	..	7·50	4·00
	a. Name double	..		
19	5 f. mauve/*pale lilac* (1896)	..	22·00	20·00
6/19	*Set of* 14	..	55·00	30·00

1898. *PARCEL POST. No.* 10 *optd at Hanoi with Type P* **6**, *in red.*
P20   10 c. black/*lilac* ..   ..   3·50   3·00

1899–1902. *PARCEL POST. Nos.* 10 *and* 24 *handstamped at Hanoi as Type P* **5**, *but without* "Indo-Chine".

P21	10 c. black/*lilac* ..	8·00	5·00
P22	10 c. rose-red (1902)	7·00	3·25

1900 (Dec)–**01.** *French Colonies Type X. Colours changed. Inscr in blue* (10 *c.) or red (others). P* 14×13½.

23	5 c. pale green ..	..	12	5
	a. Bright yellow-green (1901)	..	25	5
24	10 c. rose-red	..	40	20
25	15 c. grey	..	1·40	12
26	25 c. blue	..	3·75	40
27	50 c. brown/*azure*	..	4·50	1·75
23/27	*Set of* 5	..	9·00	2·25

15   **5**

(7)   8 "Grasset" type   (D 9)

1903. *Surch at Hanoi as T* **7**.

28	X	5 on 15 c. grey (4.12) ..	..	20	15
29		15 on 25 c. blue (6.8)	..	30	15

1904 (Mar)–**06.** *Toned or tinted paper* (1 *c. on white paper). Typo. P* 14×13½.

30	8	1 c. olive-green (6.04)	..	10	5
31		2 c. claret/*yellow* (5.04)	..	12	8
32		4 c. magenta/*azure* (6.04)	..	5	8
33		5 c. deep green (6.04) ..	..	10	8
34		10 c. rose (7.04)	..	30	5
35		15 c. brown/*azure*	..	20	5
36		20 c. red/*green* (6.04)	..	50	15
37		25 c. blue (7.04)	..	3·25	25
38		30 c. brown/*cream* (7.04)	..	90	50
39		35 c. black/*yellow* (1906)	..	3·75	25
40		40 c. black/*greyish* (8.04)	..	90	25
41		50 c. brown/*toned* (7.04)	..	1·25	45
42		75 c. red/*orange* (7.04) ..	..	11·00	6·50
43		1 f. pale olive-green (7.04)	..	5·00	95
44		2 f. brown/*yellow* (8.04)	..	11·00	9·50
45		5 f. violet (7.04)	..	55·00	45·00
46		10 f. red/*green* (8.04)	..	45·00	38·00
30/46		*Set of* 17	..	£125	90·00

1904 (26 June). *POSTAGE DUE. French Colonies (General issues) No.* D79 *surch at Hanoi with Type D* **9**.
D47   5 on 60 c. brown/*buff* ..   ..   2·25   1·60

1905 (22 July). *POSTAGE DUE. French Colonies (General issues) Nos.* D68/9 *surch at Hanoi as Type D* **9**, *in red.*

D48	5 on 40 c. black	..	6·50	1·90
D49	10 on 60 c. black	..	6·50	3·25
D50	30 on 60 c. black	..	6·50	3·25

10 Annamite   11 Cambodian   12 Cambodian

(Des A. Puyplat. Dies eng G. Johannet. Typo)

1907 (July–Oct). *T* **10**, **11** *and vert designs as T* **12**. (*Native women.*) *Heads and figures of value in black. P* 14×13½ *or* 13½×13½ (**12**).

51	10	1 c. sepia (Oct)	..	5	5
52		2 c. brown (Oct)	..	5	5
53		4 c. (Oct)	..	12	12
54		5 c. pale green	..	10	5
55		10 c. scarlet	..	12	5
		a. Centre and value double ..			
56		15 c. violet	..	25	15
57	11	20 c. violet	..	50	30
58		25 c. blue	..	95	12
59		30 c. chocolate	..	1·90	1·25
60		35 c. olive-green	..	25	12
61		40 c. brown	..	65	35
62		45 c. orange	..	2·00	1·25
63		50 c. carmine	..	2·50	1·25
64	12	75 c. orange	..	1·90	1·90
65	—	1 f. lake (Annamies)	..	10·00	3·25
66	—	2 f. green (Muong)	..	3·25	2·50
67	—	5 f. blue (Laotian) ..	..	10·00	6·50
68	—	10 f. violet (Cambodian)	..	22·00	19·00
51/68		*Set of* 18	..	50·00	35·00

These stamps perf 11 are of doubtful status.

D 13 Annamite Dragon

05 (14)

10 (15)

(Des and eng A. Puyplat. Typo)

1908. *POSTAGE DUE. P* 14×13½.

D69	D 13	2 c. black	12	12
D70		4 c. blue	12	12
D71		5 c. green	12	12
D72		10 c. carmine	50	5
D73		15 c. violet	65	45
D74		20 c. deep brown	12	12
D75		30 c. olive-green	15	12
D76		40 c. purple-brown	1·90	1·60
D77		50 c. greenish blue	75	12
D78		60 c. yellow	2·50	2·25
D79		1 f. grey	5·00	3·50
D80		2 f. yellow-brown	3·75	2·75
D81		5 f. vermilion	6·50	4·50
D69/81		*Set of* 13	20·00	14·00

1912 (Nov). *Surch as T* **14/15**.

A. Narrow spacing. B. Wide spacing

			A		B	
69	8	05 on 4 c. magenta/*azure*	1·25	1·10	£160	£160
70		05 on 15 c. brown/*azure* (R.)	5	5	5·00	5·00
71		05 on 30 c. brown/*cream*	10	10	16·00	16·00
72		10 on 40 c. black/*greyish* (R.)	15	15	11·00	11·00
73		10 on 50 c. brown/*toned* (R.)	12	12	11·00	11·00
74		10 on 75 c. red/*orange*	1·10	1·00	19·00	19·00
69/74		*Set of* 6	2·50	2·25	£200	£200

In Type A the space between "0" and "5" is 1½ mm and between "1" and "0" 2½ mm. In Type B the spacing is 2 mm and 3 mm respectively.

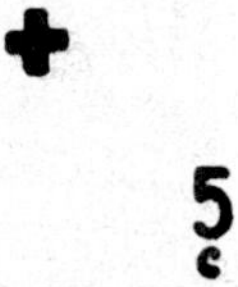

(16)

(17)

INDOCHINE 10 CENTS (18)

1914 (Nov). *Red Cross. Surch at Hanoi with T* **16**, *in red*.

75	10	10 c.+5 c. black and scarlet	12	10

1915 (Feb)–**17**. *Red Cross. Surch in Paris with T* **17**, *in red*.

76	10	5 c.+5 c. black and green (1917)	10	10
		a. Surch double	25·00	25·00
77		10 c.+5 c. black and scarlet	40	30
78		15 c.+5 c. black and violet (1917)	40	30
		a. Surch four times	25·00	25·00
		b. Surch three times	28·00	28·00

1918 (Nov)–**19**. *Nos.* 76/8 *surch in addition with new value in cents, as in T* **18**.

79	4 c. on 5 c.+5 c. black and green	75	50
	a. "4" with closed top	40·00	40·00
80	6 c. on 10 c.+5 c. black and scarlet	65	50
81	8 c. on 15 c.+5 c. black and violet (3.19)	2·50	1·90
	a. "8 CENTS" double	32·00	

1918 (Nov). *French stamps of War Orphans' Fund* (*Nos.* 372/7) *surch as T* **18**, *and sold at double the face value*.

82	10 c. on 15 c.+10 c. grey-green	5	5
	a. "10 CENTS" double	55·00	55·00
83	16 c. on 25 c.+15 c. blue	65	65
84	24 c. on 35 c.+25 c. violet and slate	90	90
	a. Surch double	48·00	
	b. "24 CENTS" double	80·00	80·00
85	40 c. on 50 c.+50 c. brown	95	95
86	80 c. on 1 f.+1 f. carmine	2·50	2·50
87	4 p. on 5 f.+5 f. blue and black	32·00	32·00
	a. "4 PIASTRES" double	£450	£450
82/87	*Set of* 6	32·00	32·00

$\frac{2}{5}$ CENT (19)

1 CENT (20)

12 CENTS (21)

1919 (Jan). *Stamps of* 1907, *surch as T* **19**.

88	10	$\frac{2}{5}$ c. on 1 c. sepia	5	5
89		$\frac{4}{5}$ c. on 2 c. brown	20	12
90		1$\frac{3}{5}$ c. on 4 c. blue (R.)	25	12
91		2 c. on 5 c. pale green	12	5
		a. Surch inverted	15·00	
92		4 c. on 10 c. scarlet (B.)	12	5
		a. "4" with closed top	95	8
		b. "4" and "CENTS" widely spaced	4·50	25
		c. Surch double	15·00	
93		6 c. on 15 c. violet	40	12
		a. Surch inverted	15·00	
94	11	8 c. on 20 c. violet	55	20
95		10 c. on 25 c. blue	40	5
96		12 c. on 30 c. chocolate	1·10	12
97		14 c. on 35 c. olive-green	12	10
		a. "4" with closed top	1·60	75
98		16 c. on 40 c. brown	1·00	30
99		18 c. on 45 c. orange	1·25	65
100		20 c. on 50 c. carmine (B.)	1·60	12
101	12	30 c. on 75 c. orange (B.)	1·60	40
102	–	40 c. on 1 f. lake (B.)	3·25	65
103	–	80 c. on 2 f. green (R.)	3·75	1·25
		a. Surch double	48·00	40·00
104	–	2 p. on 5 f. blue (R.)	22·00	19·00
105	–	4 p. on 10 f. violet (R.)	32·00	30·00
88/105		*Set of* 18	65·00	55·00

1919. *POSTAGE DUE. Surch as T* **19**.

D106	D 13	$\frac{4}{5}$ c. on 2 c. black (R.)	25	12
D107		1$\frac{3}{5}$ c. on 4 c. blue (R.)	25	20
D108		2 c. on 5 c. green	50	25
D109		4 c. on 10 c. carmine (B.)	25	20
D110		6 c. on 15 c. violet (R.)	70	65
D111		8 c. on 20 c. deep brown	1·10	25
D112		12 c. on 30 c. olive-green	1·10	25
D113		16 c. on 40 c. purple-brown	1·10	25
D114		20 c. on 50 c. greenish blue	1·90	1·00
D115		24 c. on 60 c. yellow	50	40
		a. Figure "4" with closed top	4·50	2·50
D116		40 c. on 1 f. grey	50	12
		a. Figure "4" with closed top	4·50	2·50
D117		80 c. on 2 f. yellow-brown	6·50	4·00
D118		2 p. on 5 f. vermilion (B.)	7·50	4·75
		a. Surch double	32·00	25·00
		b. Surch quadruple	32·00	22·00
D106/118		*Set of* 13	20·00	11·00

A further set of surcharges as T **20** and **21** on the 1907 issue was produced in Paris during 1922. Although specimens were supplied to the U.P.U., these stamps were not put on sale in Indo-China (*Set of* 6 £1·50 *un*).

1922 (Apr)–**23**. *As T* **10** *and* **11**, *but value in "cents" or "piastres". Head and value in black* (*except No.* 115). *P* 14×13½.

115	10	$\frac{1}{10}$ c. red and grey (6.23)	5	5
116		$\frac{1}{5}$ c. blue (10.22)	5	5
117		$\frac{2}{5}$ c. olive-brown (10.22)	5	5
		a. Centre and value double		
118		$\frac{4}{5}$ c. cerise/*bluish* (10.22)	5	5
119		1 c. brown (10.22)	5	5
120		2 c. green (10.22)	5	5
121		3 c. violet (10.22)	5	5
122		4 c. orange	5	5
		a. Centre and value double	22·00	22·00
123		5 c. carmine	5	5
		a. Centre and value double	70·00	65·00

124	**11**	6 c. red (10.22)	5	5
125		7 c. olive-green (10.22)	8	8
126		8 c. slate/*lilac* (10.22)	15	12
127		9 c. orange-yellow/*greenish* (10.22)	20	12
128		10 c. blue	5	5
129		11 c. violet	5	5
130		12 c. deep brown	5	5
		a. Centre and value double (11 c. +12 c.)	80·00	80·00
131		15 c. orange (10.22)	12	8
132		20 c. blue/*straw* (10.22)	20	10
133		40 c. scarlet/*bluish* (10.22)	40	20
134		1 p. blue-green/*greenish* (10.22)	90	80
135		2 p. purple/*rose* (10.22)	1·60	1·10
115/135		*Set of* 21	4·00	3·00

Differences in lettering of "CENTS" can be found in printings of the 4, 5, 10, 11 and 12 c.

1922 (Oct). *POSTAGE DUE. As Type* D **13**, *but values in "cents" or "piastres", in black. P* 14×13½.

D136	$\frac{2}{5}$ c. black	5	5
D137	$\frac{4}{5}$ c. scarlet	5	5
D138	1 c. buff	5	5
D139	2 c. green	12	5
D140	3 c. violet	12	5
D141	4 c. orange	10	5
	a. Value double	9·00	9·00
	b. Value omitted	£110	
D142	6 c. olive-green	15	10
D143	8 c. black/*lilac*	12	5
D144	10 c. blue	25	5
D145	12 c. orange/*greenish*	25	15
D146	20 c. blue/*buff*	25	5
D147	40 c. scarlet/*azure*	20	8
D148	1 p. purple/*rose*	75	55
D136/148	*Set of* 13	2·00	1·25

22 Ploughman and Tower of Confucius

23 Bay of Along

24 Ruins of Angkor

25 Wood-carver

26 Temple, Thuat-Luong

27 Foundling of Saigon

(T **22**/7 des Yon-Thay, P. Munier, Pham-Thong, N. Dinh Chi, Lecere and Fouqueray respectively. Dies eng A. Delzers (T **24**, **26**), A. Mignon (others). Typo)

1927 (26 Sept). *P* 14×13½.

136	**22**	$\frac{1}{10}$ c. olive-green	5	5
137		$\frac{1}{5}$ c. yellow	5	5
138		$\frac{2}{5}$ c. pale blue	5	5
139		$\frac{4}{5}$ c. brown	5	5
140		1 c. orange	10	5
141		2 c. green	12	5
142		3 c. indigo	10	5
143		4 c. pink	20	15
144		5 c. violet	12	5
145	**23**	6 c. scarlet	40	5
146		7 c. bistre-brown	10	5
147		8 c. olive-green	20	25
148		9 c. purple	25	25
149		10 c. pale blue	30	12
150		11 c. orange	30	25
151		12 c. slate	12	12
152	**24**	15 c. brown and carmine	1·60	1·50
153		20 c. slate and bright violet	65	25
154	**25**	25 c. magenta and red-brown	1·90	1·25
155		30 c. olive and blue	95	50
156	**26**	40 c. pale blue and vermilion	1·25	45
157		50 c. slate and yellow-green	1·90	65
158	**27**	1 p. black, yellow and blue	3·25	1·90
		a. Yellow omitted	28·00	
159		2 p. blue, orange and red	3·75	2·50
136/159		*Set of* 24	16·00	9·50

Nos. 144/5 in panes of 10 with inscribed margins are from booklets.

D **28** Môt Còt Pagoda, Hanoi

D **29** Annamite Dragon

(Des N. Dinh Chi, eng A. Delzers (D **28**); des Ng Thank Oo, eng A. Mignon (D **29**). Typo)

1927 (26 Sept). *POSTAGE DUE. P* 14×13½ *or* 13½×14 (D **29**).

D160	D **28**	$\frac{2}{5}$ c. orange and maroon	5	5
D161		$\frac{4}{5}$ c. black and violet	5	5
D162		1 c. slate and red	25	20
D163		2 c. olive and green	25	20
D164		3 c. pale blue and plum	25	20
D165		4 c. chocolate and slate-blue	25	20
D166		6 c. red and lake	25	25
D167		8 c. violet and olive	25	25
D168	D **29**	10 c. blue	25	12
D169		12 c. olive-brown	95	75
D170		20 c. carmine	65	12
D171		40 c. green	65	55
D172		1 p. orange-red	3·75	3·00
D160/172		*Set of* 13	7·00	5·50

4 CTS (30) **6 Cts** (31) **10 CTS =** (32)

1931 (13 Apr). *International Colonial Exhibition, Paris. As T* **18**/**20** *of French Sudan, inscr* "INDOCHINE" *and surch with T* **30**/**32**.

160	4 c. on 50 c. mauve	50	25
161	6 c. on 90 c. vermilion	65	65
162	10 c. on 1 f. 50, blue	75	40

33 Junk

34 Ruins at Angkor

35 Rice Fields

36 "Apsara", or dancing Nymph

D **37**

(Des N. Huu-Dau, G. Barlangue, N. Phan-Chanh and To-Ngoc-Van. Photo Vaugirard, Paris)

1931 (16 Nov)–**41**. (*a*) *P* 13½×13.

163	**33**	1/10 c. greenish blue	5	5
164		1/5 c. deep lake	5	5
165		2/5 c. brown-orange	5	5
166		1/2 c. red-brown	5	5
167		4/5 c. violet	5	5
168		1 c. sepia	5	5
169		2 c. green	5	5
170	**34**	3 c. brown	5	5
171		3 c. green (4.10.34)	95	10
172		4 c. deep blue	8	5
173		4 c. blue-green (8.6.38)	10	10
174		4 c. yellow (1940)	5	5
175		5 c. purple	5	5
176		5 c. green (1941)	5	5
177		6 c. vermilion	5	5
178		7 c. grey-black (8.6.38)	5	5
179		8 c. deep lake (8.6.38)	5	5
180		9 c. black/*yellow* (1941)	5	5
181	**35**	10 c. blue	15	5
182		10 c. blue/*pink* (1941)	5	5
183		15 c. sepia	1·10	5
184		15 c. deep blue (1.7.33)	5	5
185		18 c. bright blue (8.6.38)	5	5
186		20 c. carmine	5	5
187		21 c. deep green	5	5
188		22 c. blue-green (8.6.38)	5	5
189		25 c. purple	65	25
190		25 c. deep blue (1941)	5	5
191		30 c. chestnut (18.7.32)	5	5

(*b*) *P* 13½

192	**36**	50 c. sepia	5	5
193		60 c. purple (18.7.32)	5	5
194		70 c. light blue (1941)	5	5
195		1 p. bright green	12	5
196		2 p. scarlet	20	5
163/196		*Set of 34*	4·00	1·75

Nos. 175 and 177 exist in booklet panes of five stamps plus a label bearing a St. Andrew's Cross.

In 1943 30 c., 50 c., 1 p. and 2 p. stamps in these designs, but without "RF", were produced by the Pétain Government in France, but these were not sold in Indo-China.

(Des N. Duc Thuc. Die eng A. Mignon. Typo and photo Vaugirard, Paris)

1931 (16 Nov)–**41**. *POSTAGE DUE. Value in black or blue* (1 *p.*). *P* 13½×13.

D197	**D 37**	1/5 c. red/*yellow* (8.6.38)	5	5
D198		2/5 c. red/*yellow*	5	5
D199		4/5 c. red/*yellow*	5	5
D200		1 c. red/*yellow*	5	5
D201		2 c. red/*yellow*	5	5
D202		2, 5 c. red/*yellow*	5	5
D203		3 c. red/*yellow* (8.6.38)	5	5
D204		4 c. red/*yellow*	5	5
D205		5 c. red/*yellow* (8.6.38)	5	5
D206		6 c. red/*yellow*	5	5
D207		10 c. red/*yellow*	5	5
D208		12 c. red/*yellow*	5	5
D209		14 c. red/*yellow* (8.6.38)	8	8
D210		18 c. red/*yellow* (1941)	10	10
D211		20 c. red/*yellow*	8	8
D212		50 c. red/*yellow*	8	8
D213		1 p. red/*yellow*	40	40
D197/213		*Set of 17*	1·25	1·25

S
E
R
V
I
C
E

SERVICE   SᴇRᵛⁱᶜₑ SERVICE

(O 38)   (O 39)   (O 40)   (O 41)

1933 (27 Feb). *OFFICIAL. Stamps of 1931–32 surch.*

(*a*) *With Type* O **38**

O197	**33**	1 c. sepia (B.)	12	5
O198		2 c. green (B.)	12	10

(*b*) *With Type* O **39**

O199	**34**	3 c. brown (B.)	25	20
O200		a. Opt inverted	19·00	
		4 c. deep blue (R.)	25	20
		a. Opt inverted	19·00	
O201		5 c. purple (B.)	40	5
O202		6 c. vermilion (B.)	40	5

(*c*) *With Type* O **40**

O203	**35**	10 c. blue (R.)	12	10
O204		15 c. sepia (B.)	65	40
O205		20 c. carmine (B.)	50	5
O206		21 c. deep green (B.)	50	40
O207		25 c. purple (B.)	12	5
O208		30 c. red-brown (B.)	50	20

(*d*) *With Type* O **41**

O209	**36**	50 c. sepia (B.)	2·75	90
O210		60 c. purple (B.)	40	40
O211		1 p. bright green (B.)	6·50	2·50
O212		2 p. scarlet (B.)	2·25	2·00
O197/212		*Set of 16*	14·00	8·00

42 Airmail 'Plane   O **43**

(Des G. Barlangue. Photo Vaugirard, Paris)

1933 (1 June)–**49**. *AIR. P* 13½.

197	**42**	1 c. brown	5	5
198		2 c. myrtle-green	5	5
199		5 c. yellow-green	5	5
200		10 c. brown-lake	5	5
201		11 c. carmine (8.6.38)	8	5
202		15 c. blue	5	5
203		16 c. cerise (5.2.41)	5	5
204		20 c. grey-green	10	10
205		30 c. red-brown	5	5
206		36 c. carmine	40	5
207		37 c. bronze-green (8.6.38)	5	5
208		39 c. olive-green (5.2.41)	5	5
209		60 c. deep purple	8	5
210		66 c. bronze-green	10	5
211		67 c. light blue (5.10.38)	20	20
212		69 c. ultramarine (5.2.41)	5	5
213		1 p. black	5	5
214		2 p. orange	20	5
215		5 p. bright violet	40	5
216		10 p. scarlet	65	12
217		20 p. blue-green (13.6.49)	2·50	95
218		30 p. brown (13.6.49)	2·50	95
197/218		*Set of 22*	7·00	3·00

15 values in this design, but without "RF", were prepared by the Pétain Government in France during 1942–44, but these were not sold in Indo-China.

1934 (4 Oct). *OFFICIAL. As T* **11**, *but value in* "CENTS" *or* "PIASTRES", *diag optd as in Type* O **43**. *P* 14×13½.

O219		1 c. olive	12	10
O220		2 c. yellow-brown	12	12
O221		3 c. green	10	10
O222		4 c. rosine	25	20
O223		5 c. orange	5	5
O224		6 c. vermilion	1·00	65
O225		10 c. grey-green (R.)	65	50
O226		15 c. ultramarine	40	25
O227		20 c. black (R.)	25	12
O228		21 c. bright violet	1·90	1·60
O229		25 c. claret	2·25	1·10
O230		30 c. slate-violet	30	25
O231		50 c. magenta	1·90	1·60
O232		60 c. grey	2·50	1·60
O233		1 p. blue (R.)	5·50	3·75
O234		2 p. scarlet	7·50	6·50
O219/234		*Set of 16*	22·00	17·00

44 Emperor Bao Dai of Annam

45 King Sisowath Monivong of Cambodia

(Eng J. Piel. Recess)

1936 (20 Nov). *P* 13.
219	**44**	1 c. brown		12	12
220		2 c. bright green		12	12
221		4 c. bright violet		25	12
222		5 c. brown-lake		20	12
223		10 c. carmine		40	40
224		15 c. blue		40	40
225		20 c. scarlet		50	40
226		30 c. purple		65	50
227		50 c. blue-green		75	75
228		1 p. bright magenta		1·10	65
229		2 p. black		1·25	90
219/229		*Set of 11*		5·00	4·00

(Eng A. Delzers. Recess)

1936 (20 Nov). *P* 13.
230	**45**	1 c. brown		12	12
231		2 c. bright green		12	12
232		4 c. bright violet		25	25
233		5 c. brown-lake		25	25
234		10 c. carmine		65	50
235		15 c. blue		75	65
236		20 c. scarlet		50	40
237		30 c. purple		50	50
238		50 c. blue-green		50	50
239		1 p. bright magenta		65	50
240		2 p. black		75	65
230/240		*Set of 11*		4·50	4·00

Nos. 219/40 were definitive issues used concurrently throughout Indo-China.

1937 (15 Apr). *International Exhibition, Paris. As T 2/7 of French Equatorial Africa.*
241		2 c. bright violet		20	12
242		3 c. green		20	12
243		4 c. carmine		12	12
244		6 c. brown		12	12
245		9 c. scarlet		12	12
246		15 c. blue		12	12
241/246		*Set of 6*		80	65
MS246a		120×100 mm 30 c. slate-lilac (as T 7). Imperf		95	90
		b. Error. Inscription inverted		£225	

46 President Doumer

47 Môt Còt Pagoda, Hanoi

THE WORLD CENTRE FOR FINE STAMPS IS 391 STRAND

(Photo Vaugirard, Paris)

1938 (8 June). *Opening of Trans-Indo-China Railway. P* 13½.
(a) POSTAGE
247	**46**	5 c. carmine		20	12
248		6 c. reddish brown		20	12
249		18 c. bright blue		15	10

(b) AIR. Inscr "POSTE AERIENNE"
250	**46**	37 c. red-orange		5	5
247/250		*Set of 4*		55	35

1938 (24 Oct). *International Anti-Cancer Fund. As T 14 of French Equatorial Africa.*
251		18 c.+5 c. ultramarine		2·00	2·00

1939 (10 May). *New York World's Fair. As T 17 of French Equatorial Africa.*
252		13 c. lake		5	5
253		23 c. ultramarine		10	10

(Des E. Feltesse. Eng Cerutti-Maori. Recess)

1939 (12 June). *San Francisco International Exhib'··· ··· P* 13.
254	**47**	6 c. sepia		20	20
255		9 c. scarlet		12	12
256		23 c. ultramarine		12	12
257		39 c. purple		20	20
254/257		*Set of 4*		60	60

1939 (5 July). *150th Anniv of French Revolution. As T 18 of French Equatorial Africa. (a) POSTAGE*
258		6 c.+2 c. green and black		1·50	1·50
259		7 c.+3 c. brown and black		1·50	1·50
260		9 c.+4 c. red-orange and black		1·50	1·50
261		13 c.+10 c. carmine and black		1·50	1·50
262		23 c.+20 c. blue and black		1·50	1·50

(b) AIR
263		39 c.+40 c. black		5·00	5·00
258/263		*Set of 6*		11·00	11·00

JAPANESE OCCUPATION

Following the defeat of France in June 1940 Japan forced the Vichy authorities to grant bases for her troops in Indo-China. Following an attack by Thailand on southern Indo-China, during January 1941 Japan "mediated" between the Thai and Vichy French authorities, awarding the Cambodian provinces of Battambang and Siemreap, together with Laotian territory west of the Mekong, to Thailand. These areas were returned to Indo-China in October 1946.

During July 1941 the Japanese army completed the occupation of Indo-China, although the Vichy French administration was allowed to continue as a puppet regime.

A number of issues were prepared in France for Indo-China by the Pétain Government, but none of these was put on sale there.

PRINTERS. Nos. 264 to 327 were printed or surcharged by the Imprimerie d'Extrême-Orient, Hanoi.

48 King Sihanouk of Cambodia

49 Processional Elephant

(50)

1941 (15 Oct). *Coronation of King Sihanouk. Litho. No gum. P* 11½.
264	**48**	1 c. orange-red		12	12
265		6 c. violet		25	25
266		25 c. blue		5·00	3·75

1942 (29 Mar). *Fêtes of Nam-Giao. Litho. No gum. P 11½.*
267 **49** 3 c. brown 20 20
268 6 c. carmine 20 20

1942. *No. 189 surch with T 50.*
269 **35** 10 c. on 25 c. purple 5 5

10ᶜ   +2ᶜ

≡

51 Hanoi University   (52)

1942 (1 June)—**44**. *University Fund. Litho. No gum. P 11½.*
　　　　(a) Without surcharge
270 **51** 6 c.+2 c. carmine 10 10
　　　a. Perf 13½ .. .. ..
271 15 c.+5 c. purple 12 12
　(b) *No. 270 surch as T 52 but spacing arranged to fit design*
272 **51** 10 c.+2 c. on 6 c.+2 c. carm (10.6.44) 5 5
　　　a. Perf 13½
Stamps perf 13½ were a second printing made for surcharging, but 5,000 were sold without surcharge (No. 270a).

53 Marshal   54 Shield and   55 Emperor
　Pétain　　　　　　 Sword　　　　　　　 Bao Dai of
　　　　　　　　　　　　　　　　　　　　 Annam

56 King   57 Empress   58 King
　Sihanouk of　 Nam-Phuong of　　 Sisavang-Vong
　Cambodia　　　 Annam　　　　　　 of Laos

1942 (1 July)—**44**. *Litho. No gum. P 11½.*
273 **53** 1 c. brown (4.9.42) 5 5
　　　a. Perf 13½ .. .. ..
274 3 c. bistre-brown (17.6.43) .. 5 5
　　　a. Perf 13½ .. .. ..
　　　b. Perf 11½×13½ .. .. ..
275 6 c. carmine 5 5
　　　a. Perf 13½ .. .. ..
　　　b. Perf 11½×13½ .. .. ..
276 10 c. green (1.12.43) 5 5
277 40 c. blue (15.1.43) 5 5
278 40 c. slate (1.4.44) 25 25
273/278 *Set of 6* 45 45

1942 (1 Aug)—**44**. *National Relief Fund. Litho. No gum. P 11½.* (a) *Without surcharge.*
279 **54** 6 c.+2 c. carmine and blue 10 10
280 15 c.+5 c. violet-black, carmine & blue 12 12
　　　a. Imperf between (vert pair) ..
　(b) *No. 279 surch as T 52, but surch spaced to fit design*
281 **54** 10 c.+2 c. on 6 c.+2 c. carmine and
　　　blue (15.3.44) 5 5

1942 (1 Sept)—**43**. *Litho. No gum. P 13½ and (Nos. 283/8) 11½.*
282 **55** ½ c. purple-brown (1.11.42) .. 5 5
283 **56** 1 c. purple-brown (10.3.43) .. 12 10
284 **58** 1 c. bistre-brown (10.3.43) .. 5 5
285 **55** 6 c. rose 15 10
286 **56** 6 c. carmine (10.5.43) .. 5 5
287 **57** 6 c. rose 12 10
288 **58** 6 c. rose (1.6.43) 5 5
282/288 *Set of 7* 55 45

59 Saigon Fair

1942 (20 Dec). *Saigon Fair. Litho. No gum. P 11½–13½.*
289 **59** 6 c. carmine 5 5

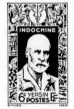

60 Alexandre   61 Alexandre de Rhodes
　Yersin

1943 (10 June)—**45**. *As T 60/1 (various portraits). Litho. No gum. P 11½.*
290 **60** 6 c. rose (5.10.43) 15 15
291 15 c. brown-purple (10.12.44) .. 5 5
292 **61** 15 c. brown-purple (10.3.45) .. 5 5
293 20 c. brown-red 15 15
294 **61** 30 c. yellow-brown (15.6.43) .. 5 5
　　　a. Perf 13½ .. .. ..
　　　b. Perf 11½×13½ .. .. ..
　　　c. Orange-brown .. ..
295 **60** $1 green (10.1.45) 5 5
290/295 *Set of 6* 50 50
Portrait: *Vert*—20 c. Pigneau de Béhaine, bishop of Adran. Nos. 292 and 295 have "EF" replaced by second face value. No. 294 has "EF" instead of "RF".

D 62   63 Do-Huu-Vi

(Des T. Chuoc. Litho)

1943–44. *POSTAGE DUE. Type D* **62** *(1 c. to 10 c.) and similar type with modified background. No gum. P 11½–13½.*
D296	1 c. red/*yellow* (10.6.44)	..	..	5	5
D297	2 c. red/*yellow* (15.7.43)	..	..	5	5
D298	3 c. red/*yellow* (15.7.43)	..	..	5	5
D299	4 c. red/*yellow* (10.6.44)	..	..	5	5
D300	6 c. red/*yellow* (26.8.43)	..	..	5	5
D301	10 c. red/*yellow* (26.8.43)	..	..	5	5
D302	12 c. blue/*salmon* (26.8.43)	..	..	5	5
D303	20 c. blue/*salmon* (26.8.43)	..	..	5	5
D304	30 c. blue/*salmon* (26.8.43)	..	..	5	5
D296/304	*Set of 9*	..	..	40	40

1943 (1 Aug)–**44.** *Famous Airmen. Litho. No gum. P 11½.*
296	**63**	6 c.+2 c. rose	..	..	8	8
297	–	6 c.+2 c. rose (15.11.43)	..	..	5	5

Nos. 296/7 surch with T **52**, *or similarly* (10.2.44)
298	**63**	10 c.+2 c. on 6 c.+2 c. rose	..	..	5	5
299	–	10 c.+2 c. on 6 c.+2 c. rose	..	..	5	5

Design: *Vert* (22×30 *mm*)—No. 297, Roland Garros.

67 De Lanessan **68** Paul Doumer

1944. *Famous Governors. As T* **67/8** (*various portraits*). *Litho. No gum. P 11½–13½.*
313	1 c. olive-brown (10.10)	..	..	5	5
314	1 c. grey-brown (10.12)	..	..	5	5
315	2 c. mauve (15.5)	..	..	5	5
	a. Imperf between (horiz pair)	..			
316	4 c. yellow-orange (10.2)	..	..	5	5
317	4 c. brown (15.6)	..	..	5	5
318	5 c. brown-purple (1.11)	..	..	5	5
319	10 c. grey-green (5.1)	..	..	5	5
320	10 c. grey-green (5.1)	..	..	5	5
321	10 c. grey-green (10.9)	..	..	5	5
322	10 c. grey-green (10.10)	..	..	10	5
323	15 c. purple (16.10)	..	..	5	5
313/323	*Set of 11*	..	..	55	50

Portraits: *Horiz*—1 c. (No. 313), 10 c. (No. 322) Van Vollenhoven; 1 c. (No. 314), 15 c., *T* **67**; 4 c. (No. 316), 10 c. (No. 319) Auguste Pavie. *Vert*—2 c., 4 c. (No. 317), 10 c. (No. 320), *T* **68**; 5 c., 10 c. (No. 321) Pierre Pasquier.

64 Doudart de Lagrée **65** La Grandière

1943 (16 Aug)–**45.** *Famous Sailors. As T* **64/5** (*various portraits*). *Litho. No gum. P 11½–13½.*
300	1 c. grey-brown (10.1.45)	..	..	5	5
301	1 c. olive-bistre (16.9.43)	..	..	10	10
302	1 c. olive-bistre	..	..	5	5
303	5 c. brown (10.1.45)	..	..	5	5
304	6 c. rose (1.9.43)	..	..	5	5
305	6 c. rose (1.9.43)	..	..	5	5
306	6 c. rose (5.10.43)	..	..	5	5
307	10 c. grey-green (10.8.44)	..	..	5	5
308	15 c. purple (10.11.44)	..	..	5	5
309	20 c. brown-red (10.8.44)	..	..	5	5
310	40 c. ultramarine (10.11.44)	..	..	5	5
311	1 p. yellow-green (27.7.44)	..	..	8	8
300/311	*Set of 12*	..	..	60	60

Portraits: *Vert*—1 c. (No. 300), 15 c., 40 c. *T* **64**; 6 c. (No. 306) Chasseloup Laubat; 10 c., 20 c., 1 p. Charner. *Horiz*—1 c. (No. 301) F. Garnier; 1 c. (No. 302), 5 c. *T* **65**; 6 c. (No. 304), Courbet; 6 c. (No. 305) Rigault de Genouilly.
Similar 3 c. and 15 c. designs, showing Courbet and Garnier, were prepared, but not issued.

69 Athlete **70** Orleans Cathedral

1944 (10 July). *Juvenile Sports. Litho. No gum. P 11½.*
324	**69**	10 c. purple and·yellow	..	..	45	45
325		50 c. brown-red	..	..	45	45

1944 (20 Dec). *Martyr Cities. Litho. No gum. P 11½.*
326	**70**	15 c.+60 c. brown-purple	..	..	20	15
327		40 c.+1 p. 10, blue	..	..	20	20

RETURN TO FRENCH CONTROL

On 9 March 1945 the Japanese declared that rule by the Vichy colonial authorities was at an end, and appointed Emperor Bao Dai of Annam head of an autonomous state of Vietnam. Cambodia had been previously declared independent by King Norodom Sihanouk in March 1944. Bao Dai continued in office until after the surrender of Japan, abdicating on 23 August 1945.

During the preceding months the Viet Minh groups of resistance fighters had been formed into a National Liberation Army under Ho Chi Minh. Based in Tongking the Liberation Army seized Hanoi on 17 August and by the end of August had extended their authority into Annam and Cochin China. On 2 September Ho Chi Minh proclaimed the independence of the Democratic Republic of Vietnam (*see Vietnam*).

French troops began to arrive in Indo-China during October 1945, replacing the British forces in Cochin China and Annam and Chinese occupation troops in Tongking which had moved into these areas following the Japanese surrender. French authority was quickly re-established over large areas, including Hanoi, and further French issues were released.

66 "Family, Homeland and Labour"

1943 (5 Nov). *Third Anniv of National Revolution. Litho. No gum. P 11½.*
312	**66**	6 c. rose	..	..	..	5	5

INDOCHINE

50 c + 50 c

(71) (72)

1945. *Map of French Colonial Empire, as T **149** of France, but with Cross of Lorraine, "1945" and surch as T **71**.* P 13

328	50 c.+50 c. on 2 f. olive-green ..	..	8	8
329	1 p.+1 p. on 2 f. red-brown ..	..	8	8
330	2 p.+2 p. on 2 f. slate-grey ..	..	15	15

1946 (8 May). *AIR. Victory. As T **32** of French Equatorial Africa.*

331	80 c. orange ..	..	..	..	12	10

1946 (6 June). *AIR. From Chad to the Rhine. As Nos.* 229/34 *of French Equatorial Africa.*

332	50 c. emerald-green	..	..	8	8
333	1 p. mauve ..	..	..	8	8
334	1 p. 50, brown-red	..	..	8	8
335	2 p. purple ..	..	..	10	10
336	2 p. 50, blue	..	..	12	12
337	5 p. brown-red ..	..	..	20	20
332/337	*Set of 6* ..	..	..	60	60

1946 (15 Aug). *Unissued stamps similar to T **24** with inset portrait of Marshal Pétain, optd with T **72**.* P 12½×12.

338	10 c. carmine ..	..	..	..	5	5
339	25 c. blue ..	..	..	..	20	20

1949 (4 July). *AIR. 75th Anniv of Universal Postal Union. As T **39** of French Equatorial Africa.*

340	3 p. blue, violet, olive and red ..	..	55	50

On 14 June 1949 Tongking, Annam and Cochin China were joined as the independent state of Vietnam, within the French Union, with Bao Dai as Head of State. Laos and Cambodia became independent states, within the French Union, on 19 July and 8 November 1949 respectively. For later issues see CAMBODIA, LAOS, VIETNAM.

PHILATELIC TERMS ILLUSTRATED

This successful STAMP MONTHLY series has now been brought together in a snappy black and yellow binding and published as a useful addition to Stanley Gibbons range of essential handbooks for keen stamp collectors. Within its 192 pages this handy limp-bound volume houses a veritable mine of useful information on the words and phrases used in philately. It describes and illustrates printing processes and watermarks, papers and perforations, errors and varieties . . . and it does all this IN COLOUR. Indeed, there are 92 full page plates in colour, plus many black and white illustrations, making it

FANTASTIC VALUE AT ONLY £1·95 POST PAID FROM

**Stanley Gibbons Publications Ltd
391 Strand, London WC2R 0LX**

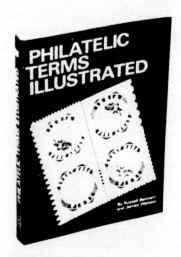

INDO-CHINESE POST OFFICES IN CHINA

1901. 100 Centimes=1 Franc

1918. 100 Cents=1 Piastre

The following are surcharged or overprinted on the "Tablet" Type X inscribed "INDO-CHINE" (see under French Post Offices in China) or on other stamps of Indo-China.

A. CANTON

An Indo-Chinese Post Office was opened at Canton, the chief city of Kwangtung province, on 15 June 1901.

CANTON

CANTON

州 廣

(1)

CANTON

仙 四

(2)

花銀八厘

(3)

1901 (15 June). *Type* X *("Tablet") inscr* "INDO-CHINE" *optd with T* **1** (="CANTON" *in French and Chinese), in carmine, at Hanoi.*

1	X	1 c. black/*azure*	..	40	40
2		2 c. brown/*buff*	..	40	40
3		4 c. purple-brown/*grey*		50	50
4		5 c. bright yellow-green		50	50
5		5 c. green/*green*	..	£110	£110
6		10 c. black/*lilac* ..		1·00	1·00
7		15 c. blue/*quadrillé*	..	65	65
8		15 c. grey	..	1·00	1·00
9		20 c. red/*green* ..		1·90	1·90
10		25 c. black/*rose* ..		1·90	1·90
11		30 c. cinnamon/*drab*		3·75	3·75
12		40 c. red/*yellow*		5·00	5·00
13		50 c. carmine/*rose*		6·50	6·50
14		75 c. brown/*orange*		8·00	8·00
15		1 f. olive-green/*toned* ..		6·50	6·50
16		5 f. mauve/*pale lilac*	..	55·00	55·00
1/16		*Set of 16*	..	£180	£180

1903–04. *As last but surch as T* **2** (*Chinese characters represent value), in black, at Hanoi.*

17	X	1 c. black/*azure*		65	65
18		2 c. brown/*buff*		65	65
19		4 c. purple-brown/*grey*		65	65
20		5 c. bright yellow-green		50	40
21		10 c. rose-red	..	50	40
22		15 c. grey	..	65	50
23		20 c. red/*green* ..		3·25	3·25
24		25 c. blue		1·40	1·00
25		25 c. black/*rose* ..		1·40	90
26		30 c. cinnamon/*drab*		3·75	3·25
27		40 c. red/*yellow*		11·00	7·50
28		50 c. carmine/*rose*		80·00	70·00
29		50 c. brown/*azure* (1904)		17·00	15·00
30		75 c. brown/*orange*		17·00	15·00
		a. "INDO-CHINE" in label inverted ..		£7000	
31		1 f. olive-green/*toned* ..		15·00	15·00
32		5 f. mauve/*pale lilac*		15·00	18·00
17/32		*Set of 16*	..	£150	£140

Only two copies are known of No. 30a.

1906 (Oct). *As last and T* **8** *but surch as T* **3***, at Hanoi.*

33	**8**	1 c. olive-green (R.)	..	40	40
34		2 c. claret/*yellow*		40	40
35		4 c. magenta/*azure* (R.)..		40	40
36		5 c. deep green (R.)	..	50	40
37		10 c. rose		65	65
38		15 c. brown/*azure*		75	75
39		20 c. red/*green*		50	50
40		25 c. blue	..	50	50
41		30 c. brown/*cream*		75	65
42		35 c. black/*yellow* (R.)		50	25
43		40 c. black/*greyish* (R.)	..	65	65
44		50 c. brown/*toned*	..	1·00	1·00
45	X	75 c. brown/*orange* (R.) ..		11·00	11·00

46	**8**	1 f. pale olive-green	..	2·50	2·50
47		2 f. brown/*yellow* (R.) ..		7·50	6·50
48	X	5 f. mauve/*pale lilac*	..	16·00	15·00
49	**8**	10 f. red/*green*	..	16·00	16·00
33/49		*Set of 17*	..	55·00	50·00

In the first printing the surcharge was applied at a separate operation; the ink is bright and clear. There were two printings in 1908 in which the overprint and surcharge were applied together and the ink is dull and paler.

CANTON

肆圓

CANTON

壹角

(4)

CANTON

(5)

1908. *Stamps of Indo-China, 1907, surch as T* **4** (1 *c. to 50 c.*) *or* **5** *(others), in Paris. Centre and value in black.*

50	**10**	1 c. sepia (R.) ..		25	25
51		2 c. brown (R.)		25	25
52		4 c. blue (R.)		40	25
53		5 c. pale green (R.)		40	25
54		10 c. scarlet (B.)		40	40
		a. With surch of 5 c.		6·50	6·50
55		15 c. violet (R.)	..	65	65
56	**11**	20 c. violet (R.)		65	65
57		25 c. blue (R.)		65	65
58		30 c. chocolate (R.)		1·25	1·25
59		35 c. olive-green (R.)		1·25	1·25
60		40 c. brown (R.)		1·50	1·50
61		50 c. carmine (B.)		1·90	1·50
62	**12**	75 c. orange (B.)		1·90	1·90
63	–	1 f. lake (B.)		3·25	3·25
64	–	2 f. green (R.)		7·50	7·00
65	–	5 f. blue (R.)		9·50	9·50
66	–	10 f. violet (R.)	..	19·00	17·00
50/66		*Set of 17*		45·00	42·00

No. 54a was surcharged in complete sheets.

⅖ CENT

肆分

(6)

貳分

(a) Normal   (b) Error

1919 (Jan). *As last, further surch in new currency as T* **6***, in Paris.*

67	**10**	⅖ c. on 1 c. sepia ..		25	25
68		⅘ c. on 2 c. brown		25	25
69		1⅗ c. on 4 c. blue (R.)		25	25
70		2 c. on 5 c. pale green		25	25
71		4 c. on 10 c. scarlet (B.) (a)..		25	25
		a. "4" with closed top		2·50	2·50
		b. Chinese "2" for "4" (b)		3·00	3·00
72		6 c. on 15 c. violet		40	25
73	**11**	8 c. on 20 c. violet		40	40
74		10 c. on 25 c. blue		50	25
75		12 c. on 30 c. chocolate		50	25
		a. "12 CENTS" double		19·00	19·00
76		14 c. on 35 c. olive-green		50	25
		a. "4" with closed top		1·50	1·50
77		16 c. on 40 c. brown		50	40
78		20 c. on 50 c. carmine (R.)		50	40
79	**12**	30 c. on 75 c. orange (B.)		50	25
		a. "30 CENTS" double		75·00	75·00
80	–	40 c. on 1 f. lake (B.)		1·90	1·10
81	–	80 c. on 2 f. green (R.)		1·90	1·90
82	–	2 pi. on 5 f. blue (R.)		2·50	2·00
83	–	4 pi. on 10 f. violet (R.)		2·50	2·00
67/83		*Set of 17*	..	12·00	9·50

This office was closed down on 31 December 1922.

Indo-China—POST OFFICES IN CHINA

B. CHUNGKING

An Indo-Chinese Post Office was opened at Chungking, the chief city of Szechwan province, on 7 February 1902.

Stamps of Indo-China, 1892–1902, overprinted "TCHONG-KING" only, in small capitals, in red or black, were sold at Chungking and used for franking letters. They were not, however, officially authorised.

TCHONGKING

四之五仙

(1)

Tch'ong
K'ing

花銀八厘

(2)

1903–04. *Type X ("Tablet") inscr "INDO-CHINE" surch as T 1, at Hanoi.*

1	X	1 c. black/*azure*	..	75	75
2		2 c. brown/*buff*	..	75	75
3		4 c. purple-brown/*grey*	..	75	75
4		5 c. pale green ..	..	75	75
5		10 c. rose-red	..	75	75
6		15 c. grey	..	75	75
7		20 c. red/*green* ..	..	75	75
8		25 c. blue	..	9·00	9·00
9		25 c. black/*rose* ..	..	1·10	1·10
10		30 c. cinnamon/*drab*	..	1·75	1·75
11		40 c. red/*yellow*	..	9·50	9·50
12		50 c. carmine/*rose*	..	50·00	50·00
13		50 c. brown/*azure* (1904)	..	28·00	28·00
14		75 c. brown/*orange*	..	9·00	9·00
15		1 f. olive-green/*toned* ..	..	9·50	9·50
16		5 f. mauve/*pale lilac*	..	15·00	15·00
1/16		*Set of 16*	..	£120	£120

1906 (Oct). *Stamps of Indo-China surch as T 2, at Hanoi.*

17	8	1 c. olive-green (R.)	..	45	45
18		2 c. claret/*yellow*	..	45	45
19		4 c. magenta/*azure* (R.)	..	45	45
20		5 c. deep green (R.)	..	45	45
21		10 c. rose	..	45	45
22		15 c. brown/*azure* ..	..	1·25	1·25
23		20 c. red/*green*	..	45	45
24		25 c. blue	..	75	75
25		30 c. brown/*cream* ..	..	70	70
26		35 c. black/*yellow* (R.)	..	70	70
27		40 c. black/*greyish* (R.)	..	1·40	1·40
28		50 c. brown/*toned* ..	..	1·40	1·40
29	X	75 c. brown/*orange* (R.)	..	7·50	7·50
30	8	1 f. pale olive-green	..	·5·00	5·00
31		2 f. brown/*yellow* (R.)	..	5·00	5·00
32	X	5 f. mauve/*pale lilac*	..	24·00	24·00
33	8	10 f. red/*green*	..	28·00	28·00
17/33		*Set of 17*	..	70·00	70·00

The note about printings under No. 49 of Canton also applies here.

贰圆

TCHONGKING

云南

(3)

TCHONGKING

(4)

1908. *Stamps of Indo-China, 1907, surch as T 3 (1 c. to 50 c.) or 4 (others), in Paris. Centre and value in black.*

34	10	1 c. sepia (R.)			5	5
35		2 c. brown (R.)	..	..	8	8
36		4 c. blue (R.)	..	..	12	12
37		5 c. pale green (R.)	..	..	30	30
38		10 c. scarlet (B.)	..	..	45	45
39		15 c. violet (R.)	..	..	60	60
40	11	20 c. violet (R.)	..	..	65	65
41		25 c. blue (R.)	..	..	65	65
42		30 c. chocolate (R.)	..	..	70	70
43		35 c. olive-green (R.)	..	..	1·10	1·10
44		40 c. brown (R.)	..	..	2·75	2·75
45		50 c. carmine (B.)	..	..	1·90	1·90
46	12	75 c. orange (B.)	..	..	1·90	1·90
47	–	1 f. lake (B.)	..	..	1·90	1·90
48	–	2 f. green (R.)	..	..	19·00	19·00
49	–	5 f. blue (R.)	..	..	5·50	5·50
50	–	10 f. violet (R.)	..	..	65·00	65·00
34/50		*Set of 17*	..	..	£100	£100

1919 (Jan). *As last, further surch in new currency as T 6 of Canton, in Paris.*

51	10	⅖ c. on 1 c. sepia ..	..	..	12	10
52		⅘ c. on 2 c. brown	..	..	12	12
53		1⅗ c. on 4 c. blue (R.)	..	..	25	20
54		2 c. on 5 c. brown	..	..	15	15
55		4 c. on 10 c. scarlet (B.)	..	..	15	12
56		6 c. on 15 c. violet	..	..	15	10
57	11	8 c. on 20 c. violet	..	..	15	10
58		10 c. on 25 c. blue	..	..	25	25
59		12 c. on 30 c. chocolate	..	..	30	25
60		14 c. on 35 c. olive-green	..	..	30	15
		a. "4" with closed top	..	..	2·75	
61		16 c. on 40 c. brown	..	..	45	30
		a. T 4 double	..	..	19·00	
62		20 c. on 50 c. carmine (B.)	..	..	1·90	1·90
63	12	30 c. on 75 c. orange (B.)	..	..	40	25
64	–	40 c. on 1 f. lake (B.)	..	..	45	45
65	–	80 c. on 2 f. green (R.)	..	..	90	80
66	–	2 pi. on 5 f. blue (R.)	..	..	1·40	1·40
67	–	4 pi. on 10 f. violet (R.)	..	..	1·40	1·40
51/67		*Set of 17*	..	..	7·50	6·50

This office was closed down on 31 December 1922.

C. HOIHOW

An Indo-Chinese Post Office was opened at Hoihow, the chief town of the island of Hainan, on 15 May 1900.

HOI HAO

州瓊

(1)

HOI HAO

仙六

(2)

HOI-HAO

花銀八厘

(3)

1901. *Type X ("Tablet") inscr "INDO-CHINE" optd with T 1 (="HOI HAO" in French and Chinese), in carmine, at Hanoi.*

1	X	1 c. black/*azure*	..	65	65
2		2 c. brown/*buff*	..	65	65
3		4 c. purple-brown/*grey*	..	65	65
4		5 c. pale green ..	..	65	65
5		10 c. black/*lilac*	..	90	90
6		15 c. blue/*quadrillé*	..	£350	£150
7		15 c. grey	..	40	40
8		20 c. red/*green* ..	..	2·50	2·50
9		25 c. black/*rose* ..	..	1·25	1·25
10		30 c. cinnamon/*drab*	..	5·00	4·50
11		40 c. red/*yellow*	..	5·00	4·50
12		50 c. carmine/*rose*	..	7·50	6·50
13		75 c. brown/*orange*	..	45·00	38·00
14		1 f. olive-green/*toned* ..	..	£150	£150
15		5 f. mauve/*pale lilac*	..	£130	£120

1903–04. *As last but surch as T 2 (Chinese characters represent value), in black, at Hanoi.*

16		1 c. black/*azure* ..	..	20	20
17		2 c. brown/*buff* ..	..	20	20
18		4 c. purple-brown/*grey* ..	..	40	40
19		5 c. pale green	..	40	40
20		10 c. rose-red	..	40	40

21	**15**	5 c. grey	.. .. ..	30	30		
22		20 c. red/*green*	.. .. ..	1·00	1·00		
23		25 c. blue	.. .. ..	50	50		
24		25 c. black/*rose*	.. .. ..	45	45		
25		30 c. cinnamon/*drab*	.. ..	65	65		
26		40 c. red/*yellow*	.. ..	7·50	7·50		
27		50 c. carmine/*rose*	.. ..	7·50	7·50		
28		50 c. brown/*azure* (1904)	..	22·00	22·00		
29		75 c. brown/*orange*	.. ..	7·50	7·50		
		a. "INDO-CHINE" inverted	..	£5000			
30		1 f. olive-green/*toned*	..	7·50	7·50		
31		5 f. mauve/*pale lilac*	..	38·00	38·00		
16/31		*Set of 16*	.. .. ..	85·00	85·00		

1906 (Oct). *As last and* **T 8** *but surch as* **T 3**, *at Hanoi.*

32	**8**	1 c. olive-green (R.)	..	40	40
33		2 c. claret/*yellow* ..	..	40	40
34		4 c. magenta/*azure* (R.)	..	50	50
35		5 c. deep green (R.)	..	75	75
36		10 c. rose	.. ..	75	75
37		15 c. brown/*azure* ..	..	80	80
38		20 c. red/*green*	..	80	80
39		25 c. blue	.. ..	95	95
40		30 c. brown/*cream* ..	..	95	95
41		35 c. black/*yellow* (R.)	..	1·25	1·25
42		40 c. black/*greyish* (R.)	..	1·90	1·90
43		50 c. brown/*toned* ..	..	2·50	2·50
44	X	75 c. brown/*orange* (R.)	..	8·00	8·00
45	**8**	1 f. pale olive-green	..	7·50	7·50
46		2 f. brown/*yellow* (R.)	..	7·50	7·50
47	X	5 f. mauve/*pale lilac*	..	25·00	25·00
48	**8**	10 f. red/*green*	..	25·00	25·00
32/48		*Set of 17*	.. ..	75·00	75·00

The note about printings under No. 49 of Canton also applies here.

HOI-HAO

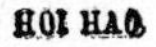

(4) 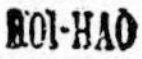   (5)

1908. *Stamps of Indo-China,* 1907, *surch as* **T 4** (1 c. *to* 50 c.) *or* **5** (*others*), *in Paris. Centre and value in black.*

49	**10**	1 c. sepia (R.)	.. ..	12	12
50		2 c. brown (R.) ..	..	12	12
51		4 c. blue (R.)	.. ..	25	25
52		5 c. pale green (R.)	..	40	40
53		10 c. scarlet (B.)	..	40	40
54		15 c. violet (R.)	..	80	80
55	**11**	20 c. violet (R.)	..	1·25	1·25
56		25 c. blue (R.)	..	80	80
57		30 c. chocolate (R.)	..	80	80
58		35 c. olive-green (R.)	..	1·25	1·25
59		40 c. brown (R.) ..	..	1·00	1·00
60		50 c. carmine (R.) ..	..	1·40	1·40
61	**12**	75 c. orange (B.) ..	..	1·50	1·50
62	–	1 f. lake (B.)	..	3·50	3·50
63	–	2 f. green (R.)	..	7·50	7·50
64	–	5 f. blue (R.)	..	13·00	13·00
65	–	10 f. violet (R.)	..	19·00	19·00
49/65		*Set of 17*	..	50·00	50·00

1919 (Jan). *As last, further surch in new currency as* **T 6** *of Canton, in Paris.*

66	**10**	⅖ c. on 1 c. sepia ..	..	20	20
67		⅘ c. on 2 c. brown	..	20	20
68		1⅗ c. on 4 c. blue (R.)	..	25	25
69		2 c. on 5 c. pale green	..	20	20
70		4 c. on 10 c. scarlet (B.) (*a*)	..	30	30
		a. Chinese "2" for "4" (*b*)	..	10·00	10·00
71		6 c. on 15 c. violet	..	30	30

72	**11**	8 c. on 20 c. violet	..	40	40
		a. "CENT" for "CENTS"	..	18·00	18·00
73		10 c. on 25 c. blue	..	1·00	1·00
74		12 c. on 30 c. chocolate ..	..	25	25
75		14 c. on 35 c. olive-green	..	30	30
		a. "4" with closed top	..	2·50	2·50
76		16 c. on 40 c. brown	..	25	25
77		20 c. on 50 c. carmine (B.)	..	40	40
78	**12**	30 c. on 75 c. orange (B.)	..	65	65
79	–	40 c. on 1 f. lake (B.)	..	1·60	1·60
80	–	80 c. on 2 f. green (R.)	..	3·75	3·75
81	–	2 pi. on 5 f. blue (R.)	..	11·00	11·00
		a. "2 PIASTRES" treble	..	75·00	
82	–	4 pi. on 10 f. violet (R.) ..	..	45·00	45·00
66/82		*Set of 17*	.. ..	60·00	60·00

This office was closed down on 31 December 1922.

D. KWANGCHOW

(French Leased Territory)

The territory of Kwangchow, with an area of 328 square miles, was leased for 99 years by France from China, as a coaling station and naval base, in April 1898. In January 1900 it was placed under the authority of the Governor-General of Indo-China.

Although Kwangchow had a different status from the towns with Indo-Chinese Post Offices, these stamps are listed here for convenience.

貳 圓

KOUANG-TCHÉOU

Kouang Tchéou·Wan

花銀八厘   毫角   KOUANG-TCHÉOU

(1)    (2)   (3)

1906 (Oct). *Stamps of Indo-China, surch as* **T 1**, *at Hanoi.*

1	**8**	1 c. olive-green (R.)	..	55	55
2		2 c. claret/*yellow* ..	..	55	55
3		4 c. magenta/*azure* (R.)	..	75	75
4		5 c. deep green (R.)	..	75	75
5		10 c. rose	..	75	75
6		15 c. brown/*azure* ..	..	1·00	1·00
7		20 c. red/*green*	..	75	75
8		25 c. blue	..	75	75
9		30 c. brown/*cream* ..	..	75	75
10		35 c. black/*yellow* (R.)	..	75	75
11		40 c. black/*greyish* (R.)	..	75	75
12		50 c. brown/*toned* ..	..	3·25	3·25
13	X	75 c. brown/*orange* (R.)	..	4·50	4·50
14	**8**	1 f. pale olive-green	..	5·00	5·00
15		2 f. brown/*yellow* (R.)	..	5·00	5·00
16	X	5 f. mauve/*pale lilac*	..	35·00	35·00
17	**8**	10 f. red/*green*	..	40·00	40·00
1/17		*Set of 17*	..	90·00	90·00

The note about printings under No. 49 of Canton also applies here.

1908. *Stamps of Indo-China,* 1907, *surch as* **T 2** (1 c. *to* 50 c.) *or* **3** (*others*), *in Paris. Centre and value in black.*

18	**10**	1 c. sepia (R.)	..	8	8
19		2 c. brown (R.) ..	..	8	8
20		4 c. blue (R.)	..	12	12
21		5 c. pale green (R.)	..	12	12
22		10 c. scarlet (B.)	..	8	8
23		15 c. violet (R.)	..	40	40
24	**11**	20 c. violet (R.)	..	75	75
25		25 c. blue (R.)	..	80	80
26		30 c. chocolate (R.)	..	1·25	1·25
27		35 c. olive-green (R.)	..	1·90	1·90
28		40 c. brown (R.) ..	..	1·90	1·90
29		50 c. carmine (B.) ..	..	1·90	1·90

30	**12**	75 c. orange (B.)	1·90	1·90
31	–	1 f. lake (B.)	3·25	3·25
32	–	2 f. green (R.)	7·50	7·50
33	–	5 f. blue (R.)	13·00	13·00
34	–	10 f. violet (R.)	19·00	19·00
		a. Surch double	£130	
		b. Surch treble	£130	
18/34		*Set of* 17	50·00	50·00

1919 (Jan). *As last, further surch in new currency as T* **6** *of Canton, in Paris.*

35	**10**	$\frac{2}{5}$ c. on 1 c. sepia	8	8
36		$\frac{4}{5}$ c. on 2 c. brown	8	8
37		1$\frac{3}{5}$ c. on 4 c. blue (R.)	15	10
38		2 c. on 5 c. pale green	15	12
		a. "2 CENTS" inverted	11·00	
39		4 c. on 10 c. scarlet (B.)	50	25
40		6 c. on 15 c. violet	12	8
41	**11**	8 c. on 20 c. violet	75	65
42		10 c. on 25 c. blue	1·90	1·40
43		12 c. on 30 c. chocolate	20	15
44		14 c. on 35 c. olive-green	45	35
		a. "4" with closed top	5·00	4·50
45		16 c. on 40 c. brown	20	10
46		20 c. on 50 c. carmine (B.)	30	20
47	**12**	30 c. on 75 c. orange (B.)	1·10	1·00
48	–	40 c. on 1 f. lake (B.)	1·25	1·10
		a. "40 CENTS" inverted		
49	–	80 c. on 2 f. green (R.)	1·90	90
50	–	2 pi. on 5 f. blue (R.)	35·00	32·00
51	–	4 pi. on 10 f. violet (R.)	4·00	3·75
35/51		*Set of* 17	44·00	35·00

OVERPRINTS. The following were all overprinted in Paris on stamps of Indo-China.

KOUANG-TCHÉOU (4)

KOUANG-TCHÉOU (5)

1923 (July). *Stamps of* 1922–23 *optd with T* **4**. *Values and centres in black (except* $\frac{1}{10}$ *c.).*

52	**10**	$\frac{1}{10}$ c. red and grey (B.)	5	5
		a. Opt omitted (pair with normal)		
53		$\frac{1}{5}$ **c. blue (R.)**	5	5
		a. Opt in black	16·00	
54		$\frac{2}{5}$ c. sepia (R.)	5	5
55		$\frac{4}{5}$ c. rosine	5	5
56		1 c. brown (B.)	8	8
57		2 c. green (R.)	12	12
58		3 c. violet (R.)	12	12
59		4 c. orange	12	12
60		5 c. carmine	12	12
61	**11**	6 c. red	15	15
62		7 c. olive-green	12	12
63		8 c. black/*lilac* (R.)	25	25
64		9 c. yellow/*greenish*	25	25
65		10 c. blue	25	25
66		11 c. violet	25	25
67		12 c. chocolate	25	25
68		15 c. yellow-orange	40	40
69		20 c. blue/*buff* (R.)	25	25
70		40 c. scarlet (B.)	55	55
71		1 pi. blue/green/*greenish*	1·60	1·60
72		2 pi. purple/*rose* (B.)	1·90	1·90
52/72		*Set of* 21	6·50	6·50

1927 (26 Sept). *Pictorial stamps of* 1927 *optd with T* **5**.

73	**22**	$\frac{1}{10}$ c. olive-green (R.)	5	5
74		$\frac{1}{5}$ c. yellow	5	5
75		$\frac{2}{5}$ c. pale blue (R.)	5	5
76		$\frac{4}{5}$ c. brown	8	8
77		1 c. orange	5	5
78		2 c. green (R.)	12	12
79		3 c. indigo (R.)	12	12
80		4 c. pink	12	12
81		5 c. violet	12	12
82	**23**	6 c. scarlet	15	15
83		7 c. bistre-brown	15	15
84		8 c. olive-green (R.)	15	15
85		9 c. purple	20	15
86		10 c. pale blue (R.)	20	15
87		11 c. orange	20	15
88		12 c. slate (R.)	20	15
89	**24**	15 c. brown and carmine	45	45
90		20 c. slate and bright violet (R.)	45	45
91	**25**	25 c. magenta and red-brown	45	45
92		30 c. olive and blue (R.)	25	25
93	**26**	40 c. pale blue and vermilion	20	15
94		50 c. slate and yellow-green (R.)	30	25
95	**27**	1 pi. black, yellow and blue (R.)	75	80
96		2 pi. blue, orange and red (R.)	75	80
73/96		*Set of* 24	5·00	5·00

1937 (15 Apr). *International Exhibition, Paris. As No.* **MS**246*a of Indo-China, colour changed, optd* "KOUANG-TCHEOU" *in black. Imperf.*

MS97		30 c. green	95	95
		a. Inscription inverted	£475	

KOUANG-TCHEOU (6)

1937 (19 May). *Pictorial stamps of* 1931–41 *optd with T* **6**.

98	**33**	$\frac{1}{10}$ c. greenish-blue	5	5
99		$\frac{1}{5}$ c. deep lake	5	5
100		$\frac{2}{5}$ c. brown-orange	5	5
101		$\frac{1}{2}$ c. red-brown	5	5
102		$\frac{4}{5}$ c. violet	5	5
103		1 c. sepia	5	5
104		2 c. green	5	5
105	**34**	3 c. green	10	10
106		4 c. deep blue (R.)	15	15
107		5 c. purple	12	12
108		6 c. vermilion	5	5
109	**35**	10 c. blue (R.)	20	20
110		15 c. deep blue (R.)	8	8
111		20 c. carmine	8	8
112		21 c. deep green	8	8
113		25 c. purple	50	50
114		30 c. chestnut	8	8
115	**36**	50 c. sepia	8	8
116		60 c. purple	12	12
117		1 pi. bright green	30	30
118		2 pi. scarlet	30	30
98/118		*Set of* 21	2·40	2·40

1939 (10 May). *New York World's Fair. As T* **20** *of Cameroun.*

119		13 c. lake	12	12
120		23 c. bright ultramarine	12	12

1939 (5 July). 150*th Anniv of French Revolution. As T* **25** *of Cameroun.*

121		6 c.+2 c. green	1·00	1·00
122		7 c.+3 c. brown	1·00	1·00
123		9 c.+4 c. red-orange	1·00	1·00
124		13 c.+10 c. carmine	1·00	1·00
125		23 c.+20 c. blue	1·00	1·00
121/125		*Set of* 5	4·50	4·50

1941–42. *Pictorial stamps of* 1931–41 *optd with T* **6**.

126	**34**	3 c. brown	5	5
127		4 c. blue-green	5	5
128		4 c. yellow	30	30
129		5 c. green	5	5
130		7 c. grey-black (R.)	5	5
131		8 c. deep lake	5	5
132		9 c. black/*yellow* (R.)	5	5
		a. Opt in black	1·25	1·25
133	**35**	10 c. blue/*pink* (R.)	5	5
134		18 c. bright blue (R.)	5	5
135		22 c. blue-green	5	5
136		25 c. deep blue (R.)	5	5
137		70 c. light blue (R.)	5	5
126/137		*Set of* 13	1·90	1·90

During 1941/44 other stamps of Indo-China were overprinted and issued in Paris but were not in use in Kwangchow.

The territory was returned by France to China in February 1943 and was promptly occupied by Japanese troops. It was eventually returned to China, after the defeat of Japan, by a Convention signed at Chungking on 18 August 1945.

THE WORLD CENTRE FOR FINE STAMPS IS 391 STRAND

E. MENGTSZ

An Indo-Chinese Post Office was opened at Mongtze (now Mengtsz), a town in the south of Yunnan province, on 25 January 1900.

Mong-Tseu

MONGTZE

仙 二　　　花銀八厘

(1)　　　　　　(2)

1903–06. Type X ("Tablet") inscr "INDO-CHINE" surch as T **1**, at Hanoi.

1	X	1 c. black/*azure*	..	1·10	1·10
2		2 c. brown/*buff*	..	95	95
3		4 c. purple-brown/*grey*	..	95	95
4		5 c. pale green ..	..	1·10	1·10
5		10 c. rose-red	..	1·25	1·25
6		15 c. grey	..	1·50	1·50
7		20 c. red/*green*	..	1·50	1·50
8		25 c. blue	..	1·75	1·75
9		25 c. black/*rose* (1906) ..	..	£140	£140
10		30 c. cinnamon/*drab*	..	1·75	1·75
11		40 c. red/*yellow*	..	13·00	13·00
12		50 c. carmine/*rose*	..	70·00	70·00
13		50 c. brown/*azure* (1906)	..	19·00	19·00
14		75 c. brown/*orange*	..	17·00	17·00
		a. "INDO-CHINE" in label inverted		£5500	
15		1 f. olive-green/*toned* ..	..	17·00	17·00
16		5 f. mauve/*pale lilac*	..	17·00	17·00
1/16		Set of 16	..	£275	£275

Only one copy is known of No. 14a.

1906 (Oct)–**08.** Stamps of Indo-China surch as T **2**, at Hanoi.

17	8	1 c. olive-green (R.)	..	40	40
18		2 c. claret/*yellow*	..	40	40
19		4 c. magenta/*azure* (R.) ..	..	40	40
20		5 c. deep green (R.)	..	40	40
21		10 c. rose	..	40	40
22		15 c. brown/*azure*	..	50	50
23		20 c. green	..	75	75
24		25 c. blue	..	75	75
25		30 c. brown/*cream*	..	1·25	1·25
26		35 c. black/*yellow* (R.)	..	90	90
27		40 c. black/*greyish* (R.)	..	90	90
28		50 c. brown/*toned*	..	3·25	3·25
29	X	75 c. brown/*orange* (R.) ..	..	8·00	8·00
		a. "INDO-CHINE" in label inverted		£8000	
30	8	1 f. pale olive-green	..	3·75	3·75
31		2 f. brown/*yellow* (R.)	..	9·50	9·50
32	X	5 f. mauve/*pale lilac* ..	..	19·00	19·00
33	8	10 f. red/*green* (opt inverted)	..	£350	£350
34		10 f. red/*green* (1908) ..	..	25·00	25·00

Only one copy is known of No. 29a.
The note about printings under No. 49 of Canton also applies here. All the first printing of the 10 f. (150) had the overprint inverted (No. 33).

捌 角

MONGTSEU

窗 墨　　　**MONGTSEU**

(3)　　　　　　(4)

1908. Stamps of Indo-China, 1907, surch as T **3** (1 c. to 50 c.) or **4** (others), in Paris. Centre and value in black.

35	10	1 c. sepia (R.)	..	..	12	12
36		2 c. brown (R.)	..	..	12	12
37		4 c. blue (R.)	..	..	12	12
38		5 c. pale green (R.)	..	..	25	25
39		10 c. scarlet (B.)	..	..	50	50
40		15 c. violet (R.)	..	..	50	50
41	11	20 c. violet (R.)	..	..	75	75
42		25 c. blue (R.)	..	..	1·00	1·00
43		30 c. chocolate (R.)	..		65	65
44		35 c. olive-green (R.) ..	..		75	75
45		40 c. brown (R.)	..	..	75	75
46		50 c. carmine (B.)	..	..	75	75
47	12	75 c. orange (B.)	..	..	1·90	1·90
48	–	1 f. carmine (B.) ..	..		1·90	1·90
49	–	2 f. green (R.)	..	..	2·50	2·50
50	–	5 f. blue (R.)	..	..	22·00	22·00
51	–	10 f. violet (R.)	..	..	22·00	22·00
35/51		Set of 17	..	..	50·00	50·00

1919 (Jan). As last, further surch in new currency as T **6** of Canton, in Paris.

52	10	½c. on 1 c. sepia ..		..	12	12
53		½c. on 2 c. brown	..	..	12	12
54		1⅓c. on 4 c. blue (R.)	..	..	40	40
55		2 c. on 5 c. green..	..	..	25	25
56		4 c. on 10 c. scarlet (B.)	..	..	50	50
57		6 c. on 15 c. violet	..	..	50	50
58	11	8 c. on 20 c. violet	..	..	65	65
59		10 c. on 25 c. blue	..	..	65	65
60		12 c. on 30 c. chocolate	..	..	65	65
61		14 c. on 35 c. olive-green	..	..	65	65
		a. "4" with closed top	..		2·50	2·50
62		16 c. on 40 c. brown	..	..	65	65
63		20 c. on 50 c. carmine (B.)	..	..	65	65
64	12	30 c. on 75 c. orange (B.)	..	..	65	65
65	–	40 c. on 1 f. carmine (B.)	..	..	1·50	1·50
66	–	80 c. on 2 f. green (R.)	..	..	1·00	1·00
		a. Surch treble, one inverted			70·00	70·00
67	–	2 pi. on 5 f. blue (R.)	..	..	28·00	28·00
		a. Surch double			80·00	80·00
		b. Surch treble, one inverted			80·00	80·00
68	–	4 pi. on 10 f. violet (R.)	..	..	3·75	3·75
52/68		Set of 17	..	..	35·00	35·00

This office was closed down on 31 December 1922.

F. PAKHOI

An Indo-Chinese Post Office was opened at Pakhoi, a seaport in Kwangtung province, on 1 February 1902.

PAK·HOI

PACKHOI

仙 二　　　花銀八厘

(1)　　　　　　(2)

1903 (Apr)–**04.** Type X ("Tablet") inscr "INDO-CHINE" surch as T **1**, at Hanoi.

1	X	1 c. black/*azure*	..	1·50	1·50
2		2 c. brown/*buff*	..	1·10	1·10
3		4 c. purple-brown/*grey*	..	75	75
4		5 c. pale green ..	..	75	75
5		10 c. rose-red	..	65	65
6		15 c. grey	..	65	65
7		20 c. red/*green* ..	..	1·25	1·25
8		25 c. blue	..	1·25	1·25
9		25 c. black/*rose* ..	..	75	75
10		30 c. cinnamon/*drab*	..	1·40	1·40
11		40 c. red/*yellow*	..	11·00	11·00
12		50 c. carmine/*rose*	..	75·00	75·00
13		50 c. brown/*azure* (1904)	..	13·00	13·00
14		75 c. brown/*orange*	..	13·00	13·00
		a. "INDO-CHINE" in label inverted		£6500	
15		1 f. olive-green/*toned* ..	..	14·00	14·00
16		5 f. mauve/*pale lilac*	..	22·00	22·00
1/16		Set of 16	..	£140	£140

Only three copies of No. 14a are known.

1906 (Oct). *Stamps of Indo-China surch as T* **2**, *at Hanoi.*

17	**8**	1 c. olive-green (R.)	..	..	30	30
18		2 c. claret/*yellow*	..	..	30	30
19		4 c. magenta/*azure* (R.)	..	..	30	30
20		5 c. deep green (R.)	..	..	30	30
21		10 c. rose		..	30	30
22		15 c. brown/*azure* ..	..	..	1·10	1·10
23		20 c. red/*green*	..	..	80	80
24		25 c. blue	..	..	80	80
25		30 c. brown/*cream* ..	..	..	80	80
26		35 c. black/*yellow* (R.)	..	..	80	80
27		40 c. black/*greyish* (R.)	..	..	70	70
28		50 c. brown/*toned*	..	..	1·10	1·10
29	X	75 c. brown/*orange* (R.)	..	..	10·00	10·00
30	**8**	1 f. pale olive-green	..	..	6·50	6·50
31		2 f. brown/*yellow* (R.)	..	..	9·00	9·00
32	X	5 f. mauve/*pale lilac*	..	..	20·00	20·00
33	**8**	10 f. red/*green*	..	..	23·00	23·00
17/33		*Set of* 17	..	..	70·00	70·00

The note about printings under No. 49 of Canton also applies here.

(1)

PAKHOI

 — *placeholder*

(3)   **PAKHOI**

(4)

1908. *Stamps of Indo-China,* 1907, *surch as T* **3** (1 *c. to* 50 *c.*) *or* **4** (*others*), *in Paris. Centre and value in black.*

34	**10**	1 c. sepia (R.)	..	..	10	10
35		2 c. brown (R.)	..	..	12	12
36		4 c. blue (R.)	..	..	15	15
37		5 c. pale green (R.)	..	..	25	25
38		10 c. scarlet (B.)	..	..	25	25
39		15 c. violet (R.)	..	..	40	40
40	**11**	20 c. violet (R.)	..	..	40	40
41		25 c. blue (R.)	..	..	40	40
42		30 c. chocolate (R.)	..	..	65	65
43		35 c. olive-green (R.)	..	..	65	65
44		40 c. brown (R.)	..	..	65	65
45		50 c. carmine (B.) ..	..	..	65	65
46	**12**	75 c. orange (B.) ..	..	..	1·10	1·10
47	–	1 f. lake (B.) ..	..	..	1·25	1·25
48	–	2 f. green (R.)	..	..	3·75	3·75
49	–	5 f. blue (R.)	..	..	18·00	18·00
50	–	10 f. violet (R.)	..	..	32·00	32·00
34/50		*Set of* 17	..	..	55·00	55·00

1919 (Jan). *As last, further surch in new currency as T* **6** *of Canton, in Paris.*

51	**10**	½ c. on 1 c. sepia	..	..	15	15
		a. "PAKHOI" double	..	..	25·00	
52		½ c. on 2 c. brown		..	15	15
53		1½ c. on 4 c. blue (R.)	..	..	15	15
54		2 c. on 5 c. green ..	..	..	25	25
55		4 c. on 10 c. scarlet (B.)	..	..	65	65
56		6 c. on 15 c. violet	..	..,	15	15
57	**11**	8 c. on 20 c. violet	..	..	65	65
58		10 c. on 25 c. blue	..	..	65	65
59		12 c. on 30 c. chocolate	..	..	30	30
		a. "12 CENTS" double	..	..	25·00	
60		14 c. on 35 c. olive-green	..	..	15	15
		a. "4" with closed top	..	..	2·10	2·10
61		16 c. on 40 c. brown	..	..	45	45
62		20 c. on 50 c. carmine (B.)	..	..	30	30
63	**12**	30 c. on 75 c. orange (B.)	..	..	30	30
64	–	40 c. on 1 f. lake (B.)	..	..	2·10	2·10
65	–	80 c. on 2 f. green (R.)	..	..	65	65
66	–	2 pi. on 5 f. blue (R.)	..	..	1·90	1·90
67	–	4 pi. on 10 f. violet (R.)	..	..	3·75	3·75
51/67		*Set of* 17	..	..	11·00	11·00

This office was closed down on 31 December 1922.

G. YUNNANFU (now KUNMING)

An Indo-Chinese Post Office was opened at Yunnansen, chief city of Yunnan province, on 15 February 1900. "Sen" and "Fu" both mean "town" in Chinese, the latter indicating a place of greater importance than the former. In 1906 Yunnansen was raised in rank, and was then known as Yunnanfu.

Yunnan·Fou

YUNNANSEN

仙四   花銀八厘

(1)   (2)

1903–04. *Type* X (*"Tablet"*) *inscr* "INDO-CHINE" *surch as T* **1**, *at Hanoi.*

1	X	1 c. black/*azure*		..	1·50	1·25
2		2 c. brown/*buff*	..	..	1·10	1·10
3		4 c. purple-brown/*grey*	..	..	1·10	1·00
4		5 c. pale green ..	..	..	1·10	90
5		10 c. rose	..	..	1·10	90
6		15 c. grey	..	..	1·25	1·10
7		20 c. red/*green*	..	..	1·60	1·25
8		25 c. blue	..	..	1·50	1·25
9		30 c. cinnamon/*drab*	..	..	1·60	1·25
10		40 c. red/*yellow*	..	..	14·00	9·00
11		50 c. carmine/*rose*	..	..	90·00	80·00
12		50 c. brown/*azure* (1904)	..	..	38·00	38·00
13		75 c. brown/*orange*	..	..	11·00	9·50
		a. "INDO-CHINE" in label inverted	..	£7000	
14		1 f. olive-green/*toned* ..	..	..	11·00	9·50
15		5 f. mauve/*pale lilac*	..	..	16·00	16·00
1/15		*Set of* 15	..	..	£170	£150

Only three copies of No. 13a are known.

1906 (Oct). *Stamps of Indo-China surch as T* **2**, *at Hanoi.*

16	**8**	1 c. olive-green (R.)	..	..	55	55
17		2 c. claret/*yellow* ..	..	..	55	55
18		4 c. magenta/*azure* (R.)	..	..	80	80
19		5 c. deep green (R.)	..	..	80	80
20		10 c. rose	..	..	75	75
21		15 c. brown/*azure*	..	..	1·00	1·00
22		20 c. red/*green*	..	..	90	90
23		25 c. blue	..	..	90	90
24		30 c. brown/*cream* ..	..	..	90	90
25		35 c. black/*yellow* (R.)	..	..	1·10	1·10
26		40 c. black/*greyish* (R.)	..	..	1·25	1·25
27		50 c. brown/*toned*	..	..	1·25	1·25
28	X	75 c. brown/*orange* (R.)	..	..	9·50	9·50
29	**8**	1 f. pale olive-green	..	..	5·00	5·00
30		2 f. brown/*yellow* (R.)	..	..	5·00	5·00
31	X	5 f. mauve/*pale lilac*	..	..	14·00	14·00
32	**8**	10 f. red/*green*	..	..	16·00	16·00
16/32		*Set of* 17	..	..	55·00	55·00

The note about printings under No. 49 of Canton also applies here.

貳圓

VUNNANFOU

貳圓 (3)   **YUNNANFOU** (4)

1908. *Stamps of Indo-China, 1907, surch as T 3 (1 c. to 50 c.) or 4 (others), in Paris. Centre and value in black.*

33	**10**	1 c. sepia (R.)	..	15	15
34		2 c. brown (R.)	..	15	15
35		4 c. blue (R.)	..	15	15
36		5 c. pale green (R.)	..	30	20
37		10 c. scarlet (B.)	..	15	12
38		15 c. violet (R.)	..	90	65
39	**11**	20 c. violet (R.)	..	90	65
40		25 c. blue (R.)	..	90	70
41		30 c. chocolate (R.)	..	1·10	95
42		35 c. olive-green (R.)	..	1·10	95
43		40 c. brown (R.)	..	1·60	1·60
44		50 c. carmine (B.)	..	1·60	1·60
45	**12**	75 c. orange (B.)	..	1·90	1·75
46	–	1 f. lake (B.)	..	5·00	5·00
47	–	2 f. green (R.)	..	5·00	5·00
		a. Error. "YUNANNFOU"	..	£325	
48	–	5 f. blue (R.)	..	14·00	14·00
		a. Error. "YUNANNFOU"	..	£325	
49	–	10 f. violet (R.)	..	16·00	16·00
		a. Error. "YUNANNFOU"	..	£325	
33/49		*Set of 17*	..	45·00	45·00

1919 (Jan). *As last, further surch in new currency as T 6 of Canton, in Paris.*

50	**10**	⅔ c. on 1 c. sepia	..	15	12
		a. "⅔ CENT" double	..	22·00	
51		⅘ c. on 2 c. brown	..	30	20
52		1⅗ c. on 4 c. blue (R.)	..	30	25
53		2 c. on 5 c. green	..	20	20
		a. "2 CENTS" treble	..	38·00	
54		4 c. on 10 c. scarlet (B.)	..	20	15
55		6 c. on 15 c. violet	..	20	15
56	**11**	8 c. on 20 c. violet	..	40	30
57		10 c. on 25 c. blue	..	55	45
58		12 c. on 30 c. chocolate	..	45	30
59		14 c. on 35 c. olive-green	..	90	80
		a. "4" with closed top	..	21·00	
60		16 c. on 40 c. brown	..	90	80
61		20 c. on 50 c. carmine	..	45	35
62	**12**	30 c. on 75 c. orange (B.)	..	95	80
63	–	40 c. on 1 f. lake (B.)	..	1·10	95
64	–	80 c. on 2 f. green (R.)	..	1·75	1·75
		a. "80 CENTS" double	..	95·00	
		b. "80 CENTS" treble, one inverted	..	48·00	
65	–	2 pi. on 5 f. blue (R.)	..	9·50	9·50
66	–	4 pi. on 10 f. violet (R.)	..	2·50	2·50
50/66		*Set of 17*	..	18·00	18·00

This office was closed down on 31 December 1922.

PHILATELIC TERMS ILLUSTRATED

This successful STAMP MONTHLY series has now been brought together in a snappy black and yellow binding and published as a useful addition to Stanley Gibbons range of essential handbooks for keen stamp collectors. Within its 192 pages this handy limp-bound volume houses a veritable mine of useful information on the words and phrases used in philately. It describes and illustrates printing processes and watermarks, papers and perforations, errors and varieties . . . and it does all this IN COLOUR. Indeed, there are 92 full page plates in colour, plus many black and white illustrations, making it

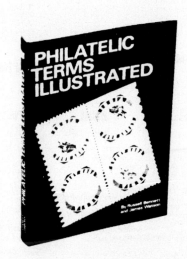

FANTASTIC VALUE AT ONLY £1·95 POST PAID FROM

**Stanley Gibbons Publications Ltd
391 Strand, London WC2R 0LX**

Ivory Coast

100 Centimes=1 Franc

French trading posts were established on the Ivory Coast in 1700, and in 1842–43 territory round them was ceded by local chiefs. Following expeditions by Marcel Treich-Laplène and, in 1887–92, by Capt. Louis Binger to the interior, further territory was ceded there to France. The Ivory Coast became a French colony by decree of 10 March 1893; stamps had been issued in 1892.

PRINTERS. All stamps were printed at the Government Printing Works, Paris, *unless otherwise stated.*

IMPERFORATE STAMPS. Stamps exist imperforate in their issued colours, but they were not valid for postage. Imperforate stamps in other colours are colour trials.

A. FRENCH COLONY

1892 (Nov). *French Colonies Type X ("Tablet") inscr "COTE D'IVOIRE", in red* (1, 5, 15, 25, 75 *c.* and 1 *f.) or blue (others). P* 14×13½.

1	X	1 c. black/azure			20	20
2		2 c. brown/buff			30	30
3		4 c. purple-brown/grey			60	50
4		5 c. green/pale green			2·00	1·25
		a. Deep green/green			2·25	1·25
5		10 c. black/lilac			3·00	1·50
6		15 c. blue (quadrillé paper)			3·25	2·00
7		20 c. red/green			3·00	1·75
8		25 c. black/rose			3·00	
9		30 c. cinnamon/drab			4·25	3·75
10		40 c. red/yellow			3·75	3·50
11		50 c. carmine/rose			12·00	10·00
12		75 c. brown/yellow			5·50	4·50
13		1 f. olive-green/toned			6·00	5·00
1/13		*Set of 13*			45·00	32·00

1900 (Dec). *Colours changed. Inscr in blue* (10 *c.) or red (others).*

14	X	10 c. rose-red			25·00	23·00
15		15 c. grey			1·90	65
16		25 c. blue			6·50	5·00
17		50 c. brown/azure			3·75	1·90
14/17		*Set of 4*			32·00	28·00

Côte d'Ivoire COLIS Postaux

(P 1)

Colis Postaux

(P 2)

Côte d'Ivoire Colis Postaux

(P 3)

1903 (Jan). *PARCEL POST. Postage Due type of French Colonies (Type U), optd locally. Imperf.*

P18	P 1	50 c. dull claret			6·50	5·50
P19	P 2	50 c. dull claret			£650	£650
P20	P 1	1 f. rose/buff			6·50	5·50
P21	P 2	1 f. rose/buff			£650	£650

One unused copy has been reported of No. P18 with "Cote d'Ivoire" omitted.

In Type P **1** four stamps in the setting of 25 are without the circumflex.

The above were printed in two panes of 25 each and Type P **2** occurred in the left-hand pane.

1903 (6 Apr). *PARCEL POST. Type U of French Colonies optd locally with Type P* **3**. *Imperf.*

P22	P 3	50 c. dull claret (Vm.)			22·00	22·00
		a. Opt inverted			45·00	45·00
P23		1 f. rose/buff (B.-Bk.)			13·00	13·00
		a. Opt inverted			38·00	38·00

Côte d'Ivoire 50ᶜ Colis Postaux (P 4)

50ᶜ A

Côte d'Ivoire fr 1 fr Colis Postaux (P 5)

fr | fr — B

fr 1 fr — C

fr | fr — D

XX 1FR — E

1FR — F

XX 1FR — G

UN FR — H

UN FR — I

1903 (17 June). *PARCEL POST. Type U of French Colonies variously surch locally as Types P* **4/5**. *Imperf.*

P24	P 4	50 c. on 15 c. green			2·25	2·25
		a. Surch inverted			25·00	25·00
		b. Wide figure "0" (Type A)			13·00	13·00
P25		50 c. on 60 c. brown/buff			6·50	5·50
		a. Surch inverted			25·00	25·00
		b. Wide figure "0" (Type A)			14·00	14·00
P26	P 5	1 f. on 5 c. blue			2·50	2·25
		a. Surch inverted			50·00	50·00
		b. Type B			3·75	3·25
		c. Type C			£750	£750
		d. Type D			£1100	£1000
		e. Type E			£700	£550
		f. Type F			£650	£500
		g. Type G			£6500	£6500
		h. Type H			17·00	17·00
		i. Type I			£550	£550
P27		1 f. on 10 c. grey-brown			3·75	3·75
		a. Surch inverted			38·00	38·00
		b. Type B			4·50	3·75
		c. Type H			£800	£800
		d. Type I			£9000	

In all values four stamps in the setting of 25 are without the circumflex.

The above were printed from several settings of 25.

In the 50 c. surcharges Type A occurred once.

There were four settings of the 1 f. on 5 c. as follows:—

1st setting containing five of Type B, the rest being normal.
2nd setting containing five of Type D, the rest being Type C.
3rd setting containing one of Type I, the rest being Type H.
4th setting containing Types E, F and G but so far as we know there is no complete setting and it has not been plated.

In the 1 f. on 10 c. there were two settings, being the 1st and 3rd settings as used for the 1 f. on 5 c. Only one pane of the 3rd setting is known, hence only one copy of No. P27d has been recorded.

Colis Postaux

Côte d'Ivoire

(P 6)

A Large Stars

Côte d'Ivoire

fr **4** fr

4 4 0,05

Colis Postaux

(P 7)   B   C   (4)

1903 (Aug). *PARCEL POST. Type U of French Colonies variously surch locally as Types P 6/7. Imperf.*

P28	P 6	4 f. on 15 c. yellow-green	25·00	19·00
		a. Type A	32·00	25·00
		b. Large star at left, small at right	35·00	35·00
P29		4 f. on 30 c. rose	25·00	19·00
		a. Type A	32·00	25·00
		b. Large star at left, small at right	35·00	35·00
P30	P 7	4 f. on 60 c. brown/*buff*	25·00	19·00
		a. Type B	45·00	38·00
		b. Type C	£160	£120

The above were each printed from one setting of 25.

Type P **6** contains four stamps without circumflex, four Type A, one Type A and without circumflex, one with large and small star and fifteen normals.

Type P **7** contains three stamps without circumflex, three Type B, one Type B and without circumflex, one Type C, and seventeen normals.

1904 (14 Jan). *Stamps of 1892 surch locally as T* **4**.

18	X	0,05 on 30 c. cinnamon/*drab*	14·00	14·00
19		0,10 on 75 c. brown/*yellow*	2·25	2·25
20		0,15 on 1 f. olive-green/*toned*	3·50	3·50

In No. 20 the "0" of "0,15" is the same size as the other figures.

C. P.   Cote d'Ivoire   Colis Postaux

Cote d'Ivoire   *C. P.*   Cote d'Ivoire

(P 9)   (P 10)   (P 11)

1904 (27 Apr). *PARCEL POST. Type U of French Colonies optd locally. Imperf.*

(a) With Type P **9**

P31	U	50 c. dull claret	5·00	5·00
P32		1 f. rose/*buff*	5·00	5·00

(b) With Type P **10**, *in blue-black*

P33	U	50 c. dull claret	5·50	5·50
		a. "Cote d'Ivoire" omitted	28·00	28·00
		b. Opt inverted	25·00	25·00
P34		1 f. rose/*buff*	7·50	7·50
		a. "Cote d'Ivoire" omitted		
		b. "C.P." omitted		
		c. Opt inverted	28·00	28·00

Types P **9** and P **10** are different settings.

1904 (July). *PARCEL POST. Type U of French Colonies surch locally as Type P* **11**. *Imperf.*

P35	U	4 f. on 5 c. bright blue	55·00	55·00
P36		8 f. on 15 c. pale green	55·00	55·00

Côte d'Ivoire

C.   Côte d'Ivoire

2 Francs

P.   *C. P.*   **4 4**

(P 12)   (P 13)   A   B

1905 (Sept). *PARCEL POST. Type U of French Colonies.*

(a) Optd locally with Type P **12**

P37	U	50 c. dull claret	6·50	6·50
P38		1 f. rose/*buff*	6·50	6·50

(b) Surch locally as Type P **13**

P39	U	2 f. on 1 f. rose/*buff*	32·00	32·00
P40		4 f. on 1 f. rose/*buff* (A)	50·00	50·00
		a. Type B	£225	£225
P41		8 f. on 1 f. rose/*buff*	£150	£150

Type B of the 4 f. occurs once in the setting of 25.

1906–7. *As T* **3/5** *of Upper Senegal and Niger (see French Sudan), inscr "CÔTE D'IVOIRE". Name in blue (10 c., 5 f.) or red (others). P 14×13½ (horiz) or 13½×14 (vert).*

22	1 c. slate		25	25
23	2 c. chocolate		25	25
24	4 c. chocolate/*blue*		40	40
	a. Inscr omitted		32·00	
	b. Inscr double		32·00	28·00
25	5 c. green		40	40
	a. Inscr omitted		13·00	9·50
26	10 c. rose		1·25	1·00
27	20 c. black/*bluish*		1·90	1·50
28	25 c. blue		1·25	1·00
29	30 c. chocolate/*flesh*		1·90	1·25
30	35 c. black/*yellow* (1907)		1·90	90
32	45 c. chocolate/*green*		2·50	2·25
33	50 c. deep violet		2·75	2·50
34	75 c. green/*orange*		2·75	2·50
35	1 f. black/*azure*		8·00	7·50
36	2 f. blue/*rose*		9·00	8·00
37	5 f. red/*straw*		16·00	16·00
22/37	*Set of 15*		£120	£120

1906–7. *POSTAGE DUE. As Type D* **6** *of Upper Senegal and Niger (see French Sudan), inscr "CÔTE D'IVOIRE" in blue (10 c., 30 c.) or red (others). P 13½×14.*

D38	5 c. green/*tinted*		55	55
D39	10 c. maroon		45	45
D40	15 c. blue/*bluish*		80	80
D41	20 c. black/*yellow* (1907)		1·50	1·50
D42	30 c. red/*cream*		1·75	1·75
D43	50 c. violet		1·25	1·25
D44	60 c. black/*buff*		6·50	6·50
D45	1 f. black/*flesh*		6·50	6·50
D38/45	*Set of 8*		17·00	17·00

05 10

(5)   (6)   7 River Scene

1912 (Nov). *Surch as T* **5/6**.

A. Narrow spacing. B. Wide spacing

				A		B	
38	X	05 on 15 c. grey (R.)		8	8	1·25	1·25
39		05 on 30 c. cinnamon/*drab* (R.)		20	20	1·90	1·90
40		10 on 40 c. red/*yellow*		12	12	7·50	7·50
41		10 on 50 c. brown/*azure* (R.)		25	25	19·00	19·00
42		10 on 75 c. brown/*orange*		1·25	1·25	45·00	45·00
38/42		*Set of 5*		1·75	1·75	65·00	65·00

In Type A the space between "0" and "5" is 1½ mm and between "1" and "0" 2½ mm. In Type B the spacing is 2 mm and 3 mm respectively.

(Des J. de la Nézière. Eng E. Froment. Typo)

1913–16. P 14×13½.

43	**7**	1 c. lilac and purple	..	5	5
44		2 c. black and brown	..	5	5
45		4 c. purple and violet	..	5	5
		a. Centre double	..	16·00	
46		5 c. green and yellow-green	..	5	5
47		10 c. rose and orange-red	..	12	12
48		15 c. carm & orge (*chalky paper*) (1916)	5	5
49		20 c. grey and black	..	5	5
50		25 c. blue and ultramarine	..	1·00	70
51		30 c. brown and chocolate	..	20	12
52		35 c. orange and violet	..	5	5
53		40 c. green and grey	..	20	12
54		45 c. brown and orange-red	..	8	5
55		50 c. lilac and black	..	55	50
56		75 c. rose and brown	..	8	8
57		1 f. black and orange-yellow	..	20	15
58		2 f. blue and brown	..	65	30
59		5 f. brown and Prussian blue	..	1·10	75
43/59		*Set of 17*	..	4·00	3·00

The 5, 10, 25 and 35 c. also exist on chalk-surfaced paper.
See also Nos. 61/79.

1915. *POSTAGE DUE. As Type D 9 of Upper Senegal and Niger (see French Sudan), inscr "CÔTE D'IVOIRE". P* 14×13½.

D60		5 c. green	..	5	5
D61		10 c. carmine	..	5	5
D62		15 c. grey	..	5	5
D63		20 c. brown	..	5	5
D64		30 c. blue	..	5	5
D65		50 c. black	..	10	10
D66		60 c. orange	..	12	12
D67		1 f. violet	..	15	15
D60/67		*Set of 8*	..	55	55

(8)   **(9)**

1915 (Apr). *Surch in Paris with T 8, in red. Ordinary or chalk-surfaced paper.*

60	**7**	10 c.+5 c. rose and orange-red	..	15	15
		a. Surch double	..	9·50	9·50

1922 (1 Jan)–**36.** *New values and colours.* P 14×13½.

61	**7**	5 c. brown and chocolate	..	5	5
62		10 c. green and yellow-green	..	5	5
63		10 c. rose/*azure* (1.2.26)	..	5	5
64		25 c. bright violet and black	..	5	5
		a. Magenta and black (1936)	5	5
65		30 c. rose and red	..	20	20
66		30 c. carmine and light blue	..	5	5
67		30 c. green and olive-green (14.11.27)	..	5	5
68		45 c. claret and carmine (20.9.34)	..	80	75
69		50 c. blue and ultramarine	..	5	5
70		50 c. bright blue & olive-green (15.4.25)	..	5	5
71		60 c. violet/*rose* (7.9.25)	..	5	5
72		65 c. olive-green and carmine (1.3.26)	..	20	20
73		75 c. ultramarine and blue (20.9.34)	..	55	50
74		85 c. black and purple (1.3.26)	..	15	15
75		90 c. carmine and brown-red (5.5.30)	..	2·25	2·25
76		1 f. 10, brown and green (25.9.28)	..	1·10	1·10
77		1 f. 50, blue and light blue (5.5.30)	..	1·25	95
78		1 f. 75, magenta & ultramarine (15.9.35)	..	2·00	95
79		3 f. magenta/*rose* (5.5.30)	..	1·25	75
61/79		*Set of 19*	..	7·00	6·00

1922 (Sept)–**34.** *Surch as T 9.*

80	**9**	50 on 45 c. claret and carmine (20.9.34)	40	30
81		50 on 75 c. ultram & bl (R.) (20.9.34)	30	30
82		50 on 90 c. rose and scarlet (20.9.34)	30	30
83		60 on 75 c. violet/*rose*	..	5	5
		a. Surch omitted	..	22·00	
84		65 on 15 c. carmine and orange (1.2.25)	12	12
85		85 on 75 c. rose and brown (1.2.25)	12	12
80/85		*Set of 6*	..	1·10	1·10

1924 (June)–**27.** *Surch as T 10.*

86	**7**	25 c. on 2 f. blue and brown (R.)	..	12	12
87		25 c. on 5 f. brown and blue	..	12	12
88		90 c. on 75 c. rose and carmine (28.2.27)	12	12
		a. Surch omitted	..	32·00	
89		1 f. 25 on 1 f. ultram & bl (R.) (14.6.26)	5	5
90		1 f. 50 on 1 f. blue & light blue (28.2.27)	20	20
91		3 f. on 5 f. blue-green & lake (19.12.27)	50	50
92		10 f. on 5 f. mauve and carmine (7.2.27)	2·75	2·75
93		20 f. on 5 f. vermilion & blue-grn (7.2.27)	3·50	3·50
86/93		*Set of 8*	..	6·50	6·50

1927 (10 Oct). *POSTAGE DUE. As No. D67 but colour changed, surch as Type D 13 of French Sudan.*

D94		2 f. on 1 f. magenta	..	12	12
D95		3 f. on 1 f. chestnut	..	12	12

1931 (13 April). *International Colonial Exhibition, Paris. As T 17/20 of French Sudan.*

94		40 c. black and green	..	40	40
95		50 c. black and mauve	..	1·10	1·10
96		90 c. black and vermilion	..	25	25
97		1 f. 50, black and blue	..	1·10	1·10
94/97		*Set of 4*	..	2·50	2·50

1933 (2 Oct). *T 3/5 of Upper Volta optd or surch as T 11.*

98	**3**	2 c. chocolate and lilac	..	5	5
		a. Opt inverted	..	3·25	
99		4 c. black and yellow	..	5	5
100		5 c. indigo and light blue	..	8	5
		a. Opt inverted	..	5·00	
101		10 c. indigo and pink	..	10	8
102		15 c. chocolate and light blue	..	10	10
103		20 c. chocolate and yellow-green	..	12	12
104	**4**	25 c. chocolate and lemon	..	40	30
105		30 c. deep green and green	..	40	30
106		45 c. chocolate and light blue	..	1·25	1·10
		a. Opt inverted	..	10·00	
107		65 c. indigo and light blue	..	65	55
		a. Opt inverted			
108		75 c. black and lilac	..	70	55
109		90 c. carmine and mauve	..	50	40
110	**5**	1 f. chocolate and apple-green	..	50	40
		a. Opt inverted	..	15·00	
111	**4**	1 f. 25 on 40 c. black and pink	..	25	20
112	**5**	1 f. 50, ultramarine and azure	..	50	40
		a. Opt inverted	..	22·00	
113	**4**	1 f. 75 on 50 c. black & yellow-green	40	35
98/113		*Set of 16*	..	5·50	4·50

The 2, 4, 5, 15, 30, 45, 65 and 75 c., 1 f. 25, 1 f. 50 and 1 f. 75 exist with overprint or surcharge double.

12 Baoulé Woman
(*wrongly described as "Femme Baloué" on stamp*)

13 Mosque at Bobo-Dioulasso

THE WORLD CENTRE FOR
FINE STAMPS IS 391 STRAND

14 Coastal Scene   **15** Comoé Rapids

(Eng D. Delzers, A. Ouvré, A. Decaris and J. Piel. Recess)

1936 (19 Oct)–42. *P* 13.

114	**12**	1 c. carmine . .	5	5
115		2 c. bright ultramarine	5	5
116		3 c. green (15.4.40)	5	5
117		4 c. brown	5	5
118		5 c. bright violet	5	5
119		10 c. turquoise-blue	5	5
120		15 c. scarlet	5	5
121	**13**	20 c. ultramarine	5	5
122		25 c. scarlet	5	5
123		30 c. emerald-green	8	5
124		30 c. chocolate (15.4.40)	5	5
125	**12**	35 c. green (16.5.38)	5	5
126	**13**	40 c. carmine . .	5	5
127		45 c. brown	10	8
128		45 c. emerald-green (15.4.40)	5	5
129		50 c. purple	5	5
130		55 c. violet (16.5.38)	5	5
131	**14**	60 c. carmine (26.3.40)	5	5
132		65 c. red-brown	5	5
133		70 c. red-brown (26.3.40)	5	5
134		75 c. violet	8	5
135		80 c. black-brown (16.5.38) . .	8	5
136		90 c. carmine . .	1·10	70
137		90 c. green (4.12.39)	10	10
138		1 f. green	55	20
139		1 f. carmine (5.12.38)	5	5
140		1 f. violet (26.3.40) . .	5	5
141		1 f. 25, scarlet	5	5
142		1 f. 40, blue (5.3.40)	5	5
143		1 f. 50, ultramarine . .	5	5
144		1 f. 50, greenish grey (1942)	5	5
145		1 f. 60, black-brown (5.3.40)	10	10
146	**15**	1 f. 75, carmine	5	5
147		1 f. 75, blue (5.12.38)	5	5
148		2 f. ultramarine	5	5
149		2 f. 25, blue (4.12.39)	5	5
150		2 f. 50, scarlet (5.3.40)	5	5
151		3 f. emerald-green	10	8
152		5 f. brown	10	8
153		10 f. bright violet	12	12
154		20 f. scarlet	30	20
114/154		*Set of 41*	3·75	3·00

30 c., 60 c., 1 f. and 20 f. stamps in these designs, but without "RF", were prepared in 1944. These were never issued.

1937 (15 Apr). *International Exhibition, Paris. As T 2/7 of French Equatorial Africa.*

155	20 c. bright violet	20	20
156	30 c. green	20	20
157	40 c. carmine	25	25
158	50 c. brown	20	20
159	90 c. scarlet	20	20
160	1 f. 50, blue	25	25
155/160	*Set of 6*	1·10	1·10
MS160*a*	120×100 mm. 3 f. sepia (as T **4**).		
	Imperf	95	95

16 General Binger

(Eng H. Cheffer. Recess)

1937 (25 Oct). *50th Anniv of Gen. Binger's Exploration. P* 13.

161	**16**	65 c. purple-brown	5	5

1938 (24 Oct). *International Anti-Cancer Fund. As T **14** of French Equatorial Africa.*

162	1 f. 75+50 c. ultramarine	2·25	1·90

1939 (5 Apr). *Death Centenary of René Caillé (explorer). As T **21** of French Sudan.*

163	90 c. orange	12	12
	a. "COTE D'IVOIRE" omitted	4·50	
164	2 f. violet	20	20
	a. "COTE D'IVOIRE" omitted	8·00	
165	2 f. 25, blue	12	12
	a. "COTE D'IVOIRE" omitted	8·00	

1939 (10 May). *New York World's Fair. As T **17** of French Equatorial Africa.*

166	1 f. 25, lake	15	15
167	2 f. 25, ultramarine	15	15

1939 (5 July). *150th Anniv of French Revolution. As T **18** of French Equatorial Africa.*

168	45 c.+25 c. green and black	1·25	1·25
169	70 c.+30 c. brown and black	1·25	1·25
170	90 c.+35 c. red-orange and black	1·25	1·25
171	1 f. 25+1 f. carmine and black	1·25	1·25
172	2 f. 25+2 f. blue and black	1·25	1·25
168/172	*Set of 5*	5·50	5·50

1940 (8 Feb). *AIR. As T **22** of French Sudan.*

173	1 f. 90, bright blue	5	5
	a. "COTE D'IVOIRE" omitted	13·00	
174	2 f. 90, rose-red . .	5	5
	a. "COTE D'IVOIRE" omitted	13·00	
175	4 f. 50, green	8	8
	a. "COTE D'IVOIRE" omitted	16·00	
176	4 f. 90, olive-bistre	8	8
	a. "COTE D'IVOIRE" omitted	16·00	
177	6 f. 90, orange	25	25
	a. "COTE D'IVOIRE" omitted	19·00	
173/177	*Set of 5*	25	25

VICHY GOVERNMENT

Nos. 178 to 179 were issued by the Pétain regime in Unoccupied France. A number of other issues exist but we only list those items which were available in Ivory Coast.

1941. *National Defence Fund. Surch as T **23** of French Sudan.*

178	**13**	+1 f. on 50 c. purple	20	20
178*a*	**14**	+2 f. on 80 c. black-brown (R.)	2·75	2·75
178*b*		+2 f. on 1 f. 50, ultramarine (R.)	2·75	2·75
178*c*	**15**	+3 f. on 2 f. ultramarine	2·75	2·75
178/178*c*		*Set of 4*	7·50	7·50

1942 (19 Oct). *AIR. As T **25** of French Sudan, inscr* "COTE D'IVOIRE".

179	50 f. brown-olive and yellow-green	30	40

Seven other values in this or a similar design were prepared, but not issued.

The Ivory Coast remained under the Vichy Government until November 1942. From 1944 to 1959 the stamps in use were those of French West Africa.

B. AUTONOMOUS REPUBLIC
(within the French Community)

The Ivory Coast became an autonomous republic on 4 December 1958.

ALBUM LISTS

Write for our latest lists of albums
and accessories.
These will be sent free on request.

17 Elephant   18 Place Lapalud, Abidjan

(Des and eng G. Bétemps. Recess)

1959 (1 Oct). *P* 13.
180	**17**	10 f. black and emerald	12	5
181		25 f. chocolate and bistre	25	15
182		30 f. deep olive and turquoise-blue	30	20

(Des and eng R. Serres (100 f.), J. Combet (200 f.), R. Cami (500 f.). Recess)

1959 (1 Oct). *AIR. T* **18** *and similar designs. P* 13.
183	100 f. chestnut, yellow-green & chocolate	1·10	40
184	200 f. purple-brown, slate-grn & turq-bl	2·00	95
185	500 f. turquoise-blue, bistre-brown & grn	5·00	2·00
180/185	*Set of 6*	8·00	3·25

Designs: *Horiz*—200 f. Houphouët-Boigny Bridge; 500 f. Ayamé Barrage.

19 Pres.   20 Bété Mask   D 21 Guéré
Houphouët-   Mask
Boigny

(Des and eng P. Munier. Recess)

1959 (4 Dec). *First Anniv of Republic. P* 13.
186	**19**	25 f. chocolate	30	20

(Des G. Francois. Eng A. Frères (50 c.), J. Miermont (1 f.), G. Aufschneider (45 f., 85 f.), R. Fenneteaux (50 f.). Des and eng N. Hertenberger (2 f., 4 f.), R. Serres (5 f., 6 f.). Recess)

1960 (5 Mar). *Native Masks. Various designs as T* **20**. *P* 13.
187	50 c. brown-purple and bistre-brown		5	5
188	1 f. violet and carmine-red		5	5
189	2 f. blue-green and ultramarine		5	5
190	4 f. orange-red and deep grey-green		8	5
191	5 f. bistre-brown and rose-red		10	10
192	6 f. ultramarine and deep maroon		12	10
193	45 f. maroon and grey-green		60	30
194	50 f. greenish blue and chocolate		75	40
195	85 f. black-green and scarlet		1·25	75
187/195	*Set of 9*		2·75	1·75

Designs: *Vert*—Masks of: 1 f. Guéré; 2 f. Guéré (diff. type); 45 f. Bété (diff. Type); 50 f. Gouro; 85 f. Gouro (diff. Type). *Horiz*—Masks of: 4 f. Baoulé; 5 f. Sénoufo; 6 f. Sénoufo (diff. type).

(Des R. Serres. Eng G. Bétemps. Recess)

1960 (5 Mar). *POSTAGE DUE. Values in black. P* 14×13.
D196	D **21**	1 f. reddish violet	5	5
D197		2 f. emerald	5	5
D198		5 f. yellow-orange	5	5
D199		10 f. ultramarine	12	12
D200		20 f. magenta	25	25
D196/200	*Set of 5*		45	45

1960 (16 May). 10th*Anniv of African Technical Co-operation Commission. As T* **26** *of Gabon.*
196	25 f. violet and turquoise-blue		40	35

21 Conseil de   21a "World Peace"
l'Entente
Emblem

(Photo Comoy, Paris)

1960 (29 May). *First Anniv of Conseil de l'Entente. P* 13.
197	**21**	25 f. multicoloured	40	40

The Ivory Coast became an independent republic on 7 August 1960.

ALBUM LISTS

Please write for our latest lists of albums and accessories. These will be sent free on request.

Laos

1951. 100 Cents = 1 Piastre
1955. 100 Cents = 1 Kip

In 1353 a Thai chieftain united the lands now known as Laos as the kingdom of Lan Chang ("the land of a million elephants"). In 1694 this disintegrated into three states, which in the years 1778 to 1827 were all conquered by Siam and made to acknowledge Siamese suzerainty. The French, who by 1885 had obtained control of Annam, Tongking, Cambodia and Cochin China, wished to extend their rule westward to the Mekong valley. On 3 October 1893 Siam was forced to sign a treaty by which all claims to territory east of the Mekong were abandoned. A French protectorate was established in 1899, and extended in 1904 by the acquisition of part of Luang Prabang west of the Mekong.

In the Second World War, French Indo-China was occupied by Japanese troops from 1941 to 1945. The French returned in 1946, and on 10 May 1947 a constitution proclaimed the unity of the Laotian provinces as the kingdom of Laos, an independent state, with King Sisavang Vong (king of Luang Prabang since 1904) as ruler. On 19 July 1949, Laos became an Associated State within the French Union, and on 22 October 1953 it became fully independent within that Union.

INTERNATIONAL COMMISSION. Indian stamps overprinted for the use of the International Commission in Laos are listed in the *British Commonwealth* Catalogue.

PRINTERS. All stamps of Laos were printed at the Government Printing Works, Paris, *unless otherwise stated.*

KINGDOM

King Sisavang Vong
10 May 1947–29 October 1959

1 River Mekong

2 King Sisavang Vong

1951 (13 Nov). *T* **1** (*various views*) *and T* **2**. Recess. *P* 13.

1	1	10 c. bright green and blue-green	5	5
2		20 c. carmine and claret	8	8
3		30 c. bright blue and indigo	45	35
4	−	50 c. purple-brown and deep brown	15	12
5	−	60 c. orange and vermilion	15	12
6	−	70 c. greenish blue and bright blue	15	12
7	−	1 p. reddish violet and violet	20	20
8	2	1 p. 50, brown-purple and deep brown	35	25
9	−	2 p. grey-green and blue-green	7·00	1·00
10	−	3 p. red and claret	35	30
11	−	5 p. bright blue and indigo	50	45
12	−	10 p. brown-purple and deep brown	90	65
1/12		Set of 12	9·50	3·50

Designs: *Horiz*— 50 c. to 70 c. Luang Prabang; 1 p., 2 p. to 10 p. Vientiane.

3 Laotian Woman

D **5** Vat Sisaket Shrine

D **6** Sampans

4 Laotian Woman Weaving

(Des M. Leguay. Eng R. Serres (T **3**), Pheulpin (T **4**). Recess)

1952 (13 Apr–19 July). *P* 13. (*a*) *POSTAGE.*

13	3	30 c. reddish violet and indigo	15	10
14		80 c. deep blue-green and emerald	15	12
15		1 p. 10, carmine-red and crimson	30	15
16		1 p. 90, blue and indigo	50	40
17		3 p. black-brown and purple-brown	50	40

(*b*) *AIR. T* **4** *and similar horiz design inscr* "POST AERIENNE"

18	−	3 p. 30, violet and deep violet (19.7)	45	30
19	4	10 p. deep blue-green and ultramarine	1·00	70
20		20 p. orange-red and crimson	1·50	1·00
21		30 p. purple-brown and brown-black	2·10	1·75
13/21		Set of 9	6·00	4·50
MS21*a*		135×55 mm. No. 18. Imperf	£200	£200

Design:—3 p. 30, Vat Pra Keo shrine.

(Des M. Leguay. Eng Dufresne (10 c. to 5 p.). Pheulpin (10 p.). Recess)

1952 (13 Apr)–**53**. *POSTAGE DUE. P* 13.

D22	D **5**	10 c. chocolate	10	10
D23		20 c. deep violet	10	10
D24		50 c. carmine-red	8	8
D25		1 p. deep green	10	10
D26		2 p. blue	10	10
D27		5 p. bright purple	40	35
D28	D **6**	10 p. indigo (14.7.53)	50	50
D22/26		Set of 7	1·25	1·25

1952. *Anniversary of First Issue of Laos Stamps. Souvenir booklet containing 26 sheets. Nos. 1/12, 13/17, 19/21 and D22/8. Imperf.*

MS21*b*	26 sheets each 130×90 mm	£150

5 King Sisavang Vong and U.P.U. Monument

(Des Pheulpin. Recess)

1952 (7 Dec). *First Anniv of Admission of Laos into U.P.U.* P 13. (a) POSTAGE.

22	**5**	80 c. deep reddish violet, blue and indigo	30	30
23		1 p. chestnut, carmine-red and lake ..	30	30
24		1 p. 20, blue and deep reddish violet ..	30	30
25		1 p. 50, purple-brown, emerald & dp grn	30	30
26		1 p. 90, deep blue-green & blackish brn	30	30

(b) AIR. Inscr "POSTE AVION"

27	**5**	25 p. indigo and ultramarine	2·00	2·00
28		50 p. blackish brown, maroon & pur-brn	2·00	2·00
22/28		Set of 7	5·00	5·00

6 Mother and Child

7 Native Musicians

(Des M. Leguay. Eng Pheulpin. Recess)

1953 (14 July). *Red Cross Fund.* P 13.

29	**6**	1 p. 50+1 p. red, brown-purple & indigo	1·00	1·00
30		3 p.+1 p. 50, red and deep blue-green ..	1·00	1·00
31		3 p. 90+2 p. 50, red, brown-pur & dp brn	1·00	1·00

(Des Leliepvre. Eng Pheulpin. Recess)

1953 (14 July). P 13.

32	**7**	4 p. 50, turquoise-blue and indigo	40	40
33		6 p. chocolate and violet-grey ..	50	50

8 Buddha

(Des M. Leguay. Eng Dufresne (4 p.), Pheulpin (others). Recess)

1953 (18 Nov). *AIR. Various statues of Buddha as T 8 and similar designs.* P 13.

34		4 p. green	60	30
35		6 p. 50, deep bluish green ..	55	50
36		9 p. blue-green	80	55
37		11 p. 50, yellow-orange, chocolate & scar	1·00	80
38		40 p. deep purple	1·90	1·50
39		100 p. yellow-olive	5·50	4·00
34/39		Set of 6	9·50	7·00

Designs: Horiz—4 p. Reclining. Vert—6 p. 90, Seated; 9 p. Standing (full-face); 40 p. Standing (facing right); 100 p. Buddha and temple dancer.

9 Vientiane

(Des M. Leguay. Eng Pheulpin. Recess)

1954 (4 Mar). *Golden Jubilee of King Sisavang Vong.* P 13. (a) POSTAGE

40	**9**	2 p. reddish violet and indigo ..	25·00	11·00
41		3 p. brown-red and deep brown	25·00	15·00

(b) AIR. Inscr "POSTE AERIENNE"

42	**9**	50 p. turquoise-blue and indigo	70·00	70·00

10 Ravana

(Des M. Leguay. Eng Pheulpin. Recess)

1955 (28 Oct). *AIR. New Currency. "Ramayana" (dramatic poem). Various designs as T 10.* P 13.

43		2 k. indigo, emerald and bluish green ..	40	35
44		4 k. red and lake-brown ..	50	50
45		5 k. yellow-olive, blackish brn & rose-red	75	50
46		10 k. black, orange and sepia ..	1·50	1·50
47		20 k. yellow-olive, deep green & brt violet	1·90	1·75
48		30 k. black, brown and ultramarine ..	2·50	2·25
43/48		Set of 6	7·00	6·50

Designs: Horiz—4 k. Hanuman, the white monkey; 5 k. Ninh Laphath, the black monkey. Vert—10 k. Sita and Rama; 20 k. Luci and Ravana's friend; 30 k. Rama.

11 Buddha and Worshippers

(Des M. Leguay. Eng Pheulpin. Recess)

1956 (24 May). *2500th Birth Anniv of Buddha.* P 13. (a) POSTAGE

49	**11**	2 k. red-brown..	2·00	1·50
50		3 k. black	2·00	1·50
51		5 k. blackish brown	2·50	2·00

(b) AIR. Inscr "POSTE AERIENNE"

52	**11**	20 k. carmine and carmine-red ..	15·00	15·00
53		30 k. yellow-olive and bistre ..	15·00	15·00
49/53		Set of 5	32·00	32·00

Laos left the French Union on 7 December 1956.

SET PRICES

Set prices are given for many issues generally those containing five stamps or more. Definitive sets include one of each value or major colour change but do not cover different perforations, die types or minor shades. Where a choice is possible the catalogue set prices are based on the cheapest versions of the stamps included in the listings.

Lebanon

100 Centiemes = 1 Piastre

The Lebanon area, inhabited mainly by Maronite Christians and Moslem Druses, came under Turkish rule in 1516 and was allowed a degree of self-government. From 1697 to 1842 it had Emirs of the Shihab family of Sunni Moslems. After a civil war, won by the Druses in 1860, the Powers intervened, and by the Organic Law of 1861, the Lebanon received autonomy under a Christian governor appointed by the Sultan.

FRENCH POST OFFICE IN TURKISH EMPIRE

A French Post Office opened in Beirut in about 1840 and from the late 1850s unoverprinted stamps of France were used there, identified by the cancellations "3706" (small figures) and "5082" (large figures). From 1885 the General Issues for French P.O.s in the Turkish Empire were used there. The stamp listed below was issued as a provisional at Beirut.

1 Piastre

Beyrouth

(2)

1905 (17 Jan). *No. 15 of French Post Offices in the Turkish Empire surch with T 2, in greenish black.*

24	1 pi. on 15 c. pale red	..	..	£325 55·00
	a. "Piastte" for "Piastre"	..	..	£1100 £170

The French Post Office in Beirut closed in 1914.

B. FRENCH MANDATED TERRITORY OF GREATER LEBANON

After the defeat of Turkey in 1918, the Lebanon came under French military administration, and on 25 April 1920 France was given a mandate by the League of Nations to administer Syria, including the Lebanon, which was given a separate status on 1 September. To the Lebanon as defined in 1861 were added Beirut and other coastal towns and the inland Bekaa area, and the whole was renamed Greater Lebanon (Grand Liban). The mandate came into effect on 29 September 1923.

Until September 1923 the French military occupation stamps of Syria were used in the Lebanon, and then, till the end of 1923, the joint issues for Syria and Greater Lebanon (Syria Nos. 97, etc.).

GRAND LIBAN 10 CENTIEMES

(1)

GRAND LIBAN 2 PIASTRES

(2)

1924 (1 Jan–June). *Stamps of France surch.*

(a) Definitive stamps. (i) *Surch as T* 1

1	11	10 c. on 2 c. claret	..	..	25	25
		a. "CE" omitted	..	..	5·00	
		b. Surch inverted	..	..	5·00	5·00
		c. Surch double	..	..	5·00	5·00
2	18	25 c. on 5 c. orange	..	..	40	20
3		50 c. on 10 c. green	..	..	30	15
		a. "R" omitted	..	..	15·00	8·00
		b. Surch double	..	..	6·00	6·00

4	15	75 c. on 15 c. olive-green	..	..	60	45
5	18	1 p. on 20 c. chocolate	..	..	40	20
		a. Surch inverted ..	..	..	6·00	6·00
		b. Surch double	..	..	6·00	6·00
6		1,25 p. on 25 c. blue	..	..	75	50
7		1,50 p. on 30 c. orange	..	..	60	40
8		1,50 p. on 30 c. scarlet (Apr)	..	..	60	40
9	15	2,50 p. on 50 c. blue	..	..	50	25
		a. Figure "0" omitted	..	..	5·00	
		b. Surch inverted ..	..	..	6·00	6·00

(ii) *Surch as T* 2

10	13	2 p. on 40 c. red and pale blue	..	75	65
		a. "2" omitted	..	..	15·00	
		b. Surch inverted	..	..	7·00	7·00
11		3 p. on 60 c. violet and blue	..	2·00	1·75
12		5 p. on 1 f. lake and yellow	..	2·50	2·00
13		10 p. on 2 f. orange and blue-green ..	4·00	3·00
		a. Surch inverted ..	..	..	12·00	12·00
14		25 p. on 5 f. deep blue and buff	..	7·00	5·00
		a. Error. "LIABN"	..	..	60·00	
		b. Surch inverted ..	..	..	23·00	23·00

(b) Pasteur type surch as T 1 (June)

15	30	50 c. on 10 c. green	..	..	25	20
		a. Surch inverted ..	..	..	5·00	5·00
16		1,50 p. on 30 c. red	..	..	60	50
17		2,50 p. on 50 c. blue	..	..	35	20
		a. Error. "250,"	..	..	10·00	10·00
		b. Surch inverted ..	..	..	7·00	7·00
		c. Surch double	..	..	8·00	8·00

(c) Olympic Games stamps (Nos. 401/4) surch as T 1 *or* 2 (June)

18	31	50 c. on 10 c. green and yellow-green	7·50	7·50
		a. Surch inverted ..	..	65·00	
19	–	1,25 p. on 25 c. deep and dull carmine	7·50	7·50
		a. Figure "1" omitted	..	15·00	
		b. Surch inverted	..	65·00	
20	–	1,50 p. on 30 c. red and black ..	..	7·50	7·50
		a. Surch inverted ..	..	65·00	
21	–	2,50 p. on 50 c. ultramarine	..	7·50	7·50
		a. Surch inverted ..	..	65·00	
1/21		*Set of 21*	..	..	45·00	42·00

All values exist with thin "G" in "GRAND" and there are many other minor varieties of type and spacing.

Poste par Avion
GRAND LIBAN
2 PIASTRES

(2a)

(Surch by Capuchin Fathers, Beirut)

1924 (1 Jan). *AIR. Stamps of France surch as T* 2a.

22	13	2 p. on 40 c. red and pale blue	..	2·75	3·00
23		3 p. on 60 c. violet and blue ..	..	2·75	3·00
24		5 p. on 1 f. lake and yellow	..	2·75	3·00
		a. Figure "5" omitted	..	..	£110	
25		10 p. on 2 f. orange and blue-green	..	2·75	3·00
		a. Surch and opt inverted	..	25·00	25·00
22/25		*Set of 4*	..	..	10·00	11·00

1924 (1 Jan). *POSTAGE DUE. Postage Due stamps of France surch as T* 1.

D26	D 11	50 c. on 10 c. pale brown ..	..	1·25	1·10
D27		1 p. on 20 c. olive-green ..	..	1·25	1·10
D28		2 p. on 30 c. carmine	..	..	1·25	1·10
D29		3 p. on 50 p. dull claret ..	..	1·25	1·10
D30		5 p. on 1 f. claret/straw ..	..	1·25	1·10
D26/30		*Set of 5*	..	..	5·50	4·50

The note after No. 21 also applies here.

Lebanon

G^d Liban   Grand Liban
1 Piastre   2 Piastres

لبنان الكبير   لبنان الكبير

عرش ١   غروش ٢٠

(3)   (4)

غرش ٢   هروش ٢

(a) (singular)   (b) (plural)

1924 (1 July)–**25**. *Stamps of France surch as T* **4** (*on T* **13**) *or as T* **3** (*others*).

(a) Postage stamps

26	**11**	0 p. 10 on 2 c. claret ..	..	8	8
		a. Figure "1" inverted	..	4·50	
		b. Surch inverted ..	..	3·75	3·75
		c. Surch double ..	..	3·75	3·75
27	**18**	0 p. 25 on 5 c. orange	..	20	20
		a. Surch inverted ..	..	4·00	4·00
		b. Surch double ..	..	4·00	4·00
28		0 p. 50 on 10 c. green	..	30	30
		a. Surch inverted ..	..	5·00	5·00
		b. Surch double ..	..	4·00	4·00
29	**15**	0 p. 75 on 15 c. sage-green ..		30	30
		a. Surch inverted ..	..	6·00	6·00
		b. Surch double ..	..	4·00	4·00
30	**18**	1 p. on 20 c. lake-brown	..	15	15
		a. Surch inverted ..	..	3·75	3·75
		b. Surch double ..	..	3·75	3·75
31		1 p. 25 on 25 c. blue ..	..	35	35
		a. Surch inverted ..	..	7·00	7·00
		b. Surch double ..	..	5·00	5·00
32		1 p. 50 on 30 c. scarlet	..	25	25
		a. Surch inverted ..	..	6·00	6·00
		b. Surch double ..	..	4·00	4·00
33		1 p. 50 on 30 c. orange (1.25)		20·00	20·00
		a. Surch inverted ..	..	85·00	85·00
34		2 p. on 35 c. violet (26.2.25)		40	40
		a. Surch inverted ..	..	7·00	7·00
35	**13**	2 p. on 40 c. red and pale blue		15	15
		a. Surch inverted ..	..	3·50	3·50
		b. Surch double ..	..	3·75	3·75
		c. 4th line of T **4** as (a) instead of (b)			
		(11.24) ..	..	45	45
		ca. Surch inverted ..	..	5·00	5·00
36		2 p. on 45 c. dp green & blue (26.2.25)	5·00	5·00
		a. Surch inverted ..	..	20·00	20·00
37		3 p. on 60 c. violet and blue ..		60	60
		a. Surch inverted ..	..	6·00	6·00
38	**15**	3 p. on 60 c. violet (26.2.25)		45	45
39		4 p. on 85 c. vermilion (2.2.25)		35	25
40	**13**	5 p. on 1 f. lake and yellow ..		90	80
		a. Surch inverted ..	..	7·00	7·00
		b. Surch double ..	..	7·00	7·00
41		10 p. on 2 f. orange and blue-green		1·50	1·50
42		25 p. on 5 f. deep blue and buff		2·00	2·00

(b) Pasteur type

43	**30**	0 p. 50 on 10 c. green	..	12	10
		a. Surch inverted ..	..	4·50	4·50
		b. Surch double ..	..	3·25	3·25
44		0 p. 75 on 15 c. green (26.2.25)		40	40
45		1 p. 50 on 30 c. red ..	..	30	30
		a. Figure "1" omitted ..	..	12·00	
		b. Line under "d" ..	..	6·00	
		c. "C" for "G" ..	..	5·00	
		d. Surch inverted ..	..	5·50	5·50
46		2 p. on 45 c. scarlet (26.2.25)		60	60
		a. Surch inverted ..	..	7·00	7·00
47		2 p. 50 on 50 c. blue ..	..	10	10
		a. Comma omitted after "2" (12.24)		30	30
		b. Surch inverted ..	..	6·00	6·00
		c. Surch double ..	..	6·00	6·00
48		4 p. on 75 c. blue (1.25)	..	60	60

(c) Olympic Games stamps (Nos. 401/4) (25.9.24)

49	**31**	0 p. 50 on 10 c. green and yellow-green	8·00	8·00
		a. Surch inverted ..	..	60·00	
50	–	1 p. 25 on 25 c. deep and dull carmine	8·00	8·00
		a. Surch inverted ..	..	60·00	

51	–	1 p. 50 on 30 c. red and black ..	..	8·00	8·00
		a. Surch inverted ..	..	60·00	
52	–	2 p. 50 on 50 c. ultramarine and blue ..	8·00	8·00
		a. Surch inverted ..	..	60·00	

(d) Ronsard stamp (12.24)

53	**35**	4 p. on 75 c. blue/*bluish*	..	45	45
		a. Surch inverted ..	..	12·00	12·00
26/53		*Set of 28*	..	60·00	60·00

G^d Liban
2 Piastres   Avion

غروش ٢   لبنان الكبير   طيارة

(4a)

1924 (1 July). *AIR. "Olivier Merson" type of France surch as T* **4a**.

54	**13**	2 p. on 40 c. red and pale blue	..	2·75	2·75
55		3 p. on 60 c. violet and blue ..	..	2·75	2·75
		a. Opt double ..	..	30·00	
56		5 p. on 1 f. lake and yellow ..		2·75	2·75
		a. Surch and opt inverted ..		27·00	
57		10 p. on 2 f. orange and blue-green		2·75	2·75
		a. Surch and opt inverted ..		27·00	
		b. Surch and opt double ..		27·00	
54/57		*Set of 4* ..	..	10·00	10·00

1924 (1 July). *POSTAGE DUE. Type D* **11** *of France surch as T* **3**.

D58	D **11**	0 p. 50, on 10 c. pale brown	..	1·25	75
D59		1 p. on 20 c. olive-green ..		1·25	75
D60		2 p. on 30 c. carmine ..		1·25	75
		a. 4th line of T **3** as (a) instead of (b)	1·50	90
D61		3 p. on 50 c. dull claret ..		1·50	90
		a. 4th line of T **3** as (a) instead of (b)	1·75	1·00
D62		5 p. on 1 f. claret/*straw* ..		1·75	1·00
D58/62		*Set of 5* ..	..	6·00	3·50

5 Cedar of Lebanon   6 Beirut

6a Beit ed-Din   6b Baalbek Ruins

6c Mouktara   7 Tripoli

(Des J. de la Nézière. 0 p. 10, litho; others photo
Vaugirard, Paris)

1925 (1 Mar). *T **5** and various views as **6** to **7**.* P 12½
(*No.* 58) *or* 13½ *(remainder).*

58	0 p. 10, violet		8	8
59	0 p. 25, olive-black		10	8
60	0 p. 50, yellow-green		8	8
61	0 p. 75, brown-red		10	8
62	1 p. bright claret		35	30
63	1 p. 25, green		40	35
64	1 p. 50, bright rose		10	8
65	2 p. sepia		25	8
66	2 p. 50, light blue		40	25
67	3 p. brown		40	25
68	5 p. bright violet		50	50
69	10 p. plum		70	65
70	25 p. bright blue		2·50	2·50
58/70	*Set of 13*		5·50	5·00

Designs: *Horiz*—0 p. 50, Tripoli; 1 p. 50, Tyre; 2 p. Zahle;
2 p. 50, Baalbek; 3 p. Deir el-Kamar; 5 p. Sidon; 25 p. Beirut
(*different*).

AVION

طيارة

(7*a*)

1925 (1 Mar). *Nos.* 65 *and* 67/9 *optd with T **7a**, in green.*

71	—	2 p. sepia		1·00	80
72	—	3 p. brown		1·00	80
73	—	5 p. bright violet		1·00	80
		a. Opt inverted		10·00	
74	**7**	10 p. plum		1·00	80
71/74		*Set of 4*		3·50	3·00

D **7** Nahr el-Kalb

(Des J. de la Nézière. Photo Vaugirard, Paris)

1925 (1 Mar). *POSTAGE DUE. As Type* D **7** *(views).* P 13½.

D75	0 p. 50, brown/yellow		15	15
D76	1 p. brown-lake/carmine		25	25
D77	2 p. black/blue		40	40
D78	3 p. deep brown/red		80	80
D79	5 p. black/green		3·00	2·00
D75/79	*Set of 5*		4·00	3·00

Designs:—1 p. Pine forest, Beirut; 2 p. Pigeon Grotto,
Beirut; 3 p. Beaufort Castle; 5 p. Baalbek.

(7*b*)

1926 (1 May). *AIR. Nos.* 65 *and* 67/9 *optd with T **7b**, in red,
reading vertically on* 10 p.

75	2 p. sepia		1·00	1·00
	a. Opt inverted		10·00	
76	3 p. brown		1·00	1·00
	a. Opt inverted		10·00	
77	5 p. bright violet		1·00	1·00
	a. Opt inverted		10·00	
78	10 p. plum		1·00	1·00
	a. Opt inverted		10·00	
75/78	*Set of 4*		3·50	3·50

Secours aux Réfugiés

Secours
aux
Réfugiés

اعانات للاجئين

Aff‌ᵗ الاجرة

0ᴾ·50 غ ½

(7*c*)

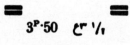

اعانات للاجئين

Aff‌ᵗ الاجرة

0ᴾ·50 غ ½

(7*d*)

1926 (1 May). *War Refugee Charity stamps.*

(*a*) POSTAGE. *Stamps of* 1925 *surch as T **7c** or **7d** (No.* 89)

79	0 p. 25+0 p. 25 olive-black (R.)		1·40	1·40
80	0 p. 50+0 p. 25 yellow-green		1·40	1·40
81	0 p. 75+0 p. 25 brown-red		1·40	1·40
82	1 p.+0 p. 50 bright claret		1·40	1·40
83	1 p. 25+0 p. 50 green (R.)		1·40	1·40
	a. Black surch		8·00	
84	1 p. 50+0 p. 50 bright rose		1·40	1·40
	a. Surch double		15·00	15·00
85	2 p.+0 p. 75 sepia (R.)		1·40	1·40
86	2 p. 50+0 p. 75 light blue (R.)		1·40	1·40
87	3 p.+1 p. brown (R.)		1·50	1·50
	a. Black surch		8·00	
88	5 p.+1 p. bright violet		1·50	1·50
89	10 p.+2 p. plum		1·50	1·50
90	25 p.+5 p. bright blue (R.)		1·50	1·50
79/90	*Set of 12*		15·00	15·00

All values exist with surcharge inverted (*Price* £12 *each
unused*).

(*b*) AIR. *Nos.* 75/8 *surch as T **7c**, in black (new value in red
on Nos.* 91/3)

91	2 p.+1 p. sepia		2·00	2·00
	a. Type **7c** inverted		7·00	
92	3 p.+2 p. brown		2·00	2·00
	a. Figure "2" omitted		£150	£150
93	5 p.+3 p. violet		2·00	2·00
94	10 p.+5 p. plum (*Type **7c** vert up*)		2·00	2·00
	a. "au" for "aux" in opt		8·00	8·00
91/94	*Set of 4*		7·00	7·00

These stamps were sold at face value plus the value indicated
by the surcharge, but were only available for postage to the
first amount, the difference going to the Refugee Fund.

C. REPUBLIC UNDER FRENCH MANDATE

The Lebanese Republic was proclaimed by the French on
23 May 1926.

═ ═
3ᴾ·50 ع ½

(7*e*)

═4ᴾ·50 ه ½═

(7*f*)

1926 (Sept–Dec). *Stamps of* 1925 *surch as T **7e** or **7f**.*

95	**7e**	3 p. 50 on 0 p. 75, brown-red	15	15
96		4 p. on 0 p. 25, olive-black (8.10)	40	40
		a. Surch double	2·50	2·50
		b. Thin "4" as in T **7f** (12.11)	25	25
		ba. Surch inverted	3·50	3·50
98	**7f**	4 p. 50 on 0 p. 75, brown-red (Dec)	40	40
		a. Arab figure omitted	1·50	1·50
		b. Surch inverted	5·00	5·00
99	**7e**	6 p. on 2 p. 50, light blue	20	20
		a. Surch inverted	5·00	5·00

100	7f	7 p. 50 on 2 p: 50, light blue (Dec)		40	40
		a. Surch inverted		5·00	5·00
101	7e	12 p. on 1 p. 25, green		25	25
		a. Surch inverted		6·00	6·00
		b. Surch back and front		3·50	3·50
102	7f	15 p. on 25 p. bright blue (Dec)		40	40
103	7e	20°p. on 1 p. 25, green (8.10)		1·25	1·25
		a. Surch back and front		4·00	4·00
95/103		Set of 8		2·75	2·75

Republique
Libanaise

━━━━━━

━━━━━━ ## République Libanaise

(8)   (9)

Two types of 15 p. on 25 p.

(a) Surcharge at top, "République Libanaise" at foot.
(b) Surcharge at foot, "République Libanaise" at top.

1927 (1 July–Oct). *Stamps of 1925 and provisionals as for 1926–27 optd as T 8 or 9.*

104	0 p. 10, violet (R.)			5	5
	a. Opt in black			6·00	6·00
105	0 p. 50, yellow-green			5	10
	a. Opt inverted			3·00	3·00
106	1 p. bright claret			8	8
	a. Opt inverted			3·00	3·00
107	1 p. 50, bright rose			20	20
	a. Opt inverted			4·00	4·00
	b. Opt double			5·00	5·00
108	2 p. sepia			35	20
109	3 p. brown			25	15
110	4 p. on 0 p. 25, olive-black			20	8
111	4 p. 50 on 0 p. 75, brown-red			25	25
	a. Opt inverted			5·00	5·00
112	5 p. bright violet			60	40
113	7 p. 50 on 2 p. 50, light blue			15	12
114	10 p. plum			70	30
115	15 p. on 25 p. bright blue (a)			1·90	1·40
116	15 p. on 25 p. bright blue (b) (10.27)			2·00	1·90
117	25 p. bright blue			2·00	1·25
	a. Opt inverted			10·00	10·00
104/117	Set of 14			8·00	6·00

The figures of the surcharges on Nos. 110 and 111 are below the cancelling bars, instead of above them as in Nos. 96b and 98

1927 (1 July). *AIR. Nos. 75/8 optd as T 9 (in two lines on 10 p.).*

118	2 p. sepia		1·50	1·50
119	3 p. brown		1·50	1·50
120	5 p. bright violet		1·50	1·50
121	10 p. plum		1·50	1·50
118/121	Set of 4		5·50	5·50

1927 (1 July). *POSTAGE DUE. Nos. D75/9 optd as T 9.*

D122	0 p. 50, brown/yellow		15	15
D123	1 p. brown-lake/carmine		30	30
D124	2 p. black/blue		50	50
D125	3 p. deep brown/red		1·00	1·00
D126	5 p. black/green		1·50	1·50
D122/126	Set of 5		3·00	3·00

الجمهورية اللبنانية

(10)

1928. *Nos. 113 and 116 additionally optd. above the surch. with T 10.*

122	7 p. 50 on 2 p. 50, light blue (R.)*		75	75
123	15 p. on 25 p. bright blue (R.)*		5·00	4·00
	a. Arabic opt inverted		40·00	

Red cancelling bars (as for No. 135), cover the Arabic inscription at foot of No. 123

1928 (May Dec). *Stamps of 1927, further opted with T 10 and with additional bars (except No. 131), above or below, obliterating former Arabic inscription.*

124	0 p. 10, violet (R.)			10	10
	a. French opt omitted			4·00	4·00
	b. Arabic opt vert			6·00	6·00
125	0 p. 50, yellow-green			30	30
	a. Arabic opt inverted			2·50	2·50
	b. Entire opt inverted			2·50	2·50
126	1 p. bright claret			10	10
	a. Entire opt inverted			3·75	3·75
127	1 p. 50, bright rose			40	40
128	2 p. sepia (R.) ⁑			60	50
	a. Error "épublique Libana"			3·00	3·00
128b	2 p. sepia (a Bk., b R.)⁺			18·00	15·00
129	3 p. brown			30	30
130	4 p. on 0 p. 25, ol-blk (a Bk., b R.)⁺			30	30
131	4 p. 50 on 0 p. 75, brown-red			45	45
132	5 p. bright violet (a Bk., b R.)⁺			65	65
132a	5 p. bright violet (R.)⁑ (14 Dec)			75	75
132b	5 p. bright violet (R.)⁑ (Dec)			90	90
133	7 p. 50 on 2 p. 50, light blue (R.)*			75	75
134	10 p. plum			75	75
	a. Entire opt inverted			5·00	5·00
	b. Entire opt double			4·00	4·00
135	15 p. on 25 p. bright blue (R.)*			1·50	1·50
136	25 p. bright blue (a Bk., b R.)⁺			2·10	2·10
136a	25 p. bright blue (R.)⁑			5·00	5·00

* There were three issues of the 7 p. 50 on 2 p. 50 and 15 p. on 25 p. In the first only the Arabic overprint is in red and is applied *above* the surcharge, whereas in the second both the French and Arabic overprints are in red *below* it. For the third, see Nos. 149/50.

⁑ The French and Arabic overprints on Nos. 128, 132a and 136a are both red. On No. 132a "République Libanaise" is above the Arabic overprint, but on No. 132b it is below it and closer. These overprints were applied, in each case, at one operation.

⁺ On Nos. 128b, 130, 132 and 136 the overprints are bicoloured, *a* and *b* denote French and Arabic overprints respectively.

1928 (May). *AIR. Nos. 118/21 further optd with T 10 and with additional bars (except on No. 139) obliterating former Arabic inscription.*

137	2 p. sepia		2·00	2·00
138	3 p. brown		2·00	2·00
139	5 p. bright violet		2·00	2·00
140	10 p. plum		2·00	2·00
137/140	Set of 4		7·00	7·00

République Libanaise

الجمهورية اللبنانية

(11)

1928 (May). *AIR. Nos. 65 and 67/9 optd as T 11.*

141	2 p. sepia (R.)		65	65
	a. Error. On 2 p., No. 71		80·00	
	b. Opt double		8·00	
142	3 p. brown (R.)		50	50
	a. Error. On 3 p., No. 72		80·00	
	b. Opt double		8·00	
143	5 p. bright violet (R.)		65	65
	a. Error. On 5 p., No. 73		80·00	
144	10 p. plum (R.)		70	1·00
	a. Error. On 10 p., No. 74		80·00	
	b. Opt reading down		5·00	
	c. Républiqne" for "République"		2·50	

The overprint on No. 144 is vertical, with the exception of the bars.

1928 (May). *POSTAGE DUE. Nos. D122/6 additionally optd as T 10 but with bars in upper corners obliterating the old Arabic inscriptions (except on 2 p.).*

D145	0 p. 50, brown/yellow (R.)		30	30
D146	1 p. brown-lake/carmine		40	40

D147 2 p. black/*blue* (R.) .. .. .. 1·50 80
D148 3 p. deep brown/*red* .. .. .. 2·00 1·10
D149 5 p. black/*green* (R.) .. .. .. 3·00 1·50
D145/149 *Set of* 5 .. .. 6·50 3·00
See also Nos. D151/3.

(12) (13)

1928 (June)–**29**. *Stamps of* 1925 *surch with T* **12** *or as T* **13**.
145 05 on 0 p. 10, violet (2.11.28) .. 5 5
  a. Surch double .. .. .. 5·00 5·00
146 0 p. 50 on 0 p. 75, brown-red (7.29) .. 20 20
147 2 p. on 1 p. 25, green (R.) .. 20 20
  a. Surch double .. .. .. 5·00 5·00
148 4 p. on 0 p. 25, olive-black (R.) .. 20 20
  a. "4" inverted .. .. .. 75·00
  b. Surch inverted .. .. 9·50 9·50
  c. Surch double .. .. 6·00 6·00
149 7 p. 50 on 2 p. 50, light blue (R.) .. 25 25
  a. Opt inverted .. .. 6·00 5·00
  b. Opt double .. .. .. 6·00 5·00
  c. Opt on back .. .. 4·00 4·00
  d. Surch "5 p. 70" instead of "7 p. 50" £130
  e. "Républiqne" for "République" .. 2·25 2·25
150 15 p. on 25 p. bright blue (R.) .. .. 3·00 3·00
  a. Surch double .. .. 8·00
145/150 *Set of* 6 .. .. .. 3·50 3·50

1928 (July–Oct). *POSTAGE DUE. Nos.* D75, D77 *and* D79
optd with T **9** *and* **10** *at one operation.*
D151 0 p. 50, black/*yellow* (R.) 40 15
D152 2 p. black/*blue* (R.) (Oct) .. .. 3·00 1·00
D153 5 p. black/*green* (R.) (Oct) .. .. 7·00 3·50
  In Nos. D145/9, bars obliterating the old Arabic inscriptions
are found on all values except the 2 p., whereas in this set the
only exception is the 5 p.

15 15

I II

1929–30. *AIR. Stamps of* 1925–28 *optd with an aeroplane
only* (*No.* 152) *or as T* **11**. *Nos.* 154/5 *have surcharges
and bars in addition.*
151 0 p. 50, yellow-green (R.) (10.6.29) .. 12 12
  a. "Républiqne" for "République" .. 75
  b. Opt inverted .. .. .. 7·50
152 0 p. 50 on 0 p. 75, brown-red (B.)
  (146) (9.29) 25 25
  a. "Républiqne" for "République" .. 80
  b. Surch normal, aeroplane inverted .. 7·50 7·50
  c. Aeroplane normal, surch inverted .. 7·00
  d. Surch double .. .. 10·00
153 1 p. bright claret (7.29) 30 30
  a. "Républiqne" for "République" .. 80
  b. Opt inverted .. .. 9·00
154 2 p. on 1 p. 25, green (R.) (1.30) .. 35 35
  a. "Républiqne" for "République" .. 75
  b. Surch inverted .. .. 8·00
  c. Surch double .. .. 8·00
155 15 p. on 25 p. bright blue (I) (R.) (7.29) 65·00 65·00
  a. "Républiqne" for "République"
  b. Type II £100 £100
156 25 p. bright blue (R.) (7.29) .. 40·00 40·00
  a. "Républiqne" for "République"
  b. Opt inverted .. ..
151/156 *Set of* 6 .. .. .. 95·00 95·00
  Beware of forgeries of No. 155.

14 Silk-worm, Larva, Cocoon and Moth

(Typo Imp Gédéon, Beirut).
1930 (11 Feb). *Silk Congress. P* 11.
157 **14** 4 p. sepia .. .. .. 3·25 3·25
158 4½ p. vermilion .. .. 2·50 2·50
159 7½ p. deep blue .. .. 2·75 2·75
160 10 p. violet .. .. 2·75 2·75
161 15 p. deep green .. .. 2·75 2·75
162 25 p. pale claret .. .. 2·75 2·75
157/162 *Set of* 6 .. .. .. 15·00 13·00
  The above exist imperforate from a limited supply used only
for presentation purposes.

IMPERFORATE STAMPS. Most of the following issues up
to 1945 exist imperforate from very limited printings.

FORGERIES. Forgeries exist of stamps as Types **15** and **20**
and of most issues between 1944 and 1955. The details of
the designs and lettering are less sharp and the colours
generally paler than in the originals.

15 Cedars of Lebanon **16** Nahr el-Kalb

16a Baalbek

A B C

D E

F

G

(Des J. de la Nézière. Ptd Vaugirard, Paris)
1930–36. *Various views and frames.*
  (*a*) *As T* **15**, *lithographed. P* 12½
163 0 p. 10, brown-orange (A) (12.30) .. 5 5
163a 0 p. 10, brown-orange (B) (1932) .. 65 65
163b 0 p. 10, yellow-orange (C) (1936) .. 5 5
164 0 p. 20, yellow-brown (10.30) .. 10 5
165 0 p. 25, blue (D) (6.31) .. 5 5
165a 0 p. 25, blue (E) (1932) .. 5 5

(b) As T **16** and **16**a in photogravure. P 13½

166	0 p. 50, red-brown (F) (7.30)		30	25
166a	0 p. 50, red-brown (G)		1·50	1·25
166b	0 p. 75, brown (8.32)		10	10
167	1 p. green (10.30)		25	12
167a	1 p. deep plum (1.10.35)		25	12
168	1 p. 50, deep plum (7.30)		50	40
168a	1 p. 50, green (11.32)		25	12
169	2 p. greenish blue (4.31)		60	30
170	3 p. sepia (5.31)		60	20
171	4 p. red-brown (9.30)		60	10
172	4 p. 50, carmine (10.30)		60	30
173	5 p. blackish green (7.30)		30	20
174	6 p. purple (10.30)		60	40
175	7 p. 50, deep blue (5.30)		60	20
176	10 p. deep green (6.30)		90	20
177	15 p. deep purple (10.30)		1·25	30
178	25 p. blue-green (9.30)		2·00	40
179	50 p. yellow-green (10.30)		7·00	3·25
180	100 p. slate-black (10.30)		6·00	3·00

Designs: As T **15**—0 p. 10, Beirut; 0 p. 25, Baalbek. As T **16** and **16**a—0 p. 50, Bickfaya; 1 p. Saida (Sidon); 1 p. 50, 5 p. Beit ed-Din (different); 2 p. Tripoli; 0 p. 75, 3 p., 7 p. 50, 100 p. Baalbek (different); 4 p. 50, Beaufort; 6 p. Tyre; 10 p. Hasbaya; 15 p. Afka Falls; 25 p. Beirut; 50 p. Deir el-Kamar.

Redrawn types exist of the 7 p. 50, 10 p. and 15 p. having larger marginal inscriptions at foot.

See also Nos. 248/51.

18 Skiing   **19** Djounié Bay

(Des M. Farrouk and P. Mourani. Photo Vaugirard, Paris)

1936 (12 Oct). AIR. Tourist Propaganda. P 13½.

191	**18**	0 p. 50, deep green		50	50
192	**19**	1 p. orange-vermilion		65	65
193	**18**	2 p. blackish violet		70	70
194	**19**	3 p. yellow-green		80	80
195	**18**	5 p. lake		1·50	1·50
196	**19**	10 p. chestnut		1·75	1·75
197		15 p. carmine-lake		11·00	11·00
198	**18**	25 p. green		30·00	30·00
191/198		Set of 8		42·00	42·00

17 Jebeil (Byblos)

(Photo Vaugirard, Paris)

20 Cedar of Lebanon   **21** President Edde

1930–31. AIR. As T **17** (views). P 13½.

181	0 p. 50, deep purple (1.31)		12	12
182	1 p. yellow-green (4.31)		15	12
183	2 p. orange (4.31)		25	25
184	3 p. carmine (4.31)		40	30
185	5 p. blackish green (6.30)		25	25
186	10 p. orange-vermilion (10.30)		45	40
187	15 p. red-brown (10.30)		40	40
188	25 p. deep violet (1.31)		50	50
189	50 p. lake (10.30)		2·00	2·00
190	100 p. brown (10.30)		2·50	2·00
181/190	Set of 10		6·50	5·50

Designs: Airplane above—0 p. 50 Rachaya; 1 p. Broumana; 2 p. Baalbek; 3 p. Hasroun; 10 p. Kadisha; 15 p. Beirut; 25 p. Tripoli; 50 p. Kabelais; 100 p. Zahle.

A redrawn type exists of the 10 p. having larger marginal inscriptions at foot.

22 Lebanese Landscape   **23** Exhibition Pavilion, Paris

(Des P. Mourani. T **20**: Die eng G. Hourriez. Typo. T **21**/2: Eng H. Cheffer and J. Piel. Recess French Govt Ptg Wks, Paris)

1937–40. P 14×13½ (T **20**) or 13 (T **21**/2).

199	**20**	0 p. 10, carmine (11.37)		5	5
200		0 p. 20, greenish blue (1940)		5	5
201		0 p. 25, rose-lilac (1940)		5	5
202		0 p. 50, cerise (1.9.37)		5	5
203		0 p. 75, brown (1940)		10	10
207	**21**	3 p. bright violet (4.11.37)		25	15
208		4 p. purple-brown (1.11.37)		10	8
209		4 p. 50, carmine (26.6.37)		12	10
211	**22**	10 p. brown-lake (1.9.37)		20	12
212		12½ p. ultramarine (1940)		15	10
213		15 p. bluish green (1938)		20	12
214		20 p. chestnut (1940)		15	12
215		25 p. rose-carmine (1940)		25	25
216		50 p. violet (1940)		55	50
217		100 p. sepia (1940)		80	1·00
199/217		Set of 15		2·75	2·50

(Des P. Mourani. Photo Vaugirard, Paris)

D 18   **D 19** Bas-relief from Sarcophagus of King Ahiram at Byblos

(Des J. de la Nézière. Photo Vaugirard, Paris)

1931 (Apr). POSTAGE DUE. As Types D **18** and D **19** (various designs). P 13½.

D191	0 p. 50, black/rose		12	12
D192	1 p. black/blue		30	30
D193	2 p. black/yellow		25	25
D194	3 p. black/green		30	30
D195	5 p. black/red		1·40	1·40
D196	8 p. black/rose		75	75
D197	15 p. black/white		80	80
D191/197	Set of 7		3·00	3·00

Designs with Arabic and French inscriptions:—1 p. Bas-relief of a ship; 2 p. Arabesque; 3 p. Garland; 5 p. as Type D **32**; 15 p. Statuettes.

For 10 p. see No. D252.

1937 (1 July). AIR. Paris International Exhibition. P 13½.

218	**23**	0 p. 50, greenish black		40	40
219		1 p. yellow-green		40	40
220		2 p. chestnut		40	40
221		3 p. blackish green		40	40
222		5 p. green		50	50
223		10 p. rose-red		2·00	2·00
224		15 p. claret		2·00	2·00
225		25 p. red-brown		2·75	2·75
218/225		Set of 8		8·00	8·00

24 Beit ed-Din   25 Ruins of Baalbek

(Des P. Mourani. Eng A. Delzers and Feltesse (10 p.). Recess.
French Govt Ptg Wks, Paris)

1937–40. *AIR. P 13.*

226	24	0 p. 50, bright blue (1.3.38)	5	5
227		1 p. brown-red (1940)	8	8
228		2 p. sepia (1940)	10	10
229		3 p. rose-carmine (1940)	30	30
230	24	5 p. light green (1940)	15	15
231	25	10 p. dull violet (1.12.37)	12	10
232		15 p. turquoise-blue (1940)	40	40
233		25 p. violet (1940)	1·00	80
234		50 p. yellow-green (1940)	1·90	95
235		100 p. brown (1940)	70	70
226/235		*Set of 10*	4·25	3·25

(26)   27 Medical College, Beirut

1938–41. *Nos. 207/8 surch as T 26.*

236	21	2 p. on 3 p. bright violet	25	10
237		2½ p. on 4 p. purple-brown	25	10
		a. Surch in red (1941)	50	30

(Des P. Mourani. Photo Vaugirard, Paris)

1938 (9 May). *AIR. Medical Congress. P 13½.*

238	27	2 p. green	60	60
239		3 p. orange-vermilion	60	60
240		5 p. deep violet	60	60
241		10 p. carmine	1·00	1·00
238/241		*Set of 4*	2·50	2·50

28 M. Noguès and Aeroplane over Beirut

(Des P. Mourani. Photo Vaugirard, Paris)

1938 (15 July). *AIR. 10th Anniv of First Air Service between France and Lebanon. P 11.*

242	28	10 p. maroon	1·00	1·00
MS242a		161×120 mm. No. 242 in block of four. P 13½	15·00	15·00

6   **٦**

(29)

12.ᴾ50   **ق ۱۲,٪**

(30)

12 ½   **۱۲٪**

—   =

(31)

1938–39. *Surch with T 29/31.*

243	29	6 p. on 7 p. 50 (No. 175) (R.)	80	40
244	30	7 p. 50 on 50 p. (No. 179)	60	45
245		7 p. 50 on 100 p. (No. 180) (R.)	60	50
246	31	12 p. 50 on 7 p. 50, blue (T 22) (R.)	80	75
247		12½ p. on 7 p. 50, blue (T 22) (R.) ('39)	30	15
243/247		*Set of 5*	2·75	2·00

(Litho Catholic Printing Press, Beirut)

1939. *As T 16a, but view of Beit ed-Din. P 11½.*

248	1 p. slate-green	25	8
249	1 p. 50, slate-purple	25	25
250	7 p. 50, rose-carmine	40	40

In Nos. 248/50, the figures and Arabic inscriptions, in the side panels, differ from those of T **16a** and the imprint "HELIO VAUGIRARD" is replaced by "IMP. CATHOLIQUE-BEY-ROUTH-LIBAN".

1940. *Nahr el-Kalb design, as No. 173, but with "DEGORCE" (engraver) at bottom. Recess. P 13.*

251	5 p. greenish blue	8	8

D 32

(Des J. de la Nézière. Eng Feltesse. Recess)

1940. *POSTAGE DUE. P 13.*

D252	D 32	10 p. dark green	2·00	1·25

British and Free French forces took control of Syria and Lebanon from the Vichy-controlled French régime in June 1941 and on 26 November 1941 Lebanon was proclaimed independent. The powers exercised by France were transferred to the republic on 1 January 1944.

The issues for the Free French Forces made in 1942–43 which were formerly listed here will be found under Free French Forces in the Levant.

ALBUM LISTS

Please write for our latest lists of albums and accessories. These will be sent free on request.

Madagascar

100 Centimes = 1 Franc

Madagascar was discovered by the Portuguese sailor Diego Dias in 1500. From 1642 to 1674 the French had a settlement at Fort Dauphin in the extreme south-east. In the late 17th and early 18th century the island was the haunt of pirates. During the years 1787 to 1810 the King of the Hovas, a Malay people who had come from overseas before the year 1000, established a strong kingdom in much of the island.

PRINTERS. All the following stamps were printed at the Government Printing Works, Paris, *unless otherwise stated.*

IMPERFORATE STAMPS. Stamps exist imperforate in their issued colours, but these were not valid for postage. Imperforate stamps in other colours are colour trials.

BRITISH CONSULAR MAIL. Stamps for the British Consular Mail in Madagascar issued between 1884 and 1895 are listed in the *British Commonwealth* Catalogue.

A. FRENCH POST OFFICES IN MADAGASCAR

In 1882 France, having previously acquired a protectorate over Diégo-Suarez in 1840, claimed a protectorate over the whole north-western part of Madagascar. The war which ensued ended with the treaty of 17 December 1885 by which the Hova kingdom ceded to France the territory round the bay of Diégo-Suarez, and gave France control of its foreign affairs. French post offices were opened at Tamatave, Tananarive, Fianarantsoa, Mahanoro, Majunga, Vatomandry and Vohemar.

05 (1)   **25** (2)

1889 (Mar–8 Dec). *French Colonies Type J* (*"Commerce"*). *P 14×13½. Handstamped at Tamatave with T 1 or 2.*
1	05 on 10 c. black/*lilac*	..	..	£175	60·00
	a. Error. "25" for "05"	..	..	£1100	£850
	b. Error corrected. "05" over "25"				
2	05 on 25. c. black/*rose* (8 Dec)	..	..	£160	50·00
3	25 on 40 c. red/*yellow*	..	..	£150	35·00

05 (3)   **5** (4)

1891 (25 Apr–July). *French Colonies Type J. P 14×13½. Handstamped at Tamatave as T 3 or 4.*
4	05 on 40 c. red/*yellow*	..	..	40·00	18·00
5	5 on 10 c. black/*lilac* (25 June)	..	50·00	25·00
6	5 on 25 c. black/*rose* (3 July)	..	50·00	25·00
7	5 on 25 c. black/*rose*	..	..	40·00	22·00

In No. 6 the handstamp is diagonal.

(Type-set at Tamatave)

1891 (29 June). *Ten varieties. Without gum. Imperf.*
9	5 c. black/*green*	..	..	18·00	6·00
10	10 c. black/*blue*	..	..	22·00	7·00
11	15 c. blue/*blue*	..	..	22·00	7·50

12	25 c. brown/*buff*	..	..	..	4·00	3·00
13	1 f. black/*yellow*	..	..	£250	80·00
14	5 f. lilac/*lilac* (*value in black*)	..	£500	£250

On the 1 f. and 5 f. there is also an orange-red pattern.

Type **10**   (6)   (7)
of France

1895 (Feb). *Stamps of France, T 10, Var (b). P 14×13½. Optd with T 6.*
15	5 c. deep green (Vm.)	..	..	2·00	75
16	10 c. black/*lilac* (Vm.)	..	..	8·00	6·00
17	15 c. blue (*quadrillé paper*) (Vm.)	..	11·00	3·50
18	25 c. black/*rose* (Vm.)	..	..	15·00	3·50
19	40 c. red/*yellow* (Vm.)	..	..	11·00	6·00
20	50 c. carmine	..	..	15·00	9·00
21	75 c. brown/*orange* (Vm.)	..	14·00	6·00
22	1 f. olive-green	..	..	20·00	9·00
23	5 f. mauve/*lilac*	..	..	25·00	12·00

The 5, 10, 25 and 50 c. as variety (*a*) and the 15 c. blue (*ordinary paper*), 20 c. and 30 c. variety (*b*) also exist with this overprint, but were not issued.

1895 (25 Feb). *Provisional Issue for Majunga. Stamps of France, T 10, Var (b). P 14×13½.*

(*a*) *Manuscript surcharge in red*
24	0.15 on 25 c. black/*rose*	..	..		£1300
25	0.15 on 1 f. olive-green/*toned*	..		£1100

(*b*) *MS surcharge partly washed out and handstamped "15" added in black*
26	15 on 25 c. black/*rose*	..		£1000
27	15 on 1 f. olive-green/*toned*	..		£950

(*c*) *Handstamped "15" only (two slightly different types)*
28	15 c. on 25 c. black/*rose*	..	..	£1100

1896 (5 Mar). *Stamps of France, T 10, Var (b). Handstamped as T 7 at Tananarive.*
29	5 c. on 1 c. black/*azure*	..	..	£1200	£500
30	15 c. on 2 c. red-brown/*buff*	..	£600	£300
31	25 c. on 3 c. grey	..	..	£725	£350
32	25 c. on 4 c. plum/*grey-blue*	..	£1200	£500
33	25 c. on 40 c. red/*yellow*	..	£275	£200

B. DIÉGO-SUAREZ

Diégo-Suarez, in the extreme north of Madagascar, was made a French protectorate by a treaty with a local chief in 1840, and was ceded to France in 1885. The islands of Nossi Bé and Ste. Marie de Madagascar were dependencies of Diégo-Suarez until 1894.

(1)   2   3

1890. _French Colonies Type_ J (_"Commerce"_). _P_ 14×13½.
Handstamped with T **1**, _in violet._
1	15 on 1 c. black/_azure_ (15.7)			50·00	13·00
2	15 on 5 c. green (15.7)			£130	12·00
3	15 on 10 c. black/_lilac_ (3.8)			50·00	12·00
4	15 on 20 c. red/_green_ (25.1)			£130	13·00
5	15 on 25 c. black/_rose_ (24.2)			20·00	6·00

This surcharge varies in position, but is always more or less diagonal.

(Litho at Diégo-Suarez)

1890 (5 Sept). _T_ **2** _and similar types. Imperf._
6	1 c. black ..			£250	70·00
7	5 c. black ..			£250	38·00
8	15 c. black ..			60·00	18·00
9	25 c. black ..			60·00	25·00

Designs:—5 c. Negress and white woman; 15 c. Two white women; 25 c. "France" (woman wearing helmet).
Very good forgeries of these four stamps exist.

(Litho at Diégo-Suarez)

1891 (18 Sept). _Imperf._
10	**3**	5 c. black		50·00	30·00

D 4　　　　　　(5)　　　　　　(6)

(Litho at Diégo-Suarez)

1891 (18 Sept). _POSTAGE DUE. Type_ D **4** _and similar design._
Imperf.
D11	—	5 c. violet			25·00	12·00
D12	D **4**	50 c. black/_buff_			25·00	12·00

Design:—5 c. Similar to Type D **4** but with lined background and curved inner frame-lines.
Beware of forgeries.

1891 (19 Nov). _French Colonies Type_ J (_"Commerce"_), _surch locally with T_ **5** (_No._ 14) _or similar type._
13	5 c. on 10 c. black/_lilac_ (R.)			32·00	18·00
	a. Surch inverted			80·00	50·00
14	5 c. on 20 c. red/_green_			32·00	9·00
	a. Surch inverted			80·00	60·00

The surcharge on No. 13 reads up from left to right and differs in type from that illustrated.

1892 (Nov). _French Colonies Type_ J (_"Commerce"_), _optd with T_ **6** _at Diégo-Suarez._
15	1 c. black/_azure_ (R.)			7·00	4·00
	a. Opt inverted			10·00	
16	2 c. brown/_buff_ ..			7·00	4·00
	a. Opt inverted			9·00	
17	4 c. purple-brown/_grey_ ..			10·00	6·50
18	5 c. green/_pale green_			22·00	18·00
	a. Opt inverted			40·00	40·00
19	10 c. black/_lilac_			7·00	4·00
	a. Opt inverted			12·00	
20	15 c. blue/_pale blue_			6·50	4·00
21	20 c. red/_green_			7·50	4·50
22	25 c. black/_rose_			5·00	3·50
	a. Opt inverted			9·00	9·00
23	30 c. cinnamon/_drab_ (R.)			£275	£225
	a. Opt inverted			£350	£250
24	35 c. black/_orange_			£300	£200
	a. Opt inverted			£375	£250
25	75 c. carmine/_rose_			15·00	10·00
26	1 f. olive-green/_toned_ (R.)			15·00	10·00

1892 (Nov). _POSTAGE DUE. French Colonies Type_ U, _imperf, optd with T_ **6** _at Diégo-Suarez._
D27	1 c. black			27·00	14·00
D28	2 c. black			27·00	14·00
	a. Opt inverted				
D29	3 c. black			17·00	10·00

D30	4 c. black			17·00	10·00
D31	5 c. black			17·00	10·00
D32	10 c. black			7·00	6·50
	a. Opt inverted				
D33	15 c. black			9·00	6·50
D34	20 c. black			45·00	25·00
D35	30 c. black			17·00	12·00
	a. Opt inverted				
D36	60 c. black			£250	£140
D37	1 f. brown			£400	£300

1892 (Nov). _As T_ **11** _of New Caledonia, inscr_ "DIEGO-SUAREZ ET DEPENDANCES" _in red_ (1, 5, 15, 25, 75 _c._, 1 _f._) _or blue_ (_others_). _P_ 14×13½.
38	1 c. black/_azure_			50	50
39	2 c. brown/_buff_ ..			50	50
40	4 c. purple-brown/_grey_			30	25
41	5 c. green/_pale green_			75	50
42	10 c. black/_lilac_			1·10	75
43	15 c. blue (_quadrillé paper_)			2·00	1·10
44	20 c. red/_green_			3·25	2·10
45	25 c. black/_rose_			2·50	2·00
46	30 c. cinnamon/_drab_			2·25	1·50
47	40 c. red/_yellow_			5·00	4·00
48	50 c. carmine/_rose_			10·00	6·00
49	75 c. brown/_yellow_			7·00	5·00
	a. Brown/_orange_			7·00	5·00
50	1 f. olive-green/_toned_			12·00	9·00
38/50	_Set of 13_			42·00	30·00

In 1894 the issue inscribed "Diégo-Suarez et Dependances" was replaced by three series, for "Diégo-Suarez", "Nossi Bé" and "Ste. Marie de Madagascar".

1894 (Jan). _As T_ **11** _of New Caledonia, inscr_ "DIEGO-SUAREZ" _in red_ (1, 5, 15, 25, 75 _c._, 1 _f._) _or blue_ (_others_). _P_ 14×13½.
51	1 c. black/_azure_ ..			15	15
52	2 c. brown/_buff_			40	40
53	4 c. purple-brown/_grey_ ..			40	40
54	5 c. green/_pale green_			50	40
55	10 c. black/_lilac_			75	60
56	15 c. blue (_quadrillé paper_)			90	70
57	20 c. red/_green_			2·00	1·25
58	25 c. black/_rose_			90	50
59	30 c. cinnamon/_drab_			1·25	80
	a. "DIEGO-SUAREZ" omitted (in pair with normal)			£600	
60	40 c. red/_yellow_			1·40	1·25
61	50 c. carmine/_rose_			2·75	1·40
62	75 c. brown/_yellow_			75	65
63	1 f. olive-green/_toned_			3·50	1·50
51/63	_Set of 13_			14·00	9·00

For Nos. 59 and 61 surcharged see Nos. 34/7 of Madagascar and Dependencies. Bisects of 10, 20, 30 and 50 c. are listed between Nos. 52a/53 of Madagascar and Dependencies.

In 1898 Diégo-Suarez became an administrative part of Madagascar and Dependencies.

C. NOSSI BÉ

In 1840 a chieftainess who had fled to the island of Nossi Bé, off the north-west coast of Madagascar, accepted French protection. and in 1841 the French took possession of the island.
Nossi Bé was an administrative dependency of Diégo-Suarez until 1894.

25 c　　　　**25**

(1)　　　　(2)

1889 (June). _French Colonies_ (_General issues_) _handstamped, in blue, at Nossi Bé._

(_a_) _In small figures as T_ **1** (5.6)
1	J	5 c. on 10 c. black/_lilac_		£700	£300
2		5 c. on 20 c. red/_green_ ..		£700	£300
3	H	25 c. on 40 c. red/_yellow_		£700	£500

(_b_) _In large figures as T_ **2**
4	J	5 c. on 10 c. black/_lilac_ (25.6)		£650	£300
5		5 c. on 20 c. red/_green_ (6-24.6)		£750	£450
6		15 on 20 c. red/_green_ (25.6)		£650	£250

7	J	25 on 30 c. cinnamon/*drab* (25.6)		£450	£250
		a. Error. "15" for "25"		£4000	£3500
		b. Error corrected. "25" over "15"		—	£3750
8	H	25 on 40 c. red/*yellow* (6-24.6)		£500	£250
9	J	25 on 40 c. red/*yellow* (6-24.6)		£400	£225

The first printing has the surcharge in pale or dull blue, the same colour as that used for the postmark, but in subsequent printings the colour is ultramarine. The obliteration on the later printings is ultramarine or indigo.

(3)

(4)

(5)

1890 (23 Oct). *French Colonies Type J ("Commerce").*
P 14×13½, surch at Nossi Bé.

(a) With T 3

10	0 25 on 20 c. red/*green*		90·00	65·00
11	0 25 on 75 c. rose-carmine/*rose*		90·00	65·00
12	0 25 on 1 f. olive-green/*toned*		90·00	65·00

(b) With T 4

13	25 c. on 20 c. red/*green*		90·00	65·00
14	25 c. on 75 c. rose-carmine/*rose*		90·00	65·00
15	25 c. on 1 f. olive-green/*toned*		90·00	65·00

(c) With T 5

16	25 on 20 c. red/*green*		£225	£140
17	25 on 75 c. rose-carmine/*rose*		£225	£140
18	25 on 1 f. olive-green/*toned*		£225	£140

Nossi-Bé   **Nossi-Bé**
chiffre-taxe   chiffre-taxe
0.30   **0.35**
A PERCEVOIR   ▲ PERCEVOIR

(D 6)   (D 7)

1891 (10 Aug). *French Colonies Type J ("Commerce").*
P 14×13½, surch at Nossi Bé.

D19	D 6	0.20 on 1 c. black/*azure*		£100	75·00
		a. Surch inverted		£150	£120
D20		0.30 on 2 c. brown/*buff*		£100	75·00
		a. Surch inverted		£150	£120
D21	D 7	0.35 on 4 c. purple-brown/*grey*		£100	80·00
		a. Surch inverted		£150	£120
D22		0.35 on 20 c. red/*green*		£100	80·00
		a. Surch inverted		£150	£120
D23	D 6	0.50 on 30 c. cinnamon/*drab*		30·00	25·00
		a. Surch inverted		£130	£110
D24	D 7	1 f. on 35 c. black/*orange*		70·00	40·00
		a. Surch inverted		£120	£110

Nossi-Bé   **Nossi-Bé**
5 C.   **0.15**
A PERCEVOIR   ▲ PERCEVOIR

(D 8)   (D 9)

1891 (15 Oct). *POSTAGE DUE. French Colonies Type J surch at Nossi Bé.*

(a) As Type D 8

D25	5 c. on 20 c. red/*green*			60·00	60·00
	a. Surch inverted			75·00	75·00
D26	10 c. on 15 c. blue/*pale blue*			60·00	60·00
	a. Surch inverted			75·00	75·00

D27	15 c. on 10 c. black/*lilac*			32·00	32·00
	a. Surch inverted			65·00	65·00
D28	25 c. on 5 c. green/*green*			32·00	32·00
	a. Surch inverted			65·00	65·00

(b) With value as Type D 8 and the rest similar to Type D 9

D29	5 c. on 20 c. red/*green*			55·00	55·00
	a. Surch inverted			70·00	70·00
D30	10 c. on 15 c. blue/*pale blue*			55·00	55·00
	a. Surch inverted			70·00	70·00
D31	15 c. on 10 c. black/*lilac*			32·00	32·00
	a. Surch inverted			65·00	65·00
D32	25 c. on 5 c. green/*green*			32·00	32·00
	a. Surch inverted			65·00	65·00

1891 (16 Nov). *POSTAGE DUE. French Colonies Type J surch at Nossi Bé as Type D 9.*

D33	0.10 on 5 c. green			4·00	3·50
D34	0.15 on 20 c. red/*green*			5·00	5·00
	a. Error. "0.25" for "0.15"			£6000	£5000
D35	0.25 on 75 c. carmine/*rose*			£140	£120
	a. Surch inverted			£300	£250

(10)

(11)

(12)

1893 (8 Feb). *French Colonies Type J ("Commerce").*
P 14×13½, surch at Nossi Bé as T 10.

36	25 on 20 c. red/*green*			8·00	6·00
37	50 on 10 c. black/*lilac*			8·50	7·00
	a. Surch inverted			50·00	40·00
38	75 on 15 c. blue			50·00	45·00
39	1 f. on 5 c. green			17·00	15·00
	a. Surch inverted			50·00	40·00

1893 (May). *French Colonies Type J ("Commerce").*
P 14×13½, handstamped at Nossi Bé.

40	11	10 c. black/*lilac* (Vm.)		3·00	2·50
		a. Carmine opt		3·00	2·50
41		15 c. blue		3·00	2·75
42		20 c. red/*green*		£100	9·00
43	12	20 c. red/*green* (B.)		17·00	9·00

1894 (1 Jan). *As T 11 of New Caledonia, inscr "NOSSI-BE" in red 1, 5, 15, 25, 75 c. and 1 f.) or blue (others). P 14×13½.*

44	1 c. black/*azure*			30	30
45	2 c. brown/*buff*			40	40
46	4 c. purple-brown/*grey*			50	40
47	5 c. green/*pale green*			75	60
48	10 c. black/*lilac*			1·25	1·00
49	15 c. blue (*quadrillé paper*)			1·40	1·00
50	20 c. red/*green*			2·00	1·25
51	25 c. black/*rose*			2·75	2·00
52	30 c. cinnamon/*drab*			2·50	2·25
53	40 c. red/*yellow*			3·00	2·25
54	50 c. carmine/*rose*			2·75	1·90
55	75 c. brown/*orange*			7·00	6·00
56	1 f. olive-green/*toned*			2·75	2·25
44/56	*Set of 13*			25·00	19·00

In 1901 Nossi Bé became an administrative part of Madagascar and Dependencies.

D. STE. MARIE DE MADAGASCAR

The island of Ste. Marie, off the east coast of Madagascar, north of Tamatave, was in French possession from 1750 to 1761 and was then ceded to France on 30 July 1850. After being in turn a dependency of Réunion, Mayotte and Diégo-Suarez the island was provided with its own stamp issue in 1894, before becoming an administrative part of Madagascar and Dependencies in 1898.

1894 (Apr). As T **11** of New Caledonia, inscr "STE. MARIE DE MADAGASCAR" in red (1, 5, 15, 25, 75 c., 1 f.) or blue (others). P 14×13½.

1	1 c. black/azure		10	10
2	2 c. brown/buff		30	30
3	4 c. purple-brown/grey		90	60
4	5 c. green/pale green		1·50	90
5	10 c. black/lilac		2·50	2·50
6	15 c. blue (quadrillé paper)		7·50	6·00
7	20 c. red/green		5·00	5·00
8	25 c. black/rose		6·00	4·00
9	30 c. cinnamon/drab		2·25	2·00
10	40 c. red/yellow		3·00	2·75
11	50 c. carmine/rose		10·00	8·00
12	75 c. brown/orange		14·00	9·00
13	1 f. olive-green/toned		7·00	6·00
1/13	Set of 13		55·00	42·00

E. MADAGASCAR AND DEPENDENCIES

In 1890 the United Kingdom and Germany agreed to a French protectorate over Madagascar. In 1894 France sent an ultimatum to the Hova government, making extensive claims. When it was rejected a French force took Tananarive and on 16 January 1896 France claimed possession of the island. A popular rising followed, but on 6 August 1896 Madagascar, with its dependent islands, was proclaimed a French colony. General Galliéni was sent to pacify the island and on 28 February 1897 he deposed Queen Rànavàlona III and ended Hova supremacy over the aboriginal tribes.

1896–99. As T **11** of New Caledonia, inscr "MADAGASCAR ET DEPENDANCES" in red (1, 5, 15, 25, 75 c., 1 f. (No. 14)) or blue (others).

1	1 c. black/azure		10	10
2	2 c. brown/buff		12	12
	a. Name in black		1·00	1·00
3	4 c. purple-brown/grey		25	20
4	5 c. green/pale green		1·25	25
5	5 c. deep green/green		1·40	35
6	10 c. black/lilac		1·60	50
7	15 c. blue (quadrillé paper)		3·00	10
8	20 c. red/green		1·25	25
9	25 c. black/rose		1·60	1·00
10	30 c. cinnamon/drab		1·60	75
11	40 c. red/yellow		1·60	40
12	50 c. carmine/rose		2·50	40
13	75 c. violet/orange		60	50
14	1 f. olive-green/toned (inscr in red)		2·40	65
15	1 f. olive-green/toned (inscr in blue) (1899)		5·00	4·00
16	5 f. mauve/pale lilac (1899)		7·00	5·00
1/16	Set of 16		28·00	13·00

Madagascar
et
DEPENDANCES
(D 1)

05
(1)

1896–97. POSTAGE DUE. French Colonies Type U, optd with Type D **1**.

D17	5 c. blue (R.)		1·25	1·25
D18	10 c. brown (R.)		1·25	1·25
D19	20 c. yellow (B.)		1·25	1·25
D20	30 c. rose (B.)		1·50	1·50
D21	40 c. mauve (R.)		12·00	10·00
D22	50 c. violet (B.)		1·75	1·75
D23	1 f. green (R.) (1897)		14·00	12·50
D17/23	Set of 7		30·00	26·00

1900–6. As Nos. 1/16 but colours changed.

17	5 c. bright yellow-green (1901)		30	25
18	10 c. rose-red		30	15
19	15 c. grey		30	15
20	25 c. blue		6·00	5·50
21	35 c. black/yellow (1906)		10·00	1·50
22	50 c. brown/azure		7·50	6·50
17/22	Set of 6		22·00	13·00

1902 (2 June). Stamps of 1896–99 surch as T **1**, at Tananarive.

23	05 on 50 c. carmine/rose		1·25	1·25
	a. Surch inverted		20·00	20·00
24	10 on 5 f. mauve/lilac		6·00	5·00
	a. Surch inverted		23·00	23·00
25	15 on 1 f. olive-green/toned (No. 14)		1·25	1·25
	a. Surch inverted		22·00	22·00
	b. Surch double		50·00	50·00

0,01　**0,01**
(2)　　　(3)　　4 Zebu and Lemur

1902 (9 Aug). Surch as T **2/3** at Tananarive.

(a) Nos. 2, 10 and 12/14 of Madagascar and Dependencies

26	**2** 0,01 on 2 c. brown/buff		1·60	1·60
	a. Name in black		1·75	1·75
	b. Surch inverted		11·00	11·00
	c. "00,1" for "0,01"		17·00	17·00
	ca. Do., inverted			
	d. Comma omitted		21·00	21·00
27	**3** 0,01 on 2 c. brown/buff		1·50	1·50
	a. Name in black		1·75	1·75
	b. Surch inverted		11·00	11·00
	c. Comma omitted		21·00	21·00
28	**2** 0,05 on 30 c. cinnamon/drab		2·25	2·25
	a. Surch inverted		18·00	18·00
	b. "00,5" for "0,05"		14·00	14·00
	ba. Do., inverted		45·00	45·00
	c. Comma omitted		21·00	21·00
29	**3** 0,05 on 30 c. cinnamon/drab		2·00	2·00
	a. Surch inverted		11·00	11·00
	b. Comma omitted		21·00	21·00
30	**2** 0,10 on 50 c. carmine/rose		2·25	2·25
	a. Surch inverted		11·00	11·00
	b. Comma omitted		25·00	25·00
31	**3** 0,10 on 50 c. carmine/rose		1·50	1·50
	a. Surch inverted		11·00	11·00
	b. Comma omitted		25·00	25·00
32	**2** 0,15 on 75 c. violet/orange		1·60	1·60
	a. Surch inverted		13·00	13·00
	b. Comma omitted		27·00	27·00
33	0,15 on 1 f. olive-green/toned (No. 14)		2·50	2·50
	a. Surch inverted		17·00	17·00
	b. Comma omitted		27·00	27·00

(b) Nos. 59 and 61 of Diègo-Suarez

34	**2** 0,05 on 30 c. cinnamon/drab		38·00	38·00
	a. Surch inverted		£190	£190
	b. "00,5" for "0,05"		£120	£120
35	**3** 0,05 on 30 c. cinnamon/drab		38·00	38·00
	a. Surch inverted		£190	£190
36	**2** 0,10 on 50 c. carmine/rose		£950	£950
37	**3** 0,10 on 50 c. carmine/rose		£950	£950

(Des and eng B. Damman. Recess Wittman, Paris)

1903. P 11½.

38	**4** 1 c. dull purple		25	25
	a. Deep lilac/bluish		1·90	1·40
39	2 c. sepia		25	25
40	4 c. brown		25	25
41	5 c. green		1·90	30
42	10 c. scarlet		2·10	25
43	15 c. carmine		4·00	25
	a. Printed on both sides		21·00	
	b. Carmine/bluish		32·00	
44	20 c. orange		1·50	45
45	25 c. blue		9·50	1·40
46	30 c. vermilion		10·00	4·50
47	40 c. grey-lilac		9·00	1·25
48	50 c. yellow-brown		15·00	6·50
49	75 c. orange-yellow		16·00	6·50
50	1 f. deep green		16·00	9·50

51	4	2 f. slate	..	..	21·00	10·00
52		5 f. black	..	..	19·00	10·00
38/52		Set of 15			£110	50·00

Stamps can be found showing part of the sheet watermark "BFK RIVES"

1904–06 PROVISIONALS. Between 1904 and 1906 many Post Offices in Madagascar experienced shortages of certain low values of the definitive series.

These shortages were overcome by bisecting the 10, 20, 30 and 50 c. stamps of previous issues of which there were sufficient stocks. Such bisects did duty at half the face value of the complete stamp and were tied to the cover by a handstamp, of which different types exist.

For Nos. 52a/53 prices in column A are for examples on cover, without further cancellation, and in column B for bisects used on cover with additional postmark.

Affranchissement

spécial

(faute de figurines.-

(4a)

1904 (Aug). *General Issue. Stamps bisected and handstamped with T 4a, in blue.*

(a) Nos. 6, 18, 8, 10 and 12 of Madagascar and Dependencies

				A	B
52a	Half of 10 c. black/*lilac*	..		50·00	40·00
52b	Half of 10 c. rose-red	..	..	22·00	16·00
52c	Half of 20 c. red/*green*	..	..	20·00	13·00
52d	Half of 30 c. cinnamon/*drab*	..		11·00	9·50
52e	Half of 50 c. carmine/*rose*	..		40·00	30·00

(b) Nos. 55, 57, 59 and 61 of Diégo-Suarez

52f	Half of 10 c. black/*lilac*	..		65·00	50·00
52g	Half of 20 c. red/*green*	..	..	55·00	40·00
52h	Half of 30 c. cinnamon/*drab*	..		50·00	38·00
52i	Half of 50 c. carmine/*rose*	..		75·00	65·00

Type 4a can be found with the bracket before "fáute" omitted.

(4b)

1905. *Ambohibe issue. No. 59 of Diégo-Suarez bisected and tied to cover by manuscript inscr and signature as T 4b.*
52j Half of 30 c. cinnamon/*drab* .. .. — £2500

A regular new issue supplement to this catalogue appears each month in

STAMP MONTHLY

—from your newsagent or by postal subscription
—details on request.

Affranchi ainsi

Faute figurine

➤※➤

(4c)

1904 (Feb). *Antalaha issue. No. 59 of Diégo-Suarez bisected and handstamped with T 4c, in blue.*
52k Half of 30 c. cinnamon/*drab* £750 £750

Affranchissement

exceptionnel

(faute de Timbres.)

(4d)

1904 (Mar). *Diégo-Suarez issue. Stamps bisected and handstamped with T 4d, in blue.*

(a) Nos. 6, 18, 8, 10 and 12 of Madagascar and Dependencies

52l	Half of 10 c. black/*lilac*	..	19·00	16·00
52m	Half of 10 c. rose-red	..	9·50	8·00
52n	Half of 20 c. red/*green*	..	12·00	11·00
52o	Half of 30 c. cinnamon/*drab*	..	10·00	8·00
52p	Half of 50 c. carmine/*rose*	..	40·00	40·00

(b) Nos. 55 and 59 of Diégo-Suarez

52q	Half of 10 c. black/*lilac*	..	70·00	75·00
52r	Half of 30 c. cinnamon/*drab*	..	19·00	19·00

Affranch.except.

faute de Timbres

(4e)

1904 (Feb). *Mahela issue. No. 59 of Diégo-Suarez bisected and handstamped with T 4e, in red.*
52s Half of 30 c. cinnamon/*drab* .. .. — £5000

Affranch.except.

faute de timbres

(4f)

1904. *Manaujary issue. No. 59 of Diégo-Suarez bisected and handstamped with T 4f, in violet.*
52t Half of 30 c. cinnamon/*drab* .. .. — £1500

Affranchi ainsi

faute figurine

➤☆☆➤

(4g)

1904 (Feb). *Vohemar issue. Stamps bisected and handstamped with T 4g.*

(a) Nos. 10 and 12 of Madagascar and Dependencies

52u	Half of 30 c. cinnamon/*drab*	..	65·00	65·00
52v	Half of 50 c. carmine/*rose*	..	£100	65·00

(b) Nos. 59 and 61 of Diégo-Suarez

52w	Half of 30 c. cinnamon/drab	..	..	£100	50·00
52x	Half of 50 c. carmine/rose	..	..	£325	£250

Type 4g only exists with the inverted "s" as shown.

1904. *Vohemar issue. No. 59 of Diégo-Suarez bisected and handstamped as T 4g, but with second line reading "faute de figurine" and single star only at foot.*

52y	Half of 30 c. cinnamon/drab	..	..	£650	£650

Affranch.t exceptionnel
faute de Timbres.-

(4h)

1904. *Vohemar issue. No. 59 of Diégo-Suarez bisected and handstamped with T 4h.*

52z	Half of 30 c. cinnamon/drab	..	..	— £2000

0,05
Affranchi ainsi
faute de figurines

(4i)

1906 (Feb). *Vohemar issue. No. 42 bisected and handstamped with T 4i, in blue.*

53	**4**	5 c. on half of 10 c. scarlet	..	..	13·00	10·00

5 Transport in Madagascar

D 6 Governor's Palace, Tananarive

(Des A. Johannet. Eng J. Puyplat. Typo)

1908 (July)—**17.** P 13½×14.

53a	**5**	1 c. olive and violet	..	..	5	5
54		2 c. olive and red	..	..	5	5
55		4 c. pale brown and olive	..	..	5	5
56		5 c. olive and green	..	..	5	5
57		10 c. purple-brown and pink	..	..	5	5
58		15 c. carmine and lilac (1917)	..		5	5
59		20 c. brown and brownish orange	..	8	5
60		25 c. black and blue	..	..	40	10
61		30 c. black and yellow-brown	..	..	65	30
62		35 c. black and dull red	..	..	12	8
63		40 c. black and chocolate	..	..	12	5
64		45 c. black and green	..	..	10	5
65		50 c. black and violet	..	..	10	5
66		75 c. black and carmine	..	..	10	5
67		1 f. olive and yellow-brown	..	..	10	5
68		2 f. olive and blue	..	..	90	20
69		5 f. chocolate and pale violet	..	2·50	1·00
53/69		Set of 17	..	..	5·00	2·00

The 1, 35, 40 and 75 c. exist on chalk-surfaced paper.
See also Nos. 90/108 and 114a.

1908 (July)—**24.** *POSTAGE DUE. Typo.* P 13½×14.

D70	D **6**	2 c. dull claret	..	..	5	5
D71		4 c. pale violet	..	..	5	5
D72		5 c. green	..	..	5	5
D73		10 c. carmine	..	..	5	5
D74		20 c. olive	..	..	5	5
D75		40 c. brown/toned	..	..	5	5
D76		50 c. olive-brown/azure	..	..	5	5
D77		60 c. red (1924)	..	..	5	5
D78		1 f. deep blue	..	..	12	12
D70/78		Set of 9	..	..	45	45

05 10 ✚5ᶜ
(6)   (7)   (8)

1912 (Nov). *Surch as T 6/7.* (a) Nos. 19, 8, 10 and 13.

	A. Narrow spacing		B. Wide spacing	
		A.		B.
70	05 on 15 c. grey (R.)	..	12 12	1·60 1·60
71	05 on 20 c. red/green	..	12 12	1·60 1·60
	a. Surch inverted	..	28·00 —	£450 —
72	05 on 30 c. cinnamon/drab			
	(R.)	..	20 20	1·60 1·60
73	10 on 75 c. violet orange	..	2·25 2·25	55·00 55·00
	a. Surch double	..	50·00	£600 —

(b) T **4**. (Narrow spacing, Type B)

74	05 on 2 c. sepia (R.)	..	..	5	5
75	05 on 20 c. orange	..	..	12	12
76	05 on 30 c. vermilion	..	..	20	20
77	10 on 40 c. grey-lilac (R.)	..	..	20	20
78	10 on 50 c. yellow-brown	..	..	65	65
79	10 on 75 c. orange-brown	..	..	1·60	1·60
	a. Surch double	..	..	50·00	

In Type A the space between "0" and "5" is 1½ mm and between "1" and "0" 2½ mm. In Type B the spacing is 2 mm and 3 mm respectively.

1915 (Feb). *Red Cross Fund. Surch in Paris with T **8**, in red.*

80	**5**	10 c.+5 c. brown and pink	..	..	15	15

MADAGASCAR ET DEPENDANCES
0ᶠʳ·10
COLIS POSTAUX
(P 8)

1919. *PARCEL POST. Receipt stamp of France (vertical format), surch at Tananarive with Type P **8**, in purple, vertically, reading upwards.* P 14×13½.

P81	0 f. 10 on 10 c. grey	..	..	..	1·00	1·00

1919. *PARCEL POST. Fiscal stamp of Madagascar surch "CONNAISSEMENTS 0 fr. 10" in red, further optd "COLIS POSTAUX" in black, both at Tananarive. Pin-perf 13½.*

P82	0 f. 10 on 1 f. rose	..	..	15·00	9·50

1919–22. *PARCEL POST. Similar design to No. P82 but without original red opt, surch as Type P **8**. Litho. Pin-perf 17½.*

P83	0 f. 10, rose	..	..	1·90	1·60
P84	0 f. 10, carmine and green (1921)	..	45	30
P85	0 f. 10, black and green (1922)	..	50	5

In Nos. P84/5 the overprint reads "Madagascar et Dependances" instead of in capital letters.

HAVE YOU READ THE NOTES AT THE BEGINNING OF THIS CATALOGUE?

These often provide answers to the enquiries we receive.

0,25

0,60 1 FR. **│cent.** **≡**

(9) (10) (11) (12)

60ᶜ

(D 13) 14 Sakalava Chief 18 General Galliéni

15 Zebus 17 Betsileo Woman

16 Hova Girl (vert)

1921 (16 Apr–9 July). *Various stamps surch at Tananarive.*

(a) 1896–99 *issue surch with T* **9/10**, *in red* (No. 81) *or black*
81	0,60 on 75 c. violet/*orange*	..	1·60	1·60
	a. Surch inverted		38·00	38·00
82	1 f. on 5 f. mauve/*pale lilac*	..	20	20

(b) 1903 *issue surch with T* **10**, *in red*
83	1 f. on 5 f. black	..	19·00	19·00

(c) 1908–17 *issue surch as T* **11/12**
84	1 c. on 15 c. carmine and lilac (14 June)	8	8
85	25 on 35 c. black and dull red (9 July)	..	1·00	75
	a. Surch in red		4·00	3·25
86	25 on 40 c. black and chocolate (9 July)	1·00	75
87	25 on 45 c. black and green (9 July)	..	75	65
88	0,30 on 40 c. black and chocolate (R.)	..	25	20
89	0,60 on 75 c. black and pink	..	60	25

The surcharge on Nos. 88/9 is similar to T **12**, but is without the bars.

1922 (1 Jan)–**28**. *New values and colours. P* 13½×14.
90	**5**	5 c. carmine and black	..	5	5
91		10 c. olive-green and green	..	5	5
92		10 c. purple and brown (16.11.25)		5	5
93		15 c. green and olive-green (5.9.27)		5	5
94		15 c. carmine and blue (25.9.28)		30	25
95		25 c. black and violet	..	5	5
96		30 c. brown and carmine	..	5	5
97		30 c. purple and green (16.11.25)		5	5
98		30 c. yellow-green and green (20.4.28)	20	20
99		45 c. scarlet and red (1.2.25)	..	5	5
100		45 c. claret and lilac (30.4.28)		15	15
101		50 c. black and blue	..	5	5
102		50 c. yellow and black (1.2.25)		5	5
103		60 c. violet/*rose* (7.9.25)	..	5	5
104		65 c. blue and black (1.3.26)	..	15	15
105		85 c. scarlet and green (1.3.26)		20	20
106		1 f. light blue (1.2.25)		12	10
107		1 f. green and magenta (25.9.28)		1·60	1·40
108		1 f. 10, green & yellow-brn (25.9.28)	25	25
90/108		*Set of* 19		3·00	3·00

For 75 c. violet/*rose* see No. 114a.

Two types of 25 c. surcharge.

25ᶜ **25ᶜ**

(I) *Enlarged illustrations* (II)

1922 (Sept)–**32**. *Surch with new value and bars over old value; some colours changed.*
109	**5**	25 c. on 15 c. carmine and lilac (1.2.25)	5	5
110		25 c. on 2 f. olive and blue (I) (6.24)	..	5	5
111		25 c. on 2 f. olive and blue (II) (4.7.32)	5	5
112		25 c. on 5 f. chocolate and violet (6.24)	5	5
113		50 c. on 1 f. olive & yell-brn (4.7.32)	5	5
114		60 c. on 75 c. violet/*rose*	..	5	5
		a. Surch omitted	..	28·00	
115		65 c. on 75 c. black & carmine (1.2.25)	8	8
116		85 c. on 45 c. black and green (1.2.25)	8	8
117		90 c. on 75 c. rose and carmine (28.2.27)	8	5
118		1 f. 25 on 1 f. lt bl & bl (R.) (14.6.26)	8	8
119		1 f. 50 on 1 f. lt blue & blue (28.2.27)	8	8
120		3 f. on 5 f. violet and green (19.12.27)	25	25
121		10 f. on 5 f. magenta & verm (28.2.27)	1·75	1·40
122		20 f. on 5 f. grey-blue & mag (28.2.27)	2·25	1·75
109/122		*Set of* 14	..	4·50	3·50

1924 (Mar)–**27**. *POSTAGE DUE. Surch as Type* D **13**.
D123	D **6**	60 c. on 1 f. red		45	45
D124		2 f. on 1 f. magenta (10.10.27)	..	15	15
D125		3 f. on 1 f. ultramarine (10.10.27)		15	15

(Des H. Cayon. Eng C. Hourriez (**14**, **16**), A. Mignon (**15**, **17**, **18**). Typo (**14** to **17**). Recess (**18**))

1930 (8 Dec)–**38**. *P* 13½×14, 14×13½, 13½ *or* 14½.
123	**18**	1 c. bright ultramarine (14.9.31)	..	8	8
124	**15**	1 c. green and ultramarine (15.3.33)	5	5
125	**14**	2 c. brown and scarlet	..	5	5
126		4 c. mauve and brown	..	5	5
127	**15**	5 c. scarlet and green	..	5	5
128	**16**	10 c. green and vermilion	..	5	5
129	**17**	15 c. scarlet	..	5	5
130	**15**	20 c. ultramarine and yellow-brown	..	5	5
131	**16**	25 c. chocolate and lilac	..	5	5
132	**17**	30 c. deep blue-green	..	5	5
133	**14**	40 c. scarlet and green	..	10	10
134	**17**	45 c. lilac	..	15	12
135	**18**	50 c. red-brown (14.9.31)	..	30	5
136	**15**	65 c. mauve and brown	..	20	10
137	**17**	75 c. chocolate	..	5	5
138	**15**	90 c. scarlet	..	20	10
139	**16**	1 f. ultramarine and yellow-brown	..	45	12
140		1 f. carmine and scarlet (5.12.38)	..	5	5
140a		1 f. 25, chocolate & ultram (25.9.33)	30	15
141	**14**	1 f. 50, ultramarine and blue	..	1·60	20
142		1 f. 50, scarlet & chocolate (5.12.38)	5	5
143		1 f. 75, scarlet & chocolate (25.9.33)	1·00	10
144	**18**	2 f. carmine-red (14.9.31)	..	1·75	80
145		3 f. emerald-green (14.9.31)	..	1·25	65
146	**14**	5 f. chocolate and mauve	..	10	10
147	**18**	10 f. red-orange (14.9.31)	..	90	45
148	**14**	20 f. ultramarine and yellow-brown	..	30	30
123/148		*Set of* 27	..	8·00	3·00

For No. 142 with frame and centre colours reversed, see No. 278.

For stamps similar to T **18**, but printed by photogravure, see Nos. 177/86a.

Stamps in these designs, but without "RF" were prepared in 1943–44, but not used in Madagascar.

1931 (13 Apr). *International Colonial Exhibition, Paris. As T* **12/15** *of Mauritania.*
149		40 c. black and green	..	..	25	12
150		50 c. black and mauve	..	..	65	15
151		90 c. black and vermilion	..	25	20
152		1 f. black and blue	..	..	65	25
149/152		*Set of* 4	..	..	1·60	65

THE WORLD CENTRE FOR
FINE STAMPS IS 391 STRAND

| 19 Aeroplane over Madagascar | 20 J. Laborde and Tananarive Palace |

(Des P. Fonterme. Eng J. C. de Cantilou. Islands and value typo, remainder photo. Vaugirard, Paris)

1935 (23 Apr)–**41**. *AIR. P* 13½.
153	19	50 c. scarlet and green			15	12
154		90 c. scarlet & yellow-green (24.2.41)			8	
155		1 f. 25, scarlet and lake			8	8
156		1 f. 50, scarlet and blue			8	8
157		1 f. 60, scarlet and blue (24.2.41)			5	5
158		1 f. 75, scarlet and orange			3·00	1·40
159		2 f. scarlet and light blue			12	8
160		3 f. scarlet and orange (24.2.41)			5	5
161		3 f. 65, scarlet and black (18.7.38)			5	5
162		3 f. 90, scarlet & blue-grn (24.2.41)			5	5
163		4 f. scarlet and carmine			12·00	60
164		4 f. 50, scarlet and black			8·00	45
165		5 f. 50, scarlet & deep olive (24.2.41)			5	5
166		6 f. scarlet and cerise (24.2.41)			8	8
167		6 f. 90, scarlet & dull purple (24.2.41)			5	5
168		8 f. scarlet and magenta			25	15
169		8 f. 50, scarlet and blue-green			30	30
170		9 f. scarlet and olive-green (24.2.41)			8	8
171		12 f. scarlet and chocolate			10	8
172		12 f. 50, scarlet and violet			35	35
173		15 f. scarlet and orange (24.2.41)			25	20
174		16 f. scarlet and grey-green			50	50
175		20 f. scarlet and brown			40	40
176		50 f. scarlet and ultramarine (18.7.38)			1·50	1·50

Stamps as *T* **19**, but without "R F" in upper label, were prepared by the Vichy Government, but were not issued in the Colony.

1936 (3 Feb)–**40**. *Photo. P* 13½.
177	18	3 c. light blue (15.4.40)			5	5
178		45 c. emerald-green (15.4.40)			5	5
179		50 c. yellow-brown			5	5
180		60 c. magenta (26.3.40)			5	5
181		70 c. scarlet (26.3.40)			5	5
182		90 c. chocolate (4.12.39)			5	5
183		1 f. 40, orange (5.3.40)			8	8
184		1 f. 60, violet (5.3.40)			8	8
185		2 f. brown-red			12	8
186		3 f. bright green			1·10	70
186*a*		3 f. grey-green (4.12.39)			15	12
177/186*a*		*Set of* 11			1·60	1·25

The 60 c. design without "R F" was prepared, but not issued in Madagascar.

1937 (15 Apr). *International Exhibition, Paris. As T* **16/21** *of Mauritania.*
187		20 c. bright violet			30	30
188		30 c. green			25	25
189		40 c. carmine			25	25
190		50 c. brown and blue			15	15
191		90 c. scarlet			40	35
192		1 f. 50, blue			40	35
187/192		*Set of* 6			1·50	1·40
MS192*a*		120×100 mm. 3 f. orange-red (as T **16**). Imperf			1·40	1·40

(Eng A. Delzers. Recess)

1938 (6 July)–**40**. *60th Death Anniv of Jean Laborde (explorer). P* 13.
193	20	35 c. green			12	8
194		55 c. violet			12	5
195		65 c. red			12	5
196		80 c. purple			12	5
197		1 f. carmine			12	5
198		1 f. 25, carmine (4.12.39)			5	5
199	20	1 f. 75, bright blue			40	8
200		2 f 15. brown			90	30
201		2 f. 25, blue (4.12.39)			8	5
202		2 f. 50, black-brown (5.3.40)			8	5
203		10 f. green (5.3.40)			20	10
193/203		*Set of* 11			2·00	80

1938 (24 Oct). *International Anti-Cancer Fund. As T* **22** *of Mauritania.*
204		1 f. 75+50 c. ultramarine			3·00	3·00

1939 (10 May). *New York World's Fair. As T* **28** *of Mauritania.*
205		1 f. 25, lake			30	30
206		2 f. 25, ultramarine			30	30

1939 (5 July). *150th Anniv of French Revolution. As T* **29** *of Mauritania.*
207		45 c.+25 c. green			2·50	2·50
208		70 c.+30 c. brown			2·50	2·50
209		90 c.+35 c. red-orange			2·50	2·50
210		1 f. 25+1 f. carmine			2·50	2·50
211		2 f. 25+2 f. blue			2·50	2·50

(*b*) *AIR. Name and value in orange*
212		4 f. 50+4 f. black			5·50	5·50
207/212		*Set of* 6			16·00	16·00

VICHY ISSUES. No. 213 was issued by the Madagascar authorities of the Pétain administration in Unoccupied France. Other issues were prepared, but were not olaced on sale in the island.

In September 1942 a British expedition seized the island, to forestall any Japanese attempt at occupation, and handed over the administration to the Free French.

50 =

(21)

1942. *No.* 136 *surch with T* 21.
213	15	50 on 65 c. mauve and brown			30	5

50 = FRANCE LIBRE

FRANCE LIBRE

(22)

2,00 ×

(23)

FRANCE LIBRE

(D 24)

1943 (Jan–Feb). *Free French Administration. Optd* "FRANCE LIBRE", *or additionally surch with new values, as in T* **22** *or* **23**. *Nos.* 214, 218, 220, 221, 223, 238 *and* 243 *have the words in one line as in T* **22**. (*a*) *POSTAGE*
214	14	2 c. brown and scarlet			20	20
215	18	3 c. light blue (R.)			20·00	20·00
216	15	0,05 on 1 c. green and ultramarine			8	8
217	20	0,10 on 55 c. violet			25	25
218	17	15 c. scarlet			2·50	2·00
219	20	0,30 on 65 c. red			12	12
220	15	0 f. 50 on 0,05 on 1 c. green and ultramarine (216)			8	8
221		50 on 65 c. mauve and brown (213)			10	10
222	18	50 on 90 c. chocolate			5	5
223	15	65 c. mauve and brown			15	15
224	18	70 c. scarlet			8	8
225	20	80 c. purple			40	40
226	16	1,00 on 1 f. 25, chocolate & ultramarine			45	45
227	20	1,00 on 1 f. 25, carmine			1·25	1·25
228	18	1 f. 40, orange			10	10
229	5	1 f. 50 on 1 f. bl & bl (119) (R.)			25	25
230	14	1 f. 50, ultramarine and blue (R.)			25	25
231		1 f. 50, scarlet and chocolate			25	25
232	18	1,50 on 1 f. 60, violet			5	5
233	14	1,50 on 1 f. 75, scarlet and chocolate			8	8
234	20	1,50 on 1 f. 75, bright blue (R.)			5	5
235	18	1 f. 60, violet			10	10
236	20	2,00 on 2 f. 15, brown			20	15
237		2 f. 25, blue (R.)			8	8
238	–	2 f. 25. ultramarine (206) (R.)			8	8

239	**20**	2 f. 50, black-brown (R.)	65	65
240	**5**	10 f. on 5 f. magenta and vermilión	1·90	1·90
241	**20**	10 f. green	1·10	1·10
242	**5**	20 f. on 5 f. grey-blue & magenta (R.)	1·90	1·90
243	**14**	20 f. ultramarine & yellow-brown (R.)	£225	£200

(b) AIR. All overprints and surcharges in black

244	**19**	1,00 on 1 f. 25, scarlet and lake	90	90
245		1 f. 50, scarlet and blue	1·10	1·10
246		1 f. 75, scarlet and orange	20·00	20·00
247		3,00 on 3 f. 65, scarlet and black	20	20
248		8 f. scarlet and magenta	35	35
249		8,00 on 8 f. 50, scarlet and blue-green	20	20
250		12 f. scarlet and chocolate	65	65
251		12 f. 50, scarlet and violet	40	40
252		16 f. scarlet and grey-green	95	95
253		50 f. scarlet and ultramarine	70	70

*(c) POSTAGE DUE. Optd "FRANCE LIBRE" in two lines as Type D **24** or additionally surch with new values, in black*

D254	D **6**	10 c. carmine	20	20
D255		20 c. olive	20	20
D256		0,30 on 5 c. green	25	25
D257		40 c. brown/*toned*	20	20
D258		50 c. olive-brown/*azure*	15	20
D259		60 c. red	20	20
D260		1 f. blue	20	20
D261		1 f. on 2 c. dull claret	1·00	1·00
D262		2 f. on 4 c. pale violet	30	30
D263		2 f. on 1 f. magenta	20	20
D264		3 f. on 1 f. ultramarine	20	15

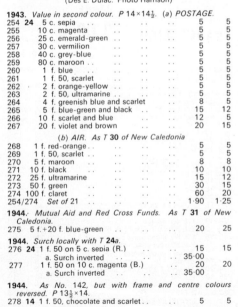

24 Traveller's Tree (24*a*) (25)

(Des E. Dulac. Photo Harrison)

1943. *Value in second colour.* P 14×14½. *(a) POSTAGE.*

254	**24**	5 c. sepia	5	5
255		10 c. magenta	5	5
256		25 c. emerald-green	5	5
257		30 c. vermilion	5	5
258		40 c. grey-blue	5	5
259		80 c. maroon	5	5
260		1 f. blue	5	5
261		1 f. 50, scarlet	5	5
262		2 f. orange-yellow	5	5
263		2 f. 50, ultramarine	5	5
264		4 f. greenish blue and scarlet	8	5
265		5 f. blue-green and black	15	12
266		10 f. scarlet and blue	12	5
267		20 f. violet and brown	20	15

*(b) AIR. As T **30** of New Caledonia*

268		1 f. red-orange	5	5
269		1 f. 50, scarlet	5	5
270		5 f. maroon	8	8
271		10 f. black	10	10
272		25 f. ultramarine	15	12
273		50 f. green	30	15
274		100 f. claret	60	20
254/274		*Set of 21*	1·90	1·25

1944. *Mutual Aid and Red Cross Funds. As T **31** of New Caledonia.*

275		5 f.+20 f. blue-green	20	25

1944. *Surch locally with T **24***a*.*

276	**24**	1 f. 50 on 5 c. sepia (R.)	15	15
		a. Surch inverted	35·00	
277		1 f. 50 on 10 c. magenta (B.)	20	20
		a. Surch inverted	35·00	

1944. *As No. 142, but with frame and centre colours reversed.* P 13½×14.

278	**14**	1 f. 50, chocolate and scarlet	5	5

1945. *Eboué. As T **32** of New Caledonia.*

279		2 f. black	5	5
280		25 f. blue-green	20	20

1946 (8 May). *AIR. Victory. As T **34** of New Caledonia.*

281		8 f. brown-red	12	8

1945. *Surch as T **25**, in London.*

282	**24**	50 c. on 5 c. sepia (R.)	5	5
283		60 c. on 5 c. sepia (R.)	10	10
284		70 c. on 5 c. sepia (R.)	5	5
285		1 f. 20 on 5 c. sepia (R.)	5	5
286		2 f. 40 on 25 c. emerald-green	5	5
287		3 f. on 25 c. emerald-green	5	5
288		4 f. 50 on 25 c. emerald-green	10	10
289		15 f. on 2 f. 50, ultramarine (R.)	8	8
282/289		*Set of 8*	35	35

1946. *AIR. From Chad to the Rhine. As Nos. 300/5 of New Caledonia.*

290		5 f. greenish blue	30	30
291		10 f. claret	30	30
292		15 f. grey-green	30	30
293		20 f. sepia	40	40
294		25 f. violet	40	40
295		50 f. brown-red	40	40
290/295		*Set of 6*	1·90	1·90

26 Southern Dancer **29** General Galliéni **34** "Flight"

27 Herd of Zebus **30** Betsimisaraka Mother and Child

28 Sakalava Couple (36×20 *mm*)

31 General Duchesne (20×37 *mm*)

32 Marshal Joffre when Lt.-Col. (20×37 *mm*)

33 Port of Tamatave

35 Aeroplane over Madagascar (50×29 *mm*)

(Des T **26/33**, J. Douy; T **34**, R. Serres; T **35**, Brenet. Photo
Vaugirard, Paris)

1946. (*a*) *POSTAGE. P* 13½.

296	26	10 c. green	..	.. .. ..	5	5
297		30 c. orange ..		.. .. ..	5	5
298		40 c. brown-olive	..	.. ..	5	5
299		50 c. brown-purple	..	.. ..	5	5
300	27	60 c. ultramarine	..	.. ..	5	5
301		80 c. blue-green	..	.. ..	5	5
302	28	1 f. sepia ..	..	.. ..	5	5
303		1 f. 20, green	..	.. ..	5	5
304	29	1 f. 50, red ..	..	.. ..	5	5
305		2 f. black ..	..	.. ..	5	5
306		3 f. purple ..	..	.. ..	5	5
307	30	3 f. 60, carmine	..	.. ..	12	12
308		4 f. ultramarine	..	.. ..	5	5
309		5 f. orange-red	..	.. ..	8	5
310	31	6 f. blue ..	..	.. ..	5	5
311		10 f. red-brown	..	.. ..	10	5
312	32	15 f. purple-brown	..	.. ..	25	5
313		20 f. ultramarine	..	.. ..	30	5
314		25 f. brown ..	..	.. ..	35	5

(*b*) *AIR. P* 13½×12½ (*horiz*) or 12½×13½ (*vert*)

315	33	50 f. blue and carmine	.. ..	50	8
316	34	100 f. brown and carmine	..	1·00	15
317	35	200 f. brown and blue-green ..	..	2·25	45
296/317		*Set of 22* ..	.. ..	5·00	1·40

38 Cacti and Succulents   **39** *Uratelornis*

40 Woman and Forest Road

TERRE ADÉLIE
DUMONT D'URVILLE
══ 1840 ══

36 Gen. Galliéni   D **37**   (**37**)
and View

(Des and eng R. Serres. Recess)

1946 (Nov). *Fiftieth Anniv of French Conquest. P* 13.
318 **36** 10 f.+5 f. brown-purple   ..   8   8

(Des J. Douy. Photo Vaugirard, Paris)

1947. *POSTAGE DUE. P* 13.

D319	D **37**	10 c. mauve	..	.. ..	5	5
D320		30 c. sepia	..	.. ..	5	5
D321		50 c. blue-green	..	.. ..	5	5
D322		1 f. orange-brown	..	.. ..	5	5
D323		2 f. claret	..	.. ..	5	5
D324		3 f. red-brown ..	..	.. ..	5	5
D325		4 f. blue	..	.. ..	10	10
D326		5 f. brown-red :.	..	.. ..	10	10
D327		10 f. olive-green ..	..	.. ..	10	10
D328		20 f. violet-blue ..	..	.. ..	25	25
D319/328		*Set of 10* ..	..	.. ..	75	75

1948 (26 Oct). *AIR. Rear-Admiral Dumont D'Urville's Discovery
of Adélie Land, Antarctica. No.* 316 *optd with T* **37**, *in red.*
319 **34** 100 f. brown and carmine   .. ..   16·00   16·00

1949 (4 July). *AIR. ·75th Anniv of Universal Postal Union.
As T* **38** *of New Caledonia.*
320   25 f. multicoloured   ..   ..   1·25   1·00

1950 (15 May). *Colonial Welfare Fund. As T* **39** *of New
Caledonia.*
321   10 f.+2 f. purple and blue-green   ..   1·10   1·10

(Des and eng R. Cami (7 f. 50); C. Hertenberger (100 f.);
J. Pheulpin (500 f.); P. Gandon (others). Recess)

1952. *P* 13. (*a*) *POSTAGE.*
322 **38**   7 f. 50, dp blue-green & indigo (20.9)   45   8
323 **39**   8 f. lake (20.9)   ..   25   8
324   15 f. blue and deep blue-green (20.9)   60   5

(*b*) *AIR. As T* **40**
325   50 f. blackish grn & dp turquoise (20.9)   95   8
326   100 f. black, dp purple-brown & bl (20.9)   1·60   40
327   200 f. black-brown & blackish grn (20.9)   3·75   75
328   500 f. brown, blk-brn & bronze-grn (30.6)   7·50   1·50
322/328   *Set of 7*   ..   .. ..   14·00   2·75
Designs: *Horiz*—50 f. Palm trees and aeroplane; 100 f.
Antsirabe Viaduct; 200 f. Lemurs.

1952 (1 Dec). *Centenary of Médaille Militaire. As T* **40** *of
New Caledonia.*
329   15 f. deep blue-green, yellow and green   75   60

1954 (6 June). *AIR. Tenth Anniv of Liberation. As T* **42** *of
New Caledonia.*
330   15 f. purple-brown and violet   ..   75   60

41 Marshal Lyautey

(Des and eng P. Gandon. Recess)

1954 (29 Nov)–**55**. *Birth Centenary of Marshal Lyautey. P* 13.
331 **41** 10 f. indigo, blue & ultramarine (2.5.55)   25   5
332   40 f. brown-lake, dp grey-blue & black   55   5

42 Galliéni School   **43** Cassava

STAMP MONTHLY
—finest and most informative magazine for all
collectors. Obtainable from your newsagent or
by postal subscription—details on request.

(Des and eng C. Hertenberger. Recess)

1956 (22 Oct). *Economic and Social Development Fund.* T **42** *and similar horiz designs inscr "F.I.D.E.S.".* P 13×12½.

333	3 f. deep brown and violet-grey	8	5
334	5 f. chocolate and orange-brown	5	5
335	10 f. indigo and violet-grey	15	5
336	15 f. green and slate-green	20	5
333/336	*Set of* 4	35	15

Designs:—3 f. Tamatave and tractor; 10 f. Canal; 15 f. Irrigation.

1956 (22 Oct). *Coffee. As T* **44** *of New Caledonia.*

337	20 f. sepia and brown	25	8

(Des and eng H. Cheffer (2 f.), P. Munier (4 f.), J. Pheulpin (12 f.). Recess)

1957 (12 Mar). *Various plants as T* **43**. P 13.

338	2 f. green, brown and blue	8	5
339	4 f. scarlet, chocolate and bluish green	10	5
340	12 f. dp bluish green, brown & dp violet	20	10

Designs:—4 f. Cloves; 12 f. Vanilla.

Madagascar became autonomous as the Malagasy Republic on 14 October 1958.

F. MALAGASY REPUBLIC

1958 (10 Dec). *Tenth Anniv of Declaration of Human Rights. As T* **48** *of New Caledonia.*

1	10 f. brown and blue	30	20

1959 (31 Jan). *Tropical Flora. As T* **47** *of New Caledonia.*

2	6 f. green, brown-purple & greenish yellow	10	8
3	25 f. multicoloured	35	10

Designs: *Horiz*—6 f. Datura. *Vert*—25 f. Pointetia.

1 Malagasy Flag and Assembly Hall

(Des and eng A. Decaris. Recess)

1959 (28 Feb). *Proclamation of Malagasy Republic, and "French Community" Commemoration* (60 f.). T **1** *and similar designs.* P 13.

4	20 f. carmine-red, emerald and brown-purple	20	12
5	25 f. red, emerald and violet-grey	30	15
6	60 f. carmine-red, blue, emerald and maroon	70	40

Designs: *Vert*—25 f. Malagasy flag on map of Madagascar; 60 f. Natives holding French and Malagasy flags.

2 *Chionaema pauliani* (butterfly)

3 Reafforestation

(Des and eng R. Cottet (30 c., 40 c.), P. Munier (50 c., 50 f.), J. Pheulpin (1 f., 200 f.), P. Gandon (3 f., 100 f.), C. Durrens (5 f.), G. Bétemps (6 f., 10 f.), R. Serres (8 f., 15 f.), C. Mazelin (30 f., 500 f.), R. Cami (40 f.). Recess)

1960 (16 Jan—25 May). *Various butterflies and other designs as* T **2**. P 13. (*a*) *POSTAGE.*

7	30 c. crimson, vio, yell & turq-bl (25 May)	5	5
8	40 c. red-brown, choc & emer (25 May)	5	5
9	50 c. turquoise-blue & brn-pur (25 May)	5	5
10	1 f. red, dull purple and blue-black	5	5
11	3 f. violet-black, orge-red & ol (25 May)	5	5
12	5 f. emerald, bistre-brown & brown-red	5	5
13	6 f. yellow and deep green	8	8
14	8 f. black, light emerald and red	10	8
15	10 f. yellow-brn, yell-grn & dp bluish grn	12	8
16	15 f. deep green and brown	20	10

(*b*) *AIR. Inscr "POSTE AERIENNE"*

17	30 f. sepia, ochre, maroon, green & black	45	10
18	40 f. olive-brown and deep bluish green	65	20
19	50 f. pur-brn, yell, red & mag (25 May)	70	20
20	100 f. emerald, black, orange and deep grey-green (25 May)	1·60	30
21	200 f. yellow & dp reddish violet (25 May)	3·00	70
22	500 f. yellow-brown, blue & dp bluish grn	6·00	1·50
7/22	*Set of* 16	12·00	3·00

Design: *Horiz*—30 c. *Colotis zoe*; 40 c. *Acrœa hova*; 50 c. *Salamis duprei*; 3 f. *Hypolimnas dexithea*; 5 f. Sisal; 8 f. Pepper; 15 f. Cotton. (48½×27 *mm*)—30 f. Sugar-cane trucks; 40 f. Tobacco plantation; 50 f. *Charaxes antamboulou*; 100 f. *Chrysiridia madagascariensis*; 500 f. Mandrarè Bridge. *Vert*—6 f. Ylang-ylang (vegetable); 10 f. Rice. *Vert* (27×48 *mm*)—200 f. *Argema mittrei*.

(Des Strand. Eng G. Aufschneider. Recess)

1960 (1 Feb). *Trees Festival.* P 13.

23	3 20 f. red-brown, green and yellow-ochre	25	20

4

5 Pres. Philibert Tsiranana

(Des and eng R. Cami. Recess)

1960 (22 Feb). *Tenth Anniv of African Technical Co-operation Commission.* P 13.

24	4 25 f. lake and blue-green	40	30

(Des and eng J. Pheulpin. Recess)

1960 (25 Mar). P 13.

25	5 20 f. chocolate and blue-green	25	8

6 Young Athletes

7 Pres. Tsiranana

(Des and eng A. Decaris. Recess)

1960 (13 Apr). *First Youth Games, Tananarive.* P 13.

26	6 25 f. chocolate, chestnut and bright blue	40	25

Malagasy Republic became independent on 26 June 1960.

Mali Federation

100 Centimes = 1 Franc

The Federation of Mali, comprising the former French Colonies of French Sudan and Senegal, came into existence on 4 April 1959. The Federation took its name from the ancient Empire of Mali which existed in the area from the 13th century until the early 17th century. The Federation became independent within the French Community on 20 June 1960, but broke up when Senegal seceded on 20 August 1960.

PRINTERS. All stamps of the Mali Federation were printed at the Government Printing Works, Paris.

4 Amethyst Merlin   **4a** C.C.T.A. Emblem

1 Map, Flag, Mali and Torch

(Des and eng P. Gandon. Recess)

1959 (7 Nov). *Establishment of Mali Federation.* P 13.
1 **1** 25 f. carm-red, buff, bluish grn & brn-pur   40   40

(Des and eng P. Munier (5 f., 20 f.), C. Hertenberger (10 f., 15 f., 25 f., 30 f., 85 f.). Recess. Des Dekayser. Photo (others))

1960. (*a*) *POSTAGE. Various horiz designs as T* **3**. P 13. (5 Mar).
3	5 f. red-orange, blue and bronze-green	..	20	10
4	10 f. black, brown and turquoise-blue	..	20	15
5	15 f. red-brown, slate and blue	..	30	20
6	20 f. black, bistre-brown and olive-green	..	40	25
7	25 f. yellow-orange, sepia & dp bluish green		45	30
8	30 f. orange-red, deep maroon and blue	..	65	40
9	85 f. crimson, blue and deep bluish green	..	1·50	1·25

(*b*) *AIR. Inscr "POSTE AERIENNE".* T **4** *and similar designs.* P 13½×12½ (200 f.) or 12½×13½ (others). (13 Feb)
10	100 f. multicoloured	..	..	1·60	1·10
11	200 f. multicoloured	..	..	3·25	1·75
12	500 f. multicoloured	..	..	8·00	6·00
3/12	*Set of 10*	..	..	15·00	10·00

Designs: Fishes—10 f. Trigger fish; 15 f. Batfish; 20 f. Threadfish; 25 f. Butterfly; 30 f. Surgeon; 85 f. Seam bream Birds. *Horiz*—200 f. Bateleur eagle. *Vert*—500 f. Gonolek.

(Des and eng R. Cami. Recess)

2

(Des and eng J. Pheulpin. Recess)

1959 (11 Dec). *AIR. 300th Anniv of St. Louis of Senegal.* P 13.
2 **2** 85 f. bistre-brown, blue, chest & brn-pur   1·10   1·00

1960 (21 May). *Tenth Anniv of African Technical Co-operation Commission.* P 13.
13 **4a** 25 f. bright purple and violet   ..   80   65
Imperforate copies of this stamp were not valid for postage.

3 Parrot Fish

ALBUM LISTS

Please write for our latest lists of albums and accessories. These will be sent free on request.

Martinique

100 Centimes = 1 Franc

The island of Martinique, in the West Indies, was owned by the French Antilles Company from 1635 to 1674, when it became a French royal domain. In 1762–63, 1793–1801 and 1809–14 it was occupied by the British.

PRINTERS. All the stamps of Martinique were printed at the Government Printing Works, Paris, *unless otherwise stated*.

IMPERFORATE STAMPS. Many stamps exist imperforate in their issued colours, but these were not valid for postage. Imperforate stamps in other colours are colour trials.

15	05 c. on 35 c. black/*yellow* (2.91)		3·25	2·50
	a. On 35 c. *black/orange*		3·75	2·50
	b. Surch inverted		45·00	45·00
16	05 c. on 40 c. red/*yellow* (2.91)		10·00	9·00
17	15 c. on 4 c. purple-brown (6.88)		£2250	£2000
18	15 c. on 20 c. red/*green* (6.88)		25·00	19·00
	a. Surch double		£100	90·00
19	15 c. on 25 c. black/*rose* (2.91)		4·50	3·75
	a. Surch inverted		60·00	60·00
	b. Surch double		65·00	55·00
20	15 c. on 75 c. rose-carmine/*rose* (2.91)		35·00	28·00

FRENCH COLONY

MARTINIQUE · MARTINIQUE

(1) · (2)

Two types of surch T **1**:—
A. "MARTINIQUE" and "5" 6¾ mm apart.
B. "MARTINIQUE" and "5" 9¾ mm apart.

1886 (18 July). *French Colonies Type J ("Commerce").* P 14×13½. *Surch with T* **1** *or* **2** *at Fort-de-France*

1	**1**	5 on 20 c. red/*green* (A)	13·00	11·00
		a. Surch double	£110	£110
		b. Type B	£800	£800
2	**2**	5 on 20 c. red/*green*	£2500	£2500

1886 (Nov)–**88**. *French Colonies Type J surch as T* **1** *at Fort-de-France.*

3	01 on 20 c. red/*green* (6.5.88)		3·00	2·50
	a. Surch double		12·00	12·00
	b. Surch inverted		65·00	65·00
4	05 on 20 c. red/*green*		1·50	1·25
5	15 on 20 c. red/*green* (1887)		38·00	32·00
	a. Surch inverted		£110	£110
6	015 on 20 c. red/*green* (1887)		11·00	10·00
	a. Surch inverted		£110	£100

MQE · MQE · MARTINIQUE / 01 c.

15 c. · 15 c.

(3) · (4) · (5)

1887 (2 May). *French Colonies Type J surch with T* **3** *or* **4** *at Fort-de-France.*

7	**3**	15 c. on 20 c. red/*green*	22·00	19·00
		a. Surch inverted	£250	£250
8	**4**	15 c. on 20 c. red/*green*	50·00	50·00
		a. Surch inverted	£325	£325

1888 (11 May).–**91**. *French Colonies Type J surch as T* **5**, *at Fort-de-France.*

9	01 on 2 c. brown/*buff* (10.88)		50	45
	a. Surch double		55·00	55·00
10	01 c. on 4 c. purple-brown (10.88)		1·50	65
11	05 c. on 4 c. purple-brown		£325	£275
12	05 c. on 10 c. black/*lilac* (2.91)		16·00	9·50
13	05 c. on 20 c. red/*green*		4·00	3·25
	a. Surch inverted		65·00	50·00
14	05 c. on 30 c. cinnamon/*drab* (2.91)		5·50	5·00

TIMBRE·POSTE · 1892 · 1892

05 c. · MARTINIQUE · 15 c.

MARTINIQUE · 15 c. · MARTINIQUE

(6) · (8) · (9)

1891 (May)–**92**. *French Colonies (General Issues) surch as T* **6**, *at Fort-de-France.*

(a) Postage Due Type U, Imperf. (i) *In black*

21	05 c. on 5 c. black (1892)		2·50	2·50
	a. "PCSTE" for "POSTE"			
22	05 c. on 15 c. black		1·90	1·75
	a. "PCSTE" for "POSTE"		6·00	5·00
	b. "POSUE" for "POSTE"			
23	15 c. on 20 c. black		2·50	1·90
	a. Surch double		45·00	45·00
	b. Surch inverted		45·00	45·00
	c. "POSUE" for "POSTE"		6·00	5·50
24	15 c. on 30 c. black		2·50	2·25
	a. Surch inverted		45·00	45·00

(ii) *In/red*

25	05 c. on 10 c. black		1·50	1·50
	a. Surch inverted		45·00	45·00
26	05 c. on 15 c. black		2·50	2·50
27	15 c. on 20 c. black		7·50	6·50
	a. Surch inverted		60·00	60·00

(b) "Commerce" Type J. P 14×13½. *In black*

28	01 on 2 c. brown/*buff* (7.91)		1 60	1 60

1892. *French Colonies Type J. P* 14×13½. *Surch as T* **8** *or* **9**, *in black at Fort-de-France.*

29	**8**	05 c. on 25 c. black/*rose*	11·00	11·00
30	**9**	05 c. on 25 c. black/*rose*	10·00	9·50
		a. "1882" for "1892"	75·00	65·00
		b. "95" for "05"	£110	95·00
31	**8**	15 c. on 25 c. black/*rose*	4·50	4·50
32	**9**	15 c. on 25 c. black/*rose*	4·50	4·50
		a. "1882" for "1892"	70·00	65·00

1892 (Nov). *As T* **11** *of New Caledonia, inscr* "MARTINIQUE" *in red* (1, 5, 15, 25, 75, c., 1 f.) *or blue* (others). *P* 14×13½.

33	1 c. black/*azure*		25	25
	a. Name in blue		90·00	90·00
34	2 c. brown/*buff*		25	25
35	4 c. purple-brown/*grey*		30	25
36	5 c. green/*pale green*		40	20
37	10 c. black/*lilac*		1·40	20
38	15 c. blue (*quadrillé paper*)		5·00	1·10
39	20 c. red/*green*		3·25	1·00
40	25 c. black/*rose*		3·75	40
41	30 c. cinnamon/*drab*		6·50	2·50
42	40 c. red/*yellow*		6·50	2·50
43	50 c. carmine/*rose*		5·50	3·25
44	75 c. brown/*orange*		5·50	3·50
45	1 f. olive-green/*toned*		4·50	2·50
33/45	*Set of 13*		38·00	16·00

Martinique 1899

1899–1906. *As Nos.* 33/45 *but colours changed and new value.*

46	5 c. yellow-green		50	12
47	10 c. rose-red (12.00)		75	12
48	15 c. grey (12.00)		1·90	25
49	25 c. blue		2·50	2·50
50	35 c. black/*yellow* (1906)		3·25	1·25
51	50 c. brown/*azure*		6·50	5·00
52	2 f. violet/*rose* (1904)		18·00	18·00
53	5 f. mauve/*pale lilac* (1903)		21·00	21·00
46/53	*Set of 8*		50·00	42·00

TIMBRE POSTE

5 F.		**1904**
MARTINIQUE	**10ᶜ**	**0ᶠ10**
COLIS POSTAUX		
(10)	(11)	(12)

1903 (Oct). *French Colonies Type* U *surch with T* **10** *at Fort-de-France. Imperf.*

53a	5 f. on 60 c. brown/*buff*		£110	£110
	b. Surch inverted		£160	£160

Although inscribed "COLIS POSTAUX" No. 53a was available for use on letters, as well as parcels.

1904 (5 Aug). *Nos.* 41 *and* 53 *surch with T* **11**

54	10 c. on 30 cinnamon/*drab*		1·60	1·60
	a. Surch double		50·00	50·00
55	10 c. on 5 f. mauve/*pale lilac*		2·50	2·50

There is a minor variety in the setting of the above surcharge, a wrong fount "c" having been used on two positions in the sheet.

1904 (18 Aug). *Nos.* 41/5 *and* 53 *surch with T* **12**, *at Fort-de-France.*

56	0 f. 10 on 30 c. cinnamon/*drab*		3·25	3·25
57	0 f. 10 on 40 c. red/*yellow*		3·25	3·25
	a. Surch double		70·00	70·00
58	0 f. 10 on 50 c. carmine/*rose*		3·25	3·25
59	0 f. 10 on 75 c. brown/*orange*		2·75	2·75
60	0 f. 10 on 1 f. olive-green/*toned*		3·25	3·25
	a. Surch double		40·00	40·00
61	0 f. 10 on 5 f. mauve/*pale lilac*		60·00	60·00

13 Martinique Woman   **15** Woman and Sugar Cane

14 Fort-de-France

(Des L. Colmet-Daage. Typo)

1908 (17 Dec)–**17**. *Central design, name, and value in purple-brown (except for* 15 *c.). P* $14 \times 13\frac{1}{2}$ *(T* **14**) *or* $13\frac{1}{2} \times 14$ *(others).*

62	**13**	1 c. red-brown		5	5
63		2 c. olive		5	5
64		4 c. brown-purple		5	5
65		5 c. green		5	5
66		10 c. carmine		10	5
67		15 c. carmine and purple (1917)		5	5
68		20 c. deep lilac		15	12

69	**14**	25 c. blue		15	8
70		30 c. Venetian red		20	12
71		35 c. deep lilac		10	10
72		40 c. pale sage-green		12	5
73		45 c. deep brown		10	10
74		50 c. rosine		15	12
75		75 c. greenish black		12	10
76	**15**	1 f. dull greenish blue		10	5
77		2 f. grey		55	20
78		5 f. Venetian red		2·00	1·90
62/78	*Set of 17*			4·50	3·00

The 35 c. and 45 c. values exist on chalk-surfaced paper.

1912 (Aug). *Nos.* 48, 39, 42 *and* 53 *surch as T* **6/7** *of Madagascar and Dependencies* (*see Malagasy Republic*).

		A. Narrow spacing	B. Wide spacing	
			A.	B.
79	05 on 15 c. grey (R.)		10	10 5·00 5·00
80	05 on 25 c. black/*rose* (R.)		25	25 13·00 13·00
81	10 on 40 c. red/*yellow*		30	30 32·00 32·00
82	10 on 5 f. mauve/*pale lilac*		30	30 32·00 32·00

For note *re* spacing, see Madagascar and Dependencies.

1915 (15 May). *Red Cross Fund. Surch as T* **8** *of Madagascar and Dependencies, in red.*

83	**13**	10 c. +5 c. purple-brown and carmine	40	30

10	**≡0,01≡**	**℅**	**0₊01**
(18)	(19)	(20)	(21)

1920 (15 June). *Surch as T* **18**, *at Fort-de-France.*

84	**13**	05 on 1 c. purple-brown and red-brown	30	30
		a. Surch inverted	5·00	5·00
		b. Surch double	5·00	5·00
		c. Small "0"	1·50	1·50
85		10 on 2 c. pur-brown and olive	20	20
		a. Surch inverted	5·00	5·00
		b. Small "0"	1·50	1·50
86		25 on 15 c. carmine and purple	20	20
		a. Surch inverted	6·50	6·50
		b. Surch double	6·50	6·50

On Nos. 84c and 85b the zero is 6 mm high, insteads of $6\frac{3}{4}$ mm.

1922 (1 Jan)–**30**. *Colours charged and new values. P* $14 \times 13\frac{1}{2}$ *(T* **14**) *or* $13\frac{1}{2} \times 14$ *(others).*

87	**13**	5 c. brown and orange		5	5
88		10 c. grey-green and green		8	8
89		10 c. carmine and dull purple (15.2.25)		5	5
90		15 c. olive and green (15.2.25)		5	5
91		15 c. vermilion and blue (30.4.28)		12	12
92	**14**	25 c. brown and orange		5	5
93		30 c. brown and red		5	5
94		30 c. red and carmine (9.24)		5	5
95		30 c. brown and light brown (15.2.25)		5	5
96		30 c. green and greenish blue (14.11.27)		10	10
97		50 c. brown and blue		15	12
98		50 c. green and dull red (22.6.25)		5	5
99		60 c. pink and blue (1.12.25)		5	5
100		65 c. brown & bright violet (19.12.27)		25	25
101		75 c. blue and deep blue (22.6.25)		5	5
102		75 c. ultramarine & red-brn (30.4.28)		45	45
103		90 c. carmine and brown-red (22.3.30)		75	75
104	**15**	1 f. blue (1.12.25)		5	5
105		1 f. olive-green & verm (14.11.27)		30	30
106		1 f. 10, brown & brt violet (25.9.28)		50	50
107		1 f. 50, light blue and brown (22.3.30)		90	90
108		3 f magenta/*rose* (22.3.30)		1·25	1·25
87/108	*Set of 22*			5·00	5·00

1922 (Dec). *Surch as T* **19**.

109	**13**	0,01 on 15 c. carmine and purple	5	5
		a. Surch double	20·00	
110		0,02 on 15 c. carmine and purple (B.)	5	5
111		0,05 on 15 c. carmine and purple (R.)	5	5

1923 (May)–**25**. *Surch as T* **20**.

112	**14**	60 on 75 c. rose and blue	5	5
113		65 on 45 c. brown & lt brown (1.2.25)	20	20
114		85 on 75 c. brown & black (R.) (1.2.25)	15	15

289

1924 (14 Feb). *Surch as T* **21**, *in red at Fort-de-France. Surch is horiz on Nos.* 115/6; *vert on others; reading upwards on Nos.* 117 *and* 120 *and downwards on Nos.* 118/9

115	**13**	0,01 on 2 c. brown and olive..	35	35
		a. Surch inverted	10·00	10·00
		b. Surch double	60·00	60·00
116		0,05 on 20 c. brown and lilac	40	40
		a. Surch inverted	9·50	9·50
117	**14**	0,15 on 30 c. brown & Venetian red..	2·25	2·25
		a. Surch inverted	5·00	5·00
118		0,15 on 30 c. brown and red ..	2·10	2·10
		a. Surch inverted	7·50	7·50
119		0,25 on 50 c. brown and rosine	65·00	55·00
120		0,25 on 50 c. brown and blue	90	90
		a. Surch inverted	5·00	5·00

25ᶜ   **1ᶠ25**   **3ᶠ**   **MARTINIQUE**

(22)   (23)   (24)   (D 25)

1924 (June)–**27**. *T* 13/15, *some with colours changed, surch with new value and bars.*

(a) As T **22**
121	**13**	25 c. on 15 c. carmine & purple (1.2.25)	5	5
122	**15**	25 c. on 2 f. brown and grey ..	5	5
123		25 c. on 5 f. brown and red (B.) ..	12	12
124	**14**	90 c. on 75 c. carmine & red (11.4.27)	45	40

(b) As T **23**
125	**15**	1 f. 25 on 1 f. blue (R.) (14.6.26) ..	5	5
126		1 f. 50 on 1 f. ultramarine & bl (11.4.27)	20	20

(c) As T **24**
127	**15**	3 f. on 5 f. green & carmine (19.12.27)	30	30
128		10 f. on 5 f. carmine & green (11.4.27)	1·90	1·75
129		20 f. on 5 f. violet and brown (11.4.27)	2·75	2·50
121/129		*Set of 9*	5·00	5·00

1927 (10 Oct) *POSTAGE DUE. Postage Due stamps of France, Type* D **11** *optd with Type* D **25**. *P* 14×13½.
D130		5 c. pale blue	25	25
D131		10 c. pale brown	40	40
D132		20 c. olive-green	40	40
D133		25 c. rosine	65	65
D134		30 c. carmine	65	65
D135		45 c. pale green	65	65
D136		50 c. deep purple	1·25	1·25
D137		60 c. green	1·25	1·25
D138		1 f. claret/straw	1·50	1·50
D139		2 f. bright violet	1·90	1·90
D140		3 f. magenta	2·50	2·50
D130/140		*Set of 11*	9·00	9·00

1931 (13 Apr). *International Colonial Exhibition, Paris. As T* **12**/15 *of Mauritania.*
130		40 c. black and green	70	70
131		50 c. black and mauve	70	70
132		90 c. black and vermilion ..	70	70
133		1 f. 50, black and blue ..	70	70
130/133		*Set of 4*	2·50	2·50

(Des C. Hourriez (**26**); C. Rollet (**27**/8). Eng H. Cheffer, C. Hourriez and J. Piel, respectively. Photo Vaugirard, Paris)

1933 (15 Jan)–**40**. *P* 13½.
134	**26**	1 c. scarlet/rose		..	5	5
135	**27**	2 c. light blue	.. ..	5	5
136		3 c. brown-purple (15.4.40)		5	5
137	**26**	4 c. bronze-green	..	5	5
138	**27**	5 c. claret	.. ..	5	5
139	**26**	10 c. black/rose	..	5	5
140	**27**	15 c. black/red	..	5	5
141	**28**	20 c. red-brown	..	5	5
142	**26**	25 c. purple	.. ..	5	5
143	**27**	30 c. green	.. ..	5	5
144		30 c. ultramarine (15.4.40)		5	5
145	**28**	35 c. blue-green (16.5.38)		5	5
146		40 c. sepia	.. ..	5	5
147	**27**	45 c. brown	.. ..	20	20
148		45 c. green (15.4.40)	..	8	8
149		50 c. scarlet	.. ..	5	5
150	**26**	55 c. red (16.5.38)	..	10	10
151		60 c. greenish blue (26.3.40)		5	5
152	**28**	65 c. scarlet/azure	..	8	8
153		70 c. bright purple (26.3.40)..		8	8
154	**26**	75 c. brown	.. ..	12	12
155	**27**	80 c. violet (16.5.38) ..		8	8
156	**26**	90 c. carmine..	..	30	30
157		90 c. bright purple (4.12.39)		5	5
158	**27**	1 f. black/green	..	30	20
159		1 f. carmine (16.5.38)	..	8	8
160	**28**	1 f. 25. violet (25.9.33)		10	10
161		1 f. 25, carmine (4.12.39)		8	8
162	**26**	1 f. 40, ultramarine (5.3.40)		8	8
163	**27**	1 f. 50, blue	.. ..	5	5
164		1 f. 60, red-brown (5.3.40)..		10	10
165	**28**	1 f. 75, bronze-green (25.9.33)		1·60	65
166		1 f. 75, blue (16.5.38)	..	8	8
167	**26**	2 f. blue/green	..	8	8
168	**28**	2 f. 25, blue (4.12.39)	..	8	8
169	**26**	2 f. 50, brown-purple (5.3.40)		8	8
170	**28**	3 f. purple	.. ..	5	5
171		5 f. scarlet/rose	..	20	10
172	**26**	10 f. blue/blue	..	10	10
173	**27**	20 f. scarlet/yellow	..	12	10
134/173		*Set of 40*	4·00	2·75

Five values as Type **27**, but without "RF", were prepared in 1942–44, but not used in Martinique.

(Des C. Hourriez. Eng E. Feltesse. Photo Vaugirard, Paris)

1933 (15 Feb). *POSTAGE DUE. P* 13½.
D174	D **29**	5 c. blue/green ..		..	5	5
D175		10 c. red-brown	..	..	5	5
D176		20 c. blue	.. ..	..	20	20
D177		25 c. scarlet/rose..	..		20	20
D178		30 c. slate-purple	..	..	15	15
D179		45 c. scarlet/yellow	..		8	8
D180		50 c. brown	.. ..		15	15
D181		60 c. green	.. ..	..	15	15
D182		1 f. black/red	..	..	35	35
D183		2 f. claret	.. ..		15	15
D184		3 f. blue/blue	.. ..		20	20
D174/184		*Set of 11*		1·50	1·50

10, 20, 25 and 30 c. values in the same design, but without "RF", were prepared in 1943, but not issued.

26 Basse Pointe Village   27 Government House, Fort-de-France

28 Martinique Women   D 29 Fruit

30 Belain d'Esnambuc, 1635   31 Schœlcher and Abolition of Slavery, 1848

(Eng J. Piel. Recess)

1935 (22 Oct). *West Indies Tercentenary. P* 13.
174	**30**	40 c. sepia	45	45
175		50 c. scarlet	45	45
176		1 f. 50, ultramarine	3·25	3·00
177	**31**	1 f. 75, carmine	3·00	3·00
178		5 f. brown	3·00	3·00
179		10 f. emerald-green	2·00	2·00
174/179		*Set of* 6	11·00	11·00

1937 (15 Apr). *International Exhibition, Paris. As T* **16/21** *of Mauritania.*
180	20 c. bright violet		25	25
181	30 c. green		25	25
182	40 c. carmine		25	25
183	50 c. brown and blue		30	30
184	90 c. scarlet		30	30
185	1 f. 50, blue		30	30
180/185	*Set of* 6		1·50	1·50

MS185a 120×100 mm. 3 f. emerald (as *T* **16**).
	Imperf	1·00	1·00
	b. Error. Inscription inverted	£375	
	c. Error. Inscription omitted	£600	

1938 (24 Oct). *International Anti-Cancer Fund. As T* **22** *of Mauritania.*
186	1 f. 75+50 c. ultramarine	2·10	2·10

1939 (10 May). *New York World's Fair. As T* **28** *of Mauritania.*
187	1 f. 25, lake	20	20
188	2 f. 25, ultramarine	20	20

1939 (5 July). *150th Anniv of French Revolution. As T* **29** *of Mauritania.*
189	45 c.+25 c. green and black	1·40	1·40
190	70 c.+30 c. brown and black	1·40	1·40
191	90 c.+35 c. red-orange and black	1·40	1·40
192	1 f. 25+1 f. carmine and black	1·40	1·40
193	2 f. 25+2 f. blue and black	1·40	1·40
189/193	*Set of* 5	6·50	6·50

VICHY ISSUES. A number of stamps were prepared by the Pétain Government of Unoccupied France for use in Martinique, but were not placed on sale there.

1944. *Mutual Aid and Red Cross Funds. As T* **31** *of New Caledonia.*
194	5 f.+2 f. violet	15	15

1945. *Eboué. As T* **32** *of New Caledonia.*
195	2 f. black	5	5
196	25 f. blue-green	15	15

(32)   33 Victor Schœlcher

1945. *As Nos.* 135/7 *and* 152, *but surch as T* **32** *and bars.*
197	**27**	1 f. on 2 c. light blue (R.)	5	5
198	**26**	2 f. on 4 c. bronze-green	5	5
199	**27**	3 f. on 2 c. light blue (R.)	8	8
200	**28**	5 f. on 65 c. scarlet/*azure*	15	15
201		DIX f. on 65 c. scarlet/*azure*	12	12
202	**27**	VINGT f. on 3 c. brown-purple (B.)	20	20

(Litho. De La Rue & Co, London)

1945. *P* 12.
203	**33**	10 c. indigo and violet	5	5
204		30 c. red-brown and brown-red	5	5
205		40 c. greenish blue and light blue	5	5
206		50 c. brown-lake and claret	5	5
207		60 c. orange and yellow	5	5
208		70 c. brown-purple and chocolate	5	5
209		80 c. green and light green	5	5
210		1 f. blue and light blue	5	5
211		1 f. 20, bright violet and claret	5	5
212		1 f. 50, red-orange and orange	5	5

213	**33**	2 f. black and grey	8	8
214		2 f. 40, scarlet and rose	20	20
215		3 f. pink and pale pink	5	5
216		4 f. ultramarine and grey-blue	8	5
217		4 f. 50, blue-green and green	10	8
218		5 f. orange-brown and brown	5	5
219		10 f. dull purple and mauve	15	10
220		15 f. carmine and pink	15	12
221		20 f. olive-green and yellow-green	25	20

1945. *AIR. As T* **30** *of New Caledonia.*
222		50 f. green	15	15
223		100 f. claret	20	20
203/223		*Set of* 21	1·75	1·50

1946 (8 May). *AIR. Victory. As T* **38** *of New Caledonia.*
224	8 f. indigo	30	30

1946 (6 June). *AIR. From Chad to the Rhine. As Nos.* 300/5 *of New Caledonia.*
225	5 f. brown-orange	10	10
226	10 f. grey-green	12	12
227	15 f. rose-red	12	12
228	20 f. chocolate	15	15
229	25 f. blue	20	20
230	50 f. blue-grey	30	30
225/230	*Set of* 6	90	90

FRENCH OVERSEAS DEPARTMENT

On I January 1947 Martinique was made an Overseas Department of France.

34 Martinique   **35** Sailing Vessels
Woman   and Rocks

36 Gathering Sugar Cane   **37** Mount Pelé

38 Fruit Products   **39** Mountains and
Palms

237	36	2 f. bright green	..	..	..	20	20
238		2 f. 50, sepia	..	..	..	20	15
239		3 f. blue	..	..	..	15	12
240	37	4 f. brown	..	..	..	15	15
241		5 f. green	..	..	..	15	15
242		6 f. magenta	..	..	..	12	8
243	38	10 f. indigo	..	..	..	20	12
244		15 f. brown-lake	..	..	..	30	25
245		20 f. sepia	..	..	..	40	35
246	39	25 f. bright violet	..	..	..	45	30
247		40 f. bright green	..	..	..	45	35

40 West Indians and Flying Boat

(b) AIR

248	40	50 f. purple	..		..	90	80
249	41	100 f. blue-green	..	..	..	1·25	1·25
250	42	200 f. bright violet	..	..	..	8·00	6·50
231/250		Set of 20	..	..	..	11·00	9·50

D 43 Map of Martinique

41 Aeroplane over Landscape   **42** Gull in Flight

(Des Lemagny, eng Cortot. Recess)

(Des Lemagny, eng Ouvré (T **34**). Des Brenet (T **35, 39/40**), eng. R. Cottet (T **35**), E. Feltesse (T **39**) and C. Mazelin (T **40**). Des M. Dassonville (T **36** and **41**), eng Dufresne (T **36**) and Feltesse (T **41**). Des and eng Barlangue (T **37/8** and **42**). Recess)

1947 (2 June). P 13. (a) POSTAGE.

231	34	10 c. brown-lake	..	..	..	5	5
232		30 c. blue	..	..	..	5	5
233		50 c. sepia	..	..	..	5	5
234	35	60 c. dull green	..	..	..	5	5
235		1 f. brown-lake	..	..	..	5	5
236		1 f. 50, violet	..	..	..	5	5

1947 (2 June). POSTAGE DUE. P 14×13.

D251	D 43	10 c. ultramarine	..		..	5	5
D252		30 c. bright green	..		..	5	5
D253		50 c. indigo	..		..	5	5
D254		1 f. red-orange	..		..	5	5
D255		2 f. brown-purple	..		..	8	8
D256		3 f. bright purple	..		..	10	10
D257		4 f. sepia	..		..	15	15
D258		5 f. red	..		..	20	20
D259		10 f. black	..		..	30	30
D260		20 f. olive-green	..		..	30	30
D251/260		Set of 10	..	..	..	1·25	1·25

After supplies of the 1947 issue were exhausted, the stamps of France were used in Martinique.

stamp monthly

Gibbons' own monthly magazine, essential reading for **every** collector !
Detailed monthly New Issue Guide to update all Gibbons catalogues for you—and a special Stamp Market feature on price changes.
Informative articles cover all facets of philately, with regular notes on new discoveries, stamp designs, postmarks, market trends and news and views of the world of stamps. Britain's LARGEST circulation of any stamp magazine—that fact speaks for itself !
Monthly from all dealers and newsagents or by post direct from Stanley Gibbons Magazines Ltd—subscription rates on application.

Mauritania

100 Centimes = 1 Franc

French influence was extended north of the Senegal river in 1898–1905 by Xavier Cappolini, and in May 1903 Mauritania was made a French protectorate. In 1904 it became a Civil Territory of French West Africa. In 1908–09 General Gouraud defeated Moroccan bands which had ravaged French territory, and added the Adrar region to Mauritania.

PRINTERS. All the stamps of Mauritania were printed at the Government Printing Works, Paris, *unless otherwise stated.*

IMPERFORATE STAMPS. Stamps exist imperforate in their issued colours, but these were not valid for postage. Imperforate stamps in other colours are colour trials.

A. FRENCH CIVIL TERRITORY

1 General Faidherbe   **2** Palm Trees

3 Dr. N. Eugène Balay   (D **4**)

(Des J. Puyplat. Typo)

1906–07. *Name in blue (10 c., 40 c., 5 f) or red (others). P 13½×14 (20 c. to 75 c.) or 14×13½ (others).*

1	**1**	1 c. slate		5	5
2		2 c. chocolate		15	12
3		4 c. chocolate/*blue*		25	15
4		5 c. green		20	8
5		10 c. rose		1·60	1·10
6	**2**	20 c. black/*bluish*		3·75	3·25
7		25 c. blue		1·50	1·50
8		30 c. chocolate/*flesh*		22·00	18·00
9		35 c. black/*yellow*		1·40	95
10		40 c. carmine/*azure*		1·40	95
11		45 c. chocolate/*green* (1907)		1·25	1·10
12		50 c. deep violet		1·10	1·10
13		75 c. green/*orange*		1·10	1·10
14	**3**	1 f. black/*azure*		3·25	3·25
15		2 f. blue/*rose*		7·50	6·50
16		5 f. red/*straw*		30·00	29·00
1/16		*Set of 16*		70·00	60·00

1906 (5 Sept). *POSTAGE DUE. Nos. 4/8, 12 and 14 handstamped with Type D **4**, in blue or black.*

D18	**1**	5 c. green		—	14·00
D19		10 c. rose		—	14·00
D20	**2**	20 c. black/*bluish*		—	20·00
D21		25 c. blue		—	22·00
D22		30 c. chocolate/*flesh*		—	55·00
D23		50 c. deep violet		—	55·00
D24	**3**	1 f. black/*azure*		—	70·00

There are many forgeries of this overprint.

D **5** Dakar and   **6** Merchants crossing
West Africans   Desert

(Des J. Puyplat. Typo)

1906–07. *POSTAGE DUE. Name in blue (10 c., 30 c.) or red (others). P 13½×14.*

D25	D **5**	5 c. green/*toned*		50	50
D26		10 c. maroon		75	75
D27		15 c. blue/*bluish*		1·90	1·60
D28		20 c. black/*yellow* (1906)		2·25	1·90
D29		30 c. red/*cream*		2·75	2·50
D30		50 c. violet		3·25	3·25
D31		60 c. black/*buff*		2·75	2·50
D32		1 f. black/*flesh*		3·50	3·50
D25/32		*Set of 8*		16·00	15·00

(Des J. de la Nézière. Eng J. Puyplat. Typo)

1913–17. *P 14×13½.*

18	**6**	1 c. brown and dull lilac		5	5
19		2 c. blue and black		5	5
20		4 c. black and pale violet		5	5
21		5 c. green and pale yellow-green		5	5
22		10 c. red-orange and rose		15	15
23		15 c. black and sepia (1917)		5	5
24		20 c. orange and grey-brown		5	5
25		25 c. ultramarine and blue		20	20
26		30 c. rose and green		12	12
27		35 c. violet and brown		10	10
28		40 c. green and brown		40	40
29		45 c. brown and orange		12	12
30		50 c. rose and dull lilac		12	12
31		75 c. brown and ultramarine		12	12
32		1 f. black and carmine		10	5
33		2 f. violet and red-orange		35	25
34		5 f. blue and violet		40	25
18/34		*Set of 17*		1·90	2·00

The 5, 10 and 15 c. exist on chalk-surfaced paper.
See also Nos. 37/56.

D **7**   (**8**)

1914. *POSTAGE DUE. Typo. P 14×13½.*

D35	D **7**	5 c. green		5	5
D36		10 c. carmine		5	5
D37		15 c. grey		5	5
D38		20 c. brown		5	5
D39		30 c. blue		5	5
D40		50 c. black		25	25
D41		60 c. orange		15	15
D42		1 f. violet		15	15
D35/42		*Set of 8*		70	70

1915 (Apr)–**18.** *Red Cross. Surch in Paris with T **8**, in red.*

35	**6**	10 c.+5 c. red-orange and rose		20	20
		a. Surch double		6·50	6·50
36		15 c.+5 c. black and sepia (1918)		12	12

No. 36 is on chalk-surfaced paper.

B. FRENCH COLONY

1 January 1921

1922 (1 Jan)–**38**. *New values and colours changed.* P 14 × 13½.

37	**6**	5 c. carmine and purple	..	5	5
38		10 c. green and yellow-green	..	5	5
39		10 c. rose/*azure* (1.2.26)	..	5	5
40		25 c. carmine and green		5	5
41		30 c. red and carmine	..	15	15
42		30 c. yellow and black (1.2.26)..		5	5
43		30 c. yellow-green and green (25.9.28)..		30	30
44		35 c. yellow-green and green (6.7.38)	..	8	8
45		50 c. ultramarine and blue		10	10
46		50 c. blue and green (1.2.26)	..	8	8
47		60 c. violet/*rose* (16.11.25)		5	5
48		65 c. pale blue and brown (1.3.26)		12	12
49		85 c. chestnut and blue-green (1.3.26) ..		20	20
50		90 c. rose and scarlet (5.5.30)		30	30
51		1 f. 10, vermilion and mauve (25.9.28)		2·00	2·00
52		1 f. 25, chocolate and blue (25.9.33) ..		30	30
53		1 f. 50, blue and light blue (5.5.30)	..	8	8
54		1 f. 75, vermilion and green (25.9.33)..		8	8
55		1 f. 75, ultramarine and blue (18.7.38)		8	8
56		3 f. magenta/*rose* (5.5.30)		20	20
37/56		*Set of 20*	.. ..	3·50	3·50

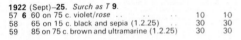

(9)

1922 (Sept)–**25**. *Surch as T* **9**.

57	**6**	60 on 75 c. violet/*rose* ..	..	10	10
58		65 on 15 c. black and sepia (1.2.25)	..	30	30
59		85 on 75 c. brown and ultramarine (1.2.25)		30	30

1ᶠ25

(10)

2ᶠ·

(D 11)

1924 (June)–**27**. *Surch as T* **10**. *Some colours changed*

60	**6**	25 c. on 2 f. violet and orange	..	20	20
61		90 c. on 75 c. rose and scarlet (11.4.27)		40	40
62		1 f. 25 on 1 f. ultram & bl (R.) (14.6.26)		8	8
63		1 f. 50 on 1 f. blue & pale blue (11.4.27)		25	25
64		3 f. on 5 f. magenta and sepia (19.12.27)		1·40	1·40
65		10 f. on 5 f. green and magenta (21.3.27)		1·25	1·25
66		20 f. on 5 f. orange & ultramarine (21.3.27)		1·40	1·40
60/66		*Set of 7*	.. .. ..	3·50	3·50

1927 (10 Oct). *POSTAGE DUE. Surch as Type* D **11**

D67	D **7**	2 f. on 1 f. magenta ..	..	50	50
D68		3 f. on 1 f. chestnut..	..	50	50

12 French Colonial Races

13 Women of Five Races

14 "France the Civiliser"

15 French Colonial Commerce

(Des J. de la Nézière (T **12**), Cayon-Rouan (T **13**), A. Parent (T **14**), G. François (T **15**). Recess Institut de Gravure, Paris)

1931 (13 Apr). *International Colonial Exhibition, Paris.* P 12½.

67	**12**	40 c. green and black ..	..	1·00	1·00
68	**13**	50 c. green and black ..	..	1·00	1·00
69	**14**	90 c. vermilion and black	..	1·00	1·00
70	**15**	1 f. 50, blue and black	..	1·00	1·00
67/70		*Set of 4*	.. ..	3·50	3·50

16 Commerce

17 Sailing Ships

18 Women of Three Races

19 Agriculture

20 France extends Torch of Civilisation

21 Diane de Poitiers

(Des J. Goujon (T **16**), Robichon (T **17**), Cayon-Rouan (T **18**), A. Decaris (T **19**, **21**), G. Barlangue (T **20**). Eng R. Cottet (T **16**), E. Feltesse (T **17**), P. Munier (T **18**), A. Decaris (T **19**, **21**), A. Delzers (T **20**). Recess)

1937 (15 Apr). *International Exhibition, Paris.* P 13.

71	**16**	20 c. bright violet	.. ..	20	15
72	**17**	30 c. green	.. ..	20	20
73	**18**	40 c. carmine	.. ..	20	20
74	**19**	50 c. brown and blue	.. ..	15	15
75	**20**	90 c. scarlet	.. ..	20	20
76	**21**	1 f. 50, blue ..	.. ..	20	20
71/76		*Set of 6*	.. ..	1·00	1·00
MS76a		120 × 100 mm **18** 3 f. blue. Imperf ..		70	70

22 Pierre and Marie Curie

(Des J. de la Nézière. Eng J. Piel. Recess)

1938 (24 Oct). *International Anti-Cancer Fund. P* 13.
76*b* **22** 1 f. 75+50 c. ultramarine . . . . 2·00 2·00

23 Man on Camel

24 Warriors

25 Encampment

26 Mauritanians

(Eng H. Cheffer (T **23**), A. Decaris (T **24**), R. Cottet (T **25**),
N. Degorce (T **26**). Recess)

1938 (17 Nov)–**40**. *P* 13.

77	**23**	2 c. slate-purple	.. .. ..	5	5
78		3 c. bright blue	.. .. ..	5	5
79		4 c. lilac	.. .. ..	5	5
80		5 c. vermilion	.. .. ..	5	5
81		10 c. brown-lake	.. .. ..	5	5
82		15 c. violet	..	5	5
83	**24**	20 c. vermilion	.. .. ..	5	5
84		25 c. bright blue	.. .. ..	5	5
85		30 c. brown-purple	.. ..	5	5
86		35 c. blue-green	.. ..	5	5
87		40 c. carmine (15.4.40)	..	5	5
88		45 c. blue-green (15.4.40)	..	5	5
89		50 c. violet	.. .. ..	5	5
90	**25**	55 c. lilac	.. .. ..	10	10
91		60 c. violet (26.3.40) ..	..	8	8
92		65 c. myrtle-green	.. ..	12	12
93		70 c. scarlet (26.3.40)	..	12	12
94		80 c. blue	.. .. ..	30	30
95		90 c. purple (4.12.39)	..	10	10
96		1 f. scarlet	.. .. ..	30	30
97		1 f. green (26.3.40)	..	10	10
98		1 f. 25, carmine (4.12.39)	..	20	20
99		1 f. 40, blue (5.3.40)	..	15	15
100		1 f. 50, bright violet	..	12	12
101		1 f. 60, black-brown (5.3.40)	..	20	20
102	**26**	1 f. 75, bright blue	..	15	15
103		2 f. lilac	.. .. ..	20	20
104		2 f. 25, bright blue (4.12.39)	..	10	10

105	**26**	2 f. 50, black-brown (5.3.40)	..	12	12
106		3 f. myrtle-green	.. .. ..	10	10
107		5 f. scarlet	.. .. ..	15	15
108		10 f. brown-purple	.. ..	30	30
109		20 f. brown-lake	.. ..	35	35
77/109		*Set of 33*	.. .. ..	3·50	3·50

Six values between 10 c. and 1 f. in similar designs, but
without "RF", were prepared in 1943–44, but were not used in
Mauritania.

27 René Caillé (explorer)

28

(Des and eng R. Cottet. Recess Institut de Gravure, Paris)

1939 (5 Apr). *Death Centenary of Caillé. P* 12½.
110	**27**	90 c. orange ..	.. .. ..	30	30
111		2 f. violet	.. .. ..	40	40
112		2 f. 25, blue	.. .. ..	30	30

(Des and eng A. Decaris. Recess Institut de Gravure, Paris)

1939 (10 May). *New York World's Fair. P* 12½.
113	**28**	1 f. 25, lake ..	.. .. ..	15	15
114		2 f. 25, ultramarine	.. ..	15	15

29 Storming the Bastille

(Des and eng L. Ouvre. Photo and typo Vaugirard, Paris)

1939 (5 July). *150th Anniv of French Revolution. P* 13½, 13.
115	**29**	45 c. +25 c. green and black	..	1·50	1·50
116		70 c. +30 c. brown and black	..	1·50	1·50
117		90 c. +35 c. red-orange and black	..	1·50	1·50
118		1 f. 25+1 f. carmine and black	..	1·50	1·50
119		2 f. 25+2 f. blue and black ..		1·50	1·50
115/119		*Set of 5*	.. .. ..	7·00	7·00

30 Aeroplane over Jungle

SECOURS
+ 1 fr.
NATIONAL

(31)

(Des D. Paul. Recess Institut de Gravure, Paris)

1940 (8 Feb). *AIR. P* 12½.
120	**30**	1 f. 90, bright blue	.. ..	5	5
121		2 f. 90, rose-red	.. ..	5	5
122		4 f. 50, green ..	.. ..	10	10
123		4 f. 90, olive-bistre	.. ..	20	20
124		6 f. 90, orange	.. ..	20	20
120/124		*Set of 5*	.. ..	55	55

Mauritania 1941

VICHY ISSUES. Nos. 124a/129 were issued by the Pétain government of unoccupied France. A number of other issues exist, but were not available in Mauritania.

1941. *National Defence Fund. Surch as T **31**, in black (No. 124d) or red (others).*

124a	**24**	+1 f. on 50 c. violet		25	25
124b	**25**	+2 f. on 80 c. blue		1·40	1·40
124c		+2 f. on 1 f. 50, bright violet		1·40	1·40
124d	**26**	+3 f. on 2 f. lilac		1·40	1·40
124a/124d		Set of 4		4·00	4·00

32 Aeroplane over
Camel Caravan

(Des and eng D. Paul. Typo and recess)

1942 (19 Oct). *AIR. As T **32**, inscr "MAURITANIE" at foot. P 12½×12.*
124e **32** 50 f. orange and greenish yellow .. 30 40
Seven other values exist, but were not used in Mauritania.

15 fr.

5 fr. ═ ═

(33) (34)

1944. (a) No. 92 surch with T **33**, in red.
125	**25**	3 f. 50 on 65 c. myrtle-green		5	5
126		4 f. on 65 c. myrtle-green		5	5
127		5 f. on 65 c. myrtle-green		20	15
128		10 f. on 65 c. myrtle-green		20	12
		a. Surch inverted		28·00	

(b) No. 110 Surch with T **8**
129	**27**	15 f. on 90 c. orange		12	12
125/129		Set of 5		55	45

Stamps of French West Africa were used in Mauritania from 1945 until 1959.

C. AUTONOMOUS ISLAMIC REPUBLIC

The Islamic Republic of Mauritania was created as an autonomous state within the French Community on 28 November 1958.

35 Flag of   **36** C.C.T.A.
Republic   Emblem

(Des and eng A. Decaris. Recess)

1960 (20 Jan). *Inauguration of Republic. P 13.*
130 **35** 25 f. bistre, emerald & lt brn/*pale rose* 35 30

(Des and eng R. Cami. Recess)

1960 (16 May). *10th Anniv of African Technical Co-operation Commission (C.C.T.A.). P 13.*
131 **36** 25 f. blue and turquoise-green .. 35 30
Mauritania became independent on 28 November 1960.

stamp monthly

Gibbons' own monthly magazine, essential reading for **every** collector!
Detailed monthly New Issue Guide to update all Gibbons catalogues for you—and a special Stamp Market feature on price changes.
Informative articles cover all facets of philately, with regular notes on new discoveries, stamp designs, postmarks, market trends and news and views of the world of stamps.
Britain's LARGEST circulation of any stamp magazine—that fact speaks for itself!
Monthly from all dealers and newsagents or by post direct from Stanley Gibbons Magazines Ltd—subscription rates on application.

New Caledonia

100 Centimes = 1 Franc

This island is in the South-west Pacific Ocean, 1000 miles east of Queensland. It was discovered by Captain James Cook on 5 September 1774 and named New Caledonia by him. A French Roman Catholic Mission was established there in 1843 and in 1853 the island was annexed by France. For some years it was a penal colony. It became French Overseas Territory in 1946.

PRINTERS. All issues were printed by the French Government Printing Works, Paris, *unless otherwise stated.*

IMPERFORATE STAMPS. Many stamps exist imperforate in their issued colours, but these were not valid for postage. Imperforate stamps in other colours are colour trials.

1 Napoleon III

(Drawn on stone by Sergeant Triquèrat. Litho)

1860 (1 Jan). *From stone of 50 varieties. No gum. Imperf.*
1 **1** 10 c. grey-black .. .. 65·00
On mail for Europe this stamp was not obliterated and stamps of New South Wales had to be applied in addition. On local mail the stamp was cancelled by pen.
It was in use until 17 September 1862 and afterwards the stamps of French Colonies (General Issues) were used.

2

3

At various times in 1876 supplies of French Colonies stamps were exhausted and the above cachets were applied directly on the mail, Type **3** being for printed matter at reduced rate. (*Prices on cover: Type* **2** (*in black, violet or orange*), £50; *Type* **3** (*in black*), £100).

NCE 05

(4)

NCE 5

(5)

1881 (1 June)–**84**. *French Colonies* (*General Issues*) *Type* H (*"Peace and Commerce"*). *Imperf. Surch by Govt Printer, Nouméa.* (*a*) *As T* **4**.
4	5 on 40 c. red/*yellow* (21.10.82)		95·00	80·00
	a. Surch inverted		£180	£180
5	05 on 40 c. red/*yellow* (15.3.83)		7·00	7·00
6	25 on 35 c. black/*yellow*		75·00	65·00
	a. On 35 c. black/*orange* (1882)		27·00	27·00
	b. Surch inverted		£160	£160
7	25 on 75 c. rose-carmine (21.10.82)		90·00	75·00
	a. Surch inverted		£160	£160

(*b*) *With T* **5**
8	5 on 40 c. red/*yellow* (29.1.84)		4·50	4·50
	a. Surch inverted		3·25	3·25
9	5 on 75 c. rose-carmine (3.12.83)		9·50	9·50
	a. Surch inverted		8·00	8·00
	b. On 75 c. deep carmine		16·00	16·00
	ba. Surch inverted		13·00	13·00

N.C.E. 5 c.

(6)

N. C.E. 5c.

(7)

1886. *French Colonies* (*General Issues*) *Types* H (*"Peace and Commerce"*), *imperf and* J (*"Commerce"*), *P* 14×13½, *surch by Govt Printer, Nouméa.*

(*a*) *With T* **6** (29 June)
10	J 5 c. on 1 f. olive-green/*toned*		5·00	5·00
	a. Surch inverted		6·50	6·50
	b. Surch double		25·00	25·00

(*b*) *With T* **7** (Aug)
11	H 5 c. on 1 f. olive-green		£2250	£2250
12	J 5 c. on 1 f. olive-green/*toned*		5·00	5·00
	a. Surch inverted		7·50	7·50
	b. Surch double, one inverted		25·00	25·00

PUZZLED?
Then you need
PHILATELIC TERMS ILLUSTRATED
to tell you all you need to know about printing methods, papers, errors, varieties, watermarks, perforations, etc. 192 pages, almost half in full colour, soft cover. £1·95 post paid.

N.-C. E. 10 c.

(8)

N·C·E· 10 centimes

(9)

1891 (23 Dec). *Types H (imperf) and J (P* 14×13½), *surch with T* **8**, *at Nouméa.*

13	H 10 c. on 40 c. red/*yellow*	5·50	5·00
	a. Surch inverted	6·50	6·50
	b. Surch double	11·00	11·00
	c. Surch double, one inverted	6·50	6·50
14	J 10 c. on 40 c. red/*yellow*	2·50	2·50
	a. Surch inverted	2·50	2·50
	b. Surch double	7·50	7·50
	c. Surch double, one inverted	7·50	7·50

Variations in the setting of the frame ornaments occur in this surcharge.

Types **8** and **9** were applied in settings of 25 and stamps in the right-hand pane always have the surcharge inverted.

1892 (25 May). *Type J (P* 14×13½), *surch with T* **9**, *at Nouméa*

15	J 10 c. on 30 c. cinnamon/*drab*	2·50	2·50
	a. Surch inverted	2·50	2·50
	b. Surch double	7·50	7·50
	c. Surch double, one inverted	7·50	7·50
	d. Surch double, both inverted	6·50	6·50

See note after No. 14c.

(10)   (10a)

1892 (24 June). *Handstamped at Nouméa with T* **10**.

(a) Type H. Imperf

16	20 c. red/*green*		£100	£100
17	35 c. black/*orange*		13·00	11·00
19	1 f. olive-green		65·00	65·00

(b) Type J. P 14×13½

20	5 c. green/*pale green*		3·25	2·50
21	10 c. black/*lilac*		25·00	14·00
22	15 c. blue		20·00	8·00
23	20 c. red/*green*		19·00	13·00
24	25 c. ochre/*yellow*		4·50	3·25
25	25 c. black/*rose*		22·00	3·25
26	30 c. cinnamon/*drab*		15·00	13·00
27	35 c. black/*orange*		40·00	38·00
29	75 c. carmine/*rose*		45·00	35·00
30	1 f. olive-green/*toned*		38·00	25·00

There are two types of T **10** which occur on all values. The first type has a very short centre stroke to the "E"s in "CALEDONIE" and is much scarcer. The second type is as illustrated and our prices refer to this.

The 1, 2, 4 and 40 c. values in both Types H and J exist with this handstamp but they were not issued.

1892 (5 Dec)–**93**. *Surch as T* **10a**, *at Nouméa.*

(a) Type H. Imperf

31	10 on 1 f. olive-green (B.)	£1000	£900

(b) Type J. P 14×13½

32	5 on 20 c. red/*green* (17.2.93)		4·75	2·75
	a. Surch inverted		19·00	19·00
	b. Surch double		18·00	18·00
33	5 on 75 c. carmine/*rose*		2·75	1·90
	a. Surch inverted		19·00	19·00
	b. Surch double		15·00	15·00
34	5 on 75 c. carmine/*rose* (B.)		2·25	1·60
	a. Surch inverted		19·00	19·00
	b. Surch double		15·00	15·00
35	10 on 1 f. olive-green/*toned*		2·25	1·60
	a. Surch inverted		90·00	90·00
36	10 on 1 f. olive-green/*toned* (B.)		3·50	3·50
	a. Surch inverted		19·00	19·00
	b. Surch double		18·00	18·00

HAVE YOU READ THE NOTES AT THE BEGINNING OF THIS CATALOGUE?

These often provide answers to the enquiries we receive.

N.C.E

11   (12)

(Des A. Dubois. Typo)

1892 (Nov). *Name in red* (1, 5, 15, 25, 75 *c.,* 1 *f.*) *or blue (others). P* 14×13½.

37	11	1 c. black/*azure*		20	12
38		2 c. brown/*buff*		30	25
39		4 c. purple-brown/*grey*		50	40
40		5 c. green/*pale green*		50	25
41		10 c. black/*lilac*		1·60	75
42		15 c. blue (*quadrillé paper*)		5·00	40
43		20 c. red/*green*		2·50	2·00
44		25 c. black/*rose*		3·75	90
45		30 c. cinnamon/*drab*		3·75	3·00
46		40 c. red/*yellow*		3·75	3·00
47		50 c. carmine/*rose*		10·00	4·50
		a. Name inverted		£5000	
48		75 c. brown/*orange*		5·00	3·75
49		1 f. olive-green/*toned*		6·50	3·75
37/49		*Set of* 13		40·00	20·00

See also Nos. 55/60.

1899 (29 Dec)–**1901**. *Surch at Nouméa as T* **10a** *(Nos.* 50/1) *or* **12** *(Nos.* 52/4).

50	11	5 on 2 c. brown/*buff* (1901)		4·00	3·75
		a. Surch inverted		20·00	20·00
		b. Surch double		20·00	20·00
51		5 on 4 c. purple-brown/*grey*		65	65
		a. Surch inverted		9·50	9·50
		b. Surch double		9·50	9·50
52		15 on 30 c. cinnamon/*drab*		95	95
		a. Surch inverted		8·00	8·00
		b. Surch double		8·50	8·50
53		15 on 75 c. brown/*orange* (1901)		3·25	2·25
		a. Surch inverted		20·00	20·00
		b. Surch double		20·00	20·00
54		15 on 1 f. olive-green/*toned* (1901)		4·75	4·50
		a. Surch inverted		25·00	25·00
		b. Surch double		25·00	25·00
50/54		*Set of* 5		12·00	11·00

The 15 on 4 c. also exists but this was not issued.

1900 (Dec)–**04**. *Colours changed. Name in blue* (10 *c. and* 50 *c., No.* 59) *or red (others). P* 14×13½.

55	11	5 c. bright yellow-green (1901)		30	25
56		10 c. rose-red		1·60	40
57		15 c. grey		1·90	80
58		25 c. blue		2·50	1·60
59		50 c. brown/*azure*		18·00	16·00
60		50 c. brown/*azure* (1904)		10·00	9·00
55/60		*Set of* 6		30·00	25·00

N.C.E.   **15** 1853   1903   **4**   **4**   4

(13)   (14)   I   II   III

1902 (8 Feb). *Surch at Nouméa as T* **13**.

61	11	5 on 30 c. cinnamon/*drab*		2·00	1·75
		a. Surch inverted		6·50	6·50
		b. Top of "5" broken		5·50	5·50
62		15 on 40 c. red/*yellow*		1·60	1·40
		a. Surch inverted		6·50	6·50
		b. Top of "5" broken		5·50	5·50

1903 (16 July). *50th Anniv of French Annexation. Optd at Nouméa with T* **14**.

63	**11**	1 c. black/*azure* (B.) ..	40	40
		a. Opt inverted	28·00	28·00
64		2 c. purple-brown/*buff* (B.)	90	65
65		4 c. purple-brown/*grey* (B.)	95	65
		a. Opt double	40·00	40·00
66		5 c. green/*pale green* (C.)	1·25	90
67		5 c. bright yellow-green (C.) ..	1·90	1·60
68		10 c. black/*lilac* (C.)	4·00	3·00
69		10 c. black/*lilac* (Bk. Gold)	2·75	2·25
70		15 c. grey (C.) ..	2·75	1·25
71		20 c. red/*green* (B.)	4·50	3·50
72		25 c. black/*rose* (B.)	4·50	3·50
73		30 c. cinnamon/*drab* (C.)	5·00	4·50
74		40 c. red/*yellow* (B.)	7·00	5·00
75		50 c. carmine/*rose* (B.)	9·00	5·00
76		75 c. brown/*orange*	14·00	10·00
		a. Opt double (Bk.+R.)	£100	
77		1 f. olive-green/*toned* (B.)	17·00	17·00
		a. Opt double (B.+R.)	£100	
		b. Opt in black	£500	
63/77		*Set of* 15	65·00	50·00

No. 69 was first overprinted in black but as this was difficult to see it was overprinted again in gold and later printings were made in carmine (No. 68).

In all values one stamp in the sheet has the "I" of "TENAIRE" omitted. This also applies to Nos. D78/85 and 78/84.

1903 (17 July). *POSTAGE DUE. French Colonies Type U optd with T* **14**, *at Nouméa. Imperf.*

D78	5 c. pale blue (C.)	40	40
D79	10 c. grey-brown (C.)	1·90	1·40
D80	15 c. pale green (C.)	4·00	1·60
D81	30 c. carmine (B.)	2·75	2·25
D82	50 c. dull claret (B.)	13·00	3·25
D83	60 c. brown/*buff* (B.)	35·00	13·00
D84	1 f. rose (Sil.)	3·25	2·75
D85	2 f. brown (B.)	£190	£190

1904 (4 Feb). *Stamps of* 1903 *surch in blue* (*sideways except on Nos.* 81 *and* 84).

78	1 on 2 c. purple-brown/*buff*		15	15
	a. Surch double		16·00	16·00
79	2 on 4 c. purple-brown/*grey*		35	35
80	4 on 5 c. green/*pale green* (I)		40	40
	a. Type II		7·00	7·00
	b. Type III		£130	£130
81	4 on 5 c. bright yellow-green (III)		65	65
82	10 on 15 c. grey		65	65
83	15 on 20 c. red/*green*		65	65
94	20 on 25 c. black/*rose*		1·00	1·00
3/84	*Set of* 7		3·50	3·50

Types I and II are found in the same setting but Type III is a different setting.

Surcharges are found misplaced or omitted (in pair with normal).

(*Des* H. Vollet. *Eng* J. Puyplat. *Typo*)

1905–07. *P* 14×13½.

85	**15**	1 c. black/*greenish* ..	5	5
86		2 c. chocolate	5	5
87		4 c. blue/*orange*	5	5
88		5 c. green ..	5	5
89		10 c. rose-red	12	5
90		15 c. bright lilac	5	5
91	**16**	20 c. brown/*toned*	5	5
92		25 c. blue/*greenish*	5	5
93		30 c. brown/*orange* ..	5	5
94		35 c. black/*yellow* (1906)	5	5
95		40 c. carmine/*greenish*	8	8
96		45 c. maroon/*toned* (1907)	8	8
97		50 c. red/*orange*	40	35
98		75 c. olive/*toned*	5	5
99	**17**	1 f. blue/*green*	10	8
100		2 f. carmine/*azure*	30	30
101		5 f. black/*orange*	1·10	1·10
		a. Black/*yellow*	1·60	1·60
85/101		*Set of* 17	2·50	3·50

See also Nos. 112/23.

(*Des* H. Vollet. *Die eng* J. Puyplat. *Typo*)

1906. *POSTAGE DUE. P* 13½×14.

D102	**D 18**	5 c. ultramarine/*toned*	5	5
D103		10 c. brown/*pale buff*	8	8
D104		15 c. green/*toned*	12	12
D105		20 c. black/*yellow*	15	15
D106		30 c. carmine	20	20
D107		50 c. ultramarine/*cream*	20	20
D108		60 c. bronze-green/*bluish*	25	25
D109		1 f. deep green/*cream* ..	30	30
D102/109		*Set of* 8 ..	1·25	1·25

1912 (July). *Type* **11** *such as T* **6** *and* **7** *of Madagascar and Dependencies* (*see Malagasy Republic*).

A. *Narrow spacing.* B. *Wide spacing*

			A	B	
102	05 on 15 c. grey (R.)	12	12	25·00	25·00
	a. Surch inverted ..	25·00	—	£550	£550
103	05 on 20 c. red/*green*	8	8	17·00	17·00
104	05 on 30 c. cinna/*drab* (R.)	15	15	48·00	48·00
105	10 on 40 c. red/*yellow*	30	30	32·00	32·00
106	10 on 50 c. brown/*azure* (R.)	40	40	35·00	35·00
102/106	*Set of* 5 ..	90	90	£140	£140

In Type A the space between "0" and "5" is 1½ mm and between "1" and "0" 2½ mm. In Type B the spacing is 2 mm and 3 mm respectively.

(18)	(19)	(20)

1915. *Red Cross Fund. No.* 89 *surch locally with T* **18**.

1C7	**15**	10 c.+5 c. rose-red (R.)	20	20
		a. Surch inverted ..	7·00	
108		10 c.+5 c. rose-red (Vm.)	15	15

Both 107 and 108 exist with broken top to the "5".

1915–16. *Red Cross Fund. Nos.* 89/90 *surch in Paris with T* **8** *of Madagascar and Dependencies* (*see Malagasy Republic*), *in red.*

109	**15**	10 c.+5 c. rose-red	15	15
		a. Surch double	10·00	
110		15 c.+5 c. bright lilac (1916)	15	15

1918. *No.* 90 *surch with T* **19**.

111	**15**	5 c. on 15 c. bright lilac (R.)	25	25
		a. Surch double	11·00	11·00
		b. Surch inverted	6·00	6·00
		c. Surch in brown-red	35	35

15 Kagu

16

17

D 18

1922 (1 Jan)–**28**. *Colours changed and new values. P* 14×13½.

112	**15**	5 c. slate-blue		5	5
113		10 c. green		8	8
114		10 c. red/rose (20.5.25)		5	5
115	**16**	25 c. red/straw		5	5
116		30 c. carmine		15	15
117		30 c. orange-red (1.12.25)		5	5
118		50 c. blue		12	12
119		50 c. grey (1.12.25)		5	5
120		65 c. blue (2.4.28)		5	5
121		75 c. blue/azure (1.6.25)		5	5
122		75 c. bright violet (14.11.27)		8	8
123	**17**	1 f. blue (21.12.25)		5	5
112/123		*Set of 12*		75	75

1922 (Dec). *No. 90 surch with T* **20**.

124	**15**	0,05 on 15 c. bright lilac (R.)		8	8
		a. Surch double		10·00	

1924–27. *Stamps as T* **15/17**, *some with colours changed, surch as T* **22/4** *of Martinique, with bars obliterating old values*

125	**15**	25 c. on 15 c. bright lilac (1.2.25)		5	5
		a. Surch double		12·00	
		b. Surch double, one inverted		18·00	
126	**17**	25 c. on 2 f. carmine/azure (6.24)		5	5
127		25 c. on 5 f. black/yellow (6.24)		15	15
		a. Surch double		16·00	16·00
		b. On 5 f. black/orange		25	25
		ba. Surch double		25·00	25·00
128	**16**	60 on 75 c. green (R.) (3.24)		5	5
129		65 on 45 c. maroon/toned (1.2.25)		15	15
130		85 on 45 c. maroon/toned (1.2.25)		15	15
131		90 on 75 c. rose-carmine (11.4.27)		12	12
132	**17**	1 f. 25 on 1 f. blue (R.) (14.6.26)		8	8
133		1 f. 50 on 1 f. blue/azure (11.4.27)		20	20
134		3 f. on 5 f. magenta (19.12.27)		20	20
135		10 f. on 5 f. bronze-green/mauve (R.) (6.9.26)		1·25	1·25
136		20 f. on 5 f. rose-car/yellow (11.4.27)		2·50	2·50
125/136		*Set of 12*		4·50	4·50

50c Colis Postaux 2F. ═

(P 21) (D 21)

1926 (6 Sept). *PARCEL POST. Surch or optd as Type* P **21**

P137	**17**	50 c. on 5 f. bronze-green/mauve		20	20
P138		1 f. blue		40	40
P139		2 f. carmine/azure		40	40

1926 (6 Sept)–**27**. *POSTAGE DUE. Surch as Type* D **21**

D137	D **18**	2 f. on 1 f. bright mauve		50	50
D138		3 f. on 1 f. red-brown (10.10.27)		50	50

22 Pointe des Palétuviers   23 Chief's Hut

24 La Pérouse and De Bougainville   D 25 Sambar Stag

(Des C. Hourriez (T **22**), A. Delzers (T **23/4**). Typo)

1928 (30 Apr)–**40**. *P* 14×13½.

137	**22**	1 c. blue and purple		5	5
138		2 c. green and brown		5	5
139		3 c. blue and lake (1940)		5	5
140		4 c. blue-green and red		5	5
141		5 c. brown and blue		5	5
142		10 c. chocolate and lilac		5	5
143		15 c. ultramarine and brown		5	5
144		20 c. brown and carmine		5	5
145		25 c. chocolate and deep green		5	5
146	**23**	30 c. blue-green and green		5	5
147		35 c. mauve and blue-black (7.33)		5	5
148		40 c. sage-green and scarlet		5	5
149		45 c. vermilion and blue		5	5
150		45 c. green and blue-green (1940)		8	5
151		50 c. chocolate and mauve		5	5
152		55 c. carmine and ultramarine (6.7.38)		45	20
153		60 c. carmine and ultramarine (1940)		12	12
154		65 c. blue and red-brown		10	5
155		70 c. brown and magenta (7.33)		5	5
156		75 c. drab and greenish blue		30	8
157		80 c. green and maroon (6.7.38)		5	5
158		85 c. brown and green (7.33)		25	20
159		90 c. rose and scarlet		12	10
160		90 c. scarlet and olive-brown (1939)		8	8
161	**24**	1 f. rose and drab		80	45
162		1 f. carmine and scarlet (1938)		25	25
163		1 f. green and scarlet (1940)		8	5
164		1 f. 10, brown and green		1·90	1·75
165		1 f. 25, yell-grn & red-brn (25.9.33)		12	12
166		1 f. 25, carmine and scarlet (1939)		8	8
167		1 f. 40, vermilion and blue (1940)		8	8
168		1 f. 50, pale blue and blue		5	5
169		1 f. 60, brown and green (1940)		15	15
170		1 f. 75, vermilion and blue (25.9.33)		15	15
171		1 f. 75, brt blue & ultram (5.12.38)		12	12
172		2 f. brown and vermilion		8	5
173		2 f. 25, brt blue & ultramarine (1939)		8	8
174		2 f. 50, brown (1940)		8	8
175		3 f. brown and magenta		10	5
176		5 f. brown and dull blue		10	5
177		10 f. brown and purple/rose		25	25
178		20 f. brown and scarlet/yellow		40	30
137/178		*Set of 42*		6·50	4·50

The 35 c. blue-green and deep blue-green will be found listed under Wallis and Futuna Islands in *Overseas 4*, as it appeared there with the overprint omitted.

(Die eng C. Hourriez. Typo)

1928 (30 Apr). *POSTAGE DUE. P* 13½×14.

D179	D **25**	2 c. chocolate and blue		5	5
D180		4 c. green and red		5	5
D181		5 c. slate-blue and vermilion		5	5
D182		10 c. blue and magenta		5	5
D183		15 c. scarlet and olive-green		8	8
D184		20 c. brown and maroon		20	20
D185		25 c. blue and bistre-brown		8	8
D186		30 c. olive and green		12	12
D187		50 c. carmine and brown		20	20
D188		60 c. scarlet and magenta		20	20
D189		1 f. blue-green and blue		30	30
D190		2 f. olive and carmine		25	25
D191		3 f. brown and mauve		40	40
D179/191		*Set of 13*		1·90	1·90

1930 (17 Feb). *PARCEL POST. Optd "Colis Postaux", as in Type* P **21**.

P179	**23**	50 c. chocolate and mauve		15	15
P180	**24**	1 f. rose and drab		15	15
P181		2 f. brown and vermilion		30	30

1931 (13 April). *International Colonial Exhibition, Paris. As T* **12/15** *of Mauritania*.

179		40 c. black and green		75	75
180		50 c. black and mauve		75	75
181		90 c. black and vermilion		75	75
182		1 f. 50, black and blue		75	75
179/182		*Set of 4*		2·75	2·75

THE WORLD CENTRE FOR FINE STAMPS IS 391 STRAND

New Caledonia 1932

PARIS-NOUMÉA
Verneilh-Dévé-Munch
5 Avril 1932
(25)

PARIS-NOUMÉA
Première liaison aérienne
5 Avril 1932
(26)

1932 (17 May). *Paris-Nouméa Flight of French Aviators, De Verneilh, Dévé and Munch. Optd with T **25**. P 14×13½.*

183	23	40 c. sage-green and scarlet ..	..	£110	£110
184		50 c. chocolate and mauve	..	£110	£110

1933 (4 Dec). *First Anniv of Paris-Nouméa Flight. Optd with T **26**. P 14×13½.*

185	22	1 c. blue and purple..	1·40	1·40
186		2 c. green and brown	1·40	1·40
187		4 c. blue-green and red	1·40	1·40
188		5 c. brown and blue (R.)	1·40	1·40
189		10 c. chocolate and lilac (R.)	1·40	1·40
190		15 c. ultramarine and brown (R.)	1·40	1·40
191		20 c. brown and carmine	1·40	1·40
192		25 c. chocolate and deep green (R.)..	1·40	1·40
193	23	30 c. blue-green·and green (R.)	1·40	1·40
194		35 c. mauve and blue-black ..	1·40	1·40
195		40 c. sage-green and scarlet ..	1·40	1·40
196		45 c. vermilion and blue	1·40	1·40
197		50 c. chocolate and mauve	1·40	1·40
198		70 c. brown and magenta	1·40	1·40
199		75 c. drab and greenish blue (R.)	1·40	1·40
200		85 c. brown and green	1·40	1·40
201		90 c. carmine and scarlet	1·40	1·40
202	24	1 f. scarlet and drab	1·40	1·40
203		1·f. 25, green and brown	1·40	1·40
204		1 f. 50, pale blue and ultramarine (R.)	1·40	1·40
205		1 f. 75, vermilion and blue ..	1·40	1·40
206		2 f. brown and vermilion	1·40	1·40
207		3 f. brown and magenta	1·40	1·40
208		5 f. brown and blue (R.)	1·40	1·40
209		10 f. brown and purple/*rose*	1·40	1·40
210		20 f. brown and scarlet/*yellow*	1·40	1·40
185/210		*Set of 26*	32·00	32·00

1937 (15 Apr). *International Exhibition, Paris. As T **16/21** of Mauritania.*

211		20 c. bright violet	20	20
212		30 c. green	20	20
213		40 c. carmine	20	20
214		50 c. brown	20	20
215		90 c. scarlet	25	25
216		1 f. 50, blue	25	25
211/216		*Set of 6*	1·25	1·25
MS216a		120×100 mm. 3 f. sepia (as T **20**).		
		Imperf	1·00	1·00

27 Flying-boat over Nouméa   (28)

(Des and eng A. Decaris. Design recess; numerals typo)

1938 (14 Mar)–**40**. *AIR. P 13.*

217	27	65 c. violet ..	15	15
		a. Value omitted		
218		4 f. 50, scarlet	20	20
219		7 f. blue-green (8.2.40)	12	12
220		9 f. bright blue	60	60
221		20 f. orange (8.2.40)	35	35
222		50 f. black (8.2.40)	40	40
217/222		*Set of 6*	1·60	1·60

1938 (24 Oct). *International Anti-Cancer Fund. As T **22** of Mauritania.*

223		1 f. 75+50 c. ultramarine	2·50	2·50

1939 (10 May). *New York World's Fair. As T **28** of Mauritania.*

224		1 f. 25, lake	12	12
225		2 f. 25, ultramarine	15	15

1939 (5 July). *150th Anniv of French Revolution. As T **29** of Mauritania.*

(a) POSTAGE. Name and value in black

226		45 c.+25 c. green	1·40	1·40
227		70 c.+30 c. brown	1·40	1·40
228		90 c.+35 c. red-orange ..	1·40	1·40
229		1 f. 25+1 f. carmine	1·40	1·40
230		2 f. 25+2 f. blue	1·40	1·40

(b) AIR. Name and value in orange

231		4 f. 50+4 f. black	3·75	3·75
226/231		*Set of 6*	9·50	9·50

VICHY ISSUES. A number of stamps were prepared by the Pétain Government of Unoccupied France for use in New Caledonia, but as the inhabitants declared for the Free French, these issues were not placed on sale there.

1941. *Adherence to General de Gaulle. Optd with T **28**, at Nouméa.*

232	22	1 c. blue and purple..	3·75	3·75
233		2 c. green and brown	3·75	3·75
234		3 c. blue and lake	3·75	3·75
235		4 c. blue-green and red	3·75	3·75
236		5 c. brown and blue	3·75	3·75
237		10 c. chocolate and lilac	3·75	3·75
238		15 c. ultramarine and brown ..	3·75	3·75
239		20 c. brown and carmine	3·75	3·75
240		25 c. chocolate and deep green	3·75	3·75
241	23	30 c. blue-green and green	3·75	3·75
242		35 c. mauve and blue-black ..	3·75	3·75
243		40 c. sage-green and scarlet ..	3·75	3·75
244		45 c. green and blue-green	3·75	3·75
245		50 c. chocolate and mauve	3·75	3·75
246		55 c. carmine and ultramarine	3·75	3·75
247		60 c. carmine and ultramarine	3·75	3·75
248		65 c. blue and red-brown	3·75	3·75
249		70 c. brown and magenta	3·75	3·75
250		75 c. drab and greenish blue ..	3·75	3·75
251		80 c. green and maroon	3·75	3·75
252		85 c. brown and green	3·75	3·75
253		90 c. rose and scarlet ..	3·75	3·75
254	24	1 f. carmine and scarlet	3·75	3·75
255		1 f. 25, yellow-green and red-brown	3·75	3·75
256		1 f. 40, vermilion and blue ..	3·75	3·75
257		1 f. 50, pale blue and blue ..	3·75	3·75
258		1 f. 60, brown and green	3·75	3·75
259		1 f. 75, vermilion and blue	3·75	3·75
260		2 f. brown and vermilion	3·75	3·75
261		2 f. 25, bright blue and ultramarine ..	3·75	3·75
262		2 f. 50, brown	5·00	5·00
263		3 f. brown and magenta	5·00	5·00
264		5 f. brown and dull blue	5·00	5·00
265		10 f. brown and purple/*rose* ..	5·00	5·00
266		20 f. brown and scarlet/*yellow*	5·00	5·00
232/266		*Set of 35*	£120	£120

France Libre

29 Kagu   **30** Airliner

(Des E. Dulac. Photo Harrison)

1942. *Free French Issue. P 14½×14.* (a) POSTAGE.

267	29	5 c. brown ..	5	5
268		10 c. blue	5	5
269		25 c. emerald-green ..	5	5
270		30 c. red-orange	5	5
271		40 c. slate-green	8	8
272		80 c. maroon ..	5	5
		a. Value omitted	80·00	

273	29	1 f. magenta				8	8
274		1 f. 50, scarlet	..	..	..	8	8
275		2 f. grey-black				8	8
276		2 f. 50, ultramarine				15	15
277		4 f. violet	..	..	..	12	12
278		5 f. yellow-bistre	..			15	15
279		10 f. red-brown		..	..	25	25
280		20 f. blue-green				30	30
		(b) AIR					
281	30	1 f. red-orange	..	..		8	8
282		1 f. 50, scarlet				8	8
283		5 f. maroon	..	..	..	15	15
284		10 f. black	..			20	20
285		25 f. ultramarine		..	..	25	25
286		50 f. green	..			40	40
287		100 f. claret	..	..		50	50
267/287		*Set of 21*	..			2·75	2·75

35 Legionaries by Lake Chad

(Des and eng A. Decaris. Recess Institut de Gravure, Paris)

1946. *AIR. From Chad to the Rhine. T* **35** *and similar horiz designs. P* 12½.

300	5 f. olive-black..				25	25
301	10 f. carmine	..		..	25	25
302	15 f. blue	..		..	25	25
303	20 f. chestnut		..	..	25	25
304	25 f. grey-green		..	..	40	40
305	50 f. purple	..		..	50	50
300/305	*Set of 6*			..	1·75	1·75

Designs:—10 f. Battle of Koufra; 15 f. Tank Battle, Mareth; 20 f. Normandy Landings; 25 f. Liberation of Paris; 50 f. Liberation of Strasbourg.

31

32 Félix Eboué

(Des E. Dulac. Photo Harrison)

1944. *Mutual Aid and Red Cross Funds. P* 14½×14.

| 288 | 31 | 5 f.+20 f. scarlet | .. | | .. | 20 | 20 |

1945. *Recess. P* 13.

| 289 | 32 | 2 f. black | .. | | .. | 8 | 8 |
| 290 | | 25 f. blue-green | .. | .. | | 25 | 30 |

(33)

1945. *Surch as T* **33,** *in black (Nos.* 295/7) *or red (others).*

291	29	50 c. on 5 c. brown		..	..	12	12
292		60 c. on 5 c. brown				12	12
293		70 c. on 5 c. brown		..		12	12
294		1 f. on 5 c. brown	..	..		8	8
295		2 f. 40 on 25 c. emerald-green		8	8
		a. Surch inverted	..			25·00	
296		3 f. on 25 c. emerald-green..		10	10
297		4 f. 50 on 25 c. emerald-green		20	20
298		15 f. on 2 f. 50, ultramarine	..		30	30
291/298		*Set of 8*	..		..	1·00	1·00

36 Two Kagus

37 Airliners over Landscape

(Des J. Duoy. Photo Vaugirard, Paris)

1948 (1 Mar). *(a) POSTAGE. T* **36** *and similar designs. P* 13½.

306	36	10 c. purple and yellow	..	..	5	5
307		30 c. purple and green			5	5
308		40 c. purple and orange-brown	..	5	5
309	—	50 c. maroon and rose		..	5	5
310	—	60 c. brown and yellow		..	5	5
311	—	80 c. green and pale green	..		5	5
312	—	1 f. violet and orange		..	8	8
313	—	1 f. 20, brown and blue	..	..	8	8
314	—	1 f. 50, blue and yellow		..	8	8
315	—	2 f. sepia and blue-green		..	12	5
316	—	2 f. 40, vermilion and claret		10	8
317	—	3 f. violet and orange		..	1·10	15
318	—	4 f. indigo and light blue		..	20	10
319	—	5 f. violet and red	..	..	30	15
320	—	6 f. lake-brown and yellow ..		30	12
321	—	10 f. blue and orange		..	35	8
322	—	15 f. lake and grey-blue	..		45	30
323	—	20 f. violet and yellow		..	50	35
324	—	25 f. blue and orange		..	60	40

(b) AIR. T **37** *and similar designs. P* 12½×13½ (100 *f.*) *or* 13½×12½ *(others)*

325		50 f. purple and orange		..	1·50	1·25
326		100 f. blue and blue-green	..		2·75	1·50
327		50 f. purple-brown and yellow		5·00	3·00
306/327		*Set of 22*	..		..	12·00	7·00

Designs: *As T* **36**—50 c., 60 c., 80 c. Ducos Sanitorium; 1 f., 1 f. 20, 1 f. 50, Porcupine Island; 2 f., 2 f. 40, 3 f., 4 f. Nickel foundry; 5 f., 6 f., 10 f. "The Towers of Notre Dame" rocks. *As T* **36** *but vert*—15 f., 20 f., 25 f. Chief's hut. *As T* **37** *but horiz*—50 f. Airliner over St. Vincent Bay; 200 f. Airliner over Nouméa.

34 "Victory"

(Des and eng A. Decaris. Recess Institut de Gravure, Paris)

1946 (8 May). *AIR. Victory. P* 12½.

| 299 | 34 | 8 f. ultramarine | .. | .. | .. | 20 | 20 |

D 38

38 People of Five Races, Aircraft and Globe

(Des Planson. Photo Vaugirard, Paris)

1948 (1 Mar). *POSTAGE DUE. P* 13.

D328	D 38	10 c. mauve	.. .. ..	5	5
D329		30 c. sepia		5	5
D330		50 c. blue-green	.. .. ..	5	5
D331		1 f. orange-brown		5	5
D332		2 f. claret	.. .. ..	8	8
D333		3 f. red-brown	..	8	8
D334		4 f. blue	.. ..	10	10
D335		5 f. brown-red	..	20	12
D336		10 f. olive-green	.. ..	20	20
D337		20 f. violet-blue	..	50	45
D328/337		*Set of 10*	.. ..	1·25	1·10

(Des and eng R. Serres. Recess)

1949 (4 July). *AIR. 75th Anniv of Universal Postal Union. P* 13.

328 **38** 10 f. multicoloured .. .. .. 1·25 1·25

39 Doctor and Patient

40

(Des and eng R. Serres. Recess)

1950 (15 May). *Colonial Welfare Fund. P* 13.
329 **39** 10 f.+2 f. brown-purple and red-brown 75 75

(Des R. Serres. Recess and typo)

1952 (1 Dec). *Centenary of Médaille Militaire. P* 13.
330 **40** 2 f. carmine-red, yellow and green .. 65 55

41 Admiral D'Entrecasteaux

(Des and eng C. Hertenberger (6 f.), P. Gandon (13 f.), J. Pheulpin (others). Recess)

1953 (24 Sept). *Centenary of French Administration. T* **41** *and similar horiz designs inscr "1853 1953". P* 13.
331 1 f. 50, carmine-lake and chestnut .. 1·60 1·10
332 2 f. indigo and turquoise-blue 95 75
333 6 f. chocolate, deep blue and carmine-red 1·90 95
334 13 f. deep turquoise-green and emerald.. 2·25 1·60
331/334 *Set of 4* .. .. 6·00 4·00
Designs:—2 f. Mgr. Douarre and church; 6 f. Admiral D'Urville and map; 13 f. Admiral Despointes and view.

42 Normandy Landings, 1944

(Des and eng R. Serres. Recess)

1954 (6 June). *AIR. 10th Anniv of Liberation. P* 13.
335 **42** 3 f. bright blue and indigo .. .. 1·25 1·25

43 Towers of Notre-Dame (rocks)

44 Coffee

45 Transporting Nickel

(Des and eng C. Mazelin (T **43**), R. Serres (T **44**), H. Cheffer (T **45**). Recess)

1955 (21 Nov). *P* 13. *(a) POSTAGE.*
336 **43** 2 f. 50, ultram, dp bl-grn & brn-blk 30 20
337 3 f. ultram, pur-brn & deep blue-green 1·90 1·10
338 **44** 9 f. indigo and deep bright blue .. 30 20
(b) AIR
339 **45** 14 f. indigo and black-brown .. 90 25
336/339 *Set of 4* .. .. 3·00 1·50

46 Dumbea Barrage

47 *Xanthostemon*

(Des and eng R. Cami. Recess)

1956 (22 Oct). *Economic and Social Development Fund. P* 13
340 **46** 3 f. deep dull green and blue 30 20

(Des M. Rolland. Photo Vaugirard, Paris)

1958 (7 July). *Flowers. T* **47** *and similar vert design. P* 12½.
341 4 f. multicoloured 60 25
342 15 f. red, yellow and green .. .. 1·10 30
Design:—15 f. Hibiscus.

48 "Human Rights"   O 49 Ancestor Pole

(Des and eng R. Cami. Recess)

1958 (10 Dec). *10th Anniv of Declaration of Human Rights.*
P 13.
343 **48** 7 f. carmine and ultramarine 40 30

(Des G. Bétemps. Eng G. Aufschneider (O **49**), A. Frères (10 f.
to 26 f.), A. Barre (50 f. to 200 f.). Typo)

1959 (1 Jan). *OFFICIAL. Type O **49** and similar vert designs*
P 14×13½.
O344 O **49** 1 f. orange-yellow 8 5
O345 — 3 f. blue-green 12 5
O346 — 4 f. reddish violet 15 8
O347 — 5 f. bright blue 25 15
O348 — 9 f. black 30 15
O349 — 10 f. bluish violet 30 15
O350 — 13 f. yellow-green 40 20
O351 — 15 f. light blue 45 40
O352 — 24 f. bright purple 55 40
O353 — 26 f. orange 70 50
O354 — 50 f. deep green .. .. 1·40 90
O355 — 100 f. brown .. .. 2·25 1·40
O356 — 200 f. scarlet .. .. 3·75 1·90
O344/356 Set of 13 .. .. 9·75 6·00
Designs:—10 f. to 26 f. and 50 f. to 200 f., Different idols.

49 *Brachyrus zebra*   49a The Carved Rock, Bourail

(Des G. François. Eng J. Pheulpin (2 f., 5 f.). Des G. François.
Eng P. Munier (3 f.). Des and eng C. Mazelin (4 f.).
Des and eng P. Gandon (others). Recess)

1959 (21 May)–**62**. *Various designs as T **49**. P* 13.
344 1 f. red-brown and blue-grey 12 8
345 2 f. lt bl, brn-pur & bronze-green (2.7.62) 20 12
346 3 f. red, blue and deep green 20 12
347 4 f. brown-purple, red & green (2.7.62) 25 20
348 5 f. bistre-brn, ultram & dull grn (2.7.62) 25 20
349 10 f. salmon, dp grn, dp turq-blue & black 45 30
350 26 f. orange, green, brown and blue .. 1·25 75
344/350 Set of 7 .. .. 2·50 1·50
Designs: *Horiz*—2 f. Melanesian pirogues; 3 f. *Lienardella
fasciata* (fish); 5 f. Sail Rock, Nouméa; 26 f. Fluorescent corals.
Vert—4 f. Fisherman with spear; 10 f. *Glaucus* and *spirographe*
(corals).

PUZZLED?

Then you need
PHILATELIC TERMS ILLUSTRATED
to tell you all you need to know about printing
methods, papers, errors, varieties, watermarks,
perforations, etc. 192 pages, almost half in full
colour, soft cover. £1·95 post paid.

(Des and eng C. Mazelin (15 f., 25 f.), P. Gandon (20 f., 100 f.),
C. Durrens (50 f. No. 354). Des and eng J. Pheulpin (50 f.
No. 355). Des G. François, eng R. Cottet (200 f.). Recess)

1959–64. *AIR. T **49a** and similar designs. P* 13.
351 15 f. dp bluish grn, sepia & red (26.1.62) 95 45
352 20 f. orge-brn & dp grey-grn (3.10.62) 1·40 75
353 25 f. black, blue and maroon (2.7.62) .. 1·75 75
354 50 f. dp chocolate, grn & bl (21.9.59) 2·00 1·25
355 50 f. chocolate, dp grn & bl (7.12.64) 1·90 1·25
356 100 f. sep, dp bluish grn & dp bl (25.9.62) 4·75 2·25
357 200 f. chocolate, dp grn & lt bl (21.3.59) 7·50 4·50
351/357 Set of 7 .. .. .. 18·00 10·00
Designs: *Horiz*—15 f. Fisherman with net; 20 f. *Nautilus*
shell; 25 f. Underwater swimmer shooting fish; 50 f. (No. 355),
Isle of Pines; 100 f. Corbeille de Yaté. *Vert*—50 f. (No. 354),
Yaté barrage.

49b Napoleon III   49c Port-de-France, 1859

(Des and eng P. Gandon (4 f., 13 f.), R. Serres (5 f., 9 f.),
G. Bétemps (12 f.). Des P. Gandon. Eng R. Cottet (19 f.,
33 f.). Recess)

1960 (20 May). *Postal Centenary. P* 14×13 (4 f., 13 f.) *or*
13 (*others*).
358 **15** 4 f. red 35 20
359 — 5 f. chestnut and lake 40 20
360 — 9 f. chocolate and deep bluish green 40 25
361 — 12 f. black and blue 45 25
362 **49b** 13 f. deep greenish blue .. .. 1·00 85
363 **49c** 19 f. rose-red, bronze-green & turq-bl 1·00 45
364 — 33 f. brown-red, bluish green and blue 1·50 90
358/364 Set of 7 .. .. .. 8·00 5·00
MS364a 150×80 mm. Nos. 358, 362 and 364 3·50 3·50
Designs (*sizes as T **49c***): *Horiz*—5 f. Girl operating cheque-
writing machine; 12 f. Telephone receiver and exchange
building; 33 f. Port-de-France, 1859, (as T **49c** but without
stamps). *Vert*—9 f. Letter-box on tree.

49d Map of Pacific and Palms   49e Map and
                                       Meteorological
                                       Symbols

(Des P. Lambert. Photo Delrieu)

1962 (18 July). *Fifth South Pacific Conference, Pago-Pago,
Samoa. P* 13×12.
365 **49d** 15 f. multicoloured 75 50

(Des Pelabon. Photo Delrieu)

1962 (5 Nov). *Third Regional Assembly of World Meteorological
Association, Nouméa. P* 12×13.
366 **49e** 50 f. multicoloured .. .. .. 2·50 2·00

50 "Telstar" Satellite and part of Globe

(Des C. Durrens. Eng P. Béquet. Recess)
1962 (4 Dec). *AIR. First Transatlantic Television Satellite Link.* P 13.
367 **50** 200 f. turquoise, chocolate & deep blue   9·00   6·50

51 Emblem and Globe   52 Relay-running

(Des and eng J. Derrey. Recess)
1963 (21 Mar). *Freedom from Hunger.* P 13.
368 **51** 17 f. deep blue and brown-purple   95   55

(Des C. Durrens. Photo Delrieu)

1963 (29 Aug). *First South Pacific Games, Suva, Fiji. T 52 and similar square designs.* P 12½.
369   1 f. brown-red and deep slate-green   20   12
370   7 f. orange-brown and steel-blue   40   25
371   10 f. light brown and green   55   40
372   27 f. ultramarine and deep purple   1·40   1·00
369/372   Set of 4   2·25   1·50
   Designs:—7 f. Tennis; 10 f. Football; 27 f. Throwing the javelin.

54a Bikkia fritillarioïdes   54b Ascidies polycarpa

(Des P. Lambert. Photo So.Ge.lm.)

1964–**65.** *Flowers. T 54a and similar multicoloured designs.* P 13×12½ (vert) or 12½×13 (horiz).
375   1 f. *Freycinettia* (22.10.64)   15   12
376   2 f. Type **54a** (27.1.64)   20   15
377   3 f. *Xanthostemon francii* (27.1.64)   30   15
378   4 f. *Psidiomyrtus locellatus* (26.7.65)   45   25
379   5 f. *Callistemon suberosum* (26.7.65)   45   20
380   7 f. *Montrouziera sphaeroidea* (27.10.64)   80   30
381   10 f. *Ixora collina* (27.10.64)   80   40
382   17 f. *Deplanchea speciosa* (27.10.64)   1·25   65
375/382   Set of 8   4·00   2·00
   The 7 f. and 10 f. are horiz.

(27 f., 37 f. des P. Lambert. Photo So.Ge.lm. Others des and eng P. Gandon. Recess)

1964 (22 Feb)–**65.** *Corals and fish from Nouméa Aquarium.*
    (a) POSTAGE. As T **54b.** P 13
383   7 f. orange-red, brown and blue   40   20
384   10 f. red and deep royal blue (6.12.65) ..   45   25
385   17 f. lake, yellow-green and deep blue ..   75   50
   (b) AIR. Inscr "POSTE AERIENNE". Multicoloured. Size 48×28 mm. P 13×12½ (17.12.64)
386   27 f. *Paracanthurus teuthis*   1·25   75
387   37 f. *Phyllobranchus*   2·50   1·10
   (c) AIR. Inscr "POSTE AERIENNE". Size 48×27 mm. P 13 (29.11.65)
388   13 f. bistre, black and red-orange   55   40
389   15 f. grey-green, yellow-olive & slate-blue   80   45
390   25 f. slate-blue and yellow-green   1·40   95
383/390   Set of 8   7·50   4·00
   Designs: Vert—10 f. *Alcyonium catalai* (coral). Horiz— 13 f. *Coris angulata* (juvenile); 15 f. *C. angulata*; 25 f. *C. angulata* (adult) (all fishes); 17 f. *Crevette hymenocera elegans.*

54c "Philately"

(Des and eng P. Gandon. Recess)
1964 (9 Apr). "PHILATEC 1964" International Stamp Exhibition, Paris. P 13.
391 **54c** 40 f. brown, green and deep violet ..   2·10   2·10

53 Centenary   54 Globe and Scales
   Emblem   of Justice

(Des and eng J. Combet. Recess)
1963 (2 Sept). *Red Cross Centenary.* P 13.
373 **53** 37 f. red, grey and blue   1·75   1·75

(Des and eng A. Decaris. Recess)
1963 (10 Dec). 15*th Anniv of Declaration of Human Rights.* P 13.
374 **54** 50 f. deep claret and indigo ..   2·25   2·00

54d Houailou Mine

(Des Signe. Photo Delrieu)

1964 (14 May). *AIR. Nickel Production at Houailou.* P 13×12.
392 54*d* 30 f. multicoloured .. .. .. 1·10 65

54*e* Ancient Greek Wrestling 55 Weather Satellite

(Des and eng C. Haley. Recess)

1964 (28 Dec). *AIR. Olympic Games, Tokyo.* P 13.
393 54*e* 10 f. deep sepia, magenta and green 5·00 4·50

(Des J. Combet. Photo Delrieu)

1965 (23 Mar). *AIR. World Meteorological Day.* P 12½.
394 55 9 f. multicoloured .. .. .. 1·25 95

56 "Syncom" Communications Satellite, Telegraph Poles and Morse Key

56*a* De Gaulle's Appeal of 18th June, 1940

(Des and eng J. Combet. Recess)

1965 (17 May). *AIR. I.T.U. Centenary.* P 13.
395 56 40 f. brt purple, orange-brown & blue 3·50 2·50

(Des and eng J. Combet. Recess)

1965 (20 Sept). *25th Anniv of New Caledonia's Adherence to the Free French.* P 13.
396 56*a* 20 f. black, red and blue .. .. 2·50 1·60

56*b* Amédée Lighthouse

56*c* Rocket "Diamant"

(Des and eng P. Béquet. Recess)

1965 (25 Nov). *Inauguration of Amédée Lighthouse.* P 13.
397 56*b* 8 f. bistre, royal blue and green .. 40 15

(Des and eng C. Durrens. Recess)

1966 (17 Jan). *AIR. Launching of First French Satellite.* T 56*c* and similar horiz design. P 13.
398 8 f. brown-lake, ultramarine & turq-bl 95 60
399 12 f. brown-lake, ultramarine & turq-bl 1·25 95
Design:—12 f. Satellite "A1".
Nos. 398/9 were issued together *se-tenant* within the sheet of 16, separated by a half stamp-size label inscribed "MISE SUR ORBITE DU PREMIER SATELLITE FRANÇAIS 26 NOVEMBRE 1965". (*Price* for strip unused or used £2).

56*d* Games Emblem 56*e* Satellite "D1"

(Des and eng C. Haley. Recess)

1966 (28 Feb). *Publicity for Second South Pacific Games, Nouméa.* P 13.
400 56*d* 8 f. black, red and blue 35 20

(Des and eng C. Durrens. Recess)

1966 (10 May). *AIR. Launching of Satellite "D1".* P 13.
401 56*e* 10 f. bistre-brn, greenish bl & orge-brn 95 65

57 Nouméa, 1866 (after Lebreton).

58 Red-headed Parrot-finch

(Des and eng M. Monvoisin. Recess)

1966 (2 June). *AIR. Centenary of Re-naming of Port-de-France as Nouméa.* P 13.
402 57 30 f. slate-blue, red and new blue .. 1·25 75

(Des P. Lambert. Litho (1 f. (403), 3 f. (406)) or photo So.Ge.Im. (1 f. (404), 2 f., 3 f. (407), 50 f.). Photo Govt Ptg Wks, Paris, (4 f., 5 f., 10 f., 15 f., 30 f., 39 f., 100 f.). Photo Delrieu (27 f., 37 f.))

1966–70. *Birds. T 58 and similar vert designs. Multicoloured.*
(*a*) POSTAGE. (i) P 13×12½.
403 1 f. Type 58 (10.10.66) 25 12
404 1 f. Caledonian warbler (14.5.68) .. 20 12
405 2 f. Caledonian whistler (14.5.68) .. 25 15
406 3 f. Giant Imperial pigeon (10.10.66) .. 40 40
407 3 f. White-collared dove (14.5.68) .. 25 25
408 4 f. Kagu (16.12.67) 40 30
409 5 f. Horned cockatiel (16.12.67) .. 50 35
410 10 f. Honeyeater (16.12.67) .. .. 1·25 60

(ii) *P* 13
411 15 f. Friar bird (19.2.70) 75 40
412 30 f. Kingfisher (19.2.70) .. .. 1·40 50

(*b*) *AIR. Inscr* "POSTE AERIENNE". (i) *P* 12½. *Size*
26×45½ *mm* (10.10.67)
413 27 f. Horned cockatiel (*different*) .. 1·10 65
414 37 f. Scarlet honeyeater .. .. .. 1·60 95

(ii) *P* 13. *Size* 27½×48 *mm*
415 39 f. Green turtle-doves (19.2.70) .. 1·60 95
416 50 f. Green fruit doves (14.5.68) .. 2·25 1·10
417 100 f. Fish eagles (19.2.70) .. .. 3·50 1·90
403/417 *Set of* 15 .. .. .. 14·00 8·00

59 U.N.E.S.C.O. Allegory   60 High-jumping

(Des and eng G. Bétemps. Recess)

1966 (4 Nov). *20th Anniv of U.N.E.S.C.O. P* 13.
418 59 16 f. purple, ochre and green 75 35

(Des and eng C. Haley. Recess)

1966 (8 Dec). *South Pacific Games, Nouméa. T* 60 *and similar horiz designs. P* 13.
419 17 f. bluish vio, myrtle-grn & brn-pur 70 70
420 20 f. blue-green, brt purple & brown-pur 1·25 80
421 40 f. myrtle-grn, bluish violet & brn-pur 2·00 1·25
422 100 f. brt purple, blue-green & brown-pur 5·00 3·50
419/422 *Set of* 4 .. .. 8·00 6·50
MS423 149×99 mm. Nos. 419/22 .. .. 15·00 8·00
Designs:—20 f. Hurdling; 40 f. Running; 100 f. Swimming.

61 Lekiné Cliffs

(Des Robin. Eng P. Gandon. Recess)

1967 (14 Jan). *P* 13.
424 61 17 f. grey-green, blue-green and blue 60 40

62 Racing Yachts

(Des and eng C. Haley. Recess)

1967 (15 Apr). *AIR. 2nd Whangarei-Nouméa Yacht Race. P* 13.
425 62 25 f. red, ultramarine & turquoise-green 90 65

STAMP MONTHLY
—finest and most informative magazine for all collectors. Obtainable from your newsagent or by postal subscription—details on request.

63 Magenta Stadium   64 New Caledonian Scenery

(Des P. Lambert. Photo So. Ge.Im.)

1967 (5 June). *Sports Centres, T* 63 *and similar horiz design. Multicoloured. P* 12½×13.
426 10 f. Type 63 .. .. 45 25
427 20 f. Ouen-Toro swimming pool .. 75 50

(Des and eng C. Haley. Recess)

1967 (19 June). *International Tourist Year. P* 13.
428 64 30 f. multicoloured .. .. .. 1·25 60

65 19th-century Postman   66 Papilio montrouzieri

(Des and eng P. Forget. Recess)

1967 (12 July). *Stamp Day. P* 13.
429 65 7 f. crimson, emerald & turquoise-green 30 25

(Des and eng J. Combet. Recess)

1967 (10 Aug)–**68**. *Butterflies. T* 66 *and similar horiz designs. P* 13. (*a*) *POSTAGE. Size* 36×22 *mm.*
430 7 f. bright blue, black and light emerald 40 25
431 9 f. indigo, brown and mauve (26.3.68) 50 30
432 13 f. bluish violet, purple-brn & orge-brn 75 45
433 15 f. yellow, purple-brown and light blue 90 50

(*b*) *AIR. Inscr* "POSTE AERIENNE". *Size* 48×27 *mm*
434 19 f. red-orange, bistre-brown and light
turquoise-green (26.3.68) 1·00 65
435 29 f. purple-brown, rose & bl (26.3.68) 1·40 75
436 85 f. chocolate, red and yellow .. .. 3·25 1·75
430/436 *Set of* 7 .. .. 7·50 4·00
Butterflies:—9 f. *Polyura clitarchus;* 13 f. *Hypolimnas bolina* (male), and: 15 f. (female); 19 f. *Danaus plexippus;* 29 f. *Hippotion celerio;* 85 f. *Delias elipsis.*

67 Garnierite (mineral), Factory and Jules Garnier

(Des and eng P. Gandon. Recess)

1967 (9 Oct). *AIR. Centenary of Garnierite Industry. P* 13.
437 67 70 f. sepia, bistre-brn, grey-bl & yell-grn 1·90 1·10

67*a* Lifou Island

(Des P. Lambert. Photo So.Ge.Im.)

1967 (28 Oct). *AIR. P* 13.
438 **67**a 200 f. multicoloured . . . . . . 5·50 3·25

67b Skier and Snow-crystal

(Des and eng G. Bétemps. Recess)

1967 (16 Nov). *AIR. Winter Olympic Games, Grenoble. P* 13.
439 **67**b 100 f. lake-brown, greenish blue and
myrtle-green . . . . . . 3·75 2·50

68 Bouquet, Sun and
W.H.O. Emblem

69 Human Rights
Emblem

(Des and eng A. Decaris. Recess)

1968 (4 May). *20th Anniv of World Health Organization. P* 13.
440 **68** 20 f. slate-blue, carmine & reddish vio 75 50

(Des and eng A. Decaris. Recess)

1968 (10 Aug). *Human Rights Year. P* 13.
441 **69** 12 f. carmine, dp green & orange-yell 50 50

70 Ferrying Mail-van across
Tontouta River

71 *Conus geographus*

(Des and eng A. Decaris. Recess)

1968 (2 Sept). *Stamp Day. P* 13.
442 **70** 9 f. chocolate, bright blue and green 40 25

(Des and eng J. Pheulpin. Recess)

1968 (9 Nov)–**72**. *Seashells. T* **71** *and similar designs. P* 13.
(a) POSTAGE
443 1 f. brown, grey & blue-grn (30.12.70) 12 12
444 1 f. maroon and bluish violet (4.3.72) 12 8
445 2 f. maroon, vermilion & blue (21.6.69) 20 15
446 3 f. yellow-brown & blue-grn (4.3.72) 15 20
447 5 f. brn-red, drab & reddish vio (21.6.69) 30 10
448 10 f. chocolate, grey and new blue . . 45 25
449 10 f. yellow, drab and carmine (4.6.70) 45 25
450 10 f. black, drab red-orge (30.12.70) 40 20
451 15 f. verm, slate & myrtle-grn (21.6.69) 75 35
452 21 f. brown, sepia & blue-green (4.6.70) 90 45

(b) AIR. Inscr "POSTE AERIENNE"
453 22 f. crim, bis-brn & new bl (30.12.70) 70 40
454 25 f. chestnut and cerise (4.3.72) . . 95 55
455 33 f. brown and turquoise-blue (4.6.70) 1·10 50
456 34 f. violet, brown & yell-orge (30.12.70) 1·10 50
457 39 f. yellow-brown, drab-grey & bl-grn 1·10 65
458 40 f. black, bistre and brown-red . . 1·40 75
459 50 f. cerise, maroon & blue-grn (4.3.72) 1·60 75
460 60 f. red-brown & light emerald (4.6.70) 1·90 80
461 70 f. yellow-brown, drab-grey and violet 2·50 1·40
462 100 f. brn-lake, blk & new bl (21.6.69) 5·00 2·50
443/462 *Set of 20* . . . . 19·00 10·00
Designs: *Vert* (22×36 *mm*)—1 f. (443) *Strombus epidromis*; 1 f. (444) *Lambis scorpius*; 3 f. *Lambis lambis*; 10 f. (450) *Strombus variabilis.* (27×48 *mm*)—22 f. *Strombus sinuatus*; 25 f. *Lambis crocata*; 34 f. *Strombus vomer*; 50 f. *Lambis chiragra. Horiz* (36×22 *mm*)—2 f. *Murex haustellum*; 5 f. *Murex triremis*; 10 f. (448) *Type* **71**; 10 f. (449) *Cypraea cribaria*; 15 f. *Murex rameux*; 21 f. *Cypraea talpa.* (48×27 *mm*)—33 f. *Cypraea argus*; 39 f. *Conus lienardi*; 40 f. *Conus cabriti*; 60 f. *Cypraea mappa*; 70 f. *Conus coccineus*; 100 f. *Murex noir.*

72 Dancers

73 Rally Car

(Des P. Lambert. Eng A. Frères. Recess)

1968 (30 Nov). *AIR. P* 13.
463 **72** 60 f. red, bright blue and myrtle-green 1·75 1·10

(Des and eng C. Haley. Recess)

1968 (26 Dec). *Second New Caledonian Motor Safari. P* 13.
464 **73** 25 f. blue, brown-red and myrtle-green 1·00 45

74 Caudron C-600 "Eaglet" and Route-map

(Des and eng J. Combet. Recess)

1969 (24 Mar). *AIR. Stamp Day. 30th Anniv of 1st Nouméa-Paris Flight by Martinet and Klein. P* 13.
465 **74** 29 f. deep cerise, new blue and violet 1·40 70

75 "Concorde" in Flight

76 Cattle-dip

(Des and eng C. Durrens. Recess)

1969 (17 Apr). *AIR. 1st Flight of "Concorde". P* 13.
466 **75** 100 f. myrtle-green and light blue-green 6·50 5·00

(Des C. Durrens. Eng C. Jumelet (9 f.), C. Durrens (others). Recess)

1969 (10 May). *Cattle-breeding in New Caledonia. T **76** and similar horiz designs. P* 13. (*a*) POSTAGE.
467   9 f. purple-brown, myrtle-green & ultram   30   15
468   25 f. reddish violet, purple-brown & emer   90   40

(*b*) *AIR. Inscr "POSTE AERIENNE"*
469   50 f. maroon, brown-red and myrtle-green   1·25   80
Designs: (36×22 *mm*)—25 f. Branding. (48×27 *mm*)—50 f. Stockman with herd.

77 Judo   79 I.L.O. Building, Geneva

78 Airliner over Outrigger Canoe

(Des and eng G. Bétemps. Recess)

1969 (7 Aug). *3rd South Pacific Games, Port Moresby, Papua New Guinea. T **77** and similar designs. P* 13. (*a*) POSTAGE.
470   19 f. dull purple, new blue and red   ..   75   30
471   20 f. black, vermilion and blue-green   ..   75   30

(*b*) *AIR. Inscr "POSTE AERIENNE"*
472   30 f. black and light blue   ..   1·00   55
473   39 f. olive-brown, blue-green and black   1·50   80
470/473   Set of 4   ..   ..   ..   3·50   1·75
Designs: *Horiz* (36×22 *mm*)—20 f. Boxing. (48×27 *mm*)—30 f. Diving. *Vert* (27×48 *mm*)—39 f. Putting the shot.

(Photo Delrieu)

1969 (2 Oct). *AIR. Birth Bicentenary of Napoleon Bonaparte. Vert design as T **72** of Mali. Multicoloured. P* 12½.
474   40 f. "Napoleon in Coronation Robes" (Gerard)   ..   ..   ..   3·75   2·50

(Des and eng C. Guillame. Recess)

1969 (2 Oct). *AIR. 20th Anniv of Regular Nouméa-Paris Air Service. P* 13.
475   **78** 50 f. myrtle-green, purple-brown & lt bl   1·50   1·00

(Des and eng J. Derrey. Recess)

1969 (24 Nov). *50th Anniv of International Labour Organization. P* 13.
476   **79** 12 f. yell-brn, dp reddish vio & salmon   30   20

80 "French Wings around the World"

(Des and eng J. Gauthier. Recess)

1970 (6 May). *AIR. 10th Anniv of French "Around the World" Air Service. P* 13.
477   **80** 200 f. orange-brown, greenish bl & vio   5·00   3·25

81 New U.P.U. Building, Berne   **82** Packet-boat *Natal*, 1883

(Des and eng J. Gauthier. Recess)

1970 (20 May). *Inauguration of New U.P.U. Headquarters Building, Berne. P* 13.
478   **81** 12 f. brown-red, dp slate & chocolate   40   25

(Des and eng G. Aufschneider. Recess)

1970 (23 July). *Stamp Day. P* 13.
479   **82** 9 f. black, blue-green & greenish blue   40   25

83 Cyclists on Map

(Des and eng G. Bétemps. Recess)

1970 (20 Aug). *AIR. 4th "Tour de Nouvelle Caledonie" Cycle Race. P* 13.
480   **83** 40 f. chocolate, light blue and new blue   1·10   65

84 Mt Fuji and Japanese Express Train

(Des R. Quillivic. Photo)

1970 (3 Sept). *AIR. "EXPO 70" World Fair, Osaka, Japan. T **84** and similar horiz design. Multicoloured. P* 13.
481   20 f. Type **84**   55   40
482   45 f. "EXPO" emblem, map and Buddha   1·10   65

85 Yachts with Spinnakers

(Des and eng C. Haley. Recess)

1971 (23 Feb). *AIR. One Ton Cup Yacht Race, Auckland, New Zealand. P* 13.
483 **85** 20 f. blue-green, red and black   ..   65   40

86 Dumbea Mail Train

(Des and eng J. Combet. Recess)

1971 (13 Mar). *Stamp Day. P* 13.
484 **86** 10 f. black, myrtle-green and red   ..   45   25

87 Racing Yachts

(Des and eng J. Pheulpin. Recess)

1971 (17 Apr). *3rd Whangarei-Nouméa Ocean Yacht Race. P* 13.
485 **87** 16 f. turq-bl, blackish grn & new bl   70   45

88 Lieut.-Col. Broche and Theatre Map

(Des P. Lambert. Photo Delrieu)

1971 (5 May). *AIR. 30th Anniv of French Pacific Battalion's Participation in Second World War Mediterranean Campaign. P* 12½.
486 **88** 60 f. multicoloured   ..   ..   1·75   1·00

89 Early Tape Machine   **90** Weightlifting

(Des and eng R. Quillivic. Recess)

1971 (17 May). *World Telecommunications Day. P* 13.
487 **89** 19 f. orange, claret and scarlet   ..   55   30

(Des C. Durrens. Eng J. Miermont (11 f.), C. Jumelet (100 f.), C₄ Durrens (others). Recess)

1971 (24 June). *4th South Pacific Games, Papeete, French Polynesia. T* **90** *and similar designs. P* 13. (*a*) *POSTAGE.*
488   11 f. purple-brown and rosine   ..   50   25
489   23 f. bluish violet, red and new blue   ..   90   45

(*b*) *AIR. Inscr* "POSTE AERIENNE"
490   25 f. blue-green and red   ..   75   40
491   100 f. ultramarine, yellow-green and red   2·75   1·50
488/491   *Set of 4*   ..   ..   ..   4·50   2·40
Designs: *Vert*—23 f. Basketball. *Horiz* (48×27 *mm*)—25 f. Pole-vaulting; 100 f. Archery.

91 Port de Plaisance, Nouméa   **92** De Gaulle as President of French Republic, 1970

(Des P. Lambert. Photo Delrieu)

1971 (27 Sept). *AIR. P* 13.
492 **91** 200 f. multicoloured ..   ..   ..   5·50   3·25

(Des G. Bétemps. Eng G. Bétemps (34 f.), J. Miermont (100 f.). Recess)

1971 (9 Nov). *1st Death Anniv of General De Gaulle. T* **92** *and similar vert design. P* 13.
493   34 f. black and plum   ..   ..   1·60   65
494   100 f. black and plum   ..   ..   3·50   1·60
Design:—100 f. De Gaulle in uniform, 1940.

93 Publicity Leaflet showing Aircraft

(Des and eng C. Haley. Recess)

1971 (20 Nov). *AIR. 40th Anniv of First New Caledonia-Australia Flight. P* 13.
495 **93** 90 f. sepia, deep blue and orange   ..   2·25   1·25

94 Downhill Skiing

(Des and eng M. Monvoisin. Recess)
1972 (22 Jan). *AIR. Winter Olympic Games, Sapporo, Japan.*
P 13.
496 **94** 50 f. myrtle-green, red and blue   1·25   70

95 St. Mark's Basilica, Venice

(Des and eng R. Quillivic. Recess)
1972 (5 Feb). *AIR. U.N.E.S.C.O. "Save Venice" Campaign.*
P 13.
497 **95** 20 f. yellow-brown, bl-grn & greenish bl   80   40

96 Commission Headquarters, Nouméa

(Des Baillais. Photo)
1972 (5 Feb). *AIR. 25th Anniv of South Pacific Commission.*
P 13.
498 **96** 18 f. multicoloured   50   30

99 Goa Door-post

(Des P. Lambert. Photo)
1972 (5 Aug)–**73**. *Exhibits from Nouméa Museum.* T **99** and
similar vert designs. *P* 12½×13. (*a*) *POSTAGE.*
501   1 f. red, myrtle-green and brownish grey
              (20.4.73)   12   8
502   2 f. black, myrtle-green and dull green   20   12
503   5 f. multicoloured   25   20
504   12 f. multicoloured   45   25
          (*b*) *AIR. Inscr* "POSTE AERIENNE"
505   16 f. multicoloured (20.4.73)   40   25
506   40 f. multicoloured (20.4.73)   90   50
501/506 *Set of 6*   ..   ..   2·00   1·25
Designs:—2 f. Carved wooden pillow; 5 f. Monstrance; 12 f.
Tchamba mask; 16 f. Ornamental arrow-heads; 40 f. Portico,
chief's house.

100 Hurdling over "H" of "MUNICH"

(Des and eng J. Gauthier. Recess)
1972 (2 Sept). *AIR. Olympic Games, Munich. P* 13.
507 **100** 72 f. bluish violet, brt purple & new bl   2·25   1·00

101 New Head Post Office, Nouméa

(Des and eng M. Monvoisin. Recess)
1972 (25 Nov). *AIR. P* 13.
508 **101** 23 f. brown, bright blue and emerald   65   30

97 Breguet Aircraft and   **98** Pacific Island
Nouméa Monument   Dwelling

(Des and eng C. Haley. Recess)
1972 (5 Apr). *AIR. 40th Anniv of 1st Paris-Nouméa Flight.*
P 13.
499 **97** 110 f. new blue, brt purple & emerald   3·75   2·50

(Des and eng J. Combet. Recess)
1972 (13 May). *AIR. South Pacific Arts Festival, Fiji. P* 13.
500 **98** 24 f. light brown, new blue and orange   70   40

102 J.C.I. Emblem

(Des Baillais. Photo)

1972 (16 Dec). 10th Anniv of New Caledonia Junior Chamber of Commerce. P 12½×13.
509 **102** 12 f. multicoloured 40 20

103 Forest Scene

(Des P. Lambert. Photo)

1973 (24 Feb). AIR. Landscapes of the East Coast. T **103** and similar multicoloured designs. P 13.
510 11 f. Type **103** 40 20
511 18 f. Beach and palms (vert) 65 30
512 21 f. Waterfall and inlet (vert) .. 95 45
For similar stamps see Nos. 534/6.

104 Molière and Characters   **105** Tchamba Mask

(Des and eng J. Combet. Recess)

1973 (24 Feb). AIR. 300th Death Anniv of Molière (playwright). P 13.
513 **104** 50 f. multicoloured .. .. .. 1·60 80

(Des P. Lambert. Eng C. Haley (12 f.). Des and eng R. Quillivic (23 f.). Recess)

1973 (15 Mar). Booklet Stamps. T **105** and similar vert design. P 13. (a) POSTAGE.
514 12 f. bright purple 50 35
(b) AIR. Inscr "POSTE AERIENNE"
515 23 f. blue .. .. 1·10 65
Design:—23 f. "Concorde" in flight.
Nos. 514/15 were each issued in booklet panes of ten.

106 S.S. El Kantara in Panama Canal

(Des and eng C. Haley. Recess)

1973 (24 Mar). AIR. 50th Anniv of Marseille-Nouméa Shipping Service via Panama Canal. P 13.
516 **106** 60 f. black, brown and olive-green .. 1·90 90

107 Globe and Allegory of Weather

(Des Caussin. Eng G. Aufschneider. Recess)

1973 (24 Mar). AIR. Centenary of World Meteorological Organization. P 13.
517 **107** 80 f. multicoloured .. .. 2·00 1·10

108 "DC-10" in Flight

(Des and eng J. Combet. Recess)

1973 (19 May). AIR. Inauguration of Nouméa-Paris "DC-10" Air Service. P 13.
518 **108** 100 f. myrtle-green, yell-brn & ultram 2·50 1·25

109 Ovula ovum   O **110** Carved Wooden Pillow
(Nouméa Museum)

(Des P. Lambert. Photo)

1973 (23 June)—**74**. Marine Fauna from Nouméa Aquarium. T **109** and similar horiz designs. Multicoloured. P 13×12½.
(a) POSTAGE
519 8 f. Chaetodon melanotus (daylight) .. 25 15
520 14 f. Chaetodon melanotus (nocturnal) .. 40 25
(b) AIR. Inscr "POSTE AERIENNE"
521 3 f. Type **109** (23.3.74) 10 5
522 32 f. Acanthurus olivaceus (adult & young) 90 55
523 32 f. Hydatina (23.3.74) 65 45
524 37 f. Dolium perdix (23.3.74) 95 50
519/524 Set of 6 .. .. .. 3·00 1·75

(Des P. Lambert. Photo)

1973 (1 July)—**76**. OFFICIAL. P 13.
O525 O **110** 1 f. grn, blk & pale greenish yell 5 5
O526 3 f. green, black & pale cinn 8 5
O527 4 f. green, black & pale lavender 10 5
O528 5 f. green, black and light mauve 12 10
O529 9 f. green, black and pale blue 20 12
O530 10 f. green, black & lt orange-red 20 15
O531 11 f. grn, blk & brt mve (1.12.76) 12 5
O532 12 f. green, black & lt turq-grn 30 20
O533 15 f. green, blk & bl-grn (1.12.76) 20 5
O534 20 f. grn, blk & rose-red (1.12.76) 25 5
O535 24 f. grn, blk & grnish bl (1.12.76) 30 10
O536 26 f. green, black & lem (1.12.76) 35 15
O537 36 f. green, black & mag (1.12.76) 45 20
O538 42 f. green, blk & ochre (1.12.76) 55 30
O539 50 f. green, blk & pale bl (1.12.76) 65 45
O540 100 f. grn, blk & orge-red (1.12.76) 1·25 80
O541 200 f. grn, blk & orge-yell (1.12.76) 2·50 1·25
O525/O541 Set of 17 .. .. 7·00 3·75

111 Office Emblem

(Des P. Sampoux. Photo)

1973 (21 July). *10th Anniv of Central Schools' Co-operation Office. P* 13.
532 **111** 20 f. ultramarine, green & brt yellow   45   25

112 New Caledonia Mail-coach, 1880

(Des and eng J. Pheulpin. Recess)

1973 (22 Sept). *AIR. Stamp Day. P* 13.
533 **112** 15 f. purple-brown, blackish grn & bl   45   30

(Des P. Lambert. Photo)

1974 (23 Mar). *AIR. Landscapes of the West Coast. Multicoloured designs as T* 103. *P* 13.
534   8 f. Beach and palms (*vert*)   25   12
535   22 f. Trees and mountains   50   25
536   26 f. Trees growing in sea   65   30

113 Centre Building

(Des P. Lambert. Photo)

1974 (23 Mar). *AIR. Opening of Scientific Studies Centre, Anse-Vata, Nouméa. P* 13.
537 **113** 50 f. multicoloured   95   65

114 "Bird" embracing Flora

(Des M. T. Veillon. Photo)

1974 (22 June). *Nature Conservation. P* 13.
538 **114** 7 f. multicoloured   20   12

115 18th-century French Sailor

116 "Telecommunications"

(Des and eng R. Quillivic. Recess)

1974 (4 Sept). *AIR. Discovery and Reconnaissance of New Caledonia and Loyalty Islands. T* 115 *and similar designs. P* 13.
539   20 f. claret, reddish violet & turquoise-blue   30   25
540   25 f. bistre-brown, blue-green and red ..   45   30
541   28 f. red-brown, turq-bl & blackish grn   50   30
542   30 f. olive-brown, new blue & lake-brown   55   35
543   36 f. olive-brown, reddish purple & indigo   65   40
539/543   Set of 5   ..   ..   ..   2·25   1·55
Designs: *Horiz*—20 f. Captain Cook, *Endeavour* and map of Grand Terre island; 25 f. La Perouse, ship and map of Grand Terre island (reconnaissance of west coast); 30 f. Entrecasteaux, ship and map of Grand Terre island (reconnaissance of west coast); 36 f. Dumont d'Urville, ship and map of Loyalty Islands.

(Des and eng J. Gauthier. Recess)

1974 (9 Oct). *AIR. Centenary of Universal Postal Union. P* 13.
544 **116** 95 f. red-orange, purple and slate ..   2·00   1·10

117 "Art"

(Des J. Gauthier. Photo)

1974 (26 Oct). *AIR. "Arphila 75" International Stamp Exhibition, Paris* (1975) (*1st issue*). *P* 13.
545 **117** 80 f. multicoloured   ..   ..   ..   1·60   95
See also No. 554.

118 Hotel Chateau-Royal

118a Animal Skull, Burnt Tree and Flaming Landscape

(Des P. Lambert. Photo)

1974 (9 Déc). *AIR. Inauguration of Hotel Chateau-Royal, Nouméa. P* 13.
546 **118** 22 f. multicoloured 30 20

(Des P. Lambert, after R. Morin. Photo)

1975 (3 Feb). *"Stop Bush Fires". P* 13.
547 **118**a 20 f. multicoloured 30 20

119 "Cricket" **120** *Calanthe veratrifolia*

(Des P. Lambert. Photo Delrieu)

1975 (24 Mar). *AIR. Tourism. T* 119 *and similar horiz designs. Multicoloured. P* 13½.
548 3 f. Type **119** 10 5
549 25 f. "Bouga" ceremony 50 25
550 31 f. "Pilou" native dance 65 30

(Des O. Baillais. Photo Delrieu)

1975 (30 May). *Orchids. T* 120 *and similar vert designs. Multicoloured. P* 13½. *(a) POSTAGE.*
551 8 f. Type **120** 20 12
552 11 f. *Lyperanthus gigas* 25 20

(b) AIR. Inscr "POSTE AERIENNE"
553 42 f. *Eriaxis rigida* 75 45

121 Global "Flower" **122** Throwing the Discus

(Des and eng R. Quillivic. Recess)

1975 (7 June). *AIR. "Arphila 75" International Stamp Exhibition, Paris (2nd issue). P* 13.
554 **121** 105 f. brt pur, bronze-grn & new bl 1.90 1.10

(Des J. Gauthier. Photo)

1975 (23 Aug). *AIR. Fifth South Pacific Games, Guam. T* 122 *and similar horiz design. Multicoloured. P* 13.
555 24 f. Type **122** 45 30
556 50 f. Volleyball 80 45

123 Festival Emblem **124** Birds in Flight

(Des N. Delange. Photo)

1975 (6 Sept). *"Melanesia* 2000" *Festival, Nouméa. P* 13.
557 **123** 12 f. multicoloured 20 15

(Des Berechel, after P. Nielly. Photo Delrieu)

1975 (18 Oct). *10th Anniv of Nouméa Archaeological Society. P* 13½×13.
558 **124** 5 f. multicoloured 10 5

125 President Pompidou **126** Two "Concordes"

(Des and eng P. Gandon. Recess)

1975 (6 Dec). *Pompidou Commemoration. P* 13.
559 **125** 26 f. slate and blackish green .. 45 25

(Des and eng C. Andréotto. Recess)

1976 (21 Jan). *First Commercial Flight of "Concorde". P* 13.
560 **126** 147 f. bright blue and red 2.25 2.25

127 Brown Booby **128** Festival Emblem

(Des O. Baillais. Photo)

1976 (26 Feb). *Ocean Birds. T* 127 *and similar multicoloured designs. P* 12½×13 (8 f.) *or* 13×12½ *(others).*
561 1 f. Type **127** 5 5
562 2 f. Blue-faced booby 5 5
563 8 f. Red-faced booby *(vert)* 25 20

(Des P. Lambert. Litho Cartor)

1976 (13 Mar). *South Pacific Arts Festival, Rotorua, New Zealand. P* 12½.
564 **128** 27 f. multicoloured 45 30

129 Lion and Lions' Emblem

130 Early and Modern Telephones

(Des P. Lambert. Photo)

1976 (13 Mar). *15th Anniv of Nouméa Lions Club. P* 13.
565 **129** 49 f. multicoloured 70 55

(Des J. Chesnot. Photo)

1976 (12 Apr). *AIR. Telephone Centenary. P* 13.
566 **130** 36 f. multicoloured 50 35

131 Capture of Penbosct

(Des and eng J. Combet. Recess)

1976 (14 June). *AIR. Bicentenary of American Revolution. P* 13.
567 **131** 24 f. brown-purple and lake-brown.. 40 25

132 Bandstand

(Des P. Lambert. Litho Cartor)

1976 (14 June). *"Aspects of Old Nouméa". T* **132** *and similar multicoloured design. P* 12.
568 25 f. Type **132** 35 20
569 30 f. Monumental fountain (*vert*) .. 40 25

133 Athletes

(Des and eng J. Gauthier. Recess)

1976 (24 July). *AIR. Olympic Games, Montreal. P* 13.
570 **133** 33 f. violet, carmine and purple .. 50 30

134 "Chick" with Magnifier

(Des Susini, after M. Peyrouze. Photo)

1976 (21 Aug). *AIR. "Philately in Schools" Stamp Exhibition, Nouméa. P* 13.
571 **134** 42 f. multicoloured 70 45

135 Dead Bird and Trees

(Des P. Lambert, after R. Morin. Photo)

1976 (21 Aug). *Nature Protection. P* 13.
572 **135** 20 f. multicoloured 30 20

PUZZLED?

Then you need
PHILATELIC TERMS ILLUSTRATED
to tell you all you need to know about printing methods, papers, errors, varieties, watermarks, perforations, etc. 192 pages, almost half in full colour, soft cover. £1·95 post paid.

136 South Pacific "Heads"

(Des C. Andréotto, after P. Neilly. Photo Delrieu)

1976 (23 Oct). *16th South Pacific Commission Conference, Nouméa. P* 13.

573 **136** 20 f. multicoloured 30 20

137 Old Town Hall, Nouméa

(Des O. Baillais. Photo)

1976 (Oct). *AIR. Old and New Town Halls, Nouméa. T* 137 *and similar horiz design. Multicoloured. P* 13 × 12½.

574 75 f. Type **137** .. .. 1·10 65
575 125 f. New Town Hall .. .. .. 1·75 1·00

138 Water Carnival   139 *Psuedophyllanax imperialis*

(Des H. Sainson, after M. Vonne. Photo)

1977 (15 Jan). *AIR. Summer Festival, Nouméa. P* 13 × 12½.

576 **138** 11 f. multicoloured 20 12

(Des and eng G. Bétemps. Recess)

1977 (21 Feb). *Insects. T* 139 *and similar horiz design. P* 13 × 12½.

577 26 f. emerald, brt green & orange-brown .. 35 20
578 31 f. chestnut, sepia and deep green .. 40 25
Design:—31 f. *Agrianome fairmairei.*

140 Miniature Roadway

(Des O. Baillais. Photo)

1977 (12 Mar). *AIR. Road Safety. P* 13 × 12½.

579 **140** 50 f. multicoloured 70 50

141 Earth Station   142 *Phajus daenikeri*

(Des O. Baillais. Photo)

1977 (16 Apr). *Earth Satellite Station, Nouméa. P* 13.

580 **141** 29 f. multicoloured 40 25

(Des O. Baillais. Photo)

1977 (23 May). *Orchids. T* 142 *and similar vert design. Multicoloured. P* 13.

581 22 f. Type **142** 30 20
582 44 f. *Dendrobium finetianum* 60 45

143 Mask and Palms

(Des S. Hnepeune. Photo)

1977 (25 June). *La Perouse School Philatelic Exhibition. P* 13.

583 **143** 35 f. multicoloured 45 35

144 Trees

(Des L. Kaliaki. Photo)

1977 (16 July). *Nature Protection. P* 13 × 12½.

584 **144** 20 f. multicoloured 30 20

145 Palm Tree and Emblem   146 Young Frigate Bird

(Des J. P. Ormand. Photo)

1977 (6 Aug). *French Junior Chambers of Commerce Congress.*
P 13.
585 **145** 200 f. multicoloured .. .. .. 2·75 1·90

(Des Verret-Le Marinier. Photo)

1977 (17 Sept). *Frigate Birds. T* **146** *and similar design.*
Multicoloured. P 13. (*a*) POSTAGE.
586 16 f. Type **146** 20 15

(*b*) AIR. *Inscr "POSTE AERIENNE"*
587 42 f. Adult male bird (*horiz*) 60 45

147 Magenta Airport and Map
of Internal Air Network

(Des G. Bétemps. Photo Delrieu)

1977 (22 Oct). AIR. *Airports. T* **147** *and similar horiz design.*
Multicoloured. P 13.
588 24 f. Type **147** 35 25
589 57 f. La Tontout International Airport,
Nouméa 80 60

22.11.77 PARIS NEW-YORK

(148)

1977 (22 Nov). AIR. *First Commercial Flight of "Concorde",*
Paris–New York. No. 560 *optd with T* **148**, *in ultramarine.*
590 **126** 147 f. bright blue, red and ultramarine 2·10 1·50

149 Horse and Foal

(Des and eng J. Combet. Recess)

1977 (Nov). *Tenth Anniv of S.E.C.C. (Horse-breeding Society).*
P 13×12½.
591 **149** 5 f. brown, yellow-green & greenish bl 5 5

150 "Moselle Bay" (H. Didonna)

(Photo Delrieu (41 f.). Eng Larrivière. Recess (42 f.))

1977 (28 Nov). AIR. *Views of Old Nouméa. T* **150** *and similar*
horiz design. P 13.
592 41 f. multicoloured 55 40
593 42 f. deep maroon and orange-brown .. 60 45
Design: (49×27 *mm*)—42 f. "Settlers' Valley" (J. Kreber).

151 *Sterna sumatrana* Raffles

(Des Verret-Le Marinier. Photo)

1978 (11 Feb). *Ocean Birds. T* **151** *and similar horiz design.*
Multicoloured. P 13×12½.
594 22 f. Type **151** 30 20
595 40 f. *Sterna fuscata* Linné 55 40

152 *Araucaria*   **153** *Halityle*
 montana   *regularis*

(Des O. Baillais. Photo)

1978 (17 Mar). *Flora. T* **152** *and similar design. Multicoloured.*
P 12½×13 (16 *f.*) *or* 13×12½ (42 *f.*). (*a*) POSTAGE.
596 16 f. Type **152** 20 15

(*b*) AIR. *Inscr "POSTE AERIENNE"*
597 42 f. *Amyema scandens* (*horiz*) .. 60 45

(Des Ky Phungchaleun. Photo Delrieu)

1978 (20 May). *Nouméa Aquarium. P* 13.
598 **153** 10 f. multicoloured 20 15

154 Turtle

(Des F. Fay. Photo)

1978 (20 May). *Protection of the Turtle. P* 13×12½.
599 **154** 30 f. multicoloured 40 25

155 *Pteropus macmilliani*

(Des Verret-Le Marinier. Photo)

1978 (10 June). *Nature Protection. P* 13.
600 **155** 20 f. multicoloured 30 20

156 "Underwater Carnival"

157 Pastor Maurice Leenhardt

(Des Gemmanick. Photo Delrieu)
1978 (17 June). *AIR. Aubusson Tapestry. P* 13.
601 **156** 105 f. multicoloured .. .. .. 1·50 95

(Des and eng E. Lacaque. Recess)
1978 (12 Aug). *Birth Centenary of Pastor Maurice Leenhardt. P* 13.
602 **157** 37 f. olive-sepia, dp yell-grn & dull orge 45 35

158 Hare chasing "Stamp" Tortoise

(Des Y. Coqueugniot; adapted P. Lambert. Litho Delrieu)
1978 (19 Aug). *AIR. School Philately. P* 13½.
603 **158** 35 f. multicoloured 45 35

(Des Petron; adapted P. Lambert. Photo)
1978 (28 Oct). *AIR. Third Caledonian Old People's Day. P* 13.
605 **160** 36 f. multicoloured 45 35

161 Footballers and League Badge

162 "Faubourg Blanchot" (after Lacouture)

(Des Ny Phungchaleun. Photo)
1978 (4 Nov). *50th Anniv of New Caledonia Football League. P* 13.
606 **161** 26 f. multicoloured 35 25

(Photo Delrieu)
1978 (25 Nov). *AIR. Views of Old Nouméa. P* 13.
607 **162** 24 f. multicoloured 35 25

159 Heads, Map, Magnifying Glass and Shell

160 Candles

163 Map of Lifou, Solar Energy Panel and Transmitter Mast

(Des and eng J. Combet. Recess)
1978 (30 Sept). *AIR. Thematic Philately at Bourail. P* 13.
604 **159** 41 f. multicoloured 55 40

(Des G. Mariscalchi. Photo)
1978 (9 Dec). *Telecommunications through Solar Energy. P* 13.
608 **163** 33 f. multicoloured 45 35

ALBUM LISTS

Please write for our latest lists of albums and accessories. These will be sent free on request.

New Hebrides

(FRENCH ISSUES)

1908. 100 Centimes = 1 Franc
1938. 100 Gold Centimes = 1 Gold Franc

These islands, in the south-west Pacific Ocean, north of New Caledonia, were discovered by the Portuguese Pedro Fernandez de Quirós in 1606, when searching for a great southern continent, and were named by him Terra Australia del Espiritu Santo. Louis de Bougainville explored the islands in 1768 and they were charted by Captain James Cook in 1774 and renamed the New Hebrides by him. One of the islands is still called Espiritu Santo. British commercial interests prevailed until 1870, after which French interests developed rapidly. By an Anglo-French Convention of 1878 the islands were declared neutral. Several native outbreaks resulted in a further convention in 1887, providing for surveillance by an Anglo-French commission of naval officers to protect life and property. An Anglo-French Condominium was created by the Convention of 20 October 1906, which made the islands a region of joint influence, in which French and British have equal rights. In 1940 the New Hebrides were the first French territory to rally to General de Gaulle, and they became a major allied base in the war against Japan.

Stamps inscribed in French and English are issued concurrently and have equal validity anywhere in the islands. The British issues (inscribed "NEW HEBRIDES") are listed in the *British Commonwealth* Catalogue.

F13	F 5	20 c. greyish slate			75	60
F14		25 c. ultramarine			1·00	90
F15		30 c. brown/*yellow*			90	75
F16		40 c. red/*yellow*			1·10	95
F17		50 c. sage-green			1·10	1·00
F18		75 c. orange			1·75	1·50
F19		1 f. red/*blue*			90	75
F20		2 f. violet			1·75	1·75
F21		5 f. red/*green*			3·25	3·25
F11/21		*Set of* 11			11·50	10·00

1913. *As last but wmk. "R F" in sheet or without wmk.*

F22	F 5	5 c. green			55	55
F23		10 c. carmine			55	55
F24		20 c. greyish slate			90	90
F25		25 c. ultramarine			90	90
F26		30 c. brown/*yellow*			90	90
F27		40 c. red/*yellow*			5·50	5·50
F28		50 c. sage-green			3·00	2·75
F29		75 c. orange			2·75	2·75
F30		1 f. red/*blue*			1·60	1·60
F31		2 f. violet			2·75	2·50
F32		5 f. red/*green*			5·50	5·50
F22/32		*Set of* 11			22·00	22·00

The above were placed on sale in Paris on 29 April 1912.

NOUVELLES HÉBRIDES (F 1)

NOUVELLES-HÉBRIDES (F 2)

1908 (21 Nov). *Types of New Caledonia optd with Types* F 1 *or* F 2 (1 f.), *by Govt Ptg Wks, Paris.*

F1	15	5 c. green			1·00	1·00
F2		10 c. carmine			1·25	1·25
F3	16	25 c. blue/*greenish* (R.)			1·25	1·25
F4		50 c. red/*orange*			1·50	1·50
F5	17	1 f. red/*green* (R.)			4·00	4·00
F1/5		*Set of* 5			8·00	8·00

CONDOMINIUM (F 3)

F 5 Weapons and Idols

1910 (Sept)–**11**. *Nos.* F1/5 *further optd with Type* F 3, *or larger* (1 f.), *by Govt Ptg Wks, Paris.*

F 6	15	5 c. green			30	30
F 7		10 c. carmine			40	40
F 8	16	25 c. blue/*greenish* (R.) (1911)			50	75
F 9		50 c. red/*orange* (1911)			1·25	1·50
F10	17	1 f. blue/*green* (R.)			4·00	4·00
F6/10		*Set of* 5			6·00	6·00

All the above were released in Paris on 16 March 1910. The 5 c., 10 c. and 1 f. were issued in New Hebrides in September but the 25 c. and 50 c. were not received until 1911 after the issue of the definitive stamps and they were placed in reserve, although some may have been issued on request.

(Des J. Giraud. Recess De La Rue)

1911 (12 July). *Wmk Mult Crown CA. P* 14.

F11	F 5	5 c. green			20	20
F12		10 c. carmine			25	25

10c. (F 6)

1920–21. *Surch as Type* F 6, *at Govt Printing Establishment, Suva, Fiji.*

(a) On stamps of 1908–11 (June 1920)

F32a	16	5 c. on 50 c. red/*orange* (F4)		£325	£325
F33		5 c. on 50 c. red/*orange* (F9)		75	75
F33a		10 c. on 25 c. blue/*greenish* (F8)		30	30

(b) On stamps of 1911–13 (10.3.21)

F34	F 5	05 c. on 40 c. red/*yellow* (F27)		7·50	7·50
F35		20 c. on 30 c. brown/*yellow* (F15)		3·25	3·25
F36		20 c. on 30 c. brown/*yellow* (F26)		3·25	3·25

(c) On British issue (10.3.21)

F37	3	10 c. on 5d. sage-green (24)		3·25	3·25

1924 (1 May). *Stamps of 1911–13 surch as Type* F 6, *at Suva.*

F38	F 5	10 c. on 5 c. green (F22)		25	25
F39		30 c. on 10 c. carmine (F23)		20	20
F40		50 c. on 25 c. ultramarine (F14)		1·25	1·25
F41		50 c. on 25 c. ultramarine (F25)		75	75
F38/41		*Set of* 4			2·25	2·25

CHIFFRE TAXE

F 7 (FD 8)

(Recess De La Rue)

1925 (June). *Wmk "R F" in sheet or without wmk. P* 14.

F42	F 7	5 c. (½d.) black			30	30
F43		10 c. (1d.) green			15	15
F44		20 c. (2d.) greyish slate			15	15
F45		25 c. (2½d.) brown			15	15
F46		30 c. (3d.) red			15	15
F47		40 c. (4d.) red/*yellow*			30	30

F48	F 7	50 c. (5d.) ultramarine	30	30
F49		75 c. (7½d.) yellow-brown	45	45
F50		1 f. (10d.) carmine/*blue*	75	75
F51		2 f. (1/8) violet	75	75
F52		5 f. (4s.) carmine/*green*	1·90	1·90
F42/52		*Set of* 11	5·00	5·00

In July 1929 a batch of mail was carried by aircraft from Port Vila to the French cruiser *Tourville*, for sorting and forwarding at Nouméa, New Caledonia. Stamps of the above issue (including those with British inscriptions) were affixed to covers and handstamped "PAR AVION" before cancellation.

1925 (June). *POSTAGE DUE. Optd with Type* FD **8**, *by De La Rue.*

FD53	F 7	10 c. (1d.) green	11·00	1·10
FD54		20 c. (2d.) greyish slate	11·00	1·10
FD55		30 c. (3d.) red	11·00	1·10
FD56		50 c. (5d.) ultramarine	11·00	1·10
FD57		1 f. (10d.) carmine/*blue*	11·00	1·10
FD53/57		*Set of* 5	48·00	5·00

Although on sale in Paris, the Postmaster would not issue any in unused condition for about a year and most used copies are cancelled to order.

F **8** Lopevi Is. and Copra Canoe   **CHIFFRE TAXE** (FD **9**)

(Des J. Kerhor. Recess Bradbury, Wilkinson)

1938 (1 June). *Gold Currency. Wmk "R F" in sheet or without wmk. P* 12.

F53	F **8**	5 c. blue-green	20	20
F54		10 c. orange	20	20
F55		15 c. bright violet	20	20
F56		20 c. scarlet	20	20
F57		25 c. reddish brown	30	30
F58		30 c. blue	30	30
F59		40 c. grey-olive	50	50
F60		50 c. purple	60	60
F61		1 f. lake/*pale green (shades)*	75	75
F62		2 f. blue/*pale green (shades)*	2·10	2·10
F63		5 f. red/*yellow*	5·50	5·50
F64		1 f. violet/*blue*	11·00	11·00
F53/64		*Set of* 12	20·00	20·00

1938 (1 June). *POSTAGE DUE. Optd with Type* FD **9**, *by Bradbury, Wilkinson.*

FD65	F **8**	5 c. blue-green	30	30
FD66		10 c. orange	30	30
FD67		20 c. scarlet	40	40
FD68		40 c. grey-olive	90	90
FD69		1 f. lake/*pale green*	1·40	1·40
FD65/69		*Set of* 5	3·00	3·00

France Libre

(F **9**)   F **10** U.P.U. Monument, Berne

1941 (15 Apr). *Adherence to General de Gaulle. Optd with Type* F **9**, *at Nouméa, New Caledonia.* (*a*) *POSTAGE.*

F65	F **8**	5 c. blue-green	2·50	2·50
F66		10 c. orange	2·50	2·50
F67		15 c. bright violet	2·50	2·50
F68		20 c. scarlet	2·50	2·50
F69		25 c. reddish brown	3·50	3·50
F70		30 c. blue	3·50	3·50
F71		40 c. grey-olive	3·50	3·50
F72		50 c. purple	3·50	3·50

F73	F **8**	1 f. lake/*pale green*	3·75	3·75
F74		2 f. blue/*pale green*	3·75	3·75
F75		5 f. red/*yellow*	5·00	5·00
F76		10 f. violet/*blue*	6·50	6·50
F65/76		*Set of* 12	38·00	38·00

(*b*) *POSTAGE DUE* (*Nos.* FD65/9)

FD77	F **8**	5 c. blue-green	2·25	2·00
FD78		10 c. orange	2·25	2·00
FD79		20 c. scarlet	2·25	2·00
FD80		40 c. grey-olive	2·25	2·00
FD81		1 f. lake/*pale green*	2·25	2·00
FD77/81		*Set of* 5	10·00	9·00

(Recess Waterlow)

1949 (10 Oct). *75th Anniv of U.P.U. Wmk "R F" in sheet or without wmk. P* 13½.

F77	F **10**	10 c. red-orange	50	50
F78		15 c. violet	75	75
F79		30 c. ultramarine	1·00	1·00
F80		50 c. purple	1·60	1·60
F77/80		*Set of* 4	3·50	3·50

NOUVELLES HEBRIDES   **TIMBRE-TAXE**

F **11** Outrigger Sailing Canoes   (FD **12**)

(Des C. Hertenberger (1 f. to 5 f.), R. Serres (others). Recess Waterlow)

1953 (30 Apr). *Type* F **11** *and similar horiz designs. Wmk "R F" in sheet or without wmk. P* 12½.

F81	F **11**	5 c. green	5	5
F82		10 c. scarlet	12	12
F83		15 c. yellow-ochre	15	15
F84		20 c. ultramarine	30	30
F85	—	25 c. olive	30	30
F86	—	30 c. brown	55	55
F87	—	40 c. blackish brown	55	55
F88	—	50 c. violet	55	55
F89	—	1 f. orange	1·25	1·25
F90	—	2 f. reddish purple	3·75	3·75
F91	—	5 f. scarlet	5·00	5·00
F81/91		*Set of* 11	11·00	11·00

Designs:—25 c. to 50 c. Native carving; 1 f. to 5 f. Two natives outside dwelling.

1953 (30 Apr). *POSTAGE DUE. Optd with Type* FD **12**, *by Waterlow.*

FD92	F **11**	5 c. green	12	12
FD93		10 c. scarlet	15	15
FD94		20 c. ultramarine	30	30
FD95	—	40 c. blackish brown	75	75
FD96	—	1 f. orange	1·75	1·75
FD92/96		*Set of* 5	2·75	2·75

F **12** Quirós' Caravel and Map   F **13** Port Vila: Iririki Islet

(Photo Harrison)

1956 (20 Oct). *Fiftieth Anniv of Condominium. Type* F **12** *and similar horiz design inscr* "1906 1956". *Wmk "R F" in sheet or without wmk. P* 14½×14.

F92	F **12**	5 c. emerald	45	45
F93		10 c. scarlet	45	45
F94	—	20 c. deep bright blue	50	50
F95	—	50 c. deep lilac	1·60	1·60
F92/95		*Set of* 4	2·75	2·75

Design:—20 c., 50 c. "Marianne", "talking drum" and "Britannia".

(Des H. Cheffer (5 c. to 20 c.), P. Gandon (others). Recess Waterlow)

1957 (3 Sept). *Type F 13 and similar horiz designs.* Wmk "R F" *in sheet or without wmk. P* 13½.

F 96	F 13	5 c. green	..	..	8	8
F 97		10 c. scarlet	..	..	12	12
F 98		15 c. orange-yellow	..	..	25	25
F 99		20 c. ultramarine	..	..	25	25
F100	—	25 c. yellow-olive	..	..	25	25
F101	—	30 c. brown	..	..	50	50
F102	—	40 c. sepia	..	..	50	50
F103	—	50 c. reddish violet	..	..	55	55
F104	—	1 f. red-orange	..	..	1·25	1·25
F105	—	2 f. mauve	..	..	3·25	3·25
F106	—	5 f. black	..	..	3·75	3·75
F96/106		*Set of* 11	..	..	10·00	10·00

Designs:—25 c. to 50 c. River scene and spear fisherman; 1 f. to 5 f. Woman drinking from coconut.

1957 (3 Sept). *POSTAGE DUE. Optd with Type FD* **12**, *by Waterlow.*

FD107	F 13	5 c. green	..	..	12	12
FD108		10 c. scarlet	..	..	20	20
FD109		20 c. ultramarine	..	..	25	25
FD110	—	40 c. sepia	..	..	50	50
FD111	—	1 f. red-orange	..	..	2·10	2·10
FD107/111		*Set of* 5	..	..	3·00	3·00

1963 (2 Sept). *Freedom from Hunger. As T* **51** *of New Caledonia.*

F107	60 c. deep bluish green and chestnut	..	1·00	1·00

1963 (2 Sept). *Red Cross Centenary. As T* **53** *of New Caledonia.*

F108	15 c. red, grey and orange	..	40	40
F109	45 c. red, grey and yellow-bistre	..	75	75

F **16** Copra

(Des V. Whiteley, from drawings by J. White (10 c., 20 c.), K. Penny (40 c., 60 c.), C. Robin (3 f.); photo Harrison. Des C. Robin (5 c., 1 f.), J. White (15 c.), G. Vasarhelyi (25 c., 5 f.), Larkins, Turrell and Thoma (30 c., 50 c., 2 f.); recess Govt Ptg Wks, Paris)

1963 (25 Nov)–**72.** *Type F* **16** *and similar horiz designs. Sizes vary slightly. No wmk. P* 12½ (10, 20, 40, 60 c.), 14 (3 f.) *or* 13 (*others*).

F110	5 c. lake, purple-brown and greenish blue (15.8.66)	..	15	15
	a. lake and greenish blue (29.2.72)	..	25	25
F111	10 c. lt brown, buff & emerald* (16.8.65)	55	45
F112	10 c. lt brown, buff & emerald (5.8.68)	10	10
F113	15 c. yellow-bistre, red-brown & dp vio	20	20
F114	20 c. black, olive-green and greenish blue* (16.8.65)	..	1·10	80
F115	20 c. blk, ol-grn & greenish bl (5.8.68)	..	15	15

F116	25 c. reddish violet, orange-brown and crimson (15.8.66)	..	..	40	40
F117	30 c. chestnut, bistre and violet	..	..	40	40
F118	40 c. vermilion and deep blue* (16.8.65)	1·75	1·25
F119	50 c. green, yellow and greenish blue	..	50	50
F120	60 c. vermilion and deep blue (5.12.67)	40	40
F121	1 f. red, blk & dp bluish green (15.8.66)	90	75
F122	2 f. black, brown-purple & yellow olive	1·90	1·90
F123	3 f. multicoloured* (16.8.65)	..	..	5·00	3·25
F124	3 f. multicoloured (5.8.68)	..	..	1·60	1·60
F125	5 f. blue, deep blue & black (24.1.67)	..	3·25	3·25
F110/125	*Set of* 16	..	..	16·00	13·00

Designs:—5 c. Exporting manganese, Forari; 10 c. Cocoa beans; 20 c. Fishing from Palikulo Point; 25 c. Picasso fish; 30 c. Nautilus shell; 40 c., 60 c. Stingfish; 50 c. Blue Lined surgeon; 1 f Cardinal honey-eater (bird); 2 f. Buff-bellied flycatcher; 3 f. Thicket warbler; 5 f. White-collared kingfisher.

*Normally all French New Hebrides issues have the "RF" inscription on the right to distinguish them from the British New Hebrides stamps which have it on the left. The stamps indicated by an asterisk have "RF" wrongly placed on the left.

1965 (17 May). *I.T.U. Centenary. As T* **56** *of New Caledonia.*

F126	15 c. blue, emerald and red-brown	..	75	50
F127	60 c. cerise, slate and deep bluish green	1·60	1·40

F **17** I.C.Y. Emblem

(Des V. Whiteley. Litho Harrison)

1965 (24 Oct). *International Co-operation Year. P* 14½.

F128	F 17	5 c. dp reddish purple & turq-grn	12	12
F129		55 c. deep bluish green and lavender	50	50

F **18** Sir Winston Churchill and St. Paul's Cathedral in Wartime

(Des Jennifer Toombs. Photo Harrison)

1966 (24 Jan). *Churchill Commemoration. P* 14.

F130	F 18	5 c. black, cerise, gold & new blue	25	20
F131		15 c. black, cerise, gold & dp green	30	25
F132		25 c. black, cerise, gold and brown	40	40
F133		30 c. black, cerise, gold & bluish vio	55	40
F130/133		*Set of* 4	..	..	1·40	1·10

PUZZLED?

Then you need
PHILATELIC TERMS ILLUSTRATED
to tell you all you need to know about printing methods, papers, errors, varieties, watermarks, perforations, etc. 192 pages, almost half in full colour, soft cover. £1·95 post paid.

F **19** Footballer's Legs, Ball and Jules Rimet Cup

(Des V. Whiteley. Litho Harrison)

1966 (1 July). *World Cup Football Championships.* P 14.
F134 F **19** 20 c. violet, yell-grn, lake & yell-brn   25   25
F135   40 c. choc, bl-grn, lake & yell-brn   40   40

F **20** W.H.O. Building

(Des M. Goaman. Litho Harrison)

1966 (20 Sept). *Inauguration of W.H.O. Headquarters, Geneva.* P 14.
F136 F **20** 25 c. black, yellow-green & lt blue   25   25
F137   60 c. black, mauve & yellow-ochre   45   45

F **21** "Education"

(Des Jennifer Toombs. Litho Harrison)

1968 (1 Dec). *20th Anniv of U.N.E.S.C.O. Type F **21** and similar horiz designs.* P 14.
F138   15 c. slate-violet, red, yellow and orange   20   20
F139   30 c. orange-yellow, violet & deep olive   25   25
F140   45 c. black, bright purple and orange . .   30   30
Designs:—30 c. Globe in retort and ears of wheat ("Science"); 45 c. Lyre and columns ("Culture").

F **22** The Coast Watchers

(Des R. Granger Barrett. Photo Enschedé)

1967 (26 Sept). *25th Anniv of the Pacific War. Type F **22** and similar horiz designs. Multicoloured.* P 14×13.
F141   15 c. Type F **22**   20   20
F142   25 c. War Zone map, U.S. marine and
             Australian soldier   30   30
F143   60 c. H.M.A.S. *Canberra*   55   55
F144   1 f. "Flying Fortress"   75   75
F141/144   *Set of 4* . .   . .   . .   2·00   2·00

HAVE YOU READ THE NOTES AT THE BEGINNING OF THIS CATALOGUE?
These often provide answers to the enquiries we receive.

F **23** Globe and Hemispheres   F **24** "Concorde" and
                                                        Vapour Trails

(Des and eng J. Combet. Recess Govt Ptg Wks, Paris)

1968 (23 May). *Bicentenary of Bougainville's World Voyage. Type F **23** and similar horiz designs.* P 13.
F145   15 c. emerald, slate-violet and red   . .   12   12
F146   25 c. deep olive, maroon & ultramarine   25   25
F147   60 c. bistre-brown, brn-pur & myrtle-grn   45   45
Designs:—25 c. Ships *La Boudeuse* and *L'Etoile*, and map; 60 c. Bougainville, ship's figure-head and bougainvillaea flowers.

(Des S. W. Moss (25 c.), R. Granger Barrett (60 c.). Litho De La Rue)

1968 (9 Oct). *Anglo-French "Concorde" Project. Type F **24** and similar horiz design.* P 14.
F148   25 c. lt blue, orange-red & dp violet-blue   1·60   1·25
F149   60 c. red, black and bright blue   . .   2·75   2·50
Design:—60 c. "Concorde" in flight.

F **25** Kauri Pine   F **26** Relay Runner receiving
                                            Baton, and Flags

(Des V. Whiteley. Litho Format International)

1969 (30 June). *Timber Industry.* P 14½.
F150 F **25** 20 c. multicoloured (*shades*)   . .   20   20
No. F150 was issued in small sheets of 9 (3×3) and is printed on a simulated wood-grain background. The sheet margins show various aspects of the timber industry.

(Des C. Haley. Photo Delrieu)

1969 (13 Aug). *3rd South Pacific Games, Port Moresby, Papua New Guinea. Type F **26** and similar horiz design. Multicoloured.* P 12½.
F151   25 c. Type F **26**   20   20
F152   1 f. Runner passing baton, and flags . .   70   65

F **27** Diver on Platform   F **28** New U.P.U. Building, Berne

(Des V. Whiteley. Litho Perkins, Bacon Ltd)

1969 (15 Oct). *Land Divers of Pentecost Island. Type F 27 and similar vert designs. Multicoloured. P 12½.*

F153	15 c. Type F **27**		20	20
F154	25 c. Diver jumping		30	30
F155	1 f. Diver at end of fall		1·25	1·25

(Des and eng J. Gauthier. Recess Govt Ptg Works, Paris)

1970 (20 May). *Inauguration of New U.P.U. Headquarters Building, Berne. P 13.*

F156	F **28** 1 f. 05, slate, red-orange & brt pur	65	65

F **29** General de Gaulle

(F **30**)

F **31** "The Virgin and Child" (G.Bellini)

(Des V. Whiteley. Photo Govt Ptg Works, Paris)

1970 (20 July). *30th Anniv of New Hebrides' Declaration for the Free French Government. P 13.*

F157	F **29** 65 c. multicoloured	55	55
F158	1 f. 10, multicoloured	1·10	1·10

1970 (15 Oct). *No. F115 surch with Type F 30.*

F159	35 c. on 20 c. blk, ol-grn & greenish bl	25	25

(Des V. Whiteley. Litho Harrison)

1970 (30 Nov). *Christmas. Type F 31 and similar vert painting. Multicoloured. P 14½×14.*

F160	15 c. Type F **31**	15	12
F161	50 c. "The Virgin and Child" (G. Cima)	45	40

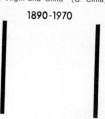

1890-1970

IN MEMORIAM
9-11-70

(F **32**)

1971 (19 Jan). *Death of General Charles de Gaulle. Nos. F157/8 optd with Type F 32, the vertical bars in black and inscriptions in gold.*

F162	F **29** 65 c. multicoloured	45	40
	a. Gold opt omitted		
F163	1 f. 10, multicoloured	1·10	90

On No. F162a the vertical black bars are still present.

ALBUM LISTS

Write for our latest lists of albums
and accessories.
These will be sent free on request.

CONDOMINIUM DES NOUVELLES-HEBRIDES

4ᵉ JEUX DU PACIFIQUE SUD - FOOTBALL

F **33** Football

(Des G. Bétemps. Photo Delrieu)

1971 (13 July). *4th South Pacific Games, Papeete, French Polynesia. Type F 33 and similar multicoloured design. P 12½.*

F164	20 c. Type F **33**	20	15
F165	65 c. Basketball (*vert*)	50	45

F **34** Kauri Pine, Cone and Arms of Royal Society

F **35** "Adoration of the Shepherds" (Louis le Nain)

(Des P. B. Powell. Litho Harrison)

1971 (7 Sept). *Royal Society Expedition to New Hebrides. P.14½×14.*

F166	F **34** 65 c. multicoloured	40	30

(Des G. Drummond. Litho Questa)

1971 (23 Nov). *Christmas. Type F 35 and similar vert design. Multicoloured. P 14×13½.*

F167	25 c. Type F **35**	25	20
F168	50 c. "Adoration of the Shepherds" (J. Tintoretto)	40	30

F **36** "Drover" Mk III Aircraft

(Des M. Goaman. Photo Delrieu)

1972 (29 Feb). *Aircraft. Type F 36 and similar horiz designs. Multicoloured. P 13.*

F169	20 c. Type F **36**	20	15
F170	25 c. "Sandringham" flying-boat	25	20
F171	30 c. DH "Dragon Rapide"	25	20
F172	65 c. "Caravelle"	45	40
F169/172	Set of 4	1·25	85

F 40 *Dendrobium teretifolium*   F 41 New Wharf from the Air

F 37 Ceremonial Headdress, South Malekula

F 38 "Adoration of the Magi" (Spranger)

(Des Jennifer Toombs. Litho Questa)

(Des Baillais (10, 20, 35 c., 2 f.), P. Lambert (others). Photo Govt Ptg Works, Paris)

1972 (24 July). *Type F 37 and similar vert designs. Multicoloured. P 12½×13.*

F173	5 c. Type F 37		5	5
F174	10 c. Baker's pigeon		10	10
F175	15 c. Drum and sculpture, North Ambrym		12	12
F176	20 c. Royal parrot-finch		15	15
F177	25 c. *Cribraria fischeri* (shell)		20	20
F178	30 c. *Oliva rubrolabiata* (shell)		25	20
F179	35 c. Chestnut-bellied kingfisher		30	25
F180	65 c. *Strombus plicatus* (shell)		50	40
F181	1 f. Drum, North Malekula, and sculpture, North Ambrym		80	65
F182	2 f. Green palm lorikeet		1·60	1·10
F183	3 f. Ceremonial headdress, South Malekula (*different*)		2·25	2·00
F184	5 f. *Turbo marmoratus* (shell)		5·00	3·75
F173/184	Set of 12		10·00	8·00

(Des G. Drummond. Litho J. Waddington Ltd)

1972 (25 Sept). *Christmas. Type F 38 and similar vert painting. Multicoloured. P 14.*

F185	25 c. Type F 38		20	15
F186	70 c. "Virgin and Child" (Provoost)		40	30

F 39 Queen Elizabeth II and Duke of Edinburgh

Multiple St. Edward's Crown CA

(Des and photo Harrison)

1972 (20 Nov). *Royal Silver Wedding. Wmk Mult St. Edward's Crown CA. P 14×14½.*

F187	F 39	35 c. multicoloured		25	20
F188		65 c. multicoloured		45	30

PUZZLED?

Then you need
PHILATELIC TERMS ILLUSTRATED
to tell you all you need to know about printing
methods, papers, errors, varieties, watermarks,
perforations, etc. 192 pages, almost half in full
colour, soft cover. £1·95 post paid.

1973 (26 Feb). *Orchids. Type F 40 and similar vert designs. Multicoloured. P 14×14½.*

F189	25 c. Type F 40		15	15
F190	30 c. *Ephemerantha comata*		20	15
F191	35 c. *Spathoglottis petri*		30	25
F192	65 c. *Dendrobium mohlianum*		40	30
F189/192	Set of 4		95	75

(Des PAD Studio. Litho Questa)

1973 (14 May). *Opening of New Wharf, Vila. Type F 41 and similar multicoloured design. P 14×14½ (25 c.) or 14½×14 (70 c.).*

F193	25 c. Type F 41		20	15
F194	70 c. View of wharf (*horiz*)		45	30

F 42 Wild Horses

(Des P. Lambert. Photo Govt Ptg Works, Paris)

1973 (13 Aug). *Tanna Island. Type F 42 and similar horiz design. Multicoloured. P 13×12½.*

F195	35 c. Type F 42		25	15
F196	70 c. Yasur Volcano		40	30

F 43 Mother and Child   F 44 Pacific Dove

(Des M. Moutouh (35 c.), T. d'Avesnières (70 c.). Adapted PAD Studio. Litho Questa)

1973 (19 Nov). *Christmas. Type F 43 and similar vert design. Multicoloured. P 14×13½.*

F197	35 c. Type F 43		25	20
F198	70 c. Lagoon and star		45	40

(Des J. & H. Bregulla. Photo Govt Ptg Works, Paris)

1974 (11 Feb). *Wild Life. Type* F **44** *and similar horiz designs. Multicoloured. P* 13×12½.
F199   25 c. Type F **44**   15   12
F200   35 c. Night Swallowtail (butterfly)   20   20
F201   70 c. Green sea turtle   40   35
F202   1 f. 15, Flying fox   65   55
F199/202   *Set of 4*   1·25   1·10

(Des P. Lambert. Photo Govt Ptg Wks, Paris)

1974 (9 Oct).   *Centenary of Universal Postal Union. P* 13×12½.
F210*a* F **48** 70 c. dp turquoise-bl, rosine & blk   40   40

(Des J. Cooter. Litho Questa)

1974 (4 Nov). *Christmas. Type* F **49** *and similar multicoloured design. P* 14×13½ (35 c.) *or* 13½×14 (70 c.).
F211   35 c. Type **49**   20   15
F212   70 c. "The Nativity" (G. van Honthorst)
          (*horiz*)   40   35

VISITE ROYALE
1974

(F **45**)   F **46** Old Post Office

1974 (11 Feb). *Royal Visit of Queen Elizabeth II. Nos.* F179 *and* F182 *optd with Type* F **45**.
F203   35 c. multicoloured (R.)   25   20
F204   2 f. multicoloured   1·25   1·10

(Des O. Baillais. Photo Govt Ptg Works, Paris)

1974 (6 May). *Inauguration of New Post Office, Vila. Type* F **46** *and similar triangular design. Multicoloured. P* 12.
F205   35 c. Type F **46**   25   20
F206   70 c. New Post Office   45   40
Nos. F205/6 were issued in *se-tenant* pairs within the sheet.

F **50** Charolais Bull   F **51** Canoeing

(Des and eng J. Pheulpin. Recess Govt Ptg Wks, Paris)

1975 (29 Apr). *P* 13×12½.
F213 F **50** 10 f. bistre-brown, yellow-grn & bl   5·00   3·50

(Des J. Cooter. Litho Questa)

1975 (5 Aug). *"Nordjamb 75" World Scout Jamboree, Norway. Type* F **51** *and similar vert designs. Multicoloured. P* 14×13½.
F214   25 c. Type F **51**   20   12
F215   35 c. Preparing meal   25   20
F216   1 f. Map-reading   55   45
F217   5 f. Fishing   2·50   1·90
F214/217   *Set of 4*   3·25   2·50

F **47** Captain Cook and Map of Tanna

(Des J. E. Cooter. Litho J. Waddington)

1974 (1 Aug). *Bicentenary of Rediscovery of New Hebrides by Captain Cook. Type* F **47** *and similar multicoloured designs. P* 11 (1 f. 15) *or* 13×13½ (*others*).
F207   35 c. Type F **47**   20   20
F208   35 c. William Wales and beach landing   20   20
F209   35 c. William Hodges and island scene   20   20
F210   1 f. 15, Capt. Cook, *Resolution* and
          map of islands (64×39 *mm*)   60   50
F207/210   *Set of 4*   1·10   1·00
Nos. F207/9 were issued together *se-tenant* in horizontal strips of three within the sheet, each strip forming a composite design.

F **52** "Pitti Madonna"   F **53** "Concorde" in
                                "Air France" Livery

(Des PAD Studio. Litho Harrison)

1975 (11 Nov). *Christmas. Type* F **52** *and similar vert designs. Multicoloured. P* 14½×14.
F218   35 c. Type F **52**   25   20
F219   70 c. "Bruges Madonna"   45   40
F220   2 f. 50, "Taddei Madonna"   1·40   1·10

(Des J. Chesnot. Typo Edila)

F **48** U.P.U. Emblem   F **49** "Adoration of the Magi"
    and Letters   (Velázquez)

1976 (30 Jan). *First Commercial Flight of "Concorde". P* 13.
F221 F **53** 5 f. multicoloured   2·50   2·25

F 54 Early and Modern Telephones   F 55 Map of the Islands

(Des J. Gauthier. Photo Delrieu)

1976 (31 Mar). *Telephone Centenary. Type* F **54** *and similar vert designs. Multicoloured.* P 13½.
F222	25 c. Type F **54**			15	12
F223	70 c. Alexander Graham Bell			30	20
F224	1 f. 15, Earth Station, Nouméa, New Caledonia			55	40

(Des O. Baillais. Photo)

1976 (29 June). *Constitutional Changes. Type* F **55** *and similar multicoloured designs.* P 13 (25 c.) *or* 13×12½ (*others*).
F225	25 c. Type F **55**			15	12
F226	1 f. View of Luganville (36×27 *mm*)		45	35
F227	2 f. View of Port-Vila (36×27 *mm*)		1·10	65

Nos. F226/7 exist with the inscription "PREMIERE ASSEMBLEE REPRESENTATIVE 1975" and the name of the city. These stamps were not available in the New Hebrides.

F 56 "The Flight into Egypt"   F 57 Royal Visit of 1974

(Des J. Cooter. Litho Walsall Security Printers Ltd)

1976 (8 Nov). *Christmas. Type* F **56** *and similar vert designs. Multicoloured.* P 13½.
F228	35 c. Type F **56**			20	12
F229	70 c. "Adoration of the Shepherds"		35	25
F230	2 f. 50, "Adoration of the Magi"		1·25	1·00

(Des BG Studio. Litho Walsall Security Printers Ltd)

1977 (7 Feb). *Silver Jubilee of Queen Elizabeth II. Type* F **57** *and similar vert designs. Multicoloured.* P 13½.
F231	35 c. Type F **57**			20	12
F232	70 c. Imperial State Crown			40	25
F233	2 f. The Blessing at the Coronation, 1953			1·00	75

25
FNH

(F 58)

1977 (1 July). *Currency Change. Nos.* F173/184 *and* F214 *surch as Type* F **58** *or with bars and "FNH" (Nos.* F234/237).
F234	5 f. on 5 c. Type F **37**			5	5
F235	10 f. on 10 c. Baker's pigeon			12	12
F236	15 f. on 15 c. Drum and sculpture, North Ambrym			20	20
F237	20 f. on 20 c. Royal parrot-finch			30	30
F238	25 f. on 25 c. *Cribraria fischeri* (shell)			40	40
F239	30 f. on 30 c. *Oliva rubrolabiata* (shell)			45	45
F240	35 f. on 35 c. Chestnut-bellied kingfisher			55	55
F241	40 f. on 65 c. *Strombus plicatus* (shell)			65	65
F242	50 f. on 1 f. Drum, North Malekula, and sculpture, North Ambrym			90	90
F243	70 f. on 2 f. Green palm lorikeet			1·25	1·25
F244	100 f. on 3 f. Ceremonial headdress, South Malekula			1·75	1·75
F245	200 f. on 5 f. *Turbo marmoratus* (shell)			3·50	3·50
F246	500 f. on 10 f. Type F **50**			9·00	9·00
F234/246	*Set of 13*			17·00	17·00

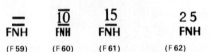

10   15   25
FNH   FNH   FNH

(F 59)   (F 60)   (F 61)   (F 62)

1977 (18 July–14 Sept). *Nos.* F173/175, F177/180, F184 *and* F213 *surch by I.P.V., Port Vila, in typography with Type* F **59/62** *or similar surcharges.*
F247	5 f. on 5 c. Type F **37** (10.8)		12	12
F248	10 f. on 10 c. Baker's pigeon (20.7)		25	25
F249	15 f. on 15 c. Drum and carving (18.7)		40	40
	a. Short bar in surcharge (5.8)			
F250	25 f. on 25 c. *Cribraria fischeri* (shell) (10.9)		80	80
	a. "FHN" for "FNH"			
F251	30 f. on 30 c. *Oliva rubrolabiata* (shell) (10.9)		90	90
	a. "FHN" for "FNH"			
F252	35 f. on 35 c. Chestnut-bellied kingfisher (10.9)		1·10	1·10
	a. "NH" for "FNH"			
F253	40 f. on 65 c. *Strombus plicatus* (shell) (12.9)		1·40	1·40
F254	200 f. on 5 f. *Turbo marmoratus* (shell) (22.8)		6·50	6·50
F255	500 f. on 10 f. Type F **50** (14.9)		11·00	11·00
F247/255	*Set of 9*		20·00	20·00

Dates are those on which the various values were surcharged.

F 63 Erromango and Kauri Pine

(Des L. D. Curtis. Litho Questa. (5, 20, 25, 50, 100, 200 f.) or J. W. (others))

1977 (7 Sept)–**78**. *Maps of the Islands. Type* F **63** *and similar vert designs. Multicoloured. P* 13½ × 13 (10 *f.*, 30 *f.*, 40 *f.*) *or* 14 (*others*).

F256	5 f. Type F **63**		5	5
F257	10 f. New Hebrides archipelago and copra industry (9.5.78)		15	12
F258	15 f. Espiritu Santo and cattle (23.11.77)		20	15
F259	20 f. Vate and Vila Post Office		30	20
F260	25 f. Malakula and headdresses (23.11.77)		40	25
F261	30 f. Aoba, Maewo and pig's tusks (23.11.77)		45	30
F262	35 f. Pentecost Islands and land divers (9.5.78)		55	40
F263	40 f. Tanna, Aniwa and volcano (23.11.77)		65	45
F264	50 f. Shepherd Islands and canoe ..		75	55
F265	70 f. Banks Islands and dancers (9.5.78)		1·10	75
F266	100 f. Ambrym and carvings		1·75	1·10
F267	200 f. Anatom and baskets		3·25	2·25
F268	500 f. Torres Islands and fishing with bow and arrow (9.5.78)		7·50	6·00
F256/268	Set of 13		15·00	11·00

F **64** "Madonna Tempi" (Raphael)

F **65** "Concorde" over New York

(Des J. W. Studio. Litho Cartor)

1977 (8 Dec). *Christmas. Type* F **64** *and similar vert designs. Multicoloured. P* 12.

F269	10 f. Type F **64**		15	12
F270	15 f. "The Flight into Egypt" (G. David)		20	15
F271	30 f. "Virgin and Child" (Pompeo Batoni)		45	40

(Des BG Studio. Litho Bruder Rosenbaum, Vienna)

1978 (9 May). *"Concorde". Type* F **65** *and similar horiz designs. Multicoloured. P* 13½.

F272	10 f. Type F **65**		15	12
F273	20 f. "Concorde" over London		30	25
F274	30 f. "Concorde" over Washington ..		45	40
F275	40 f. "Concorde" over Paris		65	50
F272/275	Set of 4		1·40	1·10

F **66** White Horse of Hanover

F **67** "Madonna and Child"

(Des Jennifer Toombs. Litho Questa)

1978 (2 June). *25th Anniv of Coronation. Type* F **66** *and similar vert designs. P* 15.

F276	40 f. sepia, turquoise-blue and silver ..		70	70
F277	40 f. multicoloured		70	70
F278	40 f. sepia, turquoise-blue and silver ..		70	70
	a. Sheetlet. Nos. F276/278 × 2 ..		4·20	

Designs:–No. F 277, Queen Elizabeth II : No. F 278, Gallic Cock. Nos. F276/278 were printed together in small sheets of 6, containing two se-tenant strips of 3, with horizontal gutter margin between.

(Des C. Abbott. Litho Questa)

1978 (1 Dec). *Christmas. Type* F **67** *and similar vert designs showing paintings by Dürer. Multicoloured. P* 14 × 13½.

F279	10 f. Type F **67**		15	12
F280	15 f. "The Virgin and Child with St. Anne"		20	15
F281	30 f. "The Madonna with the Goldfinch"		45	40
F282	40 f. "The Madonna with the Child" ..		65	50
F279/282	Set of 4		1·25	1·10

stamp monthly

Gibbons' own monthly magazine, essential reading for **every** collector !

Detailed monthly New Issue Guide to update all Gibbons catalogues for you—and a special Stamp Market feature on price changes.

Informative articles cover all facets of philately, with regular notes on new discoveries, stamp designs, postmarks, market trends and news and views of the world of stamps. Britain's LARGEST circulation of any stamp magazine— that fact speaks for itself !

Monthly from all dealers and newsagents or by post direct from Stanley Gibbons Magazines Ltd—subscription rates on application.

Niger

100 Centimes = 1 Franc

The first Europeans to enter the thinly-populated area south of the Sahara desert which is now the Niger Republic were the German explorer Hornemann in 1801 and the Scotsman Mungo Park. In 1805 the latter went down the R. Niger as far as Busso in Nigeria, where he was drowned. The area was then part of the Moslem kingdom of Sokoto. French explorers followed and by an Anglo-French Convention of 5 April 1890 the territory north of a line from Say on the Niger to Barroua on Lake Chad became a French zone of influence. The border with British territory in Nigeria was altered and defined in 1899 and 1904. On 23 July 1900 the Niger Military Territory was formed and in 1904 this was incorporated in French West Africa.

Stamps of French Sudan were used from 1894 to 1903, stamps of Senegambia and Niger from 1903 to 1906 and of Upper Senegal and Niger from 1906 to 1919; all are listed under French Sudan. The area became the Niger Territory on 4 December 1920 and the Niger Colony on 13 October 1922.

PRINTERS. All stamps were printed at the Government Printing Works, Paris, *unless otherwise stated.*

IMPERFORATE STAMPS. Stamps exist imperforate in their issued colours, but they were not valid for postage. Imperforate stamps in other colours are colour trials.

A. FRENCH TERRITORY

TERRITOIRE

DU NIGER

(1)

Type **7** of Upper
Senegal and Niger

1921 (Dec). *Type 7 of Upper Senegal and Niger optd with T 1.*
1	1 c. violet and grey-purple				5	5
2	2 c. grey-purple and grey				5	5
3	4 c. blue and black				5	5
4	5 c. chocolate and brown				5	5
	a. Surch omitted				19·00	19·00
5	10 c. green and yellow-green				20	20
6	15 c. orange-yellow and chocolate				5	5
7	20 c. black and grey-purple				5	5
8	25 c. green and black				5	5
9	30 c. carmine and red				12	12
10	35 c. violet and carmine				5	5
11	40 c. carmine and grey				10	10
12	45 c. yellow-brown and blue				10	10
13	50 c. blue and ultramarine				10	10
14	75 c. brown and orange-yellow				15	15
15	1 f. grey-purple and brown				15	15
16	2 f. blue and green				20	20
17	5 f. black and violet				40	40
1/17	*Set of 17*				1·75	1·75

See also Nos. 25/8.

TERRITOIRE

=

DU NIGER

$1^f 25$

Type D **9** of
Upper Senegal
and Niger

(D 1)

(2)

1921 (Dec). *POSTAGE DUE. Type D 9 of Upper Senegal and Niger optd with Type D 1.*
D18	5 c. green				12	12
D19	10 c. carmine				12	12
D20	15 c. grey				15	15
D21	20 c. brown				15	15
D22	30 c. blue				15	15
D23	50 c. black				20	20
D24	60 c. orange				30	30
D25	1 f. violet				35	35
D18/25	*Set of 8*				1·40	1·40

1922 (28 Sept)–**26**. *Stamps of* 1921 *surch as T* **2.**
18	25 c. on 15 c. orge-yell & choc (1.2.25)				5	5
	a. Surch inverted			19·00		
	b. Surch triple			22·00		
	c. Surch quintuple			19·00		
19	25 c. on 2 f. blue and green (R.) (6.24)				5	5
20	25 c. on 5 f. black and violet (R.) (6.24)				5	5
	a. Surch double			19·00		
21	60 on 75 c. violet/*rose*				5	5
22	65 on 45 c. yellow-brown & bl (1.2.25)				35	35
23	85 on 75 c. brown & orge-yell (1.2.25)				35	35
24	1 f. 25 on 1 f. p bl & bl (R.) (14.6.25)				5	5
	a. Surch omitted			32·00		
18/24	*Set of 7*				85	85

The new face value appears twice on Nos. 21/3.

B. FRENCH COLONY

1925 (1 Dec)–**26**. *As 1921. Colours changed and new value.*
25	10 c. rose/*azure* (1.2.26)				5	5
26	30 c. orange-vermilion and blue-green				5	5
27	50 c. ultramarine and grey				8	8
28	60 c. red (17.5.26)				12	12
25/28	*Set of 4*				25	25

3 Wells

5 Zinder Fort

4 Native Craft on the Niger

D 6 Zinder Fort

(Des J. Kerhor. Eng A. Mignon (**3**), G. Daussy (**4**) and A. Delzers (**5**). Typo)

1926 (29 Nov)–**40**. *P* $13\frac{1}{2} \times 14$ (*vert*) *or* $14 \times 13\frac{1}{2}$ (*horiz*).
29	3	1 c. olive and purple			5	5
30		2 c. carmine and slate-grey			5	5
31		3 c. chocolate and magenta (1940)			5	5

32 **3**	4 c. black and yellow-brown	..		5	5
33	5 c. yellow-green and vermilion		..	8	8
34	10 c. blue-green and blue	..		5	5
35	15 c. yellow-green and green	..		5	5
36	15 c. vermilion and lilac (30.4.28)	..		8	8
37 **4**	20 c. brown and greenish blue	..		5	5
38	25 c. rose and black	..		5	5
39	30 c. yellow-green and blue-green	..		10	8
40	30 c. magenta and yellow (1940)			5	5
41	35 c. blue and red/*bluish*			5	5
42	35 c. blue-green & dp blue-grn (16.5.38)			5	5
43	40 c. slate and claret	..		5	5
44	45 c. magenta and yellow			12	12
45	45 c. green and blue-green (1940)			5	5
46	50 c. green and scarlet/*greenish*			5	5
47	55 c. brown and rosine (16.5.38)			12	12
48	60 c. chocolate and carmine (1940)			5	5
49	65 c. rosine and sage-green	..		5	5
50	70 c. carmine and olive-green (1940)	..		15	15
51	75 c. magenta and blue-green/*rose*			20	20
	a. Double impression of centre & value	22·00			
52	80 c. green and claret (16.5.38)	..		20	20
53	90 c. red and carmine	..		12	10
54	90 c. yellow-green and carmine (1939)	..		15	15
55 **5**	1 f. yellow-green and rosine	..		1·60	1·10
56	1 f. orange and brown-red (5.12.38)	..		15	12
57	1 f. scarlet and blue-green (1940)	..		5	5
58	1 f. 10, yellow-green and brown	..		65	55
59	1 f. 25, scarlet and green (25.9.33)	..		20	20
60	1 f. 25, orange and brown-red (1939)			5	5
61	1 f. 40, chocolate and magenta (1940)			5	5
62	1 f. 50, light blue and blue	..		5	5
63	1 f. 60, yellow-green and brown (1940)			15	15
64	1 f. 75, chocolate & magenta (25.9.33)			45	45
65	1 f. 75, ultramarine and blue (5.12.38)			12	12
66	2 f. brown and orange	..		5	5
67	2 f. 25, ultramarine and blue (1939)	..		8	8
68	2 f. 50, black-brown (1940)	..		10	10
69	3 f. slate and mauve (19.12.27)	..		8	8
70	5 f. black and plum/*rose*	..		10	10
71	10 f. magenta and lilac	..		20	20
72	20 f. orange and yellow-green	..		30	30
29/72	*Set of 44*	..	..	5·50	5·00

(Des J. Kerhor. Eng A. Delzers. Typo)

1927 (28 Feb). *POSTAGE DUE. P 14×13½.*

D73 **D 6**	2 c. rose and blue ..			5	5
D74	4 c. black and vermilion	..		5	5
D75	5 c. violet and orange	..		5	5
D76	10 c. deep violet and claret ..			8	8
D77	15 c. orange and green	..		10	10
D78	20 c. sepia and rosine	..		12	12
D79	25 c. sepia and olive-black	..		12	12
D80	30 c. slate and violet	..		25	25
D81	50 c. red/*greenish* ..			12	12
D82	60 c. orange and lilac/*bluish*	..		12	12
D83	1 f. ultramarine and blue/*bluish*	..		15	15
D84	2 f. mauve and red	..		15	15
D85	3 f. blue and yellow-brown	..		20	20
D73/85	*Set of 13*	..	..	1·40	1·40

1931 (13 Apr). *International Colonial Exhibition, Paris. As T 12/15 of Mauritania.*

73	40 c. green	..	..	1·00	90
74	50 c. mauve	..	..	1·00	90
75	90 c. vermilion	..	..	1·00	1·00
76	1 f. 50, blue	..	..	1·00	1·00
73/76	*Set of 4*	..	..	3·50	3·50

1937 (15 Apr). *International Exhibition, Paris. As T 16/21 of Mauritania.*

77	20 c. bright violet	..		20	20
78	30 c. green	..		20	20
79	40 c. carmine	..		20	20
80	50 c. brown	..		20	20
81	90 c. scarlet	..		20	20
82	1 f. blue	..		20	20
77/82	*Set of 6*	..		1·10	1·10
MS82a	120×100 mm. 3 f. magenta (as T 16).				
	Imperf	..	..	1·00	1·00

1938 (24 Oct). *International Anti-Cancer Fund. As T 22 of Mauritania.*

83	1 f. 75+50 c. ultramarine ..	..	..	4·00	4·00

1939 (5 Apr). *Death Centenary of R. Caillié. As T 27 of Mauritania.*

84	90 c. orange	..	..	15	15
85	2 f. violet	..	..	15	15
86	2 f. 25, blue	..	..	15	15

1939 (10 May). *New York World's Fair. As T 28 of Mauritania.*

87	1 f. 25, lake	..	..	20	20
88	2 f. 25, ultramarine	..	..	20	20

1939 (5 July). *150th Anniv of French Revolution. As T 29 of Mauritania.*

89	45 c.+25 c. green and black	..	..	1·40	1·40
90	70 c.+30 c. brown and black	..	..	1·40	1·40
91	90 c.+35 c. red-orange and black	..	..	1·40	1·40
92	1 f. 25+1 f. carmine and black ..	..		1·40	1·40
93	2 f. 25+2 f. blue and black	..	..	1·40	1·40
89/93	*Set of 5*	..	..	6·50	6·50

1940 (8 Feb). *AIR. As T 30 of Mauritania.*

94	1 f. 90, bright blue	..	..	8	·8
95	2 f. 90, rose-red	..	..	8	8
96	4 f. 50, green	..	..	30	30
97	4 f. 90, olive-bistre	..	..	15	15
98	6 f. 90, orange ..	..	..	15	15
94/98	*Set of 5*	..	..	65	65

VICHY ISSUES. Nos. 98a/e were issued by the Pétain government of unoccupied France. A number of other stamps exist, but we list only those which were available in Niger.

1941. *National Defence Fund. Surch as T 31 of Mauritania.*

98a **4**	+1 f. on 50 c. green and scarlet/*greenish*		12	12
98b	+2 f. on 80 c. green and claret	..		1·10	1·10
98c	+2 f. on 1 f. 50, light blue and blue	..		1·60	1·60
98d	+3 f. on 2 f. brown and orange	..		1·60	1·60
98a/d	*Set of 4*	..	..	4·00	4·00

1942 (19 Oct). *AIR. As T 32 of Mauritania.*

98e	50 f. carmine and greenish yellow	..	30	

From 1944 to 1959 the stamps of French West Africa were used in Niger.

C. AUTONOMOUS REPUBLIC
(within the French Community)

Niger became an autonomous republic on 18 December 1958.

7 Giraffes

6 Manatee (sea-cow)

9 Conseil de l'Entente Emblem

8 Red Bee-eater

(Des J. Combet (**6**), J. Houssin, P. Lambert (200 f.), R. Subert (others). Eng J. Combet (**6**), G. Bétemps (1 f. to 7 f.), A. Decaris (15 f. to 30 f.), R. Cami (50 f. to 100 f.), P. Gandon (200 f.), R. Cottet (500 f.). Recess)

1959–62. *P* 13.

(a) POSTAGE. T **6/7** *and similar designs*

99	**6**	50 c. dp turquoise, grn & blk (29.1.62)		5	5
100	–	1 f. yellow, deep blue, salmon-red and bronze-green (25.7.60)		5	5
101	–	2 f. yellow, salmon-red, blue and bronze-green (25.7.60)		5	5
102	–	5 f. magenta, blk & ol-brn (25.7.60)		8	5
103	–	7 f. red, blk & bronze-green (25.7.60)		10	5
104	**6**	10 f. deep green, blue-green, chestnut and black (29.1.62)		15	5
105	–	15 f. sepia & turquoise-blue (22.2.60)		20	5
106	–	20 f. black and violet (22.2.60)		25	5
107	**7**	25 f. choc, yell, bl & blk (18.12.59)		30	8
108	–	30 f. bistre-brown, yellow-bistre and emerald (22.2.60)		35	15
109	–	50 f. indigo and chestnut (25.7.60)		65	30
110	–	60 f. sepia and yellow-green (25.7.60)		75	45
111	–	85 f. orange-brn & brn-bist (25.7.60)		1·00	50
112	–	100 f. brown-bist & yell-grn (25.7.60)		1·25	65

(b) AIR. T **8** *and similar design*

113	**8**	200 f. red, purple, ultramarine & yellow-olive (18.12.61)	2·25	1·25
114	–	500 f. green, brown and blue (11.4.60)	5·00	2·50
99/114		*Set of* 16	11·00	5·50

Designs: *Vert as T* **7**—1 f., 2 f. Crowned cranes; 5 f., 7 f. Jabirus; 15 f., 20 f. Mountain sheep; 50 f., 60 f. Ostriches; 85 f., 100 f. Lion. *As T* **8** *but vert*—500 f. Game animals.

1960 (16 May). *10th Anniv of African Technical Co-operation Commission (C.C.T.A.). As T* **36** *of Mauritania.*

115	25 f. red-brown and ochre		45	35

(Photo Comoy, Paris)

1960 (29 May). *First Anniv of Conseil de l'Entente. P* 13.

116	**9**	25 f. multicoloured		45	35

Niger became independent on 3 August 1960.

PHILATELIC TERMS ILLUSTRATED

This successful STAMP MONTHLY series has now been brought together in a snappy black and yellow binding and published as a useful addition to Stanley Gibbons range of essential handbooks for keen stamp collectors. Within its 192 pages this handy limp-bound volume houses a veritable mine of useful information on the words and phrases used in philately. It describes and illustrates printing processes and watermarks, papers and perforations, errors and varieties . . . and it does all this IN COLOUR. Indeed, there are 92 full page plates in colour, plus many black and white illustrations, making it

FANTASTIC VALUE AT ONLY £1·95
POST PAID FROM

**Stanley Gibbons Publications Ltd
391 Strand, London WC2R 0LX**

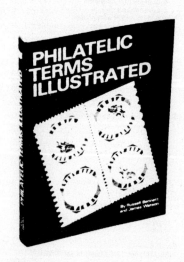

Réunion

100 Centimes = 1 Franc

The island now called Réunion, in the Indian Ocean east of Madagascar, was uninhabited when discovered by the Portuguese sailor Pedro de Mascarenhas in 1513. France took possession of the island in 1638 and settlement began after 1650 as a station for French ships on the route to India. The island was named L'lle de Bourbon in 1649. Until coffee-planting began in the 18th century it was a centre of piracy. The name was changed to Réunion in 1793 to commemorate the "reunion" of the Marseillais and the National Guard in capturing the Tuileries on 10 August 1792. After the Bourbon restoration in 1815 the island's name was changed back until 1848, since when it has been Réunion.

PRINTERS. All the stamps of Réunion were printed at the Government Printing Works, Paris, *unless otherwise stated.*

IMPERFORATE STAMPS. Stamps exist imperforate in their issued colours, but these were not valid for postage. Imperforate stamps in other colours are colour trials.

A. FRENCH COLONY

1	2	(3)

(Typo by M. Lahuppe, Saint-Denis)

1852 (1 Jan). *Type-set. Four varieties of each value. Bluish, slightly glazed paper. Imperf. No gum.*
| 1 | 1 | 15 c. black | .. | .. | £7000 | £4000 |
| 2 | 2 | 30 c. black | .. | .. | £7000 | £4000 |

Used prices for Nos. 1/2 are for pen-cancelled examples.
These stamps were reprinted five times between 1866 and 1889. The originals are framed by an inner thin line and by an outer thick line, the latter formed of two rules; the gaps between these rules being sometimes visible in the printed stamps.
The reprints, which are on unglazed paper, are framed by an inner thin line and a single outer line, not so thick as the composite outer line of the originals.

1885 (10 Dec)–86. *French Colonies General Issues surch as T 3, at Saint-Denis.*

(a) Type A. Imperf
3	5 c. on 40 c. orange	..	..	90·00	90·00
	a. Surch inverted	..	..	£225	£225
4	25 c. on 40 c. orange	..	..	11·00	9·50
	a. Surch inverted	..	..	65·00	65·00
	b. Surch double	..	..	65·00	65·00
	c. Error. 52 c. on 40 c.	..	..		

(b) Type D. Imperf
5	5 c. on 30 c. bistre-brown	..	11·00	9·50
	a. Surch double	..	..	65·00	65·00
	b. On 30 c. *deep brown*	..	10·00	8·00
	ba. Figure "5" inverted ..	..	£275	£275

(c) Type F. Imperf
6	5 c. on 40 c. orange	..	..	9·50	7·50
	a. Wide "4" (see France No. 20)	..	£350	£350
	b. On 40 c. *pale orange*	..	8·00	5·50
	c. Surch inverted	..	..	65·00	65·00
	d. Surch double	..	..	70·00	70·00

(d) Type H. Imperf
7	5 c. on 30 c. cinnamon (25.5.86)	..	1·60	1·60
8	5 c. on 40 c. red/*yellow*	..	19·00	16·00
	a. Surch inverted	..	..	60·00	60·00
	b. Surch double	..	..	60·00	60·00
9	10 c. on 40 c. red/*yellow*	..	2·50	1·90
	a. Surch double	..	..	60·00	60·00
10	20 c. on 30 c. cinnamon (25.5.86)	..	13·00	9·50

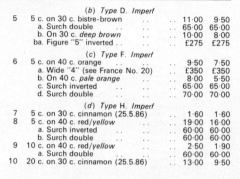

D 4	P 5	(6)

(Typo at Saint-Denis)

1889–92. *POSTAGE DUE. Type-set. Ten varieties of each value. Imperf. No gum. A. Toned paper (1889). B. Thin, bluish white paper (1892).*

				A		B	
D11	D 4	5 c. black	..	5·00	1·90	5·00	1·90
		a. Double print	..	15·00	15·00	—	—
D12		10 c. black	..	5·50	2·25	5·50	2·25
		a. Double print	..	16·00	16·00	—	—
D13		15 c. black	..	†		12·00	7·00
		a. Double print	..	†		18·00	18·00
D14		20 c. black	..	10·00	5·00	†	
		a. Double print	..	18·00	18·00	†	
D15		30 c. black	..	7·50	4·00	7·50	3·75
		a. Double print	..	18·00	18·00	—	—

(Handstamped (centre) and typo (frame) at Saint-Denis)

1890–1903. *PARCEL POST. Imperf.*
P11	P 5	10 c. black/*yellow* (Black frame)	..	40·00	22·00
P12		10 c. black/*orge* (Blue frame) (1898)	25·00	19·00
P13		10 c. black/*yell* (Blue frame) (1903)	5·50	3·75

Two varieties of overprint:
A. Without accent
B. With acute accent on "E"

SET PRICES

Set prices are given for many issues generally those containing five stamps or more. Definitive sets include one of each value or major colour change but do not cover different perforations, die types or minor shades. Where a choice is possible the catalogue set prices are based on the cheapest versions of the stamps included in the listings.

HAVE YOU READ THE NOTES AT THE BEGINNING OF THIS CATALOGUE?

These often provide answers to the enquiries we receive.

1891 (28 June). *French Colonies General Issues optd with* T **6**, *at Saint-Denis.*

(a) *Type F. Imperf*

				A	B
11	40 c. orange	..	..	—	— £110 95·00
	a. Wide "4"	..	..	—	—£1000£1000
	b. "ÉUNION"	..	..	†	£900 £900

(b) *Type G. Imperf*

12	80 c. pale rose	..	..	—	13·00 9·50
	a. "ÉUNION"	..	..	†	£100 £100

(c) *Type H. Imperf*

13	30 c. cinnamon	..	..	7·50	6·50	†
	a. "REUNIONR"	..	..	80·00	80·00	†
14	40 c. red/*yellow*	..	..	5·00	4·50	7·50 5·00
	a. "ÉUNION"	..	..	†	20·00	20·00
15	75 c. carmine	..	..	90·00	90·00	£140 £130
	a. "REUNIONR"	..	£225	£225	†	
	b. "RUÉNION"	..	†	£275	£275	
	c. "ÉUNION"	..	†	£275	£275	
16	1 f. olive-green	..	..	9·50	9·00	18·00 18·00
	a. "REUNIONR"	..	£170	£170	†	

(d) *Type J. P* 14 × 13½

17	1 c. black/*azure*	..		75	60	90	90
	a. Opt inverted	..		3·75	3·75	4·25	4·25
	b. Opt double	..		5·50	5·00	5·50	5·00
	c. "RUNION"	..		3·75	3·75	†	
	d. "REUNIONR"	..		3·75	3·75	†	
	e. "RÉUNIOU"	..		†		4·50	4·50
	f. "REUNOIN"	..		3·75	3·75	†	
	g. "RUÉNION"	..		†		3·75	3·75
	h. "ÉUNION"	..		†		3·75	3·75
	i. "ÉRUNION"	..		†		3·75	3·75
18	2 c. brown/*buff*	..		1·00	75	1·40	1·40
	a. Opt inverted	..		3·75	3·75	4·25	4·25
	b. "RUNION"	..		3·75	3·75	†	
	c. "REUNIONR"	..		3·75	3·75	†	
	d. "REUNOIN"	..		3·75	3·75	†	
	e. "RUÉNION"	..		†		4·50	4·50
	f. "ÉUNION"	..		†		3·75	3·75
	g. "RUÉNION"	..		†		3·75	3·75
	h. "REUNIN"	..		†		4·00	4·00
	i. "REUNION"	..		†		6·50	6·50
19	4 c. purple-brown/*grey*	..		1·90	1·25	3·00	2·40
	a. Opt inverted	..		11·00	11·00	13·00	13·00
	b. "RUNION"	..		5·00	5·00	†	
	c. "REUNIONR"	..		5·00	5·00	†	
	d. "REUNOIN"	..		5·00	5·00	†	
	e. "ÉUNION"	..		†		6·50	6·50
	f. "ÉRUNION"	..		†		6·50	6·50
20	5 c. green/*pale green*			1·60	1·25	3·00	2·40
	a. Opt inverted	..		5·00	5·00	7·00	7·00
	b. Opt double	..		6·50	5·50	†	
	c. "RUNION"	..		4·50	4·50	†	
	d. "REUNIONR"	..		4·50	4·50	†	
	e. "RÉUNIOU"	..		†		4·50	4·50
	f. "REUNOIN"	..		4·50	4·50	†	
	g. "RUÉNION"	..		†		10·00	10·00
	h. "ÉUNION"	..		†		5·50	5·50
	i. "ÉRUNION"	..		†		5·50	5·50
	j. "RÉUNON"	..		†		—	
21	10 c. black/*lilac*	..		5·00	1·00	4·25	95
	a. Opt inverted	..		8·50	8·50	8·50	8·50
	b. Opt double	..		8·50	8·50	8·50	8·50
	c. "RUNION"	..		9·00	9·00	†	
	d. "REUNIONR"	..		9·00	9·00	†	
	e. "REUNION"	..		11·00	11·00	†	
	f. "RUÉNION"	..		†		10·00	10·00
	g. "ÉUNION"	..		†		10·00	10·00
	h. "ÉRUNION"	..		†		10·00	10·00
22	15 c. blue/*pale blue*	..		9·50	75	8·00	70
	a. Opt inverted	..		14·00	15·00	14·00	15·00
	b. "RUNION"	..		13·00	13·00	†	
	c. "REUNIONR"	..		11·00	11·00	†	
	d. "REUNOIN"	..		11·00	11·00	†	
	e. "RUÉNION"	..		†		13·00	13·00
	f. "ÉUNION"	..		†		11·00	11·00
	g. "ÉRUNION"	..		†		11·00	11·00
23	20 c. red/*green*	..		7·00	5·00	7·00	6·00
	a. Opt inverted	..		16·00	16·00	18·00	18·00
	b. Opt double	..		16·00	13·00	†	
	c. "RUNION"	..		14·00	14·00	†	
	d. "REUNIONR"	..		13·00	13·00	†	
	e. "REUNION"	..		14·00	14·00	†	
	f. "RUÉNION"	..		†		14·00	14·00

				A	B
	g. "ÉUNION"	..	..	†	14·00 14·00
	h. "ÉRUNION"	..	..	†	14·00 14·00
	i. "REUNIN"	..	..	13·00 13·00	†
	j. "REUONIN"	..	..	17·00 17·00	†
24	25 c. black/*rose*	..		7·00	90 10·00 5·00
	a. Opt inverted	..		16·00 16·00	25·00 25·00
	b. "RUNION"	..		10·00	9·50 †
	c. "REUNIONR"	..		9·50	9·50 †
	d. "RÉUNIOU"	..		†	12·00 12·00
	e. "REUNOIN"	..		11·00 11·00	†
	f. "ÉUNION"	..		†	12·00 12·00
	g. "ÉRUNION"	..		†	12·00 12·00
25	35 c. black/*orange*	..		5·50	3·75 5·00 3·50
	a. *Black/yellow*	..		5·50	4·50 †
	b. Opt inverted	..		18·00 18·00	18·00 18·00
	c. "RUNION"	..		7·50	7·50 †
	d. "REUNIONR"	..		9·00	9·00 †
	e. "REUNOIN"	..		11·00 11·00	†
	f. "ÉUNION"	..		†	11·00 11·00
	g. "ÉRUNION"	..		†	11·00 11·00
26	40 c. red/*buff*	..		14·00 13·00	20·00 15·00
	a. Opt inverted	..		32·00 32·00	40·00 40·00
	b. "RUNION"	..		25·00 25·00	†
	c. "REUNIONR"	..		25·00 25·00	†
	d. "REUNION"	..		25·00 25·00	†
	e. "RUÉNION"	..		†	26·00 26·00
	f. "ÉUNION"	..		†	25·00 25·00
	g. "ÉRUNION"	..		†	25·00 25·00
27	75 c. rose-carmine/*rose*		£140 £130	£150 £140
	a. Opt inverted	..		£200 £200	£225 £225
	b. "RUNION"	..		£225 £225	†
	c. "REUNIONR"	..		£225 £225	†
	d. "RÉUNIOU"	..		†	£225 £225
	e. "REUNOIN"	..		£225 £225	†
	f. "ÉUNION"	..		†	£225 £225
	g. "ÉRUNION"	..		†	£225 £225
28	1 f. olive-green/*toned*		£130 £120	£150 £140
	a. Opt inverted	..		£200 £200	£225 £225
	b. "RUNION"	..		£225 £225	†
	c. "REUNIONR"	..		£225 £225	†
	d. "RÉUNIOU"	..		†	£225 £225
	e. "REUNOIN"	..		£225 £225	†
	f. "ÉUNION"	..		†	£225 £225
	g. "ÉRUNION"	..		†	£225 £225

Apart from the errors of spelling, which are listed, many varieties due to a failure to print letters or parts of letters can be found on this issue.

02c	2	2	2
(7)	(8)	(9)	(9a)

1891 (July). *French Colonies General Issues Type J surch at one operation with* T **6** (*no accent*) *and new value as* T **7**, *at Saint-Denis.*

29	02 c. on 20 c. red/*green*	..		..	1·60	1·60
	a. Surch inverted	..			6·50	6·50
	b. "RUNION"	..		..	11·00	11·00
30	15 c. on 20 c. red/*green*	..			2·50	2·50
	a. Surch inverted	..			6·50	6·50
	b. "RUNION"	..			22·00	22·00

1891 (3 Dec). *French Colonies General Issues Type J surch in one operation with* T **6** (*with accent*) *and new value as* T **8**/**9a**, *at Saint-Denis.*

31	**8** 2 on 20 c. red/*green*	..			30	30
	a. Without accent	..			1·25	1·25
	b. "RÉUNION"	..			3·50	3·50
32	**9** 2 on 20 c. red/*green*	..			65	65
	a. "RUÉNION"	..			3·50	3·50
	b. Without accent	..			3·50	3·50
33	**9a** 2 on 20 c. red/*green*	..			95	95
	a. Without accent	..			3·25	3·25

Nos. 31/33 are all from the same setting, the sheet of 150 containing seventy examples of No. 31, fifty-four of No. 32 and twenty-six of No. 33.

THE WORLD CENTRE FOR
FINE STAMPS IS 391 STRAND

10

(Des A. Dubois. Typo)

16 Map of the Island   **17** View of Saint-Denis and Arms of the Colony

1892 (Nov). *Name in red* (1, 5, 15, 15, 75 *c.*, 1 *f*) *or blue* (*others*). *P* 14 × 13½.

34 **10**	1 c. black/*azure*	30	30
35	2 c. brown/*buff*	30	30
36	4 c. purple-brown/*grey*	45	45
37	5 c. green/*pale green*	1·40	50
38	10 c. black/*lilac*	1·40	45
39	15 c. blue (*quadrillé paper*)	3·75	55
40	20 c. red/*green*	3·25	2·75
41	25 c. black/*rose*	3·25	50
	a. Name double	45·00	38·00
42	30 c. cinnamon/*drab*	3·75	2·50
43	40 c. red/*yellow*	5·00	3·75
44	50 c. carmine/*rose*	10·00	7·50
	a. Name in red and blue	55·00	55·00
45	75 c. brown/*orange*	9·00	8·00
	a. Name double	50·00	48·00
46	1 f. olive-green/*toned*	7·00	5·00
	a. Name double	50·00	45·00
34/46	*Set of 13*	45·00	29·00

See also Nos. 50/5.

18 View of St. Pierre and Crater Dolomieu   **D 19**

(Des A. Chauvet. Eng J. Puyplat. Typo)

1907 (Feb) –**17**. *P* 14 × 13½.

60 **16**	1 c. carmine and dull lilac	5	5
61	2 c. blue and brown	5	5
62	4 c. red and olive	5	5
	a. Double impression of centre	18·00	
63	5 c. red and green	5	5
64	10 c. green and carmine	25	5
65	15 c. ultramarine and black (7.17)	5	5
66 **17**	20 c. blue-green and olive	5	5
67	25 c. sepia and deep blue	55	30
68	30 c. green and yellow-brown	8	8
69	35 c. blue and olive-brown	15	5
70	45 c. rose and violet	15	10
71	50 c. blue and red-brown	40	12
72	75 c. rose and brick-red	5	5
73 **18**	1 f. deep blue and olive-brown	8	8
74	2 f. green and brick-red	70	40
75	5 f. sepia and rose	1·75	70
60/75	*Set of 16*	4·00	2·00

See also Nos. 92/114.

2ᶜ· 2ᶜ· 2ᶜ· 5ᶜ· Colis Postaux

(11)   (12)   (13)   (14)   (P 15)

1894 (7 Dec). *French Colonies General Issues Type J* ("*Commerce*") *surch as T* **11/13**, *at Saint-Denis.*

47 **11**	2 c. on 20 c. red/*green*	40	40
48 **12**	2 c. on 20 c. red/*green*	80	80
49 **13**	2 c. on 20 c. red/*green*	3·75	3·75

Nos. 47/9 come from the same setting of 25, which was used six times to surcharge each sheet of 150. Each setting contained 18 examples of No. 47, 6 of No. 48 and 1 of No. 49.

During a later shortage of stamps postage dues stamps of the French Colonies General Issue series were used as postage stamps without additional overprint or surcharge.

1900–05. *Colours changed. Name in blue* (10 *c.*, 50 *c* (No. 55), *or red* (*others*)). *P* 14 × 13½.

50 **10**	5 c. bright yellow-green	25	20
51	10 c. rose-red	40	25
52	15 c. grey	1·25	15
53	25 c. blue	5·00	4·50
54	50 c. brown/*azure*	10·00	9·50
55	50 c. brown/*azure* (1905)	11·00	9·00
50/55	*Set of 6*	25·00	21·00

1901 (20 Sept). *Surch as T* **14**, *at Saint-Denis.*

56 **10**	5 c. on 40 c. red/*yellow*	75	75
	a. Surch inverted	6·50	5·50
	b. Bar omitted	25·00	14·00
	c. Figure "5" inverted	£190	£190
57	5 c. on 50 c. carmine/*rose*	90	90
	a. Surch inverted	6·50	5·50
	b. Bar omitted	25·00	14·00
58	15 c. on 75 c. brown/*orange*	2·50	2·50
	a. Surch inverted	6·50	5·50
	b. Bar omitted	25·00	14·00
	c. Smaller figure "1"	5·50	5·00
59	15 c. on 1 f. olive-green/*toned*	2·50	2·50
	a. Surch inverted	6·50	5·50
	b. Bar omitted	25·00	14·00
	c. Smaller figure "1"	5·50	5·00
56/59	*Set of 4*	6·00	6·00

1906. *PARCEL POST. No. 51 optd with Type* P **15**.

P60 **10**	10 c. rose-red and blue	2·25	2·25

(Des A. Chauvet. Eng J. Puyplat. Typo)

1907. *POSTAGE DUE. P* 14 × 13½.

D76 D **19**	5 c. carmine/*yellow*	5	5
D77	10 c. blue/*blue*	5	5
D78	15 c. black/*grey*	12	12
D79	20 c. rose/*toned*	12	12
D80	30 c. green/*greenish*	20	20
D81	50 c. red/*yellow-green*	30	30
D82	60 c. rose/*blue*	30	30
D83	1 f. dull lilac/*toned*	45	45
D76/83	*Set of 8*	1·40	1·40

P 20   (21)   (22)

1907–23. *PARCEL POST. Receipt stamps surcharged as in Type* P **20**, *at Saint-Denis.*

P76 P **20**	10 c. brown and black	3·25	3·00
P77	10 c. brown and red (1923)	2·75	2·75

1912 (July). *Surch with T* **21/2**.

A. Narrow spacing. B. Wide spacing

			A	B
76	**10**	05 on 2 c. brown/*buff* ..	8	8 4·50 4·50
77		05 on 15 c. grey (R.) ..	8	8 4·50 4·50
		a. Surch inverted	..28·00 28·00	— —
78		05 on 20 c. red/*green* ..	20	20 55·00 55·00
79		05 on 25 c. black/*rose* (R.) ..	8	8 17·00 17·00
		a. Surch double, one inverted	..	— 30·00 —
80		05 on 30 c. cinnamon/*drab* (R.)	8	8 17·00 17·00
81		10 on 40 c. red/*yellow* ..	8	8 10·00 10·00
82		10 on 50 c. brown/*azure* (R.)	8	8 17·00 17·00
83		10 on 75 c. brown/*orange* ..	1·60	1·60 60·00 60·00

In Type A the space between "0" and "5" is 1½ mm and between "1" and "0" 2½ mm. In Type B the spacing is 2 mm and 3 mm respectively.

(23)   (24)   (25)

40
=

25ᶜ **1ᶠ25** **=2ᶠ·=**

(26)   (27)   (28)   (D 29)

1922 (1 Jan)—**33**. *Surch as T* **26**.

115	**17**	40 on 20 c. yellow and green ..	8	8
		a. Double impression of centre ..	22·00	19·00
		b. Surch double, one inverted ..	22·00	
		c. Surch omitted ..	£140	
116		50 on 45 c. red and claret (15.5.33) ..	15	12
117		50 on 45 c. red and mauve (15.5.33)	65·00	65·00
		a. Surch double ..	£275	
118		50 on 65 c. light blue & violet (15.5.33)	15	12
119		60 on 75 c. carmine and red ..	5	5
		a. Surch double ..	32·00	
120	**16**	65 on 15 c. ultram & blk (R.) (1.2.25)	20	20
121		85 on 15 c. ultram & blk (R.) (1.2.25)	20	20
122	**17**	85 on 75 c. rose and brick-red (1.2.25)	20	20
123		90 on 75 c. rose and carmine (28.2.27)	30	30

1915 (23 Jan)—**16**. *Red Cross. Surch with T* **23**, *at Saint-Denis*.

(a) In black

84	**16**	10 c.+5 c. green and carmine ..	.. 15·00	14·00
		a. Cross close to "5" ..	.. 14·00	12·00
		b. Surch inverted ..	.. 45·00	38·00

(b) In red (5.2.15)

85	**16**	10 c.+5 c. green and carmine ..	.. 75	75
		a. Cross close to "5" ..	.. 2·75	2·75
		b. Surch inverted ..	.. 21·00	20·00

(c) In carmine (17.1.16)

86	**16**	10 c.+5 c. green and carmine ..	.. 12	12
		a. Cross close to "5" ..	.. 30	30
		b. Surch inverted ..	.. 11·00	11·00

The Réunion stamps were surcharged in blocks of ten and these show small varieties. The lower borders of each sheet were also surcharged, but were not allowed to be used for postage. Ten different printings were made between 23 January 1915 and 8 February 1916, resulting in shades of the surcharge.

1916 (Apr). *Red Cross. Surch in Paris with T* **24**, *in red*.

90	**16**	10c. + 5 c. green and carmine ..	10	10

1917 (July). *Surch with T* **25**, *at Saint-Denis*.

91	**16**	0,01 on 4 c. chestnut and grey-brown ..	25	25
		a. Surch inverted ..	.. 7·50	7·50
		b. Surch double ..	.. 13·00	13·00

1922 (1 Jan)—**30**. *New values and colours changed. P* 14 ×13½.

92	**16**	5 c. violet and yellow ..	5	5
93		10 c. blue-green and green ..	5	5
94		10 c. red and lake/*azure* (1.2.26) ..	5	5
95		15 c. blue-green and green (15.4.25) ..	5	5
96		15 c. vermilion and blue (30.4.28) ..	5	5
97	**17**	25 c. blue and brown ..	5	5
98		30 c. rose and carmine ..	5	5
99		30 c. carmine and grey (1.2.26) ..	5	5
100		30 c. yellow-green and green (30.4.28)	15	12
101		40 c. brown and olive-green (1.3.25) ..	5	5
102		45 c. red and claret (15.4.25) ..	5	5
103		45 c. red and mauve (30.4.28) ..	50	40
104		50 c. ultramarine and blue ..	5	5
105		50 c. violet and yellow (1.2.26) ..	5	5
106		60 c. brown and blue (21.12.25) ..	5	5
107		65 c. light blue and violet (2.4.28) ..	15	12
108		75 c. purple and chocolate (30.4.28) ..	45	30
109		90 c. rose and carmine (22.3.30) ..	1·55	1·40
110	**18**	1 f. light blue (1.3.26) ..	10	10
111		1 f. lilac and brown (30.4.28) ..	12	10
112		1 f. 10, magenta & red-brn (25.9.28)	20	12
113		1 f. 50, lt blue & blue/*bluish* (22.3.30)	1·90	1·60
114		3 f. magenta/*rose* (22.3.30) ..	1·90	1·60
92/114		*Set of 23*	7·00	6·00

For 20 c. yellow and green, see T **17**, see No. 115c, and for 1 f. light blue and blue/*bluish* T **18**, No. 126b.

1924 (June)—**27**. *Surch as T* **27/8** *and similar figures, with three bars over old value*.

124	**18**	25 c. on 5 f. sepia and rose ..	12	12
		a. Surch double ..	16·00	
		1 f. 25 on 1 f. blue (R.) (14.6.26) ..	8	8
		a. Surch double ..	19·00	
126		1 f. 50 on 1 f. light blue and blue/*bluish* (28.2.27) ..	12	12
		a. Surch double ..	22·00	
		b. Surch omitted ..	25·00	
127		3 f. on 5 f. blue and lake (19.12.27)	45	45
128		10 f. on 5 f. lake & blue-green (7.2.27)	3·50	2·75
129		20 f. on 5 f. rose and sepia (7.2.27) ..	4·50	3·25

1927 (10 Oct). *POSTAGE DUE. Surch as Type* D **29**.

D130	D **19**	2 f. on 1 f. bright rose ..	1·40	1·40
D131		3 f. on 1 f. red-brown ..	1·40	1·40

1931 (13 Apr). *International Colonial Exhibition, Paris. As T* **23/6** *of St-Pierre et Miquelon*.

130		40 c. green and black ..	55	55
131		50 c. mauve and black ..	75	75
132		90 c. vermilion and black ..	75	75
133		1 f. 50, blue and black ..	80	80
130/133		*Set of 4*	2·50	2·50

30 Cascade, Salazie   **31** Anchain Peak, Salazie

THE WORLD CENTRE FOR
FINE STAMPS IS 391 STRAND

32 Léon Dierx Museum   D **33** Arms of Réunion

(Des R. Caulet (**30** and **32**) and C. Abadie. Recess Inst. de Gravure)

1933 (11 Sept)**–40**. *P* 12½.

134	**30**	1 c. purple	..	5	5
135		2 c. sepia	..	5	5
136		3 c. purple (15.4.40)	..	5	5
137		4 c. olive-green	..	5	5
138		5 c. red	..	5	5
139		10 c. ultramarine	..	5	5
140		15 c. black	..	5	5
141		20 c. slate-blue	..	5	5
142		25 c. red-brown	..	5	5
143		30 c. green	..	8	8
144	**31**	35 c. green (16.5.38)	..	5	5
145		40 c. ultramarine	..	5	5
146		40 c. sepia (15.4.40) ..	..	5	5
147		45 c. mauve	..	8	8
148		45 c. green (15.4.40)	..	5	5
149		50 c. red	..	5	5
150		55 c. orange (16.5.38)	..	8	8
151		60 c. ultramarine (20.3.40)	..	5	5
152		65 c. olive-green	..	30	12
153		70 c. olive-green (20.3.40)	..	5	5
154		75 c. chocolate	..	75	70
155		80 c. black (16.5.38) ..	..	5	5
156		90 c. carmine ..	..	40	30
157		90 c. purple (4.12.39)	..	5	5
158		1 f. green	..	20	5
159		1 f. carmine (16.5.38)	..	20	5
160		1 f. black (20.3.40) ..	..	5	5
161	**32**	1 f. brown (2.10.33)	..	5	5
162		1 f. 25, carmine (4.12.39)	..	12	12
163	**30**	1 f. 40, greenish blue (5.3.40)	..	5	5
164	**32**	1 f. 50, blue	..	5	5
165	**30**	1 f. 60, carmine (5.3.40)	..	10	10
166	**32**	1 f. 75, olive-green (2.10.33)	..	12	5
167	**30**	1 f. 75, ultramarine (16.5.38)	..	12	10
168	**32**	2 f. red	..	5	5
169	**30**	2 f. 25, ultramarine (4.12.39)	..	25	25
170		2 f. 50, brown (5.3.40)	..	10	10
171	**32**	3 f. violet	..	5	5
172		5 f. magenta	..	10	10
173		10 f. blue	..	12	12
174		20 f. red-brown	..	25	25
134/174		*Set of* 41	..	4·25	3·50

60 c. and 1 f. stamps, as Type **31** but without "RF", were prepared in 1944, but not placed on sale in Réunion.

(Des C. Abadie. Recess Inst. de Gravure)

1933 (11 Sept). *POSTAGE DUE*. *P* 13.

D175	D **33**	5 c. purple	..	5	5
D176		10 c. green	..	5	5
D177		15 c. brown	..	5	5
D178		20 c. vermilion	..	5	5
D179		30 c. olive-green ..	..	5	5
D180		50 c. ultramarine ..	..	10	10
D181		60 c. sepia	..	15	15
D182		1 f. violet	..	5	5
D183		2 f. slate-blue	..	5	5
D184		3 f. carmine	..	5	5
D175/184		*Set of* 10 ..	..	55	55

RÉUNION - FRANCE

par avion

«*ROLAND GARROS*»

(33)   34

1937 (23 Jan). *AIR. Pioneer Flight from Réunion to France by Laurent, Lenier and Touge. Optd with T* **33**, *in blue.*

174a	**31**	50 c. red	..	75·00	75·00
		b. Pair, one without opt ..		£375	£375
		c. Opt inverted ..	..	—	£750

1937 (15 Apr). *International Exhibition, Paris. As T* **32**/**37** *of St-Pierre et Miquelon.*

175		20 c. bright violet	..	30	30
176		30 c. green	..	30	30
177		40 c. carmine	..	30	30
178		50 c. brown and blue	..	30	30
180		1 f. 50, blue	..	30	30
175/180		*Set of* 6	..	1·60	1·60
MS180a		120 × 100 mm. 3 f. ultramarine (as *T* **32**). Imperf	..	1·10	1·10

(Recess, values typo, Institut de Gravure)

1938 (1 Mar). *AIR. P* 12½.

181	**34**	3 f. 65, blue and carmine	..	8	8
182		6 f. 65, brown and orange	..	8	8
183		9 f. 65, carmine and blue	..	8	8
184		12 f. 65, brown and green	..	20	20
181/184		*Set of* 4	..	40	40

1938 (24 Oct). *International Anti-Cancer Fund. As T* **38** *of St-Pierre et Miquelon.*

185		1 f. 75 + 50 c. ultramarine	..	3·25	3·25

1939 (10 May). *New York World's Fair. As T* **41** *of St-Pierre et Miquelon.*

186		1 f. 25, lake	..	15	15
187		2 f. 25, ultramarine	..	15	15

1939 (5 July). *150th Anniv of French Revolution. As T* **42** *of St-Pierre et Miquelon.* (*a*) *POSTAGE*

188		45 c. + 25 c. green and black	..	1·75	1·75
189		70 c. + 30 c. brown and black	..	1·75	1·75
190		90 c. + 35 c. red-orange and black	..	1·75	1·75
191		1 f. 25 + 1 f. carmine and black	..	1·75	1·75
192		2 f. 25 + 2 f. blue and black	..	1·75	1·75

(*b*) *AIR*

193		3 f. 65 + 4 f. black and orange..		3·25	3·25
188/193		*Set of* 6	..	11·00	11·00

VICHY ISSUES. A number of stamps were prepared by the Pétain Government of Unoccupied France for use in Réunion, but were not placed on sale there.

≡ 1ᶠ   **France Libre**

(35)   (36)

1943. *Surch with T* **35**, *in red.*

194	**31**	1 f. on 65 c. olive-green	..	20	5

1943. *Optd as T* **36** *in one line on horiz designs, in two lines on vert designs.* (*a*) *POSTAGE.*

(i) *On* 1907–17 *issue*

195	**16**	4 c. red and olive (B.)	..	75	75
196	**17**	75 c. rose and brick-red (B.) ..	..	20	20
197	**18**	5 f. sepia and rose (B.)	..	8·50	8·50

(ii) *On* 1933–40 *issue*

198	**30**	1 c. purple (R.)	..	8	8
199		2 c. sepia (R.)	..	8	8
200		3 c. purple (R.)	..	8	8
201		4 c. olive-green (R.)	..	8	8
202		5 c. red	..	5	5
203		10 c. ultramarine (R.)	..	8	8
204		15 c. black (R.)	..	8	8
205		20 c. slate-blue (R.)	..	8	8
206		25 c. red-brown (B.) ..	..	8	8
207		30 c. green (R.)	..	8	8
208	**31**	35 c. green	..	8	8
209		40 c. ultramarine (R.)	..	8	8
210		40 c. sepia (R.)	..	8	8
211		45 c. mauve	..	8	8
212		45 c. green	..	8	8
213		50 c. red	..	8	8
214		55 c. orange	..	8	8
215		60 c. ultramarine (R.)	..	50	50
216		65 c. olive-green	..	10	10
217		70 c. olive-green (R.)	..	30	30
218		75 c. chocolate (R.) ..	..	65	65
219		80 c. black (R.)	..	8	8
220		90 c. purple	..	8	8
221		1 f. green	..	12	12

222	**31**	1 f. carmine	15	15
223		1 f. black (R.)	30	30
224	**32**	1 f. 25, brown (B.)	12	12
225		1 f. 25, carmine	20	20
226	**30**	1 f. 40, greenish blue (R.)	25	25
227	**32**	1 f. 50, blue (R.)	8	8
228	**30**	1 f. 60, carmine	40	40
229	**32**	1 f. 75, olive-green (R.)	12	12
230	**30**	1 f. 75, ultramarine (R.)	65	65
231	**32**	2 f. red	10	10
232	**30**	2 f. 25, ultramarine (R.)	30	30
233		2 f. 50, brown (B.)	75	75
234	**32**	3 f. violet (R.)	10	10
235		5 f. magenta (B.)	20	20
236		10 f. blue (R.)	1·10	1·10
237		20 f. red-brown (B.)	1·90	1·90

(iii) *On 1939 New York World's Fair issue (Nos.* 186/7)

238	1 f. 25, lake	45	45
239	2 f. 25, ultramarine (R.)	45	45

(iv) *On 1943 provisional* (No. 194)

240	**31**	1 f. on 65 c. olive-green (R.)	10	10
195/240	*Set of 46*		18·00	18·00

(b) AIR

241	**34**	3 f. 65, blue and carmine	65	65
242		6 f. 65, brown and orange	65	65
243		9 f. 65, carmine and blue (R.)	65	65
244		12 f. 65, brown and green	65	65
241/244	*Set of 4*		2·40	2·40

37 Chief Products

(Des Edmund Dulac. Photo Harrison & Sons)

1943 (Dec). *Free French Issue.* P 14½ × 14.

245	**37**	5 c. brown	5	5
246		10 c. indigo-blue	5	5
		a. Greenish blue	5	
247		25 c. emerald-green	5	5
248		30 c. vermilion	5	5
249		40 c. grey-green	5	5
250		80 c. magenta	10	10
251		1 f. maroon	5	5
252		1 f. 50, scarlet	5	5
253		2 f. grey-black	5	5
254		2 f. 50, ultramarine	5	5
255		4 f. violet	8	8
256		5 f. orange-yellow	10	10
257		10 f. red-brown	25	25
258		20 f. blue-green	30	30
245/258	*Set of 14*		1·10	1·10

37a Airliner

(Des E. Dulac. Photo Harrison)

1944. *AIR.* P 14½ × 14.

259	**37a**	1 f. red-orange	5	5
260		1 f. 50, scarlet	5	5
261		5 f. maroon	5	5
262		10 f. black	12	12
263		25 f. ultramarine	12	12
264		50 f. green	12	12
265		100 f. claret	25	25
		a. Value doubly printed		
259/265	*Set of 7*		70	70

1944. *Mutual Aid and Red Cross Funds. As T* **49** *of St-Pierre et Miquelon.*

266	5 f. + 20 f. black	12	12

1945. *Eboué. As T* **50** *of St-Pierre et Miquelon.*

267	2 f. black	5	5
268	25 f. blue-green	12	12

= 2^Fr 40^C =

(38)

1945. *Surch with new values as T* **38**.

269	**37**	50 c. on 5 c. brown (R.)	5	5
270		60 c. on 5 c. brown (R.)	5	5
		a. Surch inverted	55·00	
271		70 c. on 5 c. brown (R.)	5	5
272		1 f. 20 on 5 c. brown (R.)	5	5
273		2 f. 40 on 25 c. emerald-green	5	5
		a. Surch inverted	65·00	
274		3 f. on 25 c. emerald-green	5	5
		a. Surch inverted	80·00	
275		4 f. 50 on 25 c. emerald-green	10	10
		a. Surch inverted	19·00	
276		15 f. on 2 f. 50, ultramarine (R.)	15	15
269/276	*Set of 8*		50	50

B. FRENCH OVERSEAS DEPARTMENT

Réunion became an Overseas Department of France on 19 March 1946.

1946 (8 May). *AIR. Victory. As T* **52** *of St-Pierre et Miquelon.*

277	8 f. grey	12	12

1946 (6 June). *AIR. From Chad to the Rhine. As Nos.* 355/60 *of St-Pierre et Miquelon.*

278	5 f. brown-red	20	20
279	10 f. brown-violet	20	20
280	15 f. olive-black	20	20
281	20 f. carmine	25	25
282	25 f. greenish blue	25	25
283	50 f. bright green	30	30
278/283	*Set of 6*	1·25	1·25

39 Cliffs

40 Banana Tree and Cliff

41 Mountain Landscape

42 Shadow of Aeroplane over Coast

10c
CFA
(44)

3ᶠ-**CFA**
(45)

=

1o0ᶠ
CFA
(46)

3ᶠ
C F A
=
(D 47)

(Des R. Mahias (Nos. 284/302), M. Rolland (Nos. 303/5).
Photo Vaugirard, Paris)

1947. (a) POSTAGE. P 13½.

284	**39**	10 c. orange and dull green	..	5	5
285	—	30 c. orange and blue	..	5	5
286	—	40 c. orange and sepia	..	5	5
287	—	50 c. brown and blue-green	..	5	5
288	—	60 c. brown and blue	..	5	5
289	—	80 c. olive and brown	..	10	10
290	—	1 f. purple and blue	..	5	5
291	—	1 f. 20, grey and blue-green	..	5	5
292	—	1 f. 50, purple and orange	..	5	5
293	**40**	2 f. blue and green	..	8	8
294	—	3 f. purple and green	..	8	8
295	—	3 f. 60, rose and carmine	..	10	10
296	—	4 f. blue and brown	..	10	10
297	**41**	5 f. mauve and brown	..	12	12
298	—	6 f. blue and brown	..	20	20
299	—	10 f. orange and blue	..	30	25
300	—	15 f. purple and blue	..	55	50
301	—	20 f. blue and orange	..	80	65
302	—	25 f. sepia and mauve	..	95	95

(b) AIR. P 13½×12½ (horiz) or 12½×13½ (vert) (24.3)

303	**42**	50 f. olive-green and blue-grey	..	2·10	1·90
304	—	100 f. orange and brown	..	2·75	2·50
305	—	200 f. blue and orange	..	3·25	3·25
284/305		Set of 22	..	11·00	11·00

Designs: Vert (20×37 mm)—50 c. to 80 c. Cutting sugar cane; 1 f. to 1 f. 50, Cascade. (28×50 mm)—100 f. Aeroplane over Réunion. Horiz (37×20 mm)—15 f. to 25 f. Ship approaching Réunion. (50×28 mm)—200 f. Réunion from the air.

D 43

(Des Planson. Photo Vaugirard, Paris)

1947. POSTAGE DUE. P 13.

D306	**D 43**	10 c. mauve	..	5	5
D307	—	30 c. sepia	..	5	5
D308	—	50 c. blue-green	..	5	5
D309	—	1 f. orange-brown	..	10	10
D310	—	2 f. claret	..	5	5
D311	—	3 f. red-brown	..	5	5
D312	—	4 f. blue	..	20	20
D313	—	5 f. brown-red	..	25	25
D314	—	10 f. olive-green	..	25	25
D315	—	20 f. violet-blue	..	25	25
D306/315		Set of 10	..	1·25	1·25

"CFA" SURCHARGES. From 1949 Réunion, together with the other Overseas Departments, used the stamps of France. In Réunion, however, the local currency, the CFA franc, continued to differ from the French franc, so that the following surcharged stamps of France were issued for use on the island. In later years some French designs were issued with the face values amended to CFA francs.

**HAVE YOU READ THE NOTES AT THE
BEGINNING OF THIS CATALOGUE?**
These often provide answers to the enquiries we
receive.

1949–53. (a) POSTAGE. (i) Nos. 909 and 914 (Ceres) surch as T **44**.

306	50 c. on 1 f. carmine-red	..	..	20	8
307	60 c. on 2 f. yellow-green	..	..	2·25	30

(ii) Nos. 972/3 (Arms) surch as T **44**

308	10 c. on 30 c. black, red & yellow (Alsace)	10	5
309	30 c. on 50 c. brown, yell & red (Lorraine)	12	8

(iii) Nos. 981, 979 and 982/a (Views) surch as T **44**, but with bars obliterating original face value

310	5 f. on 20 f. slate-blue (Finistère) (R.)	..	1·10	30
311	7 f. on 12 f. carm (Luxemburg Palace)	1·60	75
312	8 f. on 25 f. deep blue (Nancy) (R.)	..	8·00	1·40
313	10 f. on 25 f. sepia (Nancy) (R.)	..	50	15

(iv) Nos. 999, 1001, 1004/5a, 1007/b and 1007e (Marianne) such as T **45**

314	1 f. on 3 f. magenta	..	..	30	12
315	2 f. on 4 f. turquoise-green	..	1·10	15
316	2 f. on 5 f. yellow-green (1950)	..	2·75	1·40
317	2 f. on 5 f. violet (1951)	..	45	40
318	2 f. on 5 f. blue	..	5·50	3·75
319	3 f. on 6 f. carmine-red	..	65	20
320	3 f. on 6 f. green (1951)	..	1·75	70
321	4 f. on 10 f. reddish violet	..	70	12
322	6 f. on 12 f. ultramarine	..	1·25	25
323	6 f. on 12 f. red-orange (1952)	..	1·25	20
324	9 f. on 18 f. carmine (1951)	..	2·25	1·25

(v) No. 1022 (Conques Abbey) surch as T **44**, but with bars obliterating original face value

325	11 f. on 18 f. blue (R.)	..	..	2·25	75
306/325	Set of 20	..	..	31·00	11·00

(b) AIR. (i) Nos. 967/70 (Mythology) surch as T **44**, but with bars obliterating original value

326	20 f. on 40 f. blue-green (R.)	..	..	90	30
327	25 f. on 50 f. pink	..	..	1·00	30
328	50 f. on 100 f. ultramarine (R.)	..	2·75	25
329	100 f. on 200 f. red	..	..	14·00	8·00

(ii) Nos. 1056 and 1058/9 (Cities) surch as T **46**, or with slightly different figures (1000 f.)

330	100 f. on 200 f. green (Bordeaux) (1951)	40·00	16·00
331	200 f. on 500 f. vermilion (Marseilles)	..	16·00	11·00
332	500 f. on 1000 f. slate-purple and black/		
	blue (Paris) (1951)	..	..	£110	80·00
326/332	Set of 7	..	..	£170	£110

(c) POSTAGE DUE. Nos. D988/996 (Wheat Sheaves) surch as Type D **47**

D333	10 c. on 1 f. blue	..	..	5	5
D334	50 c. on 2 f. greenish blue	..	..	8	8
D335	1 f. on 3 f. brown-red	..	..	12	12
D336	2 f. on 4 f. violet	..	..	20	20
D337	3 f. on 5 f. pink	..	..	95	95
D338	5 f. on 10 f. orange-red	..	..	55	55
D339	10 f. on 20 f. olive-brown	..	..	90	90
D340	20 f. on 50 f. deep green (1950)	..	2·75	1·90
D341	50 f. on 100 f. green (30.3.53)	..	5·50	3·50
D333/341	Set of 9	..	..	10·00	7·50

1950–51. Surch as T **44** (Nos. 342/3), or with obliterating bars over original face value. (a) On Nos. 1050 and 1052 (Arms).

342	10 c. on 50 c. yell, scar & ultram (Guyenne)	8	8
343	1 f. on 2 f. scar, yell & green (Auvergne)	2·75	1·75

(b) Nos. 1067/8 and 1068b (Views)

344	5 f. on 20 f. brown-red (Comminges)	..	1·75	40
345	8 f. on 25 f. blue (Wandrille) (1951)	..	1·25	20
346	15 f. on 30 f. indigo (Arbois) (R.) (1951)	1·00	20
342/346	Set of 5	..	..	..	6·00	2·40

1951. Nos. 1123/4 (*Arms*) *surch as T* **44**.

347	50 c. on 1 f. scar, yell & ultram (Béarn)	20	5
348	1 f. on 2 f. yell, ultram & scar (Touraine)	30	15

1952. Nos. 1144 *and* 1138 (*Views*) *surch as T* **44**, *with bars obliterating original face value.*

349	5 f. on 20 f. violet (Chambord) (R.)	50	25
350	8 f. on 40 f. deep violet (Bigorre) (R.)	1·60	30

3ᶠ CFA

(48)

200ᶠ CFA

(49)

1953–54. (*a*) Nos. 1162, 1168 *and* 1170 (*Literature and Crafts*) *surch with T* **48** (*No.* 351), *or as T* **44** *with bars obliterating original face value* (*others*).

351	3 f. on 6 f. carmine-lake and rose-red (Gargantua)	30	15
352	8 f. on 40 f. brown and chocolate (Porcelain) (1954)	1·60	20
353	20 f. on 75 f. lake and carmine (Flowers) (1954)	2·25	40

(*b*) Nos. 1181/2 (*Arms*) *surch as T* **44**

354	50 c. on 1 f. yellow, verm & blk (Poitou)	8	5
355	1 f. on 2 f. yellow, ultramarine and brown (Champagne) (1954)	30	20
351/355	Set of 5	4·00	90

1954–55. (*a*) POSTAGE. (i) Nos. 1188 *and* 1190 (*Sports*) *surch as T* **44**, *with three bars obliterating the original face value.*

356	8 f. on 40 f. indigo and deep brown (Canoeing) (R.)	6·50	1·90
357	20 f. on 75 f. brown-carmine and yellow-orange (Horse-jumping) (B.)	21·00	11·00

(ii) Nos. 1205/8 *and* 1210/11 (*Views*) *surch as T* **45** (*No.* 362), **48** (359) *or* **44** (*others*), *each with bars obliterating original face value*

358	2 f. on 6 f. indigo, blue and deep blue-green (Lourdes) (R.)	20	15
359	3 f. on 8 f. deep blue-green and blue (Andelys) (R.) (1955)	40	20
360	4 f. on 10 f. brown & light blue (Royan)	65	30
361	6 f. on 12 f. deep lilac and reddish violet (Quimper)	90	25
362	9 f. on 18 f. ind, bl & dp bl-grn (Cheverny)	2·75	1·90
363	10 f. on 20 f. black-brown, chestnut and turquoise-blue (Ajaccio)	1·00	30

(iii) No. 1229 (*Arms*) *surch as T* **44**

364	1 f. on 2 f. yell, red & blk (Angoumois)	20	5
356/364	Set of 9	30·00	14·00

(*b*) AIR. Nos. 1194/7 (*Aircraft*) *surch as T* **44** *with obliterating bars* (*Nos.* 365, 367) *or as T* **48** (*others*)

365	50 f. on 100 f. red-brown and blue (Mystère IV) (B.)	80	25
366	100 f. on 200 f. deep purple and ultramarine (Noratlas) (R.)	2·25	45
367	200 f. on 500 f. scarlet and yellow-orange (Magister) (B.)	11·00	7·50
368	500 f. on 1000 f. indigo, maroon and turquoise-blue (Provence) (B.)	11·00	6·50
365/368	Set of 4	22·00	13·00

1955–57. (*a*) Nos. 1262/5, 1266, 1268 *and* 1268*b* (*Views*) *surch as T* **44**, *with bars obliterating original face value.*

369	2 f. on 6 f. carm-lake (Bordeaux) (1956)	45	20
370	3 f. on 8 f. indigo (Marseilles)	30	20
371	4 f. on 10 f. deep bright blue (Nice)	30	10
372	5 f. on 12 f. blackish brown and violet-grey (Cahors) (R.)	55	12
373	6 f. on 18 f. indigo and slate-green (Uzerche) (R.)	30	12
374	10 f. on 25 f. red-brn & chest (Brouage)	45	15
375	17 f. on 70 f. black and grey-green (Cahors) (R.) (1957)	1·90	95

(*b*) No. 1273 (*Arms*) *surch as T* **44**

376	50 c. on 1 f. yellow, red and ultramarine (Comtat Venaissin)	8	8
369/376	Set of 8	3·75	1·75

1956. Nos. 1297/1300 (*Sports*) *surch as T* **45** (*No.* 378) *or* **44** (*others*), *with bars obliterating original face value.*

377	8 f. on 30 f. blk & grey (Basket-ball) (R.)	95	12
378	9 f. on 40 f. brn-pur & dp brn (Pelota)	1·10	40
379	15 f. on 50 f. violet and purple (Rugby)	1·00	40
380	20 f. on 75 f. deep blue-green, black and indigo (Climbing) (R.)	1·10	40
377/380	Set of 4	3·75	2·10

1957–59. (*a*) POSTAGE. (i) Nos. 1198*b*, 1200*a and* 1199*c* (*Harvester*) *surch as T* **45**, *with bars obliterating original face value.*

381	2 f. on 6 f. orange-brown	15	5
382	4 f. on 12 f. bright purple	75	30
383	5 f. on 10 f. emerald	55	20

(ii) Nos. 1238*b/c* ("*France*") *surch as T* **44** *with bars obliterating original face value.*

384	10 f. on 20 f. ultramarine (R.)	30	10
385	12 f. on 25 f. scarlet (1959)	75	10

(iii) No. 1335 (*View*) *surch as T* **44** *with bars obliterating original face value*

386	7 f. on 15 f. brownish black and deep bluish green (Le Quesnoy) (R.)	45	15

(iv) Nos. 1351, 1352/3, 1354/5 *and* 1356*a* (*Views*) *surch as T* **45** (*Nos.* 387/8) *or* **44** (*others*); (*Nos.* 389 *and* 391 *have bars obliterating original face value*)

387	3 f. on 10 f. chocolate and bistre-brown (Elysée) (1958)	15	8
388	6 f. on 18 f. chocolate & indigo (Beynac)	30	15
389	9 f. on 25 f. chocolate and violet-grey (Valençay) (R.) (1958)	35	20
390	17 f. on 35 f. cerise & carm-lake (Rouen)	1·25	25
391	20 f. on 50 f. sepia & grey-grn (St. Rémy)	70	20
392	25 f. on 85 f. brown-purple (Evian-les-Bains) (1959)	1·10	45

(*b*) AIR. Nos. 1319/20 (*Aircraft*) *surch as T* **49**

393	200 f. on 500 f. black and deep blue (Caravelle) (R.)	5·00	1·90
394	500 f. on 1000 f. black, reddish violet and sepia (L'Alouette) (1958)	9·00	4·50
381/394	Set of 14	19·00	8·00

The following are surcharged on French stamps with face values in new francs.

7ᶠ CFA

(50)

12ᶠ CFA

(51)

50ᶠCFA

(52)

1960 (16 Jan)–**61.** Nos. 1461, 1464 *and* 1467 (*Views*) *surch as T* **50** (395), **51** (396) *or* **52** (397).

395	7 f. on 15 c. ind & lt bl (Laon) (6.3.61)	45	20
396	20 f. on 50 c. maroon and deep bronze-green (Tlemcen) (R.) (8.61)	5·50	1·40
397	50 f. on 1 f. bluish violet, deep green and turquoise-blue (Cilaos)	80	30

10ᶠ CFA

(53)

12ᶠCFA

(54)

10+5 CFA

(55)

1961. Nos. 1453 *and* 1455 *surch as T* **45** (399) *with bars obliterating original value, or* **53** (*others, No.* 400 *without bars*).

398	5 f. on 10 c. emerald (Harvester)	10	10
399	5 f. on 10 c. emerald (Harvester)	45	15
400	10 f. on 20 c. carmine & turquoise (Sower)	10	5

1961 (14 Jan). No. 1494 ('*Marianne*') *surch as T* **54**

401	12 f. on 25 c. grey and claret	15	5

1961 (Aug)–**67**. *AIR. Nos.* 1457, 1457*b and* 1459/60 (*Aircraft*) *such as T* **48** (402/3) *or* **49** (404/5).

402	100 f. on 2 f. deep purple and ultramarine (*Noratlas*) (R.)	1·60	50
403	100 f. on 2 f. indigo and greenish blue (*Mystère* 20) (R.) (29.1.67)	80	30
404	200 f. on 5 f. black & dp blue (*Caravelle*)	2·25	95
405	500 f. on 10 f. black, reddish violet and sepia (*L'Alouette*) (14.9.64)	5·50	2·50
402/405	*Set of 4*	9·00	4·00

1962 (8 Oct). *POSTAGE DUE. Nos.* D1474, D1476 *and* D1478 (*Wheat Sheaves*) *surch as Type* D **47**.

D406	1 f. on 5 c. cerise	50	50
D407	10 f. on 20 c. olive-brown	75	75
D408	20 f. on 50 c. deep slate-green	4·50	2·50

1962 (10 Dec). *Red Cross. Nos.* 1593/4 (*Children*) *surch as* T **55**.

409	10 f. +5 f. on 20 c. +10 c. red and chocolate (*Rosalie*)	1·10	1·10
410	12 f. +5 f. on 25 c. +10 c. red and slate-green (*Pierrot*)	1·10	1·10

1963 (2 Jan). *First Trans-Atlantic Telecommunications Satellite Link. Nos.* 1587/8 *such as* T **51**.

411	12 f. on 25 c. yellow-brown, bluish green and blue-grey (*Aerial*)	25	20
412	25 f. on 50 c. ultramarine, grey-green and deep blue (*Satellite*)	35	25

Nos. 411/12 were released in Paris on 1 Feb.

1963 (18 Mar). *Nos.* 1541 *and* 1545 (*Views*) *surch as* T **50** (413) *or* **53** (414).

413	7 f. on 15 c. slate, purple and greenish blue (*St. Paul*)	10	8
414	20 f. on 45 c. chestnut, deep blue-green and deep blue (*Sully*)	45	20

1963 (18 Mar)–**65**. *Nos.* 1498*b*/9*b and* 1499*e*/*f* (*Arms*) *surch as T* **53**.

415	1 f. on 2 c. yellow, green and deep violet-blue (*Guéret*) (19.5.64)	5	5
416	2 f. on 5 c. multicoloured (*Oran*)	5	5
417	2 f. on 5 c. red, yellow & ultram (*Amiens*)	5	5
418	5 f. on 10 c. ultramarine, yellow and brown-red (*Troyes*) (23.12.63)	5	5
419	6 f. on 18 c. multicoloured (*St. Denis*) (16.5.64)	8	8
420	15 f. on 30 c. red and ultramarine (*Paris*) (17.1.65)	20	5
415/420	*Set of 6*	40	25

No. 419 was released in Paris on 19 May, and No. 420 on 18 Jan.

1963 (8 Dec). *Red Cross Fund. Nos.* 1627/8 (*Children*) *surch as* T **55**.

421	10 f. +5 f. on 20 c. +10 c. red and black (''Child with Grapes'') (R.)	1·40	1·40
422	12 f. +5 f. on 25 c. +10 c. red and deep bluish green (''The Piper'') (R.)	1·40	1·40

Nos. 421/2 were released in Paris on 9 Dec.

1964 (8 Feb). *''PHILATEC 1964'' International Stamp Exhibition, Paris. No.* 1629 *surch as* T **48**, *but smaller.*

423	12 f. on 25 c. carmine, deep bluish green and deep grey (B.)	40	25

No. 423 was released in Paris on 10 Feb.

7f CFA

(D 56)

10+5 CFA

(57)

58 Etienne Regnault and *Le Taureau*

1964 (1 June)–**71**. *POSTAGE DUE. Nos.* D1650/4 *and* D1656/7 (*Flowers*) *surch as Type* D **56**.

D424	1 f. on 5 c. red, green and bright purple (*Knapweed*)	5	5

D425	5 f. on 10 c. blue, green and bright purple (*Gentian*)	5	5
D426	7 f. on 15 c. red, grn & brn (*Poppies*)	8	8
D427	10 f. on 20 c. purple, light green and bl-grn (*Liitle periwinkle*) (5.3.71)	20	12
D428	15 f. on 30 c. blue, green and brown (*Forget-me-not*)	10	10
D429	20 f. on 50 c. carmine, green and ultra-marine (*Clover*)	20	15
D430	50 f. on 1 f. reddish violet, green and ultramarine (*Soldanella*)	45	25
D424/430	*Set of 7*	1·00	70

1964 (14 Sept)–**67**. *Nos.* 1654/5 (*Views*) *surch as T* **51** (432) *or* **48** (431), *but smaller.*

431	20 f. on 40 c. chocolate, deep bluish green & orge-brn (*Ronchamp*) (24.9.67)	25	12
432	35 f. on 70 c. maroon, deep bluish green and indigo (*Provins*)	45	30

1964 (13 Dec). *Red Cross Fund. Nos.* 1665/6 (*Famous Doctors*) *surch as T* **57**, *in blue.*

433	10 f. +5 f. on 20 c. +10 c. red and black (*Corvisart*)	55	55
434	12 f. +5 f. on 25 c. +10 c. red and black (*Larrey*)	55	55

1965 (17 Jan) *No* 1621 (*View*) *surch as T* **48**, *but smaller.*

435	30 f. on 60 c. brown-red, deep bluish green and blue (*St. Flour*)	45	30

No 435 was released in Paris on 18 Jan.

1965 (15 Aug)–**68**. *Nos.* 1684/5 *and* 1688 (*Views*) *surch as T* **48**, *but smaller.*

436	25 f. on 50 c. grey-blue, deep bluish green and bistre (*St. Marie*)	30	10
437	30 f. on 60 c. purple-brown and greenish blue (*Aix les Bains*) (30.1.67)	30	10
438	50 f. on 1 f. grey, yellow-green and yellow-brown (*Carnac*) (B.) (26.2.68)	45	25

(Des and eng A. Decaris. Recess)

1965 (3 Oct). *Tercentenary of Colonisation of Réunion. P* 13.

439	**58** 15 f. grey-blue and lake	20	12

1965 (12 Dec). *Red Cross Fund. Nos.* 1698/9 (*Renoir's paintings*) *surch as T* **57**.

440	12 f. +5 f. on 25 c. +10 c. red and indigo (''Le Bébé à la Cuiller'')	50	50
441	15 f. +5 f. on 30 c. +10 c. red and red-brown (''Coco écrivant'')	50	50

1966 (14 Feb). *No.* 1513 (''*Marianne*'') *surch as T* **53** *with bars obliterating original value.*

442	10 f. on 20 c. carmine-red and blue	12	5

1966 (26 Mar). *Launching of First French Satellite. Nos.* 1696/7 *surch as T* **53** *with bars obliterating original value.*

443	15 f. on 30 c. new blue, greenish blue and indigo (*Rocket*) (R.)	30	25
444	30 f. on 60 c. new blue, greenish blue and indigo (*Satellite*) (R.)	40	25

Nos. 443/4 were released in Paris on 27 Mar.

1966 (11 Dec). *Red Cross Fund. Nos.* 1733/4 (*Nurses*) *surch as T* **57**.

445	12 f. +5 f. on 25 c. +10 c. red and deep bluish green (*Nurse, 1859*)	50	50
446	15 f. +5 f. on 30 c. +10 c. red and indigo (*Nurse, 1966*)	50	50

30f CFA

(59)

12+5 CFA

(60)

1967 (11 June). *World Fair, Montreal. No.* 1747 *surch as T* **59**.
447 30 f. on 60 c. turquoise-grn & greenish bl 35 25

1967 (24 Sept). *No.* 1700 (*Arms*) *surch as T* **53** *with bars obliterating original value.*
448 2 f. on 5 c. vermilion & ultramarine (Auch) 10 5

1967 (29 Oct). *50th Anniv of Lions International. No.* 1766 *surch as T* **48**, *but smaller.*
449 20 f. on 40 c. bluish violet & brn-lake (B.) 35 25

1967 (17 Dec). *Red Cross Fund. Nos.* 1772/3 (*Ivories*) *surch as T* **60**.
450 12 f.+5 f. on 25 c. red, purple-brown
       and deep reddish violet ("Flautist") . . 80 80
451 15 f.+5 f. on 30 c.+10 c. red, purple-brown
       and myrtle-green ("Violinist") . . 80 80

1968 (21 Oct). *French Polar Exploration. No.* 1806 *surch as T* **48**, *but smaller.*
452 20 f. on 40 c. light turquoise-blue, brown-
       red and greenish blue 30 15

1968 (15 Dec). *Red Cross Fund. Nos.* 1812/3 (*Seasons*) *surch as T* **60**.
453 12 f.+5 f. on 25 c.+10 c. red, indigo and
       violet ("Spring") 50 50
454 15 f.+5 f. on 30 c.+10 c. red, deep car-
       mine and yellow-brown ("Autumn") 50 50

1969 (17 Mar). *Stamp Day. No.* 1824 (*Horse-bus*) *surch as T* **60**.
455 15 f.+5 f. on 30 c.+10 c. myrtle-green,
       purple-brown and black 30 30

1969 (13 Apr). *Nos.* 1768a/b ("*République*") *surch as T* **59**. *but larger.*
456 15 f. on 30 c. emerald 15 8
457 20 f. on 40 c. cerise 20 8
See also No. 493.

1969 (22 June). *No.* 1735 (*Arms*) *surch as T* **48**, *but smaller.*
458 10 f. on 20 c. multicoloured (Saint-Lo) . 10 5

1969 (16 Aug). *Birth Bicentenary of Napoleon Bonaparte. No* 1845 *surch as T* **48**, *but smaller.*
459 35 f. on 70 c. green, reddish violet and
       light blue (Birthplace) 50 40

1969 (14 Dec). *Red Cross Fund. Nos.* 1853/4 (*Seasons*) *surch as T* **60**.
460 20 f.+7 f. on 40 c.+15 c. red, light brown
       and chocolate ("Summer") . . 45 45
461 20 f.+7 f. on 40 c.+15 c. red, greenish blue
       and reddish violet ("Winter") . . 45 45

20+5
≡ CFA
(61)

1970 (16 Mar). *Stamp Day. No.* 1866 (*Postman,* 1830) *surch as T* **61**.
462 20 f.+5 f. on 40 c.+10 c. black, ultramarine
       and carmine-red 45 30

1970 (12 Dec). *Red Cross Fund. Nos.* 1902/3 (*Frescoes*) *surch as T* **61**.
463 20 f.+7 f. on 40 c.+15 c. red and green
       ("Lord and Lady") . . . . . . 1·00 1·00
464 20 f.+7 f. on 40 c.+15 c. red and brown-
       red ("Angel with instruments of
       mortification") . . . . . . 1·00 1·00

1971 (18 Jan). *No.* 1905 ("*Marianne*") *surch as T* **53**.
465 25 f. on 50 c. cerise 20 10

1971 (29 Mar). *Stamp Day. No.* 1919 (*Field Post Office, World War* I) *surch as T* **61**.
466 25 f.+5 f. on 50 c.+10 c. blue, brown and
       bistre-brown 35 30

40ᶠ
CFA
≡
(62)

1971 (13 Apr). *French Merchant Marine. Sailing-ship era. No.* 1920 *surch as T* **62**.
467 40 f. on 80 c. reddish violet, indigo and
       new blue (*Antoinette*) 45 25

1971 (5 June). *25th Anniv of Rural Family Aid* (1970). *No.* 1928 *surch as T* **48**, *but smaller.*
468 15 f. on 40 c. blue, violet and green . . 20 10

1971 (30 Aug) –72. *Nos.* 1931/2 (*Views*) *surch as T* **53**.
469 45 f. on 90 c. brn, grn & ochre (Riquewihr) 35 20
470 50 f. on 1 f. 10, light brown, greenish blue
       and myrtle-green (Sedan) (17.1.72) 40 30

1971 (16 Oct). *40th Anniv of First Meeting of Crafts Guilds Association. No.* 1935 *surch as T* **48**, *but smaller.*
471 45 f. on 90 c. light purple and carmine . . 50 30

63 Réunion Chameleon   **64** De Gaulle in Uniform (June 1940)

(Des P. Lambert. Photo)

1971 (7 Nov). *Nature Protection. P* 13.
472 **63** 25 f. brt green, brown & greenish yell 30 15

(Des G. Bétemps. Eng E. Lacaque (Nos. 473, 476). Des and eng P. Béquet (others). Recess)

1971 (9 Nov). *De Gaulle Commemoration and First Death Anniv. T* **64** *and similar vert designs. P* 13.
473 25 f. black 25 20
474 25 f. blue 25 20
475 25 f. red 25 20
476 25 f. black 25 20
473/476 Set of 4 . . . . . . 90 70
Designs: —No. 473, Type **64**; No. 474, De Gaulle at Brazzaville, 1944; No. 475, Liberation of Paris, 1944; No. 476, De Gaulle as President of the French Republic, 1970.
Nos. 473/6 were issued in sheets of 20 stamps giving 5 horiz *se-tenant* strips with a stamp-sized label showing the Cross of Lorraine in the centre of each horiz strip.

1971 (11 Dec). *Red Cross Fund. Paintings by J. B. Greuze. Nos.* 1942/3 *surch as T* **60**.
477 15 f.+5 f. on 30 c.+10 c. red and ultra-
       marine ("Young Girl with Little Dog") 45 45
478 25 f.+5 f. on 50 c.+10 c. red and lake
       ("The Dead Bird") 45 45

A regular new issue supplement to this
catalogue appears each month in

STAMP MONTHLY

—from your newsagent or by postal subscription
—details on request.

Réunion 1972

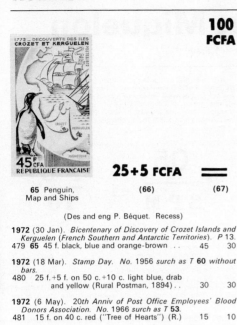

100 FCFA

25+5 FCFA ═══

65 Penguin,   (66)   (67)
Map and Ships

(Des and eng P. Béquet. Recess)

1972 (30 Jan). *Bicentenary of Discovery of Crozet Islands and Kerguelen (French Southern and Antarctic Territories).* P 13.
479 **65** 45 f. black, blue and orange-brown ..   45   30

1972 (18 Mar). *Stamp Day. No.* 1956 *surch as T* **60** *without bars.*
480   25 f. +5 f. on 50 c. +10 c. light blue, drab and yellow (Rural Postman, 1894) ..   30   30

1972 (6 May). *20th Anniv of Post Office Employees' Blood Donors Association. No.* 1966 *surch as T* **53**.
481   15 f. on 40 c. red ("Tree of Hearts") (R)   15   10

1972 (14 May). *AIR. No.* 1890 *(Pioneer Aviators) surch as T* **48**, *but smaller.*
482   200 f. on 5 f. deep blackish brown, emerald and deep greenish blue (Daurat and Vanier) (R.) ..   ..   1·90   70

1972 (2 June). *Postal Code Campaign. Nos.* 1969/70 *surch as T* **53**, *but larger figures.*
483   15 f. on 30 c. carmine-red, black & emer   12   10
484   25 f. on 50 c. yellow, black & carmine-red   20   12

1972 (16 Dec). *Red Cross Fund. Nos.* 1979/80 *(Doctors of the* 1st *Empire) surch as T* **60**.
485   15 f. +5 f. on 30 c. +10 c. red, dull green and bronze-green (Deagenettes) (R.)   35   35
486   25 f. +5 f. on 50 c. +10 c. red, scarlet and brown-lake (Broussais) (G.)   ..   45   45

1973 (24 Mar). *Stamp Day. No.* 1996 *surch as T* **60**.
487   25 f. +5 f. on 50 c. +10 c. turquoise-blue (Mail Coach, *c.* 1835) (R.)   ..   40   30

1973 (10 June). *French Merchant Marine. Sailing-ship era. No.* 2011 *surch as T* **48** *but smaller.*
488   45 f. on 90 c. greenish blue, indigo and blue (Barque *France II*) (B.)   ..   40   30

1973 (24 June). *No.* 2008 *(View) surch as T* **61**.
489   50 f. on 1 f. myrtle-green, orange-brown and light blue (Clos-Luce) (B.)' ..   35   20

1973 (13 Oct). *No.* 1960 *(View) surch as T* **48**, *but smaller.*
490   100 f. on 2 f. maroon and blackish green (Bazoches-du-Morvand) (R.)   ..   70   35

1973 (1 Dec). *Red Cross Fund.. Tomb Figures, Tonnerre. Nos.* 2021/2 *surch as T* **60**.
491   15 f. +5 f. on 30 c. +10 c. red and myrtle-green ("Mary Magdalene") (R.) ..   30   30
492   25 f. +5 f. on 50 c. +10 c. red and black (Female saint) (R.)   45   45

1973. *No.* 1843 *("Republique") surch as T* **59**, *but larger.*
493   15 f. on 30 c. emerald   12   10

1974 (20 Jan). *"ARPHILA 75" International Stamp Exhibition, Paris (1975). No.* 2026 *surch as T* **59**, *but larger.*
494   25 f. on 50 c. brn, new bl & brt pur (R.)   20   20

1974 (9 Mar). *Stamp Day. No.* 2031 *surch as T* **66**.
495   25 f. +5 f. on 50 c. +10 c. bistre-brown, brown-red and olive   25   25

1974 (23 Mar–22 Dec). *French Art. Nos.* 2033/6 *surch as T* **67**.
496   100 f. on 2 f. multicoloured ("Cardinal Richelieu" (P. de Champaigne)) ..   70   45
497   100 f. on 2 f. multicoloured ("Abstract") (Miro) (B.) (15.9)   65   45
498   100 f. on 2 f. chestnut and light blue ("Canal du Loing" (A. Sisley)) (Br.) (10.11)   65   45
499   100 f. on 2 f. multicoloured (Gobelin tapestry by Mathieu) (B.) (22.12)   65   45
496/499 *Set of 4* ..   ..   ..   2·50 1·90

1974 (28 Apr). *French Lifeboat Service. No.* 2040 *surch as T* **67**.
500   45 f. on 90 c. indigo, red and bistre (Shipwreck and Lifeboat) (R.) ..   35   25

1974 (6 Oct). *Centenary of Universal Postal Union. No.* 2054 *surch as T* **67**, *in blue.*
501   60 f. on 1 f. 20, bronze-grn, carm & ultram   40   40

30 FCFA   **30+7 FCFA** ═══

(68)   (69)

1974 (19 Oct). *Nos.* 1906*ap/bp* *("Marianne") surch as T* **68**, *in blue.*
502   30 f. on 60 c. emerald   55   45
503   40 f. on 80 c. carmine   65   50

1974 (30 Nov). *Red Cross Fund. "The Seasons". Nos.* 2059/60 *surch as T* **69**.
504   30 f. +7 f. on 60 c. +15 c. brown, blue and red ("Summer") (G.)   ..   40   40
505   40 f. +7 f. on 80 c. +15 c. slate-blue, olive-brown and red ("Winter") (R.)   ..   45   45

On 1 January 1975 the CFA franc was replaced by the French Metropolitan franc as the unit of currency. Issues surcharged in CFA currency were withdrawn, and replaced by unsurcharged stamps of France.

ALBUM LISTS

Please write for our latest lists of albums and accessories. These will be sent free on request.

St.-Pierre et Miquelon

100 Centimes = 1 Franc

The islands of St. Pierre (10 square miles) and Miquelon (83 square miles, consisting of Grande Miquelon connected by a sandy isthmus to Petite Miquelon) lie off the south coast of Newfoundland. They have been frequented by French fishermen since the early 16th century and settlement began there in the 17th century. The islands were British from 1713 to 1763, and were later under British occupation from 1778 to 1783 and 1793 to 1816, when they were returned to France. During the prohibition era, 1920 to 1935, the inhabitants lived by smuggling alcohol into the U.S.A. Since then their main means of livelihood have been cod fishing and the breeding of silver foxes, with subsidies from France.

PRINTERS. All the stamps of St. Pierre and Miquelon were printed at the Government Printing Works, Paris, *unless otherwise stated.*

IMPERFORATE STAMPS. Stamps exist imperforate in their issued colours, but these were not valid for postage. Imperforate stamps in other colours are colour trials.

FRENCH COLONY

(1)

(2)

(3)

1885 (5 Jan). *French Colonies (General issues) Type J ("Commerce") handstamped with T 1 in two operations, at St. Pierre.*

1	J 5 on 2 c. brown/*buff*	.. .. £1200	£650

On No. 1 the surcharge is always inverted.

This surcharge was applied in two operations, as were Types 2/4. The figures were struck by one handstamp and "S P M" by another. It is thought that the letters "S P M" on Types 1/4 were struck from the same handstamp.

1885 (7 Mar). *French Colonies (General issues) Type H ("Peace and Commerce") handstamped in two operations with T 2 or 3, at St. Pierre.*

2	H 25 on 1 f. olive-green (Type 2) ..	.. £1300	£700
3	25 on 1 f. olive-green (Type 3) ..	.. £750	£475

(4)

(5)

(6)

1885 (27 Mar). *French Colonies (General issues) Type J ("Commerce") handstamped with T 4 in two operations, at St. Pierre.*

4	J 5 on 4 c. purple-brown/*grey* ..	.. £100	75·00

1885 (3 Aug–6 Dec). *French Colonies (General issues) Type H ("Peace and Commerce") handstamped with T 5, at St. Pierre.*

5	H 05 on 40 c. red/*yellow* (6.12) ..	.. 25·00	12·00
6	10 on 40 c. red/*yellow* ..	.. 5·50	4·50
	a. "m" inverted ..	.. 35·00	35·00
	b. Wide surcharge (Type 6) ..	22·00	
7	15 on 40 c. red/*yellow* ..	.. 5·50	4·50
	a. Wide surcharge (Type 6) ..	22·00	

It is thought that a large number of different handstamps as Types **5** and **6** were used for these provisionals. Originally the surcharges were applied in triplets of three to panes of 50 stamps, giving an additional strike of Type 5 on the left or right margin. Later one at least of these three cliché handstamps was dismantled so that the surcharges could be struck singly or in pairs.

(7)

(8)

1885 (Dec). *French Colonies (General issues) Types H and J handstamped with T 7, at St. Pierre.*

8	J 05 on 20 c. red/*green* (30.12) ..	..	5·50	4·75
9	H 05 on 35 c. black/*yellow* (29.12)	..	25·00	19·00
10	05 on 75 c. carmine (29.12)	..	70·00	48·00
11	05 on 1 f. olive-green ..	..	5·00	4·50

Type **7** was also applied by triplet handstamps on sheets of 50, resulting in examples of the surcharge being struck in the vertical sheet margins.

1886 (11 Feb). *Handstamps as T 8 struck on plain ungummed paper at St. Pierre. Imperf.*

12	**8** 5 c. black ..	..	..	— £325
13	10 c. black ..	..	..	— £375
14	15 c. black ..	..	..	— £300

In Type **8** the letters "P D" denote "Payé à Destination". The use of Nos. 12/14 was authorised by Decree of the Colony Commandant on 22 January to offset an acute shortage of these values. The labels, which were applied by the postal clerks after the postage had been prepaid in cash, were intended for use within the colony only, although some are known used on covers to France. They were in use until 27 February 1886 when further stamp supplies were received from France. The catalogue prices are for used examples with dated postmarks between 11 and 27 February 1886.

(9)

(10)

(11)

1891 (27 Apr–10 Oct). *French Colonies (General issues) Type J ("Commerce") surch with T 9, at St. Pierre.*

15	J 15 c. on 30 c. cinnamon/*drab* ..	..	7·50	6·50
	a. Surch inverted ..	..	45·00	40·00
16	15 c. on 35 c. black/*orange* ..	..	£140	£100
	a. Surch inverted ..	..	£170	£150
	b. Surch in smaller figures (Type 10) (10.10) ..	..	£325	£190
	ba. Surch T 10 inverted ..	..	£350	£250
17	15 c. on 40 c. red/*yellow* ..	..	19·00	13·00
	a. Surch inverted ..	..	42·00	38·00

Nos. 16b/ba were produced by the postmaster without permission to fill philatelic orders from France, but it is understood that some examples were sold to the public in the normal way from the St. Pierre Post Office.

1891 (15 Oct). *French Colonies (General issues) Type J ("Commerce") optd with T 11, at St. Pierre. (a) In red.*

19	J 1 c. black/*azure* ..	..	2·25	2·25
	a. Opt inverted ..	..	3·75	3·75

20	J	2 c. brown/*buff*	.. .. ..	5·50	5·50
		a. Opt inverted	.. ..	13·00	13·00
21		4 c. purple-brown/*grey*	..	4·50	4·50
		a. Opt inverted	..	9·50	9·50
22		10 c. black/*lilac*	.. ..	3·50	3·50
		a. Opt inverted	.. ..	5·50	5·50

(*b*) *In black*

23	J	1 c. black/*azure*	.. ..	2·75	2·50
		a. Opt inverted	.. ..	5·00	5·00
24		2 c. brown/*buff*	.. ..	2·75	2·50
		a. Opt inverted	.. ..	5·00	5·00
25		4 c. purple-brown/*grey*	..	2·75	2·50
		a. Opt inverted	.. ..	5·50	5·50
26		5 c. green/*green*	.. ..	2·75	2·50
27		10 c. black/*lilac* ..	.. ..	7·50	6·50
		a. Opt inverted	.. ..	14·00	14·00
28		15 c. blue/*pale blue*	..	5·00	3·25
29		20 c. red/*green* ..	..	18·00	15·00
30		25 c. black/*rose*	.. ..	5·50	5·00
31		30 c. cinnamon/*drab*	..	23·00	20·00
32		35 c. black/*orange*	..	£100	85·00
		a. Opt inverted	.. ..	£140	£140
33		40 c. red/*yellow*	.. ..	17·00	14·00
		a. Opt double	.. ..	45·00	
34		75 c. rose-carmine/*rose* ..		25·00	21·00
		a. Opt inverted	.. ..	50·00	45·00
35		1 f. olive-green/*toned*	..	17·00	14·00
		a. Opt inverted	.. ..	38·00	35·00

Nos. 19/35 were printed from two settings. On one setting a diagonal row of 5 clichés was inverted, causing the overprint inverted errors. These were noticed during printing and the row of clichés corrected.

(12)   (13)   (14)

1891 (24 Nov)–*92. French Colonies* (*General issues*) *Type J* (*"Commerce"*) *surch as T* **12**, *at St. Pierre.*

36	J	1 c. on 5 c. green/*green*	..	2·25	1·75
37		1 c. on 10 c. black/*lilac* (29.12.91)		2·25	2·00
38		1 c. on 25 c. black/*rose* (20.6.92)		1·75	1·25
39		2 c. on 10 c. black/*lilac*	..	1·75	1·25
		a. Surch double	..	16·00	
40		2 c. on 15 c. blue/*pale blue* (29.12.91) ..		1·10	1·10
41		2 c. on 25 c. black/*rose* (20.6.92)		1·10	1·10
42		4 c. on 20 c. red/*green*	..	1·10	1·10
43		4 c. on 25 c. black/*rose* (20.6.92)		1·10	1·10
		a. Surch double	..	17·00	
44		4 c. on 30 c. cinnamon/*drab* (29.12.91)		4·50	3·25
		a. "ST-PIERRE M-on" double		30·00	30·00
45		4 c. on 40 c. red/*green* (29.12.91)		5·00	2·50
		a. "ST PIERRE M-on" double		50·00	50·00

These surcharges were normally applied in one operation onto stamps of the French Colonies (General issues). It is known, however, that for some quantities of the 4 c. on 20 c., 4 c. on 30 c. and 4 c. on 40 c. the value and "cent." were applied to sheets already overprinted with Type **11**. Stamps with the surcharge applied in two operations can often be identified by variations in spacing between the two sections.

1892 (4 Nov). *Overprinted values of* 1891 *further handstamped at St. Pierre.* (*a*) *No.* 30 *surch with thick figure as in T* **13**.

46	J	1 on 25 c. black/*rose*	.. ..	1·10	1·10
47		2 on 25 c. black/*rose*	..	1·10	1·10
48		4 on 25 c. black/*rose*	..	1·10	1·10

(*b*) *No.* 26 *surch with double-lined shaded figure as in T* **14**.

49	J	1 on 5 c. green/*green*	..	2·25	1·90
50		2 on 5 c. green/*green*	.. ..	2·25	1·90
51		4 on 5 c. green/*green*	..	2·25	1·90

HAVE YOU READ THE NOTES AT THE BEGINNING OF THIS CATALOGUE?

These often provide answers to the enquiries we receive.

                 COLIS
   Type U of   **POSTAUX**
French Colonies (General
Issues)   **(15)**   **(P 16)**

1892 (1 Dec). *French Colonies* (*General issues*) *Postage Due Type* U *optd at St. Pierre.* (*a*) POSTAGE. *With T* **15**.

52	U	10 c. black (R.) ..	.. ..	7·50	7·50
53		20 c. black (R.)	.. ..	5·00	5·00
54		30 c. black (R.)	.. ..	6·50	5·00
55		40 c. black (R.) ..	.. ..	6·50	5·50
56		60 c. black (R.)	.. ..	24·00	19·00
57		1 f. brown	.. ..	32·00	28·00
58		2 f. brown	.. ..	55·00	48·00
59		5 f. brown	.. ..	95·00	90·00

(*b*) POSTAGE DUE. *As T* **11**

D60	U	5 c. black (R.)	.. ..	9·50	8·00
D61		10 c. black (R.)	.. ..	3·25	3·25
D62		15 c. black (R.)	.. ..	3·25	3·25
D63		20 c. black (R.)	.. ..	3·25	3·25
D64		30 c. black (R.)	.. ..	3·25	3·25
D65		40 c. black (R.)	.. ..	2·50	2·50
D66		60 c. black (R.)	.. ..	13·00	13·00
D67		1 f. brown	.. ..	28·00	28·00
D68		2 f. brown	.. ..	28·00	28·00

1892 (Dec). *As T* **10** *of Réunion, inscr* "ST. PIERRE ET MIQUELON" *in red* (1, 5, 15, 25, 75 *c.*, 1 *f.*) *or blue* (*others*). *P* 14x13½.

60		1 c. black/*azure*	.. ..	25	25
61		2 c. brown/*buff*	.. ..	25	25
62		4 c. purple-brown/*grey*	..	45	40
63		5 c. green/*pale green* ..		65	65
64		10 c. black/*lilac* ..	..	1·25	1·00
65		15 c. blue (*quadrillé paper*)	..	1·75	65
66		20 c. red/*green* ..	..	4·50	3·75
67		25 c. black/*rose* ..	..	2·00	50
68		30 c. cinnamon/*drab*	..	1·90	75
69		40 c. red/*yellow*	.. ..	1·25	75
70		50 c. carmine/*rose*	..	9·00	6·50
71		75 c. brown/*orange*	..	5·50	4·50
72		1 f. olive-green/*toned* ..		4·00	2·50
60/72		Set of 13	.. ..	30·00	20·00

Although released in Paris during November, 1892, these stamps did not reach the islands until some weeks later.

1900 (Dec)–08 *As Nos.* 60/72 *but colours changed and new value. Inscr in blue* (10 *c.*) *or red* (*others. P* 14×13½.

73		5 c. bright yellow-green (1908)		75	65
74		10 c. rose-red	.. ..	75	25
75		15 c. grey	.. ..	13·00	9·50
76		25 c. blue	.. ..	3·00	2·00
77		35 c. black/*yellow* (1906)	..	1·25	90
78		50 c. brown/*azure*	.. ..	7·00	5·50
73/78		Set of 6	.. ..	23·00	17·00

1901. *PARCEL POST.* (*a*) *No.* 64 *optd with Type* P **16**, *at St. Pierre.*

P79	10 c. black/*lilac*	.. ..	10·00	10·00

(*b*) *No.* 74 *optd with Type* P **15** *of Réunion, in Paris*

P80	10 c. rose-red ..	.. ..	3·25	3·25

17 Fisherman   **18** Sea-gull

THE WORLD CENTRE FOR FINE STAMPS IS 391 STRAND

19 Fishing Boat

(Des C. J. Housez. Typo)

1909 (Feb)–**17**. *Centre, value, or tablet of value in first colour.*
P 14×13½.

79	**17**	1 c. sepia and orange-red	5	5
80		2 c. blue and sepia	5	5
81		4 c. sepia and pale violet	5	5
82		5 c. olive and blue-green	5	5
83		10 c. red and rose	5	5
84		15 c. carmine and dull purple (8.17)	5	5
85		20 c. deep purple and pale brown	15	15
86	**18**	25 c. blue and deep blue	30	25
87		30 c. purple-brown and orange	15	12
88		35 c. purple-brown and sage-green	5	5
89		40 c. grey-green and purple-brown	45	25
90		45 c. grey-green and pale violet	5	5
91		50 c. grey-green and olive-brown	20	20
92		75 c. olive and brown	15	12
93	**19**	1 f. blue and grey-green	45	40
94		2 f. brown and pale violet	55	45
95		5 f. grey-green and purple-brown	1·90	1·25
79/95		*Set of* 17	4·25	3·00

1912 (Nov). *Nos.* 61/2, 65/6, 68, 77 *and* 69/72 *surch as T* 21 *and*
22 *of Réunion.*

A. Narrow spacing. B. Wide spacing

			A		B	
96	05 on 2 c. brown/*buff*		25	25	55·00	55·00
97	05 on 4 c. pur-brn/*grey* (R.)	5	5	5·00	5·00
98	05 on 15 c. blue (R.)		5	5	9·00	9·00
99	05 on 20 c. red/*green*		5	5	3·75	3·75
100	05 on 25 c. black/*rose*	(R.)	5	5	3·25	3·25
101	05 on 30 c. cinna/*drab*	(R.)	5	5	7·50	7·50
102	05 on 35 c. black/*yellow* (R.)		10	10	2·50	2·50
103	10 on 40 c. red/*yellow*		5	5	3·25	3·25
104	10 on 50 c. carmine		8	8	3·25	3·25
105	10 on 75 c. brown/*orange*		25	25	8·00	8·00
106	10 on 1 f. olive-green/*toned*		30	30	8·00	8·00
96/106	*Set of* 11			1·10	1·10	— —

For note *re* spacing, see Réunion.

1915–17. *Red Cross. Surch as T* 24 *of Réunion, in red.*

107	**17**	10 c.+5 c. red and rose	10	10
108		15 c.+5 c. carmine & dull purple (1917)	10	10

No. 107 can be found on thin paper.

Colis Postaux

(P 20)

1917–25. *PARCEL POST. Optd with Type* P 20.

P109	**17**	10 c. red and rose	45	45
P110		20 c. dp purple & p brn (B.) (1925)	20	20
		a. Opt double	16·00	

No. P109 can be found on thin paper.

1922 (1 Jan)–**30**. *Colours changed and new values.* P 14×13½.

109	**17**	5 c. black and blue	5	5
110		10 c. olive and green	5	5
111		10 c. magenta and bistre (7.9.25)	5	5
112	**18**	25 c. green and brown	5	5
113		30 c. red and carmine	5	5
114		30 c. blue and lake (7.9.25)	5	5
115		30 c. green and olive (29.11.26)	8	8
116		50 c. pale blue and blue	12	12
117		50 c. magenta and bistre (7.9.25)	10	10
118		60 c. red and blue (21.12.25)	5	5
119		65 c. red-brown and mauve (2.4.28)	45	45
120		90 c. vermilion and scarlet (26 2 30)	3·75	3·75
121	**19**	1 f. 10, rosine and green (25.9.28)	40	40
122		1 f. 50, blue and ultramarine (22.3.30)	1·75	1·75
123		3 f. magenta/*rose* (22.3.30)	1·75	1·75
109/123		*Set of* 15	7·00	7·00

1924 (June)–**27**. *Surch with new values as T* **26/8** *of Réunion,*
and with bars over original values. Some colours changed.

124	**17**	25 c. on 15 c. carm & dull pur (1.2.25)	5	5
		a. Surch double	25·00	
		b. Surch triple	25·00	
125	**19**	25 c. on 2 f. brown and violet (B.)	5	5
126		25 c. on 5 f. grey-green and brown (B.)	5	5
		a. Surch triple	22·00	
127	**18**	65 on 45 c. grey-green & violet (1.2.25)	20	20
128		85 on 75 c. olive and brown (1.2.25)	20	20
129		90 c. on 75 c. verm & scar (11.4.27)	40	40
130	**19**	1 f. 25 on 1 f. ultramarine and blue (R.) (14.6.26)	40	40
131		1 f. 50 on 1 f. blue & lt blue (11.4.27)	50	50
132		3 f. on 5 f. magenta & sep (19.12.27)	45	45
133		10 f. on 5 f. ol-grn & rosine (11.4.27)	3·50	3·50
134		20 f. on 5 f. rosine & violet (11.4.27)	4·25	4·25
124/134		*Set of* 11	9·00	9·00

Owing to a shortage of 30 c. stamps between April and
July 1926 letters addressed to France had the postage prepaid
in cash and were then handstamped with 5 c. or 30 c. cachets
reading "GOUVERNEMENT/ PP (value)/ Saint-Pierre Miquelon/
Saint-Pierre". A similar cachet without face value was also
used.

Type D **11** of	(D 21)	(D 22)
France		

1925 (7 Sept)-**27**. *POSTAGE DUE.* Type D **11** *of France*
optd with Type D **21** *or surch as Type* D **22**.

D135		5 c. pale blue	8	8
D136		10 c. pale brown	8	8
D137		20 c. olive-green	8	8
D138		25 c. rosine	10	10
D139		30 c. carmine	15	15
D140		45 c. pale green	15	15
D141		50 c. dull claret	30	30
D142		60 c. on 50 c. yellow-brown	30	30
D143		1 f. claret/*straw*	40	40
D144		2 f. on 1 f. rose-red	50	50
D145		3 f. magenta (10.10.27)	1·25	1·25
D135/145		*Set of* 11	3·00	3·00

23 French Colonial Races　　**24** Women of Five Races

25 "France the Civiliser"

26 French Colonial
Commerce

(Des J. de la Nézière (T **23**), Cayon-Rouan (T **24**), A. Parent
(T **25**), G. Francois (T **26**). Recess Institut de Gravure, Paris)

1931 (13 Apr). *International Colonial Exhibition, Paris.* P 12½.

135	**23**	40 c. green and black	45	45
136	**24**	50 c. mauve and black	45	45
137	**25**	90 c. vermilion and black	45	45
138	**26**	1 f. 50, blue and black	45	45
135/138		*Set of* 4	1·60	1·60

27 Map of St-Pierre et Miquelon

28 Lighthouse

165 27   1 f. 50, light and deep blue .. 45 45
166 29   1 f. 75, chocolate and black (R.) .. 45 45
167 28   5 f. brown and scarlet (B.) .. 5·50 5·50
163/167 Set of 5 .. .. .. 6·50 6·50

32 Commerce

33 Sailing Ships

29 Trawler

D 30 Newfoundland Dog

(Des Gimel. Eng C. Hourriez (T 27), E. Feltesse (T 28), J. Piel (T 29), A. Mignon (Type D 30). Typo)

1932 (5 Dec)–33. P 13½×14 (vert) or 14×13½ (horiz).

(a) POSTAGE

139 27   1 c. ultramarine and claret .. 5 5
140 28   2 c. blue-green and black 5 5
141 29   4 c. brown and carmine 5 5
142   5 c. brown and mauve 5 5
143 28 10 c. black and claret 8 8
144   15 c. mauve and blue 15 15
145 27 20 c. vermilion and black 20 20
146   25 c. yellow-green and mauve .. 12 12
147 29 30 c. green and olive-green .. 15 15
148   40 c. brown and blue 10 10
149 28 45 c. green and scarlet 20 20
150   50 c. green and brown 20 20
151 29 65 c. red and brown 25 25
152 27 75 c. vermilion and green .. 25 25
153   90 c. scarlet and red 25 25
154 29   1 f. scarlet and brown-red .. 20 20
155 27   1 f. 25, carmine and blue (25.9.33).. 30 30
156   1 f. 50, light and deep blue 30 30
157 29   1 f. 75, chocolate and black (25.9.33) 35 35
158   2 f. blue-green and black .. .. 1·25 1·25
159 28   3 f. brown and green .. .. 1·75 1·75
160   5 f. brown and scarlet .. .. 3·75 3·75
161 29 10 f. mauve and blue-green .. .. 11·00 11·00
162 27 20 f. green and scarlet .. .. 11·00 11·00
139/162 Set of 24 .. .. .. 29·00 29·00

(b) POSTAGE DUE

D163 D 30   5 c. black and deep blue .. 20 20
D164   10 c. black and green 20 20
D165   20 c. black and scarlet 30 30
D166   25 c. black and purple 30 30
D167   30 c. black and orange 55 55
D168   45 c. black and light blue .. 70 70
D169   50 c. black and blue-green .. 1·10 1·10
D170   60 c. black and carmine-rose .. 1·10 1·10
D171   1 f. black and red-brown .. 3·25 3·25
D172   2 f. black and purple .. .. 4·75 4·75
D173   3 f. black and sepia .. .. 4·75 4·75
D163/173 Set of 11 .. .. 16·00 16·00

JACQUES CARTIER

1534 • 1934

(31)

1934 (18 Oct). Fourth Centenary of Cartier's Discovery of Canada. Optd with T **31** or similar opt.
163 **28** 50 c. green and brown 30 30
164 **27** 75 c. vermilion and green .. 45 45

34 Women of Three Races

35 Agriculture

36 France extends Torch of Civilisation

37 Diane de Poitiers

(Des J. Goujon (T **32**), Robichon (T **33**), Cayon-Rouan (T **34**), A. Decaris (T **35**, **37**), G. Barlangue (T **36**), Eng R. Cottet (T **32**), E. Feltesse (T **33**), P. Munier (T **34**), A. Decaris (T **35**, **37**), A. Delzers (T **36**). Recess)

1937 (15 Apr). International Exhibition, Paris. P 13.
168 **32** 20 c. bright violet 30 30
169 **33** 30 c. green 30 30
170 **34** 40 c. carmine 30 30
171 **35** 50 c. brown and blue.. .. .. 30 30
172 **36** 90 c. scarlet 30 30
173 **37**   1 f. 50, blue 30 30
168/173 Set of 6 .. .. 1·60 1·60
MS173a 120x100 mm **36** 3 f. blue. Imperf .. 70 70

38 Pierre and Marie Curie

(Des J. de la Nézière. Eng J. Piel. Recess)

1938 (24 Oct). International Anti-Cancer Fund. P 13.
174 **38**   1 f. 75+50 c. ultramarine .. .. 2·50 2·50

39 Dog-team   D 40 Codfish

(Des J. Douy (Postage), Loyer-Vigier (Postage Due). Photo Vaugirard, Paris)

1938 (17 Nov)-**40.** (a) POSTAGE. T **39** and similar horiz designs. P 13½.

175	**39**	2 c. blue-green			5	5
176		3 c. reddish brown			5	5
177		4 c. purple			5	5
178		5 c. carmine			5	5
179		10 c. yellow-brown			5	5
180		15 c. bright purple			5	5
181		20 c. bright violet			5	5
182		25 c. turquoise-blue			25	25
183	–	30 c. purple			5	5
184	–	35 c. green			8	8
185	–	40 c. slate-blue (15.4.40)			5	5
186	–	45 c. green (15.4.40)			5	5
187	–	50 c. carmine			5	5
188	–	55 c. turquoise-blue			55	55
189	–	60 c. violet (4.12.39)			5	5
190	–	65 c. brown			65	65
191	–	70 c. orange (4.12.39)			8	8
192	–	80 c. violet			15	15
193	–	90 c. ultramarine (4.12.39)			5	5
194	–	1 f. bright carmine			1·25	1·25
195	–	1 f. olive-green (26.3.40)			5	5
196	–	1 f. 25, bright carmine (4.12.39)			20	20
197	–	1 f. 40, chocolate (5.3.40)			5	5
198	–	1 f. 50, turquoise-green			5	5
199	–	1 f. 60, purple (5.3.40)			5	5
200	–	1 f. 75, light blue			20	20
201	–	2 f. bright purple			5	5
202	–	2 f. 25, light blue (4.12.39)			5	5
203	–	2 f. 50, orange (5.3.40)			10	10
204	–	3 f. sepia			5	5
205	–	5 f. vermilion			12	12
206	–	10 f. blue			15	15
207	–	20 f. grey-olive			15	15
175/207		Set of 33			4·50	4·50

Designs:—30 c. to 70 c. St. Pierre Harbour; 80 c. to 1 f. 75, Turtle Lighthouse; 2 f. to 20 f. Soldiers' Cove, Langlade.

4, 15, 20 c., 10 f. and 20 f. stamps in similar designs, but without "RF" were prepared in 1942 by the Vichy Government.

(b) POSTAGE DUE. P 13 × 13½.

D208	D **40**	5 c. black			5	5
D209		10 c. purple			5	5
D210		15 c. grey-green			5	5
D211		20 c. light blue			5	5
D212		30 c. bright carmine			5	5
D213		50 c. green			5	5
D214		60 c. blue			5	5
D215		1 f. vermilion			8	8
D216		2 f. sepia			45	45
D217		3 f. bright violet			50	50
D208/217		Set of 10			1·25	1·25

41

THE WORLD CENTRE FOR
FINE STAMPS IS 391 STRAND

(Des and eng A. Decaris. Recess Institut de Gravure, Paris)

1939 (10 May). New York World's Fair. P 12½.

208	**41**	1 f. 25, lake			15	15
209		2 f. 25, ultramarine			20	20

42 Storming the Bastille

(Des and eng A. Ouvré. Photo and typo Vaugirard, Paris)

1939 (5 July). 150th Anniv of French Revolution. P 13½×13.

210	**42**	45 c.+25 c. green and black			1·10	1·10
211		70 c.+30 c. brown			1·10	1·10
212		90 c.+35 c. red-orange			1·10	1·10
213		1 f. 25+1 f. carmine			1·10	1·10
214		2 f. 25+2 f. blue			1·10	1·10
210/214		Set of 5			5·00	5·00

VICHY ISSUES. A number of stamps were prepared by the Pétain Government of Unoccupied France for use in St. Pierre and Miquelon, but were not placed on sale there.

FREE FRENCH ADMINISTRATION

The islands were taken by a Free French naval force under Admiral Muselier on 24 December 1941.

Noël 1941

FRANCE LIBRE

F. N. F. L.

(43)

NOËL 1941

F N F L

(D 44)

"F.N.F.L." = Forces Navales Françaises Libres
(Free French Naval Forces)

1941. Free French Plebiscite. (a) POSTAGE. Stamps of 1938–40 issue optd with T **43**, or surch also. A. In red. B. In black.

					A		B	
215	**39**	10 c. yellow-brown		9·00	9·00	11·00	11·00
216		20 c. bright violet		9·00	9·00	11·00	11·00
217		25 c. turquoise-blue		9·00	9·00	11·00	11·00
218	–	40 c. slate-blue		9·00	9·00	11·00	11·00
219	–	45 c. green		9·00	9·00	11·00	11·00
220	–	65 c. brown		9·00	9·00	11·00	11·00
221	–	70 c. orange		9·00	9·00	11·00	11·00
222	–	80 c. violet		9·00	9·00	11·00	11·00
223	–	90 c. ultramarine		9·00	9·00	11·00	11·00
224	–	1 f. olive-green		9·00	9·00	11·00	11·00
225	–	1 f. 25, bright carmine		9·00	9·00	11·00	11·00
226	–	1 f. 40, chocolate		9·00	9·00	11·00	11·00
227	–	1 f. 60, purple		9·00	9·00	11·00	11·00
228	–	1 f. 75, light blue		9·00	9·00	£180	£180
229	–	2 f. bright purple		9·00	9·00	11·00	11·00
230	–	2 f. 25, light blue		9·00	9·00	11·00	11·00
231	–	2 f. 50, orange		9·50	9·50	11·00	11·00
232	–	3 f. sepia		9·50	9·50	11·00	11·00
233	**39**	10 f. on 10 c. yellow-brown	21·00	21·00	28·00	28·00
234	–	20 f. on 90 c. ultramarine	21·00	21·00	30·00	30·00
215/234		Set of 20		£190	£190	£400	£400

(b) POSTAGE DUE. Optd with Type D **31**, in black

D235	D **40**	5 c. black			3·75	3·75
D236		10 c. purple			3·75	3·75
D237		15 c. grey-green			3·75	3·75
D238		20 c. light blue			3·75	3·75
D239		30 c. bright carmine			3·75	3·75
D240		50 c. green			5·00	5·00
D241		60 c. blue			14·00	14·00

D242	D **40**	1 f. vermilion	..	.. ..	22·00 22·00
D243		2 f. sepia	..	.. ..	22·00 22·00
D244		3 f. bright violet		.. ..	22·00 22·00
D235/244		Set of 10 ..		.. ..	95·00 95·00

1941–42. *Various stamps optd "FRANCE LIBRE/ F.N.F.L." only as T* **43**. *(a) POSTAGE.* (i) *On Nos.* 111 *and* 114.

245	**17**	10 c. magenta and bistre		..	£275 £275
246	**18**	30 c. blue and lake	..		£275 £275

(ii) *On stamps of* 1932–33, *or surch also*

247	**28**	2 c. blue-green and black	..	..'	65·00 65·00
248	**29**	4 c. brown and carmine		..	8·00 8·00
249		5 c. brown and mauve		..	£225 £225
250		40 c. brown and blue		..	3·25 3·25
	a.	Opt inverted	..		
251	**28**	45 c. green and scarlet		..	40·00 40·00
252		50 c. green and brown		..	1·25 1·25
253	**29**	65 c. red and brown ..		..	8·00 8·00
254		1 f. scarlet and brown-red ..		..	95·00 95·00
255		1 f. 75, chocolate and black		..	1·60 1·60
256		2 f. blue-green and black		..	1·60 1·60
257	**28**	5 f. brown and scarlet		..	90·00 90·00
258	**29**	5 f. on 1 f. 75, chocolate & black (R.)			1·60 1·60

(iii) *On stamps of* 1938–40, *or surch also*

259	**39**	2 c. blue-green		..	£110 £110
260		3 c. reddish brown		..	32·00 32·00
261		4 c. purple ..		..	23·00 23·00
262		5 c. carmine ..		..	£250 £250
263		10 c. yellow-brown		..	3·25 3·25
264		15 c. bright purple		..	£425 £425
265		20 c. bright violet		..	48·00 48·00
266		20 c. on 10 c. yellow-brown ..		..	1·25 1·25
267		25 c. turquoise-blue ..		..	3·25 3·25
268		30 c. on 10 c. yellow-brown ..		..	1·60 1·60
269	–	35 c. green		..	£190 £190
270	–	40 c. slate-blue		..	3·25 3·25
271	–	45 c. green		..	3·25 3·25
272	–	55 c. turquoise-blue ..		..	£1800 £1800
273	–	60 c. violet		..	£150 £150
274	–	60 c. on 90 c. ultramarine		..	1·90 1·90
275	–	65 c. brown		..	3·25 3·25
276	–	70 c. orange		..	5·50 5·50
277	–	80 c. violet		..	£100 £100
278	–	90 c. ultramarine		..	3·75 3·75
279	–	1 f. olive-green		..	3·25 3·25
280	–	1 f. 25, bright carmine		..	3·25 3·25
281	–	1 f. 40, chocolate		..	3·25 3·25
282	–	1 f. 50, turquoise-green		..	£225 £225
283	–	1 f. 50 on 90 c. ultramarine ..		..	3·25 3·25
284	–	1 f. 60, purple		..	2·50 2·50
285	–	2 f. bright purple		..	11·00 11·00
286	–	2 f. 25, light blue		..	2·50 2·50
287	–	2 f. 50, orange		..	3·25 3·25
288	**39**	2 f. 50 on 10 c. yellow-brown		..	3·25 3·25
289	–	3 f. sepia ..		..	£1900 £1900
290	–	5 f. vermilion		..	£650 £650
291	**39**	10 f. on 10 c. yellow-brown ..		..	11·00 11·00
292	–	20 f. grey-olive		..	£300 £300
293	–	20 f. on 90 c. ultramarine		..	11·00 11·00

(iv) *On* 1939 *New York's World Fair issue* (*Nos.* 208/9), *or surch also*

294	**41**	1 f. 25, lake ..		..	1·90 1·90
295		2 f. 25, ultramarine		..	1·90 1·90
296		2 f. 50 on 1 f. 25, lake..		..	2·75 2·75
297		3 f. on 2 f. 25, ultramarine		..	2·75 2·75

(b) *POSTAGE DUE. On Postage Due stamps of* 1932, *or surch also*

D298	D **30**	25 c. black and purple		..	55·00 55·00
D299		30 c. black and orange		..	55·00 55·00
D300		50 c. black and blue-green		..	£190 £190
D301		2 f. black and purple		..	8·00 8·00
D302		3 f. on 2 f. black and purple		..	3·25 3·25

(c) *PARCEL POST. On No.* P110

P303	**17**	20 c. deep purple and pale brown	..	£130 £130

+ 50 c

ŒUVRES SOCIALES

FRANCE LIBRE **+**

F. N. F. L.

(45)   **(46)**

1942. *Optd or surch as T* **45**. *(a) POSTAGE. On stamps of* 1932–33.

304	**27**	20 c. vermilion and black		..	70·00 70·00
305		75 c. vermilion and green		..	3·25 3·25
306		1 f. 25, carmine and blue		..	3·25 3·25
307		1 f. 50, light blue and deep blue		..	95·00 95·00
308		10 f. on 1 f. 25, carmine and blue		..	6·50 6·50
309		20 f. on 75 c. vermilion and green		..	11·00 11·00

(b) *POSTAGE DUE. On Postage Due stamps of* 1938.

D310	D **40**	5 c. black		..	7·50 7·50
D311		10 c. purple		..	95 95
D312		15 c. grey-green ..		..	95 95
D313		20 c. light blue		..	95 95
D314		30 c. bright carmine		..	95 95
D315		50 c. green		..	95 95
D316		60 c. blue		..	95 95
D317		1 f. vermilion		..	2·75 2·75
D318		2 f. sepia		..	2·75 2·75
D319		3 f. bright violet		..	£100 £100

1942. *Social Welfare Fund. Nos.* 279 *and* 287 *further surcharged with premium as T* **46**.

320		1 f. +50 c. olive-green		..	7·00 7·00
321		2 f. 50+1 f. orange		..	7·00 7·00

47   **48** Airliner

(Des E. Dulac. Photo Harrison)

1942. *P* 14½×14. *(a) POSTAGE.*

322	**47**	5 c. blue	..		..	5 5
323		10 c. rose	..		..	5 5
324		25 c. emerald-green ..			..	5 5
325		30 c. blue-black	..		..	5 5
326		40 c. greenish blue	..		..	5 5
327		60 c. maroon ..			..	5 5
328		1 f. violet	..		..	5 5
329		1 f. 50, scarlet	..		..	12 12
330		2 f. olive-brown	..		..	8 8
331		2 f. 50, ultramarine ..			..	15 15
332		4 f. red-orange	..		..	8 8
333		5 f. purple ..			..	8 8
334		10 f. light blue	..		..	20 20
335		20 f. green ..			..	30 30
322/335		Set of 14	..		..	1·25 1·25

(b) *AIR*

336	**48**	1 f. red-orange	..		..	5 5
337		1 f. 50, scarlet	..		..	5 5
338		5 f. maroon	..		..	8 8
339		10 f. black	..		..	8 8
340		25 f. ultramarine	..		..	10 10
341		50 f. green	..		..	30 30
342		100 f. claret	..		..	35 35
336/342		Set of 7	..		..	90 90

ALBUM LISTS

Please write for our latest lists of albums and accessories. These will be sent free on request.

49   **50** Félix Eboué

(Des E. Dulac. Photo Harrison)

1944. *Mutual Aid and Red Cross Funds. P* 14½x14.
343 **49** 5 f.+20 f. ultramarine   15   15

1945. *Recess. P* 13.
344 **50** 2 f. black   5   5
345   25 f. blue-green   15   15

(51)

1945. *Surch with new values, as T* **51**.
346 **47** 50 c. on 5 c. blue (R.)   5   5
347   70 c. on 5 c. blue (R.)   5   5
348   80 c. on 5 c. blue (R.)   5   5
349   1 f. 20 on 5 blue (R.)   5   5
350   2 f. 40 on 25 c. emerald-green   . .   5   5
351   3 f. on 25 c. emerald-green. .   . .   5   5
352   4 f. 50 on 25 c. emerald-green   . .   5   5
353   15 f. on 2 f. 50, ultramarine (R.)   . .   30   30
346/353   *Set of* 8   60   60

FRENCH OVERSEAS TERRITORY

The islands became a French Overseas Territory on 19 March 1946.

52 "Victory"

(Des and eng A. Decaris. Recess Institut de Gravure, Paris)

1946 (8 May). *AIR. Victory. P* 12½.
354 **52** 8 f. claret   15   15

53 Legionaries by Lake Chad

(Des and eng A. Decaris. Recess Institut de Gravure, Paris)

1946 (6 June). *AIR. From Chad to the Rhine. T* **53** *and similar designs. P* 12½.
355 5 f. lake   12   12
356 10 f. lilac   15   15
357 15 f. brown-black.   15   15
358 20 f. violet   20   20
359 25 f. chocolate   25   25
360 50 f. olive-black   25   25
355/360 *Set of* 6   . .   . .   . .   1·00   1·00
  Designs:—10 f. Battle of Koufra; 15 f. Tank Battle, Mareth; 20 f. Normandy Landings; 25 f. Liberation of Paris; 50 f. Liberation of Strasbourg.

54 Soldiers' Cove,   **55** Allegory of Fishing
Langlade

56 Aircraft and Wrecked Vessel   **D 57** Arms and Galleon

(Des J. Lhuer (Nos. 361/75, 377/8, 380/1), P. Munier (376, 379), J. E. Bonhotal (382/4). Eng J. Jacquin (10 c. to 50 c.), Camors (60 c. to 1 f.), H. Cheffer (1 f. 20 to 2 f., 5, 6, 10 f.); R. Serres (3 f. to 4 f., 15, 20, 25 f.), P. Munier (8, 17 f.), G. Bétemps (50 f. to 200 f.). Recess Inst de Gravure, Paris)

1947 (6 Oct)–**52**. (a) *POSTAGE. T* **54/5** *and similar designs. P* 12½ *or* 12 (8, 17 f.).
361 **54** 10 c. chocolate   5   5
362   30 c. blue-violet   5   5
363   40 c. reddish purple   5   5
364   50 c. greenish blue   5   5
365 **55** 60 c. carmine.   5   5
366   80 c. ultramarine   5   5
367   1 f. grey-green   5   5
368 — 1 f. 20, emerald-green   . .   5   5
369 — 1 f. 50, black   5   5
370 — 2 f. brown-red   5   5
371 — 3 f. dull violet   20   20
372 — 3 f. 60, orange-red   12   12
373 — 4 f. brown-purple   . .   12   12
374 — 5 f. orange-yellow   . .   15   15
375 — 6 f. light blue   20   20
376 — 8 f. sepia (10.9.52)   . .   30   20
377 — 10 f. blue-green   30   30
378 — 15 f. blackish green   40   40
379 — 17 f. blue (10.9.52)   40   25
380 — 20 f. scarlet   40   40
381 — 25 f. dark blue   45   45
  Designs: *Horiz*—1 f. 20 to 2 f. Cross and fishermen; 3 f. to 4 f. Weighing fish; 5, 6, 10 f. Fishing trawler; 8, 17 f. Arctic fox; 15, 20, 25 f. Windswept mountain landscape.

  (b) *AIR. T* **56** *and similar horiz designs. P* 12½.
382 —   50 f. yellow-green and red   75   65
383 **56** 100 f. blue-green   . .   . .   1·25   1·25
384 — 200 f. indigo and rose   . .   2·50   1·60
361/384 *Set of* 24   . .   . .   . .   7·00   6·50
  Designs:—50 f. Aircraft and fishing village; 200 f. Aircraft and snow-bound sailing ship.

St.-Pierre et Miquelon

(c) POSTAGE DUE. P 13

D385	D **57**	10 c. orange	.. .. ..	5	5
D386		30 c. deep blue	.. .. ..	5	5
D387		50 c. blue-green	.. .. ..	5	5
D388		1 f. carmine	.. .. ..	5	5
D389		2 f. grey-green	.. .. ..	5	5
D390		3 f. violet	.. .. ..	8	8
D391		4 f. purple-brown	.. ..	12	12
D392		5 f. yellow-green	.. ..	15	15
D393		10 f. brownish black	.. ..	15	15
D394		20 f. vermilion	.. ..	20	20
D385/394		*Set of* 10 ..	.. .. ..	85	85

62 Refrigeration Plant   **63** Codfish

58 People of Five Races, Aircraft
and Globe

(Des and eng R. Serres. Recess)

1949 (4 July). *AIR. 75th Anniv of Universal Postal Union. P* 13.
395 **58** 25 f. multicoloured .. .. .. 2·10 2·10

64 Dog and Coastal Scene

(Des and eng R. Serres (T **62**), P. Munier (T **63**), J. Pheulpin
(4 f., 10 f.), R. Cottet (20 f.), C. Mazelin (25 f. and T **64**),
C. Hertenberger (100 f.), A. Decaris (500 f.). Recess)

1955 (4 July)–**59**. *T* **62/4** *and similar designs. P* 13.

(a) POSTAGE

399	**62**	30 c. bright blue & dp blue (22.10.56)	8	8
400	**63**	40 c. blackish choc & lt bl (4.11.57)	8	5
401	**62**	50 c. sepia, violet-grey & blk (22.10.56)	5	5
402	**63**	1 f. sepia and green (4.11.57)	5	5
403	–	2 f. indigo and light blue (4.11.57) ..	8	5
404	**62**	3 f. plum (22.10.56)	5	5
405	–	4 f. plum, carmine and lake (4.11.57)	10	8
406	–	10 f. bis-brn, dp bl & turq (4.11.57)	15	12
407	–	20 f. lake, turquoise-blue, deep green and black (14.9.59)	30	25
408	–	25 f. bistre-brn, yell-grn & ind (14.9.59)	65	45
409	**62**	40 f. deep turquoise	50	25

(b) AIR. Inscr "POSTE AERIENNE"

410	**64**	50 f. blk, bl, ind & vio-grey (4.11.57)	3·50	2·25
411	–	100 f. black and violet-grey (4.11.57)	1·60	1·10
412	–	500 f. indigo and deep blue (22.10.56)	8·00	4·50
399/412		*Set of* 14	14·00	8·50

Designs: *As T* **62/3**—4 f., 10 f. Lighthouse and fishing craft;
20 f. Ice hockey players; 25 f. Minks. *As T* **64**—100 f.
Caravelle airliner over St. Pierre and Miquelon; 500 f. Aeroplane
over St. Pierre port.

59 Doctor and patient   **60**

(Des and eng R. Serres. Recess)

1950 (15 May). *Colonial Welfare Fund. P* 13.
396 **59** 10 f.+2 f. vermilion and red-brown .. 80 80

(Des R. Serres. Recess and typo)

1952 (1 Dec). *Centenary of Médaille Militaire. P* 13.
397 **60** 8 f. deep blue, yellow and green .. 1·00 1·00

61 Normandy Landings, 1944

(Des and eng R. Serres. Recess)

1954 (6 June). *AIR. 10th Anniv of Liberation. P* 13.
398 **61** 15 f. brown-red and deep brown .. 80 80

65 Fishing Vessel

(Des and eng H. Cheffer. Recess)

1956 (20 Feb). *Economic and Social Development Fund.
P* 13×12½.
413 **65** 15 f. sepia and brown 25 12

**HAVE YOU READ THE NOTES AT THE
BEGINNING OF THIS CATALOGUE?**

These often provide answers to the enquiries we
receive.

66 "Human Rights"   **67** *Picea*

(Des abd eng R. Cami. Recess)

1958 (10 Dec). 10*th Anniv of Declaration of Human Rights. P* 13.
414 **66** 20 f. red-brown and ultramarine   ..   40   35

(Des M. Rolland. Photo Vaugirard, Paris)

1959 (5 Jan). *P* 12½.
415 **67** 5 f. multicoloured   30   20

72   Eider Ducks   73   Dr. A. Calmette

(Des P. Lambert. Eng C. Mazelin (50 c., 2 f.), J. Pheulpin (1 f., 6 f.). Recess)

1963 (4 Mar). *Birds. Vert designs as T* **72**. *P* 13.
422   50 c. yellow-brown, black and blue   ..   10   8
423   1 f. orange-brown, magenta and blue ..   10   8
424   2 f. yellow-brown, black and blue   ..   15   12
425   6 f. yellow-brown, blue & turquoise-grn   25   20
422/425   *Set of* 4   55   45
Designs:—1 f. Ptarmigan; 2 f. Ringed plovers; 6 f. Blue-winged teal.

68   Flaming Torches   69   *Cypripedium acaule*

(Des and eng R. Cami. Recess)

1959 (14 Sept). *AIR. Adoption of Constitution. P* 13.
416 **68** 200 f. dp grn, carm-lake & reddish vio   2·10   1·25

(Des P. Lambert. Eng C. Durrens (25 f., 50 f.), J. Combet (100 f.). Recess)

1962 (24 Apr). *Flowers. T* **69** *and similar designs. P* 13.
(*a*) POSTAGE
417   25 f. bright purple, yellow-orange & green   30   20
418   50 f. crimson and green   65   40
(*b*) AIR. Inscr "POSTE AERIENNE"
419   100 f. red-orange, carmine and green   ..   1·25   40
Designs: *Vert*—50 f. *Calopogon pulchellus.* Horiz (48 × 27 mm)
—100 f. *Sarracenia purpurae.*

(Des and eng P. Gandon. Recess)

1963 (5 Aug). *Birth Centenary of Dr. Albert Calmette* (*bacteriologist*). *P* 13.
426 **73** 30 f. chocolate and blue   40   35

74   Landing of Governor

(Des P. Gandon. Eng R. Cottet. Recess)

1963 (5 Aug). *AIR. Bicentenary of Arrival of First Governor, Dangeac. P* 13.
427 **74** 200 f. ultramarine, dp bluish grn & choc   2·10   1·40

70   Submarine *Surcouf* and Map

(Des P. Gandon. Photo Helio-Comoy)

1962 (24 July). *AIR. 20th Anniv of Adherence to Free French Government. P* 13½ × 12¾.
420 **70** 500 f. black, bright blue & deep carmine   25·00   25·00

75   Centenary Emblem   76   Globe and Scales of Justice

(Des and eng J. Combet. Recess)

1963 (2 Sept). *Red Cross Centenary. P* 13.
428 **75** 25 f. red, grey and ultramarine .   ..   70   55

(Des and eng A. Decaris. Recess)

1963 (10 Dec). 15*th Anniv of Declaration of Human Rights. P* 13.
429 **76** 20 f. orange, purple-brown and blue   ..   45   35

71   "Telstar" Satellite and part of Globe

(Des C. Durrens. Eng P. Béquet. Recess)

1962 (22 Nov). *AIR. First Transatlantic Television Satellite Link. P* 13.
421 **71** 50 f. bistre-brown, deep bluish green and deep sepia ..   ..   1·25   90

THE WORLD CENTRE FOR
FINE STAMPS IS 391 STRAND

77 "Philately"

(Des and eng P. Gandon. Recess)

1964 (4 Apr). "PHILATEC 1964" *International Stamp Exhibition, Paris. P* 13.
430 **77** 60 f. blue, green and purple-brown .. 1·25 1·25

78 Rabbits

(Des J. Derrey. Eng J. Derrey (3 f., 34 f.), S. Gauthier (4 f., 5 f.). Recess)

1964 (28 Sept). *Fauna. T* **78** *and similar horiz designs. P* 13.
431 3 f. chocolate, red-brown and green .., 10 10
432 4 f. sepia, ultramarine and green .. 15 12
433 5 f. orange-brown, sepia and ultramarine 20 12
434 34 f. brown, green and ultramarine .. 55 40
431/434 *Set of* 4 .. .. 90 65
Animals:—4 f. Fox; 5 f. Roebucks; 34 f. Charolais bull.

79 Airliner and Map

(Des and eng A. Decaris. Recess)

1964 (28 Sept). *AIR. First St. Pierre-New York Airmail Flight. P* 13.
435 **79** 100 f. chocolate and turquoise-blue .. 1·90 1·25

80 "Syncom" Communications Satellite, Telegraph Poles and Morse Key

(Des and eng J. Combet. Recess)

1965 (17 May). *AIR. ITU Centenary. P* 13.
436 **80** 40 f. blue, bright purple and orange-brown .. .. .. 1·75 1·50

81 Rocket "Diamant"

(Des and eng C. Durrens. Recess)

1966 (24 Jan). *AIR. Launching of First French Satellite. T* **81** *and similar horiz design. P* 13.
437 25 f. red-brown, dp ultramarine & crimson. 1·25 1·10
438 30 f. red-brown, dp ultramarine & crimson. 1·25 1·10
Design:—30 f. Satellite "A1".
Nos. 437/8 were issued together *se-tenant* within the sheet of 16, separated by a half stamp-size label inscribed "MISE SUR ORBITE DU PREMIER SATELLITE FRANCAIS 26 NOVEMBRE 1965". (*Price for strip unused or used* £3·25.)

82 Satellite "D1"

(Des and eng C. Durrens. Recess)

1966 (23 May). *AIR. Launching of Satellite "D1". P* 13.
439 **82** 48 f. light blue, blue-green and lake .. 1·25 80

83 Arrival of Settlers   84 *Journal Officiel* and Old and New Printing Presses

(Des M. Monvoisin, after M. Borotra. Photo So.Ge.Im)

1966 (22 June). *AIR. 150th Anniv of Return of Islands to France. P* 13.
440 **83** 100 f. multicoloured 95 65

(Des and eng G. Bétemps. Recess)

1966 (20 Oct). *AIR. Centenary of "Journal Officiel" Printing Works. P* 13.
441 **84** 60 f. plum, lake and Prussian blue .. 75 55

ALBUM LISTS

Write for our latest lists of albums and accessories.
These will be sent free on request.

85 Map and Fishing-boats

(Des and eng C. Durrens (25 f.), J. Combet (100 f.). Recess)

1967 (20 July). AIR. President De Gaulle's Visit. T 85 and similar horiz design. P 13.
442   25 f. olive-brown, greenish blue & scar   3·75   3·75
443   100 f. new blue, greenish blue & brt pur   6·50   6·50
Design:—100 f. Maps and cruiser Richelieu.

86 Freighter and Harbour Plan   87 Map and Control Tower

(Des and eng G. Aufschneider, after H. Sorieul. Recess)

1967 (25 Sept). Opening of St. Pierre's New Harbour. P 13.
444 86   48 f. brown, greenish blue & carm-red   50   30

(Des and eng G. Aufschneider, after H. Sorieul. Recess)

1967 (23 Oct). Opening of St. Pierre Airport. P 13.
445 87   30 f. multicoloured   30   20

88 T.V. Receiver, Aerial and   89 Speed-skating
Map

(Des and eng G. Aufschneider, after Borotra. Recess)

1967 (20 Nov). Inauguration of Television Service. P 13.
446 88   40 f. red, blackish green and olive   50   30

(Des P. Béquet. Photo So.Ge.lm)

1968 (22 Apr). AIR. Winter Olympic Games, Grenoble. T 89 and similar vert design. Multicoloured. P 13.
447   50 f. Type 89   50   30
448   60 f. Ice-hockey goalkeeper   ..   65   40

90 Bouquet, Sun and WHO Emblem

(Des and eng A. Decaris. Recess)

1968 (4 May). 20th Anniv of World Health Organization. P 13.
449 90   10 f. scarlet, orange-yellow and blue   ..   20   15

91 J. D. Cassini (discoverer of group),   92 Human Rights
Compasses and Chart   Emblem

(Des P. Béquet. Photo So.Ge.lm)

1968 (20 May). Famous Visitors to St. Pierre and Miquelon. T 91 and similar horiz designs. P 12½×13.
450   4 f. red-brown, yellow and brown-lake   30   30
451   6 f. chestnut, blue, yellow & slate-grn   40   35
452   15 f. chestnut, yellow, brown-red & dp bl   70   65
453   25 f. chestnut, yellow, blue and sepia   75   70
450/453 Set of 4   ..   ..   ..   2·00   1·75
Designs:—6 f. René de Chateaubriand and ship; 15 f. Prince de Joinville and ships; 25 f. Admiral Gauchet and flagship (Ile aux Chiens expedition).

(Des and eng A. Decaris. Recess)

1968 (10 Aug). Human Rights Year. P 13.
454 92   20 f. vermilion, new blue & orange-
yellow   20   12

93 War Memorial, St. Pierre

(Des M. Monvoisin. Photo Delrieu)

1968 (11 Nov). AIR. 50th Anniv of Armistice. P 12½.
455 93   500 f. multicoloured   ..   ..   ..   5·00   3·25

94 "Concorde" in Flight   95 Mountain Stream,
Langlade

(Des and eng C. Durrens. Recess)

1969 (17 Apr). AIR. First Flight of "Concorde" P 13.
456 94   34 f. purple-brown and olive-brown   ..   2·50   1·90

(Des and eng M. Monvoisin. Recess)

1969 (30 Apr). Tourism. P 13. T 95 and similar horiz designs.
(a) POSTAGE. Size 36 × 22 mm
457   5 f. lt brown, greenish blue & myrtle-grn   15   12
458   15 f. lt brown, myrtle-green & greenish bl   25   12

(b) AIR. *Inscr* "POSTE AERIENNE". *Size* 48 × 27 *mm*

459	50 f. maroon, olive and blue	..	..	1·40	95
460	100 f. purple-brown, indigo and new blue	2·40	1·90
457/460	*Set of 4*	..	..	4·00	2·75

Designs:—15 f. River-bank, Debon, Langlade; 50 f. Wild horses, Miquelon; 100 f. Gathering wood, Miquelon.

96 Treasury   97 *L'Estoile* and Granville, 1690

(Des and eng G. Aufschneider. Recess)

1969 (30 May). *Public Buildings and Monuments.* T **96** and *similar horiz designs.* P 13.

461	10 f. black, crimson and blue	..	..	15	12
462	25 f. brown-red, ultramarine and new blue	30	20
463	30 f. blackish brown, myrtle-grn & new bl	40	20
464	60 f. black, brown-red and new blue	..	70	55
461/464	*Set of 4*	..	..	1·40	1·00

Designs:—25 f. Maritime Fisheries Scientific and Technical Institute; 30 f. Monument of the Unknown Sailor; 60 f. St. Christopher's College.

1969 (16 June–13 Oct). *Maritime Links with France.* T **97** and *similar horiz designs.* P 13. *(a) POSTAGE. Size* 36 × 22 mm.

465	34 f. lake, myrtle-grn & lt emer (13.10.69)	45	30
466	40 f. myrtle-green, brown-red and yellow-bistre (13.10.69)	..	70	45
467	48 f. multicoloured (13.10.69)	..	80	55

(b) AIR. *Inscr* "POSTE AERIENNE" *Size* 48 × 27 *mm*

468	200 f. black, brown-lake and emerald	..	1·90	1·25
465/468	*Set of 4*	..	..	3·50	2·25

Designs:—40 f. *La Jolie* and St. Jean de Luz, 1750; 48 f. *Le Juste* and Le Rochelle, 1860; 200 f. *L'Esperance* and St. Malo, 1600.

98 Pierre Loti, Ship and Book Titles

(Des and eng J. Combet. Recess)

1969 (23 June). AIR. *Loti (explorer and writer) Commemoration.* P 13.

469	**98**	300 f. multicoloured	..	..	..	3·25	2·25

99 Seals   100 I.L.O. Building, Geneva

(Des and eng J. Combet. Recess)

1969 (6 Oct). *Marine Animals.* T **99** and *similar horiz designs.* P 13.

470	1 f. purple-brown, lt purple & brown-lake	25	20

471	3 f. indigo, blue-green and red	..	..	25	20
472	4 f. myrtle-green, lt olive-brn & carm-red	25	20
473	6 f. reddish violet, light emerald and red	30	25
470/473	*Set of 4*	..	..	95	75

Designs:—3 f. Sperm whales; 4 f. Pilot whale; 6 f. Dolphins.

(Des and eng J. Derrey. Recess)

1969 (24 Nov). *50th Anniv of International Labour Organization.* P 13.

474	**100**	20 f. lt orange-brown, slate & salmon	20	15

101 New U.P.U. Headquarters   102 Rocket and Japanese Women

(Des and eng J. Gauthier. Recess)

1970 (20 May). *New U.P.U. Headquarters Building, Berne.* P 13.

475	**101**	25 f. brown, blue and claret	..	30	20
476		34 f. slate, dp brown & brown-purple	40	25

(Des and eng G. Bétemps. Recess)

1970 (8 Sept). AIR. *World Fair "EXPO 70", Osaka, Japan.* T **102** and *similar design.* P 13.

477	34 f. bistre-brown, brown-lake and indigo	50	30
478	85 f. indigo, red and orange	..	1·00	55

Design: *Horiz:*—85 f. "Mountain Landscape" (Y. Taikan) and Expo "star".

103 Rowing Fours   104 *Rubus chamaemorus*

(Des G. Bétemps. Photo Delrieu)

1970 (13 Oct). *World Rowing Championships, St. Catherine, Canada.* P 12½ × 12.

479	**103**	20 f. chestnut, greenish blue & pale blue	25	20

(Des and eng J. Pheulpin. Recess)

1970 (20 Oct). *Fruit Plants.* T **104** and *similar vert designs.* P 12½ × 13.

480	3 f. myrtle-green, dull purple & orge-brn	12	12
481	4 f. pale yellow, rose-red & myrtle-green	12	12
482	5 f. rose, myrtle-green and violet	15	15
483	6 f. bluish violet. myrtle-green & brt pur	20	20
480/483	*Set of 4*	..	..	55	55

Plants:—4 f. *Fragaria vesca*; 5 f. *Rubus idaeus*; 6 f. *Vaccinium myrtillus*.

105 Ewe and Lamb

(Des R. Quillivic. Eng J. Miermont (48 f.), R. Quillivic (others). Recess)

1970 (10 Nov–8 Dec). *Livestock Breeding. T*105 *and similar horiz designs. P* 13.

484	15 f. lt drab, reddish pur & emer (8.12.70)	25	15
485	30 f. orange-brn, slate & yell-grn (8.12.70)	30	20
486	34 f. orge-brn, pur & lt emer (8.12.70)	40	20
487	48 f. maroon, orange-brown and new blue	40	30
484/487	*Set of 4*	1·25	75

Designs:—30 f. Animal quarantine station; 34 f. Charolais bull; 48 f. Refrigeration plant and trawler.

106 Etienne Francois, Duke of Choiseul, and Ships

(Des and eng J. Combet. Recess)

1970 (25 Nov). *AIR. Celebrities of St. Pierre and Miquelon. T* 106 *and similar horiz designs. P* 13.

488	25 f. brown-lake, greenish blue & purple	30	20
489	50 f. brown-lake, brt purple & myrtle-grn	55	30
490	60 f. brown-lake, myrtle-green & purple	70	35
488/490	*Set of 3*	1·40	75

Designs:—50 f. Jacques Cartier and landing scene; 60 f. Sebastien Le Gonard de Sourdeval and ships.

107 St. Francis of Assisi, 1900

(Des and eng C. Jumelet. Recess)

1971 (25 Aug). *Fisheries' Protection Vessels. T*107*and similar horiz designs. P* 13.

491	30 f. chestnut, greenish blue & turq-bl	30	20
492	35 f. bistre-brown, lt green & turquoise-bl	40	25
493	40 f. chocolate, greenish bl & blackish grn	45	30
494	80 f. black, emerald and greenish blue	75	40
491/494	*Set of 4*	1·75	1·00

Designs:—35 f. *St. Jehanne*, 1920; 40 f. *L'Aventure*, 1950; 80 f. *Commandant Bourdais*, 1970.

PUZZLED?

Then you need
PHILATELIC TERMS ILLUSTRATED
to tell you all you need to know about printing
methods, papers, errors, varieties, watermarks,
perforations, etc. 192 pages, almost half in full
colour, soft cover. £1·95 post paid.

108 *Aconit*   109 Ship's Bell

(Des and eng J. Pheulpin. Recess)

1971 (27 Sept).. *30th Anniv of Allegiance to Free French Movement. French Naval Patrol Vessels. T*108*and similar horiz designs. P* 13.

495	22 f. black, turquoise-green and blue	55	40
496	25 f. yellow-brown, greenish blue & blue	70	50
497	50 f. black, greenish blue & ultramarine	95	75
495/497	*Set of 3*	2·00	1·50

Designs:—25 f. *Alysse*; 50 f. *Mimosa*.

(Des O. Baillais. Photo)

1971 (25 Oct). *St. Pierre Museum. T* 109 *and similar multicoloured design. P* 13.

498	20 f. Type 109	25	20
499	45 f. Navigational instruments and charts (*horiz*)	40	25

110 De Gaulle in Uniform   111 Haddock
(June 1940)

(Des G. Bétemps. Eng J. Miermont (35 f.); G. Bétemps (45 f.). Recess)

1971 (9 Nov). *First Death Anniv of General Charles de Gaulle. T* 110 *and similar vert design. P* 13.

500	35 f. black and red	50	25
501	45 f. black and red	75	50

Design:—45 f. De Gaulle as President of the French Republic, 1970.

(Des C. Durrens. Eng G. Bétemps (2 f.); C. Durrens (3 f., 5 f.); E. Lacaque (10 f.). Recess)

1972 (7 Mar). *Ocean Fish. T* 111 *and similar horiz designs. P* 13.

502	2 f. indigo, rose-red and ultramarine	15	10
503	3 f. olive-drab and turquoise-green	20	12
504	5 f. brown-red and greenish blue	20	12
505	10 f. blackish green and emerald	30	20
502/505	*Set of 4*	75	50

Designs:—3 f. Dab; 5 f. Sea Perch; 10 f. Cod.

112 De Gaulle and Servicemen

(Des and eng P. Forget. Recess)

1972 (18 June). *AIR. General De Gaulle Commemoration.*
P 13.
506 **112** 100 f. red-brown, emer and reddish pur   1·25   80

CURRENCY. On 1 January 1973 the CFA franc used in St.
Pierre and Miquelon was replaced by the French Metropolitan
franc.

113 Long-tailed Ducks   114 Montcalm and Ships

(Des and eng J. Gauthier. Recess)

1973 (1 Jan). *P* 13. (*a*) *POSTAGE. T* 113 *and similar vert
designs, showing birds.*
507   6 c. brown, plum and turquoise-blue ..   5   5
508   10 c. black, red and turquoise-blue ..   5   5
509   20 c. bistre, ultramarine & dp violet-blue   10   5
510   40 c. brown, myrtle-green and violet ..   20   12
511   70 c. black, red and blue-green ..   20   15
512   90 c. bistre, turquoise-blue and plum ..   45   20
   Birds:—10 c., 70 c. Puffins; 20 c., 90 c. Snowy owls; 40 c.
Type 113.
(*b*) *AIR. Inscr* "POSTE AERIENNE". *T* 114 *and similar historical
designs*
513   1 f. 60, reddish violet, indigo & greenish bl   55   30
514   2 f. brt purple, myrtle-green & violet   70   35
515   4 f. deep green, magenta & bistre-brown   1·60   90
507/515   *Set of 9* ..   ..   3·50   2·00
   Designs: *Vert*—2 f. Frontenac and various scenes. *Horiz*—
4 f. La Salle, map and ships.

D115 Newfoundland Dog and   116 Swimming Pool
    Shipwreck Scene

(Des and eng C. Durrens. Recess)

1973 (1 Jan). *POSTAGE DUE. P* 13.
D516 D 115 2 c. black and brown   5   5
D517   10 c. black and reddish violet ..   5   5
D518   20 c. black and turquoise-blue ..   10   10
D519   30 c. black and lake   15   15
D520   1 f. black and new blue   40   40
D516/520   *Set of 5*   70   70

(Des and eng C. Jumelet. Recess)

1973 (25 Sept). *Inauguration of St. Pierre Cultural Centre.*
T 116 *and similar horiz design. P* 13.
521   60 c. brown, new blue and magenta ..   20   15
522   1 f. dull purple, yellow-orange & turq-bl   40   20
   Design:—1 f. Centre building.

STAMP MONTHLY

—finest and most informative magazine for all
collectors. Obtainable from your newsagent or
by postal subscription—details on request.

117 "Transall C–160" in Flight

(Des and eng C. Jumelet. Recess)

1973 (16 Oct). *AIR. P* 13.
523 **117** 10 f. multicoloured ..   ..   ..   3·75   1·90

118 Met Balloon and Weather   120 Clasped Hands on Red
     Ship   Cross

119 Gannet with Letter

(Des and eng R. Quillivic. Recess)

1974 (23 Mar). *World Meteorological Day. P* 13.
524 **118** 1 f. 60, new blue, myrtle-green and red   55   40

(Des and eng C. Andréotto. Recess)

1974 (9 Oct). *Centenary of Universal Postal Union. P* 13.
525 **119** 70 c. deep ultramarine, new blue & lake   25   20
526   90 c. deep ultramarine, carmine & lake   35   30

(Des M. Mougin. Photo)

1974 (15 Oct). *Campaign for Blood Donors. P* 12½ ×13.
527 **120** 1 f. 50, multicoloured   45   35

121 Arms and Map of Islands   122 Banknotes in "Fish"
                                           Money-box

(Des M. Louis. Photo)

1974 (5 Nov). *AIR. P* 13.
528 **121** 2 f. multicoloured   65   45

(Des and eng G. Bétemps. Recess)

1974 (15 Nov). *Centenary of St. Pierre Savings Bank. P* 13.
529 **122** 50 c. orange-brown, ultramarine & blk   20   15

123 Copernicus and Famous   **124** St. Pierre Church and
     Scientists   Sea-gull

(Des and eng J. Combet. Recess)

1974 (26 Nov). *AIR. 500th Birth Anniv* (1973) *of Copernicus* (*astronomer*). *P* 13.
530 **123** 4 f. reddish violet, vermilion & new bl   1·25   90

(Des and eng P. Forget. Recess)

1974 (9 Dec). *Island Churches. T* **124** *and similar horiz designs. P* 13×12½.
531   6 c. black, brown and emerald   5   5
532   10 c. indigo, blue and sepia   ..   5   5
533   20 c. multicoloured   10   10
531/533   *Set of* 3   20   20
    Designs:—10 c. Miquelon Church and fish; 20 c. Our Lady of the Seamen Church and fishermen.

125 *Vanessa atalanta*   **126** Cod and St-Pierre et Miquelon
                               Stamp of 1909

(Des O. Baillais. Litho Cartor)

1975 (17 July). *Butterflies. T* **125** *and similar vert design. Multicoloured. P* 12½.
534 1 f. Type **125**   30   30
535 1 f. 20, *Danaus plexippus*..   ..   40   25

(Des C. Bridoux. Eng E. Lacaque. Recess)

1975 (5 Aug). *AIR. "Arphila 75" International Stamp Exhibition, Paris. P* 13.
536 **126** 4 f. brown-red, indigo and blue   ..   1·25   90

127 "Pottery"   **128** Pointe-Plate
(Potter's wheel and products)   Lighthouse and Sea-birds

(Des and eng J. Combet. Recess)

1975 (20 Oct). *Artisan Handicrafts. T* **127** *and similar vert design. P* 12½x13.
537 50 c. dull purple, orange-brown and olive .   20   12
538 60 c. new blue and orange-yellow .   ..   20   12
    Design:—60 c. "Sculpture" (Wood-carving of Virgin and Child).

(Des and eng P. Forget. Recess)

1975 (21 Oct). *Lighthouses. T* **128** *and similar horiz designs. P* 13x12½.
539   6 c. black, bluish violet and pale yellow-
         green.   5   5
540 10 c. bright purple, bronze-green and slate   5   5
541 20 c. orange-brown, indigo and light blue .   5   5
    Designs:—10 c. Galantry Lighthouse and auks; 20 c. Cap Blanc Lighthouse and dolphin.

129 Judo

(Des and eng C. Guillame. Recess)

1975 (18 Nov). *AIR. "Pre-Olympic Year". P* 13.
542 **129** 1 f. 90, new blue, red and violet   ..   65   45

130 "Concorde" in Flight

(Des P. Lengellé. Eng C. Guillame. Recess)

1976 (21 Jan). *AIR. First Commercial Flight of "Concorde". P* 13.
543 **130** 10 f. indigo, blue and red   ..   ..   3·25   2·25

ALBUM LISTS

Write for our latest lists of albums
and accessories.
These will be sent free on request.

188	C	4 f. 75, yellow-orange	..	10	10
189	B	4 f. 90, olive-bistre (8.2.40)	..	15	15
190	C	6 f. 50, deep blue	..	20	15
191	B	6 f. 90, orange (8.2.40)	..	12	12
192	C	8 f. black	..	20	20
193		15 f. claret	..	15	15
178/193		Set of 16 ..	..	1·40	1·40

(c) POSTAGE DUE

D194	D **40**	5 c. yellow-green	..	5	5
D195		10 c. vermilion	..	5	5
D196		15 c. violet	..	5	5
D197		20 c. olive	..	5	5
D198		30 c. red-brown ..	..	5	5
D199		50 c. purple	..	12	12
D200		60 c. yellow-orange	..	30	30
D201		1 f. black	..	15	15
D202		2 f. indigo	..	12	12
D203		3 f. carmine	..	20	20
D194/203		Set of 10 ..	..	1·00	1·00

Designs:—A, Djourbel Mosque; B, African landscape; C, Aircraft over camel caravan.

Various postage values between 40 c. and 20 f. were prepared by the Vichy authorities in 1943–44, but were not placed on sale in Senegal.

1937 (15 Apr). *International Exhibition, Paris. As T 32/37 of St-Pierre et Miquelon.*

194	20 c. bright violet	..		15	15
195	30 c. green	..		15	15
196	40 c. carmine	..		15	15
197	50 c. brown and blue	..		20	20
198	90 c. scarlet	..		20	20
199	1 f. 50, blue	..		30	30
194/199	Set of 6	..		1·00	1·00
MS200	120×100 mm. 3 f. reddish purple (as T **34**). Imperf ..	..		90	90

1938 (24 Oct). *International Anti-Cancer Fund. As T 38 of St-Pierre et Miquelon.*

201	1 f. 75+50 c. ultramarine	..	..	2·25	2·25

40 René Caillié

(Des and eng R. Cottet, Recess Institut de Gravure, Paris)

1939 (5 Apr). *Death Centenary of R. Caillié (explorer). P 12½.*

202	**40**	90 c. orange ..	..	10	10
203		2 f. violet	..	10	10
204		2 f. 25, blue ..	..	12	12

1939 (10 May). *New York World's Fair. As T 41 of St-Pierre et Miquelon.*

205	1 f. 25, lake	..		10	10
206	2 f. 25, ultramarine	..		10	10

1939 (5 July). *150th Anniv of French Revolution. As T 42 of St-Pierre et Miquelon. (a) POSTAGE.*

207	45 c. +25 c. green and black	..		1·50	1·50
208	70 c. +30 c. brown and black	..		1·50	1·50
209	90 c. +35 c. red-orange and black	..		1·50	1·50
210	1 f. 25+1 f. carmine and black..			1·50	1·50
211	2 f. 25+2 f. blue and black	..		1·50	1·50

(b) AIR

212	4 f. 75+4 f. black and orange	..		2·25	2·25
207/212	Set of 6	..	..	9·00	9·00

VICHY GOVERNMENT

A British attempt on 23 to 25 September 1940 to seize Dakar, where the Governor-General of French West Africa was hostile to General de Gaulle, was repulsed. Senegal and the other colonies of French West Africa remained under the control of the Vichy government until November 1942, when Admiral Darlan ordered French resistance to the Allies to cease in Africa. In addition to Nos. 213/18 other issues were prepared in France, but were not placed on sale in Senegal.

SECOURS

+ 1 fr.

NATIONAL

(40a)

40b Aeroplane over Camel Caravan

1941. *National Defence Fund. Surch as T 40a.*

213		—	+1 f. on 50 c. vermilion	..		20	20
214	**39**	+2 f. on 80 bright violet (R.) ..		..	95	95
215		—	+2 f. on 1 f. 50, blue ..		..	95	95
216		—	+3 f. on 2 f. light blue		..	95	95
213/216		Set of 4	..	..	..	2·75	2·75

(Des and eng D. Paul. Typo and recess)

1942 (19 Oct). *AIR. As T 40 b (but inscr "SENEGAL" at foot) and similar horiz design. P 12½x12 (50 f.) or 12½ (100 f.).*

217	50 f. yellow-olive and greenish yellow ..			30	25
218	100 f. ultramarine and carmine ..		..	55	50

Design:—100 f. Aeroplane landing (48x26 mm).

Seven other values between 50 c. and 20 f. exist, but were not issued in Senegal.

FREE FRENCH ADMINISTRATION

1 fr. 50

(41)

1944. *Surch as T 41.*

219	**38**	1 f. 50 on 15 c. black (R.)	..		5	5
		a. Surch double	..	..	9·50	
220	A	1 f. 50 on 65 c. deep violet (R.)	..		5	5
221	**38**	4 f. 50 on 15 c. black (R.)	..		15	15
222		5 f. 50 on 2 c. red-brown (Bk.)	..		25	20
223	A	5 f. 50 on 65 c. deep violet (R.)	..		10	10
224	**38**	10 f. 50 on 15 c. black (R.)	..		40	30
225	A	50 f. on 65 c. deep violet (R.)	..		50	30
219/225		Set of 7	..	..		1·40	1·00

1944. *No. 202 surch as T 41.*

226	**40**	20 f. on 90 c. orange	..		30	20
227		50 f. on 90 c. orange	..		80	55

Stamps of French West Africa were used in Senegal from 1944 to 1959. On 25 November 1958 Senegal became an autonomous state within the French Community, and on 4 April 1959 it joined with French Sudan to form the independent Federation of Mali.

ALBUM LISTS

Please write for our latest lists of albums and accessories. These will be sent free on request.

Syria

1919. 40 Paras = 10 Milliemes = 1 Piastre
1920. 100 Centimes (or Centiemes) = 1 Piastre

From 1516 to 1918 Syria was part of the Turkish Empire. After the final British defeat of the Turks at Megiddo in Palestine in September 1918, Damascus, which had been entered by small Arab forces late on 30 September, was taken by an Australian Cavalry division early next day. French naval forces later landed at Beirut. For administrative purposes, Syria was divided in 1919 into a French zone of occupation comprising a coastal strip with Beirut as chief town, and the interior, administered by Arabs.

O. M. F.
Syrie
1
MILLIEME
(3)

O. M. F.
Syrie
1
MILLIEME
(4)

"O.M.F." = Occupation Militaire Française

A. FRENCH MILITARY OCCUPATION

T E. O.

4MILLIEMES

(1)

T. E. O.
1
MILLIEME

(2)

"T.E.O."—Territoires Ennemis Occupés

1919 (21 Nov). *Issued at Beirut. Stamps of France, 1900–17, surch as T 1, by Gédéon Bros, Beirut.*

1	11	1 m. on 1 c. grey		60·00	60·00
2		2 m. on 2 c. claret		£100	£100
		a. Small figure "2"		£350	£350
3		3 m. on 3 c. orange		60·00	60·00
		a. Small figure "3"		£225	£225
4	15	4 m. on 15 c. slate-green		7·00	7·00
5	18	5 m. on 5 c. blue-green		5·00	5·00
6		1 p. on 10 c. scarlet		9·50	9·50
7		2 p. on 25 c. blue		3·75	3·75
8	13	5 p. on 40 c. red and pale blue		3·75	3·75
		a. Small figure "5"		16·00	16·00
9		9 p. on 50 c. cinnamon and lavender		8·00	8·00
		a. Small figure "9"		38·00	38·00
10		10 p. on 1 f. lake and yellow		16·00	16·00
1/10		*Set of 10*		£250	£250

There are many minor surcharge varieties in this issue. All the above are on "G.C." paper except the 10 c.

1919 (1 Dec). *Stamps of French Post Offices in the Turkish Empire (French types inscr "LEVANT") surch or optd only as T 2, by Gédéon Bros, Beirut.*

(a) *Nos. 9/13 surch*

11	11	1 m. on 1 c. grey		20	15
		a. Surch inverted		3·25	3·25
12		2 m. on 2 c. claret		20	15
		a. Surch inverted		3·25	3·25
13		3 m. on 3 c. orange-red		30	25
14	14	4 m. on 15 c. pale red		15	15
		a. Surch inverted		3·25	3·25
15	11	5 m. on 5 c. green		20	15

(b) *Nos. 19/23 optd "T.E.O." only*

16	14	1 p. on 25 c. blue		15	10
		a. Opt inverted		3·25	3·25
17	13	2 p. on 50 c. brown and lavender		30	25
		a. Opt inverted		6·50	6·50
18		4 p. on 1 f. lake·and yellow-green		50	40
19		8 p. on 5 f. deep lilac and buff		1·90	1·60
		a. Opt double		13·00	10·00
20		20 p. on 5 f. deep blue and buff		£110	75·00
11/20		*Set of 10*		£110	75·00

On Nos. 17/20 the overprint reads vertically upwards at the left of the stamp.
No. 11 is on "G.C." paper and No. 12 exists on ordinary and "G.C." paper; the rest are on ordinary paper.
Nos. 16/20 were also used in Cilicia from December 1919 to March 1920.

1920 (Feb–Mar). *Stamps of France. 1900–19, surch by Gédéon Bros, Beirut.*

(a) *As T 3 ("O.M.F." thin)* (Feb)

21	11	1 m. on 1 c. grey			1·10	1·10
		a. Surch inverted			3·25	3·25
22		2 m. on 2 c. claret			1·40	1·40
		a. Surch double			3·25	3·25
23	18	3 m. on 5 c. blue-green			3·00	3·00
		a. Surch double			6·50	6·50
24	13	20 p. on 5 f. deep blue and buff			£170	£170

(b) *As T 4 ("O.M.F." thick)* (Mar)

25	11	1 m. on 1 c. grey			12	12
26		2 m. on 2 c. claret			25	25
27	18	3 m. on 5 c. blue-green			20	20
28		5 m. on 10 c. red			15	12
		a. Surch double			3·25	3·25
29	13	20 p. on 5 f. deep blue and buff			25·00	25·00
30		20 p. on 5 f. deep blue and buff (R.)			95·00	95·00

Nos. 21/23 and 25/27 are on "G.C." paper.

Syrian Currency

100 Syrian Piastres = 5 French Francs

O. M. F.
Syrie
50
CENTIMES
(5)

O. M. F.
Syrie
Ch. taxe
1 PIASTRE
(D 6)

(Surch locally by Gédéon Bros, later by French High Commission, Beirut)

1920 (1 May–July). *Stamps of France, 1900–19, surch as T 5 (Nos. 31/3 value in "CENTIMES").*

31	11	25 c. on 1 c. grey			20	20
32		50 c. on 2 c. claret			20	20
33		75 c. on 3 c. orange			20	20
34	18	1 p. on 5 c. blue-green (R.)			15	15
35		1 p. on 5 c. blue-green (5.20)			8	8
		a. Surch inverted			2·50	2·50
36		2 p. on 10 c. scarlet			8	8
		a. Surch inverted			2·50	2·50
37		2 p. on 25 c. blue (R.) (5.20)			8	8
38		3 p. on 25 c. blue (R.)			20	20
		a. Surch inverted			2·50	2·50
39	15	5 p. on 15 c. slate-green			15	15
		a. Surch inverted			2·50	2·50
40	13	10 p. on 40 c. red and pale blue			30	30
41		25 p. on 50 c. cinnamon and lavender			30	30
42		50 p. on 1 f. lake and yellow			65	65
		a. "PIASRTES"			28·00	28·00
43		100 p. on 5 f. deep blue and buff (6.20)			30·00	27·00
		a. "PIASRTES"			42·00	42·00
44		100 p. on 5 f. deep blue & buff (R.) (6.20)			6·00	6·00

Value in "CENTIEMES" (July)

45	11	25 c. on 1 c. slate			8	8
		a. Pearl-grey			8	8
		b. Error. 50 c. on 1 c. pearl-grey			50	50

46	**11**	50 c. on 2 c. claret	.. .. ..	5	5
		a. Surch inverted	.. .. ..	2·50	2·50
47		75 c. on 3 c. orange	.. .. ..	15	15
		a. Surch inverted	.. .. ..	2·50	2·50
31/47		Set of 17	.. .. ..	35·00	32·00

All are on "G.C." paper except Nos. 36 and 43/44.

There were two printings by Gédéon Bros. In both there is a short "y" and open "e" in "Syrie" but the second printing can be distinguished by the space between "Syrie" and the figures of value which is only 1 mm instead of 2 mm.

The French High Commission made printings of Nos. 34, 37 and 39/43 which can be distinguished by the longer "y" and almost closed "e" in "Syrie".

1920 (May). *POSTAGE DUE. Nos. 14 and 16/18 of French Post Offices in the Turkish Empire (French types inscr "LEVANT") surch as Type D* **6**, *by Gédéon Bros, Beirut.*

D48	**14**	1 p. on 10 c. carmine	..	32·00	32·00
D49		2 p. on 20 c. purple-brown	..	32·00	32·00
D50		3 p. on 30 c. deep lilac	..	32·00	32·00
D51	**13**	4 p. on 40 c. red and pale blue	..	32·00	32·00
		a. Thin "4" ..	.. ..	80·00	80·00
D48/51		Set of 4	.. ..	£120	£120

Nos. D49/50 are on "G.C." paper.

(Surch by Gédéon Bros, from 1921 by French High Commission, Beirut)

1920 (June). *POSTAGE DUE. Postage Due stamps of France surch as T* **5**.

D52	**D 11**	1 p. on 10 c. pale brown	..	45	45
D53		2 p. on 20 c. olive-green (R.)	..	45	45
		a. "PIASTRE" ("S" omitted)	..	£150	£150
D54		3 p. on 30 c. pale carmine	..	45	45
D55		4 p. on 50 c. dull claret	..	1·25	1·25
		a. Error 3 p. on 50 c. (in pair with normal)	.. ..	£170	£170
D52/55		Set of 4	..	2·40	2·40

No. D54 is on "G.C." paper.

No. D55a has to be in pair with normal to distinguish it from No. D63.

See final note after No. 47 for distinguishing features of the French High Commission printings.

See also Nos. D60/64.

(5a)   (6)

1920 (Oct–**1921** (Feb). *Aleppo Vilayet issue. Stamps of 1920–21 (Gédéon printings), optd with rosette, T* **5a**, *at Aleppo.*

		A. In black.	B. In red				
				A		B	
48	**11**	25 c. on 1 c. (45)	.. ..	3·25	3·25	2·50	2·50
49		50 c. on 2 c. (46)	.. ..	3·25	3·25	1·50	1·50
50	**18**	1 p. on 5 c. (35)	.. ..	2·25	2·25	2·00	2·00
51		2 p. on 25 c. (37)	.. ..	5·00	3·25	1·50	1·50
52	**15**	5 p. on 15 c. (39)	.. ..	1·75	1·75	1·50	1·50
53	**13**	10 p. on 40 c. (40)	.. ..	7·50	7·50	7·50	7·50
54		25 p. on 50 c. (41)	.. ..	17·00	17·00	17·00	17·00
55		50 p. on 1 f. (42)	.. ..	£100	£100	£100	£100
56		100 p. on 5 f. (44)	.. ..	£375	£375	£375	£375
48/56		Set of 9	.. ..	£475	£475	£450	£450

Except for Nos. 56A/B all the above are on "G.C." paper and No. 54B also exists on this paper.

All values exist with the rosette double in black, the 10 p. to 100 p. double in red and the 1 p. to 100 p. double, one in red and one in black. Nos. 48/51A exist with final "S" in the surcharge double.

Nos. 53/56 also exist overprinted in both colours on the French High Commission printings, but these were not issued.

1920 (14 Dec). *AIR. Nos. 35 and 39/40 handstamped at Beirut with T* **6**, *in violet.*

57	**18**	1 p. on 5 c. blue-green	..	55·00	13·00
58	**15**	5 p. on 15 c. slate-green	..	95·00	13·00
59	**13**	10 p. on 40 c. red and pale blue	..	£130	28·00

The above were for use on air services between Aleppo and Alexandria and between Aleppo and Déir-el-Zoor.

The handstamp was applied to the Gédéon and the High Commission printings, and there are many forgeries of it.

All values are on "G.C." paper.

1921 (May)–**22**. *POSTAGE DUE. Postage Due stamps of France surch as T* **5** *in "CENTIEMES" or "PIASTRES", by French High Commission, Beirut.*

D60	**D 11**	50 c. on 10 c. pale brown	..	15	15
		a. Error. 75 c. on 10 c.	..	18·00	
		b. "50" omitted	..	18·00	
		c. Thin "5"	..	19·00	
		d. "CENTIMES" for "CENTIEMES"		2·50	2·50
D61		1 p. on 20 c. olive-green	..	15	15
D62		2 p. on 30 c. pale carmine	..	75	75
D63		3 p. on 50 c. dull claret	..	90	90
D64		5 p. on 1 f. claret/*straw* (2.22)	..	1·75	1·75
D60/64		Set of 5	..	3·50	3·50

No. D63 is on "G.C." paper.

Currency Revaluation

5 Syrian Piastres = 1 French Franc

1921 (June–Nov). *Damascus issue. Nos. K88/95 of Arab Kingdom surch as T* **5** *(Nos. 60/61 in "CENTIEMES"), by French High Commission, Beirut.*

60	**K 3**	25 c. on 1 m. brown	..	15	15
61		50 c. on 1/10 p. yellow-green	..	20	15
62		1 p. on 3/10 p. orange-yellow	..	30	20
		a. Surch inverted	..	5·00	5·00
		b. Error "2/10" pi.	..	4·00	4·00
63	**K 4**	1 p. on 5 m. carmine (13.11)	..	45	30
		a. Rose	..	45	30
		b. Do. Tête-bêche (pair)	..	£375	
64		2 p. on 5 m. carmine	..	50	35
		a. Rose	..	35	30
		b. Do. Tête-bêche (pair)	..	35·00	35·00
		c. Surch inverted	..	5·00	5·00
65	**K 3**	3 p. on 1 p. grey-blue	..	65	50
		a. Surch inverted	..	5·00	5·00
66		5 p. on 2 p. blue-green	..	1·10	90
		a. Surch inverted	..	5·00	5·00
67		10 p. on 5 p. brown-purple	..	1·40	1·40
68		25 p. on 10 p. grey	..	1·90	1·75
		a. Surch inverted	..	5·50	5·50
60/68		Set of 9	..	5·00	4·25

O. M. F. **Syrie** **Chiffre Taxe** **50** **CENTIEMES**
(D 7)

O. M. F. **Syrie** **1 —** **PIASTRE**
(6a)

O. M. F. **Syrie** **2** **PIASTRES**
(6b)

1921 (July). *POSTAGE DUE. Damascus issue. No. KD96 of Arab Kingdom surch as Type D* **7**, *by French High Commision, Beirut.*

D69	**K 3**	50 c. on 1 p. black (R.)	..	90	90
D70		1 p. on 1 p. black (R.)	..	45	45

Both stamps exist with an inverted stop after "F".

1921 (7 July). *Ain-Tab issue. Stamps of Turkey, 1916–17, handstamped with T* **6a** *or* **6b**.

(a) In carmine

68b	**65**	1 pi. on 10 pa. on 20 pa. rose (915)	..	23·00	23·00
68c	**74**	1 pi. on 20 pa. carmine (919)	..	10·00	10·00
68d	**60**	2 pi. on 1 pi. black and violet (656)	..	£275	£225
68e	**75**	2 pi. on 1 pi. violet-blue (920)	..	9·00	9·00
68b/e		Set of 4	..	£275	£250

(b) In black

68f	**65**	1 pi. on 10 pa. on 20 pa. rose (915)	..	7·50	7·50
68g	**74**	1 pi. on 20 pa. carmine (919)	..	7·50	7·50

68h	**60**	2 pi. on 1 pi. black and violet (656) ..	£250	£225
68i	**75**	2 pi. on 1 pi. violet-blue (920) ..	19·00	19·00
68f/i		*Set of 4* ..	£250	£225

Nos. 68b/i were authorised by the District Governor of Ain-Tab for mail to Aleppo and locally and were in use until 27 August 1921. Though Ain-Tab (now Gaziantep) was in Cilicia, 20 miles north of the Syrian border, in an area where French troops were fighting the Turkish Nationalists, the stamps were overprinted "Syrie".

1921 (July). *Stamps of France surch as T* **5** (*Nos.* 69/71 *value in* "CENTIEMES"), *by French High Commission, Beirut.*

69	**18**	25 c. on 5 c. green		..	10	10
70		50 c. on 10 c. scarlet ..			10	10
71	**15**	75 c. on 15 c. slate-green			15	10
72	**18**	1 p. on 20 c. brown-lake (*shades*)			8	8
73	**13**	2 p. on 40 c. red and pale blue			20	10
74		3 p. on 60 c. violet and blue ..			25	12
75		5 p. on 1 f. lake and yellow ..			65	50
76		10 p. on 2 f. orange and blue-green		..	95	75
77		25 p. on 5 f. deep blue and buff		..	40·00	45·00
		a. Surch in red		..	£400	£400
69/77		*Set of 9* ..	..	..	38·00	38·00

All are on "G.C." paper except Nos. 70 and 76/7 and Nos. 71/2 and 75 also exist on ordinary paper.

See also Nos. 93/6d.

1921 (June). *AIR. Nos. 72 and 75/6 handstamped with T* **6**, *in violet.*

78	**18**	1 p. on 20 c. brown-lake (*shades*)		..	25·00	13·00
79	**13**	5 p. on 1 f. lake and yellow ..			£130	50·00
80		10 p. on 2 f. orange and blue-green		..	£130	50·00

The notes after No. 59 also apply here.

Nos. 79/80 are on G.C. paper and No. 80 also exists on ordinary paper.

O. M. F.
Syrie
2 PIASTRES

(7)

AVION

(8)

TAXE

(D 9)

(Surch by French High Commission, later by Capuchin Fathers, Beirut)

1921 (Oct). *Stamps of France surch as T* **7**.

81	**13**	2 p. on 40 c. red and pale blue		..	15	10
		a. Surch triple		..	11·00	
82		3 p. on 60 c. violet and blue ..			30	15
83		5 p. on 1 f. lake and yellow ..			2·00	2·00
		a. "5" with serif at top and pointed				
		tail		..	26·00	26·00
84		10 p. on 2 f. orange and blue-green		..	4·00	3·50
85		25 p. on 5 f. deep blue and buff		..	2·75	2·75
		a. "25 PIASTRES" omitted ..			21·00	
81/85		*Set of 5* ..		..	8·50	8·00

From March 1922 the Capuchin Fathers took over the printing material from the French High Commission but it is difficult to distinguish their work apart from minor differences in spacing. Numerous minor varieties occurred, mainly in these printings.

See also No. 96c.

1921 (Oct). *AIR. Nos. 72 and 75/6 optd with T* **8**, *by French High Commission, Beirut.*

86	**18**	1 p. on 20 c. brown-lake (*shades*)		..	19·00	4·50
87	**13**	5 p. on 1 f. lake and yellow ..			48·00	9·50
		a. Opt reading up ..		..	75·00	65·00
88		10 p. on 2 f. orange and blue-green		..	55·00	13·00
		a. Opt double ..		..	£100	90·00

1921 (13 Nov). *POSTAGE DUE. Damascus issue. Nos. 64/5 optd with Type* D **9**, *by French High Commission, Beirut.*

D89		2 p. on 5 m. carmine ..			1·60	1·60
		a. "A" inverted ..			15·00	15·00
D90		3 p. on 1 p. slate-blue ..		..	3·75	3·00

THE WORLD CENTRE FOR FINE STAMPS IS 391 STRAND

Poste par Avion
O. M. F.
Syrie
2 PIASTRES

(9)

1922 (May). *AIR. Stamps of France surch as T* **9**, *by Capuchin Fathers, Beirut.*

89	**13**	2 p. on 40 c. red and pale blue		..	4·00	4·00
90		3 p. on 60 c. violet and blue ..			4·00	4·00
91		5 p. on 1 f. lake and yellow ..			4·00	4·00
92		10 p. on 2 f. orange and blue-green		..	6·00	6·00
89/92		*Set of 4* ..		..	16·00	16·00

The overprint and surcharge were made by a single operation.

1922 (Nov)–**23**. *Stamps of France surch as T* **5** (*Nos.* 93/6 *in* "CENTIEMES"), *by Capuchin Fathers, Beirut.*

93	**11**	10 c. on 2 c. claret (8.23) ..		..	12	10
		a. Surch inverted ..			1·90	1·90
94	**18**	10 c. on 5 c. orange (R.) (7.23)		..	15	15
		a. Surch inverted ..			1·90	1·90
95		25 c. on 5 c. orange		..	20	20
		a. "CENTIEMES" omitted ..			3·75	3·75
		b. "N" inverted ..			2·25	2·25
		c. Surch inverted			2·00	2·00
		d. Surch double ..			2·50	2·50
		e. Surch double, one inverted			6·00	
96		50 c. on 10 c. green		..	15	10
		a. Surch double, one inverted			6·00	
96a		1,25 p. on 25 c. blue ..			30	30
		aa. "5" omitted ..			6·50	
		ab. "5" inserted by hand ..			7·50	
96b		1,50 p. on 30 c. orange			12	10
		ba. Thin, sloping "5" ..			16·00	
96c	**13**	2 p. 50 on 50 c. brown & lavender			25	25
		ca. "50" omitted ..			9·00	9·00
96d	**15**	2,50 p. on 50 c. dark blue		..	30	30
		da. "PIASTRE" ("S" omitted) ..			1·40	1·40
		db. "2" with thick straight foot ..			2·25	2·25
		dc. Surch inverted			2·25	2·25
		dd. Surch double ..			2·75	2·75
93/96d		*Set of 8* ..		..	1·40	1·10

The above are all on ordinary paper but·No. 96a also exists on "G.C." paper.

B. ARAB KINGDOM

The Emir Faisal of the Hejaz, who with Colonel T. E. Lawrence had led the Arab forces against the Turks, organised an Arab State in the interior of Syria, with Damascus as capital. At Christmas 1919 fighting began between Arabs and the French, who aimed at control of all Syria. On 8 March 1920 a Syrian National Congress declared for complete independence and on 11 March the Emir Faisal was proclaimed King of Syria.

Types of Turkish Overprints

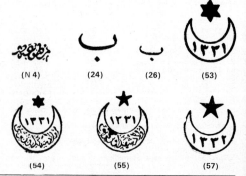

(N 4) (24) (26) (53)

(54) (55) (57)

(K 1)
("Arab Government")

(1 m.)

(2 m.)

(4 m.)

(5 m.)

(1 pi.)

1920 (Mar). *Various stamps of Turkey handstamped with Type* K **1** (*vert or horiz, according to shape*), *in black, violet, red or green, or surch also with new values as shown.*

A. *Without Turkish Star and Crescent opt*

(a) *1909 type*

K 1	28	20 pa. rose-carmine . .	. .	65·00	65·00

(b) *Pictorial issue of* 1914–15

K 2	32	1 m. on 2 pa. claret	. .	30	30
K 3	33	1 m. on 4 p̤a. sepia	. .	30	30
K 4	34	2 m. on 5 pa. dull carmine	. .	45	45
K 5	36	4 m. on 10 pa. green	. .	2·25	2·25
K 6	37	20 pa. red . .	. .	45	45
K 7	38	1 pi. bright blue	. .	1·00	1·00
K 8	39	1 pi. on 1½ pi. grey and rose (521)		£160	£160
K 9	41	2 pi. black and green	. .	25·00	25·00
K10	45	25 pi. dull yellow-green	. .	£120	£120
K11	48	25 pi. on 200 pi. black & green (535)		£130	£130
K12	47	100 pi. indigo	. .	£225	£225

(b) *As last, optd with small star*

K13	36	4 m. on 10 pa. green (516)	. .	30	30
K14	37	20 pa. red (517)	. .	£120	£120
K15	38	1 pi. bright blue (518)	. .	38·00	38·00

(c) *Postage Due stamps of* 1914

KD16	D **6**	2 m. on 5 pa. purple	. .	3·75	3·75
KD17	D **7**	20 pa. carmine	. .	3·75	3·75
KD18	D **8**	1 pi. deep blue	. .	3·75	3·75
KD19	D **9**	2 pi. grey	. .	3·75	3·75

B. *Optd with T* 53

(a) *1892 type*

K20	15	2 pi. orange-brown . .	. .	60	60

(b) *Surch with T* 19

K21	15	2 m. on 5 pa. on 10 pa. green (160)		30	30

(c) *1901 type*

K22	21	20 pa. carmine	. .	1·00	1·00
K23		1 pi. dull blue	. .	1·75	1·75
K24		25 pi. deep brown	. .	£120	£120

(d) *1905 type*

K25	23	2 m. on 5 pa. yellow-buff	. .	9·00	9·00
K26		1 pi. blue . .	. .	28·00	28·00
K27		2 pi. slate . .	. .	7·00	7·00
K28		2 pi. slate (optd with T **24**)	. .	7·00	7·00
K29		5 pi. brown . .	. .	4·00	4·00

(e) *1909 type*

K30	28	20 pa. rose-carmine . .	. .	1·00	1·00
K31		2 pi. black	. .	1·75	1·75

(f) *1913 type*

K32	30	4 m. on 10 pa. green	. .	55	55
K33		20 pa. rose	. .	4·75	4·75
K34		1 pi. ultramarine	. .	2·40	2·40
K35		5 pi. purple . .	. .	8·00	8·00

C. *Optd with T* 54

(a) *1905 type*

K36	23	10 pi. dull orange	. .	£110	£110

(b) *1909 type*

K37	28	20 pa. rose-carmine . .	. .	80	80
K38		1 pi. ultramarine	. .	4·75	4·75
K39		5 pi. slate-purple	. .	£110	£110

(c) *1913 type*

K40	30	1 pi. ultramarine	. .	. .	5·50	5·50

D. *Optd with T* 55

(a) *1892 type surch with T* 56

K41	15	4 m. on 10 pa. on 20 pa. dull rose . .	45	45

(b) *1901 type*

K42	21	5 pi. rosy mauve	. .	. .	20·00	20·00

(c) *1905 type*

K43	23	1 pi. blue	. .	. .	3·25	3·25
K44		1 pi. blue (optd with T **24**) . .		8·00	8·00

(d) *1913 type*

K45	30	20 pa. rose	. .	. .	1·10	1·10
K46		20 pa. rose (optd with T **26**)		7·50	7·50
K47		1 pi. ultramarine	. .	. .	6·50	6·50

(e) *Postal Jubilee issue of* 1916

K48	60	4 m. on 10 pa. carmine	. .	30	30
K49		20 pa. blue	. .	. .	15	15
K50		1 pi. black and violet	. .	80	80
K51		5 pi. black and brown	. .	1·75	1·75

E. *Optd with T* 57

(a) *1901 type* (*internal*)

K52	21	2 pi. orange	. .	. .	1·75	1·75

(b) *1901 type optd with Type* N **4**

K53	21	20 pa. carmine (732)	. .	£120	£120

(c) *1901 type* (*foreign*)

K54	22	20 pa. magenta	. .	. .	4·00	4·00

(d) *1901 type optd with Type* N **4**

K55	22	20 pa. magenta (737)	. .	1·40	1·40

(e) *1905 type*

K56	23	2 m. on 5 pa. yellow-buff . .	. .	24·00	24·00
K57		20 pa. rose	. .	. .	2·25	2·25
K58		1 pi. blue (optd with T **24**) . .	. .	2·50	2·50

(f) *Adrianople issue of* 1913

K59	31	4 m. on 10 pa. green	. .	2·25	2·25

(g) *Postal Jubilee issue of* 1916

K60	60	5 pi. black and brown	. .	1·75	1·75

F. *Occupation of Sinai Peninsula issue of* 1916
(*Optd with T* 59)

K61	28	20 pa. rose-carmine . .	. .	2·25	2·25
K62		1 pi. ultramarine	. .	. .	4·75	4·75

G. *Postal Jubilee issue of* 1916

K63	60	2 m. on 5 pa. green	. .	. .	£140	£110
K64		4 m. on 10 pa. carmine	. .	10·00	10·00
K65		20 pa. blue	. .	. .	45	45
K66		1 pi. black and violet	. .	45	45
K67		5 pi. black and brown	. .	1·75	1·75

H. *Pictorial issue of* 1916–17

K68	62	10 pi. violet . .	. .	. .	38·00	38·00
K69		10 pi. deep green/grey	. .	40·00	40·00
K70		10 pi. brown . .	. .	. .	£110	£110
K71	63	25 pi. carmine/buff . .	. .	32·00	32·00
K72	64	50 pi. indigo . .	. .	. .	75·00	75·00

I. *War Charity stamp of* 1917

K73	65	4 m. on 10 pa. purple	. .	45	45

J. *Provisional of* 1917 (*Surch with T* 71)

K74	65	4 m. on 10 pa. on 20 pa. rosine		45	45

K. *Pictorial stamps of* 1917–18

K75	73	4 m. on 10 pa. green	. .	45	45
K76	74	20 pa. carmine . .	. .	1·50	1·50
K77	75	1 pi. violet-blue	. .	75	75
K78	76	1 pi. on 50 pa. blue	. .	30	30

L. *Provisional of* 1918 (*Surch with T* 79)

K79	69	5 pi. on 2 pa. greenish blue . .	. .	1·50	1·50

M. *On Turkish Fiscal stamp* (*T* 7 *of Cilicia*)

K80	—	5 m. on 5 pa. red . .	. .	. .	35	30

(K 2) ($\frac{2}{10}$ pi.)  ($\frac{3}{10}$ pi.)
("Syrian Arab
Government")

1920 (Mar). *Handstamped with Type K 2 and with values as
shown in preceding issue and above for fractions, in black,
green or violet.*

	(a) On Turkish fiscal stamp, T 7 of Cilicia			
K81	1 m. on 5 pa. red	..	..	20	20
K82	2 m. on 5 pa. red	..	..	25	25
K83	$\frac{2}{10}$ pi. on 5 pa. red	..	..	20	20
K84	$\frac{3}{10}$ pi. on 5 pa. red	..	..	12	12
K85	1 pi. on 5 pa. red	..	..	45	30

	(b) T 34 of Turkey			
K86	2 m. on 5 pa. dull purple	..	..	1·60	1·60

	(c) T 74 of Turkey, with Triangle only			
K87	20 pa. carmine ..	..	..	15	15

K 3    K 4

(Litho in Damascus)

1920 (Mar). *P 11½. (a) Size 22 × 17 mm.*

K88	K 3	1 m. brown	..	..	8	8

		(b) Size 27 × 21 mm				
K89	K 3	$\frac{2}{10}$ pi. yellow-green	..	..	15	15
K90		$\frac{3}{10}$ pi. orange-yellow	..	..	8	8
		a. Error. $\frac{2}{10}$ pi.	..	..	4·75	4·75
K91	K 4	5 m. carmine	..	..	8	5
		a. Rose	..	..	8	5
		b. Do. Tête-bêche (pair)	..	7·00	7·00
K92	K 3	1 pi. grey-blue	..	..	10	8
K93		2 pi. blue-green	..	..	65	40

		(c) Size 32 × 25 mm				
K94	K 3	5 pi. brown-purple ..	..	1·25	70
K95		10 pi. grey	..	..	1·25	90
K88/95		*Set of 8*	..	..	3·25	2·25

1920 (Mar). *POSTAGE DUE. P 11½.*
KD96	K 3	1 pi. black	..	..	40	40

(Litho in Aleppo)

1920. *Fine impression. P 11½.*
K97	K 4	5 m. brown-red	..	..	75	30

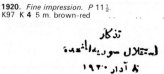

(K 5)

("Commemoration of Syrian Independence, 8 March 1920")

1920. *Optd with Type K 5.*
K98	K 4	5 m. brown-red	..	..	27·00	27·00
		a. Opt inverted	..	..	80·00	55·00

On 25 April 1920 the Supreme Council of the Allies offered to
France the mandate to administer Syria under the League of
Nations. On 25 July French troops took Damascus and
King Faisal was dethroned. In 1921 he was made king of
Iraq.
Stamps of the French Military Occupation were used in this
area.

C. FRENCH MANDATED TERRITORY

The League of Nations approved the French mandate on
24 July 1922 and it became effective on 29 September 1923.

I. ISSUES FOR LEBANON AND SYRIA

At the end of the military occupation period the stamps with
"O.M.F. Syrie" overprints were withdrawn. Great Lebanon, the
Christian area, which had had a separate status from Syria since
1 September 1920, but where "O.M.F. Syrie" stamps had been
used, now had its name joined to that of Syria on the stamps in
use.

**Syrie
Grand Liban
25
CENTIEMES**

(10)

**Syrie - Grand Liban
10 PIASTRES**

(11)

(Surch by Capuchin Fathers, Beirut)

1923 (Sept–Dec). *Stamps of France, 1900–21 surch.*

		(a) As T 10				
97	11	10 c. on 2 c. claret ..		..	8	8
98	18	25 c. on 5 c. orange (Oct)		..	8	8
99		50 c. on 10 c. green (Oct)		..	10	10
		a. "0,50" for "50"				
		b. "25" for "50" ..			9·00	
100	15	75 p. on 15 c. olive-green (Nov)		..	12	12
101	18	1 p. on 20 c. chocolate		..	10	10
102		1,25 p. on 25 c. blue (Oct)		..	12	12
103		1,50 p. on 30 c. orange (Oct)		..	12	12
104		1,50 p. on 30 c. scarlet (Dec)		..	12	12
105	15	2,50 p. on 50 c. blue (Oct)		..	10	10

		(b) As T 11				
106	13	2 p. on 40 c. red and pale blue		..	10	10
		a. Pair, one without surch		..	2·00	
107		3 p. on 60 c. violet and blue (Dec)		..	20	20
108		5 p. on 1 f. lake and yellow (Oct)		..	35	35
109		10 p. on 2 f. deep lilac and buff (Dec)		..	1·60	1·60
110		25 p. on 5 f. deep blue and buff (Dec)		..	7·50	7·50

		(c) T 30 (Pasteur) surch as T 10 (Dec)				
111	30	50 c. on 10 c. green		..	15	15
112		1,50 p. on 30 c. red		..	12	12
113		2,50 p. on 50 c. blue ..		..	15	15
		a. "5" omitted		..	1·75	
97/113		*Set of 17*		..	10·00	10·00

Nos. 100, 102, 106 and 108 exist on "G.C." paper.
Most values exist with surcharge inverted or double (*Price un*
£2 *each*).

Poste par Avion

**Syrie · Grand Liban
2 PIASTRES**

(11a)

(Surch by Capuchin Fathers, Beirut)

1923 (Nov). *AIR. Stamps of France, 1900–20, surch as T 11a.
2¼ mm between 2nd and 3rd lines.*

114	13	2 p. on 40 c. red and pale blue	..	7·50	7·50
		a. 3¾ mm between 2nd and 3rd lines	12·00	12·00
		b. Error. "Liabn"	..	..	£150	£150
115		3 p. on 60 c. violet and blue ..	..	7·50	7·50
		a. 3¾ mm between 2nd and 3rd lines	12·00	12·00
		b. Do. Error. "Liabn"	..	£150	£150
116		5 p. on 1 f. lake and yellow ..	..	7·50	7·50
		a. 3¾ mm between 2nd and 3rd lines	12·00	12·00
		b. Do. Error. "Liabn"	..	£150	£150
117		10 p. on 2 f. deep lilac and buff	..	7·50	7·50
		a. Surch double	..	..	24·00	
		b. 3¾ mm between 2nd and 3rd lines	12·00	12·00
		c. Do. Error. "Liabn"	..	£150	£150
114/117		*Set of 4*	..	..	27·00	27·00

1923 (Nov–Dec). *POSTAGE DUE. Postage Due stamps of France surch as T* **10**.

D118	D **11**	50 c. on 10 c. pale brown ..	..	25	25
D119		1 p. on 20 c. olive-green ..	..	50	50
D120		2 p. on 30 c. carmine	..	25	25
D121		3 p. on 50 c. dull claret	..	25	25
		a. "2, 50" for "3"	..	4·50	
D122		5 p. on 1 f. claret/*straw*	..	1·00	1·00
D118/122	*Set of 5*	..	..	2·00	2·00

No. D120 exists on "G.C." paper.

II. ISSUES FOR SYRIA

From 1 January 1924 separate issues of stamps were made for Great Lebanon; these are listed under Lebanon. The following issues were made for Syria only.

SYRIE

1,25

PIASTRE

(12)

SYRIE

2 PIASTRES

(13)

(Surch by Capuchin Fathers, Beirut)

1924 (Jan–June). *Stamps of France, 1900–21, surch.*

(a) As T **12**

118	**11**	10 c. on 2 c. claret ..		8	8
119	**18**	25 c. on 5 c. orange	..	8	8
		a. "25" omitted ..	..	2·25	
120		50 c. on 10 c. green	..	8	8
121	**15**	75 c. on 15 c. olive-green ..	..	12	10
		a. "YSRIE"	..	1·00	
122	**18**	1 p. on 20 c. chocolate	..	15	10
		a. "PIASTRES" ..	..	2·50	
123		1,25 p. on 25 c. blue ..	..	20	20
124		1,50 p. on 30 c. orange	..	12	12
125		1,50 p. on 30 c. scarlet (Apr)	..	15	12
126	**15**	2,50 p. on 50 c. blue ..	..	20	15

(b) As T **13**

127	**13**	2 p. on 40 c. red and pale blue	..	10	8
128		3 p. on 60 c. violet and blue	..	25	25
129		5 p. on 1 f. lake and yellow ..	..	60	60
130		10 p. on 2 f. deep lilac and buff	..	80	70
131		25 p. on 5 f. deep blue and buff	..	1·10	1·10

(c) As T **12** (June)

132	**30**	50 c. on 10 c. green	..	8	8
133		1,50 p. on 30 c. red ..	..	12	12
134		2,50 p. on 50 c. blue ..	..	8	8
118/134	*Set of 17*	..	..	3·75	3·25

Nos. 121/3 exist on "G.C." paper.

Poste par Avion
SYRIE

2 PIASTRES

(13*a*)

(Surch by Capuchin Fathers, Beirut)

1924 (Jan). *AIR. Stamps of France, 1900–20, surch as T* **13***a*.

135	**13**	2 p. on 40 c. red and pale blue	..	65	65
		a. Surch double	..	7·00	
136		3 p. on 60 c. violet and blue	..	65	65
		a. Surch inverted	..	9·50	
137		5 p. on 1 f. lake and yellow ..	..	65	65
138		10 p. on 2 f. deep lilac and buff	..	65	65
135/138	*Set of 4*	..	..	2·40	2·40

1924 (Jan). *POSTAGE DUE. Postage Due stamps of France surch as T* **12**.

D139	D **11**	50 c. on 10 c. pale brown ..	..	12	12
D140		1 p. on 20 c. olive-green ..	..	15	15
D141		2 p. on 30 c. carmine	..	20	20
D142		3 p. on 50 c. dull claret	..	30	30
D143		5 p. on 1 f. claret/*straw*	..	35	35
		a. Surch inverted	..	5·00	
D139/143	*Set of 5*	..	..	1·00	1·00

No. D141 exists on "G.C." paper.

1924 (June). *Olympic Games stamps of France surch as T* **12**.

139		50 c. on 10 c. green and yellow-green		9·00	9·00
140		1,25 p. on 25 c. deep and dull carmine ..		9·00	9·00
141		1,50 p. on 30 c. red and black	..	9·00	9·00
142		2,50 p. on 50 c. ultramarine and blue ..		9·00	9·00
139/142	*Set of 4*	..	..	32·00	32·00

Syrie
0, P. 50

سوريا

فروش ٢ *instead of* غرش ٢ العرش ٢/١،

(14)	*(a)* (singular)　　*(b)* (plural) Fourth line of surcharge ("Piastres")

(Surch by Capuchin Fathers, Beirut)

1924 (July)–**25**. *Stamps of France, surch as T* **14**.

(a) Issues of 1900–24

143	**11**	0, p. 10 on 2 c. claret	..	8	8
144	**18**	0, p. 25 on 5 c. orange	..	8	8
145		0, p. 50 on 10 c. green	..	8	8
146	**15**	0, p. 75 on 15 c. olive-green	..	10	10
		a. Comma omitted	..	50	50
147	**18**	1, p. on 20 c. chocolate	..	8	8
148		1, p. 25 on 25 c. blue	..	10	10
149		1, p. 50 on 30 c. scarlet	..	15	15
		a. With comma after "1" ..	..	40	40
150		1, p. 50 on 30 c. orange	..	7·00	7·00
151		2 p. on 35 c. violet (26.2.25)	..	15	15
152	**13**	2 p. on 40 c. red and pale blue *(b)* ..		8	8
		a. Arab surch in singular *(a)*	..	8	8
153		2 p. on 45 c. dp green & bl (26.2.25)		65	65
154		3 p. on 60 c. violet and blue	..	25	25
155	**15**	3 p. on 60 c. violet (26.2.25)	..	12	12
156		4 p. on 85 c. vermilion	..	8	8
157	**13**	5 p. on 1 f. lake and yellow ..	..	20	20
158		10 p. on 2 f. deep lilac and buff	..	30	30
159		25 p. on 5 f. deep blue and buff	..	40	40
143/159	*Set of 17*	..	..	9·00	9·00

Nos. 143/9, 152/a, 154/5 exist with surcharge inverted (*Price un* £3 *each*). Nos. 143/9 and 152/a exist with surcharge double (*Price un* £3 *each*).

(b) T **30** (*Pasteur*)

160	**30**	0, p. 50 on 10 c. green	..	15	15
161		0, p. 75 on 15 c. green (26.2.25)	..	25	25
162		1 p. 50 on 30 c. red ..	..	20	20
163		2 p. on 45 c. red (26.2.25)	..	15	15
164		2 p. 50 on 50 c. blue	..	25	25
165		4 p. on 75 c. blue	..	30	30
160/165	*Set of 6*	..	..	1·25	1·25

Nos. 160/4 exist with surcharge inverted (*Price un* £4 *each*) or double (*Price un* £4 *each*).

(c) Nos. 401/4 (Olympic Games) (26.9.24)

166		0, p. 50 on 10 c. green & yellow-green		9·00	9·00
167		1 p. 25 on 25 c. deep and dull carmine		9·00	9·00
168		1 p. 50 on 30 c. red and black	..	9·00	9·00
169		2 p. 50 on 50 c. ultramarine and blue		9·00	9·00

(d) T **35** (*Ronsard*) (12.24)

170	**35**	4 p. on 75 c. blue/*bluish*	..	15	15
		a. Surch inverted	..		
166/170	*Set of 5*	..	..	32·00	32·00

Syrie
2 Piastres

سوريا

فروش ٢

Avion

(15)

(Surch by Capuchin Fathers, Beirut)

1924 (1 July). *AIR. Stamps of France, 1900–24, surch as T* **15**.

171	**13**	2 p. on 40 c. red and pale blue	..	75	75
		a. Surch inverted ..	..	8·00	

172	**13**	3 p. on 60 c. violet and blue			75	75
		a. Surch inverted			8·00	
		b. "2" for "3"			8·00	
173		5 p. on 1 f. lake and yellow			75	75
		a. Surch inverted			8·00	
174		10 p. on 2 f. deep lilac and buff			75	75
		a. Surch inverted			8·00	
		b. "PIASTRSE"			27·00	
171/174		*Set of 4*			2·75	2·75

1924 (1 July). *POSTAGE DUE. Postage Due stamps of France surch as T* **14**.

D175	**D 11**	0 p. 50 on 10 c. pale brown			15	15
D176		1 p. on 20 c. olive-green			25	25
D177		2 p. on 30 c. carmine (*b*)			25	25
		a. Arab surch in singular (*a*)			25	25
D178		3 p. on 50 c. dull claret (*b*)			25	25
		a. Arab surch in singular (*a*)			25	25
D179		5 p. on 1 f. claret/*straw* (*b*)			40	40
		a. Arab surch in singular (*a*)			40	40
D175/179		*Set of 5*			1·25	1·25

PRINTERS AND PROCESS. Nos. 175 to 270 were designed by J. de la Nezière and printed in photogravure by Vaugirard, Paris.

D 20

D 21

D 22

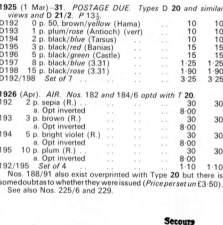

(20)

1925 (1 Mar)–**31**. *POSTAGE DUE. Types D* **20** *and similar views and D* **21**/2. *P* 13½.

D192	0 p. 50, brown/*yellow* (Hama)			10	10
D193	1 p. plum/*rose* (Antioch) (*vert*)			10	10
D194	2 p. black/*blue* (Tarsus)			10	10
D195	3 p. black/*red* (Banias)			15	15
D196	5 p. black/*green* (Castle)			15	15
D197	8 p. black/*blue* (3.31)			1·25	1·25
D198	15 p. black/*rose* (3.31)			1·90	1·90
D192/198	*Set of 7*			3·25	3·25

1926 (Apr). *AIR. Nos.* 182 *and* 184/6 *optd with T* **20**.

192	2 p. sepia (R.)			30	30
	a. Opt inverted			8·00	
193	3 p. brown (R.)			30	30
	a. Opt inverted			8·00	
194	5 p. bright violet (R.)			30	30
	a. Opt inverted			8·00	
195	10 p. plum (R.)			30	30
	a. Opt inverted			8·00	
192/195	*Set of 4*			1·10	1·10

Nos. 188/91 also exist overprinted with Type 20 but there is some doubt as to whether they were issued (*Price per set un* £3·50). See also Nos. 225/6 and 229.

16 Hama

18 Damascus

17 Merkab

A V I O N

طيارة

(19)

Secours aux Réfugiés

اعانات للاجئين

Aff¹

0ᴾ·50

الاجرة

غ ⅟₂

(21)

Secours
aux
Réfugiés

اعانات للاجئين

Aff¹

0ᴾ·50

الاجرة

غ ⅟₂

(22)

1925 (1 Mar). *T* **16**, **18** *and horiz views as T* **17**. *P* 12½ (*No.* 175) *or* 13½ (*others*).

175	0 p. 10, violet				8	8
176	0 p. 25, olive-black				20	20
177	0 p. 50, yellow-green				10	10
178	0 p. 75, brown-red				8	8
179	1 p. claret				8	8
180	1 p. 25, green				30	30
181	1 p. 50, bright rose				10	8
182	2 p. sepia				12	8
183	2 p. 50, light blue				20	20
184	3 p. brown				8	8
185	5 p. bright violet				35	8
186	10 p. plum				50	10
187	25 p. bright blue				55	45
175/187	*Set of 13*				2·50	1·75

Views: 0 p. 50, Alexandretta; 0 p. 75, Hama; 1 p. 25, Latakia; 1 p. 50, Damascus; 2 p., 25 p. Palmyra (*different*); 2 p. 50, Kaltat Yamoun; 3 p. Bridge of Daphne; 5 p., 10 p. Aleppo (*different*).

1925 (1 Mar). *AIR. Nos.* 182 *and* 184/6 *optd with T* **19**.

188	2 p. sepia (G.)				50	50
189	3 p. brown (G.)				50	50
190	5 p. bright violet (G.)				50	50
191	10 p. plum (G.)				50	50
188/191	*Set of 4*				1·75	1·75

1926 (Apr). *War Refugees Fund.*

(*a*) *POSTAGE. Stamps of* 1925 *surch as T* **21** *or with T* **22** (*No.* 199)

196	0 p. 25 on 0 p. 25, olive-black (R.)			80	80
197	0 p. 25 on 0 p. 50, yellow-green			80	80
	a. Surch inverted			12·00	
198	0 p. 25 on 0 p. 75, brown-red			80	80
	a. Surch inverted			12·00	
199	0 p. 50 on 1 p. claret			80	80
	a. Surch inverted			12·00	
200	0 p. 50 on 1 p. 25, green (R.)			80	80
	a. Surch inverted			12·00	
201	0 p. 50 on 1 p. 50, bright rose			80	80
	a. Surch inverted			12·00	
202	0 p. 75 on 2 p. sepia (R.)			80	80
203	0 p. 75 on 2 p. 50, light blue (R.)			80	80
204	1 p. on 3 p. brown (R.)			80	80
	a. Surch inverted			12·00	
205	1 p. on 5 p. bright violet			80	80
206	2 p. on 10 p. plum			80	80
	a. "au" for "aux"			6·50	
	b. "t" of "Afft" omitted			5·00	
207	5 p. on 25 p. bright blue (R.)			80	80

(b) AIR. Nos. 192/5 *surch as T* **21**

208	1 p. on 2 p. sepia		80	80
209	2 p. on 3 p. brown		80	80
	a. "2" omitted		19·00	
210	3 p. on 5 p. bright violet		80	80
	a. "Secours aux Réfugiés" omitted	55·00	
211	5 p. on 10 p. plum		80	80
	a. "au" for "aux"		6·50	
196/211	*Set of 16*		12·00	12·00

On Nos. 208/10 the surcharge is in red and the rest in black; on No. 211 the whole is in black.

The stamps were sold at face value plus the surcharge but had franking power only to the value of the surcharge, the original face value going to the war refugees fund.

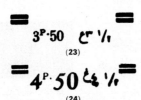

(23)

(24)

1926 (Sept–Dec). *Pictorial stamps of* 1925 *surch as T* **23** *or* **24**.

212	**23**	3 p. 50 on 0 p. 75, brown-red	12	12
213		4 p. on 0 p. 25, olive-black (8.10)	30	30
214	**24**	4 p. on 0 p. 25, olive-black (Dec)	20	5
		a. Surch double (Bk.+R.)	16·00	
		b. Surch double, one inverted	7·00	
215		4 p. 50 on 0 p. 75, brown-red (Dec)	10	8
		a. Surch double (Bk.+R.)	22·00	
216	**23**	6 p. on 2 p. 50, light blue	10	8
217	**24**	7 p. 50 on 2 p. 50, light blue (Dec)	15	8
		a. Surch double (Bk.+R.)	22·00	
218	**23**	12 p. on 1 p. 25, green	12	12
219	**24**	15 p. on 25 p. bright blue (Dec)	25	20
220	**23**	20 p. on 1 p. 25, green (8.10)	25	20
212/220	*Set of 9*		1·40	1·10

In Nos. 214/5 the "4" has a slanting foot as in T **24**. In No. 213 it is normal.

Most of the above exist with surcharge inverted or double; also with surcharge on back and front.

1928 (July)–**30**. *Pictorial stamps of* 1925 *surch.*

(a) As T **7** *of Alaouites.*

221	05 on 0 p. 10, violet (R.) (2.11.28)		5	5

(b) As T **23**

222	1 p. on 3 p. brown (6.30)		25	20

(c) As T **24**

223	2 p. on 1 p. 25, green (R.)		12	5
224	4 p. on 0 p. 25, olive-black (R.)		15	8
224a	7 p. 50 on 2 p. 50, light blue (R.)		60	55
221/224a	*Set of 5*		1·10	80

No. 224 has the "4" with slanting foot as in T **24**.

1929 (June)–**30**. *AIR. Stamps of* 1925 *optd with T* **20** *or surch in addition as T* **24**.

225	0 p. 50, yellow-green (R.)		15	15
	a. Opt inverted		6·50	
	b. Opt double		9·00	9·00
	c. Opt double, one inverted		18·00	
226	1 p. bright claret (*opt vert down*)		30	30
227	2 p. on 1 p. 25, green (R.) (1.30)		40	40
	a. Surch double		6·00	
228	15 p. on 25 p. bright blue (R.)		75	75
	a. Surch double		13·00	
229	25 p. bright blue (R.)		1·10	1·10
	a. Surch inverted		13·00	
225/229	*Set of 5*		2·40	2·40

(25)

1929 (8 Sept). *Damascus Industrial Exhibition.* *(a) POSTAGE.* *T* **17**, **18** *and similar types, optd with T* **25**.

230	0 p. 50, yellow-green (R.)		70	70
231	1 p. claret (*opt vert up*) (B.)		70	70
232	1 p. 50, bright rose (B.)		80	80
233	3 p. brown (B.)		80	80
234	5 p. bright violet (R.)		80	80
235	10 p. plum (B.)		80	80
236	25 p. bright blue (R.)		80	80
230/236	*Set of 7*		5·00	5·00

(b) AIR. Nos. 225/6, 208/11 *and* 229 *optd with T* **25**

237	0 p. 50, yellow-green (R.)		60	60
238	1 p. claret (*opt vert up*) (B.)		60	60
239	2 p. sepia (V.)		60	60
240	3 p. brown (B.)		60	60
241	5 p. bright violet (R.)		60	60
242	10 c. plum (B.)		60	60
243	25 p. bright blue (R.)		60	60
237/243	*Set of 7*		3·75	3·75

O p. 10

26 Hama   I   II

27 Damascus   **28** River Euphrates

1930 (Sept)–**36**. *Various views and frames.*

(a) As T **26**. *Litho.* P 12½

244	0 p. 10, magenta (1.31)		5	5
244a	0 p. 10, purple (I) (5.32)		5	5
244b	0 p. 10, purple (II) (3.35)		5	5
245	0 p. 20, deep blue (1.31)		5	5
245a	0 p. 20, orange-red (7.33)		5	5
246	0 p. 25, grey-green (4.31)		5	5
246a	0 p. 25, deep violet (7.33)		5	5

(b) As T **27**. *Photo.* P 13½

247	0 p. 50, bright violet (1.31)		5	5
247a	0 p. 75, orange-vermilion (8.32)		5	5
248	1 p. green (1.31)		8	5
248a	1 p. yellow-brown (1936)		8	5
249	1 p. 50, yellow-brown (1.31)		95	90
249a	1 p. 50, green (7.33)		15	15
250	2 p. violet (1.31)		5	5
251	3 p. apple-green (1.31)		25	25
252	4 p. orange		5	5
253	4 p. 50, carmine (1.31)		20	15
254	6 p. greenish black		12	10
255	7 p. 50, blue		12	12
256	10 p. brown		20	5
257	15 p. deep green		30	25
258	25 p. maroon (1.31)		30	25
259	50 p. sepia		1·60	1·40
260	100 p. orange-vermilion (3.31)		4·75	4·25
244/260	*Set of 24*		9·00	8·00

Designs: *As T* **26**—0 p. 10, 0 p. 25, Hama (*different*); 0 p. 20, Aleppo. *As T* **27**—0 p. 50, Alexandretta; 0 p. 75, 4 p. 50, Homs; 1 p., 7 p. 50, Aleppo (*different*); 1 p. 50, 4 p., 100 p. Damascus (*different*); 2 p., 10 p. Antioch (*different*); 3 p. Bosra; 6 p. Sednaya; 15 p. Hama; 25 p. St. Simeon; 50 p. Palmyra.

The 1932–36 colour changes of the 0 p. 10, 0 p. 20, 0 p. 25, and 1 p. stamps are in redrawn designs, differing in several details from the original issues.

The word "VAUGIRARD", forming part of the printer's imprint, is reversed on No. 247a.

1931 (Jan)–**33**. *AIR. T* **28** *(aeroplane in flight; views).*
P 13½.

261	0 p. 50, yellow (3.31)	..	..	5	5
261a	0 p. 50, sepia (1.7.33)		..	30	25
262	1 p. red-brown (5.31)	..	..	15	10
263	2 p. Prussian blue	..	..	65	35
264	3 p. deep blue-green	..		15	12
265	5 p. purple (3.31)	..	..	25	12
266	10 p. greenish blue	..	..	25	15
267	15 p. orange-vermilion (4.31)	..		60	60
268	25 p. brown-orange	..		60	55
269	50 p. black (5.31)	..		60	55
270	100 p. magenta	..		75	60
261/270	*Set of* 11	..	..	4·00	3·25

Views:—0 p. 50, Homs; 1 p., 10 p. Damascus *(different)*;
3 p. Palmyra; 5 p. Deir-el-Zor; 15 p. Aleppo Citadel; 25 p. Hama;
50 p. Zebdani; 100 p. Telebissé.

The designer's and printer's imprints on No. 261 measure
7½ mm and 8½ mm respectively and on 261a, 8 mm and 9 mm.

D. REPUBLIC UNDER FRENCH MANDATE

After a two-year insurrection of the Druses in 1925–27 had
been defeated, the French High Commissioner produced a
constitution for Syria on 22 May 1930. Syria and Latakia were
to be republics under French Mandate.

29 Parliament House,
Damascus

31 Aeroplane over Bloudan

30 Aboulula
el Maari

30a Pres. Mohamed
Ali Bey el-Abed

30b Saladin

(Des M. Kurcheh (T **29**, **30a**), Y. Cherif (T **30**, **30b**) and
S. Namani (T **31**). Recess (numerals typo) Institut de
Gravure, Paris)

1934 (2 Aug). *Establishment of Republic. P* 12½.

(a) POSTAGE

271	**29**	0 p. 10, olive-green	..	30	30
272		0 p. 20, black	..	30	30
273		0 p. 25, vermilion	..	30	30
274		0 p. 50, ultramarine	..	30	30
275		0 p. 75, purple	..	30	30
276	**30**	1 p. vermilion	..	95	95
277		1 p. 50, green	..	1·75	1·75
278		2 p. lake-brown	..	1·75	1·75
279		3 p. turquoise-blue	..	1·75	1·75
280		4 p. violet	..	1·75	1·75
281		4 p. 50, carmine	..	1·75	1·75
282		5 p. blue	..	1·75	1·75
283		6 p. sepia	..	1·75	1·75
284		7 p. 50, ultramarine	..	1·75	1·75
285	**30a**	10 p. sepia	..	2·50	2·50
286		15 p. blue	..	3·50	3·50
287		25 p. scarlet	..	5·00	5·00

288	**30b**	50 p. sepia	..	9·00	9·00
289		100 p. lake	..	14·00	14·00
271/289		*Set of* 19	..	45·00	45·00

(b) AIR

290	**31**	0 p. 50, brown	..	80	80
291		1 p. green	..	80	80
292		2 p. indigo	..	80	80
293		3 p. scarlet	..	80	80
294		5 p. purple	..	80	80
295		10 p. violet	..	9·00	9·00
296		15 p. orange-brown	..	9·00	9·00
297		25 p. ultramarine	..	10·00	10·00
298		50 p. black	..	14·00	14·00
299		100 p. lake-brown	..	24·00	24·00
290/299		*Set of* 10	..	65·00	65·00

(32)

33 Exhibition Pavilion

1936 (15 Apr). *Damascus Fair. Optd with T* **32**.

(a) POSTAGE as T **27**

300	0 p. 50, bright violet (R.)	..	90	90
301	1 p. yellow-brown	..	90	90
302	2 p. violet (R.)	..	90	90
303	3 p. apple-green	..	90	90
304	4 p. orange	..	90	90
305	4 p. 50, carmine	..	90	90
306	6 p. greenish black (R.)	..	90	90
307	7 p. 50, blue (R.)	..	90	90
308	10 p. brown	..	90	90
300/308	*Set of* 9	..	7·50	7·50

(b) AIR as T **28**

309	0 p. 50, sepia (R.)	..	1·10	1·10
310	1 p. red-brown	..	1·10	1·10
311	2 p. Prussian blue (R.)	..	1·10	1·10
312	3 p. deep blue-green (R.)	..	1·10	1·10
313	5 p. purple	..	1·10	1·10
309/313	*Set of* 5	..	5·00	5·00

(Des M. Kurcheh. Photo Vaugirard, Paris)

1937 (1 July). *AIR. Paris International Exhibition. P* 13½.

314	**33**	½ p. yellow-green	55	55
315		1 p. green	55	55
316		2 p. brown	55	55
317		3 p. carmine	55	55
318		5 p. orange	75	75
319		10 p. blackish green	1·10	1·10
320		15 p. blue	1·10	1·10
321		25 p. violet	1·10	1·10
314/321		*Set of* 8	5·50	5·50

34 Aleppo

35 Damascus

(Des M. Kurcheh. Eng Degorce (T **34**) and Hourriez (T **35**).
Recess)

1937 (1 Sept). *AIR. P* 13.

322	**34**	½ p. violet	5	5
323	**35**	1 p. black	10	10
324	**34**	2 p. green	12	12
325	**35**	3 p. ultramarine	12	12
326	**34**	5 p. magenta	30	30
327	**35**	10 p. lake-brown	30	30
328	**34**	15 p. purple-brown	1·10	1·10
329	**35**	25 p. blue	1·25	1·25
322/329		*Set of* 8	3·00	3·00

(36)

10 P.

(37)

1938. *Variously surch as T* **36** *and* **37.**

330	**36**	0 p. 25 on 0 p. 75, No. 247a	..	8	8
331		0 p. 50 on 1 p. 50, No. 249a (R.)	..	8	8
332		2 p. on 7 p. 50, No. 255 (R.)	..	10	10
333	**37**	2 p. 50 on 4 p. No. 252	..	8	8
334	**36**	5 p. on 7 p. 50, No. 255 (R.)	..	15	15
335		10 p. on 50 p. No. 259	..	25	25
336	**37**	10 p. on 100 p. No. 260	..	40	40
330/336		*Set of 7*	..	·1·00	1·00

38 M. Noguès and 1st Flight Route

(Des G. Ricci. Photo. Vaugirard, Paris)

1938 (20 July). *AIR.* 10th *Anniv of First Air Service Flight between France and Syria.* P 11½.

337	**38**	10 p. dull green ..	1·25	1·25
MS337a		160×120 mm. No. 337 in block of four. P 13½	9·00	9·00

12⁵⁰

(40)

39 Pres. Atasi   41 Palmyra

1938. *Surch with T* **40**. P13½.

338	**39**	12.50 on 10 p. blue (R.)	..	15	12

(Des S. Namani. Photo Vaugirard, Paris)

1938–42. P 13½.

338a	**39**	10 p. blue (1942) ..	..	15	15
339		20 p. sepia	..	20	20

PUZZLED?

Then you need
PHILATELIC TERMS ILLUSTRATED
to tell you all you need to know about printing methods, papers, errors, varieties, watermarks, perforations, etc. 192 pages, almost half in full colour, soft cover. £1·95 post paid.

(Litho Imp Catholique, Beirut)

1940. P 11½.

340	**41**	5 p. pink	..	..	..	..	15	10

42 Damascus Museum   43 Hotel de Bloudan

44 Kasr-el-Heir   45 Deir-el-Zor Bridge

(Des S. Namani. Eng G. Hourriez (**42**), C. Dufresne (**43**), E. Feltesse (**44**) and A. Degorce (**45**). Typo (**42**) or recess (others) French Govt Ptg Wks)

1940 (15 May). (a) *POSTAGE.* (i) P 13½×14.

341	**42**	0 p. 10, carmine	..	..	..	5	5
342		0 p. 20, greenish blue		..		5	5
343		0 p. 25, chestnut	..		..	5	5
344		0 p. 50, bright blue	..		..	5	5

(ii) *P* 13

345	**43**	1 p. blue ..				5	5
346		1 p. 50, brown		..		5	5
347		2 p. 50, green	..			8	5
348	**44**	5 p. violet	..		..	8	5
349		7 p. 50, scarlet	..			30	15
350		50 p. slate-purple	..			55	40
341/350		*Set of 10* ..	..		..	1·10	80

(b) *AIR.* P 13

351	**45**	0 p. 25, black	..			5	5
352		0 p. 50, greenish blue		..		5	5
353		1 p. bright blue	..			5	5
354		2 p. chestnut	..		..	8	8
355		5 p. green ..	..		..	20	20
356		10 p. carmine ..		..	..	30	30
357		50 p. dull violet	..	..	..	1·25	1·25
351/357		*Set of 7* ..	..	..	..	1·75	1·75

E. SYRIAN REPUBLIC

The outbreak of war in September 1939 delayed the application of the Franco-Syrian Treaty of 9 September 1936, by which the French mandate was to end in three years time. On 8 June 1941, however, British and Free French forces entered Syria and Lebanon to eliminate German influence there and, after some fighting against the Vichy French, occupied the area. The independence of a Syrian Republic was proclaimed, with Free French agreement, on 16 September 1941.

The stamps issued for the Free French Forces are listed under Free French Forces in the Levant.

SET PRICES

Set prices are given for many issues generally those containing five stamps or more. Definitive sets include one of each value or major colour change but do not cover different perforations, die types or minor shades. Where a choice is possible the catalogue set prices are based on the cheapest versions of the stamps included in the listings.

ALAOUITES
(STATE OF THE)

The Alawis (or Alaouites, as the French call them) are members of the Shi'ite division of Islam who inhabit the coastal region of Syria between Hatay and Lebanon. On 1 September 1920 Syria was divided by the French into the autonomous states of Aleppo, Damascus and the Alaouites. After the mandate for Syria had been given to France, an administrative reorganisation was made on 1 January 1925. The mandated territory was divided into the state of Syria (consisting of the former states of Damascus and Aleppo) and the state of the Alaouites, and separate issues of stamps were made for each state.

PRINTERS. All the overprints and surcharges of Alaouites were made by the Capuchin Fathers, Beirut.

ALAOUITES
1 PIASTRE

رعرش ١   الماو بين

(1)   **3** (I)   **3** (II)

1925 (1 Jan–26 Feb). *Stamps of France surch as T* **1**.

1	**11**	0 p. 10 on 2 claret		60	60
2	**18**	0 p. 25 on 5 c. orange		35	35
3	**15**	0 p. 75 on 15 c. olive-green		65	65
		a. Figures "75" spaced apart		6·00	6·00
4	**18**	1 p. on 20 c. chocolate		60	60
5		1 p. 25 on 25 c. blue		75	75
6		1 p. 50 on 30 c. scarlet		1·90	1·90
7		2 p. on 35 c. violet (26 Feb)		50	50
8	**13**	2 p. on 40 c. red and pale blue		75	75
9		2 p. on 45 c. dp green & blue (26 Feb)		1·90	1·90
10		3 p. on 60 c. violet and blue (I)		1·00	1·00
11	**15**	3 p. on 60 c. violet (I) (26 Feb)		1·90	1·90
		a. Surch double		13·00	
		b. Type II		21·00	21·00
12		4 p. on 85 c. vermilion (2 Feb)		20	20
13	**13**	5 p. on 1 f. lake and yellow		1·10	1·10
14		10 p. on 2 f. orange and blue-green		1·40	1·40
		a. Figures "10" spaced apart		8·00	8·00
15		25 p. on 5 f. deep blue and buff		1·90	1·90
1/15		*Set of 15*		14·00	14·00

Nos. 1 and 8 exist on "G.C." paper.
Nos. 1/7, 9 and 12/13 exist with surcharge inverted (*Price un* £2·50 *each*).

T **30** (*Pasteur*) *with similar surch*

16	**30**	0 p. 50 on 10 c. green		40	40
17		0 p. 75 on 15 c. green (26 Feb)		40	40
18		1 p. 50 on 30 c. scarlet		50	50
19		2 p. on 45 c. red (26 Feb)		50	50
20		2 p. 50 on 50 c. blue		60	60
21		4 p. on 75 c. blue		60	60
16/21		*Set of 6*		2·75	2·75

Nos. 17/20 exist with surcharge inverted (*Price un* £3·50 *each*).

ALAOUITES
2 PIASTRES   Avion

جانب   الماو بين   Avion
ع، و شر ٢

(2)

1925 (1 Jan). *AIR. Stamps of France surch as T* **2**.

22	**13**	2 p. on 40 c. red and pale blue		1·60	1·60
		a. Surch inverted		8·00	
23		3 p. on 60 c. violet and blue (I)		1·90	1·90
		a. Surch inverted		15·00	
		b. Type II		22·00	22·00
24		5 p. on 1 f. lake and yellow		1·60	1·60

25	**13**	10 p. on 2 f. orange and blue-green		1·60	1·60
22/25		*Set of 4*		6·00	6·00

No. 22 exists on "G.C." paper.

1925 (1 Jan). *POSTAGE DUE. Stamps of France, surch as T* **1**.

D26	D**11**	0 p. 50 on 10 c. pale brown		80	80
D27		1 p. on 20 c. olive-green		80	80
D28		2 p. on 30 c. carmine		80	80
		a. Opt. double			
D29		3 p. on 50 c. dull claret (I)		80	80
		a. Type II		18·00	18·00
D30		5 p. on 1 f. claret/*straw*		80	80
D26/30		*Set of 5*		3·75	3·75

ALAOUITES

ALAOUITES

بين الطو   الملو بين

(3)   (4)

1925 (1 Mar)–**30**. *As T* **16** *to* **18** *of Syria, optd as T* **3** *or* **4**

26	**3**	0 p. 10, violet (R.)		12	12
		a. Surch inverted		3·00	3·00
		b. Surch double		4·50	4·50
27	**4**	0 p. 25, olive-black (R.)		30	30
		a. Surch inverted		3·00	3·00
		b. Surch in blue		6·00	6·00
28		0 p. 50, yellow-green		20	20
		a. Surch inverted		3·00	3·00
		b. "S" omitted		5·50	5·50
		c. Surch in blue		6·00	6·00
		d. Surch in red		6·00	6·00
29		0 p. 75, brown-red		20	20
30	**3**	1 p. bright claret		30	30
		a. Surch inverted		3·00	3·00
		b. "ALACUITES"		3·75	3·75
		c. "ALAUCITES"		7·50	7·50
31	**4**	1 p. 25, green		25	25
32		1 p. 50, bright rose (B.)		25	25
		a. Surch inverted		3·00	3·00
		b. Surch in black (1930)		3·75	3·75
33		2 p. sepia (R.)		25	25
		a. Surch inverted		3·00	3·00
34		2 p. 50, light blue (R.)		30	30
35		3 p. brown (R.)		25	25
		a. Surch in blue		6·00	6·00
36		5 p. bright violet		25	25
		a. Surch in red		6·00	6·00
37		10 p. plum		40	40
38		25 p. bright blue (R.)		90	90
26/38		*Set of 13*		3·50	3·50

AVION   كمة

(5)

1925 (1 Mar). *AIR. Nos.* 33 *and* 35/7 *additionally optd with T* **5**, *in green.*

40	**3**	2 p. sepia		45	45
		a. Opt inverted		4·75	4·75
41		3 p. brown		45	45
		a. Opt inverted		4·75	4·75
42		5 p. bright violet		45	45
		a. Opt inverted		4·75	4·75
		b. Error. On 5 p. Lebanon		40·00	40·00
43		10 p. plum		45	45
		a. Opt inverted		4·75	4·75
40/43		*Set of 4*		1·60	1·60

Stamps with "AVION" overprint in *red*, either normal or inverted, are probably colour tirals.

1925 (1 Mar). *POSTAGE DUE. Nos. D192/6 of Syria optd as T **3** or **4**.*

D44	**4**	0 p. 50, brown/*yellow*	30	30
		1 a. Opt inverted	4·50	4·50
D45	**3**	1 p. brown-lake/*carmine* (B.)	30	30
		a. Opt inverted	4·50	4·50
		b. Opt in black	4·00	4·00
		c. Opt double (Bk.+B.)	7·50	7·50
D46	**4**	2 p. black/*blue* (R.)	40	40
		a. Opt inverted	4·50	4·50
D47		3 p. deep brown/*red* (B.)	65	65
D48		5 p. black/*green* (R.)	75	75
D44/48		*Set of 5*	2·10	2·10

1926 (1 May). *AIR. Nos. 33 and 35/7, all with black opt, additionally optd with T **20** of Syria (aeroplane), in red.*

44	**4**	2 p. sepia	55	55
		a. Opt on No. 40	5·50	
45		3 p. brown	55	55
		a. Opt on No. 41	5·50	
46		5 p. bright violet	55	55
		a. Opt on No. 42	5·50	
47		10 p. plum	55	55
		a. Opt on No. 43	5·50	
44/47		*Set of 4*	2·00	2·00

On No. 44 the Type **4** surcharge is in black instead of red.

= 4ᴾ·   ٤غ =

(6)

= 4ᴾ·   ٤غ =

(7)

1926 (Sept–Oct). *Postage stamps of Alaouites of March 1925 further surch as T **6**.*

48	**4**	3 p. 50 on 0 p. 75, brown-red	30	30
		a. Surch back and front	2·75	2·75
		b. Surch inverted	3·00	3·00
49		4 p. on 0 p. 25, olive-black (C.)	30	30
		a. Surch inverted	3·00	3·00
		b. Surch with T **7** (R.) (8.10)	11·00	10·00
		c. Do. Surch inverted	15·00	15·00
50		6 p. on 2 p. 50, light blue (R.)	30	30
		a. Surch inverted	3·00	3·00
51		12 p. on 1 p. 25, green	30	30
		a. Surch inverted	3·00	3·00
52		20 p. on 1 p. 25, green	45	45
48/52		*Set of 5*	1·50	1·50

ALAOUITES   = 4ᴾ·   ٤غ =

05 ·ه   Alaouites

الزريب   العلويين

(8)   (9)

1926 (Dec)–**28**. *Stamps of Syria (T **16/17**) surch at one operation as T **8** or **9**.*

53	**8**	05 on 0 p. 10, violet (R.) (2.11.28)	12	12
		a. Surch double	3·25	
54	**9**	2 p. on 1 p. 25, green (R.) (7.28)	2·25	2·00
		a. Surch inverted	5·50	
55		4 p. on 0 p. 25, olive-black (R.) (7.28)	1·60	1·50
		a. Surch inverted	4·50	
		b. Surch double	4·00	
56		4 p. 50 on 0 p. 75, brown-red	70	70
		a. Surch inverted	1·60	
		b. Surch double	4·00	
		c. Arabic fraction omitted	4·00	
57		7 p. 50 on 2 p. 50, light blue	50	40
		a. Surch inverted	5·00	
58		15 p. on 25 p. bright blue	1·25	1·25
		a. Surch inverted	3·00	
53/58		*Set of 6*	5·50	5·50

ALAOUITES

العلويين

(10)

1929 (June)–**30**. *AIR. Pictorial stamps as T **17** and **18** of Syria optd with T **10**, except Nos. 61/2, which are Nos. 54 (modified) and 58 respectively, optd with aeroplane only.*

59		0 p. 50, yellow-green (R.)	30	30
		a. Opt inverted	9·50	
		b. Opt double	7·00	
		c. Aeroplane only inverted	35·00	
60		1 p. bright claret (*opt vert up*)	1·00	1·00
61		2 p. on 1 p. 25, green (R.) (1.30)	50	50
		a. Surch inverted	3·00	
		b. Surch double	2·50	
62		15 p. on 25 p. bright blue (R.)	7·00	6·50
		a. Aeroplane only inverted		
63		25 p. bright blue (R.)	5·50	5·50
		a. Opt inverted	14·00	14·00
		b. Opt double	6·00	
59/63		*Set of 5*	13·00	12·00

LATAKIA

On 22 May 1930 the State of the Alaouites was made a republic, which on 22 September was given the name of Latakia.

LATTAQUIE   LATTAQUIE

لاذقية   لاذقية

(11)   (12)

1931 (July)–**34**. *Views as T **26** and **27** of Syria, optd with T **11** and **12** respectively.*

64		0 p. 10, magenta	15	15
65		0 p. 10, purple (I) (8.33)	15	15
66		0 p. 20, deep blue (R.)	12	12
67		0 p. 20, orange-red (8.33)	15	15
68		0 p. 25, grey-green (R.)	10	10
69		0 p. 25, deep blue (R.) (8.33)	20	20
70		0 p. 50, bright violet	30	30
71		0 p. 75, orange-vermilion (8.32)	30	30
72		1 p. green (R.)	30	30
73		1 p. 50, yellow-brown (R.)	50	50
74		1 p. 50, green (8.33)	75	75
75		2 p. violet (R.)	55	55
76		3 p. yellow-green (R.)	90	90
77		4 p. orange	90	90
78		4 p. 50, carmine (11.31)	90	90
79		6 p. blackish green (R.)	95	95
80		7 p. 50, blue (R.)	95	95
		a. Opt inverted	£100	£100
81		10 p. chocolate (R.)	1·25	1·25
		a. Opt inverted	£100	£100
82		15 p. deep green (R.)	1·60	1·60
83		25 p. maroon (11.31)	3·50	3·50
84		50 p. sepia (R.)	2·75	2·75
		a. Opt inverted	£100	£100
85		100 p. orange-vermilion (11.31)	9·00	9·00
64/85		*Set of 22*	23·00	23·00

1931. *POSTAGE DUE. Nos. D197/8 of Syria optd with T **12**.*

D86	D **21**	8 p. black/*blue* (R.) (Nov)	3·50	3·50
D87	D **22**	15 p. black/*rose* (R.) (July)	3·25	3·25

LATTAQUIE

(13)

1931 (Nov)-**33**. *AIR. Nos. 261/70 of Syria, optd with T* **13**.

86	0 p. 50, yellow ..			20	20
87	0 p. 50, sepia (R.) (8.33)			20	20
88	1 p. red brown ..			40	40
89	2 p. Prussian blue (R.)			65	65
90	3 p. deep blue-green (R.)			80	80
91	5 p. purple			1·75	1·75
92	10 p. greenish blue (R.)			2·25	2·25
93	15 p. orange-vermilion			2·75	2·75
94	25 p. brown-orange			3·25	3·25
95	50 p. black (R.) ..			6·50	6·50
96	100 p. magenta			7·50	7·50
86/96	*Set of* 11			24·00	24·00

By the Franco-Syrian Treaty of 9 September 1936, Latakia was merged with Syria, under a decree made on 5 December. At the end of February 1937, Latakian stamps were withdrawn and replaced by those of Syria.

ROUAD ISLAND (ARWAD)

(FRENCH OCCUPATION)

The island of Arwad (called Rouad by the French) lies off the coast of Syria, south of Latakia. During the First World War it was occupied in 1916 by French naval forces and used as a base from which to supply provisions and arms to the Maronite Christians of Syria, who were hostile to the Turks.

25 Centimes = 1 Piastre

ILE ROUAD

ILE ROUAD	**ILE**	**ROUAD**
(1)	(2)	(3)

Stamps of the French Post Offices in the Turkish Empire of 1902–20, overprinted

1916 (12 Jan). *Handstamped locally with T* **1**.

1	**11**	5 c. green			£130	70·00
2	**14**	10 c. carmine			£130	70·00
3		1 p. on 25 c. blue			£130	70·00

The 40 c. and 2 p. on 50 c. values were also handstamped but were not issued and used copies have been cancelled by favour.

1916 (Dec)-**20**. *Optd with T* **2** *or* **3** (*T* **13**).

4	**11**	1 c. grey			25	25
		a. Slate (1920)			25	25
5		2 c. claret			25	25
6		3 c. orange-red			20	20
		a. Surch double			19·00	
7		5 c. green			30	30
8	**14**	10 c. carmine			30	30
9		15 c. pale red			40	40
10		20 c. chocolate			45	45
11		1 p. on 25 c. blue			60	60
12		30 c. deep lilac			70	70
13	**13**	40 c. carmine and blue			95	95
14		2 p. on 50 c. brown and lavender			1·60	1·60
		a. Background colour omitted			32·00	28·00
15		4 p. on 1 f. lake and yellow			1·60	1·60
16		20 p. on 5 f. deep blue and buff			6·00	6·00
4/16		*Set of* 13			12·00	12·00

The 1, 2, 3, 20 and 30 c. exist on "G.C." paper.

After France received the mandate for Syria, Arwad became part of the State of the Alaouites. It was used by the French as a place of detention for recalcitrant Syrian politicians.

Stamp monthly

Gibbons' own monthly magazine, essential reading for **every** collector!
Detailed monthly New Issue Guide to update all Gibbons catalogues for you—and a special Stamp Market feature on price changes.
Informative articles cover all facets of philately, with regular notes on new discoveries, stamp designs, postmarks, market trends and news and views of the world of stamps. Britain's LARGEST circulation of any stamp magazine—that fact speaks for itself!
Monthly from all dealers and newsagents or by post direct from Stanley Gibbons Magazines Ltd—subscription rates on application.

Togo

100 Centimes = 1 Franc

In the First World War French troops from Dahomey and British troops from the Gold Coast invaded Togo early in August 1914 and the German forces surrendered on 26 August. Until 1919 Togo was under Anglo-French military occupation. For the stamps issued by the British authorities in this period see the *British Commonwealth* Catalogue. The French issues are listed below.

A. ANGLO-FRENCH OCCUPATION
FRENCH ISSUES
26 August 1914–7 May 1919

TOGO

Occupation

franco-anglaise

(1)

05	05	05	05	05	05
I	II	III	IV	V	VI

10	10	10
I	II	III

1914 (8 Oct). *Stamps of German Togo, optd at Porto Novo, Dahomey, with T* **1**, *the 3 pf. and 5 pf. surch. in addition. Wmk. Lozenges (No. 2) or no wmk (others).*

1	A	05 on 3 pf. brown (I)	16·00	16·00
		a. Type II	16·00	16·00
		b. Type III	16·00	16·00
		c. Type IV	19·00	19·00
		d. Type V	32·00	32·00
		e. Type VI	45·00	45·00
2		10 on 5 pf. green (I)	5·00	5·00
		a. Type II	6·00	6·00
		b. Type III	7·50	7·50
		c. Surch double	£400	£400
3		20 pf. ultramarine	15·00	15·00
		a. "TOGO" and "Occupation" spaced 3½ mm apart	£120	£120
4		25 pf. black and red/*yellow*	18·00	18·00
5		30 pf. black and orange/*salmon*	16·00	13·00
6		40 pf. black and carmine	£225	£160
7		80 pf. black and carmine/*rose*	£225	£160

The overprint was set up in groups of 50 (10×5) repeated twice on each sheet. For the two surcharges the settings were made up as follows:

05 on 3 pf. Type I—18, Type II—17, Type III—11, Type IV—2, Type V—1, Type VI—1

10 on 5 pf. Type I—25, Type II—22, Type III—3

All values have a narrow "O" in "Occupation" on positions 1, 4, 38 and 43 of the setting. The 10 on 5 pf. surcharge shows a broken serif on the figure "1" from positions 10, 16 and 23.

No. 2 is known bisected and used at Anecho.

TOGO

TOGO

Occupation

franco-anglaise

(2)

Occupation

franco-

anglaise

(3)

1915 (Jan). *Stamps of German Togo optd with T* **2** (*No.* 8 *additionally handstamped with new value*) *at the Catholic Mission, Lomé. Wmk Lozenges (Nos. 9 and 10) or no wmk (others).*

8	A	05 on 3 pf. brown		£2000	£1700
9		5 pf. green		£450	£140
10	A	10 pf. carmine		£500	£140
		a. Opt inverted		—	£4500
11		20 pf. ultramarine		£600	£300
12		25 pf. black and red/*yellow*		£2750	£2500
13		30 pf. black and orange/*salmon*		£2750	£2500
14		40 pf. black and carmine		£2500	£2250
15		50 pf. black and purple/*buff*		£4000	£3500
16	B	1 m. carmine			
17		2 m. blue		—	£7500
18		3 m. violet-black			
19		5 m. carmine and black		—	£7500

1916. *Nos. 42/58 of Dahomey optd with T* **3**. *Chalk-surfaced paper.*

20	1 c. black and violet	5	5
21	2 c. rose and chocolate	5	5
22	4 c. brown and black	5	5
	a. Opt double	45·00	45·00
23	5 c. green and yellow-green	8	8
24	10 c. rose and orange-red	8	8
25	15 c. purple and red	20	20
26	20 c. chocolate and grey	15	15
27	25 c. blue and ultramarine	12	12
28	30 c. violet and chocolate	20	20
29	35 c. black and brown	20	20
30	40 c. orange and black	25	25
31	45 c. ultramarine and grey	12	12
32	50 c. brown and chocolate	20	20
33	75 c. violet and blue	1·40	1·40
34	1 f. black and green	1·60	1·60
35	2 f. chocolate and orange-yellow	2·25	2·25
36	5 f. Prussian blue and violet	2·25	2·25
20/36	*Set of 17*	8·50	8·50

All values except the 15 c., 25 c. and 35 c. also exist on ordinary paper.

On 7 May 1919 the Supreme Council of the Allies gave a mandate to France and the United Kingdom to administer Togo, and on 10 July the two powers agreed on a division of the country. The administration of the British area was amalgamated with that of the Gold Coast, but French Togo became a separate entity. The town of Lomé was at first in the British area, but by a convention of 30 September 1920 went to France in exchange for another area further north.

B. FRENCH ADMINISTRATION
7 May 1919–26 April 1960

PRINTERS. All the stamps of Togo until No. 243 were printed at the Government Printing Works, Paris, *unless otherwise stated.*

IMPERFORATE STAMPS. Up to No. 243 some stamps exist imperforate in their issued colours, but they were not valid for postage. Imperforate stamps in other colours are colour trials.

TOGO

(4)

1921 (15 July). *Optd with T* **4**. (*a*) *POSTAGE. On T* **6** *of Dahomey.*

37	1 c. yellow-green and grey	5	5
	a. Opt omitted	38·00	
38	2 c. orange and blue	5	5
39	4 c. orange and olive	5	5
40	5 c. black and red	8	8
	a. Opt omitted	90·00	
41	10 c. yellow-green and blue-green	8	8
42	15 c. carmine and brown	12	12
43	20 c. orange and blue-green	15	15
44	25 c. orange and slate	10	10

45	30 c. scarlet and carmine	.. ..	12	12
46	35 c. yellow-green and maroon	.. ..	20	20
47	40 c. olive-grey and blue-green	..	20	20
48	45 c. olive-grey and maroon	..	25	25
49	50 c. blue	.. .. ..	12	12
50	75 c. ultramarine and red-brown	.. ..	35	35
51	1 f. ultramarine and grey	..	45	45
52	2 f. carmine and olive	..	1·00	1·00
53	5 f. black and yellow	..	1·25	1·25
37/53	Set of 17	.. ..	4·00	4·00

(b) POSTAGE DUE. On Type D 2 of Dahomey

D54	5 c. green	.. .. ..	12	12
D55	10 c. carmine	..	15	15
D56	15 c. grey	.. ..	25	25
D57	20 c. brown	.. ..	60	60
D58	30 c. blue	.. ..	60	60
D59	50 c. black	.. ..	30	20
D60	60 c. orange	.. ..	35	25
D61	1 f. violet	.. ..	1·10	80
D54/61	Set of 8	..	3·00	2·75

FRENCH MANDATED TERRITORY
20 July 1922–12 December 1946

On 20 July 1922 the League of Nations gave the United Kingdom and France mandates to administer the areas of Togo under their control.

1922 (Sept)–**25.** Stamps as T **6** of Dahomey, optd with T **4**, further surch as T **26/7** of Réunion.

54	25 c. on 15 c. carmine and brown (1.2.25)	8	8
55	25 c. on 2 f. carmine and olive (15.6.24)	8	8
56	25 c. on 5 f. black and orange (15.6.24)	8	8
	a. Opt T **4** omitted	32·00	
57	60 on 75 c. violet/rose ..	20	20
	a. Surch omitted	38·00	
58	65 on 45 c. grey and maroon (1.25)	30	30
	a. Opt T **4** omitted ..	25·00	
59	85 on 75 c. ultramarine and red-brown (1.25)	35	35
54/59	Set of 6	1·00	1·00

5 Coconut Palms   **6** Cocoa Trees

7 Palm Trees   D **8** Cotton-growing

(Des J. Kerhor. Eng. A. Delzers. Typo)

1924 (26 Dec)–**38.** P 14×13½.

60	**5**	1 c. black and yellow ..	5	5
61		2 c. black and crimson	5	5
62		4 c. black and blue ..	5	5
63		5 c. black and orange ..	5	5
64		10 c. black and magenta	5	5
65		15 c. black and green ..	5	5
66	**6**	20 c. black and drab ..	5	5
67		25 c. black and green/yellow	5	5
68		30 c. black and sage-green ..	5	5
69		30 c. green and olive-green (14.11.27) ..	8	8
70		35 c. black and yellow-brown	10	10
71		35 c. green and blue-green (6.7.38) ..	5	5
72		40 c. black and vermilion ..	5	5
73		45 c. black and crimson ..	5	5
74		50 c. black and yellow-orange/azure ..	5	5
75		55 c. carmine and ultramarine (6.7.38) ..	15	15
76		60 c. black and claret/rose ..	5	5
77		60 c. scarlet (1.3.26) ..	5	5

78	**6**	65 c. brown and lilac	5	5
79		75 c. black and blue	8	8
80		80 c. lilac and deep blue (6.7.38)	15	12
81		85 c. brown and orange ..	12	12
82		90 c. rose and deep red (28.2.27) ..	12	12
83	**7**	1 f. black and claret/azure ..	8	8
84		1 f. light blue (1.3.26) ..	8	8
85		1 f. yellow-green and lilac (25.9.28) ..	45	40
86		1 f. orange and brown-red (5.12.38) ..	5	5
87		1 f. 10, chocolate and mauve (25.9.28)	1·00	90
88		1 f. 25, rose and magenta (25.9.33) ..	20	10
89		1 f. 50, light blue (28.2.27) ..	8	8
90		1 f. 75, rose & yellow-brown (25.9.33)	2·25	40
91		1 f. 75, brt blue & ultramarine (6.7.38)	12	10
92		2 f. grey and blue-black/azure ..	15	15
93		3 f. vermilion and green (19.12.27) ..	30	30
94		5 f. black and deep orange/azure ..	35	35
95		10 f. rose and deep brown (29.11.26) ..	40	40
96		20 f. black and red/yellow (29.11.26) ..	45	45
60/96		Set of 37	7·00	5·00

(Des J. Kerhor. Eng. A. Delzers. Typo)

1925 (1 Mar). POSTAGE DUE. Centres and inscriptions, etc., in black. P 14×13½.

D 97	D **8**	2 c. blue	5	5
D 98		4 c. orange-red ..	5	5
D 99		5 c. olive-green ..	5	5
D100		10 c. crimson ..	8	8
D101		15 c. orange-yellow ..	8	8
D102		20 c. magenta ..	8	8
D103		25 c. drab ..	12	12
D104		30 c. yellow/azure ..	8	8
D105		50 c. sepia ..	10	10
D106		60 c. green ..	15	15
D107		1 f. violet ..	20	20
D97/107		Set of 11 ..	95	95

1926 (14 June). Surch as T **28** of Réunion, with bars over old value.

98	**7**	1 f 25 on 1 f. light blue (R.) ..	5	5

3ᶠ

(D **9**)   **7a** Aeroplane over African Landscape

1927 (10 Oct). POSTAGE DUE. Surch as Type D **9**.

D108	D **8**	2 f. on 1 f. mauve and red ..	80	80
D109		3 f. on 1 f. blue and brown ..	80	80

1931 (13 Apr). International Colonial Exhibition, Paris. As T **23/26** of St-Pierre et Miquelon.

99	40 c. green and black ..	1·40	1·40
100	50 c. mauve and black ..	1·40	1·40
101	90 c. vermilion and black ..	1·40	1·40
102	1 f. 50, blue and black ..	1·40	1·40
99/102	Set of 4 ..	5·00	5·00

1937 (15 Apr). International Exhibition, Paris. As T **32/37** of St-Pierre et Miquelon.

103	20 c. bright violet ..	45	45
104	30 c. green ..	45	45
105	40 c. carmine ..	45	45
106	50 c. brown and blue ..	45	45
107	90 c. scarlet ..	45	45
108	1 f. 50, blue ..	45	45
103/108	Set of 6 ..	2·40	2·40

MS108a 120×100 mm 3 f. turquoise-blue and black (as T **35**). Imperf. .. 1·50 1·50

1938 (24 Oct). International Anti-Cancer Fund. As T **38** of St-Pierre et Miquelon.

109	1 f. 75+50 c. ultramarine ..	5·00	5·00

1939 (5 Apr). Death Centenary of René Caillié (explorer). As T **40** of Senegal.

110	90 c. orange ..	25	20
111	2 f. violet ..	25	20
112	2 f. 25, blue ..	25	20

1939 (10 May). *New York World's Fair. As T **41** of St-Pierre et Miquelon.*

113	1 f. 25, lake	..	..	20	20
114	2 f. 25, ultramarine .	..	..	20	20

1939 (5 July). *150th Anniv of French Revolution. As T **42** of St-Pierre et Miquelon.*

115	45 c. +25 c. green and black	..	1·50	1·50
116	70 c. +30 c. brown and black	..	1·50	1·50
117	90 c. +35 c. red-orange and black .	..	1·50	1·50
118	1 f. 25+1 f. carmine and black	..	1·50	1·50
119	2 f. 25+2 f. blue and black	..	1·50	1·50
115/119	*Set of 5*	..	..	7·00	7·00

(Des D. Paul. Recess Institut de Gravure)

1940 (8 Feb) *AIR. P 12½.*

120	**7a**	1 f. 90, bright-blue	..	5	5
121		2 f. 90, rose-red .	..	5	5
122		4 f. 50, green	..	8	8
123		4 f. 90, olive-bistre	..	8	8
124		6 f. 90, orange . .	..	25	20
120/124		*Set of 5*	..	45	40

8 Pounding Meal   11 Young Girl   D 12 Native Mask

9 Riverside Village   10 Hunting

(Des and eng A. Degorce (T **8/9**), A. Decaris (T **10**) and P. Gandon (T **11**). Recess Inst de Gravure, Paris)

1940. *P 12½.*

125	**8**	2 c. brown-violet	..	..	5	5
126		3 c. yellow-green	..	..	5	5
127		4 c. brown-black	..	..	5	5
128		5 c. cerise	..	..	5	5
129		10 c. light blue	..	..	5	5
130		15 c. chestnut	..	..	5	5
131	**9**	20 c. plum	..	..	5	5
132		25 c. violet-blue	..	..	5	5
133		30 c. brown-black	..	..	5	5
134		40 c. deep carmine	..	..	5	5
135		45 c. blue-green	..	..	5	5
136		50 c. chestnut	..	..	5	5
137		60 c. reddish violet	..	..	5	5
138	**10**	70 c. black	..	..	5	5
139		90 c. light violet	..	..	20	20
140		1 f. yellow-green	..	..	5	5
141		1 f. 25, cerise	..	..	25	25
142		1 f. 40, orange-brown	..	..	8	8
143		1 f. 60, orange	..	..	10	10
144		2 f. light ultramarine	..	..	8	8
145	**11**	2 f. 25, ultramarine ..	..	..	25	25
146		2 f. 50, cerise	..	..	20	20
147		3 f. brown-violet	..	..	15	15
148		5 f. vermilion	..	..	15	15
149		10 f. violet	..	..	20	20
150		20 f. brown-black	..	..	50	50
125/150		*Set of 26*	..	..	2·50	2·50

Nine values, in these designs but without "RF", were prepared in 1942–44, but not placed on sale in Togo.

(Des and eng P. Gandon. Recess. Inst de Gravure, Paris)

1940. *POSTAGE DUE. P 13.*

D151	D **12**	5 c. brown-black	..		5	5
D152		10 c. yellow-green	..		5	5
D153		15 c. carmine	..		5	5
D154		20 c. ultramarine ..			10	10
D155		30 c. chestnut	..		8	8
D156		50 c. olive-green ..			30	30
D157		60 c. violet	..		8	8
D158		1 f. light blue	..		15	15
D159		2 f. orange-vermilion	..		10	10
D160		3 f. violet	..		15	15
D151/160		*Set of 10*	..		1·00	1·00

Six values without "RF" were prepared in 1943–44, but were not issued.

VICHY GOVERNMENT. Nos. 151/4a were issued by the Pétain government of Unoccupied France. A number of other issues exist, but we only list those items which were available in Togo.

1941. *National Defence Fund. Surch as T **40a** of Senegal.*

151	**9**	+1 f. on 50 c. chestnut . .	..	30	30
152	**6**	+2 f. on 80 c. lilac and deep blue	..	1·50	1·50
153	**7**	+2 f. on 1 f. 50, light blue	..	1·50	1·50
154	**10**	+3 f. on 2 f. light ultramarine (R.)	..	1·60	1·60

1942 (19 Oct). *AIR. As T **40b** of Senegal, inscr 'TOGO' at foot.*

154a	50 f. violet and greenish yellow ..		25	25

Seven other values, from 50 c. to 20 f., exist, but were not issued in Togo.

1 fr. 50 — 3 fr. 50

(16)   (17)

1944. (*a*) *Surch with T **16**.*

155	**6**	1 f. 50 on 55 c. carmine and ultramarine	15	15
156		1 f. 50 on 90 c. rose and red	..	15	15

(*b*) *Surch as T **17**.*

157	**10**	3 f. 50 on 90 c. light violet ..	..	10	10
		a. Surch inverted		6·00	
158		4 f. on 90 c. light violet (R.)	..	10	10
		a. Surch inverted ..	..	6·00	
159		5 f. on 90 c. light violet (B.)	..	30	30
		a. Surch inverted ..	..	7·00	
160		5 f. 50 on 90 c. light violet (Br.)	..	30	30
161		10 f. on 90 c. light violet (G.)	..	30	30
162		20 f. on 90 c. light violet (R.)	..	45	45
155/162		*Set of 8*	..	..	1·75	1·75

FRENCH TRUST TERRITORY

13 December 1946–15 April 1955

On 13 December 1946 the Mandated Territory was made a Trust Territory under the United Nations.

18 Oil Extraction   19 Archer   D 21
Process

20 Postal Runner and Aeroplane

(Des and eng C. Hertenberger (*Nos.* 163/5, 169/71), R. Serres (*Nos.* 166/8, 172/80), P. Camors (*Nos.* 181, 184). Des J. E. Bonhotal, eng G. Bétemps (*Nos.* 182/3). Recess Institut de Gravure, Paris)

1947 (6 Oct). (*a*) *POSTAGE. T* **18**/**19** *and similar designs.* P 12½.

163	**18**	10 c. scarlet	5	5
164		30 c. ultramarine	5	5
165		50 c. turquoise-green	5	5
166	**19**	60 c. pink	5	5
167		1 f. chocolate	5	5
168		1 f. 20, emerald-green	5	5
169	−	1 f. 50, brown-orange	12	12
170	−	2 f. olive-bistre	15	5
171	−	2 f. 50, black	30	25
172	−	3 f. indigo	12	10
173	−	3 f. 60, carmine	20	15
174	−	4 f. greenish blue	10	5
175	−	5 f. purple-brown	40	8
176	−	6 f. blue	40	30
177	−	10 f. vermilion	40	10
178	−	15 f. blue-green	55	12
179	−	20 f. blackish green	60	15
180	−	25 f. pink	65	15

Designs: *Vert*—1 f. 50, 2 f., 2 f. 50. Woman picking cotton. *Horiz*—3 f., 3 f. 60, 4 f., Drummer and village; 5 f., 6 f., 10 f., Antelopes; 15 f., 20 f., 25 f., Trees and village.

(*b*) *AIR. T* **20** *and similar horiz designs.* P 12½.

181	−	40 f. blue	1·75	1·25
182	−	50 f. mauve and violet	75	55
183	−	100 f. chocolate and emerald green	1·60	95
184	**20**	200 f. pink	2·75	1·75
163/184		*Set of 22*	10·00	6·00

Designs:—40 f. Elephants and aeroplane; 50 f. Two-engined aeroplane; 100 f. Four-engined aeroplane.

(*c*) *POSTAGE DUE,* P 13

D185	**D 21**	10 c. ultramarine	5	5
D186		30 c. brown-red	5	5
D187		50 c. blue-green	5	5
D188		1 f. chocolate	5	5
D189		2 f. carmine	8	8
D190		3 f. greenish black	8	8
D191		4 f. ultramarine	8	8
D192		5 f. purple-brown	12	12
D193		10 f. brown-orange	20	20
D194		20 f. indigo	25	25
D185/194		*Set of 10*	85	85

1949 (4 July). *AIR, 75th Anniv of Universal Postal Union. As T* **58** *of St-Pierre et Miquelon.*
185   25 f. red, purple, green and blue   ..   1·40   1·40

1950 (15 May). *Colonial Welfare Fund. As T* **59** *of St-Pierre et Miquelon.*
186   10 f.+2 f. blue and indigo..   ..   1·00   1·00

1952 (1 Dec). *Centenary of Médaille Militaire. As T* **60** *of St-Pierre et Miquelon.*
187   15 f. lake-brown, yellow and green.   ..   1·25   1·25

1954 (6 June). *AIR. 10th Anniv of Liberation. As T* **61** *of St-Pierre et Miquelon.*
188   15 f. reddish violet and indigo ·   85   85

THE WORLD CENTRE FOR
FINE STAMPS IS 391 STRAND

22 Gathering Palm Nuts   **23** Roadway through Forest

(Des and eng A. Decaris (500 f.), H. Cheffer (others). Recess)

1954 (29 Nov). P 13. (*a*) *POSTAGE.*

189	**22**	8 f. maroon, lake and deep violet	30	15
190		15 f. chocolate, blue-grey and indigo	35	20

(*b*) *AIR*
191   **23**   500 f. indigo and deep bluish green   ..   14·00   13·00

AUTONOMOUS REPUBLIC
16 April 1955–26 April 1960

On 16 April 1955 Togo became the first former colony in West Africa to receive the status of an autonomous republic within the French Community.

24 Goliath Beetle   **25** Rural School

(Des and eng J. Pheulpin. Recess)

1955 (2 May). *Nature Protection.* P 13.
192   **24**   8 f. black and deep green   50   25

(Des and eng J. Pheulpin. Recess)

1956 (22 Oct). *Economic and Social Development Fund.* P 13.
193   **25**   15 f. deep brown and chestnut   ..   1·25   65

26 Togolese Woman with Flag

(Des and eng R. Cottet. Recess)

1957 (8 June). *New National Flag.* P 13.
194   **26**   15 f. sepia, red and deep bluish green   60   20

27 Togolese Woman and "Liberty" releasing Dove

(Des and eng R. Cottet. Recess)

1957 (28 Oct). *AIR. First Anniv of Autonomous Republic. P* 13.
195 **27** 25 f. sepia, red and blue 40 40

28 Konkomba **29** Antelope **D 31** Konkomba
Helmet Helmet

30 Torch and Flag

(Des and eng G. Bétemps (T **28**, D **31**), R. Serres (T **29**).
Des H. Cheffer. Eng A. Frères, (15 f. to 40 f.). Des and
eng P. Gandon (T **30** and 500 f.). Recess)

1957 (29 Oct). *T* **28/30** *and similar designs. Inscr "REPUB-
LIQUE AUTONOME DU TOGO". P* 13. (*a*) *POSTAGE.*
196 **28** 30 c. deep lilac and lake 5 5
197 50 c. indigo and light blue 5 5
198 1 f. dp reddish lilac & brt purple 5 5
199 2 f. blackish chocolate & yellow-ol .. 5 5
200 3 f. black and green 5 5
201 **29** 4 f. black and blue 45 20
202 5 f. claret and violet-grey 45 20
203 6 f. slate and vermilion 45 20
204 8 f. violet and violet-grey 45 20
205 10 f. orange-brown & dp bluish green 45 20
206 — 15 f. multicoloured 25 20
207 — 20 f. multicoloured 30 15
208 — 25 f. multicoloured 35 25
209 — 40 f. multicoloured 50 30

(*a*) *AIR. Inscr "POSTE AERIENNE"*
210 **30** 50 f. multicoloured 70 50
211 100 f. multicoloured .. .. 1·25 60
212 200 f. multicoloured .. .. 2·40 1·40
213 — 500 f. indigo, green and blue .. 8·00 5·50
196/213 *Set of 18* .. .. .. 14·00 9·00
Designs: *Horiz*—15 f. to 40 f. Teak forest; 500 f. (48 × 27 *mm*),
Stork in flight.

(*c*) *POSTAGE DUE*
D214 D **31** 1 f. bright violet 5 5
D215 2 f. orange 5 5
D216 3 f. violet-grey 5 5
D217 4 f. scarlet 8 8
D218 5 f. bright blue 10 10
D219 10 f. deep green 20 20
D220 20 f. brown-purple 30 30
D214/220 *Set of 7* 75 75
See also Nos. D244/50.

31 "Human Rights" **32** *Bombax*

(Des and eng R. Cami. Recess)

1958 (10 Dec). *Tenth Anniv of Declaration of Human Rights.
P* 13.
214 **31** 20 f. carmine-red & dp bluish green . 45 40

(Des M. Rolland. Photo Vaugirard, Paris)

1959 (15 Jan). *Tropical Flora. T* **32** *and similar design. P* 12½.
215 5 f. multicoloured. 10 8
216 20 f. yellow green and black 15 10
Design: *Horiz*—20 f. *Tectona*.

1959 (15 Jan). *As Nos. 196/213 but new value (No.* 231*),
colours changed and inscr "REPUBLIQUE DU TOGO".*

(*a*) *POSTAGE*
217 **28** 30 c. ultramarine and black 5 5
218 50 c. blue-green and orange 5 5
219 1 f. bright purple and olive 5 5
220 2 f. olive-brown and turquoise-green 5 5
221 3 f. bluish violet and bright purple .. 8 5
222 **29** 4 f. reddish violet and bright purple 30 12
223 5 f. chocolate and deep bluish green 30 20
224 6 f. grey-blue and ultramarine .. 30 20
225 8 f. bistre and blackish green .. 30 15
226 10 f. bistre-brown and bluish violet .. 30 15
227 — 15 f. brown, orange, sepia & brn-pur 20 15
228 — 20 f. green, blue-green, black & maroon 30 12
229 — 25 f. red-brown, dp choc, vio & ol-brn 50 30
230 — 40 f. dp green, ochre, blue & red-brown 50 35

(*b*) *AIR. Inscr "POSTE AERIENNE"*
231 — 25 f. chocolate, emerald and blue .. 30 15
232 **30** 50 f. red, black, green and blue .. 60 40
233 100 f. maroon, red, green and blue .. 1·50 65
234 200 f. brown-red, scarlet, blue & green 2·50 1·25
235 — 500 f. black-brown, green & brt purple 6·00 2·75
217/235 *Set of 19* .. .. .. 12·00 6·50
Design: *Vert*—25 f. (No. 231), Togo flag and shadow of
airliner over Africa.

32a Patient on Stretcher **33** "The Five Continents"

(Des W. Wind. Recess)

1959 (17 Oct). *Red Cross Commemoration. T* **32a** *and similar
vert designs. P* 13.
236 20 f. +5 f. red, orange and slate 50 50
237 30 f. +5 f. red, brown and light blue .. 50 50
238 50 f. +10 f. red, brown and emerald .. 50 50
MS238*a* Three sheets each 78 × 106 mm. Nos.
236/8 in blocks of four .. .. 5·50 5·50
Designs:—30 f. Mother feeding child; 50 f. Nurse superin-
tending blood transfusion.

(Des C. Bottiau. Eng G. Bétemps. Recess)

1959 (24 Oct). *United Nations Day. P* 12½×13.

239	**33**	15 f. blue and brown	.. ..	20	20
240		20 f. ultramarine and bright violet	..	25	25
241		25 f. ultramarine and chestnut	..	25	25
242		40 f. ultramarine and deep bluish green		40	40
243		60 f. ultramarine and carmine	..	50	50
239/243		*Set of 5*	..	1·50	1·50

1959 (29 Oct). *POSTAGE DUE. As Nos.* D214/20, *but colours changed and inscr* "REPUBLIQUE DU TOGO".

D244	**D 31**	1 f. orange-brown	.. ..	5	5
D245		2 f. turquoise-green	.. ..	5	5
D246		3 f. yellow-orange	.. ..	5	5
D247		4 f. blue	.. ..	5	5
D248		5 f. bright purple	.. ..	8	8
D249		10 f. bluish violet	.. ..	12	12
D250		20 f. black	.. ..	20	20
D244/250		*Set of 7*	..	50	50

Togo became independent on 27 April 1960.

PHILATELIC TERMS ILLUSTRATED

This successful STAMP MONTHLY series has now been brought together in a snappy black and yellow binding and published as a useful addition to Stanley Gibbons range of essential handbooks for keen stamp collectors. Within its 192 pages this handy limp-bound volume houses a veritable mine of useful information on the words and phrases used in philately. It describes and illustrates printing processes and watermarks, papers and perforations, errors and varieties . . . and it does all this IN COLOUR. Indeed, there are 92 full page plates in colour, plus many black and white illustrations, making it

FANTASTIC VALUE AT ONLY £1·95 POST PAID FROM

Stanley Gibbons Publications Ltd 391 Strand, London WC2R 0LX

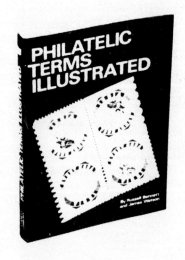

Tunisia

100 Centimes = 1 Franc

The land now known as Tunisia has, during its long history, been under the rule of Carthage, Rome (when Carthage became the second city in the Empire), the Vandals, Byzantium, the Arabs, the Normans, the Berbers, the Turks, and the Spaniards until it was recaptured by the Turks in 1574 and became part of their Empire. The Beys, originally Turkish officials, came to rule the country and in 1705 Bey Hussein ibn-Ali, son of a Cretan renegade, established a hereditary dynasty which lasted until 1957. For a long period, till the early 19th century, Tunisia was a centre of Mediterranean pirates. At the Congress of Berlin in 1878 Lord Salisbury gave France a free hand in Tunisia in return for French agreement to the British administration of Cyprus. In 1881 a French force entered Tunisia from Algeria and compelled the Bey to sign the Treaty of Bardo on 12 May 1881, by which he accepted a French protectorate. Italy, which had also had designs on Tunisia, then turned her eyes towards Ethiopia.

PRINTERS. All issues of Tunisia were printed at the Government Printing Works, Paris, *except for those in lithography or unless otherwise stated.*

IMPERFORATE STAMPS. Many stamps exist imperforate in their issued colours, but these were not valid for postage. Imperforate stamps in other colours are colour trials.

A. FRENCH PROTECTORATE

Before 1888 postal services were carried out by French post offices at Tunis and La Goulette, using French stamps with numeral cancellations "5107" and "5121" respectively, and Italian post offices at Tunis, La Goulette and Sousse, using Italian stamps with numeral cancellations "235", "3336" and "3364" respectively.

| 1 | 2 | D 3 | (3) |

(Des and eng E. Casse. Typo)

1888 (1 July). *P* 14 ×13½.
1	1	1 c. black/*azure* ..				65	45
2		2 c. purple-brown/*buff* ..				65	45
3		5 c. green/*pale green*				5·00	3·00
4		15 c. blue/*pale blue*				14·00	5·50
5		25 c. black/*rose* ..				28·00	16·00
6		40 c. red/*yellow* ..				25·00	14·00
7		75 c. rose/*pale rose*				28·00	17·00
8		5 f. mauve/*pale lilac*				£120	90·00
1/8		*Set of 8* ..				£200	£130

All values were reprinted in 1893 and 1897. The 1893 printing was on the same thin paper with greyish gum and can only be distinguished by the shades. The 1897 printing was on thick paper with white gum and all values, except the 15 c. and 40 c., can be found printed on a background of horizontal lines.

"T" PERFORATIONS. Stamps of all issues to 1901 exist perforated with a capital "T". These were used for Postage Due purposes.

(Des E. Casse. Eng E. Mouchon. Typo)

1888 (1 Oct)–**98**. *P* 14 ×13½.
9	2	1 c. black/*azure* (1.89)			30	10
10		2 c. purple-brown/*buff*	..	..	40	12
11		5 c. green/*pale green*	..	..	1·90	15

12	2	10 c. black/*lilac* (1.3.93)		..	1·90	12
13		15 c. blue/*pale blue*	..		14·00	20
14		15 c. blue (*quadrillé paper*) (1.1.93)		13·00	10
15		20 c. red/*green* (8.98)	..	..	4·00	25
16		25 c. black/*rose*			5·50	35
17		40 c. red/*yellow*			2·50	25
18		75 c. rose/*pale rose*	..	..	40·00	28·00
19		75 c. brownish violet/*yellow* (11.93)	..	5·00	1·60
20		1 f. olive-green/*toned* ..			6·50	1·60
21		5 f. mauve/*pale lilac* (2.89)	..		48·00	22·00
9/21		*Set of 13*		..	..	£130	50·00

1899 (Jan)–**1901**. *Colours changed and new values. P* 14 ×13½.
22	2	5 c. yellow-green			1·60	25
23		10 c. carmine (2.01)		..	1·60	15
24		15 c. grey (2.01)	..	..	2·50	25
25		25 c. blue (2.01)	..		3·50	35
26		35 c. brown (12.01)		..	9·50	30
27		2 f. deep lilac (12.01) ..		45·00	35·00
22/27		*Set of 6*	..	..	..	55·00	35·00

1901 (1 Apr)–**03**. *POSTAGE DUE. Typo. P* 14 ×13½.
D28	D 3	1 c. black ..		..	5	5
D29		2 c. orange		..	5	5
D30		5 c. blue ..		..	8	8
D31		10 c. brown ..		..	12	10
D32		20 c. blue-green		..	75	20
D33		30 c. carmine		..	45	20
D34		50 c. lake ..		..	35	20
D35		1 f. olive		..	25	20
D36		2 f. red/*green* (11.03)		..	90·	35
D37		5 f. black/*yellow* (10.03) ..	..	16·00	14·00
D28/37		*Set of 10* ..	..		17·00	14·00

The 5 c., 20 c., 30 c. and 50 c. exist from printings on the greyish "GC" paper made in 1917/18.

1902 (July). *Surch with T 3 at Tunis.*
28	2	25 on 15 c. blue (*quadrillé paper*)	..	75	70

4 Mosque at Kairouan

5 Agriculture

6 Ruins of Hadrian's Aqueduct

7 Carthaginian Galley

(Des L. Dumoulin. Eng J. Puyplat. Typo)

1906 (Jan)–**18**. *P* 13½ ×13 (*T* 5) *or* 14 ×13½ (*others*).
30	4	1 c. black/*yellow*	..	..	..	5	5
31		2 c. red-brown/*toned* ..		..	..	5	5
32		3 c. vermilion (1.11.18)		..	..	5	5
33		5 c. deep green/*green* ..		..	..	5	5
34	5	10 c. rose-red	..		..	5	5
35		15 c. violet (3.06)		..	..	15	5
36		20 c. brown (3.06)		..	..	5	5
37		25 c. blue/*toned* (3.06) ..		..	35	5

38	**6**	35 c. pale brown and olive	.. ..	1·90	20
39		40 c. brown-red and sepia		1·40	10
40		75 c. carmine and maroon	.. ..	15	8
41	**7**	1 f. sepia and red (3.06)		15	8
42		2 f. grey-green and pale brown (3.06) ..	1·10	40
43		5 f. blue and violet (3.06)	.. ..	2·00	1·40
30/43		*Set of* 14		6·50	2·25

The 1, 2, 3, 5, 15, 20 and 25 c. exist on greyish "GC" paper used in 1917/19.

See also Nos. 72/8 and 105, etc.

P **8** Mail **(9)** **(10)**
Carrier

(Des L. Dumoulin. Eng J. Puyplat. Typo)

1906 (1 Aug). *PARCEL POST*. P 13½ × 14.

P44	P **8**	5 c. dull purple and green ..		5	5
P45		10 c. dull pink and vermilion		30	8
P46		20 c. vermilion and deep brown		40	8
P47		25 c. brown and deep blue ..		50	8
P48		40 c. rose and grey ..	..	55	8
P49		50 c. dull violet and purple-brown		50	8
P50		75 c. blue and yellow-brown		80	8
P51		1 f. rose-red and lake-brown		75	8
P52		2 f. pale blue and deep rose		1·75	8
P53		5 f. purple-brown and violet		3·75	25
P44/53		*Set of* 10		8·50	70

For 5 c. red and brown/*rose*, see No. 114a.

1908 (Sept). *Surch as T* **9**, *at Tunis.*

44	**2**	10 on 15 c. grey (R.) ..	..	40	40
45		35 on 1 f. pale green (R.)	..	50	50
46		40 on 2 f. deep lilac (B.)	..	1·75	1·75
47		75 on 5 f. mauve/*lilac* (B.)	..	1·10	1·10
44/47		*Set of* 4	.. ..	3·50	3·50

1911. *Surch with T* **10**. *at Tunis.*

48	**5**	10 on 15 c. violet	.. ..	55	8

(D 11) (11) (12) (13)

1914 (Nov). *POSTAGE DUE. Surch with Type* D **11**.

D49	D **3**	2 f. on 5 f. black/*yellow* (B.)		35	30

1915 (Feb). *Red Cross Fund. Optd with T* **11**.

49	**5**	15 c. violet (R.) ..	.. ..	20	20

1916 (15 Feb). *Red Cross Fund. Optd with T* **12**.

50	**4**	5 c. green/*green*	.. ..	30	30

1916 (7 Aug). *Prisoners-of-War Fund. Colours changed, surch as T* **13**, *in red.*

51	**5**	10 c. on 15 c. brown/*azure*	..	12	12
52		10 c. on 20 c. brown/*yellow*		12	12
53		10 c. on 25 c. blue/*green*		65	65
54	**6**	10 c. on 35 c. violet and green ..	1·25	1·25
55		10 c. on 40 c. black and brown ..	65	65
56		10 c. on 75 c. green and maroon	..	1·60	1·60

57	**7**	10 c. on 1 f. green and red	.. ..	65	65
58		10 c. on 2 f. blue and pale brown	..	21·00	21·00
59		10 c. on 5 f. red and violet	.. ..	35·00	35·00
51/59		*Set of* 9	.. .. ..	48·00	48·00

These stamps were sold at face value, but paid postage for 10 c. only.

(14) (15)

1917 (16 Mar). *Surch with T* **14**, *at Tunis.*

60	**5**	15 c. on 10 c. rose-red ..	..	20	5
		a. Surch double	.. ..	12·00	

1918 (20 Sept). *Prisoners-of-War Fund. Surch as T* **15**, *variously spaced in red. "GC" paper.*

61	**5**	15 c. on 20 c. black/*green*	..	20	20
62		15 c. on 25 c. blue/*toned*	..	20	20
63	**6**	15 c. on 35 c. rose and olive-green	..	30	30
64		15 c. on 40 c. blue and brown	..	50	50
65		15 c. on 75 c. black and claret	..	1·25	1·25
66	**7**	15 c. on 1 f. violet and rose	..	4·50	4·50
67		15 c. on 2 f. red and brown	..	18·00	18·00
68		15 c. on 5 f. black and violet	..	45·00	45·00
61/68		*Set of* 8	.. ..	55·00	55·00

These stamps were sold at face value but paid postage for 15 c. only.

(17) **18** Ruin at Dougga

1919 (20 Apr)-**20**. *AIR. Surch or optd as T* **17**, *in red at Tunis* (69) *or Paris* (70).

69	**6**	30 c. on 35 c. pale brown and grey-green	25	25
		a. Surch double	.. ..	38·00	38·00
		b. Surch inverted	..	38·00	38·00
		c. Surch double, both inverted	..	38·00	38·00
		d. Surch double, one inverted	..	38·00	38·00
70		30 c. blue and olive	.. ..	15	15

There are numerous forgeries of the errors.

1920 (Apr)-**21**. *New values and colours changed.* P 13½ × 14 (*T* **5**) *or* 14 × 13½ (*others*).

72	**4**	5 c. orange (11.21)	.. ..	5	5
73	**5**	10 c. green (10.21)	.. ..	5	5
74		25 c. violet (11.21)	.. ..	5	5
75	**6**	30 c. violet and claret	..	15	15
76	**5**	30 c. red (11.21)	.. ..	20	15
77		50 c. blue (10.21)	.. ..	12	5
78	**6**	60 c. violet and green (12.21) ..	..	8	5
72/78		*Set of* 7	.. ..	60	45

1921 (Apr). *Surch similar to T* **15**, *but without cross, at Tunis.*

79	**5**	20 c. on 15 c. violet	.. ..	20	5

No. 79 is known on "GC" paper.

(Des H. Dabadie. Eng A. Delzers. Typo)

1922 (Dec). P 13½ × 14.

80	**18**	10 c. green	.. ..	5	5
81		30 c. carmine	.. ..	25	25
82		50 c. blue	.. ..	10	10

See also Nos. 104 and 106.

PROTECTION
DE
L'ENFANCE

10

AFFᵗ 0ᶜ

POSTES

(19)   D **20** Carthaginian   (20)
Statue

1923 (26 Feb). *War Wounded Fund.* *T* **4** to **7** and **18**.
Colours changed, surch as T **19**.

83	**4**	0 c. on 1 c. blue		5	5
84		0 c. on 2 c. brown (R.)		5	5
85		1 c. on 3 c. green (R.)		5	5
86		2 c. on 5 c. magenta		5	5
87	**18**	3 c. on 10 c. magenta/*bluish*		8	8
88	**5**	5 c. on 15 c. olive-green		8	8
89		5 c. on 20 c. blue/*rose*		25	25
90		5 c. on 25 c. magenta/*bluish*		30	30
91	**18**	5 c. on 30 c. yellow-orange		30	30
92	**6**	5 c. on 35 c. magenta and blue		45	45
93		5 c. on 40 c. brown and blue		45	45
94	**18**	10 c. on 50 c. black/*bluish* (R.)		45	45
95	**6**	10 c. on 60 c. blue and brown (R.)		45	45
96		10 c. on 75 c. green and magenta		75	75
97	**7**	25 c. on 1 f. magenta and lake		75	75
98		25 c. on 2 f. pink and blue		3·00	3·00
99		25 c. on 5 f. brown and green (R.)		15·00	15·00
83/99		*Set of* 17		20·00	20·00

Issued for the benefit of wounded soldiers, these stamps were
sold at face value, but had franking power to the value of
surcharge only. Nos. 83 and 84 had no franking value.

(Des H. Dabadie. Eng A Delzers. Typo)

1923 (Mar) –**29**. *POSTAGE DUE.* P 14 ×13½.

D100	D **20**	1 c. black		5	5
D101		2 c. black/*yellow*		5	5
D102		5 c. claret		5	5
D103		10 c. blue		5	5
D104		20 c. orange/*yellow*		5	5
D105		30 c. brown		5	5
D106		50 c. carmine		12	8
D107		60 c. mauve (10.28)		12	10
D108		80 c. bistre-brown (10.28)		8	8
D109		90 c. rosine (10.28)		20	15
D110		1 f. green		5	5
D111		2 f. olive-green		15	10
D112		3 f. violet/*rose* (9.29)		5	8
D113		5 f. violet		15	8
D100/113		*Set of* 14		1·10	90

See also Nos. D287/93.

1923 (16 Apr)–**25**. *Surch as T* **9** *at Tunis, with bars
through original value.*

100	**4**	10 on 5 c. green/*green* (R.)		8	5
		a. Surch inverted		16·00	
		b. Surch double		10·00	
		c. Surch double, one inverted		13·00	
101	**5**	20 on 15 c. violet		25	5
		a. Surch double		16·00	
102		30 on 20 c. brown (9.25)		5	5
103		50 on 25 c. blue/*toned* (R.)		30	5
100/103		*Set of* 4		60	12

No. 100 only exists on "GC" paper, and No. 101 can also
be found on this paper.

1923 (24 Sept)–**26**. *New values and colours.* P 13½ ×14
(*T* **5, 18**) *or* 14 ×13½ (*others*).

104	**18**	10 c. rose (3.26)		5	5
105	**5**	15 c. brown/*orange*		5	5
106	**18**	30 c. mauve (4.26)		5	5
107	**5**	40 c. black/*rose* (22.11.23)		15	12
108		40 c. green (6.26)		5	5
109	**6**	60 c. carmine and red (11.25)		8	5
110		75 c. scarlet and red (6.26)		5	5
111	**7**	1 f. pale blue and blue (11.25)		5	5
112		2 f. red and green/*rose* (11.25)		5	5
113		5 f. green and lilac (11.25)		15	8
104/113		*Set of* 10		60	40

1925 (7 June). *Child Welfare. Colours changed. Surch as
T* **20**.

114	P **8**	1 c. on 5 c. red and brown/*rose*		5	5
		a. Surch omitted		26·00	
115		2 c. on 10 c. blue and brown/*yellow*		5	5
116		3 c. on 20 c. carmine & purple/*mve*		12	12
117		5 c. on 25 c. red & blue-green/*green*		15	15
118		5 c. on 40 c. green and red/*yellow*		15	15
119		10 c. on 50 c. green and violet/*mauve*		45	45
120		10 c. on 75 c. sepia and green/*green*		25	25
121		25 c. on 1 f. yellow-green & bl/*bluish*		30	30
122		25 c. on 2 f. purple and carmine/*rose*		1·60	1·60
123		25 c. on 5 f. brown & carmine/*yell-grn*		11·00	11·00
114/123		*Set of* 10		13·00	13·00

Sold at face value, but with franking power to the value of
the surcharge only.

21 Arab   **22** Grand Mosque,   **23** Mosque, Place
Woman   Tunis   Halfaouine, Tunis

24 Amphitheatre,   P **25** Date
El Djem   gathering

(Des Verecque. Eng A. Mignon (**21**). Des A. Proust. Eng A.
Delzers (**22**). Des Pendrout. Eng G. Daussy (**23**). Des H.
Dabadie. Eng C. Hourriez (**24**). Des Friedling. Eng M.
Froment (P **25**). Typo).

1926 (Oct)–**41**. (*a*) *POSTAGE.* P 14 ×13½.

124	**21**	1 c. rose-red		5	5
125		2 c. sage-green		5	5
126		3 c. steel-blue		5	5
127		5 c. apple-green		5	5
128		10 c. magenta		5	5
129	**22**	15 c. lilac		5	5
130		20 c. brown-red		5	5
131		25 c. blue-green		5	5
131a		25 c. bright mauve (1.28)		20	5
132		30 c. bright mauve		5	5
133		30 c. blue-green (25.2.28)		5	5
134		40 c. bistre-brown		5	5
134a		45 c. emerald-green (1939)		15	15
135	**23**	50 c. black		5	5
135a		50 c. bright ultramarine (11.34)		10	5
135b		50 c. emerald-green (1940)		5	5
135c		60 c. vermilion (1939)		5	5
135d		65 c. bright blue (1938)		15	5
135e		70 c. scarlet (1940)		5	5
136		75 c. vermilion		12	5
136a		75 c. magenta (1.28)		20	5
137		80 c. greenish blue		15	10
137a		80 c. black-brown (1940)		5	5
138		90 c. vermilion (25.2.28)		5	5
138a		90 c. ultramarine (1939)		2·25	2·25
139		1 f. plum		20	5
139a		1 f. rose-carmine (1940)		5	5
140	**24**	1 f. 05, pink and blue		10	5
141		1 f. 25, blue and pale blue		12	10
141a		1 f. 25, rose-carmine (1940)		30	30
141b		1 f. 30, violet-blue and blue (1941)		5	5
141c		1 f. 40, bright purple (1939)		15	15

142	**24**	1 f. 50, blue and pale blue (25.2.28)		30	5
142a		1 f. 50, red-orge & rose-red (1941)		5	5
143		2 f. brown and carmine	..	40	5
143a		2 f. vermilion (1939)		5	5
143b		2 f. 25, ultramarine (1939)	..	20	20
143c		2 f. 50, green (1939)	..	15	15
144		3 f. orange and blue	..	50	5
144a		3 f. violet (1939)	..	5	5
145		5 f. green and red/*greenish*		70	12
145a		5 f. red-brown (1940)	..	25	20
146		10 f. slate and brown-red/*azure*		2·10	40
146a		10 f. pink (1940)	..	15	15
146b		20 f. red and mauve/*rose* (25.2.28)..		50	20
124/146b		*Set of 45* ..	..	9·50	5·00

For these designs printed by recess see Nos. 172/91. For designs without "RF" see Nos. 220/31 and for further stamps as T **23/4** see Nos. 257/86.

(b) *PARCEL POST.* P 13½ × 14

P147	**P 25**	5 c. blue and brown	..	5	5
P148		10 c. magenta and carmine	..	8	5
P149		20 c. black and yellow-green	..	10	5
P150		25 c. black and brown	..	12	10
P151		40 c. green and carmine	..	45	20
P152		50 c. black and bright violet	..	40	15
P153		60 c. carmine and grey-brown	..	55	20
P154		75 c. green and lilac	..	50	10
P155		80 c. brown and orange-red	..	50	10
P156		1 f. rose and greenish blue	..	40	5
P157		2 f. carmine and magenta	..	75	5
P158		4 f. black and deep red	..	90	5
P159		5 f. violet and chocolate	..	1·50	25
P160		10 f. green and red/*greenish*	..	2·50	20
P161		20 f. violet and yellow-green/*rose*		3·75	25
P147/161		*Set of 15* ..	..	11·00	1·60

1927 (24 Mar). *Surch as T* **28** *of Réunion, in red, with two bars obliterating old value.*

147	**24**	1 f. 50 on 1 f. 25, blue and ultramarine		8	8

Poste Aérienne ≡

(25)

1927 (24 Mar)–**28**. *AIR. Surch as T* **25** *or optd* "Post Aérienne" *and aeroplane, only.*

(a) *Surch as T* **25**

148	**7**	1 f. pale blue and blue (B.)	./.	20	15
149	**6**	1 f. 75 on 75 c. scarlet and red		25	12
150	**7**	1 f. 75 on 5 f. green and lilac (R.)		1·00	75
151		2 f. red and green/*rose* (R.)	..	65	55

(b) *Optd with Aeroplane and* "Poste Aérienne" *only* (25.2.28)

152	**24**	1 f. 30, mauve and orange (B.)		1·10	65
153		1 f. 80, carmine and olive-green (B.)..		1·25	30
154		2 f. 55, brown and magenta (B.)		50	25
148/154		*Set of 7* ..	..	4·50	2·50

26 First Tunis-Chad Motor Service   (27)   (27a)

(Des J. Kerhor. Eng and recess Institut de Gravure, Paris)

1928 (Feb). *Child Welfare.* P 13½.

155	**26**	40 c. +40 c. yellow-brown	..	30	30
156		50 c. +50 c. purple	..	30	30
157		75 c. +75 c. deep blue	..	30	30
158		1 f. +1 f. bright carmine	..	30	30
159		1 f. 50 +1 f. 50, turquoise-blue	..	30	30

160	**26**	2 f. +2 f. green		30	30
161		5 f. +5 f. red-brown ..	..	30	30
155/161		*Set of 7*	..	1·90	1·90

1928 (1 May) –**30**. *Surch as T* **27** *or* 27a *(No. 166).*

162	**4**	3 c. on 5 c. orange	..	5	5
163	**5**	10 c. on 15 c. brown/*orange*..	..	5	5
164	**18**	25 c. on 30 c. mauve ..		8	5
165	**23**	40 c. on 80 c. greenish blue	..	10	8
166	**22**	50 c. on 40 c. bistre-brown (12.30)	..	1·10	5
167	**23**	50 c. on 75 c. vermilion	..	10	10
162/167		*Set of 6*	..	1·25	30

1929 (18 Mar). *No. 132 precancelled* "AFFRANCHts POSTES" *and surch as T* **27**a.

168		10 on 30 c. bright mauve	..	†	30

1930 (Aug). *AIR. Surch as T* **25**, *in blue.*

169	**24**	1 f. 50 on 1 f. 30, mauve and orange..		75	35
170		1 f. 50 on 1 f. 80, carmine & olive-grn		90	25
171		1 f. 50 on 2 f. 55, brown and magenta	2·75	70

28   29   30

31

(Recess. Institut de Gravure, Paris)

1931 (15 Jan). *Designers as for T* **21** *to* **24**.

(a) *P* 13

172	**28**	1 c. indigo ..	..	5	5
173		2 c. yellow-brown	..	5	5
174		3 c. black	..	5	5
175		5 c. bright green	..	5	5
176		10 c. scarlet	..	5	5
177	**29**	15 c. dull purple	..	10	10
178		20 c. brown	..	5	5
179		25 c. scarlet	..	5	5
180		30 c. deep green	..	5	5
181		40 c. orange ..	..	5	5
182	**30**	50 c. deep ultramarine	..	5	5
183		75 c. yellow	..	30	30
184		90 c. scarlet	..	12	12
185		1 f. olive-brown	..	5	5

(b) *P* 12½ (1 f. 50, 2 f., 3 f.) *or* 11 (*others*)

186	**31**	1 f. 50, ultramarine ..	..	8	5
187		2 f. chocolate	..	12	12
188		3 f. deep green	..	3·25	3·25
189		5 f. carmine ..	..	4·75	4·75
		a. Perf 12½	..	7·50	3·75
190		10 f. black	..	11·00	11·00
191		20 f. deep red-brown..	..	14·00	14·00
172/191		*Set of 20* ..	..	38·00	35·00

25ᶜ·   **25 c.**

≡   ≡   ■ **0,65**   ≡ **65**

(32)   (32a)   (33)   (34)

1 FR.

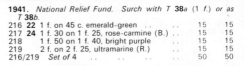

1.F.   **1**f**75**   **1**f**75**

≡   ≣   ═   ═

(34a)   (34b)   (35)   (36)

1937–41. *Stamps of 1936–41 surch.*

191a	32	25 c. on 65 c. brt blue (R.) (1939)		5	5
191b	32a	25 c. on 65 c. brt blue (R.) (1941)		5	5
192	33	0,65 on 50 c. bright ultramarine (R.)		15	5
		a. Surch double		16·00	14·00
193	34	65 on 50 c. bright ultramarine (1938)		25	5
		a. Surch double, one inverted		38·00	38·00
193b	34a	1 FR. on 90 c. ultramarine (R.) (1940)		10	5
193c	34b	1 F. on 1 f. 25, rose-carmine (1941)		5	5
193d		1 F. on 1 f. 40, bright purple (1941)		5	5
193e		1 F. on 2 f. 25, ultram (R.) (1941)		5	5
194	35	1 f. 75 on 1 f. 50, blue & pale bl (R.)		1·90	45
		a. Surch double		15·00	15·00
195	36	1 f. 75 on 1 f. 50, blue and pale blue			
		(R.) (1938)		1·90	1·90
191a/195		*Set of 10*		4·00	2·25

1888   1938   1888   1938

+ **10** e   + **3**F

(37)   (38)

1938. *50th Anniv of Tunisian Postal Service.* *Surch as T 37 or T 38 (on T 31).*

196	28	1 c.+1 c. indigo		60	60
197		2 c.+2 c. yellow-brown		60	60
198		3 c.+3 c. black		60	60
199		5 c.+5 c. bright green		60	60
200		10 c.+10 c. scarlet		60	60
201	29	15 c.+15 c. dull purple		60	60
202		20 c.+20 c. brown		60	60
203		25 c.+25 c. scarlet		60	60
204		30 c.+30 c. deep green		60	60
205		40 c.+40 c. orange		60	60
206	30	50 c.+50 c. deep ultramarine		60	60
207		75 c.+75 c. yellow		60	60
208		90 c.+90 c. scarlet		60	60
209		1 f.+1 f. olive-brown		60	60
210	31	1 f. 50+1 f. ultramarine		60	60
211		2 f.+1 f. 50, chocolate		65	65
212		3 f.+2 f. deep green		65	65
213		5 f.+3 f. carmine (p 11)		4·50	4·50
		a. Perf 12½		28·00	28·00
214		10 f.+5 f. black		10·00	10·00
215		20 f.+10 f. brown		14·00	14·00
196/215		*Set of 20*		35·00	35·00

VICHY GOVERNMENT. From July 1940 until May 1943 Tunisia was administered by officials of the Pétain government. We do not list a set of four charity stamps, produced in 1944, but sold only in Paris. However, Nos. 216/19 and 222/31 were issued by the Vichy administration.

SECOURS
NATIONAL
1941

SECOURS NATIONAL

1941

≡ **1**.F   **1**f**50** ≡

(38a)   (38b)

1941. *National Relief Fund.* Surch with T 38a (1 f.) or as T 38b.

216	22	1 f. on 45 c. emerald-green		15	15
217	24	1 f. 30 on 1 f. 25, rose-carmine (B.)		15	15
218		1 f. 50 on 1 f. 40, bright purple		15	15
219		2 f. on 2 f. 25, ultramarine (R.)		15	15
216/219		*Set of 4*		50	50

39 Grand Mosque,   40 Mosque, Place
   Tunis   Halfaouine, Tunis

41 Amphitheatre,
   El Djem

1941–45. *T 22/4 redrawn without "RF" as T 39/41. Typo. P 14 × 13½.*

220	39	30 c. carmine (1945)		5	5
221	40	1 f. 20, bluish grey (1945)		5	5
222		1 f. 50, red-brown (1942)		10	10
223	41	2 f. 40, pink and carmine (1942)		5	5
224		2 f. 50, light blue & greenish bl (12.41)		5	5
225		3 f. violet (16.2.43)		5	5
226		4 f. ultramarine and black (1942)		5	5
227		4 f. 50, brown and olive-green (1942)		5	5
228		5 f. brown-black (1.42)		5	5
229		10 f. slate-violet and purple (1.42)		10	5
230		15 f. brown-red (1942)		1·00	1·00
231		20 f. carmine and lilac		70	30
220/231		*Set of 12*		2·10	1·50

On 12 May 1943 the German and Italian troops in Tunisia surrendered to British, American and Free French forces.

41a "Victory"

(Des Fernez. Eng C. Hervé. Litho, Algiers)

1943. *P 12.*

232	41a	1 f. 50, rose		5	5

42 Allied   43 Mosque and
   Soldiers   Olive Trees

(Des C. Hervé. Litho, Algiers)

1943 (July). *Charity. Tunisian Liberation. P 12.*

233	42	1 f. 50+8 f. 50, carmine		5	5

(Des Hue. Litho, Algiers)

1944-45. *P* 11½. (*a*) 15½×19 *mm*.

234	**43**	30 c. yellow			5	5
235		40 c. red-brown			5	5
236		60 c. red-orange			5	5
237		70 c. pink			5	5
238		80 c. blue-green			5	5
239		90 c. violet			5	5
240		1 f. vermilion			5	5
241		1 f. 50, blue			5	5

(*b*) 21¼×26½ *mm*

242	**43**	2 f. 40, vermilion			5	5
243		2 f. 50, red-brown			5	5
244		3 f. violet			5	5
245		4 f. violet-blue			5	5
246		4 f. 50, yellow-green			5	5
247		5 f. grey			5	5
248		6 f. chocolate (1945)			8	8
249		6 f. brown-purple (1945)			8	8
250		15 f. red-brown			10	10
251		20 f. lilac			12	12
234/251		*Set of 18*			90	90

(43*a*)

44 Sidi Mahrez Mosque

45 Ramparts of Sfax

1944. *Forces' Welfare Fund. Surch with T* **43***a*.

252	**43**	2 f. +48 f. vermilion (21¼×26½ *mm*)		20	20

(Des Roubtzoff (1 f. 50), Mauchien (3 f.), Farion (others).
Litho, Algiers)

1945. *Forces' Welfare Fund. As T* **44/5** (*various designs surch* "POUR NOS COMBATANTS" *and new values*). *P* 11½.

253		1 f. 50+8 f. 50, red-brown (R.)		15	15
254		3 f. +12 f. green (R.)		15	15
255		4 f. +21 f. yellow-brown (R.)		15	15
256		10 f. +40 f. red (Bk.)		15	15
253/256		*Set of 4*		50	50

Designs: *Horiz*—4 f. Camel patrol at Fort Saint; 10 f. Mosque at Sidi-bou-Said.

1945-49. *Typo. P* 14×13½.

257	**23**	10 c. brown		5	5
258		30 c. olive-green		5	5
259		40 c. magenta		5	5
260		50 c. greenish blue		5	5
261		60 c. ultramarine		5	5
262		80 c. yellow-green		8	8
263		1 f. 20, sepia		5	5

264	**23**	1 f. 50, lilac		5	5
265		2 f. deep green		5	5
266		2 f. yellow-green		5	5
267	**24**	2 f. 40, rose		8	8
268	**23**	2 f. 50, yellow-brown (1947)		5	5
269	**24**	3 f. sepia		5	5
270	**23**	3 f. carmine		5	5
271	**24**	4 f. blue		12	10
272	**23**	4 f. dull violet		5	5
273	**24**	4 f. violet (1946)		5	5
273*a*	**23**	4 f. brown-orange (1949)		15	8
274		4 f. 50, blue		5	5
275	**24**	5 f. yellow-green		5	5
275*a*	**23**	5 f. blue (9.48)		15	5
275*b*		5 f. green (1949)		15	8
276	**24**	6 f. violet-blue		5	5
277		6 f. rose (1946)		5	5
278	**23**	6 f. carmine-red (1947)		5	5
279	**24**	10 f. red-orange		5	5
280		10 f. ultramarine (1946)		5	5
281		15 f. magenta		8	5
281*a*	**23**	15 f. carmine (1949)		15	5
282	**24**	20 f. grey-green		10	5
283		25 f. violet		15	12
284		25 f. orange (1946)		25	12
285		50 f. brown-red		30	5
286		100 f. carmine		50	5
257/286		*Set of 34*		2·75	1·75

1945-50. *POSTAGE DUE. New colours. P* 14×13½.

D287	D **20**	10 c. green		5	5
D288		50 c. violet		5	5
D289		2 f. rose		5	5
D290		4 f. greenish blue		10	10
D291		10 f. magenta (1946)		12	5
D292		20 f. olive-brown (1946)		25	5
D293		30 f. blue (1950)		35	20
D287/293		*Set of 7*		85	50

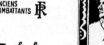

(47) (48) 49 Legionary

1945. *Anti-Tuberculosis Fund. T* **222** *of France* (*Patient in chair*) *optd with T* **47**.

287	**46**	2 f. +1 f. red-orange		5	5

1945. *Postal Employees' War Victims' Fund. T* **223** *of France* (*Refugees*) *optd with T* **47**.

288		4 f. + 6 f. purple-brown		12	12

1945 (13 Oct). *Stamp Day. T* **228** *of France* (*Louis XI*), *optd with T* **47**.

289		2 f. +3 f. green		5	5

1945. *War Veterans' Fund. As T* **21** *and* **23**, *but without* "R.F.", *surch as T* **48**, *in red*.

290	**21**	4 f. +6 f. on 10 c. blue		15	15
291	**23**	10 f. +30 f. on 80 c. green		15	15

(Des and eng G. Barlangue. Recess)

1946. *Welfare Fund for French Troops in Indo-China. P* 13.

292	**49**	20 f. +30 f. black, red and green		45	45

+
1946

+50^c

(50)

SOLIDARITÉ 1947

+40^f

(52)

1946. *Red Cross Fund. Surch as T **50**, "+1946", in red, and new values in black.*

293	23	80 c.+50 c. yellow-green	..	12	12
294		1 f. 50+1 f. 50, lilac	..	12	12
295		2 f.+2 f. deep green	.. ..	12	12
296	24	2 f. 40+2 f. rose	.. ..	12	12
297		4 f.+4 f. blue	.. ..	12	12
293/297		Set of 5	.. ..	55	55

1946 (29 June). *Stamp Day. T **241** of France (La Varane), optd with T **47**.*

298	3 f.+2 f. blue (R.)	.. ..	20	20

1947 (15 Mar). *Stamp Day. T **253** of France (Louvois), optd with T **47**.*

299	4 f. 50+5 f. 50, purple-brown (R.)	..	25	25

1947 (Apr). *Naval Charities. As T **234** of France (Warships), but colour changed, optd with T **47** and new value, in red.*

300	10+15 on 2 f.+3 f. ultramarine..	25	25

1947 (10 June). *Welfare Fund. Surch with T **52**, in red.*

301	24	10 f.+40 f. black ..	35	35

53 Arabesque Ornamentation,　**54** Neptune
Great Mosque, Kairouan

(Des M. Besson. Eng C. Mazelin (**53**), J. Piel (**54**). Recess)

1947 (24 Nov)–**51**. *P* 13.

302	53	3 f. yellow-green & blue-grn (1948)	20	15
303		4 f. carmine and purple (1948)	5	5
304	54	5 f. black and green	20	20
305	53	6 f. orange-red & red-brown (1948)	5	5
306	54	10 f. black and purple-brown	5	5
306a	53	10 f. violet (12.48) ..	10	5
306b		12 f. red-brown (12.48)	20	8
306c		12 f. brown-orange & red-brn (1.4.49)	12	5
306d		15 f. red and red-brown (1949)	12	10
307	54	16 f. blue and blackish green (7.48)	25	12
307a		25 f. greenish blue and blue (1.4.49)	30	5
307b	53	30 f. blue and deep blue (29.10.51)	30	15
302/307b		Set of 12 ..	1·75	95

AIDEZ LES

+10ᶠ

TUBERCULEUX

55 Feeding a　(56)
Fledgling

(Des Michel Grange. Eng E. Feltesse. Recess)

1947 (1 Dec). *Infant Welfare Fund. P 13.*

308	55	4 f. 50+5 f. 50, blue-green ..	45	45
309		6 f.+9 f. ultramarine..	45	45
310		8 f.+17 f. carmine ..	45	45
311		10 f.+40 f. violet ..	45	45
308/311		Set of 4	1·60	1·60

1948 (6 Mar). *Stamp Day. As T **267** of France (Etienne Arago), but colour changed, optd "TUNISIE" vert down at left.*

312	6 f.+4 f. carmine ..	30	30
	a. Opt double	18·00	

1948 (Mar). *Anti-Tuberculosis Fund. Surch with T **56**.*

313	53	4 f.+10 f. orange and olive-green	30	30

57 Triumphal Arch,　**58** Child in Cot
Sbeitla

(Des M. Besson. Eng C. Mazelin. Recess)

1948 (Nov). *Army Welfare Fund. P 13.*

315	57	10 f.+40 f. green and bistre ..	..	40	40
316		18 f.+42 f. deep blue and blue	..	40	40

1949 (26 Mar). *Stamp Day. As T **278** of France (Duc de Choiseul), but colour changed. Optd "TUNISIE" in red.*

317	15 f.+5 f. slate-black ..	..	45	45

(Des H. Farion. Eng R. Cottet. Recess)

1949 (1 June). *Child Welfare Fund. P 13.*

318	58	25 f.+50 f. deep green	..	..	60	60

59 Oued Mellegue　**60** Bird from
Barrage　Antique Mosaic

(Des M. Besson. Eng C. Mazelin. Recess)

1949 (1 Sept). *Tunisian Development. P 13.*

319	59	15 f. greenish black ..	..	75	8

Two types of 200 f.:—
I. Arabic inscr in two lines.
II. Arabic inscr in one line as T **60**.

(Des M. Besson. Eng G. Barlangue. Recess)

1949 (1 Sept)–**51**. *AIR.*

320	60	100 f. brown and blue-green (1.2.50)	90	15
321		200 f. blue-black and blue (I) ..	1·90	45
322		200 f. blue-black & blue (II) (20.1.51)	1·60	90

+ FFL 15ᶠ

61 Globe, Mounted　(61a)
Postman and
Aeroplane

(Des M. Besson. Eng C. Dufresne. Recess)

1949 (28 Oct). *75th Anniv of U.P.U. P 13. (a) POSTAGE.*

323	61	5 f. green/*blue* ..	..	30	30
324		15 f. red-brown/*blue* ..		35	35

(b) AIR. Inscr "POSTE AERIENNE"

325	61	25 f. blue/*blue* ..	50	50

1949 (8 Dec). *Free French Association Fund. Surch with T **61**a.*

326	54	10 f.+15 f. carmine and ultramarine ..	40	40

1950 (11 Mar). *Stamp Day. As T 292 of France (Postman), but colour changed. Optd "TUNISIE" vert down at right, in blue.*
327 12 f.+3 f. blue-green 45 45

62 "Tunisia Thanks   **63** Old Soldier
France"

(Des M. Besson. Eng E. Feltesse. Recess)

1950 (5 June). *Franco-Tunisian Relief Fund. P 13.*
328 **62** 15 f.+35 f. scarlet 45 45
329 25 f.+45 f. blue 45 45

(Des M. H. Farion. Eng R. Serres. Recess)

1950 (21 Aug). *Veterans' Welfare Fund. P 13.*
330 **63** 25 f.+25 f. blue 60 60

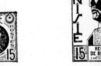

64 Horse   **65** Hermes of
(bas relief)   Berbera

(Des M. Besson. Eng R. Cortot)

1950–53. *P 13 ×14. (a) Typo. 21½ ×17½ mm.*
331 **64** 10 c. turquoise-blue (29.10.51) .. 5 5
332 50 c. yellow-brown (27.3.51) .. 5 5
333 1 f. violet (27.3.51) 5 5
334 2 f. grey (27.3.51) 5 5
335 3 f. orange-brown (25.3.52) .. 5 5
336 4 f. red-orange (27.3.51) 5 5
337 5 f. yellow-green (27.3.51) .. 5 5
338 8 f. blue (27.3.51) 10 8
339 12 f. red (29.10.51) 30 8
340 12 f. carmine (28.10.52) .. 30 5
341 15 f. carmine (26.12.50) .. 15 5
342 15 f. pale blue (28.5.52) .. 15 5

(b) Recess. 22½ ×18¼ mm
343 **64** 15 f. carmine (26.2.51) 25 12
344 15 f. bright blue (27.4.53) 25 12
345 30 f. blue (1.8.51) 30 5
331/345 *Set of 15* 1 90 70

(Des Feuille. Eng C. Dufresne. Recess)

1950 (25 Sept)–**51.** *P 13.*
346 **65** 15 f. lake 25 20
347 25 f. deep blue (27.3.51) 25 20
348 50 f. green (27.3.51) 55 12

1951 (10 Mar). *Stamp Day. T 300 of France (Sorting Van), but colour changed, optd with T 47.*
349 12 f.+3 f. grey-brown 30 25

66 Sleeping Child   **67** Gammarth
National Cemetery

(Des H. Farion. Eng R. Cottet. Recess)

1951 (19 June). *Child Welfare Fund. P 13.*
350 **66** 30 f.+15 f. blue 70 70

(Des H. Farion. Eng C. Dufresne. Recess)

1951 (1 Oct). *War Orphans' Fund. P 13.*
351 **67** 30 f.+10 f. blue 65 65

1952 (8 Mar). *Stamp Day. As T 319 of France (Mail Coach), but colour changed, optd "TUNISIE" in violet.*
352 12 f.+3 f. deep violet 35 35

68 Panel from   **69** Schoolboys   **70**
Great Mosque,   clasping   Charles Nicolle
Kairouan   Hands

(Des A. Spitz. Eng J. Pheulpin (15 f.), C. Mazelin (50 f.). Recess)

1952 (5 May). *Army Welfare Fund. T 68 and similar vert design inscr "OEUVRES SOCIALES DE L'ARMEE". P 13.*
(a) POSTAGE.
353 – 15 f.+1 f. indigo and blue 35 35
(b) AIR
354 **68** 50 f.+10 f. blue-green and black .. 75 75
Design:—15 f. Ornamental stucco, Bardo Palace.

(Des C. Riami. Eng J. Pheulpin. Recess)

1952 (15 June). *Holiday Camp Fund. P 13.*
355 **69** 30 f.+10 f. deep blue-green 50 50

(Des and eng R. Malé. Recess)

1952 (4 Aug). *Golden Jubilee of Tunisian Medical Sciences Society. P 13.*
356 **70** 15 f. blackish brown 30 15
357 30 f. deep blue 35 25

1952 (15 Oct). *Centenary of Médaille Militaire. As T 327 of France, but colour changed, and surch "TUNISIE+5F.".*
358 15 f.+5 f. emerald 35 35

1953 (14 Mar). *Stamp Day. As T 334 of France (Count D'Argenson), but colour changed and optd "TUNISIE".*
359 12 f.+3 f. vermilion 30 30

A regular new issue supplement to this
catalogue appears each month in

STAMP MONTHLY

—from your newsagent or by postal subscription
—details on request.

71 Tower and Flags   72 Tozeur Mosque

76 Bey of   76a Paris Balloon
Tunisia   Post. 1870

1953 (18 Oct). *First International Fair, Tunis. Recess. P* 13.

360	**71**	8 f. blackish brown and deep brown	40	40
361		12 f. slate-green and emerald	40	40
362		15 f. indigo and blue ..	40	40
363		18 f. deep violet and reddish violet ..	40	40
364		30 f. lake and carmine	40	40
360/364		*Set of* 5	1·75	1·75

(Des and eng R. Cottet (500 f.), A. Decaris (1000 f.), P. Gandon (others). Recess)

1953 (10 Dec)–**54**. *AIR. T* **72** *and similar horiz designs.*
P 13.

365	100 f. indigo, dp turq & dp grn (29.5.54)	1·00	25
366	200 f. sepia, brn-pur & red-brn (29.5.54)	2·00	60
367	500 f. blackish brown and blue	9·00	3·75
368	1000 f. deep green	14·00	9·50
365/368	*Set of* 4	23·00	13·00

Designs:—100 f., 200 f. Monastir; 500 f. View of Korbous.
For stamps without "RF" see Nos. 423/6.

1954 (20 Mar). *Stamp Day. As T* **346** *of France (Lavalette),*
but colour changed and optd "TUNISIE".

369	12 f.+3 f. indigo (R.)	30	30

73 Courtyard,   **74** Sidi Bou Maklouf
Sousse   Mosque, Le Kef

(Des and eng P. Gandon (50 c., 1 f., 2 f., 4 f., 15 f.), R. Cottet
(5 f., 8 f., 18 f., 20 f., 25 f.), A. Decaris (others).
Recess)

1954 (29 May). *T* **73/4** *and similar designs. P* 13.

370	50 c. emerald		5	5
371	1 f. carmine ..		5	5
372	2 f. brown-purple		5	5
373	4 f. deep turquoise-blue		5	5
374	5 f. bright violet		5	5
375	8 f. black-brown		8	5
376	10 f. deep bluish green ..		8	5
377	12 f. lake-brown		10	5
378	15 f. ultramarine (18 × 22 *mm*) ..		45	5
379	18 f. deep brown		30	30
380	20 f. deep bright blue ..		30	5
381	25 f. indigo		30	5
382	30 f. deep claret		30	10
383	40 f. deep turquoise-green		35	12
384	50 f. blackish lilac		60	5
385	75 f. bright carmine		1·10	75
370/385	*Set of* 16		3·75	1·60

Designs: *As T* **73**—1 f. T **73**; 2 f., 4 f. Takrouna ramparts;
5 f., 8 f. Mosque and dwellings, Tatahouine; 10 f., 12 f. Cave
dwellings, Matmata; 15 f. Street, Sidi Bou Said. *As T* **74**—20 f.,
25 f. Genoese Fort, Tabarka; 30 f., 40 f. Bab-El-Khadra Gate,
Tunis; 50 f., 75 f. Four-storey dwellings, Médénine.
For Nos. 370/85 but re-engraved with "R F" see Nos. 406/22.

(Des and eng P. Gandon. Typo)

1954. *As No.* 378, *but redrawn and reduced to* 17 ×21½ *mm.*
P 14 ×13½.

386	15 f. bright blue	10	5

(Des and eng R. Cottet. Recess)

1954 (16 Oct). *P* 13.

387	**76**	8 f. deep blue and blue	25	25
388		12 f. indigo and deep grey-blue ..	25	25
389		15 f. lake and carmine	25	25
390		18 f. deep brown and red-brown ..	25	25
391		30 f. deep bluish green and blue-green	40	40
387/391		*Set of* 5	1·25	1·25

(Des and eng R. Serres. Recess)

1955 (19 Mar). *Stamp Day. P* 13.

392	76a	12 f. + 3 f. red-brown		35	35

77

(Des and eng A. Decaris. Recess)

1955 (17 Apr). *50th Anniv of "L'Essor" (Tunisian Amateur*
Dramatic Society). P 13.

393	**77**	15 f. greenish bl, brn-lake & red-orge	25	25

78 Tunisian Buildings   **79** Bey of
and Rotary Emblem   Tunisia

(Des and eng A. Decaris. Recess)

1955 (14 May). *50th Anniv of Rotary International. P* 13.

394	**78**	12 f. blackish brown and purple-brown	20	20
395		15 f. blackish brown and violet-grey ..	20	20
396		18 f. deep lilac and violet	20	20
397		25 f. deep bright blue and blue ..	25	25
398		30 f. indigo and turquoise-blue ..	40	40
394/398		*Set of* 5	1·10	1·10

(Des and eng R. Cottet. Recess)

1955 (25 July). *P* 14 ×13.

399	**79**	15 f. deep blue	25	5

STAMP MONTHLY

—finest and most informative magazine for all
collectors. Obtainable from your newsagent or
by postal subscription—details on request.

B. AUTONOMOUS STATE

On 3 June 1955 France agreed to internal autonomy for Tunisia, to start on 1 September.

80 "Embroidery"   80a Francis of Taxis

(Des and eng P. Gandon (after A. Gorgi). Recess)

1955 (15–30 Oct). *3rd International Fair, Tunis.* T **80** and similar vert designs. P 13.

400	5 f. brown-lake	..	25	25
401	12 f. ultramarine (30.10)	..	25	25
402	15 f. deep turquoise-green	..	25	25
403	18 f. scarlet (30.10)	..	25	25
404	20 f. deep violet..	..	25	25
405	30 f. brown-purple·(30.10)	..	30	30
400/405	*Set of 6*	..	1·40	1·40

Designs:—12 f. T **80**; 15 f., 18 f. "Pottery"; 20 f., 30 f. "Jasmin Sellers".

1956 (1 Mar). *As Nos. 365/8 and 370/86 but re-engraved without "R F".* (a) POSTAGE.

406	50 c. emerald	..	..	5	5
407	1 f. carmine	..	..	5	5
408	2 f. brown-purple	..	..	5	5
409	4 f. deep,turquoise-blue	..	5	5
410	5 f. bright violet	..	..	5	5
411	8 f. black-brown	..	..	5	5
412	10 f. deep bluish green ..	..	8	5
413	12 f. lake-brown	..	..	5	5
414	15 f. ultramarine (18 × 22 mm) ..	45	5
415	15 f. bright blue (17 × 21½ mm)	..	8	5
416	18 f. deep brown	..	..	10	5
417	20 f. deep bright blue	..	..	12	5
418	25 f. indigo	..	..	12	5
419	30 f. deep claret	..	..	75	5
420	40 f. deep turquoise-green	..	65	10
421	50 f. blackish lilac	..	..	45	5
422	75 f. bright carmine	..	..	50	40

(b) AIR

423	100 f. indigo, dp turquoise & dp green	65	30
424	200 f. sepia, brown-purple & red-brown	1·00	70
425	500 f. blackish brown and blue	..	3·00	2·50
426	1000 f. deep green	..	..	5·00	4·00
406/426	*Set of* 21	..	..	12·00	7·00

(Des and eng J. Pheulpin. Recess)

1956 (17 Mar). *Stamp Day.* P 13.

427	80a 12 f. + 3 f. deep bluish green	35	35

On 20 March 1956 a protocol was signed in Paris giving complete independence to Tunisia.

PHILATELIC TERMS ILLUSTRATED

This successful STAMP MONTHLY series has now been brought together in a snappy black and yellow binding and published as a useful addition to Stanley Gibbons range of essential handbooks for keen stamp collectors. Within its 192 pages this handy limp-bound volume houses a veritable mine of useful information on the words and phrases used in philately. It describes and illustrates printing processes and watermarks, papers and perforations, errors and varieties . . . and it does all this IN COLOUR. Indeed, there are 92 full page plates in colour, plus many black and white illustrations, making it

FANTASTIC VALUE AT ONLY £1·95 POST PAID FROM

Stanley Gibbons Publications Ltd
391 Strand, London WC2R 0LX

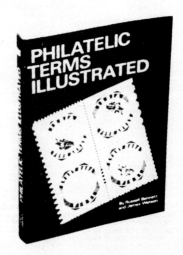

Ubangi-Shari

100 Centimes = 1 Franc

The country which is now the Central African Republic was from 1903 to 1958 the French colony of Ubangi-Shari. The explorer Savorgnan de Brazza extended French influence north of the Ubangi river in 1887 and the town of Bangui was founded in 1889. The French territory of Upper Bangui was formed in 1894 and the Shari area was occupied in 1898. After the failure of the French expedition to Fashoda on the Nile in 1898 the frontier with Sudan was fixed on 21 March 1899.

Ubangi-Shari, at first part of the French Congo, became a colony as from 1 July 1904 by a decree of 29 December 1903. Until 1915 the stamps of French Congo were used there; from 1915 to 1922 it shared a postal administration with Chad.

PRINTERS. All stamps, except for those in lithography, were printed at the Government Printing Works, Paris, *unless otherwise stated.*

IMPERFORATE STAMPS. Stamps exist imperforate in their issued colours but they were not valid for postage. Imperforate stamps in other colours are colour trials.

A. UBANGI-SHARI-CHAD

OUBANGUI-CHARI-TCHAD

(1)

1915–18. *Stamps of Middle Congo, 1907–17, optd as T* **1** *(1 c. to 20 c.) or in two lines (others).*

1	**1**	1 c. olive and brown		5	5
		a. Opt double		25·00	
2		2 c. violet and brown		5	5
3		4 c. blue and brown		5	5
4		5 c. green and blue		5	5
5		10 c. carmine and blue		8	8
5a		15 c. dull purple and pink (1918)		20	20
6		20 c. pale brown and blue		45	45
7	**2**	25 c. blue and grey-green		12	12
8		30 c. red and green		5	5
9		35 c. chocolate and blue		85	85
10		40 c. dull green and pale brown		85	85
11		45 c. violet and salmon		1·00	1·00
12		50 c. green and salmon		20	20
13		75 c. brown and blue		2·10	2·10
14	**3**	1 f. deep green and pale violet		2·25	2·25
15		2 f. violet and grey-green		2·25	2·25
16		5 f. blue and pink		8·50	8·50
1/16		*Set of 17*		17·00	17·00

The 15 c. is on ordinary paper and the rest on chalk-surfaced paper; however, the 1 c. to 10 c., 20 c., 45 c. and 50 c. also exist on ordinary paper.

See also Nos. 19/23.

➕5ᶜ   **➕5ᶜ**   OUBANGUI-CHARI

(2)   (3)   (4)

1916 (4 Jan). *No. 5 surch with T* **2**. *Chalk-surfaced paper.*

17	10 c.+5 c. carmine and blue			40	40
	a. Surch inverted			14·00	14·00
	b. Surch double			14·00	14·00
	c. Surch double, one inverted			19·00	19·00
	d. Surch vert			14·00	14·00
	e. No stop below "c"			2·25	2·25

1916 (July). *No. 5 surch with T* **3**, *in red.*

18	10 c.+5 c. carmine and blue		5	5

1922 (1 Jan). *As* 1915–18. *New colours.*

19	**1**	5 c. yellow and blue			8	8
20		10 c. green and blue-green			5	5
21	**2**	25 c. green and black			5	5
22		30 c. carmine			5	5
23		50 c. blue and green			5	5
19/23		*Set of 5*			25	25

From 1922 to 1936 separate issues of stamps were made for Ubangi-Shari and for Chad.

B. UBANGI-SHARI

1922 (Nov). *Stamps of Middle Congo, new colours, optd with T* **4** *(1 c. to 20 c.) or in two lines (others).*

24	1 c. violet and green		5	5
	a. Opt omitted		28·00	
25	2 c. green and rose		5	5
26	4 c. brown and purple		8	8
	a. Opt omitted		28·00	
27	5 c. deep blue and rose		15	15
28	10 c. green and blue-green		25	25
29	15 c. bright rose and blue		35	35
30	20 c. brown and rose		95	95
31	25 c. violet and rose		80	80
32	30 c. carmine		55	55
33	35 c. violet and green		95	95
34	40 c. slate-blue and mauve (R.)		95	95
35	45 c. brown and mauve		95	95
36	50 c. blue and pale blue		65	65
37	60 on 75 c. violet/*rose*		65	65
38	75 c. brown and rose		70	70
39	1 f. green and blue (R.)		80	80
40	2 f. green and rose		1·60	1·60
41	5 f. green and brown		2·10	2·10
24/41	*Set of 18*		11·00	11·00

AFRIQUE ÉQUATORIALE FRANÇAISE   **AFRIQUE ÉQUATORIALE FRANÇAISE**

(5)   (6)

1924 (27 Oct)–**33**. *Stamps of 1922 and similar stamps additionally optd with T* **5** *(1 c. to 20 c.) or* **6** *(others).*

42	1 c. violet and green (B.)			5	5
	a. T **4** opt omitted			19·00	
43	2 c. green and rose (B.)			5	5
	a. T **4** opt omitted			16·00	
	b. T **5** opt double			19·00	
44	4 c. brown and chocolate (B.)			5	5
	a. T **5** opt double (Bk.+B.)			19·00	
	b. T **5** opt omitted			32·00	
44c	4 c. brown (B.)			15	15
45	5 c. deep blue and rose			5	5
	a. T **4** opt omitted			22·00	
46	10 c. green and blue-green			5	5
47	10 c. orange-vermilion and blue (1.12.25)			5	5
	a. T **5** opt double			22·00	
48	15 c. bright rose and blue			5	5
	a. T **5** opt in blue (6.26)			10	10
49	20 c. brown and rose (B.)			8	8
50	25 c. violet and rose (B.)			5	5
51	30 c. carmine (B.)			5	5
52	30 c. chocolate and rose (1.12.25)			5	5
	a. "OUBANGUI-CHARI" opt omitted			25·00	
53	30 c. olive-green and green (14.11.27)			12	12
54	35 c. violet and green (B.)			5	5
55	40 c. deep blue and mauve (B.)*			8	8
56	45 c. brown and mauve (B.)			8	8
57	50 c. blue and pale blue (R.)			5	5
58	50 c. grey and ultramarine (R.) (1.12.25)			20	20

59	60 on 75 c. violet/*rose* (R.)	..	..	5	5
	a. "60" omitted	..	..	35·00	
	b. Surch double (R.+Bk.)	..	..	28·00	
60	65 c. red-brown and blue (2.4.28)	..		20	20
61	75 c. brown and rose (B.)	..		8	8
62	75 c. blue and pale blue (R.) (1.6.25)	..		5	5
	a. "OUBANGUI-CHARI" opt omitted ‡		25·00		
63	75 c. claret and brown (25.9.28)	..		20	20
64	90 c. bright rose and scarlet (22.3.30)	..		95	95
65	1 f. green and blue (B.)*	..		5	5
	a. "OUBANGUI-CHARI" in black (B.)				
	(1.2.25)	..		5	5
66	1 f. 10, yellow-brown & ultram (25.9.28)		30	30	
67	1 f. 25, magenta and green (25.9.33) ..		90	90	
68	1 f. 50, ultramarine and blue (22.3.30)		1·00	1·00	
69	1 f. 75, chocolate and orange (25.9.33)		1·60	1·60	
70	2 f. green and rose	..		15	15
	a. "OUBANGUI-CHARI" opt omitted	£225	£110		
71	3 f. magenta/*rose* (22.3.30)	..	..	1·10	1·10
72	5 f. green and brown (B.)	..		55	55
42/72	*Set of 31*	..	..	8·50	7·00

‡On No. 62a the top line of Type **6** is 10 mm from the top of the stamp but is 13 mm from the top on No. 39a of Chad.
*Nos. 55 and 65 have Type **4** in red. No. 65a was not issued without Type **6** overprint.

90   90   1ᶠ25   3ᶠ·

65   =   =   =   =

(7)   (8)   (9)   (10)

1925–27. Stamps as 1924–33 but colours changed, with "OUBANGUI-CHARI" opt in black and opt T **6** in black or colours shown, further surch in black as T **7/10**.

	(a) In figures only (1.2.25)		
73	65 on 1 f. violet and grey-brown (R.) ..	20	20
	a. "65" omitted	18·00	
74	85 on 1 f. violet and grey-brown (R.) ..	20	20
	a. Opt T **6** omitted	18·00	
	b. Opt T **6** double	22·00	
	(b) In figures with bars over old values		
75	90 on 75 c. bright rose & scarlet (11.4.27)	20	20
76	1 f. 25 on 1 f. blue and ultramarine		
	(B.+R.) (14.6.26)	10	10
	a. "1 f. 25" omitted	22·00	
77.	1 f. 50 on 1 f. ultramarine and greenish		
	blue (11.4.27)	20	20
78	3 f. on 5 f. red-brown & carm (19.12.27)	30	30
	a. No stop after "F"	2·25	2·25
79	10 f. on 5 f. vermilion & magenta (21.3.27)	3·50	3·50
80	20 f. on 5 f. magenta and grey (21.3.27) ..	4·50	4·50
	a. No stop after "F"	11·00	11·00
73/80	*Set of 8*	8·00	8·00

On No. 76 the Type **6** overprint is in blue and the surcharge in red.

**OUBANGUI-
CHARI**

A. E. F.

(D **11**)

1928 (4 Apr). *POSTAGE DUE. Type D **11** of France optd with Type D **11**. P 14×13½.*

D81	5 c. light blue	..			30	30
D82	10 c. brown	..	..		30	30
D83	20 c. olive-green				30	30
D84	25 c. rosine	..			30	30
D85	30 c. rose	..			30	30
D86	45 c. green	..	..		30	30
D87	50 c. claret	..			40	40
	a. No stop after "F" ..		..	1·90	1·90	
D88	60 c. yellow-brown/*cream*			40	40	
D89	1 f. maroon/*cream*	..			55	55
D90	2 f. rose-red	..			70	70
D91	3 f. bright violet	..			70	70
D81/91	*Set of 11*	..			6·00	6·00

D **12** Mobaye   D **13** E. Gentil

(Des and eng G. Hourriez (D **12**), A. Delzers (D **13**). Typo)

1930 (17 Feb). *POSTAGE DUE. P 14×13½ (D **12**) or 13½×14 (D **13**).*

D 92	D **12**	5 c. olive and deep blue		..	10	10
D 93		10 c. chocolate and scarlet		..	12	12
D 94		20 c. chocolate and green		..	25	25
D 95		25 c. chocolate and light blue		..	25	25
D 96		30 c. blue-green and yellow-brown			40	40
D 97		45 c. olive and blue-green		..	55	55
D 98		50 c. chocolate and magenta		..	1·00	1·00
D 99		60 c. black and lilac-blue		..	1·00	1·00
D100	D **13**	1 f. slate-black and yellow-brown			40	40
D101		2 f. chocolate and mauve		..	65	65
D102		3 f. chocolate and scarlet		..	90	90
D92/102	*Set of 11*	..		..	5·00	5·00

1931 (13 Apr). *International Colonial Exhibition, Paris. As T **9/12** of Cameroun.*

103	40 c. green	..	..	80	80
104	50 c. mauve	..	..	80	80
105	90 c. vermilion	..	..	80	80
106	1 f. 50, blue	..	..	80	80
103/106	*Set of 4*	..	..	3·00	3·00

From 16 March 1936 to 1960, stamps of French Equatorial Africa were used in Ubangi-Shari.

C. CENTRAL AFRICAN REPUBLIC

The Central African Republic, formerly Ubangi-Shari, was created as an autonomous state on 1 December 1958.

1 President Boganda   **2** C.C.T.A. Emblem

(Des P. Gandon. Eng P. Gandon (15 f.), J. Piel (25 f.). Recess)

1959 (1 Dec). *First Anniv of Republic. T* **1** *and similar design. Multicoloured centres; frame colours given below.* P 13.

1	15 f. blue	..	..	20	15
2	25 f. carmine-red	..	..	30	15

Design: Horiz—25 f. As T **1** but flag behind portrait.

(Des and eng R. Cami. Recess)

1960 (21 May). 10*th Anniv of African Technical Co-operation Commission.* P 13.

3 **2** 50 f. blue and emerald   70   55

The Central African Republic became independent on 13 August 1960.

PHILATELIC TERMS ILLUSTRATED

This successful STAMP MONTHLY series has now been brought together in a snappy black and yellow binding and published as a useful addition to Stanley Gibbons range of essential handbooks for keen stamp collectors. Within its 192 pages this handy limp-bound volume houses a veritable mine of useful information on the words and phrases used in philately. It describes and illustrates printing processes and watermarks, papers and perforations, errors and varieties . . . and it does all this IN COLOUR. Indeed, there are 92 full page plates in colour, plus many black and white illustrations, making it

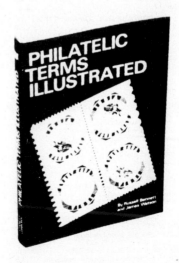

FANTASTIC VALUE AT ONLY £1·95 POST PAID FROM

Stanley Gibbons Publications Ltd
391 Strand, London WC2R 0LX

Upper Volta

100 Centimes = 1 Franc

A. FRENCH COLONY

By decree of 1 March 1919 the French colony of Upper Volta, consisting of an area to the north of Ivory Coast, Gold Coast, Togo and Dahomey, was created from territory which had been part of Upper Senegal and Niger.

PRINTERS. All the listed stamps of Upper Volta were printed at the Government Printing Works, Paris, *unless otherwise stated.*

IMPERFORATE STAMPS. Stamps exist imperforate in their issued colours, but these were not valid for postage. Imperforate stamps in other colours are colour trials.

HAUTE-VOLTA   **10,0 ═ 10,0**

(1)   (2)

1920 (Dec)–**21**. Stamps of Upper Senegal and Niger (*see French Sudan*) optd with T **1**. (*a*) POSTAGE. On T **3**.

1	1 c. violet and grey-purple	..	5	5
	a. Frame double	..	17·00	
2	2 c. grey-purple and grey (R.)	..	5	5
3	4 c. blue and black	..	5	5
4	5 c. green and yellow-green	..	8	8
5	10 c. carmine and orange-red	..	15	15
6	15 c. orange-yellow and chocolate	..	12	10
	a. Opt double	..	25·00	
7	20 c. black and grey-purple (R.)	..	30	25
8	25 c. blue and ultramarine	..	25	20
9	30 c. chocolate and brown (R.)	..	40	30
	a. Brown and olive	..	3·75	4·00
10	35 c. violet and carmine (3.21)	..	15	12
11	40 c. carmine and grey	..	12	8
12	45 c. yellow-brown and blue (R.)	..	8	8
13	50 c. green and black	..	55	35
14	75 c. brown and orange-yellow	..	8	5
15	1 f. green and brown	..	25	15
16	2 f. blue and green	..	30	25
17	5 f. black and violet .(R.)	..	60	60
1/17	*Set of 17*	..	3·25	2·50

(*b*) POSTAGE DUE. On Nos. D77/84

D18	5 c. green	..	10	10
D19	10 c. carmine	..	10	10
D20	15 c. grey	..	10	10
D21	20 c. brown (R.)	..	10	10
D22	30 c. blue	..	12	12
D23	50 c. black (R.)	..	15	15
D24	60 c. orange	..	15	15
D25	1 f. violet	..	25	25
D18/25	*Set of 8*	..	95	95

1922 (1 Jan)–**28**. As before, but colours changed. Optd with T **1**.

18	5 c. chocolate and brown	..	5	5
19	10 c. green and yellow-green	..	8	8
20	10 c. light blue and magenta (15.4.25)	..	5	5
	a. Opt omitted	..	32·00	
21	25 c. green and black	..	10	10
	a. Opt omitted	..	26·00	
22	30 c. carmine and red	..	8	8
23	30 c. lake and violet (1.12.25)	..	8	8
23a	30 c. blue-green and green (14.11.27)	..	12	12
24	50 c. blue and ultramarine	..	8	8
25	50 c. blue and orange (1.12.25)	..	15	15
26	60 c. red (17.5.26)	..	5	5
26a	65 c. blue and yellow-brown (2.4.28)	..	12	12
18/26a	*Set of 11*	..	80	80

Nos. 18/26a were not issued without Type **1** overprint.

1922 (Sept). No. 6 further surch as T **2**.

27	0,01 on 15 c. orange-yellow and chocolate	15	15
	a. Opt T **1** omitted	..	19·00	
	b. Surch double	..	18·00	18·00

28	0.02 on 15 c. orange-yellow & choc (B.)	15	15
29	0.05 on 15 c. orange-yellow & choc (R.)	15	15

1922 (Sept)–**27**. As before, further surch with new value and bars over old value as T **27/8** of *Réunion and similar types.*

30	25 c. on 2 f. blue and green (6.24)	..	5	5
	a. Surch double	..	15·00	
31	25 c. on 5 f. black and violet (6.24)	..	5	5
32	60 on 75 c. violet/*rose*	..	8	8
33	65 on 45 c. brown and blue (1.2.25)	..	12	12
34	80 on 75 c. brown and orange-yell (1.2.25)	..	12	12
35	90 c. on 75 c. rose & carmine (11.4.27)	..	20	20
	a. Surch omitted	..	48·00	
36	1 f. 25 on 1 f. pale bl & bl (R.) (14.6.26)	..	5	5
37	1 f. 50 on 1 f. ultram & blue (11.4.27)	..	40	40
37a	3 f. on 5 f. yellow-brn & rose (19.12.27)	..	45	45
38	10 f. on 5 f. rose & olive-grn (21.3.27)	..	3·50	3·50
39	20 f. on 5 f. violet & chest (21.3.27)	..	3·75	3·75
30/39	*Set of 11*	..	8·00	8·00

1927 (10 Oct). POSTAGE DUE. *As No.* D25, *colour changed and optd with* T **1**, *further surch as Type* D **29** *of Réunion, but without bars.*

D40	2 f. on 1 f. magenta	..	75	75
D41	3 f. on 1 f. red-brown	..	75	75

3 Hausa Man   4 Hausa Woman

5 Hausa Warrior   D **6**

(Des Becker. Eng G. Daussy. Typo)

1928 (16 Nov). P 13½×14 (T **3/4**) *or* 14×13½ (T **5**).

40	**3**	1 c. indigo and green	..		
41		2 c. chocolate and mauve	..	5	5
42		4 c. black and yellow	..	5	5
43		5 c. indigo and pale blue	..	8	8
44		10 c. indigo and pink	..	10	10
45		15 c. chocolate and light blue	..	25	25
46		20 c. chocolate and yellow-green	..	30	30
47	**4**	25 c. chocolate and lemon	..	35	35
48		30 c. deep green and green	..	45	45
49		40 c. black and pink	..	45	45
50		45 c. chocolate and light blue	..	50	50
51		50 c. black and yellow-green	..	50	50
52		65 c. indigo and light blue	..	55	55
53		75 c. black and mauve	..	55	55
54		90 c. scarlet and mauve	..	50	50
55	**5**	1 f. chocolate and apple-green	..	50	50
56		1 f. 10, indigo and mauve	..	55	55
57		1 f. 50, bright blue	..	75	75
58		2 f. black and light blue	..	75	75
59		3 f. chocolate and yellow	..	80	80

60	**5**	5 f. chocolate and mauve	80	80
61		10 f. black and yellow-green	4·75	4·75
62		20 f. black and pink	6·00	6·00
40/62		*Set of 23*	18·00	18·00

1928 (26 Nov). *POSTAGE DUE. Typo. P* 14 × 13½.

D63	**D6**	5 c. green	8	8
D64		10 c. carmine	12	12
D65		15 c. grey	12	12
D66		20 c. brown	12	12
D67		30 c. blue	12	12
D68		50 c. black	70	70
D69		60 c. orange	95	95
D70		1 f. violet	1·25	1·25
D71		2 f. magenta	1·90	1·90
D72		3 f. red-brown	1·90	1·90
D63/72		*Set of 10*	6·50	6·50

1931 (13 Apr). *International Colonial Exhibition, Paris. As T* **23/26** *of St-Pierre et Miquelon.*

63		40 c. green and black	70	70
64		50 c. mauve and black	70	70
65		90 c. vermilion and black	70	70
	a.	"HAUTE-VOLTA" double	32·00	
66		1 f. 50, blue and black	70	70
63/66		*Set of 4*	2·50	2·50

On 5 September 1932 the colony was divided between French Sudan, the Ivory Coast and Niger and the stamps of Upper Volta were withdrawn on 1 January 1933. Upper Volta was reconstituted as a separate territory on 4 September 1947 and used the stamps of French West Africa.

B. AUTONOMOUS REPUBLIC

After being given a limited degree of independence in 1957, Upper Volta became an autonomous republic within the French Community on 10 December 1958.

6 President Coulibaly

7 Antelope Mask

8 President Yaméogo

(Des and eng J. Pheulpin. Recess)

1959 (10 Dec). *First Anniv of Republic. P* 13.

67	**6**	25 f. reddish purple and black	30	12

(Des and eng R. Cottet (1 f., 2 f., 4 f., 30 f., 40 f., 50 f.), J. Combet (others). Recess)

1960 (11 Apr). *T* **7** *and similar vert designs. P* 13.

68	**7**	30 c. violet and carmine-red	5	5
69		40 c. brown-purple and ochre	5	5
70		50 c. olive-brown and deep turquoise	5	5
71	−	1 f. hlack, orange-brown and vermilion	5	5
72	−	2 f. blackish green, yellow-grn & emer	5	5
73	−	4 f. blue-black, bluish violet & light blue	8	5
74	−	5 f. scarlet, brown and bistre	10	8
75	−	6 f. maroon and turquoise-blue	10	8
76	−	8 f. red-brown and orange-red	12	10
77	−	10 f. maroon and yellow-green	15	12
78	−	15 f. ultramarine and orange-red	20	15
79	−	20 f. blue-green and ultramarine	25	12
80	−	25 f. dp maroon, emerald-green & lt blue	30	15
81	−	30 f. black, chocolate and turquoise	30	15
82	−	40 f. indigo, lake and ultramarine	40	20
83	−	50 f. bistre-brown, green and bright purple	50	25
84	−	60 f. blue and orange-brown	65	35
85	−	85 f. blue and grey-green	90	45
68/85		*Set of 18*	4·00	2·25

Designs: Animal masks—1 f., 2 f., 4 f., Warthog; 5 f., 6 f., 8 f., Monkey; 10 f., 15 f., 20 f. Buffalo; 25 f. Antelope; 30 f., 40 f., 50 f. Elephant; 60 f., 85 f. Secretary-bird.

(Des and eng P. Munier. Recess)

1960 (1 May). *P* 13.

86	**8**	25 f. brown-purple and grey	30	20

8a C.C.T.A. Emblem   **8b** Conseil de l'Entente Emblem

(Des and eng R. Cami. Recess)

1960 (16 May). *10th Anniv of African Technical Co-operation Commission* (*C.C.T.A.*). *P* 13.

87	**8a**	25 f. indigo and ultramarine	35	35

(Photo Comoy, Paris)

1960 (29 May). *First Anniv of Conseil de l'Entente. P* 13.

88	**8b**	25 f. multicoloured	45	35

Upper Volta became an independent republic on 5 August 1960.

ALBUM LISTS

Please write for our latest lists of albums and accessories. These will be sent free on request.

Wallis & Futuna Is.

100 Centimes = 1 Franc

The Wallis and Futuna Islands, in the south central Pacific Ocean, comprise two groups: the Wallis Islands, which were discovered by Captain Samuel Wallis in 1767, lie west of Samoa and consist of the island of Uvea and 22 islets in a coral reef; the islands of Futuna and Alofi (also called the Horn Islands), which were discovered by the Dutch explorers Jacques Le Maire and Willem Cornelisz Schouten in 1616, lie further south-west, half way between Samoa and Fiji. The first French influence was brought by missionaries in 1837 and the natives were converted by Père Bataillon. In 1842 the French government would not agree to a request for a protectorate, but from 1843 the kings of the islands were advised by a French resident. The Third Republic was, however, willing to accept the burden of empire, and the islands were made French protectorates, the Wallis Islands by decree of 5 April 1887 and Futuna and Alofi by decree of 16 February 1888. All were attached to New Caledonia for administrative purposes on 27 November 1888. Special issues of stamps began in 1920.

PRINTERS. All issues were printed by the French Government Printing Works, Paris, *unless otherwise stated.*

IMPERFORATE STAMPS. Many stamps exist imperforate in their issued colours, but these were not valid for postage. Imperforate stamps in other colours are colour trials.

FRENCH PROTECTORATE

ILES WALLIS et FUTUNA
(1)

ILES WALLIS et FUTUNA
(2)

1920 (May). *Stamps of New Caledonia optd with T* **1** *or* **2** (*franc values*).

1	**15**	1 c. black/*greenish*			5	5
		a. Opt double			13·00	
		b. Opt triple, one inverted			13·00	
		c. "et" omitted			3·50	
2		2 c. chocolate			5	5
3		4 c. blue/*orange*			5	5
4		5 c. green			5	5
5		10 c. rose-red			8	8
6		15 c. bright lilac			8	8
7	**16**	20 c. brown/*toned*			10	10
8		25 c. blue/*greenish*			12	12
9		30 c. brown/*orange*			12	12
		a. Opt double			16·00	
		b. Opt triple			19·00	
10		35 c. black/*yellow* (R.)			5	5
11		40 c. carmine/*greenish*			8	8
12		45 c. maroon/*toned*			8	8
13		50 c. red/*orange*			8	8
14		75 c. olive/*toned*			30	30
15	**17**	1 f. blue/*green*			65	65
		a. Opt triple			20·00	
16		2 f. carmine/*azure*			70	70
17		5 f. black/*orange* (R.)			1·25	1·25
1/17		*Set of 17*			3·50	3·50

1920. *POSTAGE DUE. Postage Due stamps of New Caledonia optd with T* **1.**

D18	D **18**	5 c. ultramarine/*toned*			8	8
D19		10 c. brown/*pale buff*			12	12
D20		15 c. green/*toned*			12	12
D21		20 c. black/*yellow* (R.)			12	12
		a. Opt double			16·00	
D22		30 c. carmine			12	12
D23		50 c. ultramarine/*cream*			25	25
D24	D **18**	60 c. bronze-green/*bluish*			40	40
		a. Opt double			16·00	
D25		1 f. green/*cream*			50	50
D18/25		*Set of 8*			1·50	1·50

1922 (1 Jan)–**28.** *As* 1920. *New values and colours.*

18	**15**	5 c. slate-blue			5	5
19		10 c. green			5	5
20		10 c. red/*rose* (1.12.25)			12	12
21	**16**	25 c. red/*straw*			8	8
22		30 c. carmine			5	5
23		30 c. orange-red (1.12.25)			8	8
24		30 c. green (14.11.27)			12	12
25		50 c. deep blue			15	15
26		50 c. grey (1.12.25)			15	15
27		65 c. blue (2.4.28)			40	40
28	**17**	1 f. 10, red-brown (25.9.28)			40	40
18/28		*Set of 11*			1·50	1·50

The 30 c. green and 1 f. 10 were not issued without overprint.

0,05
(3)

ILES WALLIS et FUTUNA 2ᶠ
(D 4)

1922 (Dec). *No.* 6 *surch as T* **3.**

29	**15**	0,01 on 15 c. bright lilac			8	8
30		0,02 on 15 c. bright lilac (B.)			8	8
31		0,04 on 15 c. bright lilac (G.)			8	8
32		0,05 on 15 c. bright lilac (R.)			8	8
29/32		*Set of 4*			25	25

25ᶜ 25ᶜ 65 1ᶠ25
(3a) (3b) (3c)

1924 (June)–**27.** *Stamps as* 1920, *some with colours changed, surch as T* **3** *a/c and similar type, with bars obliterating old values.*

33	**17**	25 c. on 2 f. carmine/*azure*			5	5
34		25 c. on 5 f. black/*orange*			5	5
35	**16**	65 on 40 c. carmine/*greenish* (1.2.25)			8	8
36		85 on 75 c. olive/*toned* (1.2.25)			8	8
37		90 on 75 c. rose-carmine (11.4.27)			20	20
38	**17**	1 f. 25 on 1 f. blue (R.) (14.6.26)			5	5
39		1 f. 50 on 1 f. blue/*azure* (11.4.27)			30	30
		a. Surch omitted			38·00	
		b. Surch double			32·00	
40		3 f. on 5 f. magenta (19.12.27)			45	45
		a. Surch omitted			35·00	
		b. Surch double			35·00	
41		10 f. on 5 f. bronze-green/*mauve* (R.) (24.3.27)			4·75	4·75
42		20 f. on 5 f. rose-carmine/*yellow* (24.3.27)			5·50	5·50
33/42		*Set of 10*			10·00	10·00

1927 (10 Oct). *POSTAGE DUE. As No.* D109 *of New Caledonia but colour changed, surch as Type* D **4.**

D43	D **18**	2 f. on 1 f. magenta			1·60	1·60
D44		3 f. on 1 f. red-brown			1·60	1·60

1930 (21 July)–**40.** *Stamps of New Caledonia, some with colours changed, optd with T* **1.**

43	**22**	1 c. blue and purple			5	5
		a. Opt double			16·00	
44		2 c. green and brown			5	5
45		3 c. blue and lake (1940)			5	5

46	22	4 c. blue-green and red	..	..	5	5
47		5 c. brown and blue ..	..	..	5	5
48		10 c. chocolate and lilac	..		5	5
49		15 c. ultramarine and brown	..		5	5
50		20 c. brown and carmine	..	..	5	5
51		25 c. chocolate and deep green		..	5	5
52	23	30 c. blue-green and green	..	..	5	5
53		35 c. blue-green and deep blue-green				
		(16.5.38)	..	..	8	8
		a. Opt omitted	..	..	32·00	
54		40 c. sage-green and scarlet	..		5	5
55		45 c. vermilion and blue	..		5	5
56		45 c. green and blue-green (1940)	..		5	5
57		50 c. chocolate and mauve	..		5	5
58		55 c. carmine and bright blue (16.5.38)		20	20
59		60 c. carmine and ultramarine (1940) ..		5	5
60		65 c. ultramarine and red-brown	..		15	15
61		70 c. brown and magenta (5.12.38)	..		5	5
62		75 c. drab and greenish blue	..		30	30
63		80 c. green and maroon (16.5.38)	..		8	8
64		85 c. brown and green (5.12.38)	..		50	50
65		90 c. carmine and scarlet	..		12	12
66		90 c. scarlet and olive-brown (4.12.39)		5	5
67	24	1 f. scarlet and drab ..	..	..	45	45
68		1 f. carmine and scarlet (5.12.38)	..		20	20
69		1 f. green and scarlet (15.4.40)	..		5	5
70		1 f. 10, brown and green	..	..	4·50	4·50
71		1 f. 25, yellow-green and red-brown				
		(25.9.33)	..	..	30	30
72		1 f. 25, carmine and scarlet (4.12.39)		5	5
73		1 f. 40, vermilion and blue (15.4.40)		5	5
74		1 f. 50, blue and deep ultramarine	..		12	12
75		1 f. 60, brown and green (15.4.40)	..		5	5
76		1 f. 75, vermilion & ultram (25.9.33)		1·60	1·60
77		1 f. 75, ultramarine (5.12.38)	..		30	30
78		2 f. brown and orange	..		15	15
79		2 f. 25, bright blue & ultram (4.12.39)		8	8
80		2 f. 50, brown (15.4.40)	..	..	8	8
81		3 f. brown and claret ..	..	..	15	15
82		5 f. brown and blue ..	..	..	15	15
83		10 f. brown and mauve/*rose* ..	..		40	40
84		20 f. brown and scarlet/*yellow*	..		55	55
43/84		*Set of 42*	..	..	10·00	10·00

10 c., 15 c., 1 f., 1 f. 50, 10 f. and 20 f. stamps as above but without "RF", were prepared in 1944, but not placed on sale in the islands.

1930 (21 July). *POSTAGE DUE. Postage Due stamps of New Caledonia optd with T 1.*

D85	D 25	2 c. chocolate and blue ..	..	5	5
D86		4 c. green and carmine ..	..	5	5
D87		5 c. slate-blue and scarlet	..		5	5
D88		10 c. blue and claret	..	..	5	5
D89		15 c. scarlet and deep myrtle	..		5	5
D90		20 c. brown and maroon ..	..	5	5
D91		25 c. ultramarine and brown	..		5	5
D92		30 c. brown and green ..	..	10	10
D93		50 c. carmine and brown ..	..	8	8
D94		60 c. scarlet and magenta	..		15	15
D95		1 f. blue-green and blue	..		10	10
D96		2 f. brown and carmine ..	..	10	10
D97		3 f. brown and mauve ..	..	10	10
D85/97		*Set of 13* ..	..	..	90	90

1931 (13 Apr). *International Colonial Exhibition, Paris. As T 23/26 of St-Pierre et Miquelon.*

85	40 c. green and black	..	..	80	80
86	50 c. mauve and black	..	..	80	80
87	90 c. vermilion and black	..	..	80	80
88	1 f. 50, blue and black	..	..	80	80
85/88	*Set of 4*	..	..	3·00	3·00

1937 (13 Dec). *International Exhibition, Paris. Sheet 120× 100 mm. As T 36 of St-Pierre et Miquelon. Imperf.*

MS88a	3 f. bright purple	..	..	1·10	1·10
	b. Inscription inverted	..	..	£600	

1939 (10 May). *New York World's Fair. As T 41 of St-Pierre et Miquelon.*

89	1 f. 25, lake	..	..	..	30	30
90	2 f. 25, ultramarine	..	..	30	30

1939 (5 July). *150th Anniv of French Revolution. As T 42 of St-Pierre et Miquelon.*

91	45 c.+25 c. green and black	..	1·50	1·50
92	70 c.+30 c. brown and black	..	1·50	1·50
93	90 c.+35 c. red-orange and black ..	1·50	1·50
94	1 f. 25+1 f. carmine and black	..	1·50	1·50

95	2 f. 25+2 f. blue and black	..	1·50	1·50
91/95	*Set of 5*	..	..	..	7·00	7·00

VICHY ISSUES. A number of stamps were prepared by the Pétain Government of Unoccupied France for use in Wallis and Futuna Islands, but as the inhabitants declared for the Free French, these issues were not placed on sale there.

France Libre

(4)

1941. *Adherence to General de Gaulle. Stamps of 1930–40 optd with T 4, at Nouméa.*

96	22	1 c. blue and purple..	..	..	15	15
97		2 c. green and brown	..	..	15	15
97a		3 c. blue and lake	..	..	18·00	18·00
98		4 c. blue-green and orange ..	..		15	15
99		5 c. brown and blue	..	..	15	15
100		10 c. chocolate and lilac	..		15	15
101		15 c. ultramarine and brown ..	..		15	15
102		20 c. brown and carmine	..		45	45
103		25 c. chocolate and deep green	..		45	45
104	23	30 c. grey-green	..	..	45	45
105		35 c. blue-green	..	..	15	15
106		40 c. sage-green and scarlet ..	..		45	45
107		45 c. vermilion and blue	..		45	45
107a		45 c. green and blue-green ..	..	21·00	21·00
108		50 c. chocolate and mauve ..	..		15	15
109		55 c. carmine and bright blue	..		15	15
109a		60 c. carmine and ultramarine	..	21·00	21·00
110		65 c. ultramarine and red-brown	..		15	15
111		70 c. brown and magenta	..		45	45
112		75 c. drab and greenish blue ..	..		45	45
113		80 c. brown and maroon	..		15	15
114		85 c. brown and green	..		45	45
115		90 c. carmine and scarlet	..		40	40
116	24	1 f. carmine and scarlet	..		35	35
117		1 f. 25, yellow-green and red-brown		35	35
118		1 f. 50, blue and deep blue ..	..		20	20
119		1 f. 75, ultramarine ..	..		20	20
120		2 f. brown and orange	..		40	40
121		2 f. 50, brown	..	..	35·00	35·00
122		3 f. brown and claret	..		25	25
123		5 f. brown and blue	..		1·10	1·10
124		10 f. brown and mauve/*rose* ..	..	10·00	10·00
125		20 f. brown and scarlet/*yellow*	..	13·00	13·00
96/125		*Set of 33*	..	..	£110	£110

1943. *POSTAGE DUE. Nos. D85/97 optd "FRANCE LIBRE" in two lines, at Noumea.*

D126	D 25	2 c. chocolate and blue	..		7·50	7·50
D127		4 c. green and carmine ..	..		7·50	7·50
D128		5 c. slate-blue and scarlet	..		7·50	7·50
D129		10 c. blue and claret	..		7·50	7·50
D130		15 c. scarlet and deep myrtle	..		7·50	7·50
D131		20 c. brown and maroon	..		7·50	7·50
D132		25 c. ultramarine and brown	..		7·50	7·50
D133		30 c. brown and green	..		7·50	7·50
D134		50 c. carmine and brown	..		7·50	7·50
D135		60 c. scarlet and magenta	..		7·50	7·50
D136		1 f. blue-green and blue	..		7·50	7·50
D137		2 f. brown and carmine	..		7·50	7·50
D138		3 f. brown and mauve ..	..		7·50	7·50
D126/138		*Set of 13* ..	..	..	£100	£100

5 Native Ivory Head

(Des Edmund Dulac. Litho Bradbury, Wilkinson)

1944. *Free French Administration. P 11½×12.*

126	5	5 c. olive-brown	..	..	5	5
127		10 c. greenish blue	..	..	5	5
128		25 c. emerald-green	..	..	5	5
129		30 c. orange	..	..	..	5	5
130		40 c. grey-green	..	..	8	8

131	**5**	80 c. maroon		8	8
132		1 f. purple		8	8
133		1 f. 50, scarlet		8	8
134		2 f. black		8	8
135		2 f. 50, ultramarine		8	8
136		4 f. violet		8	8
137		5 f. yellow		8	8
138		10 f. brown		8	8
139		20 f. blue-green		12	12
126/139		*Set of 14*		1·00	1·00

1944. *Mutual Aid and Red Cross Funds. As T* **49** *of St-Pierre et Miquelon.*

140	5 f.+20 f. red-orange		30	30

1945. *Surch with new values, as T* **38** *of Réunion.*

141	**5**	50 c. on 5 c. olive-brown		10	10
142		60 c. on 5 c. olive-brown		10	10
143		70 c. on 5 c. olive-brown		8	8
144		1 f. 20 on 5 c. olive-brown		8	8
145		2 f. 40 on 25 c. emerald-green		8	8
146		3 f. on 25 c. emerald-green		8	8
147		4 f. 50 on 25 c. emerald-green		12	12
148		15 f. on 2 f. 50, ultramarine (R.)		15	15
141/148		*Set of 8*		65	65

1946 (8 May). *AIR. Victory. As T* **52** *of St-Pierre et Miquelon.*

149	8 f. violet		20	20

1946 (6 June). *AIR. From Chad to the Rhine. As Nos.* 355/60 *of St-Pierre et Miquelon.*

150	5 f. violet		15	15
151	10 f. blackish green		15	15
152	15 f. purple-brown		20	20
153	20 f. ultramarine		25	25
154	25 f. brown-orange		30	30
155	50 f. rose-red		40	40
150/155	*Set of 6*		1·25	1·25

1949 (4 July). *AIR. 75th Anniv of Universal Postal Union. As T* **58** *of St-Pierre et Miquelon.*

156	10 f. multicoloured	1·40	1·40

WALLIS ET FUTUNA

(6)

1949 (4 July). *AIR. As Nos.* 325/6 *of New Caledonia, but colours changed, optd with T* **6** *(or in three lines on* 100 *f.). in blue.*

157	**37**	50 f. carmine and yellow		1·25	1·25
158	**38**	100 f. brown and yellow		2·50	2·50

1952 (1 Dec). *Centenary of Médaille Militaire. As T* **60** *of St-Pierre et Miquelon.*

159	2 f. turquoise, yellow and green		45	45

1954 (6 June). *AIR. Tenth Anniv of Liberation. As* **61** *of St-Pierre et Miquelon.*

160	3 f. purple-brown and deep brown		1·40	1·40

7 Making Tapa (cloth)

8 Father Chanel

HAVE YOU READ THE NOTES AT THE BEGINNING OF THIS CATALOGUE?

These often provide answers to the enquiries we receive.

(Des and eng R. Cami (3 f., 9 f.), J. Combet (5 f., 19 f.), G. Bétemps (7 f., 21 f.), J. Pheulpin (14 f., 17 f., 33 f.), C. Haley (27 f.). Recess)

1955 (21 Nov)–**65**. *Various designs. P* 13. *(a) POSTAGE. As T* **7**.

161	3 f. purple, mag & deep lilac (11.6.57)		12	12
162	5 f. chocolate, brown & grn (19.9.60)		15	15
163	7 f. chocolate & dp bluish grn (19.9.60)		20	20
164	9 f. blackish purple, brown-purple and blue (11.6.57)		30	30
165	17 f. crimson, purple, grn & bl (19.9.60)		45	45
166	19 f. turquoise-green and lake (19.9.60)		55	55

(b) AIR. As T **8**

167	14 f. light blue, deep blue-green & indigo		55	45
168	21 f. green, bistre-brown & blue (19.6.60)		85	85
168a	27 f. deep grey-green, blue and brown (26.11.65)		90	90
169	33 f. chocolate, ultram & turq-bl (19.9.60)		1·60	1·60
161/169	*Set of 10*		5·00	5·00

Designs: *Horiz*—3 f., 9 f. Wallisian and island view; 7 f. Preparing kava; 17 f. Dancers; 21 f. View of Mata-Utu, Queen Amelia and Mgr. Bataillon; 27 f. Wharf, Mata-Utu; 33 f. Map of Wallis and Futuna Islands and sailing ship. *Vert.*—19 f. Paddle dance.

1958 (7 July). *Tropical Flora. As T* **67** *of St-Pierre et Miquelon.*

170	5 f. carmine, green yellow and pale blue	75	65

Design: *Horiz*—5 f. *Montrouziera.*

1958 (10 Dec). *Tenth Anniv of Declaration of Human Rights. As T* **66** *of St-Pierre et Miquelon.*

171	17 f. light blue and ultramarine	1·00	1·00

FRENCH OVERSEAS TERRITORY

The Wallis and Futuna Islands were made a French Overseas Territory on 29 July 1961 after a plebiscite on 27 December 1959 had overwhelmingly supported such a change.

8a Pacific Map and Palms **9** *Charonia tritonis*

(Des P. Lambert. Photo Delrieu)

1962 (18 July). *Fifth South Pacific Conference, Pago Pago. P* 13×12.

172	**8a**	16 f. multicoloured	95	95

(Des P. Lambert. Eng J. Pheulpin (25 c., 1 f.), G. Bétemps (others). Recess)

1962 (20 Sept)–**63**. *Marine Fauna. T* **9** *and similar designs. P* 13. *(a) POSTAGE.*

173	25 c. light brown and black-green		5	5
174	1 f. brown-red and green		8	8
175	2 f. chestnut and blue		12	12
176	4 f. chestnut and turquoise-blue		45	45
177	10 f. orange, brown, violet & grn (1.4.63)		90	90
178	20 f. chestnut and ultramarine (1.4.63)		1·60	1·60

(b) AIR. Inscr "POSTE AERIENNE"

179	50 f. chestnut, turquoise-blue and bright purple (1.4.63)		2·25	2·25
180	100 f. black, dp bluish green & brown-pur		4·50	4·50
173/180	*Set of 8*		9·00	9·00

Designs: *Vert*—1 f. *Mitra episcopalis;* 2 f. *Cypraecassis rufa;* 4 f. *Murex tenuispina;* 10 f. *Oliva erythrostoma;* 20 f. *Cypraea tigris.* (26½×48 mm)—50 f. *Harpa ventricosa. Horiz* (48×26½ mm)—100 f. Fishing under water for trochus shells.

1962 (4 Dec). *AIR. First Trans-Atlantic Television Satellite Link. As T* **71** *of St-Pierre et Miquelon.*

181	12 f. blue, brown-purple & dp reddish vio		75	75

D **10** *Zanclus cornutus*

10 Throwing the Javelin

13 Art Students

(Des and eng P. Forget. Recess)

1966 (4 Nov). *AIR. 20th Anniv of U.N.E.S.C.O. P* 13.
192 **13** 50 c. purple-brown, yellow-orge & grn   1·40   1·40

(Des and eng G. Aufschneider. Typo)

1963 (1 Apr). *POSTAGE DUE. Type D* **10** *and similar fish designs inscr "TIMBRE TAXE". P* 13½×14.
D182   1 f. black, yellow-orange and light blue   5   5
D183   3 f. vermilion, green and light blue   ..   12   12
D184   5 f. orange, black and light blue   ..   20   20
    Fishes: *Horiz*—3 f. *Thalassoma lunare*; 5 f. *Amphiprion percula*.

1963 (2 Sept). *Red·Cross Centenary. As T* **75** *of St-Pierre et Miquelon.*
182   12 f. red, grey and bright purple   ..   45   45

1963 (10 Dec). *15th Anniv of Declaration of Human Rights. As T* **76** *of St-Pierre et Miquelon.*
183   29 f. ochre and carmine-red   ..   ..   1·60   1·60

1964 (15 Apr). *"PHILATEC 1964" International Stamp Exhibition, Paris. As T* **77** *of St-Pierre et Miquelon.*
184   9 f. brown-red, green and deep grey-green   75   75

(Des and eng A. Decaris. Recess)

1964 (10 Oct). *AIR. Olympic Games, Tokyo. P* 13.
185 **10** 31 f. brown-purple, vermilion & green   3·75   3·75

11 Inter-island Ship, *Reine Amelia*

12 W.H.O. Building

(Des R. Chapelet. Photo So.Ge.Im)

1965 (11 Feb). *P* 12½×13.
186 **11** 11 f. multicoloured   90   90

1965 (17 May). *AIR. I.T.U. Centenary. As T* **80** *of St-Pierre et Miquelon.*
187   50 f. chocolate, brown-red & brt purple   4·00   4·00

1966 (17 Jan). *AIR. Launching of First French Satellite. As Nos.* 437/8 *of St-Pierre et Miquelon.*
188   7 f. red, claret and vermilion   95   95
189   10 f. red, claret and vermilion   95   95
    (*Price for strip of two stamps and label unused or used* £2·25.)

1966 (2 June). *AIR. Launching of Satellite "D* 1". *As T* **82** *of St-Pierre et Miquelon.*
190   10 f. rose-red, lake and blue-green .   75   75

(Des H. H. Biais. Photo So.Ge.Im.)

1966 (5 July). *AIR. Inauguration of W.H.O. Headquarters, Geneva. P* 12½×13.
191 **12** 30 f. lake, orange-yellow and light blue   1·10   1·10

14 Athlete and Decorative Pattern

(Des Michoutouchkine. Eng P. Gandon. Recess)

1966 (8 Dec). *AIR. South Pacific Games, Nouméa. T* **14** *and similar horiz design. P* 13.
193   32 f. black, maroon, cerise and blue   ..   95   95
194   38 f. emerald and magenta   ..   ..   1·10   1·10
    Design:—38 f. Woman with ball, and decorative pattern.

15 Samuel Wallis's Ship at Uvea

(Des Dessirier. Photo So.Ge.Im.)

1967 (16 Dec). *AIR. Bicentenary of Discovery of Wallis Island. P* 13.
195 **15** 12 f. multicoloured   ..   ..   ..   1·60   1·60

1968 (4 May). *20th Anniv of World Health Organization. As T* **90** *of St-Pierre et Miquelon.*
196   17 f. purple, orange and blue-green   ..   90   90

1968 (10 Aug). *Human Rights Year. As T* **92** *of St-Pierre et Miquelon.*
197   19 f. lake-brown, plum and magenta   ..   70   70

1969 (17 Apr). *AIR. First Flight of "Concorde". As T* **94** *of St-Pierre et Miquelon.*
198   20 f. black and reddish purple   ..   ..   2·25   2·25

16 Gathering Coconuts

Wallis & Futuna Is. 1969

(Des P. Lambert. Photo)

1969 (30 Apr). *Scenes from Everyday Island Life. T* **16** *and similar horiz designs. Multicoloured. P* 13.

(*a*) *POSTAGE. Inscr "POSTES". Size* 35×22 *mm*
199 1 f. Launching outrigger canoe .. 10 10

(*b*) *AIR. Inscr "POSTE AERIENNE". Size* 47×27 *mm*
200	20 f. Type **16**	..			55	30
201	32 f. Horse-riding	..	..	..	80	40
202	38 f. Wood-carving	..	..		90	65
203	50 f. Fishing	..	..	..	1·60	90
204	100 f. Marketing fruit	..	..	..	3·25	1·50
199/204	*Set of 6*	..	..	..	6·50	3·50

1969 (24 Nov). 50*th Anniv of International Labour Organization.* As *T* **100** *of St-Pierre et Miquelon.*
205 9 f. greenish blue, light brown and salmon 40 40

1970 (20 May). *Inauguration of New U.P.U. Headquarters Building, Berne.* As *T* **101** *of St-Pierre et Miquelon.*
206 21 f. bistre-brown, indigo & bright purple 70 70

==

12ᶠ

(17)

18 Weightlifting

1971 (19 Feb). *Nos.* 166 *and* 169 *surch as T* **17.**

(*a*) *POSTAGE*
207 12 f. on 19 f. turquoise-green and lake 30 30

(*b*) *AIR*
208 21 f. on 33 f. chocolate, ultram & turq-bl 95 95

(Des C. Durrens. Eng J. Miermont (24 f.), C. Jumelet (54 f.), C. Durrens (others). Recess)

1971 (25 Oct). 4*th South Pacific Games, Papeete, Tahiti. T* **18** *and similar designs. P* 13. (*a*) *POSTAGE. Size* 22×36 *mm.*
209 24 f. brown-red, indigo and blue-green 75 75
210 36 f. bright blue, olive and red 95 95

(*b*) *AIR. Inscr "POSTE AERIENNE". Size* 47×27 *mm*
211 48 f. red-brown, turquoise-bl & slate-lilac 1·10 75
212 54 f. carmine-red, purple and blue .. 1·40 1·10
209/212 *Set of 4* .. .. .. 4·00 3·25
Designs: *Vert*—36 f. Basketball. *Horiz*—48 f. Pole-vaulting; 54 f. Archery.

1971 (9 Nov). 1*st Death Anniv of General Charles de Gaulle.* As *Nos.* 500/1 *of St-Pierre et Miquelon.*
213 30 f. black and new blue .. .. 1·10 90
214 70 f. black and new blue .. .. 2·00 1·60

19 Commission Headquarters, Nouméa, New Caledonia

(Des O. Baillais. Photo)

1972 (5 Feb). *AIR.* 25*th Anniv of South Pacific Commission. P* 13.
215 **19** 44 f. multicoloured .. .. .. 1·40 1·10

20 Pacific Island Dwelling   21 Child's Pirogue

(Des and eng J. Combet. Recess)

1972 (15 May). *AIR. South Pacific Arts Festival, Fiji. P* 13
216 **20** 60 f. reddish violet, blue-green & carm 1·40 1·10

(Des P. Lambert. Photo)

1972 (16 Oct). *Sailing Pirogues. T* **21** *and similar horiz designs. Multicoloured.* (*a*) *POSTAGE. Size* 35×25 *mm. P* 13×12½.
217 14 f. Type **21** 35 20
218 16 f. Children with model pirogues .. 35 20
219 18 f. Racing pirogue 55 30

(*b*) *AIR. Inscr "POSTE AERIENNE". Size* 47×27 *mm. P* 13
220 200 f. Pirogue race .. .. .. 4·50 3·50
217/220 *Set of 4* .. .. .. 5·00 4·00

22 La Pérouse and *La Boussole*

(Des and eng R. Quillivic. Recess)

1972 (20 July). *AIR. Explorers of the Pacific. T* **22** *and similar horiz designs. P* 13.
221 22 f. brown, slate and red 50 40
222 28 f. myrtle-green, brown-red and blue .. 65 50
223 40 f. chocolate, blue and bright blue .. 90 75
224 72 f. brown, new blue and reddish violet 1·75 1·25
221/224 *Set of 4* .. .. .. 3·50 2·50
Designs:—28 f. Samuel Wallis and *Dolphin*; 40 f. Dumont D'Urville and *L'Astrolabe*; 72 f. Bougainville and *La Boudeuse.*

23 General De Gaulle

(Des Dessirier. Eng J. Larrivière. Recess)

1973 (9 Nov). *AIR. 3rd Death Anniv of General Charles de Gaulle. P* 13.
225 **23** 107 f. maroon and orange-brown   ..   2·25   1·90

24 *Plumeria rubra*

(Des P. Lambert. Photo)

1973 (6 Dec). *AIR. Flora of Wallis Islands. T* **24** *and similar square designs. Multicoloured. P* 13.

226	12 f. Type **24**	..	30	25
227	17 f. *Hibiscus tiliaceus* ..	..	40	30
228	19 f. *Phaeomeria magnifica*	..	50	40
229	21 f. *Hibiscus rosa sinensis*	..	50	40
230	23 f. *Allamanda cathartica*	..	55	45
231	27 f. *Barringtonia asiatica*	..	65	55
232	39 f. Bouquet in vase	..	90	75
226/232	*Set of 7*	..	3·50	2·75

25 *Oryctes rhinoceros*

26 "Flower Hand" holding Letter

(Des P. Lambert. Photo)

1974 (29 July). *Insects. T* **25** *and similar square designs. Multicoloured. P* 13.

233	15 f. Type **25**	..	30	20
234	25 f. *Cosmopolites sordidus*	..	45	35
235	35 f. *Ophideres fullonica*	..	50	45
236	45 f. *Pantala flavescens* ..	..	80	55
233/236	*Set of 4*	..	1·90	1·40

(Des and eng C. Andréotto. Recess)

1974 (9 Oct). *AIR. Centenary of Universal Postal Union. P* 13.
237 **26** 51 f. bright purple, brown & blue-green   95   95

27 "Holy Family"
(Kamalielf-Filimoehala)

(Des P. Lambert. Photo)

1974 (9 Dec). *AIR. Christmas. P* 13.
238 **27** 150 f. multicoloured ..   ..   2·75   2·25

28 Tapa Pattern

(Des P. Lambert. Photo)

1975 (3 Feb). *AIR. Tapa Mats. T* **28** *and similar horiz designs, each blackish brown, gold and orange-yellow. P* 13.

239	3 f. Type **28**	..	12	5
240	24 f. "Villagers" ..	..	50	40
241	36 f. "Fishes"	..	65	50
242	80 f. "Fishes and Dancers"	..	1·60	1·25
239/242	*Set of 4*	..	3·00	2·00

29 Aircraft in Flight   **30** Volleyball

(Des and eng J. Combet. Recess)

1975 (13 Aug). *AIR. First Regular Air Service to New Caledonia. P* 13.
243 **29** 100 f. multicoloured ..   ..   1·75   1·40

(Des J. Chesnot. Photo)

1975 (10 Nov). *AIR. Fifth South Pacific Games, Guam. T* **30** *and similar vert designs. Multicoloured. P* 13.

244	26 f. Type **30**	..	50	40
245	44 f. Football ..	..	75	65
246	56 f. Throwing the javelin	..	95	75
247	105 f. Aqua-diving	..	1·90	1·50
244/247	*Set of 4*	..	3·75	3·00

1975 (1 Dec). *Pompidou Commemoration. As T* **131** *of St-Pierre et Miquelon.*
248   50 f. slate and ultramarine ..   ..   1·25   95

31 Lalolalo Lake, Wallis

(Des P. Lambert. Photo)

1975 (1 Dec). *AIR. Landscapes. T* **31** *and similar horiz designs. Multicoloured. P* 13.

249	10 f. Type **31**	..	25	20
250	29 f. Vasavasa, Futuna	..	50	45
251	41 f. Sigave Bay, Futuna ..	..	75	65

252	68 f. Gahi Bay, Wallis			1·50	1·10
249/252	Set of 4			2·75	2·00

32 "Concorde"

(Des P. Lengelle. Eng J. Combet. Recess)

1976 (21 Jan). *First Commercial Flight of "Concorde". P* 13.
253 **32** 250 f. multicoloured   ..   ..   4·50   3·75

33 Washington and Battle of Yorktown

(Des and eng C. Guillame. Recess)

1976 (28 June). *Bicentenary of American Revolution. T* **33** *and similar horiz design. P* 13.
254   19 f. bronze-green, ultramarine and rosine   40   25
255   47 f. reddish purple, red and new blue   ..   75   65
Design:—47 f. Lafayette and sea-battle of the Virginia Capes.

34 Throwing the Hammer

(Des and eng J. Combet. Recess)

1976 (2 Aug). *AIR. Olympic Games, Montreal. T* **34** *and similar horiz design. P* 13.
256   31 f. brown-purple, blue and orange-red ..   55   45
257   39 f. cerise, brown-red and maroon   ..   70   65
Design:—39 f. High-diving.

35 *Conus ammiralis*

(Des and eng J. Pheulpin. Recess)

1976 (1 Oct). *Seashells. T* **35** *and similar horiz designs. Multicoloured. P* 13.
258   20 f. Type **35**   35   25

259	23 f. *Cyprae asellus*			35	30
260	43 f. *Turbo petholatus*			70	45
261	61 f. *Mitra papalis*			1·00	75
258/261	Set of 4			2·25	1·60

36 Father Chanel and Sanctuary Church, Poi

(Des P. Lambert. Litho Cartor)

1977 (28 Apr). *Rev Father Chanel Memorial. T* **36** *and similar horiz design. Multicoloured. P* 12
262   22 f. Type **36**   35   30
263   32 f. Father Chanel and map   ..   45   35

1977 (18 June). *AIR. Fifth Anniv of General de Gaulle Memorial. As T* **806** *of France.*
264   100 f. multicoloured   ..   ..   1·40   1·10

37 Tanoa (bowl), Lali (musical instrument) and Ipu (coconut shell)

(Litho Cartor)

1977 (26 Sept). *Handicrafts. T* **37** *and similar horiz designs. Multicoloured. P* 12½.
265   12 f. Type **37**   15   12
266   25 f. Wallis and Futuna Kumetes (bowls) and Tuluma (box)   35   25
267   33 f. Milamila (comb), Ike (club) and Tutua (model outrigger)   ..   45   35
268   45 f. Kolo (Futuna clubs)   ..   60   45
269   69 f. Kailao (Wallis and Futuna lances) ..   95   70
265/269   Set of 5   ..   ..   ..   2·25   1·75

PARIS NEW-YORK
22.11.77

1ᵉʳ VOL COMMERCIAL

(38)

1977 (26 Nov). *AIR. First Commercial Flight of "Concorde", Paris–New York. No.* 253 *optd with T* **38**.
270 **32** 250 f. multicoloured   ..   ..   3·50   2·75

39 Post Office, Mata-Utu

Wallis & Futuna Is. 1977

(Des P. Lambert. Lithó Edila)

1977 (12 Dec). *Buildings and Monuments. T* **39** *and similar horiz designs. Multicoloured. P* 13.

271	27 f. T **39**			40	30
272	50 f. Sia Hospital, Mata-Utu			65	45
273	57 f. Government Buildings, Mata-Utu			80	60
274	63 f. St Joseph's Church, Sigave			90	65
275	120 f. Royal Palace, Mata-Utu			1·75	1·10
271/275	*Set of* 5			4·00	2·75

JAMES COOK
Bicentenaire de la
découverte des Iles
Hawaii 1778-1978
(40)

1978 (22 Jan). *Bicentenary of Captain Cook's Discovery of Hawaii. Nos.* 254/5 *optd with T* **40**.

276	19 f. bronze-green, ultramarine and rosine	75	65
277	47 f. reddish purple, red and new blue	1·60	1·25

41 *Balistes niger*

(Des P. Lambert. Litho Edila)

1978 (31 Jan). *AIR. Fishes. T* **41** *and similar horiz designs. Multicoloured. P* 13.

278	26 f. Type **41**			35	25
279	35 f. *Amphiprion akindynos*			45	35
280	49 f. *Pomacanthus imperator*			65	50
281	51 f. *Zanclus cornutus*			70	55
278/281	*Set of* 4			1·90	1·50

42 Map of Futuna and Alofi

(Des and eng P. Béquet. Recess)

1978 (7 Mar). *AIR. Maps of Wallis and Futuna Islands. T* **42** *and similar design. P* 13.

282	300 f. dp blue-green, turq-bl & ultram		4·00	3·50
283	500 f. sepia, new blue and ultramarine		7·00	5·50

Design: *Vert*—500 f. Map of Wallis Island.

43 Father Bataillon and Churches

(Des P. Lambert. Litho Edila)

1978 (28 Apr). *AIR. Arrival of First French Missionaries. T* **43** *and similar horiz design. Multicoloured. P* 13×12½.

284	60 f. Type **43**	90	65
285	72 f. Monsgr. Pompallier and Map	95	70

44 I.T.U. Emblem and Antennae

(Des C. Bridoux. Litho Edila)

1978 (17 May). *AIR. World Telecommunications Day. P* 13.

286	**44** 66 f. multicoloured	90	65

45 *Triomphant*

(Des H. Sainson. Photo)

1978 (18 June). *Free French Pacific Naval Force, 1940–1944. T* **45** *and similar horiz designs. Multicoloured. P* 13.

287	150 f. Type **45**		1·75	1·10
288	200 f. *Cap des Palmes* and *Chevreuil*	∴	2·50	2·25
289	280 f. *Savorgnan de Brazza*		4·00	3·50

46 *Solanum seaforthianum*   **47** Grey Egret

(Des O. Baillais. Photo)

1978 (11 July). *Tropical Flowers. T* **46** *and similar square designs. Multicoloured. P* 13.

290	16 f. Type **46**		15	12
291	24 f. *Cassia alata*		35	25
292	29 f. *Gloriosa superba*		40	30
293	36 f. *Hymenocallis littoralis*		45	35
290/293	*Set of* 4		1·25	90

(Des Verret-Le Marinier. Photo)

1978 (5 Sept). *Ocean Birds. T* **47** *and similar vert designs. Multicoloured. P* 13.

294	17 f. Type **47**		15	12
295	18 f. Red-footed booby		15	12
296	28 f. Brown booby		40	30
297	35 f. White tern		45	35
294/297	*Set of* 4		1·00	80

403

48 Costumed Carpet-sellers

(Des P. Lambert. Photo)
1978 (3 Oct). *Costumes and Traditions. T* **48** *and similar horiz designs. Multicoloured. P* 13×12½.

298	53 f. Type **48**	..	..	..	70	55
299	55 f. "Festival of God" procession		..		80	60
300	59 f. Guards of Honour	..	..	..	80	60

49 Nativity Scene

(Des P. Lambert. Photo)
1978 (4 Dec). *AIR. Christmas. P* 13.

301	**49**	160 f. multicoloured	..	1·75	1·10

50 Human Rights Emblem

(Des L. Arquer. Litho Edila)
1978 (10 Dec). 30th *Anniv of Declaration of Human Rights. P* 12½.

302	**50**	44 f. multicoloured	..	..	60	45
303		56 f. multicoloured	..	..	80	60

PHILATELIC TERMS ILLUSTRATED

This successful STAMP MONTHLY series has now been brought together in a snappy black and yellow binding and published as a useful addition to Stanley Gibbons range of essential handbooks for keen stamp collectors. Within its 192 pages this handy limp-bound volume houses a veritable mine of useful information on the words and phrases used in philately. It describes and illustrates printing processes and watermarks, papers and perforations, errors and varieties . . . and it does all this IN COLOUR. Indeed, there are 92 full page plates in colour, plus many black and white illustrations, making it

FANTASTIC VALUE AT ONLY £1·95 POST PAID FROM

**Stanley Gibbons Publications Ltd
391 Strand, London WC2R 0LX**

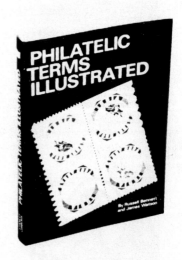

Andorra

This small state in the Pyrenees has two nominal heads of state—the French President and the Spanish Bishop of Urgel. It uses both Spanish and French currency.

French and Spanish stamps were probably first used in Andorra in 1877. During the 1880s, French interest in Andorra increased, and the earliest known postmark is a French style circular date-stamp "ANDORRA-VAL D'ANDORRE" of 15 October 1882. The U.P.U. allocated Andorran postal administration to Spain; however, in 1887, France organized a courier service (using contemporary French stamps) which, in improved form, existed from 1892 to 1931. No postmarks were available, but date-stamps of French telegraph offices in Andorra occur on cover. The Spanish P.O. in Andorra opened on 1 January 1928, and used Spanish stamps (types **66**, **68**, **69** and E**53**) until 28 March, when a provisional set of overprints was issued. The French Postal Service commenced on 16 June 1931.

Internal mail is carried free.

I. FRENCH POST OFFICES

100 Centimes=1 Franc

PRINTERS. All the following were printed at the Government Printing Works, Paris.

F **3** Notre Dame de Meritxell

F **4** St. Anthony's Bridge

F **5** St. Miguel d'Engolasters

F **7** Andorra-la-Vella   F **6** Gorge of St. Julia

(Des A. Delzers (F **3**), J. Piel (F **4**), Hourriez (F **5**), H. Cheffer (F **6**) and A. Mignon (F **7**), eng. A. Mignon. Recess)

ANDORRE ANDORRE
(F **1**)   (F **2**)

1931 (16 June). *Contemporary types of France optd.*

(a) Optd with Type F **1**

F 1	**11**	½ c. (R.) on 1 c. slate (No. 379)	..	25	25
F 2		1 c. grey	.. .. ..	25	25
		a. Opt double	.. .. ..	£225	£225
F 3		2 c. claret	.. .. ..	40	40
F 4		3 c. orange	.. .. ..	40	40
F 5		5 c. green	.. .. ..	50	50
F 6		10 c. lilac	.. .. ..	75	75
F 7	**18**	15 c. chocolate	.. ..	1·60	1·60
F 8		20 c. magenta	.. ..	2·75	2·75
F 9		25 c. ochre-brown	..	2·75	2·75
F10		30 c. green	.. ..	2·25	2·25
F11		40 c. deep ultramarine	..	4·50	4·50
F12	**15**	45 c. violet	.. ..	6·50	6·50
F13		50 c. vermilion	.. ..	4·50	4·50
F14		65 c. sage-green	.. ..	6·50	6·50
F15		75 c. magenta	.. ..	8·50	8·50
F16	**18**	90 c. scarlet	.. ..	9·00	9·00
F17	**15**	1 f. blue	.. ..	11·00	11·00
F18	**18**	1 f. 50, blue	.. ..	14·00	14·00

(b) Optd with Type F **2**

F19	**13**	2 f. red and blue-green	..	16·00	16·00
F20		3 f. mauve and carmine	..	45·00	45·00
F21		5 f. deep blue and buff	..	65·00	65·00
F22		10 f. sage-green and red	..	£120	£120
F23		20 f. magenta and green	..	£150	£150
F1/23		*Set of 23*	.. ..	£425	£425

Beware of forged overprints.

1931 (16 June)–**32.** *POSTAGE DUE. Postage Due stamps of France optd with Type F* **1**. *(a) Type D* **11**.

FD24	5 c. pale blue	.. ..	65	65
FD25	10 c. brown	.. ..	65	65
FD26	30 c. pale carmine	..	15	15
FD27	50 c. dull claret	..	65	65
FD28	60 c. green	.. ..	3·75	3·75
FD29	1 f. claret/*straw*	..	30	30
FD30	2 f. mauve	.. ..	3·25	3·25
FD31	3 f. magenta	.. ..	65	65
FD24/31	*Set of 8*	.. ..	9·00	9·00

(b) Type D **43**

FD32	1 c. grey-green ('32)	..	30	30
FD33	10 c. rosine	.. ..	95	95
FD34	60 c. red	.. ..	11·00	9·00
FD35	1 f. greenish blue ('32)	..	22·00	16·00
FD36	1 f. 20 on 2 f. pale blue (R. and Bk.)	9·50	7·50
FD37	2 f. sepia ('32)	..	32·00	20·00
FD38	5 f. on 1 f. bright violet	..	25·00	22·00
FD32/38	*Set of 7*	.. ..	90·00	65·00

1932 (16 June)–**1943.** *P* 13.

F24	F **3**	1 c. slate	..	..	..	15	12
F25		2 c. violet	..		..	30	25
F26		3 c. chocolate	..		..	15	12
F27		5 c. blue-green	..		..	30	20
F28	F **4**	10 c. lilac	..		..	50	35
F29	F **3**	15 c. vermilion	..		..	65	65
F30	F **4**	20 c. carmine-rose	..		..	5·00	3·50
F31	F **5**	25 c. chocolate	..		..	2·25	1·25
F32	F **4**	25 c. brown-lake ('37)	..		..	4·50	2·50
F33		30 c. yellow-green	..		..	90	65
F34		40 c. ultramarine	..		..	3·75	3·25
F35		40 c. sepia ('39)	..		..	50	50
F36		45 c. vermilion	..		..	4·50	3·25
F37		45 c. green ('39)	..		..	2·50	1·60
F38	F **5**	50 c. claret	..		..	5·50	4·50
F39	F **4**	50 c. bright violet ('39)	..		..	2·50	1·60
F40		50 c. yellow-green ('40)	..		..	1·10	75
F41		55 c. violet (6.38)	..		..	7·50	5·00
F42		60 c. brown (6.38)	..		..	35	30
F43	F **5**	65 c. blue-green	..		..	20·00	15·00
F44	F **4**	65 c. blue ('38)	..		..	5·50	3·75
F45		70 c. rose-red ('39)	..		..	1·00	65
F46	F **5**	75 c. violet	..		..	2·10	1·40
F47	F **4**	75 c. bright ultramarine ('39)	..		..	1·90	1·25
F48		80 c. blue-green (6.38)	..		..	9·50	7·00
F49	F **6**	80 c. blue-green ('40)	..		..	15	12
F50		90 c. carmine	..		..	2·25	1·75
F51		90 c. myrtle-green ('39)	..		..	1·90	95
F52		1 f. blue-green (3.37)	..		..	9·50	5·50
F53		1 f. scarlet (6.38)	..		..	10·00	8·00
F54		1 f. bright blue ('39)	..		..	15	12
F55		1 f. 20, violet ('42)	..		..	15	12
F56	F **3**	1 f. 25, claret ('33)	..		..	7·00	4·50
F57		1 f. 25, carmine ('39)	..		..	2·50	1·10
F58	F **6**	1 f. 30, sepia ('40)	..		..	15	12
F59	F **7**	1 f. 50, ultramarine	..		..	9·00	7·50
F60	F **6**	1 f. 50, crimson ('40)	..		..	15	12
F61		1 f. 75, violet ('35)	..		..	48·00	38·00
F62		1 f. 75, deep blue (6.38)	..		..	17·00	13·00
F63		2 f. purple	..		..	2·00	1·25

F64	F **3**	2 f. carmine ('40)	.. ..	75	55
F65		2 f. green ('42)	..	15	12
F66		2 f. 15, violet (6.38)	..	20·00	16·00
F67		2 f. 25, ultramarine ('39)	...	3·75	2·50
F68		2 f. 40, scarlet· ('42)	..	15	12
F69		2 f. 50, black ('39)		3·75	2·50
F70		2 f. 50, ultramarine ('40)	..	1·10	75
F71	F **6**	3 f. orange-brown		2·00	1·25
F72	F **3**	3 f. red-brown ('40)	..	15	12
F73		4 f. deep blue ('42)	..	15	12
F74		4 f. 50, violet ('42)	..	50	20
F75	F **7**	5 f. brown	..	25	15
F76		10 f. violet	..	30	20
F77		10 f. purple	..	3·75	3·75
F78		15 f. blue ('42)	..	40	20
F79		20 f. carmine	..	30	20
F80		20 f. red	..	65	65
F81	F **4**	50 f. greenish blue ('43)		75	45
F24/81		*Set of* 58		£200	£150

F **10**

F **11** St. Jean de Caselles Church

F **12** "House of the Valleys"

F **13** Andorre la Vieille

FD **7**

(F **8**)

F **9**

1935. *POSTAGE DUE. Typo.* P 14 × 13½.
FD82 FD **7** 1 c. grey-green 40 25

1935 (25 Sept). *No.* F38 *surch with Type* F **8.**
F82 F **5** 20 c. on 50 c. claret .. .. 1·10 95
    a. Surch double £160

(Eng Ouvré. Recess)

1936 (Dec)**–42.** *P* 14×13.

F83	F **9**	1 c. black (3.37)	..	5	5
F84		2 c. light blue (1.37)	..	5	5
F85		3 c. brown	..	5	5
F86		5 c. magenta	..	5	5
F87		10 c. ultramarine (1.37)	..	5	5
F88		15 c. mauve (1.37)	..	15	15
F89		20 c. green (3.37)	..	5	5
F90		30 c. scarlet (6.38)	..	12	12
F91		30 c. black ('42)	..	8	8
F92		35 c. blue-green (6.38)	..	17·00	17·00
F93		40 c. red-brown ('42)	..	5	5
F94		50 c. deep green ('42)	..	5	5
F95		60 c. greenish blue ('42)	..	5	5
F96		70 c. violet ('42)	..	5	5
F83/96		*Set of* 14	..	17·00	17·00

FD **10**

FD **11** Wheat Sheaves

1937–41. *POSTAGE DUE. Typo.* P 14×13½.

FD 97	FD **10**	5 c. pale blue	..	2·25	1·90
FD 98		10 c. brown ('41)	..	2·25	1·90
FD 99		2 f. violet ('41)	..	1·25	65
FD100		5 f. orange ('41)	..	95	65
FD97/100		*Set of* 4 ..	..	6·00	4·75

(Des P. Gandon. Die eng H. Cortot. Typo)

1943–46. *POSTAGE DUE.* P 14×13½.

FD101	FD **11**	10 c. black	..	5	5
FD102		30 c. purple	..	25	25
FD103		50 c. green	..	40	40
FD104		1 f. blue	..	15	15
FD105		1 f. 50, scarlet	..	65	65
FD106		2 f. greenish blue	..	30	30
FD107		3 f. brown	..	50	50
FD108		4 f. violet ('46)	..	75	75
FD109		5 f. carmine	..	75	75
FD110		10 f. orange ('46)	..	75	75
FD111		20 f. olive-brown (27.5.46)	1·10	1·10
FD101/111		*Set of* 11	..	5·00	5·00

F **14** Councillor

(Des Lucas. Eng J. Piel (Type F **10**) and Ouvré (remainder).
Recess)

1944–51. *(a) P* 14 × 13.

F 97	F **10**	10 c. violet	..	5	5
F 98		30 c. carmine	..	5	5
F 99		40 c. blue	..	5	5
F100		50 c. orange	..	5	5
F101		60 c. black	..	5	5
F102		70 c. magenta	..	5	5
F103		80 c. green	..	5	5
F104		1 f. ultramarine (28.3.49)	..	30	25

(b) P 13.

F105	F **11**	1 f. dull purple	..	10	5
F106		1 f. 20, blue	..	8	5
F107		1 f. 50, red-orange	..	10	5
F108		2 f. blue-green	..	5	5
F109	F **12**	2 f. 40, carmine-rose	..	12	8
F110		2 f. 50, rose-carmine (27.5.46) ..	20	10
F111		3 f. purple-brown	..	5	5
F112	F **11**	3 f. vermilion (9.7.51)	..	1·60	1·40
F113	F **12**	4 f. ultramarine	..	10	5
F114		4 f. turquoise-green (26.7.48)	45	45
F115	F **11**	4 f. sepia (28.3.49)	..	1·00	80
F116	F **12**	4 f. 50, greenish blue (8.3.47) ..	95	90
F117	F **13**	4 f. 50, sepia	..	10	8
F118		5 f. ultramarine	..	8	5
F119		5 f. blue-green (27.5.46)	..	20	12
F120	F **12**	5 f. emerald-green (28.3.49)	..	95	90
F121		5 f. violet (9.7.51)	..	80	50
F122	F **13**	6 f. carmine (1.11.45)	..	20	8
F123		6 f. purple (26.7.48)	..	20	15
F124	F **12**	6 f. emerald-green (9.7.51)	..	80	55
F125	F **13**	8 f. indigo (4.12.48)	..	55	50
F126	F **12**	8 f. red-brown (28.3.49)	..	30	30
F127	F **13**	10 f. blue-green	..	5	5
F128		10 f. ultramarine (27.5.46)	..	8	5
F129		12 f. scarlet (26.7.48)	..	40	40
F130		12 f. blue-green (1.2.49) ..	..	45	45
F131	F **14**	15 f. bright purple	..	20	12
F132	F **13**	15 f. carmine (1.2.49)	..	25	25
F133		15 f. purple-brown (9.7.51)	..	75	65
F134	F **14**	18 f. blue (26.7.48)	..	90	50
F135	F **13**	18 f. scarlet (9.7.51)	..	3·50	2·75
F136	F **14**	20 f. blue	..	20	20
F137		20 f. violet (26.7.48)	..	75	65
F138		25 f. rose-carmine (27.5.46)	..	45	40
F139		25 f. ultramarine (1.2.49)	..	55	55
F140		30 f. ultramarine (9.7.51)	..	4·50	2·50
F141		40 f. green (27.5.46)	..	45	45
F142		50 f. purple-brown	..	45	40
F97/142		*Set of* 46 ..	..	21·00	16·00

1946–53. *POSTAGE DUE. As Type* FD **11**, *but inscr* "TIMBRE-TAXE". *Typo.* P 14×13½.

FD143	10 c. sepia (25.9.46)	..	..	40	40
FD144	1 f. ultramarine ('47)		..	15	15
FD145	2 f. greenish blue ('47)	..	..	15	15
FD146	3 f. red-brown ('47)		..	65	65
FD147	4 f. purple ('47)	..		95	95
FD148	5 f. rose-carmine ('47)		..	25	25
FD149	10 f. orange ('47)	..	..	90	90
FD150	20 f. olive-brown ('47)	..	1·40	1·40
FD151	50 f. deep green ('50)	..	..	6·50	6·50
FD152	100 f. green (30.3.53)	..	..	16·00	16·00
FD143/152	*Set of* 10	..	..	24·00	24·00

See also Nos. FD185/8.

F **15** Chamois and Pyrenees   F **16** Les Escaldes

F **17** St. Coloma Belfry (*Horiz*)

F **18** Gothic Cross, Andorre-la-Vieille (*Vert*)

F **19** Les Bons Village (*Horiz*)

F **20** East Valira River (*Vert*)

(Des and eng Barlangue. Recess)

1950 (10 Feb). *AIR.* P 13.
F143	F **15**	100 f. indigo	..	..	..	15·00	15·00

(Des Decaris. Eng Hertenberger (F **16**), Frères (F **17**), Dufresne (F **18**), Decaris (F **19/20**). Recess)

1955 (15 Feb)–**58.** P 13. (*a*) *POSTAGE.*
F144	F **16**	1 f. deep grey-blue		5	5
F145		2 f. green	..	5	5
F146		3 f. bright scarlet	..	5	5
F147		5 f. chocolate	..	5	5
F148	F **17**	6 f. deep bluish green	..	15	12
F149		8 f. lake	..	..	15	15
F150		10 f. bright reddish violet		30	20
F151		12 f. indigo	..	40	20
F152	F **18**	15 f. vermilion	..	45	25
F153		18 f. turquoise-blue	..	45	25
F154		20 f. deep violet	..	50	25
F155		25 f. blackish brown	..	65	30
F156	F **19**	30 f. deep bright blue	..	11·00	5·50
F157		35 f. greenish blue (19.8.57)	5·00	3·50
F158		40 f. deep green	..	13·00	11·00
F159		50 f. carmine	..	1·25	90
F160		65 f. reddish violet (10.2.58)	2·75	2·75
F161		70 f. light brown (19.8.57)	2·75	2·75
F162		75 f. violet-blue	..	18·00	14·00
F144/162	*Set of* 19	..	..	55·00	38·00

(*b*) *AIR. Inscr* "POSTE AERIENNE"
F163	F **20**	100 f. deep green	..	2·50	2·25
F164		200 f. carmine	..	5·50	3·75
F165		500 f. deep blue (20.3.57)	28·00	22·00
F163/165	*Set of* 3	..	..	32·00	25·00

New currency. 100 (old) francs=1 (new) franc

F **21**   F **22** Gothic Cross, Meritxell

(Des R. Louis; die eng A. Barre. Typo. (Type F **21**). Des and eng Mazelin (Type F **22**), Gandon (65 c., 85 c., 1 f.), Durrens (2 f. to 10 f.). Recess)

1961 (17 June)–**71.** *Type* F **21** *and horiz views as Type* F **22**. P 14×13½ (*Type* F **21**) *or* 13 (*others*). (*a*) *POSTAGE.*
F166	F **21**	1 c. grey, sl-pur & dp bl (16.5.64)	5	5
F167		2 c. yell-orge, orge & blk (16.5.64)	5	5
F168		5 c. pale green, emerald & black	5	5
F169		10 c. rose, red and black	..	5	5
F170		12 c. yellow, emer & mar (16.5.64)	5	5
F171		15 c. light blue, blue and black	..	5	5
		*a. Light blue and black**		5	5
F172		18 c. pink, light reddish violet and black (16.5.64)	5	5
F173		20 c. pale lemon, yellow and brown	5	5
		a. Pale lemon, yellow-orange and brown ('69)	5	5
F174	F **22**	25 c. pl bl, vio, emer & blcksh grn	10	10
F175		30 c. brown-pur, lake, grn & olive	15	15
F175a		40 c. bronze-green and orange-brown (24.4.65)	30	30
F176		45 c. blue, indigo & yellow-green	4·50	2·50
F176a		45 c. deep slate-blue, olive-brown and deep violet (13.6.70)	30	25
F177		50 c. sepia, purple, green & ol-brn	65	65
F177a		60 c. dp brn & orge-brn (24.4.65)	30	30
F178	–	65 c. turq-blue, brown-ol & choc	5·00	4·50
F179	–	85 c. mauve, purple, vio & dp pur	4·25	3·75
F179a	–	90 c. blue-green, yellow-brown and bright blue (28.8.71)	30	25
F180	–	1 f. turquoise-grn, indigo & sepia	65	50
F166/180	*Set of* 19	..	..	15·00	12·00

(*b*) *AIR*
F181	–	2 f. red. sepia and maroon	75	50
F182	–	3 f. dp blue, brn-pur & blackish grn	1·10	75
F183	–	5 f. mauve, orange and lake	1·75	1·25
F184	–	10 f. dp green & turq-bl (25.4.64)	3·50	2·50
F181/184	*Set of* 4	..	..	6·50	4·50

Designs:—60 c. to 1 f. Engolasters Lake; 2 f. to 10 f. Inclès Valley.

*On No. F171a the colour of the frame matches the colour of the shield background.

1961 (17 June). *POSTAGE DUE. As Nos.* FD143/52 *but new values and colours.*
FD185	FD **11**	5 c. crimson	..	..	75	75
FD186		10 c. orange-red	..	..	1·10	1·10
FD187		20 c. olive-brown	..	..	1·90	1·90
FD188		50 c. blackish green	..	..	2·50	2·50
FD185/188	*Set of* 4	..	..	5·50	5·50

F **23** "Telstar" Satellite and part of Globe

(Des Durrens. Eng Béquet. Recess)

1962 (29 Sept). *First Trans-Atlantic Television Satellite Link.* P 13.
F185	F **23**	50 c. reddish violet and bright blue	90	90

F **24** "La Sardane" (dance)

(Des and eng Durrens (20 c.), Decaris (others). Recess)

1963 (24 June). *Andorran History* (1*st issue*). *Type* F **24** *and larger horiz designs inscr* "1963". P 13.
F186		20 c. reddish purple, magenta & ol-grn	1·50	1·50
F187		50 c. lake and slate-green	..	..	2·25	2·25

F188 1 f. dp bluish green, black & red-brn 3·25 3·25
F186/188 Set of 3 .. .. .. 6·50 6·50
Designs: (48½ × 27 mm)—50 c. Charlemagne crossing
Andorra; (48 × 27 mm)—1 f. Foundation of Andorra by Louis
le Débonnaire.

F 25 St. Coloma Belfry and Grand Palais, Paris

F 26 The Virgin of St. Coloma

(Des and eng Combet. Recess)

1964 (18 Jan). *"PHILATEC 1964" International Stamp Exhibition, Paris. P* 13.
F189 F **25** 25 c. green, brown-purple & sepia 55 30

(Des and eng Decaris. Recess)

1964 (25 Apr). *Andorran History (2nd issue). Horiz designs as Nos. F187/8 inscr "1964". P* 13.
F190 60 c. dp bluish green, chestnut & brown 3·25 3·25
F191 1 f. blue, sepia and orange-brown .. 3·75 3·75
Designs: (48½ × 27 mm)—60 c. "Napoleon re-establishes the Andorran Statute, 1806"; 1 f. "Confirmation of the Co-Government, 1288".

1964 (15 June)**–71.** *POSTAGE DUE. Designs as Nos. D1650/7 of France, but inscr "ANDORRE". P* 14×13½.
FD192 5 c. red, green & brt purple (26.4.65) 5 5
FD193 10 c. blue, green & brt purple (26.4.65) 5 5
FD194 15 c. red, green and brown .. 5 5
FD195 20 c. pur, lt green & blue-grn (15.3.71) 8 8
FD196 30 c. blue, green and brown .. 10 10
FD197 40 c. yell, cerise & blue-grn (15.3.71) 12 12
FD198 50 c. carmine, green & ultram (26.4.65) 20 20
FD192/198 Set of 7 .. .. .. 60 60

(Des and eng Durrens. Recess)

1964 (25 July). *Red Cross Fund. P* 13.
F192 F **26** 25 c.+10 c. red, green and blue 9·00 9·00

F 27 I.T.U. Emblem, "Syncom", Morse Key and House", Paris Pleumeur-Bodou Centre

F 28 "Andorra and House", Paris

F 29 Chair-lift

(Des and eng Decaris. Recess)

1965 (17 May). *I.T.U. Centenary. P* 13.
F193 F **27** 60 c. violet, light blue and crimson 1·90 1·60

(Des and eng Béquet. Recess)

1965 (5 June). *Opening of "Andorra House", Paris. P* 13.
F194 F **28** 25 c. orange-brown, olive-brn & bl 35 30

(Des and eng J. Combet. Recess)

1966 (2 Apr). *Winter Sports. Type F* **29** *and similar design. P* 13.
F195 25 c. myrtle-green, brn-pur & new bl 30 30
F196 40 c. sepia, bright blue and crimson .. 45 40
Design: *Horiz*—40 c. Ski-lift.

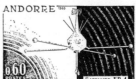

F 30 Satellite "FR 1"

F 31 Europa "Ship"

(Des and eng C. Durrens. Recess)

1966 (7 May). *Launching of Satellite "FR 1". P* 13.
F197 F **30** 60 c. new blue, emer & myrtle-grn 70 45

(Des G. and J. Bender. Eng J. Combet. Recess)

1966 (24 Sept). *Europa. P* 13.
F198 F **31** 60 c. brown 70 45

F 32 Cogwheels

F 33 "Folk Dancers" (statue)

F 34 Telephone and Dial

(Des Bonnevalle. Eng Cami. Recess)

1967 (29 Apr). *Europa. P* 13.
F199 F **32** 30 c. deep indigo and light blue .. 45 40
F200 60 c. brown-red and bright purple 80 65

(Des and eng Béquet (after Viladomat). Recess)

1967 (29 Apr). *Centenary of the New Reform (1966). P* 13.
F201 F **33** 30 c. myrtle-green, olive-grn & slate 25 20

(Des and eng Combet. Recess)

1967 (29 Apr). *Inauguration of Automatic Telephone Service. P* 13.
F202 F **34** 60 c. black, violet and carmine .. 45 40

F 35 Andorran Family

F 36 "The Temptation"

(Des and eng Decaris. Recess)

1967 (23 Sept). *Institution of Social Security. P* 13.
F203 F **35** 2 f. 30, lake-brown & purple-brown 2·10 1·50

(Des and eng Combet. Recess)

1967 (23 Sept). *16th-Century Frescoes in the "House of the Valleys" (First Series). Type F* **36** *and similar vert designs. P* 13.
F204 25 c. Venetian red and black 30 25
F205 30 c. bright purple & deep reddish violet 45 30

F206 60 c. greenish blue and deep blue   ..   50   25
F204/206 *Set of 3* ..   ..   ..   1·10   75
Designs: Frescoes—30 c. "The Kiss of Judas"; 60 c. "The Descent from the Cross".
See also Nos. F210/12.

F **37** Downhill Skiing   F **38** Europa "Key"

(Des and eng Combet. Recess)
1968 (27 Jan). *Winter Olympic Games, Grenoble. P* 13.
F207 F **37** 40 c. purple, yellow-orange & red   40   30

(Des H. Schwarzenbach. Eng P. Béquet. Recess)
1968 (27 Apr). *Europa. P* 13.
F208 F **38** 30 c. new blue and deep slate   55   40
F209   60 c. reddish violet and brown   .. 1·10   90

(Des and eng Combet. Recess)
1968 (12 Oct). *16th-Century Frescoes in the "House of the Valleys"* (2nd Series). *Horiz designs similar to Type* F **36.**
P 13.
F210 25 c. bronze-green and myrtle-green..   30   30
F211 30 c. plum and chocolate   ..   40   40
F212 60 c. chocolate and lake   ..   70   70
F210/212 *Set of 3* ..   ..   1·25   1·25
Frescoes:—25 c. "The Beating of Christ"; 30 c. "Christ Helped by the Cyrenians"; 60 c. "The Death of Christ".

F **39** High-jumping   F **40** Colonnade

(Des and eng Bétemps. Recess)
1968 (12 Oct). *Olympic Games, Mexico. P* 13.
F213 F **39** 40 c. red-brown and new blue   .. 45   40

(Des L. Gasbarra and G. Belli. Eng Béquet. Recess)
1969 (26 Apr). *Europa. P* 13.
F214 F **40** 40 c. slate, greenish blue & dp cerise 70   65
F215   70 c. brown-red, olive and indigo 1·10 1·00

F **41** Canoeing   F **42** "The Apocalypse"

(Des and eng J. Combet. Recess)
1969 (2 Aug). *World Kayak-Canoeing Championships, Bourg-St. Maurice. P* 13.
F216 F **41** 70 c. grey-blue, blue & myrtle-grn 60   60

(Des and eng J. Combet. Recess)
1969 (27 Sept). *European Water Charter. Vert design similar to T* **639** *of France. P* 13.
F217 70 c. black, greenish blue & ultramarine 65   65
(Des and eng J. Combet. Recess)

1969 (18 Oct). *Altar-screen, St. Jean-de-Caselles* (1st Series). *"The Revelation of St. John". Type* F **42** *and similar vert designs, showing further sections of the screen. Dated "1969". P* 13.
F218 30 c. brown-red, dp reddish violet & brn 30   30
F219 40 c. bistre-brown, purple-brn & slate 35   35
F220 70 c. bright purple, lake & carmine-red 50   50
F218/220 *Set of 3* ..   ..   1·00 1·00
See also Nos. F225/7, F233/5 and F240/2.

F **43** Handball Player   F **44** "Flaming Sun"

(Des and eng G. Bétemps. Recess)
1970 (21 Feb). *7th World Handball Championships. P* 13.
F221 F **43** 80 c. new blue, chocolate & indigo 65   55
(Des L. le Brocquy. Eng Bétemps. Recess)
1970 (2 May). *Europa. P* 13.
F222 F **44** 40 c. yellow-orange   ..   45   25
F223   80 c. bluish violet..   ..   65   50

F **45** Putting the Shot   F **46** Ice-skaters

(Des and eng G. Bétemps. Recess)
1970 (11 Sept). *1st European Junior Athletic Championships, Paris. P* 13.
F224 F **45** 80 c. maroon and new blue   .. 65   55

(Des and eng J. Combet. Recess)
1970 (24 Oct). *Altar-screen, St. Jean-de-Caselles* (2nd Series). *Vert designs as Type* F **42,** *but dated "1970". P* 13.
F225 30 c. reddish violet, purple-brn & cerise 30   30
F226 40 c. myrtle-green and violet ..   40   40
F227 80 c. rose, indigo and deep olive .. 55   55
F225/227 *Set of 3* ..   ..   1·10 1·10
(Des and eng Forget. Recess)

1971 (20 Feb). *World Ice-skating Championships, Lyon. P* 13.
F228 F **46** 80 c. reddish violet, brt purple & red 55   40

F **47** Grouse   F **48** Europa Chain

(Des J. Combet. Photo (No. F229). Des and eng Combet. Recess (No. F230)

1971 (24 April). *Nature Protection. T **47** and similar vert design. P* 13.
F229 F **47** 80 c. multicoloured 65 45
F230 – 80 c. chocolate, myrtle-grn & new bl 65 45
Design:—No. F230, Pyrenean bear.
See also Nos. F238, F251/2 and F259/60.

(Des H. Haflidason. Eng Bétemps. Recess)

1971 (8 May). *Europa. P* 13.
F231 F **48** 50 c. rose-red 45 30
F232 80 c. turquoise-green 70 55

(Des and eng Combet. Recess)

1971 (18 Sept). *Altar-screen, St. Jean-de-Caselles (3rd Series). Vert designs similar to Type F **42**, but dated "1971". P* 13.
F233 30 c. emerald, olive-brown & myrtle-grn 30 30
F234 50 c. olive-brown, red-orange & lake 40 40
F235 90 c. new blue, plum & blackish brown 60 60
F233/235 Set of 3 .. .. 1·10 1·10
Designs:—30 c. to 90 c. Further scenes from "The Revelation of St. John".

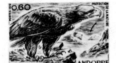

F **49** "Communications" F **50** Pyrenean Golden Eagle

(Des P. Lambert, after P. Huovinen. Photo)

1972 (29 Apr). *Europa. P* 13.
F236 F **49** 50 c. multicoloured 40 30
F237 90 c. multicoloured 70 55

(Des and eng P. Forget. Recess)

1972 (27 May). *Nature Protection. P* 13.
F238 F **50** 60 c. olive, bluish green and purple 50 40

F **51** Rifle-shooting F **52** General De Gaulle

(Des and eng G. Bétemps. Recess)

1972 (8 July). *Olympic Games, Munich. P* 13.
F239 F **51** 1 f. plum 65 50

(Des and eng J. Combet. Recess)

1972 (16 Sept). *Altar-screen, St. Jean-de-Caselles (4th series). Vert designs as Type F **42**, but dated "1972". P* 13.
F240 30 c. bright purple, slate & greenish olive 30 30
F241 50 c. grey and ultramarine 40 40
F242 90 c. slate-green and greenish blue .. 55 55
F240/242 Set of 3 .. .. 1·10 1·10
Designs:—30 c. to 90 c. Further scenes from "The Revelation of St. John".

(Des and eng P. Béquet. Recess)

1972 (23 Oct). *5th Anniv of Gen. De Gaulle's Visit to Andorra. Type F **52** and similar vert design. P* 13.
F243 50 c. deep ultramarine 55 55
F244 90 c. brown-lake 70 70
Design:—90 c. Gen. De Gaulle in Andorre-la-Vieille, 1967.
Nos. F243/4 were issued together in sheets of 10 stamps, made up of 5 horizontal pairs each separated by a stamp-sized label in brown-lake, orange-yellow and deep ultra-marine showing Andorra Arms; thus forming a triptych.

F **53** Europa "Posthorn"

(Des P. Lambert, after L. Anisdahl. Photo)

1973 (28 Apr). *Europa. P* 13.
F245 F **53** 50 c. multicoloured 30 30
F246 90 c. multicoloured 45 45

F **54** "Virgin of Canolich" F **55** Lily
(wood-carving)

(Des and eng P. Forget. Recess)

1973 (16 June). *Andorran Art. P* 13.
F247 F **54** 1 f. lilac, greenish blue and drab .. 70 70

(Des P. Lambert. Photo)

1973 (7 July). *Pyrenean Wild Flowers. (1st series). Type F **55** and similar vert designs. Multicoloured. P* 13.
F248 30 c. Type F **55** 20 20
F249 50 c. Columbine 30 30
F250 90 c. Wild pinks 55 55
See also Nos. F253/5 and F264/6.

F **56** Blue Tit F **57** "The Virgin of Pal"

(Des H. Heinzel. Photo)

1973 (27 Oct). *Nature Protection. Birds. Type F **56** and similar vert design. Multicoloured. P* 13.
F251 F **56** 90 c. Type F **56** 40 40
F252 1 f. Woodpecker 45 45
See also F259/60.

(Des P. Lambert. Photo)

1974 (6 Apr). *Pyrenean Wild Flowers* (2nd series). *Vert designs as Type F* **55.** *Multicoloured. P* 13.
F253   45 c. Iris   20   20
F254   65 c. Tobacco plant   30   30
F255   90 c. Narcissus   45   45

(Des and eng A. Decaris. Recess)

1974 (27 Apr). *Europa. Church Sculptures. Type F* **57** *and similar vert design. Multicoloured. P* 13.
F256   50 c. Type F **57**   30   25
F257   90 c. "The Virgin of St. Coloma"   .. 50   40

F **61** "Arphila" Motif

F **62** Pres. Pompidou (Co-Prince of Andorra)

(Des O. Baillais. Eng G. Bétemps. Recess)

1975 (7 June). *"Arphila 75" International Stamp Exhibition, Paris. P* 13.
F267 F **61** 2 f. carm-lake, greenish bl & emer   65   65

(Des and eng J. Pheulpin. Recess)

1975 (23 Aug). *President Pompidou of France Commemoration. P* 13.
F268 F **62** 80 c. black and deep violet   .. 30   30

F **58** Arms of Andorra

F **59** Letters crossing Globe

(Des and eng P. Béquet. Recess)

1974 (24 Aug). *Co-Princes' Meeting, Cahors. P* 13.
F258   F **58** 1 f. ultramarine, reddish violet and reddish orange   40   40

(Des H. Heinzel. Photo)

1974 (21 Sept). *Nature Protection. Birds. Vert designs as Type F* **56.** *Multicoloured. P* 13.
F259   60 c. Citril finch   35   35
F260   80 c. Bullfinch..   35   35

(Des and eng P. Béquet. Recess)

1974 (5 Oct). *Centenary of Universal Postal Union. P* 13.
F261 F **59** 1 f. 20, brn-lake, slate & yell-brn   50   50

F **63** "La Pubilla" and Emblem

F **64** Skier

(Des H. Sainson. Eng J. Pheulpin. Recess)

1975 (8 Nov). *International Women's Year. P* 13.
F269 F **63** 1 f. 20, black, deep reddish purple and new blue   40   40

(Des and eng P. Forget. Recess)

1976 (31 Jan). *Winter Olympic Games, Innsbruck. P* 13.
F270 F **64** 1 f. 20, bl-blk, ol-grn & greenish bl   40   40

F **60** "Calvary"

(Des P. Lambert. Photo)

1975 (26 Apr). *Europa. Type F* **60** *and similar multicoloured design. P* 11½×13 (*vert*) *or* 13×11½ (*horiz*).
F262   80 c. Type F **60**   40   40
a. Black (inscr. & face value) omitted
F263   1 f. 20, "Coronation of St. Marti" (*horiz*)   55   55

1975 (10 May). *Pyrenean Flowers* (3rd series). *Vert designs as Type F* **55,** *but inscribed "ANDORRE-ANDORRA". P* 13.
F264   60 c. multicoloured   20   20
F265   80 c. multicoloured   30   30
F266   1 f. 20, lemon, rose and deep green   .. 40   40
Designs:—60 c. Gentian; 80 c. Anemone; 1 f. 20, Colchicum.

F **65** Telephone and Satellite

F **66** Catalan Forge

(Des and eng M. Monvoisin. Recess)

1976 (20 Mar). *Telephone Centenary. P* 13.
F271 F **65** 1 f. deep yell-grn, blk & bright carm   30   30

(Des P. Lambert. Eng M. Monvoisin. Recess)

1976 (8 May). *Europa. Type F* **66** *and similar horiz design. P* 13.
F272   80 c. dull pur-brn, vio-bl & slate-grn   25   25
F273   1 f. 20, carmine-red, bottle grn & blk   40   40
Design:—1 f. 20, Andorran folk-weaving.

F **67** Thomas Jefferson

F **68** Ball-trap (clay-pigeon) Shooting

F **73** Book and Flowers

(Des and eng C. Durrens. Recess)

1977 (11 June). *1st Anniv of Institute of Andorran Studies.* P 13.
F282 F **73** 80 c. red-brown, slate-grn & royal bl   25   25

(Des and eng R. Quillivic. Recess)

1976 (3 July). *Bicentenary of American Revolution.* P 13.
F274 F **67** 1 f. 20, slate-grn, ol-brn & bl-grn   40   40

(Des and eng C. Haley. Recess)

1976 (17 July). *Olympic Games. Montreal.* P 13.
F275 F **68** 2 f. bistre-brn, reddish vio & grn   65   65

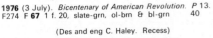

F **69** Rebuilt Chapel

F **74** St. Romain

F **75** Council-General Assembly Hall

(Des and eng J. Pheulpin. Recess)

1976 (4 Sept). *Reconstruction of Notre Dame Chapel, Meritxell.* P 13.
F276 F **69** 1 f. yellow-grn, mar and orge-brn   30   30

(Des and eng P. Béquet. Recess)

1977 (23 July). *Reredos of Sant Roma, Les Bons.* P 12×13.
F283 F **74** 2 f. multicoloured   65   65

(Des and eng C. Haley (1 f. 10), P. Gandon (2 f.). Recess)

1977 (24 Sept). *Andorran Institutions. Type F **75** and similar design.* P 13.
F284   1 f. 10, dull scarlet, brt blue & chocolate   40   40
F285   2 f. sepia and deep carmine   65   65
Design: *Vert*—2 f. Don Guillem D'Arény Plandolit.

F **70** *Parnassius apollo*

F **71** Ermine

F **72** Church of St. Joan de Caselles

F **76** Red Squirrel

F **77** Pont des Escalls

(Des H. Heinzel. Photo)

1976 (16 Oct). *Nature Protection. Butterflies. Type F **70** and similar vert design. Multicoloured.* P 13.
F277   80 c. Type F **70**   25   25
F278   1 f. 40, *Euvanessa antiopa*   40   40

(Des H. Heinzel. Photo)

1977 (2 Apr). *Nature Protection.* P 13.
F279 F **71** 1 f. brownish grey, black & chalky bl   30   30

(Des H. Sainson. Eng M. Monvoisin (1 f.), C. Guillame (1 f. 40). Recess)

1977 (30 Apr). *Europa. Type F **72** and similar vert design.* P 13.
F280   1 f. purple, dp yellow-green & dp turq-bl   30   30
F281   1 f. 40, indigo, yellow-olive & ultram   40   40
Design:—1 f. 40, St. Vicens Château.

(Des and eng J. Pheulpin. Recess)

1978 (18 Mar). *Nature Protection.* P 13.
F286 F **76** 1 f. purple-brown, blue-grn & brn-ol   30   30

(Des and eng C. Andréotto. Recess)

1978 (8 Apr). *700th Anniv of Parity Treaties (1st issue).* P 13.
F287 F **77** 80 c. deep yellow-green, reddish brown and deep turquoise-blue   25   25

See also No. F292.

F 78 Church at Pal

F 79 "Virgin of Sispony"

(Des P. Lambert. Eng M.-N. Goffin (1 f.), E. Lacaque (1 f. 40). Recess)

1978 (29 Apr). *Europa. Type* F **78** *and similar design.* P 13.
F288 1 f. chocolate, dp yellow-green & scarlet ... 30 ... 30
F289 1 f. 40, indigo, greenish blue and scarlet ... 40 ... 40
Design: *Vert*—1 f. 40, Charlemagne's House.

(Des and eng P. Béquet. Recess)

1978 (20 May). *Andorran Art.* P 12×13.
F290 F **79** 2 f. multicoloured ... ... 65 ... 65

F 80 Tribunal Meeting

(Des and eng C. Haley. Recess)

1978 (24 June). *Tribunal of Visura.* P 13×12½.
F291 F **80** 1 f. 20, multicoloured ... ... 40 ... 40

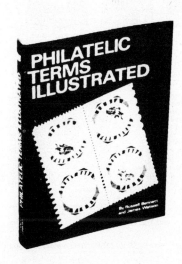

F 81 Treaty Text

(Des and eng J. Combet. Recess)

1978 (2 Sept). *700th Anniv of Parity Treaties* (2nd issue). P 13×12.
F292 F **81** 1 f. 70, agate, green & deep carmine ... 40 ... 40

PHILATELIC TERMS ILLUSTRATED

This successful STAMP MONTHLY series has now been brought together in a snappy black and yellow binding and published as a useful addition to Stanley Gibbons range of essential handbooks for keen stamp collectors. Within its 192 pages this handy limp-bound volume houses a veritable mine of useful information on the words and phrases used in philately. It describes and illustrates printing processes and watermarks, papers and perforations, errors and varieties ... and it does all this IN COLOUR. Indeed, there are 92 full page plates in colour, plus many black and white illustrations, making it

FANTASTIC VALUE AT ONLY £1·95 POST PAID FROM

**Stanley Gibbons Publications Ltd
391 Strand, London WC2R 0LX**

II. SPANISH POST OFFICES

100 Centimos=1 Peseta

PRINTERS. All the following were printed at The Government Printing Works, Madrid.

CORREOS

◄ CORREOS ►

ANDORRA   **A N D O R R A**
(1)   (E 2)

1928 (28 Mar). *Types of Spain (King Alfonso XIII), optd with T 1.* A. *P* $12 \times 11\frac{1}{2}$ *(comb)* or $13 \times 12\frac{1}{2}$ *(comb)* B. *P* 14 *(line).*

				A		B	
1	**68**	2 c. sage-green (R.)	..	20	15	30·00	12·00
2		5 c. crimson	..	25	25	30·00	12·00
3		10 c. yellow-green (R.)		25	25	25·00	9·00
4		10 c. blue-green (R.)	..	8·00	8·00	20·00	6·00
5		15 c. greenish blue (R.)		1·00	95	30·00	12·00
6		20 c. violet (R.)		1·00	95	12·00	9·00
7		25 c. scarlet	..	1·00	95	—	—
		a. Opt inverted	..	45·00	35·00	/	†
8		30 c. sepia (R.)	..	7·00	7·00	24·00	9·00
		a. Opt inverted	..	45·00	35·00		†
9		40 c. blue (R.)	..	5·00	2·00	14·00	4·75
10		50 c. red-orange	..	5·00	2·40	30·00	14·00
		a. Opt inverted	..	25·00	21·00		†
11	**69**	1 p. greenish black (R.)		6·00	4·00	24·00	12·00
12		4 p. carmine-lake	..	40·00	30·00	40·00	24·00
13		10 p. brown	..	65·00	40·00	40·00	40·00
1/13		*Set of 13*	..	£130	85·00	£300	£160

All except No. 1 have blue control figures on back. The 40 c., 4 p. and 10 p. exist perf 11, without control figures on back.
Fakes and forgeries exist.

1928 (18 Mar)–**29.** *EXPRESS LETTER. Type E 53 of Spain (Pegasus), optd with Type E 2. P 14.*

E14	20 c. rose (blue figs on back)	..	..	10.00	5·00
E15	20 c. red (without figs) ('29)	..	..	24·00	15·00

2 La Vall   **3** General Council   E **4** Eagle over
            of Andorra   Pyrenees

1929–38 (25 Nov). *As T* **2** *(various designs) and* **3.** *Blue control figures on back of all except No.*14. *Recess.* A. *P* $11\frac{1}{2}$. B. *P* 14.

				A		B	
14	**2**	2 c. sage-green	..	2·25	15	80	30
15	–	5 c. claret	..	3·50	80	1·00	35
16	–	10 c. yellow-green	..	3·50	60	1·00	55
17	–	15 c. slate-blue	..	11·00	8·00	1·00	55
18	–	20 c. violet	..	3·25	1·90	1·00	60
19	–	25 c. carmine	..	3·25	1·90	2·75	80
20	**2**	30 c. sepia	..	55·00	22·00	38·00	12·00
21	–	40 c. blue	..	5·50	4·00	2·25	55
22	–	50 c. red-orange	..		†	2·25	60
23	**3**	1 p. greenish black	..	14·00	8·00	3·25	1·60
24		4 p. bright purple	..	£160		— 28·00	8·00
25		10 p. brown	..:		†	32·00	12·00

Designs:—5 c., 40 c. St. Juan de Caselles. 10 c., 20 c., 50 c. St. Julia de Loria. 15 c., 25 c. St. Coloma.
The 2 c., 10 c., 20 c., 50 c. and 10 p. exist perf 13 and Nos. 15/25 and E26 exist without control figures, perf 14.
The 2 c., 20 c. and 1 p. to 4 p. are known in imperf between pairs.

1929 (26 Nov). *EXPRESS LETTER. Blue figures on back. Recess.* A. *P* $11\frac{1}{2}$. B. *P* 14.

				A		B	
E26	E **4**	20 c. scarlet ..	..	£160		— 8·00	2·25

This also exists perf 13.

1935–43. *Without control figures. P* $11\frac{1}{2}$.

26	**2**	2 c. red-brown ('37)	..	..	80	25
27	–	5 c. sepia ('36)		..	80	25
28	–	10 c. yellow-green ('39)		..	48·00	7·00
29	–	10 c, blue-green ('43)		..	1·60	55
30	–	15 c. blue-green ('37)	..	..	2·00	55
31	–	15 c. yellow-green ('39)		..	3·25	80
32	–	20 c. violet ('39)		..	2·75	55
33	–	25 c. lake ('37)		..	1·00	40
34	**2**	30 c. carmine ('35)		..	1·60	40
35	–	40 c. blue ('42)		..	£130	6·50
36	**2**	45 c. carmine ('37)		..	80	25
37	–	50 c. red-orange ('38)	..		3·25	80
38	**2**	60 c. blue ('37)		..	2·75	40
38a	**3**	1 p. greenish black	..		£800	£400
39		4 p. bright purple('43)			12·00	6·50
40		10 p. brown ('43)	..		16·00	6·50
26/40		*Set of 15* (excl. 38a) ..			£190	32·00

Designs:—As for similar values above.

1937. *EXPRESS LETTER. Without control figures. P* $11\frac{1}{2}$.

E41	E **4**	20 c. red	..	..	..	4·00	1·00

7 Councillor   **8** Arms   **9** Market Place,
                                     Ordino

10 Shrine near   **11** Map
Meritxell Chapel

1948 (16 Feb)–**53.** *Photo (2 c., 5 c., 10 c.), recess (others). P* $12\frac{1}{2}$, *(2 c., 5 c., 10 c., 25 c.),* 10 *(4 p., 10 p.) or* $9\frac{1}{2} \times 10\frac{1}{2}$ *(others).*

41	–	2 c. olive (12.6.51)	..	..	35	20
42	–	5 c. orange (8.1.53)	..	..	35	20
43	–	10 c. deep blue (8.1.53)	..		35	20
44	**7**	20 c. purple	..	..	3·75	50
45		25 c. yellow-orange (8.1.53)		..	2·40	30
46	**8**	30 c. deep green	..	..	3·75	50
47	**9**	50 c. green	..	..	5·50	75
48	**10**	75 c. blue	..	..	7·00	75
49	**9**	90 c. claret	..	..	2·75	75
50	**10**	1 p. orange-red	..	..	5·50	75
51	**8**	1 p. 35, violet-blue	..	..	2·75	1·00
52	**11**	4 p. bright blue (8.1.53)	..		5·50	1·40
53		10 p. brown-purple (12.6.51)	..		7·50	2·40
41/53		*Set of 13*	..	..	42·00	9·00

Design:—2 c. to 10 c. Edelweiss (frame as T **7**).

E **12** Squirrel (after Dürer)   **12** Shrine
and Coat-of-Arms

1949 (1 Aug). *EXPRESS LETTER. Recess. P* 10.

E54	E **12**	25 c. orange-red	..	..	2·40	1·00

1951 (27 June). *AIR. Recess. P* 11.

54	**12**	1 p. slate-purple	..	..	..	8·00	1·00

13 St. Anthony's Bridge

14 Narcissus
(*N. pseudonarcissus*)

1963 (20 July–**64**. *T* **13** *and similar designs. Recess. P* 13.

55	25 c. bistre-brown and grey-black	..	5	5
56	70 c. black-olive and deep bluish green	..	5	5
57	1 p. reddish violet and grey-blue	..	20	5
58	2 p. reddish violet and violet	..	20	5
59	2 p. 50, reddish purple (29.2.64)	..	40	12
60	3 p. deep slate-green and black (29.2.64)		60	12
61	5 p. dull purple and sepia (29.2.64)	..	80	35
62	6 p. carmine-red and sepia (29.2.64)	..	1·00	35
55/62	*Set of 8*	..	3·00	1·00

Designs: *Vert*—70 c. Aryos meadows (spelt wrongly on stamp); 1 p. Canillo; 2 p. St. Coloma belfry; 2 p. 50, Andorran arms; 6 p. Madonna of Meritxell. *Horiz*—3 p. Andorra-la-vieja; 5 p. Ordino.

1966 (10 June). *Pyrenean Flowers. T* **14** *and similar vert designs. Recess. P* 13.

63	50 c. blue and slate-blue	..	12	5
64	1 p. maroon and yellow-brown		15	5
65	5 p. slate-blue and blue-green	..	40	20
66	10 p. deep slate-violet and violet		1·00	25
63/66	*Set of 4*	..	1·50	45

Designs:—1 p. Carnation; 5 p. Narcissus (*N. poeticus*); 10 p. Anemone (*Pulsatilla vernalis*) (*wrongly inscribed* "HELEBORUS CONI").

15 "Communications"

16 Encamp Valley

1972 (2 May). *Europa. Photo. P* 13.
67 **15** 8 p. multicoloured .. .. .. 48·00 35·00

1972 (4 July). *Tourist Views. T* **16** *and similar multicoloured designs. Photo. P* 13.

68	1 p. Type **16**	..	10	5
69	1 p. 50, La Massana	..	25	15
70	2 p. Skis and snowscape, Pas de la Casa	..	40	15
71	5 p. Lake Pessons (*horiz*)	..	55	25
68/71	*Set of 4*	..	1·25	55

17 Volleyball

18 St. Anthony's Auction

1972 (26 Aug). *Olympic Games, Munich. T* **17** *and similar multicoloured design. Photo. P* 13.
72 2 p. Type **17** 25 15
73 5 p. Swimming (*horiz*) 25 15

1972 (5 Dec). *Andorran Customs. T* **18** *and similar multicoloured designs. Photo. P* 13.

74	1 p. Type **18**	..	5	5
75	1 p. 50, "Les Caramelles" (choir)	..	5	5
76	2 p. Nativity play	..	10	5
77	5 p. Giant cigar (*vert*)	..	20	5
78	8 p. Carved shrine, Meritxell (*vert*)	..	25	15
79	15 p. "La Marratxa" (dance)	..	60	25
74/79	*Set of 6*	..	1·10	55

19 "Peoples of Europe"   **20** "The Nativity"

1973 (30 Apr). *Europa. T* **19** *and similar horiz design. Photo. P* 13.
80 2 p. black, red and blue 12 10
81 8 p. red, black and pale brown 35 30
Design:—8 p. Europa "Posthorn".

1973 (14 Dec). *Christmas. Frescoes from Meritxell Chapel. T* **20** *and similar vert design. Multicoloured. Photo. P* 13.
82 2 p. Type **20** 5 5
83 5 p. "Adoration of the Kings" 20 10

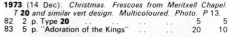

21 "Virgin of Orchino"   **22** Oak Cupboard and Shelves

1974 (29 Apr). *Europa. Sculptures. T* **21** *and similar vert design. Multicoloured. Photo. P* 13.
84 2 p. Type **21** 5 5
85 8 p. Cross 30 10

1974 (30 July). *Arts and Crafts. T* **22** *and similar vert design. Multicoloured. Photo. P* 13.
86 10 p. Type **22** 25 10
87 25 p. Crown of the Virgin of the Roses .. 60 25

23 Universal Postal Union
Monument, Berne

1974 (9 Oct). *Centenary of Universal Postal Union. Photo. P* 13.
88 **23** 15 p. multicoloured 45 20

| 24 "The Nativity" | 25 19th-Century Postman |

| 30 Slalom Skiing | 31 "The Nativity" |

1974 (4 Dec). *Christmas. Carvings from Meritxell Chapel. T 24 and similar horiz design. Multicoloured. Photo. P 13.*
89   2 p. Type **24**   5   5
90   5 p. "Adoration of the Kings"   ..   15   5

1975 (4 Apr). *"Espana 75" International Stamp Exhibition, Madrid. Photo. P 13.*
91 **25** 3 p. multicoloured   12   5

1976 (9 July). *Olympic Games, Montreal. T 30 and similar multicoloured design. Photo. P 13.*
99   7 p. Type **30**   15   8
100   15 p. Canoeing (*horiz*)   35   12

1976 (7 Dec). *Christmas. Carvings from La Massana Church. T 31 and similar horiz design. Multicoloured. Photo. P 13.*
101   3 p. Type **31**   8   5
102   25 p. "The Adoration"   45   15

| 26 "Peasant with Knife" | 27 Cathedral and Consecration Text |

| 32 Ansalonge | 33 Cross at Terme |

1975 (28 Apr). *Europa. 12th-century Romanesque Paintings from Ordino Church. T 26 and similar vert design. Multicoloured. Photo. P 13.*
92   3 p. Type **26**   10   5
93   12 p. "Christ"   30   15

1975 (4 Oct). *1100th Anniv of Urgel Cathedral Consecration. Photo. P 13.*
94 **27** 7 p. multicoloured   75   50

1976 (2 May). *Europa. T 32 and similar horiz design. Multicoloured. Photo. P 13.*
103   3 p. Type **32**   5   5
104   12 p. Xuclar   20   8

1977 (2 Dec). *Christmas. T 33 and similar vert design. Multicoloured. Photo. P 13×12½.*
105   5 p. Type **33**   5   5
106   12 p. St. Miquel's Church, Engolasters   15   8

| 28 "The Nativity" | 29 Copper Cauldron |

| 34 Map of Andorran Post Offices | 35 House of the Valleys |

1975 (2 Dec). *Christmas. Paintings from Ordino Church. T 28 and similar horiz design. Multicoloured. Photo. P 13.*
95   3 p. Type **28**   15   8
96   7 p. "Adoration of the Kings"   ..   20   12

1976 (3 May). *Europa. T 29 and similar multicoloured design. Photo. P 13.*
97   3 p. Type **29**   12   5
98   12 p. Wooden chest (*horiz*)   ..   20   10

1978 (31 Mar). *50th Anniv of Spanish Post Offices. Sheet 105×149 mm containing T 34 and similar vert designs. Multicoloured. Photo. P 13.*
MS107   5 p. Type **34**; 10 p. Postman delivering letter, 1928; 20 p. Spanish Post Office; 25 p. Post House Arms, 1928   ..   ..   1·40   60

1978 (2 May). *Europa. T 35 and similar horiz design. Multicoloured. Photo. P 13.*
108   5 p. Type **35**   5   5
109   12 p. Church of Sant Joan de Caselles   20   8

36 Crown, Mitre and Crook

1978 (July). *700th Anniv of Parity Treaties. Photo.* P 13.
110 **36** 5 p. multicoloured   5   5

37 "Holy Family"

1978 (5 Dec). *Christmas. T 37 and similar vert design showing frescoes in the Church of St. Mary d'Encamp. Multicoloured. Photo.* P 13.
111   5 p. Type **37**   5   5
112   25 p. "Adoration of the Kings"   45   15

PHILATELIC TERMS ILLUSTRATED

This successful STAMP MONTHLY series has now been brought together in a snappy black and yellow binding and published as a useful addition to Stanley Gibbons range of essential handbooks for keen stamp collectors.
Within its 192 pages this handy limp-bound volume houses a veritable mine of useful information on the words and phrases used in philately. It describes and illustrates printing processes and watermarks, papers and perforations, errors and varieties . . . and it does all this IN COLOUR. Indeed, there are 92 full page plates in colour, plus many black and white illustrations, making it

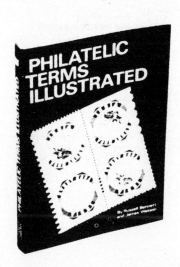

FANTASTIC VALUE AT ONLY £1·95 POST PAID FROM
Stanley Gibbons Publications Ltd
391 Strand, London WC2R 0LX

Monaco

100 Centimes=1 French Franc

The sovereignty of Monaco was recognised by France in 1512; in 1793, during the French Revolution, it was annexed by the French, and in 1815 the treaty of Vienna placed it under Sardinian protection. By a treaty of 2 February 1861 Monaco became completely independent.

Between 1851 and 1860, the first four issues of Sardinia were used in Monaco. French postal services commenced in June 1860, using French stamps (T 3–10), with Sardinian cancellations until September 1860, then various French cancellations (numerals in a lozenge of dots and circular date-stamps). From 1 July until 31 March 1886, French stamps could only be used together with T 1 of Monaco.

Prince Charles III
20 June 1856–10 September 1889

PRINTERS. All Monaco stamps were printed at the French Government Printing Works, Paris, *except where otherwise stated.*

| | 1 | | | 2 | |

(Des D. Depuiš. Eng E. Mouchon. Typ.)

1885 (1 July–Sept). *P* 14 × 13½.
1	**1**	1 c. olive-green (Sept)			5·00	5·00
2		2 c. dull lilac (Sept)			14·00	10·00
		a. *Slate-purple*			16·00	11·00
3		5 c. blue			20·00	15·00
4		10 c. red-brown/*straw* (Sept)			25·00	16·00
5		15 c. rose			80·00	6·00
		a. *Pale rose*			80·00	6·00
6		25 c. blue-green			£225	18·00
7		40 c. indigo/*rose* (Sept)			22·00	16·00
8		75 c. black/*rose* (Sept)			50·00	25·00
9		1 f. black/*yellow* (Sept)			£475	£220
10		5 f. carmine/*green* (Sept)			£1200	£825

Prince Albert
10 September 1889–26 June 1922

(Eng E. Mouchon. Typo)

1891 (Mar)–**94**. *P* 14 × 13½.
11	**2**	1 c. olive-green (15.4.91)			25	25
		a. *Bronze-green*			25	25
12		2 c. maroon (15.4.91)			25	25
		a. *Slate-lilac*			25	25
		b. *Slate-purple*			25	25
13		5 c. pale blue (8.91)			15·00	1·25
		a. *Blue*			15·00	1·25
14		10 c. brown/*yellow* (10.93)			40·00	6·50
		a. *Purple-brown/yellow*			40·00	7·00
15		15 c. bright rose (6.91)			45·00	1·60
		a. *Dull rose*			45·00	1·60
16		25 c. deep grey-green (7.91)			£100	10·00
		a. *Pale grey-green*			£100	10·00
17		40 c. *lilac/pale rose* (20.11.94)			2·00	95
		a. *Bluish black/rose*			2·00	90
18		50 c. brown/*orange* (shades) (5.91)			2·25	1·40
		a. *Violet-brown/orange*			4·25	3·75
19		75 c. violet-brown/*buff* (1.94)			8·00	5·00
		a. *Lilac-brown/buff*			9·00	5·00
20		1 f. black/*yellow-green* (3.91)			4·50	3·75
		a. *Black/yellow*			5·50	3·75
21		5 f. rose/*greenish* (8.4.91)			32·00	22·00
		a. *Deep carmine/greenish*			50·00	28·00

1901–21. *Colours changed.*
22	**2**	5 c. yellow-green			30	25
23		10 c. carmine-red			40	30
		b. *Vermilion* (3.21)			40	30

24		15 c. purple-brown/*yellowish*			75	45
25		15 c. myrtle-green (1921)			1·20	1·20
26		25 c. blue (*shades*)			2·25	60
27		75 c. brown/*buff* (1921)			4·00	3·50
28		5 f. mauve (1920)			80·00	80·00
29		5 f. grey-green (1921)			12·00	12·00

A mark consisting of the letters "OL" (="origine locale") in a dotted circle is a control applied to stamps used on letters posted in Monte Carlo Supérieur (French territory), correspondence from which district was dealt with, by arrangement, by the Monaco postal authorities. It was in use until 1904. In 1908 the French Government established its own post office.

| D 3 | | D 4 |

1905–09. *POSTAGE DUE.* Typo. *P* 14 × 13½.
D29	D **3**	1 c. olive			20	20
		a. *Deep olive*			20	20
D30		5 c. green			35	20
D31		10 c. carmine-red			15	15
		a. *Carmine*			15	15
D32		10 c. sepia (1909)			£150	50·00
D33		15 c. purple/*cream*			90	40
D34		30 c. blue			15	15
D35		50 c. brown/*buff*			1·60	1·10
		See also Nos. D113/21.				

1910. *POSTAGE DUE.* Typo. *P* 14 × 13½.
D36	D **4**	1 c. olive			12	12
D37		10 c. lilac			20	20
D38		30 c. bistre			90·00	75·00

| (3) | (D **5**) | **4** War Widow and Monaco |

1914 (Oct). *Red Cross Fund.* Surch with T **3**, *in red.*
30		10 c.+5 c. carmine-red			2·25	1·60

1919. *POSTAGE DUE.* Surch as Type D **5**.
D39	D **4**	20 c. on 10 c. lilac			75	65
D40		40 c. on 30 c. bistre			75	65

1919 (20 Sept). *War Orphans Fund.* Typo. *P* 14 × 13½.
31	**4**	2 c.+3 c. dull purple			6·50	6·50
32		5 c.+5 c. bluish green			5·00	5·00
33		15 c.+10 c. carmine			5·00	5·00
34		25 c.+15 c. blue			12·00	12·00
35		50 c.+50 c. brown/*orange*			50·00	50·00
36		1 f.+1 f. black/*yellow*			£150	£150
37		5 f.+5 f. rose-red			£550	£550
31/37		*Set of 7*			£700	£700

20 mars
1920

28
DÉCEMBRE
1920

5ᶜ +5ᶜ

25ᶜ·

| (5) | (6) | (7) |

1920 (20 Mar). *Marriage of Princess Charlotte. Surch as T **5** or optd only.*

38	**4**	2 c.+3 c. on 15 c.+10 c.	..	15·00	15·00
39		2 c.+3 c. on 25 c.+15 c.	..	15·00	15·00
40		2 c.+3 c. on 50 c.+50 c.	..	15·00	15·00
41		5 c.+5 c. on 1 f.+1 f.	..	15·00	15·00
42		5 c.+5 c. on 5 f.+5 f.	..	14·00	14·00
43		15 c.+10 c. carmine	..	9·50	9·50
44		25 c.+15 c. blue	..	4·50	4·50
45		50 c.+50 c. brown/*orange*	..	19·00	19·00
46		1 f.+1 f. black/*yellow*	..	19·00	19·00
47		5 f.+5 f. rose-red	..	£2250	£2250

1921 (5 Mar). *Baptism of Princess Antoinette. Optd as T **6** or surch also.*

48	**2**	5 c. yellow-green	..	25	25
49		75 c. brown/*buff*	..	2·50	2·50
50		2 f. on 5 f. mauve	..	17·00	17·00

1922. *Surch as T **7**.*

51	**2**	20 c. on 15 c. myrtle-green	..	80	65
52		25 c. on 10 c. rose-red	..	45	40
53		50 c. on 1 f. black/*yellow*	..	3·75	3·00

Prince Louis II, 26 June, 1922–9 May, 1949

8 Prince Albert I   **9** Viaduct and St. Dévote

(Des H. Cheffer. Recess Maison Braun, Paris (early ptgs) and French Govt Ptg Works)

1922 (15 July)—**24.** *T **8** and various views as T **9**. P 11.*

54		25 c. olive-brown	..	2·50	2·50
55		30 c. myrtle-green (11.22)	..	65	65
56		30 c. vermilion (1923)	..	25	25
57		40 c. chestnut (1.24)	..	25	25
58		50 c. bright blue	..	2·75	2·75
59		60 c. sepia-grey (11.22)	..	15	15
60		1 f. black/*yellow* (12.22)	..	15	15
61		2 f. scarlet (12.22)	..	1·25	1·25
		a. Vermilion (1923)	..	25	
62		5 f. deep brown	..	22·00	22·00
63		5 f. deep green/*blue* (10.24)	..	3·25	2·50
64		10 f. carmine (1922)	..	7·00	5·00
		a. Rose (1924)	..	7·00	7·00
54/64a		*Set of 11*	..	35·00	35·00

Designs: *Horiz*—30 c., 50 c. Oceanographic Museum; 60 c., 1 f., 2 f. The Rock; 5 f., 10 f. Prince's Palace, Monaco.

12 Prince Louis   **13** Prince Louis and Palace

(Designer, etc, as last)

1923 (14 June)—**24.** *P 11.*

65	**12**	10 c. green (1.24)	..	25	25
66		15 c. carmine (3.24)	..	45	45
67		20 c. deep red-brown (1923)	..	25	25
68		25 c. purple	..	20	20
69	**13**	50 c. blue	..	20	20
65/69		*Set of 5*	..	1·25	1·25

Nos. 65/9 and 59 may be found showing portions of the paper-maker's watermark "BFK RIVES" (Blanchet Frères et Kleber, Rives).

1924 (5 Aug). *Surch as T **7** (two bars only).*

70	**2**	45 on 50 c. brown/*buff*	..	45	45
71		75 on 1 f. black/*yellow*	..	30	30
72		85 on 5 f. grey-green	..	30	30

14   **15**   **16**

1
franc
à percevoir

17 Viaduct and St. Dévote   D **18**   (D **19**)

(T **14** des Brefort; remainder H. Cheffer. Die eng G. Daussy. Typo)

1924 (1 Dec)—**33.** *T **14** to **17** and similar type. P 14×13½.*

73	**14**	1 c. grey-black	..	8	8
74		2 c. red-brown ('25)	..	10	10
75		3 c. bright magenta ('33)	..	80	20
76		5 c. orange (1.26)	..	20	20
77		10 c. light blue	..	15	15
78	**15**	15 c. yellow-green	..	15	15
79		15 c. violet ('29)	..	1·10	65
80		20 c. magenta	..	12	8
81		20 c. carmine-pink ('26)	..	20	15
82		25 c. carmine-pink	..	10	8
83		25 c. red/*yellow* ('26)	..	20	15
84		30 c. orange	..	15	15
85		40 c. brown	..	10	8
86		40 c. light blue/*azure* ('26)	..	15	12
87		45 c. grey-black ('26)	..	45	25
88	**16**	50 c. blue-green ('25)	..	20	15
89	**15**	50 c. brown/*yellow* ('26)	..	15	8
90	**16**	60 c. yellow-brown ('25)	..	15	15
91	**15**	60 c. green/*greenish* ('26)	..	15	8
92		75 c. green/*greenish* ('26)	..	15	15
93		75 c. carmine/*pale yellow* (6.26)	..	15	15
94		75 c. grey-black ('27)	..	40	20
95		80 c. red/*yellow* ('25)	..	25	20
96		90 c. carmine/*pale yellow* (9.2.27)	..	40	30
97	**17**	1 f. black/*yellow* (1.25)	..	15	15
98		1 f. 05, magenta (12.25)	..	15	15
99		1 f. 10, blue-green (4.27)	..	5·00	2·50
100	**15**	1 f. 25, blue/*azure* (6.26)	..	15	15
101		1 f. 50, blue/*azure* ('27)	..	65	45
102	—	2 f. sepia and bright violet ('25)	..	70	55
103		3 f. lavender and red/*yellow* ('27)	..	3·50	2·50
104	—	5 f. rose and green ('25)	..	3·50	2·25
105	—	10 f. blue and brown ('25)	..	5·50	4·00
73/105		*Set of 33*	..	23·00	15·00

Design: As T **17**—2 f. to 10 f. View of Monaco. No. 95 is on chalk-surfaced paper.

1924 (Dec)—**32.** *POSTAGE DUE. Typo. P 14×13½.*

D106	D **18**	1 c. olive-green (1925)	..	10	10
D107		10 c. violet (1.25)	..	12	12
D108		30 c. bistre	..	12	12
D109		60 c. red (1.25)	..	20	15
D110		1 f. pale blue (1932)	..	50·00	38·00
D111		2 f. scarlet (1932)	..	65·00	45·00

1925 (Nov). *POSTAGE DUE. Surch with Type D **19**.*

D112	D **3**	1 f. on 50 c. brown/*buff*	..	25	20
		a. Surch double	..	£160	

30

(19)

20 Princes Charles III, Louis II and Albert I

1926–31. *Surch as T **19**.*

106	**15**	30 on 25 c. carmine-pink (20.2.26)	..	15	12
107		50 on 60 c. green/*greenish* (11.28)	..	40	15

108	**17**	50 on 1 f. 05, magenta (10.28) ..		30	25
109		50 on 1 f. 10, blue-green (1931) ..		1·60	95
110	**15**	50 on 1 f. 25, blue/*azure* (R.) (10.28)		40	25
111		1 f. 25 on 1 f. blue/*azure* (1.5.26) ..		30	20
112	—	1 f. 50 on 2 f. sepia and bright violet (No. 102) (11.28) ..		1·25	65
106/112		*Set of 7*		4·00	2·25

1926—43. *POSTAGE DUE.* P 14 × 13½.

D113	D **3**	20 c. bistre/*buff*		8	8
D114		40 c. bright magenta		8	8
D115		50 c. blue-green (1.27) ..		8	8
D116		60 c. grey-black		25	25
D117		60 c. magenta (11.34)		5·00	5·00
D118		1 f. maroon/*cream*		10	10
D119		2 f. orange-vermilion (10.27) ..		20	20
D120		3 f. rosine (10.27)		20	20
D121		5 f. blue (1943)		20	20
D113/121		*Set of 9*		5·50	5·50

Nos. D113 and D118 are on chalk-surfaced paper.

(Des H. Cheffer. Recess)

1928 (18 Feb). *International Philatelic Exhibition, Monte Carlo.* P 11.

113	**20**	50 c. crimson		75	75
114		1 f. 50, blue		75	75
115		3 f. deep violet		75	75

Sold at Exhibition only (entrance fee 5 f.).

20*a*

21 Palace Entrance   **22** St. Dévote's Church

21*a* The Prince's Residence (*horiz*)

23 Prince Louis II   **24** The Rock of Monaco

25 Palace Gardens (*horizontal*)

26 Fortifications and Harbour (*horizontal*)

(Des J. G. Goulinat (T **21** to **26**). Eng G. Hourriez (**21** and **24**); A. Delzers (**20***a*, **22**, **25** and **26**); and J. Piel (remainder). Recess)

1933 (17 Jan)—**39.** *P* 13 *or* 14 × 13 (*T* 20*a* and 23).

116	**20***a*	1 c. plum (4.38)		5	5
117		2 c. emerald-green (7.38) ..		5	5
118		3 c. bright purple (7.38) ..		5	5
119		5 c. scarlet (1937)		8	5
120		10 c. ultramarine (1937) ..		5	5
121		15 c. bright violet (24.8.39) ..		45	40
122	**21**	15 c. carmine		40	15
123		20 c. yellow-brown ..		40	15
124	**21***a*	25 c. sepia		50	25
125	**22**	30 c. bright green ..		65	25
126	**23**	40 c. chocolate		1·00	65
127	**24**	45 c. red-brown		1·60	40
		a. Brick-red		£110	£110
128	**23**	50 c. violet		90	30
129	**25**	65 c. deep blue-green ..		1·60	25
130	**26**	75 c. blue		1·90	1·10
131	**23**	90 c. scarlet		1·90	95
132	**22**	1 f. red-brown (6.33) ..		6·50	3·75
133	**26**	1 f. 25, claret		2·50	1·90
134	**23**	1 f. 50, ultramarine ..		7·50	3·75

135	**21***a*	1 f. 75, claret		9·50	1·90
136		1 f. 75, carmine (1937) ..		11·00	1·90
137	**24**	2 f. indigo..		3·75	1·90
138	**21**	3 f. violet		5·00	2·50
139	**21***a*	3 f. 50, orange (1935) ..		25·00	13·00
140	**22**	5 f. purple		11·00	7·50
141	**21***a*	10 f. blue		38·00	23·00
142	**25**	20 f. brown-black		70·00	40·00
116/142		*Set of 27*		£300	£190

For later issues in T 20*a*, see Nos. 249/255.

(27)

1933 (22 Aug). *AIR. No.* 104 *surch with T* **27.**

143		1 f. 50 on 5 f. rose and green ..		13·00	9·00

28 Palace Gardens   **29** Prince Louis II

(Des E. Clerissi (views). Eng Degorce and H. Cheffer (views) and Ouvré (portrait). T **29.** Photograph by Taponier. Recess)

1937 (Apr). *As T* **28** (*views*) *and T* **29.** *P* 13.

144	**28**	50 c.+50 c. bright green ..		1·25	1·25
145		90 c.+90 c. scarlet ..		1·25	1·25
146	—	1 f. 50+1 f. 50, ultramarine ..		2·50	2·50
147	**29**	2 f.+2 f. bright violet ..		3·25	3·25
148		5 f.+5 f. dull lake		35·00	35·00
144/148		*Set of 5*		40·00	40·00

Designs:—90 c. Exotic gardens; 1 f. 50 Bay of Monaco.

(30)

31 Prince Louis II   30*a*

1937 (20 Dec)—**38.** *Nos.* D107/11 *surch or optd as T* **30.** (*Surch on No.* 149 *has two obliterating bars.*)

149		5 on 10 c. violet		45	45
150		10 c. violet		45	45
151		15 on 30 c. bistre		45	45
152		20 on 30 c. bistre		45	45
153		25 on 60 c. red		70	65
154		30 c. bistre		1·10	1·00
155		40 on 60 c. red		95	95
156		50 on 60 c. red		1·25	75
157		65 on 1 f. pale blue		95	75
158		85 on 1 f. pale blue		1·90	1·60
159		1 f. pale blue		1·90	1·60
160		2 f. 15 on 2 f. scarlet ..		2·75	2·50
161		2 f. 25 on 2 f. scarlet (1.38) ..		3·75	3·25
162		2 f. 50 on 2 f. scarlet (1.38) ..		5·00	4·50
149/162		*Set of 14*		20·00	16·00

Monaco 1938

(Des Taponier. Eng H. Cheffer. Recess)

1938 (17 Jan). *National Fête Day. Sheet* 100 × 120 *mm.*
Imperf.
MS163 **30**a 10 f. bright purple .. .. 14·00 13·00

(Des Taponier. Eng H. Cheffer. Recess)

1938 (May)—**39**. *P* 14 × 13.
164	**31**	55 c. red-brown			..	1·25	65
165		65 c. bright violet	..	..	..	9·00	3·75
166		70 c. red-brown (21.2.39)	..		10	10
167		90 c. bright violet (1.39)	..	..	5	5
168		1 f. scarlet ..	..	..	..	2·10	1·25
169		1 f. 25, scarlet (21.2.39)	..	..	20	15
170		1 f. 75, bright blue ..	..	..	3·50	2·10
171		2 f. 25, bright blue (21.2.39)	..	20	15
164/171		*Set of* 8	..	..	..	15·00	7·50

32 Pierre and Marie Curie   **33** Monaco Hospital

(Eng Degorce and A. Delzers. Recess)

1938 (15 Nov). *Anti-Cancer Fund. 40th Anniv of Discovery
of Radium. P* 13.
172	**32**	65 c.+25 c. green	..	..	3·50	3·50
173	**33**	1 f. 75+50 c. ultramarine ..	..	3·75	3·75

34 The Cathedral   **35** Place St. Nicholas

36 Palace Gateway (*vertical*)

37 Palace of Monaco (*vertical*)

38 Monaco Harbour

39 Aerial View of Monaco (*horizontal*)

(T **34, 36**. Des and eng H. Cheffer. T **35, 38**. Des Tournay,
eng Degorce. T **37**. Des and eng A. Delzers. T **39**.
Des Tournay, eng J. Piel. Recess)

1939 (21 Feb)—**41**. *P* 13.
174	**34**	20 c. magenta	..	..	..	10	10
175	**35**	25 c. brown ..	..	..	..	25	15
176	**36**	30 c. green ..	..	..	..	20	15
177	**35**	40 c. brown-red	..	..	..	40	25
178	**39**	45 c. bright purple	..	..	..	15	15
179	**37**	50 c. green	..	..	..	15	15
180	**36**	60 c. carmine	..	..	..	25	20
181		60 c. green	..	..	..	15	15
182	**38**	70 c. bright lilac (1941)	..	..	15	10
183		75 c. deep green	..	..	..	15	15
184	**37**	1 f. olive-black	..	..	..	15	15
185		1 f. 30, sepia (1941)	..	..	15	15
186	**35**	2 f. purple ..	..	..	..	20	20
187	**39**	2 f. 50, scarlet	..	..	..	9·00	5·00

188	**39**	2 f. 50, ultramarine (1940)	..	45	15
189	**38**	3 f. brown-red	..	..	..	20	15
190	**34**	5 f. turquoise-blue ..	..	..	65	25
191	**39**	10 f. green ..	..	..	..	75	25
192	**36**	20 f. bright blue	..	..	..	95	25
174/192		*Set of* 19	..	..	..	13·00	7·50

For later issues in T **34/9**, Nos. 250/70, 362/74 and 391/407.

40 Louis II Stadium

(Des J. Fissore. Eng Degorce. Recess)

1939 (23 Apr). *Inauguration of Louis II Stadium, Monaco.
P* 13.
198 **40** 10 f. green .. .. 70·00 65·00

41 Lucien   **42** The Rock of Monaco

(Eng H. Cheffer (5 c., 10 c., 5 f.). Degorce (45 c., 2 f. 25).
A. Delzers (70 c., 2 f.). J. Piel (90 c.). Ouvré (1 f., 3 f.).
Recess)

1939 (26 June). *National Relief. As T* **41** (XVI—XVII *century
portraits*) *and T* **42** (5 *f.*). *P* 13.
199		5 c.+5 c. black			65	65
200		10 c.+10 c. purple	..	..	65	65
201		45 c.+15 c. emerald-green	..	1·25	1·25
202		70 c.+30 c. magenta ..	..	2·75	2·75
203		90 c.+35 c. bright violet	..	2·75	2·75
204		1 f.+1 f. ultramarine ..	..	9·00	9·00
205		2 f.+2 f. brown-red ..	..	9·50	9·50
206		2 f. 25+1 f. 25, turquoise-blue	..	14·00	14·00
207		3 f.+3 f. carmine	..	..	20·00	20·00
208		5 f.+5 f. scarlet	..	..	40·00	40·00
199/208		*Set of* 10	..	..	90·00	90·00

Portraits:—10 c. Honoré II; 45 c. Louis I; 70 c. Charlotte de
Gramont; 90 c. Antoine I; 1 f. Marie de Lorraine; 2 f. Jacques I;
2 f. 25, Louise-Hippolyte; 3 f. Honoré III.

1939 (14 Aug). *VIII International University Games. As T* **40**,
but inscr "VIIIeme JEUX UNIVERSITAIRES INTERNATION-
AUX 1939". *Recess. P* 13.
209		40 c. blue-green	..	..	75	75
210		70 c. sepia	..	..	..	80	80
211		90 c. violet	..	..	..	1·00	1·00
212		1 f. 25, red	..	..	..	1·00	1·00
213		2 f. 25, deep blue	..	..	1·75	1·75
209/213		*Set of* 5	..	..	4·75	4·75

(43)   **44** Prince Louis II

1940 (10 Feb). *Red Cross Ambulance Fund. As Nos.* 174 *etc.,
but in new colours and surch as T* **43**, *in scarlet.*
214	**34**	20 c.+1 f. violet	..	..	1·60	1·60
215	**35**	25 c.+1 f. green	..	..	1·60	1·60
216	**36**	30 c.+1 f. brown-red	..	..	1·60	1·60
217	**35**	40 c.+1 f. blue	..	..	1·60	1·60
218	**39**	45 c.+1 f. carmine	..	..	1·60	1·60
219	**37**	50 c.+1 f. reddish brown	..	1·90	1·90
220	**36**	60 c.+1 f. green	..	..	1·90	1·90

221	**38**	75 c.+1 f. olive-black	..	..	1·90	1·90

221 **38** 75 c.+1 f. olive-black .. .. 1·90 1·90
222 **37** 1 f.+1 f. scarlet .. .. 1·90 1·90
223 **35** 2 f.+1 f. greenish slate .. .. 2·25 2·25
224 **39** 2 f. 50+1 f. green .. .. 4·50 4·50
225 **38** 3 f.+1 f. blue .. .. 5·50 5·50
226 **34** 5 f.+1 f. olive-black .. .. 6·50 6·50
227 **39** 10 f.+5 f. turquoise-blue .. 7·50 7·50
228 **36** 20 f.+5 f. maroon .. .. 9·00 9·00
214/228 *Set of* 15 .. .. .. 45·00 45·00

(Des A. Somos Talbor. Eng Ouvré. Recess)

1941 (May)—**46**. *P* 14 × 13.
229 **44** 40 c. brown-carmine 10 10
230 80 c. green 10 10
231 1 f. rose-violet 10 10
232 1 f. 20, green (1942) 8 8
233 1 f. 50, rose 8 8
234 1 f. 50, violet (1942) 8 8
235 2 f. green (1946) 10 10
236 2 f. 40, carmine (1942) 8 8
237 2 f. 50, bright blue 20 20
238 4 f. ultramarine (1942) 8 8
229/238 *Set of* 10 .. .. 90 90

45 **46**

(Des J. Julien. Eng J. Piel (T **45**) and H. Cheffer (T **46**).
Recess)

1941 (15 May). *National Relief Fund. P* 13.
239 **45** 25 c.+25 c. bright purple 90 90
240 **46** 50 c.+25 c. dark brown 90 90
241 75 c.+50 c. rose-violet .. .. 1·10 1·10
242 **45** 1 f.+1 f. dark blue.. .. .. 1·10 1·10
243 **46** 1 f. 50+1 f. 50, rose-red .. .. 1·40 1·40
244 **45** 2 f.+2 f. dark green .. .. 1·40 1·40
245 **46** 2 f. 50+2 f. bright blue .. .. 1·40 1·40
246 **45** 3 f.+3 f. red-brown .. .. 1·40 1·40
247 **46** 5 f.+5 f. blue-green .. .. 1·90 1·90
248 **45** 10 f.+8 f. sepia .. .. 3·25 3·25
239/248 *Set of* 10 .. .. .. 13·00 13·00

1941–46. *New values and colours. P* 13 or 14 × 13 (*T* **20a**).
249 **20a** 10 c. black 5 5
250 **36** 30 c. red 20 15
251 **20a** 30 c. blue-green 10 10
252 40 c. carmine 5 5
253 50 c. violet 5 5
254 60 c. greenish blue 5 5
255 70 c. red-brown 8 8
256 **34** 80 c. blue-green 8 8
257 **39** 1 f. lilac-brown 8 8
258 **38** 1 f. 20, ultramarine (1946) .. 15 15
259 **35** 1 f. 50, ultramarine (1946) .. 15 15
260 **38** 2 f. ultramarine (1943) .. 8 8
261 **37** 2 f. emerald-green (1946).. .. 10 10
262 **35** 3 f. black 8 8
263 **34** 4 f. bright purple (1946) .. 25 25
264 **37** 4 f. 50, violet 10 10
265 **36** 5 f. green 10 10
266 **37** 6 f. bright violet (1946) .. 30 30
267 **34** 10 f. blue 10 10
268 **38** 15 f. carmine 20 15
269 **39** 20 f. sepia 20 15
270 **38** 25 f. green (1946) 70 50
249/270 *Set of* 22 .. .. .. 3·00 2·50

For later issues in T **34/9**, see Nos. 362/74 and 391/407.

STAMP MONTHLY

—finest and most informative magazine for all
collectors. Obtainable from your newsagent or
by postal subscription—details on request.

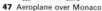

POSTE AÉRIENNE

47 Aeroplane over Monaco   **48** Propeller and Palace

49 Arms, Aeroplane and Globe

(Des Badia 5 f., 10 f., S. Tonetti 15 f., P. Bret, 20 f., Courvoisier
50 f., M. Ravarino 100 f. Eng Degorce 5 f., 10 f., Gandon 15 f.,
Serres 20 f., Piel 50 f., Cheffer 100 f. Recess)

1942 (15 Apr). *AIR. T* **47/9** *and similar designs. P* 13.
271 5 f. green 15 15
272 10 f. ultramarine 15 15
273 15 f. sepia 15 15
274 20 f. red-brown 30 30
275 50 f. bright purple .. .. 1·40 1·00
276 100 f. red and purple .. .. 1·40 75
271/276 *Set of* 6 .. .. .. 3·25 2·25
Designs: *Vert*—10 f. as T **47**; 20 f. Pegasus. *Horiz*—50 f.
Albatross over Bay of Monaco.

50 Charles II   **52** Prince Louis II

(Eng Serres 2 c., 20 f., Cottet 5 c., Feltesse 10 c., Gandon 20 c.,
Delzers 30 c., 3 f., Barlangue 40 c., Munier 50 c., Mazelin
75 c., Cheffer 1 f., Ouvré 1 f. 50, 10 f., Degorce 2 f. 50, 5 f.
Recess)

1942 (10 Dec). *National Relief Fund. Royal Personages.
Portraits as T* **50**. *P* 13.
277 2 c.+3 c. ultramarine 12 12
278 5 c.+5 c. red 12 12
279 10 c.+5 c. black 12 12
280 20 c.+10 c. emerald-green 12 12
281 30 c.+30 c. brown-purple 12 12
282 40 c.+40 c. carmine 12 12
283 50 c.+50 c. mauve 12 12
284 75 c.+75 c. bright purple 12 12
285 1 f.+1 f. blue-green 12 12
286 1 f. 50+1 f. brown-lake 12 12
287 2 f. 50+2 f. 50, violet 75 75
288 3 f.+3 f. greenish blue 90 90
289 5 f.+5 f. brown-black 90 90
290 10 f.+5 f. purple 90 90
291 20 f.+5 f. ultramarine .. .. 1·00 1·00
277/291 *Set of* 15 .. .. .. 5·00 5·00
Portraits: *Vert*—2 c. Rainier Grimaldi; 10 c. Jeanne Grimaldi;
20 c. Charles Auguste, Goyon de Matignon; 30 c. Jacques I;
40 c. Louise-Hippolyte; 50 c. Charlotte Grimaldi; 75 c. Marie
Charles Grimaldi; 1 f. Honoré III; 1 f. 50, Honoré IV; 2 f. 50,
Honoré V; 3 f. Florestan I; 5 f. Charles III; 10 f. Albert I; 20 f.
Princess Marie-Victoire.

(Eng Degorce. Recess)

1943–44. *P* 13.
292 **52** 50 f. violet 45 45
a. Lilac (1944) 75 75

53 St. Dévote

54 Blessing the Sea

55 Arrival of St. Dévote at Monaco   **(56)**

$$1^f + 4^f$$
$$=$$

(Des P. Gandon, 50 c., 70 c., 1 f 50, 5 f., 20 f.; Degorce, 80 c., 1 f., 2 f., 10 f. Eng. Ch. Mazelin, 50 c.; E. Feltesse, 70 c.; P. Munier, 80 c.; Degorce, 1 f., 10 f.; A. Delzers, 1 f. 50; Barlangue, 2 f.; P. Gandon, 5 f., 20 f. Recess)

1944 (27 Jan). *Festival of St. Dévote. T **53/5** and similar festival scenes. P* 13.

293	50 c.+50 c. sepia	..	..	15	15
294	70 c.+80 c. ultramarine	..	..	15	15
295	80 c.+70 c. green	..	..	15	15
296	1 f.+1 f. purple	..	..	15	15
297	1 f. 50+1 f. 50, scarlet	..	..	25	25
298	2 f.+2 f. brown-purple	..	..	25	25
299	5 f.+2 f. violet	..	..	25	25
300	10 f.+40 f. light blue	..	..	25	25
301	20 f.+60 f. blue	..	..	2·50	2·50
293/301	*Set of* 9	..	..	3·75	3·75

Designs: *Vert*—70 c., 1 f. various processional scenes; 1 f. 50, Burning the boat; 10 f. Trial scene. *Horiz*—80 c. Procession; 5 f. St. Dévote's Church.

1945 (27 Mar). *AIR. For War Dead and Deported Workers. As Nos.* 272/6, *colours changed, variously surch as T **56**.

302	1 f.+4 f. on 10 f. carmine	..	12	12
303	1 f.+4 f. on 15 f. red-brown	..	12	12
304	1 f.+4 f. on 20 f. sepia	..	12	12
305	1 f.+4 f. on 50 f. ultramarine	..	12	12
306	1 f.+4 f. on 100 f. bright purple	..	12	12
302/306	*Set of* 5	..	55	55

57   Prince Louis II   **58**

(Des and eng Mazelin. Recess)

1946. *P* 14 × 13 *or* 13 (*T* **58**).

307	**57**	2 f. 50, green	..	..	5	5
308		3 f. bright purple	..	..	8	5
309		6 f. scarlet	..	..	10	8
310		10 f. ultramarine	..	..	10	8

311	**58**	50 f. blue-grey	..	..	1·25	1·00
312		100 f. scarlet	..	..	1·90	1·50
307/312	*Set of* 6	..	..	..	3·25	2·50

For other values in T **57**, see Nos. 361/72 and 389/96.

59 Child Praying   **60** Nurse and Baby

(Eng Gandon. Recess)

1946 (18 Feb). *Child Welfare Fund. P* 13.

313	**59**	1 f.+3 f. blue-green		..	15	15
314		2 f.+4 f. carmine	..	..	15	15
315		4 f.+6 f. blue		..	15	15
316		5 f.+40 f. mauve	..		25	25
317		10 f.+60 f. brown-lake		..	25	25
318		15 f.+100 f. indigo	..		40	40
313/318	*Set of* 6	..	..	..	1·25	1·25

(Des Gandon. Eng Mazelin. Recess)

1946 (18 Feb). *Anti-tuberculosis Fund. P* 13.

319	**60**	2 f.+8 f. light blue	..		10	10

POSTE AÉRIENNE

(61)

1946 (20 May). *AIR. Optd with T **61** in blue.*

320	**58**	50 f. blue-grey	..	75	75
321		100 f. scarlet	..	1·10	1·10
		a. Opt inverted	..	£3500	

62 Steamship and Chart   **63**

(Des R. Hugon. Eng Cottet. Recess)

1946 (20 May). *Stamp Day. P* 13.

322	**62**	3 f.+2 f. blue	..	10	10

(Des R. Hugon. Eng J. Piel. Recess)

1946 (20 May)**–49.** *AIR. P* 13.

323	**63**	40 f. scarlet	50	35
324		50 f. brown-lake	60	40
325		100 f. turquoise-green	1·00	60
326		200 f. bright violet	1·40	90
326a		300 f. deep blue & ultram (10.3.49)	28·00	20·00
326b		500 f. green & dp bl-grn (10.3.49)	19·00	16·00
326c		1000 f. brt vio & purple-brn (10.3.49)	35·00	25·00
323/326c	*Set of* 7	..	75·00	55·00

D 64   **D 65**

(Eng Cottet. Recess)

1946 (20 May)–**57**. *POSTAGE DUE. P* 14×13 *or* 13 (*Type* D **64**).

D327	D **64**	10 c. blackish brown	10	10
D328		30 c. violet	10	10
D329		50 c. blue	10	10
D330		1 f. green	10	10
D331		2 f. yellow-brown	10	10
D332		3 f. magenta	20	20
D333		4 f. carmine	25	25
D334	D **65**	5 f. yellow-brown	20	20
D335		10 f. blue	30	30
D336		20 f. blue-green	35	35
D337		50 f. carmine & mag (28.9.50)	3·75	3·25
D338		100 f. red & deep green (11.5.57)	2·50	2·50
D327/338		*Set of* 12	7·50	7·50

64 Pres Roosevelt and Palace of Monaco

65 Pres Roosevelt and Map of Monaco   **66** Pres Roosevelt

(5 f. des and eng Barlangue, remainder des Gandon. Eng Mazelin (10 c.), Barlangue (30 c.), Piel (60 c,), Serres (1 f., 3 f.), Cottet (2 f.), Feltesse (10 f.), Dufresne (15 f.). Recess)

1946 (13 Dec). *President Roosevelt Commemoration. As T* **64**/**5** (*portrait and views*) *and T* **66**. *P* 13. (*a*) *POSTAGE. Inscr* "POSTES"

327	10 c. magenta	12	12
328	30 c. blue	12	12
329	60 c. blackish green	12	12
330	1 f. brown-purple	30	30
331	2 f.+3 f. greenish blue	40	40
332	3 f. violet	50	50

(*b*) *AIR. Inscr* "POSTE AÉRIENNE"

333	5 f. carmine	35	30
334	10 f. black	30	25
335	15 f.+10 f. red-orange	55	50
327/335	*Set of* 9	2·40	2·40

Designs: *Horiz*—30 c. without and 5 f. with aeroplane, the Rock of Monaco; 2 f. Viaduct and St. Dévote. *Vert*—3 f. without and 10 f. with aeroplane, as *T* **65**. *Triangular*—10 c. as *T* **66**.

67 Prince Louis II   **68** Pres Roosevelt as a Philatelist

69 Statue of Liberty and New York Harbour   **70** Prince Charles III

(Des T **67**, De Laszlo, other types Gandon. Eng, *Postage*— 10 f. (No. 336), Piel; *Air*—50 c. Barlangue, 1 f. 50 P. Munier, 3 f. Feltesse, 10 f. (No. 340) Mazelin, 15 f. Dufresne. Recess)

1947 (9 May). *Participation in the Centenary International Philatelic Exhibition, New York. P* 13. (*a*) *POSTAGE*.

336	**67** 10 f. greenish blue	1·10	1·10

(*b*) *AIR. Designs inscr* "1847 1947". 50 *c. to* 3 *f. as T* **68**; 10 *f. and* 15 *f. as T* **69**.

337	50 c. violet	15	15
338	1 f. 50, mauve	20	20
339	3 f. brown-red	20	20
340	10 f. ultramarine	1·10	1·10
341	15 f. carmine	95	95
336/341	*Set of* 6	2·40	2·40

Designs: (36½×22½ *mm.*)—1 f. 50, G.P.O., New York; 3 f. Oceanographic Museum, Monte Carlo (47×36 *mm.*)—10 f. Bay of Monaco.

Nos. 341, 336 and 340 were printed in that order, in sheets of 15 (5 × 3); each horizontal row containing one stamp of each value. The total (35 f.) represents the franking value of a registered air mail letter between Monaco and U.S.A. (*Price* £3·50 *un. or us.*)

1947. *Twenty-fifth Year of Reign of Prince Louis II. Sheet* 85 × 98 *mm. As T* **67**. *Imperf*.

MS341*a*	200 f.+300 f. blackish brown	4·00	4·00

(Des D. Dupuis. Eng J. Piel. Recess)

1948 (6 Mar). *Stamp Day. P* 14 × 13.

342	**70** 6 f.+4 f. green/*blue*	15	15

71 Diving   **72** Tennis

73 Hurdling   **74** Yachting

(Des Gandon and Ouvré (6 f.). Eng Cottet, Mazelin, Piel, Barlangue, Munier, Gandon, Ouvré, Serres and Dufresne. Recess)

1948 (12 July). *Participation in the Olympic Games, Wembley. As T* **71**/**4** (*inscr* "JEUX OLYMPIQUES 1948"). *P* 13.

(*a*) *POSTAGE. Inscr* "POSTES".

343	50 c. turquoise-green	15	15
344	1 f. lake	15	15
345	2 f. greenish blue	35	35
346	2 f. 50, scarlet	40	35

347 4 f. slate   45   40
Designs: *Vert*—1 f. Running; 2 f. Throwing the discus;
2 f. 50, Basket-ball.

        (b) *AIR. Inscr* "POSTE AÉRIENNE".
348 5 f. + 5 f. blackish brown ..   ..   4·00   4·00
349 6 f. + 9 f. violet ..   ..   ..   5·00   5·00
350 10 f. + 15 f. carmine ..   ..   6·00   6·00
351 15 f. + 25 f. blue ..   ..   ..   9·00   9·00
343/351 *Set of 9* ..   ..   .. 23·00 23·00
Designs: *Vert*—5 f. Rowing; 6 f. Skiing

75 The Salmacis Nymph   **76** Hercules struggling
                                 with Achelous

77 F. J. Bosio   **78** The Salmacis Nymph
(wrongly inscr "J.F.")

(Des Gandon. Eng Piel (50 c., 15 f.); Munier (1 f., 5 f.);
Dufresne (2 f., 6 f.); Mazelin (2 f. 50, 10 f.) and Cotte (
(4 f.). Recess)

1948 (12 July). *Death Centenary of Francois Joseph Bosio
(sculptor).* As T **75/8** (*designs inscr* "F. J. BOSIO 1769-
1845"). P 13. (a) *POSTAGE. Inscr* "POSTES".
352 50 c. blue-green   10   10
353 1 f. scarlet   10   10
354 2 f. blue   15   15
355 2 f. 50, bluish violet   20   20
356 4 f. mauve   30   30

        (b) *AIR. Inscr* "POSTE AÉRIENNE"
357 5 f. + 5 f. greenish blue ..   .. 2·50   2·25
358 6 f. + 9 f. green ..   ..   .. 2·50   2·50
359 10 f. + 15 f. scarlet ..   ..   3·25   3·25
360 15 f. + 25 f. brown-lake.. ..   4·00   4·50
352/360 *Set of 9* ..   ..   .. 12·00 12·00
Designs: *Vert*—2 f., 6 f. Aristæus (Garden God); 5 f. T **76**.
Horiz—2 f. 50, 10 f. Hyacinthus awaiting his turn to throw a
quoit.

1948 (July). *As Nos. 174/92 and 307/10, but new values
and colours.*
361 **57** 30 c. black   15   8
362 **34** 50 c. sepia   15   15
363 **35** 60 c. pink   15   15
364 **36** 3 f. bright purple   25   20
365 **35** 4 f. emerald-green   25   20
366 **57** 5 f. red-brown   25   15
367   6 f. purple   65   15
368 **37** 8 f. lake-brown   90   50
369 **57** 10 f. orange-yellow   50   8
370 **37** 10 f. red-brown ..   .. 1·25   45
371 **57** 12 f. carmine.. ..   .. 1·60   50
372   18 f. blue ..   ..   .. 2·25 1·50
373 **39** 20 f. carmine..   65   15
374 **38** 25 f. black ..   ..   9·00 3·50
361/374 *Set of 14* ..   .. 16·00 7·00
For later issues in T **34/9**, see Nos. 391/407.

80 *Princess Alice II*

79 Exotic Gardens

81 Constitution Day, 1911   **82** Prince Albert I
(Des Serres. Eng Dufresne (2 f, 100 f.); Munier (6 f.); Mazelin
(20 f, 200 f.); Feltesse (25 f.); Barlangue (40 f.) and Piel (50 f.).
Recess)

1949 (5 Mar). *Birth Centenary of Prince Albert I. Various
designs as T* **79/82.** *P* 13.

         (a) *POSTAGE. Inscr* "POSTES".
375 2 f. light blue   10   10
376 3 f. yellow-green   15   15
377 4 f. sepia and greenish blue ..   15   15
378 5 f. scarlet   15   15
379 6 f. deep violet   35   35
380 10 f. sepia   30   30
381 12 f. magenta   40   40
382 18 f. red-brown and brown .. 1·25 1·25

        (b) *AIR. Inscr* "POSTE AERIENNE"
383 20 f. red-brown   65   65
384 25 f. slate   65   65
385 40 f. bluish green   65   65
386 50 f. deep green, brown and black .. 95   95
387 100 f. carmine ..   ..   1·90 1·90
388 200 f. orange ..   ..   4·00 4·00
375/388 *Set of 14* ..   .. 11·00 11·00
Designs: *Horiz*—2 f. *Hirondelle I* (1870); 4 f. Oceanographic
Museum, Monaco; 10 f. *Hirondelle II* (1914); 25 f. Albert
harpooning whale; 18 f. Buffalo (Palaeolithic mural); 25 f.
Institute of Palaeontology, Paris; 200 f. Effigy of Albert on 200 f.
gold piece. *Vert*—6 f. Statue of Albert at tiller; 40 f. Anthropo-
logical Museum; 100 f. Oceanographic Institute, Paris.

1949 (15 Mar)—**59**. *As Nos. 174/92 and 307/10, but new
values and colours.*
389 **57** 50 c. olive-bistre   12   8
390   1 f. violet-blue   15   12
391 **35** 3 f. turquoise (22.12.51) ..   40   20
392 **39** 5 f. turquoise-green ..   25   12
393 **36** 5 f. brown-red (5.59) ..   30   25
394 **38** 10 f. orange-yellow.. ..   50   8
395 **57** 12 f. deep turquoise-blue .. 2·25 1·50
396   15 f. brown-red ..   .. 2·25 1·50
397 **36** 25 f. light blue ..   .. 5·50 2·75
398 **37** 25 f. vermilion (12.4.54) ..   75   35
399 **36** 30 f. indigo (22.12.51) .. 2·50 1·40
400 **37** 35 f. deep blue (5.59) .. 1·25   65
401 **34** 40 f. scarlet.. ..   .. 2·75 1·50
402   50 f. violet ..   ..   .. 1·75   50
403 **39** 65 f. bright violet (13.11.57) .. 2·25 1·90
404 **34** 70 f. orange-yellow (6.11.57) .. 2·50 1·90
405 **35** 75 f. deep green (12.4.54) .. 6·50 2·75
406   85 f. brown-purple (5.59) .. 2·00 1·25
407 **39** 100 f. turquoise-blue (5.59).. 1·90 1·60
389/407 *Set of 19* ..   .. 32·00 18·00

       Prince Rainier III, 9 May, 1949

82a Princess Charlotte   **83** Palace of Monaco and Globe

Monaco 1949

(Des and eng R. Serres (10 f. +5 f., 40 f. +5 f.), C. Mazelin
(15 f.+5 f., 25 f.+5 f.). Recess)

1949 (27 Dec). *Red Cross Fund. Sheet* 150×172½ *mm., containing vert portraits as T* 82a.
MS408 10 f.+5 f. red-brown and red, and
    40 f.+5 f. myrtle-green and red;
    15 f.+5 f. red, and 25 f.+5 f. deep blue
    and red. Each ×4. P 13   ..   ..   65·00   65·00
MS409 As MS408 but imperf.   ..   65·00   65·00
Designs:—10 f., 40 f., T **82a**; 15 f., 25 f., Prince Rainier.
The miniature sheet contains four sets arranged in *se-tenant*
blocks of four separated by inscribed gutter margins.
(Eng Gandon. Recess)

1949 (27 Dec)**–50**. *75th Anniv of Universal Postal Union.*
P 13. *(a) POSTAGE. Inscr* "POSTES".
410 **83**   5 f. green   15   15
411   10 f. yellow-orange (12.9.50)   1·60   1·60
412   15 f. carmine   20   20
    (b) AIR. Inscr "POSTE AERIENNE"
413 **83**   25 f. blue   45   45
414   40 f. sepia and red-brown (12.9.50) ..   65   55
415   50 f. ultramarine & blue-grn (12.9.50)   80   65
416   100 f. greenish blue & claret (12.9.50)   1·60   1·50
410/416   *Set of* 7   ..   ..   ..   5·00   4·50

84 Prince Rainier III and   **85** Prince
     Monaco Palace   Rainier III

86 Prince Albert I

(Des and eng R. Serres. Recess)

1950 (11 Apr). *Accession of Prince Rainier III.* P 13.
    (a) POSTAGE. Inscr "POSTES".
417 **84**   10 c. purple and scarlet   ..   10   10
418   50 c. brown, red-brown and orange ..   10   10
419   1 f. violet   10   10
420   5 f. blue-green   45   45
421   15 f. carmine   70   70
422   25 f. blue, olive and ultramarine   ..   1·25   1·25
    (b) AIR. Inscr "POSTE AERIENNE"
423 **84**   50 f. lake-brown and black   ..   1·50   1·25
424   100 f. blue, sepia and lake-brown   ..   2·25   1·90
417/424   *Set of* 8   ..   ..   ..   6·00   5·50
1950 (Apr)**–51**. *P* 14 × 13. *(a) Recess.* 18 × 22½ *mm.*
425 **85**   5 c. violet   8   5
426   1 f. brown   10   8
427   6 f. green (22.12.51)   30   25
428   8 f. green   95   65
429   8 f. yellow-orange (22.12.51)   ..   40   25
430   12 f. light blue   45   35
431   15 f. carmine   65   30
432   15 f. indigo (22.12.51)   ..   45   20
433   18 f. carmine (22.12.51)   ..   1·25   70

    (b) Typo. 17¾ × 22 *mm.* (31.3.51)
434 **85**   5 f. emerald-green   ..   ..   1·60   1·40
435   10 f. orange   ..   ..   ..   3·25   2·25
425/435   *Set of* 11   ..   ..   ..   8·50   6·00
(Des and eng F. Cogne and H. Cheffer. Recess)
1951 (11 Apr). *Unveiling of Prince Albert I Statue. P* 13.
436 **86**   15 f. blue   ..   ..   ..   3·25   3·25

87 Edmond and Jules de Goncourt

1951 (11 Apr). *50th Anniv of Goncourt Academy. Recess.*
P 13.
437 **87**   15 f. purple   ..   ..   ..   3·25   3·25

88 St. Vincent de Paul   **90** St. Peter's Keys and
                                    Papal Bull

89 Judgment of St. Dévote

91 Mosaic   **92** Rainier of Westphalia

(Des Serres (10 c., 50 c., 2 f., 12 f., 25 f., 40 f., 50 f.), Gandon
(1 f., 5 f., 15 f., 20 f., 100 f.). Eng Serres (10 c., 50 c.),
Gandon (1 f., 5 f., 100 f.), Combet (2 f.), Ouvré (12 f.),
Cottet (15 f.), Munier (20 f.), Mazelin (25 f.), Dufresne
(40 f.), Pheulpin (50 f.). Recess)

1951 (4 June). *Holy Year. Designs as T* **88**/**92** *inscr* "ANNO
SANTO". P 13.
438 **88**   10 c. blue, ultramarine and red   ..   15   15
439 —   50 c. violet and claret   15   15
440 **89**   1 f. green and red-brown   ..   20   20
441 **90**   2 f. vermilion and purple   ..   30   30
442 **91**   5 f. emerald-green   30   30
443 —   12 f. reddish violet   45   45
444 —   15 f. vermilion   ..   ..   1·90   1·90
445 —   20 f. red-brown   ..   ..   2·50   2·50
446 —   25 f. light blue   ..   ..   2·75   2·75
447 —   40 f. violet and magenta   ..   3·25   3·25
448 —   50 f. purple-brown and olive-brown ..   3·25   3·25
449 **92** 100 f. purple-brown   ..   ..   10·00   10·00
438/449   *Set of* 12   ..   ..   ..   22·00   22·00
Designs: *Triangular* (as T **88**)—50 c. Pope Pius XII. *Vert*
(as T **90**)—12 f. Prince Rainier III in St. Peter's; 15 f. St. Nicholas
of Patara; 20 f. St. Romain; 25 f. St. Charles Borromeo; 40 f.
Coliseum; 50 f. Chapel of St. Dévote.

93 Wireless Mast and
     Monaco

94 Seal of Prince Rainier III

95 Gallery of Hercules

Monaco 1951

(Des M. Camia. Eng Gandon. Recess)
1951 (22 Dec). *Monte Carlo Radio Station.* P 13.
450	**93**	1 f. orange, vermilion and light blue	15	15
451		15 f. bright purple, vermilion & violet	60	15
452		30 f. brown and deep blue	1·10	65

(Des and eng Gandon. Recess)
1951 (22 Dec). P 13.
453	**94**	1 f. violet	35	25
454		5 f. black-brown	1·25	50
455		8 f. claret	1·90	1·25
456		15 f. bright green	2·25	1·90
457		30 f. indigo	3·25	1·90
453/457		*Set of 5*	8·00	5·50

For later issues in T **94**, see Nos. 512/6.
1951 (22 Dec). Nos. **MS**408·9 *surch* 1 f. on 10 f.+5 f., 3 f. on 15 f.+5 f., 5 f. on 25 f.+5 f., 6 f. on 40 f.+5 f.
MS458	As above perf 13	.. ..	..	65·00	65·00
MS459	As above imperf	.. ..	..	65·00	65·00

(Des and eng Cheffer. Recess)
1952 (26 Apr). *Monaco Postal Museum.* P 13.
460	**95**	5 f. brown-red and brown ..	35	35
461		15 f. violet and bright purple	40	20
462		30 f. indigo and bright blue	50	45

96 Football

(Des B. Minne (1 f. to 15 f.), Molné (others). Eng Cottet (1 f.), Barlangue (2 f.), R. Serres (3 f. and 15 f.), Dufresne (5 f.), Gandon (8 f.), Pheulpin (100 f.) and P. Munier (200 f.). Recess)
1953 (23 Feb). *Fifteenth Olympic Games, Helsinki.* T **96** and similar designs inscr "HELSINKI 1952". P 11.
(a) POSTAGE.
463	1 f. magenta and deep violet ..	25	20
464	2 f. greenish blue and deep emerald ..	25	20
465	3 f. pale blue and deep bright blue ..	25	20
466	5 f. deep blue-green & blackish brown	60	35
467	8 f. rose-red and lake	90	60
468	15 f. purple-brown, deep blue-green & bl	70	45

(b) AIR. Inscr "POSTE AERIENNE"
469	40 f. blue-black	4·50	3·75
470	50 f. reddish violet	5·00	4·50
471	100 f. deep grey-green	5·50	5·00
472	200 f. carmine-red	6·50	5·50
463/472	*Set of 10*	22·00	19·00

Designs:—1 f. Basket-ball; 3 f. Yachting; 5 f. Cycling; 8 f. Gymnastics; 15 f. Louis II Stadium, Monaco; 40 f. Running; 50 f. Fencing; 100 f. Rifle, target and arms of Monaco; 200 f. Olympic torch.

97 "Journal Inédit"

(Des and eng Gandon. Recess)
1953 (29 June). *Centenary of Publication of Journal by E. and J. de Goncourt.* P 13.
473	**97**	5 f. deep green	40	30
474		15 f. red-brown	65	40

98 Physalia, Yacht, Prince Albert, Richet and Portier

(Des and eng H. Cheffer. Recess)
1953 (29 June). *Fiftieth Anniv of Discovery of Anaphylaxis.* P 13.
475	**98**	2 f. violet, slate-green and chocolate	15	10
476		5 f. scarlet, carmine-lake & slate-grn	30	25
477		15 f. deep lilac, dp brt blue & slate-grn	1·25	90

D **99**

(Pairs des Serres and Minne. Eng Serres (1 f., 4 f., 50 f.), Cheffer (2 f.), Mazelin (3 f.), Cottet (5 f.), Gandon (10 f.), Dufresne (20 f.), Barlangue (100 f.). Recess)
1953 (29 June)—**54**. *POSTAGE DUE. Designs showing old and new forms of transport as Type* D **99**. P 11.
D478	1 f. red and green (12.4.54)	5	5
D479	1 f. green and red (12.4.54)	5	5
D480	2 f. deep turquoise-green & dp brt bl	5	5
D481	2 f. deep bright bl & dp turquoise-grn	5	5
D482	3 f. carmine-lake and slate-green ..	10	10
D483	3 f. slate-green and carmine-lake ..	10	10
D484	4 f. blackish green and black-brown ..	12	12
D485	4 f. black-brown and blackish green ..	12	12
D486	5 f. deep violet and blue	25	25
D487	5 f. blue and deep violet	25	25
D488	10 f. deep blue and deep bright blue ..	3·25	3·25
D489	10 f. deep bright blue and deep blue ..	3·25	3·25
D490	20 f. reddish violet and indigo ..	95	95
D491	20 f. indigo and reddish violet ..	95	95
D492	50 f. deep brown and rose-red ..	2·75	2·75
D493	50 f. rose-red and deep brown ..	2·75	2·75
D494	100 f. green and purple-brown	5·00	5·00
D495	100 f. purple-brown and green	5·00	5·00
D478/495	*Set of 18*	23·00	23·00

Designs:—No. D478, Pigeons released from mobile loft, No. D479, *Sikorsky* helicopter; D480, Sailing ship; D481 S.S. *United States*; D482, Old railway engine; D483, Streamlined locomotive; D484, Old monoplane; D485, *Comet* airliner; D486, Old motor-car; D487, *Sabre* racing-car; D488, Leonardo da Vinci's flying machine; D489, Postal rocket; D490, Balloon; D491, Airship *Graf Zeppelin*; D492, Postilion; D493, Motor-cycle messenger; D494, Mail-coach; D495, Railway mail van.
The two designs in each value are arranged in *tête-bêche* pairs throughout the sheet.

99 F. Ozanam

100 St. Jean-Baptiste de la Salle

(Des J. E. Lorenzi. Recess)
1954 (12 Apr). *Death Centenary of Ozanam (founder of St. Vincent de Paul Conferences).* T **99** and another vert design inscr "CONFERENCES DE ST. VINCENT DE PAUL". P 13.
478	**99**	1 f. vermilion	8	8

479 – 5 f. deep bright blue 30 30
480 **99** 15 f. black 55 55
Design:—5 f. Outline drawing of Sister of Charity.

(Des J. E. Lorenzi. Recess)

1954 (12 Apr). *De la Salle Commemoration. T* **100** *and another vert design inscr "ST. J-B DE LA SALLE". P* 13.
481 **100** 1 f. lake 8 8
482 – 5 f. brown-black 30 30
483 **100** 15 f. deep bright blue 55 55
Design:—5 f. Outline drawing of De La Salle and two children.

101

102

103

104 Seal of Prince Rainier III

(Des J. E. Lorenzi. Typo)

1954 (12 Apr). *Arms of Monaco. Various designs as T* **101/3**. *P* 13 × 14 (50 c., 80 c., 5 f.) *or* 14 × 13 (*others*).
484 – 50 c. red, black and magenta 5 5
485 – 70 c. red, black and turquoise-blue .. 5 5
486 **101** 80 c. red, black and deep green 5 5
487 – 1 f. red, black and ultramarine 5 5
488 **102** 2 f. red, black and red-orange 5 5
489 – 3 f. red, black and emerald 8 5
490 **103** 5 f. red, black, maroon and green .. 12 8
484/490 *Set of* 7 .. .. 40 30
Arms designs: *As T* **101**—50 c.; *As T* **102**—70 c., 1 f., 3 f.

(Des B. Minne. Eng R. Serres. Recess)

1954 (12 Apr)**–59**. *Precancelled. P* 13.
491 **104** 4 f. deep orange-red .. 40 12
492 – 5 f. deep violet-blue (6.11.57) .. 15 10
493 – 8 f. deep green .. 35 25
494 – 8 f. bright purple (5.59) .. 30 15
495 – 10 f. yellow-green (6.11.57) .. 15 10
496 – 12 f. deep reddish violet 65 45
497 – 15 f. orange (6.11.57) .. 40 30
498 – 20 f. emerald (5.59) .. 45 40
499 – 24 f. lake-brown .. .. 1·60 1·10
500 – 30 f. blue (6.11.57) 55 40
501 – 40 f. deep chocolate (5.59) .. 65 50
502 – 45 f. scarlet (6.11.57) 75 55
503 – 55 f. ultramarine (5.59) .. .. 1·25 65
491/503 *Set of* 13 .. .. 7·00 4·50
See also Nos. 680/3.

105 Lambaréné

106 Dr. Albert Schweitzer

(Des Gandon. Eng R. Serres (2 f.), H. Cheffer (5 f.), Gandon (*others*). Recess)

1955 (14 Jan). *80th Birthday of Dr. Schweitzer* (*humanitarian*). *T* **105/6** *and other designs. P* 11 (5 f., 15 f.) *or* 13 (*others*).
(*a*) POSTAGE.
504 **105** 2 f. bronze-grn, dp blue-grn & indigo 15 15
505 **106** 5 f. deep greenish blue and emerald 50 50
506 – 15 f. brown-purple, black & deep grn 1·25 1·25

(*b*) AIR. *Inscr "POSTE AERIENNE"*
507 – 200 f. slate-blk, dp blue-grn & pale bl 11·00 9·50
Designs: *As T* **106**—15 f. Lambaréné Hospital. *Horiz* (48 × 27 mm.)—200 f. Schweitzer and jungle scene.

107 Cormorants

(Des Gandon. Eng Mazelin (200 f.). Des and eng Gandon (500 f., 1,000 f.). Recess)

1955 (14 Jan)**–58**. *AIR. T* **107** *and similar designs. P* 11.
508 – 100 f. indigo and blue .. .. 9·50 5·00
    a. Perf 13 ('58) .. .. 9·00 4·50
509 – 200 f. black and light blue .. .. 11·00 6·50
    a. Perf 13 ('58) .. .. 90·00 19·00
510 – 500 f. violet-grey and slate-green .. 11·00 9·50
511 – 1,000 f. brown-blk, turq-grn & slate-grn 90·00 75·00
    a. Perf 13 ('58) .. .. 35·00 22·00
Designs:—100 f. Sea swallows; 200 f. Seagulls; 500 f. Albatrosses.

1955 (14 Jan). *As Nos.* 453/7. *New value* (6 f.) *and colours changed. Recess. P* 13.
512 **94** 5 f. reddish violet .. .. .. 1·10 45
513 – 6 f. red .. .. .. 1·00 70
514 – 8 f. red-brown .. .. 1·10 80
515 – 15 f. ultramarine .. .. 2·50 1·50
516 – 30 f. deep green .. .. 3·25 1·90
512/516 *Set of* 5 .. .. 8·00 5·00

108 Eight Starting Points

109 Prince Rainier III

(Des Dufresne. Eng B. Minne. Recess)

1955 (14 Jan). *25th Monte Carlo Car Rally. P* 13.
517 **108** 100 f. scarlet and blackish brown .. 30·00 30·00

(Des and eng H. Cheffer. Recess)

1955 (7 June)**–59**. *P* 13.
518 **109** 6 f. deep dull purple & dull emerald 15 8
519 – 8 f. violet and scarlet 15 8
520 – 12 f. slate-green and carmine .. 20 8

521	**109**	15 f. deep bright blue & bright purple	30	15
522		18 f. blue and red-orange	40	30
523		20 f. turquoise-blue (6.11.57)	40	35
524		25 f. black and orange (5.59)	30	25
525		30 f. brown-black and ultramarine	2·25	1·25
526		30 f. deep violet (5.59)	55	30
527		35 f. light brown (6.11.57)	1·60	65
528		50 f. lake and blue-green (5.59)	65	45
518/528		*Set of* 11	6·00	3·50

See also Nos. 627/41.

110 "La Maison à Vapeur"

111 "The 500 Millions of the   113 U.S.S. *Nautilus*
Begum"

112 "Round the World in Eighty Days"

(Des B. Minne. Eng Dufresne (1 f.), Gandon (2 f., 8 f.),
J. Piel (3 f.), R. Serres (5 f.), Miermont (6 f.), Cottet (10 f.),
Mazelin (15 f.), Cheffer (25 f.), Busiere (30 f.), A. Frères
(200 f.). Recess).

1955 (7 June. *50th Death Anniv of Jules Verne* (author).
Designs as T **110/113**. *P* 11 (30 f.) *or* 13 (*others*). (*a*)
POSTAGE.

529	1 f. indigo and lake-brown	8	8
530	2 f. blackish brown, indigo and pale blue	8	8
531	3 f. indigo, black and red-brown	10	8
532	5 f. blackish brown and carmine	10	8
533	6 f. violet-grey and blackish brown	25	20
534	8 f. turquoise-blue and olive-green	30	25
535	10 f. blackish brown, turquoise-bl & ind	75	65
536	15 f. vermilion and brown-lake	70	65
537	25 f. black, deep green and slate-green	1·25	95
538	30 f. black, deep purple & turquoise-blue	2·75	2·50

(*b*) AIR. *Inscr* "POSTE AERIENNE"
| 539 | 200 f. indigo, blue and deep bright blue | 19·00 | 19·00 |
| 529/539 | *Set of* 11 | 22·00 | 22·00 |

Designs: *As T* **111**—*Vert*—1 f. "Five Weeks in a Balloon".
Horiz—5 f. "Michael Strogoff"; 8 f. "Le Superbe Orénoque".
As T **110**—2 f. "A Floating Island"; 10 f. "Journey to the
Centre of the Earth"; 25 f. "20,000 Leagues under the Sea";
200 f. "From Earth to Moon".

114 "The Immaculate Virgin" (F. Brea)

(Des and eng R. Serres (15 f.). Recess)

1955 (7 June). *Marian Year. T* **114** *and other designs. P* 11
(15 f.) *or* 13 (*others*).
540	5 f. slate-green, violet-grey & purple-brn	30	30
541	10 f. slate-green, violet-grey & purple-brn	30	30
542	15 f. brown and brown-black	40	40

Designs: *As T* **114**—10 f. "Madonna" (L. Brea). *As T* **113**—
15 f. Bienheureux Rainier.

115 Rotary Emblem

(Des B. Minne. Eng Fenneteaux. Recess)

1955 (7 June). *50th Anniv of Rotary International. P* 13.
| 543 | **115** | 30 f. greenish blue & orange-yellow | 70 | 70 |

116 George Washington   118 President Eisenhower

117 Abraham Lincoln

119 Monaco Palace in the Eighteenth Century

(Des and eng J. Piel (1 f., 40 f.), Gandon (30 f., 100 f.). Des Gandon (2 f., 3 f., 5 f.), B. Minne (15 f., 50 f.). Eng Miermont (2 f.), Dufresne (3 f.), Mazelin (5 f.), A. Frères (15 f.), Munier (50 f.). Recess).

1956 (3 Apr). *Fifth International Philatelic Exhibition, New York. T 116/9 and similar designs inscr "F.I.P.E.X. 1956". P 13.*

544	1 f. reddish violet and deep lilac	5	5
545	2 f. deep lilac and brown-purple	5	5
546	3 f. deep blue and deep violet	8	5
547	5 f. deep brown-red	20	20
548	15 f. blackish brown and chocolate	45	45
549	30 f. black, indigo and blue	85	85
550	40 f. chocolate	80	70
551	50 f. vermilion	95	80
552	100 f. deep bluish green	1·25	1·25
544/552	*Set of 9*	4·25	4·00

Designs: *As T 117*—2 f. Franklin D. Roosevelt. *As T 119*—30 f. Landing of Columbus. *As T 118*—40 f. Prince Rainier III. Horiz (48 × 36 mm.)—50 f. Monaco Palace in the eighteenth century; 100 f. Louisiana landscape in the eighteenth century.
Nos. 551, 550 and 552 were printed in that order, in sheets of 15 (5 × 3); each horizontal row containing one stamp of each value.

120

(Des and eng B. Minne (15 f.). Des B. Minne, eng Fenneteaux (30 f.). Recess)

1956 (3 Apr). *Seventh Winter Olympic Games, Cortina d'Ampezzo and Sixteenth Olympic Games, Melbourne. T 120 and similar horiz design. P 13.*

553	15 f. slate-green, sepia and brown-purple	80	65
554	30 f. red-orange	1·40	1·40

Design: 15 f. "Italia" Ski-jump.

1956 (3 Apr). *Nos. D482/95 optd with bars or additionally surch with new values, for postal use.* (a) POSTAGE.

555	2 f. on 4 f. blackish green & blk-brn (B.)	
556	2 f. on 4 f. blk-brn & blackish brn (R.)	
557	3 f. carmine-lake and slate-green (R.)	
558	3 f. slate-green and carmine-lake (R.)	
559	5 f. on 4 f. blackish grn & blk-brn (B.)	
560	5 f. on 4 f. black-brn & blackish grn (R.)	
561	10 f. on 4 f. blackish green & blk-brn (B.)	
562	10 f. on 4 f. black-brn & blackish grn (R.)	
563	15 f. on 5 f. deep violet and blue (B.)	
564	15 f. on 5 f. blue and deep violet (B.)	
565	20 f. reddish violet and indigo (R.)	
566	20 f. indigo and reddish violet (R.)	
567	25 f. on 20 f. reddish violet and indigo	
568	25 f. on 20 f. indigo & reddish violet	
569	30 f. on 10 f. dp bl & dp bright bl (B.)	
570	30 f. on 10 f. deep bright bl & dp bl (R.)	
571	40 f. on 50 f. deep brown & rose-red (R.)	
572	40 f. on 50 f. rose-red & deep brown (R.)	
573	50 f. on 100 f. green and purple-brown	
574	50 f. on 100 f. purple-brown and green	

(b) AIR. *Surch "POSTE AÉRIENNE", bars and new value*

575	100 f. on 20 f. reddish violet & indigo (R.)		
576	100 f. on 20 f. indigo & reddish violet (R.)		
555/576	*Set of 22*	35·00	35·00

121 Route Map from Glasgow

(Des B. Minne. Eng Dufresne. Recess)

1956 (3 Apr). *Twenty-sixth Monte Carlo Rally. P 13.*

577	**121**	100 f. red-brown and red	11·00	11·00

122 Princess Grace and Prince Rainier III

(Eng J. Piel. Recess)

1956 (19 Apr). *Royal Wedding. P 13.* (a) POSTAGE.

578	**122**	1 f. black and deep green	5	5
579		2 f. black and deep rose-red	5	5
580		3 f. black and ultramarine	5	5
581		5 f. black and bright yellow-green	5	5
582		15 f. black and red-brown	25	25

(b) AIR. *Inscr "POSTE AERIENNE"*

583	**122**	100 f. deep brown and deep lilac	50	50
584		200 f. deep brown and carmine-rose	75	75
585		500 f. deep brown and violet-grey	1·90	1·90
578/585	*Set of 8*		3·00	3·00

123 Princess Grace

124 Princess Grace with Princess Caroline

1957 (11 May). *Birth of Princess Caroline. Recess. P 13.*

586	**123**	1 f. violet-grey	5	5
587		2 f. olive-green	5	5
588		3 f. yellow-brown	5	5
589		5 f. crimson	5	5
590		15 f. rose-pink	10	8
591		25 f. deep turquoise-blue	15	12
592		30 f. deep reddish violet	15	15
593		50 f. red	25	20
594		75 f. yellow-orange	40	40
586/594	*Set of 9*		1·10	1·00

(Des and eng J. Piel. Recess)

1958 (15 May). *Birth of Prince Albert. P 13.*

595	**124**	100 f. black	2·25	1·90

THE WORLD CENTRE FOR FINE STAMPS IS 391 STRAND

125 Order of St. Charles   **126** Route Map from Munich

(Des and eng R. Serres. Recess)

1958 (15 May). *Centenary of National Order of St. Charles.* P 13.
596 **125** 100 f. lake, dull grn, ochre & carm ..   1·40   1·40

(Des B. Minne. Eng Dufresne. Recess)

1958 (15 May). *Twenty-seventh Monte Carlo Rally.* P 13.
597 **126** 100 f. red, sepia, brown-red & green   3·50   2·75

127 Statue of the Holy Virgin, and Popes Pius IX and Pius XII

(Des and eng J. Piel (1 f.), Gandon (3 f.), Hertenberger (5 f.), R. Cami (35 f.), Decaris (100 f.), P. Munier (200 f.). Des Lagaze (2 f.), B. Minne (8 f.), P. Jouve (10 f., 12 f.), Poullain (20 f.), M. Chassard (65 f.). Eng R. Serres (2 f.), Bétemps (8 f.), Mazelin (10 f., 12 f.), Gandon (20 f.), Cottet (50 f.), A. Frères (65 f.). Recess)

1958 (15 May). *Centenary of Apparition of Virgin Mary at Lourdes. Various designs inscr "1858–1958".* P 12½ × 13 (2 f., 3 f., 5 f., 20 f., 35 f.), 13 × 12½ (65 f.) *or* 13 (*others*).
(*a*) POSTAGE.

598	1 f. violet-grey and chocolate	..	5	5
599	2 f. violet and light blue	..	5	5
600	3 f. sepia and green ..	..	5	5
601	5 f. grey-blue and deep sepia	..	10	5
602	8 f. multicoloured	..	20	12
603	10 f. multicoloured	..	20	12
604	12 f. multicoloured	..	20	12
605	20 f. blackish green and maroon	..	30	15
606	35 f. blackish green, bistre & olive-brown	40	35
607	50 f. indigo, bronze-green and lake	..	50	45
608	65 f. turquoise-blue and indigo	..	80	65

(*b*) AIR. Inscr "POSTE AERIENNE"

609	100 f. violet-grey, bronze-green & dp bl	1·40	1·25
610	200 f. bistre-brown and orange-brown ..	2·10	1·90
598/610	Set of 13	6·00	5·00

Designs: *Vert*—(26½ × 36 mm.) 2 f. St. Bernadette; 3 f. St. Bernadette at Bartres; 5 f. Miracle of Bourriette; 20 f. St. Bernadette at prayer; 35 f. St. Bernadette's canonization; (22 × 36 mm.) 8 f. Stained-glass window. As T 127: 50 f. St. Bernadette. Pope Pius XI, Mgr. Laurence and Abbé Peyramale. *Horiz*—(48 × 36 mm.) 10 f. Lourdes grotto; 12 f. Interior of Lourdes grotto; (36 × 26½ mm.) 65 f. Shrine of St. Bernadette; (48 × 27 mm.) 100 f. Lourdes Basilica; 200 f. Pope Pius X and subterranean interior of Basilica. Nos. 602/4 are printed together in the form of a triptych, in sheets.

128 Princess Grace and Clinic

(Des B. Minne. Eng J. Piel, A. Freres. Recess)

1959 (16 May). *Opening of new hospital block in "Princess Grace" Clinic, Monaco.* P 13.
611 **128** 100 f. grey, chocolate and green   ..   80   65

129 U.N.E.S.C.O. Headquarters, Paris, and Cultural Emblems

(Des B. Minne. Eng Gandon (25 f.); J. Piel (50 f.). Recess)

1959 (16 May). *Inauguration of U.N.E.S.C.O. Headquarters Building, Paris.* T **129** *and a similar design.* P 13.
612   25 f. blue, brown, orange-red and black ..   25   20
613   50 f. deep blue-green, black and olive-grn   45   40
Design:—50 f. As T **129** but with heads of children and letters of various alphabets in place of the emblems.

130 Route Map from Athens   **131** Prince Rainier and Princess Grace

(Des B. Minne. Eng Bétemps. Recess)

1959 (16 May). *Twenty-eighth Monte Carlo Rally.* P 13.
614 **130** 100 f. ultram, red & blksh grn/*azure*   3·75   3·75

(Des and eng J. Piel. Recess)

1959 (16 May). *AIR.* P 13.
615 **131** 300 f. violet   ..   ..   ..   3·00   2·50
616   500 f. blue   ..   ..   ..   5·00   4·00
See also Nos. 642/3.

Monaco   1959

132 "Princess Caroline" Carnation

(Des B. Minne. Eng Serres (5 f.), Combet (10 f.), Munier (15 f.), Bétemps (20 f.), Mazelin (25 f.), Cottet (35 f.), Hertenberger (50 f.), J. Piel (85 f.), Gandon (100 f.). Recess)

1959 (16 May). *Flowers as T* **132**. *P* 13.
617	5 f. magenta, deep bluish green & brown	12	10
618	10 f. on 3 f. rose-red, deep green & brown	15	12
619	15 f. on 1 f. yellow and deep green	15	12
620	20 f. bright purple and bronze-green	30	25
621	25 f. on 6 f. vermilion, yell-grn & dp grn	35	30
622	35 f. rose-pink and deep green	55	40
623	50 f. deep green and sepia	70	40
624	85 f. on 65 f. lav, bronze-green & dp grn	95	65
625	100 f. rose and green	1·10	90
617/625	*Set of* 9	4·00	3·75

Flowers: *As T* **132**—10 f. "Princess Grace" carnation; 100 f. "Grace of Monaco" rose. *Vert* (22 × 36 *mm.*)—15 f. Mimosa; 25 f. Geranium. *Horiz* (36 × 22 *mm.*)—20 f. Bougainvillea; 35 f. "Laurier" rose; 50 f. Jasmine; 85 f. Lavender.

Currency Revaluation. 100 (old) Francs = 1 (new) Franc

133 "Uprooted Tree"   **134** Oceanographic Museum

(Eng Decaris. Recess)

1960 (7 Apr). *World Refugee Year. P* 13.
626	**133**	25 c. olive-green, blue and black	15	15

1960 (1 June)—**71**. *P* 13.
627	**109**	25 c. black and orange	10	5
628		30 c. deep violet	20	8
629		40 c. rosine and olive-brn (13.1.69)	12	8
630		45 c. orange-brn & dp slate (1969)	20	10
631		50 c. cerise and blue-green	35	12
632		50 c. claret & orange-brown (1969)	20	10
633		60 c. deep sepia & black-grn (3.65)	35	15
634		60 c. sepia and bright purple (7.71)	30	20
635		65 c. deep grey-blue and brown	75	30
636		70 c. violet-blue and plum (1969)	30	15
637		85 c. emerald and deep violet (1969)	40	25
638		95 c. ultramarine (19.5.64)	55	20
639		1 f. 10, bright blue and sepia (7.71)	45	35
640		1 f. 30, deep sepia & crimson (3.65)	90	50
641		2 f. 30, bright purple and yellow-orange (12.12.66)	90	30
627/641	*Set of* 15		5·50	2·75

1960 (1 June). *AIR. P* 13.
642	**131**	3 f. violet	13·00	6·50
643		5 f. blue	13·00	9·50

(Des R. D'Agof. Eng Decaris (5 c.). Des Spitz. Eng Mazelin (No. 645). Des B. Minne. Eng R. Cami (No. 646). Des B. Minne. Eng Durrens (40 c., 45 c., 80 c., 1 f. 40). Des Gandon. Eng Piel (70 c., 85 c., 90 c., 1 f. 15, 1 f. 30), Gandon (1 f.). Recess)

1960 (1 June)—**71**. *T* **134** *and similar designs. P* 12½×13 (*No.* 645) *or* 13×12½ (*others*).
644	5 c. green, black and light blue	5	5
645	10 c. chocolate and blue	30	20
646	10 c. blue, deep violet and green (6.6.62)	8	5
647	40 c. brn-pur, bl-grn & bronze-grn (3.65)	25	12
648	45 c. brown, green and blue	25	20
649	70 c. chocolate, orge-red & grn (19.5.64)	40	20
650	80 c. brown-red, green & light blue ('69)	40	25
651	85 c. black, yellow-brown and slate	65	40
652	90 c. brown-lake, bright blue & blk (7.71)	45	30
653	1 f. red, dp bluish grn, blk & dp blue	55	20
654	1 f. 15, blk, brown-lake & light bl ('69)	50	35
655	1 f. 30, bistre-brown, grey-green and light blue (15.12.70)	45	25
656	1 f. 40, orange, green and violet (7.71)	70	50
644/656	*Set of* 13	4·50	3·50

Designs: *Horiz*—5 c. Palace of Monaco; 10 c. (No. 646), Aquatic Stadium; 40 c., 45 c., 80 c., 1 f. 40, Aerial view of Palace; 70 c., 85 c., 90 c., 1 f. 15, 1 f. 30, Court of Honour, Monaco Palace; 1 f. Palace floodlit. *Vert*—10 c. (No. 645), T **134**.

134a St. Dévote   **135** Sea Horse
(Des and eng Serres. Recess)

1960 (1 June)—**61**. *AIR. P* 13.
668	**134a**	2 f. bluish violet, blue and green	1·25	75
669		3 f. olive-brown, bluish green and ultramarine (3.6.61)	1·90	1·10
670		5 f. carmine (3.6.61)	2·50	1·90
671		10 f. purple-brown, slate and green	3·75	3·25
668/671	*Set of* 4	8·50	6·50

(Des after Millot. Eng Fenneteaux (No. 672). Des P. Lambert. Eng Béquet (No. 673). Des and eng Decaris (Nos. 674/5). Des E. Clérissi (others). Eng Freres (Nos. 676, 679), Miermont (Nos. 677/8). Recess)

1960 (1 June)—**64**. *Marine Life and Plants. Various designs as T* **135**. *P* 13. (*a*) *Marine Life.*
672	1 c. brown-red & dp bluish grn (19.5.64)	5	5
673	12 c. chestnut and violet-blue (19.5.64)	12	5
674	15 c. deep bluish green & brown-orange	25	12
675	20 c. red, red-brown, bistre & deep brown	20	12

Designs: *Horiz*—1 c. *Macrocheira kampferi* (crab); 20 c. *Pterois volitans. Vert*—12 c. *Fasciolaria trapezium* (shell).

(*b*) *Plants*
676	2 c. multicoloured (19.5.64)	5	5
677	15 c. yellow-orange, choc & olive-green	25	10
678	18 c. multicoloured (19.5.64)	15	8
679	20 c. carmine, olive-green and red-brown	20	12
672/679	*Set of* 8	1·10	65

Designs: *Vert*—2 c. *Selenicereus sp.;* 15 c. *Cereus sp.;* 18 c. *Aloe ciliaris;* 20 c. *Nopalea dejecta.*

1960 (1 June). *Precancelled. P* 13.
680	**104**	8 c. bright reddish purple	40	15
681		20 c. bright emerald	50	15
682		40 c. deep chocolate	50	30
683		55 c. ultramarine	75	35

ALBUM LISTS
Write for our latest lists of albums and accessories.
These will be sent free on request.

136 Route Map from Lisbon **137** Stamps of Monaco, 1885, France and Sardinia, 1860

(Des Minne. Eng Serres. Recess)

1960 (1 June). *29th Monte Carlo Rally. P* 13.
684 **136** 25 c. black, carmine-red & blue/*blue*   1·10   1·10

(Des and eng Piel. Recess)

1960 (1 June). *75th Anniv of First Stamp. P* 13.
685 **137** 25 c. bistre, Prussian blue and violet   80   75

138 Aquarium

(Des Spitz. Eng Mazelin (5 c.). Des and eng Mazelin (10 c.), Durrens (15 c.), Munier (20 c.), Decaris (25 c.), Piel (50 c.). Recess)

1960 (1 June). *50th Anniv of Oceanographic Museum.
T* **138** *and similar designs inscr* "1910–1960". *P* 13.
686   5 c. black, blue and maroon . .   20   15
687   10 c. grey, red-brown and green   35   20
688   15 c. black, bistre and blue   25   20
689   20 c. black, blue and magenta . .   45   30
690   25 c. turquoise-blue   . .   90   75
691   50 c. chocolate and blue   .:   1·00   90
686/691   *Set of* 6   . .   . .   3·00   2·25
Designs: *Vert*—5 c. Oceanographic Museum. *Horiz*—15 c. Conference Hall; 20 c. Hauling-in catch; 25 c. Museum, aquarium and research equipment; 50 c. Prince Albert, *Hirondelle I* and *Princess Alice.*

139 Horse-jumping

(Des Gandon. Eng Cottet (5 c.), Durrens (10 c.), Busière (15 c.), Aufschneider (20 c.), Gandon (25 c.). Des Minne. Eng Gandon (50 c.). Recess)

1960 (1 June). *Olympic Games. Designs as T* **139**. *P* 13:.
692   5 c. deep chocolate, red and emerald . .   20   20
693   10 c. red-brown, blue and green   20   20
694   15 c. crimson, bistre-brown and maroon   20   20
695   20 c. black, light blue and yellow-green   1·60   1·60
696   25 c. maroon, turquoise & deep bluish grn   55   55
697   50 c. maroon, deep blue and turquoise . .   75   75
692/697   *Set of* 6   . .   . .   3·50   3·50
Designs:—10 c. Swimming; 15 c. Long-jumping; 20 c. Throwing the javelin; 25 c. Free-skating; 50 c. Skiing.

D **140** 18th-Century Felucca

(Des Spitz. Eng Cottet (1 c.), Mazelin (2 c.). Des and eng Cottet (5 c.), Munier (10 c., 20 c.), Gandon (50 c., 1 f.). Des Minne. Eng Cottet (30 c.). Recess)

1960 (1 June)—**69**. *POSTAGE DUE. Pictorial designs as Type* D **140**. *P* 13.
D698   1 c. bistre-brown, bluish green and blue   25   25
D699   2 c. sepia, blue and grey-green   . .   8   8
D700   5 c. brown-purple, black & turq-blue   8   8
D701   10 c. black, green and ultramarine   . .   8   8
D702   20 c. brown-purple, green and blue   . .   20   20
D703   30 c. bistre-brown, bl & lt blue-grn ('69)   10   10
D704   50 c. blue, bistre-brown & blackish green   30   30
D705   1 f. bistre-brown, blackish green & blue   40   40
D698/705   *Set of* 8   . .   . .   1·40   1·40
Designs:—2 c. *La Palmaria* (steamboat); 5 c. Arrival of first railway train at Monaco; 10 c. 15th-16th-century armed messenger; 20 c. 18th-century postman; 30 c. *The Charles III* (steamboat); 50 c. 17th-century courier; 1 f. Mail-coach (19th-century).

140 Rally Badge, and Old and Modern Cars

(Des B. Minne. Eng R. Fenneteaux. Recess)

1961 (3 June). *50th Anniv of Monte Carlo Rally. P* 13.
698 **140** 1 f. violet, rose-red & orange-brown   1·25   1·10

141 Route Map from Stockholm   **142** Marine Life

(Des B. Minne. Eng R. Fenneteaux. Recess)

1961 (3 June). *30th Monte Carlo Rally. P* 13.
699 **141** 1 f. red, carmine, green & blue-violet   1·40   1·40

(Des J.-E. Lorenzi. Eng Gandon. Recess)

1961 (3 June). *World Aquariological Congress. Orange network background. P* 13.
700 **142** 25 c. carmine-red, sepia and violet . .   20   15

143 Leper in Town of Middle Ages
144 Semi-submerged Sphinx of Ouadi-es-Saboua

147 Racing Car and Race Circuit

(Des and eng Mazelin. Recess)

1961 (3 June). *Sovereign Order of Malta.* P 13.
701 **143** 25 c. sepia, carmine-red & yellow-brn 20 15

(Des B. Minne. Eng P. Béquet. Recess)

1962 (6 June). *20th Monaco Motor Grand Prix.* P 13.
718 **147** 1 f. bright purple .. .. .. 1·25 1·00

(Des and eng Decaris. Recess)

1961 (3 June). *U.N.E.S.C.O. Campaign for Preservation of Nubian Monuments.* P 13.
702 **144** 50 c. deep maroon, blue & yellow-brn 75 75

148 Route Map from Oslo
149 Louis XII and Lucien Grimaldi

145 Insect within Protective Hand
146 Chevrolet, 1912

(Des and eng C. Mazelin (25 c.). Des R. Louis. Eng A. Freres (50 c.); Eng R. Cami (1 f.). Recess)

1962 (6 June). *31st Monte Carlo Rally.* P 13.
719 **148** 1 f. red, ultramarine, brown-pur & grn 1·10 95

(Des J.-E. Lorenzi. Eng Gandon. Recess)

1961 (3 June). *Nature Preservation.* P 13.
703 **145** 25 c. magenta and bright purple .. 20 15

(Des B. Minne (1 c., 3 c., 5 c., 15 c.), H. Malartre (others). Eng J. Miermont (1 c.), Cottet (2 c., 25 c.), Combet (3 c.), A. Freres (4 c.), J. Piel (5 c.), Gandon (10 c., 30 c.), Mazelin (15 c.), Bétemps (20 c., 50 c., 1 f.), Durrens (45 c., 65 c.). Recess)

1962 (6 June). *450th Anniv of Recognition of Monegasque Sovereignty by Louis XII.* T **149** *and similar horiz designs inscr "1962".* P 13.

1961 (13 June). *Veteran Motor Cars. Horiz designs as T* **146**. *P 13.*

704	1 c. chocolate, green and chestnut ..	10	10
705	2 c. deep blue, purple and vermilion ..	10	10
706	3 c. brown-purple, black & indigo-purple	10	10
707	4 c. brown-purple and blackish violet..	10	10
708	5 c. grey-green, carmine & yellow-olive	10	10
709	10 c. yellow-brown, red and indigo ..	15	15
710	15 c. deep grey-green and turquoise ..	15	15
711	20 c. sepia, red and reddish violet ..	20	20
712	25 c. violet, red and chocolate ..	25	25
713	30 c. deep lilac and yellow-green ..	40	40
714	45 c. deep green, purple & orange-brown	75	75
715	50 c. violet-blue, red and sepia ..	75	75
716	65 c. sepia, carmine-red and slate ..	75	75
717	1 f. indigo, red and violet ..	1·10	1·10
704/717	*Set of* 14	4·50	4·50

Motor Cars:—2 c. Peugeot, 1898; 3 c. Fiat 1901; 4 c. Mercedes, 1901; 5 c. Rolls-Royce, 1903; 10 c. Panhard-Levassor, 1899; 15 c. Renault, 1898; 20 c. Ford "S", 1908; 25 c. Rochet-Schneider, 1894; 30 c. FN-Herstal, 1901; 45 c. De Dion Bouton, 1900; 50 c. Buick, 1910; 65 c. Delahaye, 1901; 1 f. Cadillac, 1906.

720	25 c. black, red and violet-blue ..	30	25
721	50 c. chocolate, lake and deep blue ..	25	25
722	1 f. carm-red, bluish grn & dp pur-brn	50	45

Designs:—50 c. Parchment bearing declaration of sovereignty; 1 f. Seals of two Sovereigns.

150 Mosquito and Swamp

(Des B. Minne. Eng R. Cottet. Recess)

1962 (6 June). *Malaria Eradication.* P 13.
723 **150** 1 f. yellow-green and olive-brown .. 60 50

151 Sun, Bouquet and "Hope Chest"
152 Harvest Scene

STAMP MONTHLY

—finest and most informative magazine for all collectors. Obtainable from your newsagent or by postal subscription—details on request.

(Des and eng A. Decaris. Recess)

1962 (6 June). *National Multiple Sclerosis Society, New York.* P 13.
724 **151** 20 c. red, yellow, pur, grn, brn & blue 20 15

(Des and eng A. Decaris (T **152**), P. Gandon (2 f.). Recess)

1962 (6 June). *Europa.* *T* **152** *and similar horiz design.* *P* 13.

(*a*) POSTAGE.
725	**152**	25 c. chestnut, deep green & deep bl		15	15
726		50 c. yellow-olive & deep turq-green		30	30
727		1 f. yellow-olive and bright purple		50	50

(*b*) AIR. Inscr "POSTE AERIENNE"
728	–	2 f. greenish slate, choc & yell-grn		1·10	95
725/728		*Set of* 4		1·90	1·75

Design:—2 f. Mercury in flight over Europe.

153 Atomic Symbol and Scientific Centre, Monaco

154 Wagtails

(Des B. Minne. Eng J. Piel. Recess)

1962 (6 June). *AIR. Scientific Centre, Monaco.* *P* 13.
729	**153**	10 f. violet, brown and light blue ..		7·50	7·00

(Des P. Lambert. Eng Cottet (5 c., 1 f.), Mazelin (10 c., 20 c.), Bétemps (15 c.), Munier (25 c.), Durrens (30 c.), Gandon (45 c.), Piel (50 c.), Béquet (85 c.). Recess)

1962 (12 Dec). *Protection of Birds Useful to Agriculture.* *Vert designs as* T **154.** *P* 13.
730		5 c. yellow, brown and green..	..	10	10
731		10 c. red, bistre and maroon	..	12	12
732		15 c. purple, yellow, green and blue	..	20	15
733		20 c. deep sepia, yell-grn & bright purple		25	20
734		25 c. black, brown, red & reddish purple		25	20
735		30 c. brown, blue and deep grey-green..		25	25
736		45 c. orange-brown and bluish violet	..	40	35
737		50 c. black, olive-yellow and turquoise..		55	45
738		85 c. verm, red-brown, greenish yell & grn		55	50
739		1 f. deep sepia, red and green..	..	70	70
730/739		*Set of* 10	..	3·00	2·75

Birds:—10 c. Robins; 15 c. Goldfinches; 20 c. Warblers; 25 c. Woodpeckers; 30 c. Nightingale; 45 c. Brown owls; 50 c. Starlings; 85 c. Cross-bills; 1 f. White storks.

155 Galeazzi's Diving Turret

156 Donor's Arm and Globe

(Eng Durrens (5 c., 45 c.), Bétemps (10 c.), Béquet (25 c., 85 c.). Des Minne. Eng Béquet (50 c.), Combet (85 c.). Recess)

1962 (12 Dec). *Underwater Exploration.* *Designs as* T **155** *inscr* "1962". *P* 13.
740		5 c. black, bluish violet & turquoise-blue		8	8
741		10 c. blue, reddish violet and brown	..	12	12
742		25 c. yellow-bistre, deep grn & turq-blue		15	15
743		45 c. black, deep ultramarine and green		35	35
744		50 c. olive-green, bistre and blue	..	35	35
745		85 c. deep violet-blue and turquoise-blue		60	60
746		1 f. chocolate, black-green and blue..		70	70
740/746		*Set of* 7	..	2·10	2·10

Designs: *Horiz*—5 c. Divers; 25 c. Williamson's photosphere (1914) and bathyscape *Trieste*; 45 c. Klingert's diving-suit (1797) and modern diving-suit; 50 c. Diving saucer; 85 c. Fulton's *Nautilus* (1800) and modern submarine; 1 f. Alexander the Great's diving bell and Beebe's bathysphere.

(Des B. Minne. Eng Forget. Recess)

1962 (12 Dec). *Third International Blood Donors' Congress, Monaco.* *P* 13.
747	**156**	1 f. crimson, sepia and orange	..	50	45

157 "Ring-a-ring o' Roses"

158 Feeding Chicks

159 Ship's Figurehead

(Des Béquet (5 c.), Navone (10 c.), Abramoff (15 c.), Raynaud (20 c.), Santi (25 c.), Ginocchio (50 c.), Fontana (95 c.), Lambert, after painting by A. Vidal-Quadras (1 f.). Eng Béquet (5 c.), Gandon (10 c., 15 c., 20 c.), Mazelin (25 c.), Hertenberger (50 c., 95 c.), Cottet (1 f.). Recess)

1963 (3 May). *U.N. Children's Charter.* *T* **157/8** *and similar designs.* *P* 13.
748		5 c. red, blue and ochre	..	5	5
749		10 c. emerald, olive-brown and blue	..	8	8
750		15 c. ultramarine, red and emerald	..	12	10
751		20 c. multicoloured	..	15	15
752		25 c. blue, purple and chestnut ..		20	20
753		50 c. blue, emerald, violet and magenta		35	30
754		95 c. multicoloured	..	45	45
755		1 f. maroon, red and turquoise	..	65	65
748/755		*Set of* 8	..	1·90	1·75

Designs:—As T **157**: 1 f. Prince Albert and Princess Caroline. Children's paintings as T **158**: *Horiz*—15 c. Children on scales; 50 c. House and child. *Vert*—20 c. Sun and Children of three races; 25 c. Mother and child; 95 c. Negress and child.

(Des P. Lambert. Eng Gandon (50 c.), Piel (1 f.). Recess)

1963 (3 May). *Red Cross Centenary.* *T* **159** *and similar design.* *P* 13.
756		50 c. carmine, red-brown and turquoise..		40	40
757		1 f. myrtle-grn, red, maroon & grey-blue		55	55

Design: *Horiz*—1 f. Moynier, Dunant and Dufour, and centenary emblem.

160 Racing Cars

161 Emblem and Charter

(Des B. Minne. Eng C. Haley. Recess)

1963 (3 May). *European Motor Grand Prix.* *P* 13.
758	**160**	50 c. multicoloured ..	.. ..	45	40

(Des B. Minne. Eng Miermont. Recess)
1963 (3 May). *Founding of Monaco Lions Club.* P 13.
759 **161** 50 c. blue, bistre and violet 40 40

162 Hôtel des Postes, Paris, and U.P.U. Monument, Berne

(Des P. Lambert. Eng J. Piel. Recess)
1963 (3 May). *Centenary of Paris Postal Conference.* P 13.
760 **162** 50 c. lake, blue-green and yellow . . 40 40

163 "Telstar" Satellite and Globe **164** Route Map from Warsaw

(Des and eng C. Durrens. Recess)
1963 (3 May). *First Trans-Atlantic Television Satellite Link.* P 13.
761 **163** 50 c. pur-brn, emerald-grn & dp pur 50 45

(Des B. Minne. Eng R. Fenneteaux. Recess)
1963 (3 May). *Thirty-second Monte Carlo Rally.* P 13.
762 **164** 1 f. ultram, light bl, sepia & chestnut 90 75

165 Feeding Chicks **166** Allegory

(Des Chiavassa and A. Decaris. Eng Decaris. Recess)
1963 (3 May). *Freedom from Hunger.* P 13.
763 **165** 1 f. chestnut, myrtle-grn, ol-brn & bl 45 45

(Des P. Lambert. Eng J. Piel. Recess)
1963 (3 May). *2nd Ecumenical Council, Vatican City.* P 13.
764 **166** 1 f. turquoise-bl, yellow-grn & brn-red 45 45

167 Henry Ford and Ford "A" Car of 1903   **168** H. Garin (winner of 1903 race) cycling through Village

(Des and eng R. Cami. Recess)
1963 (12 Dec). *Birth Centenary of Henry Ford (motor pioneer).* P 13.
765 **167** 20 c. deep bluish grn & bright purple 25 20

(Des and eng C. Durrens (25 c.), J. Pheulpin (50 c.). Recess)
1963 (12 Dec). *50th "Tour de France" Cycle Race.* T **168** and similar horiz design. P 13.
766 25 c. deep green, red-brown and blue . . 15 12
767 50 c. sepia, grey-green and blue . . 25 20
Design:—50 c. Cyclist passing Desgranges Monument, Col du Galibier, 1963.

169 P. de Coubertin and Discus-thrower   **170** R. Garros and Aircraft

(Des P. Lambert. Eng J. Piel. Recess)
1963 (12 Dec). *Birth Centenary of Pierre de Coubertin (reviver of Olympic Games).* P 13.
768 **169** 1 f. yellow-brown, carmine and carmine-lake 45 45

(Des and eng G. Bétemps. Recess)
1963 (12 Dec). *AIR. 50th Anniv of First Aerial Crossing of the Mediteranean Sea.* P 13.
769 **170** 2 f. purple-brown and deep blue . . 1·10 80

171 Route Map from Paris **172** Children with Stamp Album

(Des B. Minne. Eng R. Fenneteaux. Recess)
1963 (12 Dec). *33rd Monte Carlo Rally.* P 13.
770 **171** 1 f. red, deep bluish green and blue . . 75 75

(Des B. Minne. Eng P. Béquet. Recess)
1963 (12 Dec). *"Scolatex" International Stamp Exhibition, Monaco.* P 13.
771 **172** 50 c. ultramarine, violet and red . . 30 30

173 "Europa"   **174** Wembley Stadium

Monaco
1963

(Des P. Lambert. Eng R. Cottet. Recess)

1963 (12 Dec). *Europa.* P 13.

772	**173**	25 c. brown, carmine and green	20	20
773		50 c. purple-brown, carmine & black	35	30

(Des B. Minne. Eng J. Miermont (4 c). Des and eng P. Gandon (1 c.), G. Bétemps (2 c., 3 c.), J. Pheulpin (10 c., 15 c.), C. Durrens (20 c., 25 c.), J. Combet (30 c., 50 c.), P. Béquet (95 c., 1 f.). Recess)

1963 (12 Dec). *Centenary of (English) Football Association.* T **174** *and various designs.* P 13.

774	1 c. violet, yellow-green and red		5	5
775	2 c. red, black and green		5	5
776	3 c. orange, olive-brown and red		5	5
777	4 c. black, carmine-red, green and blue		5	5

Multicoloured. Horiz designs depicting (a) "Football Through the Centuries".

778	10 c. "Calcio", Florence (16th cent)		8	8
779	15 c. "Soule", Brittany (19th cent)		10	10
780	20 c. English military college (after Cruickshank, 1827)		12	12
781	25 c. English game (after Overend, 1890)		15	15

(b) "Modern Football"

782	30 c. Tackling			20	20
783	50 c. Saving goal			30	30
784	95 c. Heading ball			65	65
785	1 f. Corner kick			75	75
774/785	*Set of 12*			2·10	2·10

Designs: As T **174**—4 c. Louis II Stadium, Monaco. This stamp is optd in commemoration of the Association Sportive de Monaco football teams in the French Championships and in the Coupe de France, 1962–63. *Horiz* (36 × 22 *mm*)—2 c. Footballer making return kick; 3 c. Goalkeeper saving ball. Nos. 778/81 and 782/5 were respectively issued together in sheets and arranged in blocks of 4 with a football in the centre of each block.

175 Communications in Ancient Egypt, and Rocket

(Des and eng A. Decaris. Recess)

1964 (22 May). *"PHILATEC 1964" International Stamp Exhibition, Paris.* P 13.

786	**175**	1 f. orange-brown, indigo & deep bl	75	75

176 Reproduction of Rally Postcard Design

(Des and eng Pheulpin (1 c., 2 c., 4 c.), Cottet (3 c., 10 c.), Gandon (5 c., 15 c.), Béquet (20 c., 30 c.), Durrens (25 c., 1 f., 5 f.), Combet (45 c., 50 c.), Gauthier (65 c.), Bétemps (95 c.). Recess)

1964 (22 May). *50th Anniv of First Aerial Rally, Monte Carlo.* T **176** *and similar designs.* P 13.

(a) POSTAGE

787	1 c. olive-brown, blue and green		5	5
788	2 c. bistre, brown-red and blue		5	5

789	3 c. olive-brown, blue & yellow-green	5	5
790	4 c. brown-red, deep bluish grn & blue	5	5
791	5 c. olive-brown, carmine and violet	5	5
792	10 c. violet, olive-brown and blue	10	5
793	15 c. orange, brown and blue	12	10
794	20 c. sepia, bright emerald and blue	15	12
795	25 c. olive-brown, blue and carmine	20	15
796	30 c. deep olive-green, brown-purple & greenish blue	25	20
797	45 c. sepia, turquoise-blue & red-brown	45	40
798	50 c. yellow-ochre, yell-ol & reddish vio	45	45
799	65 c. vermilion, slate and turquoise-blue	50	50
800	95 c. deep bluish green, brown-red and yellow-brown	80	70
801	1 f. chocolate, blue & deep bluish grn	80	75

(b) AIR. Inscr "POSTE AERIENNE 1964"

802	5 f. deep sepia, blue and bistre-brown	3·50	3·25
787/802	*Set of 16*	7·00	6·00

Designs: *Horiz* (48 × 27 *mm*)—Rally planes: 2 c. Renaux's 'Farman'; 3 c. Espanet's "Nieuport"; 4 c. Moineau's "Breguet"; 5 c. Garros' and B. des Moulinais' "Morane-Saulnier"; 10 c. Hirth's "Albatros"; 15 c. Prevost's "Deperdussin". Famous planes and flights: 20 c. "Vickers-Vimy" (Ross Smith: London-Port Darwin, 1919); 25 c. Douglas—"Liberty" (U.S. World Flight, 1924); 30 c. Savoia "S-55" (De Pinedo's World Flight, 1925); 45 c. Fokker "F-7" (First Flight over North Pole, Byrd and Bennett, 1925); 50 c., Ryan—"Spirit of St. Louis" (First solo crossing of N. Atlantic, Lindbergh, 1927); 65 c. "Breguet-19" (Paris-New York, Coste and Bellonte, 1930); 95 c. "Laté-28" (Dakar-Natal, first S. Atlantic airmail flight, Mermoz, 1930); 1 f. Dornier "DO-X" (Germany-Rio de Janeiro, Christiansen, 1930); 5 f. Convair B-58 "Hustler" (New York-Paris in 3 hours, 19' 41" Major Payne, U.S.A.F., 1961).

177 Aquatic Stadium   **178** Europa "Flower"

(Des B. Minne. Eng Cottet. Recess)

1964 (13 July)—**67.** *Precancelled.* P 13.

803	**177**	10 c. multicoloured		55	5
803a		15 c. multicoloured (28.4.67)		30	5
804		25 c. slate-blue, deep blue and black		30	5
805		50 c. reddish violet, blue and black		50	12
803/805	*Set of 4*			1·50	25

The "1962" date has been obliterated with two bars. See also Nos. 949/51a and 1227/1230.

(Des G. Bétemps. Recess)

1964 (12 Sept). *Europa.* P 13.

806	**178**	25 c. red, emerald and indigo		25	20
807		50 c. red-brown, bistre and blue		45	45

179 Weightlifting

437

(Des P. Lambert. Eng Piel (1 c., 2 c.), Cottet (3 c.), Mazelin (4 c.). Des and eng Durrens (5 f.). Recess)

1964 (3 Dec). *Olympic Games, Tokyo and Innsbruck. T* **179** *and similar designs. P* 13.

(a) POSTAGE

808	1 c. brown-red, brown and ultramarine		5	5
809	2 c. brown-red, deep bluish green & olive		5	5
810	3 c. blue, bistre-brown and brown-red		5	5
811	4 c. deep bluish green, olive & brown-red		5	5

(b) AIR. Inscr "POSTE AERIENNE"

812	5 f. brown-red, olive-brown and blue		2·25	2·25
808/812	*Set of* 5		2·25	2·25

Designs: 2 c. Judo; 3 c. Pole-vaulting; 4 c. Archery; 5 f. Bobsleighing.

180 Pres Kennedy and Space Capsule

(Des P. Lambert. Eng Mazelin. Recess)

1964 (3 Dec). *President Kennedy Commemoration. P* 13.

813	**180**	50 c. indigo and blue	70	65

181 Monaco and Television Set   **182** F. Mistral and Statue

(Des and eng Decaris. Recess)

1964 (3 Dec). *Fifth International Television Festival, Monte Carlo. P* 13.

814	**181**	50 c. chocolate, blue and crimson	30	30

(Des P. Lambert. Eng Mazelin. Recess)

1964 (3 Dec). *50th Death Anniv of Fréderic Mistral (poet). P* 13.

815	**182**	1 f. chestnut and deep yellow-olive	45	45

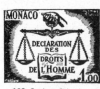

183 Scales of Justice   **184** Route Map from Minsk

(Des and eng Decaris. Recess)

1964 (3 Dec). *15th Anniv of Declaration of Human Rights. P* 13.

816	**183**	1 f. bronze-green and yellow-brown	50	45

(Des B. Minne. Eng Gandon. Recess)

1964 (3 Dec). *34th Monte Carlo Rally. P* 13.

817	**184**	1 f. chocolate, turquoise and ochre	60	55

185 FIFA Emblem

1964 (3 Dec). *60th Anniv of International Federation of Football Associations. (FIFA). Recess. P* 13.

818	**185**	1 f. bistre, blue and red		70	70

186 "Syncom 2" and Globe

(Des and eng Miermont (5 c.), Fenneteaux (10 c.), Cottet (12 c., 50 c., 1 f.), Frères (18 c.), Durrens (25 c., 60 c.), Bétemps (30 c., 70 c.), Pheulpin (95 c.). Des Serres. Eng Piel (10 f.). Recess)

1965 (17 May). *I.T.U. Centenary. T* **186** *and similar designs. P* 13. *(a) POSTAGE.*

819	5 c. grey-green and ultramarine		8	5
820	10 c. orange-brown, olive-brn & deep bl		8	5
821	12 c. brown-purple, carmine & slate-grey		12	12
822	18 c. brown-purple, carmine and indigo		15	15
823	25 c. reddish violet, bistre & brown-purple		20	20
824	30 c. bistre, orange-brown and sepia		25	25
825	50 c. indigo and yellow-green		30	30
826	60 c. blue and red-brown		30	30
827	70 c. deep sepia, orange and blue		45	45
828	95 c. black, indigo and light blue		55	55
829	1 f. brown and bright blue		70	70

(b) AIR. Inscr "POSTE AERIENNE"

830	10 f. deep bluish grn, bl & yellow-brown		4·50	4·50
819/830	*Set of* 12		7·00	7·00

Designs: *Horiz* (As T **186**)—10 c. "Echo 2"; 18 c. "Lunik 3"; 30 c. A. G. Bell and telephone; 50 c. S. Morse and telegraph; 60 c. E. Belin and "belinograph". (48½ × 27 mm) —25 c. "Telstar" and Pleumeur-Bodou Station; 70 c. Roman beacon and Chappe's telegraph; 95 c. Cable-laying ships *Great Eastern* and *Alsace*; 1 f. E. Branly, G. Marconi and English Channel. *Vert* (As T **186**)—12 c. "Relay"; 10 f. Monte Carlo television transmitter.

187 Europa "Sprig"   **188** Monaco Palace (18th Century)

(Des H. Karlsson. Eng C. Haley. Recess)

1965 (25 Sept). *Europa. P* 13.

831	**187**	30 c. brown-red and emerald		15	15
832		60 c. violet and brown-lake		35	30

Monaco   1966

(Des and eng C. Durrens (10 c.), C. Mazelin (18·c., 1 f. 30).
Des R. Serres, eng J. Piel (12 c.). Des A. Spitz, eng J.
Piel (30 c.). Des R. Serres, eng A. Frères (60 c.). Recess)

1966 (1 Feb). 7 with Anniv of Monaco Palace. T **188** and
similar horiz designs. P 13 × 12½.

833	10 c. violet, myrtle-green and grey-blue	10	10
834	12 c. bistre-brown, blue and black ..	10	10
835	18 c. green, black and blue ..	15	15
836	30 c. purple-brown, black and ultramarine	20	20
837	60 c. green, new blue and bistre-brown	25	25
838	1 f. 30, purple-brown and myrtle-green	60	60
833/838	Set of 6	1·25	1·25

Different views of Palace:—12 c. 17th cent; 18 c. 18th cent;
30 c. 19th cent; 60 c. 19th cent; 1 f. 30, 20th cent.

189 Dante

(Des P. Lambert. Eng R. Cottet (30 c.), Monvoisin (60 c.,
1 f.), G. Bétemps (70 c.), C. Durrens (95 c.). Recess)

1966 (1 Feb). 700th Anniv of Dante's Birth. T **189** and similar
horiz designs. P 13.

839	30 c. green, blackish green and scarlet ..	40	40
840	60 c. deep slate-blue, greenish blue & grn	75	75
841	70 c. black, slate-green and carmine-red	75	75
842	95 c. light blue, reddish violet & brt purple	1·60	1·60
843	1 f. turquoise-blue, greenish blue & blue	1·60	1·60
839/843	Set of 5	4·50	4·50

Designs: Scenes from Dante's works—60 c. Dante harassed
by the panther (envy); 70 c. Crossing the 5th circle; 95 c.
Punishment of the arrogant; 1 f. Invocation of St. Bernard.

190 "The Nativity"

191 Route Map from London

(Des and eng C. Durrens. Recess)

1966 (1 Feb). World Association of Children's Friends
(A.M.A.D.E.). P 13 × 12½.

844	**190** 30 c. bistre-brown	20	20

(Des B. Minne. Eng Fenneteaux. Recess)

1966 (1 Feb). 35th Monte Carlo Rally. P 13.

845	**191** 1 f. indigo, purple and carmine-red	55	55

192 Princess Grace with Children

(Des and eng R. Cottet. Recess)

1966 (1 Feb). AIR. Princess Stéphanie's First Birthday.
P 13.

846	**192** 3 f. red-brown, greenish blue and		
	reddish violet	1·75	1·40

193 Casino in 19th Century

194 Europa "Ship"

(Des and eng J. Pheulpin (12 c., 30 c.), J. Gauthier, after
Mulder (60 c.), P. Gandon, (70 c.), M. Monvoisin (95 c.,
1 f. 30), C. Durrens (5 f.). Des B. Minne. Eng G. Bétemps
(25 c., 40 c.). Recess)

1966 (1 June). Centenary of Monte Carlo. T **193** and similar
designs. P 12½ × 13 (12 c.), 13 × 12½ (25 c., 40 c., 95 c.,
1 f. 30) or 13 (others). (a) POSTAGE.

847	12 c. black, crimson and blue ..	12	12
848	25 c. grey-blue, red-brown, green & blue	15	15
849	30 c. reddish purple, grn, orange-brn & bl	20	20
850	40 c. vermilion, orange-yellow, ultra-		
	marine and yellow-olive ..	20	20
851	60 c. new blue, orange-red, brn-pur & grn	30	30
852	70 c. Prussian blue and slate ..	30	30
853	95 c. black and purple	55	55
854	1 f. 30, purple-brown, ol-brn & orge-brn	70	70

(b) AIR. Inscr "POSTE AERIENNE".

855	5 f. lake, ochre and turquoise-blue ..	2·25	2·25
847/855	Set of 9	4·25	4·25

Designs: Sizes as T **193**—Vert—12 c. Prince Charles III.
Horiz—40 c. Charles III Monument; 95 c. Massenet and Saint-
Saëns; 1 f. 30, Fauré and Ravel. (48 × 27 mm)—30 c. F. Blanc,
originator of Monte Carlo and view of 1860; 60 c. Prince Rainier
III and projected esplanade; 70 c. René Blum and Diaghilev,
ballet character from "Petrouchka". (36 × 36 mm)—5 f. Interior of Opera House, 1879.

(Des G. and J. Bender. Eng J. Combet. Recess)

1966 (26 Sept). Europa. P 13.

856	**194** 30 c. yellow-orange	15	15
857	60 c. emerald	35	35

195 Prince Rainier and Princess Grace

197 "Learning to Write"

196 Prince Albert I and Yachts Hirondelle I and Princesse Alice

(Des and eng R. Cottet, after H. Lagriffoul. Recess)
1966 (12 Dec)–**71**. *AIR.* *P* 12½ × 13.
358	**195**	2 f. slate and rose	..	80	30
859		3 f. slate and light emerald	..	2·00	65
860		5 f. slate and light blue ..	..	2·25	95
860*a*		10 f. slate and bistre (7.12.67)	..	3·75	2·50
860*b*		20 f. bistre-brn & red-orge (7.71)	11·00	5·00
858/860*b*		Set of 5 ..	..	..	18·00	8·50

(Des and eng J. Piel. Recess)
1966 (12 Dec). *First International Oceanographic History Congress, Monaco.* *P* 13.
861 **196** 1 f. slate-lilac and blue 55 50

(Des B. Minne, after Z. Domenico. Eng P. Gandon. Recess)
1966 (12 Dec). *20th Anniv of U.N.E.S.C.O.* *P* 12½ × 13.
862 **197** 30 c. brown-purple and magenta .. 12 12
863 60 c. light brown and light blue .. 25 25

198 TV Screen, Cross and Monaco Harbour   **200** W.H.O. Building

199 "Precontinent III"

(Des B. Minne. Eng R. Cami. Recess)
1966 (12 Dec). *Tenth Meeting of International Catholic Television Association (U.N.D.A.), Monaco.* *P* 12½ × 13.
864 **198** 60 c. red, light purple and crimson .. 25 20

(Des J. Roux. Eng A. Frères. Recess)
1966 (12 Dec). *First Anniv of Submarine Research Craft, "Precontinent III".* *P* 13.
865 **199** 1 f. ol-yell, blackish brn & greenish bl 40 35

(Des B. Minne. Eng P. Gandon. Recess)
1966 (12 Dec). *Inauguration of W.H.O. Headquarters, Geneva.* *P* 13×12½.
866 **200** 30 c. bistre-brown, blue-green & blue 12 10
867 60 c. choc, carm-red & blackish grn 20 20

201 Bugatti, 1931   **202** Dog (Egyptian bronze)

(Des and eng Hertenberger (1 c.), Combet (2 c.), Béquet (5 c.), Monvoisin (10 c.), Gauthier (18 c.), Mazelin (20 c., 30 c.), Haley (40 c., 50 c.), Guillame (60 c.). Des Spitz. Eng Pheulpin (25 c.). Des Bétemps. Eng Lambert (70 c.). Des Minne. Eng Mazelin (1 f.), Béquet, (2 f. 30), Fenneteaux (3 f.). Recess)
1967 (28 Apr). *25th Motor Grand Prix, Monaco.* (*a*) *POSTAGE.* *T* **201** *and similar horiz designs. Multicoloured.* *P* 13 × 12½.
868	1 c.	Type **201**	.		5	5
869	2 c.	Alfa Romeo, 1932	..		5	5
870	5 c.	Mercedes, 1936	..	..	8	5
871	10 c.	Maserati, 1948	..	..	8	8
872	18 c.	Ferrari, 1955	..	..	12	12
873	20 c.	Alfa Romeo, 1950	..		12	12
874	25 c.	Maserati, 1957	..		15	12
875	30 c.	Cooper-Climax, 1958	..		20	15
876	40 c.	Lotus-Climax, 1960	..		20	20
877	50 c.	Lotus-Climax, 1961	..		25	20
878	60 c.	Cooper-Climax, 1962	..		35	30
879	70 c.	B.R.M., 1963–6	..		35	30
880	1 f.	Walter Christie, 1907	..		55	50
881	2 f.	30, Peugeot, 1910	..		95	90

    (*b*) *AIR.* *Inscr* "POSTE AÉRIENNE". *P* 13.
882 3 f. black and deep greenish blue .. 1·40 1·25
868/882 *Set of* 15 .. .. .. 4·50 4·00
Design: *Diamond* (50 × 50 *mm*)—3 f. Panhard-Phénix, 1895.

(Des and eng J. Combet. Recess)
1967 (28 Apr). *International Cynological Federation Congress, Monaco.* *P* 12½ × 13.
883 **202** 30 c. black, purple-brown and green 20 15

203 View of Monte Carlo

(Des B. Minne. Eng C. Haley. Recess)
1967 (28 Apr). *International Tourist Year.* *P* 13.
884 **203** 30 c. yellow-brn, myrtle-grn & new bl 15 12

204 Chessboard

(Des B. Minne. Eng Monvoisin. Recess)
1967 (28 Apr). *International Chess Grand Prix, Monaco.* *P* 13.
885 **204** 60 c. black, plum and blue 45 40

205 Melvin Jones (founder). Lions Emblem and Monte Carlo

(Des and eng Cottet. Recess)
1967 (28 Apr). *50th Anniv of Lions International.* *P* 13.
886 **205** 60 c. slate-blue, ultramarine & choc .. 30 25

206 Rotary Emblem and Monte Carlo

(Des B. Minne. Eng Miermont. Recess)
1967 (28 Apr). *Rotary International Convention.* P 13.
887 **206** 1 f. bistre, new blue & light yellow-grn 40 35

207 Fair Buildings

(Des B. Minne. Eng R. Cami. Recess)
1967 (28 Apr). *World Fair, Montreal.* P 13.
888 **207** 1 f. orange-red, slate and blue 40 30

208 Squiggle on Map of **209** Cogwheels
Europe

(Des and eng Decaris. Recess)
1967 (28 Apr). *European Migration Committee (C.I.M.E.).*
P 13.
889 **208** 1 f. chocolate, lt bistre & greenish bl 35 25

(Des O. Bonnevalle. Eng A Frères. Recess)
1967 (28 Apr). *Europa.* P 12½ × 13.
890 **209** 30 c. violet, purple and carmine-red 15 12
891 60 c. green, turquoise-green & emer 25 20

210 Dredger and Coastal Chart

(Des B. Minne. Eng G. Aufschneider. Recess)
1967 (7 Dec). *Ninth International Hydrographic Congress, Monaco.* P 13.
892 **210** 1 f. olive-brown, blue and emerald .. 40 30

HAVE YOU READ THE NOTES AT THE BEGINNING OF THIS CATALOGUE?
These often provide answers to the enquiries we receive.

211 Marie Curie and Scientific Equipment

(Des P. Lambert. Eng J. Pheulpin. Recess)
1967 (7 Dec). *Birth Centenary of Marie Curie.* P 13
893 **211** 1 f. bright blue, olive-brown & brown 40 35

212 Skiing

(Des B. Minne. Eng G. Bétemps. Recess)
1967 (7 Dec). *Winter Olympic Games, Grenoble.* P 13.
894 **212** 2 f. 30, lake-brown, new blue & slate 95 80

213 Prince Rainier I **214** Putting the Shot
(E. Charpentier)

(Des and eng C. Durrens (No. 895), P. Gandon (No. 896).
Recess)
1967 (7 Dec). *Paintings. "Princes and Princesses of Monaco".*
T **213** *and similar vert design. Multicoloured.* P 12½ × 13.
895 1 f. Type **213** .. . . 1·25 95
896 1 f. Lucien Grimaldi (A. di Predis) .. 1·25 95
See also Nos. 932/3, 958/9, 1005/6, 1023/4, 1070/1, 1108/9, 1213/14, 1271/2, 1325 and 1368/1369.

(Des Peyrié. Eng Miermont (20 c.), Monvoisin (30 c.). Des and eng Gandon (60 c.), Durrens (70 c.), Forget (1 f.), Bétemps (2 f. 30), Combet (3 f.). Recess)
1968 (29 Apr). *Olympic Games, Mexico.* T **214** *and similar square designs.* P 13. (*a*) *POSTAGE.*
897 20 c. new blue, brown and emerald .. 15 15
898 30 c. brown, deep violet-blue and plum .. 20 20
899 60 c. blue, bright purple and carmine-red 30 30
900 70 c. brown-red, greenish blue & ochre 30 30
901 1 f. slate-blue, brown and orange-brown 45 45
902 2 f. 30, olive, deep violet-blue and lake .. 95 95

(b) AIR. Inscr "POSTE AÉRIENNE"
903   3 f. turquoise-blue, bluish vio & lt emer   1·40   1·25
897/903   Set of 7   ..   ..   ..   3·25   3·25
Designs:—30 c. High-jumping; 60 c. Gymnastics; 70 c. Water-polo; 1 f. Greco-Roman wrestling; 2 f. 30, Gymnastics (diff); 3 f. Hockey.

215 "St. Martin"

216 "Anemones" (after Raoul Dufy)

(Des P. Lambert. Eng C. Haley. Recess)

1968 (29 Apr). *20th Anniv of Monaco Red Cross. P* 13.
904 **215**   2 f. 30, greenish blue and red-brown   95   90

1968 (29 Apr). *Monte Carlo Floral Exhibitions.* Photo. *P* 12 × 13.
905 **216**   1 f. multicoloured   50   40

217 Insignia of Prince
Charles III and Pope Pius IX

218 Europa "Key"

(Des and eng Frères (10 c.). Des Peyrié. Eng Bétemps (20 c.). Monvoisin (60 c.). Des and eng Hanniquet (30 c.), Gandon (1 f.). Recess)

1968 (29 Apr). *Centenary of "Nullius Diocesis" Abbey. Designs as T* 217. *P* 13 × 12½ (1 f.) *or* 12½ × 13 (*others*).
906   10 c. light brown and scarlet   ..   8   5
907   20 c. red, myrtle-green and yellow-brown   15   15
908   30 c. olive-brown and bright blue   ..   20   15
909   60 c. light brown, new blue & myrtle-grn   25   25
910   1 f. indigo, bistre and blue   40   40
906/910   Set of 5   ..   ..   ..   1·00   90
Designs: *Vert*—20 c. "St. Nicholas" (after Louis Brea); 30 c. "St. Benedict" (after Simone Martini); 60 c. Subiaco Abbey. *Horiz*—1 f. Old St. Nicholas' Church (on site of present cathedral).

(Des H. Schwarzenbach. Recess)

1968 (29 Apr). *Europa. P* 13.
911 **218**   30 c. carmine and bright red-orange   15   12
912   60 c. bright blue and carmine   ..   20   15
913   1 f. lake-brown and emerald   ..   45   40

219 Steam Locomotive, Type 030 (1868)

(Des I. Vidal. Eng Miermont (20 c.), Gauthier (30 c.), Fenneteau (60 c.), Durrens (70 c.), Jumelet (1 f.), Bétemps (2 f. 30). Recess)

1968 (12 Dec). *Centenary of Nice-Monaco Railway. T* **219** *and similar horiz designs. P* 13.
914   20 c. black, blue and dull purple   12   10
915   30 c. black, blue and yellow-olive   ..   15   12
916   60 c. black, blue and ochre   20   20
917   70 c. black, bluish violet and lake-brown   30   25
918   1 f. black, blue and brown-red   40   30
919   2 f. 30, greenish blue, black & rose-red   ..   95   95
914/919   Set of 6   ..   ..   1·90   1·75
Locomotives:—30 c. Steam, Type C-220 (1898); 60 c. Steam, Type 230-C (1910); 70 c. Steam, Type 231-F (1925); 1 f. Steam, Type 241-A (1952); 2 f. 30, Electric, Type BB (1968).

220 Chateaubriand and Combourg Castle

(Des P. Lambert. Eng Monvoisin (10 c., 20 c.), Forget (25 c.), Hanniquet (30 c.), Cami (60 c.), Haley (2 f. 30). Recess)

1968 (12 Dec). *Birth Centenary of Chateaubriand (novelist). T* **220** *and similar horiz designs. P* 13.
920   10 c. plum, blue-green and myrtle-green   10   8
921   20 c. bluish violet, bright purple & new bl   15   12
922   25 c. bistre-brn, dp reddish vio & slate-bl   20   15
923   30 c. deep reddish violet, choc & yell-brn   20   20
924   60 c. chocolate, blue-green & brown-red   30   20
925   2 f. 30, bistre-brown, magenta and blue   95   90
920/925   Set of 6   ..   ..   1·60   1·50
Scenes from Chateaubriand's novels:—20 c. "Le Génie du Christianisme"; 25 c. "René"; 30 c. "Le Dernier Abencérage"; 60 c. "Les Martyrs"; 2 f. 30, "Atala".

221 Law Courts, Paris and statues—"La France et la Fidelité".

(Des and eng Gandon (20 c.), Hanniquet (25 c.), Pheulpin (30 c.), Cami (2 f. 30). Des Peyrié. Eng Haley (60 c.). Recess)

1968 (12 Dec). *Birth Centenary of J. F. Bosio (Monegasque sculptor). T* **221** *and similar designs. P* 13.
926   20 c. bistre-brown and purple-brown   ..   10   5
927   25 c. chocolate and red   12   10
928   30 c. ultramarine and blackish green   ..   15   12
929   60 c. bronze-green and myrtle-green   ..   25   20
930   2 f. 30, black and slate   80   75
926/930   Set of 5   ..   ..   1·25   1·10
Designs: *Vert* (26 × 36 *mm.*)—25 c. "Henry IV as a Child"; 30 c. "J. F. Bosio" (lithograph); 60 c. "Louis XIV". *Horiz* (*as T* **221**)—2 f. 30, "Napoleon I, Louis XVIII and Charles X".

222 W.H.O. Emblem

(Des M. Louis. Photo)
1968 (12 Dec). *20th Anniv of World Health Organization.*
P 13.
931 **222** 60 c. multicoloured   20   20

(Des and eng Combet (1 f.), Pheulpin (2 f. 30). Recess)
1968 (12 Dec). *Paintings. "Princes and Princesses of Monaco". Vert designs as T* **213**. *Multicoloured. P* 13.
932   1 f. "Prince Charles II" (after Mimault) ..   45   45
933   2 f. 30, "Princess Jeanne Grimaldi"
     (Mimault)   95   95

223 The Hungarian March

(Des and eng Decaris. Recess)
1969 (26 Apr). *Death Centenary of Hector Berlioz* (*composer*).
T **223** *and similar designs. P* 13. (*a*) *POSTAGE.*
934   10 c. brown, reddish violet & turq-green   8   8
935   20 c. brown, magenta & deep olive-brn   10   8
936   25 c. chocolate, indigo and magenta   ..   12   10
937   30 c. black, yellow-green and slate-blue   15   12
938   40 c. brown-red, black and slate   ..   20   15
939   50 c. deep olive-brown, slate and purple   25   20
940   70 c. brown, slate and myrtle-green   ..   30   30
941   1 f. black, magenta and brown   ..   40   40
942   1 f. 15, black, new blue & turq-blue ..   50   50

(*b*) *AIR. Inscr* "POSTE AERIENNE"
943   2 f. black, bright blue & myrtle-green ..   90   80
934/943   *Set of* 10   ..   ..   ..   2·75   2·40
Designs: *Horiz* (Scenes from Berlioz's "The Damnation of Faust")—20 c. Mephistopheles appears to Faust; 25 c. Auerbach's tavern; 30 c. Sylphs' ballet; 40 c. Minuet of the goblins; 50 c. Marguerite's bedroom; 70 c. "Forests and Caverns"; 1 f. The journey to Hell; 1 f. 15, Heaven. *Vert*—2 f. Bust of Berlioz.

224 "St. Elisabeth of Hungary"   **225** "Napoleon I"
                                                    (P. Delaroche)

(Des P. Lambert. Eng C. Haley. Recess)
1969 (26 Apr). *Monaco Red Cross. P* 13.
944 **224** 3 f. indigo, olive-brown and red   ..   1·25   1·25

(Des G. Bétemps. Photo)
1969 (26 Apr). *AIR. Birth Bicentenary of Napoleon Bonaparte.*
P 12 × 13.
945 **225** 3 f. multicoloured   ..   ..   ..   1·40   1·25

ALBUM LISTS

Write for our latest lists of albums
and accessories.
These will be sent free on request.

226 Colonnade

227 "Head of Woman"
(Da Vinci)

228 Marine Fauna, King Alfonso   **229** I.L.O. Emblem
XIII of Spain and Prince Albert I
of Monaco

(Des Gasbarra and Belli. Eng Fenneteaux. Recess)
1969 (26 Apr). *Europa. P* 13.
946 **226** 40 c. carmine-red and purple   ..   15   12
947   70 c. new blue, bistre and black   ..   30   20
948   1 f. ochre, brown & light greenish bl   40   30

1969–71. *Precancelled. Design as T* **177**, *but without the obliterated date at top. P* 13×12½.
949   22 c. chocolate, blue and black   ..   20   5
949*a*   26 c. reddish violet, brt bl & blk (7.71)   20   5
949*b*   30 c. multicoloured (7.71)   20   5
950   35 c. multicoloured   20   10
950*a*   45 c. multicoloured (7.71)   20   10
951   70 c. black and ultramarine   ..   30   15
951*a*   90 c. yellow-olive, turq-bl & blk (7.71)   45   15
949/951*a*   *Set of* 7   ..   ..   ..   1·60   60

(Des from photographs. Eng R. Cami (30 c., 3 f.), J. Pheulpin (70 c., 80 c.). Des A. Peyrié. Eng Lacaque (40 c.), Miermont (1 f. 15). Recess)

1969 (25 Nov). *450th Death Anniv of Leonardo da Vinci.*
T **227** *and similar vert designs. P* 13.
952   30 c. bistre-brown   12   10
953   40 c. rose-red and brown   15   12
954   70 c. myrtle-green   25   20
955   80 c. sepia   30   25
956   1 f. 15, chestnut   50   45
957   3 f. light bistre-brown ..   ..   1·00   95
952/957   *Set of* 6   ..   ..   2·00   1·90
Da Vinci's drawings:—40 c. Self-portrait; 70 c. "Head of an Old Man"; 80 c. "Head of St. Madeleine", 1 f. 15, "Man's Head"; 3 f. "Condottiere".

(Des and eng G. Bétemps (1 f.), R. Cottet (3 f.). Recess)

1969 (25 Nov). *Paintings. "Princes and Princesses of Monaco". Vert designs as T* **213**. *Multicoloured. P* 13.
958   1 f. "Prince Honoré II" (Champaigne) ..   50   50
959   3 f. "Princess Louise-Hippolyte" (Champaigne)   ..   ..   ..   1·25   1·25

(Des A. Peyrié. Eng J. Pheulpin. Recess)

1969 (25 Nov). *50th Anniv of International Commission for Scientific Exploration of the Mediterranean, Madrid. P* 13.
960 **228** 40 c. greenish blue and black   ..   20   20

(Des B. Minne. Eng R. Fenneteaux. Recess)
1969 (25 Nov). *50th Anniv of International Labour Organization. P* 13.
961 **229** 40 c. multicoloured   20   20

230 Aerial View of Monaco and TV Camera

231 J.C.C. Emblem

(Des A. Peyrié. Eng R. Fenneteaux. Recess)

1969 (25 Nov). *10th International Television Festival.* P 13.
962 **230** 40 c. bright purple, brn-lake & new bl .. 20 .. 20

(Des B. Minne. Eng C. Haley. Recess)

1969 (25 Nov). *25th Anniv of Junior Chamber of Commerce.*
P 13.
963 **231** 40 c. deep violet-blue, bistre & new bl .. 20 .. 20

232 Alphonse Daudet and Scenes from "Lettres"

(Des P. Lambert. Eng Fenneteaux (30 c.), Lacaque (40 c.),
Forget (70 c.), Jumelet (80 c.), Bétemps (1 f. 15). Recess)

1969 (25 Nov). *Centenary of Daudet's "Lettres de Mon
Moulin".* T **232** *and similar horiz designs.* P 13.
964   30 c. lake, reddish violet and blue-green   20   20
965   40 c. olive-green, purple-brown & ultram   30   30
966   70 c. brn, blackish brn, reddish vio & vio   35   35
967   80 c. bluish vio, lake-brn & blackish grn   40   40
968   1 f. 15, bistre-brn, brn-orange & blue   50   50
964/968   *Set of 5* .. ..   1·60   1·60
    Designs: Scenes from the book—40 c. "Installation"
(Daudet writing); 70 c. "Mule, Goat and Wolf"; 80 c. "Gaucher's
Elixir" and "The Three Low Masses"; 1 f. 15, Daudet drinking,
"The Old Man" and "The Country Sub-Prefect".

233 Conference Building, Albert I and Rainier III

234 Baby Seal

(Des and eng J. Pheulpin. Recess)

1970 (21 Feb). *Interparliamentary Union's Spring Meeting,
Monaco.* P13.
969 **233** 40 c. black, red and maroon .. 20 .. 15

(Des A. Peyrié. Eng C. Jumelet. Recess)

1970 (16 Mar). *Protection of Baby Seals.* P 13.
970 **234** 40 c. drab, light greenish bl & brt pur .. 20 .. 15

235 Japanese Print

236 Dobermann

(Des A. Peyrié. Eng E. Lacaque (20 c., 40 c., 70 c.). Des and
eng C. Jumelet (30 c., 1 f. 15). Recess)

1970 (16 Mar). *Expo 70.* T **235** *and similar designs.* P 13.
971   20 c. chocolate, yellow-green & dp carm   10   10
972   30 c. brown, buff and yellow-green   ..   15   15
973   40 c. bistre and deep reddish violet   ..   20   20
974   70 c. brownish grey and red   40   40
975   1 f. 15, red, myrtle-green and claret   ..   55   55
971/975   *Set of 5* .. ..   1·25   1·25
    Designs: *Vert*—30 c. Ibises (birds); 40 c. Shinto temple
gateway. *Horiz*—70 c. Cherry blossom; 1 f. 15, Monaco Palace
and Osaka Castle.

(Des and eng Jumelet. Recess)

1970 (25 Apr). *International Dog Show, Monte Carlo.* P 13.
976 **236** 40 c. black and orange-brown   ..   20   15

237 *Parnassius apollo*

238 "St. Louis" (King of France)

(Des and eng P. Gandon (30 c., 80 c.), P. Forget (40 c., 1 f.),
G. Bétemps (50 c., 1 f. 15). Recess)

1970 (4 May). *20th Anniv of World Federation for Protection
of Animals.* T **237** *and similar designs.* P 13.
977   30 c. black, red and greenish blue   ..   15   12
978   40 c. red-brown, new blue & myrtle-grn   20   15
979   50 c. brown, light ochre & light blue   20   15
980   80 c. bistre-brn, turq-blue & myrtle-grn   35   25
981   1 f. chocolate, light bistre and slate   ..   45   30
982   1 f. 15, blackish brn, yell-grn & light bl   50   40
977/982   *Set of 6* .. ..   1·75   1·25
    Designs: *Horiz*—40 c. Basque ponies; 50 c. Seal. *Vert*—80 c.
Izards (antelopes); 1 f. Ospreys; 1 f. 15, Otter.

(Des P. Lambert. Eng C. Haley. Recess)

1970 (4 May). *Monaco Red Cross.* P 13.
983 **238** 3 f. myrtle-green, olive-brn & dp sl   1·25   1·25
    See also Nos. 1022, 1041, 1114, 1189 and 1270.

239 "Roses and Anemones" (Van Gogh)

1970 (4 May). *Monte Carlo Flower Show. Photo.* P 12 × 13
984 **239** 3 f. multicoloured .. ..   1·25   1·25
    See also Nos. 1042 and 1073.

THE WORLD CENTRE FOR
FINE STAMPS IS 391 STRAND

240 Moon Plaque, Pres Kennedy and Nixon

(Des J. Pheulpin (80 c.). Photo)
1970 (4 May). *First Man on the Moon* (1969). *T* **240** *and similar horiz design. Multicoloured. P* 13.
985 40 c. Type **240** 20 15
986 80 c. Astronauts on Moon 45 30

241 New U.P.U. Building, **242** "Flaming Sun" and Monument

(Des B. Minne. Eng R. Quillivic. Recess)
1970 (4 May). *New U.P.U Headquarters Building P* 13.
987 **241** 40 c. olive-brown, black & turq-grn 20 15
(Des M. Louis, after L. le Brocquy. Eng R. Fenneteaux. Recess)
1970 (4 May). *Europa. P* 13.
988 **242** 40 c. bright purple 20 10
989 80 c. blue-green 30 12
990 1 f. blue 40 25

243 Camargue Horse

(Des and eng R. Cottet (10, 40 c.), G. Bétemps (20, 50 c.), J. Pheulpin (30 c., 1 f. 15), P. Gandon (70, 85 c.), C. Durrens (3 f.). Recess)
1970 (15 Dec). *Horses. T* **243** *and similar designs. P* 13×12½.
(a) POSTAGE
991 10 c. slate-blue, olive and new blue .. 8 5
992 20 c. brown, olive and ultramarine .. 10 8
993 30 c. light brown, myrtle-green and blue 15 10
994 40 c. grey, bistre-brown and slate .. 20 15
995 50 c. chocolate, olive and blue 25 20
996 70 c. bistre-brown, orge-brn & myrtle-grn 35 20
997 85 c. slate-blue, blackish green and olive 40 35
998 1 f. 15, black, yellow-green & grnsh bl 50 45
(b) AIR
999 3 f. brown-red, black, olive and brown 1·40 95
991/999 *Set of 9* .. .. .. 3·00 2·10
Horses: *Horiz (as T* **243**)—20 c. Anglo-Arab; 30 c. French saddle-horse; 40 c. Lippizaner; 50 c. Trotter; 70 c. English thoroughbred; 85 c. Arab; 1 f. 15, Barbary. *Diamond* (51×51 *mm*)—3 f. Rock-drawings of horses, Lascaux cave.

244 Dumas, D'Artagnan and the Three Musketeers

(Des and eng P. Forget. Recess)
1970 (15 Dec). *Birth Centenary of Alexandre Dumas (père)* (*author*). *P* 13.
1000 **244** 30 c. slate, red-brown and new blue 12 10

245 H. Rougier and Blériot Aircraft

(Des and eng P. Gandon. Recess)
1970 (15 Dec). *60th Anniversary of First Mediterranean Flight. P* 13.
1001 **245** 40 c. bistre-brown, blue and slate.. 20 12

246 De Lamartine and scenes from "Méditations Poétiques"

(Des P. Lambert. Eng C. Jumelet. Recess)
1970 (15 Dec). *150th Birth Anniv of A. de Lamartine* (*writer*). *P* 13.
1002 **246** 80 c. purple-brn, greenish bl & turq 30 25

247 Beethoven

248 Cocker Spaniel

(Des and eng P. Gandon. Recess)
1970 (15 Dec). *Birth Bicentenary of Beethoven. P* 13.
1003 **247** 1 f. 30, sepia and claret 65 55

(Des and eng G. Bétemps. Recess)
1970 (15 Dec). *50th Death Anniv of Modigliani. Vert painting as T* **213**. *Multicoloured. P* 12×13.
1004 3 f. "Portrait of Dédie" (Modigliani) .. 1·25 1·25

(Des J. Pheulpin. Eng J. Combet (1 f.). Des and eng C. Durrens (3 f.). Recess)
1970 (15 Dec). *Paintings "Princes and Princesses of Monaco". Vert designs as T* **213**. *P* 12×13.
1005 1 f. red and black 45 45
1006 3 f. multicoloured .. .. .. 1·25 1·25
Portraits:—1 f. "Prince Louis I" (F. de Troy); 3 f. "Princess Charlotte de Gramont" (S. Bourdon).

(Des P. Lambert. Photo)
1971 (6 Sept). *International Dog Show, Monte Carlo. P* 13×12½.
1007 **248** 50 c. multicoloured 30 20
See also Nos. 1036, 1082, 1119, 1218 and 1239.

249 Polluted Sea-bird   **250** Hand holding Emblem

(Des F. Bel and G. Vienne. Eng C. Jumelet. Recess)

1971 (6 Sept). *Campaign Against Pollution of the Sea.* P 13.
1008 **249** 50 c. indigo and blue 25 20

(Des B. Minne. Eng P. Gandon. Recess)

1971 (6 Sept). *7th International Blood Donors Federation Congress.* P 13×12½.
1009 **250** 80 c. red, violet and pale grey . . 30 25

251 Sextant, Scroll and Underwater Scene

(Des B. Minne. Eng E. Lacaque. Recess)

1971 (6 Sept). *50th Anniversary of International Hydrographic Bureau.* P 13.
1010 **251** 80 c. bistre-brn, turq-grn & slate-grn   30 25

252 Detail of Michelangelo   **253** Europa Chain
Painting (''The Arts'')

(Des J. Pheulpin (1 f.). Des and eng C. Jumelet (others).
Photo (1 f.) or recess (others))

1971 (6 Sept). *25th Anniversary of U.N.E.S.C.O.* T **252** and
similar designs. P 13×12½ (horiz) or 12½×13 (vert).
1011   30 c. light brown, new blue and violet . .   15   8
1012   50 c. indigo and orange-brown   . .   20   12
1013   80 c. brown and light emerald   . .   35   20
1014   1 f. 30, grey-green   50   40
1011/1014   Set of 4   . .   . .   . .   1·10   75
Designs: *Vert*—50 c. Alchemist and dish aerial (''Sciences'');
1 f. 30, Prince Pierre of Monaco (National U.N.E.S.C.O. Commission). *Horiz*—80 c. Ancient scribe, book and T.V. screen
(''Culture'').

(Des H. Haflidason. Eng R. Fenneteaux. Recess)

1971 (6 Sept). *Europa.* P 13×12½.
1015 **253** 50 c. carmine   20   12
1016   80 c. new blue   30   20
1017   1 f. 30, slate-green   50   25

254 Old Bridge, Sospel

(Des B. Minne. Eng Jumelet (50 c.), Miermont (80 c.),
Fenneteaux (3 f.). Recess)

1971 (6 Sept). *Protection of Historical Monuments.* T **254** and
similar designs. P 13.
1018   50 c. bistre-brown, grey-blue & grey-grn   20   12
1019   80 c. brown, blackish green and grey . .   30   15
1020   1 f. 30, red, blackish green and brown   45   30
1021   3 f. slate, greenish blue and olive   . .   1·10   75
1018/1021   Set of 4 . .   . .   1·90   1·10
Designs: *Horiz*—80 c. Roquebrune Chateau; 1 f. 30,
Grimaldi Château, Cagnes-sur-Mer. *Vert*—3 f. Roman ''Trophy
of the Alps'', La Turbie.

(Des P. Lambert. Eng C. Haley. Recess)

1971 (6 Sept). *Monaco Red Cross. Design similar to T **238**,
but showing St. Vincent de Paul.* P 13.
1022   3 f. purple-brown, olive-brn & blue-grn   1·25   1·10

(Des and eng Bétemps (1 f.), Durrens (3 f.). Recess)

1972 (18 Jan). *Paintings. ''Princes and Princesses of Monaco''.
Vert designs similar to T **213**. Multicoloured.* P 12×13.
1023   1 f. ''Prince Antoine I'' (Rigaud)   . .   40   35
1024   3 f. ''Princess Marie de Lorraine'' (18th-
cent French School)   . .   . .   1·25   1·00

255 La Fontaine and   **256** Saint-Saëns and Scene from Opera,
Animal Fables (350th)   ''Samson and Delilah''

(Des and eng Gandon. Recess)

1972 (18 Jan). *Birth Anniversaries (1971).* T **255** and similar
vert design. P 13.
1025   50 c. olive-brown, emerald and grey-grn   20   12
1026   1 f. 30, deep maroon, black and red . .   55   45
Design:—1 f. 30, Baudelaire, nudes and cats (150th).

(Des and eng Bétemps. Recess)

1972 (18 Jan). *50th Death Anniv (1971) of Saint-Saëns.*
P 13.
1027 **256** 90 c. light bistre-brown and sepia . .   40   25

PUZZLED?

Then you need
PHILATELIC TERMS ILLUSTRATED
to tell you all you need to know about printing
methods, papers, errors, varieties, watermarks,
perforations, etc. 192 pages, almost half in full
colour, soft cover. £1·95 post paid.

257 Battle Scene

(Des and eng Gandon. Recess)

1972 (18 Jan). *400th Anniversary of Battle of Lepanto, 1571.*
P 13.
1028 **257** 1 f. new blue, chocolate and red .. 45 30

258 "Christ before Pilate" **259** "The Cradle" (B. Morisot)
(engraving by Dürer)

(Des and eng Cami. Recess)

1972 (18 Jan). *500th Birth Anniv (1971) of Albrecht Dürer.*
P 13.
1029 **258** 2 f. black and brown 80 55

(Des and eng Combet. Recess)

1972 (18 Jan). *25th Anniversary (1971) of Foundation of
U.N.I.C.E.F.* P 12×13.
1030 **259** 2 f. multicoloured 80 55

260 "Gilles" (Watteau) **261** Santa Claus

(Des and eng Miermont. Recess)

1972 (18 Jan). *250th Death Anniv (1971) of Watteau.*
P 12×13.
1031 **260** 3 f. multicoloured .. .. .. 1·25 1·00

(Des and eng Forget. Recess)

1972 (18 Jan). *Christmas (1971).* P 12½×13.
1032 **261** 30 c. red, indigo and ochre .. 12 8
1033 50 c. red, green and yellow-orange 20 12
1034 90 c. red, greenish blue and ochre .. 35 25

262 Steam Locomotive and Modern Express

(Des and eng P. Forget. Recess)

1972 (17 Apr). *50th Anniv of International Railway Union.*
P 13.
1035 **262** 50 c. maroon, lilac and carmine .. 20 12

(Des P. Lambert. Photo)

1972 (27 Apr). *International Dog Show, Monte Carlo. Horiz
design similar to T **248** but showing Great Dane and inscr
"1972".* P 13×12½.
1036 60 c. multicoloured 30 20

263 "Pollution Kills"

(Des Chesnot. Eng C. Jumelet. Recess)

1972 (27 Apr). *Anti-Pollution Campaign.* P 13.
1037 **263** 90 c. brown, emerald and black .. 40 25

264 Ski-jumping **265** "Communications"

(Des and eng P. Forget. Recess)

1972 (27 Apr). *Winter Olympic Games, Sapporo, Japan.* P 13.
1038 **264** 90 c. black, red and turquoise-green 45 30

(Des P. Huovinen. Eng G. Bétemps. Recess)

1972 (27 Apr). *Europa.* P 12½×13.
1039 **265** 50 c. deep blue and red-orange .. 20 12
1040 90 c. deep ultramarine and green .. 40 25

(Des P. Lambert. Eng C. Haley. Recess)

1972 (27 Apr). *Monaco Red Cross. Design similar to T **238**
but showing St. Francis of Assisi.* P 13.
1041 3 f. chestnut and plum .. .. 1·25 1·00

1972 (27 Apr). *Monte Carlo Flower Show. Design similar to
T **239** but showing "Vase of Flowers" (Cezanne). Photo.*
P 12×13.
1042 3 f. multicoloured .. .. .. 1·00 75

266 "SS. Giovanni e   267 Dressage
Paulo" (detail, Canaletto)

(Des and eng J. Pheulpin. Recess)

1972 (27 Apr). *U.N.E.S.C.O. "Save Venice" Campaign. T 266
and similar vert designs. P* 13.

1043	30 c. rosine and carmine-red	..	..	25	20
1044	60 c. reddish violet	..	..	..	30	20
1045	2 f. turquoise-blue	..	..	..	70	50

Designs: (27×48 *mm*)—60 c. "S. Pietro di Castello"
(F. Guradi). (*As T* 266)—2 f. "Piazzetta S. Marco" (B.
Bellotto).

(Des and eng P. Forget. Recess)

1972 (27 Apr). *Olympic Games, Munich. Equestrian Events.
T 267 and similar vert designs. P* 13.

1046	60 c. brown, ultramarine and lake	..	40	35
1047	90 c. lake, brown and ultramarine	..	65	60
1048	1 f. 10, ultramarine, lake and brown	..	75	70
1049	1 f. 40, brown, lake and ultramarine	..	1·10	1·00
1046/1049	*Set of 4*	..	..	2·75	2·40

Designs:—90 c. Cross-country; 1 f. 10, Show-jumping
(wall); 1 f. 40, Show-jumping (parallel bars).
Nos. 1046/49 were issued together *se-tenant* in blocks of
four within the sheet, which also included vert strip of *se-tenant*
stamp-sized labels bearing commemorative inscriptions.

268 Escoffier and Birthplace   269 Drug Addiction

(Des and eng G. Bétemps. Recess)

1972 (6 May). *125th Birth Anniv of Auguste Escoffier* (*master
chef*). *P* 13×12½.

| 1050 | **268** 45 f. black and bistre | .. | .. | 20 | 12 |

(Des and eng. C. Jumelet. Recess)

1972 (3 July). *Campaign Against Drugs. P* 12½×13.

1051	**269** 50 c. scarlet, bistre-brn & red-orge	20	12
1052	90 c. blackish green, bistre-brown
	and indigo	..	..	35	25

See also Nos. 1088/91 and 1280/1.

A regular new issue supplement to this
catalogue appears each month in

STAMP MONTHLY

—from your newsagent or by postal subscription
—details on request.

270 Globe, Birds and Animals   271 Lilies in Vase

(Des and eng A. Decaris. Recess)

1972 (25 Sept). *17th International Congress of Zoology,
Monaco. T 270 and similar symbolic designs. P* 13.

1053	30 c. blue-green, olive-brown and red	12	10
1054	50 c. orange-brown, dull purple and
	lake-brown (*horiz*)	..	..	20	15
1055	90 c. new blue, olive-brown & lake-brn	35	25

(Des P. Lambert (30 c., 50 c.), Yolef (90 c.). Photo Delrieu)

1972 (13 Nov). *Monte Carlo Flower Show,* 1973. (1*st issue*).
T 271 and similar vert designs. Multicoloured. P 13.

1056	30 c. Type 271	..	..	..	12	8
1057	50 c. Bouquet	..	..	..	20	15
1058	90 c. Flowers in vase	..	..	..	35	20

See also Nos. 1105/4, 1143/4, 1225/6, 1244, 1282/3 and
1316/17.

272 "The Nativity" and   274 "Gethsemane"
Child's Face

273 Blériot and Aircraft

(Des and eng P. Forget. Recess)

1972 (13 Nov). *Christmas. P* 13×12½.

1059	**272** 30 c. grey, deep blue & brt purple	..	12	8
1060	50 c. carmine, brt purple & lake-brn	20	10
1061	90 c. bluish violet, plum and reddish
	violet	..	..	..	35	20

(Des and eng G. Bétemps (30 c.), M. Monvoisin (50 c.), Des
Chesnot. Eng Fenneteaux (90 c.). Recess)

1972 (4 Dec). *Birth Anniversaries. T 273 and similar horiz
designs. P* 13.

1062	30 c. new blue and chocolate	..	..	12	8
1063	50 c. steel-blue, turquoise & new blue	20	15
1064	90 c. purple-brown and buff	..	..	40	30

Designs and anniversaries:—30 c. T **273** (birth centenary);
50 c. Amundsen and polar scene (birth centenary); 90 c.
Pasteur and laboratory (150th birth anniv).

Monaco

(Des and eng G. Bétemps (30 c.), C. Haley (50 c.), M. Monvoisin (90 c.), E. Lacaque (others). Recess)

1972 (4 Dec). *Protection of Historical Monuments. Frescoes by J. Canavesio, Chapel of Notre-Dame des Fontaines, La Brigue. T **274** and similar vert designs. P* 12×13.

1065	30 c. cerise	..	..	15	10
1066	50 c. slate	..	..	30	20
1067	90 c. myrtle-green	..	..	40	35
1068	1 f. 40, vermilion	..	..	50	45
1069	2 f. plum	..	..	90	75
1065/1069	*Set of 5* ..	..	..	2·00	1·75

Designs:—50 c. "Christ Outraged"; 90 c. "Ascent to Calvary"; 1 f. 40, "The Resurrection"; 2 f. "The Crucifixion".

(Des and eng C. Slania (1 f.), E. Lacaque (3 f.). Recess)

1972 (4 Dec). *"Princes and Princesses of Monaco". Vert designs similar to T **213**. Multicoloured. P* 12×13.

1070	1 f. "Prince Jacques I" (N. Largillière)		50	40
1071	3 f. "Princess Louise-Hippolyte" (J. B. Vanloo)	..	1·25	1·00

275 "St. Dévote" (triptych by Louis Bréa)

276 Europa "Posthorn"

(Des and eng C. Durrens. Recess)

1973 (May). *25th Anniv of Monaco Red Cross. Sheet* 100×130 *mm. P* 13.
MS1072 **275** 5. f. brown-red .. .. 9·00 9·00

1973 (May). *Monte Carlo Flower Show* (2nd issue). *Vert design similar to T **239** but showing "Bouquet of Flowers" (Bosschaert.) Photo. P* 12×13.
1073 3 f. 50, multicoloured .. .. .. 1·40 1·00

(Des and eng G. Bétemps, after L. F. Anisdahl. Recess)

1973 (May). *Europa. P* 13×12½.
1074	**276**	50 c. orange	..	20	12
1075		90 c. blue-green	..	40	20

277 Molière and Characters from "La Malade Imaginaire"

278 Colette, Cat and Books

(Des and eng C. Durrens. Recess)

1973 (May). *300th Death Anniv of Molière. P* 13.
1076 **277** 20 c. red, brown and deep ultram .. 20 12

(Des and eng P. Gandon (30 c., 45 c.); Des P. Lambert, Eng C. Guillaume (50 c.). Des and eng C. Jumelet (90 c.). Recess)

1973 (May). *Birth Anniversaries. T **278** and similar designs P* 12½×13 (50 c.) *or* 13×12½ (*others*)

1077	30 c. black, deep blue and vermilion	..	20	12
1078	45 c. multicoloured	.. ..	20	12
1079	50 c. lilac, bright purple & ultramarine		20	12
1080	90 c. multicoloured	.. ..	40	30
1077/1080	*Set of 4* ..	..	90	60

Designs and anniversaries: *Horiz*—30 c. T **278** (nature writer, birth centenary); 45 c. J.-H. Fabre and insects (entomologist, 150th birth anniv); 90 c. Sir George Cayley and early flying machines (aviation pioneer, birth bicentenary). *Vert*—50 c. Blaise Pascal (philosopher and writer, 350th birth anniv). ..

279 E. Ducretet, "Les Invalides" and Eiffel Tower   **281** Telecommunications Equipment

280 C. Péguy and Chartres Cathedral

(Des and eng J. Pheulpin, Recess)

1973 (May). *75th Anniv of Eugene Ducretet's First Hertzian Radio Link. P* 13×12½.
1081 **279** 30 c. brown-red, slate-lilac and deep olive 20 12

(Des P. Lambert. Photo)

1973 (May). *International Dog Show, Monte Carlo. Horiz design similar to T **248** but showing Alsatian and inscr* "1973". *P* 13×12½.
1082 45 c. multicoloured 20 12

(Des and eng J. Combet. Recess)

1973 (May). *Birth Centenary of Charles Péguy* (writer). *P* 13.
1083 **280** 50 c. olive-brown, claret & slate .. 25 15

(Des A. Peyrié. Eng Lacaque. Recess)

1973 (May). *5th World Telecommunications Day. P* 13×12½.
1084 **281** 60 c. bluish violet, lt blue & brn-lake 25 15

282 Stage Characters   **283** Ellis and Rugby Tackle

Monaco   1973

(Des Chesnot. Eng J. Larrivière. Recess)

1973 (May). *5th World Amateur Theatre Festival. P* 13.
1085 **282** 60 c. lilac, light blue and red   30   15

(Des and eng P. Forget. Recess)

1973 (May). *150th Anniv of Founding of Rugby Football by William Webb Ellis. P* 13×12½.
1086 **283** 90 c. cerise. lake and brown   40   30

284 St. Theresa

(Des Chesnot. Eng E. Lacaque. Recess)

1973 (May). *Birth Centenary of St. Theresa of Lisieux. P* 13.
1087 **284** 1 f. 40, multicoloured   65   45

285 Drug Addiction

(Des A. Peyrié. Eng C. Haley (Nos. 1088, 1090), P. Forget (others). Recess)

1973 (May–2 July). *Campaign Against Drugs. T* **285** *and similar horiz design. P* 13×12½.
1088 **285** 50 c. crimson, blackish grn & new bl   20   10
1089 —   50 c. multicoloured (2.7)   20   20
1090 **285** 90 c. reddish violet, light emerald
                  and red-orange   40   25
1091 —   90 c. multicoloured (2.7)   40   30
1088/1091 *Set of 4* . .   1·10   75
Design:—Nos. 1089, 1091, Children, syringes and addicts.

286 "Institution of the Crèche" (Giotto)

(Des P. Lambert (30 c., 45 c., 50 c., 2 f.), C. Haley (1 f.) and M. Monvoisin (3 f.). Eng E. Lacaque (30 c.), P. Forget (45 c.), J. Combet (50 c.) and P. Béquet (2 f.). Recess)

1973 (12 Nov). *750th Anniv of St. Francis of Assisi Crèche. T* **286** *and similar designs. P* 12×13 (*vert*) or 13×12 (*horiz*).
     (*a*) POSTAGE
1092   30 c. plum   20   15
1093   45 c. crimson   20   20
1094   50 c. orange-brown   25   20
1095   1 f. myrtle-green   45   45
1096   2 f. olive-brown   95   90
     (*b*) AIR. *Inscr* "POSTE AERIENNE"
1097   3 f. turquoise-blue . .   . .   1·10   95
1092/1097 *Set of 6* . .   . .   . .   3·00   2·50
Designs: *Horiz*—45 c. "The Nativity" (School of F. Lippi); 50 c. "The Birth of Jesus Christ" (Giotto). *Vert*—1 f. "The Nativity" (15th-century miniature) ; 2 f. "The Birth of Jesus" (Fra Angelico); 3 f. "The Nativity" (Flemish School).

287 Country Picnic

(Des B. Minne. Eng C. Haley (10 c. 50 c.) P. Forget (20 c., 45 c.), N. Hanniquet (30 c.), C. Guillame (60 c.), M. Monvoisin (1 f.). Recess)

1973 (12 Nov). *50th Anniv of National Committee for Monegasque Traditions. T* **287** *and similar designs. P* 13.
1098   10 c. blue, myrtle-grn & bistre-brown . .   10   10
1099   20 c. reddish vio, new bl & dp olive   . .   12   12
1100   30 c. sepia, light brown & brt green   . .   15   15
1101   45 c. carmine-red, reddish violet and
                  dull purple   25   25
1102   50 c. multicoloured   25   25
1103   60 c. cerise, bluish violet & new blue . .   30   30
1104   1 f. violet, bluish violet & olive-brn . .   50   50
1098/1104 *Set of 7* . .   . .   . .   1·50   1·50
Designs: *Vert*—20 c. Maypole dance. *Horiz*—30 c. "U Brandi" (local dance); 45 c. "St. Jean Fire Dance"; 50 c. Blessing the Christmas loaf; 60 f. Blessing the sea (Festival of St. Dévote); 1 f. Corpus Christi procession, Good Friday.

(Des P. Lambert. Photo Delneu)

1973 (12 Nov). *Monte Carlo Flower Show, 1974. Vert designs similar to T* **271**. *Multicoloured. P* 13.
1105   45 c. Roses and strelitzia   . .   20   12
1106   60 c. Mimosa and myosotis   . .   30   25
1107   1 f. "Vase of Flowers" (Odilon Redon)   45   35

(Des and eng P. Gandon (No. 1108), C. Durrens (1109). Recess)

1973 (12 Nov). *"Princes and Princesses of Monaco". Vert designs as T* **213**. *Multicoloured. P* 12×13.
1108   2 f. "Charlotte Grimaldi" (in day dress.
                  P. Gobert)   . .   1·10   95
1109   2 f. "Charlotte Grimaldi" (in evening
                  dress, P. Gobert) . .   . .   1·10   95

288 Prince Rainier III

289 U.P.U. Emblem and Symbolic Heads

(Des and eng C. Slania. Recess)

1974 (8 May). *25th Anniv of Prince Rainier's Accession. Sheet* 100×130 *mm. Imperf.*
MS1110 **288** 10 f. black   . .   . .   7·00   7·00

(Des and eng A. Decaris. Recess)

1974 (8 May). *Centenary of Universal Postal Union. T* **289** *and similar vert designs. P* 12½×13.
1111   50 c. maroon and orange-brown   . .   20   15
1112   70 c. multicoloured   30   25
1113   1 f. 10, multicoloured   55   45
Designs:—70 c. Hands holding letters; 1 f. 10, "Countries of the World" (famous buildings).

(Des Chesnot. Eng J. Larrivière. Recess)

1974 (8 May). *Monaco Red Cross. Design similar to T* **238**, *but showing St. Bernard of Menthon. P* 13.
1114   3 f. turquoise-blue, deep grn & maroon   1·25   1·10

290 Farman and Aircraft of   **291** Marconi, Circuit Plan
      1909 and 1919   and Ships

(Des and eng J. Gauthier. Recess)

1974 (8 May). *Birth Centenary of Henri Farman* (*aviation pioneer*). *P* 13×12½.
1115   **290**   30 c. bistre-brown, plum & slate-bl   15   10

(Des and eng P. Gandon. Recess)

1974 (8 May). *Birth Centenary of Guglielmo Marconi* (*radio pioneer*). *P* 13×12½.
1116   **291**   40 c. brown-red, steel-blue & new bl   20   12

292 Duchesne and *Penicillium*   **293** Forest and Engine
     glaucum

(Des and eng J. Pheulpin. Recess)

1974 (8 May). *Birth Centenary of Ernest Duchesne* (*microbiologist*). *P* 13×12½.
1117   **292**   45 c. black, new blue and purple   20   12

(Des and eng J. Pheulpin. Recess)

1974 (8 May). *60th Death Anniv of Fernand Forest* (*motor engineer and inventor*). *P* 13×12½.
1118   **293**   50 c. plum, lake and black   20   12

(Des P. Lambert. Photo)

1974 (8 May). *International Dog Show, Monte Carlo. Horiz design similar to T* **248**. *but showing Schnauzer and insc* "1974". *P* 13×12½.
1119   60 c. multicoloured   25   15

294 Ronsard and Characters from "Sonnet to Hélène"

(Des P. Lambert. Eng C. Haley. Recess)

1974 (8 May). *450th Birth Anniv of Pierre de Ronsard* (*poet*). *P* 13.
1120   **294**   70 c. deep brown and rose   ..   30   20

ALBUM LISTS

Write for our latest lists of albums
and accessories.
These will be sent free on request.

295 Sir Winston Churchill   **297** "The King of Rome"
   (after bust by O. Nemon)   (Bosio)

296 Interpol Emblem, and Views of
      Monaco and Vienna

(Des and eng G. Bétemps. Recess)

1974 (8 May). *Birth Centenary of Sir Winston Churchill. P* 12½×13.
1121   **295**   1 f. bistre-brown and grey   45   30

(Des and eng C. Haley. Recess)

1974 (8 May). *60th Anniv of 1st International Police Judiciary Congress and 50th Anniv of International Criminal Police Organization* (*Interpol*). *P* 13.
1122   **296**   2 f. blue, brown-purple & myrtle-grn   75   50

(Des and eng P. Forget. Recess)

1974 (8 May). *Europa. Sculptures by J. F. Bosio. T* **297** *and similar vert design. P* 12½×13.
1123   45 c. myrtle-green and bistre-brown   40   30
1124   1 f. 10, bistre-brown and brown   65   50
MS1125 170×140 mm, Nos. 1123/4×5   10·00 10·00
     Design:—1 f. 10, "Madame Elizabeth".

298 "The Box" (A. Renoir)   **299** Tigers and Trainer

(Des and eng C. Durrens (1126), G. Bétemps (1127, 1131), P. Gandon (1128), J. Pheulpin (1129), R. Cami (1130). Recess)

1974 (12 Nov). *The "Impressionists". Paintings. T* **298** *and similar multicoloured designs. P* 12×13 (*vert*) *or* 13×12 (*horiz*).
1126   1 f. Type **298**   40   25
1127   1 f. "The Dance Class" (E. Degas)   40   25
1128   2 f. "Impression—Sunrise" (C. Monet)
     (*horiz*)   80   50
1129   2 f. "Entrance to Voisins Village" (C.
     Pissarro) (*horiz*)   80   50
1130   2 f. "The Hanged Man's House" (P.
     Cezanne) (*horiz*)   80   50
1131   2 f. "Floods at Port Marly" (A. Sisley)
     (*horiz*)   80   50
1126/1131   *Set of* 6   ..   ..   ..   3·75   2·25

(Des and eng A. Decaris. Recess)

1974 (12 Nov). *1st International Circus Festival, Monaco.*
T **299** *and similar designs.* P 13×12½ *(horiz)* or 12½×13
(vert).

1132	2 c. orange-brn, bronze-grn & new bl				5	5
1133	3 c. maroon and deep mauve		..		5	5
1134	5 c. indigo, cerise and deep brown		..		5	5
1135	45 c. chocolate, grey-black and cerise				20	10
1136	70 c. multicoloured	..	..	..	40	30
1137	1 f. 10, chocolate, bottle-grn & cerise				55	40
1138	5 f. bright emerald, deep turq-bl & red			1·90	1·25
1132/1138	*Set of 7* ..		..		3·00	2·00

Designs: *Vert*—3 c. Performing horses; 45 c. Equestrian act;
1 f. 10, Acrobats; 5 f. Trapeze act. *Horiz*—5 c. Performing
elephants; 70 c. Clowns.
See also Nos. 1221, 1284, 1319 and 1363/1367.

300 Honore II on Medal

301 Marine Flora and Fauna

(Des and eng P. Gandon. Recess)

1974 (12 Nov). *350th Anniv of Monegasque Numismatic Art.*
P 13.

1139	**300**	60 c. deep olive and rosine	..	25	20

(Des and eng P. Lambert. Photo)

1974 (12 Nov). *24th Congress of International Commission for*
Scientific Exploration of Mediterranean. T **301** *and similar*
designs showing marine flora and fauna. P 13×12½ (45 c.)
or 13 *(others)*.

1140	45 c. multicoloured	..	..	20	12
1141	70 c. multicoloured (52×31 mm)	..	30	15
1142	1 f. 10, multicoloured (52×31 mm)	..	40	25

(Des P. Lambert. Photo Delrieu)

1974 (12 Nov). *Monte Carlo Flower Show* (1975). *Vert*
designs similar to T **271**. *Multicoloured.* P 13.

1143	70 c. Honeysuckle and violets	..	30	20
1144	1 f. 10, Iris and chrysanthemums	..	45	25

302 Prince Rainer III

303 Prince Rainer III
(F. Messina)

(Des and eng C. Slania. Recess)

1974 (23 Dec)–**78**. (*a*) *POSTAGE.* P 13.

1145	**302**	60 c. slate-green	..	..	20	10
1146		80 c. rosine	..	..	25	12
1147		80 c. bright blue-green (10.1.77)	..	20	8
1148		1 f. brown	..	..	30	12
1149		1 f. bright carmine (10.1.77)	..	25	10
1149a		1 f. slate-green (1978)	..	25	10
1150		1 f. 20, blue-violet	..	40	20
1150a		1 f. 20, orange-vermilion (1978)	..	40	20
1151		1 f. 25, bright new blue (10.1.77)	..	35	15
1151a		1 f. 50, grey-black (1978)	..	40	25
1151b		1 f. 70, deep turquoise-blue (1978)	..	45	40
1152		2 f. deep reddish lilac	..	55	40
1152a		2 f. 10, olive-brown (1978)	..	55	40
1153		2 f. 50, black (10.1.77)	..	60	30
1153a		9 f. bright violet (1978)	..	2·00	1·10

(*b*) *AIR.* P 12½×13.

1154	**303**	10 f. violet ..	..	..	2·25	1·25
1155		15 f. brown-red	..	..	3·50	1·90
1156		20 f. ultramarine	..	..	4·75	2·75
1145/1156	*Set of 12*	..	..	16·00	9·00

304 Coastline, Monte Carlo

305 *Haageocereus*
chosicensis

(Des and eng C. Jumelet. Recess)

1974 (23 Dec)–**78**. T **304** *and similar designs.* P 13×12½ *(horiz)*
or 12½×13 *(vert)*.

1161	25 c. multicoloured		12	10
1161a	25 c. dp brown, lt green & new bl (1978)	12	10
1162	50 c. sepia and blue		12	10
1162a	65 c. new blue, orge-brn & emer (1978)	20	12
1163	1 f. 10, sepia, bronze-green and new		
	blue (10.1.77)		25	12
1163a	1 f. 30, brown, dp olive & new bl (1978)	35	15
1164	1 f. 40, choc, dull yellowish grn & slate	40	25
1165	1 f. 70, multicoloured ..		45	40
1165a	1 f. 80, orange-brown, yellowish green		
	and new blue (1978)		45	40
1166	3 f. red-brown, slate and deep green	..	85	55
1167	5 f. 50, red-brown, deep green and blue	1·40	1·10
1168	6 f. 50, drab, new blue and bronze-		
	green(1978)		1·75	1·25
1161/1168	*Set of 12* ..		6·00	4·25

Designs: *Vert*—50 c. Palace clock tower; 1 f. 30, Monaco
Cathedral; 1 f. 40, Prince Albert 1 statue and Museum; 3 f. Fort
Antoine. *Horiz*—25 c. As No 1165; 65 c., 1 f. 10, T **304**; 1 f. 70, "All
Saints" tower; 1 f. 80, As No. 1167; 5 f. 50, La Condamine; 6 f. 50,
Aerial view of hotels and harbour.

Numbers have been left for future additions to this series.

(Des P. Lambert. Photo)

1974 (23 Dec). *Plants.* T **305** *and similar vert designs.*
Multicoloured. P 12½×13.

1180	10 c. Type **305**	..	..	5	5
1181	20 c. *Matucana madisoniarum*	..	5	5
1182	30 c. *Parodia scopaioides*	..	8	5
1183	85 c. *Mediolobivia arachnacantha*	..	20	10
1184	1 f. 90, *Matucana yanganucensis*	..	40	25
1185	4 f. *Echinocereus marksianus*	..	90	60
1180/1185	*Set of 6* ..		1·50	1·00

306 "Portrait of a Sailor"
(P. Florence)

307 "St Bernardin de Sienne"

(Des and eng J. Pheulpin. Recess)

1975 (13 May). *Europa.* T **306** *and similar vert design.*
P 12½×13.

1186	80 c. deep magenta	..	..	30	20
1187	1 f. 20, new blue	..	..	45	25

Monaco

MS1188 170×130 mm. Nos. 1186/7×5 .. 4·50 4·50
Design:—1 f. 20, "St. Devote" (L. Brea).

(Des P. Lambert. Eng C. Haley. Recess)
1975 (13 May). *Monaco Red Cross.* P 13.
1189 **307** 4 f. deep turquoise-blue & deep pur 1·60 1·10

308 "Prologue"   309 Saint-Simon

(Des and eng A. Decaris. Recess)
1975 (13 May). *Centenary of "Carmen" (opera by Georges Bizet).* T **308** *and similar designs.* P 12½×13 (*vert*) or 13×12½ (*horiz*).
1190	30 c. black, deep brown & reddish violet	12	8
1191	60 c. slate, dull yellowish grn & car-lake	20	12
1192	80 c. olive-brown, deep green & black	30	15
1193	1 f. 40, blackish pur, ochre & deep brn	55	30
1190/1193	Set of 4	1·00	60

Designs: *Horiz*—60 c. "Lilla Pastia's Tavern"; 80 c. "The Smuggler's Den"; 1 f. 40, "Confrontation at Seville".

(Des and eng P. Gandon. Recess)
1975 (13 May). *300th Birth Anniv of Louis de Saint-Simon (writer).* P 12½×13.
1194 **309** 40 c. blue-black 20 12

310 Dr Albert   311 "Stamp" and Calligraphy
Schweitzer

(Des and eng P. Gandon. Recess)
1975 (13 May). *Birth Centenary of Dr Albert Schweitzer (Nobel Peace Prize-winner).* P 12½×13.
1195 **310** 60 c. deep rose-red 20 15

(Des and eng C. Jumelet. Recess)
1975 (13 May). *"Arphila 1975" International Stamp Exhibition, Paris.* P 13.
1196 **311** 80 c. bistre-brown & orange-brown 40 25

312 Seagull and Sunrise   313 Pike smashing Crab

(Des P. Lambert. Photo)
1975 (13 May). *International Exposition, Okinawa.* P 13×12½.
1197 **312** 85 c. orge, bright bl & deep turq-grn 40 30

(Des and eng J. Gauthier. Recess)
1975 (13 May). *Anti-Cancer Campaign.* P 13×12½.
1198 **313** 1 f. multicoloured 40 20

314 Christ with   315 Villa Sauber,
Crown of Thorns   Monte Carlo

(Des P. Lambert. Eng E. Lacaque. Recess)
1975 (13 May). *Holy Year.* P 12½×13.
1199 **314** 1 f. 15, slate-black, olive-brown and deep reddish purple .. 45 25

(Des and eng C. Slania. Recess)
1975 (13 May). *European Architectural Heritage Year.* P 13×12½.
1200 **315** 1 f. 20, deep dull grn, sep & new bl 45 30

316 Woman's Head and Globe

(Des P. Lambert. Eng P. Forget. Recess)
1975 (13 May). *International Women's Year.* P 13×12½.
1201 **316** 1 f. 20, multicoloured 45 30

317 Rolls-Royce "Silver Ghost" (1907)

(Des and eng P. Forget (5 c., 5 f. 50,), J. Combet (10 c., 20 c.), C. Durrens (30 c., 1 f. 40,), G. Bétemps (50 c., 60 c., 1 f. 20,), M. Monvoisin (80 c.), C. Guillame (85 c.). Recess)
1975 (12 Nov). *History of the Motor-car.* T **317** *and similar horiz designs.* P 13.
1202	5 c. indigo, deep green and ochre ..	5	5
1203	10 c. indigo and new blue ..	5	5
1204	20 c. new blue, deep ultramarine & bl-blk	8	5
1205	30 c. deep purple and deep mauve .·.	15	5
1206	50 c. indigo, purple and cerise	20	8
1207	60 c. carmine-red ..	20	10
1208	80 c. indigo and deep turquoise-blue ..	30	15
1209	85 c. sepia, orge-brn & dp yellowish grn	30	20
1210	1 f. 20,deep ultramarine, lake-brown and deep yellowish green ..	40	30
1211	1 f. 40, dull yellowish green & new bl	50	30
1212	5 f. 50, new blue and light green ..	1·60	95
1202/1212	Set of 11	3·50	2·00

Designs:—10 c. Hispano Suiza "H.6B" (1926); 20 c. Isotta Fraschini "8A" (1928); 30 c. Cord "L.29"; 50 c. Voisin V12 (1930); 60 c. Duesenberg "SJ" (1933); 80 c. Bugatti "57 C" (1938); 85 c. Delahaye "135 M" (1940); 1 f. 20, Cisitalia "Pininfarina" (1945); 1 f. 40, Mercedes-Benz "300 SL" (1955); 5 f. 50, Lamborghini "Countach" (1974).

(Des and eng C. Slania. Recess)

1975 (12 Nov). *Paintings. "Princes and Princesses of Monaco". Vert designs similar to T **213**. Multicoloured. P* 12½×13.
1213	2 f.	Prince Honore III	..	75	50
1214	4 f.	Princess Catherine de Brignole	..	1·50	75

318 Dog behind Bars   **319** Maurice Ravel

(Des and eng P. Gandon. Recess)

1975 (12 Nov). *125th Birth Anniv of General J. P. Delmas de Grammont (author of Grammont's Law for protection of animals). T **318** and similar designs. P* 12½×13 (80 c.) or 13×12½ (others).
1215	60 c. black and brown	..	..	20	12
1216	80 c. black and brown	..	..	30	15
1217	1 f. 20, slate-green and carmine	..	45	25

Designs: *Vert*—80 c. Cat chased up tree. *Horiz*—1 f. 20, Horses being ill-treated.

(Des P. Lambert. Eng C. Haley. Recess)

1975 (12 Nov). *International Dog Show, Monte Carlo. Horiz design similar to T **248**. P* 13×12½.
1218	60 c. black and magenta	..	..	20	12

Design:—60 c. French Poodle.

(Des and eng P. Gandon. Recess)

1975 (12 Nov). *Birth Centenaries of Musicians. T **319** and similar vert design. P* 12½×13.
1219	60 c. bistre-brown and lake-brown	..	20	12
1220	1 f. 20, blue-black and lake-brown	..	45	25

Design:—1 f. 20, Johann Strauss (the younger).

320 Circus Clown   **321** Monaco Florin Coin, 1640

(Des P. Lambert and D. Bazzoli. Photo)

1975 (12 Nov). *2nd International Circus Festival, Monaco. P* 12½×13.
1221	**320**	80 c. multicoloured	..	..	30	15

(Des and eng J. Pheulpin. Recess)

1975 (12 Nov). *Monaco Numismatics. P* 13.
1222	**321**	80 c. drab and indigo	..	..	30	15

See also No. 1245.

322 André Ampère with Electrical Meter

323 "Lamentation for the Dead Christ"

(Des and eng M. Monvoisin. Recess)

1975 (12 Nov). *Birth Bicentenary of André Ampère (physicist). P* 13×12½.
1223	**322**	85 c. indigo and ultramarine	..	30	15

(Des and eng C. Durrens. Recess)

1975 (12 Nov). *500th Birth Anniv of Michelangelo. P* 13.
1224	**323**	1 f. 40, olive-drab and black	..	50	35

(Des P. Lambert. Photo Delrieu)

1975 (12 Nov). *Monte Carlo Flower Show. Vert designs similar to T **271**. Multicoloured. P* 13½×13.
1225	60 c. Bouquet of wild flowers	..	20	10
1226	80 c. Ikebana flower arrangement	..	30	15

(324)   **325** Prince Pierre de Monaco

1975 (12 Nov). *Precancels. Designs as T **177**, but without obliterated date. Surch as T **324**. P* 13×12½.
1227	42 c. on 26 c. reddish vio, bright bl & blk	20	10
1228	48 c. on 30 c. multicoloured	..	..	20	12
1229	70 c. on 45 c. multicoloured	..	..	35	25
1230	1 f. 35, on 90 c. yell-ol, turq-bl & blk	50	40
1227/1230	*Set of 4* ..	..	..	1·10	80

(Des and eng P. Gandon (10 c., 60 c.), J. Pheulpin (20 c., 25 c.), G. Bétemps (30 c., 50 c.). Des P. Lambert. Eng E. Lacaque (80 c., 1 f. 20,). Recess)

1976 (3 May). *25th Anniv of Literary Council of Monaco. T **325** and similar designs. P* 13.
1231	10 c. black	..	..	..	5	5
1232	20 c. indigo and rosine	..	..	5	5
1233	25 c. deep blue and rosine	..	8	8
1234	30 c. chocolate	..	..	8	8
1235	50 c. deep ultramarine, rosine & black	15	12
1236	60 c. sepia, deep green and light brown	20	15
1237	80 c. deep reddish purple and indigo	..	25	15
1238	1 f. 20, deep violet, indigo & magenta	40	25
1231/1238	*Set of 8* ..	..	..	1·10	85

Designs: *Horiz*—20 c. Maurois and Colette; 25 c. Jean and Jérôme Tharaud; 30 c. Henriot, Pagnol and Duhamel; 50 c. Heriat, Superville and Pierard; 60 c. Dorgeles, Achard and Bauër; 80 c. Hellens, Billy and Grente; 1 f. 20, Giono, Pasteur-Vallery-Radot and Garcon.

326 Dachsunds

(Des P. Lambert. Photo)

1976 (3 May). *International Dog Show, Monte Carlo. P* 13.
1239	**326**	60 c. multicoloured	..	..	20	15

327 Bridge Table and Monte Carlo Coast

328 Alexander Graham Bell and Early Telephone

(Des B. Minne. Eng J. Pheulpin. Recess)

1976 (3 May). *5th Bridge Olympics, Monte Carlo. P* 13×12½.
1240 **327** 60 c. multicoloured 20 15

(Des and eng P. Forget. Recess)

1976 (3 May). *Telephone Centenary. P* 13×12½.
1241 **328** 80 c. red-brown, slate and bistre .. 25 15

329 Federation Emblem on Globe

(Des and eng A. Decaris. Recess)

1976 (3 May). *50th Anniv of International Philatelic Federation.
P* 13.
1242 **329** 1 f. 20, scarlet, ultram & bronze-grn. 40 20

330 U.S.A.
2 c. Stamp, 1926

(Des B. Minne. Eng P. Béquet. Recess)

1976 (3 May). *Bicentenary of American Revolution. P* 13.
1243 **330** 1 f. 70, black and deep carmine-red 55 30

331 "The Fritillaries" (Van Gogh)

332 Diving

(Des P. Lambert. Photo)

1976 (3 May). *Monte Carlo Flower Show. P* 12½×13.
1244 **331** 3 f. multicoloured .. .. .. 1·00 75

(Des and eng P. Forget (60 c., 1 f. 70,), J. Gauthier (80 c.),
R. Quillivic (85 c.), G. Bétemps (1 f. 20,). Recess)

1976 (3 May). *Olympic Games, Montreal. T* **332** *and similar
designs. P* 12½×13 (*vert*) *or* 13×12½ (*horiz*).
1245 60 c. brown-lake and deep ultramarine 20 12
1246 80 c. deep ultram, brn-lake & bottle-grn 25 15
1247 85 c. bottle-grn, deep ultram & brn-lake 30 20
1248 1 f. 20, brn-lake, bottle-grn & dp ultram 35 20
1249 1 f. 70, brn-lake, dp ultram & bottle-grn 55 30
1245/1249 Set of 5 .. .. 1·50 80
MS1250 150×145 mm. Nos. 1245/9. .. 1·75 1·75
Designs: *Vert*—60 c. Diving; 80 c. Gymnastics; 85 c.
Hammer-throwing. *Horiz*—1 f. 20, Rowing; 1 f. 70, Boxing.

333 Decorative Plate

334 Palace Clock Tower

(Des P. Lambert. Photo)

1976 (3 May). *Europa. Monegasque Ceramics. T* **333** *and
similar vert design. Multicoloured. P* 12½×13.
1251 80 c. Type **333** 25 12
1252 1 f. 20, Grape Harvester (statuette) .. 40 25
MS1253 170×140 mm. Nos. 1251/2×5 .. 3·50 3·50

(Des and eng C. Jumelet. Recess)

1976 (3 May)–77. *Precancels. P* 12½×13 (54 c., 68 c., 1f. 05, 1f.
85) *or* 13 (*others*).
1254 **334** 50 c. brown-lake 12 5
1255 52 c. brown-orange (1.7.76) .. 15 10
1256 54 c. light yellowish green (1.4.77) .. 20 15
1257 60 c. deep green 15 10
1258 62 c. deep mauve (1.7.76) .. 20 12
1259 68 c. orange-yellow (1.4.77) .. 25 20
1260 90 c. violet 25 15
1261 95 c. carmine (1.7.76) 30 20
1262 1 f. 05, bistre (1.4.77) 40 30
1263 1 f. 60, new blue 40 25
1264 1 f. 70, blue-green (1.7.76) .. 45 35
1265 1 f. 85, orange-brown (1.4.77) .. 75 55
1254/65 Set of 12 .. .. 3·25 2·25

335 "St Louise de Marillac" (altar painting)

336 Saint Vincent-de-Paul

(Des P. Lambert. Eng C. Haley. Recess)

1976 (Nov). *Monaco Red Cross. Monegasque Art. P* 13.
1270 **335** 4 f. multicoloured .. .. .. 1·25 95

(Des and eng C. Slania. Recess)

1976 (Nov). *Paintings. "Princes and Princesses of Monaco".*
Vert designs similar to T **213.** *P* 12×13.
1271 2 f. agate 65 45
1272 4 f. multicoloured .. .. .. 1·25 1·00
Designs:—2 f. Prince Honore IV; 4 f. Princess Louise
d'Aumont Mazarin.

(Des P. Lambert. Eng C. Haley. Recess)

1976 (Nov). *Centenary of Saint-Vincent-de-Paul Conference,*
Monaco. P 13×12½.
1273 **336** 60 c. slate-black, brown & turq-bl 20 12

337 Marie de Rabutin
Chantal

338 Monaco 2 g. "Honore II"
Coin, 1640

(Des and eng P. Gandon. Recess)

1976 (Nov). 350*th Birth Anniv of Marie de Rabutin Chantal,*
Marquise de Sevigne (writer). *P* 12½×13.
1274 **337** 80 c. brnish blk, dp reddish vio & car 25 12

(Des and eng J. Pheulpin. Recess)

1976 (Nov). *Monaco Numismatics. P* 13.
1275 **338** 80 c. greyish blue & deep dull green 25 15

339 Admiral R. E. Byrd with
Fokker Trimotor Aircraft and
Roald Amundsen with *Norge*
Airship

340 Gulliver and
Lilliputians

(Des and eng M. Monvoisin. Recess)

1976 (Nov). 50*th Anniv of First Flights over North Pole. P* 13.
1276 **339** 85 c. black, new blue & brown-olive 30 15

(Des and eng P. Forget. Recess)

1976 (Nov). 250*th Anniv of Publication of "Gulliver's Travels"*
by Jonathan Swift. P 13.
1277 **340** 1 f. 20, multicoloured 40 25

341 Girl's Head and
Christmas Decorations

342 "Drug" Dagger piercing
Man and Woman

(Des and eng P. Forget. Recess)

1976 (Nov). *Christmas. P* 13×12½.
1278 **341** 60 c. multicoloured 20 12
1279 1 f. 20, orge, bronze-grn & brt mag 40 25

(Des Gonzague. Eng J. Larrivière. Recess)

1976 (Nov). *Campaign against Drug Abuse. P* 13×12½.
1280 **342** 80 c. dull ultram, reddish orge & dp grn 20 15
1281 1 f. 20, dp lil, dp clar & reddish brn 40 25

(Des P. Lambert. Photo Delrieu)

1976 (Nov). *Monte Carlo Flower Show* (1977). *Vert designs*
similar to T **271.** *Multicoloured. P* 13½×13.
1282 80 c. Flower arrangement 25 12
1283 1 f. Bouquet of flowers 30 20

343 Circus Clown

344 Schooner *Hirondelle*

(Des Gonzague. Photo)

1976 (Nov). 3*rd International Circus Festival, Monaco. P* 13.
1284 **343** 1 f. multicoloured 30 20

(Des and eng P. Gandon (10 c.), C. Slania (20 c.), C. Haley
(30 c., 1 f. 40,), M. Monvoisin (80 c.), G. Bétemps (1 f., 2 f.
50,), P. Forget (1 f. 25,). Recess)

1977 (3 May). 75*th Anniv of Publication of "La Carriere d'un*
Navigateur" by Prince Albert 1. *Illustrations by L. Tinayre. T* **344**
and similar designs. P 13.
1285 10 c. bistre-brn, deep bl & dp turq-bl 5 5
1286 20 c. black, red-brown and brown-red 8 5
1287 30 c. deep green, deep vio-bl & orge 15 10
1288 80 c. brownish blk, deep turq-bl & carm 25 15
1289 1 f. deep purple-brown and black .. 35 20
1290 1 f. 25, brown-olive, deep grey-green
and reddish violet 40 30
1291 1 f. 40, agate, brown-olive & bluish grn 45 30
1292 1 f. 90, blue-black, blue and scarlet .. 55 40
1293 2 f. 50, agate, bright blue and deep
turquoise-blue 90 70
1285/1293 *Set of* 9 .. .. 3·00 2·00
Designs: *Vert*—20 c. Prince Albert 1; 1 f. Helmsman; 1 f.
90, Bringing in the trawl. *Horiz*—30 c. Crew-members: 80 c.
Hirondelle in a gale; 1 f. 25, Securing the lifeboat; 1 f. 40,
Shrimp fishing; 2 f. 50, Capture of a moon-fish.
See also Nos. 1305/13.

345 Pyrenean Sheep and
Mountain Dogs

346 "Maternity"
(M. Cassatt)

(Des P. Lambert. Photo)

1977 (3 May). *International Dog Show, Monte Carlo. P* 13.
1294 **345** 80 c. multicoloured 25 15

(Des and eng P. Gandon. Recess)

1977 (3 May). *World Association of the "Friends of Children".*
P 12½×13.
1295 **346** 80 c. sepia, orange-brown & black 25 15

347 Archers

(Des and eng P. Forget. Recess)

1977 (3 May). *10th International Archery Championships, Monte Carlo.* P 13.

1296 **347** 1 f. 10, black, olive-brown and deep
violet-blue 30 25

348 Charles Lindbergh and
Spirit of St. Louis

(Des and eng J. Gauthier. Recess)

1977 (3 May). *50th Anniv of Lindbergh's Transatlantic Flight.* P 13.

1297 **348** 1 f. 90, greenish blue, olive-sepia and
deep ultramarine 65 40

349 "Harbour, Deauville"

350 "Portrait of a
Young Girl"

(Des P. Lambert. Photo)

1977 (3 May). *Birth Centenary of Raoul Dufy (painter).* P 13.

1298 **349** 2 f. multicoloured 65 40

(Des and eng J. Pheulpin (80 c., 1 f.), P. Gandon (1 f. 40,). Recess)

1977 (3 May). *400th Birth Anniv of Peter Paul Rubens (painter).* T **350** and similar vert designs. P 12½×13.

1299 80 c. orange-brown, olive-brown and black .. 25 15
1300 1 f. carmine-red 30 20
1301 1 f. 40, dull orange and carmine-red 40 25
Designs:—1 f. "Duke of Buckingham"; 1 f. 40, "Portrait of a Child".

351 "L'Oreillon" Tower

352 Santa Claus
and Sledge

(Des B. Minne. Eng J. Pheulpin. Recess)

1977 (3 May). *Europa. Monaco Views.* T **351** and similar vert design. P 12½×13.

1302 1 f. agate and deep turquoise-blue .. 30 20
1303 1 f. 40, deep turq-bl, olive-brn & agate 40 25
MS1304 169×130 mm. Nos. 1302/3×5 .. 3·50 3·50
Design:—1 f. 40, St. Michael's Church, Menton.

(Des and eng J. Pheulpin (10 c., 1 f. 90), E. Lacaque (20 c., 1 f. 40), C. Haley (30 c., 1 f., 3 f.), G. Bétemps (80 c.), P. Forget (1 f. 25). Recess)

1977 (Nov). *75th Anniv of Publication of "La Carriere d'un Navigateur" by Prince Albert* 1 *(2nd issue). Illustrations by L. Tinayre. Designs similar to T* **344**. P 13.

1305 10 c. black and blue 5 5
1306 20 c. deep turquoise-blue 5 5
1307 30 c. Prussian blue, bright greenish blue
and blackish olive.. .. .. 10 5
1308 80 c. orange-brown, black & bl-grn 20 12
1309 1 f. indigo and bright turquoise-green.. 30 15
1310 1 f. 25, black, brownish black & dp lilac 35 20
1311 1 f. 40, blackish purple, dull ultramarine
and olive-brown 40 25
1312 1 f. 90, olive-black, Prussian blue and
bright greenish blue 55 30
1313 3 f. new blue, olive-brown & bottle grn 80 50
1305/13 *Set of 9* .. .. 2·50 1·50
Designs: *Horiz*—10 c. *Princess Alice II* at Kiel; 20 c. Ship's laboratory; 30 c. *Princess Alice II* in ice floes; 1 f. Polar scene; 1 f. 25, Bridge of *Princess Alice II* during snow storm; 1 f. 40, Arctic camp; 1 f. 90, Ship's boat amongst floating ice; 3 f. *Princess Alice II* passing an iceberg. *Vert*—80 c. Crewmen in Arctic dress.

(Des and eng P. Forget. Recess)

1977 (Nov). *Christmas.* P 13×12½.
1314 **352** 80 c. carmine, dp green & blackish bl 20 12
1315 1 f. 40, multicoloured 40 20

(Des P. Lambert. Photo)

1977 (Nov). *Monte Carlo Flower Show. Vert designs similar to* T **271**. *Multicoloured.* P 12½×13.
1316 80 c. Snapdragons and campanula .. 20 12
1317 1 f. Ikebana 30 15

353 Face, Poppy
and Syringe

354 Clown and Flags

(Des P. Lambert. Eng C. Haley. Recess)

1977 (Nov). *Campaign against Drug Abuse.* P 12½×13.
1318 **353** 1 f. black, carmine & brt bluish violet 30 15

(Des Gonzague. Photo)

1977 (Nov). *4th International Circus Festival, Monaco.* P 12½×13.
1319 **354** 1 f. multicoloured 30 15

355 Gold Coin of Honoré II

(Des and eng J. Pheulpin. Recess)

1977 (Nov). *Monaco Numismatics. P* 13.
1320 **355** 80 c. olive-brown and carmine-lake .. 20 12

356 Mediterranean divided
by Industry

(Des and eng C. Jumelet. Recess)

1977 (Nov). *Protection of the Mediterranean Environment. P* 13.
1321 **356** 1 f. multicoloured 30 15

357 Dr Guglielminetti and Road
Tarrers

(Des and eng P. Forget. Recess)

1977 (Nov). *75th Anniv of First Experiments at Road Tarring in Monaco. P* 13.
1322 **357** 1 f. 10, slate-blk, brn-ol & reddish brn 25 15

358 F.M.L.T. Badge and Monte
Carlo

(Des B. Minne. Eng Guédron. Recess)

1977 (Nov). *50th Anniv of Monaco Lawn Tennis Federation. P* 13.
1323 **358** 1 f. dp turq-bl, rosine & lake-brn .. 30 15

359 Wimbledon and First
Championships

(Des and eng C. Jumelet. Recess)

1977 (Nov). *Centenary of Wimbledon Lawn Tennis Championships. P* 13.
1324 **359** 1 f. 40, slate, bright yellowish green
and red-brown.. .. .. 40 20

(Des M. Verroust. Eng C. Slania. Recess)

1977 (Nov). *Paintings. "Princes and Princesses of Monaco". Vert design similar to T* **213.** *Multicoloured. P* 12×13.
1325 6 f. Prince Honoré V .. .. .. 1·75 90

360 St Jean Bosco   (**361**)

(Des P. Lambert. Eng C. Haley. Recess)

1977 (Nov). *Monaco Red Cross. Monegasque Art. P* 13.
1326 **360** 4 f. dp grey-green, brn-ol & new bl .. 1·10 65

1978 (17 Jan). *Precancels. Nos.* 1256, 1259, 1262 *and* 1265 *surch as T* **361.**
1327 58 c. on 54 c. light yellowish green .. 12 5
1328 73 c. on 68 c. orange-yellow 15 10
1329 1 f. 15 on 1 f. 05, bistre 30 20
1330 2 f. on 1 f. 85, orange-brown 45 30
1327/30 *Set of* 4 .. .. .. 90 60
The stamps were only issued precancelled, the mint prices being for stamps with full gum.

362 Aerial Shipwreck from "L'Ile
Mysterieuse"

(Des and eng P. Forget. Recess)

1978 (2 May). *150th Birth Anniv of Jules Verne. T* **362** *and similar horiz designs. P* 13.
1331 5 c. chocolate, carmine and olive-brown 5 5
1332 25 c. dp turquoise-blue, dp slate & carm 5 5
1333 30 c. dull ultram, bistre-brn & new bl .. 5 5
1334 80 c. black, greenish grey and orange .. 15 12
1335 1 f. olive-brn, lake-brn & dp ultram .. 20 15
1336 1 f. 40, bistre-brown, sepia & dp green 30 20
1337 1 f. 70, maroon, new blue & dp ultram 40 25
1338 5 f. 50, deep reddish violet and indigo 1·10 70
1331/8 *Set of* 8 .. .. .. 2·10 1·40
Designs:—25 c. The abandoned ship from "L'Ile Mysterieuse"; 30 c. The secret of the island from "L'Ile Mysterieuse"; 80 c. "Robur the Conqueror"; 1 f. "Master Zacharius"; 1 f. 40, "The Castle in the Carpathians"; 1 f. 70, "The Children of Captain Grant"; 5 f. 50, Jules Verne and allegories.

A regular new issue supplement to this
catalogue appears each month in

STAMP MONTHLY

—from your newsagent or by postal subscription
—details on request.

363 Aerial View of Conference Centre

365 Antonio Vivaldi

364 Footballers and Globe

(Des B. Minne. Eng C. Haley. Recess)

1978 (2 May). *Inauguration of Monaco Congress Centre.* T **363** and similar horiz design. P 13 × 12½.
1339 1 f. maroon, blue and yellowish green .. 20 15
1340 1 f. 40, new blue, bistre-brown & dp olive 30 20
Design:—1 f. 40, View of Congress Centre from the sea.

(Des and eng J. Combet. Recess)

1978 (2 May). *World Cup Football Championship, Argentina.* P 13.
1341 **364** 1 f. dp turquoise bl, slate-blk & dp ol 20 15

(Des and eng P. Gandon. Recess)

1978 (2 May). *300th Birth Anniv of Antonio Vivaldi (composer).* P 12½ × 13.
1342 **365** 1 f. chocolate and vermilion 20 15

366 Control Ship and Grimaldi Palace

367 Monaco Cathedral

(Des Rosticher. Eng G. Bétemps. Recess)

1978 (2 May). *Environment Protection. "Ramoge" Agreement.* T **366** and similar horiz design. P 12½ × 13 (80c.) or 13 (1 f.).
1343 80 c. multicoloured 15 12
1344 1 f. lake-brown, ultramarine & dp olive 20 15
Design:—1 f. Map of coastline between St. Raphael and Gênes.

(Des B. Minne. Eng J. Pheulpin. Recess)

1978 (2 May). *Europa. Monaco Views.* T **367** and similar vert design. P 12½ × 13.
1345 1 f. bottle green, sepia and Prussian blue 20 15
1346 1 f. 40, sepia, myrtle green and blue .. 30 20
MS1347 170 × 143 mm. Nos 1345/6 × 5 .. 2·50 2·50
Design:—1 f. 40, View of Monaco from the east.

368 "Cinderella"

(Des P. Lambert. Eng C. Jumelet (5 c., 1 f. 70), J. Pheulpin (30 c., 1 f. 40), E. Lacaque (80 c., 1 f., 1 f. 90), J. Larrivière (others). Recess)

1978 (Nov). *350th Birth Anniv of Charles Perrault (writer).* T **368** and similar horiz designs. P 13.
1348 5 c. red, deep olive and reddish violet .. 5 5
1349 25 c. black, bistre and magenta 5 5
1350 30 c. bronze-green, lake-brn and reddish brown 5 5
1351 80 c. multicoloured 15 12
1352 1 f. rosine, bistre-brown and olive-green 20 15
1353 1 f. 40, dp mauve, ultram & new bl .. 30 20
1354 1 f. 70, bottle green, dp ultram & slate 40 25
1355 1 f. 90, multicoloured 55 30
1356 2 f. 50, dp ultramarine, brt orge & bl-grn 75 45
1349/1356 *Set of 9* .. 2.25 1.50
Designs:—25 c. "Puss in Boots"; 30 c. "The Sleeping Beauty"; 80 c. "Donkey's Skin"; 1 f. "Little Red Riding Hood"; 1 f. 40, "Bluebeard"; 1 f. 70, "Tom Thumb"; 1 f. 90, "Riquet with a Tuft"; 2 f. 50, "The Fairies".

369 "The Sunflowers" (Van Gogh)

370 Afghan Hound

(Des P. Lambert. Photo)

1978 (Nov). *Monte Carlo Flower Show, 1979.* 125th Birth Anniv of Vincent Van Gogh. T **369** and similar vert design. Multicoloured. P 12½ × 13.
1357 1 f. Type **369** 20 15
1358 1 f. 70, "The Iris" (Van Gogh) 40 25

(Des P. Lambert. Photo)

1978 (Nov). *International Dog Show, Monte Carlo,* T **370** and similar horiz design. Multicoloured. P 13 × 12½.
1359 1 f. Type **370** 20 15
1360 1 f. 20, Borzoi 40 30

371 Girl with Letter

372 Catherine and William Booth

(Des P. Lambert. Eng J. Combet. Recess)

1978 (Nov). *Christmas.* P 12½ × 13.
1361 **371** 1 f. bistre, blue and carmine 20 15

(Des P. Lambert. Eng E. Lacaque. Recess)

1978 (Nov). *Salvation Army Centenary. P* 13.
1362 **372** 1 f. 70, multicoloured 40 25

374 Henri Dunant and Battle Scene

(Des P. Lambert. Eng C. Slania. Recess)

1978(Nov). 150*th Birth Anniv of Henri Dunant (founder of Red Cross). Sheet* 100×130 *mm. P* 13.
MS1370 **374** 5 f. chocolate, crimson and red .. 1·10 70

373 Juggling Seals

(Des and eng A. Decaris. Recess)

1978 (Nov). *Fifth International Circus Festival, Monaco. T* **373** *and similar designs. P* 12½×13 (1 *f.) or* 13×12½ (*others*).
1363 80 c. dull orange, black & dp turquoise-bl 15 12
1364 1 f. multicoloured 20 15
1365 1 f. 40, chocolate, magenta & olive-brn 30 20
1366 1 f. 90, dp ultram, dp lilac & dp mve .. 55 30
1367 2 f. 40, multicoloured 75 45
1363/1367 *Set of* 5 .. .. 1·75 1·10
Designs: *Horiz*—1 f. 40, Horseback acrobatics; 1 f. 90, Musical monkeys; 2 f. 40, Trapeze. *Vert*—1 f. Lion tamer.

375 Congress Centre

(Des B. Minne. Eng C. Haley. Recess)

(Des and eng C. Slania. Recess)

1978. *Precancels. P* 13×12½.

1978 (Nov). *Paintings. "Princes and Princesses of Monaco". Vert designs similar to T* **213**. *Multicoloured. P* 12×13.
1368 2 f. "Prince Florestan 1" (G. Dauphin) .. 55 30
1369 4 f. "Princess Caroline Gibert de La Metz"
(Marie Verroust) .. .. .. 1·50 75

1371 **375** 61 c. orange-vermilion 15 12
1372 78 c. deep magenta 15 12
1373 1 f. 25, brown 40 30
1374 2 f. 10, ultramarine 55 30
1371/1374 *Set of* 4 .. .. 1·10 75

Stamp monthly

Gibbons' own monthly magazine, essential reading for **every** collector!
Detailed monthly New Issue Guide to update all Gibbons catalogues for you—and a special Stamp Market feature on price changes.
Informative articles cover all facets of philately, with regular notes on new discoveries, stamp designs, postmarks, market trends and news and views of the world of stamps.
Britain's LARGEST circulation of any stamp magazine—that fact speaks for itself!
Monthly from all dealers and newsagents or by post direct from Stanley Gibbons Magazines Ltd—subscription rates on application.